THE TRUE PROOF OF GOD

ALSO BY DAVID L ROPER

Proving Shakespeare
The Popes of Saint Malachy
Shakespeare: To Be or Not To Be ?

THE TRUE PROOF OF GOD

CREATION AND THE COUNTERFEIT UNIVERSE

WITH A RATIOCINATION OF THE SCIENCES

AND

THE FUTURE HISTORY

OF THE WORLD

David L Roper

First-proofs.com

First published in 2015 by
FIRST-PROOFS.COM

FIRST EDITION

British Library Cataloguing in Publications Data
A catalogue record of this book
is available from the
British Library

ISBN
978 0 9543873 7 2

There's a divinity that shapes our ends,
Rough-hew them how we will.

                       William Shakespeare

*Human beings, vegetables, or cosmic dust, we all dance
to a mysterious tune, intoned in the distance by an
invisible player.*

                       Albert Einstein

Acknowledgements

Scripture quotations taken from The Holy Bible, New International Version (Anglicised edition) Copyright © 1979, 1984, 2011 by Biblica (formerly International Bible Society)' Used by permission of Hodder & Stoughton Publishers, an Hatchette UK company
All rights reserved
'NIV' is a registered trademark of Biblica (formerly International Bible Society).
UK trademark number 1448790

Verse quotations in their original French are from Bonhomme 1555, Du Rosne 1557, Rigaud 1568, and Leffen 1650. Translated material can be referenced from Randle Cotgrave's Dictionary of the French and English Tongues 1611; Emile de Littré's Le Dictionnaire de la langue français 1863-72; dictionnaire de l'ancien français jusqu'au milieu du XIVe siècle, par A. –J. Greimas; also from Cassell's compact French – English English - French Dictionary compiled by J.H. Douglas, Denis Girard, W. Thompson.

CONTENTS

INTRODUCTION

Is all that you see around you reality? Simple though this question sounds it harbours one of the profoundest questions in the universe—'Do we make this reality, or does it make us? The assumption is that it makes us. It then uses us, and at the end of our lives dispenses with us. Surprisingly, science points in the opposite direction; it is we who make reality. Solid steel, for example, is mostly empty space. Its volume is occupied by atomic particles that collectively account for just one ten-trillionth part of the dimensions that define its existence. Its resistance to touch is caused by the electrical forces between the particles. The steel we perceive is actually a construct of the human mind. As for the particles, they can be defined by mathematical points on a world line, which completes the circle, since mathematics is likewise a mental construct.

Consider therefore, our ears and eyes. These act as antenna for disturbances: either in the air, resulting from sound waves, or from the field of electromagnetic radiation arriving as light waves. Once these means of communication have been received, they are transmitted to the brain in the form of electro-chemical impulses, which are then processed to form visible and audible knowledge. Then, together with the addition of further data arriving as impulses from touch, taste and smell, a world of knowledge completes the picture to become the environment that not only surrounds each person, it includes them within the only world they will ever *directly* know.

Neuroscientists would dearly love to understand how impulses received by the brain become *changed* into personal experiences of an external, four-dimensional world in which they, themselves, together with everyone else, live for the duration of their lives. Does the problem even have a scientific solution?—the barrier to an answer, being, itself, the actual acquisition of knowledge. For, it is the mind that reveals science; hence, science can never reveal the mind.

According to the scientific explanation, briefly outlined above, mankind does not possess an actual *outlook* onto the colourful, illuminated, material world that is experienced by sense. Instead, that world, although possessing a spatial relationship to the percipient, is a personal, therefore insightful world, constructed by the brain, and is composed entirely from the data it receives. From where did that data originate? Certainly not from any object that appears within the percipient's spatial awareness, for that is already part of a cerebral composition, constructed from data that was earlier received. So, from where did it originate?

Scientists are by no means ignorant of this problem, and their response has been to theorise a real world of space and objects that exist in unison with that which has been constructed in the brain. But no scientist can ever observe, measure, or experiment upon anything in this theoretical world. Instead, work must be conducted upon the only things that are available to the senses, and these are confined to the insightful world of conscious awareness. Consequently, the result of any measurement or experiment can only ever *knowingly* belong to, and pertain to, the world of a percipient's conscious awareness.

The scientific response to this irritating embarrassment is to argue the necessity for a cause of the data received, and that cause is inferred to be something called 'matter'. But this does not answer the problem of where it exists, or, as is believed, how it could possibly coexist in unison with spatial objects composed by the brain. Would the same claim be made for the brain's other spatial constructs, such as those composed in a dream or in a virtual reality scenario? It is a question which presents a major difficulty for science, and one that is made worse by the fact that while the necessity for an origin to the data is undeniable, to propose that this can be satisfied solely by something called 'matter' is very far from being a sufficient explanation.

Instead, let us restate the problem by first asking: 'where does the world, perceived by sense, exist? Since it is a fabrication of cerebral processes, the answer must be 'in the mind'. In which case, since it exists 'in the mind', why not deduce the existence of another mind, but one vastly superior that created the data, which it then relays to mankind? This would be akin to an author writing a novel. The finished book exists from beginning to end; the words are the author's data; it is only when they are relayed to a reader that the words come alive in that person's mind. At which point, they replicate a world of activity created by the author. There are differences, of course. The author requires intelligence, paper, ink and a printing press, whereas a superior being would require no more than an immensely powerful mind. But the concept is certainly plausible. The inference that God is to be identified as that superior, all-powerful mind, and the cause of the world composed of sense data is not new. Reasons were prominent, logical and persuasively made in a treatise written by the philosopher, George Berkeley in 1709, before he became Bishop of Cloyne. As Bertrand Russell remarked in *The Problems of Philosophy* (p.4), "Berkeley retains the merit of having shown that the existence of matter is capable of being denied without absurdity, and if there are any things that exist independently of us they cannot be the immediate objects of our sensations." This continues to remain the present situation, and the scientific implications of quantum physics and relativity have recently begun to renew interest in Berkeley's work.

The same lack of absurdity cannot be said for 'matter' at the quantum level. Professor Michio Kaku, himself a particle physicist, quoted Richard Feynman as saying, "There was a time when the newspapers said that only twelve men understood the theory of relativity. I do not think there ever was such a time. [...] On the other hand, I think I can safely say that nobody understands quantum mechanics." Feynman then continued by saying that quantum mechanics "describes nature as absurd from the point of view of common sense." To which, Kaku added his own rejoinder "The quantum theory is incomplete and rests on shaky philosophical grounds. This quantum controversy forces one to re-examine the work of philosophers like Bishop Berkeley, who in the eighteenth century claimed that objects exist only because humans are there to observe them." (*Parallel Worlds*, p.157).

None of this is pleasing to the ears of the evolutionist. Their adopted theory works on the premise that neither 'purpose', 'meaning' or 'design' must be imported into its structure—which makes atheists of everyone who embraces their way of thinking. Their colleagues in the physics and cosmological departments work upon the same principle, but increasingly find themselves thwarted by discoveries that again and again challenge the notion of chance and lack of design.

There was a period of time at the dawn of empirical science, when natural philosophers, who were mostly Christian stalwarts, believed they were working to discover the 'Laws of God'. If they were alive today, they would be congratulating themselves upon having achieved their goal. As Stephen Hawking remarked (*The Grand Design*, p.205) "Were it not for a series of startling coincidences in the precise details of physical law, it seems, humans and similar life-forms would never have come into being." Fellow physicist and author, Paul Davies, enlarged upon this.

> What impresses many scientists is not so much the fact that alterations in the value of the fundamental constants would change the structure of the physical world, but that the observed structure is remarkably sensitive to such alterations. Only a minute shift in the strength of the forces brings about a drastic change in the structure [...]. The delicate fine-tuning in the value of the constants, necessary so that the various different branches of physics can dovetail so felicitously, might be attributed to God. It is hard to resist the impression that the present structure of the universe, apparently so sensitive to minor alterations in the numbers, has been rather carefully thought out   (*God And The New Physics*, p. 188-9)

Sir Fred Hoyle also came to that conclusion after discovering the triple alpha process, which so astounded him because it required the unstable beryllium nucleus to exist for one hundred-billion-billionths of a single second—the time required for carbon to exist—without which, there would be no life. This discovery impelled him to say, "I do not believe that any scientist who examined the evidence would fail to draw the inference that the laws of nuclear physics have been deliberately designed with regard to the consequences they produce inside the stars." (Hawking, *The Grand Design*, p.202). Hoyle may well have been correct about the formation of carbon, but was not so well informed about the attitude of his fellow scientists. Prominent among them is an attitude that believes chance to be more probable than design.

Consider a machine that has been manufactured for randomly selecting letters of the alphabet, including six punctuation marks and the space bar. Now set the machine in motion and consider obtaining Shakespeare's Sonnet 18 by chance. To obtain a perfect version of just the first two lines of this sonnet by chance is 33^{80} (1 followed by 121 noughts). Antony Flew used a similar argument to expose the stupidity of supposing that monkeys could reproduce the *entire* works of Shakespeare by chance, given enough time. But Sir Roger Penrose did something remarkably similar with regard to the chance formation of the universe. He calculated the probability of a low-energy universe emerging from the big bang. The result is a probability so vast (10^{10} raised to a further power of 123) that it dwarfs the number of particles (10^{80}) in the entire universe. Even this number of particles is less than the chance of obtaining two lines from Shakespeare's Sonnet 18. Evolution theory, which is dependent upon the chance mutation of carbon having first occurred, is therefore a non-starter, insofar as probability theory is concerned.

It is with this that we return to the importance of Berkeley's insistence that if it were not for the mind's ability to perceive the sensible world, it would not then exist. What has brought this to the forefront in recent time is the result of an experiment, repeated in physics laboratories across the world, in which Berkeley's conclusion always proves true. One is therefore tempted to call it 'God's Stamp of Authority' upon the conclusion reached by Berkeley.

The experiment concerns light that passes through a slit in a screen to form a pattern of alternate bands of light and shade upon a second screen. The bands are consistent with the crests and troughs of the wave. It is therefore unremarkable that when a second slit is introduced beside the original slit, the wave passes through both slits and forms two separate patterns of bands that intersect as they spread out.

But light can be reduced in its luminosity to become photons, which are individual particles. Consequently, each time a photon passes through one of the two slits, it leaves its mark on the second screen. One would therefore expect the screen to appear pock-marked after a time, with no discernible pattern in the number of hits it received. This is not the case. If left over time, "the collective effect is to produce a wave interference pattern – despite the fact that a particle should be able to pass through only one slit." Instead, it is acting in a manner consistent with passing through both slits at the same time.

If tennis balls are thrown randomly, one at a time, through any one of two adjacent windows onto a wall outside, leaving marks where they make contact, it would be absurd to suppose these marks always formed the same pattern on the wall, wherever in the world this practice took place. Yet, that is precisely what individual particles of light manage to achieve when projected randomly through either one of two adjacent slits. But the unaccountable oddness of this result is only the first step towards what happens next.

> However – and this is crucial – the interference pattern will emerge only if the experimenter makes no attempt to determine which slit any given photon went through. Any sneaky apparatus stationed near the slits to glimpse the photon taking one path or the other will mess up the experiment. If the experimenter succeeds in detecting a photon going through a given slit, that photon will not contribute to the interference pattern.
> The two-slits experiment dramatically illustrates the key role that the experimenter or observer, plays in determining the nature of quantum reality.   (Paul Davies, *The Goldilocks Enigma*, p.277)

Uninterrupted waves carry the potential of another actuality. It is only when a conscious mind intercepts them that they 'oblige' the percipient by exhibiting the content of their potential; whence, it follows that to be is to be perceived—*esse* is *percipi* as Bishop Berkeley so aptly put it.

With regard to this book, it is now many years ago when, as a young *Idealist*, I began studying the problem of perception. I little realized then the implications that would arise from it. In sharing these with the reader, it comes at a time when the Christian religion is under attack from politicians swayed by the ideology of creating a Godless society. Already, the greater part of Christian morality has been overturned in just five decades, thus preparing the way for an easier assault upon what remains. This book questions the logic of scientific materialism, which is the guiding force to many political decisions. It does so by advancing Berkeley's ideas with a new demonstration that the theory of 'matter' can be replaced by the theory of 'world-lines': yet—without changing anything whatsoever, except the way in which the world is understood.

PROLEGOMENA

The subject of this foregoing book is the result of a long, rigorous, and often arduous enquiry. The intention of which has been to place the existence of God beyond reasonable doubt. It has been said that one cannot prove the existence of God. But against this, it has come to my knowledge that neither can one prove anything at all to a person who is emotionally and habitually attached to an opposing belief. Within such cases, the barrier against acceptance is no longer that of logic, nor of neutrality, but of pride born from having been attached to a mistruth for so long that it is no longer humanly possible to doubt its veracity. In the course of this book, the conflict between evidence-based reasoning and the attachment to formerly held beliefs will surface many times, possibly causing the inveterate disbeliever too much discomfort to continue reading further. This book is therefore directed at those for whom verifiable truth is, as it should be, the preserve and pursuit of all who place scholarship at the head of reason, and are willing to contemplate a possible new dawn to their understanding.

The evidence set out in this book is based solely upon current, scientific discoveries in company with verifiable, historical records. The combination of these two disciplines will then be shown as both necessary and sufficient for the establishment of a formal proof for the existence of God—a God of eternity, creativity and omniscience; a Spirit that is also divine, omnipotent and immutable. For this, I ask only that the reader first examine the evidence with an impartial outlook, that they may become wholly acquainted with matters of fact that media outlets seldom give attention to. For this reason, I request the reader's indulgence: that their final judgment remains suspended until all the evidence has been assimilated, whereafter it can be reviewed in its entirety as a perfectly consistent union between man and God, and one that offers a valid alternative to the atheistic model of the world which presently infects cultures that have been westernized by secular education.

The importance for requesting this indulgence lies in the fact that it is an easy matter to extract text from its place of settled consistency within these pages, and submit it to a hostile environment, where it becomes prey to misinterpretation, inconsistency and misrepresentation. The truth of what is placed before the reader, within the full range of this book, is of prime concern to every living person. As for the novelty and singularity it contains, for this there is no apology. It is an unfortunate soul that discards a fact only because it challenges a strongly held alternative belief. An impartial approach is therefore an essential commitment, if only to weigh fairly the balance of what is soon to pass before each reader's judgement. For, once the entire case has been understood, judgement cannot long afterwards be delayed.

In the present age, scientific methodology has replaced religion in the classroom as the true basis for understanding the world. Yet, unbeknown to a majority of the population, the authority wielded by scientists is actually very tenuous. It succeeds, because it has been painstakingly built upon the trust people have in the authority of scientists. But what if that trust and authority is misplaced? Suppose the theories that structure scientific knowledge are designed to build a counterfeit plan of the universe, instead of discovering its true nature. Can this be possible? It would seem so, when we consider that scientific investigation began in its infant days by seeking to understand the world created by God. "Newton, Galileo and other early scientists treated their investigations as a religious quest. They thought by exposing the patterns woven into the processes of nature they truly were glimpsing the mind of God." (Paul Davies, *The Goldilocks Enigma* 2006: p.5) This can no longer be said to be the case. A new breed of scientists has taken over, with intentions that are opposed to those of their predecessors.

> Many scientists who are struggling to construct a fully comprehensive theory of the physical universe openly admit that part of the motivation is to finally get rid of God, who they view as a dangerous and infantile delusion. And not only God, but any vestige of God-talk, such as 'meaning' or 'purpose' or 'design' in nature. [...] They concede no middle ground, and regard

science and religion as two implacably opposed world views. Victory is assumed to be the
inevitable outcome of science's intellectual ascendency and powerful methodology.

(ibid. pp. 16-17)

Observable facts permit no denial. It is the theories generated to explain these facts that fall short
of truth. For although they have been elaborately and ingeniously constructed to mimic nature,
they also eliminate the existence of anything spiritual, religious or supernatural. Scientific
theories are therefore constructed upon a chosen premise that excludes the soul, the mind,
consciousness, and God. These terms have been replaced by non-spiritual terminology that has
the effect of banishing them altogether from possessing any meaningful existence. But by taking
this stance, the Achilles heel of scientific investigation is exposed. Scientific theories can never be
said to be sufficient, no matter how necessary they may appear when describing nature. To be
sufficient, a theory must exclude all possibility of God's presence as an alternative explanation.

Perception and Reality

Factually speaking, scientific knowledge can only be obtained, at source, by reference to the five
senses. Knowledge is therefore dependent upon data reaching the *conscious understanding* of the
mind. But for reasons that are seldom made public, and even then, only in evasive language, the
scientific theory for the acquisition of human knowledge involves 'circular reasoning', since the
conclusion is contained in the premise—a taboo in logic, yet permitted by scientists.

Why should that be? It is because it allows the continuation of results that are deemed desirable
to society, as well as upholding the dignity and authority of the scientific community responsible
for furthering its influence in public. Nevertheless, a structure built upon an unstable foundation
will inevitably fail. Eventually, the ingenuity of theories devised to explain ever increasing
complexities will either stall for want of sense, or struggle against absurdity. Some believe this
situation was reached in physics more than a half century ago.

There is also the added fact that the general public is continuously being misled by magazine
articles, news reports, and television documentaries: all of which take it for granted that scientific
theories apply to the world perceived by the senses. Scientists certainly expect the public to
believe this—in fact, they would even like to believe it themselves. But, for everyone who inclines
to this belief, there is no possible appeal against the logic that denies it. Put simply, the world you
actively perceive is *not*, nor ever can be, the world that scientists are *really* referring to; that world,
as they have come to realize from their theories, is imperceptible; it is literally *out of sight*.

Virtual Reality is the effect produced on the brain by relaying to it data that simulates those
sensory impulses which it would otherwise receive naturally. When this artificial data is received,
the recipient becomes conscious of a three-dimensional world in which they are situated at a
focal point to what is then witnessed as their new environment.

Let it be perfectly understood what this means. Within scenes of virtual reality, subject to its
author's program, the viewer will perceive light, colour, distance, extended objects, motion, and
an obedience of everything happening in strict accordance to the familiar laws of nature.

The subject of this experience will then interpret, subconsciously, the data being received,
thereby experiencing, consciously, everything in an artificial environment, exactly as that person
would otherwise do in the familiar world of everyday life. They will do so, because the data
received has been pre-planned to become the subject's *virtual reality*. To achieve this effect,
visual, audio and tactile data will have been co-ordinated to simulate life in the familiar world
perceived by the senses. The data will also have been designed to produce a pre-ordained effect. If
this virtual reality experience were sustained and previous memories erased, why should that
person not accept they were part of that world?

Although virtual reality is often associated with gaming, its greater potential is to the military, to
education and to commerce and industry. In the near future, one may experience visiting any
place in the world without ever leaving home. For, although it will have been a virtual visit, the

reality of the experience can be so overwhelming that the percipient returns to normal life with a vivid memory of actually having participated as a visitor to that place.

This type of personal interaction with virtual realities has long been recognized, and not just anecdotally, but experimentally. Subjects have been presented with the virtual reality of a plank laid across a bottomless pit. Although the subject remains well aware that an experiment is taking place and they are standing in a room on a solid floor, in no danger whatsoever, this safe reality becomes overpowered by evidence from the visual sense: to wit, the view of a plank spanning a pit. It has been repeatedly shown that when the percipient is instructed to walk across the plank, the accompaniment of fear associated with the experience in a real-life situation is always present.

The reason for emphasising virtual reality is because of its logical implications. These are to be found within the pages that follow. But first, the question alluded to above—how does the perception of scenes occurring in day-to-day life differ from those occurring in a virtual reality? According to the American neuroscientist, David Eagleman, Director of the Laboratory for Perception and Action, "We are trapped in a virtual reality machine." Essentially, he is admitting that there is no qualitative difference between what is perceived normally and what is perceived by artificial means. To each and every percipient, whether involved in a virtual reality experience or going about their daily routine, the perception of the world in which they find them self at any moment has been constructed from an input of sensible data. This was also the conclusion reached by Stephen Hawking.

> (O)ur brains interpret the input from our sensory organs by making a model of the outside world. We form mental concepts of our home, trees, other people, the electricity that flows from wall sockets, atoms, molecules and other universes. These mental concepts are the only reality we can know.   (Stephen Hawking, *The Grand Design* p.217)

Let us take these two scientists at their word, and by doing so, we find ourselves immersed in a world wherein we live and move and have our being, but which does not exist in the physical sense that we have always taken for granted. Mental concepts exist only because they are—well, mental. They exist because they are perceived to exist. Their '*esse* is *percipi*' as Bishop Berkeley so aptly put it three hundred years ago, when contemplating the same question of perceived reality. Stephen Hawking was equally forceful in his exposition. "There is no model-independent test of reality. It follows that a well-constructed model creates a reality of its own." (Ibid)

Professor Vilayanur Ramachandran, a leading brain research scientist and Director of the Center for Brain and Cognition at the University of California, indicated where current research is heading; "the first step in understanding perception is to get rid of the idea of images in the brain and to begin thinking about symbolic descriptions of objects and events in the external world." (*Phantoms in the Brain*, p.66) "What is meant by a symbolic description in the brain?" he asks. It is, he replies, "the language of nerve impulses."

Recent discoveries indicate that our eyes are capable of intercepting approximately 11,000,000 impressions per second from light rays. These are then transferred to the 250.000,000 photoreceptors in the eyes. There they form patterns that are passed, via the optic nerve, to the brain's cortex for processing. Upon arrival they can only be dealt with at the rate of 40 per second: the remainder are said to be shelved in the subconscious. So what happens to the impulse patterns selected by the cortex? Ramachandran's response indicated his perplexity.

> The central mystery of the cosmos [...] Why are there always two parallel descriptions of the universe—the first person account ("I see red") and the third-person account ("He says that he sees red when certain pathways in the brain encounter a wavelength of six hundred nanometres")? How can these two accounts be so utterly different yet complementary? Why isn't there only a third-person account, for according to the objective worldview of the physicist and neuroscientist, that's the only one that really exists? [...] By what magic is matter transmuted into the invisible fabric of feelings and sensations? This problem is so puzzling that not everyone agrees it is even a problem.   (Ibid. p.229)

Ramachandran is understandably bemused because his thinking is rigidly founded upon an error. Unanswerable questions are those that have arrived at a cul-de-sac of confused thinking. This most often occurs from having adopted a fake premise. All logical structures eventually collapse if they are founded upon a basic premise which is false. And this has occurred within the problem remarked upon by Professor Ramachandran. In fact, the error is demonstrated in his own book. It occurred when he admitted to his interest in asking people how *they believe* they see things— and how the brain is involved in their perception (ibid p.65). For, therein lies the error affecting anyone attempting the same investigation. It is impossible to explain anything *correctly*, without *first defining* what it is that the explanation is intended to justify. Ramachandran failed to do this; as, indeed, do others who commit the same error.

Look around you, and pick anything in sight, then ask the question, how do I see it? The answer you will receive, or have already been taught, will follow the explanation Ramachandran gave. You will be informed that light reflects off the object, enters the eye, forms an inverted image on the retina, and by a series of electro-chemical impulses along the optic nerve, these are transmitted to the cortex region of the brain, where a cerebral 'computer' takes up the task of decoding these impulses into knowledge comprising the world perceived by the senses.

Knowledge of the external world is therefore understood to take the form of mental concepts. It is the result of the internal workings of the brain. Ramachandran's task, as he has made clear, is to discover how the brain *decodes* these impulses, so that they transform into the knowledge that reveals the world we perceive in our day-to-day lives, and which is referred to by scientists as a well-constructed model of reality.

But this raises an important question. From *where* did the data come from? Certainly not from any of the mental concepts of which we are already aware. It is for this reason that one has no need to ask from where the data that forms dreams or virtual realities come from. In neither case do they come from material replicas that exist in unison with what is witnessed. The fact is, of course, this consideration is unnecessary because what is witnessed in dreams and virtual realities are accepted as mental concepts created by the mind. It is the same conclusion reached by Dr. Eagleman (p.3) and other cognitive scientists concerning our 'well-constructed model of reality'. It consists of mental concepts. Hence, the question that asks how we see mental concepts—as though they were *not* mental concepts, but material objects existing externally in a parallel world of matter, only to conclude thereafter that they *are* mental concepts, is absurd.

Space—A Physical Reality or a Mental Concept?

Imagine that you are walking along the seashore, or by the side of a large lake, on a moonlit night. The moon appears somewhere above the water and casts an illuminated path across the darkness of the waves to where you are walking. You notice, as you continue your stroll, that this path of light keeps pace with you, while either side of it all is in darkness. There are other people also enjoying a late evening stroll; some are ahead of you and others behind. Do they see a path lit by the moon across the water to where they are walking? It would be incomprehensible if they did not: yet, the water on either side of your moonlit path is black; it shows no sign of the paths leading to the people either in front of you or behind. You therefore conclude that each person has their own personal view of the illuminated path across the water. In which case, the path of light is not actually *out there*. Nevertheless, the light does illuminate the water, which means it cannot be an illusion. A figment of the mind cannot illuminate a large stretch of water. Therefore, the stretch of moonlit water must be as real as the water that has been illuminated. Moreover, since this water is inseparable from the waves on either side of the path of light, it implies acceptance that the entire scene is, as Hawking maintained, a mental construct. But, if that is so, then this entire scene cannot have been projected out into physical space, even though that is where the scene is situated. Instead, space must likewise be a mental construct, which also includes the moon that shed its light. One can rationalise this conclusion by becoming aware that if anything did not exist as a mental concept, then how could it be known to exist? To *know* something is to possess it as knowledge: and where is knowledge retained if not in the mind?

This previous paragraph is simply a further illustration of the importance attached to perception and the definition of what is perceived as knowledge. However, it also leads to an important question. Can knowledge exist externally to the mind?

Nothing perceived by the mind can be known to exist outside of it, for then, contrarily, it would be *in* the mind of the knower. This means that scientists are compelled to admit that everything known about the world and experienced by mankind originates from outside their human awareness. And, without *direct* awareness of its origin, its existence can only be theorised by creating a manmade model of what is *thought* to be its cause and origin.

Intelligent thought in mankind has therefore moved from a position in which it was believed that *Homo sapiens* possessed visual *out-look,* which enabled the instant perception of a material world: and has now arrived at a state in which the world perceived 'out there' is not a material world at all. Instead, it is a mental construction cognized singly within each person's *insightfulness.*

The physical sciences are chief amongst those that are attempting to discover the essential nature of this unobservable world, from which our sense data is believed to originate. But it can only be undertaken by means of observation, measurement and experiment. This method is therefore *restricted* to that which exists solely in the *perceived world.* Whence, it is from this standpoint that scientists work to counterfeit the world perceived by the senses; which is to say, they are creating their own manmade world, composed of theories that are intended to explain *everything* within the perceived world by what is *theorised to exist* in a world that is external to the mind.

Thus, scientists readily observe and record how 'nature' reacts to that which they perceive to be present within the personal knowledge of their own mentally, constructed world. They do so in the firm belief that what is being observed, mentally, in their *insightfulness,* is duplicated *outside* of their minds in a non-mental, imperceptible world of space, time and matter. Their ultimate aim is to achieve the creation of this *causal* world, consisting of interlocking theories that are capable of rationally explaining how this unobservable world came into existence; and how it is also able to replicate itself by impressions received in brains that are capable of life and intelligent thought—all of which, they presume, happened by a combination of random events, accidental mutations, and arbitrary 'motions' occurring in a universe that appeared from nowhere.

This enterprise raises many difficult questions. Not least among these is that which questions the assurance that can be given regarding the actual existence of a non-mental, duplicate world. Is such a replicated world of space, time and matter actually possible from a logical perspective? Is it not the case that a mental concept can be like nothing but another mental concept? If not, how can it be otherwise? To replicate mental concepts and then claim that these are not mental concepts after all, but material objects that exist in their own right within a non-mental, spatial setting, cannot be considered an entirely rational deduction. Yet, it persists as science.

The question as to whether or not a mental concept can exist outside the mind has already been answered in the negative above. But, distance is also a mental concept, since it forms an essential part of our knowledge. And, it is with distance that we infer the existence of space. Hence, it is permissible to enquire if space exists, other than within the mind's insightfulness?

> It is not only colours and sounds and so on that are absent from the scientific world of matter, but also *space* as we get it through sight and touch. It is essential to science that its matter should be in *a* space, but the space in which it is cannot be exactly the space we see or feel. To begin with,

> space as we see it is not the same as space as we get it by the sense of touch; it is only by experience in infancy that we learn how to touch things we see, or how to get a sight of things which we feel touching us. But the space of science is neutral as between touch and sight; thus it cannot be either the space of touch or the space of sight.
>
> (Bertrand Russell: *The Problems of Philosophy* p.14)

Bertrand Russell has confirmed that mankind's knowledge of space is learned at infancy by a child's experience of coordinating its tactile sense data with its visual sense data. This enables the mind to form a mental concept of distance, from which space is then inferred as an *abstract idea*. Abstract ideas are a contentious subject, and it has been argued that they have no existence in themselves except that they serve as a linguistic means for communicating ideas. Thus, one may talk of a triangle without needing to say whether by triangle we mean scalene, equilateral, isosceles or right angled. The point being that a single triangle cannot be all of these, nor can it be none of these. Similarly, when we refer to space, we are referring to distance: but to what length, far or near? It cannot be both: and nor can it be neither. But when we define distance, we do so according to our personal knowledge of the world we perceive. Anything else is an abstraction of the mental concept we have of distance.

In the fifth century B.C., Zeno of Elea considered the same problem. In his famous paradox *the Dichotomy,* he concluded that it is impossible to traverse space within a finite time interval. His argument, in its simplest terms is that the distance between any two points in space will always include a halfway point. For example, before travelling one mile, it is necessary to reach the half-mile stage. And before setting off to reach the half-mile stage, it is then necessary to arrive at the quarter-mile stage. And although these distances become increasingly less, the number of halfway points that must be reached before commencing the journey never terminates. It is therefore impossible to traverse these *infinite* stages in a *finite* period of time. Consequently, physical space serves no purpose. If it existed, nothing would be capable of movement within the timescale of a human lifetime. It is with this in mind that we turn to the current, scientific view of space.

Spacetime

In 1905, Albert Einstein published his groundbreaking paper concerning the theory of relativity. This has since become the foundation for a scientific understanding of the cosmos and a basis for experimental research in physics. But the theory has also shown the necessity for space-time.

Hermann Minkowski, Einstein's former tutor at the Eidgenossische Technische Hochschule, first alerted the world to spacetime when, in 1907, he gave a memorable lecture at Göttingen University. It was in this address that he explained the geometry of space-time.

> The views of space and time which I wish to lay before you have sprung from the soil of experimental physics, and therein lies their strength. They are radical. Henceforth space, by itself, and time, by itself, are doomed to fade away into mere shadows, and only a kind of union of the two will preserve an independent reality.　　(Abraham Pais: *Subtle is the Lord,* 2005, p.152)

Minkowski was stating that three-dimensional space and one dimensional time are now to be understood as a four-dimensional space-time. The accepted meaning of this is that time occurs *in* space-time. If we were to take a sheet of paper and draw a straight line from left to right, then this would represent the history and direction of an event. Consequently, any point on that line represents a three-dimensional 'still frame' of the said event at a particular moment in time. If that point is traced along the line, then the event becomes activated in a manner similar to that seen from a roll of cinematographic film when it is passed through a projector. Professor Roger Penrose confirmed this meaning when writing *The Emperor's New Mind* in 1990.

> The thing to bear in mind about a spacetime diagram is that each point in the picture represents an *event* – that is, a point in space at a single moment, a point having only an *instantaneous* existence. The entire diagram represents the whole of history, past, present, and future. (p. 250).

Sir James Jeans reached the same conclusion in *The Mysterious Universe* (1930, pp. 138–39.)

> Just as a cable is formed of a great number of fine threads, so the world-lines of a large body like the sun is formed of innumerable smaller world-lines, the world-lines of the separate atoms of which the sun is composed. [...] The world-lines of the earth is a smaller cable, made up of several strands, these representing the mountains, trees, aeroplanes, human bodies, and so on, the aggregate of which makes up the earth. Each strand is made up of many threads—the world-lines of the atoms.

Einstein was able to put this conclusion into a succinct sentence when comforting the grieving widow of Michael Besso, his recently deceased friend and colleague from the patent office where they had once worked together.

> For us faithful physicists, the separation between past, present and future has only the meaning of an illusion, though a persistent one. Time is not all what it seems. It does not flow in one direction, and the future exists simultaneously with the past.   (L. Dossey: *Healing Words*, 2009)

Scientists are by no means happy with the implications of relativity theory, as Professor Russell Stannard remarked in *Relativity: A Very Short Introduction* (2008, p.30).

> One of the disconcerting features about four-dimensional spacetime is that nothing changes. Changes occur in time. But spacetime is not in time; time is in spacetime. [...] It appears to be saying that all of time – past present and future – exists on an equal footing. In other words, events that we customarily think of as no longer existing because they lie in the past, do exist in spacetime. In the same way, future events which we normally think of as not yet existing do exist in spacetime.

As we see from this passage, by attempting to create a counterfeit model of the universe, scientists have discovered a problem that stabs right at the heart of what they wish to achieve—'nothing changes'. If nothing changes in spacetime, then 'cause and effect' are defunct notions. Recall Einstein's commiseration with the widow of Michael Besso—past and future coexist. This contradicts 'cause and effect', since a cause must precede its effect in real time: that is, if it is to be considered genuine. Space-time does not permit this. Thus, by conferring a redundancy notice upon 'cause and effect' all scientific theories lose their efficacy. This especially affects the attempt being made to compile a set of theories that counterfeit the world perceived by the senses, and then explain it in terms of space, time and matter. Instead of a dynamic universe, bursting with activity, one of the most fundamental theories in physics has provided science with what is called a *block universe:* a universe that is timeless and immutable—the very same two qualities that theologians apply to the Mind of God.

Understandably, materialists want no part of this concept of relativity, and are desperate to reinvent time by reintroducing it into the universe. Despite this wish, a devastating setback was dealt in 1967, when the block universe received further confirmation by American theorist, Bryce DeWitt and fellow theorist John Wheeler. Together they produced '*The Equation That Killed Time*'— so-called, because t = time is absent in the equation intended to explain the universe.

$$\frac{\partial^2 \Psi}{\partial a^2} - \frac{6}{ka}\frac{\partial^2 \Psi}{\partial \Phi^2} - \frac{144\pi^4}{k^2}\left(a^2 - \frac{k}{3}a^4 V(\Phi)\right)\Psi = 0$$

[Psi = wave function; a = cosmic scale-factor; k = quantity linked to the Planck scale; phi = scalar field; V = scalar potential]

As Professor Lee Smolin remarked, albeit acidly (*Time Reborn*), "According to the Wheeler DeWitt equation, the quantum state of the Universe is just frozen. [...] The quantum Universe is a Universe without change. It just simply is." In which case, as previously maintained, cause and effect become redundant as a valid explanation. From whence it follows that the brain can no longer be considered the *cause* of consciousness. Instead, consciousness must be part of this static universe.

The block universe was also considered by Professor Gerald Whitrow, former President of the International Society for the Study of Time, with tenure at Imperial College, London.

> In a block universe [...] past, present and future do not apply to physical events, and so they neither come into existence nor cease to exist – they just are. But whatever kind of universe we

inhabit; mental events certainly come to be and cease to be in our personal experience. Therefore, if we inhabited a block universe, mental events would have a completely different kind of experience from physical events. This would have the most peculiar consequences for cause and effect. In purely physical causation, an effect would not actually be produced by its cause, it would merely be further on in time.   (Gerald J. Whitrow, *The Nature of Time*: p. 143)

Compare this passage with that of mathematician, physicist and theologian, Reverend Dr. John C. Polkinghorne.

Classical theology, in the great tradition that stretches from Augustine and Boethius (fourth to sixth centuries), through Thomas Aquinas in the later Middle Ages and on through Reformers like John Calvin to the present day, pictured God as existing in eternity, wholly outside time and looking down on the whole history of creation, laid out before the divine eye 'all at once' so to speak. According to classical theology, God does not have foreknowledge of the future, for all events are equally contemporaneous to the atemporal gaze of divinity. In other words, for the classical theologians, God knows creation exactly as the block-universe theorists describe it. Since theologically it is clear that God must know creation in true accordance with its actual nature, this would seem to imply a theological endorsement of the fundamental correctness of the block universe point of view! This claim is one that is seldom actually made in the theological literature, but it seems an unavoidable implication of classical theology.

(*On Space and Time:* p. 282)

Perception, Consciousness and Spacetime

In so far as what has gone before, a rather negative view has been reported, although more so to the materialists than to the religious. It would seem that despite the efforts of those most gifted in the sciences, their intelligence has failed to proceed very far with a rational counterfeit universe. The efforts made in that direction have succeeded only by circumventing logical obstacles instead of removing them—if, indeed, this were actually possible, which may be doubted. A further obstacle that has since been encountered is that of finding an explanation for consciousness. The following passage by Professor Stannard will help explain why this has become important.

We are presented with a world where it is not only true that all of space exists at each point in time, but also all of time exists at each point in space. [...] Where does the perceived special nature of the moment 'now' come from, and where do we get that dynamical sense of the flow of time? This is a big unsolved mystery, and might remain that way for all time. It does not seem to come out of the physics – certainly not from the block universe idea – but rather from our *conscious perception* of the physical world. For some unknown reason, consciousness seems to act like a searchlight scanning progressively along the time axis, momentarily singling out an instant of physical time as being that special moment we label 'now' – before the beam moves on to pick out the next instant to be so labelled.   (*Relativity - A Very short Introduction*, pp. 30, 32)

We may discern from this passage that when our conscious awareness interacts with a point in space-time, we experience it as the moment 'now', even though past and future states of the world coexist on either side. In which case, this would then mean that every point in a block universe contains sense data that is capable of being relayed to a conscious mind as a 'now moment': albeit, solely within the experience of a percipient.

Recall, therefore, the words of Sir James Jeans and Sir Roger Penrose, both of whom referred to the history of events and atoms in space-time as consisting of world-lines. It then becomes a simple matter to accept their explanation, but also to refine it by insisting that these world-lines contain *only* data for events, rather than the actual events themselves. This allows the conclusion that when a conscious mind receives this data from a world-line, it becomes a 'perceived' event.

Stephen Hawking, for his own purpose, maintained, "These mental concepts are the only reality we can know." In which case, it presents no difficulty to conclude that the data for these mental concepts – which form 'the only reality we can know' – are relayed to mankind's conscious awareness from world-lines existing in a block universe, and *not* from the imperceptible world of space, time and matter that scientists believe exists, but can never indubitably prove. As Hawking reminded his readers, "There is no model-independent test of reality." Thus, where there is no visual *out-look* onto an external world, everything outside the mind is forever unknowable.

What does this mean for people? It means that the world continues to be experienced exactly as it always has, with everything perceived by the senses appearing as normal. Essentially, nothing whatever has changed, except understanding. For it is now no longer necessary to accept that sense data can only originate from an *out-of-sight* parallel world of matter lacking colour, light, sound, heat, taste, smell and tactility:—these being mental qualities. Instead, it is conceptually possible that this same data originates from world-lines existing in space-time.

———————❧———————

When scientists discovered the existence of space-time, with its coeval events frozen on world-lines that existed timelessly; that is, where past and future were immutably united—were they not, in fact, discovering the Creation of the universe present in the Mind of God? Not so, if they were following an atheistic, agenda of total materialism; it would impel in them a need to assign these divine qualities—timelessness, immutability, and creativity of events, down to the smallest particle—to world-lines, existing in space-time. Yet, the comparison appears strikingly obvious, as are the efforts to explain it away by using secular terminology.

> However, your world line strictly speaking isn't a line: it has non-zero thickness and is not straight. Let's first consider the roughly 10^{29} elementary particles (quarks and electrons) that your body is made of. Together, they form a tube like shape through spacetime, analogous to the spiral shape of the Moon's orbit but more complicated, reflecting the fact that your motion from birth to death is more complicated than the Moon's. For example, if you're swimming laps in a pool, that part of your spacetime tube has a zigzag shape, and if you're using a playground swing, that part of your spacetime has a serpentine shape.

(Max Tegmark, *Our Mathematical Universe*, 2014, p.282)

The Mind of God, which now appears to be counterfeited by spacetime, will also have world-lines. But these contain sense data that when consciously perceived become the consensual world of familiar objects identified by the five senses. It is therefore an *insightful* world, constructed from mental concepts, for which there is no external reality beyond God and the minds of others. Professor Tegmark's explanation is drawn from his *belief* that he can construct a mathematical model of an external reality from these same passive, mental, constructs that furnish his conscious awareness. The problem with this is that he is restricted to testing his results upon the models he used to construct his equations. This limits him to defining the world of his perception, using mathematics, to the only world he knows. It does not prove his counterfeit world actually exists. Instead, it describes the world of mental constructs mathematically. And since there is no intrinsic difference between mental constructs, whether composed from data conveyed by God or from a parallel world of matter, a theoretical model of the latter does not disprove the former.

There are also other reasons for doubting the validity of a wholly mathematical theory of the universe. The gatekeeper for much of what is intended by this approach, rests upon the value of $\sqrt{-1}$, an invaluable asset to quantum theory, but which has no counterpart, value, or existence in the physical world. It is there just to open the gate to a specious set of equations that appear to be attributable to reality, but only by neglecting the fact that the square root of minus one has no actual, *physical* counterpart in this reality. The square root of minus one is an *imaginary number*. What, therefore, can one expect from imaginary numbers but imaginary results? There is also the fact that mathematics, when stripped of its operational symbols (+, x, − , ÷, √)—all of which require mental activity—becomes meaningless.

A further negation of the scientific conclusion regarding the origin of sense data is borne out by a recent discovery. It is one that enables a comparison to be drawn between sense data that is consciously interpreted as the familiar world of sense, when obtained directly from a world–line, and sense data arriving from a physical world existing imperceptibly and externally to the mind.

Based firmly upon scientific principles, Benjamin Libet (1916 – 2007), a research physiologist at the University of California, devised an experiment to determine the brain's response to stimuli. He and his team discovered that a mild electric impulse to the back of the hand, when lasting less than half a second (500 milliseconds) produced no conscious awareness in the subject. It was only when the stimulus lasted longer than a half second that the subject became consciously aware of its presence.

> What is surprising is that the subject's conscious awareness of the stimulus began not after 500 milliseconds but when the stimulus started. In other words, it took half a second for the stimulus to be experienced subjectively, but this subjective experience moved backwards to when the stimulus was first applied.
> (Rupert Sheldrake, *The Science Delusion*. p.123)

Sheldrake was quoting from an article in *Brain* (1979), written by B. Libet, W. Elwood, B. Feinstein, and D.K. Pearl, 'Subjective Referral of The Timing For A Conscious Sensory Experience' p. 202):

> There is an automatic subjective referral of the conscious experience backwards in time [...] The sensory experience would be "antedated" from the actual delayed time at which the neuronal state becomes adequate to elicit it; and the experience would appear subjectively to occur with no significant delay.

Consider this result from what has been stated above with regard to world-lines. A stimulus is applied to subjects who have ...

> consented to having electrodes placed in part of the brain concerned with receiving sensory signals from certain parts of the skin. In conjunction with this direct stimulation, there would be occasions when the corresponding point on the skin would be stimulated. The general conclusion of these experiments was that it would take something like half a second of neural activity (but with some variation, depending on circumstances) before the subjects could become consciously aware of any sensations at all, yet in the case of the direct skin stimulation, they would have the impression that they had already been aware of the stimulus at the earlier time when the skin was actually stimulated.
> (Roger Penrose, *Shadows of the Mind*, p.386)

The data experienced by these subjects existed on their personal world-line, which enabled their minds to perceive the stimulus when it was applied. Whereas, in conjunction with the application of the stimulus, the experimenter's personal insightfulness of the mental constructs existing in his/her mind perceived the brains of these subjects from data on their world-line half a second later. This would not be inappropriate for a mind and brain that were separate but also conjoined. The subject perceives the stimulus as normal: whereas, the experimenter perceives the correlated effect in the subject's brain a fraction of a second later.

The separation between brain and conscious awareness has, in recent times, received public attention from an increasing number of near-identical experiences related by those who have 'died', and after being resuscitated, have reported how their conscious awareness vacated their body and was able to continue perceiving the world without any sensory input to the brain, which, in its deceased state, had already shut down. Even those born blind have reported the experience of vision while 'floating' out of their body after their apparent, or closeness to death.

In, *The Truth in the Light – An Investigation of over 300 Near-Death Experiences*, Dr Peter Fenwick MB B.Chir (Cantab) DPM FRCP Psych and his wife, Elizabeth MA (Cantab), wrote:

> The near-death experience (NDE) is intriguing for two major reasons. First, it is very common and secondly, it is cross-cultural. The results of one NOP survey in America suggest that over 1 million Americans have 'seen the light'. Any experience that is so common must have had some influence on the way we think about life and death. Indeed, it could be the very engine that drives our ideas of an afterlife.
> (Fenwick & Fenwick, 1995: p.1)

Needless to say, these accounts totally contradict the materialistic teaching that dominates the acquisition of knowledge in western society. In the main, scientists either ignore these reports, or take shelter from them by passing them off as the effect of a 'dying' brain. At the same time, they carefully 'forget' to include any mention of conscious lucidity and long-term memory: both of which play an important part in these experiences.

The capacity to hold on to habitual beliefs when confronted by opposing evidence is a common feature of the human condition, and scientists are by no means exempt from this condition.

Consider the NDE of Hal, an Australian schoolboy. During a break period in the school playground, he suffered a series of heart attacks. After recovering, he related the following account to Dr Cherie Sutherland.

> "I was out of the body, and I thought to myself 'I must be dead'. So I went up to Miss Smith [one of his teachers] and told her not to bother, I was dead. She took no notice of me. I made a few more attempts to speak to her and to Miss Brown then gave up."

Hal then added this further detail to his explanation.

> "I went to take her arm and my hand went right through her. [...] I went to open a door but my hand went through the handle. I then tried the bricks [brick wall] beside the door, pushed with my hand, and then went straight through the bricks to the outside. I remember going through the bricks two or three times just to try it out."   (*Transformed by the Light*, 1992: p.6)

In common with many similar reports, Hal could see, think, and move about in the world that was familiar to him before he collapsed. But he had lost the sense of touch. The world of matter was no longer tangible. He could walk through walls, which he did several times, just for the sheer novelty of the experience.

The NDE would be a natural consequence of God's Creation; with each conscious mind being attached to a world-line containing the data that enabled it to form visually, but not tangibly, the world perceived by this one sense. From this, it follows that when a person dies, their conscious awareness will first detach from the body it occupied, but without severing the connexion.

By detaching from the body (which may well be 'brain-dead'), the mind is still able to perceive the environment in which it newly exists, although from a different vantage point. This indicates that sensory brain activity, involving the cerebral computation of frequency vibrating impulses, is distinct from the perceptions to which they are coordinated. And this, of course, is confirmed by the half second interval between the subject's awareness and the effect of sensory stimuli to the brain, as discovered by Benjamin Libet (see above).

We may also recall that neurologist, Professor Ramachandran, considered the connexion between perception of the world and the wave lengths that convey this information to be "the central mystery of the cosmos." It will continue to remain so, as long as NDEs are ignored, and brain activity is believed to be the cause of consciousness. A thought also echoed by Eban Alexander, MD, a neurosurgeon who experienced his NDE when infected by "a very rare strain of bacterial meningitis". He was therefore able to analyse his experience first-hand. (*The Map of Heaven*, pp. 83-4)

> To those still seduced by the simplistic notion that "the brain creates consciousness"—those who might recoil when I mention that destruction of my neocortex greatly heightened my awareness—I would remind you of two commonly witnessed clinical phenomena that defy the simplistic brain-creates-mind model: 1) *terminal lucidity* (in which demented elderly patients close to death often have astonishing oases of cognition, memory, insight, and reflection as they approach death, often at periods when they are fully aware of departed souls there to escort them to the spiritual realm); and 2) the *acquired savant syndromes* (in which some form of brain damage—such as that seen in autism, head injury, or stroke—allows for some superhuman mental capability such as advanced calculation abilities, intuition, musical abilities, or perfect memory of numbers, names, dates, or visual scenery). There is no explanation within our simplistic neuroscientific ideas of the brain to explain such extraordinary and counterintuitive observations.

The importance of conscious awareness was also emphasised by physicist, Sir Roger Penrose.

> A scientific world-view which does not profoundly come to terms with the problem of conscious minds can have no pretensions of completeness. Consciousness is part of our universe, so any physical theory which makes no proper place for it falls fundamentally short of providing a genuine description of the world.   (*Shadows of the Mind*, p.8)

The conscious mind and the existence of the soul had long ago received attention from another mathematician: one who lived in the 17th century. René Descartes (1596–1650) gave what he considered to be an indubitable reason for the soul's existence. When seeking for something that was impossible to doubt, he realized that it was not possible to doubt at a time when he actively doubted. In which case, he must also be thinking, for one cannot doubt without thinking of ways to doubt. It was this realization that produced his famous dictum – *Cogito ergo sum* (I think, therefore I am). But what is this 'I' to which he referred? Mind, soul and spirit are usually employed in giving an answer. Biologists reject this response because nothing fitting that description has ever been discovered in the human body, which is why the materialist's reaction is to assign these things to activity of the brain. This is a mistaken response. Descartes' dictum indicates quite logically that brain activity is an *effect* of thinking; its *cause* is "I": the spiritual, conscious mind of a soul that imposes its personality upon the brain. One may determine the same conclusion from research conducted on 1,114 men and women by Sengul Kupell-Holt of Southampton University. Upon delivering her paper to the British Psychological Society in Liverpool in May 2015, she remarked, "Many people simply do not have an age on the inside—they are ageless." The mind *is* ageless because it is not an *object* formed by sense data existing on a world-line. It is, instead, the perceiving agent of that data: therefore, like God, timeless.

The NDE confirms the division between body and mind, especially when those experiencing this phenomenon report that their focal point of observation was removed—and sometimes far removed—from where their inert body was located. Yet, they were still able to think, remember, understand and perceive, despite the separation in distance between their mental awareness and their corporeal body. This reaffirms the soul and mind's independence from the body it occupies.

By ignoring the implications of space-time, although not space-time itself, scientists render themselves prone to error. Brains are perceived. Consequently they cannot be exempted from appearing within the neuroscientist's 'well-constructed model of reality'; for which, 'no model-independent test exists'; (Hawking). As such, the perceived brain is essentially a passive organ: one that is no more capable of activity than any other mental concept.

Although it is unlikely that any neuroscientist would willingly concur with this conclusion, the evidence is both clear and concise. Does the human condition permit visual *out-look* onto a world that exists externally to the brain? The neuroscientist must answer negatively. In which case, without visual *out-look;* the brain perceived is formed by the percipient's sense data. But sense data is passive and inert; it is therefore incapable of any activity. Moreover, sense data is located in space-time, where every instant is frozen in a motionless state. As a matter of fact, according to physicists, time does not flow at all.

> In fact it is *only* the phenomenon of consciousness that requires us to think in terms of a 'flowing' time at all. According to relativity, one has just a 'static' four-dimensional space-time, with no 'flowing' about it. The space-time is just *there* and time 'flows' no more than does space. It is only consciousness that seems to need time to flow, so we should not be surprised if the relationship between consciousness and time is strange in other ways too.
>
> (Roger Penrose, *Shadows of the Mind*, p.384)

Instead, there is synchronization between what is perceived as a subject's brain 'activity' and the objects of sense with which it is associated. Both the objects and the brain's activity are perceived from sense data that becomes translated and witnessed within the mind's *insightfulness*. These are detected from static instants that are rapidly accessed from a world-line in spacetime (*aka* the Mind of God). The swift succession of these instants, when translated by consciousness, becomes the familiar world of sense, which provides an outlook view of apparent motion and activity. Without this succession, there can be no witness of activity, motion, or synchronization.

To the unwary, this observed 'activity' of mental concepts becomes misinterpreted as causal; this is entirely due to the rapid passage of 'data instants' interpreted by consciousness. These are conveyed to the mind in such swift succession, as to inflict upon the understanding the same illusion of motion that occurs in the cinema when watching a 'movie'. Both *time* and observation deceive the observer into believing that what is actually passive is not passive at all, but active.

Scientists become drawn into this delusion, which is beneficial to their authority, and conclude from their own mental activity that thinking occurs just as naturally as the motion perceived in the world around them—since they also believe this exists externally to their conscious awareness. From this they infer that the mind is an *effect* of the brain's activity. It is an error of judgment. The essence of mind is not an *object* of knowledge. A mind is the *subject* of knowledge. A subject cannot be perceived as the object of its own knowledge. It cannot coexist as both subject and object. This is because one is passive and the other is active. It would be as much a contradiction to believe odd was even as to believe that mind and brain are one and the same.

Without visual *out-look*, brains can only ever be perceived *insightfully*; they are therefore perceived from data contained on world-lines; as such, they are quite incapable of activity. Minds are imperceptible. They actively perceive, think and understand, and are incapable of inactivity. Consequently, they are not, nor could they be, included on a world-line of static data. For this reason they remain imperceptible to the five senses.

Time and Data Instants

The Creation, with its tapestry of world-lines existing in a state of timeless duration, is the source of the world perceived by sense. Our conscious awareness receives data from the line to which it is attached. At each point on that line there exists a combination of sense data which, when processed by the mind, becomes perceived as a personalised view of a three-dimensional world in which body, mind and soul dwell. In this scenario, space and time are inseparably united, since it is impossible to move through space without moving through time. Motion and time are united; time and space are united; therefore *space and motion are united*—as occurs on a strip of film.

> All your subjective perceptions exist in spacetime, just as every scene of a movie exists on its DVD. Specifically, spacetime contains a large number of braidlike patterns corresponding to subjective perceptions both at different places, corresponding to different people, and at different times. Let's refer to each such perception as an "observer moment".

(Max Tegmark, *Our Mathematical Universe*, p.285)

At this point, Professor Tegmark is broadly in agreement with the *Idealist* interpretation of the universe and *Homo sapiens* ability to perceive it. But he is also a materialist, and it has brought him a problem. This is because, for him, the mind does not exist, other than as a phenomenon of the brain: and since the brain is now confined to a succession of single, separate scenes (observer moments), as in a movie, then how is one scene connected to the other. For, as one scene 'dies' the adjacent one is 'born', how can one scene 'inherit' the content of its predecessor and yet be just sufficiently different as to maintain the development of what is happening?

Tegmark was seemingly aware of the hole he had dug for himself.

> You know from experience that some of these observer moments feel connected and fused together into a seemingly seamless sequence, corresponding to what you call your life. However, this feeling raises tough questions. *How does the connecting work?* Specifically, is there some sort of rule for which observer moments feel connected, and why does this connected sequence of observer moments subjectively feel like time flowing? (Ibid.)

Once again, the world-lines of an idealist philosophy provide the simplest answer. Neither time nor motion is perceptible unless witnessed relative to a background at rest. The mind, being timeless and therefore at rest, provides the required background for the sense data it receives to become a succession of 'observer moments'. The data, having been created by God, forms a rapid succession of 'observer moments'. These are united together by the mind's comprehension.

Tegmark struggles with his own attempt at providing a materialistic explanation, but ends by having to admit, in his own way, that it requires duplicating the universe.

> Moreover, you too are in the movie, since your reality model includes a model of yourself—that's
> why you're not merely aware but also self aware. This means that when you feel you're looking at
> this book, what's really going on is that your brain's reality model has its model of you looking at
> the model of the book.   (Ibid. p. 289)

This rather bizarre conclusion is the logical outcome of a materialistic *faith*. It has to be a 'faith' because without visual *out-look,* and because the materialist has 'no model-independent test of reality' (Hawking), faith-based conclusions are all that remain.

———————— ❧ ————————

Sense data streamed directly from world-lines in the Mind of God to the minds of men produce the same effect as Max Tegmark's explanation: in which he replaced God with a theoretical, 'external, universe'. This, he conjectured, exists of replicas to the mental concepts (models) formed by an imperceptible brain—and to which he has alluded in the passage quoted above.

Zeno of Elea would not have been impressed by these attempts to explain motion in the universe. He anticipated the problem in a treatise written in the fifth century B.C. Apart from his paradox of the *Dichotomy* (see above), he also argued that at any instant an arrow is either at rest or not at rest: that is, it is moving. If the instant is indivisible, the arrow cannot move, for if it did, the instant would be divisible; thus contradicting its definition of being indivisible. But, since time is composed of a succession of instants (observer instants), and with motion impossible at any one of them, then nothing actually moves.

This, it will be recalled, was also the inference drawn from the Wheeler-DeWitt Equation (p.7), in which time was absent in the universe; and without time, there can be no motion. The same result is also implicit in Einstein's theory of special relativity, in which the coeval nature of past and present at any given instant labelled 'now', leads directly to a block universe: one, wherein events are 'just there', frozen in eternity.

Cause and Effect

The absence of motion in space-time is at one with the absence of change. This presents the physical sciences with an insuperable problem. It means essentially that physical *causes* and their *effects* have no *true* meaning, in so far as investigations into nature are concerned.

To take a simple example, consider the 'litmus test'; that is, the use of litmus paper to indicate the acidity or alkalinity of a solution. Cause and effect would no longer apply to this test—by which, I mean *in truth*—since the entire test consists of data instants perceived as a succession of observer moments ('data instants' are situated on world-lines; 'observer moments' are limited to those that are perceived.) each one of which is inert. Thus, the same can be said for every scientific theory. Henceforth, for those who place truth above expediency, physical causes in the sciences are redundant notions: and although stated for convenience, are inappropriate terms.

Laws of nature are also affected by this, for the same reason. These should be consigned to history: and replaced by *laws of succession*. If event 'B' consistently follows event 'A', then this becomes a 'law of succession', and is no more causal than the letter 'u' that invariably follows the letter 'q', when confined to English grammar: proper nouns and their derivatives excluded.

———————— ❧ ————————

Undoubtedly, there will be strong opposition to any diminution of scientific authority, for it is founded four square upon cause and effect, as determined by the laws of nature. Nevertheless, any attempt at resurrecting the idea that time consists of 'fleeting moments' ends in delusion.

Imagine a universe that exists only for the present moment, so that neither past nor future states physically exist. The universe is therefore destroyed at each instant, only to be replaced by the next, and the next, in a never-ending sequence of destruction and re-creation. But, does anything move during each fleeting instant. If it does, then it is not an instant but a composite instant, wherein motion can be timed; whence, it is not a 'fleeting instant' as was required. On the other hand, if nothing moves during a 'fleeting instant', then nothing is achieved by proposing it.

The physicist may still counter, by asserting that differential calculus measures velocity and acceleration, at any given instant, and since both velocity and acceleration describe motion, this overcomes the difficulty. Quite the contrary, it proves the opposite. Consider the derivative for the function of a particle that appears to move along a quadrilateral curve. It will certainly provide equations for solving the particle's velocity and acceleration at a given instant. But that instant will be a 'data instant' on the particle's world-line. It will therefore be motionless.

Time is therefore continuous in the sense that each world-line consists of 'data instants': in much the same way that a line is continuous yet consists of infinite points. If world-lines consist of infinite 'data instants' then consciousness, being distinct from the limitations of 'data instants' will pass over them, as happens when encountering a line of infinite points. As Russell Stannard remarked (p.8) "For some unknown reason, consciousness seems to act like a searchlight scanning progressively along the time axis, momentarily singling out an instant of physical time as being that special moment we label 'now' – before the beam moves on to pick out the next instant to be so labelled."

The result of this scanning operation is the familiar world of the senses, which circumvents the need for 'matter' to intervene. Although Bishop Berkeley's logical analysis of reality recognized the same conclusion, it was written two centuries before Einstein's special theory of relativity paved the way for it to be reconsidered by physicists.

It then enabled Arthur Eddington (1882 – 1944) to arrive at his conclusion: "the stuff of the world is mind stuff." (K. Wilber, *Quantum Questions*, p.185). And a similar inference was drawn by Sir James Jeans (1877 – 1946). "The universe can be best pictured [...] as consisting of pure thought." (Ibid, p.137). Ernst Mach (1838 – 1916), was another led in the same direction with a remark that later greatly influenced Einstein. "Properly speaking, the world is not composed of 'things' [...] but of colours, tones, pressures, spaces, times, in short what we ordinarily call individual sensations." (D. Skrbina, *Journal of Conscious Studies*, 'Panpsychism as an Underlying Theme in Western Philosophy' p. 27).

Memory (1)

Memory is such a familiar feature to the way of life that it only becomes mentioned when it fails to deliver. But how does it operate? Surprisingly, no one actually knows. The neuroscientist is aware that certain areas of the brain 'light up' when memory occurs, but this is an observation, not an explanation. Neuroscience works by assuming that memories are stored in the brain: as indeed do most people. But cells are replaced at frequent intervals—sometimes in days or weeks. And studies have so far failed to reveal any mechanism for transferring memories from redundant cells to their replacement. Worse still, when different areas of the brain are surgically removed from a subject, and more especially from animals, memories of past habits that have been learned are retained. In short, it has not been possible to locate any one part of the brain where memories are located, nor has it been possible to explain how they survive cell exchange.

> All religions take it for granted that some aspect of a person's memory survives that person's bodily death. [...] In Christianity there are several different theories of survival, but all imply a survival of memory. According to the Roman Catholic doctrine of Purgatory, after death believers enter an ongoing process of development, comparable to dreaming. This process would make no sense unless the person's memories played a part in the process. Some Protestants believe that after death everyone goes to sleep, only to be resurrected just before the Last Judgement. But this theory too requires survival of memory because the Last Judgement would be meaningless if the person being judged had forgotten who he was and what he had done.
>
> (Rupert Sheldrake, *The Science Delusion*, p. 210)

It seems evident from this, and from the failure of neuroscience to establish the location of memory as part of the brain's function, that world-lines are best prepared to provide the answer. Let it therefore be brought to mind that the entire store of every person's life is contained on his or her world-line of sense data. In which case, what need is there to store it inside the brain? Each act of memory would then involve drawing upon the data contained on that world-line.

While people in general have different levels of ability when recalling memories, there are some, like Jill Price whose ability is extraordinary. Jill underwent an extended series of observations and experiments carried out at the University of California in Irvine, and by Harvard University, because she 'suffers' from hyperthymestic syndrome, (meaning remembering more than normal).

> Jill Price never misplaces her keys. Never forgets where she parked her car. She never mislays her mobile phone, loses the TV remote control or misses a friend's birthday. She remembers every TV show she has ever watched and recalls in intricate detail events dating back to her childhood. The 42-year-old school administrator has been the secret subject of an eight-year investigation by scientists trying to unravel her rare blessing: having a near-perfect memory of every event in every day of her life.   (Peter Sheridan, *Daily Express*, 12 May 2008 p. 31)

Research into her condition began in 2000, but it failed to throw any meaningful light on the elusive area of brain where her memories lay hidden. Scientists "found that her brain recalls memories in different ways from most of us but not why. Brain scans revealed no obvious cause although there are some unusual structural qualities and her brain 'appears larger than normal', reported Professor Jim Mc Gaugh of Irvine. (Ibid)

Jill describes her experience in the following way.

> In my job I see a lot of birth dates, so whenever I do, such as April 11, 1995, I will automatically 'see' the day in my head, as if someone put a tape in a VCR. The day just plays in my head. I know that day was a Tuesday and what I was doing. This happens a million times a day, even while I am functioning in the present.   (Ibid)

It would appear that Jill Price is replaying the data contained on her world-line. This data is not only static, passive and inert; it is also timeless and therefore indestructible. Access to this data would account for her hyperthymestic syndrome far better than any alternative so far suggested. In which case, is there further evidence to support this conclusion? There is, and it is found in Dr Jeffrey Long's book, advertised as the "largest NDE study ever conducted." In chapter 7 he recorded a selection of experiences by those who responded to resuscitation after 'dying'; each of which, includes the same detailed memory as that displayed by Jill Price.

> "I then began to see my whole life unfolding before me like a film projected on a screen, from babyhood to adult life. It was so real! I was looking at myself, but better than a 3-D movie as I was also capable of sensing the feelings of the persons I had interacted with through the years. I could feel the good and bad emotions I made them go through."

> "I saw everything from birth till then in fast motion. Also, while this was happening I could feel the feelings of these events. I could also feel any pain I gave out to others. I also felt the goodness I'd given out."

> "While in the light I had a life review and saw everything I [...] ever did in my life; every thought, word, deed, action, inaction was shown to me."

> "The review was very fast, but I seemed to comprehend everything easily despite the speed."

> "At that moment, I'm not sure exactly when, someone or something began giving me an examination of conscience, and in the blink of an eye images from my life began passing before me, beginning with my childhood."

> "Everything I ever thought, did, said, hated, helped, did not help, should have helped was shown in front of me, the crowd of hundreds, and everyone like [in] a movie. How mean I'd been to people, how I could have helped them, how mean I was (unintentionally also) to animals! Yes! Even the animals had had feelings. It was horrible."

> "All of a sudden in my mind from left to right like an IMAX movie, I saw all the very important moments of my life up to the present time. Most of the earlier moments in my life [...] I had long forgotten about until this happened."

> "I saw my childhood and felt the emotions my actions created in others."

"Everything in my life, including long-forgotten details, made sense."

"The being of light knew everything about me. It knew all I had ever thought, said, or done, and it showed me my whole life in a flash of an instant. I was shown all of the details in my life, the one I'd already lived, and all that was to come if I returned to earth. It was all there at the same time, all the details of all the cause-and-effect relations in my life, all that was good or negative, all of the effects my life on earth had had on others, and all of the effects the lives of others that had touched me had had on me."

(Jeffrey Long M.D. with Paul Perry, *Evidence of the Afterlife*, pp. 111 – 116)

These reports defy a materialist explanation, and make redundant the neuroscientists' search for a repository of memories held within the brain. However, they are all in perfect accord with the sensible data that exists on each person's world-line. In particular, the experience reported in the final passage above, in which the subject was given information that extended into the future; this could only be accessed from a world-line that extended into the subject's future.

The Mind of God being timeless and the counterfeit model of the universe having arrived at the timelessness of space-time, when seen together, have conveniently established both a religious and a scientific basis for world-lines that are coeval. The reader is therefore asked to keep this in mind when reading the ten chapters that follow. These provide veridical evidence that world-lines contain the appropriate sense data for the mind's conscious formation of future events.

Memory (2)

For a theory to be accepted in science, it usually requires not only evidence that support its claim, but also a prediction that is unique to it. Consequently, if we accept that world-lines act as both the origin of sensory experiences and a repository for memories of those experiences, then we must concede that each line is composed of strands that relate to different bodily parts. It will therefore be true to say that when an organ transplant occurs; a strand from the world-line of the donor will become joined to the world-line of the recipient. Whereafter, this may present serious and dramatic repercussions.

Consider this true case in which an organ donor committed suicide, and left his wife a widow. The heart of her husband was then donated to another man. The recipient of the heart then married the donor's widow, and subsequently committed suicide: just as the heart donor had done twelve years before. (Reported in the UK: *Daily Mail*, 8 April, 2008).

Could this be just one unhappy coincidence? Aided by William Novak, Claire Sylvia wrote of her own extraordinary experience, in *"A Change of Heart"* (1997). In her book, she related how she had been given the heart and lungs of a young man who had been killed in a motor cycle accident. Upon recovering from her operation, the first thing that came to mind, when asked for anything that she wanted, was to say, "Actually. I'm dying for a beer right now." As she confessed afterwards—before her operation, she disliked beer. But this was only the beginning of her change in taste. After leaving hospital and being able to "eat like a normal person, I found, bizarrely, I'd developed a sudden fondness for certain foods I hadn't liked before: Snickers bars, green peppers, Kentucky Fried Chicken takeaway." Her daughter even said she walked like a man: "lumbering—like a muscle-bound football player."

Matters began to come to a head "when she had the most unforgettable dream of my life." She dreamt of a young man, with whom she was on extremely friendly terms, whose name was Tim L. She thought the surname could be Leighton, but upon waking, was unsure. Convinced that this was her donor, she first attempted to discover his identity from the hospital. When this information was refused, she and a friend travelled to Boston to begin searching the newspapers for a young man killed in a motor cycle accident, prior to her transplant. The search revealed a young man named Tim Lamirande, who fitted the description. Convinced that this was her donor, she contacted his family, from whom she learned that he was a beer drinker and "yes, Tim had loved green peppers—'but what he really loved were chicken nuggets'. This explained my trips to Kentucky Fried Chicken. I was dumfounded," she said. (Ibid. 9 April 2008).

These cases are far from being isolated examples of behavioural changes and altered preferences that take place after receiving a major donated organ from a deceased person. Conversely, there appear to be no reports of similar, dramatic changes to a recipient's behaviour that have nothing in common with the donor. It is always the donor's character that is noticeably identified in the behavioural and mood changes that occur in the recipient.

Paul Pearsall, PhD (1942 – 2007) was a clinical neuropsychologist, and clinical professor at the University of Hawaii, and a member of the heart transplant study team at the University Of Arizona School Of Medicine. In his book, *The Heart's Code*, he reported the result of his research into the function of the heart as the seat of cellular memories. These included the role of the heart in forming a connexion between mind, body and spirit. What appear most intriguing are the case studies that repeatedly identify the donor's character by a personality change in the recipient.

Forty-one-year-old male heart patient (received heart of nineteen-year-old girl killed when her car was struck by a train).

Wife of recipient: – "He's a kid again. He used to struggle to breathe and had no stamina at all, but now he's like a teenager. [...] He is sure that his donor was driving a big truck that hit a bigger truck."

Thirty-six-year-old female heart-lung transplant recipient (received the heart and lungs of a twenty-year-old girl who was killed while running across the street to show her fiancé a picture of her new wedding dress).

(Recipient): – "Almost every night, I had this dream about her. I knew she was young and pretty and very happy. I've always been sort of somewhat down type of person yet, somehow, I have this new happiness in me I never experienced before. [...] The medication makes me feel angry and depressed sometimes, but inside I feel this strange kind of happiness, excitement, and joy that I cannot fully explain or put in words. I just want to go around telling everybody about it, but I'm afraid they'll think I've totally lost it."

Thirty-five year old female heart transplant recipient (donor a twenty-four-year-old prostitute killed in a stabbing).

Husband of recipient: – "Not that I'm complaining, mind you, but what I have now is a sex kitten. It's not that we do it more, but she wants to talk about sex more and wants to see sexually explicit tapes which I could never talk her into before. When we do have sex, it is different. Not worse or better, just different. She never talked much during sex, but now she practically narrates the whole thing. She uses words I never heard her use before, but it turns me on, so who's complaining? [...] well before she knew who her donor was. I was joking and at a passionate moment said that she must have gotten the heart of a whore. We didn't talk for weeks."

Fifty-two-year-old male heart transplant recipient (donor a seventeen-year-old boy killed by a hit-and-run driver).

(Recipient): – "I loved quiet classical music before my new heart. Now, I put on earphones, crank up the stereo, and play loud rock and roll music. I love my wife, but I keep fantasizing about teenage girls. My daughter says I have regressed since my new heart and that I act like a sixteen-year-old."

Daughter of recipient: "It is really embarrassing sometimes. When my friends come over they ask if my dad is going through his second childhood. He's addicted to loud music and my mom says the little boy in him is finally coming out."

Forty-seven-year-old female heart transplant recipient (donor a twenty-three-year-old gay man shot to death in a robbery and died from severe wound to lower back.

Husband of recipient: – "I was surprised when one of the first things "X" asked me when we started having sex again after her surgery was whether or not I ever had gay fantasies. She has completely changed how she dresses now. She wears very feminine and revealing clothes where before she wore unisex clothes. Sometimes during the night she will awake suddenly and scream. I used to think she was having a heart attack, but she would point to her back and say it was like a shooting pain right in the middle of her back." (Paul Pearsall, *The Heart's Code*, pp. 88 – 90)

Before commenting upon the above cases, the reaction of those involved in performing organ transplants is noteworthy. Pearsall writes, "Psychiatrist Pietro Castelnuovo-Tedesco interviewed many of the world's leading heart transplant surgeons." (Cardiac Surgeons Look at Transplantation—Interviews with Drs. Cleveland, Cooley, DeBakey, Hallman, and Rochelle, *Seminars in Psychiatry* Vol, 3 (1971): pp. 5 – 16)," To which he added the following comments.

> In addition to seventy-three heart and heart-lung transplant recipients and sixty-seven other transplant recipients I interviewed for this book, I also interviewed three transplant surgeons, all of whom asked to remain anonymous stating, "*I don't want my colleagues to think I'm nuts,*" and "*I'm afraid I would frighten my patients.*" I have also interviewed six nurses who assist in heart transplantation, and all but two asked to be anonymous, primarily because they felt the doctors with whom they worked would be uncomfortable.   (Ibid. p.91)

The interviews conducted by Dr. Castelnuovo-Tedesco with the five doctors named above showed a similar quiescence with regard to comments concerning the adoption of the donor's characteristics. For example, Dr DeBakey maintained, "The heart is a pump, a magnificent pump, but just a pump." He also "felt it inappropriate and fallacious to try to erect a special mystique about heart transplantation." To this, he also added, "physicians have different personal interests and concerns than other people [...] talk about the significance of the heart may "*appeal to the lay and press*" but is not something physicians should concern themselves with." (Ibid. p.93).

The Religious Aspect of Memory

As we have seen, all religions include survival of the soul in some form. Catholic Christians define the soul as "the subject of human consciousness [...] individual and immortal [...] The soul does not die with the body, from which it is separated by death." (Catechism of the Catholic Church). The soul is therefore by contrast *spirit*: antithetic to what is understood by *matter*.

Since the soul possesses ability for conscious thought, it must be supposed to possess memory; it therefore coincides with the repository for memory being a world-line in the Mind of God.

Organ transplantation would then be expected to create a branch line formed by a strand from the donor's world-line, which connects to the world-line of the recipient. It is therefore not an impossible concept that the recipient of a transplanted organ may, by way of consciousness (or sub-consciousness), access the memory store of the organ donor. This could occur via the branch line connecting the two world-lines of donor and recipient. It would then explain the pressing belief among some organ recipients that they have *intimations* of who their donor was.

However, according to the religious aspect of memory, which is non-material, there is another possibility. The disembodied spirit of the donor may be in a position to use the fact that their heart, or other organ, is still alive inside another body. If that were to be the case, there would be a temptation, particularly by souls that were cut off from life at an early age, to 'possess' the body of the recipient, by re-establishing the connexion they once had with their donated organ.

If they could establish that possession, it would conceivably allow them to enjoy a revival of their previous, pleasurable, emotions, which they recalled when being alive in the world. This, of course, would entail memory of such pleasures on their part. But the branch line between donor and recipient provides access between their store of memories, and the recipient of their organ.

———————— ✌✧ ————————

Materialists will unquestionably denounce this explanation, because of its religious association. They will plead for public patience and more funding, so that they can continue to search for what has already been found, but which they cannot accept. As for those with a Christian interest in the religious explanation, they will find assurance that disembodied spirits do, indeed, roam the earth.

> "When evening came, many who were demon-possessed were brought to him, and he drove out the spirits with a word and healed all the sick." (Matthew, 8:16). "Jesus called his twelve disciples to him and gave them authority to drive out impure spirits and to heal every disease and sickness." (Ibid, 10: 1). "When an impure spirit comes out of a person, it goes through arid places

seeking rest and does not find it. Then it says, 'I will return to the house I left.' When it arrives, it finds the house unoccupied, swept clean and put in order. Then it goes and takes with it seven other spirits more wicked than itself, and they go in and live there." (Ibid. 12: 43 – 45).

"Whenever the impure spirits saw him, they fell down before him and cried out, "You are the Son of God." (Mark, 3: 11). "He gave them permission, and the impure spirits came out and went into the pigs. The herd, about two thousand in number, rushed down the steep bank into the lake and were drowned." (Ibid. 5:13). "All the people were amazed and said to each other, 'What words these are! With authority and power he gives orders to impure spirits and they come out!'" (Luke, 4: 36). "The twelve were with him, and also some women who had been cured of evil spirits and diseases: Mary (called Magdalene) from whom seven demons had come out."   (Ibid. 8: 1– 2)

———————— ৵৽ ————————

In the present age, the Christian religious can be forgiven the conjecture that evil spirits are still roaming the earth. How many, it may be wondered, suffer from multiple personality disorder, when possession is the true cause? Materialists detest the implied suggestion that possession may be involved and have renamed the affection 'dissociative identity disorder' (DID). Re-labelling a jar does not change its content, and the language of medics still refers to *alter egos, or alters*. The materialists' explanation believes the cause to be a 'coping mechanism' that enables the affected person to dissociate from their conscious self.

> One fascinating aspect of DID is the fact that the distinct alters often exhibit markedly different symptoms or physiological features. [...] For example, some of these studies have shown that one alter [a host personality among several other host personalities] can experience anaesthesia or pain relief, but the others cannot. There have been reports of one alter being deaf or suffering from auditory hallucinations, while the others hear normally. Changes in handedness or handwriting have also been reported across alters.
> Additionally, alter egos can respond differently to medications. For instance, a woman who had diabetes needed different amounts of insulin depending on which alter was in charge.

Understandably, "Researchers are still puzzled by this tantalizing phenomenon. The bodily alterations associated with switches support the view that changes in mental states and events are accompanied by modifications in physiological activity. In other words, *change the mind and you change the brain and the body.*" (Mario Beauregard, *Brain Wars*, pp.104 – 106).

This was very much in evidence for one woman suffering DID. In her case, an alter emerged as a heroin addict, while the other alters were not addicts. The effect this had upon the woman was that she "exhibited needle track marks when she switched to that alter." (Ibid. p.105; see also E.W. Kelly, *"Psychophysiological Influence.* in 'Irreducible Mind Toward a Psychology for the Twenty-First Century' pp.117-239).

Perception, Mind and Body

> A debate about the nature of vision was going on in ancient Greece 2,500 years ago. It was taken up in the Roman Empire and in the Islamic world, and continued in Europe throughout the Middle Ages and the Renaissance. The debate played an important part in the birth of modern science, and is still alive today.   (Rupert Sheldrake, *The Science Delusion*, p. 214).

The naïve realist is a person who looks out upon the world during any single day and sees it as existing before their eyes. Placed in a city street, s\he will readily confirm that what they see are solid buildings of brick and concrete, mechanised vehicles noisily travelling along the road, and pedestrians attending to their everyday business. To perceive the world as such is simply to stare out at it, and view what is seen as the only reality that exists. It is also the world of government.

If that were only the case, then to stare at a mirror and see it for what it 'is' would reveal no more than a sheet of glass with one side coated. Reflections in the mirror require light waves. So, what if light waves are needed—what difference does that make? The difference it makes begins with a camera, which also requires light waves. By taking a photograph of the night sky, the camera is displaying a pattern of stars for which the light arriving at the apparatus has taken years – often many thousands of years – to arrive. It has also taken the same time to reach the lens in your eyes. This means you see the same pattern of stars as recorded by the camera. You cannot therefore be seeing the actual stars that shed that light. After so much time having passed, these heavenly bodies will either have moved position or ceased to shed light altogether.

But, perhaps you protest that the same cannot be said for what is immediately seen in the city street. In which case, take a good look at what is before you. A bus, perhaps, that is just moving away to your left. Now, imagine donning a pair of spectacles that have been manufactured with prisms designed to divert the passage of light passing through them. To your amazement (for so it may be assumed), the bus you saw moving away to your left is now moving away to your right. The entire scene, which you believed contained the very essence of a material world, has suddenly dissolved into the fabric of an illusion. What was seen to your right now appears to your left and *vice versa*.

If you think it is all a trick of the apparatus that could never happen otherwise, then consider once again the city street. It is midday. The sun is shining. It is a warm day; children are playing in the park nearby. All seems right with the world. Alas, unbeknown to you, one minute earlier in the same instant that enabled the Big Bang to occur, the sun exploded, and is no more. You, on the other hand, are unaware of this cosmological disaster and continue to enjoy your stroll along the road. You glance at the sky; the sun is still brightly shining and shedding its warmth—nothing whatever has changed. And that will be the case for the next six or seven minutes, which is the time it takes for the final rays from the sun to arrive before the world goes dark and cold.

Clearly, since the sun ceased to exist during those final minutes, the sun *witnessed* afterwards by those on Earth cannot be made of matter. How could it be otherwise? Yet it was seen as usual, and its warmth continued. What was seen, therefore, were *immaterial* objects of sense existing at different distances: the same effect that occurred in the city street with its traffic, when the scene was viewed through special prisms. And this can also be said for everything you see around you. Visually speaking it is immaterial. It exists because it is perceived to exist. In which case, the tangible qualities associated with it are coordinated impressions from the same world-line. Together with appropriate data from the other senses, the mind, after receiving this data, experiences the result as a visual field containing objects that respond to the number of senses employed in their composition. As such, they appear solid and independent, having been formed from the relevant sense data. Their appearance, as such, is possible because the percipient had no conscious role in their construction. For, although sensible objects cannot exist independently of a percipient, the sense data can, because it has been created by God, wherein it continues to exist.

Let us look again at this from a different perspective. Each object of sense is composed from data existing on the percipient's world-line: which, at varying points along that line, contain data for its several, different, sensible qualities and potential. When these are interpreted by the conscious mind as objects, perceived to exist, complete with their recognizable qualities, and to all appearances with the added property of continuing to sustain themselves independently, whether or not they are perceived, common sense concludes they have an independent existence of their own; and one that has no bearing upon whether or not these qualities are being perceived.

The effect this 'added property' has upon the human understanding is to cause it to rationalize what it witnesses. An inference is therefore concluded that the qualities and potentials witnessed belong to something that John Lock famously declared to be "something, I know not what."

We may surmise what led Locke to this conclusion. He had become wholly aware that what he perceived were particular qualities (ideas) that allowed him to recognize what he was aware of in his surrounding vicinity, and that these were mind-dependent. But he was also aware that these objects were, at the same time, divorced from his mind, because they were self-sustaining; that is to say, they continued to exist independently from his perception of them. In his attempt to rationalise this divorce between mind-dependence and sustained independence, he distinguished between *secondary* qualities that existed mentally and *primary* ones that were the property of objects existing independently of the mind. Berkeley later exposed the weakness of this division by proving that Locke's primary qualities were no different in principle to secondary qualities.

So where did Locke err? His error was to ignore *time*. Like so many scientists and philosophers of eras past and present, he reached his conclusion by believing that *time* is a sequence of fleeting instants that measure duration, having no further bearing upon the questions of existence. This error of omission is apparent in his *Essay Concerning Human Understanding*, in which he admitted: "I confess there is another idea which would be of general use for mankind to have [...] and that is the idea of substance, which we neither have nor can have by sensation or reflection." (Chapter III, 19) To add to this, he deduced, 'there must be substance, since we cannot intelligently suppose mere qualities to exist in their own right, on their own, *sine re substante*.' This was his rationalization of the implication that such qualities must belong to something that he labelled 'matter'. Whereas, instead, the qualities perceived, and their potential to connect with other qualities, are the result of sense data existing on world-lines. These also sustain their existence; and when coordinated into a perceptual composition, appear to our senses as the substantial world of commonsense.

———————— *৶৹* ————————

Science, in its quest for a wholly material world, is seeking to explain the perceived world of mental constructs by referring to 'matter', which it examines as a theoretical substratum to which mental qualities adhere. But to suppose that mental qualities could combine with a non-mental substratum strikes one as ridiculous. The problem is, of course, that scientists have no alternative other than to work with 'matter' which they equate with the sense data belonging to a world-line. The brain, which is the neuroscientist's principal object of research remains, from a visual point of view, immaterial. But, in common with other objects of sense, it is co-ordinated to the tactile sense, and therefore fit for inspection at the hands of the scientist. Even so, lest it be overlooked, the hands of the scientist are—even from his or her own visual point of view—no less immaterial than the brain s/he inspects. All things sensible are so well co-ordinated on their existing world-lines that *mind matter* (collected qualities of *a thing*) is assumed to be 'matter' in the raw: thus allowing scientists to speak about it as such. The fact that the brain is co-ordinated to the perceptions of the percipient has also led scientists to infer it as the *cause* of what is perceived. But in a static universe, where world-lines exist timelessly, *cause* and *effect* coexist.

> After four hundred years of mechanistic science, there has been almost no progress in understanding how the brain produces subjective experiences, although many details have been discovered about the activities of different regions of the brain. The orthodox assumption is that the brain constructs a picture or model of the world *inside itself.* [Author's emphasis]
>
> (Rupert Sheldrake, *The Science Delusion* p.217).

The *Essentials of Neural Science*, Kandel *et al* (1995) p.368, describes the process as follows. "[T]he brain constructs an internal representation of external physical events after first analyzing them into component parts." This is circular reasoning. Since, one would first have to KNOW *where* these external physical events were located. To position them, by implication, in the same place as the models formed by the brain begs the question, because the conclusion is in the premise. The 'explanation' then proceeds to say, "In scanning the visual field the brain simultaneously but separately analyzes the form of objects, their movement, and their colour, all before putting together an image according to the brain's own rules." But 'form', 'motion', and 'colour', even 'brains', are mental concepts, as too, is 'distance', even when referring to the 'visual field'. The authors appear to have no real grasp of the difficulties involved, and have opted for a 'folk-science' approach to the problem, which is hopelessly flawed by ignoring the known restraints imposed by logic.

———————— *৶৹* ————————

Because of these flaws, the orthodox theory of perception, as stated by Kandel *et al*, when taken seriously, leads to the most bizarre conclusion. As Hamlet remarked, "O God, I could be bounded in a nutshell and count myself a king of infinite space." Shakespeare appears to have been alerted to Kepler's research on optics in 1603. (Kepler was the first to recognize images on the retina are inverted and reversed by the eye's lens. This caused him to suggest the image was later corrected "in the hollows of the brain" due to the "activity of the Soul.") This is essentially what is at issue, according to the orthodox theory of perception. If the entire world you perceive surrounding you is 'inside your brain' then your real skull – assuming that your skull is modelled upon a material skull – is somewhere beyond the outer region of space; that is, the space you perceive as presently existing. We may recall that Professor Max Tegmark has already adopted this model: "your reality model includes a model of yourself [...] This means that when you feel you're looking at this book [...] your brain's reality model has its model of you looking at the model of the book." (p.14). He is not alone. Steven Lehar, a Harvard University professor, also advocated that belief.

> I propose that out beyond the farthest things you can perceive in all directions, i.e. above the dome of the sky, and below the solid earth under your feet, or beyond the walls and ceiling of the room you see around you, is located the inner surface of your true physical skull, beyond which is an unimaginable immense external world of which the world you see around you is merely a miniature internal replica. In other words, the head you have come to know as your own is not your true physical head, but only a miniature perceptual copy of your head in a perceptual copy of the world, all of which is contained within your real head. (Steven Lehar, *Gestalt Theory*, 'Gestalt Isomorphism and the Quantification of Spatial Perception' pp. 21 122-39).

Bishop Berkeley's robust rebuttal to Hylas may be repeated against those who adopt this weird if-worldly concept of reality.

> "I am of a vulgar cast, simple enough to believe my senses, and leave things as I find them. To be plain, it is my opinion, that the real things are those very things I see and feel and perceive by my senses. These I know, and finding they answer all the necessities and purposes of life, have no reason to be solicitous about any other unknown beings. A piece of sensible bread, for instance, would stay my stomach better than ten thousand times as much of that insensible, unintelligible real bread you speak of. It is likewise my opinion that colours and other sensible qualities are on the objects. I cannot for my life help thinking that snow is white, and fire is hot. You, indeed, who by snow and fire mean certain external, unperceived, unperceiving substances, are in the right to deny whiteness or heat to be affections inherent in them. But I, who understand by those words the things I see and feel, am obliged to think like other folks. And as I am no sceptic with regard to the nature of things, so neither am I as to their existence. That a thing should be really perceived by my senses, and at the same time not really exist, is to me a plain contradiction; since I cannot prescind or abstract, even in thought, the existence of a sensible thing from its being perceived. Wood, stones, water, flesh, iron, and like things, which I name and discourse of, are things that I know. And I should not have known them, but that I perceived them by my senses; and things perceived by the senses are immediately perceived; and things immediately perceived are ideas and ideas cannot exist without the mind; their existence therefore consists in being perceived; when therefore they are actually perceived, there can be no doubt of their existence." (George Berkeley, *Three Dialogues Between Hylas and Philonous*, 1713, pp. 265-6).

This must surely coincide with the experiences of most people of a rational disposition. Does a mother give birth to her baby, only to be informed by scientists and philosophers that the *real* mother, being of *real* flesh and blood, is beyond the realm of anyone's immediate knowledge, and that her baby is not really *there*, where she sees it, since the infant she perceives is caused by blobs of 'jelly' and a network of electric circuitry in the *real* brain of her *material* body—which, unfortunately, is imperceptible to everyone? In which case, one does wonder how conception ever occurred.

Scientific materialists can only scratch their heads and perhaps shuffle a little their feet: knowing that this is exactly where their belief in a totally materialistic reality has led. For, it is essentially the only *direct* knowledge possible inside a computerised automaton, which happens to be what they model their mind and brain upon.

The root cause of every perception is sense data. The evidence proposed in this book is that this data originates from God, its Creator. It then becomes perceived as the world in which each percipient lives, moves and has their being. Notice therefore how the perception of this world is always from a personal perspective, with its point of focus from the percipient's viewpoint. For that reason alone, whatever is perceived exists for as long as it remains perceived. When it ceases to be perceived, the data continues to be maintained by God, within whom it exists. The sense data therefore exists on what may be called world-lines. They exist with the Creator, and are therefore timeless, having neither past nor future, but are eternally present within His Mind.

It is a system that is similar to a book. When it is read, the words enliven the mind with the ideas of the author. But when it is closed the words remain passive, in wait to be transformed into an active means of conveying the author's thoughts and ideas to the reader.

It is a small step from this towards understanding how the data that is contained on world-lines act in a similar fashion. When the data is activated by consciousness, they open up a world of sensible impressions. At this point on the world-line, the ideas of the Author-Creator are relayed into the percipient's awareness. And lo, the percipient is presented with a temporal setting of the world that is consistent with his/her situation.

A world that has been constructed from mental concepts by the mind, from data it did not create, implies the existence of a far greater and superior mind in which this data originated.

Prayer

There is also an important corollary to this transfer of sensible data. The world-line attached to each mind and soul born into the world is connected to its Creator. It is because of this union with God that mankind has direct access to Him through the medium of prayer. Consequently, prayers are never wasted words, for they are implanted upon each person's world-line, and those world-lines are with God. All prayers are therefore known by the Creator. If they are not there, He has nothing to consider. If they are there, He has taken account of them.

The Tapestry of God

The Creation of the world can be likened to a two-dimensional tapestry embroidered by God. Each thread represents a world-line of prose, with every word replaced by a sense datum that will contribute towards fulfilling the life, wishes and eventual destiny of the person for whom it was intended. Those, for whom each thread has been made, are the conscious minds of the people who populate the world. Each mind is attached to a world-line that interweaves among those joined to other minds. Destiny for each person is the outcome of the development of data contained on these interwoven lines, according to the mind's habits and its freewill.

Placed upon His seat in eternity, nothing is unknown to God. In His timeless existence, He has neither past nor future. Were it otherwise, He would be a servant of time, and His future unknowable. Instead, in this timeless manner, He oversees the whole of His Creation. "By faith we understand that the universe was formed at God's command, so that what is seen was not made out of what was visible." (Hebrews, 11: 3). This text adequately describes the world that has been constructed by the minds of souls, from the sense data created by the thoughts of God.

> The heavens declare the glory of God: the skies proclaim the work of his hands. Day after day they pour forth speech; night after night they reveal knowledge. They have no speech, they use no words; no sound is heard from them. Yet their voice goes out into all the earth, their words to the ends of the world.   (Psalm 19: 1-3)

These biblical texts inform us we perceive the world that God has created. We do so, because the data that fills our insightfulness with 3-dimensional scenery are the result of thoughts contained in His mind. These are imprinted upon the tapestry threads of all living creatures. "Are not two sparrows sold for a penny? Yet not one of them will fall to the ground outside your Father's care." (Matthew 10: 29). For such is God's Creation that "even the very hairs of your head are all numbered."

The natural world we perceive is also comprehensible; it conveys knowledge—from the One Mind of its Maker to the lesser minds of men. If it were otherwise, the world would be unintelligible and intelligence would be unknown.

World-lines also make heaven an accessible reality. The death of the body leaves mind, soul, and consciousness free to become attached to a new world-line composed of heavenly data. A new existence therefore beckons those judged worthy to enter, with Jesus reigning supreme.

The Counterfeit Universe

Materialists oppose this view of the world. They deny the existence of anything pertaining to *spirit*. It must therefore be a puzzle to them when they view the surrounding world. Of what is it composed? It cannot be the *matter* from which they take their title. For, this would imply they possess visual *out-look* (the ability to see by direct observation that which exists externally to the mind). The scientific theory of perception denies them any such privilege. Instead, they must content themselves with an internal, immaterial model of reality: but for which, "There is no model-independent test of reality:" (p.3). How, then, can they know, with the certainty they protest, that the data from which their model of the world is constructed, did not come from God?

Instead, what they do, and which presently engages the activities of those devoted to the sciences, is to harbour the desire for re-constructing the universe according to scientific theories. To achieve this end, they commence with the premise that the reality which they perceive is caused by an external and independent source called 'matter'. Although they are perfectly aware that the mental imagery of their model cannot co-exist with this externally existing 'matter', any more than it can do so in a dream or a virtual reality, they are content to ignore this troublesome fact. And so they treat their mental constructs and their supposed corporeal archetypes as single units. This is a clever piece of deception, for it allows scientists to speak with that forked tongue referred to above. They can switch from one to the other—from mental imagery to 'matter'—depending upon the subject under discussion.

The application of science is therefore to remove objects from their perceived reality and theorise how they could exist in an unperceived state.

How far this effort to counterfeit God's Creation has progressed may now be judged. The Standard Model of Cosmology represents the scientists' attempt at explaining the universe in terms of a model that exists externally to the insightful world perceived by the senses. It is intended to describe a system that is capable of operating independently of any mind perceiving it. The system is governed by 'natural laws' that operate upon a non-mental 'substance'. It is therefore strange, even contradictory, that materialists should argue that an immaterial spirit cannot act upon 'matter', but insensate laws can! Further to this, by introducing *nature* as an invisible cause, it avoids mentioning an equally invisible deity, such as a 'law giver'.

Despite these irritants, the materialists have another serious problem. The existence of a universe counterfeited by theories copied from the only one that is definitely known to exist – the one perceived by the senses – can never be positively confirmed. Every observation, measurement, and experiment ever conducted by science is limited to the furniture of the world perceived by the senses. The results emanating from scientific research can only ever be further on in time within the same perceptible universe where research and experiments have been conducted. The results obtained do not therefore prove that an imperceptible universe exists. It is important therefore to note that this conclusion is supported by general relativity.

> According to general relativity, 'time' is merely a particular choice of coordinate in the description of the location of a space-time event. There is nothing in the physicists' space-time descriptions that singles out 'time' as something that 'flows'. [...] According to relativity, one has just a 'static' four-dimensional space-time, with no flowing about it.
>
> (Roger Penrose, *Shadows of the Mind*, p.384)

However, the situation is one in which, through experience, people do believe that time 'flows': in much the same way they have come to accept that the sun rises and sets. It is this personal bias that allows scientists involved in modelling the universe to include time-flow as part of their counterfeit universe: whereas, the 'laws of nature' are indifferent to its existence.

———— ✦ ————

At this point, it would be remiss if one failed to mention that in seeking to construct a model of the universe, scientists are perfectly aware of their limitations, and that their proposed model could never do more than represent a theoretical alternative to the world that is perceived from sense data originating from world-lines. These accord with their own theories, and are admitted to exist. This is seldom made clear to the public, but it remains implicit in their conclusions.

Scientific language also serves to counterfeits the activity of the mind. A simple example will illustrate this point. Few people will be unaware of the tennis master who wins points by serving aces to hit the sidelines of the court, or the basketball player to lobs the ball into the net from any position. The language of science can analyse both of these to explain what happened. But the language will be one of mathematical equations that involve angles, forces, heights, distances, etc. Sportsmen and women do not use the language of science to achieve the skills described above. They use their minds to adjust for error on the practice court. That is an elementary difference between mind and science achieving the same result.

In the book of Genesis, we are told that God created the universe in an instant. The counterfeit universe is in agreement with that result, but its atheistic remit requires a different cause.

The present model of the counterfeit universe begins with Monsignor Georges Lemaître, a Roman Catholic priest, and professor of physics at the Catholic University of Leuven. He was responsible for a paper, published in France in 1927, titled "A homogeneous Universe of constant mass and growing radius accounting for the radial velocity of extragalactic nebulae." Fred Hoyle derisively called it the Big Bang.

Since then, scientists have been busy secularising it for their own model of how the universe began. But, in the absence of God's eternity, the theory quickly runs into difficulties. The most obvious problem is that the Big Bang cannot have originated *within* space, because *space* only came into existence with the Big Bang. That is to say, "space itself is *created* by the explosion, and there is, or was, no central point." (Roger Penrose, *The Emperor's New Mind*, p. 423). Consequently, wherever it began, it was *not* within any part of space. This leaves the scientist having to explain that it originated out of *nothing* — " 'nothing' is not a surrounding void [...] nothing before the big bang really is 'no thing' – neither matter, nor space. *Nothing*." (Paul Davies, *The Goldilocks Enigma*, p. 78). If there is one thing that can be said with certainty about *nothing*, it is that any state of *nothing* has to be timeless. Because, where nothing exists, there is no future. But, without a future, there could never be a time – an occasion – when anything, especially the 'big bang', could have occurred. So there is something logically wrong with the creation of the universe from nothing.

⋙⋘

This is not the only flaw with the secular version of the Big Bang. A second failing is the lack of accommodation in which it could occur. For the universe to expand (or inflate) there must be room in which this is able to take place. Yet, *nothing* existed into which it was able to inflate. If there had been something, whatever that *something* was, it would have existed *before* the Big Bang. And this too, would exempt it from having been the beginning of the universe.

At this point, it may be mentioned that the Big Bang's explosion, from where nothing whatever existed, also requires that it occurred in less than a single second (actually, one quadrillionth part of a second, and there are 1,000,000,000,000,000,000,000,000 of these micro-seconds in just one single second). How does the speed of this hypothetical universe's appearance compare with that made by God? Well, "God said, 'Let there be light,' and there was light:" (Genesis 1: 3)—in which case, why not suppose it occurred in a quadrillionth part of a second?

The credibility of accepting that the universe created itself spontaneously, out of nothing, *in* that same instant of time in which it also created that *same* instant of time should strike the reader as a *non sequitur:* but it passes muster in the imagination of scientists. Clearly, it could never happen outside their mind, because nothing can create time without first possessing the time needed for its creation. Those who imagine otherwise have failed to understand that the mind is *not* 'nothing'. It is something that allows imagination to conceive of an explosion happening from apparently nothing, and all within the miniscule of a fraction of a second. But because a thing can be imagined does not confer upon it the ability to either be, or become a reality outside of the mind that conceived it.

Some may raise the objection that if 'nothing can create time without first possessing the time needed for its creation', then how could God accomplish this? The answer is that God did not create time for Him to dwell in. He created time for the minds of His subjects to experience sense data as a sequence of separate 'frames', instant by instant, which collectively become time.

———————⟨✦⟩———————

As for *light*, this is taken so much for granted and with such impunity that it desperately needs to be reconsidered. For this reason, the analysis provided by Bertrand Russell is informative.

> [T]he light which we immediately see, which we know directly by means of our senses, is *not* a form of wave-motion, but something quite different—something which we all know if we are not blind, though we cannot describe it so as to convey our knowledge to a man who is blind. [...] Now this something, which all of us who are not blind know, is not, according to science, really to be found in the outer world: it is something caused by the action of certain waves upon the eyes and nerves and brain of the person who sees the light. When it is said that light *is* waves, what is really meant is that waves are the physical cause of our sensations of light. But light itself, the thing which seeing people experience and blind people do not, is not supposed by science to form any part of the world that is independent of us and our senses.   (*The Problems of Philosophy*, p. 14)

The model universe counterfeited by scientists therefore exists in perpetual darkness. Light, as we know it, occurs only to a consciously, perceiving mind. Light waves that form part of the Standard Model are therefore not to be confused with illumination. This belongs solely to the world perceived by the senses. Unsurprisingly, the nature of light is a scientific enigma.

The problem concerning light began with the question of whether light was conveyed by waves or by particles. One experiment 'proved conclusively' that light occurs in waves. But a separate experiment also 'proved conclusively' that light travels as particles.

> In this way it appears that the seventeenth century, which regarded light as mere particles, and the nineteenth century, which regarded it as mere waves, were both wrong—or, if we prefer, both right. Light, and indeed radiation of all kinds, is both particles and waves at the same time.
> (Sir James Jeans, *The Mysterious Universe:* 1943 revised ed. p. 46)

The acceptance of these paradoxical results eventually exposed a further conundrum. By reducing the light emitted from a source, so that only one particle at a time is directed toward a screen containing two slits of identical size, it was discovered that ...

> each individual photon behaves like a wave entirely on its own! In some sense, each particle travels through *both slits at once* and it interferes with *itself!* [...] the import of this extraordinary fact [...] is that *each individual particle* behaves in a wavelike way entirely on its own.
> (Roger Penrose, *The Emperor's New Mind:* 1989: p. 304)

In an attempt to shed further light on the problem (no pun intended), a particle detector was installed to discover which slit the photon actually passed through: or to see if the photon split into two parts, with each part passing through a separate slit. The result was dramatic.

> [W]hen the detector is present at one of the slits, so that an observer can *tell* which slit the photon went through, the wavy interference at the screen disappears. In order for the interference to take place, there must apparently be a 'lack of knowledge' as to which slit the particle went through.   (Ibid. p. 305)

This extraordinary result makes it appear that the photon *always knows when it is being watched, or measured,* and it responds accordingly by the way it acts. Consequently, when it 'knows' it is not being observed, measured or interfered with, it records a wave effect. Scientists regard this strange 'behaviour' as one of the enigmas of quantum physics—which is not at all surprising.

In the experiments described above, photons were used. But this is not essential.

> Electrons or any other kind of particle, or even whole atoms would do equally well. The rules of quantum mechanics appear even to insist that cricket balls [similar to baseballs] and elephants ought to behave in this odd way.   (Ibid, p. 306)

To account for what is happening scientists have been forced to conclude that the particle, in its unobserved state, exists as a wave; thus, occupying no single point. But, the instant the wave is *observed* by a sentient being, which includes measurements being taken, or interference to it of any sort, the wave 'obliges' the observer by collapsing into a single state, occupying a unique position in the observable world.

This can be restated to mean that before being *observed*, objects exist in a state of potential: as if in wait for an observer to arrive. Then, in response to the observer's conscious awareness of its potential to metamorphose, the wave transforms into a classic state of existence, which conforms to the observer's perceived surroundings.

But this is precisely the same conclusion reached for objects appearing in the perceived world when a conscious mind encounters data existing on its world-line: a world-line, which is a thread upon the tapestry of God's Creation. The conscious mind 'collapses' (or translates) the data to form a classical view of the world. When the data is unobserved by any mind, it remains in a potential state of being.

———————◦✧◦———————

It is apparent from what has been said heretofore that with each attempt to construct a working model of the universe without intervention by God, the opposite has occurred. Relativity theory has given the scientist a universe in which time exists in space-time. The definition of space-time is that of a timeless state in which world-lines contain the past, present and future of the world as co-existing. Change and motion are therefore meaningless terms, unless viewed in succession by a conscious mind.

Compare this with the Mind of God, which is defined as eternal, therefore timeless. He knows the end from the beginning, which includes the past, present and future of every living being. God is also immutable. He cannot change, because eternity has no future in which change could occur. And when quantum theory enters into the counterfeit model of the universe, it, too, points towards the tapestry of God.

The Wheeler-DeWitt equation, for example, defines a quantum universe and reaffirms that it exists in a timeless state. The so-called 'Copenhagen interpretation', which is advocated wherever quantum physics is taught, teaches that "if something is *not* being observed, then its wave function changes according to the Schrödinger equation, but if it is being observed, then its wavefunction collapses so that you find the object only in one place [...] and explains our familiar classical world where we see things in only one place at a time." (Max Tegmark, *Our Mathematical Universe*, p. 178)

To accept that everything in the world exists in its classical state only when it is perceived as such seems counter-intuitive, but then so does being told that the sun does not rise at dawn and set at dusk. Instead, it is the Earth's rotation that makes it appear so. Therefore, let this quantum proposal be considered afresh, since its conclusion belongs as much to the world perceived from strands of data existing on the tapestry of God, as it does to the counterfeit universe.

> Take a good look at the book you're now holding in your hand. Now put it down on the table and close your eyes for ten seconds or so and open them again. Chances are good that the book will still be there on the table. But was it there when you were not looking? If you answer, 'Of course it was there; the book's behaviour doesn't depend on whether I'm looking or not,' then you haven't yet come to terms with quantum theory.   (John L. Casti, *Paradigms Regained*: 2001: p.248)

Now take the book and place it before a mirror. Observe its reflection and then close your eyes. Does the reflection of the book still exist? If not, then how can the book itself still exist with your eyes shut? According to scientists, you saw both the book and its reflection from the same light waves that entered your eyes. How, then, can one disappear and not the other?

The customary reply is to change the subject by referring to the history of your relationship with the book. You recall holding the book, its weight, its intangibility, the fact that you bought it, or it was given to you, that it was manufactured from ink and paper &c. The point is that everything you observe in the world of *insightfulness* is likely to have a history attached to it, learned from past experiences, and which have become resident in your mind. For this reason, it is nigh impossible to dissociate these memories from the visible appearance of the book. But the question was—how can one book visibly exist when the other does not if the same light waves are responsible for the perception of both?

It must therefore be the collection of associated memories that together give a material presence and reality to what is seen, which a single observation is unable to do. The materiality of the book and a belief in its continued existence, when there is no one to perceive it, comes from past experiences of its qualities and the memories attached to them. By contrast, the single appearance of the book reflected in the mirror, which has neither history, nor a direct association with any other sense, presents no concern if told that it visibly disappears when not consciously perceived. In which case, it must be asked, where does that history, spoken of above, exist? It is, of course, in the memory. And where do memories exist? On world-lines, as argued previously. Hence, that which materialists call 'matter' is nothing other than a collection of sensible qualities, existing on a world-line, attached to memories perceived in the past. Any one of these qualities, if required, can be made to appear at a particular moment in time, according to the percipient's situation. But when these qualities are not perceived, they exist as data from which any one or more has the potential state of becoming translated into a sensible experience.

———————— ❧ ————————

As previously indicated, scientists are subject to the same persuasion, but insists upon pursuing a different line of thought in order to explain objects of sense in terms of a universe existing externally and materially, yet conjoined to the insightful world of sense experience. The American philosopher and psychologist, William James (1842 – 1910), explained the dilemma.

> [T]he whole philosophy of perception from Democritus' time downwards has been just one long wrangle over the paradox that what is evidently one reality should be in two places at once, both in outer space and in a person's mind. 'Representative' theories of perception avoid the logical paradox, but on the other hand they violate the reader's sense of life which knows no intervening mental image but seems to see the room and the book immediately as they physically exist.

(M. Velmans, Understanding Consciousness – Quoting James, 1904: p. 185)

John Locke (1632 – 1704), the English philosopher famous in his time, thought and wrote upon this question, but was compelled to admit there could be no idea of substance: "Matter is something, I know not what," he said. (*Essay Concerning Human Understanding*, 1689). In order to justify the pursuit of scientific progress in the age of Newton, Hook, Boyle &c. he was therefore compelled to introduce a form of representationalism. "When Locke says that some ideas resemble the qualities they stand for, it is only plausible to take his meaning according to the picture-original model, if one has already taken an idea to be a special kind of mental thing." (Ibid. pp. 33) Descartes, too, appears to have leaned towards this explanation for obtaining knowledge of the external world, and his work had been the inspiration for Locke's *Essay*.

The reason for reintroducing Locke's diversity between *primary* and *secondary* qualities, for which the former are to be understood as belonging to substance, whereas the latter belong to the mind of the percipient, is because biologists are so in need of an explanation for justifying their knowledge by perception, that Locke provides an easy referential authority for this absence. Indeed education in the schoolroom usually begins with representationalism as a means of circumventing the logical difficulties that attend explanations. But there is a further reason. Physics, chemistry and biology have witnessed such advancement in the past that the general trend of philosophy has been atheistic: more intent upon rationalising the progress of the sciences than challenging its conclusions, while theologians have remained mute. Consequently, the questions surrounding the philosophical implications of modern science are scarcely if ever heard. Let us therefore return to Berkeley in order to understand how he disproved Locke's explanation.

> [8] But say you, though the ideas themselves do not exist without the mind, yet there may be things like them, whereof they are copies or resemblances, which things exist without the mind in an unthinking substance. I answer, an idea can be like nothing but an idea; a colour or figure can

be like nothing but another colour or figure. If we look but never so little into our own thoughts, we shall find it impossible for us to conceive a likeness except only between our ideas. Again I ask whether those supposed originals or external things, of which our ideas are the pictures or representations, be themselves perceivable or no? If they are, then they are ideas and we have gained our point: but if you say they are not, I appeal to anyone whether it be sense to assert a colour is like something which is invisible; hard or soft, like something which is intangible; and so of the rest.

[9] Some there are who make a distinction betwixt *primary* and *secondary* qualities. By the former they mean extension, figure, motion, rest, solidity, impenetrability, and number; by the latter they denote all other sensible qualities, as colours, sounds, tastes and so forth. The ideas we have of these last they acknowledge not to be the resemblances of anything existing without the mind, or unperceived, but they will have our ideas of the primary qualities to be patterns or images of things which exist without the mind, in an unthinking substance which they call Matter.—By Matter, therefore, we are to understand *an inert, senseless, substance, in which extension, figure and motion do actually subsist.* But it is evident, from what we have already shewn, that extension, figure and motion are only ideas existing in the mind, and that an idea can be like nothing but another idea, and that consequently neither they nor their archetypes can exist in an unperceiving substance. Hence it is plain that the very notion of what is called *Matter* or *corporeal substance* involves a contradiction in it.   (*The Principles of Human Knowledge*, 1710)

In the passage above, Berkeley drives home his objection. The sensible qualities that are perceived – be they *primary* or *secondary* – exist in the mind. How, then, can these same qualities exist in an unthinking substance called 'matter'? Attempts have been made to override this conclusion by insisting that unification occurs between the insightful world composed from sense data and a material, causal agent that exists externally to the content of the mind's perception, but in the same place. It is wishful thinking. If it were possible, then dreams and virtual reality experiences would come under the same umbrella of that explanation. What exists in the mind cannot be united by replication and location to something existing in a world that is sustained externally to the mind, therefore free from it, and composed of non-mental (unimaginable) 'archetypes'.

Prophecy and freewill

Despite the lack of a single substantive reason to justify the existence of a world existing externally to the mind and composed of causal matter, mainstream scientists totally ignore philosophical reasoning in order to identify further qualities that add to those of the groups under inspection. They do this, because their act of *faith* is directed toward a *belief* that sensible qualities *belong* to, or are generated by a substratum they refer to as 'matter'. Furthermore, they admit this *material substratum* exists outside of their purview, but that they possess a competent knowledge of its existence, while also concluding there is no model-independent test of its reality. The evidence from world-lines is far more enticing. Prophetic foresight of a world event would utilise the linkage between adjacent 'observer instants' on a world-line, because world-lines stretch into both the *past* and the *future* from any *present* point on the line. Retrocognition and precognition are therefore both conceptual possibilities. This would also complement the conclusion that 'space' and 'motion' are mental concepts. A true prophecy would also consist of the same sense data belonging to both the event and its prediction: for it would be derived from part of a world-line that was situated farther along its length, where the event existed. Evidence for the same sense data describing both prediction and its fulfilment would validate prophecy.

The world-lines described in the foregoing pages mean that *every event* in the world, including the people to whom the sense data relates, is timelessly known to God. Biblical text also asserts this to be true (Psalm 139). Importantly, this divine knowledge permits our every expression of freewill to conform fully to the world God has created for our lives—be it good or bad. His design is that we be allowed to judge ourselves after death, by the effect our freewill has had upon the world and the people we lived amongst. The world has been created to concur with freewill.

When life on earth ends, we take with us the content of our world-line: against which, there can be no appeal. It contains full knowledge of the choices we made during our lifetime, and portrays our character, *exactly* as others witnessed and knew us. It also enables our *inner being* to comprehend who we really are, by how we have reacted to the situations that confronted us.

Of no less importance is the fact that if it is in a person's character to change direction in their life, the opportunity to do so, exists on their world-line, and subsequent sense data will conform to whatever choice of direction is made. God does not prevent freewill by predestination. Instead, He reveals freewill by his prior knowledge of each person; for nothing is new or old in eternity: it is just there.

Some religious groups may possibly take offence at this, since their belief in Judgement Day is viewed as something akin to a present-day court of law, with God sitting in judgement at some future time. But, if this creates a problem, then it has a logical solution. All things are known to God, or they are not! If they are not, then God has an unknown future, and He, becomes subject to time, which means He cannot have created it. But time and space are united; therefore He cannot have created space either. All of which defies biblical text. On the other hand, if He created time, He knows the end from the beginning. In which case, freewill and predestination can be united, given that His intelligence is sufficient to accomplish what is required. I dare to say that few, if any, will doubt that this ability already exists. In fact, it is precisely such ability that brings the dichotomy between world-lines and matter, as the true source of sense data, to a point where the confliction can be resolved.

Stephen Hawking, who is sometimes fêted as the leading scientific mind of the present age, stated categorically in his book, *The Grand Design*, that "We form mental concepts of our home, trees, other people, the electricity that flows from wall sockets, atoms, molecules and other universes. These mental concepts are the only reality we can know. There is no model-independent test of reality. It follows that a well-constructed model creates a reality of its own." (p. 217).

I maintain such a test does exist. If Hawking is correct, and matter is the source of sense data, then accurate prophecies of future world events are impossible to predict. This is because the precise arrangement of 'matter' required to source the future sense data of an event, cannot be supposed to exist in the universe *at any time prior* to when this event actually occurs. But, if world-lines are the source of sense data, then the problem goes away. The reason for this is very simple. World-lines are timeless. They contain a full set of sense data that accurately describes God's Creation for every event occurring between any two points on that world-line.

In the following ten chapters, the evidence for world-lines being the true model for the source of sense data has been set out. Close to five hundred years of historically, validated prophecies (fully referenced), including a significant number that contain their date of fulfilment, or else provide the names of those involved in the predicted events, long before they were born, are available for inspection. Freewill and predestination are inherent within their context, and the fact that they have been tested for historical accuracy and found to be without error represents a powerfully, persuasive reason for their *fons et origo* to exist within the Mind of God.

This poses the question why. Why should God reveal His existence to the world as its Creator at this particular point in the history of mankind? The answer to this may lie in the single direction that world leaders have taken. If we look back in history, whether ancient or modern, there have always been periods of time when a country or an empire has exercised its anti-religious bias and political ideas upon the people it governed. Usually, the 'madness' of the time, captivates the people by sweeping away ancient, social norms, and replacing them with what are always labelled 'progressive' freedoms. The more outlandish changes never survive a generation or two, and the countries affected eventually fall into line with those that had remained unaffected.

The age in which this book is written poses a different situation. No longer is it a single country, or even an empire, but the entire western world that has begun overturning its Christian heritage – and continues to overturn it – by abandoning the cultural norms of its recent ancestry. But, is it really 'social madness' or is it social progress? People captivated by the age in which they live will be expected to call it progress. Who then benefits? Has poverty been eliminated? Quite the opposite—the gap between rich and poor has grown. Soup kitchens, food banks, charity shops, and those sleeping rough have become the norm. Is medical aid more freely available than before? The answer is no, it has largely remained unaffected by the change in social norms. If anything, several advances in medicine have now become too expensive to be made available to the general public. So, who has benefitted from the social upheaval that has spread across the western world? What has God discerned in the future direction mankind has set its sight upon, which He deems irreversibly destructive if left to proceed without divine intervention?

Of course, it is not possible to see the world through the eyes of the Creator. But it is possible to be aware of what He witnesses happening in the world, particularly when it contrasts with the culture that previously did not require His intervention. The so-called 'Sexual Revolution', for instance, which has made commonplace the legalised murder of unborn babies, fornication, divorce, single sex marriages: these are very obvious contrast between the present age and past generations. The next stage will be to introduce polygamy as a human right. For, if it is the human right of a man to be free to marry another man, how can it not be a human right for a man to marry two men—or, for that matter, two women, or even a man and a woman? All it requires is that the parties involved are willing participants.

Another change within society has occurred in the entertainment' industry, where the relaxing of past legislation controlling gambling, drugs, pornography, games involving violence, blasphemy, censorship, alcohol, and gutter language in media outlets, is in complete contrast to life in the western world as it was lived, up until the mid twentieth century, when these changes began.

These so-called 'progressive', 'liberal' trends, which history has shown to be ultimately destructive to the welfare of societies now long past, may well have been left for future generations to repair and reform. In the past, this was usually achieved by the reaction of a religious revival. But, in the present age, which is now in the process of being deconstructed by politicians intent upon replacing it with the counterfeit model constructed by scientific theories, means that religion no longer has the same ascendency over the minds of the population that it once held.

By counterfeiting the formation and operation of the universe, science uses its intellectual and authoritative structures to displace God. But, without a deity, moral authority is replaced by crowd control. Let it be recalled that Jesus was crucified because Pilate yielded to crowd control. Moral relativism is the latest development of this brand of ethics. It allows individual members of the 'crowd' to invent their own standards of behaviour without reproach. Who is there left to say what is correct when 'right' and 'wrong' have different meanings to different classes of people?

Anarchy is the absence of political order. Moral relativism has now become the first step towards 'moral anarchy': the absence of moral order. Western politicians have already gained ground in leading their people in that destination. But in the absence of moral order, political disorder and economic disarray are bound to follow—to be replaced by the imposed morality of a tyranny.

Euthanasia (euphemistically renamed 'assisted suicide') is already legal in countries on the continent of Europe, and efforts are underway to spread the practice to their neighbouring governments. Eventually, it will become freely available. The removal of limitations upon those requesting their own death is also part of the process. It is even allowing children to make their own decision about ending their lives. In which case, this will strengthen the argument for paedophilia to be made legal. For, how can it be denied that if a child has the human right to decide to terminate its own life in the hands of an adult, then it has the human right for the lesser decision of deciding to have a sexual relationship with person of adult age? One decision simply opens the door to another. The Greeks knew more about Pandora's Box than this age!

After abortion and euthanasia, the next step in this downward progression is eugenics. In 1916, Madison Grant, an easy-going companion for men like Herbert Hoover and President Roosevelt, wrote *The Passing of the Great Race*, "one of the seminal works of scientific racialism," in which he subscribed to the notion that "life is valuable only when it is of use to the community or race." This greatly appealed to Hitler, who read it while in the midst of writing *Mein Kampf.* He was therefore able to include it among the ideas he held. "He who is not physically and mentally healthy and worthy must not perpetuate his misery in the body of his child." Afterwards, he wrote to Grant, praising the book and referring to it as "my bible." It was Hitler's introduction to eugenics.

Eugenics can be described as an accelerated evolutionary process toward a desired goal directed by intelligent design. Once Hitler had been elected to the office of Chancellor, the opportunity presented itself for the implementation of his much favoured eugenics programme. "In 1934 Germany established a nationwide system of eugenic courts to decide who should be sterilized [...] After 1935, with the passage of the Nuremberg Laws, the same courts would arbitrate race cases, deciding who should be allowed to marry whom." (Dennis Sewell, *The Political Gene*, p. 137)

As a result of this policy, "four hundred thousand Germans were sterilized, about half of them in the first four years of operation of the racial-hygiene system." (Ibid.)

Germany was not alone in implementing a eugenics programme. In the late 1960s and early 1970s the United States was operating a similar policy.

> Federal District Judge Gerhard Gesell estimated that during the previous few years [prior to 1973] somewhere close to a hundred and fifty thousand poor people had probably been sterilized under federal programmes. [...] A common method of coercion, it appeared, had been the threat to withdraw welfare payments if the victims did not agree.
>
> The sheer scale of the assault launched against America's poor by eugenics is astonishing [...] there are tens of thousands more whose names we do not know.   (Ibid. p.104)

The political incentive for embarking upon eugenics stems from the atheistic conclusions reached by Charles Darwin. "A host of writers from Hannah Arendt to Richard Weikart and nearly all of Hitler's respected biographers have made some form of Hitler-Darwin connection." (Ibid. p.132). One of these authors, David Klinghoffer, also "linked the ideology that produced Auschwitz [...] [to] moral relativism aligned with a rejection of the sacredness of human life, a belief that violent competition in nature creates greater and lesser races, that the greater will inevitably exterminate the lesser [...] these ideas may be found in Darwin's writing." (David Klinghoffer, *National Review Online*, 18 April 2008).

As Darwin, himself, admitted: "A man who has no assured and ever-present belief in the existence of a personal God, or of a future existence with retribution and reward, can have for his rule of life, as far as I can see, only to follow those impulses and instincts which are the strongest or which seem to him the best ones." (*Autobiographies*, Charles Darwin, eds. Michael Neve & Sharon Messenger, p. 54).

The strength of Darwin's irreligion found fertile soil among those who came after him. Lee M. Silver, a Princeton microbiologist and Professor of Public and International Affairs at Woodrow Wilson School of Public and International Affairs, foresaw a future composed of a 'class of genetic aristocrats' that form a 'political economic and media elite.' Those excluded from this group were relegated to second-class citizens.

Peter Singer, a Professor of Bioethics, also at Princeton, is another anti-religionist who uses his authority as a platform to air his atheism. As a laureate and professor in the centre for applied philosophy and ethics, he has a reputation for downgrading human life: believing its sacredness to be 'hokum'. "Indeed, he goes further, arguing that it is not wrong to kill disabled children even some time after they are born." (Sewell p.160) "[It] is, rather, characteristics like rationality, autonomy, and self-consciousness that make a difference. Infants lack these characteristics. Killing them, therefore, cannot be equated with killing normal human beings." (Peter Singer, *Practical Ethics*, pp. 175-217).

Francis Crick (1916 – 2004) a molecular biologist, biophysicist, and neuroscientist, and Nobel laureate was another voice anxious to promote Darwinian ideas, together with a fascination to murder the imperfectly born. "No new-born infant should be declared human until it has passed certain tests regarding its genetic endowment," wrote Crick. "If it fails these tests it forfeits the right to live." (Ted Howard & Jeremy Rifkin, *Who Should Play God?* p.81). No pity, therefore, for the grieving parents who witnessed their offspring sacrificed on the 'altar' of science.

> Historically, eugenicists in both Britain and the United States frequently voiced their frustration at being constantly restrained by outdated religious ideas and by the timidity of God-fearing politicians. One might imagine a society in which they would have been happier: where biologists and evolutionary scientists were unshackled; where they did not need to concern themselves with the prattling of prelates; where they were free of the ethical restraints of sentimental humanitarianism, and where there was no cause to make the kinds of fudges and compromises that a pluralist, democratic society imposes; a society in which they could remake public policy along rational, scientific lines and according to the most up-to-date thinking in their field. But there is no need to imagine such a place. Nazi Germany made it a reality.   (Sewell, p.132)

As the third decade of the twenty-first century draws near, westernised societies must come to a political decision concerning the world in which human lives are experienced. Either the world we perceive is the result of sense data created by an unimaginably, superior intellect: one whose creative thoughts are the language existing along the world-lines that timelessly subsist within the eternity of His Mind, and from where they are conveyed to us. Or, the world we perceive is the result of sense data transmitted to the mind from an external world of random events, blackened in an eternal night, imperceptible, unlocatable, and which can only be modelled by mathematical equations, based upon the mental concepts of which we are consciously aware.

If this second alternative is believed, then we are forever confined to ignorance concerning this other world, and a moral decline that will end the accidental emergence of life in the universe.

Alternatively, by choosing the first option, ignorance of the world and its reality is avoided. There is no external world of archetypal, corporeal substance. Instead, the qualities and aspects of whatever is witnessed in the world (including light, motion and distance, which are also mental concepts), come into existence by an act of perception. Hence, that which is commonly regarded as 'matter' is in reality a collection of nouns: each of which identify the group of sensible qualities to which they are attached. The universe then becomes comprehensible as a masterful thought in the Mind of God, where it continues to be sustained.

The theory of evolution is of course devitalised by this new outlook to existence. It becomes just another part of the data occurring on world-lines, but which were never perceived by human kind to exist in reality: because there were no percipients at the world's beginning other than the Creator. Scientists can have their theory of evolution in this diminished form, but only as the language of God; that is, without any causal component other than the Creator's intentions: because the actual language of God – like words – is passive. It is the effect it has upon the mind that motivates mental activity. The religious faithful are therefore able to retain a Judeo-Christian account of Creation, with both sides in the debate justified in their respective beliefs.

The remaining part of this book is devoted to solid evidence for everything that has this far been said—most especially, the existence of timeless, world-lines containing sense data from which the world obtains its perceptual reality. This evidence consists of several thousand historical incidents that occurred during the previous five centuries: all of which were predicted to occur. These incidents have been linked together to form units of prophecy, for which very many cross-references occur to expand their prophetic content. Some predictions also contain dates that are far in advance of their fulfilment. Others include the name or names of those involved in the predicted event. All, however, can be recognized by their complete correlation to past records, written by independent historians. These authors were – and some still are – scholars of history who, at the time of writing, were quite unaware that what they were committing to print as narrative had, at one time in the distant past, been written as prophecy.

The reader may therefore be completely reassured that what is contained in the forthcoming chapters is a rational and logical extension of evidence for world-lines. It is also in keeping with relativity theory, which requires space-time to be the location where both past and future events coexist timelessly, and where time does not flow. It also harmonises with "the Copenhagen interpretation, which says nothing is real until it is observed, or measured." Neither is there any conflict between prophecy and Christianity. For, Paul confirmed that prophecy is a gift from the Holy Spirit, and predestination is determined by God. In the Hebrew Bible, the psalmist, David, confirmed that God knows everything about everyone before it happens, and for which there is no escape from such knowledge. Isaiah many times foresaw the future: even naming a future King called Cyrus. He also confirmed that the Lord has genuine prophets whose predictions He causes to come true. Daniel, too, was a prophet. He foresaw the battle between Alexander the

CENTURY ONE

The Bible is a rich source of prophecy. Indeed, so rich that on the road to Emmaus, Jesus was able to recount to Cleopas and his companion, the prophecies that had been made of his coming. "And beginning with Moses and all the Prophets, he explained to them what was said in all the Scriptures concerning himself." (Luke, 24: 27) We can see from this that Jesus's biographical data line existed centuries before he made his appearance in the world. But this would only be possible if it was coordinated with the data lines of his apostles and those he met during his lifetime. Once a data line is established, it indicates that others, too, exist.

This same conclusion is also made clear by the prophet Isaiah. "It is I who made the earth and created mankind on it. My own hands stretched out the heavens; I marshalled the starry hosts. I will raise up Cyrus in my righteousness: I will make all his ways straight. He will rebuild my city and set my exiles free, but not for a price or reward, says the LORD Almighty." (45: 12, 13) It would seem that Isaiah became well acquainted with the future life of Cyrus. "Cyrus, 'He is my shepherd and will accomplish all that I please; he will say of Jerusalem, 'Let it be rebuilt,' and of the temple, Let its foundations be laid.'" (44: 28) Then, in the next chapter, again speaking as the voice of God, Isaiah states: "This is what the LORD says to his anointed, to Cyrus, whose right hand I take hold of to subdue nations before him and to strip kings of their armour, to open doors before him so that gates will not be shut:" (45: 1).

Isaiah flourished in the 8th century B.C., during the reigns of Uzziah, Jotham, Ahaz, and Hezekiah, kings of Judah; hence, his prophetic work dates from c. 740 B.C. Therefore, since he lived in Jerusalem during the First Temple period, his prophecies regarding Cyrus, the rebuilding of Jerusalem, relaying the foundations of the temple and return of the exiles, would have had no immediate meaning to his contemporaries.

The first temple in Jerusalem is credited to King Solomon who built it in 957 B.C. It was razed to the ground four centuries later, in 586 B.C., when the Babylonian army invaded Jerusalem and began exiling its citizens to Babylonia, where they were put to work as slaves. A little calculation informs us, therefore, that something approaching 150 years had to pass before Isaiah's prophecy stirred the thoughts of those in exile. But it was another prophet, Jeremiah, who resumed Isaiah's earlier prediction. "This is what the LORD Almighty, the God of Israel, says to all those I carried into exile from Jerusalem to Babylon. [...] When seventy years are completed for Babylon, I will come to you and fulfil my good promise to bring you back to this place. For I know the plans I have for you,' declares the LORD, plans to prosper you and not to harm you, plans to give you hope and a future." (Jeremiah 29: 4, 10, 11).

Between the years 560 and 547 B.C., King Croesus ruled Lydia, a kingdom that had dominion over all Asia Minor west of the River Halys, except Lycia. His reign ended when he decided to expand his empire by attacking Persia (modern day Iran). Although he had been promised aid from Egypt and Babylon, he also wanted to be assured of success. Croesus therefore sent envoys to seven oracles renowned for their ability to predict the future; these were to "Delphoi, to Abai in Phokia, and to Dodona, while others were despatched to Amphiaraos and Trophonios, and others to Brankhidae in the Milesian country. These are the Greek oracles to which Kroisos sent for divination: and he told others to go inquire of Ammon in Libya." [1] At each shrine his representative was required to ask the priestess what King Croesus was doing on the one-hundredth day of this mission. The false answers he received are now lost, but the responses he obtained from the oracles at Delphi and Amphiaraus were both correct: although only the one received from Delphi has survived.

> I count the grains of sand on the beach and measure the sea;
> I understand the speech of the dumb, and hear the voiceless.
> The smell has come to my sense of a hard-shelled tortoise
> Boiling and bubbling with lamb's flesh in a bronze pot:
> The cauldron underneath is of bronze, and of bronze the lid. [2]

Croesus had thought this recipe of boiled lamb and tortoise cooked inside a bronze cauldron would be among the most unlikely of all combinations, and he made it the answer to his test. It was because of the successful replies he received that envoys were then dispatched to both oracles: one at Oropos, a border city between Boeotia and Attica, and the other to Delphi, with the same question—should he march against Persia: and would it be wise to seek an alliance?

The answers he received were identical. If Croesus attacked the Persians he would destroy a great empire. The oracles also advised him to reach an understanding with the most powerful of the Greek states. Yet, still he wanted to hear more, and so he consulted the oracle at Delphi again. This time his question sought personal reassurance; for, "On this occasion he asked if his reign would be a long one. The priestess answered:"

> When comes the day that a mule shall sit on the Median throne,
> Then, tender-footed Lydian, by pebbly Hermus
> Run and abide not, nor think it shame to be a coward. [3]

Filled with confidence at this response, since a mule on the Median throne could never happen, Croesus took the oracle's advice and sought an alliance with Sparta, the most powerful of the Greek states. With his preparations in place, Croesus attacked Persia in 547 B.C.

The main battle took place to the north of Sardis, and ended with the siege of the city and its eventual fall. The Lydian army had been swept aside. A great empire had been defeated— Croesus's own empire. His triumphant victor was the new King of Persia: a man named Cyrus: the same Cyrus whose name had been foretold by Isaiah as the ruler of empires, who would also free the people of Judah from their bondage.

> Cyrus the Great was the founder of the Archaemenid Empire. Under his rule, the empire embraced all the previous civilized states of the ancient Near East, expanded vastly and eventually conquered most of Southwest Asia and much of Central Asia and the Caucasus. From the Mediterranean Sea and Hellespont in the west to the Indus River in the east, Cyrus the Great created the largest empire the world had yet seen. [...] His regal titles in full were The Great King, King of Persia, King of Anshan, King of Media, King of Babylon, King of Sumer and Akkad, and King of the Four Corners of the World. [4]

Cyrus ruled his empire between 559 and 530 B.C. It was a complete fulfilment of the prophecy given to Isaiah by God two hundred years earlier. Cyrus's conquest of the Babylonian Empire also led to the fulfilment of the second part of Isaiah's prophecy. His edict, freeing the captives from Judah, allowed them to return to their homeland and begin the task of rebuilding Jerusalem and laying the foundations for the construction of Zerubabel's Temple.

Work began on the temple in 537 B.C.; and the "Construction of the Second Temple was completed in 516 BCE, during the reign of Darius the Great, seventy years after the destruction of the First Temple." [5] This time span of 70 years therefore fulfils the prophecy given by Jeremiah.

As for the city of Babylon, it continued under the reign of Cyrus and his successor, but gradually deteriorated.

> By the time the Parthian Empire ruled the region in 141 BCE Babylon was deserted and forgotten. The city steadily fell into ruin and, even during a brief revival under the Sassanid Persians, never approached its former greatness. In the Muslim conquest of the land in 650 CE whatever remained of Babylon was swept away and, in time, was buried beneath the sands. [6]

This, too, had been predicted by Isaiah (14: 22-23).

> 'I will rise up against them,' declares the LORD almighty. 'I will wipe out Babylon's name and survivors, her offspring and descendants,' declares the LORD. 'I will turn her into a place for owls and swampland; I will sweep her with the broom of destruction,' declares the LORD Almighty.

If we return now to Croesus, he had been taken prisoner by Cyrus at the fall of Sardis, and sentenced to death by burning. But the sentence was later lifted. And when questioned by Cyrus, as to the motivation for his attack against Persia, the defeated king blamed the oracles he had consulted. Intrigued by this, Cyrus permitted Croesus to send envoys back to Delphi, so that he could enquire why this oracle had deceived him.

The oracle's response was that Croesus had been told that if he attacked the Persians, an empire would be destroyed. He should have sent again to enquire which empire was meant by this. Since he did not, the fault was his. As for the question he posed regarding the length of his reign, he failed to understand its content. The mule was Cyrus, who was the child of different races. His mother was a Mede: the daughter of Astyages, king of Media; but his father was Persian.[7]

The true academic will perhaps be aware of a breed of scientists who abandon all sense of truth, rigour, and propriety in their desperation to eliminate prophecy from serious consideration; no doubt, this is because of the threat it poses to the materialistic ambitions and teaching they promulgate. In seeking to accomplish this end, they cite the single case of the ambiguity contained in the first oracles received by Croesus: albeit independently from Delphi and from Oropos. Scientists well know that a general rule cannot be obtained from a single example, but when it pleases their argument, they do it with aplomb.

The prophetic instances given above relate to the ancient world. It is now time to seek similar accounts that have occurred in the modern world. On 27 June 1558, a letter was addressed to Henri II of France which gave warning to the King of what lay ahead for the French people, and for the world in general. One sentence in particular stood out: "et sera le commencement comprenant ce de ce que durera et commencement icelle année sera faite plus grande persecution à l'Église Chrétienne, que n'a été en Afrique, et durera cette ici jusque'à l'an mille sept cent nonante deux que l'on euidera être une renovation de siècle."[8]

> And it will be the beginning, comprising this for that, which will endure; also, the commencement in the same year will effect greater persecution to the Christian Church than was in Africa, and it will endure in this place, here, even to the year 1792, when men will deem it to be a renewal of time. (*Translation is based upon Cotgrave's 1611 French Dictionary*)

On 20 September 1792, Prussian troops commanded by the Duke of Brunswick attempted to march on Paris, which was then in the throes of its revolution. In the battle that took place that day, the French army stopped the advance near the northern village of Valmy.

> The battle was considered a "miraculous" event and a "decisive defeat" for the vaunted Prussian army. After the battle, the newly assembled National Convention was emboldened enough to formally declare the end of monarchy in France and the establishment of the First French Republic. Valmy permitted the development of the Revolution and all its resultant ripple effects, and for that it is regarded as one of the most significant battles of all time.[9]

The great German author, poet and statesman, Johann Wolfgang von Goethe, was a witness to the battle, and he described the event in words eerily reminiscent of those in the letter to Henri II. "At this place, on this day, there has begun a new era in the history of the world."[10]

These words proved to be prophetic. On the next day, 21st September, the National Convention decreed the commencement of the new Revolutionary Calendar, starting with Year One.

> The dawn of the new era, Year one of the Republic, had already been declared as having begun with the abolition of the monarchy on 22 September 1792. That year, and all subsequent years, were now to be divided into twelve months of thirty days each, with five days left at the end of the year to be known as *sans-culottides* and to be celebrated as festivals.[11]

This "renewal of" recorded "time" was part of the de-Christianization of France and it had been designed to replace the Gregorian calendar, because of its connexion to Pope Gregory XIII.

> In Paris Religious monuments outside churches were destroyed; various religious ceremonies were suppressed; ecclesiastical plate and other treasures were seized in the name of the people; images of the Madonna were replaced by busts of Marat; surplices were cut up to make bandages and soldiers' shirts; and it was henceforth forbidden to sell in the streets 'any kinds of superstitious jugglery such as holy napkins, St Veronica's handkerchiefs, Ecce Homos, crosses, Agnes Deis, rings of St Hubert or any medicinal waters or other adulterated drugs'. Theatres began to offer such plays as *L'Inauguration du Temple de la Verité* in which a parody of the High Mass was performed. [...] From Paris the de-Christianization movement spread all over France.[12]

The prophecy addressed to Henri II indicated that the de-Christianization of France would begin sometime before 1792; and it was compared with what took place in Africa.

The reference made to Africa was to the Vandals, from whom the word 'vandalism' is derived. "Renaissance and Early Modern writers characterized the Vandals as barbarians, 'sacking and looting' Rome. This led to the use of the term vandalism, to describe any senseless destruction, particularly the barbarian defacing of artworks." [13] The similarity to what befell Christian churches in France during the Revolution is at once both relevant and convincing.

The Vandals entered Africa in 429 A.D., leaving in their wake a trail of death and destruction. Among those affected was Saint Augustine; who, together with his Christian priests, suffered a siege inside the Algerian, walled city of Hippo Regius, "knowing full well that the fall of the city would spell conversion or death for many Roman Christians." [14] The city finally succumbed to the Vandals when, after fourteen months of resistance, hunger and disease took their toll.

Thereafter, at Carthage, the Vandals hacked 500 hostages to pieces and threw the body parts into the sea. It was a grim forerunner to the September Massacres of the French Revolution in 1792, when, "By 6 September, half the prison population of Paris had been executed: some 1200 to 1400 prisoners. Of these, 233 were nonjuring Catholic priests who refused to support the government;" [15] – hence, the comparison: "death or conversion." In fact, 'execution' is a misnomer. "A quick sword thrust" following a guilty verdict in a room piled high with blood-stained corpses was the norm. Others, like the Princesse de Lamballe were, quite literally, hacked to pieces.

The de-Christianization of France, which reached full fury in 1792, had been gathering force since the fall of the Bastille three years before. Church property was nationalized in November 1789, and then sold to raise revenue. The clergy were also required to swear allegiance to the new Constitution. Many refused. In 1790, the Civil Constitution of the Clergy split the country and the religious community in two, causing Pope Pius VI to condemn it. In response, the Pope was burnt in effigy many times, convents were attacked, nuns assaulted, and churches were daubed with revolutionary slogans. Under this new law, priests and bishops had to be elected, and then swear to the new Constitution. Those who preached outside the law were subject to arrest for civil disobedience.

In August 1792, a new law was passed which required priests to leave the country unless they swore on oath to defend the Constitution. It was because of their refusal that the prisons began to be filled with priests, and which then led to their murder a month later.

But even before the French Revolution, the Age of Enlightenment had begun to thread doubts into the centuries-old fabric, woven by the church fathers.

In France, Enlightenment was based in the salons and culminated in the great *Encyclopédie* (1751–72) edited by Denis Diderot (1713–1784) and (until 1759) Jean le Rond d'Alembert (1717–1783) with contributions by hundreds of leading intellectuals who were called philosophes, notably Voltaire (1694–1778), Rousseau (1712–1778) and Montesquieu (1689–1755). [16]

By the time of the French Revolution, science and reason had gained ascendancy in intellectual thinking, and the de-Christianizing of society was making formidable progress.

It was in the midst of the turmoil, fury and social disorder of revolutionary France that the letter addressed to Henri II, 234 years earlier, was suddenly recognized for its accurate prediction of events taking place in 1792—with this year actually named, "A contemporary magazine *(Journal historique et littéraire*, Vol. I [February 1, 1792]. p. 233) mentions that the following was printed in a royalist newspaper called the *Journal de la ville:*"

New Year's gift for the Jacobins, drawn from Page 18 of the letter of Nostradamus to Henri II, dated from Salon, June 27, 1558, printed in the Prophecies of the same author, Lyon edition by Pierre Rigaud.

"Plus grande persecution sera fait à l'Église chrétienne . . . et continuels changements."

N.B. This copy of Nostradamus, in which this prediction is found, will remain exposed in our office for eight days, so that the curious will be able to verify it for themselves. [17]

This raises the question, who was this 'Nostradamus' and what do we really know about him, aside from crass comments? The best response is to ignore totally the world-wide-web with its internet spiders, intent upon trapping both the unwary and ill-informed. Instead, seek an answer from a reputable academic, who has given a professional opinion to this question from an historical point of view. Professor Emeritus Norman Davies, PhD., F.B.A., F.R.Hist.S.,D.Litt. author of the best-selling book *Europe A History* (1996), which received rave reviews from the Press, calling it 'A noble monument of scholarship'; 'Monumental authoritative [...] it will answer hundreds of enquiries'; 'it brims with learning [...] and abounds in good judgement.' &c. It also includes a noteworthy response to the question posed above.

> Michel de Nostredame (1503–66), called Nostradamus, was well known in the Midi as an unconventional healer. He came from a family of Jewish *converses* at St Rémy-en-Provence, and had graduated in medicine at Montpellier. He was learned in potions and remedies, concocting an elixir of life for the Bishop of Carcassonne and a diet of quince jelly for the Papal Legate. He worked in plague-stricken Marseilles and Avignon when all other doctors had left, refusing to bleed patients as was customary, and insisting on fresh air and clean water. More than once, as a suspected wizard, he attracted the notice of the Inquisition and fled abroad...
> The prophecies of Nostradamus were composed late in life. [...] They were written in quatrains and organized in centuries. They were published in two parts, in 1555 and 1568; and were an immediate sensation. [18]

De Nostredame's account of how he received his prophecies denounces both 'magic' (whatever is meant by that word) and astrology. He even went to the extent of burning such books as those that came into his hands. Repeatedly and insistently, there is contained within his published letters, the declaration that his gift of prophecy was a divine gift from God. In this respect, we may give pause to consider the importance of the words of Isaiah concerning such claims.

> I am the LORD, the Maker of all things, who stretches out the heavens, who spreads out the earth by myself, who foils the signs of the prophets and makes fools of diviners, who overthrows the learning of the wise and turns it into nonsense, who carries out the words of his servants and fulfils the predictions of his messengers. (44: 24-26)

These words of Isaiah, emanating from God, can now be used in support of de Nostredame as a true prophet. In the passage of time since his predictions were first published, close to two hundred and fifty of his four-lined verses have already foreshadowed the historical event they portended, and without a single error having been detected. As prophecies, they are word perfect, and their origin is literally 'out of this world', although not outside a 'block universe'.

Professor Davies confirmed the accuracy of four quatrains in his 1365-page tome on the history of Europe. Three appear in this present chapter (Nos. 3, 35 and 63); the fourth occurs in chapter ten as No. 39. Davies referred to 63 as "uncanny", for the "short description of life in the twentieth century" which it gave. And, while admitting that, "many come too close for comfort," he described others as "wonderfully obscure and suggestive, and can be made to fit all manner of coincidences."

The facts are somewhat different. The prophecies referred to are as much from God as those predicted by the biblical prophets. No mortal can foretell the future. A 'true prophet' can only report what s/he has been told or shown by God. or His divine messenger. Thus, all prophecies in these ten chapters are understood to be of divine origin. Each one is shown to be flawless in its accuracy, which is the hallmark of God, the Creator of Time. The 16th–century author of the prophecies then explained to King Henri II that "such secret events should not transpire, except in enigmatic sentences, having but one sense and one only meaning." [19] This requirement is preceded by the same sentiment expressed in Proverbs 25: 2. "It is the glory of God to conceal a matter."

This need for secrecy was also hinted at when Croesus received his reply from the priestess at Delphi, during his captivity. "It is said that when the Lydian messengers reached Delphi and asked the questions they had been told to ask. The Priestess replied that not God himself could escape destiny." [20] This, surprisingly, accords with Christian teaching. God is perfect; therefore to alter perfection would imply an imperfection. Moreover, God is eternal, from whence it follows that He has no future in which to impart change. But mankind, who dwells in *time*, does have a future, and the freewill to impose his wishes upon it. For this reason, any event lying in mankind's future, which could be altered if known beforehand, is denied his foreknowledge. Hence, the future can only be foretold by cryptic phrases, which become understood after the predicted event has occurred. Even then, it has long been understood that interpreting a divine work is unlikely to meet with success when placed in the hands of the impious—theologians included. This was made clear by Philo Judæus, a contemporary of the apostle Paul. It was Philo who "laid the foundations for the development of Christianity in the West and in the East, as we know it today. Philo's primary importance is in the development of the philosophical and theological foundations of Christianity." [21]

> A prophet says nothing of his own, but everything that he says is strange, and prompted by someone else; and it is not lawful for a wicked man to be an interpreter of God, as also no wicked man can be properly said to be inspired; but this statement is only appropriate to the wise man alone, since he alone is a sounding instrument of God's voice. [22]

These words are certainly applicable to the prophetic words and personal confessions of Michel de Nostredame, whose prophecy for 1792 was recognized at the time of the French Revolution, and bears comparison with Isaiah's foreknowledge of Cyrus. Well before then, and in an era of *faith*, later replaced by the Enlightenment, de Nostredame's divine gift was acknowledged by King Charles IX. During the young monarch's grand tour of France in 1564, the court stopped at Salon de Crau, and the King visited the house of the Seer. After which, he conferred upon him the title, Counsellor and Physician-in-Ordinary to the King of France. But Charles was not alone among the monarchs who paid homage to the Seer. In 1622, Louis XIII visited Salon to pay his respect at the Seer's tomb. And in 1660, it was the turn of his son, Louis XIV, to do likewise, accompanied by the Queen-regent, Anne of Austria and Cardinal Mazarin. These visits indicate that the monarchy was already recognizing events in France's recent history as having earlier appeared among the quatrains in de Nostredame's book of Prophecies.

And what had de Nostredame to say about himself and his ability? The two letters that preface his prophetic books, which appeared in two parts, allow him to affirm, "I fully confess that all proceeds from God, and for that I return Him thanks, honour and immortal praise." These words are in harmony with those proceeding from the LORD Almighty through the mouth of Isaiah, who condemned false prophets and declared He would frustrate their predictions.

Since the two-part publication of *Les Propheties* (in 1555 and 1558) first appeared, not less than 245 (to date) of de Nostredame's compound predictions have been fulfilled without error. His words are always meaningful because they can be understood in the linguistic context of the age for which they were intended, but remain baffling when presaged for a future generation. He also foresaw this would affect his readers, and appealed for their greater understanding—"Possum non errare, falli, decipi (I am not able to err, fail, or be deceived); though I am the greatest sinner in this world and heir to every human affliction."

This aspect of unfailing accuracy over a period of five centuries is indicative of the divine origin of these prophecies. It also means that at times past, what was then the future, contained details written down by the Seer concerning incidents that would later become part of the history of the world. Hence, there is no reason to suppose that this will now cease to continue. Rather, it implies that those quatrains remaining, and are as yet uninterpreted, can be considered true prophecies of what future generations will look back upon as *their* recent history.

It is with this thought in mind that what was once, and still is in part, the future history of the world, can be laid open for inspection until the end of its *time,* insofar as mankind is concerned.

Since the first two quatrains, Nos. 1 and 2, are given as the Seer's preface to these prophecies, and in which he explains how he prepared himself in tranquility to receive the divinity who would present the future to him, they have been excluded.

The purpose of this book is *not* to promote this man as a Seer, but to present verifiable evidence for a block universe. The manner in which that evidence was obtained lies outside the remit of this work, which is essentially a philosophical enquiry into science and religion, based principally upon logic, epistemology and, most particularly, historical records of prophetic foresight.

The prophecy numbered 3, below, is the first of the four quatrains confirmed by Norman Davies as being historically correct. Others will be identified in the order of their appearance. It was not until the French Revolution that the words and sentence structure of this prophecy became meaningful in the linguistic context of what was happening at that time.

> 3   *Quand la lictiere du tourbillon versée,*
> *Et seront faces de leurs manteaux couuers:*
> *La republique par gens nouueaux vexée,*
> *Lors blancs & rouge iugeront à l'enuers.*
>
> When the litter is overturned by the whirlwind,   1789
> And faces will be covered by their cloaks:
> The republic is vexed by new people,
> Then whites and reds will judge on the wrong side.

When the litter is overturned by the whirlwind

This well constructed allegory foretells the coming of the French Revolution: a time when political turmoil in the country was both sudden and ferocious. The effect it had is compared to a whirlwind. This word is taken from Hosea 8: 7; "They sow the wind, and reap the whirlwind;" and refers to the civil anarchy in Israel, that occurred when the people rebelled against God by setting up their own leaders in opposition to those appointed—much like what happened in France, when it overruled the priesthood and replaced the country's monarch and princes. Symbolically, the overturning of litters by a whirlwind represents the overthrow of nobility by revolution. [1]

And faces will be covered by their cloaks

Continuing with the same allegory, the prophecy next identifies the nobility *by their cloaks*. In sixteenth-century France, as in England, the wearing of a cloak was a privilege to be enjoyed only by the nobility. Across the Channel there were even sumptuary laws that forbade cloaks to be worn by anyone other than the titled classes. The Seer predicts that the nobility, the wearers of cloaks, will strive to avoid being recognized at the time of the *whirlwind*, for fear of their lives.

After laws proscribing the nobility had been passed by members of the new government, those affected by the legislation were compelled to conceal their identity or else flee the country. [2] This behaviour was far removed from life in sixteenth-century France, when these words were written. And it would be more than 200 years after then, before changes in society made it possible.

The republic is vexed by new people

On 21 September 1792, the monarchy in France was formerly replaced by a republic. Previously, during the elections of September 1791, in which the resigning members of the government had legislated against their own re-appointment, the *new people* elected to take their place were to become figureheads of the *First French Republic*. But first, they had to prove themselves. "Inside the Convention, the struggle for power developed between the Girondins and the more active and extreme Mountain, so called because its members took their seats on the highest tiers of benches."

It was to be these new people, elected into office, that were soon to *vex the republic*. [3] For, between November 1793 and July 1794: "the Jacobins tried to set up a system of government based on the absolutist aspects of Rousseau's *Contrat Social*," but the growing instability this caused was to lead to the Great Terror in the following year, which attempted to redress the problem.

Then whites and reds will judge on the wrong side

[I]n 1791 [...] the crowd attacking the Tuileries picked up a blood-soaked royal standard. Henceforth, 'red' and 'white' were the accepted colour codes for revolution and counter-revolution. [4]

White was the colour of the King's Bourbon flag. The oracle uses both colours to represent the royalists and revolutionaries attending the trial of Louis XVI, when he stood accused of treason.

The King was put on trial for his life, following the abolition of the monarchy and the establishment of France's First Republic. After the court hearing, three votes were taken to determine guilt, punishment and reprieve. At the first vote, a verdict of guilty was read out. A second ballot was then called for, to decide if the sentence should be death or exile. The result was death. There was then a third vote to settle the question of a reprieve.

The Seer makes a political judgement, by asserting that the voters on both sides – the *reds and the whites* – *will judge* the King guilty; that is, to be *on the wrong side* of him.[5] As a piece of cross-referencing, these same words are again employed when predicting the outcome of Charles I's trial in 1649. However, instead of 'reds and whites', the oracle refers to 'salt and wine' (Century 9: N°. 49).

Louis XVI received his death sentence with a placid show of inner courage. He did however harbour the regret that his own relative, the newly named Philip Égalité, had voted for his death.

Summary: *This first quatrain rightly begins with the French Revolution, which it links to the 'whirlwind' referred to by the biblical prophet Hosea: and it signifies civil unrest. The colours of the Revolution: red for those in revolt, against the white of the Bourbon monarchy, are correctly named. The overturning of the nobility, identified by their litters, which led to titled aristocrats concealing their faces, for fear of imprisonment, is also correctly alluded to. And the outstanding fact that this was first published 238 years before France became the republic named in the prophecy, is validated by the revolutionaries and the pro-monarchists having joined together to judge the King guilty at his trial in January 1793.*

4   *Par l'vniuers sera faict vng monarque,*
Qu'en paix & vie ne sera longuement:
Lors se perdra la piscature barque,
Sera regie en plus grand detriment.

This quatrain is left for the future. The second and third lines are certainly suggestive of events during the Napoleonic era, but neither the first line nor the fourth appears to be sufficiently appropriate for the First French Republic. As for its possible fulfilment, read Daniel, 11: 36.

5   *Chasséz seront sans faire long combat*
Par le pays seront plus fort greués:
Bourg & cité auront plus grand debat,
Carcas. Narbonne auront cœurs esprouués.

greués (OF. tourmenter, blâmer sévèrement); Carcas. (*portmanteau and abbreviation*) car + cas; [cas (OF) offence], *also* Carcas[sonne]; cueur (OF) heart, affection, mind, thought opinion.

They will be pursued without making a long struggle,   1791
Through the country they will be very much grieved:
Borough and city will have the greatest debate,
Because of the offence, Carcassonne, **NARBONNE** will have affections tested.

They will be pursued

When Paris awoke on the morning of June 21st to find that Louis XVI and the Queen had fled the capital during the night, panic broke out. Riders were dispatched in every direction with orders to *pursue* and detain the fugitive monarch and his family until an escort party could be arranged to bring them back. In the early hours of the morning of June 22nd, two envoys, Romeuf and Bayon, arrived in Varennes, a town in north-eastern France, after having successfully following the trail left by the lumbering *berline:*[1] this was the carriage chosen to take the royal family to safety in Austrian held Belgium.

Without making a long struggle

The appearance in Varennes of the two dusty riders from Paris coincided with the arrival of a detachment of troops loyal to the King. The army at once offered to escort the royal family to the Belgian border. A heated discussion then followed between the National Guard, who had been summoned to detain the King, and the army commissioned to escort the royal party to safety. It was during this altercation that a shot was fired and swords brandished. In the mêlée a man was wounded. Without wishing to cause more bloodshed by extending the conflict, Louis relented, and agreed to return to Paris under guard. It was to prove a fatal decision. [2]

Through the country they will be very much grieved

On their return journey through the countryside, angry demonstrations and a barrage of insults met the royal party at every stop. Acts of atrocious disrespect were aimed at the King and Queen each time the coach stopped over for the night. And this continued throughout the four-day journey back to Paris. At Sainte-Ménéhould, the mayor publicly blamed the King for leaving Paris. At Dormans, they were tormented by a hostile crowd that kept them awake all night with their anti-royalist chanting. At Épernay there was a threat to assassinate Marie Antoinette, and during a struggle that developed inside the hotel her dress was ripped. At Châlons, the dregs of Rheims arrived to intercept the coach, and then confront the royal party with their obscenities: most of which were directed at the Queen. At Chouilly, a hostile crowd surrounded the *berline*, shaking their fists at the occupants; one man even leaned into the coach and spat into the King's face. [3]

Borough and city will have the greatest debate

Once the King and Queen had arrived back in Paris, every borough and city across France became embroiled in the great debate. Could the King be considered a traitor for having tried to leave the country? And, had it been his intention to prepare the way for an invasion of France in order to restore him to power?

Different solutions were suggested to resolve the disquiet, including his deposition in favour of the Dauphin and a Regent. Some argued that the suspension of the King had already made the monarchy a redundant force. [4]

Because of the offence Carcassonne, Narbonne will have affections tested

Even as the coach trundled its way back to captivity, news of the flight was travelling around the country. Since it took three to four days for news to reach the farthest corners of the country, panics broke out, especially at the frontiers. [5]

"At Bayonne," on the French border with Spain, "there were reports of a Spanish invasion, to occur immediately." [7] Although the anticipated invasion did not materialise, the border towns were placed under duress in anticipation of an invasion. Carcassonne was also similarly affected.

Carcassonne became a border fortress between France and the Kingdom of Aragon [in north eastern Spain] under the Treaty of Corbeil (1258). [...] Its strategic importance was quickly recognized by the Romans who occupied its hilltop until the demise of their western empire. [6]

Apart from Carcassonne, Narbonne was another who had his heart tested: although with the Seer's forewarned deviousness to conceal the future, he never distinguishes between place and person when they both share the same name.

The Comte de Narbonne-Lara always maintained his fidelity towards the King; a true idealist, he hoped for a Constitutional Monarchy. [...] He became field marshal in 1791, and, through the influence of Madame de Staël, was appointed Minister of War of Louis XVI. In this office he tried at all cost to impose his constitutional project. [...] Narbonne-Lara and his friends [also] hoped to bring on the war with Austria, by which they hoped to restore the prestige of the monarchy. [8]

Summary: *This predicted episode from the French Revolution includes the pursuit and capture of the King and Queen at Varennes and their ignominious return to Paris, confronted daily by insults from the unruly crowds in the towns where they were forced to stay. The effect of their attempted escape is foretold by the heated debates that took place almost everywhere in France afterwards. Predicted, too, is the threat of invasion caused by their escape bid. This alerted the frontier towns, of which Carcassonne, near the Spanish border, is named. Nearby is Narbonne, which is also named, but is actually intended for Count Narbonne, whose affection for the King was likewise tested at that time.*

6   *L'œil de Rauenne sera destitué,*
         Quand à ses pieds les œisles failliront,
         Les deux de Bresse auront constitué,
         Turin, Verseil que Gaulois fouleront.

7   *Tard arrivé l'execution faicte,*
         Le vent contraire, lettres au chemin prinses:
         Les coniures. xiiij. d'vne secte:
         Par le Rosseau senez les entreprinses.

8   *Combien de foys prinse cité solaire,*
         Seras, changeant les loys barbares & veines.
         Ton mal s'aproche: Plus seras tributaire
         La grand Hadrie reourira tes vaines.

9   *De l'Orient viendra le cœur punique,*
         Fascher Hadrie & les hoirs Romulides:
         Acompaigné de la classe Libyque,
         Trembler Mellites: & proches isles vuides.

Libicque (L Libycus) African, ["Libya" used by the Greeks for all of North Africa, except Egypt] vuide (OF) free of

The Punic heart will arrive from the East,   1799
Displeasing Adria and the heirs of Romulus,
Accompanied by the African fleet,
The Maltese trembling: & the neighbouring islands free.

The Punic heart will arrive from the East

This is the first quatrain to refer to Napoleon. It is also written in reverse time order to obscure a premature understanding of what was to occur.

In October 1799, Napoleon returned to France from his conquest of Egypt: *arriving from the East*, at the port of Fréjus. He had learned of the political unrest in France, and his intention was to establish himself in the eyes of the people as a step towards governing the country.

What, then, is the connexion between Napoleon and *the Punic heart?* The answer is to attract attention to the Punic Wars fought between Carthage and Rome. From this, it is a short step to the original Punic heart, Hannibal the Carthaginian who crossed the Alps and invaded Rome. For, this had also become Napoleon's purpose after returning to France His plan was to re-conquer Italy, which had been lost to France during his campaign in Egypt. To achieve that end, he decided to follow Hannibal's example and embark upon a surprise attack cross the Alps. By this route, he expected to arrive in Italy without warning. The planned invasion began in May 1800, and it involved 50,000 soldiers; by 2 June, Bonaparte was in Milan.

Displeasing Adria

The Napoleonic Wars that followed after France regained control of Italy included the Adriatic Campaign. This took place when Napoleon seized the ancient port of *Adria*, which he needed as an outlet to the Adriatic Sea.

> Control of the Adriatic brought numerous advantages to the French Navy, allowing rapid transit of troops from Italy to the Balkans and Austria for campaigning in the east and giving France possession of numerous shipbuilding facilities, particularly the large naval yards of Venice. [1]

And the heirs of Romulus

The heirs of Romulus were the Holy Roman Emperors. Their empire commenced in 962 A.D., and, very much to the point of this prophecy,

> The Holy Roman Empire explicitly proclaimed itself to be the successor of the Western Roman Empire under the doctrine of *translation imperii*. [2]

It is in this context that the Holy Roman Emperors were *the heirs of Romulus*: the founder of Rome. The oracle has therefore correctly predicted that *the heirs of Romulus will be displaced by the 'Punic heart':* and they were given every reason for displeasure. After 844 years in existence, Napoleon finally brought the Holy Roman Empire and their reign to an end.

The last Holy Roman Emperor was Francis II, who abdicated and dissolved the Empire in 1806 during the Napoleonic Wars. [3]

Accompanied by the African fleet, the Maltese trembling

On board his flagship *Orient,* at the head of his African fleet – named after the North African coastline to which it was bound – Napoleon was accompanied by his *Armée d'Orient.* He first headed for Malta. After being allowed to enter the harbour, the French squadron turned their guns on the Maltese city of Valetta – *the Maltese trembling* – and the French army lost no time in conquering the island. Napoleon stayed in Malta for only six days, but in that time he removed the power of the Knights Hospitaler, and left behind a substantial garrison to administer and protect the changes he had instituted for governing the island.

And the neighbouring islands free

The irreligious French army occupying Malta soon became unpopular. And, by seeking aid from Naples and Sicily, the dissident Maltese were supplied with arms, which they used to rebel against the French. Britain also intervened, by sending its navy to set up a blockade around Malta's neighbouring islands. The French were therefore forced to retreat: abandoning their places of occupation, they sought refuge behind the fortifications in Valetta, from where General Vaubois surrendered to the British in 1800. The Maltese then created a Declaration of Rights, in which they agreed to come —

"under the protection and sovereignty of the King of the free people, His Majesty the King of the United Kingdom of Great Britain and Ireland." The Declaration also stated that "his Majesty has no right to cede these Islands to any power [...] if he chooses to withdraw his protection, and abandon his sovereignty, the right of electing another sovereign, or of the governing of these Islands, belongs to us, the inhabitants and aborigines alone, and without control." [4]

Summary: *The prediction of Napoleon as the Punic heart arriving from the East is most aptly confirmed by what else has been predicted. His conquest of Italy by crossing the Alps, as Hannibal had done before him; his capture of the port of Adria; his ending of the Holy Roman Empire; his garrison's occupation of Malta and the island's fight to free itself; followed by a signed declaration to guarantee the freedom of Malta and its neighbouring islands; these are events unquestionably related to Napoleon after his return from Egypt.*

10   *Serpens transmis dans la caige de fer,*
          Ou les enfans septains du roy sont pris:
          Les vieux & peres sortiront bas de l'enfer,
          Ains mourir voir de son fruict mort & crys.

Serpens (L) serpent; fer (OF) metal; ains (OF ainçois) before; mort (OF) decease.

A serpent transferred inside the metal cage,   1610
Where the seven children of the King are taken:
The old men & fathers will emerge from the bottom of hell
Before perishing, to see of its fruit decease and shrieks.

A serpent

"Catherine de' Medici was well versed in the arts of Machiavelli – and of poison." Her cabinet of toxic substances inside her closet at the Château de Blois has been preserved. There was also her 'Flying Squad': a bevy of court beauties, which she took with her to soften-up visiting dignitaries and make them more compliant to her policies. Upon visiting Chenonceaux in 1572, Jeanne d'Albret, the Queen of Navarre, was shocked at the women's licentious behaviour. Small wonder, therefore, that Catherine's youngest son, Alençon, called his mother, 'Madame la Serpente'. [1]

Transferred inside the metal cage

Catherine de' Medici died of pleurisy at 1.30 pm on 5 January 1589. After her death, the body was sent for embalming, but the operation was bungled through a lack of the relevant herbs. Without these, the body began to putrefy. Because of this, the corpse was *transferred to a lead-lined coffin*. The oracle derisorily calls it a metal cage, and it was interred in an unmarked grave at the church of Saint-Sauveur. The doyens of Paris steadfastly refused to accept the dead queen's body, believing her to be complicit in the Duke of Guise's murder. Consequently, for the next twenty-one years it laid buried at Blois [2] Eventually, in 1610, Anne de France the illegitimate daughter of Catherine's husband, arranged for the body to be re-interred at Saint-Denis. Her body was then transferred inside the metal cage to the Valois rotunda.

Where the seven children of the king are taken
Catherine de' Medici had made elaborate plans for her last resting place alongside her husband, Henri II, and *their seven children*. They were to be interred inside a specially constructed circular chapel at the north end of the transept in the abbey at Saint-Denis. [3] Construction began in 1563, but it was never completed. Despite this, sufficient work had been carried out for the initial burials to take place. But, inevitably, the passage of years took its toll, and the building fell into a state of decay. In 1719 it was demolished, and the bodies were removed to another tomb inside the basilica. [4]

The old men and fathers will emerge from the bottom of hell
As a practising Catholic, the Seer would have been aware of Jesus Christ's vision of hell, which is frequently referred to in the gospels as a place where unclean spirits go after their bodily death, to wail and gnash their teeth through having surrendered to the pleasures that kill the soul. The Seer's words in the third line of this oracle may therefore be taken as a judgment upon the Valois forefathers and their offspring as they faced their future: doomed to the abyss.

Before perishing, to see of its fruit decease and shrieks
The oracle concludes by indicating the failure and final judgement that awaited those of the House of Valois: a family that ruled France for 261 years (1328 – 1589). The four sons of Henri II and Catherine de' Medici died without legitimate heirs or honour. Francis II, aged sixteen, was an almost perpetual invalid, and unable to countermand the greater experience and authority of the Duke of Guise. As a result, he expressed little interest in the government of France, and his health gave way after just one year. Charles IX's part in that 'carnival of butchery', known as the Massacre of St. Bartholomew's Eve, will be forever remembered in the annals of infamy. Henri III's reign is likewise acknowledged for the blood of the Huguenots he spilled during the Wars of Religion; for his political ineptness, which included his loss of power when confronted by the Duke of Guise, and for the fratricidal hatred of his brother, which threatened the monarchy. His final crime was to order the assassination of the duc de Guise and Cardinal Lorraine.

One historian's epitaph for Henri III said pointedly, "**The worst ruler of the worst dynasty that has ever governed.**" The fourth son, Alençon, never became king. This did not stop him from presiding over the murder of 3,000 citizens in the town of Issoire, or for organizing the 'French Fury' in Antwerp, for which, afterwards, he was branded a common criminal. [5] All four sons, however, had one thing in common, their mother, 'Madame la Serpente'.

Summary: *Although Catherine de Medici was known to the author of this prophecy, her death occurred more than two decades after that of the seer. Likewise her seven surviving children (she actually gave birth to ten, three of whom died in infancy) were all born during the life of the seer. The element of prophecy therefore exists in the apparent foreknowledge that her coffin would be transferred, and that her sons would suffer the torment of hell for their crimes, while also ending the Valois line of kingship. The vision of hell, which accompanies this prophecy, seeing that all genuine foreknowledge is of divine origin, should serve as a stark warning to political leaders of all colours; for they are not excluded from sharing the same fate as those of the House of Valois, if they continue to offend God with anti-Christian policies that aid and abet sinfulness among those they govern. One recalls the question Jesus posed, "What good will it be for someone to gain the whole world, yet forfeit their soul?" (Matt. 16: 26)*

11   *Le mouuement de sens, cœur, pieds, & mains*
      Seront d'acord. Naples, Leon, Secille:
      Glaisues, feus, eaux: puis aux nobles Romains
      Plongés, tués, mors par cerueau debile.

12   *Dans peu dira faulce brute, fragile,*
      De bas en hault esleué promptement:
      Puis en instant desloyale & labile
      Qui de Veronne aura gouuernement.

13   *Les exilés par ire, haine intestine,*
      Feront au roy grand coniuration:
      Secret mettront ennemis par la mine,
      Et ses vieux siens contre eux sedition.

14   *De gent esclaue chansons, chantz & requestes,*
      Captifz par princes & seigneur aux prisons:
      A l'aduenir par idiotz sans testes,
      Seront receuz par diuins oraisons.

esclaue (OF) slavish; seigneur (OF) Lord; testes (AF Livre des Évangiles) the gospels; Cross-reference: gent esclaue, C.V: 26.

Concerning the slavish people, songs, chants and demands,   1917
Captives through Princes (**MIKHAIL & LVOV**) and the Lord (**NICHOLAS**) to prisons:
In the befalling, through idiots without the gospels,
They will be received by divine speeches.

Concerning the slavish people

The word slavish – 'servily following or conforming' – is derived from the old French word 'esclave', originally a Slav. (Chambers English Dictionary). In Medieval Latin, it is 'Sclavus'– from which we get the word Slav – people of Russia. (OED). Hence, the phrase: "The Russian people have long been inured to tyranny," [1] is descriptive of the 'slavish people'.

Songs, chants and demands

In just three words, the oracle correctly describes the three events that signalled the outbreak of the Russian Revolution. In Petrograd, "discontented workers began a demonstration carrying banners that said 'We want bread.'" This was accompanied by shouts of: "Down with the war [...] soon there were speeches on street corners, choruses of the French revolutionary song and national anthem, the Marseillaise – sung in Russian. [2] [...] By Monday March 12 the tide of revolution was at its full, and there would be no stopping it." [3]

Captives through Princes

Up until this time, Nicholas II had ruled as Czar of Russia. But, within the space of seven violent days he was forced to abdicate, as the upsurge in public protest became a full-scale revolt. In his place, he named Prince Mikhail as his successor; [4] he also appointed Prince Georgy Lvov to preside over the Council of Ministers. Both appointments were intended to save him from arrest, but the plan failed. *Prince Mikhail* refused to accept the succession, and *Prince Lvov's* provisional government resolved to place the deposed Czar, together with his family, under house arrest. [5]

And the Lord to prisons

Nicholas II, referred to as 'the Lord', was a feudal lord: [6] therefore an apt description for the ruler of Russia. After his arrest, the Czar was taken with his wife and children to Czarskoe Selo: the first of three prisons. There, he was held under guard until the family could be transferred to a mansion house in Tobalsk: where, for eight months they continued under house arrest. In April 1918, Nicholas and his family were transferred to a merchant's house in Ekaterinburg. A high wooden fence had been hurriedly placed around the property, including the garden. The windows were also painted over to shield the occupants from public view. The Romanov family arrived there on May 3rd to begin their last days alive as captives of the Revolution. [7]

In the befalling, through idiots without the gospels

After the brutal murder of the Romanov family, a long period of Communist rule replaced Czarist Russia. The oracle speaks disparagingly about the people living under this mode of government. The descriptive vocabulary of the Seer is reflected in the following text.

> The Soviet Union was the first state to have as an ideological objective the elimination of religion. [...] The main target of the anti-religious campaign in the 1920s and 1930s was the Russian Orthodox Church, which had the largest number of faithful. Nearly all of its clergy, and many of its believers, were shot or sent to labour camps. Theological schools were closed, and church publications were prohibited.[8]

> Lenin's decree on the separation of church and state in early 1918 deprived the formerly official church of its status of legal person, the right to own property, or to teach religion in both state and private schools or to any group of minors. The decree abolished the privileges of the church and thus ended the alliance between church and state.[9]

They will be received by divine speeches

The prophecy concludes with the arrival of Lenin, although not without a tinge of the Seer's characteristic wit. For, as one former Soviet citizen remarked to me, "We were taught at school that we had no need of God because Lenin provided us with everything." Historians have taken a similar view with regard to the way Lenin was welcomed by the populace; "semi-divine honours were readily paid to his every speech." Or, as the Seer said: *the people will be received by divine speeches.* And, for the entire generation that followed – "The works of Karl Marx and Friedrich Engels were like prophetic works in the Bible for most [Bolsheviks]; and Lenin as well as Marx and Engels were beatified."[10]

Summary: *This quatrain focuses upon the Russian Revolution in 1918, which began, as predicted with songs, chants and demands. The imprisonment of the Czar and his family, for which the Princes, Mikhail and Lvov were partly responsible, has also been correctly foretold. The oracle then looks at the aftermath, in which it describes the people after the Revolution who were made to live under the atheistic rule of communism. Finally, and no less remarkably, it foretells in biblical terminology how the founders of the communistic system were greeted by the people of Russia.*

15   *Mars nous menasse par sa force bellique,*
        Septante foys fera le sang espandre:
        Auge & ruyne de l'Ecclesiastique,
        Et plus ceux qui d'eux rien voudront entendre.

Mars (Gk Myth.) god of war; sang espandre (see. epandre) blood to shed: whence, bloodshed; auge (L auge\o) increase, honour.

> Mars menaces us by his martial strength,   1796
> Seventy times he will cause bloodshed:
> Increase and ruin for the Ecclesiastic (PIUS VII),
> And those more, that will want to hear nothing from them.

Mars menaces us by his martial strength

Napoleon's military conquests began in the spring of 1796 with his appointment as Commander of the Army of Italy. By the following year he had established himself as one of the foremost military figures in Europe, accomplished by the strength of his armed forces.

> [B]etween March 1804 and April 1815 practically two million native-born Frenchmen saw active service in his successive armies; there were no less than thirty two levies on the various annual classes over the same period, and probably a further million men were procured from allied or satellite states.[1]

Seventy times he will cause bloodshed

By the time Napoleon left the field at Waterloo, he had, during his career, *caused blood to be shed* in battle *seventy times.* Alan Palmer records the names of all *seventy battles* in *An Encyclopaedia of Napoleon's Europe:*

> Aboukir Bay; Acre; Albuera; Alexandria; Almeida; Arcis-sur-Aube; Arcole; Aspern; Auerstädt; Austerlitz; Badajoz; Bassano; Bautzen; Baylen; Bayonne; Berezina; Bidassoa; Borghetto; Borisov; Borodino; Burgos; Caldiero [2]; Castiglione; Champeaubert; Ciudad Rodrigo; Corunna; Dego; Dresden; Eckmühl; Eylau; Friedland; Fuentes de Oñoro; Hohenlinden; Jena;

Katzbach; Krasnoe; Kulm; Laon; La Rothière; Leipzig; Ligny; Lodi; Lützen; Maloyaroslavets; Mantua; Marengo; Montmirail; Oporto; Orthèz; Polotsk; Pultusk; Pyramids; Quatre Bras; Salamanca; San Sebastian; Saragossa; Smolensk; Talavera; Toulouse; Ulm; Vauchamps; Vilna; Vimiero; Vitebsk; Vitoria; Wagram; Waterloo; Wavre; Zurich. (p.xxiii). [2]

N.B., two battles occurred at Caldiero. The first one was fought on 12 November 1796 in a failed attempt at preventing the Austrian General, Joseph Alvintzi, reaching Verona. The second battle took place on 30 October 1805, and was fought between Archduke Charles of Austria and Bonaparte's Marshal, André Masséna.

Increase and ruin for the Ecclesiastic

Pius VII (Barnaba Niccolò Maria Luigi Chiaramonti,) began his ministry six months after the unhappy demise of Pius VI, and with an *increase* in good fortune for the Church. The Concordat of 1801, agreed between Bonaparte and the Pope, acknowledged Catholicism to be the preferred religion of France. It also guaranteed every citizen the freedom of worship. The French government also arranged to pay the clergy from state funds, and it redrew the boundaries of many dioceses to help implement this arrangement.

In 1808, the predicted *ruin for the Ecclesiastic* began. Rome became incorporated into the French Empire. Pius objected by excommunicating those responsible. Napoleon's retaliation was swift. He ordered the Pope's arrest and deportation. Pius was first taken to Grenoble and then transferred to Savona. He did not see Rome again until 24 May 1814. [3]

There is a reason why Pius VII is described as an 'Ecclesiastic', complete with a capital letter for emphasis. It is because, "Chiaramonti was also a monk, theologian, and bishop throughout his life." [4] In other words, he remained a Clergyman who happened to occupy the papal seat.

And those more, that will want to hear nothing from them

The Napoleonic wars that were fought after the Concordat – which had been agreed between Napoleon and Pius VII – were in opposition to the Church's teaching. Nevertheless, wealth and territory acquired by conquest, greatly helped build the French Empire, and it increased for a time, but ended in ruin. The Battle of Leipzig, fought in the middle of October 1813, foreshadowed the Empire's collapse. Soldiers, once triumphant in conquest, returned from the wars disillusioned and without employment. The lands won by French blood were afterwards (by order of the Congress of Vienna), returned to their 1792 borders. The gains obtained by those who fought for the French Empire had eventually come to nothing.

Summary: *This quatrain commences by predicting the exact number of battles; i.e., seventy, fought by France during the time of Napoleon. It then turns to the Church in Rome, during the papal reign of Pius VII, whom it correctly foresees as continuing in office as a Clergyman. Next, it predicts the rise and fall of the Church's administration, which occurred during this period, and it then correctly contrasts this with the far worse rise and fall of France under Napoleon.*

16   *Faulx à l'estang ioinct vers le Sagitaire,*
       En son hault AVGE de l'exaltation,
       Peste, famine, mort de main militaire:
       Le siecle approche de renouation.

Faulx (OF fauls) a sham; estang (OF) a great pond; ioinct (OF) joined; AVGE (*apocope*) AUGE[REAU] *also* (L) AUGE\o honour; exaltation (OF) high-raising, exalting, renowning.

A sham at the great pond joined toward Sagittarius,   1797
At his height, **AUGEREAU**, honour from the raising-up:
Plague, hunger, death by the military hand,
The century approaches renewal.

A sham at the great pond, joined toward Sagittarius

The only thing certain about this line of prophecy is the time of year. The sun sign, Sagittarius – 23 November–21 December – is intended to mark the time of year when 'deceit at the great pond' will occur.

The word 'estang' also appears in Century Three N°. 12, where it refers to Lake Geneva: one of the largest lakes in Western Europe situated in the canton of Vaud. (It is also known as Lac Léman in the Pays de Vaud). From this information and using the known facts appearing as predictions in the remaining three lines of this quatrain, the year in question can be placed shortly before the turn of the 18th century.

Following the outbreak of the French Revolution, Frédéric-César de la Harpe began *plotting an uprising* designed to free the Pays de Vaud from its domination by Bern. For this, he and other exiles sought the help of the Paris Directory.

> La Harpe published his *Essay on the Constitution of the Vaud*, an anti-Bernese tract. On the 10 December 1797 he addressed the French Directory, stating that commitments made by the Duke of Savoy in treaties signed with Bern at Lausanne in 1564 were now the responsibility of the French and thus gave them the right to assist the people of Vaud against the Bernese. [1]

> The French Directory, which was interested in acquiring Swiss money and the Swiss passes over the Alps, agreed with La Harpe's interpretation of the treaty. In late 1797, the Directory ordered Bern to restore the Pays de Vaud region to its former independence. The citizens of Pays de Vaud, reacted to the French announcement with excitement and declared the creation of the Lémanic Republic. Bern, on the other hand, looked with dismay on the events, and in January 1798, sent Colonel Weiss with troops into the province. France replied by immediately sending portions of André Masséna's army under an officer named Mesnard from Italy to occupy the southern shore of Lake Geneva. [2]

Note the date of the address made by La Harpe to the Directory, 10 December 1797, and the Directory's response in late 1797, ordering Bern to restore the Pays de Vaud region to its former independence. This, having all taken place near Sagittarius; soon afterwards it was followed by French troops arriving at Lake Geneva – the great pond – in January 1798.

At his height Augereau, honour from the raising-up

The Paris Directory consisted of five executive members. It was created in 1795, after the former National Convention had been dissolved, and it "included a bicameral legislature known as the Corps Législatif." But two years later,

> The Directory, fearing that it was losing favour in the country, called upon Napoleon Bonaparte to send a general to command troops guarding the legislature at the Tuileries. On 18 Fructidor, year V (Sept. 4, 1797), Gen. Pierre-François Charles Augereau, commanding the troops, purged more than 130 royalists and counterrevolutionaries from the Corps Législatif. [3]

Augereau "carried out the coup d'état of 18 Fructidor (September 4, 1797) and was elected a deputy and secretary of the Assembly in 1799." [4] He was therefore *at his height, from the raising up*. His elevation to governmental rank was an honour that stood in direct contrast to his background. "General Augereau was a product of the Paris gutters," wrote military historian, David Chandler (p. 55). His father was a stonemason and his mother worked as a serving girl; both parents were poor.

Plague, hunger

In the summer of 1799, Napoleon was still in Egypt, having failed to take the fortress at Acre. Realising that the task before him was now beyond him, he ordered his army to begin the arduous trek back to Cairo. The retreat was long and gruelling, with his soldiers being forced to march across the barren desert beneath a hostile sun.

"Plague ridden, burdened by wounded, starved," [5] the French soldiers at last reached Katia where they "fell like starved vultures on the drink and supplies stored there." [6]

Death by the military hand

Shortly before the close of Bonaparte's campaign in Egypt (July 1799), his *Armée d'Orient* came under attack from a Turkish expeditionary force that had landed in Aboukir Bay.

> It was not a bloodless victory [...] the French lost 150 killed and 750 wounded [...] of the Turkish force 2000 were killed on the field [...] and no less than 10,000 shot or drowned as they vainly attempted to swim to their ships. Another 1800 were found killed and 300 wounded in the fort. [7]

The century approaches renewal

This final line requires little explanation. All of the events described above, took place between 1797 and 1799 inclusive: *as the century approached renewal.*

Summary: *This quatrain predicts for the three years leading to the turn of the 18th century. It foresees a plot to recover the Pays de Vaud at Lake Geneva, even naming the time of the year. It also capitalises one half of General AUGEreau's name, when predicting his rise in government office. In the same timeframe it switches to Bonaparte's Egyptian campaign and the French retreat from the Siege at Acre. At which time, as predicted, his men were suffering from plague and hunger as they crossed the desert to Cairo. At Aboukir Bay they were met by a Turkish army, which resulted in 'death by the military hand' and a French victory.*

17   *Par quarante ans l'Iris n'aparoistra,*
        Par quarante ans tous les iours sera veu:
        La terre aride en siccité croistra,
        Et grans deluges quand sera aperceu.

Siccité (L) siccitas; croire (OF) to commit into the hands of, to credit

        For forty years the rainbow will not be perceived,
        For forty years it will be seen every day:
        The ground arid, it will be committed to drought,
        And great deluges whenever it will be perceived.

This prophecy concerns the effect of climate change. In his introduction to the first edition of the prophecies, the Seer wrote of a time when very few parts of the world would be above water. The rainbow is a biblical symbol. It refers to God's promise that he would never again flood the world, as in the days of Noah. According to this oracle, He comes very close to doing so.

18   *Par la discorde negligence Gauloise*
        Sera passaige à Mahommet ouuert:
        De sang trempé la terre & mer Senoise
        Le port Phoce de voilles & nefz couuert.

19   *Lors que serpens viendront circuir l'are,*
        Le sang Troyen vexé par les Espaignes:
        Par eux grand nombre en sera faicte tare,
        Chef fuit, caché aux mares dans les saignes.

20   *Tours, Orleans, Bloys, Angiers, Reims, & Nantes*
        Cités vexées par subit changement:
        Par langues estranges seront tendues tentes
        Fluues, dards Renes, terre, & mer tremblement.

21   *Profonde argille blanche nourir rochier,*
        Qui d'vn abisme istra lacticineuse,
        En vain troubles ne l'oseront toucher
        Ignorans estre au fond terre argilleuse.

22   *Ce que viura & n'ayant aucun sens,*
        Viendra à leser à mort son artifice:
        Austun Chalon, Langres & les deux Sens,
        La gresle & glace fera grand malefice.

23   *Au mois troisiesme se leuant le Soleil.*
        Sanglier, Liepard, au champ Mars pour combatre.
        Liepard laissé au ciel extend son œil,
        Vn Aigle autour du Soleil voit s'esbatre.

Liepard (OF. liepart) leopard; laisse (OF laisser) leaves; extend (L. extendo) to stretch; s'ebatre (OF) dally.
Cross-reference: Aigle, C.III: 37; C.IV: 70; C.VIII: 4; C.VIII: 46

        In the third month, the sun rising,   1815
        Boar, leopard, in the martial field for combat.
        Leopard leaves; stretches his sight to the sky,
        An eagle is seen to dally about the sun.

This quatrain is filled with symbolism. It has been suggested by previous commentators that these symbols can be understood to refer to the armies that took part in the Battle of Waterloo, in which the Duke of Wellington, aided later in the day by General Blücher, fought against Napoleon in a field outside Brussels; military records are supportive of this conjecture.

In the third month
The third month indicates March, but these oracles frequently use the earlier, legalistic form of dating in which 25th March began the New Year. In which case, *the third month* is understood to mean June. [1]

The sun rising
On the morning of 18 June 1815, the sun rose *early* above the saturated countryside at Waterloo. Torrential rain over the past eighteen hours had waterlogged the ground. But with the clouds gone, the sky was clear. [2] [This is one of several long range weather forecasts made by the Seer].

Boar, leopard
The boar is a legendary beast associated with northern Europe, in particular Prussia. [3] It is also of interest to note the boar signifies one of the twelve years in the Chinese horoscope: the present case being especially relevant, because 1815 was the year of the boar.
The leopard, which is also a heraldic beast, was identified by the French as a creature related to England, because English heralds had described their device as a "lion leopard". [4]

In the martial field for combat
> The battlefield of Waterloo is extremely small in area. The opposing armies occupied two low ridges, separated by a gentle valley extending over a distance of some 1,500 yards. In width, the battle zone barely extended over 5,000 yards. [5]

On the day of the battle, the area was filled by "almost 140,000 troops and more than 400 guns." [6] Fighting began at noon on the 18th, with Wellington– *the leopard* – pitting his troops against Napoleon– *the eagle*. It was not until Blücher– *the boar* – arrived that evening, with his Prussian troops still fresh, that the exhausted French realised the battle could no longer be won.
Napoleon was defeated at Waterloo because he delayed the start. This gave Blücher time to reach the battlefield, and change the course of events. But the weather too played an important part. Had Napoleon not been hindered by torrential rain on the eve of battle, he would have caught up with Wellington, who was retreating from a battle fought at Quatre Bras, and was now seeking to reposition his army on the field at Waterloo.
In which case, had it not been for the rain, the battle of Waterloo would very likely never have been fought; and with the British army defeated, the future would be different to what it is now.

Leopard leaves, stretches his sight to the sky
On the eve of Waterloo, with Wellington having *left* Quatre Bras pursued by the French, "a colossal thunderstorm burst overhead, and within minutes the ground was turned into a quagmire. This ruled out any moves across country, and the French pursuit was consequently confined to the roads." [7]
Despite these adverse conditions, the French attempted to make up the ground that lay between the two armies, and almost caught up with Lord Uxbridge's rear guard. But, "'The tracks were so deep in mud after the rain that we found it impossible to maintain any sort of order in our columns,' noted Sergeant Mauduit of the Imperial Guard." [8]
By 6.30 in the evening it had become clear that Wellington, having given due regard to the *sky* took advantage of what he saw, had escaped to the safety of a ridge at Mont-St.-Jean. It was from there that he made plans to engage the French in battle next day. "'What would I not have given to have had Joshua's power to slow down the sun's movement by two hours,' said Napoleon afterwards." [9]

An eagle is seen to dally about the sun
On the morning of the 18th, Bonaparte – *the eagle* – was informed of intelligence just received,

revealing that Wellington and Blücher intended to join forces. But the Emperor dismissed the account as nonsense. In a similar mood, he declined to recall Grouchy. It was only when General Drouot suggested delaying the battle to let the sun dry out the sodden ground, that he took note.

Napoleon immediately agreed, and ordained that the main action should commence only at 1:00 p.m. This decision proved the most fatal one of the day for the French. For had even an adequately supported infantry attack been launched against Wellington during the morning, the French must surely have won; for Blücher would have been too late arriving on the field to affect the issue. [10]

Thus, ended the Battle of Waterloo; it was won by Wellington and Blücher because their adversary, *the eagle, dallied too long about the sun.*

Summary: *As a prediction of the Battle of Waterloo, it accurately describes the war-like field prepared by*
                Wellington, the time of year, and the participants, albeit by heraldic symbols. It foretells, also, that the
                leopard will give regard to the sky as he leaves—but does not indicate why, or from where. But it does allow
                the eagle to attend to the sun, which caused the dalliance that led to Napoleon's defeat.

> 24   *A cité neufue pensif pour condemner,*
>   *L'oisel de proye au ciel se vient offrir:*
>   *Apres victoire à captifz pardonner,*
>   *Cremo. & Mant. grands maulx aura souffert.*
>
> 25   *Perdu trouué, caché de long siècle,*
>   *Sera pasteur demi Dieu honoré.*
>   *Ains que la Lune acheue son grand siecle*
>   *Par autres veux sera deshonoré.*

siecle (OF- une longue période de temps); Pasteur (Louis Pasteur. *also* 'pastor') Ains (OF ainçois) ere,; veux (AF veue) view

> Lost, found, hidden for a long period of time: 1822
> A pastor (**PASTEUR**) will be honoured a demy-god:
> Ere the moon completes its great cycle,
> By other views, he will be dishonoured.

To those familiar with the life of Louis Pasteur, the second and fourth lines will suggest comparison. The third line is understood to be an astronomical reference. This leaves the opening line, which appears to indicate an archaeological discovery. In which case, it should be recognizable for its importance. At the same time, it would need to have some bearing upon the life of Pasteur. In fact, these requirements have all been met in the commentary below.

Lost, found, hidden for a long period of time
One of the greatest archaeological finds of all time was undoubtedly the discovery of the Rosetta stone, which dated back to the second century B.C. It was discovered in August 1799, during Napoleon Bonaparte's conquest of Egypt. Ancient hands had employed three writing systems – hieroglyphics, demotic script and Greek – in order to inscribe the stone with a decree made by Ptolemy V (Epiphanes). After its discovery at Rosetta, a location some 35 miles from Alexandria, the inscription promised to provide scholars with the key to understanding many ancient and, what were up until then, undeciphered hieroglyphs. [1] But deciphering the stone proved to be far from simple, despite one third of it being in Greek. Several decades elapsed before Jean-François Champollion found the key; and his discovery gave rise to a new science, that of Egyptology.

A pastor (Pasteur)
The internationally famous chemist, Louis *Pasteur*, was born in France in 1822: the same year that Champollion discovered the key to deciphering the Rosetta stone. It may therefore be said, that this oracle has cleverly combined one of the greatest archaeological discoveries of the age with the birth year of one of France's greatest scientists. [2]

Pasteur proved to be an excellent scholar, and it was not long before he was appointed Dean at Lille University, and later Director of Scientific Studies at the *École Normale Supérieure*. It was also a period in his life when he took on a *pastoral* role, "by instituting evening classes for the many young workmen of the industrial city, conducting his regular students around large factories in the area, and organizing supervised practical courses." [3]

Will be honoured a demy-god

By 1892 his fame had grown so great that "the whole of France assisted by representatives of many nations united to honour her greatest scientist." The festival of appreciation took place at the Sorbonne in Paris, and was attended by delegates "from London, Ireland, Brussels, Liege, Ghent, Leyden, Stockholm, Copenhagen, Genoa, Berlin, Cologne, Posen, Warsaw, Geneva, Berne, Lausanne, Athens and Bucharest."

Pasteur had also been given a seat "among the 'Immortals': the forty Frenchmen most distinguished in letters and in science." And when a popular vote was taken amongst the people of France, Louis *Pasteur* was voted, "the greatest Frenchman of all time". [4]

Ere the moon completes its great cycle, by other views he will be dishonoured

In January 1887, a spate of criticisms broke out aimed at the chemist. These concerned the serum he used to cure Rabies: "many were sceptical and a few were positively hostile." Monsieur Peter, prominent among the other physicians, took a leading role in *dishonouring* Pasteur. He maintained, "that the anti-rabic cure was useless [even] dangerous when applied in intensive form." The Press took up the attack, and very soon Pasteur found himself at the focal point of "all that envy and hatred could invent," as wave after wave of protests poured in from across the country.

It was while he was convalescing at Bordighera, to recover from these verbal attacks that the Academy of Sciences retaliated on Pasteur's behalf. They did so by issuing a pamphlet exonerating him from any blame. These leaflets were delivered to every village across France, and proved very successful. By the time the chemist returned to Paris in March that year, the controversy had faded away. [5] It had lasted barely a month: *ere the moon completed its great cycle*.

Summary: *This quatrain clearly names Louis Pasteur 267 years before his birth. The doubters are left with having to claim a coincidence existing between a quatrain, which includes the name Pasteur (meaning 'pastor'), and a prophecy that predicts the international level of acclaim received by the great chemist of that same name. To add to the alleged coincidence, the prophecy then foretells the short-lived criticism that he received towards the end of his career by referring to 'other views'. Incidentally, 'veux' as a paragram becomes 'vieux', which would then incorporate the 'other elders' who had opposed Pasteur.*

26   *Le grand du fouldre tumbe d'heure diurne,*
        Mal & predict par porteur postulaire
        Suiuant presaige tumbe d'heure nocturne,
        Conflit Reims, Londres, Etrusque pestifere.

27   *Dessoubz de chaine Guien du ciel frappe,*
        Non loing de la est caché le tresor,
        Qui par longs siecles auoit este grappé.
        Trouue moura: l'œil creué de ressort.

28   *La tour de Bouq gaindra* (craindra) *fuste Barbare,*
        Vn temps long temps après barque hesperique,
        Bestail, gens, meubles tous deux feront grand tare
        Taurus & Libra quelle mortelle picque!

29   *Quand le poisson terrestre & aquatique*
        Par sorte vague au grauier sera mis,
        Sa forme estrange suave & horrifique,
        Par mer aux murs bien tost les ennemis.

forme (OF) appearance; suave (L suavis); estrange (OF) foreign, bizarre.

When the terrestrial and aquatic fish (**AMPHIBIOUS TANK**)   1944
By a strong wave will be placed on the shingle,
Its bizarre appearance pleasing, also hair-raising,
Very soon by sea, the adversaries at the walls.

During the Second World War, there was no tighter secret held by the allied forces than the date of the D-Day landings and their location. Yet, in retrospect, it can be seen that this was no secret to a gifted seer. In a block universe, everything is potentially open to the conscious mind. But those who 'see' across time are also part of the temporal scenery. This necessarily means that their ability has been encoded into the data that leads toward what they foresee.

When the terrestrial and aquatic fish

For the Allied invasion of France during World War II, the US army had been assigned a part of Normandy's coastline on either side of the River Vire. These sections of beach were codenamed 'Utah' and 'Omaha'. Among the assault craft used by the Americans was the Sherman D D (duplex drive) amphibious tank. The oracle refers to its amphibious nature by calling it *the fish that is both terrestrial and aquatic.*

Referring to the Sherman tank as a *fish* is consistent with the *ferocious beasts* – in Century Two Nº. 24 – that gave their name to German tanks. We shall meet up with these later. [1]

By a strong wave

Early on the morning of 6 June 1944, the first "Sherman DD (duplex drive) amphibious tanks reached the shore with the first wave." [2]

Will be placed on the shingle

The weather condition that morning was poor. "It was not until 10.00 when the rising tide was approaching the shingle," that US army engineers managed to make progress. "Each seaborne landing was timed for one hour after low water." However, "Gaps had to be made in the bank of loose stones to allow tanks and other vehicles to pass through." [3]

Its bizarre appearance pleasing, also hair-raising

The oracle describes the amphibian's *appearance* as *bizarre.* One can well understand a 16th-century observer's initial reaction at first sight of these 20th century mechanised amphibious tanks emerging from the sea. Apart from the tank having been American, therefore *foreign,* it had "propellers and a canvas skirt to protect it from the water. When the tank made it to the shore, the canvas was lowered." [4]

SHERMAN DD AMPHIBIOUS TANK

For occupied France, the Sherman was a *pleasing;* sight; it was also *hair-raising* in its destructive capability, as it dealt with the German artillery. "As the morning wore on more tanks [...] landed, and began to take out gun positions and pillboxes." [5]

Very soon by sea, the adversaries

The initial landings were to be made by 156,000 men, mostly Britons, Americans and Canadians. The line-up included an armoured division from France, one Belgian brigade, one Polish division, as well as multi-national seaborne forces. [6]

At the walls

The Atlantic Wall comprised "an extensive system of coastal fortifications built by the German Third Reich during the Second World War along the western coast of Europe (1942 –44) in order to defend against an anticipated Anglo-American invasion of the continent." By the end of what became called 'The Longest Day', the Normandy landings had been accomplished, and the Atlantic Wall breached. [7]

Summary: *Although neither date nor place, other than the sea, has been given, the events predicted were precisely those that occurred during the first part of the D -Day landings on the beaches of Normandy during the allied invasion of France by 'friendly' adversaries. The amphibian tanks employed in the ultimate liberation of France, described in the prophecy as 'bizarre and hair -raising', are of special note.*

30   *La nef estrange par le tourment marin*
       Abourdera pres de port incongneu,
       Nonobstant signes de rameau palmerin
       Apres mort, pille: bon auis tard venu.

Abourdera (*epenthesis:* Abordera, OF) draw near: also Arabic phonetic – Abourdera for Abour[k]era i.e., Aboukir; incongneu
(L incognitus); pille (OF. pillé) bereaved of all.

         The foreign ship, by reason of the marine torment   1799
         Will draw near close to port unrecognised,
         Notwithstanding signs of the palm bough:
         Afterwards a death, bereft of all: good intelligence arrived late.

The foreign ship, by reason of the marine torment

The foreign ship refers to the Venetian-built galley that brought Napoleon back to France in October 1799. [1] It was through the loss of almost his entire fleet in the battle of the Nile (August 1798), referred to here as *the marine torment,* that Napoleon found himself stranded in Egypt. By the time he was ready to leave the country, two vessels had been prepared for the voyage. Of these, it was *La Muiron* that carried him back to France. [2]

Will arrive close to port unrecognised

On Wednesday 9 October, *La Muiron* arrived at the French coastal town of Fréjus. The vessel had been observed arriving, but was *unrecognised* when it first appeared *close to port*. But, upon learning that Bonaparte was on board, news of his return quickly spread across the country. [3]

Notwithstanding signs of the palm bough

In medieval Europe, a *palm bough* was traditionally carried by a 'palmer': a pilgrim returning from the Holy Land. It was also from where Napoleon and his fellow officers had just returned. But the palm has another meaning: 'To bear the palm' is to be the best. "The allusion is to the Roman custom of giving the victorious gladiator a branch of the palm tree." (Brewer) Both descriptions describe Napoleon's return from the east. He had arrived from the Holy Land, where on one occasion he "had set up his quarters in the Monastery of Nazareth, and had read the Bible to his officers under a Syrian sky in places sanctified by Christ and His apostles." Secondly, he had returned as a recent victor from his triumph 'against the Turks at Aboukir'. In each of these respects, *not withstanding signs of the palm bough,* he was allowed to disembark, even though he had arrived unannounced, and without official papers. [4]

Afterwards a death, bereft of all

Bonaparte's departure from Egypt (22 August) left General Jean-Baptiste Kléber in overall control of France's conquests in the east. But, soon afterwards he was assassinated (14 June 1800), by "a Syrian Muslim, Sulayman al-Halabi." [5] After Kléber's death, Cairo was overrun by a British-led invasion, and the city was retaken. Alexandria, too, was recaptured three months later, when the French army finally capitulated. This, and Kléber's death, left France *bereft of all* the conquests it had made during the past two years. [6]

Good intelligence arrived late

Following the capitulation of Cairo, negotiations for a peaceful settlement were begun between England and France. However, because of the extra distance required for information to travel from Paris to London, news of the fall of Alexandria was able to be delayed by several days. France realised its negotiating power would be severely compromised once the loss of Alexandria was discovered. Hence, by skilful political manoeuvring, the French managed to get the preliminaries to the peace treaty signed, so that "the news reached Whitehall, too late to influence the deliberation at the conference table." [7] As a consequence, *good intelligence arrived late*.

Summary: *This quatrain correctly predicts the surprise return of Napoleon from his campaign in Egypt aboard an unrecognized ship: its acquisition having been necessitated by the loss of the French squadron at the battle of the Nile. The symbolism of the palm bough is also apt for the return of Napoleon. The remaining part of the quatrain accurately foretells what happened after Bonaparte vacated Egypt. This includes the death of General Kléber, who had been left in control of France's conquests, and the delay of information reaching London, concerning France's loss of Alexandria: thereby favourably affecting its peace negotiations with Britain.*

31   *Tant d'ans les guerres en Gaule dureront,*
      Oultre la course du Castulon monarque,
      Victoire incerte trois grands couronneront
      Aigle, coq, lune, lyon, soleil en marque.

32   *Le grand empire sera tost translaté*
      En lieu petit qui bien tost viendra croistre:
      Lieu bien infime d'exigue comté
      Ou au milieu viendra poser son sceptre.

The great (**FRENCH**) empire will soon be transferred   1814
Into a little place (**ELBA**), which very soon will come to increase:
The place very tiny, of scanty reckoning,
Where in the midst he (**NAPOLEON**) will arrive to lay down his sceptre.

The majority of these prophecies concern France. Those which refer to other nations are invariably indicated. The oracle above does not specify any nation. It is therefore to French history that we must look for recognition of its fulfilment.

The great empire will soon be transferred

In 1804, Napoleon Bonaparte became Emperor of the French. At its height, his empire stretched from the Mediterranean to the Baltic, and eastwards to encompass parts of Poland. But in 1814, the Emperor was forced to abdicate.

By the Treaty of Fontainebleau, the allies granted him the island of Elba as a sovereign principality with an annual income of 2,000,000 francs to be provided by France and a guard of 400 volunteers; also, he retained the title of emperor. [1]

Into a little place, which very soon will come to increase

Elba has an area of 86 square miles. [2] Although the land, itself, might not be able to *increase*, Napoleon's personal magnetism made certain that his following did. General Cambronne joined him in exile and brought seven hundred men to add to the four hundred that had earlier arrived. Officially, they were there to act only as his personal body guard. [3]

The place very tiny, of scanty reckoning

This is an apt description for Elba [4] to judge by its many changes of ownership. During the middle Ages, Elba was ruled by Pisa who passed it to Genoa. Afterwards, it became the property of the dukes of Piombino. They transferred ownership to Cosimo I. Thereafter, Spain acquired partial ownership until Naples became its new ruler. Finally, in 1802, France took possession. [5]

Where, in the midst, he will arrive to lay down his sceptre

The sceptre refers to the staff of imperial office. It therefore confirms the possessor to be an emperor. After Napoleon's defeat, and his abdication from office, the title of Emperor was returned to him, but his dominion was to be Elba. It was there that Napoleon *arrived in the midst to lay down his sceptre* and take control of the island's affairs. For less than a year he remained on the island in exile, devoting his energy towards expanding his tiny kingdom's economy. The iron-ore industry was revived; agricultural output increased; new roads constructed, and sanitation introduced. [6]

Summary: *The uniqueness of this prophecy exists in the fact that it foresees an empire having been transferred from one place to another. It also describes the emperor's destination as that of a tiny, insignificant place. Napoleon's little empire on the island of Elba therefore fulfils this prophecy in a way for which history has no duplicate to offer. The prophecy also foresees that it will expand, which it did as a growing number of people were drawn to join him in his exile, while he busied himself expanding the island's economy.*

33   *Prés d'vn grand pont de plaine spatieuse,*
      Le grand lyon par forces Césarées
      Fera abbatre hors cité rigoreuse,
      Par effroy portes luy seront reserées.

plaine (OF) spacious level ground without tree or house; reserrer (OF) to close, to stop.

Close to a great (**ARNHEM**) bridge, from the spacious plain,   1944
The great (**BRITISH**) lion, by Caesarean forces
Outside, it will try to overthrow the rigorous city,
Through fear, the entrances to it will be closed.

On 17 September 1944, after the D-Day landings, Operation Market Garden attempted to take the bridge at Arnhem. The film, from the book, *A Bridge Too Far,* later dramatised the operation.

Close to a great bridge, from the spacious plain

The idea proposed by Field Marshall Montgomery to Supreme Allied Commander Dwight Eisenhower in September 1944 was to "thrust through the Netherlands that would enable Allied forces to bypass much of the defensive Siegfried Line and swing into Germany from the north."[1] A major part of this plan was for the British to capture *the great bridge* over the Nederrijn at Arnhem. There was also to be no invasion over land. Instead, "It was to be the biggest airborne assault of all time."[2] It was essential, therefore, that the paratroopers landed on open ground and not in trees or on housetops; hence, the oracle's deliberate mention of 'spatieuse plain' *the spacious plain.*

This, however, proved to be a weak part of the plan, since the paratroops then had to march seven miles from the *open plain* where they had come down, in order to reach *the bridge.* This delay enabled the German army to mobilise their defences in time to meet the expected attack.

The great lion, by Caesarean forces

The great lion is a symbolic reference to Great Britain, which still retains the lion on its heraldry. Market Garden had been put together by Montgomery, with the United States agreeing to take part. This involved the American 82nd and 101st airborne divisions. Their task was to secure the river crossings near Eindhoven and Nijmegen. In total, 30,000 British, Polish and American troops were dropped behind enemy lines. On the first day, 500 gliders and 1500 aircraft were employed to equip the troops with tanks and trucks—described in the quatrain as the *Caesarean forces* taking part in this operation.

Outside, it will try to overthrow the rigorous city

Outside Arnhem, which the prophecy refers to as 'the rigorous city', because of the stern defence it maintained against attack, battles were being desperately fought by the paratroops as they attempted to reach Arnhem.

"Three miles from Arnhem British paratroopers were holding a pocket of land at the village of Oosterberck."[3] But they were separated from those who had reached the city, and with the Germans controlling the bridge, there was no reinforcements available from that direction.

The plan had been for British troops to reach the bridge at Arnhem. The 1st Airborne division was actually the only group to arrive inside the town, and they were able to take up positions inside buildings on both sides of the river. But the German tanks proved too strong, and without reinforcements arriving, and with insufficient ammunition, they fell prey to the German mobile land force. The British troops were therefore forced to retreat. As a result, "The Parachute division had left behind nearly 1,500 dead, and more than 6,500 prisoners, many badly wounded."[4]

Through fear, the entrances to it will be closed

Operation Market Garden was not successful, and it resulted in the battle of Arnhem: one of the great conflicts in WW II. The German army had only to deal with an advance party of troops, and this gave them time to organize a rigorous defence of the city. Thereafter, through fear that another attempt would be made to gain access to the bridge, *the entrances* to Arnhem remained *closed* up until April 1945, when the city was finally liberated by British and Canadian troops.

Summary: *Here, we are presented with another prophecy referring to WW II: Operation Market Garden, which came after the D-Day landings recounted above. The spacious ground required for the paratroops to land has been predicted in conjunction with the bridge at Arnhem, which was the allies' target. The failure of the mission is also foretold, as is the defence of the city, which remained closed until the end of the war.*

34   *L'oyseau de proye volant à la senestre*
      Auant conflict faict aux Francoys pareure
      L'vn bon prendre, l'vn ambigue sinistre,
      La partie foyble tiendra par bon augure.

35   *Le lyon ieune le vieux surmontera,*
      En champ bellique par singulier duelle,
      Dans caige d'or les yeux luy creuera:
      Deux classes vne, puis mourir, mort cruelle.

lyon (Dictionnaire de français "Littré" – lion *Fig.* Homme hardi et courageux) Man bold and courageous; classe (OF) rank or order according to degree.

The young lion (**MONTGOMERY**) will overcome the aged one (**HENRI II**),   1559
In a martial field, by single combat,
The eyes inside a cage of gold, it will puncture him,
Two ranks one, then dying, a cruel death.

This is the second of the four quatrains confirmed by historian Norman Davies as being historically correct.

This, undoubtedly, is the most often quoted quatrain from all those contained in the Centuries. Although scorn has been aimed at it by the benighted, it was fully appreciated at the time of its fulfilment, as confirmed by Antonia Fraser in her biography *Mary Queen of Scots*. It appears that a group of Parisians were so incensed by de Nostredame's prediction of the King's accident that they went in search of him. But, finding that he lived in Provence, they burnt his effigy instead.

The prophecy foretells what happened one day during a week of festivities, organized by the King to celebrate a double wedding. The King's sister, Princess Marguerite, was to marry the Duke of Savoy. At the same time, the King's daughter, Elisabeth, was to marry the King of Spain. As part of the celebrations, a tournament had been arranged in which the King would compete.

The young lion will overcome the aged one

The victor, referred to as *the young lion*, describes Montgomery. He was the twenty-nine-year-old captain in the King's Scot's Guards: a regiment for which Scotland's heraldic beast is the red *lion*. Equally notable is the reference to Henri II as *the old one*. This recalls the forty-year-old King's leonine character, and dates back to the time when he first became King. The people of Lyons had recognized his leonine character, both as a monarch and a hunter. To mark this feature, the dignitaries of the city honoured his arrival to their city by presenting him with a magnificent mechanical lion, emblazoned with the heraldic arms of his wife, Catherine de' Medici. [1]

In a martial field by single combat

On Friday 30 June 1559, *in a martial field, by single combat,* [2] Henri II fulfilled the prophecy made by de Nostredame. The King rode three challenges on that day. Two were against the dukes of Nemours and Guise; the third was against Gabriel de Lorges, Comte de Montgomery. The first two jousts went in the King's favour, but on the third run, he was almost unseated by the young count, causing the monarch to demand a re-match. His decision proved to be fatal. The two combatants met midfield, but on impact, Montgomery's lance shattered and the King was thrown to the ground.

The eyes inside a cage of gold, it will puncture him

Henri II laid there for a moment unconscious, and then dazed upon reviving. A long splinter jutted from his tilting helm. After removing the headpiece, more splinters were discovered. The longest had penetrated his forehead just above the right eye and pierced the left one, puncturing it. [3] Five further splinters were later removed. Spectators present at the time recalled "that the tilting helm strangely resembled a cage, and that the king's visor was actually gilded." [4]

Two ranks one

The injured King was then carried from the tournament field "to the near-by Hôtel des Tournelles, and here lay in a state of virtual unconsciousness for nine days." [5] On 8 July, the King rallied, and was sufficiently lucid to order that his sister's wedding should go ahead. At the stroke of midnight in the nearby church of St Paul, *two ranks* in the hierarchy of nobility became *one*, as the Princess and the Duke were united in marriage. [6]

Then dying: a cruel death

On the morning of July 10th, Henri's state of health began to deteriorate fast, and it was evident he was now dying. [7] Both hands and feet had become grossly swollen from the infection that had set in from the wounds to his head and eye, and he was clearly in dreadful pain. His passing proved to be a particularly *cruel death.* [8]

As an interesting aside to this prophecy, the Queen's six-year-old daughter, Princess Marguerite de Valois, later remembered that on the night before the accident her mother had a premonitory dream in which she saw her husband, the King, lying injured with blood covering his face. Next morning she begged Henri not to enter the lists that day, but to his peril, he refused to listen.

Summary: *The fulfilment of this prediction has been retold many times, but past translations from the French have tended to colour its content with minor inaccuracies. Both Professor Norman Davies and Antonia Fraser, each greatly respected as authors in their own field of history, refer to it. And there can be no doubt whatsoever that its relevance to the death of Henri II, on that June afternoon in 1559, was widely acknowledged at the time.*

36   *Tard le monarque se viendra repentir*
           De n'auoir mis à mort son aduersaire:
           Mais viendra bien à plus hault consentir
           Que tout son sang par mort fera defaire.

venir (AF - convenir) agree; bien (OF adverb) content; que (OF) then

           Later, the King (**HENRI III**) will come to regret   1588
           For not having put his adversary (**GUISE**) to death:
           But he will agree content, consenting to the tallest,
           Then all his lineage will be rid of, through death.

Quatrain 10 above, predicted the death of the French Queen, Catherine de Medici. This quatrain sets the scene shortly before she died. It refers to her last surviving son, Henri III and his response to the fear and anger he felt at what he perceived was an attempt to usurp his power.

Later, the king will come to regret

The cause of Henri III's regret occurred at a meeting of the Estates-General held at Blois in December 1588. Henri Duke of Guise had already asserted himself as the self-styled 'King of Paris' and was seen by Catholics as the most likely successor to the French throne – should the king die. Earlier that year, Guise had entered Paris, contrary to Henri III's orders to stay away.

A revolt against the King then ensued inside the capital, and he had been forced to flee the city in fear for his life. Now, inside his château at Blois, information had been passed to him that Guise's sister, the Duchess Montpensier, had been toasting her brother at a private dinner party, as the next king of France. To make matters worse, both King and Duke had previously been seen together, embroiled in a heated argument.

For not having put his adversary to death

Their dispute had grown bitter in May that year, when Guise arrived in Paris, having disregarded the King's command to stay away. His arrival in the city then resulted in a revolt, which became known as the 'The Day of the Barricades'. This insurrection proved sufficiently serious to force Henri to take refuge inside the Louvre. It was then and there that he first consulted with his bodyguards, concerning a planned assassination of Guise. The idea was greeted positively by the Comte d'Ornano, who said, "If your majesty will issue the command, I will bring you the head of the duc de Guise, or secure his person." [1] Henri is said to have mused upon the manner this could be achieved, since he knew Guise to be "tall and strong", but further thoughts were interrupted by the appearance of the queen-mother, Catherine de Medici, and the King was forced to dismiss the plan he had prepared.

But he will agree content, consenting to the tallest

Seven months later, inside the castle at Blois where a meeting of the Estates-General had been convened, the King was again confronted by the duc de Guise.

> Exasperated, the king asked his small circle of trusties, "Who will kill these evil Guises for me?" His loyal 'quarante-cinq', the special bodyguard created for him by d'Épernon had no scruples in accepting the task. [2]

The assassination was set for the morning of 23 December. On the night before, "Henri was a picture of good humour and munificence. [...] Henri is said to have taken the duke into his arms and kissed him." Next morning, the Duke was summoned to a meeting with the King. The trap was then sprung, and upon his arrival, Guise was cut down outside the King's chamber. After hearing the clamour had subsided, Henri emerged from his room, and upon observing the duke lying dead on the floor, acquiesced with the remark – "Look at him, the King of Paris. Not so tall now!" [3]

Then all his lineage will be rid of, through death

The House of Valois ruled France for 260 years. Its end came with the death of Henri III, the last of the Valois kings. The assassination of Henri Duke of Guise, which was followed next day by the murder of his brother, Cardinal Louis of Lorraine, sent shock waves across Europe. It also invited the deceased's sister to plan her revenge.

On 1 August 1589, Henri III was assassinated by a mentally unstable monk in the employ of the House of Guise. With his death came an end to the lineage of the Valois kings

Summary: *This quatrain provides a prophetic account of events that took place during Henri III's final year on the throne, and which were to portend his own death. It begins by foretelling the thoughts he had concerning ridding the realm of the duc de Guise, who had disobeyed him by entering Paris with an armed escort. Although the King at first dismissed the idea of sanctioning the Duke's murder, he revived the idea later in the year when they met at Blois, and the Duke again disrespected him. The assassination was then carried out. Thereafter, the prophecy predicts that death will end the royal lineage. This occurred in the following year when Henri was, himself, assassinated in revenge for the murder he had sanctioned.*

37   *Vng peu deuant que le soleil s'esconse*
        Conflict donné, grand peuple dubieux:
        Profligés, port marin ne faict responce,
        Pont & sepulchre en deux estranges lieux.

38   *Le Sol & l'aigle au victeur paroistront:*
        Responce vaine au vaincu l'on asseure,
        Par cor ne crys harnoys n'arresteront
        Vindicte, paix par mort si acheue à l'heure.

39   *De nuict dans lict le supresme estrangle*
        Pour trop auoir subiourné, blond esleu.
        Par troys l'empire subroge exancle,
        A mort mettra carte, pacquet ne leu.

40   *La trombe faulse dissimulant folie*
      Fera Bisance vn changement de loys:
      Hystra d'Egypte qui veult que l'on deslie
      Edict changeant monnoyes & aloys.

41   *Siege en cité, & de nuict assaillie,*
      Peu eschapés: non loing de mer conflict.
      Femme de ioye, retours filz defaillie
      Poison & lettres cachées dans le plic.

42   *Le dix Kalendes d'Apuril de faict Gotique*
      Resuscité encor par gens malins:
      Le feu estainct, assemblée diabolique
      Cherchant les os du d'Amant & Pselyn.

43   *Auant qu'aduienne le changement d'empire,*
      Il auiendra vn cas bien merueilleux,
      Le champ mué, le pilier de porphyre
      Mis, translaté sus le rochier noilleux.

Avant (OF. adverb) before, or ere; aviendra (OF. avaindre) to bring or lead forth; changement (OF) a varying, a transforming; cas (AF événement) event; mué (AF verb, muer) modify; porphyre, (L Porphyrion) one of the giants; translaté (AF- transporter); sus (OF) above, upon; rochier (AF) quarry of stones; noilleux (OF *syncope* no[üa]illeux) full of joints

Ere that could happen, the transforming of the Empire: 1889
It will lead with good reason to a marvellous event:
The field (**CHAMP DE MARS**) modified: the pillar of Porphyrion (**EIFFEL TOWER**)
Placed: transported above the quarry of stones, full of joints.

Ere that could happen, the transforming of the empire

The end of the Second Empire was made necessary by the capture of Napoleon III at the battle of Sedan in September 1870. "The news of Sedan precipitated the fall of the Second Empire and the proclamation of the Third Republic in Paris."

However, the actual date of the Third Empire is subject to doubt, and is given by Claude Lebédel in his *Chronologie de l'Histoire de France* as, "La IIIᵉ République: 1875–1940." He states that it is difficult to date the début of the Third Republic, since three dates have been suggested. The first is 4 September 1870, because of the military defeat and invasion of France. The second is February 1871, through the reunion at Bordeaux of the new National Assembly under the presidency of Adolphe Thiers. The third is January 1875, when the Assembly voted the Wallon amendment with a scanty majority. Before then, there had been a compromise of between five and ten years. [1]

The oracle reveals what happened after the empire had been transformed from the second to the third. To commemorate the centenary of the French Revolution, and to create a signpost for the Great Exposition, planned for 1889, an idea was proposed that was intended, "To distract minds and hearts from France's territorial loss, the central theme was the colonial empire." (The theme of *empire* links the first two lines of this oracle). It was therefore decided to hold a competition for the design of a monument to mark the exhibition. The winning entry – although foreseen 334 years earlier – was the Eiffel Tower.

It will lead with good reason to a marvellous event

At the time of its completion, the Eiffel Tower was the tallest man made construction in the world. "Each of the 18,000 pieces used to build the tower was calculated specifically for the project and prepared in Eiffel's factory on the outskirts of Paris." [2] It stood "twice as high as the dome of St. Peter's in Rome or the Great Pyramid of Giza;" and was seen worldwide as a, "technological masterpiece in building-construction history." [3]

The field modified

The location chosen for the monument was *the Champ de Mars*. This Field still occupies a huge area of open ground on the left bank of Paris, stretching back to the *École Militaire*. In the past, the field had been the scene of several rallies held during the French Revolution; the first of which was the Festival of the Federation (1790); another was the Festival of the Supreme Being (1794). But, before the Tower could be constructed, *the Field* had to be *modified*. Two acres of ground were levelled for the site, in order to allow the foundations to be put in place. [4]

The pillar of Porphyrion placed

Porphyrion appears in Greek Mythology as the giant offspring of Uranus and Gaia. The Seer likens the giant's stature to a *pillar*, thus equating it with the Eiffel Tower placed at the far end of the field, with its four arches at the base acting as entrances to the exhibition. [5]

Transported above the quarry of stones

The construction of the Tower, which had been designed to reach the height of 300 metres with a weight of 10,000 tons [6] required a solid foundation. This was resolved by allowing, "The uprights [to] rest on concrete foundations installed a few metres below ground-level on top of a layer of compacted gravel." [7]

Full of joints

The final design called for more than 18,000 pieces of puddle iron, a type of wrought iron used in construction, and 2.5 million rivets. Several hundred workers spent two years assembling the framework of the iconic lattice tower, which at its inauguration in March 1889 stood nearly 1,000 feet high. [8]

PILLAR OF PORPHYRION
'CHAMP DE MARS'

Summary: This oracle foretells the change of empire in France that followed Napoleon III's defeat at Sedan. As a means of boosting public morale, the great Paris Exhibition of 1889, celebrating a hundred years since the French Revolution, became a worldwide event. It was made all the more marvellous by Gustav Eiffel's giant tower. This has been predicted by referring to the mythological giant Porphyrion, who is likened to the tower situated in the Champ de Mars. The fact that it is transported to a height of 300 metres and has its foundations built upon a bed of compacted stones, with its 18,000 pieces of ironwork held together by two and a half million rivets is indicated in the prophecy.

44   *En brief seront de retour sacrifices,*
         Contreuenants seront mis à martyre:
         Plus ne seront moines abbés ne nouices:
         Le miel sera beaucoup plus cher que cire.

In short, there will be a recurrence of renunciations;   1792
Contraveners will be put to martyrdom:
There will be no more monks, priests, nor novices,
Honey will be plentiful, more liked than beeswax.

The victims of the September Massacres, during the French Revolution, were mainly priests, monks, nuns and novices, drawn from monasteries, seminaries, churches, etc. The intention of the revolutionaries was to complete the de-Christianising of France, which commenced at the start of the revolt. This quatrain concerns the effect it had upon the Catholic Church in France.

In short, there will be a recurrence of renunciations

The Enlightenment, which had begun to gather force during the early part of the eighteenth century, was the initial reason for some members of the clergy abandoning their vows. Not long afterwards, both the training and the work of priests became the responsibility of the State. "Monasteries – particularly purely contemplative houses – were dissolved, and their wealth confiscated. [...] In many states, the Jesuits were expelled."

This is predicted in the opening line of the quatrain, which refers to *a recurrence* of priests and other religious abandoning their vows. Those who remained either became state-sponsored priests, or else they fled the country.

The move towards de-Christianising France began on 2 November 1789, when the National Assembly voted by 568 to 346 that Church property be transferred to the nation. This led the Constituent Assembly to abolish all monastic vows; and a banning order was introduced to cover congregations. Priests and other religious were strongly urged to *renounce their vows* and become productive citizens. An oath of allegiance to nation, law, king and constitution was subsequently required from any French priest wishing to remain active in the Church. [1]

Contraveners will be put to martyrdom
On 26 August 1792, a law was drafted requiring all dissident priests; that is, *contraveners*, to leave the country or be deported to Guyana. [2] One week later, priests still in Paris were rounded up and imprisoned. There, they would await the outbreak of violence that was to follow. Their arrest was followed by a new decree, condemning to death within 24 hours all non-juring priests remaining in France. That autumn, it proved to be a forerunner to a new wave of atrocities that broke out in September, when priests were *put to martyrdom* wherever they were found.
In Nantes, Jean-Baptiste Carrier drowned eighty-four non-juring priests in the river Loire by confining them below decks in a river transporter, and then scuttling the boat. At Lyons, Marseilles, Bordeaux, and other towns across France, murder and the guillotine substantially added to the death toll of priests and nuns caught up in the frenzy of judicial murder. [3]

There will be no more monks, priests nor novices
A significant number of clergy had refused to swear the oath, preferring instead to obey Pope Pius VI, who condemned the Civil Constitution. These recalcitrant priests left France to take refuge in Spain, England and Ireland. In Spain alone, an estimated 6,000 priests sought asylum in that country. In France, monasteries and convents lay silent, with church services conducted only by state registered clerics. *No longer were there any monks, priests or novices* in France. [4]

Honey will be plentiful, more liked than beeswax
Church candles were made from expensive *beeswax*. "Beeswax was one of the most valuable of commodities in the Middle Ages and taxes could be paid in beeswax to the Church." [5] But with demand having declined, the product of the hive switched to *honey*. [6] Wealthy families were therefore heard to apologise to visitors for the 'tallow candles' as 'wax candles' were no longer available.

Summary: *The de-Christianizing that occurred in France during its revolution at the end of the 18th century has been predicted in this quatrain. It also acts as a future warning of the violence that erupts when a secular society gains so great a following that it can no longer tolerate religious opposition to its anti-Christian laws.*

45   *Secteur de sectes grand preme au delateur:*
      Beste en theatre, dressé le ieu scenique:
      Du faict antique ennobli l'inuenteur,
      Par sectes monde confus & scismatique.

46   *Tout aupres d'Aux, de Lectore & Mirande*
      Grand feu du ciel en troys nuicts tumbera:
      Cause auiendra bien stupende & mirande:
      Bien peu après la terre tremblera.

47   *Du Lac Leman les sermons facheront:*
      Des iours seront reduicts par les sepmaines:
      Puis mois, puis an, puis tous defailliront,
      Les magistrats damneront leur loys vaines.

Lac Leman (L. Lemannus lacus) Geneva; sermons (OF) discours; magistrats (L. magistratus); sepmaines (OF) semaines

Concerning Geneva (**LEAGUE OF NATIONS**) the speeches will anger: 1920
Of the days, they will be dimmed by the weeks,
Then months, then a year, then all will fail,
The officials will condemn their ineffectual laws.

The two decades that occurred between the end of World War I and the beginning of World War II began with the intention of procuring a peaceful relationship between nations. There was an earnest desire to avoid furthering conflict by discussing contentious issues before they erupted into outright war. Policing this unity, although only at a political level, was the League of Nations. It has been said that 'the road to hell is paved with good intentions', and so it proved. Bickering, defiance, unilateralist policies and political vanity eventually blighted a host of those important issues that the League was designed to resolve. In the end, the entire fabric of this international organization collapsed, allowing a Second World War to complete the League's breakdown. The effect of its failure resulted in the deaths of a further forty-seven million of the world's population, which were added to the 8.5 million killed during World War I.

Concerning Geneva
The four lines of the oracle predict the decline of the League of Nations: an international peacekeeping body whose headquarters were situated at Geneva. The League was important because it was formed after the First World War: its intention being that member states would air their grievances inside an international forum, and seek solutions that secured a peaceful settlement. [1] But as the oracle foretold, this noble idea was doomed to failure.

The speeches will anger
The first Assembly met on 15 November 1920, with forty-one nations represented. More than twenty nations later joined, but there were also numerous resignations: notably, those resulting from *angry disagreements voiced* by countries wanting to act independently; e.g., Brazil, Spain, Japan, Paraguay, Germany, Italy and USSR. [2]

Of the days, they will be dimmed by the weeks, then months, then a year
Prolonged attempts at settling disputes bedevilled the League. Meetings frequently made little progress, and matters of immediate concern in international politics were deliberated upon endlessly without resolution.

The political questions and issues occurring after 1931 readily fall into this category, and were to become the subject of many endless disputes: an example was the Japanese occupation of Manchuria in 1931. This preceded a decade of political turmoil among the nations affected, and the disputes arising challenged the League's principles down to its very roots. Additionally, the League was ineffective at coping with the rising power of Germany; or with Italy's invasion of Ethiopia and Albania, or with the economic distress caused by the Great Depression. [3]

Then all will fail, the officials will condemn their ineffectual laws
By the early 1930s, the principles of the League's covenant had been abandoned. The League of Nations finally folded in 1939 with the outbreak of World War II. Further meetings ceased, and the League was officially disbanded in April 1946: its good intentions having long since failed. [4] *The officials* responsible for the statutes governing the League's operation had finally conceded that *their laws* were *ineffectual.* [5]

Summary: *This prophecy accurately, although briefly, outlines the reason for the failure of the League of Nations, whose headquarters were situated in Geneva.*

48   *Vingt ans du regne de la lune passés*
       Sept mil ans autre tiendra sa monarchie:
       Quand le soleil prendra ses iours lassés
       Lors accomplir & mine ma prophetie.

       Twenty years passed from the reign of the moon,   3797±
       Seven thousand years another will hold his kingdom:
       When the sun shall undertake its days fatigued,
       In that time to accomplish and finish my prophecy.

In a letter addressed to his son César (1 March 1555), which formed the preface to his first book of prophecies, the Seer maintained that his oracles "extend from now to the year 3797." In which case, it is reasonable to infer this quatrain is intended for that time, since the end of his prophetic career is included in the prediction. But there is no mention in the quatrain of any screams, as might be expected if the sun should become too fatigued to restrain the moon from wandering from its orbit. However, screams are mentioned in the next quatrain, which continues on from the present verse.

It may also be noted that 3797 A.D. is equivalent to 7557 in the Jewish calendar. Interestingly, it was c. 557 B.C. in the Hebrew Bible that marked the time when Nehemiah rebuilt Jerusalem, purified the priesthood, and enforced the Law of Moses. Consequently, a further 7000 years added to this date carries the time forward to the year mentioned in the prophecy.

Elsewhere in these prophecies, there is a prediction of Saturn arriving late in its orbit. A loss to the Sun's mass would weaken its gravitational effect on the planets in the solar system while also dimming its light. This would explain its 'fatigue' and the irregularity in the orbit of Saturn.

At the time this was written, Saturn was the furthest planet known. However any gravitational deviation of the Sun affecting Saturn would affect the Earth and its satellite moon. It is therefore open to a possibility that our moon will stray from its course as the Earth becomes affected by the Sun's weakened state.

The tidal effect would then be disastrous for those living at this time; and would account for the screams of fear and despair at what was about to befall mankind.

Oceans and seas would be in turmoil, uncontrolled by the absent moon's gravitational effect. Consequently, there would be massive flooding worldwide. Moreover, because motion is relative, any wayward straying of the Earth from its natural orbit would make it appear as though it were the stars that were falling. Alternatively, the Earth could pass through a meteor shower, which would make it appear that these were the stars predicted to fall.

If we now turn to the gospels of Mark (13: 24, 25) and Luke (21: 25, 26), it is to read something so similar, it can scarcely be ignored. Moreover, it precedes the return of Jesus, and also coincides with the Seer ending his prophecies.

> But in those days, following that distress, the sun will be darkened, and the moon will not give its light; the stars will fall from the sky, and the heavenly bodies will be shaken.

> There will be signs in the sun, moon and stars. On earth, nations will be in anguish and perplexity at the roaring and tossing of the sea. People will faint from terror, apprehensive of what is coming on the world, for the heavenly bodies will be shaken.

49   *Beaucoup beaucoup auant telles meneés*
      Ceux d'Orient par la vertu lunaire
      L'an mil sept cent feront grands emmenées
      Subiugant presques le coing Aquilonaire.

telles (OF) de cette nature, de ce genre; meneés (OF) cris prolongés; vertu (L. verti) (war) overthrown, destroyed; emmenées (AF amenée) sommation – Military challenge; Aquilonaire (L. aquilonius)

> Much, much before prolonged wails of this sort,   1700
> Those of the east, through the overthrown moon:
> The year **1700**, they will make great military challenges,
> Almost subjugating the northerly corner.

At the time this oracle was written, the Ottoman Empire was at its peak. Its decline came later, towards the end of the seventeenth century: when, between 1683 and 1699, Turkey fought the armies of the Holy League– Austria, Poland, Venice, and Russia. The war was finally brought to an end by the *Treaty of Karlowitz* (26 January 1699), which gave considerable concessions to the League: Poland receiving a large part of what is now Ukraine. Russia's reward came the following year, when Turkey signed the *Treaty of Constantinople* (1700). Under this agreement, Turkey was compelled to surrender the Russian province of Azov.

Much, much before prolonged wails of this sort

Unusually for these prophecies, the opening line continues on from the last line of the previous quatrain. By so doing, it confirms the wails of terror described in Luke's gospel. The remaining three lines are then able to predict for the emblematic moon of the Ottoman Empire.

Those of the east, through the overthrown moon

The oracle has, upon several occasions, employed the phrase *those of*, and then followed it by naming a particular region. Each time this occurred, it directed attention towards the victors, or occupiers of the region, rather than to its indigenous people. In 1699, Russia and Poland, as part of the Holy League, defeated the Ottoman Empire.[1] In this sense, Russia and Poland became *those of the east, through the overthrown moon*; that is to say, the emblematic moon, representative of the Turkish Empire, was overthrown.

> The city of Byzantium, at the mouth of the Black Sea, was dedicated to the Greek goddess Artemis, whose symbol was the crescent moon. The flag of Byzantium thus became a white crescent moon against a field of red. In 330 AD, Roman Emperor Constantine I made Byzantium the capital of what historians today call the Byzantine Empire. An eight-pointed star was added to the city's flag during Constantine's rule, possibly as a symbol of the Virgin Mary.
>
> After Constantine's death, Byzantium was renamed Constantinople. In 1453, Constantinople was conquered by Ottoman Turks, and Sultan Mehmed II adopted its flag for his own. In 1844, the eight-pointed star was replaced with a five-pointed star.[2]

The year 1700

In the year 1700, the Great Northern War began. The first blows involved Russia and Poland assisted by Denmark, and was directed against Charles II of Sweden, who had formed an alliance with Turkey. During the 16th and 17th centuries, Sweden had been pursuing a policy of adding to its territory along the coastlands. Eventually, the neighbouring states reacted by going to war.

They will make great military challenges

In March of that year, the leaders of the northern region *began making military challenges*. The first strike was made by Christian V of Denmark, who conquered the neighbouring region of Holstein-Gottorp: its ruling duke having allied himself to Sweden.

Two months later, Poland struck at Livonia (now part of Estonia and Latvia with the result that Riga became occupied. Another two months passed, and it was Charles XII who came to the fore by invading Zealand: Denmark's largest island in the Baltic Sea. Charles next advanced on Copenhagen, forcing the Danes to hand back Holstein-Gottorp, and compelling them to sue for peace (*Treaty of Traventhal*, August 1700). Victorious, he then turned his army towards occupied Riga, compelling Augustus II of Saxony-Poland to withdraw his forces. Buoyant with these successes, Charles turned his attention next to Peter I of Russia, and at Narva in Estonia, on 20 November 1700, with only 9,000 men he scattered a Russian army that was more than twice his strength.[3]

Almost subjugating the northerly corner

After suffering defeat at Narva, Czar Peter, another of the State leaders in that part of the world, retaliated and retook the Baltic provinces from Charles XII. Later, in 1703, he founded the city of St. Petersburg, from where he was able to subdue the Cossacks in what became known as the Third Peasant War. Then, aided by Augustus, he went on to destroy the Swedish army sent to attack Moscow. Turning next to the northwest, he subdued Finland before making several renewed and successful attacks by land and sea against Sweden.

Having *almost subjugated the northerly corner*, Peter finally brought the wars to an end. It was as a result of Czar Peter's efforts that Russia was able to take its first step towards becoming one of the great political powers in the modern world.[4]

Summary: *This prophecy continues from the preceding one, using the 'overthrow of the moon' as a link that pertains to both quatrains. In 1700, the overthrow of the moon was a prediction for the downfall of the Ottoman Empire It also signaled the commencement of the Great Northern War. The success of Peter the Great in the northern corner of Europe, as predicted, was also an important step towards raising Russia's status to that of a world power. The next oracle also predicts the beginning to a world power—one that would rival Russia.*

50   *De l'aquatique triplicité naistra*
      D'vn qui fera le ieudy pour sa feste:
      Son bruit, loz, regne, sa puissance croistra,
      Par terre & mer aux orients tempeste.

triplicité (Late Latin): triplicitatem; los (OF), reputation; bruit (OF) renomée, tempeste (OF) combat violent.

It will be born composed of the aquatic triplicity,   1776
For one that will take Thursday for its festival (**THANKSGIVING DAY**):
Its renown, reputation, rule, and its power will grow
By land and sea, violent combat to the easterners.

After having introduced the political events that led to Russia becoming an emerging nation, long after these prophecies were written, the very next oracle does the same for its cold war arch rival, America. The opening line of the quatrain helps to identify the geographical location for its fulfilment. The second line describes a feature that is unique to the United States.

It will be born composed of the aquatic triplicity

The United States of America, Hawaii excepted, are bounded by *the aquatic triplicity*. This comprises the Pacific Ocean on the west coast, the Atlantic Ocean on the east coast, and the Gulf of Mexico, fed by the Caribbean Sea, to the south. [1] Along America's northern border lies Canada. The term: 'United States' was *born* from a phrase used in the Declaration of Independence (1776), and later repeated in the preamble to the Federal Constitution of 1787. [2]

For one that will take Thursday for its festival

In 1863, President Abraham Lincoln, while engaged in the American Civil War, decreed that the last Thursday in November should be celebrated as the *United States* 'Thanksgiving Day'. It was not until 1941 that this was amended, so that the *festival of Thanksgiving* would always fall on the fourth *Thursday* of November. [3]

Its renown, reputation, rule and its power will grow

The United States' renown, rule, and power have grown enormously in recent time, and the nation presently enjoys the reputation of a super-power. Its political rule and military might are impressive, and its influence has spread around the globe, affecting many people's lives in lands ranging from the smallest to the largest. [4] But this has not always been welcomed.

By land and sea, violent combat to the easterners

Currently, America's reputation for military fire-power *by land and sea* is sufficient to maintain its supremacy – *its renown* – wheresoever the rule of law requires its presence. [5]

Historically, in December 1941, the Japanese air force attacked the American fleet anchored at Pearl Harbour, thereby impelling the nation to declare war against Japan, *the easterners*. In June 1950, war broke out between North and South Korea, with the US becoming engaged in the conflict. Once again, the nation found itself pitted against *the easterners*, having taken up arms against North Korea: a country heavily supported by Chinese arms and men. In 1955, another war broke out, this time between North and South Vietnam. Again, America became involved in fighting against *the easterners*; this time it was the communist guerrillas of North Vietnam. Then, in January and February of 1991, the United States led a coalition force against Iraq – more *easterners* – in an effort to curtail the territorial ambitions of Saddam Hussein.

In 2001, it became the turn of *the easterners* inside Afghanistan to bear the weight of America's armed forces, as an aerial onslaught was undertaken to root out and destroy the terrorist organization thought to be responsible for attacking the World Trade Center in New York. And, in March 2003, America once again declared war against *the easterners:* when it targeted Iraq for a second time. The *violent combat predicted for the easterners* seems somewhat understated. [6]

Summary: This prophecy was written at a time when Northern America was inhabited by the Sioux, Apaches, and Comanches together with other indigenous tribes. Settlers from Europe were only just beginning to arrive. Yet it has been placed next to a similar prophecy that predicts the political beginning of Russia, its arch rival for world supremacy. The identification of what has become the USA is correctly foreseen by the seas that border it on three sides; as, too, is its political and military domination in the world. Furthermore, the day of the week selected for the nation's Festival of Thanksgiving has been named. Added To which, the country's violent combat with easterners is foreseen, and which has since been fulfilled many times over.

51   Chef d'Aries, Iuppiter & Saturne,
       Dieu eternal quelles mutations!
       Puis par long siècle son maling temps retourne,
       Gaule & Itale quelles esmotions!

52   Les deux malins de Scorpion conioints,
       Le grand seigneur meurtri dedans sa salle:
       Peste à l'eglise par le nouueau roy ioint,
       L' Europe basse & Septentrionale.

53   Las qu'on verra grand peuple tormenté
       Et la loy saincte en totale ruine:
       Par aultres loyx toute Chrestienté,
       Quand d'or d'argent trouue nouuelle mine.

Chrestienté (OF) Christianity

Alas that one shall see a great people tormented   1790
And the sacred law in total ruin:
All Christianity, by other laws,
When for gold, money discovers a new source (**ASSIGNATS**).

This quatrain returns to the time of the French Revolution, and the commencement of its anti-Christian laws. The nationality of the Seer requires that he identify those of his nation as 'a great people'. It is a phrase that we shall encounter on other occasions within these prophecies.

Alas that one shall see a great people tormented
Legislation attacking the Christian Church was passed in two stages, in 1789 and then with greater severity in 1790. This second piece of legislation introduced the Civil Constitution of the Clergy, [1] and its announcement split the country in two. At which point, *one was able to see a great people tormented* at having to behold the nation's Christian heritage being legally destroyed.

And the sacred law in total ruin
Under this new legislation, the clergy were required to swear, on oath, their allegiance to the new Constitution. Many refused, taking courage from those in their congregation who supported them. On 10 March 1791, Pope Pius VI condemned the Civil Constitution of the Clergy. But this only brought fresh outbreaks of violence against the papacy. While those supporting Louis XVI, added to the ferment when the King declared that his conscience forbade him receiving Holy Communion from a constitutional priest. For this, Louis was declared a traitor, but he stuck to his decision.

Within France, this controversy continued, often accompanied by violent demonstrations. Effigies of the Pope were made and then set alight, convents were attacked and nuns assaulted, churches were daubed with revolutionary graffiti, and the King was repeatedly importuned to sanction the constitutional priests. [2] Everywhere, *the sacred laws were in total ruin.*

All Christianity by other laws
Underpinning this change in attitude to the Church was the legislation passed by the National

Assembly in 1790; that is to say, *other laws* were passed to govern the Church. These included the requirement that priests and bishops could only be elected, and thereafter, they had to swear their allegiance to the new Constitution. Those who preached outside the law were to be arrested for civil disturbance. At the same time, the privileges of the monarchy were also being diffused. The King no longer had the power to make decrees, and his rule was replaced by France's first written constitution based upon the Rights of Man. [3]

On 13 April, Pope Pius VI once again denounced the Civil Constitution, urging the *Christian community* not to collaborate with anyone obeying these *other laws*. The Constitution, he declared, was 'schismatical', and he condemned all priests and prelates who had taken the oath of allegiance in defiance of his order. [4] (Incidentally, this was the pope who, ten years earlier in 1781, had condemned these prophecies. Quite clearly, he had failed to understand their truth.)

When for gold, money discovers a new source.
The lands belonging to the Church were nationalised on 2 November 1789, during the first wave of anti-Christian legislation. It was intended that money raised from the acquisition of land would pay the wages of the constitutional clergy.

However, the land that had been acquired this way soon led to *a new source of money.* Initially, Church property to the value of 400 million *livres* was offered for sale. Unlike money, whose value was based on gold, these bonds (*assignats*; i.e., 'assigned') were guaranteed by land, and bore interest. Consequently, *assignats* soon began changing hands, in much the same way that money changes hands in the present day. In 1790, the government bowed to pressure and *assignats* were declared legal currency. [5]

Summary: *The anti-Christian laws that were put in place during the French Revolution were in complete opposition to the religious sentiments of those brought up in the faith. And the effect this had upon the Church was felt most painfully in the monasteries, convents and churches. The seer then adds a further line of prophecy, which sets this oracle apart from any other time. He refers to the appropriation of Church lands by the new government. These were to become assets under the new laws, and were to be valued by bonds that quickly became legalised as a currency replacement for money. The value of assignats was therefore a new source of money based not upon gold, but upon the value of the land it described.*

54   *Deux reuolts faits du malin falcigere,*
       De regne & siecles faict permutation:
       Le mobil signe à son endroict si ingere
       Aux deux egaux & d'inclination.

55   *Soubz l'opposite climat Babylonique*
       Grande sera de sang effusion,
       Que terre & mer, air, ciel, sera inique:
       Sectes, faim, regnes, pestes, confusion.

Soubz (Romance from Latin, sub) under the reign of; l'opposite (OF) adverse; regnes (OF) royaumes; confusion (OF) confusion, disorder.

Under the reign of the adverse Babylonian region   1991
Great will be the effusion of blood:
When land, sea, air, & sky will be iniquitous,
Sects, hunger, governments, pestilences, disorder.

Under the reign of the adverse Babylonian region
This description most aptly fits Iraq's former president, Saddam Hussein, for he noticeably displayed the trait of opposition during his reign. It had, in fact, become evident upon a number of occasions, particularly when opposing world opinion after he launched an attack against neighbouring Kuwait. The United Nations issued a directive, requiring that he immediately withdraw his army from Kuwait. Stubbornly, he refused to comply. As a result, his refusal led to Iraq becoming the target for military action, consisting of a joint international task force.

Historically, Babylonia was the ancient empire of southern Mesopotamia: the capital of which once occupied what is now central Iraq. From 1979 to 2003, the country came under the rule of President Saddam Hussein.

> Saddam formally rose to power in 1979, although he had been the *de facto* head of Iraq for several years prior. He suppressed several movements, particularly Shi'a and Kurdish movements seeking to overthrow the government or gain independence, and maintained power during the Iran-Iraq War and the Gulf War. [1]

Great will be the effusion of blood

The Iran–Iraq War began when Iraq invaded Iran by air and on land on 22 September 1980. It continued until the United Nations peace-keepers exercised control over the ceasefire in August 1988.

> The bloody eight-year war ended in a stalemate. There were hundreds of thousands of casualties with estimates of up to one million dead. Neither side had achieved what they had originally desired and at the borders, [these] were left nearly unchanged. [2]

Three years in later in 1991, Iraq began a second war, this time by invading Kuwait. The death toll arising after the UN had intervened was estimated to be:—

> United States 148 killed, 458 wounded. Great Britain 47 killed, 43 wounded. France 2 killed, 25 wounded. Egypt 14 killed, 120 wounded. Iraq 60,000 to 100,000 military personnel are estimated to have been killed or wounded in action. 2,000 to 3,000 civilians are estimated to have been killed, and from 5,000 to 7,700 injured. [3]

This huge loss of life occurred because Saddam Hussein refused to withdraw from Kuwait under a UN mandate to comply. As a result, armed forces from across the world agreed to remove Iraq by force.

> Hussein defied United Nations Security Council demands to withdraw from Kuwait by mid-January 1991, and the Persian Gulf War began with a massive U.S.-led air offensive known as Operation Desert Storm. After 42 days of relentless attacks by the allied coalition in the air and on the ground, U.S. President George H.W. Bush declared a cease-fire on February 28; by that time, most Iraqi forces in Kuwait had either surrendered or fled. Though the Persian Gulf War was initially considered an unqualified success for the international coalition, simmering conflict in the troubled region led to a second Gulf War–known as the Iraq War–that began in 2003. [4]

In the Iraq War of 2003: the third to involve the Babylonian region, "The number of Iraqis killed through 2007 ranges from 'a conservative cautious minimum' of more than 85,000 civilians, to a survey estimate of more than 1,000,000 citizens." [5]

When land, sea, air and sky will be iniquitous

Both the Second Gulf War and the Third Gulf War were unequal conflicts between American led coalition forces, armed with the latest technological weaponry, against a weaker opposition.

> Early on the morning of January 17, 1991, a massive U.S.-led air offensive hit Iraq's air defences, moving swiftly on to its communications networks, weapons plants, oil refineries and more. The coalition effort, known as Operation Desert Storm, benefited from the latest military technology, including Stealth bombers, Cruise missiles, so-called "Smart" bombs with laser-guidance systems and infrared night-bombing equipment. The Iraqi air force was either destroyed early on or opted out of combat under the relentless attack. [6]

> By mid-February, the coalition forces had shifted the focus of their air attacks toward Iraqi ground forces in Kuwait and southern Iraq. A massive allied ground offensive, Operation Desert Sabre, was launched on February 24, with troops heading from north-eastern Saudi Arabia into Kuwait and southern Iraq. Over the next four days, coalition forces encircled and defeated the Iraqis and liberated Kuwait. At the same time, U.S. forces stormed into Iraq some 120 miles west of Kuwait, attacking Iraq's armoured reserves from the rear. [7]

> The Royal Navy made a significant contribution to Allied efforts in the early stages of the war. In particular, Royal Navy Westland Lynx helicopters were responsible for the destruction of almost the entire Iraqi Navy. Additionally, Royal Navy mine hunters cleared Iraqi mines near the Kuwaiti

coast, allowing the US battleships Wisconsin and Missouri to move in close enough to launch devastating bombardments against Iraqi ground forces. HMS Gloucester intercepted an Iraqi Silkworm Missile bound for the US Battleships. [8]

Overall, the coalition air campaign (consisting mostly of U.S. pilots) accumulated a total of 109,876 sorties over the 43-day air war — averaging 2,555 sorties per day. Of those, more than 27,000 sorties struck enemy Scuds, airfields, air defences, electrical power, biological and chemical weapons caches, headquarters, intelligence assets, communications, the Iraqi army, and oil refineries. [9]

In the end, the out-numbered and under-equipped Iraqi army proved unable to compete on the battlefield with the highly mobile coalition land forces and their overpowering air support. Some 175,000 Iraqis were taken prisoner and casualties were estimated at over 85,000. [10]

The third Gulf War followed a similar pattern between Saddam Hussein's Iraq and an allied force led by the US. It began on 20 March 2003, making it the first war of the 21st century.

Coalition troops launched air and amphibious assault on the Al-Faw peninsula to secure the oil fields there and the important ports, supported by warships of the Royal Navy, Polish Navy, and Royal Australian Navy. The United States Marine Corps' 15th Marine Expeditionary Unit attached to 3rd Commando Brigade and the Polish Special Forces unit GROM attacked the port of Umm Qasr, while the British Army's 16th Air Assault Brigade secured the oil fields in southern Iraq. [11]

Sects

Ethnically and linguistically the Iraqi population includes Arabs, Kurds, Turkmen, Chaldeans, Assyrians, and Armenians. The religious mix likewise is varied and consists of Shi'a and Sunni Muslims (both Arab and Kurdish) [...] Civil uprisings occurred in previous years, especially in Kurdish areas in the north and Shi'a areas in the south. The minority Arab Sunni regime reacted with extreme repression against those who oppose or even question it. [12]

Following the defeat of Iraq in 2003, and the removal of Saddam Hussein who was executed, frequent attempts to bring peace to the country have been less than successful.

Behind the power struggle between Sunnis and Shi'ites in modern Iraq, therefore, lie two sectarian groups that are quite similar. The divisions between them are primarily political rather than ethnic or cultural, and reflect the competition of the two groups over the right to rule and to define the meaning of nationalism in the country. [13]

Hunger, pestilences

The two recent wars also caused Iraqis to suffer hunger and disease. The country was unable to provide enough food for its citizens, even using strict rationing controls. Iraq needed to import 70% of its grain, but draconian measures imposed upon the government by United Nations' sanctions made this impossible.

[Very soon] garbage collectors in Baghdad reported a sinister change in the loads carted to the city dump [...] after almost twelve months of war and sanctions, the scraps had entirely disappeared. Food, any food, had become too precious to throw away. Even the skins of melons were being saved and devoured. People were beginning to go hungry. [14]

Disease, too, took its toll among the Iraqi population, as "Typhoid, hepatitis, meningitis and gastroenteritis" reached epidemic proportions. An outbreak of "plague threatened by rats feeding on unburied garbage" was also reported, along with an epidemic of cholera.
In the 1990s, the Tigris changed colour again.

It was now a rich café-au-lait brown because raw sewage from 3.5 million people in Baghdad, not to mention effluent from cities upstream, was entering the river [...] The end results were visible in the children's' wards of the hospitals . [...] The dirty water that brought gastroenteritis and cholera in its train found its little victims easier to overcome because they were already weak. [15]

Governments

Iraq was occupied by foreign troops beginning with the 2003 invasion of Iraq, with military forces coming primarily from the United States and the United Kingdom. [...] The occupation yielded to a transitional administrative law, which was replaced by the Constitution of Iraq following approval in a referendum held on October 15, 2005. A permanent 275-member Council of Representatives was elected in the December 2005 Iraqi legislative elections, initiating the formation of the Government of Iraq, 2006-2010. [16]

The [2010] election was rife with controversy. Prior to the election, the Supreme Court in Iraq ruled that the existing electoral law/rule was unconstitutional, and a new elections law made changes in the electoral system. On 15 January 2010, the Independent High Electoral Commission (IHEC) banned 499 candidates from the election due to alleged links with the Ba'ath Party. Before the start of the campaign on 12 February 2010, IHEC confirmed that most of the appeals by banned candidates had been rejected and 456 of the initially banned candidates would not be allowed to run for the election. [17]

Afterwards, Parliamentary elections were held in Iraq on 30 April 2014. These decided the 328 members of the Council of Representatives who will in turn elect the Iraqi President and Prime Minister.

According to Transparency International, Iraq's is the most corrupt government in the Middle East. [...] The 2011 report "Costs of War" from Brown University's Watson Institute for International Studies concluded that U.S. military presence in Iraq has not been able to prevent this corruption, noting that as early as 2006, "there were clear signs that post-Saddam Iraq was not going to be the linchpin for a new democratic Middle East." [18]

Disorder

After the second Gulf War had been won by the US alliance, there was an air of *disorder*, even amongst the victorious nations. Saddam Hussein had survived, and continued to remain sufficiently popular with his people to ensure his continued rule over Iraq. Not wishing to indulge in the illegality of regime change, which is forbidden by international law, the US had confidently supposed that Saddam would be overthrown from within. It did not happen; it took the Third Gulf War in 2003 to dispose of Iraq's president. But more than a decade later, the country continues to suffer from the aftermath of its wars, with frequent acts of violence adding weekly to the number of deaths and injuries sustained by its citizens, and a fresh outbreak in 2014 of terrorist activities from an organization called Islamic State.

Summary: *This quatrain is so packed with detail that it appears to have been intended to be read by those living at the time it was fulfilled, since much of what has been predicted will have been recognized by them. The oracle began with a comment concerning Saddam Hussein's character. It was this that led to the 'effusion of blood' from the gulf wars that followed. The nature of the warfare, too, has been predicted, so as to include land, sea, sky (bombings and strafing) and air (air-to-air missiles). Aerial warfare is far removed from the 16th century, when this was written. Moreover, the words predicted for the aftermath of the Gulf Wars have also proved to be incredibly accurate, with emphasis placed upon hunger, disease, sects, governments and disorder—all of which proved to be true. (Century Ten No 72 also refers to the Iraq war).*

56   *Vous verrés tost & tard faire grand change*
      Horreurs extremes, & vindications,
      Que si la lune conduicte par son ange
      Le ciel s'approche des inclinations.

57   *Par grand discord la trombe tremblera.*
      Accord rompu dressant la teste au ciel:
      Bouche sanglante dans le sang nagera:
      Au sol sa face ointe de laict & miel.

trombe (*cf* 'tourbillon in No, 3 above); sol (L solum) soil

Through great discord the waterspout will shake,   1792
Accord broken, raising the head (of **LOUIS XVI**) to the sky:
Bloody mouth (**MARAT**) will swim in his blood,
His face (**LOUIS XVI**) anointed with milk and honey to the soil.

For the fulfilment of this prophecy we return to the French Revolution.

Through great discord the waterspout will shake

The French Revolution eventually reached a stage when the destructive forces within it began to spiral out of control: *through great discord the waterspout* – equivalent to *the whirlwind* in Century One N°. 3, and a metaphor for the Revolution – began to *shake* out of control. The year was 1792: a time when the elections of the previous September had given voice to men like, "Robespierre, Marat, Robert, Santerre, Danton, Fabre, Desmoulins and the actor Collot d'Herbois." Before their election, the previous administration had reached an agreement with the King, in which he had been assured that by upholding the Constitution, his position would be secure.

Despite this earlier promise, made in the summer of 1792, the Palace of the Tuileries in the centre of Paris was twice overrun; the second time with such ferocity and carnage that the royal family were only saved by their timely removal to the Assembly Hall. In the following month, the September Massacres forced open the prison doors for the slaughter of the clergy and other inmates. [1] The Revolution was violently *trembling* and about to spiral out of control.

Accord broken

The accord, so carefully planned, and which was intended to avoid any further interruption between king and *parlement*, was broken by both verbal and physical attacks made against Louis XVI. Thereafter, there would be no turning back. The monarchy was officially abolished on 21 September 1792, and three months later, the King was put on trial for his life. [2]

Raising the head to the sky

The verdict was never really in doubt; the assembled deputies voted firstly for the King's guilt, and then for his execution. The beheading of Louis XVI took place on 21 January 1793 at the *Place de la Révolution*. As a final gesture to this act of regicide, and in keeping with the practice of the time:—

> The executioner leaned over the basket and firmly picked up the severed head. He raised it on high and walked along the four sides of the platform showing it to the sovereign people. [3]

Bloody mouth

EXECUTION OF LOUIS XVI

One of the principal fomenters of unrest at that time was Jean Paul Marat. His popular paper, *L'Ami du Peuple*, the forerunner of modern tabloid journalism, acted as a disseminator for his sanguinary views. A favourite saying of his had been, "We must cement liberty in the blood of the despot." Previously, in the summer of 1790, he had declared to his readers that five or six hundred heads cut off would be a price worth paying if it bought them freedom and happiness.

During the September Massacres, it was Marat who urged the good citizens of Paris to go to the prison where the priests were being held, and to run a sword through them. But Marat's bloodthirsty speeches had also attracted enemies; some were already calling for Marat's own blood to be spilt. "In Caen, Pézenas wrote 'Purge France of this man of blood [who] sees the Public Safety only in a river of blood.'" [4]

On 13 July 1793, Marat's opponents had their wish granted, when a well-educated young woman, Marie-Anne-Charlotte Corday d'Armont, aged 24, arrived in Paris from Caen. Her objective was to meet Marat under the pretence of providing information of several plots being planned by the Girondins in her hometown.

Will swim in his blood

Marat suffered from prurigo, a skin complaint he had contracted in the past while hiding in the Paris sewers. To alleviate his discomfort, he took to having frequent baths. It was while bathing, and still immersed in a tub of water, that he agreed to see Charlotte Corday. The decision was to prove fatal. After entering the room and engaging Marat in conversation, Charlotte Corday drew a knife from the fold of her dress and stabbed him below the neck, severing an artery. *Bloody mouth* – as the Seer has labelled Marat – was now *swimming in his blood*. His cries for help, as he threshed about in the water, were to no avail. Nothing could be done for him; and he died from loss of blood. [5]

His face anointed with milk and honey to the soil

Six months previously, Louis XVI's body and severed head had been interred in a deep grave dug for him at the Madeleine, and the remains covered with quicklime. In later years, an attempt was made to recover his body, but *the soil* around the grave, to which the head and trunk had been committed, revealed only a grey chalky compound. [6]

In this respect, it was suggested by author and scholar James Laver that a clue exists in the oracle's phraseology for dating the King's execution. Louis XVI was beheaded on 21st January, the Feast Day of St Agnes. As with Louis XVI, Agnes, too, was beheaded. But the connexion appears to go deeper, for the words taken from the Church's celebratory 'Office of St Agnes' read: "Mel et lac ex ore ejus suscepi, et sanguis ejus ornavit genas meas ..." [7] That is to say, they contain the same words as those appearing in this oracle; that is, 'mel et lac' – *milk and honey*; 'ore' – *face* or *mouth*; sanguis – *blood*. [8]

Summary: *This prophecy was fulfilled during the French Revolution. It refers to the accord reached between the government and the monarchy, but which was later broken when a new intake of deputies was elected in their place. This resulted in the King being made to stand trial for his life. The oracle predicts his execution and the fate of his remains. It has also signalled the exact day of the year on which the execution would take place. One of the bloodthirsty anti-royalists urging death had been Marat. His own death, while in his bath is also predicted.*

58   *Trenché le ventre, naistra auec deux testes,*
        Et quatre bras: quelques ans entier viura:
        Iour qui Alquilloye celebrera ses festes
        Fouslan, Turin, chief Ferrare suyura.

59   *Les exiles deportés dans les isles*
        Au changement d'vng plus cruel monarque,
        Seront meurtrys: & mis deux des scintilles
        Qui de parler ne seront estés parques.

60   *Vn Empereur naistra pres d'Italie,*
        Qui à l'Empire sera vendu bien cher,
        Diront auec quels gens il se ralie
        Qu'on trouuera moins prince que boucher.

ralie (AF rassembler) to gather together: whence, se ralier – to gather to himself

An Emperor will be born close to Italy (**NAPOLEON 1**)   1769
Who will be sold very expensively to the Empire:
They will remark with what people he gathers to himself,
When one will discover, less prince than a butcher.

An Emperor will be born close to Italy

The quatrain begins with an announcement that is surely familiar to most people. Napoleon Bonaparte *was born close to Italy* on the island of Corsica. We are therefore given notice of his place of birth, which occurred in 1769 at Ajaccio where his birthplace is now a museum.

Corsica is situated 56 miles (90 km) from the Tuscan coast of Italy and north of the Italian isle of Sardinia, thus confirming what had been predicted more than two centuries earlier. [1]

The science of genetics may very well triumph at having discovered the human genome. But 'the *Prophetic Creation*, authored by God, excludes birth as a truly random cause.

Who will be sold very expensively to the empire

It was through a series of spectacular battles, from which he emerged victorious, that Napoleon was able to establish the French Empire. It stretched from Spain to the Baltic and included Italy, the Illyrian provinces, as well as much of what is now Poland.

In 1804, Bonaparte became Emperor. [2] But *the French paid a heavy price* for their empire. "Estimates of casualties over the eleven years fluctuate enormously; some authorities place them as high as 1,750,000." (Chandler). The monetary deficit was equally massive. On one occasion: "At least [three-hundred-million francs] for the army alone," was requested from the Treasury. Even this was considered "paltry compared with the vast revenues Napoleon had been used to." (Coote). In 1812, it was reported that he spent nearly three times that sum. [3]

They will remark with what people he gathers to himself

Unlike rulers in the past, Napoleon did not fraternize with members of the existing nobility. Instead, he chose talented, classless individuals who shared his ideals. He recognized their value, and the contribution they were capable of making to the French Empire: and so he rewarded them with positions of power. Pierre Augereau rose from being the son of a stonemason to become Duke of Castiglione; André Masséna was a cabin boy whom Napoleon made Prince of Rivoli; Joachim Murat started life in an inn, but subsequently rose to become King of Naples, and Michel Ney, the son of a blacksmith, received the title, Prince of Moscowa. [4]

When one will discover, less prince than a butcher

In this final line, the oracle predicts Napoleon's darker side. This became apparent during the Commander's Egyptian campaign. It was also before Napoleon became Emperor of France and King of Italy, which then explains why he is called *a Prince*.

It was while conducting his military expedition in Egypt, from May 1798 to October 1799, that evidence of his *butchery* began to emerge. In October 1798, he ordered his chief of staff to cut the throats of all the prisoners, and dispose of their bodies in the Nile. While, in Cairo, his Correspondence recorded that he was cutting off heads at the rate of five or six a day. But it was during March of the following year, when the worst excess of his butchery came to light. Three thousand men, holding out against the French army agreed to surrender on condition that their lives would be spared. The French officer in charge of negotiations agreed terms, but Napoleon countermanded these, and ordered that the rebels be executed. For good measure, he added another 1400 prisoners to the list of condemned men. "He later attempted to explain this foul butchery in terms of military necessity." [5]

Summary: *This oracle provides a straightforward prophecy of Napoleon Bonaparte. It commences by correctly indicating the closeness of his birth to Italy. Thereafter, the oracle proceeds to emphasise the enormous cost to France, in blood and finance that the establishment of his empire cost the country. It also predicts that unlike other emperors, Napoleon gathered to his side men of low standing in society and raised them to dukes, princes and even kings. Against this, his dark side is also predicted—his butchery.*

61   *La republique miserable infelice*
        Sera vastée du nouueau magistrat:
        Leur grand amas de l'exil malefice
        Fera Sueve rauir leur grand contract.

62   *La grande perte las que feront les letres:*
        Auant le cicle de Latona parfaict,
        Feu, grand deluge plus par ignares sceptres
        Que de long siècle ne se verra refaict.

63   *Les fleaux passés diminue le monde*
        Long temps la paix terres inhabitées
        Seur marchera par ciel, terre, mer, & onde:
        Puis de nouueau les guerres suscitées.

fleau (OF) scourge, *or* judgement of God; seure (OF) secure; susciter (OF) incite

The judgements of God having passed, the world is diminished,   1950 ±
A long time the peace, lands inhabited,
Secure, one will proceed by sky, land, sea and wave:
Then afresh, wars incited.

This is the third of four quatrains mentioned by historian Norman Davies, and which he described as 'uncanny', because of its description of life in the twentieth century.

The judgements of God having passed

The scourges or judgements of God referred to in this opening phrase dominated the first half of the 20th century. The First World War (1914–18) was followed by the Second World War (1939–45). In between these two conflicts, there was a pandemic known as 'Spanish Flu', followed by the Russian Revolution and the pogrom of its people by Stalin. There then came the Spanish Civil War. These scourges all occurred within the space of 31 years, producing a death toll counted in many millions. [1]

The Seer has chosen the word *'scourges'* to describe the terrible loss of life that occurred during the first half of the 20th century. In fact, the *OED* defines its archaic use as "whip for chastising persons" and it then continues by stating: "person or thing regarded as instrument or manifestation of divine [...] punishment (e.g. barbarian, conqueror, pestilence, war.)"

Within the prophecies given to the little shepherds of Fatima in 1917 by the Holy Mother, and approved by the Catholic Church, Mary confirmed that God would scourge the world if it failed to adhere to His commandments. But world leaders always imagine that they know better. One can see where this has led the world by referring to the final line of this oracle.

The world diminished

Military losses during the Second World War [...] Total (estimate) 14 362 177. [...] Civilians killed during the Second World War. [...] Total (estimate) 27 077 614. [...] The Holocaust: the genocide of Jews by the Nazis, 1939-45 Total (average) 5 571 300. (Norman Davies).

But *diminishing the world* can also be applied to the terrain. Air travel greatly reduced the time taken to cross both land and sea, which meant the world became smaller. This leads to the next line of prophecy. [2]

A long time the peace

For almost half a century, following the Second World War Europe experienced *a long time of peace*. In mainland Europe this was achieved by forming a European Union of member nations: living together and trading peacefully between themselves in accordance with the treaties of Rome (1957). [3]

Lands inhabited

While across the world, during this *time of peace*, massive immigration programmes were set up by America, Canada, Australia and New Zealand. These were to become *lands* newly *inhabited* by immigrants who were keen to add to the country's workforce, and increase its population; Australia even offered assisted passages as an extra inducement. [4]

Secure, one will proceed by sky, land, sea, and wave

A further feature to appear in post-war Europe concerned travel time. Distances that had once taken days, weeks or even months to traverse were reduced to hours—thus, was the world made smaller. Foreign countries soon became the province of the workingman on holiday. Secure in his mind that he and his family could now travel by sky, land, sea and wave to destinations that previous generations had only read about, he embarked upon his holiday abroad.

Charter flights took holidaymakers across the *skies*. [5] Passenger coaches, high speed trains and motor vehicles criss-crossed the *land*. [6] Ferries bridged the English Channel, and liners offered cruise holidays at *sea*. [7] Also, the hovercraft and hydrofoil skimmed over the *waves* [8] to give added meaning to the distinction between *sea and wave*.

Travel in the 16th century was very much different to how *secure* it became four hundred years later. On land, the risk to a traveller had once been that of murder or highway robbery; at sea, the danger was from pirates, or that the ship might founder in heavy weather. Consequently, one did not undertake journeys to distant places without apprehension: or without considerable thought to their safety.

Then afresh, wars incited

The return of the wars predicted in the oracle and affecting Europe began during the final decade of the twentieth century, when the combined forces of the United Nations took military action against Iraq as a reprisal for its invasion of Kuwait. The fact that Iraq had earlier invaded Iran without exciting the U.N.'s involvement may be considered noteworthy.

This break in Europe's *long time peace* was followed by further *wars* inside the former Yugoslav Republic, especially involving French troops as part of a United Nations peacekeeping force. Then, as the twentieth century gave way to the twenty-first, a new type of war emerged, one directed against terrorist organizations based in regimes nurturing harmful intentions towards western interests. Led by the US and backed by Great Britain, with countries around the world being cajoled into giving their support, military action was taken against Afghanistan, and thereafter, for a second time, against Iraq. [9]

In 2006, 2008 and 2014, this was followed by Israel's attack on Gaza and, with greater destructive consequences, against Hezbullah in Lebanon. Civil war in 2014 also broke out in Ukraine, incited by Russia's occupation of Crimea. There were also uprisings in, Tunisia, Egypt, Libya Yemen, and Syria: as well as in Africa and Asia; further 'scourges', more deadly still, are no doubt awaiting their perception by mankind, on the world-lines that occupy spacetime.

Summary: *This prediction provides a snapshot of life in Europe during the second half of the 20th century. Its accuracy in the descriptive phrases used by the seer was the reason it drew attention from Professor Davies. Apart from its obvious accuracy, the only question remaining is whether the terrible events that occurred in the first half of that century were simply scourges or divine chastisements sent by God. If the latter, woe to the forthcoming future, for even worse must follow when one takes stock of the antichristian laws promulgated by western leaders, with deaths from abortions soon to surpass the number of dead from two world wars.*

64   *De nuit soleil penseront auoir veu*
        Quand le pourceau demy-homme on verra,
        Bruict, chant, bataille, au ciel battre aperceu
        Et bestes brutes à parler l'on orra.

65   *Enfant sans mains iamais veu si grand foudre:*
        L'enfant royal au ieu d'œsteuf blessé.
        Au puy brises: fulgures allant mouldre:
        Trois sous les chaines par le milieu troussés.

mains (OF *judicial meaning*, sauvegarde) safeguard; œsteuf (OF esteuf) tennis ball; puy (AF montagne) mountain; brises (OF) crushed; fulgures (L fulgur) thunderbolt; mouldre (OF) to grind to pieces; par le milieu (Littré - Au milieu de l'assemblée).

Child without safeguards (**LOUIS-CHARLES**), never seen so great a calamity: 1793
The royal child hurt by the game of tennis.
Crushed by the Mountain: thunderbolts proceeding to grind into pieces:
Three in bonds trussed-up in the surroundings.

The French word '*maine*' has several different usages, according to context. In the present case, since it applies to a 'royal child', the context is taken in its judicial sense, which is, '**sauvegard**'.

Child without safeguards, never seen so great a calamity

The child without safeguards, as we shall now discover, was the Dauphin, Louis Charles. He was taken to the Temple Tower, together with his parents, the King and Queen of France, in the summer of 1792, aged seven. But on 3 July 1793 he was separated from his mother, and would never see her again. The decision had been taken to re-educate the child as a 'citizen' of the Revolution. To accomplish this transition, he was placed in the care of Antoine Simon and his wife. Although only a child, the little prince was encouraged to drink wine, given brandy to stop him crying for his mother, and for his amusement, he was provided with pornographic picture books. At other times, he was taught how to blaspheme and curse at his own family to amuse the guards: "Haven't those confounded bitches [his mother, sister and aunt] up there been guillotined yet?" The Paris whores that entertained the palace guards were also brought to him. A doctor was therefore called to examine the child for any sign of a sexually transmitted disease, but nothing was found. After the guillotining of his parents in 1793, the Prince's welfare became ignored, and he was left to waste away in a dirty, lice-infested little room inside the Tower. He died there from tuberculosis and neglect on 8 June 1795, aged ten and a quarter. [1] *'Never seen so great a calamity,'* wrote the Seer—doubtless comparing it with the regal upbringing of the Valois children.

The royal child hurt by the game of tennis

The oracle then looks back to where this abuse against *the royal child* began, and it lights upon the Oath of the Tennis Court. The Oath was sworn by deputies of the Third Estate at a meeting held in Versailles in 1789. The deputies had originally intended to meet inside the Assembly Hall, but upon their arrival, they found it locked. Fortunately, someone remembered an indoor tennis court nearby, and it was inside the 'Jeu de Pomme' (i.e., *at the game of tennis*) that members of the Third Estate swore never to separate until a "constitution of the kingdom" had been established. [2] Historians have long pointed out that this was the definitive beginning of the revolution that followed. For, in effect, they were declaring war against the old regime, which included the absolute power of the monarch. If successful, this would hurt the *royal child,* since he was being raised to rule France in accordance with the traditions of the ancient regime.

Crushed by the Mountain

The Mountain was the name given to the political party peopled by revolutionaries voicing extremist views, and whose members were seated at the highest point in the Assembly Hall. It was through legislation inspired by their inflammatory oratory that won for them the approval of the people, and which afterwards translated into the violent acts that crushed the monarchy. [3]

Thunderbolts proceeding to grind into pieces

What was left of the old order was blown away in the tourbillion that followed. From having once occupied the ultimate seat of power, Louis XVI's position was systematically reduced by a series of sudden thunderbolts. These began with the Oath of the Tennis Court; then the Storming of the Bastille; next, the women's march to Versailles; the King's arrest at Varennes, the assault on the Palace; the slaughter of the Swiss guards and palace staff; the September Massacres; then finally, the royal family's incarceration in the Temple Tower. Apart from these *thunderbolts,* the King was also hounded by the Press, by the Assembly and by the unrestrained *sans-culottes:* each fresh blow *grinding into pieces* the King's power base until nothing further remained. [4]

Three in bonds (the white hairs) trussed up in the surroundings

The oracle concludes with a reference to *three* prisoners *in bonds,* including one *with the white hair.* They are identifiable as "the three royal martyrs, Louis XVI and Madame Elisabeth as well as Marie Antoinette," The Queen is identified by her *white hair.* All *three* were imprisoned together inside the Temple. On the day of their individual executions, they were *trussed-up,* with hands tied behind their backs: this was a formality that victims of the guillotine underwent before being lowered into position beneath the great blade suspended high above their neck; and all of this took place in the midst of curious onlookers, drawn to witness the most grisly of spectacles. [5] As for the Queen's white hair: this, she discovered after returning to the palace from her ordeal at Varennes, when "she took off her cap to reveal hair that had gone quite white through her sufferings."

(Fraser pp. 535-6 & 420)

Summary: *These events predicted for the French Revolution begin with the young Dauphin, Louis Charles, who was*
physically and sexually abused after having been separated from his family, inside the Temple. The Oath of
the Tennis Court is then alluded to as having begun the series of events that led to his suffering. The
political group known by their seats in the Assembly Hall as the Mountain are predicted by its name:
together with its responsibility for having 'crushed' the monarchy, by hounding the King and Queen, and
being part of the calamities that destroyed them. The fate of the child's mother, father and aunt is also
presaged.

66   *Celui qui lors portera les nouuelles,*
        Apres vn peu il viendra respirer.
        Viuiers, Tournon, Montserrant & Pradelles,
        Gresle & tempestes les fera souspirer.

67   *La grand famine que ie sens approcher,*
        Souuent tourner, puis estre vniuersele,
        Si grande & longue qu'on viendra arracher
        Du bois racine, & l'enfant de mammelle.

68   *O quel horrible & malheureux tourment*
        Troys innocens qu'on viendra à liurer.
        Poyson suspecte, mal garde tradiment:
        Mis en horreur par bourreaux enyures.

69   *La grand montaigne ronde de sept estades,*
        Apres paix, guerre, faim, inundation,
        Roulera loing abysmant grands contrades,
        Mesmes antique, & grand fondation.

70   *Pluye, faim, guerre en Perse non cessee*
        La foy trop grande trahira le monarque:
        Par la finie en Gaule commencee:
        Secret augure pour à vn estre parque.

faim (Dictionnaire de français: Littré – Fig. *Ceux qui ont faim de la justice*) Those who have a longing for justice; Perse (Persia –
modern-day Iran since 1935); cesser (AF arrêter) to check; pour (OF) with regard to; estre (AF) situation, condition; parquer (OF)
to pen in, *or* hem in.

Rain, a great longing for justice, war in Iran unchecked,   1980
The faith too great, it will mislead the monarch (**SHAH PAHLAVI**):
By reason of the finish, commenced in France,
A private omen, with regard to one being hemmed in.

Rain

The geography of Iran renders it prone to earthquake activity, as well as drought and periodic
flooding. Among the country's ten worst disasters listed in recent times, and one following a
period of *intense rainfall,* was "**the great flood of July 1980**," which affected 950,000 citizens,
causing many to become homeless. [1]

A great longing for justice

This torrential rainfall came within weeks of two manmade disasters. "**At the end of January 1980
Abol Hassan Bani-Sadr was elected President but by the mid-summer there were pitched battles between
extremist groups in Tehran and other cities.**" [2]

These militant demonstrators were caused by *a great longing for* Iran to become an Islamic
Republic, but to achieve this they had to overcome those who were still supporting Shah Pahlavi.

War in Iran unchecked

The third blow to strike Iran during the summer of 1980 occurred "**when Iraq launched a war to
secure control of the Shatt al Arab waterway in September 1980.**" *War in Iran* would rage *unchecked*
for eight years, and cost the lives of one million men. [3]

The faith too great: it will mislead the monarch

Up until Shah Pahlavi's exile in January 1979, he had been implementing a policy of social reform, aimed at providing both the working and middle classes with the benefits of the country's new oil wealth. This included sweeping changes to the educational system, financial support for university students, a lowering of income taxes, an ambitious health insurance plan, and the implementation of a program introduced in 1972 under which, industrialists were required to sell 49 percent of the shares of their companies to their employees. But it was not enough to placate the Islamic extremists.

In December 1978, following demonstrations that had taken place on 5 November, and even greater ones on December 9 and 10, when several hundred thousand people participated in marches in Tehran and the provinces, Shah Pahlavi finally conceded to the demand for his removal. Until then, he had believed himself safe. But *the faith* which powered the revolution for an Islamic state proved *too great*.[4] And failure to recognise this *misled the monarch* into a belief that his programme of social reform, and the appointment of Shahpur Bakhtiar as Prime Minister would appeal to enough people, so as to overcome those among his opponents who were calling for his removal.[5]

By reason of the finish, commenced in France

Prior to this, in 1964, the Shah had viewed the Ayatollah Khomeini as a troublemaker, and had ordered his exile. Moving from Turkey into Iraq, Khomeini continued what he had begun, urging his followers to ferment unrest as a means of undermining the Shah, and to agitate for Iran to become an Islamic state. Eventually, Saddam Hussein deported this troublesome cleric, and the Ayatollah was allowed to enter France.

At Neauphle-le-Château, outside Paris, Khomeini set up his headquarters, and aided by modern communication technology, he soon had the ear of the world's Press. It was undoubtedly this move – *commenced in France* – that gave him the *opportunity to finish* plans for changing Iran into an Islamic state. On 1 February 1979 – the Shah having departed – "Ayatollah Ruhollah Khomeini returned to Iran from exile in France".[6] Two months later, following a referendum on the new constitution, it was finished: the country finally took a major step forward to becoming an Islamic state.

A private omen

These words further identify Mohammad Reza Shah Pahlavi by his nickname, KHOSHGHADAM. It was given to him by his father after his birth, and used privately within the family circle. "Reza Shah was always convinced that his sudden quirk of good fortune had commenced in 1919 with the birth of his son who was dubbed *khoshghadam* (bird of good *omen*)."[7]

With regard to one being hemmed in

On 4 January 1979, Shahpur Bakhtiar was named Prime Minister; Shah Pahlavi had made the appointment in a last-ditch effort to forestall the Islamic fundamentalist revolution that was gripping Iran. Although Bakhtiar accepted the post, he did so, only on condition that Pahlavi left the country until matters became more settled.

Hemmed in by a "Widespread dissatisfaction among the lower classes, the Shi'ite clergy, the bazaar merchants, and students,"[8] which had begun to gather force since 1978, Shah Pahlavi finally left Iran. He realized the situation no longer offered him anywhere else to turn to, and he departed the country never to return. On 1 February, Ayatollah Khomeini arrived in Tehran to be greeted by the cheers of more than a million onlookers.

Summary: This prophecy is located by name in Iran, and is dated by three major events that took place in 1980. It concerns the overthrow of Shah Pahlavi and the creation of an Islamic State, engineered by the Ayatollah Khomeini. The prophecy actually names France as the place where the transition of Iran's statehood began to take effect. The oracle also benefits from having foreseen the private nickname given to Pahlavi by his father. This has been used to confirm him as the person hemmed in by the revolutionary forces at that time.

71   *La tour marine troys foys prise & reprise*
      Par Hespagnoles, barbares, Ligurins:
      Marseille & Aix, Arles par ceux de Pise
      Vast, feu, fer, pillé Auignon des Thurins.

72   *Du tout Marseille des habitans changée,*
      Course & poursuitte iusques au pres de Lyon.
      Narbon. Tholoze par Bourdeaux outragée:
      Tués captifz presque d'vn million.

73   *France à cinque pars par neglect assailie*
      Tunys, Argiels esmeus par Persiens,
      Leon, Seuille, Barcelonne faillie
      N'aura la classe par les Venitiens.

74   *Apres seiourné vogueront en Epire:*
      Le grand secours viendra vers Antioche,
      Le noir poil crespe tendra fort à l'empire:
      Barbe d'œrain le roustira en broche.

75   *Le tyran Siene occupera Sauone:*
      Le fort gaigné tiendra classe marine:
      Les deux armées par la marque d'Ancone
      Par effraieur le chef s'en examine.

76   *D'vn nom farouche tel proferé sera,*
      Que les troys seurs auront fato le nom:
      Puis grand peuple par langue & faict duira
      Plus que nul autre aura bruit & renom.

farouche (OF sauvage) wild; avoir (OF) use, possess; fato (L ablative case from fat/um) destiny; duira (OF) lead.

By a wild name, such a one will be pronounced (**NAPOLEON**),   1769
That the three sisters (**THE FATES**) will use the name with destiny:
Then a great nation will lead by tongue and deed,
More than none other, he will have fame and renown.

In quatrain N°. 70, the Seer made clear that he knew the private nickname of Shah Pahlavi. In this quatrain, the Seer reaffirms that ability by alluding to Napoleon's name.

By a wild name, such a one will be pronounced

The name Napoleon is obtained from Saint Néopol, martyred during the reign of the Emperor Diocletian. But the name gradually underwent change, and in its present form it can translate as Lion of Napoli—hence the wild name. Lord Byron may have had a similar thought in mind when writing of Napoleon in *Childe Harold's Pilgrimage* – "Conqueror and captive of the earth art thou! / She trembles at thee still, and thy wild name."[1] Author, Stewart Robb, who commented on this oracle, observed that Napoleon (pronounced in French as Na-poll-y-on) and A-poll-y-on (a Greek name that interprets as 'Destroyer': see *Book of Revelation* 9:11) sound sufficiently close when *pronounced* in the French tongue, thus allowing an agreeable comparison to be made.

That the three sisters will use the name with destiny

In Greek Mythology, the Fates took human form as *three sisters*. Together, they decided each person's *destiny*. Napoleon, too, accepted this fatalistic viewpoint, as he came to admit. "All that is to happen is written down. Our hour is marked and we cannot prolong it a minute longer than fate has predestined."[2] For this reason, biographers often portray him as a "Man of Destiny".

Then a great nation will lead by tongue and deed

As one would expect from a French author, France is referred to as *a great nation*. In the age of Napoleon, France certainly earned a reputation for leadership over its growing empire, both verbally, through its administration, and by deed, when enforcing its laws using martial strength.

Certain areas [...] were simply incorporated into the *Grande Nation:* Avignon (1791), Belgium (1795), Nice and Savoy (1796), Geneva and Mulhouse in Alsace (1798). The left-bank Rhineland, annexed. [...] Other areas, Dutch, Swiss and Italian, submitted to the organization of satellite republics under constitutions worked out by local admirers of the Revolution. [...] Practically everywhere they went, from Amsterdam to Mainz and from Basel to Naples, the armies of France could count on a welcome from critics of the Old Régime in each locality. [3]

More than none other, he will have fame and renown

The prophecy concludes by foretelling the greatness of Napoleon in a manner often expressed by his biographers.

The greatest personality of all time, superior to all other men of action by virtue of the range and clarity of his intelligence, his speed of decision, his unswerving determination, and his acute sense of reality, allied to the imagination on which great minds thrive. [4]

Alan Schom voiced a similar opinion to that of Octave Aubry above.

Due to his success in these wars, often against numerically superior enemies, he is generally regarded as one of the greatest military commanders of all time, and his campaigns are studied at military academies throughout much of the world. [5]

Summary: *We have in this quatrain a prophecy that describes the chief characteristic of Napoleon's name and his adherence to fatalism. At the same time there is a clear prediction that he will bring about, or at least contribute to the greatness of France. The nonpareil reputation of the man for whom the prophecy has been written is likewise foreseen.*

77   *Entre deux mers dressera promontoire*
        Que puis mourra par le mords du cheual:
        Le sien Neptune pliera voyle noire,
        Par Calpre & classe aupres de Rocheual.

Que (OF) to the end that; mords (OF) sting; cheual (Harraps Dictionary & Harraps Dictionary of Slang and Colloquialisms). lout, jailbird; Calpre (L *epenthesis* Calp[r]e) Gibraltar; Rocheval (*hybrid:* Roche+val: val\ens is Latin for strong: *and* in French, 'fort'; whence: Roche+val = Roche+fort; i.e., Rochefort. Cross reference: dressera promontoire, C.VI: 79.

Between two seas he will lay out a promontory   1805
To the end that he (**NELSON**): will then die by the sting of a lout,
His own **NEPTUNE** will fold the black sail
Into **GIBRALTAR**, and the fleet close to **ROCHEFORT**.

Although Napoleon was a master tactician in field warfare, it was left for others to match his achievements at sea. This fell not to a French admiral but to a British seaman, Admiral Lord Nelson. His death in victory at the Battle of Trafalgar is described in this oracle.

Between two seas

The Strait of Gibraltar flows *between two seas,* the Mediterranean and the Atlantic Ocean. [1] In October 1805, this area became the scene of the battle of Trafalgar: an affray that took its name from Cape Trafalgar on the Spanish mainland nearby. At the head of the British fleet was Horatio Nelson in the *Victory.* His adversary was Pierre-Charles Villeneuve in his flagship, the *Bucentaure.*

He will lay out a promontory

Nelson's battle formation was unusual in that he lined up his ships in the form of a spear: the oracle refers to this formation as *a promontory.* At its head, he placed his own ship *Victory,* and with the *Temeraire* on one side and *Neptune* on the other, he led his fleet into battle. In Century Six N°. 79 the oracle predicted that Napoleon would also 'lay out a promontory'. This prediction was fulfilled when Bonaparte drove a wedge between the Austrian army and the Piedmontese during his first Italian campaign. Nelson's plan was similarly designed, to *lay out a promontory* on the ocean and drive a wedge between the enemy's ships. [2]

To the end that he will then die

The French flagship *Bucentaure* was among the first to be put out of action by cannon fire, but this early success was quickly followed by tragedy. Nelson had been seen on deck by one of the sharpshooters high up on the mast of the *Redoubtable*. The marksman fired, and Nelson fell to the deck fatally wounded. He died a little while afterwards, holding on to life just long enough to be told that the battle had been won. [3]

By the sting of a lout

Perhaps, because of its content, this oracle is extremely cryptic with its words. Thus, when taken literally in old French, *le mords du cheval* could mean 'the bit of the horse'. However, Harraps *Dictionary of Slang and Colloquialisms* states that 'cheval' can be used to mean a 'jailbird' or a 'common lout'. Cotgrave's dictionary of 1611 defines 'cheval du poste' as a 'lout' or 'blockhead'. The Seer has apparently played with these words for fear of revealing too much before the event. This is because the two words *cheval* and *mords,* when understood in their cryptic form, conceal the truth of what happened on board the *Victory* in 1805.

It was a time when men used by the French navy, if not swept up from the gutters, were often released from jail on condition they would fight in the navy. "The work of the press gangs went on continuously in France [...] for many of these men-unskilled, vagrants, jailbirds – life on land had been even harder than life at sea." [4] The snipers perched precariously on the mast tops fell into this category: having been placed there because it was the most dangerous, and accident-prone place to be, whilst serving on board a fighting ship. Hence, the bullet (sting) of a lout ended Nelson's life.

His own Neptune will fold the black sail into Gibraltar

Nelson's body was taken on board a ship from *his* fleet, H.M.S. *Neptune,* and carried in solemn state *to Gibraltar*. Reference to *the black sail* is included in the prophecy because of the similarity it has to a familiar tale from Greek Mythology. Theseus, the son of Aegeus, king of Athens, hoisted *a black sail* before setting off to destroy the Minotaur, which was the name given to a beast that was half bull and half man.

Now compare this to the French ship, *Bucentaure* a name meaning half bull and half man (Βουξ + κενταυροξ), which was destroyed by Nelson at Trafalgar. Theseus had said that if he returned alive, only then would he change *the black sail* for a white one. Nelson, of course, did not return alive, hence the reference to *the black sail.*

Theseus returned home, "on the eighth day of Pyanepsion – (a period in October)." Again, compare this with the date of Nelson's victory at Trafalgar – "21 October". Unfortunately, upon his return voyage, Theseus forgot to hoist a white sail. When those on land saw his ship approaching with a black sail, they fell into mourning for the death of their hero.

Once again, this can be compared to the reception which greeted the body of Nelson, when *his Neptune* brought the admiral's body *into Gibraltar.* [5] A painting exists of this scene, and hangs at the National Maritime Museum in Greenwich. It was completed by William Clarkson Stansfield R.A. (1793–1867), and the inscription reads–

> Lord Nelson's flagship, with much of her masts and rigging shot away, being towed by H.M.S. Neptune into Gibraltar Bay on 28 October 1805.

The fleet close to Rochefort

After the Battle of Trafalgar, Rear-Admiral Dumanoir le Pelley, with four French ships under his command, took evasive action. To avoid being detected by the British Navy, *his fleet set course for Rochefort:* a place of "refuge, defence and supply" serving the French navy. As le Pelley crossed the Bay of Biscay, he encountered a lone British frigate. This was the *Phoenix*, searching the Bay for a squadron of ships that was known to have left *Rochefort* under the command of Rear-Admiral Allemand. With odds of four to one, le Pelley gave chase, but as his ships headed south in pursuit, they encountered five British ships commanded by Captain Sir Richard Strachan in the 80-gun *Caesar*. In the sea battle that followed all four French ships were captured. [6]

Summary: As a prophecy of the Battle of Trafalgar, this contains a wealth of detail. It describes a location that is historically appropriate; the strategy employed by Nelson; this same admiral's death by a sharpshooter; the name of the ship that carried his body into Gibraltar; the similarity of the battle to a tale from Greek Mythology, and the French squadron that escaped towards Rochefort.

78   *D'un chief viellard naistra sens hebete,*
           Degenerant par sauoir & par armes
           Le chef de France par sa sœur redouté:
           Champs diuisés, concedés aux gendarmes.

79   *Bazaz, Lectore, Condon, Ausch. & Agine*
           Esmeus par loys, querele & monopole.
           Car Bourd. Thoulouze, Bay. metra en ruine:
           Renouueler voulant leur tauropole.

80   *De la sixiesme claire splendeur celeste*
           Viendra tonner si fort en la Bourgoigne:
           Puis naistra monstre de tres hideuse beste.
           Mars, apuril, May, luing grand charpin & rongne.

81   *D'humain troupeau neuf seront mis à part*
           De iugement & conseil separés:
           Leur sort sera diuisé en depart
           Καπ. θhita λambda mors, bannis esgarés.

82   *Quand les colomnes de bois grande trémblée*
           D'Auster conduicte couuerte de rubriche
           Tant vuidera dehors grand assemblée,
           Trembler Vienne & le païs d'Austriche.

columnes (L. columna) columns; grande (great one - feminine) great lady; Auster (OF âpre) cruel, austere; Tant (L. tantum) vuidera (OF vuidier – purger de); païs (OF) country, land

      When the columns of wood have trembled the great lady (**MARIE ANTOINETTE**),   1793
      Conducted by the merciless one, clothed with rubric, (**ROBESPIERRE**)
      He will purge so many out from the great (**NATIONAL**) **ASSEMBLY**:
      Vienna trembling and the land of Austria.

This quatrain concerns Marie Antoinette and Maximilien de Robespierre. Both were major figures during the French Revolution, and both appear separately in other quatrains. This particular oracle is also noteworthy for having combined two separate predictions: both of which occurred on the same day.

THE GUILLOTINE
WITH ITS COLUMNS OF WOOD

When the columns of wood

The guillotine became the official method of execution in France after the penal code became law in October 1791. It consisted of two tall upright *columns of wood* with a blade suspended beneath a crossbar at the top. At the base were two slats of wood, with semicircles cut from each edge: when closed, they formed a circle – Sanson's little window as it became called. A plank of wood, laid lengthwise before the slats, supported the victim's body. When the slats were clamped together, the neck lay directly beneath the blade. The entire machine was placed on an elevated platform in full view of onlookers.

Have trembled the great lady

The prospect of facing execution by beheading is not one that is likely to encourage much thought.

But on 16 October 1793, Marie Antoinette, the *great lady* and former Queen of France was preparing for this ordeal. A show trial had previously provided judicial authority for executing her. Inside the Conciergerie, she prepared herself, as she awaited her fatal journey to the scaffold.

> Prepared for death with her hair cut, she flinched on seeing the open cart, for she had been expecting, or at least hoping for, the same closed carriage that had carried Louis to the place de la Révolution. [...] Sitting erect and gaunt as she was driven through the streets, she was sketched by Jacques-Louis David as an object of curiosity, and only at the very last minute on the scaffold itself did she begin to tremble. [1]

Conducted by the merciless one

Between October 1793 and April 1794, Maximilien de Robespierre, although aided by Georges Couthon and Louis Antoine de Saint-Just, rose to become the virtual dictator of France. Known as 'the Incorruptible', he was austere, *merciless* and quite ruthless in pursuing his single-minded ambition, which was to mould the country according to his wishes. For dissenters, he had a simple solution – the guillotine.

At the trial of Louis XVI, Robespierre had urged the court not to give special consideration to the Queen: "send her before the courts, like all other persons charged with similar crimes," he insisted. On 27 March 1793, having accused Marie Antoinette of being: "no less guilty" than the late King, Robespierre "suggested to the Convention that the former Queen should be brought before the new Revolutionary Tribunal, which had been set up on 10 March, for her crimes against the State." This proposal, made clearly by the man whom the Seer has termed *the merciless one*, was acted upon, and on 3 August the Queen was *conducted* to the Conciergerie in Paris to await her trial. [2]

Clothed with rubric, he will purge so many out from the great Assembly

Further confirmation that Robespierre was indeed *the merciless one* is contained in the Seer's words 'clothed with rubric'. When making his speeches, Robespierre had the reputation of being "a fanatical believer in the inspired text" and the public adored his oratory. It is therefore of note that *clothed* has been chosen to describe his *rubric*, because Robespierre was also known to be a fastidious dresser. "Green was the shade he most often favoured in the choice of the clothes he wore, with such attention to their immaculate neatness and precision of cut." [3] And so, when, these clues are combined, *clothed with rubric* is a phrase applying specifically to Robespierre. But there is more.

Still further confirmation as to his identity arises from his actions. Among the political factions at the time were a group known as Girondins. They were a loosely formed party of moderates from the Gironde department who made up part of the Legislative Assembly. They had joined together in 1791, and in 1793 they began attacking the Mountain, whose chief spokesman was Robespierre. But these attacks led to their unpopularity, and *twenty-two were purged from the Assembly,* to be later tried for treason. The guilty verdict was a foregone conclusion, and on 31 October 1793, "It took 36 minutes to cut off 22 heads."

In March 1794, Hébert was next to invite the enmity of Robespierre. Hébert had been a vigorous instrument in bringing to trial both Marie Antoinette and the Girondin leaders. But his irreligious campaign irritated Robespierre, who accused the Hébertists of plotting a conspiracy. Hébert, together with *nineteen of his colleagues,* were then *purged from the Assembly,* and on 24 March, they, too, were guillotined.

In the following month, it was the Dantonists who fell under Robespierre's vengeful eye. Convinced by a belief that liberty could only be obtained if criminals lost their heads, the *austere one* saw Danton's indulgent attitude as a dangerous opportunity for counter-revolution. On the 30 March 1794, the Committee of Public Safety ordered Danton's arrest, and on 5 April, after a trial cut short to ensure a conviction, Danton, and *seventeen of his followers* were taken to the place de la Révolution, and guillotined. In the space of just six months, following the execution of Marie Antoinette, Robespierre had managed to *purge so many from the* Legislative *Assembly,* these included the Girondins, the Hébertists, and the Dantonists; a total of sixty in all. [4]

Vienna trembling and the land of Austria

On 16 October 1793 all *Vienna* was *trembling* as the people of the city allowed their thoughts to dwell upon what was taking place in Paris. Marie Antoinette, the daughter of Maria Theresa and Francis I, as well as being the sister of Emperors Joseph II and Leopold II, was inside the Conciergerie, having stood trial for treason and then been judged guilty. Her execution was to take place at noon that day.

At the same time, the Prince of Saxe-Coburg was besieging Maubeuge in a move that was taking Austria and its allies (Holland, Britain and Prussia) towards the French border. But, on 15 October General Jourdan commanding the French Army of the North, attacked along the entire Allied line, having quickly realized the danger to France if Maubeuge fell. [5]

> On the following day, that on which Marie Antoinette was executed, Jourdan followed his own judgment, concentrated overwhelming strength on his right, and, not without difficulty, turned the Battle of Wattignies [...] into a victory, relieving Maubeuge. [6]

Thus, in the prophetic sense, all of *Austria* was *trembling* that day. The French army's victory at Wattignies (16 October) forced Prince Saxe-Coburg to lift the siege of Maubeuge for the loss of 2,500 men, and to suffer a further 500 captured.

Summary: *This prophecy covers a six month period between the middle of October 1793, when Marie Antoinette was executed and the first week in April 1794, when Danton and his followers met the same fate. Other strong points occur in the minor details that were nevertheless reported: such as, the Queen trembling at the last moment, as she stood before the instrument of her approaching death; the unity between Robespierre's oratory and his clothing, and the fact that he used his authority to promote the Queen's trial and execution. There is also the prediction of the Assembly, which was fulfilled by the Legislative Assembly, and the purging of sixty of its members opposed to Robespierre. Finally, there is the unexpected separation between Austria and its capital Vienna, each fearful on the same day, but trembling for different reasons.*

83   *La gent estrange diuisera butins,*
        Saturne en Mars son regard furieux:
        Horrible strage aux Tosquans & Latins,
        Grecs, qui seront à frapper curieux.

84   *Lune obscurcie aux profondes tenebres,*
        Son frere passe de couleur ferrugine:
        Le grand caché long temps sous les latebres,
        Tiedera fer dans la plaie sanguine.

85   *Par la response de dame, roy troublé:*
        Ambassadeurs mespriseront leur vie:
        Le grand ses freres contrefera doublé
        Par deus mourront, ire, haine, enuie.

Ambassadeurs (figurative) envoys, messengers; mespriseront (O.Fr. mespriser) neglect, make light of; contrefera (AF agir d'une manière contraire à) to act in a manner contrary to; doublé (OF) twice as big; as great again; of as much worth again.

> Through the response of the woman, the King (**HENRI III**) troubled,   1588
> Envoys will make light of their life:
> The great man (**MAYENNE**) will act contrary to his brothers, of twice as much worth:
> Through anger, hatred, envy, two will die (**GUISE & LORRAINE**).

This prophecy follows directly from the events predicted in N°. 36 above. Henri III of France had ordered the assassinations of two brothers, the Duke of Guise and Cardinal Lorraine; both of whom he saw as a threat to his throne. The House of Guise was at that time the most powerful family in France, and its members were outraged. This oracle reflects the impact the two murders had upon the family, especially upon Madame de Montpensier, the sister of the murdered Duke and Cardinal. She was known as 'The Fury of the League': that is to say, the Holy Catholic League, in which her ducal brother had been its leader.

Through the response of the woman, the King troubled

In Paris, Madame de Montpensier, sister of the murdered duc de Guise and Cardinal Lorraine, was incandescent with rage, and quite inconsolable.

> When informed of the assassination of her brother, her ungovernable passion nearly destroyed her life. Her face for a few minutes became suffused. Then she lay motionless and livid. After an interval her cries of despair, horror and rage resounded through [...] the vast hotel. She tore her hair, and in words of appalling purport cursed the tyrant. [...] The duchess then vehemently harangued the Seize [the sixteen council members]. She exhorted them to rise and avenge the cruel perfidy of the king, to whom she applied epithets the most degrading and ignominious. Raising her hands aloft, the duchess then vowed that henceforth her own life should be devoted to revenge. [1]

It was *through the* vehement *response of this woman* that *the King* now had good reason to be *troubled*. For within a short while of making her outburst, Madame de Montpensier had engaged the services of Jacques Clément: a man of unstable mind whom she began to groom as a regicide.

Envoys will make light of their life

Elsewhere, as a response to the brutal murders that had taken place inside the Château de Blois, the city of Orleans erupted in protest. To further inflame their already raised passions, the citizens next learned that the detested M. d'Entragues had been chosen to govern them in place of the young duc de Guise. Believing that the King's mind could yet be changed, a delegation was dispatched to Blois to petition Henri into accepting the Prince de Joinville (the palace at Joinville was the stately home of the Guise family) as their preferred choice. But when they arrived at Blois they were met by a furious Henri III, who admonished them with "harsh words. 'I command you to receive and obey M. d'Entragues as your governor,' said the King. 'If you do it not willingly, I will soon compel your obedience.'" [2]

Now that Guise and the Cardinal had been removed from the scene, Henri was in no mood to listen to those still influenced by the deceased brothers. In fact, by coming to Blois to make their objections heard, *the envoys had neglected, or made light of their lives*. This became very evident when the King dispatched the Maréchal d'Aumont to Orléans at the head of his Swiss troops, accompanied by a further detachment of his *gardes du corps*, intent upon seeing that dissenters, like those who had just approached him, were to be ruthlessly dealt with.

The great man will act contrary to his brothers, of twice as much worth

Charles duc de Mayenne was the third Guise brother. On 12 February 1589, the *Seize* appointed him Lieutenant General of the kingdom. But to their dismay,

> He possessed no gifts of eloquence like his deceased brother, nor had he that gracious and affable address and princely bearing which conduced so greatly to the duke's popularity; he was, on the contrary, dry, phlegmatic, and practical [...] before declaring himself the mortal foe of his sovereign, Mayenne desired to ascertain whether that course would be most conducive to his interests. [3]

In the event, Mayenne, although he had since become the great man of France in his role as Lieutenant General of the kingdom, lost twice on the battlefield to his rival, Henri of Navarre. Also, acting contrary to his two ambitious brothers: they having been of twice his worth when in power, he not long afterwards resigned his office. From then on, he avoided all further plans to become France's next Catholic King.

Through anger, hatred, envy, two will die

The final line of this oracle looks back at the deaths of Henri of Lorraine, 3rd Duke of Guise, and Cardinal Lorraine: they being the *two* who *were to die*. The reason for their murders has been summed up in three words. Firstly, *anger*; it was Guise's overriding ambition to be the next Lieutenant General of the realm and become the people's choice to replace him as king that had so angered Henri III, especially if aided by the Queen-mother's renewed regency. Secondly,

Henri's *hatred* against Guise grew from the Duke's use of the League, which usurped the power of his kingship—even to the extent of forcing him to flee Paris in fear for his life. And thirdly, there was *envy*, especially at the adulation and enormous support that Guise attracted around him, which the King had been taught to accept as being his royal prerogative. [4] As a part of Guise's support team, there was also the influence invested in the League by Cardinal Lorraine, and so together, they were permanently 'removed' from the threat this posed to the King.

Summary: *As with so many of these prophecies, the accuracy of their fulfilment is recognized from knowledge of the future history that has been predicted. In the present case, this oracle is one in a chain of events that led to Henri III planning two murders that would eventually result in his own assassination, and the end of the Valois line of kings. (The chain runs along these oracles, Century Nine, No. 96, Century Three, No 51, Century One Nos 36 85, & 97.) This particular link in the chain predicts the effect that the murder of the Guise brothers had upon his family, and upon the people who were to suffer rule under the Duke's replacement. Also, in just three words, the seer names the reasons behind these murders.*

86   *La grande royne quand se verra vaincu,*
       Fera exces de masculin courraige:
       Sus cheual, fleuue passera toute nue,
       Suite par fer: à soy sera oultrage.

toute (OF) every whit; nue (*as* nu) destitute;

The great Queen (**MARY STUART**) when she shall see herself vanquished,   1568
Will make excess of masculine courage:
On a horse, she will cross a river, every whit destitute:
Retinue in iron: to herself, she will offend.

This prophecy coincides with events in the life of Mary Stuart. The oracle takes up her life story with the attempt made by her supporters to recover her title as the legitimate Queen of Scotland. It concludes with her escape into England, and the final act that led to her execution.

The great Queen

Mary Stuart's association with the Earl of Bothwell and the murder of Lord Darnley, her legitimate, second husband but also Bothwell's rival in love, had turned the Scottish nobility against her. In 1567, under pressure, she was forced to abdicate. And, in an attempt to separate her from further political influence, she was confined behind castle walls on the island of Lochleven. Ten months later, an escape was planned. On 2 May 1568, with the help of devoted friends, Mary Stuart donned a disguise and was smuggled out of her castle prison. From there, she was taken over the water to an army assembled in wait for her to join them in battle.

Just eleven days after her escape from Lochleven, *the great queen* – formerly Queen of both France, and Scotland – arrived at Langside south of Glasgow to recover her lost kingdom.

When she shall see herself vanquished

On a hillside overlooking the battlefield, Mary was able to watch the fighting as her forces engaged the earl of Moray's army. But it was soon apparent that her side was losing, and very soon *she would see herself vanquished.*

Will make excess of masculine courage

It was then, *with an excess of masculine courage* that she mounted a charger and would have – "like another Zenobia ridden into the battle, to encourage her troops to advance." In words written by her servant to Catherine de' Medici: "she would have led them to the charge in person." [1] But upon arriving amongst her men, she found them in a quarrelsome mood, more interested in fighting each other than engaging the enemy.

On a horse, she will cross a river

Realizing that all was now lost, Mary quit the field of battle and headed south. Her flight on horseback took her to Dumfries and *across the River* Dee, [2] "where her escort destroyed the ancient wooden bridge to avoid pursuit." Finally, she arrived on the shoreline of the Solway Firth. On 16 May, she crossed by boat into England, believing that her cousin, Queen Elizabeth, would provide her with sanctuary. She was to be disappointed.

Every whit destitute

Up until her arrival in England, everything had been done without pause. Firstly, there had been her clandestine escape across water from Lochleven. Next, the hurried preparations that she made to equip herself for battle at Langside. Finally, she had been forced to take flight into England. It was because of the haste in which all this had happened that Mary had been forced to travel without clothes of her own. She was destitute. Everything, even the disguise she had worn when escaping from Lochleven, down to her undergarments were borrowed: "a hurried escape from danger, in disguise, had left her with nothing in the way of a change of clothes."[3]

Retinue in iron

The boat carrying Mary into England landed at Workington in Cumberland. Upon coming ashore, she then spent the night at Workington Hall; after which, she was taken into protective custody and transferred to nearby Carlisle Castle. From then onwards, Mary was kept constantly under armed guard; this was to become her *retinue in iron* for the remainder of her life.[4]

After vainly appealing to Elizabeth for aid, she was removed to the castle at Bolton. From there, she was taken to the medieval fortress of Tutbury. Her next place of confinement was the moated manor of Chartley Hall. Finally, she was transferred to Fotheringay, where she remained until her trial and execution.

To herself, she will offend

After eighteen years of captivity, Mary's final act was to *give offense to herself*. A Catholic admirer had been plotting to free her, and at the same time assassinate Queen Elizabeth. Coded letters passed between the former Scots Queen and Sir Anthony Babington, her would-be rescuer. But, unbeknown to them both, their messages were being intercepted. The code she used had been broken, and the secrets passing between her and her correspondent were read. The letters in her handwriting convicted her, and she was tried for treason and beheaded on 8 February 1587.[5]

Summary: *This oracle identifies Mary Queen of Scots by the events it predicts; these foreshadow her history from the point where she escaped from Lochleven to fight her final battle for the crown of Scotland. As such, they include facts that would later come to pass, such as her attempt to join her army in battle; her subsequent defeat, and escape on horseback across the river Dee; also, her state of destitution upon arriving in England, followed by her permanent confinement, which lasted until the offence by her own hand, and execution.*

87   *Ennosigée feu du centre de terre*
        Fera trembler au tour de cité neufue:
        Deux grands rochiers long temps feront la guerre
        Puis Arethusa rougira nouueau fleuue.

88   *Le diuin mal surprendre le grand prince*
        Vn peu deuant aura femme espousée,
        Son puy & credit à vn coup viendra mince,
        Conseil mourra pour la teste rasée.

puy (AF appui) support; conseil (OF) judgement; mourra (OF) decay; raser (AF tondre de près) crop close; teste (OF) head.
Cross-reference: teste rasée, C.VII: 13; C.V: 60.

The divine sickness surprising the great prince: 1802
A little before; he will have wed a married woman (**NAPOLEON**):
His support & esteem, at a stroke, will become small;
Judgement will decay for the nearly-cropped head.

This oracle is composed of two parts. The first part predicts two related events that occurred before Napoleon became Emperor. The second part predicts the decline in his abilities that finally brought his rule to a close. The central part of Napoleon's career is therefore omitted, and has been left for other quatrains to complete. The time lapse of more than a decade was therefore sufficient to allow interest in the expected fulfilment of the second part of the prophecy to fade.

The divine sickness surprising the great prince

Most biographies of Bonaparte confirm that he suffered from 'petit-mal'—*the divine sickness.* "At worst the turns could only have been of the lesser, petit mal, type." On one notable occasion, prior to his becoming Emperor of the French – hence, *great prince* – the divine sickness overcame him. It occurred in 1802, while enjoying an intimate moment with Mlle George (Josephine Weimer aged fifteen), an actress from the Comédie Française. During his moment of passion, he "passed into a dead faint in bed." His young conquest screamed in horror, pulled the bell-chord, and ran naked from the bedroom, passing Joséphine and other concerned members of the household who were hurrying to investigate the cause of the commotion. [1]

A little before, he will have wed a married woman

Bonaparte's sexual interests are continued in the second line by referring to his marriage with Joséphine de Beauharnais, whom *he wed* on 9 March 1796. Joséphine was a *married woman* who had since become widowed. Her husband, Alexandre de Beauharnais was guillotined during the Great Terror and his estate forfeited. She therefore found herself alone and destitute in Paris with two children to support. It was while in this state that she met Napoleon in October of 1795. [2]

His support and esteem

Napoleon became First Consul in 1799. In 1802 he accepted the title Consul for life, and in 1804 he was raised to Emperor. "From 1799 to 1814 he was the autocrat of France and the dependent territories his conquests secured for her."

> Napoleon became "first consul" for ten years, with two consuls appointed by him who had consultative voices only. His power was confirmed by the new constitution ("Constitution of the year VIII"), originally devised by Sieyès to give Napoleon a minor role, but rewritten by Napoleon, and accepted by direct popular vote (3,000,000 in favor, 1,567 opposed). [3]

At a stroke

A *coup* had brought Napoleon to power, and it was *a coup* that terminated it. Following France's military reversals in Russia, Spain and Leipzig, he was confronted by his chief minister, Charles Talleyrand. With the backing of the Senate and accompanied by the military, Talleyrand was able to inform Bonaparte that a Provisional Government had been formed to replace him, and he no longer had the support of the military, who were absolved from the allegiance they had given to their Emperor.

Will become small

As a consolation for the loss of his former imperial status, Napoleon was allowed to retain the title of Emperor, although his dominion was now confined solely to the little island of Elba [4]

Judgement will decay

Bonaparte's failing powers had begun to appear evident in the military defeats he suffered in the years from 1812 to 1814.

> Napoleon can therefore be charged with being completely unrealistic in his conduct during 1814 [...] with eternal optimism he dreamed of regaining all his old prestige and position. On several occasions he rejected offers of reasonable terms when any wholly sane man would have accepted them. By 1814 he had become entirely out of tune with the mood of his subjects and of his time, and even with reality itself. [5]

As a result of this decay in his former ability to make astute judgments, his fate was sealed. And he was finally and permanently removed from the political scene after his defeat at Waterloo.

For the nearly cropped head

On the battlefield, Napoleon was frequently referred to by his men as "**Le Tondu**" (the Shorn).
Keeping his *hair shorn or nearly-cropped* had become the Emperor's preferred hairstyle at a time
when other men were fashionably choosing a more elegant appearance. [6]

Summary:　　*The marriage of Napoleon to a previously married woman is aptly predicted together with one of his extra-
marital affairs, which occurred in the year before he became emperor. Hence, he is called a 'prince'. This
affair has allowed the prediction of Bonaparte's petit-mal to be included. With Napoleon identified, the
events occurring before his reign as Emperor are then joined to his declining ability at the end of his reign;
particularly his lack of judgment that led to his enforced abdication and exile to the little kingdom of Elba.
Finally, there is the prediction that also identifies Napoleon by his preferred hair style as the 'crop head'.*

89　　*Tous ceux de Ilerde seront dedans Moselle,*
　　　Mettant à mort tous ceux de Loyre & Seine:
　　　Secours marin viendra pres d'haulte velle.
　　　Quand Hespaignolz ouurira toute vaine.

90　　*Bourdeaux, Poitiers, au son de la campane,*
　　　A grande classe ira iusques à l'Angon:
　　　Contre Gauloys sera leur tramontane,
　　　Quand monstres hideux naistra pres de Orgon.

91　　*Les dieux seront aux humains apparence,*
　　　Ce qu'ils seront auteurs de grand conflit:
　　　Auant ciel veu serain espée & lance,
　　　Que vers main gauche sera plus grand afflit.

92　　*Sous vn la paix par tout sera clamée,*
　　　Mais non long temps pille & rebellion,
　　　Par refus ville, terre & mer entamée,
　　　Morts & captifz le tiers d'vn milion.

93　　*Terre Italique pres des monts tremblera,*
　　　Lyon & coq non trop confederés:
　　　En lieu de peur l'vn l'autre s'aidera,
　　　Seul Castulon & Celtes moderés.

94　　*Au port Selin le tyran mis à mort*
　　　La liberté non pourtant recouurée:
　　　Le nouueau Mars par vindicte & remort:
　　　Dame par force de frayeur honorée.

95　　*Deuant monstier trouué enfant besson*
　　　D'heroic sang de moine & vestutisque:
　　　Son bruit par secte langue & puissance son
　　　Qu'on dira sort eleué le vopisque.

96　　*Celui qu'aura la charge de destruire*
　　　Temples, & sects, changés par fantasie,
　　　Plus aux rochiers qu'aux viuans viendra nuire
　　　Par langue ornée d'oreilles ressaisies.

97　　*Ce que fer flamme n'a sceu paracheuer,*
　　　La doulce langue au conseil viendra faire.
　　　Par repos, songe, le roy fera resuer.
　　　Plus l'ennemi en feu, sang militaire.

sceu (sceau); paracheuer (OF) accomplish; doulce (OF *as* doux) sweet - clemencie, also clément, *synonym* for doux (Cassell's
French English Dictionary); conseil (OF) délibération; resuer (OF) délirer; feu (OF qui a accepté son destin) who has accepted his
destiny.

　　　　　　That which iron, flame, have not sanction to accomplish,　　　　　　　　　　1589
　　　　　　The clement (**CLÉMENT**) tongue will arrive to do at the deliberation:
　　　　　　Through sleep, dreaming, the King (**HENRI III**) will make delirious,
　　　　　　More the enemy from having accepted his destiny: military blood.

This quatrain completes the run of historical events predicted for Henri III. In N°. 36 above, the King sanctioned the deaths of the Duke of Guise and his brother, the Cardinal of Lorraine. In N°. 85, the effect this had on the brothers' sister, Madame de Montpensier caused the King to fear her. And in this quatrain, the last act is played out when the duchess obtained her revenge, and had Henri assassinated.

That which iron, flame, have not sanction to accomplish

Many times on the battlefield, before becoming King of France, Henri III could very easily have met with an early death. He had led the fight against Condé at Jarnac (13 March 1569), and at the battle of Moncontour in Poitou (3 October 1569) he was nearly killed when he was unhorsed: only being rescued by the prompt action of his bodyguard. Henri also emerged unscathed along the approach roads to La Rochelle: a dangerously hostile area for Catholics, because of its location close to the Huguenot's stronghold. After taking Niort, Henri had laid siege to Saint-Jean d'Angély and was repulsed three times before the town fell. [1] But, according to this oracle: *iron and flame would not have sanction to accomplish* Henri's death in battle. That event would be left to the action of an assassin.

The clement (Clément) tongue will arrive to do at the deliberation

Twenty-two-year-old Jacques *Clément* was an ex-soldier from the village of Serbonnes, outside Sens, who abandoned military life to become a Dominican friar. It was during this stage in his life that he was invited to join Madame Montpensier's household. She had heard reports of his visions, and so began appealing to them as a means of exacting her revenge against the King.

In July 1589 Clément left Paris for St. Cloud carrying an important document that he wished to bring to the King's notice in person. Upon *arriving* at the palace, a meeting was arranged for August 1st, so that *Clément* could pass the document over to Henri for his *deliberation*. [2]

It was at this meeting that Clément produced a knife from his cloak and thrust it into the King's abdomen. Whereupon, the assassin was quickly seized and thrown out of the upper window to his death. In a letter written to the Queen, Louise of Lorraine, the King explained to her what happened.

> "After presenting me with letters from the said president, the said monk, pretending that he had some secret communication to make, I desired the said Bellegarde and my attorney-general to retire a little. This wicked wretch then gave me a stab with a knife, thinking to kill me." [3]

When Henri dictated this letter, he had initially been persuaded that his injury was not life threatening, but shortly afterwards, his condition worsened. In fact, the knife had penetrated his intestines, causing internal bleeding. The wound proved fatal. "At four o'clock on the morning of Tuesday, August 2nd, Henri III. ceased to exist." And with the King's last dying breath, the Valois dynasty expired.

Through sleep, dreaming, the King will make delirious

The Duchess of Montpensier had wanted Henri III dead. She was a Catholic zealot of the most extreme kind, and had seen in Clément a possible tool for her aim. She had therefore given him her hospitality and nurtured in him a desire to kill the King. But this had had an effect upon the unstable mind of the would-be regicide.

> To merit the favor of his Sybil, therefore, the young monk assiduously dreamed his dreams, denounced the tyrant Henri de Valois, and advocated his assassination. [4]

But the magnitude of the enterprise, urging him to murder the King, eventually took effect.

> The brain of Clement appears to have given way under the terrible excitements to which he was subjected. Mysterious voices whispered in his ears at night when alone in his cell, adjuring him to avenge the oppressed people. He was assured that, as soon as the decisive blow had been struck, angels would bear him away from the scene of his crime; and that his body, invisible to mortal eyes, would be miraculously borne back to his convent. [5]

More the enemy from having accepted his destiny

The Duchess of Montpensier deliberately played upon Clément's dreams, and his delirium at the thought of killing the King.

> [She] appealed to his visions in proof that he was destined to accomplish some great achievement [...] Clement at length applied to his superiors, and asked them whether 'he might kill the king?' They replied by falling at his feet transported at the contemplation, as they declared, of the holy and chosen instrument of Divine vengeance. [6]

It is plain to see from this that Clément had become *more the enemy from accepting a destiny*, urged upon him, than from a murderous act of his own devising.

Military blood

One month after the King's assassination, and with the succession to the throne under dispute, *military blood* was spilt at Arques (21 September 1589) and then at Ivry (14 March 1590). [7]

This fresh outbreak of civil war began when Henri of Navarre sought recognition from the people of France to be acknowledged as the legitimate successor to Henri III. Opposed to him were the Catholic League led by Charles, Duke of Mayenne. Both battles, fought at Arques and Ivry, ended in victory for Navarre thus strengthening his claim to the throne. However, the interregnum proved to be a lengthy affair and its prediction occurs in Century Nine, N°. 50.

Summary: *Henri III is introduced as the intended subject; having survived death on the field of battle, only to be assassinated by a person attending a council meeting, and for whom, 'sweet' is a synonym for 'clement', the actual name of the regicide. The oracle then very competently predicts the dreams and delirium experienced by the assassin, as the man's mind worked feverishly upon the killing of the King. The fact that Clément was groomed to carry out the crime is also implied in the prophecy. Once the deed had been completed, and with no obvious successor to the throne, two major battles were fought, and the spilling of 'military blood' was therefore correctly foreseen.*

> 98   *Le chef qu'aura conduit peuple infini*
>   *Loing de son ciel, de meurs & langue estrange:*
>   *Cinq mil en Crete & Thessale fini,*
>   *Le chef fuiant sauué en marine grange.*

Crete (AF *homonym*: ferme) resolute; Thessale (Gk. Θεσσαλός) Thessalonian

> The chief that will have conducted innumerable people,   1798
> Far from his sky for foreign customs and language (**NAPOLEON**):
> Five thousand within, resolute, and the Thessalonian (**VELESTINLIS**) finished,
> The chief fleeing, concealed in a nautical barn.

The chief that will have conducted innumerable people

The Commander-in-Chief[1] who conducted innumerable people across the sea is identified as Napoleon, for that was how he described his Army of the Orient in a letter sent to the Sultan Sahib Tippoo of Mysore in January 1799. "You have already learned of my arrival on the banks of the Red Sea with an innumerable and invincible army, filled with the desire to deliver you from the iron yoke of the British." [2]

Far from his sky

The phrase, *'far from his sky'* is similar to that in Century Three, N°. 75 ('far distant blades,'), which predicted events concerning Napoleon's Army of the Orient in Egypt and Syria.

For foreign customs and language

Napoleon encountered many *foreign customs* upon arriving in the Islamic world. After capturing Alexandria and then Cairo, he made his famous Arabic Declaration – his *foreign speech*. In this, he addressed the people of Egypt, assuring them that he was, and would continue to be, a friend to the Islamic religion. He then set up a council of Moslem leaders to ensure full cooperation was maintained between them and his administration; also, to reassure them that the existing *customs* of their people would be preserved. [3]

Five thousand within, resolute

Although this quatrain has introduced Napoleon during his campaign in Egypt, the prophetic content is actually concerned with his departure from the country (see line 4). This was precipitated by the Commander-in-Chief's failure to take the fortress at Acre.

The Seer is profoundly cryptic when describing this event. Crete, of course, draws attention to the island rather than to an archaic word in the French tongue meaning 'resolute', 'firm of purpose'. He has also given the word a capital letter. But whether this was intended by the Seer as a diversion, or it occurred through a typesetter's 'correction' is impossible now to ascertain.

> [T]he walls of Acre were more imposing in appearance than in actual strength, and had the French possessed heavy guns from the beginning of the siege a practicable breach would soon have been effected. Under the particular circumstances however, for the first six weeks the French had to employ their field artillery in this vital role, and the results were far from satisfactory. The 5000 men of the garrison, on the other hand, were well provided with artillery of all calibres. [...] Only one realistic course remained open to the French army: to raise the siege and retreat to Egypt. [4]

And the Thessalonian finished

The oracle next turns its attention to Thessaly, which then belonged to the Ottoman Empire. Rigas Velestinlis, a *Thessalonian*, had been so enthralled by the success of the French Revolution that he had begun planning for Turkey to adopt *The Rights of Man*.

> Rigas Velestinlis [...] had come under the influence of the French Revolution, as is manifest in a number of revolutionary tracts he had printed, intending to distribute them in an effort to stimulate a Pan-Balkan uprising against the Ottomans.

Among Velestinlis's targets for political reform were —

> the principalities of Moldavia and Wallachia. The latter proposed the establishment of what, in essence, would have been a revived Byzantine Empire [...] in which monarchical institutions would have been replaced by republican institutions on the French model. [5]

Historically, under Diocletian, Thessaly had become part of this Byzantine Empire, hence the reference made in the oracle. But after the arrival of the Walachians: "Thessaly came to be called Great Walachia. (Megale Vlachia)."

Sadly, Velestinlis's efforts failed. In the summer of 1798 he was strangled by Ottoman assassins in Belgrade, and the Thessalonian's plan for a French-style, political system was finished.

The chief fleeing

Having begun with Napoleon's campaign in Egypt, the oracle concludes with his retreat from Acre. It was there that news of the political unrest in France reached him. Eager to return to Paris, and in company with a few chosen officers, he left Egypt in a secret flight back to France.

Concealed in a nautical barn

For the greater part of his return voyage aboard *La Muiron* he remained *concealed* below deck, lest a passing ship should recognize him and report his presence to the British navy. His sister ship was *La Carrère* "But both frigates were Venetian-built and very bad sailors." [6]

Even more interesting, as Italian scholar Ruggero Orilia discovered, the Seer has compared Napoleon to Pompey, Rome's military and political leader (52 – 51 B.C.).

It was upon his return to Rome that Pompey became a consul, but with the ambition to become emperor. Napoleon's aspiration upon returning to Paris completely mirrored that of Pompey, and he was able to achieve it.

Orilia also discovered that Pompey had once deserted his army, taking with him a small band of followers, just as Napoleon would do eighteen centuries later when leaving Egypt. Upon reaching the shoreline, Pompey had then boarded a *"navis frumentaria"*— a grain boat or *nautical barn*. The Seer has therefore constructed this analogy between Pompey and Napoleon, by likening Napoleon's ship, *La Muiron* to Pompey's grain boat.

Summary: *This prophecy covers the years 1798 and 1799, at a time when Napoleon was campaigning in Egypt. It refers to the Army of the Orient, using the same descriptive word employed by Bonaparte in his letter to the Sultan of Mysore. And, most importantly, it states the exact number besieged at Acre: declaring them to be firm of purpose, which they were, thus affirming the reason for Napoleon's decision to return to Paris. His subsequent flight to France is predicted, and likened to a similar occurrence drawn from classical history. This involved Pompey's own flight by ship, and his elevation to Consul. In the midst of this, a mention is also made of the Thessalonian who attempted, but failed, to convert Napoleon's Turkish enemy to the Rights of Man, a political philosophy by Rousseau, which had helped to underpin the French Revolution.*

99   *Le grand monarque que fera compaignie*
      Avecq deux roys vnis par amitié:
      O quell souspir fera la grand mesnie:
      Enfants Narbon à l'entour quel pitie!

100   *Long temps au ciel sera veu gris oiseau*
      Au pres de Dole & de Tousquane terre,
      Tenant au bec vn verdoiant rameau,
      Mourra tost grand, & finira la guerre.

This concludes *Century One* of the proposed one thousand prophetic quatrains.

References Century 1

1   http://www.theoi.com/Khthonios/Amphiaraos.html
2   Herodotus, *The Histories:* translated by Aubrey Sélincourt, 58
3   Ibid 60
4   wikipedia.org/wiki/Cyrus_the_Great
5   Ancient History Encyclopedia: http://www.ancient.eu.com/jerusalem/
6   Ibid http://www.ancient.eu.com/babylon/
7   Herodotus, 78-9
8   Edgar Leoni, *Nostradamus and His Prophecies:* 340
9   wikipedia.org/wiki/Battle_of_Valmy
10 Ian Littlewood, *The Rough Guide Chronicle France:* 202
11 Christopher Hibbert, *The French Revolution:* 231
12 Ibid 231-32
13 wikipedia.org/wiki/Vandals
14 Ibid
15 wikipedia.org/wiki/September_Massacres
16 wikipedia.org/wiki/Age_of_Enlightenment
17 Leonie, 690
18 Norman Davies, *Europe A History:* 546-7
19 Charles A. Ward, *Oracles of Nostradamus:* 57 (Nu Vision, 2007)
20 Herodotus, 78
21 Internet Encyclopedia of Philosophy http://www.iep.utm.edu/philo/
22 Philo, *Heir of Divine Things,* § 52, Bohn, ii 146

Nº. 3
1   French Revolution, *Compton's Encyclopedia 2000: Broderbund,* CD-ROM
2   Christopher Hibbert, *The French Revolution,* 162
3   S. Hopewell, *Europe from Revolution to Dictatorship,* 15; & Franklin L. Ford, *Europe 1780-1830,* 119; & Simon Schama, *Citizens,* 646; & Alan Palmer, *Dictionary of Modern History 1789 – 1945,* 122-3
4   Norman Davies, *Europe - A History,* 710
5   Hibbert, 185

Nº. 5
1   Christopher Hibbert, *The French Revolution,* 124-5
2   Antonia Fraser, *Marie Antoinette,* 317–8
3   Ibid 319; & Ian Dunlop, *Marie Antoinette,* 319; & Christopher Hibbert, *The French Revolution,* 128; & J. Hearsey, *Marie Antoinette,* 153; & J Haslip, *Marie Antoinette,* 239
4   S.K. Padover, *Life and Death of Louis XVI,* 266-7; & Simon Schama, *Citizens,* 561
5   Simon Schama, *Citizens.* 557
6   wikipedia.org/wiki/Carcassonne
7   Schama, 557
8   wikipedia.org/wiki/Louis,_comte_de_Narbonne-Lara37

Nº. 9
1   Wikipedia, 'Adria'
2   Ibid. 'Holy Roman Empire'
3   Ibid
4   wikipedia.org/wiki/Malta#Knights_of_Malta_and_Napoleon

Nº. 10
1   H.A.L. Fisher, *A History of Europe Vol. 1,* 574; & H. Williamson, *Catherine de' Medici,*
2   R.J. Knecht, *Catherine de' Medici,* 269
3   Ibid 306
4   Leonie Frieda, *Catherine de' Medici,* 382
5   Ibid 125–6, 336, 349–50; & Fisher, 580–1, 582

Nº.14
1   Jonathan White, Russia 1905 – 1941, 9-10; & H.A.L. Fisher, *A History of Europe,* 1317
2   E.M. Halliday, Russia In Revolution, 15
3   Ibid 15, 17
4   Ibid 24-5
5   Russian Revolution of 1917, *Encyclopædia Britannica* 2001: CD-ROM; & Nicholas II – abdication and death, Ibid
6   White, 10
7   Robert K. Massie, *Nicholas and Alexandra,* 425, 446, 451, 482
8   https://en.wikipedia.org/wiki/Persecution_of_Christians_in_the_Soviet_Union#Anti-religious_campaign _1917.E2.80.931921
9   http://www.loc.gov/exhibits/archives/anti.html
10 Fisher, 1288–9; & Robert Service, *A History of Twentieth-Century Russia,* 136

Nº. 15

1   David Chandler, *The Campaigns of Napoleon*, xxix
2   Alan Palmer, *An Encyclopaedia of Napoleon's Europe*, xxiii
3   Ibid 91, 221, 222
4   wikipedia.org/wiki/Pope_Pius_VII

Nº. 16

1   wikipedia.org/wiki/Canton_of_Léman
2   Ibid
3   britannica.org/coup of 18 Fructidor
4   Ibid Pierre-François Charles Augereau duke of Castiglione
5   6 'Plague ridden, burdened by wounded, starved'- (Eyewitness accounts: Bernard, Bonaparte's A.D.C. – Raguse VII 121 & C. Barnett, *Bonaparte*, 64; & Chandler, 241
6   Ibid
7   J.M. Thompson, *Napoleon Bonaparte*, 131-2

Nº. 23

1   Alan Palmer, *Dictionary of Modern History* 1789 – 1945, 302
2   David Chandler, *The Campaigns of Napoleon*, 1064
3   R. Cavendish (ed.) *The Illustrated Encyclopedia of Mythology, Religion and the Unknown*, 297
4   E. Cobham Brewer, *The Dictionary of Phrase and Fable*, 744
5   Chandler, 1064
6   Ibid 1064
7   id 1061
8   id 1062
9   id 1062
10 id 1067

Nº. 25

1   Ian Crofton, *Collins Gem Encyclopedia*, 301–2; & Champollion, Ibid 195
2   Louis Pasteur, *Encyclopædia Britannica 2001*: CD-ROM
3   Ibid
4   *The death of spontaneous generation*, Ibid; & Joanna Richardson, *The Young Pasteur*, 126–8 & Piers Compton, *The Genius of Louis Pasteur*, 342–3, 353
5   René Vallery-Radot, *The Life of Pasteur* (trans. Mrs. R.L. Devonshire), 424

Nº. 29

1   John Macdonald, *Great Battles of World War II*, 136-7
2   Ibid 138
3   Ibid 136-7
4   Ibid 137; & Karen Farrington, *Handbook of World War II*, 69&www.Sherman_DD_Tank_Courseulles-sur-Mer
5   Macdonald, 136-7
6   Farrington, 62
7   *Wikipedia* – Atlantic Wall

Nº. 30

1   J.M. Thompson, *Napoleon Bonaparte*, 134; & Carola Oman, *Napoleon's Viceroy & Eugene de Beauharnais*, 98
2   Jeremy Black and Roy Porter (ed.) *A Dictionary of Eighteenth-Century History*, 1; & Christopher Lloyd, *Sea Fights Under Sail*, 93
3   David Chandler, *The Campaigns of Napoleon*, 245
4   Ibid 244, 245; & H.A.L. Fisher, *A History of Europe, vol 2*, 915
5   Thompson, 133; & Kléber, *Encyclopædia Britannica 2001*: CD-ROM
6   Egypt – French occupation and its consequences, Ibid
7   Chandler, 303

Nº. 32

1   Elba, *Encyclopædia Britannica 2001*: CD-ROM
2   Ibid
3   Denis Richards, *An Illustrated History of Modern Europe, 1789-1974*, 55; and J. Marshall-Cornwall, *Napoleon*, 260
4   Elba, *Encyclopædia Britannica 2001*: CD-ROM
5   Ibid
6   Marshall-Cornwall, 260

Nº. 33

1   historyextra. com/feature/A bridge too far
2   Ibid
3   BBC – History – World Wars: The Battle of Arnhem (Operation Market Garden)
4   Ibid

Nº. 35

1   Leonie Frieda, *Catherine de Medici*, 86, 87
2   R.J. Knecht, *Catherine de' Medici*, 57; Antonia Fraser, *Mary Queen of Scots*, 117
3   Knecht, 57

4   Fraser, 118. Henri II's armour and gilt embossed helm were displayed at the Tower of London in the early 1970s, and witnessed by the author. Also a suit of armour belonging to Henri II, similarly embossed, was displayed at the Louvre in 2008. The helmet belonging to Charles IX was made of iron and plated with gold. Itwas made by Pierre Redon, goldsmith to the Court, and is owned by the Louvre.

5   Fraser, 117-18

6   Ibid

7   Ibid

8   Ibid

N⁰. 36

1   M. Freer, *Henry III, King of France and Poland*, London, 1858

2   Leonie Frieda, *Catherine de Medici*, 376

3   Ibid 379

N⁰. 43

1   Alan Palmer, *Dictionary of Modern History 1789-1945*, 259; & Claude Lebédel, *Chronologie de l'Histoire de France*, 22

2   http://www.livescience.com/29391-eiffel-tower.html

3   The Eiffel Tower, *Encyclopædia Britannica 2001:* CD-ROM; & Alistair Horne, *Seven Ages of Paris*, 327

4   Paris, Neighbourhood and Sights, *Encyclopædia Britannica 2001:* CD-ROM

5   The Eiffel Tower, Ibid; & Brewer, *Dictionary of Phase and Fable*, 998; & Ian Littlewood, *The Rough Guide Chronicle France*, 263

6   http://www.livescience.com/29391-eiffel-tower.html

7   http://www.toureiffel.paris/en/everything-about-the-tower/themed-files/69.html

8   http://www.history.com/topics/eiffel-tower

N⁰. 44

1   E.N. Williams, *Dictionary of English and European History 1485 – 1789*; 135

2   Simon Schama, *Citizens*, 698

3   Ibid 633-4; & Christopher Hibbert, *The French Revolution*, 170

4   Schama, 777–8

5   Gwenen Apiaries Info (Tida-Apa, Portreath.Cornwall)

6   Hibbert, 255–6

N⁰. 47

1   League of Nations, *Encyclopædia Britannica 2001:* CD-ROM

2   Ibid

3   Ibid

4   Alan Palmer, *Dictionary of Twentieth-Century History 1900-1982*, 234

5   Ibid 383; & 'The United Nations', *Encyclopædia Britannica 2001:* CD-ROM

N⁰. 49

1   Treaty of Carlowitz', *Encyclopædia Britannica 2001:* CD-ROM; and Ottoman Empire; also – Military defeats and the emergence of the Eastern Question.

2   cliffsnotes.com/cliffsnotes/history/what-is-the-history-and-meaning-of-turkeys-fla

3   E.N. Williams, *Dictionary of English and European History 1485-1789*, 190–1

4   Ibid 191-3

N⁰. 50

1   United States, *Encyclopædia Britannica 2001:* CD-ROM

2   Alan Palmer, *Dictionary of Modern History 1789–1945*, 293

3   Thanksgiving Day, *Encyclopædia Britannica 2001:* CD-ROM

4   The United States, Ibid

5   The United States at War, Ibid

6   Roosevelt – attack on Pearl Harbour, Ibid; & History of the United States – TheKorean War; & The Vietnam War, Ibid; & the George Bush Administration, Ibid

N⁰. 53

1   Christopher Hibbert, *The French Revolution*, 111–2

2   Ibid 117–8

3   Jeremy Black and Roy Porter (ed.) *A Dictionary of Eighteenth-Century History*, 174; & Simon Schama, *Citizens*, 548

4   J.N.D. Kelly, *The Oxford Dictionary of Popes*, 302

5   Schama, 487; & Black and Porter, 46

N⁰. 55

1   wikipedia.org/wiki/Saddam_Hussein

2   wikipedia.org/wiki/Saddam_Hussein#Iran.E2.80.93Iraq_War

3   Derrik Mercer (ed.) *20th Century Day by Day*, 1341; & Persian Gulf War, *Encyclopædia Britannica 2001:* CD ROM & Bruce W. Watson (ed.) *Military Lessons of the Gulf War*, 247

4   http://www.history.com/topics/persian-gulf-war

5   Opinion Research Business, January 2008

6   http://www.history.com/topics/persian-gulf-war

7   Ibid

8   wikipedia.org/wiki/Operation_Granby
9   (http://www.u-s-history.com/pages/h2020.html)
10   wikipedia.org/wiki/Saddam_Hussein#Iran.E2.80.93Iraq_War
11   wikipedia.org/wiki/Iraq_War#Poison_gas
12   Ethnic and Religious Groups in Iraq – US Iraq War ProCons.org
13   Ibid
14   The invasion and war, *Encyclopædia Britannica 2001*: CD-ROM; Cockburn, 114
15   BBC News at Midnight – 12 March 1991; & Cockburn, 130, 132
16   Wikipedia.org/wiki/Politic of Iraq
17   wikipedia.org/wiki/Politics_of_Iraq#Iraqi_parliamentary_election.2C_2014
18   Ibid

N°. 57

1   Christopher Hibbert, *The French Revolution*, 146–7
2   Franklin L. Ford, *Europe 1780-1830*, 119
3   Hibbert, 189; & S.K. Padover, *The Life and Death of Louis XVI*, 335
4   Simon Schama, *Citizens*, 630, 730; & Marat, *Encyclopædia Britannica 2001*: CD-ROM
5   Schama, 736–7
6   Padover, 335
7   Ibid 82
8   James Laver, *Nostradamus orThe Future Foretold*, 155

N°. 60

1   John Belcham and Richard Price (ed.) *A Dictionary of Nineteenth-Century History*, 78
2   J.M. Thompson, *Napoleon Bonaparte*, 93, 135-6, 187-8
3   Stephen Coote, *Napoleon and the Hundred Days*, 186-7; & David Chandler, *The Campaigns of Napleon*, xxix
4   Chandler, 55, 1122–3; & Murat, *Encyclopædia Britannica 2001*: CD-ROM; & Ney, Ibid
5   Thompson, 117; & Corelli Barnett, *Bonaparte*; & Chandler, 236

N°. 63

1   Alan Palmer, *The Dictionary of Twentieth-Century History 1900-1982*, 402-3
2   Norman Davies, *Europe A History*, 1328-9
3   Ibid 1057
4   Melbourne, the People, Patterns of Immigration, *Encyclopædia Britannica 2001*: CD-ROM; & Zimbabwe, Immigration, Ibid; & Washington, the People, Ibid; & Montreal, the People, Ibid; & South Africa, the People, Ibid; & New Zealand, the People, Ibid
5   History of Transportation, the Jet Era, Ibid
6   The Railroad in Continental Europe, Ibid; & France, Roads, Ibid
7   P & O Cruises 2003, 6
8   Hydrofoil - *Encyclopædia Britannica 2001* - CD-ROM; & Hovercraft, Ian Crofton (ed.) *Collins Gem Encyclopedia*, 480
9   Norman Davies, *Europe A History*, 1124; & Operation Desert Storm, *20th Century Day By Day*: CD-ROM; & Eye witness accounts of current events.

N°. 65

1   Meade Minnigerode, *The Son of Marie Antoinette*, 183–6
2   June 20th 1789 – W. Edwards, *Notes on European History,* Vol. III; & Simon Schama, *Citizens*, 359
3   Franklin L. Ford, *Europe 1780 –1830*, 120; & C. Hibbert, *The French Revolution*, 180–1
4   Hibbert, 330–2
5   Ibid 188, 222; & Schama, 311, 653, 799

N°. 70

1   EM-DAT: The OFDA/CRED International Disaster Database: Université Catholique de Louvain, Brussels, Belgium.
2   Alan Palmer, *Dictionary of Twentieth Century History 1900-1982*, 200
3   Ibid 200
4   'The protests, moreover, aimed at more fundamental change: in slogans and leaflets, the protesters attacked the shah and demanded his removal, and they depicted Ayatollah Khomeini as their leader and an Islamic state as their ideal' Ibid
5   Milton Viorst, a Middle East specialist, and author of *In the Shadow of the Prophet*, *Time Magazine*, Monday, April 13, 1998; & The shah was aware of the rising resentment and dissatisfaction in the country and the increasing international concern about the suppression of basic freedoms in Iran … ' *Library of Congress*.
6   Khomeini moved to Paris in France … ' *Encyclopaedia of the Orient*, – Iran History by Tore Kjeilen.
7   Ferydoun Hoveyda, *The Shah and the Ayatollah: Iranian Mythology and Islamic Revolution 2003*, 5.
8   Mohammad Reza Shah Pahlavi (shah of Iran) – Encyclopedia Britannica

N°. 76

1   Lord Byron, *Childe Harold's Pilgrimage*, 37th stanza of the 3rd canto; & Saint John, *Book of Revelation*, 9:11
2   David Chandler, *The Campaigns of Napoleon*, xxv–xxvi, xxviii; & Stephen Coote, *Napoleon and the Hundred Days*, 147
3   Alan Palmer, *Dictionary of Modern History 1789-1945*, 109; & Franklin L Ford, *Europe 1780–1830*, 158-9
4   Octave Aubry, *Napoléon*, Paris, 1969
5   Alan Schom, *Napoleon Bonaparte*, 1997

Nº. 77

1 Ian Crofton (ed.) *Collins Gem Encyclopedia*, 406
2 Christopher Lloyd, *Sea Fights Under Sail*, 99–100
3 Ibid 100; & Peter Padfield, *Nelson's War*, 186–7
4 Alan Palmer, *An Encyclopaedia of Napoleon's Europe*, 207; & Franklin L. Ford, *Europe 1780-1830*, 240–1
5 Geoffrey Bennett, *The Battle of Trafalgar*, 128, 250; & *After Trafalgar: the crippled 'Victory' being towed into Gibraltar*, a painting by William Clarkson Stansfield, R.A. (1793-1867) held by the National Maritime Museum, Greenwich.
6 Bennett, 226

Nº. 82

1 Simon Schama, *Citizens*, 799
2 Alan Palmer, *Dictionary of Modern History 1789-1945*, 246; & H.A.L. Fisher, *A History of Europe*, 904; & Antonia Fraser, *Marie Antoinette The Journey*, 486, 491
3 Schama, 579
4 Ibid 805; & Jeremy Black and Roy Porter (ed.) *A Dictionary of Eighteenth-Century History*, 288; & Christopher Hibbert, *The French Revolution*, 235-6, 239, 243
5 historyofwar.org/articles/battles_wattignies.html
6 Battle of Wattignies - Wikipedia

Nº. 85

1 M. Freer, *Henry III, King of France and Poland*, London, 1858
2 Ibid
3 Ibid
4 Leonie Frieda, *Catherine de Medici*, 375-6

Nº. 86

1 Antonia Fraser, *Mary Queen of Scots*, 433
2 Ibid 434
3 Ibid 436
4 E.N. Williams, *A Dictionary of English and European History 1485-1789*, 300
5 Ibid 300-1

Nº. 88

1 Francine Barker, *Napoleon: The First European*, 26, The Observer 26/1/1969; & Alistair Horne, *Seven Ages of Paris*, 221
2 J.M. Thompson, *Napoleon Bonaparte*, 56-8
3 wikipedia.org/wiki/Napoleon
4 Thompson, 356
5 David Chandler, *The Campaigns of Napoleon*, 1004; and xl
6 Napoleon I, the Consulate, *Encyclopædia Britannica 2001* - CD-ROM

Nº. 97

1 Robert J. Knecht, *The French Religious Wars 1562–1598*, 58
2 R. Mousnier, *The Assassination of Henry IV* (trans. Joan Spencer), 214–5
3 M. Freer, *Henry III, King of France and Poland*, 1858
4 Ibid
5 Ibid
6 Ibid
7 Knecht, 62-3

Nº. 98

1 J.M. Thompson, *Napoleon Bonaparte*, 92, 120
2 Paul Strathern, *Napoleon in Egypt*, 273 & Thompson, 97
3 Egypt – French occupation and its consequences, *Encyclopædia Britannica 2001*: CD-ROM
4 David Chandler, *The Campaigns of Napoleon*, 237, 240
5 Rigas Velestinlis, *Encyclopædia Britannica 2001*: CD-ROM; & Thessaly, Ibid
6 Julius Caesar, *De Bello Civili* 3:96; Chandler, 242; & H.A.L. Fisher, *Napoleon*, 70; & Carola Oman, *Napoleon's Viceroy – Eugene de Beauharnais*, 98

CENTURY TWO

T he second 'century' of the intended 1000 oracles commences with a prophecy that became
fulfilled during World War I.

> 1   *Vers Aquitaine par insults Britanniques*
> *De par eux mesmes grandes incursions*
> *Pluyes, gelées seront terroirs iniques,*
> *Port Selyn fortes fera inuasions.*

insults (OF), assaults; de par eux (OF) by them; terroir (AF terr[e]oir) territory; Port (L port\a); Selyn (*paragram & synecdoche*), Sely[m] – Turkey. Cross-reference: par eux, C.X: 13.

> Towards Aquitaine, for British assaults: 1914
> Great sudden attacks by the same them:
> Rains, frosts, the territories will be iniquitous;
> The entrance to Turkey will bring about robust invasions.

Towards Aquitaine

Aquitaine was the Roman name for Gaul. Originally, it was identified by the land from the Pyrenees to the River Garonne. The relevance of Aquitaine to this oracle occurred in 1914, when, "the French government left the capital for the safety of Bordeaux." This city is situated on the river Garonne, *towards* the northern border of *Aquitaine*.

For British assaults

The reason for transferring the government from Paris to Bordeaux was fear of invasion, caused by the retreat of the French Army. It had joined with an Expeditionary Force sent by Britain in an attempt to drive the German army out of France.

The German Army eventually reached to within 30 miles of the French capital, before being halted at the battle of Marne (5-12 September 1914). It was where the French and British forces were victorious, causing the German army to 'dig in' and begin four years of trench warfare. [1]

The French army thereafter became reinforced by a continuous flow of British recruits, keen to push the Hun back across its border—and so began the first wave of *British assaults*.

During the conflict that followed the German retreat at Marne, a large expanse of northern France became the scene of indescribable carnage as the German army sought to extend its hold on France. For four years, war on the 'Western Front' – a battle line stretching from Switzerland to the sea – was fought with such ferocity that deaths and mutilations were, at times, counted in thousands per second.

Great sudden attacks by the same them

Trench warfare involved *sudden attacks by British soldiers* ordered to 'go over the top' in a mass charge at a German defence position. At Mons, where the two opposing armies met in August 1914, the fighting ended with the British being forced to retreat. At Ypres, the first battle took place during the months of October and November when the two armies arrived outside the town at the same time. The second battle of Ypres took place in April of the following year, with poison gas making its opening début in what became euphemistically called the 'theatre of war'. The battle of the Somme began in July 1916, and lasted for two and a half months. After pounding the German line with mortar shells for a week, supposedly to diminish the opposition, the British launched a major attack from the trenches, and very quickly lost 20,000 men on the first day. By the end of the battle the number of British casualties had risen to more than 420,000, whereas the German casualty figure was put at 190,000. Passchendaele, also known as the third battle of Ypres, was fought during the late summer of 1917. At Passchendaele, five miles of territory was won for the loss of 325,000 men—equivalent to 37 dead per yard gained. [2]

Rains, frosts, the territories will be iniquitous

To make matters far worse, there was the *rain*. In October, during the battle of the Somme, torrential rain turned the battlefield into a quagmire. At Passchendaele the *rains* were even worse. Men floundered up to their waists in mud; heavy artillery sank beneath the surface of the ground, and tanks were submerged in the mire. The effect upon the human body from continuously standing in mud and water was 'trench foot', with the possibility of the toes, or even the foot, being amputated.

Frosts, too, proved hazardous to trench life. Apart from many incidences of frostbite, a sudden thaw could melt the frost, causing the parapet of the trench to collapse, with potentially dangerous consequences for those attending to its repair. It was also difficult to dig trenches in ground that had frozen solid. During the course of the Great War, the number of British soldiers admitted to hospital suffering from either trench foot or frostbite totalled 75,000. [3]

The entrance to Turkey

The final line of prophecy continues predicting events during World War I, but shifts the scene to Turkey. Both Selym I and Selym II were rulers over the Ottoman Empire during the lifetime of the Seer: Selym II having ruled during Turkey's greatest military triumphs.

The entrance to the Turkish capital is through the Dardanelles, a narrow strait in the northwest of the country that leads to the Sea of Marmara. In fact, the Strait and the Sea combined give it the appearance of a *port*, although many times enlarged. [4]

Will bring about robust invasions

In February and March 1915, an Anglo-British fleet launched a preliminary attack upon the fortifications lying on both sides of the Strait. The plan was to reach Constantinople and make contact with Russia. The first landings occurred on 25 April at Cape Helles, on the tip of the Gallipoli peninsula. Another landing, made by the Australian and New Zealand Army Corps (ANZAC), took place about 15 miles to the north of there, at Ari Burnu. The French, on the other side of the Strait, also made a landing, so that all told, *the entrance to Turkey* had begun to *bring about robust invasions*. [5] After three months of bitter conflict, three further British divisions landed to help make a planned, coordinated assault against the defending Turks. But the plan failed. Casualties totalled 252,000 among the Allies, and as many again for the Turks.

Summary: Anyone who is aware of the history of World War One will recognize the salient references in this prophecy—the French government in retreat to Bordeaux, as Paris came under threat of occupation, the assaults and incursions by the British, who were fighting on French soil for France, the torrential rain suffered by the soldiers in the trenches: also the battles fought by ANZAC, among others, in Turkey. References to all these appear in this oracle, although it was written more than 360 years before WWI began. Einstein's block universe explains its background, as does the Mind of God.

2   La teste blue fera la teste blanche.
       Autant de mal que France a fait leur bien:
       Mort a l'anthenne, grand pendu sus la branche,
       Quand prins des siens le roy dira combien.

3   Pour la chaleur solaire sus la mer,
       De Negrepont les poissons demis cuits:
       Les habitans les viendront entamer,
       Quand Rod. & Gennes leur faudra le biscuit.

4   Depuis Monech iusques au pres de Sicile
       Toute la plage demoura desolée,
       Il n'y aura fauxbourg, cite, ne vile
       Que par Barbares pillée soit & vollée.

5   *Qu'en dans poisson, fer & letre enfermée*
        Hors sortira qui puys fera la guerre,
        Aura par mer sa classe bien ramée,
        Apparoissant pres de Latine terre.

6   *Au pres des portes & dedans deux citéz*
        Seront deux fleaux onques n'aperceu vn tel,
        Faim dedans peste, de fer hors gens boutés,
        Crier secours au grand Dieu immortel.

fleaux (OF *singular* flael *also* châtiment envoyé par Dieu) flail, chastisement sent by God; oncques (OF relating to time) never; aperceu (OF appercevoir) to behold; bouts (OF bouter) to force, thrust or push forward.

Close by the gates, and within two towns (**AUSCHWITZ BIRKENAU**)   1942
Will be two scourges, a like never before beheld,
Hunger, disease inside; outside, the people forced forward by iron,
Crying help to the great immortal God.

One of the greatest horrors of the Second World War occurred at Auschwitz. All across occupied Europe, Jews were being rounded up to be sent by cattle trucks to concentration camps under German control. Some were extermination centres designed to eliminate the Jewish people, *en masse*, as well as other people termed undesirable. The most notorious was Auschwitz.

Close by the gates

"The entrance gate that prisoners called the 'Gate of Death' was located in the main SS guardhouse building. Trains carrying deportees entered here after May 1944 on the railroad spur that extended into the camp." Before then, the trains had stopped outside the entrance gate.

Inside the compound were two further gates: above one of which, there had been placed the most infamous message in history:

ARBEIT MACHT FREI – (Work Brings Freedom). It was the sign above the iron gates of Auschwitz. It was placed there by [SS-Hauptsturmführer] Rudolf Höss, commandant of the camp. He seems not to have intended it as a mockery, nor even to have intended it literally, as a false promise that those who worked to exhaustion would eventually be released, but rather as a kind of mystical declaration that self-sacrifice in the form of endless labour does in itself brings a kind of spiritual freedom. [1]

And within two towns

Near these gates was the prison compound of Auschwitz, with its large extermination camp. The name, 'Auschwitz-Birkenau' was obtained from *two* Polish *towns* Auschwitz from the "Silesian town of Oswiecim" Birkenau from neighbouring Brzezinka. It was inside this hugely extensive prison compound, with its electrified fences, that row upon row of prison huts had been erected to house the masses, as they spilled each day from the cattle trucks arriving from across occupied Europe; men, women and children: families torn from their homes to end their lives degraded, numbered and despised.

Will be two scourges

KL Auschwitz I – Gas Chamber I. Beginning in 1942, Auschwitz began to function in another way. It became the center of the mass destruction of the European Jews. The Nazis marked all the Jews living in Europe for total extermination, regardless of their age, sex, occupation, citizenship, or political views. They died only because they were Jews. After the selections conducted on the railroad platform, or ramp, newly arrived persons classified by the SS physicians as unfit for labor were sent to the gas chambers: the ill, the elderly, pregnant women, children. In most cases, 70-75% of each transport was sent to immediate death.

KL Auschwitz II – Birkenau. The Crematorium II building, which contained a gas chamber and furnaces for burning corpses. Several hundred thousand Jewish men, women and children were murdered here with poison gas, and their bodies burned. The bodies of Jewish and non-Jewish prisoners who died in the concentration camp were also burned here. According to calculations by the German authorities, 1,440 corpses could be burned in this crematorium every 24 hours. According to the testimony of former prisoners, the figure was higher. [2]

As to whether the source of the oracle intended the meaning of *fleaux* to be read as 'chastisements sent by God' or simply 'scourges' (which can also mean instruments of divine punishment), is unknown. Alluding to God as the cause of travail has a strong biblical foundation. In the seventeenth-century, Londoners believed the Great Plague and the Great Fire were punishments from God, for their government's act of regicide. In 1703, the Great Storm of London caused a similar reaction, and even occasioned the government to declare 19 January 1704 as a 'day of fasting'. Even in 1984, Archbishop Habgood's ordination of Bishop Jenkins, followed by a bolt of lightning igniting the Minster, was thought by some to be divine judgement for his blasphemy.

A like never before beheld

As for the hell on earth that was Auschwitz, this defied even Dante's imagination – "There has never been a more horrific place than Auschwitz, the Nazi concentration camp in Poland where the biggest mass murder ever took place. More than a million men, women and children died there." These words seem to be rather eerily like those mentioned in the oracle, written four centuries earlier. The camp was a death factory, with purpose-built gas chambers for exterminating as many men, women and children as could be accommodated inside.

Immediately upon arrival, the intended victims would be divided between those who were to be killed, and those who were to be used for enforced labour. See also N°. 20 below.

Others were chosen for experimentation in the medical laboratories of Josef Mengele and his accomplices. Those condemned to die were never aware of what lay ahead. Their destination was a building containing 'showers' for delousing – or so they were told. Once they had been stripped naked and forced inside the building, the doors were closed and barred, and Zyklon B tablets were then inserted into a chamber on the roof that led down to the people pressed together below. When mixed with air, the tablets became lethal. The bodies of the dead were then removed for cremation in one of the ovens nearby, specifically designed to incinerate as many corpses as possible. [3]

Hunger

Feeding those who were allowed to live and work was not considered a priority at Auschwitz, and what passed for food was scarce. When, finally, Russian soldiers stumbled across the site in January 1945, "they saw living skeletons moving slowly in a landscape of corpses sprawled in the snow." [4]

Disease inside

Disease, too was rife among those detained, with scabies most prevalent. When the Germans finally abandoned the camp, they "left only a few hundred inmates behind in the camp's hospital block, most of them sick with diphtheria, scarlet fever or typhus." [5]

Outside, the people forced forward by iron

Outside the extermination camp, in the occupied countries of Europe, *the people* with immediate Jewish ancestry were being systematically and forcibly rounded-up under gunpoint. After their arrest they were collected together in groups, and housed in ghettoes to await transportation, either to Auschwitz, or one of the other death camps. "Trains brought Jews to Auschwitz-Birkenau from as far north as Norway, as far west as the Atlantic coast of France, as far south as Rome, Corfu and

Athens, as far east as Transylvania and Ruthenia." It is estimated that, "More than two and a half million Jews were deported to Birkenau, and at least two and a quarter million murdered there." In addition, it may be noted that the French word for railway is *Chemin de Fer* (Path of Iron) which presents an easily discernible allusion to those *forced forward by iron*. [6]

Crying help to the great immortal God

The Bible contains many stories from ancient times that tell of God's help, and His intervention in the history of the Jewish people. E.g. "The people of Judah came together to seek help from the Lord (2 Chronicles 20:4) [...] If calamity comes upon us, whether the sword of judgment, or plague or famine, we will stand in your presence before this temple that bears your Name and will cry out to you in our distress, and you will hear us and save us." (Ibid. 20:9)

Inside the compound at Auschwitz, Jewish religious ceremonies continued to be observed by the work force, although an increasing number were to find their faith insufficient to support former beliefs. Once locked inside the death chamber, the pleas, prayers and *cries for help to the great immortal God* from those condemned to suffocate in the poisonous blue haze, which they inhaled, was to become a haunting memory within the minds of the *Sonnerkommandos*. These were compatriots of the condemned, but who had been assigned to remove and dispose of the corpses after the gas had cleared. The anguished screams of those dying and their fading cries for help were a chilling part of the horrors taking place inside. [7] Today, "[many] Jews can no longer subscribe to the biblical idea of God who manifests himself in history, who, they say with Weisel, died in Auschwitz." (Armstrong). Nevertheless, it is noteworthy that, despite the horror 'of a like never before beheld', the Seer, though also being Jewish, did not share in this future disbelief.

Summary: *This prophecy foresees a horror 'never before beheld' that was Auschwitz. The entrance to the camp is described by its now famous portals, as too are the two townships by which the death camp became known. The hunger and the disease that were an endemic part of life among the prison population have also been recorded. And the fate of those outside, driven by iron to share the fate of those inside, is also foreseen. The religious calling of those affected is indicated by their appeals to an 'ever living God' for help. The word 'immortal' could suggest a sharp comparison with those about to die.*

7   *Entre plusieurs aux isles deportés*
     L'vn estre nay à deux dens en la gorge:
     Mourront de faim les arbres esbroutés,
     Pour eux neuf roy novel edict leur forge.

plusieurs (OF) a great number, many; deporté (OF) exempted; esbroutéz (OF es+brouter) to nibble at buds, sprigs,bark; edict (L edict/um) edict; forger (OF) to compose,make, frame;. Cross-reference: à deux dents en la gorge, C.III: 42.

Among a great number exempted, to the Isles: 1685
The one to be born with two teeth in his mouth (**LOUIS XIV**):
They will die of hunger, the trees nibbled bare,
For them a new King (**WILLIAM III**): a recent order fabricates for them.

Among a great number exempted to the Isles

Louis XIV's revocation of the *Edict of Nantes* (Edict of Fontainebleau, 18 October 1685) caused *a great number* of French citizens to be *exempted* from the legal protection which, since 1598 under Henri IV, had guaranteed their freedom to worship separately. These were Huguenots, and after their exclusion from the protection of the law, they became easy prey to the cruellest of treatments: even possible execution. [1] Their response was to leave France in huge numbers.

Counted among those moving abroad to escape persecution, were many skilled artisans who crossed the Channel to seek refuge *in the* British *Isles*. "A whole quarter of London was populated with French silk operatives; others brought to that city the perfected art of glass-cutting, an art that was henceforth lost to France." [2]

The one to be born with two teeth in his mouth

The one to be born with two teeth in his mouth identifies Louis XIV. This minor detail relating to his birth was foreseen almost 150 years earlier, and it provides a means of recognizing the King responsible for the huge migration of talent that left France: many arriving in England. The scholarly Hugo Grotius saw it as an omen of Louis XIV's future intentions.

> Neither the pope nor the lay princes appreciated the fears of the Swedish minister, the learned Hugo Grotius, who upon hearing that the child had been born with two fully developed teeth and that one wet nurse after another proved to be unable to sustain the punishment of feeding him, wrote to his master, "The Dauphin is not satisfied to dry up his nurses he tears them to pieces with his bites. It is for the neighbours of France to fear this precocious voracity." [3]

They will die of hunger, the trees nibbled bare

Seven years after Louis XIV's shattering persecution of the Huguenots, France was struck by "a terrible winter [1693 – 94] followed by a poor harvest." Together, this reduced the stock of available food, causing "widespread famine" across much of the land. [4] The oracle refers to *people dying from hunger*. Deaths happened as the year wore on, with crops withering on the ground, and the trees failing to bud properly as a result of the bitterly, harsh spring that year.

For them, a new king

The Huguenot refugees who crossed over to England – *the Isles* – fared much better. *For them* there was *a new king*. Instead of James II (who shared Louis XIV's Catholic faith and political ideals), William III had been elected in 1689 to replace the unpopular King James. [5] In keeping with the refugees arriving from France, William was also a Protestant who opposed Louis XIV's 'French aggrandizement'. Thereafter, "France became and long remained Britain's enemy."

A recent order fabricates for them

William III of Orange was a Dutch Protestant, married to his cousin Mary Stuart, daughter of James, Duke of York. From his seat across the Channel, William had frequently corresponded with members of the House of Commons opposed to James II's Catholicism. And when the Queen of England produced a male heir to the throne, it threatened to prolong the period of Catholic rule. A decision was therefore reached by parliament to depose James II, and replace him by inviting William to seize the vacant throne for himself.

> The Invitation to William was a letter sent by seven notable Englishmen, later named the Immortal Seven [...] the letter asked William to force the ruling king, his uncle and father-in-law James II of England, by military intervention to make William's Protestant wife Mary, James's eldest daughter, heir, on the grounds that newborn Prince of Wales was allegedly an impostor. [...] The Invitation briefly rehashed the grievances against King James, claimed that the King's son was supposititious (fraudulent) and that the English people generally believed him to be so. [6]

As a result of this fabrication, Britain's Catholic monarch, James II, who supported Louis XIV, was replaced by the Protestant King and Queen, William and Mary. This guaranteed the safety of those arriving from France: "a prodigious number of people proscribed, naked, fugitive [having] wandered, innocent of any crime, seeking asylum far from their native land." [7] Those arriving in Britain were therefore able to benefit from the fabricated order that gave them a new King.

Summary: *The definition of 'edict', which exists in both English and French, sets the scene for the fulfilment of this prophecy, simply by referring to the concise Oxford English Dictionary (4th edition); viz. "edict, an. Order proclaimed by authority; E- of Nantes, issued by Henry IV of France to grant toleration to Protestants, and revoked by Louis XIV." The prophecy is based upon this period of history. It foretells the exemption of Protestants by Louis XIV. It actually identifies him as having been born with two teeth in his mouth (not one, not three, but two). The famine that followed is also foretold; as, too, is the destination of the exiles. It was also a time when Britain was making plans to depose King James II and enthrone a new king, who had been invited to take the crown by a fabrication. That, too, has been predicted.*

8   *Temples sacrés prime façon Romaine,*
     Reieteront les goffes fondements,
     Prenant leurs loys premieres & humaines,
     Chassant, non tout, des saints les cultements.

goffe (OF) dull, heavy handed; prenant (OF) embracing, accepting.

> Consecrated churches, chiefly the Roman form:
> They will abandon the heavy-handed foundations
> Embracing their early and humane laws,
> Rejecting, not all, the veneration of the saints.

This has not yet been fulfilled by the Catholic Church, although it is becoming apparent in Protestant churches. It will be expected to please some people, but is less likely to bring joy to the traditionalists, who may deem it to be a backward step.

9   *Neuf ans le regne le maigre en paix tiendra,*
           Puis il cherra en soif si sanguinaire:
           Pour luy grand peuple sans foy & loy mourra,
           Tué par vn beaucoup plus de bonnaire.

10   *Auant long temps le tout sera range,*
           Nous esperons vn siècle bien senestre:
           L'estat des masques & des seulz bien changé
           Peu troueront qu'a son rang veuille estre.

estat (OF) the state or pomp of persons; veuille (OF) clasping tendrels – as of a vine; estre (OF ce qui est à.l'extérieur) that which is at the exterior

> Before a long time, everything will be ordered,
> We shall look forward to a period most sinister:
> The pomp and state of persons masked, and for the self, thoroughly changed,
> Little will they find that has its order external to 'clasping tendrils'.

An age of social engineering and government surveillance is predicted, not unlike that foreseen by George Orwell in his novel, 1984. In fact, much has already been put in place to achieve this end, with closed circuit television. Freedom of expression will also be curtailed and truth denied wherever it is considered to be politically incorrect.

Recently, we learned that our governments, working in concert, have created a world of wide surveillance, watching everything we do. Great Britain's George Orwell warned us of the dangers of this type of information. The types of collection in the book, microphones and video camera, TVs that watch us are nothing with what we have available today. We have sensors in our pockets that track us everywhere we go. Think about what this means for the privacy of the average person.
A child born today will grow up with no conception of privacy at all. They'll never know what it means to have a private moment to themselves, and unrecorded, unanalysed thought; and that's a problem, because privacy matters. Privacy is what allows us to determine who we are and who we want to be. The conversation occurring today will determine the amount of trust we can place in both the technology that surrounds us and the government that regulates it.
[Broadcast 25/12/2013]

11   *Le prochain fils de l'asnier paruiendra*
           Tant esleué iusques au regne de fors,
           Son aspre gloire vn chascun la craindra.
           Mais ses enfants du regne getés hors.

12   *Yeux clos, ouuerts d'antique fantasie,*
           L'habit des seulz seront mis à neant,
           Le grand monarque chastiera leur frenesie:
           Rauir des temples le tresor par deuant.

Fantasie (Gk - φαντασια) making visible, *also* (L) idea notion, fancy; habit (L habit/us) condition, *also* moral culture; seule (AF état séculier) secular state; devant (pp of devoir) being obliged to – alternatively, (OF par ci devant) heretofore, in former times.

> Closed eyes opened by an ancient notion,
> The moral culture of the secular states will be put to nought:
> The great monarch will chastise their raving,
> Forcibly taking away the wealth from churches through being obliged to.

13   *Le corps sans ame plus n'estre en sacrifice.*
           Iour de la mort mis en natiuité.
           L'esprit diuin fera l'ame felice,
           Voiant le verbe en son eternité.

The body without a soul never again being its sacrifice.
The day of death is set in the form of a birth.
The Holy Spirit will make the soul blissful,
Seeing the word in its eternity.

Evidence for the fulfilment of this prophecy may have already begun to emerge. Few reading this will be unaware of the NDE (near death experience) that countless people worldwide have experienced while being clinically dead. At present, mainstream scientists are avoiding the phenomenon by referring to its cause as fluctuations in a dying brain. This so-called 'explanation' is limited by its inability to explain a subject's acquisition of visual and audible knowledge, which s/he reports having observed, both locally and non-locally, during their 'brain' death.

Ironically, it the scientists that have become brain dead when this evidence is placed before them. Their state of denial concerning religion and the spiritual nature of mankind, and their fear of admitting anything that runs contrary to the groupthink beliefs of their colleagues, prevents them (at least openly) contemplating areas of a non-material reality.

The Seer's reference to 'the *word* in its eternity' is from Saint John, (1: i). "In the beginning was the Word, and the Word was with God, and the Word was God." In the Greek of John, *logos* indicated mind, reason, intellect. By this interpretation, it is understood that God created the universe by mind, reason and intellect, and this has nothing to do with imperceptible 'matter'.

14   A Tours, Iean, garde seront yeux penetrants
      Descouuriront de loing la grand sereyne,
      Elle & sa suitte au port seront entrants,
      Combat, poulsés, puissance souueraine.

15   Vn peu deuant monarque trucidé?
      Castor Pollux en nef, astre crinite.
      L'œrain publiq par terre & mer vuidé,
      Pise, Ast, Ferrare, Turin, terre interdicte.

16   Naples, Palerme, Secille, Syracuses.
      Nouueaux tyrans, fulgures feuz celestes:
      Force de Londres, Gand, Brucelles, & Suses,
      Grand hecatombe, triumphe, faire festes.

17   Le camp du temple de la vierge vestale,
      Non esloigné d'Ethne & monts Pyrenées:
      Le grand conduict est caché dans la male,
      North. getés fluues & vignes mastinées.

Ethne, fire (a Celtic name); north (A .Fr) nort.

18   Nouuelle & pluie subite, impetueuse
      Empeschera subit deux exercites.
      Pierre, ciel, feuz faire la mer pierreuse,
      La mort de sept terre & marin subites.

19   Nouueaux venus, lieu basti sans defense,
      Occuper place par lors inhabitable.
      Préz, maisons, champs, villes prendre a plaisance,
      Faim, peste, guerre, arpen long labourable.

venuë (OF) a place of arrival; arpent (arpen) an acre - but larger than the English acre; long (L long/us) long

      Unused, venues: place built without defence,   1955 ±
      Occupying a site uninhabitable then,
      Nearby, houses, fields, towns, taking to pleasure,
      Hunger, disease, war: the long arable acre.

Contrary to what is often thought about these prophecies, they are not entirely concerned with 'the evils that men do'. Periods of peace were foreseen and recorded. In the present instance, the years following World War II are of some prophetic interest, for this was a relatively tranquil period, while also being a time of immense change.

Unused, venues: place built without defence

In France, following soon after the end of World War II, new towns were built in previously unused locations. This also happened in England at the same time. But to the amazement of the 16th century Seer, they were being built *without a walled defence*. [1]

During the era in which he lived, when travelling to another city, it was often necessary to arrive before the gates closed for the night. Remnants of these old defensive walled cities have been retained, sometimes only by name, as historic monuments. For example, both London and Paris still preserve the names of their former gates.

Occupying a site uninhabitable then

With the commencement of the post-war period, the foundations for new towns, such as Sarcelles, near Le Bourget airport, were laid. Other land developments followed, with five new regions close to Paris, and still more outside the cities of Marseilles, Lyons, Rouen, and Lille, often *occupying a site* which *until then* had been *uninhabited*.

> L'Ile-d'Abeau, south-east of Lyon, set out along a valley slope in the form of a series of villages, is especially attractive. [...] (A)nother success is Evry, south of Paris, with its cheerful multi-coloured flats. [...] Cergy-Pontoise, twenty miles north-west of Paris, is taking shape on a splendidly spacious site overlooking a loop in the river Oise. [2]

Nearby, houses, fields, towns, taking to pleasure

The absence of any defensive walls is contrasted with the present-day, when people expect to *take pleasure* in their neighbourhood. New towns are planned with purpose-built leisure complexes that have been purposefully designed as an integral part of the community. Towns have their theatres, libraries, museums, cinemas, sports centres, and peripheral sports fields. These facilities have now become the norm for a modern *nouveau ville*.

> The largest multi-purpose centre in France has been completed there [at Evry], the Agora, with three theatres, a skating rink, dance halls, a library, youth centre and hypermarkets [...] (A)t Cergy-Pontoise [...] the new town has theatres and concerts. [...] On a visit [to] Massy [...] the big modern sports centre with its five swimming-pools was crowded. [...] Massy has fifty clubs and associations of a social or cultural kind — from chess to Sinology, from amateur choirs to the Cercle Celtique. [3]

Hunger

Having painted a word picture that would have been unrecognisable in the sixteenth century; the Seer moderates his forecast with words that would have found immediate rapport with the late medieval mind: to wit, *hunger, disease and war*. Despite massive progress in the way societies live, these three horsemen of the apocalypse have not been defeated. The effect of climate change continues to make frequent news, with fresh outbreaks of droughts, floods, and fires around the globe: thus posing a future threat to the world's food supply: African nations have been the first to be hit by *famine*. [4]

Disease

Disease, too, has yet to be conquered. The fear of a pandemic spreading across the world by mutating viruses, as well as cancer, influenza, malaria — familiar in ancient times — are now accompanied by AIDS and Ebola, which, at the time of writing, continue to increase their death toll. [5] Hence, there exists an ever-present need for the World Health Organization to maintain its vigilant outlook.

War

A different type of disease, one that affects politicians, is war. This too, has not gone away. Instead, it has become more deadly than anything seen in previous ages. It is also practised not only with verve, but is now aided by electronic and technological devices that can maim and kill at a distance, leaving those who instigated the attack detached from any physical or emotional consequences. In recent times, French troops have participated in wars occurring in the Balkan countries, in Iraq, Libya, and central Africa. [6]

The long arable acre

The final phrase in this oracle concerns France's agricultural system. This became especially relevant during the second half of the twentieth century. The modernisation programme introduced after the war was intended to update the antiquated agricultural practices of the past. The average French farm was therefore expanded from thirty-five acres, in 1955, to an acreage that totalled more than double that number.

Before WW II, most large estates indulged in the lethargy of *Paysantisme*. It was a state of mind in which nothing was permitted to upset 'the eternal order of the fields'. But the young farmers who replaced their parents looked to technology for ideas. By turning to economic management and marketing cooperatives, it provided them with new and exciting answers to crop yield, and harvest distribution. The small farms, with their cultivated strips of land that were once so evident before the war, became replaced by the *long arable acre* that occupies much of France's agricultural countryside today.

> In the decades after the war, French farming went through what even cautious scholars described as a 'revolution'. In no other aspect of French life was change so dramatic, or the conflict between old and new so sharp. After 1945, farm mechanization soon began to make economic nonsense of France's vast peasant community. [...] A new generation of modern-minded young farmers, with a totally different outlook from their parents [...] promoted a new creed, entirely novel in this individualistic milieu, a creed of technical advance, producer groups and marketing co-operatives. [7]

Summary: *This prophecy fits neatly into the period following the Second World War. It foresees the emergence of the new towns that sprang up in previously unoccupied places. And it describes the differences these had to what was familiar in the sixteenth century: at a time when this oracle was written. To confirm that this was the correct time for its fulfilment, the prophecy adds to what has been written by correctly foretelling the massive change in agricultural methods that would replace a system that had existed for centuries, both before and after this quatrain was first published.*

> 20   *Freres & seurs en diuers lieux captifs*
> *Se trouueront passer pres du monarque,*
> *Les contempler ses rameaux ententifz,*
> *Desplaisant voir menton, front, nez, les marques.*

se trouver (OF) to be present; pres (AF dans le temps ou l'espace) in the time or space; desplaisant (OF) offensive; monarque (Gk μοναρχης) sole ruler; ententif (OF) firmly resolved; marque (OF) mark, seizure of body, or goods

> Brothers and sisters, (**JEWISH**)captives in various places,   1942
> To be present, departing in the time of the sole ruler (**HITLER**):
> Contemplating them, his subdivisions firmly resolved,
> Offensive to see the chin, forehead, nose, the marks/seizure of goods.

Brothers and sisters

This prophecy enlarges upon the content of quatrain 6 above. Despite having been expelled from their land by the Romans in 70 AD, the Jewish nation has survived as a people for almost 1900 years. They achieved this by remaining a tight-fit, religious community, and by marrying among their own people. Thus, by referring to 'brothers and sisters', the prophecy is implying family members who are adults as well as children. Thus, when taken as a whole, its meaning suggests extended families living together as a community.

Captives in various places

After the Diaspora of 70 AD, Jewish people spread out across Europe, settling in communities, but remaining in contact. During these years of dispersion, they survived many attempts to forcibly convert them to Christianity, or deport them. But nothing could match what occurred at the outbreak of World War II, when German armed forces began occupying most countries in mainland Europe. Jews who were living in those places occupied by Germany were soon arrested and moved into ghettoes: whereafter, they were transported to concentration camps. Most notorious among these prison centres was Auschwitz in Poland, which became operative in the spring of 1942. It was where approximately 1.1 million Jews were subsequently exterminated.

To be present, departing in the time of the sole ruler

The 'sole ruler' is inferred to be the man responsible for making 'captives' of the 'brothers and sisters' 'in various places'. Adolf Hitler fits that title, following his occupation of much of Europe.

> In 1942, Germany dominated most of Europe. Greater Germany had been enlarged at the expense of its neighbours. Austria and Luxembourg were completely incorporated. Territories from Czechoslovakia, Poland, France, Belgium, and the Baltic states were seized by Greater Germany. German military forces occupied Norway, Denmark, Belgium, northern France, Serbia, parts of northern Greece, and vast tracts of territory in eastern Europe. Italy, Hungary, Romania, Bulgaria, Slovakia, Finland, Croatia, and Vichy France were all either allied to Germany or subject to heavy German influence. Between 1942 and 1944, German military forces extended the area under their occupation to southern France, central and northern Italy, Slovakia, and Hungary. [1]

> The experience of Jews in countries that were invaded and occupied by the Nazis was often quite similar to that of the Jews within Germany. However, what was different was the speed at which the Nazis enacted anti-Jewish measures. [2]

> Between 1941 and 1944, Nazi German authorities deported millions of Jews from Germany, from occupied territories, and from the countries of many of its Axis allies to ghettos and to killing centres, often called extermination camps, where they were murdered in specially developed gassing facilities. [3]

The Seer refers here to the Jewish people of the Diaspora that were 'present in this time'. Departing from the ghettoes, they would be transported to concentration camps for processing, as part of Hitler's 'Final Solution'—the elimination of the Jewish civilization.

Contemplating them: his subdivisions firmly resolved

The journey by rail often took several days, sometimes even more than a week. The passengers were crammed together in wagons without seats, toilets or food. A bucket of water was considered sufficient for drinking purposes and another bucket for human waste. Upon arrival, they were roughly pushed from the trucks and commanded to form lines for inspection. [4]

> When the trains stopped at Auschwitz II: Birkenau, the newly arrived were told to leave all their belongings on board and were then forced to disembark from the train and gather upon the railway platform, known as "the ramp".
> Families, who had disembarked together, were quickly and brutally split up as an SS officer, usually a Nazi doctor, ordered each individual into one of two lines. Most women, children, older men, and those that looked unfit or unhealthy were sent to the left, while most young men and others that looked strong enough to do hard labour were sent to the right. Unbeknownst to the people in the two lines, the left line meant immediate death at the gas chambers and the right meant that they would become a prisoner of the camp. [5]

Offensive: seeing the chin, forehead, nose

The subdivision of prisoners made upon arrival was subject to a further inspection by the prison doctors. This was achieved by propping up the chin (*soustenir le menton* AF). If a child or adult was deemed suitable for biological experimentation, then he or she was set aside. It must also be mentioned that, "Jews are commonly caricatured as having large noses." [6] In fact, "Hitler did try to assign physical characteristics to Jews, even creating charts of hair and eye colour and measuring noses and heads." [7] Much less fortunate were those chosen as subjects to be experimented upon.

> [Josef Mengele was] one of the more notorious characters to emerge from the Third Reich in World War II as an SS medical officer who supervised the selection of victims of the Holocaust, determining who was to be killed and who was to temporarily become a forced labourer, and for performing bizarre and murderous human experiments on prisoners. [8]

Marks / Seizure of goods

Once the selections had been concluded, a select group of Auschwitz prisoners (part of "Kanada") gathered up all the belongings that had been left on the train and sorted them into huge piles, which were then stored in warehouses. These items (including clothing, eye glasses, medicine, shoes, books, pictures, jewellery, and prayer shawls) would periodically be bundled and shipped to Germany. Those that had been sent to the right during the selection process [...] were then registered, had their arms tattooed with a number, and transferred to one of Auschwitz's camps for forced labour. [9]

When Auschwitz was finally liberated by the 322nd Rifle Division of the Russian army, it found 8.5 tons (7.7 tonnes) of human hair, 837,000 items of women's clothing and 370,000 men's suits, and stacks piled high with shoes. These had been taken from the personal belongings left on the train, and from those forced to disrobe before entering the gas chamber, as well as from the labourers that survived, after being shorn and forced to wear striped clothing and ill-fitting wooden clogs.

Summary: *This oracle returns to the horror of Auschwitz (see No. 6 above). It foretells of families in communities that will become captives, and then taken from various places. It also identifies Hitler as the 'Sole Ruler' at that time: thus describing his occupation of most of Europe. The oracle continues with the captives' arrival at Auschwitz, where they will be inspected and divided into two main groups. As part of the inspection process, their chin, nose and forehead are examined. Finally, they are given a number tattooed onto their arm. The belongings they brought with them are also seized. The similarity this prophecy has with the Jews who were sent to Auschwitz, exactly foreshadows what happened under Hitler's Nazi regime.*

21   *L'embassadeur enuoyé par biremes*
       A mi chemin d'incogneuz repoulses:
       De sel renfort viendront quatre triremes,
       Cordes & chaines en Negrepont troussés.

22   *Le camp Asop d'Eurotte partira,*
       S'adioignant proche de l'isle submergée
       D'Arton classe phalange pliera,
       Nombril du monde plus grand voix subrogée.

23   *Palais, oyseaux, par oyseau dechasée,*
       Bien tost après le prince preuenu,
       Combien qu'hors fleuue enemis repoulsé
       Dehors saisi trait d'oyseau soustenu.

24   *Bestes farouches de faim fluues tranner:*
       Plus part du camp encontre Hister sera,
       En caige de fer le grand fera treisner,
       Quand Rin enfant de Germain obseruera.

faim (OF) an exceeding desire; tranner (L trano) to pass through, to swim over; camp (AF pays plat) flat country; Hister (paragram, 'I' for 's' *with transposition of* 'It'), Hitler; caige (OF *epenthesis*: cage – but with *epenthesis* c[ar]aige *and with transposition of* 'ai'); cariage (OF) carriage; treisner (AF trainer - retard) to delay; enfant (AF enfant de pié – fantassin) infantryman; Germain (OF) German. Cross-references: Hister, C.IV: 68; C.V: 29; also, camp, C.V: 85.

Ferocious beasts with an exceeding desire to pass through rivers,   1940
Greater part of the flat country will be against Hister (**HITLER**),
In an iron carriage, the great man (**PÉTAIN**) will make to delay:
While the Rhine infantryman will watch the German.

This quatrain is another that refers to World War II. The conquest of mainland Europe was achieved against defending armies by Blitzkrieg tactics. In particular, two tanks played a central role. The *Tiger,* for which designs began in 1937, and the *Panther* which went into production after the *Tiger* had shown the need for a lighter tank.

Ferocious beasts with an exceeding desire to pass through rivers

Hitler's use of Blitzkrieg tactics during the Second World War involved a ground assault force headed by armoured tanks. These aptly came to be named: *Tigers* and *Panthers* (hence the ferocious beasts). The development of the Tiger proved particularly useful when crossing a large expanse of land. This was because they were capable of *crossing rivers,* even to the extent of remaining submerged for up to two and a half hours.

> The Tiger tank was too heavy for small bridges, so it was designed to ford four-meter deep water. This required unusual mechanisms for ventilation and cooling when underwater. At least 30 minutes of set-up time was required, with the turret and gun being locked in the forward position, and a large snorkel tube raised at the rear. [1]

But *The Panther* was considered to be Germany's best tank for speed, weight and firepower. [2] It had also been commissioned for cross country warfare. Hence, "The engine compartment space was designed to be watertight so that the Panther could be submerged and cross waterways." [3]

Greater part of the flat country will be against Hister (Hitler)

The flat country refers to the lowlands of Belgium and Holland, and was conquered, with little opposition in May 1940. But, as the oracle has correctly foreseen: *the greater part* of the Dutch and Belgian people *will be against Hitler.* "When the Germans invaded the Low Countries in 1940, they did not find large groups of people who supported their aims [...] the vast majority [...] were utterly hostile to Germany's plan to absorb them into the Pan-German Reich." [4]

The transliteration occurring to the word Hister, the ancient name for the Danube, allows 'st' to become 'ts' which, when followed by a paragram with 's' exchanged for 'l', reforms Hister into Hitler. This result then becomes one of identification by association, since the education and formative years of Hitler occurred in the Austrian town of Linz on the banks of the Hister.

In an iron carriage

By June 1940, France had fallen to its German invader, and Hitler was able to travel to Rethondes in the forest of Compiegne, and seat himself inside "the railroad car in which Marshal Foch had forced the Germans to surrender" in 1918, after their defeat in the First World War. *Inside the* same *iron carriage* the roles were now reversed, and it was Hitler who, as Chancellor of Germany, dictated the terms of surrender to the French. [5]

The great man will make to delay

At the head of the French delegation was General Charles Huntziger, acting on behalf of France's new Prime Minister, Philippe Pétain the former hero of Verdun: a heroic background that identified him as *the great man* of France. In obedience with orders, Huntziger *wanted to delay* proceedings by negotiating a more favourable settlement. For one whole day, and well into the next, the French protested that the German terms were too 'merciless', and far harsher than those imposed by France in 1918. But the German deputation eventually grew tired of these delaying tactics and threatened to resume hostilities unless a settlement was reached. At this, the French delegation capitulated, and the terms of surrender were quickly agreed. [6]

While the Rhine infantryman will watch the German

As a means of defence against a possible attack from neighbouring Germany, the French government had constructed a line of fortresses along its frontier, where the river Rhine divides the two countries. The ancient French language has subtly concealed the predicted failure of these forts, known collectively as the Maginot Line. For, when the attack came, the *infantrymen* stationed along *the Rhine* could do no more than keep *watch on the German* side of the river, in case a secondary attack was launched; the main thrust of the invasion force having circumvented the Maginot Line by pouring soldiers and armaments into the Belgian lowlands. [7]

Summary: *This oracle foretells the beginning of Germany's invasion of France, beginning with its blitzkrieg advance through the lowlands of Belgium and Holland. The use of tanks that were designed to cross rivers, and the name of Hitler, albeit cryptically hidden, has also been given in relation to the predicted opposition from the people of Belgium and the Netherlands. The negotiations for peace, between France and Germany, which took place in a railway carriage has likewise been presaged, including the attempt to delay proceedings. Finally, the failure of the Maginot Line is implied by the content of the last line.*

25   *La garde estrange trahira forteresse:*
Espoir & vmbre de plus hault mariage:
Garde deceue, fort prince dans la presse
Loyre, Son. Rosne, Gar. à mort oultrage.

26   *Pour la faueur que la cité fera,*
Au grand qui tost perdra camp de bataille:
Puis le rang Po, & Thesin versera,
De sang, feuz, morts, noyes de coup de taille.

27   *Le diuin verbe sera du ciel frapé,*
Qui ne pourra proceder plus auant.
Du reserant le secret estoupé,
Qu'on marchera par dessus & deuant.

verbe, mot, parole; reserrant, restrictive, stopping, closing.

28   *Le penultime du surnom du prophete,*
Prendre Diane pour son iour & repos:
Loing vaguera par frenetique teste,
Et deliurant vn grand peuple d'impos.

jour (Dictionnaire de français – Littré, Fig. Facilité, moyen pour venir à bout de quelque affaire) way of succeeding in some affair; *also:* "an important day, particularly one upon which some violent action of significance occurred." (Hibbert). repos (Littré – L'état des morts dans le tombeau) the state of deaths in a grave; impos (L impos\tura) deceit

The one before last with the additional name of the prophet (**MOHAMMED**),   1997
Taking **DIANA** for his **DAY**, and deaths:
A long time he (**FAYED**) will move from place to place, through a frenetic head,
And to deliver a great people from deceit.

The one before last with the additional name of the prophet

The name of the Prophet is recognized worldwide to be that of Muhammad, the Prophet of Islam. In this oracle, the Seer is referring to *the last but one,* within a family bearing *the additional name of the Prophet* Mohamed (Muhammad, Mohamed, Mohammed are variant spellings of the same name). The definition of a surname is that of an additional name given to a person, in common with other members of the family. Consequently, in this prophecy, there must be two men possessing the name of the Prophet: the penultimate and the ultimate; that is father and son. Two men meet this requirement, given that they also have a connexion with Diana, they are Emad El-Din Mohamed Abdel Moneim Fayed and his father Mohamed Al-Fayed. The latter being an extremely wealthy and widely known businessman whose son would likely have married the mother of the future King of England, and which introduces the second line of the oracle.

Taking Diana for his day, and deaths

HRH Diana Princess of Wales was, at the time of her title, married to Prince Charles, heir to the throne of England. Unhappily, violation of God's seventh commandment by both parties resulted in an acrimonious divorce. By July 1997, Diana had become romantically involved with Emad El-Din Mohamed, and one month later, in August, evidence was produced by a jeweller that an engagement ring had been purchased, implying that the couple were soon to announce their intention to marry. A photograph of Diana also showed visible signs of her pregnancy.

Despite their hopes, it ended in tragedy. On the morning of 1 September 1997, the world awoke to the news that Diana Princess of Wales had met her death in a car accident. It occurred during the night before in the Alma tunnel, an underpass in Paris. Her partner, Emad El-Din Mohamed, had also been killed, together with their chauffeur.

A long time he will move from place to place, through a frenetic head

With Mohamed, the son, having died, the oracle moves to Mohamed al Fayed, the father. He was not convinced the car crash was an accident. He "argued that Diana and Dodi (his son) were killed in an Establishment plot to prevent them marrying." He also "pledged to fight 'tooth and nail' to prevent a cover-up."[1] The conformist section of the British press was quick to pour scorn on what seemed to them *frenetic* allegations. For example, these are some of al Fayed's accusations.

"The couple were executed by British intelligence agents." – "MI6 engineered the bogus car crash." – "the Duke of Edinburgh, was at the heart of the conspiracy." – "The driver of the car was not drunk; his blood sample had been contaminated or switched." – "Then he talked darkly about secret intelligence material gathered by the CIA and, three years after the deaths, filed a law suit in Washington demanding that the US government turn over its classified documentation."[2]

Nevertheless, almost ten years passed before members of an inquest jury were allowed to look at selected evidence leading to the deaths of Princess Diana and Dodi Fayed. During that time, the number of coroners appointed – four in total – changed suspiciously often. To the outside observer, it could have appeared that the coroners appointed had reservations about handling such a high-powered case. During this *long* intervening *period*, Mohammed al Fayed made his own investigations, which took him *from place to place* across the UK, France and the USA.

And to deliver a great people from deceit

For the Seer, as before, 'a great people' refers to the people of his native France. And it was in May 2011 that the first steps towards fulfilling the final line of this prophecy began. The event was the Cannes Film Festival in which a feature length documentary film, *Unlawful Killing* was premiered. The film was made by Keith Allen, who received financial backing from Mr al Fayed.

> Unlawful Killing is not about a conspiracy before the crash, but a provable conspiracy after the crash. A conspiracy [...] collectively by the British establishment – judges, lawyers, politicians, police chiefs, secret services, even newspaper editors – all of whom have been appointed to their positions because they are "a safe pair of hands" [...] these people instinctively know what is expected of them when the state's interests are under threat and they act accordingly, quietly suppressing uncomfortable evidence or undermining the credibility of witnesses whose evidence contradicts the official narrative.[3]

The film's aim was to expose the hidden truths that had been kept from the six-month inquest that took place a decade after the crash. Controversially, a picture of Diana in the wreckage of the car is shown. She can be seen conscious and alert – "It is not a picture of a dying woman." But the inquest jury were not permitted to see it. The film was also banned in the UK.

In 2013 Mohammed al Fayed made a further attempt to reveal the truth of what happened when a former member of the SAS claimed, "Diana was murdered in an Establishment plot for fear she would undermine the monarchy by marrying Dodi Fayed."[4] The former SAS member then hurriedly left the country for south-east Asia, before being returned for questioning by the authorities.

In 2014, author John Morgan published *How They Murdered Princess Diana: The Shocking Truth*. The book was also used as the basis for "an explosive West End play," in which a reporter uncovers the truth behind the Princess's murder.

Summary: *The death of Princess Diana continues to be a controversial subject. The prophecy relates the facts, with each prediction becoming verified by the turn of events. Would the existence of Moslem step-brothers and/or sisters be sufficient embarrassment to England's future monarchy for this possibility to be eliminated? Unbelievable or not, the entire set of facts were already evident to the source of this prediction almost four and a half centuries before it became world news.*

29   *L'oriental sortira de son siege,*
       Passer les monts Appenins, voir la Gaule:
       Transpercera du ciel les eaux & neige:
       Et vn chascun frapera de sa gaule.

30   *Vn qui les dieux d'Annibal infernaulx,*
       Fera renaistra, effrayeur des humains:
       Oncq' plus d'horreurs, ne plus pire iournaux
       Qu'auint viendra par Babel aux Romains.

31   *En Campanie Cassilin sera tant*
       Qu'on ne verra que d'eaux les champs couuerts
       Deuant après la pluye de long temps
       Hors mis les arbres rien l'on verra de vert.

32   *Laict, sang, grenoilles escoudre en Dalmatie,*
        Conflit donné, peste pres de Balenne:
        Cry sera grand par toute Esclauonie
        Lors naistra monstre pres & dedans Rauenne.

33   *Par le torrent qui descent de Verone*
        Par lors qu'au Po guindera son entrée,
        Vn grand naufraige, & non moins en Garonne
        Quant ceux de Gennes marcheront leur contrée.

descent (L descendo) come down; quant (OF) as for; marcher (OF) proceed; Cross-references: Po (Na *po* leon,) C.II: 94; C.III: 75; C.IV: 70; C.VI: 79; C.VIII: 1.

In the torrent that descends from Verona,   1796
For at the time that he (**NAPOLEON**) will force his entrance to the Po,
A great shipwreck and not less in Garonne:
As for those of Genoa, they will proceed to their country.

In the torrent that descends from Verona

During Napoleon's First Italian Campaign, the city of Verona (situated in a loop of the river Adige) became Bonaparte's headquarters. From there, "He intended to rush all available troops from Verona to seize Villa Nova, using the Adige to cover his advance, in order to seize the field park and convoys of the Austrian army." [1] On 14 November 1796, leading 18,000 men in his planned 'rush', he *descended from Verona*. His destination was Ronco, 18 miles along the Adige, where a pontoon bridge was built to take his troops across the river on their way to Mantua.

With detachments led by Augereau and Masséna pouring across the river to secure the marshlands on the north bank, Napoleon was able to mount an assault against Joseph d'Alvintzi at Arcola. The Austrian general had earlier arrived in the town, intent upon retaking *Verona* as a means of relieving Mantua, which had been besieged by the French since July. But d'Alvintzi's subsequent defeat at Arcola put an end to this plan, and it ultimately led to General Würmser lifting the siege and surrendering Mantua to Bonaparte.

For at the time that he will force his entrance to the Po

It was at the time when the French army *descended from Verona*, by following the course of the Adige to Ronco that Napoleon defeated the Austrians at Arcola. This victory enabled his army to proceed to Mantua, while leaving General Joubert to defeat the Austrians in a battle fought at Rivoli on 14 January 1797. "Mantua is surrounded on three sides by artificial lakes, created during the 12th century, as the city's defence system. These lakes receive the water of River Mincio, a tributary of the Po which descends from Lake Garda.". [2] [N.B. The Mincio joins the Po six miles downstream.]

Mantua had been under siege for eight months. But with the Austrian defeat at Arcola and then at Rivoli, Napoleon was at last able *to force an entrance* to Mantua by defeating General Provera at La Favorita. "The destruction of d'Alvintzi and Provera meant the fall of Würmser's Mantua. Without hope of relief, the old warrior held out until the end of the month, but on February 2, 1797, the great fortress finally passed into French hands." [3] With the fall of Mantua, the Austrian army was driven back across the Alps, and northern Italy was left in the hands of the French.

Although Napoleon is not directly identified as the subject of this piece of history, in other quatrains he is given the nickname 'Po'. The river Po is the longest river in Italy, and it features several times in Napoleon's north Italian campaigns. It will also be recalled from N° 24 above that Hitler was identified by the river Danube's former name, Hister. That these two tyrants and conquerors of most of Europe would each be given a nickname from the two great rivers with which they were associated, suggests intent upon the part of the author.

A great shipwreck

The oracle now moves forward by another year to 1 August 1798, when Horatio Nelson led his British squadron into Aboukir Bay, where Napoleon's fleet lay at anchor. In what became known as the *Battle of the Nile*, Nelson totally destroyed the French fleet.

On 3 August the last two remaining French ships stranded in the bay were defeated, one surrendering and the other deliberately set on fire by its crew. The almost total destruction of the French fleet reversed the strategic situation in the Mediterranean, giving the Royal Navy control of the sea which it retained until the end of the Napoleonic Wars in 1815. [4]

And not less in Garonne

The oracle has referred to the French defeat at Aboukir Bay as *a great shipwreck*, but the river *Garonne* is not navigable. The oracle is therefore referring, instead, to the region of *Garonne* where, in the summer of 1799, a royalist uprising occurred. From June through to August, the rebels achieved some notable successes. But from the 5th to the 20th of August, a counter-revolutionary force led by General Aubugeois and aided by General Commes successfully crushed the uprising with a series of ruthless operations directed against the royalist forces. The rebellion finally came to an end at Montréjeau in Haute-*Garonne*. [5]

As for those of Genoa, they will proceed to their country

Again, the oracle moves forward one more year to April 1800. The French had captured the city of *Genoa* in 1796, the same year that *Verona* was taken. But the Austrians were determined to retake the city as a preliminary to invading France. In the spring of 1800, General Peter Ott launched a surprise attack against Masséna, the victor of Arcola, causing the French to take cover inside *Genoa*. Ott then threw a cordon of 24,000 men around the city to begin a siege, not unlike that which had occurred at Mantua.

The expression, *those of Genoa* therefore refers to the French troops that occupied Genoa and who were now besieged by an Austrian force numbering 24,000. At the same time, Napoleon, like another Hannibal, had crossed the Alps and was marching towards Milan, believing that Masséna would hold Genoa until he arrived. [6] He was mistaken. On 4 June General Masséna was impelled by starvation, and the Royal Navy's blockade of the port, to surrender the city, and he and his men were allowed to vacate it with honour.

On 4 June, with one day's rations remaining, Masséna's negotiator finally agreed to evacuate the French army from Genoa. However, "if the word capitulation was mentioned or written," Masséna threatened to end all negotiations. Two days later, a few of the French left the city by sea, but the bulk of Masséna's starving and exhausted troops marched out of the city with all their equipment and followed the road along the coast toward France, ending one of the most remarkable sieges in modern military history. [7]

Summary: *This quatrain is of interest, because it contains five different predictions that took place in five consecutive years. It commences in 1796 with the French army descending from their headquarters in Verona to defeat the Austrian army at the battle of Arcola. This victory enabled Napoleon, in 1797, to force his entry into Mantua, which had been placed under siege since June in the previous year. Mantua is situated on a tributary to the great River Po. The Po is specially mentioned in the prophecy because it identifies Napoleon where the same identification is repeated on five further occasions. Next, in 1798, Nelson totally destroyed Napoleon's fleet anchored in the bay at Aboukir, which is predicted as a 'great shipwreck'. This is followed in 1799 by the royalist uprising in the Garonne, which was brutally put down. And in 1800, French troops besieged in Genoa were starved into submission, and allowed to march out with honour and return to France to be repatriated.*

34   *L'ire insensée du combat furieux,*
           Fera à table par freres le fer luire,
           Les despartir mort, blessé, curieux:
           Le fier duelle viendra en France nuire.

35   *Dans deux logis de nuit le feu prendra,*
           Plusieurs dedans estousés & rostis.
           Pres de deux fleuues pour seur il auiendra,
           Sol, l'Arq, & Caper tous seront amortis.

36   *Du grand Prophete les letres seront prinses*
      Entre les mains du tyrant deuiendront:
      Frauder son roy, seront ses entreprinses,
      Mais ses rapines bien tost le troubleront.

37   *De ce grand nombre que l'on enuoyera*
      Pour secourir dans le fort assiegés,
      Peste & famine tous les deuorera
      Hors mis septante qui seront profligés.

38   *Des condemnés sera fait vn grand nombre,*
      Quand les monarques seront conciliés:
      Mais à l'vn d'eux viendra si malencombre
      Que guerres ensemble ne seront raliés.

39   *Vn an deuant le conflit Italique,*
      Germain, Gaulois, Hespagnols pour le fort:
      Cherra l'escolle maison de republique,
      Ou, hors mis peu, seront suffoqués morts.

40   *Vn peu apres non point longue interualle.*
      Par mer & terre sera fait grand tumulte,
      Beaucoup plus grande sera pugne nauale,
      Feus, animaux, qui plus feront d'insulte.

41   *La grand' estoile par sept iours bruslera,*
      Nuée fera deux soleils apparoir:
      Le gros mastin toute nuit hurlera,
      Quand grand pontife changera de terroir.

42   *Coq, chiens, & chats, de sang seront repeus,*
      Et de la plaie du tyrant trouué mort,
      Au lict d'vn autre iambes & bras rompus,
      Qui n'avoit peur mourir de cruel mort.

repeus (OF) fed; lict (OF) bed, couch, pallet; Qui (AF – Au sens de "si l'on")

Cock, dogs and cats will be fed with blood,   1794
And with the wound of the tyrant (**ROBESPIERRE**), death is judged:
On the bed of one other, legs & arms broken (**COUTHON**):
However much the one had not fear (**SAINT-JUST**), dying by a cruel death.

The opening line presents a recognizable picture of France during the Terror. This was a time when the revolution finally peaked with an orgy of decapitations resulting from Robespierre's 'Law of Suspects'. This piece of legislation authorized the arrest of anyone suspected of counter-revolutionary involvement. The death sentence was usually applied as a matter of course.

Cock, dogs and cats will be fed with blood
The Latin word 'gallus' means both 'Gaul' and '*cock*': hence, "the 'Red Cock' – that symbol of pillage and arson of the French Revolution."[1] This begins a prophecy that became fulfilled when *the cock was fed* by the *blood* shed during the Great Terror. So many decapitations were occurring in Paris that *dogs and cats* in the neighbourhood of the guillotine *were lapping up the life-blood* of its victims, pumped free by the systematic fall of the Paris blade.[2]

And with the wound of the tyrant
This extensive slaughter finally came to an end in July 1794 when Robespierre was himself taken into custody by deputies who feared they might be next in line for the guillotine. The circumstances of his arrest are given in a separate oracle, including a reference to *the wound of the tyrant*. Robespierre incurred this wound when he received a bullet through the cheek. The shot was claimed to have been fired by Constable Méda who was first on the scene.[3] However, an alternative version says that the wound was actually caused by Robespierre, himself, in a bungled suicide attempt.

Death is judged

After a painful night spent suffering his injury, during which several teeth were removed, Robespierre was brought before the court next morning. Although unable to speak, he was tried upon recognition, and in accordance with the Law of Suspects, his death was judged to be the appropriate sentence. It was carried out that evening, but only after the guillotine was hastily re-erected at the *Place de la Révolution*: to be especially set up for his execution. [4]

Robespierre did not die alone. His two closest companions, Couthon and Saint-Just – men who shared his vision and power – joined him on the scaffold. They are both described in this oracle.

On the bed of one other, legs and arms broken

Georges Couthon, although politically active, was a paraplegic. At some stage in his life he had suffered paralysis in both legs – probably as a result of meningitis – and could only move about *on a* mobile *bed;* possibly a horizontal tricycle type of wheelchair that supported his legs but with a raised back.

At the time of Robespierre's arrest, Couthon was with the tyrant inside the Hôtel de Ville. But, alarmed at seeing his own arrest was imminent, he attempted to escape by manoeuvring his bed down a flight of stairs. He failed, with terrible consequences. His wheelchair hurtled out of control, and he was thrown from it, ending up helplessly at the foot of the stairs: "in appalling pain, his bent limbs smashed from the fall." [5] His execution alongside Robespierre was a protracted affair, because of his bent and broken limbs. It took the executioner a quarter of an hour, amidst Couthon's screams of agony, before his wrecked body could be fitted beneath the blade.

However much the one had not fear, dying by a cruel death

The third member of this trio was Louis Antoine Léon de Saint-Just: handsome, young, and with a reputation for icy coolness in every situation. He was arrested, along with Robespierre and Couthon, and next day was executed *having* acknowledged not the least sign of *fear*, even though *dying by a cruel death*. "Saint-Just went to his death every bit the Roman stoic, in which role he had evidently cast himself." [6]

Summary: *The Great Terror was a pitiless episode in French history, during which so much blood was spilt that residents nearby asked for the guillotine to be erected somewhere else. This was carried out, but when Robespierre, the tyrant that had caused the slaughter, was himself sentenced to death, the guillotine was brought back to where so many of his victims had been executed. The wound Robespierre suffered on the night before his arrest, together with his judgement next morning, and the accident that befell Couthon in his attempt to escape his fate are included together in this oracle; as, too, is the demeanour of Saint-Just who met his death exactly as predicted.*

> 43   *Durant l'estoyle cheuelue apparente,*
> *Les trois grans princes seront faits ennemis,*
> *Frappes du ciel, paix terre tremulente;*
> *Po, Tymbre vndants, serpant sus le bord mis.*

Durant (OF) during that age; gran (AF triste) dejected, sorrowful; tremulente (L tremulus); also (Late Latin – tremulare) trembling; undant (Latin, present indicative of undare) they surge; mis (OF) brought.

> During that age, the long-haired star (**HALLEY'S COMET**) visible,   1910
> The three dejected princes (**GEORGE, NICHOLAS , WILHELM**) will be made enemies:
> Struck from the sky, quiet, the ground trembling.
> Po, Tiber surge: a serpent placed on the shoreline.

During that age, the long-haired star visible

With these opening words, a period of time is implied for the remaining lines of this prophecy to transform into history. A reference to Halley's Comet would seem to provide the most obvious link, and the Seer would have seen the comet himself in August 1531, although it was not then known by that name, since Edmond Halley was not born until 1656. Its identity, orbit and date of return were therefore unknown at the time.

In 1910 the comet returned with spectacular effect. "The comet was at its closest, therefore its brightest, between May 14 and 22." The Earth also passed through the Comet's tail causing panic among some people, alarmed by press reports portending doom.

The three dejected princes will be made enemies

That same year 1910, takes us to the next part of the prophecy. On 6 May, King Edward VII died from bronchitis after catching a chill, and was succeeded to the throne by his son George V. There were now *three princes* ruling over more than half the world. They were King George V, ruler of the British Empire, Kaiser Wilhelm II, King of Prussia and ruler of the German Empire, and Nicholas II, King of Poland and Emperor of Russia. Nicholas was also a second cousin to George V and Wilhelm II: these latter two being the grandsons of Queen Victoria and Prince Albert.

In the summer of 1914, the First World War began, having been triggered by the assassination in Sarajevo of Archduke Franz Ferdinand on 28 June. After a month of political wrangling between the great powers, the matter came to a head when "Germany refused to negotiate [further], declaring war against Russia on 1 August 1914." [1] Wilhelm II and Nicholas II were therefore, officially, *made enemies* with each other.

> Germany's war plan, the Schieffen Plan, relied on a quick, massive invasion of France to eliminate the threat on the West, before turning east against Russia. [...] Britain declared war on Germany on 4 August 1914, following an 'unsatisfactory reply' to the British ultimatum that Belgium must be kept neutral. [2]

Because of this response, George V and Wilhelm II had also been *made enemies* with each other. It is therefore noteworthy that the oracle does not say the three princes *will be* enemies. Instead, the Seer predicates their opposition by referring to their dejection at having been made enemies. And that is precisely what occurred when their respective governments took up arms on different sides, and patriotism took precedence over family connexions.

Struck from the sky, quiet, the ground trembling

The prophecy then directs attention to a unique event occurring in the First World War—the emergence of an airship as part of the hostilities.

> The first zeppelin bombardments occurred in Antwerp in September 1914, as Belgian troops were there to perform attacks on the German troops marching through Belgium. [...] The first Zeppelin raid on England took place in January 1915. From then until the end of World War I the German Navy and Army Air Services mounted over 50 bombing raids on the United Kingdom. These were generally referred to as 'Zeppelin raids', although both Zeppelin and Schütte-Lanz airships were used. [3]

The airship was also quiet, as foretold in the prophecy. It made its way silently across the sky, before releasing its bomb load onto the ground below: hence, *the ground trembling*. During the First World War, "More than 5,000 bombs were dropped on towns across Britain, causing £1.5 million in damage." [4]

Po, Tiber surge

The oracle next moves on to predict for the two most important rivers in Italy, the Po and the Tiber. In an "Analysis of extraordinary flood events in the river Po," conducted in February 2011, it was observed that, "In the last decades, while the total amount of water flowing from the Po tributaries is decreased, the values of discharges during flood events are increased compared to the past." The report then lists "Some of the most important maximal discharges of the last 100 years (ARPA, 2009)." Heading the list is the flood that occurred in, "1917, June: 8,900 m^3/sec." [5]

There was also a major flood of the river Tiber during World War I. "[T]he floods of 1900, 1915 and 1937 represent floods of longer duration at flood levels but with lower peaks [...] the flood of 1915 maintained the same level for a duration of 61 hours." [6]

By including these separate floods in the oracle, the Seer has reaffirmed the close timing of the references he has made to the other predictions: the use of an airship in World War I, the implied relationship between three Princes, and the appearance of Halley's Comet.

A serpent placed on the shoreline

The word 'serpent', 'serpens' or 'serp.' appear six times in these oracles: of which, three – 'serpent' in Chapter Four N°. 93 and 'serpens' in Chapter One N°. 10 – have since become part of a fulfilled prophecy. Catherine de Medici was so-called in 1/10 because her youngest son referred to her as *Madame la Serpente*. In Christian art the serpent is trampled underfoot by the saints. The part she played in forcing her other son, Charles IX, to murder his friend, Admiral Coligny, which caused the St Bartholomew's Day Massacre, in which many thousands of men, women and children were slaughtered in Paris and elsewhere would surely justify her nickname.

The Duke of Buckingham was also referred to as a serpent by the Seer. He fulfilled his prophetic designate by entering the French Queen's bedroom at night to engage her in a romantic liaison. Whence, the temptation of Eve in Genesis, Chapter 3 provides the background for his aptronym. In the present case, it is the serpent's refusal to heed the voice of one who would control it, which it achieves by stopping up its ears (Psalm 58, iv & v). The analogy refers to Sir Frederick William Stopford who, on 6 August 1915, was placed in command during World War I for the landing at Suvia Bay, which was part of the battle of Gallipoli.

> At Suvia Bay 20,000 men were put ashore almost without loss; only a thousand Turks without machine guns, barred their way. Here Stopford was in command. He did not go ashore; instead he congratulated the men on their successful landing, and settled down to his afternoon nap. On shore the men were told to relax; they went off to bathe, with no Turks between them and victory.

General Sir Ian Standish Hamilton, who had agreed the appointment of General Stopford, came upon the scene as he cruised along the coast and discovered Stopford asleep in his ship.

> Hamilton urged immediate advance. Stopford said things must wait until next day. Hamilton withdrew. On the following day the British troops ashore dug defences. By then the Turks were too strong for them. The attack at Gallipoli had failed – this time for good. Stopford was recalled. [7]

Summary: *This prophecy is remarkable for the number of incidents it predicts: all within the space of seven years and mostly in chronological order. Halley's Comet precedes the dejection of the three related princes that reigned over much of the world, and then discovered that despite their family ties, the First World War had divided them. The airships that were used to bomb cities, which made their first appearance in the same war; and the flooding of the two great Italian rivers, the Po and the Tiber. Finally, the Battle of Gallipoli and the lost opportunity of victory, squandered by General Stopford on the shoreline at Suvia Bay.*

44   *L'aigle pousée en tour des pauillons*
          Par autres oyseaux d'entour sera chassée,
          Quand bruit des cymbres, tubes & sonnaillons
          Rendront le sens de la dame insensée.

45   *Trop le ciel pleure l'Androgyn procrée,*
          Pres de ce ciel sang humain respandu,
          Par mort trop tarde grand peuple recrée
          Tard & tost vient le secours attendu.

46   *Apres grand trouble humain, plus grand s'aprest,*
          Le grand mouteur les siecles renouuele.
          Pluie, sang, laict, famine, fer, & peste
          Au ciel veu, feu courant longue estincele.

47   *L'ennemi grand viel dueil meurt de poison:*
          Les souuerains par infinis subiuguez.
          Pierres plouuoir, cachés sous la toison:
          Par mort articles en vain sont allegues.

48   *La grand copie que passera les monts.*
          Saturn en l'Arq tournant du poisson Mars:
          Venins cachés sous testes de saulmons:
          Leurs chief pendu à fil de polemars.

49 *Les conseilliers du premier monopole,*
Les conquerants seduits pour la Melite:
Rodes, Bisance pour leurs exposant pole:
Terre faudra les poursuiuants de suite.

50 *Quand ceux d'Ainault, de Gand & de Brucelles,*
Verront à Langres le siege deuant mis
Derrier leurs flancz seront guerres crueles,
La plaie antique sera pis qu' ennemis.

51 *Le sang du iuste à Londres fera faute*
Bruslés par fouldres de vint trois les six.
La dame antique cherra de place haute:
De mesme secte plusieurs seront occis.

Bruslés (OF) consumed with fire; vint (OF vingt) twenty; les six (the sixes – 1666); cherra (future tense of choir); occis (L occi/do) kill; plusieurs (OF) many, a great number. Cross-references: sang du iuste and La dame, C.II: 53; du iuste, C.IX: 11.

The blood of the just one (**CHARLES II**) will make a mistake in London,   1665
Consumed with fire by the calamities of **TWENTY-THREE '666**.
The antique dame will fall from her high place:
Of the same sect a great number will be killed.

The blood of the Just One

The blood of the Just One literally means the natural child of the Just One. Together with two other quatrains, N°. 53 below and Century Nine N°. 11, the 'Just One' is identified as Charles I, the lawful King of England. It was his execution in 1649, when Britain came under the rule of Oliver Cromwell that Charles acquired his prophetic aptronym 'the Just One'; whence his son, Charles II, becomes *the blood of the Just One.*

Will make a mistake in London

It was in March 1665 that Charles II *made a* costly *mistake*. He embarked upon a needless and fruitless war with Holland. It not only cost the treasury many millions of pounds to pursue, thereby draining the country's finances, but it also united France, Spain and Denmark in their hostility towards England. Worse still, Charles was eventually defeated. This cost him the only colony held by England on the mainland of South America. Apart from which, The King was also forced to relinquish Nova Scotia, as well as several strategic forts in Africa. He did, however, manage to retain New Amsterdam, which he renamed New York. At home, he was required to meet the compensation claims of English merchants, and to agree concessions for Dutch carriers arriving at English ports. [1] Taken as a whole the war had proved to be a disastrous mistake.

When Charles II declared war on the Netherlands in March 1665, he was still resident *in London*. Prophetically, this is important, because two months later, the capital was hit by the worst outbreak of Plague in its history: whereupon, the King, at its first appearance, withdrew to Hampton-court. But because the palace was considered to be too close to the capital for his personal safety, he moved to Salisbury. [2]

Consumed with fire by the calamities

In 1666, Charles II suffered a further blow. *London* ignited into a furnace that burned out of control for four days. Few people died, but many premises were *burnt* to cinders *by the suddenness of the calamities* that followed. Numbered among these were 89 parish churches, 13,200 dwellings, shops and warehouses, the great Livery Halls; even St. Paul's Cathedral did not escape the inferno. [3]

The Fire began in the bakery of Thomas Farrynor of Pudding Lane. The oven fire had not been properly damped down on the night before, and the next day, it being Sunday, the fire reignited to spread to other parts of the bakery unnoticed.

Soon there was no stopping it. A wind had also blown up overnight and was fanning the fire, causing it to spread quickly and in several directions at once. Sparks then began to sweep through the air in great profusion, and these fell onto the timbered houses and thatched roofs of premises nearby, engulfing them in flames and spreading the catastrophe at an alarming rate.

GREAT FIRE OF LONDON
[WEEK 23 – 2 SEPTEMBER 1666]

Of twenty-three, '666

According to the legalistic style of dating, which operated when this prophecy was made, New Year's Day began on 25 March, This form of dating did not change in Britain until 1752.

The British decreed that the day following Sept. 2, 1752 should be called Sept. 14, a loss of 11 days. All dates preceding were marked O.S. for Old Style. In addition New Year's Day was moved to Jan. 1 from Mar. 25. [The World Almanac and Book of Facts: 1977, p. 784].

	1666	Week Nos.
March	25 New Year's Day	-
April	1, 8, 15, 22, 29,	1 – 5
May	6, 13, 20, 27,	6 – 9
June	3, 10, 17, 24,	10 – 13
July	1, 8, 15, 22, 29	14 – 18
August	5, 12, 19, 26,	19 – 22
SEPTEMBER	**2,**	**23**

The date of "Great Fire of London, 2 September 1666"[4] is equivalent to 'Week 23 the Sixes'.

BRITANNIA - THE ANTIQUE DAME

The antique dame

In this time frame, the 'Dame of Antiquity' is identified as Britannia: "it was the Romans who first named the island of England and Scotland Britannia. [...] It were the Romans too who [...] first portrayed Britannia on coinage."[5] Hence, we have the reason for the Seer to have referred to her as *the antique dame*. During Charles II's reign, the idea of representing the British people by Britannia was revived, and the King's great love Frances Steward was asked to pose for Britannia in what was to become, "a fitting symbol used on the reverse of copper coins of Charles II.

Will fall from her high place

The oracle's reference to 'falling from a high place' is biblical. It occurs several times in the Bible and refers to idols being toppled. It is therefore an apt reference, since Britannia was an icon, intended as a symbol for Britain's growing power at sea. The spear, for example, originally held by Britannia, was replaced by Neptune's trident.

It was during Charles II's Dutch Wars that *Britannia fell from her high place;* that is to say, the high regard in which she was meant to be held. As historian H.A.L. Fisher wrote, "Whoever deserved to rule the waves in Charles II's first Dutch wars, it was not Britannia" In June 1667, Dutch ships entered the Thames unchallenged, and then sailed up the River Medway, even as far as Upnor Castle to inflict terrible damage on the King's ships anchored at Chatham. [6]

Of the same sect, a great number will be killed

This naval setback came only one year after Admiral De Ruyter had achieved a glorious victory over an English fleet commanded by Sir William Berkley. In a four-day battle that took place in the English Channel the Dutch inflicted over 8,000 casualties on the English. Tragically, a great number of the victims were family men who had been pressed into service as they left church. After the battle, their bodies "were found floating in the water dressed in their Sunday black just as they had been caught after church by the press gang." [7]

Since the Seer was Catholic, he has specifically identified the fact that *a number will be killed from the same sect*—the sect being the Church of England, which had broken away from Rome under the reign of Henry VIII.

Summary: *This prophecy is an example of one that perfectly fits the age for which it was written: as indeed do many others. Charles II, as the son of 'The Just One', Charles I; his disastrous error of judgement when engaging in a fruitless war with the Netherlands, followed immediately by the Great Fire of London, which the seer actually dates to the exact day, is accompanied by the revival of Britannia as a symbol of Britain's superiority at sea. And then, finally, the downfall of Britannia, at the hands of the Dutch navy concludes the oracle.*

52   *Dans plusieurs nuits la terre tremblera:*
        Sur le prinstemps deux effors suite:
        Corynthe, Ephese aux deux mers nagera:
        Guerre s'esmeut par deux vaillans de luite.

53   *La grande peste de cite maritime,*
        Ne cessera que mort ne soit vengée
        Du iuste sang, par pris damne sans crime
        De la grand dame par feincte n'outraigée.

damné (OF) judged unto death; que (OF) unless;

The great plague at the maritime city (**LONDON**)   1665
Will not cease, unless death be not well and truly avenged
For the just blood (**CHARLES 1**): seized, judged unto death, without crime
By the great dame through pretence, not having offended.

The great plague at the maritime city will not cease

London has long been known as *a maritime city*. In the past this had been the cause of many outbreaks of plague imported into the city. Rats infested with fleas carrying the virus were apt to scurry aboard ships in Eastern ports, eventually coming ashore in London's dockland.

In May 1665, London began experiencing the first signs of what was to become the most devastating outbreak of the disease in the city's history. [1] For eleven months, "The Great Plague of London" took its toll on the population until it had carried off an estimated: "one hundred thousand souls." [2]

Unless death be not well and truly avenged for the Just blood

It is not unusual in some societies, even in these modern times, for terrible calamities to be seen as 'Acts of God'. Indeed, the Bible records God's anger at the disobedience of His people, and the punishments they were made to suffer.

In London, at the height of the plague, it was likewise suggested that the city was undergoing a similar chastisement for having executed Charles I: a monarch descended from the lawful Stuart bloodline, hence *the Just Blood*. Many therefore believed that the mounting death toll from Plague would continue until death had reaped vengeance for the crime London had committed against the nation's lawful King. [3]

Seized, judged unto death without crime

The King *was seized* on 30 November 1648, [4] and two months later he was executed. Parliament, having made Charles its prisoner, had also posed a problem for his captors. If they were to release him, there would then be a danger that he would, in turn, punish them, and in all likelihood respond by sentencing the ringleaders to death for treason.

On the other hand, continued imprisonment would invite attempts to free him, as had already been tried by an army sent from Scotland. The only practical alternative was execution, but this would require a framework of legality to justify the death sentence.

> On 6 January, the Rump of the commons set up a 'High Court of Justice' to try the King; the hitherto obscure John Bradshaw was to preside. [...] Bradshaw's tribunal, its legality highly questionable, duly found Charles guilty of 'High Treason and other High crimes', and ordered that he be put to death by the severing of his head from his body.

The verdict was actually a contradiction in terms. High treason is an offence committed *against* the King. But Charles was the King; he was therefore *judged unto death without crime.* [5]

By the great dame

The oracle blames this act of regicide upon the British people by equating them with Britannia: claiming that the crime against the King was *by the great dame*: the *Dame of Antiquity* that was revived from Roman times to represent the British people

This reference to Britannia is itself prophetic, for as previously mentioned in N°. 51, it was during the reign of Charles II that plans to symbolise the British people by this Roman figure were finally completed. "She has never been absent from the coinage since the reign of Charles II and now, she is universally recognised as the personification of Britain." [6]

Through pretence

The *pretence* that is alluded to in this prophecy was that the King had engaged in a cruel and costly war against Parliament, and by doing so he had actively committed treason. [7] In fact, Charles had been forced to take this action in order to defend what he believed to be his divine right to rule; that is, being answerable only to God. This was a former principle of government according to biblical teaching (see Romans 13: 1-7), and it is reaffirmed in this oracle.

Not having offended

Although Charles I had indeed been engaged in a civil war, the majority of people in Britain confessed to a liking for their King, and he was *not* widely seen as *having offended* them. [8] His fate was to come up against the wishes of Parliament's forceful and ambitious leader, Oliver Cromwell. As can often happen at such times, the population found itself swept along by the sheer force of one man's charismatic personality.

Summary: *This prophecy is a companion to No, 51 above: for the Plague of London and the Fire of London are seldom referred to separately. Even here they are partitioned only by a single quatrain, which is unlikely due to coincidence. Although London is not mentioned by name, the 'maritime city' combined with the 'just blood'—which is referred to elsewhere in line with mention of 'London', does rather allay any doubt as to the intended location. Moreover the sham trial to provide legitimacy to commit murder provides further evidence that collectively, the facts stated in this prophecy comply with the history of that time.*

> 54   *Par gent estrange, & de Romains loingtaine*
>   *Leur grand cité apres eaue fort troublee:*
>   *Fille sans maine, trop different domaine,*
>   *Prins chief, farreure n'auoir esté riblee.*

> 55   *Dans le conflit le grand qui peu valloyt,*
>   *A son dernier sera cas merueilleux:*
>   *Pendant qu'Hadrie verra ce qu' il salloyt,*
>   *Dans le banquet pongnale l' orgueilleux.*

pongnale (AF) pongneur, as piqueur

56   *Que peste & glaiue n' a peu seu definer,*
      Mort dans le puys, sommet du ciel frappe.
      L' abbé mourra quand verra ruiner
      Ceulx du naufrage l' escueil voulant grapper.

57   *Auant conflit le grand mur tombera:*
      Le grand à mort, mort trop subite & plainte:
      Nay imparfaict: la plus part nagera:
      Aupres du fleuue de sang la terre tainte.

58   *Sans pied ne main par dend ayguë & forte,*
      Par globe au fort deporc & laisné nay:
      Pres du portail desloyal se transporte
      Silene luit, petit grand emmené.

59   *Classe Gauloyse par apuy de grand garde*
      Du grand Neptune, & ses tridents souldars
      Rousgée Prouence pour sostenir grand bande:
      Plus Mars Narbon. par iauelotz & dards.

garde (OF) guardian, official in charge; souldar (OF souldart) soldier; rongé, fretted;

French fleet, by support of the great guardian (**COLBERT**),   1707
For the great Neptune (**BRITAIN**) and his trident soldiers:
Provence tormented for sustaining the great band,
Further war, Narbona, by javelins and darts.

French fleet

The formation of the French Navy received a massive impetus under the reign of Louis XIV.

> The rise of a new French navy was as rapid as that in Holland. When France's greatest bureaucrat, Jean Baptiste Colbert, began to take an interest in naval affairs in 1665 he found only two or three ships fit for service. By the time of his death in 1683 there were 200 and a force of 53,000 seamen, apart from scores of agile privateers from the old corsair ports of Nantes, St Malo and Dunkirk. An immense effort was made to provide France with the finest navy as well as the finest army in Europe. [1]

Colbert's interest in naval affairs was sparked by the commencement of the Anglo-Dutch Wars: the first, fought in 1662, was followed by a second that lasted from 1664 until 1667. The third, enjoined by France, continued from 1672 until 1674.

By support of the great guardian

Colbert was the most important minister in France, and is identified as the 'great Guardian'.

> Nothing escaped his watchful and supervising eye, neither art nor letters, neither industry nor commerce. [...] His regulations were so minute as to take the spring out of industry. His vigorous arm stretched so far as to clasp the most distant settlements of the crown. [2]

In 1661, he became the leading member of the Council of Finances; and three years later he was made Superintendant of Royal Buildings, Arts and Manufacturers. In 1665, he was given the title of Controller-General of Finances, and in 1668, he was made Secretary of State for the Navy. Added to this, "He was chiefly responsible for the consolidation of the new bureaucratic machinery under the Intendants, for the improved policing of Paris, and for the new law codes." [3] As a result, "In March [1667], the *lieutenant general de Police* is created in Paris, under the control of Gabriel Nicolas de La Reynie. La Reynie will exercise wide powers of social control and surveillance." [4]

For the great Neptune

The great Neptune refers to the English navy, which had gained superiority at sea, primarily due to Oliver Cromwell (1653 – 1658), and his desire to extend his prowess as a land commander to that of the sea. During Charles II's First Anglo-Dutch War, fought at sea, Robert Blake defeated his Dutch adversary, Marten Tromp, to obtain mastery over the ocean.

And his trident soldiers

BRITANNIA WITH
NEPTUNE'S TRIDENT

Charles II's decision to revive Britannia as a female personification of England (she is the Great Dame in quatrain 53 and the Antique Dame in quatrain 51), also involved replacing Britannia's spear with *a trident*; hence the prophetic reference to Neptune's trident soldiers at precisely this period in European history.

The execution of Charles I forced the rapid expansion of the navy, by multiplying England's actual and potential enemies, and many vessels were constructed from the 1650s onward. [...] Forty new ships were built between 1650 and 1654. [...] The Interregnum saw a considerable expansion in the strength of the navy, both in number of ships and in internal importance within English policy. The Restoration Monarchy inherited this large navy and continued the same pol icy of expansion of the navy, focusing on making a strong navy full of large ships in order to provide a strong defence under Charles II. [...] In 1655 Blake routed the Barbary pirates and started a campaign against the Spanish in the Caribbean, capturing Jamaica. In 1664 the English captured New Amsterdam (later New York City) resulting in the Second Dutch War (1665–1667). In 1666 the Four Days Battle was a defeat for the English but the Dutch fleet was crushed a month later off Orfordness. [5]

The French navy participated with some success in the third Anglo-Dutch War; also, when combating Dutch ships off the coast of Sicily. However, in May 1692, defeat at the battle of Barfleur La Hougue, in which Louis XIV planned to invade England and restore James II to the throne, "marked the end of Colbert's navy. It was the Trafalgar of the seventeenth century. The *Grand Monarque* (Louis XIV) was so disgusted that he turned all his resources to his armies." [6]

Provence tormented for sustaining the great band

In 1707 the Duke of Savoy and Prince Eugene crossed the Col of Tenda and entered *Provence* together with their *great band* of followers. Their mission was to seize the port of Toulon by attacking from the south. English ships under the command of Admiral Sir Cloudesley Shovell would then simultaneously launch an attack from the Mediterranean. The plan was to provide free access for the British navy in the Mediterranean. In some discomfort, Mme Maintenon, the second wife of Louis XIV, wrote, "now we have the Duke of Savoy burning everything and marching on Toulon: you will believe me if I say that I already see the city on fire, all the King's vessels burnt and our enemies established in Provence." [7]

In fact, the plan failed to achieve its desired end, and Prince Eugene was forced to retreat with the loss of 10,000 men. Nevertheless, to prevent their ships falling into the enemy's hands, Louis had ordered the sinking of more than 46 ships in the hope of later refloating them. Of these, 15 ships of the line were subsequently discovered to be beyond repair, and this fatally hampered France's hope of retaining sea power in the Mediterranean, having already lost it in the Atlantic. "The siege of Toulon was raised, and soon afterward the enemy evacuated Provence, and Dauphiny was out of danger." [8] Thus ended the torment of Provence for having to sustain the great band of men brought over from Italy by Savoy and Eugene for a plan that eventually failed.

Further war, Narbona, by javelins and darts

Further war refers to the War of the Spanish Succession, where battles were also being fought to secure the Spanish throne for Louis XIV's great-grandson. The Seer refers to this connexion in cryptic fashion, which is achieved by abbreviating Narbon. This was an alternative spelling for Narbonne before the French language became standardized. The abbreviation also implies a different way of thinking, e.g.

Narbonne (Narbona in Catalan and in Occitan, commonly Narbo especially when referring to the Ancient Rome era) is a town and commune of south -western France. [...] It was part of the Emirate of Cordoba until conquered by the Franks a fter which it became part of the Carolingian Viscounty of Narbonne. [9]

Hence, Narbon. (abbrev.) Narbona in Catalan directs attention to *further war* in Spain.

Valencia fell to the French on 8 May and Saragossa on 26 May. The Catalan town of Lerida capitulated to the Franco-Spanish forces on 14 October. Meanwhile, near the Portuguese border, Ciudad Rodrigo also passed into Philip's hands on 4 October after a siege of nearly three weeks. By the close of 1707 Philip held most of Spain.[10]

The weapons of war at this time, which the oracle compares to the *javelins and darts* of his day, were "flintlock fusils and bayonets." The cavalry relied upon swords. Also, "Cannon hurled various packets of death across the field with the big 24pdr siege cannon highly effective at 600 yds (550 m) and capable of inflicting casualties at 2,000 yds (1830 m). Artillery began battles at long range.[11] Together, the mid-sixteenth century language referring to these later weapons is justified.

Summary: *This prophecy found its fulfilment in the reign of Louis XIV. The first half of the prophecy concentrates upon the growth in both the navies of France and Britain. Colbert was indeed, at one time, a great guardian figure in France, who was responsible for developing France's navy. At the same time Britain's naval victories and conquests were becoming more evident. In the second half of the oracle, the naval loss to Louis XIV at Toulon is foreseen by the invasion of Provence, which coincided in time with the prediction of further war in Spain.*

60   *La foy Punicque en Orient rompue*
        Gang. Iud. & Rosne, Loyre, & Tag changeront,
        Quand du mulet la faim sera repue,
        Classe espargie, sang & corps nageront.

61   *Euge, Tamins, Gironde & la Rochele:*
        O sang Troien! Mars au port de la flesche
        Derrier le fleuue au fort muse l'eschele,
        Pointes a feu gran meurtre sus la bresche.

62   *Mabus puis tost alors mourra, viendra*
        De gens & bestes vne horrible defaite:
        Puis tout à coup la vengence on verra
        Cent, main, soif, faim, quand courra la comete.

63   *Gaulois, Ausone bien peu subjugera.*
        Po, Marne, & Seine fera Perme l'vrie
        Qui le grand mur contre eux dressera
        Du moindre au mur le grand perdra la vie.

64   *Seicher de faim, de soif, gent Geneuoise*
        Espoir prochain viendra au defaillir,
        Sur point tremblant sera loy Gebonoise.
        Classe au grand port ne se peult aculir.

65   *Le parc enclin grande calamité*
        Par l'Hesperie & Insubre fera:
        Le feu en nef, peste & captiuité:
        Mercure en l'Arq Saturne fenera.

66   *Par grans dangiers le captive echapé:*
        Peu de temps grand la fortune changée.
        Dans le palais le peuple est atrapé
        Pat bon augure la cité assiegée.

67   *Le blonde au nez forche viendra commetre,*
        Par le duelle & chassera dehors:
        Les exiles dedans fera remetre
        Aux lieux marins commetant les plus forts.

blonde (OF homonym) fair, susceptible; forche (OF fourche) pitchfork; duelle (duel) struggle; remettre (AF fondre) dissolve.

The susceptible one with the pitchfork nose (**AUGEREAU**) will arrive to empower 1797
Through the struggle, he will also expel abroad:
The exiles within, he will dissolve,
Committing the strongest to maritime places.

The susceptible one with the pitchfork nose

General *Augereau* first made his reputation as a soldier in the conquest of Northern Italy. "Contemporaries described him as [...] 'an able tactician and thorough soldier' [...] his towering height and huge hooked nose made him an imposing figure." [1] It was because of his capability in the field that Napoleon saw him as being *susceptible* to carrying out his plan for a *coup d'état* against the moderates in Paris.

Will arrive to empower

Augereau arrived in Paris at the head of his troops, prepared to execute a *coup d'état*. With customary candour he declared that he had arrived "to kill the royalists": men that Napoleon, his Commander-in-Chief, had said were too dangerous to be allowed to live. [2]

GENERAL PIERRE-FRANÇOIS
AUGEREAU

Three Directors, Barras, Rewbell and La Révellière-Lépeaux, staged the *coup d'état* with support from the military. Royalist candidates had gained the great majority of seats in the recent elections, where a third of the seats were at stake. They were poised to win the next round of elections and assume control of the Directory. [3]

This *coup* confirmed the power of the army, and helped to prepare the way for Napoleon's rule.

Through the struggle, he will also expel abroad

After Augereau's *coup d'état,* known as Fructidor (4 September 1797) by the Revolutionary Calendar then in force, more than 130 royalists and counter-revolutionaries from the *Corps Législatif,* together with many non-juring priests were rounded up in *the struggle* and forcibly *expelled abroad.* [4] This effectively terminated the threatened counter-revolution by royalists.

It is also noteworthy that the oracle uses the word *duelle*, which, as 'duel' in modern French, has the same meaning as in English. Before embarking upon his military career, Augereau had been a 'duellist': earning his living as a fencing master in Dresden.

The exiles within, he will dissolve

Before Augereau's *coup,* the Directory had tolerated the gradual return of those who had been exiled under the harsher regime of France's former revolutionary government. Augereau , acting under military orders from Napoleon, whose help had been sought by Barras, reversed this by reinforcing the hard-won gains made by the Revolution. He therefore dissolved the power of the old 'noblesse' by introducing new legislation. This allowed former exiles to stay in France, but as 'foreigners'. They were therefore obliged to apply for naturalisation in order to enjoy the rights of full citizenship. [5]

Committing the strongest to maritime places

However, counted "Among the victims of this September violence were some of the noblest names in France." These were numbered among *the strongest* and who were identified as those agitating for a return of the monarchy. They were banished to Guiana and the coastal town of Cayenne— *maritime places.* [6]

Summary: *This oracle is centred upon the coup d'état known as Fructidor, which took place in Paris in 1797. It was led by General Augereau, whose name first appeared as 'Auge' in Century One No. 16. But it was not only his name that was foreseen two hundred years before he was born, it was also his physical feature of a 'huge hooked nose'. Today, we are taught to accept that this is a genetic feature, involving the complexities of DNA. The truth supporting this theory resides in the passage of time: whereas, the greater truth exists in the timelessness of God—otherwise known as the 'block universe': a tapestry of world events woven together by the Creator, in which past and future have only a relative meaning that depends upon any given present point in the overall picture. It is this that has allowed the events that followed Fructidor to be correctly predicted two centuries before the consciousness of those involved were able to perceive it as a present event.*

68   *De l'Aquilon les effors seront grands:*
      Sur l'Ocean sera la porte ouuerte,
      Le regne en l'isle sera reintegrand:
      Tremblera Londres par voile descouuerte.

Aquilon (L Aquil/onis) north; porte (OF) a port or gate;

From the North the efforts will be great: 1648
On the Ocean, the port will be opened,
The reign in the Isle will be reinstated:
London will tremble through discovered sail.

The key to interpreting this oracle is indicated by 'London', added to which there is a further reference to the 'Isle'. Both words therefore direct attention to Britain.

From the North the efforts will be great

In 1648, the Scottish parliament voted for a force of 30,000 men to be enlisted: "to rescue the king's person." Parliament was holding Charles captive at Holdenby House in Northamptonshire and Scotland had prepared an army to rescue him. Once across the border, 5000 Englishmen joined them with this same aim in mind. But Cromwell's Ironsides countered the threat by hurrying *north* to Preston. In August 1648, the two sides met head on, and in the battle that followed, the Scots and their English allies were heavily defeated. *From the North the efforts had been great*, but insufficient to overcome the might of Cromwell's model army. [1]

On the Ocean, the port will be opened

Fast forward by six years, and we discover "The Anglo-Portuguese alliance, offering the English fleet the splendid harbour of Lisbon." This occurred in July 1654. "Lisbon is the key to the Mediterranean The city is also situated at the mouth of the river Tagus *on the Atlantic Ocean,* and with its *port opened* to British ships, it enabled them to repair and restock: instead of making an extra day's journey to either Plymouth or Portsmouth. [2] The port was also an important acquisition for the Royal Navy; since it helped British ships maintain a commanding presence in the Mediterranean.

The reign in the Isle will be reinstated

Fast forward a further six years and we arrive at *the reinstatement of the reign in the* British *Isle. This* has occurred only once since these oracles were published. Oliver Cromwell abolished the monarchy in 1649 at the time of Charles I's execution. After Cromwell's death in 1658, his son, Richard, attempted to follow in his father's footsteps as Lord Protector, but he was neither popular nor successful. Consequently, in May 1660, Charles II, son of the executed former king, was invited to return to England from his exile in the Netherlands and reinstate the monarchy. [3]

London will tremble through discovered sail

Finally, we go forward seven more years to 8 June 1667, this time to find *London trembling* with fear. News had been brought to the capital that *sails* had been *discovered* belonging to a Dutch fleet, and its ships were already entering the mouth of the Thames. This was a time when England was at war with the Dutch, and it was feared that an invasion of the capital was about to begin. Widespread panic quickly followed, and the roads leading out of the city were soon clogged with barrows and carts laden with the belongings of those seeking refuge in the country. But, in the event, the Dutch fleet left the Thames, preferring instead to sail up the River Medway, where several ships at anchor were then destroyed close to the port of Chatham. [4]

Summary: *The events predicted in this oracle are spread over nineteen years. Yet, there is a unity of purpose in both their content and dating. Lines one and three refer to the British monarchy: firstly, its overthrow and then its restoration. Lines two and four refer to the British navy: its acquisition of the port in Lisbon followed by its abject failure to defend either London or the port at Chatham.*
            If we now take each of the years in which these four predictions were fulfilled; that is, 1648, 1654, 1660 1667, and then difference them to obtain the years in between, we get the numbers 6 6 7. And 1667 is the year in which the final line of this oracle was fulfilled.

69   *Le roy Gauloys par la Celtique dextre*
      Voiant discorde de la grand Monarchie,
      Sus les trois pars fera fleurir son sceptre,
      Contre la cappe de la grand Hirarchie.

70   *Le dard du ciel fera son extendue*
      Mors en parlant: grande execution.
      La pierre en l'arbre, la fiere gent rendue,
      Brut, humain monstre, purge expiation.

      The sky dart will make its outreach,
      Deaths through speaking: a great execution,
      The rock in the tree like thing, the arrogant/savage people restored/repaid,
      Brutal person, an affable outward appearance, purges satisfaction.

These are the bare bones of a future prophecy. The reason for its inclusion is because of the words used. A 'sky dart' would be understood as an arrow in previous ages and perhaps a shell at a later date. But in the present time, by attaching it to 'estendue', it suggests an intercontinental ballistic missile. There is also the word 'arbre'. This usually means 'a tree'. However, it can also mean 'a tree-like thing'. For example, the cloud arising from the explosion of a nuclear device is tree-like. There is also the word 'pierre'. In other quatrains, as we shall later discover, this word translates as 'pope', since 'pierre' was the name given to Peter, the first pope. It is, however, left for the event to become history, in order to ascertain for certainty its precognised reality.

71   *Les exilés en Secile viendront*
      Pour deliurer de faim la gent estrange:
      Au point du iour les Celtes luy faudreont:
      La vie demeure a raison: Roy se range.

72   *Armée Celtique en Italie vexée,*
      De toutes pars conflit & grande perte:
      Romains fuis, ô Gaule repoulsée,
      Pres du Thesin, Rubicon pugne incerte.

73   *Au lac Fucin de Benac le riuaige*
      Prins du Leman au port de l'Oguion:
      Nay de troys bras predict bellique image,
      Par troys couronnes au grand Endymion.

74   *De Sens, d'Autun viendront iusques au Rosne*
      Pour passer outre vers les monts Pyrenées:
      La gent sortir de la Marque d'Anconne:
      Par terre & mer le suiura à grans trainees.

75   *La voix ouye de l'insolit oyseau,*
      Sur le canon du respiral estaige,
      Si haut viendra du froment le boisseau,
      Que l'homme d'homme sera Anthropophage.

76   *Foudre en Bourgoigne fera cas portenteux,*
      Que par engin ne pourroit faire
      De leur senat sacreiste fait boiteux.
      Fera sauoir aux ennemis l'affaire.

Bourgoigne (*epenthesis*) Burgo<i>ngne; engin (OF engien) craft, artifice, also (*syncope*) for Eng[h]ien; portenteux (L) portentosus; cas (OF) case, matter, crime; pourroit (conditional form of pouvoir); fera savoir - to explain.

      Within **BOURGOGNE**, a thunderbolt will make a portentous crime,   1812
      Except through craft (**ENGHIEN**) it would not be able to occur:
      At their governing body, a sacristan made lame (**TALLEYRAND**)
      Will make the affair known to the adversaries.

Apart from indicating a region of France, 'Bourgogne' was also the name of a quite remarkable sergeant in Napoleon's army. What made A.J.B.F. Bourgogne so significant was the vivid, first-hand, personal history of his experiences while serving under the Emperor Napoleon. Louis

Philippe, King of the French from 1830 to 1848, later honoured the old soldier with the commission of *Major de Place* in his hometown of Valenciennes, where he had retired to write his memoirs; these included a first mention of the following event.

Within Bourgogne

In his book, literally *within Bourgogne*, the ex-sergeant described a dramatic event that he had personally witnessed, involving Napoleon during his Russian campaign in 1812. The description he gave was seen by the Seer as having so much similarity with a crime that Napoleon had earlier committed, as to justify the wrong as having been portentous. [1]

A thunder bolt will make a portentous crime

What *Bourgogne* described, had been totally unexpected: a *bolt from the blue*. A troop of Cossack riders appeared without warning, and made directly for a small group of French militia surrounding Bonaparte. It was a planned attack by the Russian cavalry to take the French by surprise, kidnap the Emperor, and take him into captivity. The attempt only just failed. Nevertheless, Napoleon was haunted by the possibility that a future attempt might be successful, and from then onwards he kept a phial of poison hung round his neck, believing that suicide would be preferable to capture.

Except through craft (Enghien) it would not be able to occur

Eight years earlier, in March 1804, a party of French cavalry officers suddenly, and just as unexpectedly, appeared at Ettenheim where the Duke of Enghien, prospective heir to the French throne, was in exile. The plan was for the cavalry to kidnap the Duke and bring him back to France. The stratagem worked. Enghien was captured and taken to the Chateau of Vincennes, where he was summarily tried for conspiracy, and then executed by firing squad. [2]

Except for the *craft* that led to the kidnapping and death of *Enghien*, his removal as a potential rival to Napoleon's power [3] would not otherwise have been successful. In the aftermath of the Duke's murder, especially as heir to the French throne, its repercussions not just shook France, but it also horrified the whole of Europe.

At their governing body, a sacristan made lame

Behind the stratagem to kidnap Enghien was a leading member *from the governing body*: a person who was also *a sacristan and lame*. This was Charles Maurice de Talleyrand, Napoleon's Foreign Minister. He had become *crippled* after a childhood accident, and this may have steered him towards his early career in the Church. But during the French Revolution, he changed sides and became involved in politics. His abilities, and past career in the Church were soon recognized, and he was put *in charge of Church property*; that is, he became *a sacristan*. And, importantly, it was Talleyrand in 1804 that calmed Napoleon's qualms regarding a possible Royalist revival, by having the Duke of Enghien kidnapped and then executed. [4]

Will make the affair known to the adversaries

It was also Talleyrand who later, betrayed Napoleon He did so, *by making known* to Czar Alexander of Russia details of the secret *affair* that he had previously been discussing with Bonaparte. The Czar was therefore given knowledge in advance of what was to be discussed during his forthcoming talks next day, when he resumed his discussion with Napoleon.

'Affair' is also the same word that Napoleon used to describe the secret treaty he wished to negotiate with the Czar. "It was an affair, he added, which must be treated between themselves." But, unbeknown to Bonaparte, after each session with Alexander, the Czar would arrange to meet with Talleyrand in order to discuss the proposals that had taken place earlier that day. "There can be no doubt that by any usual standard, Talleyrand's behaviour at Erfut constituted treason to France and treachery to Napoleon." [5]

Summary: *The truth contained within this extremely detailed prophecy is impossible to unravel, unless the distinction*
between the region of Burgundy (Bourgogne) and the book written by Sergeant Bourgogne are understood.
Only then can the similarity between the Russian cavalry's attempt to kidnap Napoleon be understood as
portended by the French cavalry's similar effort when kidnapping Enghien, Napoleon's rival for the
throne. The remaining part of the oracle is less cryptic, since the facts about Talleyrand's lameness, and that
he was a former sacristan who became prominent in the political affairs of Napoleon are more readily
accessible. The prophecy also includes an easily understood reference to Talleyrand's betrayal, in which he
made known to the Russian Czar, secret details of a matter that Napoleon considered confidential and,
which he intended to discuss with the Czar at their next meeting.

77   *Par arcs feuz poix & par feuz repoussés:*
Cris, hurlements sur la minuit ouys.
Dedans sont mis par les ramparts cassés
Par cunicules les traditeurs fuis.

Poix, weights,; minuit, midnight; cunicules, holes inside; traiteur (L) traditor – traitor.

By bows, fires, weights & by fire driven back: 1575?
Shouts, yelling, yeas about midnight.
Inside, they are taken by reason of the broken ramparts,
By the holes inside, the traitors escape.

The word 'arcs' translates as 'bows'. The problem with this is that the bow and arrow was
replaced in the 16th century by the arquebus (a muzzle loaded firearm). This may suggest that
'arcs' is intended as an abbreviation for these later weapons.

The alternative suggestion that the battle of Arques (1589) is the intended meaning fails after the
opening line. There was, however, an attack made in 1575 by Protestants on the Cathar Castle in
Arques, known as the Château d'Arques The interest in this as a possible solution resides in the
fact that *the ramparts were broken* during the attack; also, the fortress contained numerous
murder-*holes inside* (meurtrière), which would then link it to the 'cunicules' in the fourth line of
the oracle. But there the trail grows cold. A detailed account of the attack is required to
determine *if* the remaining details are able to confirm or deny it as a prophecy for this event.

78   *Le grand Neptune du profond de la mer*
De gent Punique & sang Gauloys mesté,
Les Isles à sang, pour le tardif ramer:
Plus luy nuira que l'occult mal celé.

79   *La barbe crespe & noire par engin*
Subiuguera la gent cruele & fiere.
Le grand CHYREN *ostera du longin,*
Tous les captifs par Seline baniere.

80   *Apres conflit du lesé l'eloquence,*
Par peu de temps se tramme faint repos:
Point l'on n'admet les grands à deliurance:
Les ennemis sont remis à propos.

81   *Par feu du ciel la cité presque aduste:*
L' Vrne menasse encore Deucalion:
Vexée Sardaigne par la Punique fuste,
Apres que Libra lairra son Phaëton.

82   *Par faim la proye fera loup prisonnier,*
L'assaillant lors en extreme detresse.
Le nay aiant au deuant le dernier,
Le grand n'eschappe au milieu de la presse.

83   *Le gros trafficq du grand Lyon change*
La plus part tourne en pristine ruine,
Proye aux souldars par pille vendange
Par Iura mont & Sueue bruine.

84   *Entre Campaigne, Sienne, Flora, Tuscie*
     Six moys neufz iours ne plouura vne goute.
     L'estrange langue en terre Dalmatie,
     Courira sus: vastant la terre toute.

85   *Le vieux plain barbe sous l' estatut seuere,*
     A Lyon fait dessus l' Aigle Celtique:
     Le petit grand trop outre perseuere:
     Bruit d' arme au ciel: mer rouge Lygustique.

86   *Naufraige a classe pres d'onde Hadriatique:*
     La terre esmeuë sus l'air en terre mis:
     Egypte tremble augment Mahommetique,
     L'Herault soy rendre à crier est commis.

87   *Apres viendra des extremes contrées,*
     Prince Germain sus le throsne doré:
     La seruitude & eaux rencontrées
     La dame serue, son temps plus n'adoré.

88   *Le circuit du grand faict ruineux,*
     Le nom septiesme du cinquiesme sera:
     D'vn tiers plus grand l'estrange belliqueux.
     Mouton, Lutece, Aix ne garantira.

circuit (AF voyage circulaire) round trip; nom (OF titre) title; Lutece (L) Lutetia, Latin name for Paris; garantira (AF fournir une garantie) to furnish a guarantee;

The round trip of the great one (**CHARLES IX**) made ruinous,   1564
The seventh title will be from the fifth:
Of a third (**CHARLES III**) more great; the foreigner (**PHILIP II**) war-like,
Ram, Paris, Aix will not furnish a guarantee.

The round trip of the great one

The grand tour, or *round trip of* France arranged by the Queen-mother, Catherine de' Medici, for her thirteen-year-old son, King Charles IX– *the great one* – left Paris on 24 January 1564.[1] It would continue until 1 May 1566. The idea was to present the young King to the people, and encourage their allegiance to the monarchy. This seemed especially necessary at the time, because of the bloodletting that had occurred during the recent civil war (April 1562–March 1563).

Made ruinous

While on tour, it was Catherine's intention to visit her daughter Elisabeth, and her son-in-law Philip II. But her real aim was to propose two marriages. The first of which, involved a union between her son Edouard (later Henri III) and Philip's sister Juana. The other intended marriage was between her daughter Marguerite and the King's son Don Carlos. But to Catherine's intense annoyance, Philip refused even to meet with her. Instead, he sent his emissary, the Duke of Alba, who dismissed both marriages out of hand.

Worse was to follow. Alba urged the Queen to renounce the peace treaty that had been made with the Huguenots, the *Edict of Amboise*. This was a peace settlement, made on 2 March 1560, which pardoned all past crimes of religion in France on condition that the accused abjure their heresy. Spain did not approve. Alba strongly believed that religious dissidents were heretics who had to be terrorized, and this was best achieved by executing their leaders.

Catherine therefore left Bayonne having gained nothing. On the contrary, she had aroused suspicions amongst the Huguenots, and placed in serious jeopardy the one fragile chance she had of bringing a lasting peace to France. Further disappointment awaited her at Navarre.

Catherine arrived in this southern border kingdom, which divided France from Spain in the southwest, with the intention of forming a friendship with its Queen, Jeanne d'Albret: a stalwart defender of the Huguenot cause. But their coming together only caused further friction, and the unresolved enmity between these two Queens was to become yet another factor in the Wars of Religion that were to bedevil France for the next thirty years.

In short, the Queen-mother's two major initiatives had not merely failed; they had, in fact, proved *ruinous* for any future prospect of peace. [2] Indeed, it was because of Alba, "at Bayonne [and his] conversations with Catherine de Medici which led to the 2nd of the French Wars of Religion." [3]

The seventh title will be from the fifth

The second and third lines of this quatrain deviate from the King's tour, in order to predict the future of the Queen-mother's other children. Thus, *the seventh* child born to Catherine de' Medici and Henri II was Hercule (b. 18. 3. 1555), duc d'Alençon. *The fifth* child was Edouard-Alexandre (b. 20 .9. 1551) duc d'Anjou. When Charles IX died in 1574, the crown passed to his brother Edouard who chose to be known as Henri III. This released *the* ducal *title* d'Anjou, and it passed down the male line to his brother Hercule, *the seventh* child. Consequently, *the title* of *the seventh* child had *resulted from* that of *the fifth:* [4] as foretold in the oracle.

Of a third more great

Princess Claude was *the third* of Catherine's children, and she married another *third*, Charles III of Lorraine. During the reign of Charles IX, his youngest brother Alençon had been promised the position of Lieutenant-General of France—the title had been surrendered by Edouard in December 1573, when he left France to become King of Poland. But Charles feared that Alençon might misuse the military power that went with this title, and perhaps seize the crown for himself. He therefore retracted his promise, and gave the position of Lieutenant-General to his brother-in-law, Charles III; 'the Great Duke of Lorraine' therefore became even *greater.* [5]

The foreigner warlike

The other son-in-law of the Queen-mother was King Philip II of Spain, *the foreigner* in the family. He had married Catherine's eldest daughter Elisabeth on 22 June 1559. Mother and daughter did not meet again until at Bayonne, during Charles IX's progress across France.

The year after this meeting, Philip adopted a *warlike* mood, and proposed to Catherine that he march 20,000 Spanish militia through eastern France, *en route* for Flanders. [6] The Queen-mother was appalled, believing it "would set fire to the kingdom," and she declined his request. Philip was therefore forced to send the Duke of Alba at the head of 10,000 men through "Savoy, Milan, and Lorraine," in order to reach the Netherlands.

Whilst there, Alba, acting on behalf of his King; that is, Catherine's son-in-law, executed or deported 1105 of the 12,302 he brought to trial.

Ram

The reign of Charles IX is noted for two catastrophic events. The first of these was the outbreak of the French Wars of Religion, which began in April 1562; the second was his involvement in the Paris massacres, which started ten years later, on the Eve of St Bartholomew's Day. Both of these are alluded to in this prophecy.

The first word, 'Ram', is another name for the constellation of Aries. Attention is therefore directed to the four weeks between March 21 and April 19. For it was halfway between these dates that the Wars of Religion began (2 April 1562). [7] These conflicts, although deadly serious, amounted to little more than a series of "petty and inconclusive civil wars between great noble connections fighting for the control of the crown." [8] There would be nine wars in all, and they would persist until 1598.

Paris

Charles's second great tragedy was the part he played in the massacres that began on the Eve of St. Bartholomew's Day. The killing spree broke out in *Paris* on the night of 24 August 1572, and quickly spread across France. [9] Three thousand people perished in the capital alone, and another ten thousand in towns across France. Paris would not experience such bloodshed again until the French Revolution, two centuries later.

Aix will not furnish a guarantee

The Edict of Amboise (2 March 1560), which had been the cause of contention between Alba and the Queen-regent in Bayonne, met with new opposition in the south of France. The parliament at *Aix-en-Provence* condemned it as unacceptable to them.

In support of their opposition, the members made a defiant stand against the treaty by *refusing* outright *to furnish a guarantee* that they would pardon anyone who had committed a crime of religion. Retribution for this defiance towards the Crown was swift. On 23 October 1564, while still on his grand tour of France, the King suspended the *parlement* at *Aix*, and replaced it with a special commission of Parisian *parlementaires*. [10]

Footnote: Charles IX's progress through France is of special note to those interested in the life of Michel de Nostredame. Among the royal guests who visited him at Salon-de-Crau in October 1564, was Henri de Bourbon Prince of Navarre and Béarn. This ten-year-old was the second cousin to King Charles IX. During her visit to Salon, Catherine de' Medici with three young sons of her own, one of whom was already King of France, and with the Valois line of succession secure, as she supposed, requested the elderly doctor to predict Prince Henri's future. "The master of Henri's household was therefore amazed when Nostradamus visited him secretly, begging to see the young Prince. Afterwards the old Seer told him: 'if you live, you will have for a master a King of France and Navarre.'" [11]

The young prince fulfilled this prophecy in 1589, when he became Henri IV, following the assassination of Henri III—the last of the Valois. Henri IV later united his kingdom of Navarre with that of France and became one of the country's greatest kings.

Summary: *The predicted grand tour of France, undertaken by Charles IX and his court, including its failure, came to an end two months before the death of the man who wrote this prophecy. The oracle is largely concerned with Charles's reign, and includes the transfer of his ducal title to his youngest brother, his brother-in-law's rise in greatness, Spain's warlike intentions, the month in which the French Wars of Religion would begin, and the emphasis given to Paris, which was turned into a bloodbath by Charles, who allowed it to appear as if he had sanctioned the murder of Protestants. Aix is also foreseen as the location for a revolt against the terms included in the Edict of Amboise, which Charles dealt with, peremptorily.*

89   *Du iou seront demis les deux grandz maistres*
     Leur grand pouuoir se verra augmenté:
     La terre neufue sera en ses haults estres:
     Au sanguinaire le nombre racompté.

90   *Par vie & mort changé regne d'Ongrie:*
     La loy sera plus aspre que seruice,
     Leur grand cite d'vrlements plaincts & crie:
     Castor & Pollux ennemis dans la lyce.

aspre (OF) severe; service (OF) état de servage. Cross-reference: life and death, C.VIII: 15.

Through life and death, the reign in Hungary is changed: 1868
The law will be more severe than a state of bondage,
Their great city with howls, complaints and outcry:
Castor & Pollux adversaries in the tilt-yard.

It is a fact, relevant to these oracles, that Hungary played a major role in the events leading to World War I. To acknowledge this, the prophecies move away from France in order to predict the political beginning of Hungary, particularly when it became part of the vast Austro-Hungarian Empire. For it was in this position that the country played a crucial part in the events leading to the outbreak of the First World War.

Through life and death, the reign in Hungary is changed

On 8 June 1867, Emperor Francis Joseph of Austria was crowned king of Hungary. One year later, the Nationalities Law decreed that all citizens of Hungary, whatever their nationality, were to become a political part of "a single nation, the indivisible, unitary Hungarian nation." For the previous twenty years Hungary had been in a state of political unrest, having rebelled against its

Habsburg rulers, and for a short time gaining independence. But Vienna had retaliated, and with the aid of its ally Russia, Hungary was restored to Austria. Weeks of bitter, bloody fighting followed, with savage reprisals against the rebel leaders. [1] The final outcome was the 'Ausgleich', which, through the rebels resolve to fight for a better life, and the deaths of those who fell trying to achieve it, changed the reign in Hungary to that of the Dual Monarchy—Austria-Hungary. [2]

The law will be more severe than a state of bondage
One feature of the new regime was the infamous Agricultural Law of 1876, which covered farm workers of both sexes. This legislation, "not only curtailed their legal equality and personal freedom, but placed the often inadequately accommodated, low-paid labourer [...] under the 'authority of his master'." The effect of 'the law' was soon seen to be 'more severe than a state of bondage', especially when it was succeeded by the notorious 'Slave Law' (Law II of 1898).[3]
During this period of time, problems in the labour market began to cause growing anger, especially related to the harsh treatment dealt out to the country's workforce. The legal rights of manual workers had been deliberately restricted, and their personal freedom curtailed. Employers were even allowed to administer corporal punishment to a worker if the circumstances warranted it; and a troubled employer could always call upon the police to maintain order if workers protested: or, even if they wished to change their place of employment.

Their great city with howls complaints and, outcry
In May 1905, the first signs of mass defiance against the hardships experienced under these *slave laws* appeared. Manual workers poured onto the streets of Budapest. 30,000 metal workers joined forces with 25,000 agricultural labourers demanding higher wages and more civil rights. The military and the gendarmerie responded with multiple arrests and enforced conscription. For a little while the trouble was suppressed. But, in May 1912, a new wave of street battles broke out in Budapest. Once again, 'their great city' descended into a scene of 'howls, complaints and outcry', as disgruntled workers clashed with the police force. This time the workers' protest was in response to the country's electoral reform programme and its defence bill. [4]

Castor and Pollux
Castor and Pollux are the celestial twins that form the constellation Gemini, in which the sun enters on 22 May. Its importance to this prophecy is firstly that it coincides with the uprising in Budapest, which began on 23 May. Secondly, *Castor and Pollux* are significant for their twinning identity, which is comparable to the twinning of Austria and Hungary—the 'Dual Monarchy', 'König und Kaiser' (King and Emperor).[5]

Adversaries in the tilt-yard
Disputes between the two parts of the Empire had begun as far back as 1867, with a disagreement over which of the two languages were to be used when commanding the different parts of the army units. Austria and Hungary therefore became *adversaries in the tilt-yard* concerning this question, which then broadened to further questions concerning national and military superiority. By 1906, the quarrelling had developed into a constitutional crisis, with Hungary's position recently strengthened by its nationalist coalition.

> (Law XII of 1867, para. 11) not only caused friction between Vienna and Budapest, but also occasioned increasingly acrimonious internal quarrels within Hungary about the nature and role of the army. The mutual antipathy, which existed between the Hungarians and the army [...], was the cause of continual conflicts which weakened the cohesion of the Dual Monarchy. [6]

The dispute was eventually resolved, but only with the dissolution of the twin monarchy in 1918, following the disastrous loss of life in the First World War.

Summary: *The political awakening of Hungary is now added, presciently, to the countries destined to exercise their presence on the world stage. The oracle outlines several major incidents in undeniable detail that resulted from Hungary's union with Austria. While this covers several decades, it also serves its purpose, since it is a prophecy primarily about a nation, rather than about the people who made the nation.*

91   *Soleil leuant vn grand feu l'on verra,*
      Bruit & clarté vers Aquilon tendant:
      Dedans le rond mort & cris lont orra
      Par glaive, feu, faim, mort les attendants.

92   *Feu couleur d'or du ciel en terre veu:*
      Frappé du hault, nay, fait cas merueilleux:
      Grand meurtre humain: pris du grand le nepueu,
      Morts d'expectacles eschappé l'orguilleux.

nay (OF nai) ship; expectacles (OF) 'espectative', to stand waiting: also 'spectacle', a public sight: also (L) 'expectatus' anxiously awaited;

          Fire, colour of gold from the sky seen on earth:
          Struck from a high place, a ship, an astonishing thing done:
          A great human murder: the nephew of the great man seized,
          Deaths from the public sight anxiously awaited, the arrogant one escaped.

The explosion of a nuclear device explains the first line and the first part of each remaining line.

93   *Bien pres du Tymbre presse la Libytine:*
      Vng peu deuant grand inundation:
      Le chef du nef prins, mis a sentine:
      Chasteau, palais en conflagration.

94   GRAN. *Po, grand mal pour Gauloys receura,*
      Vaine terreur au maritin Lyon:
      Peuple infini par le mer passera,
      Sans eschapper vn quart d'vn million.

Gran. (abbrev.) grandiose; Cross-references; Po, C.II: 33; C.III: 75; C.IV: 70; C.VI: 79; C.VIII:

          Grandiose (**NAPOLEON**) will accept a great wrong from the French,   1798
          Vain dread for the maritime Lion (**BRITAIN**):
          Innumerable people will cross by sea,
          A quarter of a million without escaping,

Po has previously been identified as Napoleon Bonaparte (see N° 33).

Grandiose Napoleon, will accept a great wrong from the French

Throughout the greater part of the summer of 1797, the victorious young general ruled his Italian conquests with an almost regal authority from the castle of Mombello [...] aided by Josephine, his adored if frivolous wife and a brilliant coterie of soldiers and scholars.[1]

While at Mombello, he received new instructions from Paris.

The Directory sent him ferocious instructions. "The Roman religion", they wrote, "will always be the irreconcilable enemy of the Republic; first by its essence, and next, because its servants and ministers will never forgive the blows which the Republic has aimed at the fortune and standing of some, and the prejudices and habits of others. The Directory requests you to do all that you deem possible, without rekindling the torch of fanaticism, to destroy the papal Government, either by putting Rome under some other power or" which would be still better "by establishing some form of self government which would render the yoke of the priests odious."[2]

The order Napoleon received conflicted with his much preferred option, which was to follow up his victory over the Austrians and pursue them to their capital, Vienna.

And so on 11 February 1798 General Berthier, who had succeeded Bonaparte as commander-in-chief, marched into Castel Sant' Angelo, billeting his officers in Roman palaces and his soldiers in Roman convents. The Pope's troops were disarmed, and several of his cardinals arrested. Others were expelled or deposed, while the Pope himself was abruptly informed on 17 February that he would have to leave Rome within three days. He was then eighty years old [...] and mortally ill.[3]

Pius VI died on 29 August 1799, after an extended journey ending at the citadel in Valence.

Vain dread for the maritime Lion

In October of the following year, the Directory gave Bonaparte a new command: he was to head the *Armée d'Angelterre* and make plans for the invasion of England. The oracle refers to Britain as 'the maritime lion', an expression uniting the nation's symbolic lion with its growing mastery at sea; something that was not at all obvious when this prediction was written.

Convinced that an invasion was soon to take place, Martello towers were constructed along the southeast coast of England, and the military were given preparatory training for the expected attack. Bonfires were also prepared on a chain of hilltops to signal the invasion when it came. But the dread of a forthcoming raid, and the precautions taken turned out to be in *vain;* the threat planned by the French was abandoned. Napoleon, after visiting the Channel ports on a tour of inspection, discovered that the French navy would be no match 'for the maritime lion'. He therefore abandoned his intended invasion of England, and instead, turned his attention towards Egypt and the Holy Land. [4]

Innumerable people will cross by sea

On 19 May 1798, at the head of a great fleet, Napoleon left Toulon bound for the eastern end of the Mediterranean. After setting sail, he was joined by even more ships from Corsica, Genoa and Civita Vecchia. His armada eventually numbered approximately 300 ships, with an estimated 55,000 men on board. Eight months later, he wrote to Sahib Tippoo Sultan at Seringapatam, informing him: "an innumerable and invincible army" had left France 'by sea' to liberate him from "the iron yoke of England." [5] [Refer also to Century One N°. 98]

A quarter of a million without escaping

A little more than a month after the French arrived in the East, there occurred one of the greatest disasters in France's naval history. On 1 August 1798, Horatio Nelson's squadron discovered the French ships anchored in Aboukir Bay. What followed was the annihilation of Napoleon's armada. "This terrible disaster [...] imprisoned Bonaparte in his conquest, without hope of escape." (Lefebvre). It would be two years before the estimated 30,000 men who survived Bonaparte's eastern venture were able to return to France.

Meanwhile, in France, itself, the absence of these soldiers caused General Jourdan to introduce a new *levée en masse* across the country, to replenish its armed forces. "The mass conscription [...] was expected to lead to the enlistment of 223,000 men." (Sydenham). In the summer of 1799, legislation was passed requiring all young men to register for military service. Under a previous law it had been possible for conscripts to escape military service by paying another to take their place. This was now forbidden and there would be 'no escape' for the expected 223,000 men who were to be called-up for service. [6] 220,000 conscripts, plus 30,000 men left stranded in Egypt (calculated to the nearest 10,000), meant that a 'quarter of a million' men were 'without escape' at the same time, for one reason or the other. [7]

Summary: *The structure of this oracle has been to predict several outstanding events that follow each other in chronological order. These can easily be identified, beginning with Napoleon's disappointment at not being able to pursue the Austrian army in retreat; the occupation of Rome and Bonaparte's aborted plan to invade England; the departure from France by a great army across the sea; and the subsequent loss of this fleet, which left the French without the means of returning home; and, finally, the conscription of young men in France to replace the army absent in the east.*

95   *Les lieux peuples seront inhabitables:*
        Pour champs auoir grande diuision:
        Regnes liurés a prudents incapables:
        Lors les grands frères mort & dissention.

96   *Flambeau ardent au ciel soir sera veu*
        Pres de la fin & principe du Rosne:
        Famine, glaiue: tard le secours pourueu,
        La Perse tourne enuahir Macedoine.

97   *Romain Pontife garde de t'approcher*
    De la cité qui deux fleuues arrouse,
    Ton sang viendras au pres de la cracher,
    Toy & les tiens quand fleurira la rose.

arouse (OF arouser) to wet, water gently; la (là) there;

    Roman Pontiff, take guard from drawing near
    The city, which two rivers water:
    You will arrive near there, spitting your blood,
    You and your companions when the rose will blossom.

The prophecy is too clear to be ambiguous. Reigning popes have made visits to cities that are watered by two rivers before now and returned safely. However, a time for this event has been ordained. It will not occur until the rose blossoms.

'The rose' is mentioned in two other quatrains. In Century Five, N°. 31, 'the rose' is described as a successor to the philosophers of Greece, whose time for worldwide prominence will coincide with what appears to be the subject matter of the present oracle. In some, as yet, unexplained manner, it appears to be saying that the fate of Greece will coincide with what takes place.

65 quatrains later, 'the rose' is given another quatrain. Again, this person is described as receiving world prominence at a time when blood is spilt publicly, thus linking it with the blood spilt by the pope and his entourage. But a further clue has been given to date it. It will occur when to speak the truth, one will have to keep a closed mouth. Does this refer to biblical truth or political truth? And why does the oracle refer to this person as 'the rose'? It is a flower adopted by the English as their national emblem, but it may instead be a play on a person's name.

The prophecy above is likely to be fulfilled by the one Sister Lucia recorded. Lucia was the eldest of three Portuguese children at Fatima who received an apparition of the virgin mother of Jesus in 1917. But it was only to Lucia that Mary gave a secret: one that was not to be revealed until a much later date. Known as the third secret of Fatima, this is an extract taken from it.

[T]he Holy Father passed through a big city half in ruins and half trembling with halting step, afflicted with pain and sorrow, he prayed for the souls of the corpses he met on his way; having reached the top of the mountain, on his knees at the foot of the big Cross, he was killed by a group of soldiers who fired bullets and arrows at him, and in the same way there died one after another the other Bishops, Priests, men and women Religious, and various lay people of different ranks and positions.

98   *Celuy du sang resperse le visaige,*
    De la victime proche sacrifiée:
    Tonant en Leo augure par presaige:
    Mis estre à mort lors pour la fiancée.

resperse (L respers/us from respargo) sprinkle over; proche (AF prochaine) next; Tonant (L) epithet of Jupiter also *syncope* – ton[n]ant; pour (OF) upon; fiancée (OF: fiance) assurance, confidence (A ma fiancé: - Upon my word)

    The one with the blood sprinkled over his face (**ROBESPIERRE**)   1794
    With the casualty sacrificed next,
    The Thunderer (**MAXIMILIEN**) inveighing in Leo, he augurs by presage.
    To be put to death at that time upon the assurance.

The one with the blood sprinkled over his face

The manner of this presentation carries with it an expectation that the subject is already known within these prophecies, and can be recognized by his blood-spattered face. It should therefore be recalled that in N°. 42 above, Robespierre was the 'tyrant' with the wound' for whom 'death is judged'. In his time, as dictator of France, it is estimated that he was responsible for guillotining 17,000 individuals: many of whom were totally innocent of any crime. [1]

His own life came to its timely close with *his face spattered by blood* when a gendarme named Charles-André Méda, having been sent to arrest him, shot at him, hitting him in the face: "the bullet struck Robespierre, passed through his cheek, and shattered his jaw." (Madelin). The next morning 'the incorruptible' was hauled before the court with a blood soaked bandage holding his shattered jaw in place. [2]

With the casualty sacrificed next

How perfectly ironic it was that Robespierre should have concluded his major speeches with the words: "I offer my personal sacrifice for the good of the patrie." Because, on 28 July 1794, he was allowed to do exactly what he said would do. After being found guilty upon recognition by the court, where he was hurriedly tried on the morning after the shooting, he was sentenced to immediate execution. [3] The 'sacrifice' was carried out that same evening.

Thunderer (Maximilien)

'Tonant' in Latin means, "Thunderer (epithet for Jupiter)". Jupiter, the Roman god for whom "the cult of Jupiter Optimus Maximus ('the best and greatest') began under the Etruscan kings.") [4] Consequently, Jupiter's cognomen, Maximus is the Latin version of Maximilien: Robespierre's first name. "Maximilian [...] is derived from the Latin word maximus." [5]

Inveighing in Leo, he augurs by presage

The French word 'tonnant' translates as 'inveighing against'. The word is therefore entirely relevant to the scenes that took place in the last week of July: coinciding with the Sun entering the star sign Leo (24 July – 23 August). "Robespierre was now having difficulties with his colleagues."

> He made up his mind to deliver a speech to the Convention in which he would clearly set forth his views and denounce all his enemies, all those 'perfidious rogues' who were responsible for the ills of the nation. [...] And on 26 July (8 Thermidor) he marched in to confront the deputies [...] He mounted the rostrum and remained there speaking for over two hours. [...] he characterized and anathematized his opponents on the Committees, referring in particular and unmistakably to Billaud-Varenne and Carnot. He attacked Fouché, Collot d'Herbois and Vadier as well as Jean Lambert Tallien [...] He castigated Tallien with particular vehemence before turning on all the deputies who had derided the Festival of the Supreme Being. He spoke darkly of purifying the Committee of Public Safety and dismissing the members of the Committee of General Security. He accused those responsible for military affairs of having dealings with the enemy, and Cambon of ruining the poor, depriving the people of national assets and disrupting the economy. [6]

Having inveighed against those responsible for obstructing his political aims, he concluded with the augur that presaged his end. "Let them prepare hemlock for me. I will wait for it on these sacred seats. I have promised to leave a formidable testament to the oppressors of the people. I bequeath to them truth... and death." [7]

To be put to death at that time, upon the assurance

One month earlier in June 1794, the Committee of Public Safety had passed Robespierre's 'law of 22 Prairial'. This was the law that finally brought down the legislator – 'hoist by his own petard'. What the law did was to hasten the process of execution, but it also threatened the safety of almost everyone.

> Defence lawyers were dispensed with; so were witnesses unless the 'formality' of calling them was considered 'necessary to discover accomplices' [...] The Tribunal was no longer required to interrogate the accused before their public trial, since this merely 'confused the conscience of the judges'; now, in the absence of positive proof, juries must be satisfied with 'moral proof'. [8]

As Couthon remarked, "For a citizen to become a suspect, it is sufficient that rumour accuses him." That is, 'to be put to death at that time, upon the assurance' given by another.

Summary: *The wound to the face suffered by Robespierre is accurately foreseen; as, too, is the speed with which he was tried and executed on the following day. Moreover, the zodiacal period of the year in which this would occur is correctly given together with Robespierre's forename, Maximilien, and the final inveighing that the oracle predicted would presage his end. Finally, the law of suspects, which had been passed by Robespierre, and under which he was, himself, condemned, is also foreseen.*

99   *Terroir Romain qu'interpretoit augure,*
      Par gent Gauloyse sera par trop vexée:
      Main nation Celtique craindra l'heure,
      Boreas, classe trop loing l'auoir poulsee.

100   *Dedans les isles si horrible tumulte,*
       Rien on n'orra qu'vne bellique brigue,
       Tant grand sera des predateurs l'insulte,
       Qu'on se viendra ranger à la grand ligue.

brigue (OF) canvass; predateurs (L praedator) predator; se venir (OF convenir – to agree, to admit;

Within the (**BRITISH**) Isles, such a terrible hubbub: 1914
Nothing one will hear without a warlike canvass,
So very great will be the insult of the predators (**YOUNG BOSNIA**),
That men will collect, setting to rights at the great **LEAGUE** (**OF NATIONS**).

Within the Isles, such a terrible hubbub

It was 28 June 1914, when Archduke Franz Ferdinand and his wife, Countess Sophie Chotek were assassinated. One month later, the major countries of Western Europe were at war. "Austria-Hungary declared war on Serbia on 28 July 1914. [...] Germany declared war on Russia on 1 August and on Russia's ally, France, on 3 August, invading Belgium on the same day as part of the Schlieffen Plan; Britain declared war on Germany on 4 August."

'Within the Isles', that is the British Isles, the onset of war caused 'such a terrible hubbub' that it seemed to act as a magnet: its ghastly fascination drawing to it the cream of youthful Britain.

> Five hundred thousand volunteered in the first month; and the recruitment rate ran at over one hundred thousand a month for eighteen months thereafter. Altogether, Great Britain raised more than three million volunteers. [...] Leading politicians stumped the country, winning popularity for themselves and implanting the passion of war in their audiences. [...] By such means, public feeling in England was brought to white heat. [1]

Nothing one will hear without a warlike canvass

"All over Europe conscripts were joining their units. Troop trains were rolling to their allotted destinations.

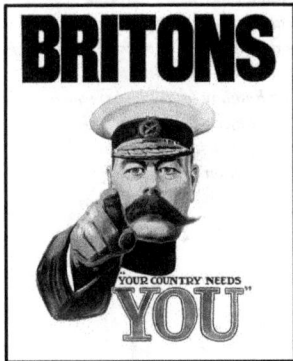

Crowds demonstrated enthusiastically in every capital, crying 'To Paris' or 'To Berlin'."

It was in Britain that the *warlike canvass* was most extreme. "Therefore the British talked, from the beginning, in idealistic terms. This was 'a war to end all wars'; 'to make the world safe for democracy'." Posters decorated the walls in every town and city as, "Fevered enthusiasm swept the land." Lord Kitchener's poster, with his forefinger pointing at every onlooker on every street corner: reminding them, with his imperious declaration, "Your country needs YOU." His call was answered by an ever-growing number of the young men it drew to the recruiting office. It is fair to say that most of those responding to this call to arms, believed the war would be over by Christmas: and very soon afterwards they would all be back at work, having given the Hun a bloody nose. [2]

So very great will be the insult

Having begun with a prediction of the preparations being made for war, the prophecy now moves to its cause, which was 'the very great insult' suffered by Austria-Hungary; to wit, the assassination in Sarajevo on 28 June 1914 of the future King of Hungary and Emperor of Austria, Archduke Franz Ferdinand. "It was more than a crime. It was a challenge to the position of Austria-Hungary as ruler of Bosnia; a challenge also to her prestige as a Great Power, which had been declining in recent years." [3]

Of the predators

The assassin was Gavrilo Princip, one of a group of seventeen young men calling themselves 'Young Bosnia' and with connections to a secret organization called the Black Hand. They had gone onto the streets of Sarajevo as 'predators', fully armed with the intention of seeking out and killing their quarry, Archduke Franz Ferdinand and his wife, who were visiting the city that day.

One member of the gang, upon encountering the Archduke as he rode by, attempted to shoot, but his pistol jammed. Another took aim, but was overcome with pity for the Countess Sophie Chotek, sitting beside her husband, and he went home instead. Another tossed a grenade, which was aimed to fall inside the Archduke's car. Instead, it hit the side, bounced off and exploded, injuring a number of bystanders.

It was Princip who dealt the fateful blow, although only by chance. The Archduke's car had taken a wrong turning. While reversing, the car stalled close to where Princip had just emerged from a café. Seizing the moment, the young man mounted the side of the car and shot dead both the Archduke and the Countess. [4] Austria immediately insisted that the Serbian government was behind the assassination, and on 23 July, it delivered an ultimatum to the country. Serbia refused to comply with the demands put to it. Five days later, a rebuffed Austria declared war on Serbia, thus precipitating the First World War.

That men will collect, setting to rights at the great League (of Nations)

After predicting the build-up to hostilities, followed closely by the cause of the war, the prophecy leaves the actual warfare to other quatrains. The final line is instead devoted to the formation of the League of Nations, which is aptly named 'the great league'.

This was set up in 1919 at Geneva, following the end of hostilities. After the terrible carnage of the Great War, countries finally agreed to collect together as an international body, believing this would guard against future national grievances and disputes becoming the cause of another deadly conflict, like that which had just ended. "The constitution of the League ('Covenant') was adopted by the Paris Peace Conference in April 1919 and written into each of the peace treaties." [5]

The eventual failure of the League of Nations is predicted in Century One, N°. 47.

Summary: *It is interesting to note that this, the final prophecy in the Second Century, concerns the outbreak of World War One, thus complementing the first prophecy of this particular chapter. The prophecy also strikes the right note with its description of the atmosphere in Britain during 1914, in which queues of men gathered outside enlistment offices right across the country, in answer to the politicians call to take up arms. This prophecy is also backed-up by describing the 'Young Bosnians' as predators, which they were, when seeking to kill Archduke Ferdinand during his visit to Sarajevo. And finally, there is the accurate foresight of a League of Nations, referred to as the 'great League', with the nations' representatives from each member country, collecting together with the intention of forestalling future conflicts from breaking out.*

References Century 2

Nº. 1

1   historylearningsite.co.uk/first_battle_of_the_marne.htm (last visited 14/3/2009); & Aquitaine, *Encyclopædia Britannica 2001:* CD-ROM

2   See battles fought under their respective names, *Encyclopædia Britannica 2001:* CD-ROM

3   A.J.P. Taylor, *The First World War – An Illustrated History,* 140, 191; & Neil Demarco, *Britain and the Great War,* 11

4   Dardanelles, *Encyclopædia Britannica 2001:* CD-ROM

5   R Ernest Dupuy and Trevor N Dupuy, *An Encyclopedia of Military History,* 953-4

Nº. 6

1   Friedrich, 2-3 (see commentary) and Norman Davies, *Europe – A History,* 1026–7, & auschwitz-muzeum.oswiecim.pl/new/index. (Last visited 20 Oct. 2006)

2   Copyright ©1999-2006 Auschwitz-Birkenau State Museum, Poland; refer: http://www.auschwitz-muzeum.oswiecim.pl/new/index. (Last visited 20 Oct. 2006)

3   Ibid & I.C.B. Dear (ed.) *The Oxford Companion to the Second World War,* 78; & *What's On TV* (8- 14 January, 2005), 29

4   Auschwitz, *Compton's Encyclopedia 2000:* CD-ROM; & Derrik Mercer (ed.) *Chronicle of the Second World War,* 601

5   Mercer, 601

6   Dear, 369

7   Bible, 2 *Chronicles*: 20: 6-9; & *Psalm*: 119: 24-27; & K. Armstrong, *A History of God,* 430

Nº. 7

1   Voltaire, *The Age of Louis XIV* (trans. Martyn P. Pollack)

2   Ibid

3   John B. Wolf, *Louis XIV,* 5

4   Ian Littlewood, *The Rough Guide Chronicle - France,* 168

5   Neil Grant, *Kings and Queens:* 192

6   wikipedia.org/wiki/Invitation_to_William

7   Wolf, 277

Nº. 19

1   John Ardagh, *France Today,* 290, 292

2   Ibid 293

3   Ibid 295

4   *The Guardian*: Saturday October 27, 2001

5   Ibid

6   Giles Foden, *The Guardian,* Saturday September 4, 1999

7   Ardagh, 200, 202, 205

Nº. 20

1   www.jewishvirtuallibrary.org/jsource/Holocaust/occmap.html

2   http://www.theholocaustexplained.org/ks3/life-in-nazi-occupied-europe/jews-in-occupied-countries/which-countries-did-the-nazi-occupy/#.VcmfprWrGPE

3   http://www.ushmm.org/wlc/en/article.php?ModuleId=10005143

4   theholocaustexplained.org/ks3/the-final-solution/auschwitz-birkenau/transport-and-arrival/#.Urlk3fv-Img

5   history1900s.about.com/od/holocaust/a/auschwitz.htm

6   Y.R. Kamalipour, Theresa Carilli (1998). Media Stereotypes of Jews. *Cultural Diversity and the U.S. Media.* 99–110

7   answers.yahoo.com/question/index?qid=20110723163722AAV5igu

8   en.wikipedia.org/wiki/Josef_Mengele

9   about.com/od/holocaust/a/auschwitz.htm

Nº. 24

1   en.wikipedia.org/wiki/Tiger_I]

2   John Keegan (ed.) *Encyclopedia of World War II,* 194-5, 235

3   en.wikipedia.org/wiki/Panther_tank

4   The Western Front, *Encyclopædia Britannica 2001:* CD-ROM; & J.A. Kossmann-Putto and E.H. Kossmann, *The Low Countries,* 53

5   Derrik Mercer (ed.) *20th Century Day By Day,* 533; & Alan Palmer, *Dictionary of Twentieth Century History: 1900-1982,* 33; & Peter Furtado, *World War II 1939 – 1945,* 29

6   Ibid 98

7   The Invasion of the Low Countries, *Encyclopædia Britannica 2001:* CD-ROM; & Alan Palmer, *Dictionary of Modern History 1789-1945,* 188

Nº. 28

1   Daily Express, 24 July 2006: 7.

2   independent.co.uk/news/people/profiles/mohamed-alfayed-the-outsider-396133.html

3   Guardian, Keith Allen: 7 May 2011

4   Daily Star, 5 October 2013: 5

Nº. 33

1   David Chandler, *The Campaigns of Napoleon,* 105

2 wikipedia.org/wiki/Mantua
3 Chandler, 121
4 wikipedia.org/wiki/Order_of_battle_at_the_Battle_of_the_Nile
5 River Garonne, *Encyclopædia Britannica 2001*: CD-ROM; & M.J. Sydenham, *The First French Republic 1789-1804*; & 20 August 1799 - Haute-Garonne - Jean Favier (ed.) *Chronicle of the French Revolution*
6 Genoa, *Encyclopædia Britannica 2001*: CD-ROM; & André Masséna, Ibid; & Chandler, 271, 274, 285
7 wikipedia.org/wiki/André_Masséna

N⁰. 42

1 Marcel Liebman, *The Russian Revolution* (trans. Arnold J. Pomerans), 142
2 Christopher Hibbert, *The French Revolution*, 246, 248; & Simon Schama, *Citizens*, 836
3 Louis Madelin, *The French Revolution*, 430; & Hibbert, 266-7
4 Hibbert, 267
5 Schama, 845-6
6 Franklin L. Ford, *Europe 1780-1830*, 126; & Schama, 845, 846

N⁰. 43

1 wikipedia.org/wiki/World_War_I
2 Ibid
3 wikipedia.org/wiki/German_strategic_bombing_during_World_War_I
4 Ibid
5 feem-project.net/water2adapt/files/W2A_Flood-events_eng.pdf
6 Gregory S. Aldrete, *Floods of the Tiber in Ancient Rome*, pps 56, 65
7 Taylor, A.J.P. *The First World War – An Illustrated History*, 95-6

N⁰. .51

1 William H. Mountague, *A New and Universal History of England*, – Vol. II, 180–1; & Ronald Hutton, *Charles II*, 249
2 Mountague, 181
3 John Bedford, *London's Burning* (quoting from Samuel Pepys Diary)
4 *The Diary of Samuel Pepys*, Vol. II: (ed.) R.C. Latham and W. Mathews, xi
5 *The New Caxton Encyclopedia*; & Royal Mint 'A New Britannia for 2005'
6 *2 Kings* Ch.18, v 4; *2 Chronicles* Ch. 14, v 3; etc. and H.A.L. Fisher, *A History of Europe*, 676
7 Fisher, 676

N⁰.53

1 John E.N. Hearsey, *London and the Great Fire*.
2 William H. Mountague, *A New and Universal History of England*, - Vol. II, 181
3 Robert Gray, *A History of London*, 168
4 Mountague, 154
5 Ibid 158; and J.G. Muddiman, *Trial of King Charles The First*, 129
6 Muddiman, 129 and the *New Caxton Encyclopedia*; & Royal Mint, *A New Britannia for 2005*
7 Mountague, 158
8 Godfrey Davies, *The Early Stuarts 1603-1660 (2nd edition)*, 159

N⁰. 59

1 Christopher Lloyd, Sea Fights Under Sail, 1970 47
2 H.A.L. Fisher, A History of Europe, 672-3
3 E.N. Williams, Dictionary of English and European History 1485-1789: 98
4 Ian Littlewood, Rough Guide Chronicle France: 159
5 wikipedia.org/wiki/History_of_the_Royal_Navy#Expansion_of_the_fighting_force.2C_1642.E2.80.931689
6 Lloyd. 50-51
7 Ian Dunlop, Louis XIV, 1999   395
8 Voltaire, The Age of Louis XIV, Vol. XII – Chapter XX.
9 Nearly Everything About The Aude, Languedoc, France (Yahoo)
10 John A. Lynn, The French Wars 1667 – 1714 67
11 Ibid. 30 - 32

N⁰. 67

1 David Chandler, *The Campaigns of Napoleon*, 55
2 Ibid 206–7; & H.A.L. Fisher, *A History of Europe*, 912
3 wikipedia.org/wiki/Coup_of_18_Fructidor
4 Fructidor, year V (Sept. 4, 1797), *Encyclopædia Britannica 2001*: CD-ROM
5 wikipedia.org/wiki/Coup_of_18_Fructidor
6 Fisher, 912

N⁰.68

1 William H. Mountague, *A New and Universal History of England*, Vol. II, 156
2 H.A.L. Fisher, *A History of Europe*, 667
3 Mountague, 176
4 Ibid 184
5 Ian Wilson, *Nostradamus The Evidence*, 333-34

N⁰. 76

1   Alan Palmer, *An Encyclopaedia of Napoleon's Europe*, 55; & David Chandler, *The Campaigns of Napoleon*, 822; &
    A.J. B.F. Bourgogne, *The Memoirs of Sergeant Bourgogne*, 59-60
2   J.F. Bernard, *Talleyrand - A Biography*, 251; & Chandler, 309
3   Talleyrand, during consulate and empire, *Encyclopædia Britannica 2001:* CD-ROM
4   Franklin L. Ford, *Europe 1780 – 1830*, 260–1; & Simon Schama, *Citizens*, 482–3
5   Bernard, 292–4

N⁰. 88

1   R.J. Knecht, *Catherine de' Medici*, 101
2   Ibid. 107-8; 217
3   E.N. Williams, *Dictionary of English and European History 1485-1789*, 14
4   Ibid 170-1
5   Ibid 170-1
6   A. Pettegree, *Europe in the Sixteenth Century*, 217–9
7   Williams, 85, 169
8   Knecht, 167
9   Ibid 170
10 Knecht, 106
11 L'Estoile, *Mémoires pour servir à l'histoire de France*: vol ii: 2

N⁰. 90

1   Hungary, *Encyclopædia Britannica 2001:* CD-ROM
2   Ibid
3   Jörg K Hoensch, *A History of Modern Hungary 1867 – 1994* (trans. Kim Traynor) 53, 70
4   Ibid 71, 73; & Derrik Mercer (ed.) *20th Century Day by Day*, 165
5   Francis Joseph – the Hungarian Compromise and the Dual Monarchy, *Encyclopædia Britannica 2001:* CD-ROM
6   Hoensch, 50-1

N⁰. 94

1   David Chandler, *The Campaignsof Napoleon*, 206
2   http://home.newadvent.org/cathen/10687a.htm
3   Thompson, 81; & Ford, 155-6; & Christopher Hibbert, *Rome The Biography of a City*, 233
4   General Sir James Marshall-Cornwall, *Napoleon As Military Commander*, 80; & Ford, 245
5   Marshall-Cornwall, 82, 89, quoting from Correspondence de Napoléon Ier 3901; & Chandler, 213
6   Thompson, 122; & Georges Lefebvre, *The French Revolution From 1793–1799* (trans. John Hall Stewart and James
    Friguglietti), 220; & M.J. Sydenham, *The First French Republic 1792-1804*, 187, 200
7   Sydenham, 201; & Chandler, 245

N⁰. 98

1   H.A.L. Fisher, *A History of Europe*, 904; & Stanley Loomis, *Du Barry*, 254; & Louis Madelin *The French Revolution*,
    430; & Simon Schama, *Citizens*, 792
2   Madelin, 430
3   Christopher Hibbert, *The French Revolution*, 267–8
4   *Encyclopedia of World Mythology*, 2006, 58
5   *An A-Z of baby names*, Sywell, 2006, 78
6   Hibbert, 259-60
7   Ibid 260
8   Id. 245-6

N⁰. 100

1   Alan Palmer, *Dictionary of Twentieth-Century History 1900-1982*, 401; & A.J.P. Taylor, *The First World War*, 53-6
2   Taylor, 22-3
3   Ibid 14
4   Wikipedia, 'Princip'
5   Palmer, 233-4

CENTURY THREE

1   *Apres combat & bataille nauale,*
       Le grand Neptune à son plus haut beffroy
       Rouge auersaire de fraieur viendra pasle,
       Mettant le grand ocean en effroy.

2   *Le diuin verbe donrra à la sustance*
       Comprins ciel terre, or occult au fait mystique
       Corps, ame, esprit aiant toute puissance,
       Tant sous ses pieds, comme au siege celique.

donrra (*syncope* donnerra); sustance (*syncope*) substance; occult (OF) concealed; mystique (OF) sacred; fait (OF) action; celique; (OF) celestial, heavenly; siege (OF) seat, throne.

> The divine word will bestow to the substance:
> Heaven and earth understood, gold concealed by the sacred action,
> Body, soul, spirit having total power,
> As much under one's feet, as if at the heavenly throne.

The 'divine word' is mentioned in Century Two, N°. 27, where it appears to refer to the actual person relaying the scriptural information. The same two words reappear in Century Four N°. 5 and again in Century Seven N°. 36. There is also a further connexion in Century Two N°. 13. It cannot, however, escape notice that the oracle appears to be confirming not just the existence of the world, but also that of heaven as a divine act of conscious perception. This world and the next are therefore parallel worlds composed of sense data. Consequently, heaven is as real (if not more real) than the world we inhabit. But it has been prepared only for those who accept Jesus as Lord. Whence, it follows that each world perceived by the mind is a world in which the Word of God has created substance, in the form of mental concepts for the conscious minds perceiving it.

A time is therefore expected, according to this prophecy, when both heaven and earth will be understood as a logical reality. And gold, the focus of attention for worldly pursuits, will be regarded as being no different from any other material, in that it exists because it is perceived to exist, and were there no minds to perceive it, then it would not exist at all.

In many respects, the Prolegomena preceding these 'Centuries' has prepared the way for this prophecy. The power of the mind is the power of spirit and soul, directing a body that interacts with the world perceived to exist——be it this one or the next. A time will therefore arrive when all this will become an acknowledged fact, and the cause of peace to the Cross.

3   *Mars & Mercure & the argent ioint ensemble*
       Vers le midi extreme siccité:
       Au fond d'Asie on dira terre tremble,
       Corinthe, Ephese lors en perplexité.

4   *Quand seront proches le defaut des lunaires,*
       De l'vn a l'autre ne distant grandement,
       Froid, siccité, danger vers les frontieres,
       Mesmes ou l'oracle a prins commencement.

5   *Pres, loing defaut de deux grand luminaires*
       Qui suruiendra entre l'Auril & Mars.
       O quell cherté! mais deux grands debonaires,
       Par terre & mer secourront toutes pars.

6   *Dans temples clos le foudre y entrera.*
       Les citadins dedans leurs forts greués:
       Cheuaux, bœufs, hommes. L'onde mur touchera,
       Par faim, soif sous les plus foibles arnés.

arner (AF) éreinter

7   Les fuitiss, feu du ciel sus les piques:
        Conflit prochain des corbeaux s'esbatans,
        De terre on crie aide secour celiques,
        Quand pres des murs seront les combatans

8   Les Cimbres ioints auecques leurs voisins,
        Depopuler viendront presque l'Hespaigne:
        Gents amassés Guienne & Limosins
        Seront en ligue, & leur feront compaignie.

9   Bourdeaux, Rouen & la Rochele ioints
        Tiendront au tour la grand mer oceane:
        Anglois, Bretons & les Flamans conioints,
        Les chasseront iusques au-pres de Roane.

10   De sang & faim plus grande calamité
        Sept fois s'apreste à la marine plage,
        Monech de faim, lieu prins, captiuité,
        Le grand mené croc en ferrée caige.

11   Les armes batre au ciel longue saison,
        L'arbre au milieu de la cité tumbé:
        Vermine, rongne, glaiue en face tyson,
        Lors le monarque d' Hadrie succombé.

12   Par la tumeur de Heb. Po, Tag. Timbre & Rosne
        Et par l'estang Leman & Aretin,
        Les deux grans chefs & cites de Garonne
        Prins, morts, noies. Partir humain butin.

13   Par foudre en l'arche or & argent fondu:
        Des deux captifs l'vn l'autre mangera:
        De la cité le plus grand estendu,
        Quand submergée la classe nagera.

14   Par le rameau du vaillant personage
        De France infime: par le pere infelice
        Honneurs, richesses trauail en son viel aage
        Pour auoir creu le conseil d'homme nice.

15   Cueur, vigueur, gloire le regne changera
        De tous points contre aiant son aduersaire.
        Lors France enfance par mort subiuguera.
        Le grand regent sera lors plus contraire.

cueur (OF) heart, mind, courage; contre (OF) in opposition; aiant (OF ayant) being.

Heart, vigour, glory; the reign will change,   1715
At all points, his adversary being in opposition.
In that time through death, France will subdue a childhood (**LOUIS XV**).
The great regent (**PHILIPPE**) at that time will be very contrary.

Heart, vigour, glory

In his Memoirs, Louis XIV wrote — "In my heart I prefer fame above all else. [...] Love of glory has the same subtleties as the most tender passions. [...]" In fact, Louis XIV — "pursued his gloire, with such concentration that it became an even more fundamental theme of French policy."[1] To this, one may add the report made by John de Witt, the Sun King's Dutch adversary — "a twenty-six year-old king, vigorous of body and spirit, who knows his own mind and acts on his own authority."[2] With just three words: *heart, vigour, glory,* the oracle has identified the character of Louis XIV, as admitted by both the King and his contemporaries.

The reign will change

In 1715, Louis XIV, the Great Monarch, died and the *reign changed.* "After the experience of his reign, there was a general determination never to be treated in the same manner again, and the Regency opened in a mood of full-scale reaction." Moreover, the Sun King's death had come at a time when France was suffering financial difficulties, and these were set to continue.

> [An] intense social crisis caused by the burden of taxation [...] almost twenty-five years of war was finally concluded by a state of mutual exhaustion. [...] [The] remainder of the eighteenth century [...] was to be characterised by economic and demographic recovery, and long periods of internal peace and order. [3]

At all points, his adversary being in opposition

Louis XIV had left precise instructions in his will for a Council of Regency to rule France during his great-grandson's minority. But Philippe, duc d'Orléans, *his adversary* while he lived, continued to oppose him after his death: especially with his opinions *differing at all points* in the government of the country. His first action was to remove the duc de Maine and the Comte de Toulouse from the Council (both appointed by the former King) so that he alone could be Regent. [4]

Secondly, the groups representing Louis XIV had been, "the Sword, the Parlements and the Jansenists." D'Orléans opposed all three. And, "In 1720 he was forced to exile the Paris Parlement to Pontoise. [...] He [also] insisted on enforcing the papal Bull Unigenitus (1713) against the Jansenists." Thirdly, in 1718, he dissolved the *Polysynodie*, through which he had originally sought to give the nobility of the Sword a role in government. [5]

In that time through death, France will subdue a childhood

It had been *through* the *deaths* of his grandfather, his parents, and his only surviving brother that five-year-old Louis XV became King of France. [6] With so many recent deaths in the royal family, and he being the last in the bloodline, the country took the utmost care to ensure that the little boy reached manhood safely. Because of this, *his childhood was subdued.*

> He had been brought up by obsequious courtiers, subject to tedious and rigid ceremonies. He ate in public, watched in worshipful silence by those who had the privilege of entering his presence. He rose and went to bed accompanied by elaborate ceremonies and disputes among nobles as to which duke had the right to hold his shirt, which the candlestick. [...] The boy became silent and withdrawn, increasingly moody and sullen. [7]

The great regent at that time will be very contrary

Philippe, duc d'Orléans, a nephew of Louis XIV was *the great regent.* He was also the only male to have occupied the position of regent since these prophecies were written. Catherine de Medici had acted as Queen-regent on several occasions for two of her sons; firstly, Charles IX, and then Henri III during the time he was King of Poland. Marie de Medici was also regent during the minority of her son, Louis XIII. And Anne of Austria was regent from the time when Louis XIV was five years of age up until the death of her advisor, Cardinal Mazarin in 1661. After which, there was only one further regent, a male. Hence, this prophecy can only be for Philippe duc d'Orléans.

But Philippe was a flawed character. "His irreverence, habitual drunkenness, and licentious behaviour had earned him an unsavoury reputation." Nevertheless, he possessed ambition and political acumen. In the wake of Louis XIV's death, he made plans for the succession of his own dynasty, should his young charge die prematurely.

> On 2 September, the Duke of Orleans went to meet the *parlementaires* in the *Grand-Chambre du Parlement* in Paris in order to have Louis XIV's will annulled and his previous right to the regency restored. [...] Philippe disapproved of the hypocrisy of Louis XIV's reign and opposed censorship, ordering the reprinting of books banned during the reign of his uncle. Reversing his uncle's policies again, Philippe formed an alliance with England, Austria, and the Netherlands, and fought a successful war against Spain that established the conditions of a European peace. [8]

This was viewed as *very contrary* to the previous policies adopted by Louis XIV, who had engaged in many wars and maintained a tight control over the State, seeing himself as its embodiment.

Summary: *The death of Louis XIV, identified by words that encapsulate the manner in which he portrayed himself, is*
followed by the transition that took place in the way the country was ruled afterwards, and which has been
aptly predicted within this oracle. The only male regent to have ruled in France since the publication of
these prophecies is also described by precisely the characteristics that identify Philippe duc d'Orléans, regent
to Louis XV. Added to which, the subdued manner in which the King was nurtured during his childhood is
also foresee as part of the prophecy.

16   *Le prince Anglois Mars à son cueur de ciel,*
Voudra poursuiure sa fortune prospere
Des deux duelles l'vn percera le fiel:
Hay de lui, bien-aymé de sa mere.

Mars, god of war; cueur, (OF) heart, thought, affection; duelle (L duell\um) hostility;

The prince, English, warlike, with his affection for the sky,   20**?
He will want to go on with his thriving fortune:
Of two hostilities, one will pierce the gall:
Detestation for him: well loved by his mother.

Of the two English princes, William and Harry, both have pilot licences, but it is William that the first line might appear to indicate, since he became employed as a full-time pilot with the Search and Rescue Force. Nevertheless, the presence of Mars in the prophecy, the god of war, would be more appropriate to Harry, since he trained for an army life at the Sandhurst Military Academy, and eventually as a tank commander. In 2007-2008, he even took part in the Afghan War, The Prince then turned to flying, and in May 2010, he was awarded his flying 'wings', having passed the test to fly helicopters. In 2011, it was announced that he had now passed the test to fly Apache attack helicopters. "It was reported that Prince Harry was said to be a natural pilot who was reportedly top of his class in the extensive training he had undertaken at the Naval Air Facility, El Centro, California." (*The Daily Telegraph* (UK). 19 October 2011.) In 2012 Prince Harry returned to Afghanistan, serving with the Army Air Corps as co-pilot and gunner in Apache helicopters.

Prince Harry has also gained a reputation for taking a less than serious attitude to his leisure hours. From being caught smoking cannabis to emerging bleary eyed in the early hours of the morning from night clubs to being photographed in a naked romp with a female in Las Vegas. These have all contributed to what could be meant by the second line of this prophecy.

Beyond this, the third line of prophecy remains unfulfilled. The 'piercing of the gall' need not be taken literally. It could simply presage some event that will cause the prince deep bitterness.

Finally, Princess Diana's love for Harry was well publicised during her brief lifetime, "and [she] would privately describe him to friends as 'good king Harry'." (*Daily Mail,* 28 February 2015, p. 5).

17   *Mont Auentine brusler nuit sera veu:*
Le ciel obscur tout à vn coup en Flandres,
Quand le monarque chassera son nepueu:
Leurs gens d'Eglise commetront les esclandres.

18   *Apres la pluie laict assés longuete,*
En plusieurs lieux de Reins le ciel touché:
Helas quel meurtre de seng pres d'eux s'appreste,
Peres & filz rois n'oseront aprocher.

'Helas quell meurtre' in Bonhomme appears as 'O quell conflit' in other first editions.

19   *En Luques sang & laict viendra plouuoir:*
Vn peu deuant changement de preteur,
Grand peste & guerre, faim & soif fera voyr
Loing, ou mourra leur prince recteur.

20   *Par les contrées du grand fleuue Bethique,*
Loing d'Ibere, au regne de Granade,
Croix repoussées par gens Mahumetiques,
Vn de Cordube trahira la contrade.

contrade (Provençal) country

21   *Au crustamin par mer Hadriatique*
       Apparoistra vn horride poisson,
       De face humaine, & la fin aquatique,
       Qui se prendra dehors de l'ameçon.

22   *Six iours l'assaut deuant cité donné:*
       Liurée sera forte & aspre bataille:
       Trois la rendront & à eux pardonné,
       Le reste a feu & sang tranche traille.

23   *Si France passes outre mer lygustique,*
       Tu te verras en isles & mers enclose:
       Mahommet contraire: plus mer Hadriatique:
       Cheuaux & d'asnes tu rougeras les os.

24   *De l'entreprinse grande confusion,*
       Perte de gens, thresor innumerable:
       Tu n'y dois faire encore extension
       France a mon dire fais que sois recordable.

25   *Qui au royaume Nauarrois paruiendra,*
       Quand de Secile & naples seront ioints:
       Bigorre & Landes par Foyx Loron tiendra,
       D'vn qui d'Hespaigne sera par trop conioint.

parvenir (AF atteindre le but) attain the end; ioint (AF — joint: élégant) stylish; Loron (aphaeresis - Oloron;)

He who will attain his end to the Navarrese Kingdom (**HENRI IV**),   1594
When for Sicily and Naples they will be stylish:
He will hold Bigorre and Landes by reason of Foyx, Oloron,
From one (**MAYENNE**), who, with Spain, will be too much conjoined.

He who will attain his end to the Navarrese Kingdom

At the time this prophecy was published, Navarre was still a kingdom ruled over by Queen Jeanne d'Albret (1555 – 1572). She was succeeded by her son, who became Henri III of Navarre. Seventeen years later, he would fight to win the throne of France, following the assassination of his cousin, Henri III, by Jacques Clément (see Century One N°. 97).

Henri of Navarre's path to the French throne was not an easy one. Much of France had remained Catholic during the Wars of Religion, and Henri was a Protestant. To become king, he first had to defeat the main Catholic contender, the Duke of Mayenne. This was achieved at the battle of Arques in 1589: and again at Ivry, in 1590. But it was not until Paris opened its gates to him in 1594, following his coronation at Chartres and his conversion to the Catholic faith, that Henri III of 'the Navarrese Kingdom attained his end' by becoming Henri IV of France.

When for Sicily and Naples they will be stylish

The word *ioint* has the potential to be what translators call a false friend. In old French the word was spelt *ioinct*, and meant 'united' or 'joined'. *Ioint*, on the other hand was an adjective from the ancient French language that meant, in modern French, stylish. And it is this which the Seer had in mind when predicting the Baroque era, which began in Italy during the reign of Henri IV. Baroque is described as –

> ... a period of artistic style that used exaggerated motion and clear, easily interpreted detail to produce drama, tension, exuberance, and grandeur in sculpture, painting, architecture, literature, dance, and music. The style began around 1600 in Rome, Italy and spread to most of Europe. [1]

The year 1600 was the midpoint of Henri IV's reign (1589 – 1610), and it provides a connexion between the two cities mentioned in the oracle. Naples was then part of the Spanish Empire, and the Baroque style had made a major impact on the city, as observed by two of Spain's viceroys.

> [T]he most important of these viceroys was Pedro Alvarez de Toledo, who was responsible for considerable social, economic and urban reforms in the city. [...] By the 17th century, Naples had

become Europe's 2nd-largest city – second only to London – and the largest European Mediterranean city, with around 250,000 inhabitants. The city was a major cultural centre during the Baroque era. [2]

Historically, "Conflict between the Hohenstaufen house and the Papacy in 1266 led to Pope Innocent IV crowning the French prince Charles, count of Anjou and Provence, as the king of both Sicily and Naples." [3]

After a brief rule by the French, who were defeated at the battle of Garigliano, the city was "Won by the Spanish in 1504, Naples and Sicily were [thereafter] ruled by viceroys for two centuries." [4]

As noted above, the period dating from the reign of Henri IV embraced the Baroque period, with *Naples* at the centre of this cultural movement. The Neapolitan city's union with Sicily was therefore conducive to the spread of this artistic style.

He will hold Bigorre and Landes by reason of Foix, Oloron

The place names mentioned in the oracle are situated in the southern part of France, close to its borders with Spain and Navarre. The latter was, at the time, an independent kingdom situated on both sides of the French border with Spain. Geographically, "Béarn [where Henri IV was born] is bordered by Basque provinces Soule and Lower Navarre to the west, by Gascony (Landes and Armagnac) to the north, by Bigorre to the east, and by Spain (Aragon) to the south." [5] [Author's emphasis]

Historically, "In the eastern part of the province are two small exclaves belonging to Bigorre. They are the result of how early Béarn grew to its traditional boundaries: some old lesser viscounties were added by marriage, and absorbed into Béarn: Oloron to the south/southwest ca. 1050." [6]

The county of Foix is also named in the prophecy. "When Catherine, wife of Jean d'Albret, succeeded her brother Francis Phoebus, the House of Foix-Grailly was merged into that of Albret, and later into that of Bourbon with Henry III of Navarre, son of Antoine de Bourbon and Jeanne d'Albret." [7]

The point which the oracle is making by referring to these regions is that when Henri IV becomes King of France, he will unite his realm to the place names in the prediction.

Henry III of Navarre became King Henry IV of France in 1589. In 1607, he united to the French crown his personal fiefs that were under French sovereignty (i.e. County of Foix, Bigorre, Quatre Vallées, and Nébouzan, but not Béarn and Lower Navarre, which were sovereign countries outside of the kingdom of France), and so the county of Foix became part of the royal domain. [8]

From one, who with Spain, will be too much conjoined

This subheading identifies Charles Duke of Mayenne who opposed Henri IV's claim to the throne by seeking help from Spain. After the murder of Henri III in 1589, Mayenne tried to prevent Henri of Navarre taking the crown by waging war against him, but he was defeated at Arques. "In 1590 Mayenne received additions to his army from the Spanish Netherlands, and took the field again, only to suffer complete defeat at Ivry (14 March 1590)." [9]

Henri IV then began besieging Paris, which was the centre of activity against his reign, on account of his Protestant religion. But, "with the assistance of Alexander Farnese, Duke of Parma, sent by Philip II of Spain, [Mayenne] raised the siege of Paris, which was about to surrender to Henry IV." [10]

Mayenne's next move occurred in 1593, when "he summoned the States-General to Paris and placed before them the claims of the Infanta." [11] This was Isabella Clara Eugenia of Spain, the daughter of Elisabeth of Valois and a granddaughter of Henri II of France. But Mayenne's proposals were rejected for two reasons. Firstly, France recognized the Salic law, which forbade women a seat on the French throne. Secondly, France feared the ambitions of Philip II. Mayenne was therefore forced into seeking an agreement with Henri IV: after which, he ceased to oppose him.

Summary: *The names listed in this remarkable prophecy enable the correct period for its fulfilment to be identified. What adds to its prophetic content is the fact that the oracle also predicts the Baroque style which commenced during the reign of Henri IV. Names of people and places, dates of events, appropriate signs in the heavens have already provided evidence of prophetic veracity; they now have added to them the timing device of when a particular culture began. The prophecy concludes by identifying the Duke of Mayenne's reliance upon Spain in his bid to prevent Henri IV becoming King of France.*

26   *Des roys & princes dresseront simulacres,*
        Augures, creuz esteués aruspices:
        Corne, victime d'orée, & d'azur, d'acre,
        Interpretés seront extispices.

27   *Prince Lybyque puissant en Occident,*
        Francois d'Arabe viendra tant enflammer:
        Scauans aux letres sera condescendent,
        La langue Arabe Francois translater.

puissant (OF) powerful, wealthy.

A Libyan potentate, powerful in the West (**GADAFFI**),   2011
He will come to enflame so many, French with Arab:
Cunning with the letters, he will be condescending,
The Arabian tongue translating French.

A Libyan potentate

Muammar al-Gadaffi was born in Libya in 1942. He subsequently became leader of his country following a *coup d'état* in 1969, when he removed King Idris from power to become his successor. Thereafter, he remained in control of the country for the next forty-two years.

Taking power in a 1969 coup d'état, he ruled as Revolutionary Chairman of the Libyan Arab Republic from 1969 to 1977 and then as the "Brother Leader" of the Great Socialist People's Libyan Arab Jamahiriya from 1977 to 2011.[1]

Powerful in the West

Libyan leader Colonel Gadaffi [...] with the country's oil income estimated at $1 billion a week, no other dictator so cannily combined such stupendous wealth with the implied threat of terror to turn Western powers into cowed appeasers.[2]

Gadaffi's control of the country's oil supplies ensured Libya of its wealth, and its importance to the West's energy supply. For many years amiable relations were maintained between Gadaffi and Western politicians.

He will come to enflame so many, French with Arab

The Libyan Civil War or Libyan Revolution, which began in March 2011, was fought between those supporting Gadaffi and those fighting to remove him from office. The protests rapidly escalated into a rebellion that spread across the country, This uprising by the Libyan people, and the brutal way in which Gaddafi used tanks and air power to suppress and kill his own people, not only enflamed those demanding political reform and more freedom, but also brought in outsiders that included both the French and several Arab states.

It was the French that first announced their country's recognition of the National Libyan Council as the legitimate government of Libya. And France was also the first foreign power to enforce the No-Fly Zone over the country. Furthermore, France also provided its aircraft carrier, General De Gaulle, to assist NATO forces who were helping the rebel army to depose Gadaffi. To enforce this, Mirage 2000 and Rafale warplanes were flown out from Corsica and Southern France to carry out raids on Gadaffi's loyalists.

Countries in The Arab League, who were also 'enflamed' by Gaddafi, joined in the demand for a No-Fly Zone to be introduced for the protection of Libya's citizens. Several states including Kuwait, Qatar and Bahrain then came forward to offer their country's facilities to the U.S. for an invasion of Libya.

Cunning with the letters, he will be condescending

After the fall of its capital, Tripoli, in August 2011, the rebel army fighting for the NTC (National Transition Council) discovered letters secretly sent by Gaddafi in a desperate bid to save his regime. In a three-page letter to Barack Obama, in which he called the US President "our son" and "Excellency", and making a point of using Obama's middle name, Hussein, he implored the President not to wage war against his small country, which was still developing. Gaddafi also used flattery, calling Obama a man of courage, able to annul a wrong, and with a willingness to serve world peace. Another letter sent to Dennis Kucinich, a Democratic congressman who voted against the NATO attack on Libya, contained an invitation for him to visit Tripoli on a "peace mission", with all expenses paid. Kucinich confirmed he had received several such requests. [3]

The Arabian tongue translating French

The final line of this prophecy foresees the end of the Libyan uprising. On 1 September 2011, sixty world leaders, including Hilary Clinton and David Cameron, gathered together at the Elysée Palace (President Sarkozy's government headquarters in Paris), to meet the Libyan head of the NTC, Mustafa Abdel Jalil—hence, *the Arabian tongue translating French*. There, they discussed with him how to help rebuild Libya. As a result of this meeting, on 16 September, "the National Transitional Council was recognised by the United Nations as the legal representative of Libya, replacing the Gadaffi government." [4] Gadaffi, was killed on 20 October, while attempting to flee the country. Three days later, "The National Transitional Council 'declared the liberation of Libya' and the official end of the war on 23 October 2011." [5]

Summary: *Before Colonel Gadaffi made his appearance in Libya, no previous commentator appears to have offered a solution to this prophecy. The emergence of Gadaffi, his power and influence in the West, brought about by his oil-rich country, combined with his antagonism towards the French and several Arab states, places him as the subject of this oracle. And when Libya came under attack, causing him to write condescending letters of appeal to several correspondents, including the President of the USA, it is extremely unlikely that history will ever repeat itself in quite the same way again. The final line, which is typical of the word games played by the seer at the close of a prophecy, was fulfilled, as stated,*

28   *De terre foible & pauure parentele,*
       Par bout & paix paruiendra dans l'empire.
       Long temps regner vne ieune femele,
       Qu'oncq, en regne n'en survint vn si pire.

parentelle (OF) kindred; bout (OF bouté) thrust; paix (OF) peace, quiet, accord, parvenir (AF atteindre le but); survint (past historic of survenir appear; pire (AF moindre) least; 'en regne' (anagram & paragram – e[i] [u]egne) Eugenie

       From feeble estate and poor kindred,   1853
       By thrusting forward and accord, she will attain her purpose in the Empire:
       Long time reigning, a young female,
       That one time in the reign (**EUGENIE**), never within had one so least appeared.

This prophecy foretells the rise of the Empress Eugenie. From an impoverished background she emerged to become the wife of an Emperor and, for a time, the ruler of France.

From feeble estate and poor kindred

Eugenie's father was Don Cipriano de Guzmán y Palafax y Portocarrero, Count of Teba. Despite this impressive title, and an ancestry that went back to the Visigoth kings, "he inherited very little." Soon after Eugenie's birth, he came close to ruin. This was because of his earlier support for a Liberal revolt, for which he was placed under house arrest at his 'little estate' at 12 Calle de Garcia in Granada. His wife, Doña Maria Manuela Kirkpatrick de Closeburn was the daughter of a Scottish fruit merchant who had taken up residence in Spain, but thereafter had become bankrupt. Eugenie's biographer explains how: "Cipriano made his children wear the same linen dresses winter and summer and would not buy them silk stockings for parties. Nor would he keep a carriage." [1]

By thrusting forward and accord

Napoleon III, France's popular new ruler, and Europe's most eligible bachelor might yet be won—so thought Eugenie's mother. With her title derived from her husband's position in the Spanish nobility, "Doña Maria Manuela immediately set about obtaining invitations to the Prince President's official receptions at the Elysée and Saint-Cloud, and found no difficulty in doing so."

Napoleon had met Eugenie before. In the summer of 1849, he had attempted to seduce her, following a private dinner party arranged for that purpose. Mother and daughter were offended, and left France soon afterwards. Reconciliation with Napoleon after an absence of three years was quickly accomplished, and it allowed Eugénie to play her role to perfection, and a fondness began to develop between the two. Napoleon had now discovered that his new found friend was intelligent in conversation, politically astute, and attentive to his wishes: except when it came to compromising her position by agreeing to become his mistress. The Prince President began to be aroused by a quite unexpected passion for this young woman. Very soon, his thoughts began to contemplate marriage. [2]

She will attain her aim in the empire

It was not long before news of Napoleon's intentions became more widely known. The British Ambassador, Lord Cowley reported to London: "[Eugénie] has played her game with him so well, that he can get her in no other way but marriage, and it is to gratify his passions that he marries her." On the day before the civil wedding, Cowley again "informed London that the emperor 'has been captured by an adventuress'." The civil marriage took place in the royal palace of the Tuileries on 29 January 1853. Next day it was solemnized in the Cathedral of Notre Dame. Eugenie had '*attained her aim in the Empire*'. She was now Empress of the French. [3]

Long time reigning, a young female

"From 1853 to 1870 Eugénie de Montijo was Empress of the French, sharing the Second Empire with her husband Napoleon III." She therefore *reigned* as Empress for seventeen years. Three times during the Emperor's absence she was appointed Regent (1859, 1865, and 1870), possessing absolute power and "chairing the Council of Ministers once a week [...] besides receiving copies of reports on internal and external affairs." Her control of the government at the time France was facing defeat in the war against Prussia was acclaimed by all: for which, it was said, "The Second Empire belonged as much to her as it did to him (Napoleon III)." [4]

Eugenie was 26 years-of-age when she became Empress, having been born on 28 May 1826. [5]

That one time in the reign (Eugenie), never within had one so least appeared

This subheading aptly describes the Empress. Ever since the reign of France began, the country has been placed, albeit temporarily, in the hands of just a few women, who acted as regents. Catherine de' Medici was an Italian noblewoman, daughter of Lorenzo II and widow of Henri II; she was regent to Charles IX. Marie de Medici was the daughter of Joanna, Archduchess of Austria and the Grand Duke of Tuscany. After the death of her husband, Henri IV, she became regent to Louis XIII. Anne of Austria was the daughter of King Philip III of Spain and Portugal. After the death of Louis XIII, she became regent to their son Louis XIV.

By comparison, the Empress Eugenie's birth was of very little significance. Yet she reigned as regent on three separate occasions: even sharing the reign of the Second Empire with her husband. As predicted in the oracle, never before within the reign of France had a female with so meagre a birthright been given such a powerful role.

Summary: *The identity of Empress Eugenie is clearly predicted in this quatrain. Her poor kindred, yet the manner in which she approached her courtship of Napoleon III, enabled her to develop a love affair between them, which fulfils this prophecy perfectly. Added to which, her youth and her long reign as Empress, adds further confirmation to the truth already contained within the oracle. There is also the fact, as predicted, that no woman from such a low estate had ever before become regent of France.*

29   *Les deux nepueus en diuers lieux nourris:*
        Nauale pugne, terre, peres tumbés
        Viendront si haut esleués enguerris
        Venger l'iniure: ennemis succombés.

30   *Celuy qu'en luite & fer au fait bellique,*
      Aura porté plus grand que lui le pris,
      De nuit au lit six lui feront la pique,
      Nud sans harnois subit sera surpris.

luite (AF lutte) contest; fer (AF arme) weapon; pris (OF) honour; pique (OF) quarrel, grudge; subit (OF) swift, quick, hasty;

The one that in contest and weapon at the martial act (**MONTGOMERY**):   1574
Will have taken the honour greater than he (**HENRI II**)
At night in bed, six will take the grudge to him;
Swiftly he will be surprised naked, without armour.

The one that in contest and weapon at the martial act

This verse begins with a recognizable description of Count Montgomery's victory over Henri II in the summer of 1559. The event took place *in a contest* held to celebrate the marriages of the King's daughter Elisabeth, and his sister, Marguerite. It was during a joust – *the martial act* – between the King and Montgomery that the young challenger's lance shattered on impact. The jagged splinters pierced the King's visor; fatally wounding him. (Century One N°. 35 predicts this incident in some detail).

Will have taken the honour greater than he

Montgomery is therefore *the one* who *will have taken the honour* for defeating his opponent; that is, King Henri II: a man *greater than he*.[1] Before he died, he King absolved Montgomery of any blame. But, not so his widow: Catherine de Medici, bore a grudge against the young count that contradicted all reason. "Montgomery had to be punished. [...] Filled with hatred for the man who had 'killed' her husband, it became her obsession that he should be brought to justice for his 'regicide'."[2]

At night in bed, six will take the grudge to him

After the accident, Montgomery wisely left France to spend time in voluntary exile, eventually settling in England, where he studied theology before converting to the Protestant faith. While in England, Catherine de Medici requested his extradition from Queen Elizabeth, but this was denied her. After the passage of some fourteen years, although not without event, he judged it safe to return to France. His intention was to join the Protestant cause in the French Wars of Religion, and in this he began with several early victories. It was while defending the medieval fortress at Domfront, with its walls several metres thick and well able to withstand an attack that he found himself outnumbered and besieged by Marshall Matignon.

15,000 Royalist (and more significantly Catholic) troops laid siege to 110 Protestant rebels holding the fortress of Domfront. The rebel leader Count Gabriel de Montgomery withstood the assault until treacherously captured in the early hours of May 26th.[3]

His betrayal came at night, in bed, when, "Unarmed, Montgomery was captured in his bedchamber after a traitor had opened the gates during the night to the Royalist troops."[4] Balthazar Guynaud, equerry and governor of the pages in the King's chamber, and who dedicated his History and Concordance of Henri III to Louis XIV, described the capture of Montgomery. "He was arrested in his castle at Domfront, during the night of 27 May 1574, by six noblemen of the Royal Army, from the number of whom, were the knights of Matignon, of Fervaques and of Vassé."[5]

Guynaud also explained that it was carried out "under an express order of Catherine de Medici."[6]

Swiftly he will be surprised, naked without armour

Montgomery's capture, while asleep in bed (*naked and without armour*) was both swift and surprising. The reason for surprise arose because he had previously agreed terms with Matignon that he and his men would vacate the castle (presumably with dignity in full armour), and by doing so, "the capitulation was guaranteeing him a safe life."[7]

One day after receiving news of Montgomery's arrest, Charles IX died, having previously and conveniently signed an approval that his mother should act as Regent, until Henri III arrived from Poland to take the crown. On 3rd June, three days after the death of Charles IX, the Paris *Parlement* ratified Catherine's new powers as regent. Three weeks later, armed with the executive power that went with her position as ruler of France, she ordered Montgomery's trial to commence. "On 26 June 1574, as he was about to be beheaded, Montgomery was informed that a royal edict had proclaimed that his property would be confiscated and his children deprived of their titles." [8] On 27 June 1574, he "was decapitated and écartelé (quartered)." [9] The rectangular cage lying on the floor of the Conciergerie in Paris can still be seen, where Montgomery was confined until his execution.

Summary: *This prophecy identifies the Count of Montgomery by reference to his victory over the King in the lists. It correctly follows this by foreseeing, in some detail, his betrayal at night, leading to his capture in bed. The revenge exercised by Catherine de Medici can be seen as the driving force behind his arrest at Domfront, and his subsequent trial and execution in Paris.*

31   Aux champs de Mede, d'Arabe & d'Armenie,
     Deux grands copies trois foys s'assembleront:
     Pres du riuage d'Araxes la mesnie,
     Du grand Solman en terre tomberont.

32   Le grand sepulchre du peuple Aquitanique
     S'aprochera aupres de la Tousquane,
     Quand Mars sera pres du coing Germanique,
     Et au terroir de la gent Mantuane.

33   En la cité ou le loup entrera,
     Bien pres de là les ennemis seront:
     Copie estrange grand païs gastera.
     Aux murs & Alpes les amis passeront.

34   Quand le defaut du soleil lors sera,
     Sus le plain iour le monstre sera veu:
     Tout autrement on l'interpretera.
     Cherté n'a garde: nul n'y aura pourueu.

35   Du plus profond de l'Occident d'Europe,
     De pouures gens vn ieune enfant naistra,
     Qui par sa langue seduira grande troupe:
     Son bruit au regne d'Orient plus croistra.

36   Enseueli non mort apopletique
     Sera trouue auoir les mains mangées:
     Quand la cité damnera l'heretique,
     Qu'auoit leurs loys si leur sembloit changées.

37   Auant l'assaut oraison prononcée:
     Milan prins d'aigle par embusches deceuz:
     Muraille antique par canons enfoncée,
     Par feu & sang à mercy peu receuz.

prononcer (OF) to deliver openly; deceu (OF) beguiled; Cross-reference Aigle: C.I: 23; C.IV: 70; C.VIII: 4; C.VIII: 46

Before the assault, a speech is delivered openly: 1796
Milan taken by the Eagle (**NAPOLEON**) beguiled by ambushes:
The ancient high wall forced open by cannons,
By fire and blood, with little mercy received.

The Eagle, as a cognomen for Napoleon, has already become part of these oracles. It first appeared in Century One N°. 23, which predicted the battle of Waterloo: at other times, Napoleon is called 'Po' or the 'crop head'.

Before the assault, a speech is delivered openly

Napoleon's first appointment of command began with an inspirational speech delivered to his ragged and dispirited army in Nice, before embarking upon the assault against Milan.

Soldiers! You are hungry and naked; the government owes you much but can give you nothing. The patience and courage, which you have displayed among these rocks, are admirable; but they bring you no glory - not a glimmer falls upon you. I will lead you into the most fertile plains on earth. Rich provinces and opulent towns will be in your power, and in them you will find honour, glory and wealth. Soldiers of Italy, will you be lacking in courage or steadfastness? [1]

Milan taken by the Eagle (Napoleon)

Within a matter of weeks this same ragged army had become the new conquerors of Italy, entering Milan on 15 May 1796.

The eagle was to become a symbol of Napoleon's power. Eagles were subsequently given to the commanders of his Imperial Army. An eagle with outstretched talons was also placed on the wall above the emperor's desk at his residence in the Château de Malmaison, and a cast of the bird was made for his sceptre. It was while directing his first campaign in Italy that we learn how "The young eagle had found his wings; the future lay with Destiny." [2]

Beguiled by ambushes

Napoleon's entry into Italy was later explained to have been successful through the early use of ambushes. Colonel Thomas Graham, a British officer attached to the 90th Foot, and an observer of Napoleon's campaign at the time, wrote an account of the practice and its success, which he included in his biography.

> Some French sharpshooters, concealed by the bushes at the edge of the river [...] kept up a very constant and annoying fire on the fine regiment of Kehl (three battalions).[...] 150 men killed and wounded was the consequence. [3]

The ancient high wall

The success of *the 'Eagle's'* entry into Milan was nevertheless incomplete. This was because the retreating Austrian army had left behind a detachment of troops. They had firmly established themselves behind the high wall of the city's ancient citadel, the *Castello Sforzesco*: built in the fifteenth century by Francesco Sforza. Unable to dislodge the besieged Austrians, the main body of Napoleon's army left Milan in pursuit of General Beaulieu, who had retreated to Mantua.

Forced open by cannons

It was while in Tuscany that the French army had the good fortune to capture some cannons from Fort Urban. Napoleon realised these cannons would assist Marshal Sérurier's assault on Mantua, "but first the guns were sent to Milan to enforce the capitulation of the castello." On 29 June 1796, the strategy succeeded. The castle was finally forced open by the newly arrived cannons, and the Austrian garrison, besieged since Beaulieu's departure, surrendered their position. [4]

By fire and blood, with little mercy received

Soon after Napoleon had led the main part of his army out of Milan, opposition to the French occupation began to gather force inside the city, and the people's unrest quickly spread to the towns and villages outside the city. Within a short time, the authority established by Bonaparte had almost completely disappeared.

Upon discovering this lapse in command, Bonaparte lost no time in re-establishing his authority. He also decided to teach the people a lesson in brutality. The village of Binasco was punished by setting it on fire and its men folk shot. [5] In Pavia, soldiers of the French army were given free rein to loot, rape and destroy at leisure; "many innocent townsfolk died in the process," *with little mercy received.* [6]

Summary: *Napoleon's first Italian campaign, which began with an opening speech, afterwards led to the capture of Milan. This is correctly foreseen, as too is his identity as the Eagle. The resistance inside the Castello, which was eventually overcome by cannons, and the strategic use of ambushes, before Milan fell, are correctly predicted as part of the conquest. Also, the villages that joined in the revolt against the French are identified by the punishments they received.*

> 38   *La gent Gauloise & nation estrange*
>   *Outre les monts, morts prins & profligés:*
>   *Au mois contraire & proche de vendange*
>   *Par les seigneurs en accord rediges.*

> 39   *Les sept en trois mis en concorde*
>   *Pour subiuguer des alpes Apennines:*
>   *Mais la tempeste & Ligure couarde*
>   *Les profligent en subites ruines.*

tempeste (AF combat violent) violent combat; Ligure (*epenthesis* – Ligue); couade (OF) dastardly, cowardly; profligent (L proflig\o) destroy.

> The seven into three had been placed in harmony   1576
> For the subduing of the Alps and Apennines:
> But the violent combat and **THE LEAGUE**, dastardly,
> Destroying them in sudden ruin.

We have already met the seven children of Henri II and Catherine de' Medici in Century One Nº. 10. After the deaths of four of their number, there occurred much friction and distrust among the remaining three. As a result of this increasing disunity between her three children, the Queen-mother, Catherine de Medici, set about accomplishing a peaceful reunion by bringing her two sons together for a meeting. The result of her diplomacy was the treaty of the *Peace of Monsieur*. But, it was achieved only at the expense of a compromise. Which is to say, as so often happens when helping one side in a disagreement, it aggravates the other side.

The seven into three
By 1575, *the seven* children of Henri II and Catherine de' Medici—those that had survived into adulthood were reduced *to three;*[1] they were Henri III, King of France, his younger brother Hercule-François, Duke of Alençon and Marguerite Queen of Navarre: also called Margot.
Alençon not only hated his brother Henri, but had even plotted to take the crown for himself. Henri, in turn, detested his sister Margot. This dysfunctional situation worsened in 1576 when Margot's husband, Henri of Navarre, escaped from the close supervision imposed upon him at court. As a result, Margot was arrested as an accomplice. For some time afterwards she feared the King would take advantage of her captivity, and have her murdered.

Had been be placed in harmony
It was to heal these family wounds that their mother stepped in with a remedy. The state was disintegrating fast. If the nation and the Valois dynasty were to be saved, then the King must act; he must make peace with his brother. On 6 May 1576, an agreement between the two brothers was reached, and the *Peace of Beaulieu*, also known as the *Peace of Monsieur* was signed. Six months later, the two brothers met at a country manor called Ollainville, where they, "kissed and embraced each other," agreeing to put aside their differences.[2]
In June of the following year, to complete this contrived harmony between the Queen-mother's three surviving children; Margot agreed to join her two brothers at Chenonceaux for a banquet that had been arranged by their mother to celebrate Alençon's military success at La Charité-sur-Loire. We shall read more of this victory further down.

For the subduing
In 1576, the year that coincided with the reconciliation between the brothers and their sister, an attempt was made, based upon this new concord, *for the subduing* of the conflicts that were dividing France through its wars of religion – Calvinism versus Catholicism.
The plan relied for its success upon the treaty Henri III and his brother d'Alençon had just signed up to. But included on the document were sixty-three articles, some contentious, that gave Huguenots an assurance of virtual parity with Catholics. The treaty also condemned the St. Bartholomew's Day Massacre as a criminal act.[3] It was not popular with the Catholics.

Of the Alps and Apennines

Particular notice is drawn to the two mountain ranges referred to in this oracle. Each one is an allegorical reference to the rock-hard centre for the religion it supported. *The Savoy Alps* overlook Geneva, [4] where John Calvin had established his base for the Protestant revolt against Rome, and which eventually led to France's thirty-six years of intermittent religious warfare. *The Apennines,* which stretch through central Italy and include the Umbrian-Marchigian range, is from where the river Tiber flows into Rome, the heart of the Catholic religion. [5]

The attempt at brokering a peaceful solution between these two rock-hard, religious factions failed. The Catholics saw it as being too favourable to the Huguenots, and in 1576, they made known their displeasure by forming the Holy Catholic League. Its intention was to draw members of the Roman Church together under the leadership of the powerful duc de Guise. He was to act as a rallying point for the recruitment of men, arms, and money in an effort to encourage allegiance to the Catholic Church in France. In fact, it acted as a trigger for the Sixth War of Religion (March – December 1577). [6]

But the violent combat

On 2 May, in the midst of this new outbreak of religious warfare, the Huguenot town of Charité-sur-Loire became the scene of *violent combat* when it was overrun by the Dukes of Nevers and Anjou. (N.B. After the reconciliation between Henri III and his brother, Alençon was given the ducal title Anjou. See Century Two N°. 88). It was for the conquest of this town, by her youngest son, that the Queen-mother arranged a banquet at Chenonceaux, which Margot was invited to attend to complete the unity between her three remaining children.

With Charité-sur-Loire in the League's hands, Anjou had demanded that all Huguenots should be executed. But the duc de Guise intervened to prevent the massacre. Anjou therefore turned his attention to another Protestant town, Issoire in the Auvergne.

And the League dastardly, destroying them in sudden ruin

On 12 June, Issoire, amidst further violent combat, was forced to surrender to Anjou's Catholic army, now part of *the League*. Again, Anjou demanded the deaths of all Huguenots. But there was no one now to deny him his bloodlust. And, while *destroying them,* he also reduced the town to *sudden ruin*. In all, some three thousand citizens were murdered. [7]

Anjou's murderous onslaught was particularly *dastardly*, because his victims shared the same religious beliefs that only a few months previously he had willingly accepted as his own. After fleeing the court, during his fratricidal hatred for his brother, d'Alençon (as he was then) had joined the Huguenots at Dreux to support their religiously inspired martial efforts.

Summary: *The events predicted were fulfilled a decade after the seer's death. Nevertheless, in 1566, the Queen-mother still had six children alive. Consequently, there is implicit within this oracle the prescient knowledge that three of those surviving would die before the events predicted became fulfilled. In the event, Elisabeth, whose marriage had been celebrated at the tournament in which her father, Henri II, was killed, died from a miscarriage in 1568. Charles IX died from tuberculosis on 30 May 1574, one day after his mother learned that she could exact her revenge against the Count of Montgomery, if she became Regent of France before her other son returned from Poland as Henri III. And Claude de Valois died from childbirth on 21 February 1575. The disunity existing between the three surviving Valois offspring is historical record, and it occurred during the French Wars of Religion. The Queen-mother's attempt at reconciliation is correctly foretold; as, too, is the violent conflict that erupted afterwards, in which several Protestant towns suffered ruin: and at Issoire, there was a massacre.*

40   *Le grand theatre se viendra redresser:*
     Le dez geté, & les rets ia tendus.
     Trop le premier en glaz viendra lasser,
     Par arcs prostraits de longtemps ia fendus.

41   Bosseu sera esleu par le conseil,
*   Plus hideux monstre en terre n'aperceu.*
*   Le coup volant prelat creuera l'œil:*
*   Le traistre au roy pour fidele receu.*

conseil (OF) council;

A hunchback will be elected by the (**PRIVY**) **COUNCIL**,   1561
A more hideous monster on earth was not perceived (**CONDÉ**).
The prelate, the flying blow will pierce the eye,
The traitor (**COLIGNY**) to the King (**CHARLES IX**) received as for a faithful friend.

A hunchback

Louis de Bourbon, Prince of Condé was *a hunchback*.[1] He was also the leader of the Protestant religion in France; that is to say, he was a *Prelate* as well as the commander of the Huguenot army. After his conversion to Protestantism, he became involved in a plot to kidnap the young King, Francis II, and overturn the power of the Duke of Guise. The conspiracy failed, and many Huguenots were arrested and executed. Condé was also arrested and sentenced to death.

Will be elected by the council

It was, however, precisely his opposition to the duc de Guise that Catherine de Medici, the Queen-mother, required, to help combat the duke's political ambitions. Consequently, after she had first pardoned the Prince for his treason against her recently deceased son, Francis II, she next arranged for Condé to be *elected by the Conseil Privé*, with its seat on the King's Council (August 1561). After his acceptance, he was granted the governorship of Picardy.[2]

A more hideous monster on earth was not perceived

Despite retaining his affiliation to the Protestant religion, Condé continued to lead a licentious lifestyle, which he coupled with political ambition.[3] The Seer clearly disliked this deformed, duplicitous man, as is evident from this prophecy. It was also a sentiment shared by Condé's Calvinist supporters, for they subsequently denounced their leader as one who had sold his principles in return for political privileges. "Calvin condemned Condé as a 'wretch who, in his vanity, had betrayed his God.'"[4] Nevertheless, it was in this revived new government role that Condé took an active part in the Wars of Religion, although never for reasons of conscience. Instead, it was because he believed himself to be the rightful regent of France during Charles IX's minority. Condé was, in fact, the leading adult prince of the French blood royal. And it was with this position in mind that he took up arms in the Second War of Religion.

The prelate, the flying blow will pierce the eye

It was while fighting at the battle of Jarnac (13 March 1569) in the Third War of Religion – a conflict, which proved to be the bloodiest of them all – that Condé was captured.
The King's brother, the duc d'Anjou, had joined the battlefield that day, and to the credit of, Marshal Gaspard de Tavannes's surprise cavalry charge, it helped Anjou win a splendid victory against the Huguenot army. With Condé having also been made a prisoner-of-war, Anjou decided the opportunity had arrived to rid himself of this detestable man.
After first parading Condé before his victorious army, tied to the back of an ass that he might be ridiculed, Anjou confided to his chief guard, Montesquioi that the prisoner should not survive captivity. In obedience to orders, while crossing the River Charente, Montesquioi fired his pistol at Condé's head, with the bullet—*the flying blow*[5] – "exiting from his right eye."[6] The Seer has also acknowledged Condé's position in the Protestant religion by referring to him as a 'prelate', since he was head of the Protestant Church in France.

The traitor to the King

The oracle's final line turns to Condé's successor as the new head of the Huguenots, This was Gaspard de Châtillon Comte de Coligny: a man who, for the past ten years, had fought against the Catholic armies of Charles IX; that is to say, he had been *a traitor to the King*.[7] He also fought at Jarnac, but escaped captivity. But in 1571, in pursuit of peace, and in an attempt to end the religious wars, Charles IX and the Queen-mother invited Coligny to return to Court.

Received as for a faithful friend

After receiving their assurances for his safety, the new Huguenot leader accepted the King's invitation, and lost little time in winning the affection of this fatherless monarch. That is to say, the King *received* Coligny *as a faithful friend*, even to the extent of calling him "Mon Père."[8]

Summary: This prophecy began to be fulfilled five years before the death of its author, but it had also appeared in print six years before then. Condé, the hunchback, was generally disliked by everyone it would seem. The seer detested him; the Catholics fought against him, and even Calvin, the leading spirit behind the Protestant movement, reviled him. Catherine de Medici, for her own political reasons, appointed him to her council. Interestingly, as a hunchback, Condé ran the risk of being recognized when these prophecies were first published. However, when he was sentenced to death for treason, interest in him as the subject of this quatrain would have faded. His predicted murder, followed by his replacement - a one-time enemy of the King, - is foretold in language that indicates the same man will also become a 'faithful friend' to the monarch. Both Coligny and Condé fulfilled their respective parts of this oracle to the letter.

42   l'enfant naistra à deux dents à la gorge
        Pierres en Tuscie par pluie tomberont:
        Peu d'ans apres ne sera bled, ne orge.
        Pour saouler ceux qui de faim failliront.

Pierre (Peter, the first Pope); Tuscie (L Tusc\us; i.e., Etruscan) Tuscany; par (AF égal) alike; peu (AF past participle of 'paistre' - repu, bien nourri.) well nourished; Cross-reference: born with two teeth, Century 2: 7

The infant will be born with two teeth in his mouth (**LOUIS XIV**):   1638
Peters in Tuscany will fall down like rain:
Well fed for years, afterwards there will be no corn, no barley
For repleting those who will be failing from famine.

The infant will be born with two teeth in his mouth

The birth [of Louis XIV 5 September 1638] took place at twenty-two minutes past eleven on Sunday morning. The child was a big, well-formed boy, weighing forty-eight marks – nine pounds. [...] Louis [XIII] [...] came up immediately to the bedroom. [...] Then Dame Péronne, midwife in charge, handed him his son and proudly pointed out that the child had been born with two teeth. [1]

Peters in Tuscany will fall down like rain

Reference to the state of Tuscany, with its boundary extending to the north of the Tiber implies that *Pierres* should be interpreted as 'popes', for Rome was the city formerly occupied by the Etruscan people, and it was they who laid the cultural foundations upon which the Eternal City grew and prospered. [2]

Pierre (French for Peter, and Petros in Greek, meaning 'a rock') has biblical connotations: refer Matthew 16: 18. Popes are all called 'Peters'; they take this name from Peter the fisherman: Jesus's apostle, whom he likened to the rock on which he built his Church.

Throughout the life of Louis XIV – he became king at the age of four – no less than nine popes occupied the seat of St. Peter; they were, Urban VIII, Innocent X, Alexander VII, Clement IX, Clement X, Innocent XI, Alexander VIII, Innocent XII and Clement XI. [3] The dark humour of the Seer can therefore be discerned in the second line of this verse, 'Peters falling down like rain'. It implies that a long life lay ahead for the *child born with two teeth* (Louis XIV died four days short of his seventy-seventh birthday).

By likening the fall of these popes to the fall of rain, the oracle is able to use the analogy to form a connexion to rainfall. During the kingship of Louis XIV, there was a particularly disastrous season of wet weather, followed by freezing conditions, which caused a widespread famine. This became the cause of a great number of deaths, especially among the aged and infirm.

Well fed for years

For most of Louis' time in power, perhaps with one exception, France enjoyed good harvests, and *for years* his people were sufficiently well fed to occasion no complaint. But towards the end of his reign the situation dramatically changed.

Afterwards there will be no corn, no barley

In 1709, the Great Winter occurred causing the harvests to fail. The frosts arrived early in October 1708, but it was during a brief respite in the first week of January 1709 that the countryside became saturated, with France undergoing a period of seemingly incessant rainfall. Then, immediately after the rain had stopped, the land was covered by a heavy frost, which instantly froze the rainwater into the ground, thereby vastly exacerbating the problems that were to come. It also heralded the beginning of what was to become the harshest winter on record, and it arrived with a severity that continued unabated until the middle of March. [4]

With no corn for bread, and no barley for brewing beer: a staple drink at that time, and the yield everywhere withering in the rock-hard ground, many thousands of people across France died: if not from hunger, then from hypothermia.

For repleting those who will be failing from famine

In response to the famine, the French *Parlement* introduced emergency legislation, accompanied by levies to help cope with the crisis. Even the King was required to contribute—a situation without precedent. With the revenue collected, grain was able to be purchased from abroad, and granaries were set up across the country, run by government officials, specifically '*for repleting those*' whose lives were '*failing from famine*'. [5]

Summary: Louis XIV is again introduced as the infant born with two teeth, thus setting the scene for what follows.
             This time it is a cryptic allusion to the longevity of his reign, indicated by the number of popes that would
             reign during his sovereignty. It is also predicted that his subjects would be 'well nourished' under his rule
             except for one occasion. That one occasion was the Great Winter of 1709, which froze the ground so hard
             that the harvest failed and there was widespread famine across the land. See Century 6 No. 2 for the year.

43   *Gents d'alentour de Tarn, Loth, & Garonne,*
         Gardés les monts Apennines passer,
         Vostre tombeau pres de Rome & d'Anconne
         Le noir poil crespe fera trophée dresser.

44   *Quand l'animal à l'homme domestique*
         Apres grands peines & faults viendra parler:
         Le foudre à vierge sera si maleficque,
         De terre prinse, & suspendue en l'air.

peine (OF): pain, labour, toil; venir (OF) to happen; suspendue (OF) discharged;

When the animal domestic to man,   ca. 1620
After great toil & errors will happen to speak,
The thunderbolt by the maiden will be so harmful:
Taken from the ground & discharged into the air.

When the animal domestic to man

The oracle is referring to a dog: but not a quadruped. It is the Seer's cryptic manner of using a familiar word to conceal a hidden meaning. This quatrain is actually a prediction of the Doglock Musket. The American colonies contain references to doglocks in records kept of their armouries during the French and Indian War, and all the way up to the eve of the American Revolution. [1]

> Much like the later flintlock devices, it contained the flint, frizzen, and pan, yet had an external catch as a half-cock safety, known as the "dog". This type of lock had no internal, half-cock loading position as the later flintlock mechanism contained. To load a firearm with a dog lock, the cock was secured with the external dog, preventing it from moving forward to strike the frizzen and begin the firing sequence. The user could then safely load the musket or pistol. To fire, the cock was moved to the full-cock position, which caused the dog to fall backward and no longer prevent the lock from firing. A pull of the trigger would then fire the piece. [2]

After great toil and errors will happen to speak

Muskets were muzzle loaded, and the process was very slow. First, powder was dropped down the barrel and tapped down with a scouring stick (a wooden rod, later to be called a ramrod). Then the lead ball would be dropped down, and if there was time wadding of some kind would be added to hold it in place. This would ideally be rammed down to ensure the best range. [3]

The musket was used during the English Civil War (1642–1651) in which the soldiers in Cromwell's Model Army were shown nine pictures of the steps required to load and prepare their muskets for firing.

In wet or windy weather the priming powder might not ignite, and sometimes even if it did there would be 'a flash in the pan' which would not set off the main charge. Ungainly soldiers might forget to remove their ramrods and fire them off. And it was not uncommon for a man whose musket failed to function to believe, in the chaos of battle, that it had in fact fired, and to set about reloading.
A subsequent ignition would be likely to blow the weapon to pieces. [4]

A well drilled soldier could fire his musket – in the cryptic language of the oracle, make it speak – at the rate of three shots per minute.

The thunderbolt by the maiden

The explosion from the musket, when it is fired, produces what the prophecy refers to as a thunderbolt. There is also a reference to the musket as a 'maiden'. In barrack room jargon, this attribution is derived from the use of the ramrod, which is inserted into the barrel of the musket.

Will be so harmful

By 1700, the doglock had evolved into a beautiful and sleek arm unique to the English. While flintlocks without dog catches started to surface at this time, the doglock would have been one of the principal English weapons in Marlborough's army when he defeated the French at the Battles of Blenheim in 1704, Ramillies in 1706, Oudenaarde in 1708, and Malplaquet in 1709. [5]

Taken from the ground and discharged into the air

In this final line of prophecy, the seer refers to the cause of the musket's explosive force as having been 'taken from the ground'. He is referring to gunpowder, which is made from a mixture of saltpetre (literally in Latin, sal petrae – the salt of rock) carbon and sulphur: all of which can be *taken from the ground*. Hence, when the '*dog*' is released and the trigger pulled, the musket ball is *discharged into the air*.

Summary: *This prophecy is really one for the physicists. Their practical minds are now presented with the invention of the Doglock Musket, first used circa 1620, but described in a book of prophecies published in 1555. It is further evidence, that Relativity theory, in which both past and future are coeval, and the Wheeler-DeWitt equation in which time has no place in the universe, have reached a valid conclusion, for which evidence is now replete. We really do live in a block universe.*

45   *Les cinq estranges entrés dedans le temple,*
      Leur sang viendra la terre prophaner:
      Aux Thoulousains sera bien dur exemple
      D'un qui viendra ses loys exterminer.

46   *Le ciel (de Plancus la cité) nous presaige*
      Par clairs insignes & par estoiles fixes,
      Que de son change subit s'aproche l'aage,
      Ne pour son bien, ne pour ses malefices.

47   *Le vieux monarche deschassé de son regne*
      Aux Orients son secours ira querre:
      Pour peur des croix pliera son enseigne:
      En Mitilene ira pour port et terre.

48   Sept cents captifs estaches rudement
        Pour la moitie meurtrir, donné le sort,
        Le proche espoir viendra si promptement,
        Mais non si tost qu'une quinzieme mort.

49   Regne Gauloys tu seras bien changé:
        En lieu estrange est translaté l'empire:
        En autres mœurs, & loys seras rangé:
        Rouan, & Chartres te feront bien du pire.

50   La republicque de la grande cité,
        A grand rigeur ne voudra consentir:
        Roy sortir hors par trompete cité,
        L'eschele au mur, la cité repentir.

The republic of the great city (**PARIS**),   1585
With great strictness will not be willing to consent:
The King (**HENRI III**) departing outside, through trumpet city (**BORDEAUX**),
The ladder at the wall, the city regretting.

The republic of the great city

Although it is well known that France became a republic during the French Revolution, it is less well known that Paris effectively, and alone, transformed itself into a *republic* during the French Wars of Religion; hence, 'the republic of the great city' is a direct reference to Paris.

The transition of Paris to a republic began in 1584 with the formation of the Holy Catholic League, led by the duc de Guise and governed by a Committee of Sixteen. The League saw itself as the last bastion of the true faith in a kingdom whose ruler was not only too lenient, but who had also nominated a Protestant, Henri of Navarre, to succeed him. "Better a Republic than a Huguenot King" was the defiant cry that thrilled the hearts of the Paris League. [1]

With great strictness will not be willing to consent

Faced with the choice of who should succeed Henri III, the Committee of Sixteen were *not willing to consent* to the King's choice of a Protestant successor. Instead, it was *with great strictness*, that they insisted Henri must sign the Treaty of Nemours (7 July 1585). According to its terms, Cardinal Charles de Bourbon would take the French crown as Charles X; that is, if Henri remained childless. As an additional safeguard, they insisted that the King's choice of Navarre together with all Protestants, be deprived of their right to hold public office. [2]

The King departing outside

On 9 May 1588, the dispute between the King's authority and the Leaguers demands came to a head. In defiance of Henri III's order to the Duke of Guise that he must stay away from Paris, Guise defied the King and entered the city with an armed escort.

Henri, fearing for his life, and that a *coup* had been planned, responded by bringing his own troops into the city. In what became known as the Day of the Barricades, Paris rose up and rebelled against the King, forcing him to shelter inside his palace. After four days had passed, and still in fear, the King managed to escape from the city, vacating Paris for the safety of Chartres. [3]

Through trumpet city

A major reason for the attrition between King and the Paris Leaguers had begun six months earlier. It occurred when the King sent Anne de Joyeuse– a favourite with the Paris Leaguers – to his death, together with 300 other noblemen: who were killed fighting against Henri of Navarre's Huguenots, outside the city of Bordeaux, guarded by Château-Trompette (Castle Trumpet).

On 12 September 1587, Henri III had joined his army stationed along the river Loire. His aim was to defeat a troop of 8,000 German *reiters* before they could join up with Navarre's army in the Midi. At the same time, he had ordered Joyeuse to confront Navarre's army approaching from the south. Joyeuse obeyed, and his army met the opposing force on the plains of Bordeaux (battle of Coutras, 20 October 1587).

In the two-hour long battle that took place, the guns of the Protestant army wreaked havoc among Joyeuse's infantry. When the fighting was over, the bodies of both the duke and his brother Claude were found amongst three hundred other noblemen who had lost their lives.

In complete contrast, Henri failed to intercept the German insurgents. But, worse still, it had been the League's leader, the duc de Guise, who had actually intercepted the Germans: defeating their entire company at Auneau.

In Paris, the League blamed the King for Joyeuse's defeat at Coutras and the loss of so many noblemen. The *Seize* insisted it should have been Henri who met Navarre instead of sending Joyeuse to his death. [4]

The military disaster on the plains of Bordeaux then became an increasingly acerbic reason for heaping further disgrace upon the King, by an already dissatisfied League.

The ladder at the wall

With Henri III absent, Paris was free to operate as a republic, and the gates were barred against the King's return. Henri was therefore compelled to lay siege to the city in an attempt to starve the League into submission and regain his authority. But, on 1 August 1589 he was assassinated, and it was left to his successor, Henri of Navarre, to prove himself by continuing the struggle.

At nightfall, with Paris in the midst of suffering the privations of a second siege, which began in May 1590, Henri IV made an effort to enter the capital by placing a *ladder at the wall*. [5] "During the night of 10th September 1590, Henri IV attempted to take Paris by scaling the walls near the papal gate, between Porte Saint-Jacques and the Porte Saint-Marcel." [6] But a disturbance in the night air attracted the attention of four guards. Together with a librarian and a lawyer, and armed only with pickaxe handles, the six men beat off the attempt. [7]

The city regretting

As the siege inside Paris continued, hunger became the dominant factor. "Donkeys began to disappear, then – as would happen in 1870 – cats and dogs, and even rats." [8] There were also reports of "little children disguised as meat [... and] experiments in milling bones out of the graveyards for flour." [9] With the city regretting having to suffer "the most crippling siege in the history of any major European city since that of Constantinople by the Turks," [10] help at last arrived from Spain. The Duke of Parma succeeded in floating food supplies down the river Seine, while also forcing Henri to withdraw. By then, the privations through hunger and disease had cost the lives of between 40,000 and 50,000 citizens.

Summary: *This is one of several prophecies that augur the approaching assassination of Henri III. It is noticeable that it immediately precedes another that brings the time of Henri III's death even nearer. In this oracle, the reason for the growing antagonism between the King and Paris – a city that had begun defying the King by operating as a republic – is foretold. The events that occurred are plainly stated, but it is left to the historian to put meat on the bones by providing the background to what occurred. At the centre of the dispute was the League, headed by the Duke of Guise. His triumph over the German reiters and the losses that were suffered at the Battle of Coutras placed the King between victory and defeat. And the status of Guise grew because of this, as foretold in the next quatrain.*

51   *PARIS coniure vn grand meurtre commetre,*
      Bloys le fera sortir en plain effet:
      Ceux d'Orleans voudront leur chef remetre,
      Angiers. Troye, Langres leur feront grand forfait.

coniure (OF) entreat; mesfait (AF coupable) culpable;

     PARIS entreats a great man (**HENRI III**) to commit murder;   1588
     Blois will cause him (**GUISE**) to depart, in effect, flat:
     Those of Orleans will want their chief restored,
     Angers, Troyes, Langres, will commit a great crime.

The historical events contained within this quatrain continue those foretold in N°. 50 above. When the quatrains, relating to Henri III, are placed together, they can be seen to have foretold the sequence of events that led to his assassination; (refer C.9 N°. 96; C.3 N°, 51; C.3 N°. 50; C.1 N°. 85; C.1 N°. 97. It therefore indicates that this predicted piece of French history was pre-viewed as a continuous stream of incidents, while the subject was either a child or as yet unborn. The Seer then composed his prophecies in verse form, using their content, but also scrambling the order in which they appeared in his book to avoid premature detection.

Paris entreats a great man to commit murder

In May 1588, barricades were erected in Paris and the Duke of Guise had the look of triumph about him. "The King, meanwhile, fell into a murderous rage that Guise had disobeyed his command and come to Paris." He sought advice from Villequier, d'Ornano and Cheverny: three men who were with him at the time. Alphonse, Comte d'Ornano, suggested that an attempt be made to assassinate Guise. "If your majesty will issue the command, I will bring you the head of the duc de Guise, or secure his person." (Freer, 1858)

Three others then joined the party: the Comte de Guiche, Bellièvre and the abbé d'Elbêne, who brought fresh news that the Queen-mother wanted to arrange a meeting between her son and the duc de Guise. Henri paused irresolute; the abbé d'Elbêne and Ornano, detecting the fierce impulse which actuated the king's mind, approached, and boldly advised his majesty to receive the duke in that very cabinet, and cause him to be assassinated on the spot as just retribution for his rebellion and disobedience.

The abbé d'Elbêne confirmed the advice with a Latin aphorism. "Percutiam pastorem et dispergentur oves." [Kill the shepherd and disperse the sheep]. "The counsel seemed pleasing to the king, who thereupon fell into a fit of musing." A plan for Guise's murder was then put together. [1]

Lognac and his five Gascons took up positions, while Henri angrily dealt with the remonstrations and prayers of his ministers. These had made little impression upon him, for he declared that Guise would not live to confront him again, but that he would cause him to be shot, and his head severed from his body, and placed on a pike in front of the Louvre before the expiration of another hour. Henri then gave Lognac the signal, upon the hearing of which, he was to rush into the queen's chamber and do just execution on the rebel. But Catherine de Medici appeared at that moment accompanied by Guise, and astutely divined from her son's manner that some dreadful catastrophe was about to take place. Skilfully, she talked the Duke of Guise out of the room and out of immediate danger.

Blois will cause him to depart, in effect, flat

Having failed to rid himself of his enemy, the King sought a new opportunity. In December 1588, the duc de Guise arrived at the Château de Blois, the residence of Henri III, to attend a meeting of the Estates-General.

On the morning of December 23rd, Guise was summoned for a private audience with the King. As he entered the chamber adjoining the royal bedroom, a group of Henri's bodyguard, led by Lognac and his Gascons, fell upon the Duke, and stabbed him to death. [2] Guise's lifeless body was then carried from the castle, 'in effect, departing flat', exactly as it was foretold. There are conflicting stories of the manner by which the body of Guise was disposed.

Those of Orleans will want their chief restored

When the citizens of Orleans heard what had taken place at Blois, and who was to replace Guise as the head of their city, they seized the gates. And in their anger, a deputation of eight citizens was forthwith elected to proceed to the King at Blois, and confront him with their request. They were to urge Henri III to remove Entragues: a man whom the citizens so detested that they would refuse to accept him as their new governor. They were then to explain to the King that the man they wanted for their chief must be from the family of Guise.

It was with this objective that they arrived at Blois to plead their cause to Henri: praying that the captive prince of Joinville, who had now become the new duc de Guise, might be made their governor. [3] In Century One N°. 85, it was predicted that these envoys would be careless of their lives for making this request. The King outraged by their plea, sent them back under guard.

Angers, Troyes, Langres will commit a great crime

Orleans was not alone in being affected during this time of upheaval and uncertainty. Each of the three places referred to above is a location where a dreadful crime was committed. [4]

In *Angers*, the Huguenots were among the first to suffer when the Duke of Montpensier, Guise's brother-in-law decided to rid the city of Protestants by decapitating all those in captivity.

At *Troyes*, in April 1590, about two thousand citizens repelled a Royalist assault. This led to over one hundred deaths, and was followed by an assault on the Royalist prisoners held inside the city's prison. Thirty-seven inmates were subsequently killed when the jailer, Pierre Gourdault opened the prison gates to allow a mob, led by town councillor Laurent Dautruy, to enter and begin murdering those targeted.

Vassy or Wassy, situated in the Haute-Marne, a diocese of *Langres*, was also the scene of an atrocious crime. On 1 March 1562, the duc de Guise, travelling with an armed escort, espied a company of Huguenots worshipping inside a barn. "The duke's men broke into the barn and a slaughter ensued." When news reached the capital, Condé left the city to raise forces intent upon retaking Orleans. It was this crime that lit the fuse which started France's Wars of Religion. [5]

Summary: *The prophecy correctly foretells that a great man, in this case Henri III, will first be persuaded to commit murder in Paris. Afterwards, the deed will be carried out at Blois. As a result of this murder, the city of Orleans will make application to the King for a leader of their choice. Three cities are also named for the great crimes – all of which were mass murders – that would be perpetrated in these places.*

> 52   *En la Campaigne sera si longue pluie,*
> *Et en la Pouile si grande siccité.*
> *Coq verra l'aigle, l'aesle mal accomplie:*
> *Par Lyon mise sera en extremité.*

> 53   *Quand le plus grand emportera le pris,*
> *De Nuremberg d'Auspurg, & ceux de Basle*
> *Par Aggripine chef Francqfort repris*
> *Transuerseront par Flamans iusques en Galle.*

pris (OF) honour; Agripine (L) Cologne; Galle (L) Gall\us – Gaul, i.e., France.

> When the greatest (**HITLER**) shall gain the honour,   1933
> Concerning Augsburg, Nuremberg, and those of Basel.
> By reason of Cologne, the chief, Frankfurt retaken,
> They (**GERMANS**) will traverse through Flanders, even into France.

When the greatest shall gain the honour

On 30 January 1933, Adolf Hitler was made Reich Chancellor of Germany following the resignation of the Schleicher cabinet two days earlier. In the turmoil caused by the cabinet's resignation, leading politicians were counselled for their preferences; it was from these soundings that an agreement was reached among them, naming Adolf Hitler as the one politician most members would be willing to serve under. Up until then, only Nazi fanatics had believed this could happen. Nevertheless, against the odds, Hitler was seen to be the best candidate at that time and to him was given the honour of leading the German nation. [1]

Concerning Augsburg, Nuremberg

Hitler's rise to power began with his dictatorial control of the NSDAP (abbreviated to Nazi Party). His appointment occurred on 26 July 1921, but only after he had first resigned from the party, and then allowed its administrators to persuade him to reconsider his decision. It was the promise of leadership with 'dictatorial powers' that induced him to return.

Members of the *Augsburg and Nuremberg* branches of the Deutsche Werkgemeinschaft had earlier caused Hitler irritation. It occurred when he was informed that they were engaged in talks with Dr Otto Dickel, author of *The Resurrection of the Western World*, and a potential party leader. Hitler was then invited to attend the NSDAP to consider the merger proposal favoured by Dickel. Unwilling to consent to the proposal, Hitler flew into one of his rages, and threatened "the Augsburg and Nuremberg representatives that he would see a merger was stopped." Dickel, however, persisted in having his way, causing Hitler to storm out of the meeting in disgust, having first tendered his resignation. The NSDAP soon realised that Hitler, with his personal magnetism and considerable rhetorical power, was too valuable a member to lose, and so a way was paved for him to return as the Nazi Party's Führer. [2]

And those of Basel

Six months after becoming Chancellor (9 August 1933), Hitler ordered his 'Nazi police' to cross the Swiss border into *Basel* and search for Communist propaganda. Demonstrations by Nazi supporters on both sides of the frontier followed. This was the first international incident involving Hitler's 'Nazi Polizei' crossing another country's frontier, and it sent out a warning to Germany's neighbours of what was to follow. [3]

By reason of Cologne

The city of Colonia Claudia Ara Agrippinensium, shortened to *Cologne*, was named after the birthplace of *Agrippina* the younger. She married the Emperor Claudius, and became mother to Nero, who repaid her in adult life by having her murdered. Cologne's name has therefore been concealed behind that of Agrippina.

In March 1936, *Cologne* made international news. Hitler had torn up two treaties, those of *Versailles* (1919) and *Locarno* (1925), and he was preparing to march his army into the demilitarised zone of the Rhineland. His chosen point of entry was the 'Hohenzollern Bridge in Cologne'. Thirty thousand troops were amassed there, waiting to be sent into what was, by international agreement, a forbidden region. Their orders were to take up positions along the banks of the Rhine. Further to this, a detachment of 3,000 troops were then ordered to venture further into the region and secure it. [4]

The chief

Eighteen months before the outrage at Cologne, Hitler had been appointed 'Chief'; that is, '*Führer of the German Reich*', following Hindenburg's death on 2 August 1934. His move toward reclaiming the Rhineland was hailed by the German people as a triumph, particularly since it followed the country's humiliation after losing the First World War.

Frankfurt retaken

This reference to Frankfurt is employed as a grammatical device: a synecdoche for the recovery of the Rhineland. As long ago as 843 AD the Rhineland had become the western border region of the East Frankish, or German kingdom: hence, the name *Frankfort,* which originally meant 'Ford (crossing place) of the Franks'.

Consequently, by referring to *Frankfurt* the intention is to direct attention to the Rhineland's Frankish origin. When this is substituted for the Rhineland, which was *retaken* by Germany in 1936, it fulfils this part of the prophecy, and is keeping with the prediction remaining. [5]

They will traverse through Flanders, even into France

Hitler's invasion of the Lowland is familiar to anyone acquainted with the history of the Second World War. "From 14 May 1940, the German Panzer forces bridged the River Meuse and poured into Belgium" on their way to France; which is to say, 'they will traverse through Flanders, even into France'. Hitler's territorial ambitions for a 'Greater Germany' had begun, [6] and the Second World War was about to make history.

Summary: *The locations mentioned in this prophecy are truly startling. Augsburg, Nuremberg, Basel, Cologne,*
Frankfurt, Flanders and France form a group which, chronologically, can be seen as stepping stones along
the path of Adolf Hitler's rise to power. From his membership of the Nazi Party, up to his invasion of the
Low Countries and the occupation of France, the prophecy has kept step with the places that paved the way.

54   *L'vn des plus grands fuira aux Hespaignes,*
      Qu'en longue plaie apres viendra saigner:
      Passant copies par les hautes montaignes
      Deuastant tout & puis en paix regner.

55   *En l'an qu'vn œil en France regnera,*
      La court sera à vn bien fascheux trouble:
      Le grand de Bloys son ami tuera:
      Le regne mis en mal & doute double.

In the year that one eye (**HENRI II**) will reign in France,   1559
The court will be in a most troublesome dispute.
The great man of Blois (**CHARLES IX**) will kill his friend (**COLIGNY**):
The kingdom placed in harm and double doubt.

In the year that one eye will reign in France

There is subtlety in the first line. It specifically focuses upon *the year* that a person with one eye
will reign in France. But this does not necessarily mean that this person will reign for the entire
year. Henri II, with his sight reduced to 'one eye, reigned in France' from the time of his accident
on 30 June, until his death on 10 July. [1] This ten-day period therefore identifies the year as 1559.
From this single fact, it becomes possible to recognize the trouble occurring at court. For, it
began just before the King's fatal accident, and continued for some time after his death.

The court will be in a most troublesome dispute

A most troublesome dispute did, indeed, break out on 10 June 1559, three weeks before the
King's tragic death. [2] It began at the quarterly meeting of the judiciary, when Henri II and
Cardinal Lorraine arrived to witness proceedings. There, they heard a young magistrate, Anne du
Bourg, openly criticizing the sentencing to death of several members of the Paris *Parlement*
because of their Calvinistic – that is, heretical – beliefs. Why, he asked those assembled, should
these people be condemned to death for their personally held belief in Christ, when adulterers
and murderers often escaped punishment?
Henri II instantly recognized himself as a serial adulterer, therefore a target for this oratory. His
response was to order the arrest of du Bourg and several other councillors who had expressed
sympathy with this opinion. However, before any action could be taken against those arrested,
the King lay dead, having suffered blindness in one eye from the jousting accident that led to his
death ten days later.
The death of Henri II did not save du Bourg. Under the influence of the powerful Guise family,
fifteen-year-old King Francis II was persuaded to pursue his father's policies against the
Huguenots. The harshness of the decision caused widespread dissent, thus furthering the trouble
at court. To make matters even worse, in September and again in November, legislation was
passed, which decreed the burning of all houses used for Huguenot meetings, and the death
penalty for anyone failing to reveal the location of these dwellings.
One month after these edicts were passed, Anne du Bourg was, burnt at the stake (23 December
1559). His death sent shudders amongst those at Court to see such a highborn figure dealt with
so harshly.
A gap of thirteen years follows this half of the prediction. A very good reason exists for the
interlude. The man who wrote the prophecy was still alive in 1559 and the King's accident,
which blinded him in one eye, would have focussed attention upon the further outcome of this
quatrain. The Seer prevents this happening by creating a thirteen year time lapse before the
second half became fulfilled.

Despite this time lapse, the Seer did manage to create a bridge between the two halves of the prophecy. This was achieved by focusing upon another man who, like du Bourg, held Protestant opinions; and, like du Bourg, was wrongfully killed by order of the King.

The great man of Blois will kill his friend

In 1570, Gaspard de Coligny, although a convert to the Protestant faith, had become a close friend and confidante of the twenty-year-old King, Charles IX. So close was their friendship that Charles even called Coligny 'Mon Père'. But on St Bartholomew's Eve, after having been harangued by the Queen-mother for hour after hour until she broke his resolve, *the great man of Blois* (King Charles) *agreed to kill his friend.* [3] "Kill them all, so that not one will be left to reproach me for it," [4] he is said to have exclaimed in exasperation.

Catherine de Medici at once conveyed the King's command to the duc de Guise, assured in the knowledge that the duke fully believed a confession extracted under torture from his father's assassin, implicated Coligny in this murder. Guise responded with immediate action by ordering Coligny's murder. The Admiral's death was a brutal affair, and it triggered the slaughter of many thousands of Huguenots, in what became known as the St Bartholomew's Day Massacre.

The kingdom placed in harm and double doubt

After the Massacre had run its course, and with the kingdom greatly harmed as a consequence of this pogrom of the Protestants, Catherine's role as Queen-mother steadily declined, as did the influence of the King. The Huguenot community now had good reason to doubt their personal safety, and they became unwilling to give Charles IX their total allegiance.

The suspicions concerning the role played by the King's mother in the murder of Coligny and the influence she had brought to bear on the King soon spread to other parts of the country. In both France and the courts of pro-Catholic Europe these doubts continued to increase: especially concerning Catherine de Medici's professed innocence.

As a result of the massacre and the mounting doubts concerning both Charles and his mother, "Huguenots, began to leave France in legions." [5]

Summary: *The two halves of this prophecy foretell the harm done in France, because of the deaths of two men linked by the Protestant faith. The first half is clearly indicated by the year in which a one-eyed king would reign. The second half, separated by a lapse of thirteen years, foretells the unique instance of a King, with a residence at Blois, who murdered his faithful friend. Students of French history would have no problem in identifying Henri II and the legislation against the Huguenots that followed the death of du Bourg. Likewise, the same students could hardly miss identifying Charles IX's father-son relationship with Admiral Coligny and the massacre that followed his murder.*

   56   *Montauban, Nismes, Auignon, & Besier,*
           Peste, tonnerre & gresle à fin de Mars:
           De Paris pont, Lyon mur, Montpellier,
           Depuis six cent & sept xxiii. pars.

Mars, (god of war, hence synecdoche) War; 607 (abbrev.) the year 1607; depuis (AF) for; par (AF, côté, part, participation) part

Montauban, Nîmes, Avignon, & Béziers   1560
Plague, thunder & hail to the end of war:
A bridge for Paris, Lyons a wall, Montpellier.
For **1607** 23 parts.

Montauban, Nîmes, Avignon, & Béziers

These four cities in the south of France indicate that they have something in common, apart from location. In fact they were strongholds during the French Wars of Religion. Avignon was Catholic. The other three cities were Protestant. Each was guilty of an atrocity.

Avignon, "Often referred to as the 'City of Popes' because of the presence of popes and antipopes from 1309 to 1423," was not under the rule of France during the Wars of Religion. "The popes bought Avignon from the Angevin ruler for 80,000 florins in 1348." [1] In 1583, Henri III attempted to buy it back, but Pope Gregory XIII declined to part with it.

Eleven years earlier, during the reign of Henri's brother, Charles IX, Pope Gregory had celebrated a *Te Deum* to celebrate the 'Overthrow of the Huguenots' and the 13,000 that were slaughtered in Paris during the St Bartholomew's Day massacre of 1572: for which the Pope also ordered a medal to be struck.

Nîmes, on the other hand, was one of the Protestant strongholds. On 29 September the city rioted in what became called the Michelade.

> The massacre of Catholics, including 24 Catholic priests and monks, by Protestant rioters in Nîmes on Michaelmas (29 September) 1567, following their failure to abduct the king and queen mother in the so-called Surprise of Meaux the previous day and in retaliation for the suppression of their Huguenot beliefs. With Meaux, it helped trigger the Second War of Religion. [2]

Montauban was another Huguenot stronghold.

> In 1560 the bishops and magistrates embraced Protestantism, expelled the monks, and demolished the cathedral. Ten years later it became one of the four Huguenot strongholds under the Peace of Saint-Germain and formed a small independent republic. [3]

Catholics also came under attack from Huguenots in *Beziers*. "In 1562, the reformed people take the city and wreck the Catholic buildings." [4]

Plague, thunder & hail to the end of war

The phrasing of the oracle in this line allegorizes the outbreaks of religious conflict across the Protestant part of France. These skirmishes continued intermittently up until the end of the war in 1598. By referring to *thunder,* the roar of cannon fire heard across the land accompanied by the *hail* of shot, introduces the emergence of firepower that began to be used at that time.

Plague has also been added to the prophecy, which proved to be apt for that time. The Huguenot strongholds referred to above were no great distance from each other, and confrontations and recriminations "continued until the middle of the 17th century, adding to the misery of periodic outbreaks of plague." [5]

A bridge for Paris

Civil liberty for religious worship was finally made legal in April 1598 by the Edict of Nantes, bringing to an end the major conflicts between Catholics and Protestants. In 1599, Maximilien, duc de Sully began a massive building programme, which included bridges, roads and canals, designed to stimulate the economy.

> While lacking the artistic tastes of the Valois, Henri beautified Paris, building the great gallery of the Louvre, finishing the Tuileries, building the Pont Neuf, the Hôtel-de-Ville and the Place Royale. [6]

The Pont Neuf – New Bridge – "Completed in 1607 [...] spans the widest part of the river, and was the first Paris bridge to be built without houses attached to it." [7] In December 1607, Henri IV rode across the bridge to celebrate its completion.

Lyons a wall

After the Wars of Religion had ended, Henri IV's name appears several times in the history of Lyon. His first major task was to unite the former enemies inside the city. Henry therefore brought his troops into the city to restore and maintain order. Then, "in 1600, he married Marie de Medici at the Cathédrale Saint Jean. Catholics and Protestants were reconciled." [8]

Also, after the destruction caused by the civil war, a massive rebuilding programme began.

> At the end of the 16th century, the royalty and clergy of France, inspired by the Counter-Reformation, set out on the revival of Roman Catholicism by creating new monasteries and enlarging existing ones. [9]

In Lyon Henri IV "declared himself the founder of the Carthusian monastery and confirmed its exemptions and privileges, which were reconfirmed by Louis XIII and Louis XIV." [10]

The oracle employs 'mur' (wall) several times in these prophecies as a synecdoche for a building. On this occasion it refers to the monastery founded by Henri IV.

Montpellier

This prophecy has so far made predictions for the French Wars of Religion involving Catholics and Huguenots, and followed these with the building programme that took place after the Edict of Nantes officially ended these wars. The city of Montpellier has been included to tie both these strands of prophecy together.

> [I]n the 16th century, many of the inhabitants of Montpellier became Protestants (or Huguenots as they were known in France) and the city became a stronghold of Protestant resistance to the Catholic French crown. [11]

> [Also] The War of Religions, which took control of the area during the 16th century, had many impacts on the city's architecture. The subsequent two centuries saw many of these architectural achievements remodelled and renovated. [12]

> Lavish private mansions [...] were built in the city, homes that were signs of their owner's prosperity. Noblemen and rich traders built nearly one hundred such luxurious buildings in the centre. [13]

For 1607, 23 parts

> From the late fifteenth century up to the late seventeenth century (and again in the 1760s) France underwent a massive territorial expansion and an attempt to better integrate its provinces into an administrative whole. [14]

In 1607, Henri added the County of Foix to France's provinces. This brought the total to 23.

> 1. Roussillon, 2. Cerdagne, 3. Conflent, 4. Vallespir, 5. Capcir, 6. Calais, 7. Béarn, 8. Navarre, 9. County of Foix, 10. Flanders, 11. Artois, 12. Lorraine, 13. Alsace, 14. Trois-Évêchés, 15. Franche-Compté, 16. Savoy, 17. Bresse, 18. Bugey, 19. Gex, 20. Nice, 21. Provence, 22. Dauphiné, 23. Brittany. [15]

Further territories were added later for administrative purposes, such as Navarre in 1620.

Summary: *This is the third quatrain to include the year in which a predicted event would occur (see 1:49 & 2:51 for the first two). It is also the first of three oracles that name 1607 (see 6: 54 & 8: 71 for the other two), although only this oracle actually applies to 1607 AD. The cities named in the prediction were among those that took action on one side or the other during the French Wars of Religion. The building programme that began after the wars ended include the Pont Neuf in Paris, which was finished in the year named in this prophecy. Henri IV's other achievement, the Carthusian Monastery in Lyon, is also indicated, as too, is the significance of Montpellier. And, of course, its crowning achievement was to name the exact year in which the precise number of 23 provinces would be obtained by the monarchy for administrative purposes.*

Footnote: The fact that Henri IV added the County of Foix to French held provinces, bringing the number to 23 in 1607, is far too trivial for a dated prophecy. It has to be connected to the other two quatrains that also name 1607 (Century Six N°. 54 and Century Eight N°. 71).

These are the two prophecies that reveal, respectively, the exact year in which Jesus Christ was crucified and the year in which he was born; in both cases, these dates are obtained by using 1607 as the key to unlocking the mystery. Only one part of this double revelation is absent, the actual day and month of Jesus's birth. For this reason, I suggest that the information has been cryptically concealed in the part of the verse that reads: *à fin de Mars... xxiii.* (at the end of March... 23.)

> 57 *Sept foys changer verrés gent Britannique,*
>   *Taintz en sang en deux cent nonante an:*
>   *Franche non point par apui Germanique.*
>   *Aries doute son pole Bastarnan.*

verrés (vous verrez); Taintz (OF teint) stained; Franche (AF affranchir) absolve; non point (adverb used with negative) not at all; apui (appui) fear, mistrust; doubte (OF) fear, mistrust; pole (OF peuple, foule, multitude);

You will see the British people changing seven times,
Stained by blood within two hundred and ninety years:
Not at all absolved from German support,
Aries fears his Bastarnae people.

You will see the British people changing seven times

The probability of fulfilling this prophecy by chance is too remote for consideration. Only a true prophet could have looked into the forthcoming three centuries, and given the exact number of years when the final change would occur. Since this oracle was published in 1555, at a time when the Tudors ruled England, the seven changes referred to must be allowed to begin from the time of their reign. [1]

The House of Tudor (1485 – 1603) changed at the end of this period. Thereafter came the *seven changes*.

1 *Stuarts*: James I; Charles I.

2 *Cromwell* Oliver; Richard.

3 *Stuarts*: Charles II; James II; Mary II.

4 *Orange*: William III.

5 *Stuarts*: Anne.

6 *Hanover*: George I; George II; George III; George IV; William IV.

7 *Saxe-Coburg & Gotha*: Victoria; Edward VII; George V Edward VIII; George VI; Elizabeth II.

In 1837 the Crown descended to Queen Victoria, six generations removed from George I— while Hanover, where female succession was forbidden, passed to a male descendant of George III. In 1840, Victoria married Prince Albert of Saxe-Coburg & Gotha, whose family name was Wettin. In 1917, when Britain was at war with Germany, and the country was suffering bombing raids by airships, George V adopted Windsor for the royal family's dynastic surname.

Stained in blood

The oracle then goes on to predict that during these *seven changes, the British people* will be *stained in blood*. Ever since the reign of Edward VI (1547 – 1553, when this oracle appears to have been written), blood has been spilt in great profusion by the British. It began with the slaughtering of religious martyrs in the 16th century, and then proceeded to the war with Spain. This was followed by the Civil War of 1642, and those fighting for their independence in Ireland. Across the Channel there was even more carnage when England fought against Spain, Holland, France, Germany, Italy and Portugal: then, further afield, in Canada, North America, India, Egypt, China, &c.

Within two hundred and ninety years

The oracle next wraps these bloody conflicts up into a passage of time lasting 290 years, which is predicted to be the time that would elapse to bring about these seven changes. Hence, based upon the list given above, the exact number of years can be calculated as follows.

On 28 January **1547**, Edward VI became King of England following the death of his father Henry VIII. Since the preface in the first edition of these prophecies is dated 1 March 1555, just nineteen months after the death of Edward VI (6 July 1553), there is every reason to believe that these oracles were being written during his reign. In which case, the count commences from 1547.

On 20 June **1837**, Victoria ascended the throne. This brought about the seventh and final change, because it allowed her to marry into the House of Wettin: the House of Hanover having split from the succession in that same year.

Consequently, 1837 − 1547 = 290. This is precisely the number of years predicted for the seven changes in the reign to occur. [2]

Not at all absolved from German support

The prophecy next delves into the composition of the English monarchy by predicting that the chain of succession will *not be absolved from German support*. The marriage of Queen Victoria in 1840 to Albert, son of Duke Saxe-Coburg-Gotha retained the German connection that began with the House of Hanover. This particular line of German succession had lasted since 1714. It eventually terminated when the next in line for the throne, William IV's brother Ernest, decided upon the Hanover crown, rather than the British one. His choice was made necessary because succession in Germany forbade a woman taking the crown. The Hanoverian succession therefore ceased after Queen Victoria's marriage and was replaced by that of Saxe-Coburg-Gotha. [3]

Queen Elizabeth II is descended from Queen Victoria and Prince Albert. In 1947, she married Prince Philip, Duke of Edinburgh who was descended from the House of Schleswig-Holstein-Sonderburg-Glücksburg, and a great-great-grandson of Queen Victoria, but retained the name of Windsor.

Aries fears his Bastarnae people

After the coronation of Queen Victoria (28 June 1838), parts of Europe became caught up in the turmoil of political change. The prophecy concludes by referring to one outbreak in particular.

In 1848, the Transylvanian part of Eastern Europe, including Hungary, rose up in revolt against the landowners. Existing among the revolutionaries was a group of young intellectuals led by the poet Sandor Petofi. Together, the rebels managed to abolish censorship and to formulate a set of laws. These became known as the 'April Laws'. [4]

Many conservatives resented everything the 'April Laws' stood for, and their resentment found willing allies among the people of Romania; that is, the *Bastarnae* who refused to accept the new administration. The *Bastarnae* were a German tribal people known to the Romans, and who had formerly "settled in Europe east of the Carpathian Mountains from the upper valley of the Dniester River to the Danube River delta." This area is presently occupied by Romania and Moldavia, and includes the *Aries* River and *Aries* Valley.

On 2 December 1848, Emperor Ferdinand I of Austria, King of Hungary and Grand Prince of Transylvania, *fearing his Bastarnae people*, who were venting their fury over the 'April Laws', [5] was persuaded to abdicate in favour of his nephew Franz Josef. Under this new regime, the 'April Laws' were abolished. [6]

Ferdinand has been given the cognomen of *Aries* because, firstly, he was born on 19 April 1793, which falls in the period that comes under the sun sign Aries; secondly, it was because part of his realm included people from the Aries Valley, and thirdly, the 'April Laws' (again Aries) were the cause of his abdication.

The significance which this final part of the prophecy has to the British throne, with its German support, centres upon the fact that Ferdinand's successor, the Austrian Emperor, Franz Josef, played an important role in the commencement of the First World War, which was fought, principally between Britain and Germany.

> In the period 1908-14 Francis Joseph held fast to his peace policy in the face of warnings by the chief of the general staff, Franz, Count Conrad von Hötzendorf, who repeatedly advocated a preventive war against Serbia or Italy. Yet, without having fully thought out the consequences, he let himself in July 1914 be persuaded by Count Leopold Berchtold, the foreign minister, to issue the intransigent ultimatum to Serbia that led to World War I. [7]

It can therefore be understood how these two, apparently unconnected parts of the prophecy came together at the start of the First World War I, in which millions of lives were lost.

Summary: *The seven successive changes to the families ruling Britain, commencing with James I who united England and Scotland to give credence to the 'British people', as mentioned in the prophecy, is then confirmed by the exact number of 290 years in which these changes would occur. The blood spilt in warfare during that time also earned Britain the reputation of being a martial country. The prophecy has also foreseen the support*

provided to the British monarchy by the German people, which has continued for the past three centuries.
Finally, this well of foreknowledge is made to include the succession of Emperor Franz Josef, whose
ultimatum to Serbia served as the spark that ignited the 1914-18 war between Britain and Germany.

58   *Aupres du Rin des montaignes Noriques,*
        Naistra vn grand de gents trop tard venu:
        Qui defendra SAVROME & Pannoniques,
        Qu'on ne saura qu'il sera deuenu.

59   *Barbare empire par le tiers vsurpé,*
        La plus grand part de son sang metra à mort:
        Par mort senile par luy le quart frapé,
        Pour peur que sang, par le sang ne soit mort.

60   *Par toute Asie grande proscription,*
        Mesmes en Mysie, Lysie & Pamphylie:
        Sang versera par absolution
        D'vn ieune noir rempli de felonnie.

        Through all Asia, a great exposing to slaughter,
        The same in Mysia, Lycia & Pamphylia:
        Blood will pour out through the discharge of offences
        By a ghastly young man/(king) replenished by treachery.

61   *La grande bande & secte crucigere*
        Se dressera en Mesopotamie:
        Du proche fleuue compaignie legiere,
        Que telle loy tiendra pour ennemie.

bande (OF) company of soldiers; secte (OF) faction (most commonly of bad opinion); se dresser (OF) advancing itself; legiere (AF diminuer les charges) diminish the charges; crucigere (*hybrid:* cruci + gere - cruci (L) cruci\are, to torture, + gere\re (L) to bring; loy (AF coutume) practice; tiendra (OF) will make good; pour (OF) against;

        The great company of soldiers & torture bringing faction   2003
        Will raise itself up in Iraq:
        By the adjoining river, the company diminish accusations,
        When such practice will hold for the enemy.

The great company of soldiers

The second invasion of Iraq in 2003 brought *a great company of soldiers* into Baghdad, led by the United States coalition force.

> The 2003 invasion of Iraq, from March 20 to May 1, 2003, was spearheaded by the United States, backed by British forces and smaller contingents from Australia, Spain, Poland and Denmark. Four countries participated with troops during the initial invasion phase, which lasted from March 20 to May 1. These were the United States (248,000), United Kingdom (45,000), Australia (2,000), and Poland (194). [...] In preparation for the invasion, 100,000 U.S. troops were assembled in Kuwait by February 18. The United States supplied the vast majority of the invading forces, but also received support from Kurdish troops in northern Iraq.[1]

And torture bringing faction

During the following year, accounts began to emerge that the US army was practising torture against Iraqi captives: particularly those held in the Abu Ghraib prison. These were acts specifically carried out by personnel of the 372nd Military Police Company.

> New photos and videos revealed by the Pentagon to lawmakers in a private viewing on the 12th of May showed attack dogs snarling at prisoners, Iraqi women forced to expose their breasts, and naked prisoners forced to have sex with each other, the lawmakers revealed.

Another statement from a guard who kept a video diary of what was happening inside the prison, "recounts having venomous snakes bite the prisoners, sometimes resulting in death, throwing stones at the prisoners, and prisoners being shot for minor misbehaviour." Pictures also appeared on televisions around the world showing "A hooded and wired Iraqi prisoner, believed to be Satar Jabar, who reportedly was told that he would be electrocuted if he fell off the box. " A list of the different abuses and tortures practiced at Abu Ghraib, and published in the New York Times (12 January 2005),

included: urinating on detainees; forcefully jumping on a detainees' limbs wounded by gunfire; beating wounded limbs with a metal baton; pouring phosphoric acid on detainees; sodomizing detainees with a baton; tying ropes to detainees' legs or penises, and dragging them across the floor. [2]

The US also operated a programme called "Extraordinary rendition, which involves transferring suspects to a third country where there is no prohibition on the use of torture during interrogation. " [3]

In a lengthy statement to parliament, Defence Secretary John Hutton confirmed that Britain handed over two suspects captured in Iraq in 2004 to U.S. custody and that they were subsequently transferred to Afghanistan, breaching U.S.--British agreements. The Ministry of Defence has been repeatedly asked over the past five years about its involvement in rendition, the unlawful transfer of suspects to a third country, and consistently denied it played any role in the U.S.-administered programme. [4]

Confinement inside a 1 cubic metre box, and the use of water-boarding was reported to have been a popular method of extracting information. This was practised by the Spanish Inquisition during the sixteenth-century, and involved the partial drowning of the victim, followed by resuscitation. When repeated continually: information – whether true or false – was extracted.

Will raise itself up in Iraq

Despite evidence that torture was occurring, and that the war in Iraq was illegal—

Former Vice President Dick Cheney said in his first television interview since leaving office that the Iraq invasion was "worth doing" and the U.S. succeeded with its goals. [...] Cheney said on CNN's "State of the Union with John King:" "We have succeeded in creating, in the heart of the Middle East, a democratically governed Iraq. And that's a big deal. And that is, in fac t, what we set out to do." [...] Cheney said. "But I would ask people in the press to take an honest look at the circumstances in Iraq today and how far we've come – the defeat of al Qaeda in Iraq, the writing of that democratic constitution, a series of elections that involve power sharing among all the various groups, the end of sectarian viol ence." [5]

N.B. *Mesopotamia* is a name from the Greek language, equivalent to 'the land between two rivers'. It is also the ancient name of modern-day Iraq, which is watered by two rivers, Euphrates and Tigris.

By the adjoining river

The River Tigris flows through Baghdad. Because of the danger inside the city from abductions, murder and suicide bombers, which occur red at frequent intervals, the US administration created a 'green zone' *adjoining the river:* from where it was able to operate and house its staff.

The International Zone (formerly known as the Green Zone) is the heavily guarded diplomatic/government area of closed-off streets in central Baghdad where US occupation authorities live and work. The Green Zone in the central city includes the main palaces of former President Saddam Hussein. The area houses the civilian ruling authority run by the Americans and British and the offices of major US consulting companies. [6]

The company diminish accusations

In response to the list of tortures that had been practised upon prisoners held by the US, "former Justice Department counsel John Yoo says that though he doesn't think the Geneva Conventions covered the prisoners at Abu Ghraib, he believes the soldiers and their commanding officers felt the interrogation techniques used fell within the Geneva Conventions. " A similar diminution of the charges was made by the Vice President Dick Cheney, who "according to more than two dozen current and former officials, created a distinction between forbidden 'torture' and the use of 'cruel, inhuman or degrading' methods of questioning which they advanced as permissible." Defence Secretary Donald Rumsfeld refused to acknowledge that US soldiers had engaged in torture. He stated. "What has been charged so far is abuse, which I believe technically is different from torture. I'm not going to address the 'torture' word." [7]

When such practice will hold for the enemy

When the British Ministry of Defence was asked about the practice of transporting prisoners to other countries, a spokesperson replied, "There was nothing illegal about Britain's involvement in the rendition process." (Swissinfo.ch)

On 5 December 2005, The US Secretary of State, Condoleezza Rice stated, "Rendition is a vital tool in combating trans-national terrorism. Its use is not unique to the United States, or to the current administration. [...] [However] the United States does not permit, tolerate or condone torture under any circumstances." [8]

Yet, under the same administration, outgoing Vice President Dick Cheney admitted:

> "I supported it," he said regarding the practice known as 'water-boarding', a form of simulated drowning. [...] "I was aware of the program, certainly, and involved in helping get the process cleared, as the agency in effect came in and wanted to know what they could and couldn't do," Cheney said. "And they talked to me, as well as others, to explain what they wanted to do. And I supported it." He added, "It's been a remarkably successful effort, and I think the results speak for themselves." [9]

In April 2009, President Obama published email correspondence sent to the CIA specifying the different tortures that were deemed acceptable, because of the perceived threat to the nation. These included "sleep deprivation for up to 11 days, forced nudity [while suspended from chains] and stress positions such as water-boarding."

Other methods of torture also included male and female rape. Despite the illegality of these operations, but the president confirmed there would be no charges brought against those responsible. Former CIA chief, Michael Hayden claimed: "The use of these techniques against these terrorists really did make us safer, it really did work." (Daily Telegraph, 21/4/2009, p.15).

Summary: *The Second Iraq War was noted for the torture committed by US troops against Iraqi prisoners, particularly at the Abu Ghraib prison; and the uncensored stories made headlines across the world. Four and a half centuries earlier, the first published account of this torture appeared in this oracle. We can now see that it went on to predict the Green Zone by the River Tigris, which was made a safe area for administration workers to carry out their duties in governing Iraq. The prophecy also foretold with similar candour the efforts made to downplay the cruel treatment against prisoners, and the pains taken by authorities at the highest level to excuse the practice, because of the enemy they were combating.*

62   *Proche del duero par mer Tyrrene close*
        Viendra percer les grands monts Pyrenées.
        La main plus courte & sa percée gloze,
        A Carcassonne conduira ses menées.

63   *Romain pouuoir sera du tout abas,*
        Son grand voysin imiter ses vestiges:
        Occultes haines ciuiles, & debats
        Retarderont aux bouffons leurs folligges.

folligges (fol + liges), whence, fol (OF) foolish, simple, fond; lige (OF) fidelity without restriction.

        Roman power will be with entire humiliation,
        His great neighbour imitating his footsteps:
        Secret, civil loathings, & disagreements
        Will loosen to the sycophants their fond, unrestricted fidelity.

64   *Le chef de Perse remplira grande* ΟΛΧΑΔΕζ
        Classe trireme contre gent Mahumetique:
        De Parthe, & Mede: & piller les Cyclades:
        Repos long temps au grand port Ionique.

> The Chief of Iran will replenish the great OLCHADES,
> The trireme fleet against the Mahommedan people:
> Of Parthia & Media: and ravaging the Cyclades:
> Rested a long time at the great Ionian port.

Triremes played a vital role in the Persian Wars, the creation of the Athenian maritime empire, and its downfall in the Peloponnesian War. Therefore, in the knowledge that the Seer sometimes uses history to predict a future event, this may be something to watch for. It is also noteworthy that Media and Parthia represent the names of two ancient Persian empires.

> The triremes equivalent in the modern world would be the US Navy's Oliver Hazard Perry class frigate. Like the trireme, the Perry class frigates are built for speed and mobility and like the trireme many sacrifices were made to make the Perry class frigates fast and mobile. The most obvious is the ship's armor. Both the trireme and the Perry class frigates have a relatively thin coat of armor. The trireme's had wood, good enough to stop arrows and spears but not the battering ram of another ship. The Perry class has a sheet of steel, good enough to stop naval gunfire, small mines or torpedoes but not strong enough to withstand a hit from one of today's sea-skimming cruise missiles. [richeast.org/htwm/greeks/kapost/ship.html]

The capital letters in the first line of the verse imply importance, but the Greek delta is a curious insert. This Greek is not repeated in any of the later editions, but is replaced by Olchade. The pronunciation is not too dissimilar to Al-Qaeda; that is Ol-chade, which would tie in with the Mahommedan people. But the Greek lettering points in a different direction.

65	*Quand le sepulcre du grand Romain trouué,* *Le iour apres sera esleu pontife,* *Du senat gueres il ne sera prouué* *Empoisonné son sang au sacré scyphe.*

66	*Le grand baillif d'Orleans mis à mort,* *Sera par vn de sang vindicatif:* *De mort merite ne mourra, ne par sort:* *Des pieds & mains mal le faisoit captif.*

baillif (OF as bailli - gouverneur) governor; sort (OF) suffrage; mal (OF adverb) evilly;

> The great governor of Orleans (**CONDÉ**) put to death,   1569
> It will be by one of vindictive blood (**D'ANJOU**):
> He will not die a worthy death, nor by vote,
> By feet and hands, evilly they were making him captive.

The great governor of Orleans put to death
The great governor of Orleans who was put to death, and for whom the following three lines confirm as being solely applicable to him, was Louis, Prince of Condé. Before the First War of Religion began in France, Orleans was a Catholic city. But in 1563, after it was placed under siege by the Huguenots, for whom Condé was their chief, it was captured, and it became a Huguenot stronghold, which meant that Condé exercised control over the city. [1] Three years later, he cemented his union with the city by marrying Françoise d'Orléans. But in 1569, Condé was captured during the battle of Jarnac (13 March 1569), and *put to death*. [2]

It shall be by one of vindictive blood
The duc d'Anjou, who would later become Henri III, was known to possess a spiteful mind. It was a trait that had been passed down to him by his mother, Catherine de' Medici. Her reputation for vindictiveness was well-known, (*cf* N° 30 above).
Before the battle at Jarnac, Condé had suffered an injury to his arm, and was forced to wear a sling. Even worse befell him while he was preparing for battle, his horse threw him and broke his leg. It was in this injured state that he was defeated, when he surrendered himself to Anjou. [3]

He will not die a worthy death, nor by vote

The capture of Condé was a huge triumph for the King's Catholic forces: although what happened next was entirely illegal. Condé was a Prince of the Blood: a legitimate descendant of Hugh Capet. This meant that a nobleman such as Condé, with his background, breeding and royal bloodline had the right of nobility. This prerogative required that he be tried by *Parlement*, and if found guilty, a sentence could then be passed after a *vote* had been taken and agreed upon by his fellow peers. In Condé's case, that right was deliberately denied to him. Instead, *he died an unworthy death, without the vote* [4] His life ended with a single gunshot to the head, fired by Joseph-François Montesquieu, captain of Anjou's guards, and acting under orders.

By feet and hands, evilly they were making him captive

It was during the 3rd War of Religion, while attempting to give support to Coligny's army at Jarnac in Poitou, that Condé suffered his injury and was *taken captive*. Although having a broken leg and an injured arm, the Prince was nevertheless *bound hand and foot* and *spitefully* thrown head first over the back of a donkey. In this ignominious position, humiliated and in acute pain, he was led from the battlefield as a figure of ridicule. [5] Not content with this, Anjou exposed him for two days on a table in the castle of Jarnac, [6] before ordering his death.

Summary: *This oracle concerns the death of Louis I de Bourbon, Prince of Condé. He was Chief of the Huguenots in France, but also a Prince of the Blood, having traced his descent from Hugh Capet. His governorship in Orleans, a Catholic city when this prophecy was published, has been foreseen, as too have the circumstances leading to his death at the hands of Catherine de Medici's favourite son, the future Henri III. The details predicting the manner of Condé's death are accurate, but the dates given differ by two days. See No.41.*

> 67   *Vne nouuele secte de Philosophes,*
>   *Mesprisant mort, or, honneurs & richesses,*
>   *Des monts Germains ne seront limitrophes:*
>   *A les ensuiure auront apui & presses.*

> 68   *Peuple sans chef d'Espagne & d'Italie*
>   *Morts, profligés dedans le Cherronnesse:*
>   *Leur duyct trahi par legiere folie*
>   *Le sang nager par tout à la trauerse.*

> 69   *Grand exercite conduict par iouuenceau,*
>   *Se viendra rendre aux mains des ennemis:*
>   *Mais le viellard nay au demi pourceau,*
>   *Fera Chalon & Mascon estre amis.*

> 70   *La grand Bretagne comprinse l'Angleterre,*
>   *Viendra par eaux si hault à inunder:*
>   *La ligue neufue d'Ausonne fera guerre,*
>   *Que contre eux mesmes ils se viendront bander.*

>   Great Britain contained within the compass of England,
>   Through waters, will come to flood so high:
>   The new league of Ausonia will make war,
>   When against the same them, they will join in league.

In the winter of 2014, England suffered the wettest period since records began. The floods in the Somerset levels and in the Thames Basin were the result of a conveyer belt of fierce Atlantic storms, caused by a shift in the jet stream. Coincidentally, there was also a new prime minister elected in Italy. This prophecy, however, is for a future time, and is predicted to exceed the preventive measures put in place after the floods of 2014. Note also, the absence of Scotland.

> 71   *Ceux dans les isles de long temps assiegés,*
>   *Prendront vigueur force contre ennemis:*
>   *Ceux par dehors morts de faim profligés,*
>   *En plus grand faim que iamais seront mis.*

72   Le bon viellard tout vif enseueli,
        Pres du grand fleuue par fauce souspeçon:
        Le nouueau vieux de richesse ennobli
        Prins au chemin tout l'or de la rançon.

73   Quand dans le regne paruiendra le boiteux
        Competiteur aura proche bastard:
        Luy & le regne viendront si fort rogneux,
        Qu'ains qu'il guerisse son fait sera bien tard.

74   Naples, Florence, Fauence & Imole,
        Seront en termes de telle facherie,
        Que pour complaire aux malheureux de Nolle,
        Plainct d'auoir fait à son chef moquerie.

Fauence (L Faventia) Faenza; complaire (OF) to please, like, serve, be obedient to, Plainct (OF) donné à regret;

        Naples, Florence, Faenza & Imola   1821
        Will be in states of so much angry feeling,
        When, on account of being pleasing to the unfortunate ones of Nola,
        [PEPE] Given to regret for having made a mockery to his chief (FERDINAND 1).

Naples, Florence, Faenza & Imola
Florence, Faenza and Imola are three major cities located in what was formerly known as the Papal States. Together with *Naples* in the south, they were centres for lodges of the Carbonari: a political movement that came into being during the early part of the nineteenth century. [1]

Will be in states of so much angry feeling
In 1821, members of the Carbonari, the more especially within the locations mentioned in this prophecy, found themselves *in states of so much angry feeling*. Their members had only recently emerged from secret meeting places to demand greater political freedom, by campaigning with open demonstrations against Austrian influence. Included amongst their grievances were appeals for political reform. But, at the heart of these protests was a call for a representative government: one that was free from foreign influence and interference. [2]

When, on account of being pleasing to the unfortunate ones of Nola
To add to their anger, the Carbonari had been supporting General Guglielmo Pepe, a disaffected officer garrisoned at Nola. This anger had increased when they discovered that King Ferdinand had subsequently deceived Pepe by reneging upon an agreement he had made with the General, regarding a new constitution. [3]
Pepe had initiated an armed uprising at Nola in pursuit of political reform. The revolt had been successful, and King Ferdinand agreed to accede to the rebels' demands. But, under the pretext of obtaining international approval for the constitution, the King visited Prince von Metternich in Laibach, and appealed to him for military aid. The Austrian statesman responded by sending troops into Italy to confront General Pepe and his rebels. On 7 March 1821, at Rieti, the two sides came together, and in the ensuing conflict, 'the unfortunate ones of Nola' were defeated. [4]

Given to regret for having made a mockery to his chief
The final line of the oracle looks further into the reasons for what happened at Rieti. Ferdinand I believed Pepe *had made a mockery of* his position as King, by having compelled him to accept the rebel army's demands. Because of this, he "saw Pepe as the criminal leader of a criminal movement, and it was with the strongest mental reservation, and under what he considered duress, that he consented to swear to a Constitution he abhorred." [5]
Ferdinand's reaction was to seek revenge against Pepe, and he found in Metternich a sympathetic ally. After losing the battle at Rieti, Pepe was *given to regret* the confrontation he had made *to his chief:* and for his own safety he fled to Spain. Later, he sought asylum in England. [6]

Summary: *This reference to Nola, a city in southern Italy in the province of Naples, which is also mentioned in the oracle alongside Florence, Faenza and Imola, provides the direction in which fulfilment of the prophecy will take. The cities were once centres for the political reform movement known as the Carbonari, which rose in prominence during the early nineteenth century. A revolt did break out in Nola, and King Ferdinand, under duress did agree to the rebels' demands, which he later rescinded, thus angering the Carbonari. The leader of the rebels subsequently escaped, after his army was defeated at Rieti, and he sought exile, having regretted cowering the King into signing a constitution he would later renege upon.*

75   *PAV. Veronne, Vicence, Sarragousse,*
        De glaisues loings terroirs de sang humides:
        Peste si grande vienda à la grand gousse
        Proches secours, & bien loing les remedes.

PAU. (AF petit *also* à peine) the little one *also* in grief; glaives (AF) swords, massacres, epidemics; terroirs (OF) lands;
Cross-references: PAV (as Napoleon)- C.II: 33; C.II: 94; C.IV: 70; C.VI: 79; C.VIII: 1

        The little one (**NAPOLEON**), Verona, Vicenza, Saragossa,   1799
        Concerning massacres, distant lands, humid with blood:
        Plague so great will arrive with the large pod,
        Help nearby, and the remedies very far away.

The little one (Napoleon)

The prophecy begins by capitalizing PAV for emphasis; 'v' and 'u' are equivalent in the classical Latin alphabet. *Pau*, in ancient French, means 'petit', the 'short one', and refers to Bonaparte's height of 5 feet 2½ inches (1·587 metres). This prophetic attribute, which defines Napoleon's stature, was confirmed by his men, who called him 'Le Petit Caporal' (The Little Corporal).

Verona, Vicenza, Saragossa

All three cities listed in the opening line of this oracle figured in campaigns directed by Napoleon. But since the latter part of the oracle concerns lands at the eastern end of the Mediterranean, rather than continental Europe, the Seer's intention must be to use these three cities as parallels for what would occur in Egypt. For example, during Bonaparte's First Italian Campaign, *Verona* was captured, subsequently lost, and later recaptured. Similarly, in Egypt, *Alexandria* was captured, subsequently lost, and later recaptured.[1] In the same Italian campaign, the occupation of *Vicenza* allowed the French to go on and make further conquests. Likewise, when *Cairo* was occupied, it allowed the French to go on and make further conquests.[2] In Spain, at the Siege of *Saragossa*, the French were eventually forced to withdraw. Likewise, in Syria, at the Siege of *Acre*, the French were eventually forced to withdraw.[3] In short, *Verona* and *Alexandria*; *Vicenza* and *Cairo*; *Saragossa* and *Acre*, when paired together, share the same characteristics. By citing them for comparative purposes, the prophetic content of the oracle is therefore doubled.

Concerning massacres, distant lands humid with blood

Between the time Napoleon landed in Alexandria (1 July 1798) and the time he departed (23 August 1799), the massacres that took place in the humid lands of Egypt and Syria are told as follows.

Alexandria was captured with little difficulty, but on 21 July the French army had to fight hard to win the battle of the Pyramids. Less than two weeks later the French fleet was destroyed by Nelson's naval attack in the battle of the Nile at Aboukir Bay. Eight days later, Napoleon's land army was more successful at the battle of Salheyeh (10 August). In October, fresh fighting brought another French victory at the battle of Sédiman. There was then a lull in the fighting as Bonaparte led his army towards Syria and into the New Year. On 2 January the Siege of El Arish ended with a further French victory.

On 7 March the French began the Siege of Jaffa, which ended in yet another victory. On 8 April, General Andoche Junot won a sterling battle, despite being outnumbered six to one at Nazareth. Three days later Napoleon defeated Turkish opposition at the battle of Cana, and then went on to assist General Kléber in his victory over Ahmed al-Jazzar Pasha at the foot of Mount Tabor.

At Acre, on 20 March, Napoleon placed the fortress under siege. His attempt to take the fort would last until 21 May, but would end in an Ottoman victory. This defeat cost Napoleon his ambitions in the East, and he returned to Alexandria, where his army was met by Turkish reinforcements. 15,000 men had been shipped over from Rhodes, and on 25 July, the battle of Aboukir was fought. It ended with a final French victory just before Napoleon left Egypt on his return voyage to France.

It is not possible to say exactly how many lives were lost as a result of Napoleon's visit to the eastern Mediterranean. French losses at Acre alone were numbered at 2,300; whereas, at the battle of the Pyramids, the Mamelukes lost 20, 000 men, and at Aboukir the Turkish death count was 13,000. All told, the loss to life of French, Turkish and Egyptians was somewhere between 50 and 100,000.

Plague so great will arrive with the large pod
It was during the French occupation of Jaffa that an outbreak of plague struck with frightening rapidity. In a matter of days the death toll had mounted to nearly 300 dead or dying. Even after the soldiers left Jaffa, the death toll continued to diminish their number. [4]

Upon reaching Acre, but failing after several vain attempts to take its heavily defended fortress, Bonaparte realised that his ambition to emulate Alexander the Great and continue on to India had become impossible. He therefore resolved to return to Cairo. But with many of his men now victims of the plague, and too weak to make the journey back across the desert sands, Bonaparte "gave orders that they should be given a fatal dose of opium." A broth laced with the "narcotic drug that is obtained from the [large] unripe seed pods of the opium poppy" was therefore administered to the *plague* victims. [5]

Help nearby and the remedies very far away
At the time this was taking place, *help was nearby*. Admiral Perrée had recently arrived at Acre with a small flotilla, and his ships were in a position to transport many of the sick and wounded men back to Alexandria. But he declined—presumably for fear that he and his crew might become infected by plague. [6] The main body of French troops were therefore left to carry their sick and injured comrades on the long trek back across the desert to Egypt, or leave them to die: knowing that the much needed *remedies were very far away*. [7]

Summary: *Napoleon reappears in this prophecy as 'the little one': a play on words, since he was known amongst his men as 'the little corporal'. The prophecy draws attention to his Egyptian campaign, with words such as 'distant' and 'humid'. It was also a campaign that cost many thousands of lives, which is also indicated by 'massacres' and 'blood'. Another feature of the prophecy is its reference to Napoleon's use of 'mercy killing', which he ordered for those suffering from the plague, and those who were unable to take part in his retreat back to Cairo. The apparent contradiction in the final line is explained by the response of the flotilla's captain, who declined to provide transport for the sick.*

76   *En Germanie naistront diuerses sectes,*
        S'approchans fort de l'heureux paganisme,
        Le cueur captive & petites receptes,
        Feront retour à payer le vray disme.

77   *Les tiers climat soubz Aries comprins,*
        L'an mil sept cens vingt & sept en Octobre,
        Le roy de Perse par ceux d'Egypte prins:
        Conflict, mort, perte: à la croix grand opprobre.

climat (OF),a division in the sky *or* a portion of the world between south and north; soubz (OF sous) under; comprins (OF) comprehended;

                The third region under Aries, comprehended (**PERSIA**),   1722
                The year **1727** in **OCTOBER**,
                The King of Persia seized through those of Egypt:
                Conflict, death, loss: a great opprobrium to the cross.

The third region under Aries comprehended

The key to understanding this opening phrase occurs in the two words, 'Aries comprehended'. For this we need to consult Claudius Ptolemy's *Tetrabiblos*, written in the middle of the second century AD: for which there existed a Latin translation available in the sixteenth century, at the time this prophecy was written.

In Book II of the *Tetrabiblos*, Ptolemy wrote, "there are four triplicities of the entire earth, distinguishable in the zodiac. The first, composed of Aries, Leo, and Sagittarius, is the north-west triplicity." He then continues by defining the "second, consisting of Taurus, Virgo, and Capricorn," which he places in the south-east. The third region he notes is in the north-east, which he refers to as the northern part of Magna Asia. The remaining region he sets in Western Æthiopia, and refers to it as Libya. From this, we are to understand that *the third region under Aries* is the northern part of Magna Asia (Aries marks the commencement of the zodiacal year).

"Magna, Asia, East of the Euphrates" [1] consists of present day Iran, which was called Persia up until March 1935, when the Shah asked for the country to be internationally recognized as Iran. Asia Minor, on the other hand, was to the west of the Euphrates.

The year 1727 in October

On 12 October 1722, Mir Mahmud, leading an army of Afghans, successfully conquered Persia from the east. The Ottoman Turks, who already held Syria and Palestine, seized this as an opportunity to add further to their own empire. Consequently, "In 1723 [...] the Ottomans invaded from the west ravaging western Persia." [2]

In Russia, Peter I responded to the conquests occurring in Persia by proposing an agreement. In return for lands on the southern and western shores of the Caspian Sea, he would provide military aid to the beleaguered Persians. After this, the southern part of Russia became involved in *the third region under Aries*.

An agreement followed this interception in which a large part of Persia became divided between the Ottomans and the Russians. This led to the *Treaty of Constantinople* (23 June 1724), which was formerly signed by Turkey and Russia. The treaty authorised extensive territorial gains to the west at the expense of Persia, which was forced to surrender its extensive borderlands to Turkey.

Three years later, Persia made its own agreement with the Ottoman Empire; this resulted in the "Treaty of Hamedan [...] signed in October 1727." [3] The city of Hamedan had been forced to surrender to the Ottomans, but it was subsequently recaptured by Shah Afshari. According to the treaty, the Ottomans agreed that it could be retained by Persia. Furthermore, under this new alliance, Persia also agreed to join forces with the Ottoman Turks against their Russian occupiers. In return for their assistance, they were promised recognition from Turkey. [4]

The King of Persia seized through those of Egypt

The Shah (King) of Persia's negotiating strength in the face of Turkish opposition was mainly due to the alliance he had earlier formed in 1726 with Nader Quli Beg, leader at the head of a band of 5000 tribal brigands. Beg proved his worth as a brilliant general, transforming the Persian army into a disciplined body of men that eventually gained victory over the Afghan rebels holding Isfahan. He also forced the Turks to abandon the western regions of Persia. Thereafter, by threatening war against the Russians, he forced them to withdraw. By doing so, they abandoned territory that had earlier been seized. [5]

Turning to Egypt, which had been conquered by the Ottomans in 1517 (hence 'those of Egypt') were the Turks – the oracle foretells what happened next.

> Relations between Nader and the Shah had declined, as the latter grew jealous of his general's military successes. While Nader was absent in the east, Tahmasp tried to assert himself by launching a foolhardy campaign to recapture Yerevan. He ended up losing all of Nader's recent gains to the Ottomans, and signed a treaty ceding Georgia and Armenia in exchange for Tabriz. Nader saw that the moment had come to ease Tahmasp from power. He denounced the treaty, seeking popular support for a war against the Ottomans. [6]

It was therefore *through* the Ottomans – *those of Egypt* - that Beg was able to take the first step towards *seizing the king of Persia.*

Before replacing Tahmasp II, he invited him to the palace which he owned, where he had organized a banquet. It was the first step planned towards his *coup d'état.* His second step was to inveigle his royal guest into intoxicating himself. Beg then paraded the Shah before his people as a drunken figure, fit only for mirth and ridicule. The Court members agreed, and Tahmasp was replaced by Abbas III, the Shah's infant son. [7]

In this manner, Beg was appointed Regent to Abbas III (7 September 1732). Three and a half years later (8 March 1736), having been the effective ruler of the country during this time, Beg "had himself crowned as Nader Shah. This marked the official end of the Safavid dynasty. Abbas was sent to join his father in prison in Sabzevar, Khorasan." [8] Three years later, having been told there was a plot to restore the former Shah to the throne, Nader had both Tahmasp II and Abbas III murdered.

Conflict, death, loss

Having achieved his ambition to obtain control over Persia, Nader set out to expand both his wealth and his rule as an empire builder.

> First, after a long siege in 1736, he recovers Kandahar - the stronghold of the Afghan chieftains who have until recently been in possession of Isfahan. With Afghanistan safely back under imperial control, Nadir Shah is next tempted further east (like Timur before him) into the fabulously wealthy empire of India. [9]

In December 1738 Nader crossed the Indus at Attock and defeated the army of the Moghul emperor, Mohammed Shah. In March he occupied Delhi, losing 900 Persians, to an Indian counter attack. As a reprisal he ordered the massacre of approximately 30,000 Indians. In 1740 he attacked and conquered Bukhara in a continuing campaign of conflict and conquest. This included Bahrain, which had been held by the Arabs: and Oman, with its capital Muscat.

In 1743 Nader started another war against the Ottoman Empire. But he also began to suffer increasingly from paranoia. In the end his guards, fearing his suspicions would be directed at them, decided to strike first.

> Nader Shah was assassinated on 20 June 1747, at Quchan in Khorasan. He was surprised in his sleep by Salah Bey, captain of the guards, and stabbed with a sword. [...] After his death the entire Empire of Nader Shah fell into anarchy [... and] quickly disintegrated. [10]

Nader Shah's lost Empire had encompassed what is now part of, or includes, Iran, Iraq, Afghanistan, Pakistan, Tajikistan, Turkmenistan, Uzbekistan, India, Georgia, Russia, Armenia, Azerbaijan, Oman and the Persian Gulf. These lands also coincide with the region alluded to in the opening line of this prophecy.

A great opprobrium to the cross

This final prediction reveals another of the Seer's enigmatic stratagems. It jumps tracks while still pursuing a Persian theme. The prediction refers to a satirical book portraying French life as seen through the eyes of two Persian travellers. The book, written by Charles Louis Montesquieu under the title: 'Lettres Persanes' (*Persian Letters*) was published in 1722: the same year that Mir Mahmud overran Persia (see above).

The years following the book's publication were to see it bring much 'opprobrium to the cross' So much harm was suffered by the Catholic Church from the derisory comparisons which it drew between Islam and Christianity, with the book especially satirizing Catholic doctrine.

It also criticized the papal bull, *Unigenitus*, which Clement XI had issued against Catholic dissidents and the followers of Cornelius Jansen. [11]

The author of the *Persian Letters* was part of a new and growing intellectual movement called the Enlightenment (the Age of Reason). It was anti-religion, anti-revelation, and anti-inspiration; in fact, anti anything that failed a rational (material?) explanation. Its origins sprang from the growth of ideas that surrounded 'Newtonian materialism'. In its time, it attracted many scientists, philosophers, politicians, and artists who were opposed to Christianity

Summary: *This is the fourth quatrain to include the year in which a part of the prediction would be fulfilled (see 1/49; 2/51; 3/56). In this prophecy, the seer once again steps outside of French history, as he did before, for Britain, Hungary, Russia and the United States. It may therefore be concluded that those nations, which will later appear on the world stage as protagonists in some major event, or events, have been given space for their political history (post 1555) to become part of these oracles. In which case, this verse outlines Persia's history in the early 18th century, when it became entwined with that of Turkey and Russia.*

78   Le chef d'Escosse auec six d'Alemagne
     Par gens de mer Orientaux captifs,
     Transuerseront le Calpre & Hespagne
     Present en Perse au nouueau roy craintif.

79   L'ordre fatal sempiternal par chaisne
     Viendra tourner par ordre consequent:
     Du port Phocen sera rompue la chaisne:
     La cité prinse, l'ennemi quand & quand.

80   Du regne Anglois l'indigne deschassé,
     Le conseillier par ire mis à feu:
     Ses adherans iront si bas tracer,
     Que le bastard sera demi receu.

feu (AF. famille) family, kindred; tracer (OF) inquire, seek out; bas(OF) abject, dejected

     Concerning the English reign, the unworthy one cast out.
     The counsellor through anger expended at the family:
     His adherents, inquiring, will be so dejected
     That the unlawfully begotten will be half accepted.

This foretells of trouble to the reign in England. But without names, it is dangerous to speculate further. Its resolution is therefore left until the future fulfils its meaning; for as in Proverbs: *Only he that hath witt, may know the secrets of the Lord.*

81   Le grand criard sans honte audacieux,
     Sera esleu gouuerneur de l'armée.
     La hardiesse de son contentieux,
     Le pont rompu, cité de peur pasmée.

82   Freius, Antibol, villes au tour de Nice,
     Seront vastées fer, par mer & par terre:
     Les sauterelles terre & mer vent propice,
     Prins, morts, trousses, pilles sans loy de guerre.

83   Les lons cheueux de la Gaule Celtique
     Accompagnés d'estranges nations,
     Metront captif la gent Aquitanique,
     Pour succomber à internitions.

84   La grand cité sera bien desolée
     Des habitans vn seul n'y demeurra:
     Mur, sexe, temple, & vierge violée
     Par fer, feu, peste, canon peuple mourra.

     The great city (**PARIS**) will be thoroughly desolated,
     Of the inhabitants, not one soul will linger there:
     Wall, sex, church, & virgin violated,
     By iron, fire, pestilence, cannon, a people will perish.

Apart from a neutron bomb, chemical warfare would be the other option for rendering an entire *city desolate*. These oracles have so far been consistent in identifying Paris as *the great city*: and sometimes, by just calling it *the city*.

85   *La cité prinse par tromperie & fraude,*
        Par le moyen d'vn beau ieune atrapé:
        Lassaut donné Roubine pres de l'AVDE
        Luy & touts morts pour auoir bien trompé.

86   *Vn chef d'Ausonne aux Hespagnes ira*
        Par mer sera arrest dedans Marseille:
        Auant sa mort vn long temps languira:
        Apres sa mort l'on verra grand merueille:

87   *Classe Gauloyse n'aproches de Corseigne*
        Moins de sardaigne, tu t'en repentiras
        Trestous mourres frustrés de l'aide Grogne:
        Sang nagera: captif ne me croyras.

grogne (AF *apocope:* grognerie) headland, cape, promontory

French fleet do not approach Corsica,   1655
Much less Sardinia, you will repent of it:
You will all die frustrated by the headland aid;
Blood will float. Captive, you will not believe me.

Anatole le Pelletier gave a brief, yet detailed explanation of the history that does appear to fulfil this prophecy. Le Pelletier was a nineteenth-century French scholar, with a deserved reputation for researching these prophecies, and especially the man behind them. Unfortunately, his grasp of history did not stretch to providing sources for the explanations he gave. Moreover, there is also a gloss of superficiality related to many of the explanations that he cites as prophetic fulfilments. At a deeper level of inspection, these are apt to show, conclusively, that his account, even if it is historically correct, which is not always evident, fails to fit with *exactitude* the prophecy to which he refers. Optimistic commentary is a common fault with all previous commentators, and it mars their reputation while at the same time throwing doubt upon the credibility of the Seer.

In the present case, I have attempted to confirm Le Pelletier's explanation, but without success. This, I am willing to accept falls entirely upon my shoulders. And I am content that a researcher in the future will account for my shortcoming by citing the reference(s) that persuaded le Pelletier of its accuracy. One thing only have I learned. It is that le chevalier de Ferrière was of a titled French family with their coat of arms (de gueules à la barre d'argent, chargée de trios fleches de sable), and that 150 years after the naval event described by le Pelletier, two members of the Ferrière family, Hector and Louis-Joachim, both served in the navy against the English during the Napoleonic Wars—the latter having fought at Trafalgar. But enough said, I shall now recount the explanation provided by le Pelletier in the words of his English advocate, the Victorian, classical scholar, Charles Ward.

M. le Pelletier tells us of a French squadron, commanded by the Chevalier de la Ferrière in 1655, that foundered in the Gulf of Lyons in coasting Corsica and Sardinia. All hands perished: they did not, he says, pass Cape Pourceau. He points out that *Grogne* is the synonym of Pourceau, which is a cape with a little port in the Mediterranean. This may have more to support it than appears at first sight, but I think it much simpler to take it for what it says. *Grogne* is the same as Groin, cape or headland which runs out into the sea. In other words: nothing will put off to you from the headland where you founder; there will you all be drowned; for what better will your master pilot be for this advertisement of mine? Jean de Rian was the master pilot, and *Le Captif* was his nickname, as he had been a slave. [1]

The verb, *grogner*, does mean 'to grunt'; hence, the connexion to Pourceau (a pig). The Universal Dictionary of Maritime Geography, volume 3, refers twice to *les Pourceau*. They are rocks close to Cadiz in south-west Spain, therefore washed by the Atlantic Ocean; alternatively, they are rocks on the coast of Norway at some distance from Oslo. This is not sufficient to disprove le Pelletier, but there is another problem—'blood will float'. Drowning does not normally cause such an outpouring of blood that it becomes worthy of a mention. And, it is there, although not entirely convincingly, that the matter must be left.

> 88   *De Barcelonne par mer si grand armee,*
>   *Toute Marseille de frayeur tremblera:*
>   *Isles saisies de mer aide fermée,*
>   *Ton traditeur en terre nagera.*
>
>   From Barcelona so great an army by sea,   1591
>   All Marseilles will tremble with fear,
>   Islands seized, aid from the sea shut off:
>   Your traitor (**CASAULX**) will swim on land.

From Barcelona, so great an army by sea

This prophecy concerns the coastal city of Marseilles, during a period when Henri IV had yet to be recognized as the legitimate King of France. Arrayed against him were supporters of the Catholic League. Among its members was Charles Casaulx, the captain of the city's bourgeois militia. In February 1591, he became the Head of the Holy Catholic League, seizing power and imposing a "dictatorship marking the temporary defeat of the local merchant aristocracy." Together with the city's Magistrate, Louis d'Aix, the two men formed a powerful duumvirate. [1]

On March 2, 1591, the Countess of Sault, who had helped Casaulx to achieve his position as captain of the militia, arrived with the Duke of Savoy in Marseille, intending to meet and discuss matters with Casaulx. After inspecting the fortress on the island of If, the Duke sailed for Spain to ask his father-in-law, Philip II, to aid the League in its defence of a Catholic monarch. This suited Philip, since he was proposing the Spanish Infanta as the queen of France.

That summer, "15 galleys and 1000 Spanish soldiers" arrived in the Bay of Marseilles: having been sent "from Barcelona", Spain's major Mediterranean port.

All Marseilles will tremble with fear

The people of Marseilles therefore had reason to be fearful, for "During the wars of religion, Marseilles took part against the Protestants, and long refused to acknowledge Henri IV." Consequently, armed conflict against Protestants seemed imminent. But this was not all that the citizens had reason to fear. In the autumn of 1591, the Duke of Savoy decided to replace Casaulx, and rule the city himself. With the aid of Baron Claude Antoine Méolhan, who commanded the fort of Our Lady of the Guard, Savoy occupied the Abbey of Saint Victor. But the Marseillais counter-attacked, and were able to recover the abbey (November 20, 1591). This victory increased the authority of Casaulx. And when the Duke of Savoy suffered a new defeat on 15 December at Vinon-sur-Verdon, by the troops of Bernard of Valletta, he withdrew back to his estates.

Marseille then suffered a fresh attack on 6 August 1592 when the troops of Gaspard Ponteves, Comte of Carcés, and an enemy of the Countess of Sault (then living in the city), attempted to invade Marseilles. During the affray, a soldier accidentally caused an explosion which wounded or killed about fifty of the invaders. It was subsequently called the "Day of the Scorched" and the attack was repulsed by Casaulx's militia.

Islands seized, aid from the sea shut off

The Château d'If in the Bay of Marseilles was an island fortress built by Francis I to defend Marseilles from an attack by sea. If is the smallest island in the Frioul archipelago: a group of islands that includes Pomègues, Ratonneau, If and Tiboulen. But with Spanish ships anchored in the Bay to protect the Catholic League, *the islands* had effectively been *seized* and Marseilles was "shut off from approaches by sea." This meant that *aid* intended for the land forces sent by Henri IV to Marseilles, was unable to be received by them.

Your traitor will swim on land

On 25 July 1593, Henri IV converted to the Catholic faith, and became recognized as the rightful King of France. But it took the parliament at Aix-en-Provence until 5 January 1594 to profess the same recognition.

Casaulx, who remained stubbornly opposed to this recognition, found that he had now become increasingly isolated, and when Pope Clement VIII removed the excommunication from Henri, Casaulx's cause was lost; worse still, it became his duty to rally the people of Marseilles to express loyalty to their new King. Instead, in November 1595, Casaulx sent a delegation to the King of Spain, headed by his brother, François de Casaulx, pleading for assistance.

Casaulx had now made himself *a traitor* to the King. On 7 December 1595, Etienne Bernard, a former member of the Catholic League, arrived in Marseille to preside over the sovereign court of the city, and especially to persuade Casaulx to recognize Henri IV. But Casaulx refused to be convinced: although still wanting to retain his position as First Consul of Marseilles, even though it would be in opposition to the King.

On 28 December, more Spanish ships and soldiers arrived. These were reinforced by a further flotilla in January, all under the command of Charles Doria.

On 6 June 1596, Charles de Lorraine, duc de Guise, who had been appointed Governor of Provence marched his troops to the gates of Marseilles and attempted a first assault, which was repulsed by Casaulx. Guise therefore sought the help of two disaffected citizens inside the city; these were Geoffroy Dupre, a notary who had been dismissed by Casaulx for his royalist opinions, and Nicolas de Bausset, a lawyer who had escaped from prison where he had been locked up for his loyalty to the King. They approached the captain of the Reale Gate, a thirty-three-year-old Corsican named Pierre de Libertat. He was informed that the duc de Guise and Etienne Bernard were promising to reward him with the position of Magistrate of Marseille, Commander of the Reale Gate, and of Notre-Dame fortress, as well as providing him with two galleys and a gratuity of 160.000 ecus, if he would open the city gate to Guise's troops. [2]

The bribe worked, and an attack took place on 17 February 1596. The cavalry of the duc de Guise arrived at the Plain of Saint-Michel, which caused a warning to be given inside the city. Casaulx with 16 guards went to inspect the Reale Gate. Upon their arrival, Libertat stepped up to Casaulx and struck him down with two surprise blows from his sword. The gates were then thrown open and the city was quickly taken by the Duke's troops. "As for the stinking carcass of Casaulx, which was in sight, rudely handled, and swimming in a stream of his blood," [3] it was dragged to the churchyard of St Martin and interred amidst shameful impieties and blasphemies.

Four days later, twelve Spanish galleys arrived in the Bay of Marseilles bringing with them 1200 men and the delegates sent by Casaulx. News of the First Consul's death was conveyed to the squadron, and it returned, to Barcelona.

Summary: Unlike the previous quatrain, this prophecy abounds with independently written, verifiable accounts that confirm what took place in Marseilles, 25 years after the death of the seer. The arrival of ships from Spain, blockading the city's port and its offshore islands to prevent aid arriving by sea to assist Henri IV is foretold. Opposing the King was the head of Marseilles' Catholic League, Charles Casaulx. His death at the hands of Pierre de Libertat, who then opened the city gates to the King's army, earned Libertat a statue in Marseilles, which still stands.

89   *En ce temps la sera frustré Cypres*
      De son secours, de ceux de mer Egée:
      Vieux trucidés: mais par masles & lyphres
      Seduict leur roy, royne plus outragée.

90   *Le grand Satyre & Tigre de Hyrcanie,*
      Don presente à ceux de l'Ocean:
      Le chef de classe istra de Carmanie
      Qui prendra terre au Tyrren Phocean.

91   *L'arbre qu'auoit par long temps mort seché,*
         Dans vne nuit viendra à reuerdir:
         Cron. roy malade, prince pied estaché,
         Craint d'ennemis fera voile bondir.

92   *Le monde proche du dernier periode,*
         Saturne encore tard sera retour:
         Translat empire deuers nation Brodde:
         L'œil arraché à Narbon par Autour.

         The world draws near for its last period,
         Saturn again will return late:
         The empire reduces towards an effeminate speaking nation:
         The eye annexed to Narbon by reason of Goshawk.

This is another prophecy that refers to the approach of the end of the world. The extended time taken by Saturn to complete its orbit appears to confirm the exhaustion of the Sun, which is predicted in Century One, N°. 48. Saturn was then the farthest known planet in the Zodiac. The third and fourth lines therefore refer to matters still in the future, hence their meaning remains uncertain. Moreover, Brodde (in old French – Brode) has more than one meaning.

93   *Dans Auignon tout le chef de l'empire,*
         Fera arrest pour Paris desolé:
         Tricast tiendra l'Annibalique ire:
         Lyon par change sera mal consolé.

94   *De cinq cent ans plus compte on tiendra,*
         Celuy qu'estoit l'aornement de son temps:
         Puis à vn coup grande clarté donrra
         Que par ce siecle les rendra trescontens.

compte (OF) an unlikely tale, or fib; tenir (OF) judge, deem; estoit (etait) was; aornement (AF- aorement) prière, also paragram and anagram – aorneme[d]t Notredame; trescontens (AF tres contens - lutte) very contested (N.B. Text from Leffen's copy)

         For five hundred years plus, men will deem him an unlikely tale,   20..?
         He that was the request (**NOTREDAME**) of his time:
         Then, at a stroke, he will give great clarity
         That for this age, it will render them very contested.

For five hundred years plus, men will deem him an unlikely tale

Michel de Nostredame was born on Thursday 14 December 1503 (O.S.) and he died on Tuesday 2 July 1566. Consequently, 500 years plus brings his fame into the 21st century.

Since the publication of his prophecies, stories of incidents that took place during his lifetime have frequently been recounted. In fact, to celebrate the fifth centenary of the Seer's birth, several major biographies were published between 2003 and 2004. [1]

Despite this passage of time, his prophecies have continued to remain in print, keeping alive his memory, although rarely for reasons of solid scholarship. There have also been abrasive criticisms of the man, which deemed him and his prophecies an unlikely tale. It can now be safely said that any errors pinned upon the Seer have been exposed as presumptuous bias. The genuine critic is limited to just three directions from which to mount an attack. (1) Is the original text genuine? (2) Can the words legitimately mean what they say: allowing the variety of their sources? (3) Does history confirm everything written within the prophecy? Because all three conditions have already been met by the author in each of the quatrains that appear within these ten chapters, is anticipated that this degree of accuracy will not suddenly cease after five centuries. Future generations will therefore have a firm basis for the remaining prophecies.

He that was the request (Notredame) of his time

Soon after publication of *Les Prophéties,*

      The repute of Nostradamus grew [...] until it came to the ears of Queen Catherine de Medici and Henry II. [...] In the following year, 1556, they sent for him to attend the Court in Paris. [...] The

Lord Constable Montmorency attended him at his inn, and presented him to the King in person. The King showed him high favour, and ordered him to be lodged at the palace of the Cardinal de Bourbon, Archbishop of Sens, during his stay in the capital.

While at Court, his biographer claims he was "loaded with honours and consulted on high matters (de choses importantes)." Another biographer, Jean Aimes Chavigny remarked, "that those who came to France sought Nostradamus as the only thing to be seen there."[2]

The poet, Pierre de Ronsard wrote a poetic tribute to de Nostredame, see page 36.

Then, at a stroke, he will give great clarity

At some time during the 21st century, according to his timing, the predictions he published in the middle of the sixteenth century will appear in public; and with a suddenness, so that at a stroke they will reveal such obvious clarity, it will be impossible to ignore their meaning.

This invites the question—Why the twenty-first century? The answer is that it is the right time. Western society has undergone a massive, moral sea change since the 1960s: with the result that people have either forgotten God, or are deliberately ignoring Him in order to devote their admiration to the sciences and its 'high priests'. Prophecy sweeps away the foothold of the sciences by destroying physical *cause and effect* – the mainspring of the sciences. An effect that exists before the activity of its 'pysical cause' requires a different explanation for its existence.

That for this age, it will render them very contested

The Hebrew Bible already has its prophets, and Christianity has its New Testament prophecies. By the grace of God, secular societies have now been given their own seer, for which reason prophecy will become a contentious subject. The reason for this should surprise no one. Once the truth of prophetic knowledge becomes an accepted fact, its implications will contradict and eventually expose the materialistic outlook on the world as a sham. With this, the validity of *all* scientific reasoning, as currently taught in the classrooms and lecture halls, will no longer hold a place in the causality of the world.

To add to their dilemma, scientists have also stripped themselves of direct access to knowledge of 'matter', by admitting their lack of a visual outlook. Instead, they must now rely upon mental concepts and the notion of 'matter' as being one and the same thing, since both emerge from the same time-line. Failure to comprehend this will result in circular reasoning, in which the notion of 'matter' is held to be the cause of its own effect.

Time is a one-track route across eternity along which the conscious mind progresses, and from which the data that forms the external world is received and decoded. Time, space and the stuff of the world are inseparable and immutable against a timeless background. It is this that feeds the foresight of temporal events, before they have added to mankind's history of the world.

> 95   *La loy Moricque on verra defaillir:*
> *Apres vne autre beaucoup plus seductiue,*
> *Boristhenes premier viendra faillir:*
> *Pardons & langue vne plus attractiue.*

loy (AF manière de vivre) way of living; Moricque (In French, 'More' allows a double meaning; it is either the name, MORE or a Moor, hence: Moresque, can be More-like or Moorish); defaillir (OF) decaying; seductiue (L seducere) to lead away; Pardons (AF dons) donations, gifts; Boristhenes (L) River Dnieper, *also* Boris + anagram, –Yeltsin (see commentary).

One will see the More-like way of living (**COMMUNISM**) decaying,	1991
Afterwards, one other much more enticing (**CAPITALISM**),	
The Dnieper (**BORIS YELTSIN**) above others will come to fail:	
One more attractive through donations and language.	

One will see the More-like way of living

Sir Thomas More's book *Utopia* was written in Latin, and published in December 1516. It would therefore have been known to the Seer. The book "depicts an ideal state ordered by reason." This has drawn commentators to compare it with the communist state of the twentieth century.

Karl Kautsky, for example, author of *Thomas More and his Utopia* (1890), regarded More as "an embryo Marxist." Another, where a similar comparison is drawn, is the Encyclopædia Britannica. It describes Lenin's brochure, *The State and Revolution*, as his most "Utopian" work, and his "doctrinal springboard to power." Notably, "The basis of Utopian economy was common ownership. [...] Without private ownership the vices of greed and pride would have nothing on which to feed [...] common ownership is the prerequisite for a happy community." [1]

Decaying

Communism became embraced as a political philosophy in Russia soon after the October Revolution of 1917. But, with the final decade of the twentieth century about to begin, the Soviet Union's economy collapsed, hastened by a breakdown in every sector. Industrial output fell by almost one fifth, and agriculture by nearly as much. Its greatly vaunted energy programme also saw a reduction of one tenth. And, whereas the country's GDP had shown a deficit of 4% in 1990, this increased to nearly 14% one year later. The government therefore found itself on the verge of bankruptcy, and unable to sustain the country's level of imported goods. Food prices continued to soar in Russian state-controlled shops until they had almost doubled, and outlying villages were unable to obtain sufficient fuel for everyday living. "Gorbachëv had scarcely any credit left with Soviet society. The economy was collapsing in every sector." [2]

Afterwards

Up until this time, Mikhail Gorbachev, the General Secretary of the Communist Party in the Soviet Union, had been enjoying widespread popularity, both at home and abroad. But, *after the collapse of the Russian economy* in August 1991 an attempt was made to replace him, and he was put under house arrest at his dacha in the Crimea. [3]

One other much more enticing,

With Gorbachev out of the way, Boris Yeltsin became Russia's new Premier. Among Yeltsin's first actions was the banning of the Russian Communist Party and seizure of its property. He followed this by removing state control from the sale of goods. No longer would the government fix prices. Nationalization together with subsidies gave place to privatisation.

A system of vouchers was introduced, enabling citizens to buy into companies that had formerly been state owned. Yeltsin's premiership proved to be *much more enticing* than that which had been passed on to Gorbachev, as evidenced by the revival of the free market. "For most people the replacement of communism with capitalism was most obviously manifested in the tin kiosks erected in all towns and cities." [4]

The Seer then looks back at the break-up of the Soviet Union, and the overthrow of the communist order, by predicting Ukraine's failing would be a major cause of revolt.

The Dnieper (Boris Yeltsin) above others will come to fail

The River Dnieper flows through Ukraine's capital city, Kiev. It was there, on 1 December 1991, that its citizens held a referendum to decide their future. "The people of Ukraine, including most of its Russian inhabitants, disagreed with Gorbachëv, and on 1 December they voted for independence in a referendum." When the votes were counted, a majority of nine to one had decided to leave the Soviet Union. [5] It was this decision – above that of other countries in the USSR – that helped Yeltsin break with the communist system. For, without the support of "fifty-three million Ukrainians," Gorbachev was rendered powerless and unable to continue in government.

On 25 December, the former president of communist Russia announced his departure. It was at this point that the Soviet Union ceased to exist. [6]

It is noteworthy that Ukraine has been indicated by *Boristhenes*, to which has been added the word 'premier'. Boris Yeltsin became the first President of the Russian Federation on 10 July 1991. It is therefore remarkable that not only can *Boristhenes* be split to read BORIS THENES, but these letters can also be rearranged as, BORIS ENTSEH. By converting them into Cyrillic script, and allowing one letter to change, as permitted with paragrams, Борис Ельцин – pronounced BORIS YELTSIN is obtained. The third line of the oracle then reads, 'Premier Boris Yeltsin will come to fail.'

> On 31 December 1999, in a surprise announcement. [...] Yeltsin said he had resigned. [...] Yeltsin said: "I want to beg forgiveness for your dreams that never came true. And also I would like to beg forgiveness not to have justified your hopes." [7]

Two complementary statements are therefore obtained from a single prophetic phrase.

One more attractive through donations and language

"In early 1992 Yeltsin toured Western Europe and signed friendship treaties with Britain and France in exchange for aid and credits." In America, similar concessions were obtained, and it was through these donations that Communism's former leaders succumbed to a language more attractive.

> After a personal appeal from former President Richard Nixon, the Bush administration also approved an economic assistance package for Russia, and Congress voted funds to help Russia dismantle its nuclear weapons.

The huge financial packages received from two US presidents, George H. W. Bush and Bill Clinton were further embellished with the latter donating more than one and a half billion dollars. America also agreed to a fixed rate of currency exchange for Russia's former satellite states so as to stabilize their economies. [8]

Summary: *This prophecy is a further instalment in the political history of Russia. It began with Peter the Great in Century One No. 14. In Century Eight No. 15, we shall meet Catherine the Great. Czar Nicholas and the Russian Revolution were previously discussed in Century One No. 14, and will be followed by Lenin and the October Revolution in Century Five No. 26. The failure of Communism, which became bankrupt in 1990, brings the prophetic history of Russia up-to-date, It is noteworthy that Ukraine has been singled out as the country that was foremost in leaving the USSR, and the country is indicated by the Latin name for the River Dnieper. This has allowed Boris Yeltsin's name to emerge from a paragram.*
In a timeless universe, this type of foresight is 'present knowledge' to an 'external' observer Even so; the cryptic manner in which the name is concealed by the Cyrillic alphabet must surely extend beyond the ability of a sixteenth-century scholar, which implies an unseen intelligence at work.

> 96   *Chef de FOVSSAN aura gorge couper*
>   *Par le ducteur du limier & leurier:*
>   *Le faict patré par ceux du mont TARPEE*
>   *Saturne en Leo XIII. de Feurier.*

> 97   *Nouuelle loy terre neufue occuper*
>   *Vers la Syrie, Iudee, & Palestine:*
>   *Le grand empire barbare corruer,*
>   *Auant que Phebés son siecle determine.*

barbare (OF) barbarous, uncivil, ignorant; corruer (L corru\ere) falling together; Auant que (OF adverb) previously; Phebés (L Phoeb\es) the moon; determine (OF) to finish;

> A new law occupying a new land,   1948
> Towards Syria, Judea and Palestine:
> The great barbarous empire falling together,
> Before that, the moon finishes its cycle.

A new law

The *new law* mentioned in the prophecy concerns the State of Israel: that is, "The Law of Return, which gave every Jew the right to immigrate." The state of Israel was founded in 1948 under new legislation that replaced the old oral and written laws of the Talmud and the Torah. Although Judaism continued to be based upon the teaching of the Hebrew prophets, politicians incorporated more modern ideas into the fabric of state legislature, principally that of political equality and social justice for all citizens, without distinction of race, creed or sex. [1]

Occupying a new land, towards Syria Judea and Palestine

The three nations referred to in the prophecy were those expressing concern at Israel's occupation of this 'new land', which they saw as having been thrust into their midst. *Judea* was formerly the name of southern Israel; *Palestine* was consolidated into Israel around 1000 BC, while *Syria*, overlooking Israel's northern frontier from the Golan Heights, was historically the nation's old enemy. [2]

The great barbarous empire falling together

It was therefore predictable that the Arab nations surrounding the recovered Jewish state would become increasingly hostile toward this intrusion. The United Nations had done its diplomatic best to ensure peace in the region, but it was not enough. In June 1967, a major war erupted. Egypt's President Nasser, backed by the United Arab Republic, and referred to in the oracle as 'barbarous', openly vowed to wipe Israel off the map. A full-scale war then developed with Egypt, Jordan and Syria the chief allies in a coalition that included other Arab states. [3] It began with a ring of steel encircling beleaguered Israel. Yet, remarkably, the war ended inside a week, in what became known as the Six Day War. During those six hectic days, the entire Arab coalition collapsed together, leaving Israel in command of the occupied territories, including Jerusalem. [4]

Before that, the moon finishes its cycle

The completion of the moon's cycle refers to the nineteen years it takes for a 'Metonic Cycle' to occur. Meton of Athens (ca. 440 BC) noticed that 235 lunar months made up almost exactly 19 solar years. The oracle has therefore predicted that *before the barbarous empire collapses, the moon will have completed its nineteen year cycle.* And that is precisely what happened. On 5 June 1967, the combined forces of the Arab countries attacked Israel. Five days later, on 10 June, the armies attacking the new land of Israel had all been defeated.

On 14 May 1948 the State of Israel was founded. Therefore, by allowing the moon (showing 34% of its image at an altitude of 55° in the constellation of Cancer) to commence its Metonic cycle, it will finish its series of changes 19 years later on 14 May 1967, which proved to be the case. Three weeks later, the Six Day War was fought, which resulted in the collapse of the Arab nations fighting against Israel—exactly as had been predicted 412 years before. [5]

Summary: *This oracle may be seen as the commencement of a prophecy made by Isaiah. "In that day the Root of Jesse will stand as a banner for the peoples. [...] He will raise a banner for the nations and gather the exiles of Israel; he will assemble the scattered people of Judah from the four quarters of the earth." (11: 10, 12). Ezekiel also predicted the return of the Jews to the land of their ancestors. "This is what the Sovereign LORD says. I will take the Israelites out of the nations where they have gone. I will gather them from all around and bring them back into their own land. I will make them one nation in the land, on the mountains of Israel." (37: 21, 22). The oracle given here has set the scene for these two biblical prophecies to be fulfilled. And to show the veracity of his own prophetic source, the seer has accurately combined his prophecy with the cycle of the moon over a period of 19 years. He has also gone to the Latin language for the precise word to describe what happened– corru\ere, which translates as 'falling together'.*

98   *Deus royals freres si fort guerroyeront,*
            Qu'entre eux sera la guerre si mortelle,
            Qu'vn chacun places fortes occuperont:
            De regne & vie sera leur grand querels.

            Two royal brothers (**LOUIS XIII & GASTON**) will make such powerful war,   1631
            That between them the conflict will be so deadly,
            When one each will occupy powerful places:
            Their huge quarrels will be about the reign and life.

Two royal brothers will make such powerful war

Gaston Duke of Orléans first came into conflict with his brother, the King, in 1626, when his mother and Cardinal Richelieu, forced him to marry Marie de Bourbon-Montpensier. She later died in childbirth. Gaston's reaction was to plot the death of Richelieu. However, the conspiracy was discovered and those involved were executed; that is, except the organiser, Gaston, who escaped punishment because of his relationship to the King, who was still childless. [1]

In November 1630, a bitter conflict broke out between Marie de Medici (the Queen-mother), and Cardinal Richelieu, which resulted in her exile to the château Compiègne. Gaston, in support of his mother, began raising troops. But during this enterprise he was forced to take refuge in the duchy of Lorraine. It was while there, that in January 1632 he secretly married Marguérite, the fifteen-year-old sister of Charles IV, Duke of Lorraine, who was then allied to Austria, which made him a foe of France. The King responded by marching against Lorraine. In preparation for the expected attack, Lorraine's troops poured over the French border to meet the King's army, but were soundly defeated. Gaston, now fearing for his life, fled to Brussels, which was then the capital city of the Spanish Netherlands.

To add further to Gaston's troubles, his marriage to Marguérite de Lorraine was denounced as an act of treason, because his new wife was the sister of the Duc de Lorraine, hostile to France. But worse, still, he had shown contempt for the King, by marrying without royal consent. [2]

That between them the conflict will be so deadly

The second war between the two royal brothers was fought after Gaston had allied himself with the Spanish Infanta, Isabella Clara Eugenia. She provided the troops for him to continue with his armed struggle against his brother, so that he might further his political ambition, which would then benefit Spain.

Gaston re-entered France with his troops in July 1631 to join the Duc de Montmorency, governor of Languedoc. Montmorency had agreed to support Gaston's rebel army by leading an uprising in the south. But Louis XIII's army met and defeated Gaston's rebel force soon after they crossed the border into France. Gaston once again escaped and fled back to the Netherlands. The royal army then marched south and defeated Montmorency at the battle of Castelnaudary. We shall meet Montmorency again in Century Nine N°. 18. [3]

When one each will occupy powerful places

Among the powerful places occupied by Gaston was firstly, the fortified city of Nancy, where Gaston had fled after supporting his mother against Richelieu. It was defended by troops loyal to the Duke of Lorraine, but defeated by the army of Louis XIII. Gaston's second powerful place was in the Spanish Netherlands, from where he received aid and troops from the Spanish Infanta. But again he was defeated; and thirdly, in Languedoc, where the Duke of Montmorency had amassed his personal army in support of Gaston's incursion from the north. But on each occasion the King's brother was overcome and defeated.

Their huge quarrels will be about the reign and life

The oracle also furnishes the reasons for these quarrels, encapsulating them into two topics, *the reign and life.*

Gaston was the son of Henri IV; he had also inherited a major part of his father's character. It was therefore natural for him to resent the position obtained by Cardinal Richelieu: believing instead that it should be he who served as principal advisor to the King. His mother, who had grown to hate Richelieu, encouraged her son to replace him. This had led to her exile, and to Gaston seeking help from Lorraine.

It was while in Lorraine that a different trouble was revived. This time it concerned his personal life. Against his will he had been forced to take a wife who had then died nine months later, leaving him with a daughter, Anne-Marie-Louise.

Freed from his marriage, he fell for the charms of the pretty young sister of the duke, of Lorraine, and a marriage took place between the couple without royal assent. This infuriated the King, and Gaston was forced to seek safety under Spain's protection. It was this that led to another war waged against his brother, and with it, he suffered a further defeat.

Summary: *This prophecy does not leave much room for doubt as to who the two royal brothers were that made such deadly war against each other. While it is true that Henri III and his brother the duc d'Alençon wanted to kill each other at one time, their short-lived animosity never became the pitched battles that occurred between Gaston and Louis III. This prophecy was undoubtedly recognized by the King's son, Louis XIV, because not only were several books of the seer's prophecies dedicated to the Sun King, but in 1660, before taking over the reign of France, Louis and his mother, together with Cardinal Mazarin, paid homage to de Nostredame by visiting his place of burial in Salon.*

99   *Aux champs herbeux d'Alein & du Varneigne,*
        Du mont Lebron proche de la Durance,
        Camp de deux pars conflict sera sy aigre:
        Mesopatamie defaillira en la France.

100   *Entre Gaulois le dernier honoré.*
        D'homme ennemi sera victorieux:
        Force & terroir en moment exploré,
        D'vn coup de trait quand mourra l'envieux

References Century 3

N°.15

1 John A. Lynn, *The French Wars* 1667 – 1714, 16; & Louis XIV, Early Life and Marriage, *Encyclopædia Britannica 2001*: CD-ROM
2 Lynn, 15-17
3 Robin Briggs, *Early Modern France* 1560–1715, 158; & Roger Price, *A Concise History of France*, 62
4 E.N. Williams, *Dictionary of English and European History* 1485 – 1789, 274
5 Ibid 274
6 Christine Pevitt Algrant, *Madame de Pompadour*, 25
7 Ibid 25
8 *Wikipedia*, Philippe II, Duke of Orleans

N°. 25

1 wikipedia.org/wiki/Baoque
2 wikipedia.org/wiki/Naples
3 wikipedia.org/wiki/Sicily
4 britannica.com/EBchecked/topic/402903/Kingdom-of-Naples
5 wikipedia.org/wiki/Béarn
6 Ibid
7 wikipedia.org/wiki/Foix
8 Ibid
9 10, 11, wikipedia.org/wiki/Charles,_Duke_of_Mayenne

N°.27

1 wikipedia.org/wiki/Gadaffi
2 Reported in*The Daily Express* 'Storyville' review: 3 February 2014, p. 47
3 Reported in *Daily Mail* 7 April 2011 p. 6 &*The Guardian* 26 August 2011
4 wikipedia.org/wiki/Libyan_civil_war
5 Ibid

N°. 28

1 Desmond Seward, *Eugénie The Empress and Her Empire*, 1-4
2 Ibid 24, 30
3 Ibid 38-40
4 Ibid back cover, xii, 113
5 Ibid 1

N°. 30

1 A. Dumas, *Queen Margot*, xii
2 Leonie Frieda, *Catherine de Medici*, 165
3 *Le Comte de Montgomery* and *Domfront Castle*, Historic Walking Tour 3, see: http://members.lycos.co.uk/medieval_festivals/castle1.htm last visited 13.10.2008
4 Ibid
5 Balthazar Guynaud, la Concordance règne de Henri III, 122
6 Ibid
7 id
8 wikipedia.org/wiki/Gabriel,_comte_de_Montgomery
9 Ibid 303; Refer, also to L. Marlet, *Le Comte de Montgomery* (Paris, 1890)

N°. 37

1 David Chandler, *The Campaigns of Napoleon*, 53
2 Ibid 85, 130
3 Ibid 86-7; & A.N. Delavoye, *Life of Thomas Graham, Lord Lynedoch*, 115
4 Chandler, 86, 92
5 Ibid 86
6 id

N°. 39

1 R. Knecht, *Catherine de' Medici*, 183–4
2 Leonie Frieda, *Catherine de Medici*, 331, 334, 336
3 Knecht, 184
4 *Encyclopædia Britannica, 2001*, CD-ROM, 'Haute-Savoie'
5 Ibid Apennine Range – Physiography
6 Knecht, 185–67 ;
7 Frieda, 335–6

N°. 41

1 *Encyclopædia Britannica 2001* CD-ROM, Louis I de Bourbon, Ier Prince de Condé
2 R. Knecht, *Catherine de' Medici*, 73–4
3 E.N. Williams, *Dictionary of English and European History 1485-1789*, 103–4

4   Leonie Frieda, *Catherine de Medici*, 170
5   Ibid 125
6   Ibid, 214
7   Knecht, 272
8   Williams, 101

N°. 42

1   V. Cronin, *Louis XIV*, 21; & Ian Dunlop, *Louis XIV*, 2
2   C. Hibbert, *Rome The Biography of a City*, 8
3   N. Davies, *Europe A History*, 1225
4   Dunlop, 419-21
5   Ibid 420-1

N°. 44

1   militaryheritage.com/musket13.htm
2   wikipedia.org/wiki/Doglock
3   hoghtons.co.uk/wikka.php?wakka=Musket
4   bbc.co.uk/history/trail/wars_conflict/weapons/musket_to_breech_04.shtml
5   militaryheritage.com/musket13.htm

N°. 50

1   H.A.L. Fisher, *A History of Europe*, vol.1, 581–3
2   R. Knecht, *The French Religious Wars 1562 – 1598*, 86–7; & *Catherine de' Medici*, 258
3   Ibid (first source) 60; & Ibid (second source) 258
4   Ibid (first source) 60
5   R. Mousnier, *The Assassination of Henry IV* (trans. Joan Spencer) 215
6   Ibid 215
7   A. Horne, *Seven Ages of Paris*, 81-2
8   Ibid 81
9   Ibid
10   Ibid 81 - 2

N°. 51

1   E.N. Williams, *Dictionary of English and European History 1485-1789*, 172; & Leonie Frieda, *Catherine de Medici*,367;
     & M. Freer, *Henry III King of France and Poland*
2   A. Pettegree, *Europe in the Sixteenth Century*, 165
3   Freer, 274
4   P. Roberts, *A City In Conflict*, 172–3, 174–5, 178–9; & Freer, 264
5   Robert J. Knecht, *The French Religious Wars 1562-1598*, 20

N°. 53

1   Stephen P Halbrook, *Target Switzerland*, 23; & Ian Kershaw, *Hitler 1889 – 1936: Hubris*, 419–20
2   Kershaw, 162-5
3   Halbrook, 27
4   Kershaw, 588; & Rhineland, *Encyclopædia Britannica 2001*: CD-ROM
5   Ibid Rhineland
6   Karen Farrington, *Handbook of World War II*, 19-20

N°. 55

1   R. Knecht, *Catherine de' Medici*, 295; & Antonia Fraser, *Mary Queen of Scots*, 117
2   A. Pettegree, *Europe in the Sixteenth Century*, 153–4
3   Knecht, 157; & E.N. Williams, *Dictionary of English and European History 1485-1789*, 101; & Pettegree, 159
4   A. Horne, *Seven Ages of Paris*, 76
5   Leonie Frieda, *Catherine de Medici*, 275

N°. 56

1   wikipedia.org/wiki/Avignon#After_the_departure_of_the_popes
2   wikipedia.org/wiki/Michelade
3   wikipedia.org/wiki/Montauban
4   www.sunnyfrance.net/histoiredebeziers/historique_UK.htm
5   wikipedia.org/wiki/Nîmes
6   nndb.com/people/836/000093557/
7   Ian Littlewood, *The Rough Guide Chronicle France*, 2002: p. 135
8   worldfacts.us/France-Lyon.htm
9   wikipedia.org/wiki/Saint-Bruno_des_Chartreux
10   Ibid
11   wikipedia.org/wiki/Montpellier
12   tripadvisor.co.uk/Travel-g187153-s203/Montpellier:France:History.html
13   ot-montpellier.fr/en/historical-center-510
14   wikipedia.org/wiki/Ancien_R%C3%A9gime
15   Ibid

Nº. 57
1   Neil Grant, *Kings & Queens*, 53, 185, 192, 194 & 196
2   Ibid 210
3   Ibid 196
4   Turda, *Encyclopædia Britannica 2001:* CD-ROM; & Hungary - revolution, reaction and compromise, Ibid; & Felipe Fernàndez Armento (ed.) *The Times Guide to The Peoples of Europe* (revised edition), 219
5   Ibid 219
6   Bastarnae, *Encyclopædia Britannica 2001:* CD-ROM; & Hungary - revolution, reaction and compromise
7   Francis Joseph – The Emperor's peace policy, Ibid

Nº. 61
1   http://en.wikipedia.org/wiki/2003_invasion_of_Iraq
2   http://en.wikipedia.org/wiki/Abu_Ghraib_prisoner_abuse
3   www.Swissinfo.ch
4   Ibid
5   www.politico.com/news/stories/0309/20014.html
6   www.globalsecurity.org/military/world/iraq/baghdad-green-zone.htm
7   http://en.wikipedia.org/wiki/Abu_Ghraib_prisoner_abuse#More_evidence_of_torture
8   http://en.wikipedia.org/wiki/Extraordinary_rendition
9   http://rawstory.com/news/2008/Cheney_admits_authorizing_detainees_torture

Nº. 66
1   Robert J. Knecht, *The French Religious Wars 1562–1598*, 29
2   E.N. Williams, *Dictionary of English and European History 1485-1789*, 104
3   Knecht, 43
4   R. Knecht, *Catherine de' Medici*, 72
5   Knecht, 43
6   fr.wikipedia.org/wiki/Louis_Ier_de_Bourbon-Condé

Nº. 74
1   Florence, Faenza and Imola… part of the Papal States. *Encyclopædia Britannica 2001* CD-ROM; & Carbonari, Ibid; & *Encyclopædia Britannica:* 15th edition
2   Franklin L. Ford, *Europe 1780–1830*, 306
3   Ibid 306
4   Ibid 306–7
5   Harold Acton, *The Bourbons of Naples (1734–1825)*
6   Ford 306–7

Nº. 75
1 Vincent Cronin, *Napoleon*, 142
2 Alan Palmer, *An Encyclopaedia of Napoleon's Europe*, 28
3 Ibid 245
4 Chandler, 231, 236-7, 239-40
5 Thompson, 130; & Opium, *Encyclopædia Britannica 2001:* CD-ROM
6 Chandler, 241
7 Ibid 241; & Thompson, 131

Nº. 77
1   www.bible-history.com/maps/romanempire/Asia.html
2   Iran *Encyclopædia Britannica 2001*, CD-ROM
3   R. Collings, *Chronology of World History;* & Dreyss, *Chronologie Univeselle;* & Derrik Mercer (ed.) *Chronicle of theWorld*, 606; and, https://en.wikipedia.org/wiki/Treaty_of_Hamedan
4   R.E. & T.N. Dupuy, *An Encyclopedia of Military History*, 649
5   historyworld.net/wrldhis/PlainTextHistories.asp?groupid=649&HistoryID=aa65&gtrack=pthc#ixzz2u00mid7Y
6   Ibid
7   Michael Axworthy, *The Sword of Persia*, London 2006: p. 125-6
8   wikipedia.org/wiki/Abbas_III_of_Persia]
9   historyworld.net/wrldhis/PlainTextHistories.asp?groupid=649&HistoryID=aa65&gtrack=pthc#ixzz2u00mid7Y
10 wikipedia.org/wiki/Nader_Shahas 8
11 Charles Louis de Secondat, Baron de la Brède et de Montesquieu, *Encyclopædia Britannica 2001:* CD-ROM; & Mercer, 605

No. 87
1   Charles A. Ward, *Oracles of Nostradamus*, 120

Nº. 88
1   fr.wikipedia.org/wiki/Charles_de_Casaulx
2   Ibid
3   L'histoire et chronique de Provence, César de Nostredame, 1614: p. 1030

Nº. 94
1   Ian Wilson, *Nostradamus The Evidence;* & John Hogue, *Nostradamus A Life and Myth*.
2   Charles A. Ward, *The Oracles of Nostradamus;* & Jean-Aimé de Chavigny, *La Première face du Janus*.

Nº. 95

1 E.E. Reynolds, *The Field is Won*, 108–9

2 Robert Service, *A History of Twentieth-Century Russia*, 495-6; & Michael Dobbs, *Down With Big Brother*, 450

3 Ibid 448-9

4 Service, 509, 517

5 Collapse of the Soviet Union, *Encyclopædia Britannica 2001*: CD-ROM; & Service, 506-7

6 Yeltsin, *Encyclopædia Britannica 2001*: CD-ROM

7 wikipedia.org/wiki/Boris_Yeltsin

8 Relations with Russia, Ibid

Nº. 97

1 Chaim Bernant. *Israel*, 69; & *Encyclopædia Britannica 2001*: CD-ROM

2 Bernant 71-2

3 Ibid 128

4 Ibid 129

5 Metonic cycle – *Encyclopædia Britannica 2001*: CD-ROM

Nº. 98

1 britannica.com/EBchecked/topic/432795/Gaston-duke-dOrleans

2 K.A. Patmore, *The Court of Louis XIII*, London, 1909 p. 150

3 Ibid pp, 151-2 & 156-7

CENTURY FOUR

1   *CELA du reste de sang non espandu:*
Venise quiert secours estre donné:
Apres auoir bien long temps attendu.
Cité liurée au premier corn sonné.

2   *Par mort la France prendra voyage à faire,*
Classe par mer, marcher monts Pyrenées,
Hespagne en trouble, marcher gent militaire:
Des plus grand dames en France emmenées.

prendre (OF) undertake; gent (AF – people, nation) nation; emmener (OF) to fetch or bring in; classe (L classis) army, fleet.

Through a death (**CARLOS 11**), France will undertake a journey to exploit,   1700
Army by sea, treading the Pyrenean Mountains,
Spain in trouble: the military nation (**ENGLAND**) marching:
For the greatest one (**LOUIS XIV**), the ladies of France brought in.

Through a death

As the seventeenth century drew to its close, the approaching death of King Carlos II of Spain was occupying the thoughts of many European leaders. This was because the King had no heir, and a successor from outside Spain would likely alter the balance of power in Europe. At the time, there were two principal claimants for the Spanish throne when it became vacant. France and Austria were both anxious to add the Iberian Peninsula to their country's empire.

Carlos II died on 1 November 1700. In his will, he left the throne to Louis XIV's grandson, Philip d'Anjou. But the Holy Roman Emperor, Leopold I, disputed the bequest, proposing instead that his son Archduke Charles should succeed Carlos. It was 'through the death' of Spain's king, and the disagreement it bred between Louis XIV and Leopold I that the War of the Spanish Succession broke out: a conflict that was to bring in many other European countries. [1]

France will undertake a journey to exploit

When Louis XIV's grandson left France to become Philip V of Spain, he took France with him. The fact that France was recognised at the time as having *undertaken this journey* prompted the Spanish ambassador to remark, "the Pyrenees had just melted away, and henceforth the two nations would no longer be separated." Louis XIV shared the same sentiment, for he saw his grandson's enthronement as an opportunity to exploit the situation as a further means of enlarging French imperialism. [2]

Army by sea

By 1704, the War of the Spanish Succession had not only begun, it had also spread to other countries, and Louis XIV's naval army soon found itself engaged in battle against British and Dutch fleets. "At the beginning of the 18th century Louis XIV remained the most powerful monarch in Europe. Although in 1700 his fleet of 108 ships of the line could not match the combined strength of the Maritime Powers. [...] At sea the English dominated having 127 ships of the line notionally available for service in 1700; the Dutch having 83. [3]

> The 18th century (1704) saw one of the most important naval battles of the War of Succession. A Franco-Spanish fleet and the combined forces of the English and Dutch navies locked horns in a fierce battle involving 146 ships and almost 50,000 men. [4] (Battle of Valez-Málaga)

> On 22 August [1705] an English fleet with sixty warships, and thirteen 'bomb boats' equipped with high-trajectory mortars, arrived at Barcelona and laid siege to it. [...] Barcelona was duly taken and Catalonia came out in support of the Archduke. [5]

Treading the Pyrenean Mountains

Fighting on the Spanish mainland also began in 1704, when Archduke Charles arrived in Lisbon to gather support for his claim to the Spanish throne. Engaging him in battle were the forces of Louis XIV, whose army had 'marched across the Pyrenean Mountains' to back Philip V.[6]

Spain in trouble

The French occupation of *Spain* was soon *in trouble*. Barcelona had been taken, an Allied army from Lisbon had also captured Madrid and forced Louis' grandson, Philip V, to flee the capital. [7] As a consequence of these victories, the Austrian Emperor became aware that he was holding the upper hand, and was backed by the United Provinces.

The military nation marching

The military nation, by reputation, refers to Britain, which formed an alliance with the Dutch Republic and Emperor Leopold against France, (7 September 1701). In command of the British forces on the continent was John Churchill, Duke of Marlborough.

> At the end of May (1704) Marlborough set out from near Bonn for his epic 250-mile march to the banks of the Danube. [...] Captain Robert Parker has left [an] account of the experience. 'We frequently marched three, sometimes four days successively. [...] surely never was a march carried on with more order and regularity and with less fatigue both to man and horse.' [8]

The march took five weeks to cover the 400 kilometres, but it was not until 12 August that the French and Bavarian armies were observed by Marlborough, having taking up position outside the village of Blenheim. Battle commenced on the following day. By evening, Marlborough was able to claim victory. The battle of Blenheim was the turning point in the War of Succession.

For the greatest one

Louis XIV was 'Le Grand Monarque': *the greatest monarch* of that age, and it is with this title that the final line of the prophecy commences. In August 1715, the King lay dying from a leg infected with gangrene. [9]

The ladies of France brought in

At the side of the King, as he lay on his bed shortly before he died, were *the ladies of France*. Those closest to him in life had been *brought in*, so they could make their final farewells.

> The King now turned to the princesses who were present. "He summoned me next," wrote Madame, "as well as the duchesse de Berry and all his other daughters. [...] He bade me adieu in words of such tenderness that I marvel that I did not fall over backwards unconscious." [8]

Also among this group of ladies were Françoise Marquise de Maintenon, Louis' wife, and Mlle d'Aumale, both women had remained by the King's bedside for the greater part of his illness. Louis XIV died at 08:15 on Sunday 1 September.

Summary: *This prophecy takes us through the final years of Louis XIV's reign. It therefore includes the War of the Spanish Succession, caused by the death of Carlos II, and the effort made by Louis to install Philip V, his grandson, on the Spanish throne. The oracle concludes with the death of Louis XIV, and a touching scene in which the 'ladies of France' – those closest to him by blood, marriage and attendance - were brought in to see him on the day before he died.*

3   *D'Arras & Bourges, de Brodes grans éseignes*
        Vn plus grand nombre de Gascons batre à pied,
        Ceulx long du Rosne saigneront les Espaignes:
        Proche du mont ou Sagonte s'assied.

4   *L'impotent prince faché, plainctz & querels.*
        De rapts & pilles par coqz & par libyques:
        Grand est par terre, par mer infinies voiles,
        Seure Italie sera chassant Celtiques.

5   *Croix, paix, sous vn accompli diuin verbe,*
        L'Hespaigne & Gaule seront vnis ensemble.
        Grand clade proche, & combat tres acerbe:
        Cueur si hardi ne sera qui ne tremble.

6   *D'habits nouueaux après faicte la treuue,*
        Malice tramme & machination:
        Premier mourra qui en fera la preuue
        Couleur venise insidiation.

7   *Le mineur filz du grand & hay prince,*
        De lepre aura à vingt ans grande tache:
        De dueil sa mere mourra bien triste & mince,
        Et il mourra la ou tombe chef lasche.

8   *La grand cité d'assaut prompt & repentin*
        Surprins de nuict, gardes interrompus:
        Les excubies & veille saint Quintin,
        Trucidés, gardes & les pourtails rompus.

prompt (L prompt\us) exposed to view; excubies (L excubi\ae) watchmen; trucidés (OF) massacred; garde (OF) a defence

The great city (**PARIS**) exposed to view by attack, & regretting.   1918
Surprised at night, the guards interrupted,
The watchmen and **SAINT-QUENTIN** night vigil
Slaughtered: defences and the entrances, broken.

By convention, 'the great city' is always Paris. However, the town of Saint-Quentin in northern France is also mentioned in this oracle. And it is the connexion between these two cities that precisely times the fulfilment of this prophecy. For both venues became directly linked by the events that took place in March 1918, during the closing stages of the First World War.

The great city exposed to view by attack

On the 23rd of March, *Paris came under attack;* that is to say it was exposed to view from gunners in the forest of Coucy behind German lines. They were firing a barrage of artillery shells aimed at the French capital from a distance of almost one hundred kilometres (65 miles). In fact, seven 'Paris Guns' were employed. The bombardment was deliberately timed to begin immediately after the fall of Saint-Quentin; hence the connexion between these two cities. [1]

And regretting

Complete accuracy was quite impossible at such a range, and the indiscriminate fall of exploding shells, "seriously hurt the morale of the Parisians." [2] The bombardment continued until August and killed 250 people, wounding a further 620.

Surprised at night, the guards interrupted

The Battle of Saint-Quentin, also known as the Second Battle of the Somme, began at night on 20 March 1918. Four and a half hours after midnight, the guards on night watch were suddenly interrupted by the instantaneous firing of six-thousand German guns. [3]

> Some 3.2 million shells were destined to land on the British-held front during that first day of the attack. To the German's advantage there was fog in the Somme battlefield sector, enabling the infantry to appear in the British forward positions without being seen to leave the German trenches. [4]

The watchmen and Saint-Quentin night vigil slaughtered

Within moments, the watchmen and night vigil patrolling the city's outposts were in a desperate situation. Apart from a steady hail of machinegun fire, there was also poison gas to contend with.

> The back areas especially being drenched with gas which hung like a pall in the moist and heavy air. [...].The men on the outpost line, beaten to the ground by the bombardment, and struggling amid clouds of gas were in desperate case. [...] Presently the outposts were gone. [5]

Defences and the entrances broken

"On the 22nd the enemy broke right through into open country north-west of St. Quentin." With the defences and entrances broken, the German army moved deeper into northern France. "[Next] morning (23 March 1918) as if to signalise their triumph, they had begun the shelling of Paris with long range guns." [6]

Summary: *The attack on Paris, exposed to the Paris Guns and coinciding with the fall of St Quentin, is the key to understanding this prophecy. The combination of these events occurred uniquely during the First World War. And the assault made at night against the sentries posted to keep watch at St Quentin, serves to furnish further proof of the exactitude with which these oracles correspond to the reality they portend.*

9   *Le chef du camp au milieu de la presse,*
       D'vn coup de fleche sera blessé aux cuisses,
       Lors que Geneue en larmes & detresse,
       Sera trahie par Lozan & Souisses.

10   *Le ieune prince accuse faulsement,*
       Mettra en trouble le camp & en querelles:
       Meurtri le chef pour le soustenement:
       Sceptre apaiser, puis guerir escroueles.

11   *Celuy qu'aura gouuert de la grand cappe,*
       Sera induict à quelque cas patrer:
       Les XII rouges viendront souiller la nappe,
       Soubs meurtre, meurtre se viendra perpetrer.

gouvert (OF) government; cappe (OF) a cloak – also, *anagram & paragram* Cape[t]; cas (OF) crime; patrer (L patr\o), to bring about; nappe (AF dissimulation, from Latin mappa) a cloth; Cross-reference: la grand cappe, C.VIII: 19; C.IX: 20; C.IX: 26.

The one that will obtain government (**DANTON**) from the great cloak (**CAPET**),   1792
Will be induced by some to bring about a crime (**SEPTEMBER MASSACRES**):
The twelve reds will arrive to soil the cloth,
Under murder, a murder will occur perpetrating itself.

The one that will obtain government from the great cloak (Capet)

Georges Jacques Danton began his career as a lawyer, but soon acquired popularity for his political ideas, which he debated as a member of the radical Cordeliers Club. It was in this capacity that he was able to draw support from the Paris Commune. His rousing speech to the Five-Hundred from Marseilles, prior to their attack on the Tuileries, led to him being offered a government post, and he was: "Appointed justice minister in the provisional executive council set up on the overthrow of Louis XVI in August 1792."

The King, by this time had been placed under guard inside the Temple. Outside, on the streets of Paris, activists were busily distributing pamphlets with the heading: "The Great Treason of Louis Capet."[1] It was because of this incitement against the King and the recent murders inside the Tuileries that "The Assembly, terrified by the slaughter, took the king into protective custody, [and] turned executive power over to a committee of six ministers led by Danton." Hence, of the six ministers appointed, *the one that will obtain government from the great Capet* "was Danton."[2]

It may be recalled from Century One No. 3 that the wearing of a cloak was a privilege confined to the nobility. From this it follows that *the great cloak*, is Louis XVI, who was derisorily referred to as Capet because Hugh Capet, Duke of France, was the first King of the Franks "The male-line descendants of Hugh Capet ruled France continuously from 987 to 1792 and again from 1814 to 1848." In revolutionary France, everyone was a citizen to be addressed by their surname.

Will be induced by some to bring about a crime

It was while holding his ministerial position of power that Danton was *induced by some* of the more bloodthirsty revolutionaries to legitimise the notorious September Massacres.[3]

It was a crime that brought international condemnation to the Revolution. Therefore, to justify the murders, Danton deemed them to be a dispensation of the 'people's justice', and they were given a flimsy veil of legality by allowing the hasty formation of citizens' tribunals. These were composed of groups of revolutionaries sitting in judgement. It was intended to give each prisoner the formality of a hearing before a verdict of guilty was given, often attended by a sword thrust.[4]

The twelve reds

Earlier that year, on 23 April, Antoine Merlin de Thionville had suggested to the Legislative Assembly that all non-juring priests should be deported. In response to this suggestion, it was decided that a committee of *twelve* revolutionaries (*reds*) should be formed in order to investigate the degree of unrest caused by non-juring priests. [5] (This committee is not to be confused with another committee of twelve, convened on 17 June 1792, with a directive to oversee the activities of new ministers.)

Will arrive to soil the cloth

One month after studying their remit, the 'twelve reds' reported back, having reached their conclusion that non-juring priests were enemies of the Revolution. A motion was then passed, which decreed that any priest failing to swear an oath to the constitution could be deported if twenty active citizens requested it. This ruling was to be enforced by the department in which the plea was made. Thereafter, the prisons slowly filled up with clergy. [6] These were men of *the cloth* who would soon find their *cloth soiled* by blood, once the September Massacres commenced.

The slaughter of prisoners began on 2 September 1792. In the course of five days, approximately 1,400 prisoners were murdered: the majority being men of *the cloth*. Mostly, these were simple clerics who had been forcibly removed from their seminaries, their churches or their colleges.

It is sometimes noticeable that the words used in these prophecies appear to have been selected for a deeper reason. For example, after the massacre of the priests had been completed, the Minister of the Interior, Jean-Marie Roland de la Platière, who shared in the guilt of the murders, expressed his concern by announcing: "the children of liberty" (those who had murdered the men of *the cloth*) "must not soil themselves."

Even more interesting is the fact that Roland was the author of a book on the mechanical production of cotton, and he "knew the cloth industry to perfection." Is this just coincidence?

Under murder, a murder will occur perpetrating itself

Inside the Temple Tower, Marie Antoinette had been allowed the companionship of the Princesse de Lamballe, who acted as her lady-in-waiting. The revolutionaries very quickly decided that this loyalty to the Queen was suspicious, and in less than a week after arriving at the Temple, the Princess was arrested and taken to the prison of La Petite Force for questioning. From there, on 3 September, at the height of the massacres, the Princesse de Lamballe was transferred to the murder centre at L'Abbaye.

Inside a room strewn with the corpses of murdered priests, she was asked to swear an oath of her hatred for the King and Queen. She declined. A door opened and the Princess was pushed through. It closed behind her. [7]

In the street outside were a group of men in wait. They stripped her, raped her, cut off her breasts, impaled her genitals on the end of a pike, charged a cannon with one of her legs and paraded her severed head on the end of a pole past the windows of the Temple cell where the Queen was imprisoned, so that she could gaze on her companion's face for one last time. [8]

The Princesse de Lamballe was born Marie Thérèse de Savoie-Carignan. "Her rank at court derived from her marriage into a legitimated princely house, not her birth." But it was because of her royal connexions, and her reputation for purity that the revolutionaries decided to use the September Massacres as a convenient means for disposing of her without need of a court trial. [9] Thus, *under* cover of the *murders* taking place at the time, another *murder occurred, perpetrating itself.*

Summary: *This is the first of four oracles that refers to Louis XVI by the surname of his ancestor, Hugh Capet. It confirms his loss of power to Danton, who, as Minister of Justice, legalised the September Massacres. The Committee of Twelve, who had previously deliberated upon the question of priests who refused to swear an oath to the constitution, is also foretold. And the execration surrounding the horrific murder of the Princess de Lamballe can be none other than that predicted to occur, thus perpetrating itself.*

> 12   Le camp plus grand de route mis en suite,
>   Gueres plus oultre ne sera pour chassé:
>   Ost recampé, & legion reducte,
>   Puis hors des Gaules du tout sera chassé.

route (OF) breaking of a troop, defeat; suite (OF suitte) a chase, pursuit; gueres (OF as guere) not long; ost (OF) army; recampé (Provençal, recampar) reassemble; legion (L legione *ablative*) army, body of troops; des Gaules (paragram and transposition of 's') de[ ] Gaul[s]e) – de Gaulle.

> The greatest army (**WEHRMACHT**) from a rout, beset by pursuit,   1944
> Not long, for it will not be chased much farther:
> The army reassembled, and the body of troops reduced (**BATTLE OF THE BULGE**),
> Afterwards, except for the French (**DE GAULLE**), all will be expelled.

The greatest army from a rout, beset by pursuit

In 1939, Hitler's *Wehrmacht* was acknowledged to be the most efficient fighting force of its time: hence, 'the greatest army'. But after five years of continuous warfare, the effectiveness of the *Wehrmacht* began to show signs of tiredness. This became apparent in the wake of the D-Day landings in France (June 1944). By the end of the year the advancing armies of America and Britain had imposed a heavy *defeat* upon the German forces in France.[1] and were pursuing them in their retreat to the German frontier.

Not long, for it will not be chased much farther

The impetus of this allied offensive against the retreating German army proved to be so successful that those leading the assault eventually outdistanced the supply line supporting them. This caused the attack to falter, and the pursuit came to a halt,[2] to allow the supply team to re-establish contact.

The army reassembled

This temporary break in the allied attack allowed the retreating German army to regroup, and it quickly reassembled. Its plan was to mount a sudden counter-attack and not only regain the ground it had just lost, but also sever the American supply line.[3]

And the body of troops reduced

What followed became known as the 'Battle of the Bulge'. Germany planned to reach Antwerp. If the plan succeeded, it would cut-off the Allied supply lines. But the sheer effort and manpower required for this proved too great, and Germany overreached itself in the attempt. "It was [also] the largest and bloodiest battle fought by the United States in World War II."

> On 16 December 1944, at 05:30, the Germans began the assault with a massive, 90-minute artillery barrage using 1,600 artillery pieces across a 130-kilometre (80 mi) front on the Allied troops facing the 6th Panzer Army. [...] They then assaulted Losheim Gap and Elsenborn Ridge in an effort to break through to Liège and Antwerp.[4]

Casualty figures vary. Germany's loss of dead, wounded and missing has been put at 100,000, with America's losses, by comparison, totalling 89.600. British casualties were less at 1,400.[5]

Afterwards, except for the French (de Gaulle)

After the battle of the Bulge had been won, the liberation of France followed. Even before then, on 10 September 1944, Charles de Gaulle had declared himself leader of the Provisional Government of the French Republic. And when the war ended eight months later, de Gaulle expected to represent French interests in the peace negotiations. But to his intense chagrin, he was repeatedly excluded by the 'Big Three'.

> As of 1942, the "Big Three" leaders of Britain, the Soviet Union, and the United States controlled Allied policy; relations between Britain and the U.S. were especially close, the latter replacing France as Britain's prime partner after the Entente Cordiale dissolved in the aftermath of the fall of France, despite [...] efforts to save it by turning it into a fully fledged Franco-British Union.[6]

The Yalta Conference held between 4th and 11th of February 1945 was the second of three wartime conferences among the Big Three. It was preceded by the Tehran Conference in 1943, and followed by the Potsdam Conference in July 1945. The Yalta Conference was intended to plan the re-establishment of nation states affected by the ravage of war.

De Gaulle had not been invited to any of the 'Big Three' Conferences, although the decisions made by Stalin, Churchill and Roosevelt in dividing up Europe were of huge importance to France. [...] Roosevelt in particular refused to allow any discussion about de Gaulle participating in the Big Three conferences that would shape Europe in the post war world [...] de Gaulle never forgave the Big Three leaders for not inviting him to the summit and continued to rage against it as having been a negative factor in European politics for the rest of his life.[7]

This proved particularly irksome for France "During the Potsdam Conference in July [17 July to 2 August 1945], to which de Gaulle was again not invited." For, apart from discussing the establishment of post-war order, peace treaty issues, and countering the effects of war, the Conference also made "a decision to divide Vietnam, which had been a French colony for over a hundred years, into British and Chinese spheres of influence."[8]

All will be expelled

The end of the Second World War was accompanied by a massive movement of people, some were welcomed as the allied forces returned to their own countries, prisoners of war were likewise repatriated and the concentration camps emptied. As part of the Potsdam Conference, it was agreed that the "'Orderly and humane' expulsions of the German populations remaining beyond the new eastern borders of Germany; from Poland, Czechoslovakia and Hungary." were to commence. As a result, nine million Germans were expelled from its former occupied eastern territories, "as well as the expulsion of 3 million Germans from the Sudetenland in Czechoslovakia to Germany. By the 1950s, every fifth West German was a refugee from the east. The Soviet Union also took over the Polish provinces east of the Curzon line, from which 2 million Poles were expelled."[9]

Summary: *This oracle is yet another that adds to the prophecies made for the Second World War. Others include the actual date war was declared by Britain; the evacuation of children in Britain; the breaching of the Maginot Line; the Atlantic War; the D-Day Landing; Operation Market Garden; Auschwitz-Birkenau; the liberation of Paris; Remagen, together with Hitler's name appearing three times, and the death of Mussolini, referred to as the Duce. With so much information within these oracles it is not surprising to discover Charles de Gaulle has also been named. The battle of the Bulge was the last great conflict before Hitler's suicide brought the war in Europe to an end. It is correctly indicated in this prophecy, together with the German Wehrmacht, and its defeat by the Americans. The situation exempting de Gaulle from all major conferences, and the discharge and expulsions of people across Europe after the War's end provides an accurate conclusion to this oracle.*

13   *De plus grand perte nouuelles raportées.*
       Le raport fait le camp s'estonnera:
       Bandes vnies encontre reuoltées:
       Double phalange grand abandonnera.

14   *Le mort subite de premier personnaige,*
       Aura changé & mis vn autre au regne:
       Tost, tard venu à si haut & bas aage,
       Que terre & mer faudra qu' on le craigne

15   *D'ou pernsera faire venire famine,*
       De la viendra le rassasiement:
       L'œil de la mer par auare canine,
       Pour de l'vn l'autre donnra huyle, froment.

canine (L canis) dog; par (OF) by, through, of, for, on, by reason of; donnra (syncope) donn[e]ra

From where one will think to make famine appear,   1940
From there the satiety will arrive (ATLANTIC OCEAN):
The EYE OF THE SEA on the avaricious canine (WOLF PACK):
For the one (BRITAIN), the other (USA) will give oil and wheat.

From where one will think to make famine appear

During World War II, Germany attempted to starve England into submission. The oracle points to the great expanse of water surrounding the British Isles as the place *from where one will think to make famine appear.* Hitler had thought this when he planned to destroy all shipping headed for the British Isles, thus effectively besieging the nation.

In February 1940, German submarine commanders were ordered to sink without warning all ships bringing food and supplies into Britain. This strategy was the beginning of the battle of the Atlantic; and it was soon apparent that German U-boats were destroying almost one hundred vessels every month. [1]

From there the satiety will arrive

The United States responded to Britain's need for food and fuel during this crucial time by passing the 'Lend-Lease Act' (March 1941). Although America was officially a neutral country in 1941, the Act allowed food and arms to be sent to any nation whose protection was deemed to be vital to the defence of the US. The problem therefore became not one of supply, but of transportation. To reach Britain, ships had to cross the Atlantic Ocean. Thus, the instrument of hunger was *from where the satiety will arrive*. [2]

The eye of the sea on the avaricious canine

German submarines were constantly lying in wait for merchant ships heading for Britain. Under the command of Admiral Dönitz, fleets of U-boats, called 'wolf packs', would situate themselves out at sea, but within radio contact of their headquarters at Kerneval in northwest France. Once a convoy had been sighted, information was then relayed to Kerneval. This enabled German naval headquarters to notify commanders in that area, giving them the convoy's position and with orders to intercept. "This was the process known as 'the forming of the wolf pack', the gathering together of as many U-boats as possible." [3]

THE EYE OF THE SEA

Quite remarkably, the oracle has actually referred to the periscope: the *lens above the waves*, used for observing ships while staying submerged. The Seer calls it *the eye of the sea*. [4] The invention allowed submarines to stay submerged and yet observe their target.

The prophecy also connects 'avaricious canine' with the periscope. The dog has been bred from the wolf, and the submarines hunted in wolf packs. Moreover, their targets were the ships carrying food, hence the reference to their avaricious nature. "By the close of 1940, more than 4,700,000 tons of British shipping had been lost in the form of 1,281 vessels, about one fifth of the pre-war merchant fleet." [5]

For the one, the other will give oil and wheat

In 1940, Britain was not an oil-producing nation. Its need for this commodity had therefore to be met by importing it. America, with its Lend-Lease Agreement, was therefore *the one able to give the other oil and wheat*.

> The most serious danger was the loss of the UK's oil supply, which by 1942 came almost entirely from the USA and the Caribbean, 65% of it shipped from the eastern seaboard of the USA where it was, at that time, particularly vulnerable to interception by submarines. [6]

In September 1940, for example, German submarines intercepted convoy SC7, and subsequently sank 27 ships with the loss of "10,000 tonnes of food [and] 5,000 tanks of petrol." In October, a further 32 ships were torpedoed, and soon the allies were losing, on average, 96 ships every month. It was not until the spring of 1943 that successful counter measures became effective.

Summary: *This oracle is another that obtained its fulfilment from the Second World War. It foretells the battle of the Atlantic. The attempt by Hitler to starve Britain into submission became a conflict between the German submarines and the Merchant Navy escorted by British destroyers. America as the chief supplier of much needed oil and food is indicated. And what is most extraordinary about this oracle is its reference to the periscope, for what else could the 'eye of the sea' mean, given the context of the prophecy?*

16   *La cité franche liberté fait serue:*
      Des profligés & resueurs faict asyle.
      Le roy changé à eux non si proterue:
      De cent seront deuenus plus de mille.

17   *Changer à Beaune, Nuy, Chalons & Dijon,*
      Le duc voulant amender la Barrée:
      Marchant pres fleuue, poisson, bec de plongeon,
      Verra la queue: porte sera serrée.

18   *Des plus letrés dessus les faits celestes*
      Seront par princes ignorant reprouués:
      Punis d'Edict, chassés, comme scelestes,
      Et mis à mort la ou seront trouués.

Prince (L Prince\ps & AF chef) chief, head, leader – see also Judges 5: 8-10, Psalm 45: 15-17 and Isaiah 23: 7-9; sceleste (L scelest\us) scoudrel.

Concerning the most well-read upon divine works,   1790
They will be condemned by ignorant rulers:
Punished by Edict, pursued, even as scoundrels,
And then put to death where they will be found.

Concerning the most well-read upon divine works

Before the French Revolution, the Church in France numbered among its serving members as many as 100,000 souls. It also —

> ... owned over one tenth of the land, that is to say about 20,000 square miles. [...] Nearly all schools were in the hands of the Church which had, in addition, its own courts of law. It also controlled most sources of information, since it had taken upon itself the responsibilities of censorship. For those who could not read, the clergy were the means by which Government decrees and intentions became known. [1]

A dramatic change was to affect the Church soon after those present at the Oath of the Tennis Court (20 June 1789) declared they would never separate until a new constitution was agreed. The outcome was the transition of the Third Estate (middle class members of the professionals) into the National Assembly. The Assembly was then able to claim that it represented the people of France. The other two Estates, composed of the nobility and the clergy, were soon afterwards swept aside before being swallowed up in a drive towards social equality.

They will be condemned by ignorant rulers

One of the first steps taken towards achieving equality of the masses was to diminish the authority of the priesthood. On 2 November 1789 the National Assembly nationalised all Church property. It was then sold off in the form of *assignats*, which quickly became the currency of the Revolution (see Century 1 N°. 53).

The next three steps followed in 1590. On 13 February, "Religious orders, except those engaged in teaching or charitable work, [were] suppressed." This was followed five months later by the Civil Constitution of the Clergy, which ordered a reduction in the number of bishoprics in France, and the abolition of ties with papal authority. It also gave people the power to elect their bishops and priests. Then, on 27 November a decree was issued imposing a civic oath upon the clergy. [2] This legislation was intended to complete the destruction of the monastic orders, by legislating them out of existence; whereupon, about half of the lower clergy refused to sign the oath. This split the Church into non-juring priests and those who swore an oath to the constitution.

Punished by edict

At the end of November 1791, the Legislative Assembly having by then become concerned at the disruptive influence caused by refractory priests – those who refused to take the oath of loyalty to the Civil Constitution – passed an *edict*, "Nonjuring priests were to have their stipends cut off forthwith [...] and on November 29 those who remained defiant against the laws of the nation were to be given just eight days to comply on pain of being declared in conspiracy against the *patrie*." [3]

Pursued, even as scoundrels

The effect of this legislative order compelled many priests to leave the country. Others, who stayed, went into hiding. But in August 1792, a revolutionary police state came into existence.

(M)ore than a thousand people were taken into custody on the flimsiest of warrants. The vast majority of them were refractory priests taken from seminaries, colleges and churches— sometimes from private houses where they had been hidden in lay dress." [4]

And then put to death where they will be found

On 2 September a party of six carriages arrived in Paris transporting priests that had been arrested in Brittany, Avignon and Marseilles. The carriages were attacked by a mob with swords, before it could reach its prison destination. Within minutes, "blood was dripping from all the carriages as the horses dragged them on their way to the doors of the prison." [5] That same afternoon in Paris, another mob invaded a Carmelite Convent, which had been used to imprison 150 priests, including the Archbishop of Arles. After murdering a few, the remainder were offered the opportunity of swearing to the Constitution. They refused and were killed on the spot. Some were thrown down a well, where their broken skeletons were discovered seventy years later. [6]

This marked the beginning of four more days of indiscriminate killing.

(M)ost murders were committed with appalling ferocity. [...] As the heaps of corpses mounted, carts drawn by horses from the King's stables were obtained to take them away to the Montrouge quarries." [7]

Summary: *This prophecy was fulfilled during the French Revolution, and foretells, in separate steps, the plight of those attached to the Catholic Church. It is one of several that predict the de-Christianization of France during the final decade of the eighteenth century. The punishment meted out against priests who refused to obey 'ignorant leaders' has particular relevance in this present age.*

19   *Deuant ROVAN d'Insubres mis le siege,*
    Par terre & mer enfermés les passages.
    D'Haynault, & Flandres, de Gand & ceux de Liege
    Par dons lœnees rauiront les riuages.

20   *Paix vberté long temps lieu louera,*
    Par tout son regne desert la fleur de lis:
    Corps morts d'eau, terre la l'on aportera,
    Sperants vain heur d'estre la enseuelis.

21   *Le changement sera sort difficile:*
    Cité, prouince au change gain fera:
    Cueur haut, prudent mis, chassé lui habile.
    Mer, terre, people son estat changera.

22   *La grand copie qui sera deschassée,*
    Dans vn moment fera besoing au roy:
    La foy promise de loing sera fauscée,
    Nud se verra en piteux desarroy.

23   *La legion dans la marine classe,*
    Calcine, Magnes soulphre, & poix brussera:
    Le long repos de l'asseurée place:
    Port Selyn, Hercle feu les consumera.

24   *Ouy sous terre sainct d'ame, voix fainte,*
    Humaine flame pour diuine voyr luire,
    Fera des seuls de leur sang terre tainte
    Et les saints temples pour les impurs destruire.

25   *Corps, sublimes sans fin à l'œil visibles,*
    Obnubiler viendront par ses raisons:
    Corps, front comprins, sens chief & inuisibles,
    Diminuant les sacrées oraisons.

sublime (OF) lofty; obnubiler (AF) obscurcir, to obscure; front (OF) forehead; chief (OF adj.)chief, principal.

Bodies, lofty, visible to the eye, without end,   1608
Through these reasons, they will come to obscure:
Matter, the forehead comprehended, the chief sense, also invisible:
Diminishing the sacred prayers.

Bodies, lofty, visible to the eye, without end

This is indeed an interesting prophecy, because it appeared when the Ptolemaic system that mapped the heavens was still in use. This system placed the world at the centre of the universe with just Mercury, Venus, Mars, Jupiter and Saturn travelling through the Zodiac. The stars visible to the naked eye numbered approximately two thousand. However, the Seer predicted they exist without end. The realization that there were more than meets the naked eye came with the discovery of the telescope. In 1608, Hans Lippershey, a Dutch spectacle maker invented the telescope by placing a convex lens behind a concave lens and inserting both inside a tube. By the following year, Galileo had reinvented this. And, using this modified telescope, he pointed it to the night sky. Now, in the world of the twenty-first century, the number of stars visible by modern telescopic means is reckoned to be approximately 10,000,000,000,000,000,000,000. [1]

Through these reasons they will come to obscure

Once it was understood that that light travelled from the stars to the human eye, taking what are now called light years to arrive, the science of optics was born and with it came the realization that by the time light has reached the eye, the star that emitted it may either have ceased to exist, or else it will have moved to a different part of the sky. Hence, the actual star that emitted the light is never directly observed—as remarked upon in the Prolegomena.

Matter, the forehead comprehended, the chief sense, also invisible

Philosophers struggled to come to terms with this new development in understanding the nature of reality. *Matter*, according to the philosopher John Locke, became "something we know not what." (*An Essay Concerning Human Understanding*, 1689), His reasoning was based upon the fact that we cannot see by sight – *the chief sense* – any object until light has been reflected from it and reaches the human eye. Signals are then sent from the retina behind the lens of the eye, along the optic nerve, to the brain. It is then decoded into the human experience of pictorial knowledge. From this, it was inferred that 'matter' is never directly observed. Instead, the brain represents that which we call matter by decoding the data into mental imagery. *Matter* is therefore *invisible*.

It is now known that the prefrontal cortex (known as Area 46) situated in the *forehead*, plays a major part in the brain's visual activity. Together with Area 9, which is adjacent to it, the upper and lower visual pathways from the parietal and temporal lobes terminate in these areas.

Diminishing the sacred prayers

Sight had always been regarded as the sense which was most easily deceived. [...] Scepticism was particularly appropriate when it came to the use of lenses. What most lenses do is magnify and distort: they are deceptive rather than veridical. The fundamental realisation that our own capacity to see depends upon a lens within the eye came only with Kepler's *Optics* of 1604, just before the invention of the telescope. [...] Galileo was well aware that the revolution he was seeking to bring about required a new attitude to the senses, and to vision in particular. [2]

To illustrate this point, Galileo used dialogue as a rhetorical device and a character called Sagredo to describe an anatomical investigation carried out by an anatomist.

The anatomist showed that the great trunk of nerves leaving the brain and passing though the nape, extended on down the spine and then branched out through the whole body, and that only a single strand as fine as a thread arrived at the heart.

Before then, Aristotle had written, "that the nerves originate in the heart." But with this new knowledge, Galileo used the final pages of *The Assayer* to propound his own theory of knowledge. He argued that it was through the tactile sense that we perceive reality.

Our other senses do not tell us how the world really is, but how it is for us. On this theory, smells are merely particles of a particular shape which enter our noses. The smell is not in the particles but in our noses [...] if someone tickles me with a feather the tickle is in me, not the feather. Sounds are our way of interpreting some sort of movement in space. Colour is something our eyes read into the world – if there were no eyes, there would be no colours. And heat and cold (Galileo's original topic) are the means by which our skin interprets the impact of certain particles upon us. [3]

Prior to the telescope, unaided sight permitted people to conclude that the world was situated at the centre of the universe, and the Sun and Moon, together with five heavenly bodies, revolved around it: all against a background of star-studded crystalline spheres. But this belief, which had become part of the biblical story of the Creation, suddenly became challenged.

Copernicus and Galileo had provided evidence that the Earth was just a planet among the five others, and all six were encircling the Sun, which now replaced Earth as the stable body. Moreover, it was now known that there were many more stars in the universe, invisible to the naked eye, than could be seen without visual aid. Mankind's special relationship with his Creator suddenly seemed less certain than heretofore, thus *reducing the sacred prayers* offered up to God. Then, as the Age of Reason increasingly gained in authority, so the Church went into retreat.

The power of the Pope was reduced: taxes to Rome were cut; papal Bulls needed royal permission [...] agents from Rome lost their powers of visiting monasteries [...] the training and the work of the clergy were taken over by the State, which regarded priests more as agents of education, health and welfare than as a means of eternal salvation. [4]

Added to which, some monasteries were closed down, and censorship, which had formally been the prerogative of the Church, was taken over by the State.

Summary: *This is a prophecy directed at philosophers. It is for them to understand that the controversy concerning reality and sensible knowledge, which began with Kepler and Galileo, and then extended to Descartes Malebranche, Locke, Berkeley, Hume and Kant, and which has now been hijacked by neuroscience, was foreseen and written about long before any of these men were even born.*

26   *Lou grand eyssame se leuera d'abelhos,*
        Que non sauran don te siegen venguddos:
        De nuech l'embousque; lou gach dessoubz las treilhos,
        Cieutad trahido per cinq lengos non nudos.

[Provençal having ancient French root]– Lou, the; eyssame (AF. eyssement) action of leaving; se lever (OF) arise; abelhos (AF. abeloier) embellir; don (AF dons) where, from where; sauran (AF saure) forgive, aquit, exonerate; siegen (AF siege) to establish, settle; venguddos (AF vengement) taken vengeance of, avenged; te (dir. obj.) you; nuech (from the Latin noctem) night; embousque (Mod. Fr.) embusque; gach (AF. gaschier) as gâcher; dessoubz, under, below; las (3rd person plural) them; treilhos (AF treille from the Latin trichida) summerhouse; cieutad (from the Latin civitatem) city; trahido (Mod. Fr) trahir; lengos (AF langoros) languid; nudos (from the Latin nudus) naked

The great man departing will raise himself for embellishment (**NAPOLEON**),   1799
When none will exonerate, where you take vengeance at the established seat:
At night the ambuscade: the muddle below them, the summerhouse,
City betrayed by five languid: not naked.

This quatrain stands alone as the only one that is written in the Provençal language. The reason for this is because it became part of the event it predicted. When Napoleon hurriedly left Egypt on his return voyage to France in 1799, he arrived unannounced at Fréjus in "the Provence-Alpes-Côte d'Azur region in southeastern France. [...] The history of the city is very similar to that of Provence." [1] One month later, he was elected First Consul of France. The Napoleonic Era was about to begin.

The great man departing will raise himself for embellishment

The great man, Commander-in Chief of the Eastern Army in Egypt, Napoleon Bonaparte, set sail from Alexandria, homeward bound for France on 23 August 1799. His ship, the *Muiron*, dropped anchor at Fréjus on 9 October. Then began a week's travel, which took him through Aix-en-Provence; Avignon in Provence-Alpes-Côte d'Azur, Valence; Lyon; Chalons, and Never.

He reached Paris on 16 October, and one month later, he was ready to strike down the government and raise himself in its place.

> In alliance with the director Emmanuel Joseph Sieyès, his brother Lucien; the speaker of the Council of five Hundred, Roger Ducos; another Director, Joseph Fouché; and Talleyrand, he overthrew the Directory by a coup d'état on November 9, 1799 ("the 18th Brumaire" according to the revolutionary calendar), and closed down the council of five hundred. Napoleon became "first consul" for ten years, with two consuls appointed by him who had consultative voices only. His power was confirmed by the new constitution ("Constitution of the year VIII"), originally devised by Sieyès to give Napoleon a minor role, but rewritten by Napoleon, and accepted by direct popular vote (3,000,000 in favour, 1,567 opposed). [2]

When none will exonerate, where you take vengeance at the established seat

At the time of the *coup*, the First French Republic was bankrupt. Blame was directed at the ruling Directory, which was not only ineffective but also corrupt.

> The Directory had very little popular or elite support left. [...] It was a government of self-interest rather than virtue, thus losing any claim on idealism. It never had a strong base of popular support; when elections were held, most of its candidates were defeated. [3]

Consequently, when Bonaparte exacted his country's 'vengeance' against the Directory, by springing his *coup d'état*, there was no one to exonerate them. After they had been removed from office, which occurred at their seat of government at Saint-Cloud, Napoleon was free to establish his own seat of government, which he did by occupying the *Palais de Tuileries*, having out-manoeuvred Sieyès to become First Consul.

At night the ambuscade

Bonaparte's *coup d'état* on 19th *Brumaire* (9 November) was concluded *at midnight*. It began with a plot to move the councils (the Ancients and the Five Hundred) from Paris to Saint-Cloud. This succeeded. But, on the following afternoon Bonaparte was forced out of the hall with daggers drawn. His brother Lucien reacted to this by summoning the guards, and they cleared the hall at bayonet point.

This purging of deputies brought the Ancients to the conference, and they "voted the suppression of the Directory, [and] the creation of an executive commission of three." By nine p.m. that evening: "a 'rump' of the Five Hundred, Lucien presiding [...] named Sieyès, Ducos and Bonaparte as provisional Consuls of the French Republic. Before midnight the three took an oath of loyalty to the Republic." [4] *The ambuscade* had achieved the desired result. By *midnight*, Napoleon had become one of the Consuls; it was from this position that he was able to rule France.

The muddle below them

But not everything had gone entirely to plan. "The events of [that] following day, November 10, were almost catastrophic, and responsibility for the near-débâcle lies heavily at Bonaparte's door." His speech to the Ancients in the *Galérie de Mars* was ill-received, some reports even called it 'incoherent'. Bonaparte then left the hall to attend a meeting of the Five Hundred in the Orangery, where he was received with shouts of: 'outlaw him', and 'down with the military dictator'. At this point, with the situation now in a total *muddle*, "They drove a dishevelled General Bonaparte and his perspiring escort of grenadiers out of the hall, down the stairs and into the courtyard below." [5] His anguished protest that daggers had been drawn against him led to Joachim Murat and his Guards breaking into the assembly hall, with drums beating and bayonets fixed. The Deputies fled through the open windows, allowing Bonaparte to return and complete his *coup*. [6]

The summerhouse

And so — "On a dull November evening the last scene of the French revolution was enacted in the orangery and park of St. Cloud. [7] The Orangery had been originally designed to grow fruit in a cool climate. Hence, it is referred to in the oracle as 'the summerhouse'.

City betrayed by five languid

From August 1795 up until Napoleon's *coup d'état de Brumaire*, France had been governed by the Directory. This consisted of "five 'Directors', jointly responsible for the conduct of affairs." However, "Many of the Directors were personally corrupt." [8] By 1799, as disclosed above, they had by then become largely ineffective: in fact, a spent force.

The City, by convention in these oracles, is Paris unless evidence exists to the contrary. On 9 November 1799, *the City was betrayed by* its *five* Directors: four of whom (Gohier, Moulin, Sieyès and Ducos) provided their signatures to a conspiratorial decree that had secretly been discussed. This gave their agreement to move proceedings from Paris to Saint-Cloud. The fifth Director, Paul Barras resigned from office and sought police protection.

It was this agreement that opened the way for the conspirators to take control of the government. For, by moving its members to the small township of Saint-Cloud, Bonaparte was able to proceed with his *coup*, which had been planned to take place there.

Not naked

When preparing his *coup d'état* for November 9th –

> Bonaparte found himself almost necessarily drawn into consultation with three men who, like himself [...] were now convinced of the need for a new constitution. [...] By a curious chance the three men upon whom Bonaparte relied to make him master of the state were all ex-ecclesiastics: Fouché, Talleyrand, and Sieyès. [9]

These three ex-ecclesiastics had each been stripped of their clerical authority during the French Revolution. Though *unfrocked* by the Church, Napoleon ensured they were *not naked*. Sieyès was appointed Consul; Fouché was made Minister of Police and Minister of the Interior; Talleyrand accepted the post of Minister for Foreign Affairs. [10]

Summary: *This prophecy is uniquely interesting because it is written in the language of Provence. Provence was where Napoleon disembarked upon his return from Egypt, and from where he began his path to become Emperor and ruler of the greater part of Europe. The coup d'état planned to take place one month after his return from Egypt is indicated by the public's dislike of the 'five' Directors he replaced, and by the events that occurred at Saint-Cloud during the actual transfer of power. The final line incorporates the typical humour of the seer by correctly identifying three unfrocked clerics who took part in the coup as 'naked'.*

27   *Salon, Mansol, Tarascon de* SEX. *L'arc,*
      Ou est debout encore la piramide,
      Viendront liurer le prince Dannemarc
      Rachat honni au temple d'Artemide.

Dannemarc could possibly be a typesettting error for d'Annemarc (see Century 6 No. 41 and Century 9 No. 33).

28   *Lors que Venus du sol sera couuert,*
      Souz l'esplendeur sera forme occulte,
      Mercure au feu les aura descouuert
      Par bruit bellique sera mis à l'insulte.

29   *Le sol caché eclipse par Mercure*
      Ne sera mis que pour le ciel second.
      De VulcanHermes sera faite pasture:
      Sol sera veu pur rutilant & blond.

30   *Plus XI fois Moon & Sun ne voudra,*
      Tous augmentés & baissés de degré:
      Et si bas mis que peu or l'on coudra:
      Qu'apres faim, peste descouuert le secret.

31   *La lune au plain de nuit sus le haut mont,*
      Le nouueau sophe d'vn seul cerueau la veu:
      Par ses disciples estre immortel semond
      Yeux au mydi. En seins mains, corps au feu.

32   *Es lieux & temps chair au poiss. donra a lieu,*
      La loy commune sera faicte au contraire:
      Vieulx tiendra fort, puis ofte du milieu,
      Le Παντα χοινα φιλον mis fort arriere.

33   *Iuppiter ioint plus Venus qu' à la Lune*
      Apparoissant de plenitude blanche:
      Venus cachée soubs la blancheur Neptune,
      De Mars frappé par granée branche.

granée (L gran\us). It has been suggested that 'the grained division' refers to the Milky Way.

Jupiter joined more to Venus than to the Moon:
Appearing of white solidity:
Venus hidden under Neptune's whiteness,
For Mars, struck by the grained division.

There are several points of interest to observe in this prophecy, both for the sceptic and the religious. The prophecy is devoid of anything other than the state of the heavens. Only the Sun, Mercury and Saturn have been omitted, and they have their own predictions elsewhere in these quatrains. At which point, sceptics may do well to shuffle their feet in discomfort. Neptune was first observed by Johann Gottfried Galle and Heinrich d'Arrest on 23 September 1846. And it was not until more than three months later that this new planet received its name 'Neptune'; and, even then, only after several different names had been proposed and rejected. Yet, this prophecy was published in 1555! Incidentally, Neptune appears as a blue planet, "in part due to methane absorption of red light."

As for those with knowledge of the Scriptures, they may recall the words in Luke's gospel. "There will be signs in the sun, moon, and stars. On earth, nations will be in anguish and perplexity at the roaring and tossing of the sea. People will faint from terror, apprehensive of what is coming on the world, for the heavenly bodies will be shaken." (21: 25-26)

34   *Le grand mené captive d'estrange terre,*
      D'or enchaîné au roy CHYREN *offert,*
      Qui dans Ausonne, Millan perdra la guerre,
      Et tout son ost mis à feu & fer.

mené (OF) led, conducted; Chyren (Latin anag. Henryc\us, also Chyr[o]n (L) tutor of heroes; Ausonne *for* Ausonia, in which the Kingdom of Naples became situated; qui (OF) that which; ost (OF) troops

The great man (**MONTMORENCY**) led captive of a foreign land,   1557
Enchained by gold, offered to the King (**HENRI 11**), tutor of heroes
That which within Naples, Milan, he will lose [&] the war,
And all his troops put to fire and iron (**BATTLE OF ST QUENTIN**).

The great man led captive of a foreign land
The Battle of Saint-Quentin was fought by France under the command of Henri II's favourite, Anne de Montmorency, Constable of France since 1538, and made a duke in 1551. "[O]n 10 August 1557 battle was joined, and the Constable suffered a catastrophic defeat." Spain's victory was not only the cause of devastating French losses; it also resulted in the capture of Anne de Montmorency, *the great man* of France. He was taken prisoner by Emmanuel-Philibert, the Duke of Savoy, and *led* across the French border to Ghent, where he was held hostage—*captive of a foreign land.* [1]

Enchained by gold, offered to the King (Henri), tutor of heroes
In the negotiations that followed, Savoy *offered* to return Montmorency *to the King* in exchange for a huge ransom in *gold*, which *Henri* could not immediately afford to pay. The Constable was therefore, figuratively speaking, *enchained by gold.* [2]

Henri eventually managed to raise the money and accepted Savoy's ransom offer, but payment had to be delayed for a year until instalments could be agreed. The Grand Master of France was finally released by Spain in December 1558.

NB: The anagram derived from Chyron (tutor of heroes) marks the obsequiousness given to monarchs and members of the nobility in the sixteenth century; apart from which, Henri II was a warrior king, who regularly competed in jousting tournaments.

That which within Naples, Milan, he will lose [&] the war

In December 1555, Naples and Milan were given to Henri II's two eldest sons, Francis and Charles, by Pope Paul IV. Two years later, François de Lorraine, 2nd duc de Guise, invaded Italy and seized control of Naples. But he was then forced to abandon Italy when Henri hurriedly recalled him to France, following the country's defeat at Saint-Quentin. But his recall had been too late to change the course of events.

Henri realised *the war was lost*, and he would have to agree a peace settlement.

> The Peace of Cateau-Cambrésis was signed between Henry II of France and Philip II of Spain on 3 April 1559, at Le Cateau-Cambrésis, around twenty kilometres south-east of Cambrai. [...] Spain retained Franche-Comté, but, more importantly, the treaty confirmed its direct control of Milan, Naples, Sicily, Sardinia, and the State of Presidi, and indirectly (through dominance of the rulers of Tuscany, Genoa, and other minor states) of northern Italy. [3]

And all his troops put to fire and iron

France had suffered a heavy defeat at Saint-Quentin. 18,000 French infantry men, plus 6,500 cavalry had taken the field of which 14,000 were killed or injured. Spain and Savoy, however, fought with just 6,000 infantry and were aided by 4,000 cavalry. Their dead or wounded numbered just 200. [4] Henri was therefore forced into submitting to the proposals contained in the peace treaty offered by Spain at Cateau-Cambrésis on 2/3 April 1559. Upon signing the treaty, firstly with England and then with Spain, the Hapsburg-Valois War came to an end.

Summary: *The events predicted in this oracle were all fulfilled during the lifetime of the seer, although his prophecy appeared in print two years before the battle of Saint-Quentin was fought. If its predictions had been recognized, would this have prevented the battle being fought? It would seem not, for true predictions always take into account the steps that lead to their fulfilment. In the present case, the capture of Montmorency, his captivity in Ghent, and the ransom paid are features that combine to authenticate the veracity of this oracle, as does the horrific defeat of the French army, which so sickened Philip II that he withdrew from the battlefield, declining to pursue his victory any further.*

35   *Le feu estaint, les vierges trahiront,*
        La plus grand part de la bande nouuelle:
        Fouldre à fer, lance les seuls roy garderont:
        Etrusque & Corse, de nuit gorge allumelle.

36   *Les ieux nouueaux en Gaule redressés,*
        Apres victoire de l'Insubre champaigne:
        Monts d'Esperie, les grands liés, troussés:
        De peur trembler la Romaingne & Espaigne.

37   *Gaulois par saults, monts viendra penetrer:*
        Occupera le grand lieu de l'Insubre:
        Au plus profond son ost fera entrer:
        Gennes, Monech pousseront class rubre.

Gaulois (OF) a Frenchman; penetrer (L penetr\o;) penetrate ost (AF armée) army, troops; Monech (L Monœcis) Monacans; rubre (L rubr\us) red. Cross-reference: Gaulois, C.X: 34

> A Frenchman, by bounds, will arrive penetrating the mountains: (**NAPOLEON**)   1800
> He will occupy the great place of the Insubres:
> His army will make access to the greatest depth,
> Genoa, Monacans will repel the **RED FLEET**.

A Frenchman

"Napoleone di Buonaparte (he habitually signed his name after the Italian fashion until 1796)" was entitled to French nationality after France's annexation of Corsica shortly before his birth. [1]

By bounds, will arrive penetrating the mountains

In May 1800, accompanied by an army of 50,000 soldiers, the First Consul began the long climb over the Alps: *penetrating the mountains* that separate France from Italy. But the snow was still deep in the higher regions, and his personal descent from the Great St. Bernard Pass was unconventional, which is to say—he descended *by bounds*. According to the official bulletin, "The First Consul came down from the top of the St. Bernard Pass, sliding and rolling in the snow." [2]

He will occupy the great place of the Insubres

After successfully crossing the mountains, Bonaparte was able to *occupy* the Po Valley, which was once occupied by the Insubres. "Around 400 BC, the Celtic Insubres settled in Milan and the surrounding region." [3] And Milan – *the great place of the Insubres* – was the target that Napoleon had set himself.

Interestingly, the Insubres were a race that had previous links with Hannibal after he, too, had crossed the Alps like Napoleon. Hannibal had then urged the people there to free themselves from Rome's domination. [4] Presumably, it was these similarities to Napoleon's situation that caused the Seer to name these people.

> June 2 found Bonaparte in Milan "in the midst of demonstrations of general joy. The inhabitants of all ages and both sexes flocked around the man who had brought them freedom and good fortune a second time," recorded Brossier. [5]

After leaving Milan on 14 June, and arriving approximately 25 miles north of Genoa, the French army of the Reserve met and fought the Austrians at Marengo. The battle was fiercely contested, and might have been lost by the French, but for Bonaparte's reserve force. But, by the end of the day, the First Consul emerged victorious.

His army will make access to the greatest depth

In the wake of this success, and with the recapture of Genoa accomplished, Napoleon was able to drive the Austrians out of Italy. By December, Joachim Murat, leading the French army down the leg of Italy, had recovered the Papal States, and occupied Tuscany: having *gained access to* the Carolingian kingdom of Italy. [6]

> Napoleon's victory at Marengo, in June 1800, is the start of the French recovery of Italy. The process is completed in stages up to 1809, by which time every part of the peninsula is under French control. [7]

Genoa

Genoa, which was captured by Napoleon after the battle of Marengo, had been besieged since the middle of April, aided by a British naval blockade. But when General Ott secured the seaport, the British blockade was no longer required, and the fleet sailed away. Inside the fort, André Masséna had held out, in wait for Napoleon to arrive and end the siege. But starvation forced him to surrender the city and he was allowed by the Austrian commander to withdraw to Nice. [8] This caused Bonaparte to rage against Masséna for not holding out until he arrived.

Monacans will repel the red fleet

This final line centres upon Lord George Keith-Elphinstone, "(Admiral of the Red, &c.)". In 1798, Lord Keith was second in command under Earl St. Vincent. "Early in the beginning of the following year, he was promoted to the rank of vice-admiral of the red, and on the occasion of a temporary indisposition of earl St Vincent, assumed the entire command of the fleet." In November, he was sent to the Mediterranean in command of a squadron, and to assist Lord Nelson. His ships then proceeded to blockade "the ports of Toulon, Marseilles, Nice, and the coast of the Riviera; and, co-operating with the Austrians, who were besieging Genoa, he so effectually cut off all supplies from the French garrison in that place by the activity of his blockade, that they were compelled to surrender;" [9] (4 June 1800). On 23 May, "The British fleet, which had been helping with a blockade, made an attack on Monaco," [10] which was resisted.

N.B: From 1191 to 1793, Monaco existed as a colony of Genoa. It was captured by France during the French Revolution, but liberated after the downfall of Bonaparte. [11]

Summary; *This oracle links Napoleon's crossing of the Alps in 1800, in order to reach Milan, with that of the Insubres, founders of that city. Bonaparte's intention was to re-establish French control in Milan before relieving General Masséna, besieged in Genoa. At the time, the French army under Masséna was trapped inside Genoa, with a British fleet blockading the seaward side to the city. The oracle particularly mentions the 'red fleet', which foretold the history that would later be realized in the blockading of Genoa by Britain's Lord Keith, Admiral of the Red Fleet, whose ships subsequently sailed along the coast of French occupied Monaco to harass it. In 1800, Italy was not then a united nation. But under Napoleon's cavalry leader, General Murat, the northern and central part of what was then Italy was entered and subdued.*

38   *Pendant que duc, roy, royne occupera*
        Chef Bizant du captive en Samothrace:
        Auant l'assaut l'vn l'autre manger:
        Rebours ferré suyura du sang la trasse.

39   *Les Rodiens demanderont secours*
        Par le neglet de ses hoyrs delaissée.
        L'empire Arabe reualera son cours
        Par Hesperies la cause redressée.

40   *Les forteresses des assieges sarrés*
        Par pudre à feu profondés en abysme:
        Les prodituers seront touts vifs serrés
        Onc aux sacristes n'auint si piteux scisme.

41   *Gymnique sexe captiue par hostaige*
        Viendra de nuit custodes deceuoyr:
        Le chef du camp deceu par son langaige
        Lairra à la gente, fera piteux à voyr.

42   *Geneue & Langres par ceux de Chartres & Dolle*
        Et par Grenoble captif au Montlimard
        Seysset, Losanne par fraudulente dole,
        Les trahiront par or soyxante marc.

43   *Seront oys au ciel les armes batre:*
        Celuy au mesme les diuins ennemis
        Voudront loix sainctes iniustement debatre
        Par foudre & guerre bien croyans à mort mis.

        They will be heard in the sky, the weapons striking,
        Those at the very same: divine enemies,
        They will want to debate sacred laws unreasonably:
        By a thunderbolt and war, the decent believing put to death.

44   *Lous gros de Mende, de Roudés & Milhau*
        Cahours, Limoges, Castres malo, sepmano
        De nuech l'intrado, de Bourdeaux vn cailhau
        Par Perigort au toc de la campano.

45   *Par conflit roy, regne abandonera:*
        Le plus grand chef faillira au besoing:
        Mors profligés peu en rechapera,
        Tous destranchés, vn en sera tesmoing.

profliges (L – proflig\atus) profligate (recklessly extravagant); destrancher (OF) cut off, hew from, hack asunder, mangle;

Through conflict, the King (**CHARLES X**) will abandon the reign: 1830
The greatest chief (**MARMONT**) will fail at the emergency:
Profligate deaths, few will escape from it.
All hewed, one will be a testimony of it.

Through conflict, the King will abandon the reign

Charles X was the third brother to occupy the throne of France. His eldest brother, Louis XVI, had died beneath the guillotine in 1793. His other brother, Louis XVIII, had been installed as King after the exile of Napoleon. Consequently, after this brother died childless in September 1824, Charles Philippe, duc d'Artois, became France's new King.

In the event, his pro-royalist reign failed to meet the expectations of those who had lived through the Revolution and the age of Napoleon. In 1830 increasing dissent amongst the people finally erupted in another revolution. Conflict on the streets of Paris reached such a pitch that the King was in despair. Upon turning to Talleyrand for advice, he confessed,

> "I see no middle way between the throne and the scaffold." The old cynic, who had seen it all, replied, "Your majesty forgets the post-chaise!" Charles took Talleyrand's advice, and the post-chaise – to dreaded England. He ended up in Gorizia (in Austrian-occupied northern Italy), where he died of cholera in 1836. [1]

The greatest chief will fail at the emergency

Auguste Frédéric Louis Viesse de Marmont (20 July 1774 – 22 March 1852) was a French general and nobleman who rose to the rank of Marshal of France and was awarded the title *Duc de Raguse* (duke of Ragusa). He is also known for having deserted Napoleon in 1814, and supporting Louis XVIII; after which, he served under Charles X.

> He was made a peer of France and a major-general of the royal guard, and in 1820 a knight of the Order of the Holy Spirit and a grand officer of the Order of St Louis. He was the major-general of the guard on duty in July 1830 during the July Revolution, and was ordered to put down with a strong hand any opposition to the ordinances. Himself opposed to the court policy, he yet tried to do his duty, and only gave up the attempt to suppress the revolution when it became clear that his troops were outmatched. [2]

Profligate deaths, few will escape from it

The July Revolution, also known as *Les Trois Glorieuses* (The Three Glorious Days) took place in Paris from 27 to 29 July 1830. "With barricades in the streets, regiments of the army in open mutiny, and Paris in the hands of the rebels," [3] it gave every appearance that the days of the republic were about to return.

On the day before the violence occurred, a group of protesters against the King had gathered outside the gardens of the *Palais*, but were subsequently dispersed by the police. But, on the next day an even larger crowd took to the streets, this time erecting barricades. In the conflict that followed, '4,000 barricades' were erected and more than 'a thousand lives' lost.

> Several rioters were killed. Among the dead was a young woman shot down in the Rue Saint-Honoré with a stray bullet in the forehead [...] the spectacle aroused the crowd to calls for vengeance. During the night fresh barricades were run up [...] and workers from Saint-Antoine plundered gunsmiths for weapons and seized the Arsenal. [...] Elsewhere, on the Place de Grève and in the Rue Saint-Antoine, there was bitter fighting with numerous casualties. [...] Marmont gave the order to withdraw from the inner city. The game was lost. But the fighting continued savagely on the 29th. [...] By the afternoon of the 29th, the insurgents – bewildered by the completeness of their success – found themselves in control of the whole city. [4]

All hewed

Here we have another interesting use of words employed by the Seer for an oracle. In order to build the barricades, "Trees were felled." [5] And when preparing to abdicate, Charles remarked to Talleyrand, "I would rather hew wood than be a king like the King of England." [6] The fact is that Charles X never understood that the subservience to his former relatives, Louis XV and Louis XIV had been destroyed forever by the Revolution and the reign of Napoleon.

> So little did he understand the seriousness of the situation that, when the laconic message "All is over!" was brought to him, he believed that the insurrection had been suppressed. On realizing the truth he hastily abdicated. [7]

One will be a testimony of it

The July Revolution of 1830 was immortalized by Delacroix, who painted *Liberty Leading the People*. For this, he was heard to remark, "And if I haven't fought for my country at least I'll paint for her."

A woman personifying the concept and the goddess of Liberty leads the people forward over the bodies of the fallen, holding the flag of the French Revolution – the tricolour flag which is still France's flag today – in one hand and brandishing a bayoneted musket with the other. The figure of Liberty is also viewed as a symbol of France and the French Republic known as Marianne.

Delacroix depicted Liberty as both an allegorical goddess-figure and a robust woman of the people. The mound of corpses acts as a kind of pedestal from which Liberty strides, barefoot and bare-breasted, out of the canvas and into the space of the viewer. The Phrygian cap she wears had come to symbolize liberty during the first French Revolution, of 1789–94. [8]

LIBERTY LEADING THE PEOPLE

Summary: *These oracles include prophecies for every King of France, from the time of their publication, up until the termination of the monarchy in 1848. Charles X was the penultimate King and the last of the Bourbon monarchs. He was preceded by Louis XVIII, Napoleon I, Louis XVI, Louis XV, Louis XIV, Louis XIII, Henri IV, Henri III, Charles IX, Francis II and Henri II. The abdication of Charles X, predicted by revolution, includes the failure of General Marmont to summon reserves for the defence of the king, and the testimony of Delacroix's painting symbolising 'Liberty'.*

46   *Bien defendu le faict par excellence,*
      Garde toy Tours de ta proche ruine.
      Londres & Nantes par Reims fera defense
      Ne passés outre au temps de la bruine.

47   *Le noir farouche quand aura essayé*
      Sa main sanguine par feu, fer, arcs tendus:
      Trestout le people sera tant effrayé:
      Voyr les plus grands par col & pieds pendus

noir (AF livide, triste: also *Fig.* Noir, par opposition à blanc, se dit, en parlant des personnes, de la noirceur morale , See Dictionnaire de français "Littré". & *anagram-paragram* – roi<n>) king; col (OF) the neck.

The ghastly, savage (**KING, CHARLES IX**), when he will have tried   1572
His bloody hand, with fire, iron, and stretched bows:
Absolutely all of the people will be so afraid:
Witnessing the greatest, (**COLIGNY**), hung by neck and feet

The ghastly, savage (King)

The colour *black* was used in art to signify 'evil, falsehood, error'; [1] (see also Littré above, which appends 'black' to persons of base morality. The Seer uses the same word in Century Nine, N°. 20, also in Century Three N°. 60. But it was Charles IX, who was first described as 'black'. This was because the King gave permission for the assassination of Coligny: a man who until then had been his faithful friend. The murder ignited anti-Protestant passions in Paris to so great a degree that there was no containing the violence released from it. [2] Even the King took an active part. The killing thereafter quickly spread to other towns and cities across France. By the time it had subsided, many thousands of lives had been lost.

When he will have tried his bloody hand with fire

In Paris, the murders happened, "under the eye of the king, himself, who enjoyed the sacrifice, and with a fowling-piece, from the windows of the palace, diverted himself with killing the few stragglers, who were attempting to make their escape." [3]

Iron and stretched bows

Those coming under the eye of the King were a band of people terrified by what was happening, and who had entered the palace courtyard while trying to escape their would-be killers, prowling the streets outside. But upon entering the square, they were confronted by the *iron and stretched bows* of "the King's archers, who pushed the terrified men and women on to the halberds of the Swiss guards, who impaled their unarmed quarry with grim efficiency." [4]

Absolutely all of the people will be so afraid

This orgy of burning and killing lasted for three days, terrifying the people as the numbers of dead rapidly increased. Three thousand people were murdered in Paris, alone, and another ten thousand in the provinces, most notably Bordeaux, Toulouse, Rouen, Lyons, Troyes and Orleans. [5]

Witnessing the greatest hung by neck and feet

Admiral Coligny, the warlord, the statesman, the Huguenot chief, and King Charles's favourite councillor was not only 'the greatest' and most influential figure at court, he was also the first to die. Whilst lying in bed at the Hôtel de Béthisy, recovering from the wound inflicted during Catherine de Medici's bungled attempt at having him assassinated, a partisan of the duc de Guise named Besme, broke into the room, and stabbed him. He was then disembowelled and thrown from the upstairs window of the Hôtel. The mob in wait below dragged the still breathing man away and *hung him by the neck* from a gibbet. But, being discontented with what they had done, they took him down and cut off his head: this was later dispatched to Pope Gregory XIII as a Catholic trophy. Coligny's decapitated body was then tossed into the Seine, but then quickly recovered so that it could again be hung from the gibbet at Montfaucon. However, since the torso was headless, the body had to be *hung by its feet*. [6]

Summary: *This oracle provides sufficient detail to identify it with the atrocity in Paris known as the Massacre of St Bartholomew's Eve'. The instigator was the Queen-mother, who had become envious of Coligny's influence over her son. She wanted him dead, but the assassination attempt only wounded Coligny. Fearful that her part in the plot would be uncovered, she harangued the King until he agreed to have his favourite murdered. But Coligny's death triggered three days of terrifying slaughter that spread across France, in which the King also participated. The hanging of Coligny by his neck and then by his feet is particularly illustrative of the foresight contained in this prophecy.*

48   *Planure Ausonne fertile, spacieuse*
        Produira taons si trestant sauterelles:
        Clarté solaire deuiendra nubileuse,
        Ronger le tout, grand peste venir d'elles.

49   *Deuant le peuple sang sera respandu,*
        Que du haut ciel ne viendra eslogner:
        Mais d'vn long temps ne sera entendu
        L'esprit d'vn seul le viendra tesmoignes.

50   *Libra verra regner les Hesperies,*
        De ciel, & terre tenir la monarchie:
        D'Asie forces nul ne verra peries
        Que sept ne tiennent par rang la hierarchie.

51   *La duc cupide son ennemi ensuiure*
        Dans entrera empeschant sa phalange:
        Astes à pied si pres viendront poursuiure,
        Que la iournée conflite pres de Gange.

52   *La cité obsesse aux murs hommes & femmes*
        Ennemis hors le chef prestz à soy rendres
        Vent sera fort encontre les gens-darmes:
        Chassés seront par chaux, poussiere & cendre.

53   *Les fugitifz & bannis reuoquez,*
        Peres & fils grand garnissant hautx puit:
        Le cruel pere & les siens suffoquez,
        Son filz plus pire submergé dans le puits.

puit (3rd person of puier) and puits are two different words.

54   *Du nom qui onques ne fut au Roy gaulois,*
    Iamais ne fut vn fouldre si craintif,
    Tremblant l'Italie, l'Espagne, & les Anglois:
    De femme estrangiers grandement attentif.

Iamais ne, not ever: i.e., never; femme (OF) femelle; grandement (OF) hugely, exceedingly.

By a name (**NAPOLEON**) which at any time was not of a French King,   1803
No never was a thunderbolt so fearful,
Italy, Spain and the English trembling,
Exceedingly attentive concerning female foreigners.

By a name which at any time was not of a French King

Napoleon was the first ruler of France, since Francis I came to power in 1515, to bear a name that was different from those who had reigned before him. After France became a republic, it was first the Convention, and then the Directory that governed the country. But in 1799, Napoleon's *coup d'état* changed the power structure, and by 1804 he, had become Emperor of the First French Empire.[1]

No, never was a thunderbolt so fearful

The era termed Napoleonic defines a succession of wars from 1796 to 1815 in which, proportionately, more people were killed than during the First World War, with its estimated military deaths of 8·5 million. Many of the battles fought by France during an era of almost continuous warfare, have since given their names to history; e.g. Nile, Marengo, Trafalgar, Austerlitz, Jena, Borodino, Wagram, Waterloo; etc.[2] *Never before in the history of France had there been such a thunderbolt;* and by one with *a name that was never before given to a French king.*

Italy, Spain, and the English trembling

The prophecy continues by naming three nations that would be most affected by Bonaparte's rule. These were, *Spain, Italy and England* each of which, subsequently lent their name to one of the Napoleonic armies; that is to say, *L'Armée D'Italie* (April 1796), *L'Armée de l'Angleterre* (1803), and *L'Armée D'Espagne* (November 1808).

Italy was invaded and conquered by Napoleon on two occasions. The first campaign was undertaken in 1796 and the second in 1800.[3] *Spain* was forced to endure the Peninsula War from 1808 until 1815.[4] And between 1799 and 1815, *the English* were engaged is a series of five separate coalitions against the French Emperor: during which time, two outstanding victories were achieved: one at sea (Trafalgar), the other on land (Waterloo).[5]

It is also noteworthy that in Century One N°. 82, the Seer uses '*trembling*' to mean an awareness of approaching danger.

Exceedingly attentive concerning female foreigners

The oracle now shifts attention to Bonaparte's sexual interests. Napoleon married twice. His first wife Joséphine was born into an aristocratic Creole family on the island of Martinique. His second wife, Marie-Louise was an Austrian princess: daughter of the Emperor Francis II. His mistress, by whom he had a son, was the Polish countess Maria Walewska, countess. His other mistress, Giuseppina Grassini, was an Italian opera singer, whose career he continued to sponsor, even long after their affair had ended. He also fostered a close friendship with the Swiss intellectual, Germaine de Staël.[6]

Summary: *The details contained in this oracle coincide completely and quite uniquely with Napoleon Bonaparte. No monarch, between the time these prophecies were published, and the reign of Napoleon I as Emperor, was known as the 'first' of that name: viz. Henri II; Francis II; Charles IX; Henri III; Henri IV; Louis XIII; Louis XIV; Louis XV; Louis XVI; republic, Napoleon I. The three countries identified as being fearful of him, all had a specific army named after them. Even Napoleon's love life, devoted mostly to foreign women, was known to the seer. Only data existing within the timelessness of a 'block universe' can explain this.*

55   *Quant la corneille sur tour de brique ioincte,*
      Durant sept heures ne fera que crier:
      Mort presagee de sang statue taincte,
      Tyran murtry, aux Dieux people prier.

56   *Apres victoire de rabieuse langue,*
      L'esprit tempté en tranquil & repos:
      Victeur sanguin par conf,ict faict harangue,
      Roustir la langue & la chair & les oz.

57   *Ignare enuie du grand Roy supportée,*
      Tiendra propos deffendre les escriptz:
      Sa femme non femme par vn autre tentée,
      Plus double deux ne fort ne crys.

58   *Soleil ardant dans le gosier coller,*
      De sang humain arrouser terre Etrusque:
      Chef seille d'eaue mener son fils filet,
      Captiue dame conduicte en terre turque.

59   *Deux assiegés en ardante ferueur,*
      De soif estainctz pour deux plainnes tasses
      Le fort limé, & vn viellart resueur,
      Aux Geneuois de Nira monstra trasse.

60   *Les sept enfans en hostaige laissés,*
      Le tiers viendra son enfant trucider:
      Deux par son filz seront d'estoc percés,
      Gennes, Florence lors viendra encunder.

61   *Le vieulx mocqué, & priué de sa place,*
      Par l'estrangier qui le subornera:
      Mains de son fils mangees deuant sa face
      Le frère à Chatres, Orl. Rouan trahira.

62   *Vn coronel machine ambitien,*
      Se saisira de la plus grande armée,
      Contre son prince fainte inuention,
      Et descouuert sera soubz la ramée.

63   *L'armée Celtique contre les montagnars,*
      Qui seront sceuz & prins à la lipee:
      Paysans fresz poulseront tost faugnars,
      Precipitez tous au fil de l'epee.

64   *Le deffaillant en habit de bourgeois,*
      Viendra le Roy tempter de son offence:
      Quinze souldarts la pluspart Vstagois,
      Vie derniere & chef de sa cheuance.

65   *Au deserteur de la grand forteresse,*
      Apres qu'aura son lieu abandonné:
      Son aduersaire fera si grand prouesse,
      L'Empereur tost mort sera condemné.

For the deserter of the great fortress,   1870
That afterwards will have abandoned his seat:
His adversary (**WILHELM 1**) will achieve such great prowess;
The Emperor (**NAPOLEON III**) soon dead will be condemned.

For the deserter of the great fortress

This prophecy addresses the final years of Napoleon III's reign. It does so by firstly identifying him as the person who deserted the *fortress* of Ham in northern France. This prediction not only serves the purpose of identification, it also connects with the remaining content of the oracle.

In August 1840, Charles-Louis Napoleon was arrested for a failed *coup,* and sentenced to life imprisonment. For six years he remained confined behind the castle walls of Ham. Then, on 25 May 1846, *he deserted the great fortress.* "He successfully accomplished his design by the simple expedient of walking out of the gaol disguised as a workman." [1]

That afterwards will have abandoned his seat

After making his escape, Louis was able to pave the way to become Emperor Napoleon III. But in September 1870, having embarked upon a war, with Prussia, he was forced to take refuge with his army inside the fortress at Sedan: reputed to be the largest in Europe. Inside the castle, his men were in desperate plight. An incessant hail of bullets, accompanied by a bombardment of shells proved indefensible, and to avoid further injury, the French were compelled to surrender.

> Napoleon III realized that the position was hopeless. He surrendered, and the next morning he and 83,000 French soldiers became prisoners of war. The French had lost 3,000 men killed, 14,000 wounded, and 21,000 missing or captured. German losses totalled 9,000 men killed and wounded. [2]

After Napoleon's release by Prussia, and having *abandoned his seat* as Emperor of France, in response to the political animosity born from his defeat, he joined his family in England.

His adversary will achieve such great prowess

Napoleon III's adversary, Wilhelm I of Germany, was, however, triumphant: having inflicted upon France one of its worst military defeats. Outside Paris, Wilhelm not only set up his 'Royal Headquarters' inside the Palace of Versailles, but on 18 January, inside the Hall of Mirrors, he had himself proclaimed 'Kaiser' of the German Empire. [3]

Before the onset of autumn, the French governing body was compelled to concede to the terms for peace offered by Germany's new Kaiser. These involved the loss to France of Alsace and most of Lorraine, a payment of five billion francs, and the expense of maintaining a German presence in the east, until the indemnity had been paid in full.

Before withdrawing his army from Paris, Kaiser Wilhelm insisted upon a victory parade. On the morning of 1 March, 30,000 triumphant German soldiers either marched or rode on horseback down the Champs-Elysées to the steady beat of their drums. In the afternoon, a second victory parade took place, this time with the massed troops striding onto the *Place de la Concorde.* [4]

The Emperor soon dead

Not long after his captivity by the Prussian Army, following France's surrender at Sedan, *the Emperor* was released. But the political atmosphere had drastically changed in France since the country's defeat. And so, on 20 March 1871, once more an exile, Napoleon sailed to England and took up residence with his wife and son at Camden Place in Chislehurst, Kent: occupying himself with plans for a fresh *coup d'état.* But less than two years later, while preparing to undergo a third operation to remove bladder stones, his condition suddenly deteriorated, and on 9 January 1873, he died. [5]

Will be condemned

> Sedan was a defeat even more bitter than Waterloo. [...] it delivered France into the hands of Prussia, and generations of Frenchmen have never forgiven Napoleon III for their country's humiliation. [6]

Summary: *The battle of Sedan, which brought about the Emperor Napoleon III's downfall, was lost inside the fortress at Sedan. The seer identifies this by connecting it to the fortress from which Napoleon escaped. It was this bid to free himself, albeit into exile, which provided him with the opportunity to pursue his ambition of emulating his illustrious uncle, Napoleon Bonaparte—but for whom no emulator had been predicted. The triumph of Germany's victory over France is also clearly demonstrated by the victorious celebration of Wilhelm I. This contrasts with the predicted death of the former Emperor, soon after his release from captivity. It may be a chastening thought to realize that in a block universe, everyone's birth and death have been assigned their place and time, but always in harmony with their freewill in the world.*

66   *Soubz couleur faincte de sept testes rasees*
Seront semés diuers explorteurs:
Puys & fontaines de poison arrousees,
Au fort de Gennes humains deuorateurs.

67   *L'an que Saturne & Mars esgaulz combust,*
L'air fort seiché, longue traiection:
Par feux secretz, d'ardeur grand lieu adust,
Per pluie, vent, chault, guerres, incursions.

68   *En l'an bien proche esloigné de Venus,*
Les deux plus grands de l'Asie & d'Affrique:
Du Ryn & hister, qu'on dira sont venus,
Crys, pleurs à Malte & coste ligustique.

bien (OF adv.) as it should be, aptly; esloigné (AF allonger) elongated; Hister (paragram + transposition) Hit[l]er; venus (OF syncope) venu[ẽ]s) localities; coste (AF côte) coast. Cross-references: Hister, C.ll: 24; C.V: 29.

In the year approaching as it should be, with Venus elongated (**1939**),   1939
The two great men of Asia and of Africa (**HIDEKI & MUSSOLINI**):
Concerning the Rhine and Danube (**HITLER**), which men will say are venues,
Screams, tears at Malta, and the Ligurian Coast.

In the year approaching as it should be, with Venus elongated

On 3 September 1939, Venus and Earth were in superior conjunction; that is to say, Earth, Sun and Venus were in a straight line, with Venus behind the Sun. Venus was therefore at full length; or, in words chosen by the Seer, Venus was elongated. On that same day, 3 September 1939, England and France, separately but in unison, declared war on Germany. [1]

The two great men of Asia and of Africa

The actual date when France and Great Britain declared war on Germany, together with a reference to two great men from Africa and Asia, directs attention firstly towards Benito Mussolini. This is because since May 1936, Italy's conquest of Eritrea, Ethiopia and Somalia had given the country an East African empire, while also raising Mussolini's status in Africa. In addition to this, he had been Italy's Prime Minister since 1922.

At the same time as the Italian army was fighting to gain control in Africa, Japanese troops were marching into Peking in support of a *coup* organized by Tokyo (26 November 1935). The successful outcome of this incursion allowed Japan to begin a full-scale invasion of northern China, and by October 1938, the entire eastern seaboard was in Japanese hands. Thereafter, with the outbreak of war in Western Europe, General Tojo Hideki, former Chief of Staff of the Kwantung Army, became Japan's War Minister, and subsequently Prime Minister of Japan.

On 27 September 1940, both Mussolini and Hideki joined Hitler in Berlin to sign up to the Tripartite Act. Together, these three countries, Italy, Japan and Germany, comprising more than 250 million people, had become the mightiest alliance in the world. [2]

Concerning the Rhine and Danube, which men will say are venues

Having introduced both *Africa* and *Asia*, which were to become major battlegrounds in the Second World War, the oracle next brings in two of Europe's mightiest rivers, the *Rhine* and the *Danube*. Both of these waterways flow through countries of mainland Europe that were caught up in the Second World War; e.g. Austria (Danube and Rhine); Czechoslovakia (Danube); The Netherlands (Rhine); France (Rhine, Romania (Danube); Bulgaria (Danube); Hungary (Danube); Yugoslavia (Danube); Germany (Danube and Rhine); Ukraine (Danube); the USSR. (Danube). [3] The Rivers *Rhine and Danube* were therefore 'venues'. In other words, they acted as locations for countries bordered by their waters that became drawn into the Second World War.

(Hitler)

In addition to this, by using the River Danube's ancient name of *Hister*, it allows the name of

Hitler to emerge as a paragram (formed by transposing 't' and 's' and exchanging 's' for an 'l'). Equally noteworthy is the fact that Hitler's name was so closely identified with Nazi Germany during the war that it became used in England as a synecdoche for the enemy. One spoke of fighting *Hitler*, or bombing *Hitler*, etc., when, in fact, Germany was the intended target. In this sense, Hitler, too, became a *venue*.

It will be recalled from Century Two N°. 24 that Hitler had lived on the outskirts of Linz, in a little farmhouse in Leonding and it was in Linz, watered by the Danube, that he grew up.

Screams, tears at Malta

The Mediterranean was another major venue in the Second World War, with *Malta* situated halfway between two Allied land bases: one at Alexandria, the other at Gibraltar. Because of its strategic position, the island was recognised to be of immense importance by both sides in the war. "Malta was first attacked by Italian aircraft on 11 June 1940." Once the Luftwaffe had established itself on the island of Sicily, raids against *Malta*, especially between January and April 1941, intensified. Attacks by the Italian Navy were also made against Valetta harbour, but these failed to achieve a breakthrough.

> [Air] raids were renewed in December with even greater intensity. During January 1942 there were 262, during February 236, and in March and April twice the tonnage of bombs that London had suffered during the Blitz was dropped on Malta. [4]

And the Ligurian Coast

It was not long after the bombing of Malta that the Ligurian Coast suffered a similar pounding. In February 1941, the British Navy joined with the Royal Air Force in carrying out a massive assault upon Genoa. This attack was repeated on 24 October 1942, when it was reported that during the night, "100 Lancasters attacked Genoa." Further air raids described, how, "For many months the Allies had been bombing Genoa, Turin, Milan and other Italian ports and cities." [5]

Summary: The declaration of war against Germany that commenced WWII is correctly dated by the elongation of Venus on 3 September 1939. One year later the two great men of Asia and Africa, Hideki and Mussolini met Hitler to form the Tripartite Agreement. The oracle then uses the rivers Rhine and Danube to indicate the countries these flow through will be involved in the predicted war. In the Mediterranean, Malta's importance was the cause for it to be bombed mercilessly, while Italy also received bombing raids from the UK. Thus, when Africa and Asia are brought into the prophecy, it makes good sense to understand how the oracle has set out the clues for having predicted the start of world war two.

69   *La cité grande les exilés tiendront,*
      Les citadins mors, murtris, & chassés:
      Ceulx d'Aquilée à Parme promettront,
      Monstrer l'entrée par les lieux non trassés.

70   *Bien contigue des grans monts Pyrenees,*
      Vn contre l'aigle grand copie addresser:
      Ouuertes vaines, forces exterminees,
      Que iusque à Pau, le chef viendra chasser.

Cross-references: aigle, C.I: 23; C.III: 37; C.VIII: 4; C.VIII: 46; Pau, C.II:33; C.II:94; C.III: 75; C.VI:79; C.VIII:1.

Completely contiguous with the great Pyrenean Mountains,   1813
One against the Eagle (**NAPOLEON**), directing a great army:
Veins open, troops exterminated,
Then until to Pau, the chief (**WELLESLEY**) will come pursuing,

The many cross-references for the Eagle are an indication of the number of times in which the Emperor Napoleon appears in these prophecies. In 1808, the British Government sent Sir Arthur Wellesley (later made Duke of Wellington) to the Iberian Peninsula to lead an Anglo-Spanish assault against the French War Lord, Bonaparte. The Peninsula War, as it became labelled, lasted five years. In the end, France was defeated, and its army driven back across the Pyrenees.

Completely contiguous with the great Pyrenean Mountains

As the year 1813 drew to a close, the Emperor Napoleon was to find his occupation of Spain under threat. "Amid the Pyrenees, the armies of Marshal Soult and Suchet (sharing 100,000 men between them) were steadily giving ground before the advance of Lord Wellington's Anglo-Spanish forces (125,000 strong)." [1]

One against the Eagle

The one referred to in this prophecy is identifiable as the future Duke of Wellington. "When in 1808 the Portuguese rose against Napoleon, Wellesley was ordered to support them." In the event: "[Wellesley won nineteen pitched battles and innumerable combats [...] sustained ten sieges and [took] four great fortresses [...] twice expelled the French from Portugal, once from Spain."

The eagle – as with Caesar before him and Hitler in the 20th century – also became Napoleon's adopted symbol. The tapestry that once decorated Bonaparte's study at the Tuileries, and then at Malmaison, was decorated by an eagle clutching thunderbolts in its talons, with the symbolic letter 'N' around it. [2]

Directing a great army

In the final stages of the Peninsula War,

[Wellington] rode over to San Sebastian to discuss with Graham how best to renew the siege. [...] A little later he instructed a troop of Horse Artillery from Santa Barbara to move to Sumbilla. [...] Wellington was back at Lesaca in time for dinner at eight and approved the precautions that Murray had taken. [...] Wellington wrote to Graham before going to bed instructing him to re-embark the bulk of the siege material which would be an encumbrance. [...] He also sent orders for one of the two Spanish divisions blockading Pamplona to move north to support Picton and Cole and for the cavalry to move to Pamplona. [...] The Sixth division was to send two of its brigades to touch in on Hill's new position. The third division was to remain in Santesteban to secure the town. [...] the Seventh division was to march to Sumbilla where it would be closely in touch with the Sixth. The Light division will place itself on the left bank of the Bidassoa. [...] Having made these dispositions, Wellington at four in the morning, rode over to the valley of Baztan where he found Hill strongly posted with 9000 men in hand and no contact with the French. [3]

Veins open

In the 19th century, British armed forces were known by their numbers, and not by the county names they later acquired. It was also common for some brigades to be given nicknames: "Regiments also acquired nicknames, some of which have stuck and some have not. [...] the 29th Foot [...] were known as 'The Vein Openers'." [4]

Troops exterminated

In point of fact, the 29th Foot – *the Vein Openers* – suffered particularly badly during Wellesley's efforts to remove the French from Spanish soil. In one memorable battle, the 29th Foot lost four-fifths of their number (*troops exterminated*). Although, apart from this one regiment, there were others, "killed, wounded or captured [numbering] two hundred thousand enemies – leaving of their own number forty thousand dead, whose bones whiten the plains and mountains of the Peninsula." [5]

Then, until to Pau, the chief will come pursuing

Rivers and waterways are the natural feature of any terrain at the foot of a huge mountain range. The largest of those footing the Pyrenees is the *Gave de Pau*. This was reached by Wellesley at the same time the coalition forces were converging upon Paris (March 1814). [6]

It is in this sense that *Pau* allows a double meaning, for it represents both Napoleon *in absentia*, whom Wellesley– *the chief* – had come pursuing. [7] But, geographically, it also describes the *Pau* region in southern France, reached by Wellesley's army at the time of Bonaparte's abdication. After arriving at Pau, further conflict was rendered unnecessary, although it took time for the news to reach the south of France.

Summary: *The end of the Peninsula War, fought between the French, who were occupying Spain and Portugal, and a coalition force comprised of British and Spanish troops, is the subject of this prophecy. The war ended with Wellesley having pushed the French back over the Pyrenees. Napoleon is again identified as the 'Eagle'. But notice too, how the 'Vein Openers' have been crafted into the prophecy. And were that not enough, there is the added information that pursuit of the French will cease upon reaching the Pau region.*

71   *En lieu d'espouse les filles trucidees,*
       Murtre à grand faulte ne sera superstie:
       Dedans le puys vestules inondees,
       L'espouse estaincte par hausse d'Aconile.

72   *Les Artoniques par Agen & l'Estore,*
       À sainct Felix seront le parlement:
       Ceul de Basas viendront à la mal'heure,
       Saisir Condon & Marsan promptement.

73   *Le nepueu grand par forces prouuera,*
       Le pache faict du cœur pusillanime:
       Ferrare & Ast de Duc esprovera,
       Par lors qu'au soir sera le pantomime.

74   *Du lac Lyman & ceulx de Brannonices,*
       Tous assemblez contre ceulx d'Aquitaine:
       Germain beaucoup encore plus Souisses,
       Seront deffaictz auec ceulx d'Humaine.

75   *Prest à combatre fera defection,*
       Chef aduersaire obtiendra la victoire:
       L'arriere garde fera defension,
       Les deffaillans mort au blanc territoire.

prest (OF); furnished; defection (L – defectio\nis)a falling away, defection; servir de défence) assist with defence

Furnished to do combat, he (**NAPOLEON**) will make a defection,   1812
Chief adversary (**CZAR ALEXANDER**) will obtain the victory:
The rear guard (**MARSHAL NEY**) will assist with defence,
The faltering ones dead in the white territory.

Furnished to do combat

In preparation for his forthcoming war with Russia, Napoleon began the massive task of planning what would be needed for the battles ahead: "The aim of all my moves will be to concentrate 400,000 men at a single point. We can hope for nothing from the countryside and accordingly must take everything with us."

> Twenty-six transport battalions were formed accordingly, four consisting of 600 light carts (each with a capacity of 600 kilos), another four of 600 heavy wagons (1,000 kilos apiece), the rest being equipped with 252 four-animal wagons (loading 1,500 kilos apiece). [...] For meat rations, vast herds of cattle and oxen were collected ready to accompany the army eastwards. [...] In round numbers, the Grande Armée was accompanied by no less than 200,000 animals [...] besides a total of some 25,000 vehicles. [...] He also placed great reliance on restocking his convoys and forward magazines by means of the great rivers of western Russia, and accordingly two naval squadrons, each of 100 river boats, were held in readiness to convey stores from Tilsit to Kovno, by way of the River Niemen.[1]

He will make a defection

The treaty of Tilsit (7–9 July 1807) was signed after Napoleons' victories at Jena, Auerstadt, Eylau and Friedland. In the treaty there was a secret article made between Napoleon and Tsar Alexander I of Russia, which agreed to their alliance against Great Britain, should it be called upon. In the event, Napoleon soon became disappointed. It appeared that Alexander was not complying with this agreement, and when several terse diplomatic exchanges between the two brought no improvement, his patience ended. On 22 June 1812, Napoleon made the following address. "Soldats! [...] At Tilsit, Russia swore eternal friendship with France and also war against England. Today she has broken her undertakings!"

Alexander's *laissez-faire* attitude towards confronting the British had finally caused Napoleon's patience to snap, and his response was to *make a defection* from the treaty by preparing for war. [2]

Chief adversary will obtain the victory

It can be seen from this that Bonaparte's *chief adversary* was Czar Alexander I the 'little father' of the Russias. [3] His ambassador in London, Vorontzov, wrote a letter on 5 June 1812, which provided, in remarkable detail, the eventual course that the war would take.

> Even if, at first, military operations go against us, we can win, by persistent defence and retreat. If the enemy pursues us, it is all up with him: for, the further he advances from his bases of supply and munitions into a trackless and foodless country, starve d and encircled by an army of Cossacks, his position will become more and more dangerous; and he will end by being decimated by the winter, which has always been our most faithful ally.

During the next six months Vorontzov's prediction became accurately fulfilled. On 5 December 1812, at Smorgoni near Vilnius, Bonaparte "dictated the 29th Bulletin announcing the defeat and dissolution of the Grand Army." He had finally been forced to admit *victory* had been *obtained by* the Czar, *his chief adversary*. [4]

The rear guard will assist with defence

A feature of Napoleon's defeat and the army's retreat from Moscow was Marshal Ney's *rear guard defence* against the Cossack forces, who made repeated attacks against the tail of the French army. "Ney, who had fought a series of stubborn rear-guard actions since Krasnoi on November 7th, was the last Frenchman to leave Russian soil." It was Ney's gallantry in providing a defence for the retreating French army that subsequently earned him the title: 'bravest of the brave'. [5]

NAPOLEON'S RETREAT FROM MOSCOW

The faltering ones dead in the white territory

In temperatures as low as minus 30 degrees *the faltering ones*, numbering as many as 30,000, were at their weakest and most vulnerable. The first snow fell on 3 November and this was followed by severe frosts. In the midst of this icy *white territory*, vast numbers, literally thousands of men, *froze to death*. [6]

> The sufferings of the retreat were now as horrible as anything imagined in Dante's C ircle of Ice. [...] men dropped and froze by the roadside, or lay down and froze around the camp-fires at night. [...] The 350 tattered and exhausted men who returned with him over the ice were all the effectives left of the 250,000 who had led the invasion across the river six months before. [7]

Summary: *In the space of just four lines of verse, the seer indicates the enormous preparations and supplies needed for taking an army into Russia; also, the reason for going to war. The oracle then correctly predicts the victory will go to his adversary. Napoleon's defeat and his army's retreat from Russia in temperatu res far below zero is one of the most pitiful accounts in history. To complete the report, the oracle includes the rear guard action of Marshal Ney, whose bravery allowed Napoleon to elude being overtaken by the pursuing Cossacks.*

76   *Les Nictobriges par ceulx de Perigort,*
        Seront vexez tenant iusques au Rosne:
        L'associe de Gascons & Begorn,
        Trahir letemple, le prestre estant au prosne.

77   *Selin monarque l'Italie pacifique,*
        Regnes vnis Roy chrestien du monde:
        Mourant voudra coucher en terre blesiq ue,
        Apres pyrates auoir chassé de l'onde.

78   *La grand armee de la pugne ciuille,*
       Pour de nuict Parme à l'estrange trouuee:
       Septante neuf murtris dedans la ville,
       Les estrangiers passez tous à l'epee.

79   *Sang roy fuis Monthurt, Mas, Eguillon,*
       Remplis seront de Bourdelois les Landes:
       Nauarre, Bigorre, pointes & eguillons,
       Profondz de faim vorer de liege glandes.

80   *Pres du grand fleuue grand fosse terre egeste,*
       En quinze pars sera l'eaue diuisee:
       La cité prinse, feu, sang, crys, conflit meste,
       Et la plus part concerne au collisee.

egeste (L egest\us) carry away; meste (AF triste) sorrowful; collisee (L collis\io) shock, collision, striking together,.

Close by the great river a huge trench, earth carried away (**MAGINOT LINE**),   1927
It will be in fifteen parts, the water divided:
The city (**PARIS**) taken: fire, blood, shouts: a sorrowful conflict,
And the greatest part relates to the coming together.

Close by the great river, a huge trench, earth carried away

The great river refers to "the Rhine, the second most important river in Europe. [...] [It] touches French territory along the Alsace-Baden frontier for about 125 miles (200 kilometres)." In 1927, André Maginot, the French Minister for War, sought approval to begin excavating for the construction of an underground line of fortifications alongside the left bank of the Rhine. The proposed undertaking was enormous, consisting of *a huge trench* approximately fourteen miles long.

After the excavation, the construction of the fortification was to continue until 1936, with every type of facility catered for, to ensure the comfort of those occupying the Line. These included, "air conditioning, clean messes, shower baths, reading rooms and cinemas." [1]

It will be in fifteen parts

When it was finally completed, the construction consisted of a line of "fortified regions for about twenty kilometres of front, on 15 depths." [2]

The water divided

Alongside the river, the Maginot Line had been divided into sections, with each subdivision overlooked by separate observation casements and machinegun nests. [3] Despite this massive engineering project for the country's defence, it quickly became obsolete.

The city taken

When hostilities did break out between Germany and France, as they did in 1940, the German army simply sidestepped this line of fortresses, and attacked France through the Low Countries. Hitler's forces were therefore able to advance through Belgium, Holland and into France. Their goal was Paris, which was taken on 14 June 1940. [4]

Fire, blood, shouts

In an effort to frustrate the German advance into Paris as much as possible, the oil refinery situated on the outskirts of the city was deliberately set on fire to deny the German army access to fuel. [5] And, of course, the taking of Paris inevitably involved bloodshed. Those who were killed were either shot as the German army advanced into Paris, or died from exploding bombs, as happened on 3 June with the cost of 250 lives. There was also isolated sniper fire. [6]

Having conquered the city, the triumphant German army marched into the centre of Paris, along the Champs Elysée, beneath an emblem of the swastika. There, they were met by shouts of derision and abuse from an angry crowd that had gathered to watch the German army occupy their capital. [7]

A sorrowful conflict

"For the third time in seventy years, Paris was under siege." Inside the capital everywhere closed down as people sought to leave the city "[A]n endless stream of refugees poured out along the Boulevard Raspail." Along the Champs Elysée, a similar bleak appearance could be observed, where buses stood forlorn, having been positioned along this normally bustling thoroughfare, to deter airborne troops invading the city from the clouds. Finally, on the night of 11 June: "General Maxime Weygand declared Paris an 'open city'." The great capital had given up with little conflict. [8]

And the greatest part relates to the coming together

Up until the time Paris fell, the French people had felt perfectly safe behind the Maginot Line. "They developed a 'Maginot line complex'." It was born from a "confidence that these fortifications would stop the Germans the next time with little loss of life to the defenders." As historian, William Shirer said, "The complex took hold of almost everyone." It therefore came as a total shock to the French people when the Line failed to prevent the German invasion by such a simple strategy. [9]

Summary: This oracle is a prediction of the occupation of Paris, which occurred in 1940. For the seer, 'the city' is always the capital of France. The prophecy speaks of the sorrowful conflict that preceded its fall to the enemy, which would be expected in most circumstances, but he also refers to the Maginot Line along the bank of the River Rhine, with the exact number of 15 levels in the main fortress. That is prophecy! And he elaborates upon it by predicting its uselessness as a means of protecting France from a German onslaught: much to the predicted astonishment of the people when this actually occurred.

81   Pont on fera promptement de nacelles,
       Passer l'armee du grand prince Belgique:
       Dans profondréz: & non loing de Brucelles,
       Oultre passés detrenchés sept à picque.

82   Amas s'approche venant d'Esclauonie,
       L'Olestant vieulx cite ruynera:
       Fort desolee verra la Romanie,
       Puis la grand flame estaindre ne scaura.

83   Combat nocturne le vaillant capitaine,
       Vaincu fuira, peu de gens profligez:
       Son peuple esmeu sedition non vaine,
       Son propre fils le tiendra assiegé.

84   Vn grand d'Auserre mourra bien miserable,
       Chassé de ceulx qui soubz luy ont esté:
       Serré de chaisnes, après d'vn rude cable,
       En l'an que Mars, Venus, Sol mis en esté.

85   Le charbon blanc du noir sera chassé,
       Prisonnier faict mené au tombereau:
       More Chameau sur piedz entre lassez,
       Lors le puisnay sillera l'aubereau.

86   L'an que Saturne en eaue sera conioinct,
       Auecques Sol, le Roy fort & puissant:
       A Reims & Aix sera recue & oingt,
       Apres conquestes murtrira innocent.

87   Vn fils du Roy tant de langues aprins,
       A son aisné au regne different:
       Son pere beau au plus beau fils comprins,
       Fera perir principe adeerant.

88   Le grand Antoine du moindre fait sordide,
       De Phintriase à son dernier rongé:
       Vn qui de plombe vouldra esrre cupide,
       Passant le port d'esleu sera plonge.

89   *Trente de Londres secret coniureront,*
        Contre leur roy sur le pont l'entreprise:
        Leuy, satalistes la mort degousteront,
        Vn roy esleu blonde, natif de Frize.

secret (L secret\o) secretly; pont (L pont\us) sea; leuy (L levi-fidus) of small credit; sataliste (L. satell\itis) attendant, follower;
blonde (AF - susceptible) capable; degousteront (Middle French - desgouster), abhor; Frize (L Frisii) Friesland.

In London, thirty will secretly conspire: 1689
The enterprise on the sea against their King (**JAMES II**),
Of small credit (**MONMOUTH**), the attendants will abhor his death,
A King elected (**WILLIAM III**), capable, a native of Friesland.

At the beginning of 1689, Prince William of Orange was King in all but name. He still needed to persuade Scotland to accept him as the country's monarch. In the previous December, William's father-in-law, James II had abandoned the thrones of England and Scotland, and sought asylum in France. But, until Parliament decreed otherwise, he was still, legitimately, the King of both countries, and Scotland remained reluctant to accede to English demands.

In London, thirty will secretly conspire

To seek a resolution to this problem, William called a meeting *in London,* consisting of *thirty* Scottish sympathizers. His aim was to find a way to overcome the difficulty, so that a consensus might be obtained concerning how best to deal with the present situation.

> There being at that time many Scotsmen of rank in London, he summoned them together, and asked their advice in the present state of affairs. This assembly, consisting of thirty noblemen [...] chose duke Hamilton for their president. [1]

Whereupon, after much discussion, an agreement was reached that William would arrange a convention north of the border in order to settle the matter. This was convened in Edinburgh on 22 March 1689.

The enterprise on the sea against their King

Before William of Orange arrived in England to become the nation's King, it had first required Parliament to take action against James II. This had involved several members of the British government sending an invitation to Prince William, requesting him to invade England and take the Crown. [2]

To ensure success of the enterprise against their King, the British government even provided the Prince with a fleet of ships to facilitate his journey on the sea. Up to fifty men-of-war were eventually assembled along the coast of Holland, together with a large number of transports, so that when the Prince left Helvoet Sluice bound for England, he had under his command almost five hundred vessels.

On 5 November 1688, William landed safely and unopposed at Torbay in Devon. [3] A picture of the fleet's arrival and the disembarkation of Prince William and his armed forces can be seen in a contemporary print owned by the Ann Ronan Picture Library.

Of small credit the attendants will abhor his death

In 1685, when James II became King, the Duke of Monmouth, King Charles II's illegitimate son, attempted to defeat James and seize the crown for himself. To help him accomplish this, a small army had been raised against the King, but it was heavily defeated at the battle of Sedgemoor, on 6 July 1685.

It was while attempting to escape the battlefield that Monmouth was captured. He was then taken to the Tower of London and tried for treason. After a guilty verdict had been passed, he was beheaded on 15 July 1685.

King James had offered his nephew clemency in return for information concerning those plotting against him, but the offer was declined. Monmouth was therefore executed, but in a most gruesome manner. The headsman, Jack Ketch (mentioned in Dickens' novels) was known for his botched executions, and his first blow was so weak that Monmouth was able to look up at the headsman with a reproaching stare. Twice more the axe fell, but without achieving much

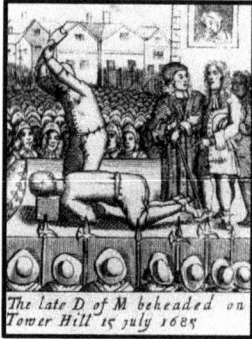

progress. At this point, Ketch threw down his axe, confessing that he could do no more. Monmouth was therefore left in a semi-conscious and blood-soaked state, collapsed over the headsman's block, awaiting the next blow. The sheriff, attending the execution, remonstrated with Ketch, demanding that he return to his task.

Braced by the sheriff's entreaties and the yells of the crowd, Ketch picked up the axe and struck once more, but still with little effect. At last, overcoming his reserve, and with one final blow, Ketch managed to separate the head from the body, but it was achieved only after numerous attempts. [4] It was an execution so grotesque that those witnessing it could only abhor it. As for the number of strikes made by the headsman, reports vary from 5 to 8.

EXECUTION OF DUKE OF
MONMOUTH

A King elected

The enthronement of the Prince of Orange as the nation's new monarch occurred on 13 February 1689, but only after he was *elected King* by Parliamentary vote.

> [T]he so-called Convention Parliament, summoned in January 1689, declared that James had abdicated and offered the vacant throne, with an accompanying Declaration of Right, to William and Mary. They were proclaimed in February and crowned on April 21. [5]

Capable

Once established on the throne, William III quickly proved himself capable of dealing with the demands required of a king. He defeated James II in the battle of the Boyne (1690); and afterwards, devoted much energy to "a gruelling war against France at sea and in the Netherlands, eventually forcing France to sign the Treaty of Rijswijk (1697) in which she abandoned all her war aims." [6] William was also successful in defeating several counter-revolutionary attempts made by James II, which attracted support in both Ireland and Scotland.

A native of Friesland

The oracle concludes by predicting that England's *elected King* would be *a native of Friesland*. William Prince of Orange was indeed *elected*, and *a native of Friesland*. Friesland or Frisia was the ancient name given to the Netherlands where William had been 'Stadholder'. It was also the land where he lived for the first thirty-eight years of his life. [7]

Summary: *This oracle is filled with detail but presented in a mixed chronological order. It begins in 1589, with the future William III recognized as King of England but not of Scotland. It then slips back one year to the Glorious Revolution planned by Parliament to replace James II (the legitimate King of England) with William of Orange and his wife Mary (eldest daughter of the soon-to-be deposed James II). The prophecy then slips back to 1685, when James II became King of England. In that same year, the Duke of Monmouth challenged James for the throne, but failed in the attempt, and was tried for treason. His loathsome execution is included in this prophecy, which identifies him, and his connexion to the events at the time. Finally, the prophecy confirms two important facts—a King would be elected and be a native of Friesland. Both predictions were fulfilled by William III.*

90   *Les deux copies aux murs ne pourront ioindre,*
        Dans cest instant tremble Milan, Ticin:
        Faim, soif, doutance, si fort les viendra poindre,
        Chair, pain, ne viures n'auront vn seul bocin.

91   *Au duc gaulois contraint battre au duelle,*
La nef Meselle Monech n'approchera:
Tort accusé, prison perpetuelle,
Son fils regner auant mort tascbera.

92   *Teste tranchee du vaillant capitaine,*
Sera getté deuant son aduersaire:
Son corps pendu de sa classe à l'antenne,
Confus suira par rames à vent contraire.

93   *Vn serpent veu proche du lict royal,*
Sera par dame, nuict chiens n'abayeront:
Lois naistra en France vn prince tant royal,
Du ciel venu tous les princes verront.

abayeront (AF aboieront); lors (OF) in that time, season, age, etc. voir (OF veoir) regard, heed.

A serpent (**BUCKINGHAM**) seen close to the royal bed,   1625
Night time, it will be by reason of the woman, the dogs will not bark:
In time a Prince will be born in France, (**LOUIS XIV**), so regal,
All the Princes will regard that he arrived from heaven.

The allusion to *a serpent* brings to mind the temptation of Eve in the Book of Genesis. The oracle appears to have intended this, for a similar temptation occurred in France, in 1625, at the marriage ceremony between Louis XIII's sister, Henrietta Maria, and Charles I of England.

Charles's representative at the proxy wedding was the dashing George Villiers, 1st Duke of Buckingham. When the Duke first saw Louis XIII's wife, Anne of Austria, an immediate attraction was kindled between them, and for the first time in her life the Queen gave way to a flirtation. Thereafter, during Buckingham's short stay in France, he sought the company of Anne at every opportunity. On his way back to England, the wedding party stopped at Amiens. It was there, while walking in the garden, that Buckingham made his first amorous approach. The Queen's attendants quickly intervened, and Anne retired to her bedroom leaving Buckingham to continue on his journey to Dover. However, contrary winds meant that sailing was deferred, this allowed Buckingham to give way to the temptation of seeing Anne for one more time, and he hurriedly returned to Amiens.

Night time, it will be by reason of the woman: the dogs will not bark

Immediately upon arrival, although it was by then *night time*, Buckingham sought an audience with the Queen-mother, requesting her permission to visit Anne in her bedroom.[1] After having obtained royal consent—that is, *by reason of the woman, the dogs will not bark*—the Duke was able to enter the Queen's bed chamber, and kneeling before Anne, he declared his love for her.

A serpent seen close to the royal bed

The Queen's ladies-in-waiting, who had been informed of the night time visitor's movements, hurriedly appeared, and being alarmed at *the Duke, seen close to the royal bed,* and being aware of the situation that was fast developing, they quietly persuaded the would-be lover to leave the room.[2]

So regal

The Seer now takes this little episode in the life of the French Queen, and joins it to the birth of her son, the future Sun King, Louis XIV, whose reign would, as predicted, be 'so regal'. By using the word *lors* the Seer is also able to conceal the period of time involved, because in its original meaning, it could be interpreted as anything from six months to twenty years.

In time, a prince will be born in France

It was not until 1638 that Anne gave birth to a prince and heir to the throne. The birth caused joy to the population but disappointment amongst the existing Princes. Before then, Gaston, the King's brother had been heir to the throne and had likely seen himself as the future King of

France. Henri de Bourbon 3rd Prince of Condé, whose lust for power had so much troubled the regency of Marie de' Médicis was also thwarted in furthering his political ambition. [3]

All the Princes will regard that he arrived from heaven

Louis XIII was soon made aware of a possibility for future dissent amongst the Princes, and he wisely ordered that all Princes must observe true allegiance to the new Prince of France. [4] Because the marriage between Louis XIII and Anne of Austria had long been barren, the King having preferred the company of men to that of women, their child was looked upon by many as having arrived from heaven. The baby's mother thought so too, and commanded that a chapel be built at Val-de-Grâce to "immortalize the miracle". Thereafter, the infant was referred to as, "Dieudonné" (the God-given).

Interestingly, there is a connection between Buckingham's amorous advances at the bedside of the French Queen, which occurred in 1625, and the birth of Louis XIV thirteen years later. This is because Buckingham's attempt at seduction became so widely talked about that it was seriously suggested his features had become imprinted on the baby's face as a direct result of the mother's love for her English admirer. [5] "Michelet says that Louis XIV resembled Buckingham, then dead ten years, as the consequence of a 'maternal impression'." This was also widely rumoured in the many innuendos that circulated after the baby's birth. The same belief appears in the Gnostic Gospel of Philip. "If the wife sleeps with her husband but thinks of her lover, the child will look like him."

Summary: *This prophecy's main source of interest was for the people of the age in which it occurred. Apparently, the story of Buckingham's attempt to bed the Queen of France was still a source of gossip thirteen years later. The details of her night visitor certainly correspond to the historical facts of that time. At a different level of understanding, the conditions under which the prophecy came to its resolution, including the inclement weather preventing Buckingham's departure from France, indicates how everything in the world is united together, thereby ensuring that a genuine prophecy cannot fail to be fulfilled.*

94   *Deux grands frères seront chassés d'Espaigne,*
      L'aisne vaincu sounz les monts Pyrenees:
      Rougir mer, Rosne, sang Leman d'Alemaigne,
      Narbon, Bliterre, d'Atheniens contaminees.

95   *Le regne à deux laissé bien peu tiendront,*
      Trois ans sept mois passés feront la guerre:
      Les deux vestals contre rebelleront,
      Victor puis nay en Armonique terre.

96   *La sœur aisnee de l'isle Britannique,*
      Quinze ans deuant le frère aura naissance:
      Par son promis moyennant verrifique,
      Succedera au regne de balance.

97   *L'an que Mercure, Mars, Venus retrograde,*
      Du grand Monarque la ligne ne faillir:
      Esleu du people l'vsitant pres de Gandole,
      Qu'en paix & regne viendra fort enuieillir.

esleu (AF eslever) to raise in rank; vsitant (AF vsiter) to accustom, to inure; Gaudole (Gandia,) *also* Gandole anagram & pargram: Gand n le – England: Note that 'Gandole' deliberately fails to rhyme with 'retrograde'; fort (AF pénible) painful; enuieillir (OF) to wax old.

The year when Mercury, Mars, Venus are retrograde,   1710
The line not failing for the great Monarch (LOUIS XIV):
Raised in rank (TO PHILIP V), inuring him for the people, near Gandia (ENGLAND),
When in peace and reign, he (LOUIS XIV) will grow painful, drawing towards his end.

The legalistic Old Style of dating, which was in use at the time these prophecies were written, governs the understanding of this oracle. It means that each New Year began on 25 March.

The year when Mercury, Mars, Venus are retrograde
On New Year's Day, 25 March 1710, the planet *Venus* was in *retrograde* motion. On 22 December 1710, *Mars,* too, went *retrograde*. And on 2 February 1710 (O.S.), it was *Mercury's* turn to go *retrograde*. [1] Thus, all three planets were retrograde in 1710 (O.S.). It is also of minor interest to observe how the oracle has correctly named the planets in the *reverse* order to that in which their *retrograde* motion occurred.

In April 1711, two months after *Mercury* went *retrograde*, the Dauphin, aged fifty, contracted smallpox and died. This left Louis XIV's grandson, the Duke of Burgundy, as the new heir to the throne. Ten months later, the Duke's wife, Marie Adélaïde fell ill and was dead within five days. Her husband, who had been by her bedside for the short duration of her illness, caught the infection and he, too, died.

The inheritance of the crown therefore went to the eldest of his two surviving sons, the duc de Bretagne. But he, together with his brother the duc d'Anjou, both succumbed to the infection that had killed their parents. Bretagne died on 7 March, leaving Anjou's death expected any day. But the little boy recovered to become King Louis XV. [2]

The line not failing for the great Monarch
In quick succession the next in line for the throne passed through three generations, from Louis XIV's son to his grandson, to his eldest great-grandson, and then to his other great-grandson. But, as the oracle correctly foretold, *the line* of succession would *not fail* for *the great Monarch*. That is, Louis XIV, who was known as 'Le Grand Monarque' (the Great Monarch). [3]

Raised in rank
Louis XIV had one other grandson, Philip. But he had earlier been *raised in rank* from Duke of Anjou to King Philip V of Spain. It was this Spanish title that debarred him from succeeding to the French throne. For this reason the succession skipped a generation to the King's two great-grandsons: the elder of the two succumbing to smallpox.

Inuring him for the people
Philip V was just sixteen years of age, and a Frenchman, when he became King of Spain. It was therefore necessary for Louis XIV and his councillors to inure him [4] for acceptance by the people of Spain. [5] But there was a rival for the Spanish throne. This was the Archduke Charles, Emperor Leopold's son. It was through this rivalry that the War of the Spanish Succession (1701–14) broke out. In the battle for preferment between the two claimants, France was able to take comfort from knowing that the greater part of Spain accepted Philip: only Catalonia, Aragon and Valencia preferred Charles.

Near Gandia
The control of Valencia, a city *near Gandia,* was the aim of those fighting at the battle of Almanza (25 April 1707). This conflict proved to be one of the most important in the War of the Spanish Succession, because it brought to an end Charles's hold on Valencia (8 May), [6] it also changed the direction of the war in France's favour.

It is especially noteworthy that Gandia has been named instead of Valencia. By writing the name as Gandole (a typesetting error caused by inverting 'n' to make 'u' appears in some texts, but not in that of Du Rosne), the Seer has allowed the anagrammatic spelling to become a paragram. When these letters are rearranged, *England* is obtained—the English being one of the countries brought into the Spanish conflict, and at war with France.

(England)
In London, during March 1707, the Act of Union between Scotland and England was passed. As one nation, Great Britain was now able to bring economic and cultural advantages to both

countries. But, just as importantly, it also removed the threat that Scotland might one day choose a different king from England, and pursue policies contrary to those being followed in the War of the Spanish Succession. [7]

When in peace and reign, he will grow painful, drawing towards his end

In 1714, the War was finally brought to an end with a series of peace treaties. Philip V kept Spain as well as Spanish America. The Emperor received Milan, Naples, Sardinia, and control over the Spanish Netherlands. Louis XIV's extensive *reign* continued just long enough for him to oversee the *peace* settlement reach its conclusion. But, as the oracle predicted, his life was also drawing to an end.

In an era when life expectancy was below fifty, the King had already reached the age of 76. He died on 1 September 1715, just four days short of his seventy-seventh birthday, with his leg painfully black from gangrene. [8]

Summary: *The date given by the retrograde motion of Mercury, Mars and Venus is in complete harmony with the threat posed to the line of succession during the reign of Louis XIV, also known as the 'The Great Monarch'. It also serves to introduce the King's sixteen-year-old grandson, who had been made King of Spain. The War of the Spanish Succession that followed is allowed to focus upon Gandia (misspelled to allow the letters to reform into England), thus embellishing the oracle with the Act of Union between England and Scotland. With peace restored, a painful death for the King is predicted. That too occurred one year later.*

   98   *Les Albanois passeront dedans Rome,*
           Moyennant Langres de miples affublés:
           Marquis & Duc ne pardoner à home,
           Feu, fang morbile, point d'eau, faillir les blés.

   99   *L'aisné vaillant de la fille du Roy,*
           Repoulsera si profond les Celtiques:
           Qu'il mettra fouldres combien en tel arroy,
           Peu & loing puis profond es Hesperiques.

   100   *De feu celeste au royal edifice.*
           Quant la luniere de Mars deffaillira:
           Sept mois grand guerre, mort gent de malefice,
           Rouan, Eureux au Roy ne faillira.

deffaillira (OF) to be wanting; malefice (L malefic\ium) an evil deed; faillir (AF – manquer) to lose.

Concerning the celestial fire at the royal building (**TUILERIES**),   1871
When the light of Mars will be wanting:
Seven months a great war (**FRANCO-PRUSSIAN**); people dead by an evil deed.
Rouen! Evreux will not lose to the King (**WILHELM 1**).

Concerning the celestial fire at the royal building

On the night of 23 May 1871, the sky above Paris became illuminated with such a brilliant light that it dwarfed all the firework displays that had been previously seen in the capital. *The royal building* in the centre of Paris, the *Palais de Tuileries* was *on fire*, and its glow could be seen for miles around.

Jules Bergeret, a Communard leader who had recently been released from prison, decided upon the vengeful act of blowing up the royal palace. Barrel after barrel of gunpowder was stacked inside the palace, and then ignited to send a huge fireball into the night sky. The central dome of the royal palace vanished in an instant, and another prediction by the Seer became history. [1]

When the light of Mars will be wanting

On the day of the palace's destruction, Mars was invisible to the naked eye; that is to say, *the light of Mars will be wanting*. The explanation for this was quite natural: the planet was below the horizon until about 1 pm. It then climbed unseen in daylight, to an altitude of 42 degrees, descending again below the horizon as night approached. Its light was therefore invisible to the French. [2] Mars also serves as an allegory for the fruitless war that France had embarked upon.

Seven months, a great war

The Franco-Prussian War, which preceded the destruction of the Tuileries, began on 19 July 1870, when Napoleon III declared war against Prussia. In quick succession, six main battles were fought—Wissembourg, Spicheren, Wörth, Mars-La-Tour, Gravelotte, and Sedan: as well as the sieges at Metz and Paris.

The war proved to be a disaster for France. During the conflict, French soldiers were so decisively defeated that the nation was compelled to accept the demanding terms set out in Bismarck's armistice agreement. This was signed on 27 January 1871. [3]

The time period set out in the prophecy of *seven months* began in July and ended in January with the surrender of the French army at Sedan and the abdication of Napoleon III.

In the aftermath of this defeat and the resignation of the Emperor, who left France for England, the Third Republic was declared.

Under Adolphe Thiers's Government of National Defence, troops were conscripted and a renewed effort was made against the German occupation of France. It proved no match for the superiority of the German forces and the Treaty of Frankfurt was signed on 10 May 1871.

People dead by an evil deed

After the treaty was signed, French anger and suspicion at the humiliation dealt out by Bismarck's success turned inwards, and Paris underwent an intense period of civil strife. The capital was taken over by the Paris Commune, and the legitimate government evacuated to Versailles. During the infamous 'semaine sanglante' (bloody week), which put an end to the Commune during the last week of May, between 20,000 and 25,000 people were killed inside the capital. Added to this atrocity was the fate of the Communards who were arrested. They were dealt with so savagely that many failed to survive long enough to be shot by the firing squad.

> That Whitsun morning, in revenge, the Versailles troops marched 147 of the captured Communards out to Père Lachaise and summarily shot them against a wall of the cemetery. Inside La Roquette [...] some 1,900 prisoners are said to have been shot in two days, and at the Mazas prison another 400.

The London Times (1 June 1871) described the fate of these people: dead by the evil deeds of their captors as "wholesale executions inflicted by the Versailles soldiery, the triumph, the glee, the ribaldry [...] sicken the soul." [4]

Rouen!

Rouen is the port city and capital of Seine-Maritime. It lies to the northwest of Paris on the River Seine. During the Franco-Prussian War, German forces under the command of General Edwin Freiherr von Manteuffel "continued to advance westward, capturing Rouen on 5 December." [5] The fall of Rouen is used in the prophecy to compare it with Evreux, 25 miles away.

Evreux will not lose to the King

During the *Siege of Paris* (19 September 1870 – 28 January 1871), King Wilhelm I, ensconced at the Palace of Versailles, "decided to proclaim himself emperor of a Germany united over the corpse of a defunct French empire." [6] At the same time, the citizens inside the capital adopted the idea of using a balloon to communicate with the rest of the country. On 23 September, the Prussian army was astonished to see a balloon passing overhead – "Its pilot Durouf landed safely at Evreux beyond the enemy's reach with 125 kilograms of despatches, after a three-hour flight." [7] The successful landing at Evreux resulted in "some sixty-five manned balloons" [8] subsequently leaving the besieged city.

Dispatched from Paris as the republican government's emissary, Léon Gambetta passed over the German lines in a balloon inflated with coal gas from the city's gasworks, and organized the recruitment of new French armies.

News about an alleged German "extermination" plan infuriated the French and strengthened their support to their new government. Within a few weeks, five new armies totalling more than 500,000 troops were recruited. [9]

Summary: This prophecy commences with the destruction of the Tuileries in Paris. It then foretells the war that preceded it. The two events are inter-connected, since Prussia's victory over France led to insurrection in Paris at the hands of the Communards, whose leader was responsible for destroying the royal palace. Their fate is predicted as an 'ill act'. The seven months, during which the major battles were fought in the Franco-Prussian War, coincide with the absence of Mars in the night sky: together, they accurately tie the events to this prophecy. The comparison drawn between Rouen and Evreux therefore makes a fitting end to this prediction, especially by its inclusion of a reference to Germany's King Wilhelm before he became emperor.

References Century 4

Nº. 2

1   Ian Dunlop, *Louis XIV*, 354, 358
2   Ibid 361–2
3   wikipedia.org/wiki/War_of_the_Spanish_Succession
4   Ibid 400–1; & http://www.malagaholidays.com/en/costa_del_sol/travelinformation.asp?regionID=12
5   Dunlop, 377
6   John A. Lynn, *The French Wars 1667 – 1714*, 67
7   Ibid
8   Dunlop, 381
9   Louis XIV (le Grand Monarque) 1643 – 1715: *Royalty Peerage and Nobility of the World (Annuaire de la Noblesse de France)* 91st Volume, 383
10 Dunlop, 465–6, 468

Nº. 8

1   R. Ernest Dupuy and Trevor N. Dupuy, *The Encyclopedia of Military History*, 978
2   Ibid 978
3   C.R.M.F. Cruttwell, *A History of the Great War 2nd ed.* (Battle of St. Quentin); & *Nelsons History othe War* – Vol. 22
4   http://www.greatwar.co.uk/battles/somme/somme-battles.htm
5   Crutwell; & *Mein Kreigstagbuch* - Vol. II: Kronprinz Rupprecht, 344; & *Nelson* Vol. XXII
6   Crutwell; & *Nelson*

Nº. 11

1   Franklin L. Ford, *Europe 1780-1830*, 119
2   Ibid 119; & *A Dictionary of Eighteenth-Century History* (ed.) Jeremy Black and Roy Porter, 186; & Christopher Hibbert, *The French Revolution*, 162
3   Simon Schama, *Citizens*, 633
4   Hibbert, 174, 176
5   Jean Favier (ed.) *Chronicle of the French Revolution*, 260; & Norman Davies, *Europe A History*, 710
6   Favier, see: Paris, May 27 1792; & Schama, 624
7   Hibbert, 170-1
8   Ibid 175
9   Antonia Fraser, *Marie Antoinette The Journey:* 78-9

Nº. 12

1   World War II, Forces and Resources of the Combatants, 1939, *Encyclopædia Britannica 2001:* CD-ROM
2   John Macdonald, *Great Battles of World War II*, 145
3   Ibid 156-7
4   wikipedia.org/wiki/Battle_of_the_Bulge
5   Macdonald, 166
6   wikipedia.org/wiki/Allies_of_World_War_II
7   wikipedia.org/wiki/Charles_de_Gaulle
8   wikipedia.org/wiki/Potsdam_Conference
9   wikipedia.org/wiki/World_War_II#Allies_close_in_.281944.29

Nº. 15

1   Derrik Mercer (ed.) *Chronicle of the Second World War*, 63; & A. Palmer, *Dictionary of Twentieth-Century History*, 30
2   Palmer, 235–6
3   Richard Humble, *Fighting Ships: U-boat*, 18; & Palmer, 30
4   Ian Crofton (ed.) *Collins Gem Encyclopedia*, 211
5   Karen Farrington, *Handbook of World War II*, 116
6   Mercer, 108; & I C.B. Dear (ed.) *Oxford Companion to the Second World War*, 1995; & Ken Hills, *Wars that Changed the World— World War II*, 14

Nº.18

1   Christopher Hibbert, *The French Revolution*, 30, 31
2   Ibid 330
3   Simon Schama, *Citizens*, 585
4   Ibid 624
5   Hibbert, 170
6   Ibid
7   id 173-4

Nº.25

1   David Waltham, *Lucky Planet*, 43
2   David Wooton, *Galileo Watcher of the Skies*, 26
3   Ibid 167
4   Enlightenment, *Encyclopædia Britannica 2001*; & Pierre Bayle, *Dictionnaire*;

Nº. 26

1   wikipedia.org/wiki/Fréjus

2   wikipedia.org/wiki/Napoleon#Ruler_of_France 3 Ibid 1003 – 1004
3   wikipedia.org/wiki/French_Directory
4   J.M. Thompson, *Napoleon Bonaparte*, 142
5   David Chandler, *The Campaigns of Napoleon*, 261
6   Christopher Hibbert, *The French Revolution*, 304
7   H.A.L. Fisher, *A History of Europe*, 916
8   Alan Palmer, *Dictionary of Modern History 1789-1945*, 99-100
9   Thompson, 137
10   Palmer 117, 261, 279

Nº. 34

1   R.J. Knecht, *Catherine de' Medici*, 48
2   Leonie Frieda, *Catherine de Medici*, 107-9
3   wikipedia.org/wiki/Italian_War_of_1551–1559
4   Ibid 49-50 & wikipedia.org/wiki/Battle_of_St._Quentin_(1557)

Nº. 37

1   David Chandler, *The Campaigns of Napoleon*, 3; & J.M. Thompson, *Napoleon Bonaparte*, 7
2   Chandler, 280
3   wikipedia.org/wiki/Milan
4   N.G.L. Hammond and H.H. Scullard (ed.) *The Oxford Classical Dictionary: 2nd edition*, 548
5   Chandler, 283
6   Franklin L. Ford, *Europe 1780 – 1830*, 192; & Chandler, 297, 302
7   historyworld.net/wrldhis/PlainTextHistories.asp?groupid=2699&HistoryID=ac52&gtrack=pthc
8   Chandler, 271
9   electricscotland.com/history/other/keith-elphinstone.htm
10   Edgar Leoni, *Nostradamus and his Prophecies*, 626
11   wikipedia.org/wiki/Monaco

Nº.45

1   Alistair Horne, *Seven Ages of Paris*, 254
2   wikipedia.org/wiki/Auguste_de_Marmont
3   Ian Littlewood, *The Rough Guide Chronicle France.* 235
4   Horne, 253-4
5   Ibid 253
6   id 254
7   nndb.com/people/833/000093554/
8   wikipedia.org/wiki/Liberty_Leading_the_People

Nº. 47

1   Brewer, *Dictionary of Phrase and Fable,* Classic Edition, 276
2   William Mountague, *A New and Universal History of England: Vol. II*, 38; & Leonie Frieda, *Catherine de Medici*, 269
3   Mountague, 38
4   Frieda, 269
5   R. Knecht, *Catherine de' Medici*, 159; & A. Dumas, *Queen Margot*, 166-7
6   Mountague, 38

Nº. 54

1   'NAPOLEON EMPEROR ET ROI' — J.M. Thompson, *Napoleon Bonaparte*, 178f
2   John Belcham and Richard Price (ed.) *A Dictionary of Nineteenth-Century History*, 78-9
3   Franklin L. Ford, *Europe 1780-1830*, 155–6
4   Ibid 209
5   id 24
6   Jeremy Black and Roy Porter (ed.) *A Dictionary of Eighteenth-Century History*, 86; & Francine Barker, *Napoleon – The First European*, Observer Supplement 26/1/1969, 13

Nº. 65

1   William H.C. Smith, *Napoleon III*, 14
2   britannica.com/EBchecked/topic/532104/Battle-of-Sedan
3   Alistair Horne, *Seven Ages of Paris*, 284
4   Ibid 285, 300
5   Smith, 128
6   Desmond Seward, *Eugénie The Empress and her Empire*, xii, 243

Nº. 68

1   SKY DIARY, EVENTS, *RedShift 4, Maris Mutimedia Ltd*; & Alan Palmer, *Dictionary of Modern History 1789-1945*, 309
2   I.C.B. Dear (ed.) *The Oxford Companion to the Second World War*, 1123; & Mussolini – Dictatorship, *Encyclopædia Britannica 2001:* CD-ROM; & Tojo Hideki, Ibid
3   *World War II – German occupied Europe*; & *The Blast of World War II*, Ibid
4   Dear, 713
5   Jasper Ridley, *Mussolini*, 320, 338; & Derrik Mercer (ed.) *Chronicle of the Second World War*, 342; & Savona, *Encyclopædia Britannica:* CD-ROM

Nº. 70

1   David Chandler, *The Campaigns of Napoleon*, 945–6
2   Wellington, *Encyclopædia Britannica 2001* - CD-ROM
3   & Michael Glover, *Wellington's Peninsula Victories*, 137
4   Byron Farwell, *Queen Victoria's Little Wars*, 357; & Jac Weller, *Wellington in the Peninsula 1808–1814*, 175, 178, 182–3 quoting from *Fortescue*, VIII, 200-1, and from *Maxwell'sPeninsula Sketches*, II, 331,
5   *English Battles and Sieges in the Peninsula*, Lt. Gen. Sir William Napier; & Weller, 359
6   D.S. Richards, *The Peninsula Veterans*, 165; & Pau, *Encyclopædia Britannica 2001* - CD-ROM.
7   Alan Palmer, *An Encyclopaedia of Napoleon's Europe*, 31

Nº. 75

1   David Chandler, *The Campaigns of Napoleon*, 757-8
2   Ibid 739; & *A Dictionary of Nineteenth Century History* (ed.) John Belcham and Richard Price, 616-7
3   J.M. Thompson, 325-7; & Alan Palmer, *Dictionary of Modern History 1789-1945*, 204–5
4   Thompson, 338–9
5   Ibid 337; & Ney, *Encyclopædia Britannica 2001*: CD-ROM
6   Chandler, 826
7   Thompson, 337, 338; & Chandler, 845

Nº. 80

1   The Maginot Line, *Encyclopædia Britannica 2001*: CD-ROM; & *Encyclopædia Britannica Vol 7* (15th ed.) 589
2   Maginot (LIGNE) nom donné au système fortifié construit de 1927 à 1936, sur le frontière française du Nord-Est … la création de régions fortifées d'une vingtaine de kilomètres de front sur 15 de profondeur.' *Grand Larousse Encyclopedique* Vol 6
3   John Keegan (ed.) *Encyclopedia of World War II*, 160
4   Thomas Parrish (ed.) *The Encyclopædia of World War II*, 480; & Arthur J. May, *Europe Since 1939*, 54
5   William L. Shirer, *The Collapse of the Third Republic*, 751
6   Ibid 752
7   Derrik Mercer (ed.) *Chronicle of the Second World War*, 96
8   Alistair Horne, *Seven Ages of Paris*, 395-6
9   Shirer, 167–8

Nº. 89

1   William Henry Mountague, *A New and Universal History of England: Vol. 2*, 231
2   Ibid 225, 227
3   id 225
4   id 219
5   E.N. Williams, *Dictionary of English and European History 1485 – 1789*, 387; & The Bill of Rights, *Encyclopædia Britannica 2001*, CD-ROM
6   Ibid William III
7   Ibid; & Frisia, Ibid

Nº. 93

1   K. Patmore, *The Court of Louis XIII*, 109-10
2   V. Cronin, *Louis XIV*, 19
3   Patmore, 300, 302–3; Ian Dunlop, *Louis XIV*, 2
4   Patmore, 302; Cronin, 25
5   Patmore, 303

Nº. 97

1   Object Information, Planets, *RedShift 4*, CD-ROM, Maris Mutimedia Ltd
2   E N Williams, *Dictionary of English and European History 1485-1789*, 273; & Ian Dunlop, *Louis XIV*, 437, 440
3   Louis XIV (le Grand Monarque), 1643 – 1715; (383) *Royalty Peerage and Nobility of the World (Annuaire de la Noblesse de France)* 91st Volume
4   Williams, 272; & Dunlop, 361
5   Williams, 272; & Dunlop, 358
6   Gandia, *Encyclopædia Britannica 2001*: CD-ROM; & John A Lynn, *The French Wars 1667- 1714*, 67
7   Lynn, 23; Williams, 439
8   Dunlop, 437

Nº. 100

1   Alistair Horne, *Seven Ages of Paris*, 309
2   Planets, *Red Shift 4*, CD-ROM, Maris Mutimedia Ltd
3   Stephen Badsey, *The Franco-Prussian War 1870-1871*, 9
4   Horne, 310, 311; & Ian Littlewood, *The Rough Guide Chronicle France*, 255
5   Badsey, 71
6   Horne, 299
7   Ibid, 289
8   Id, 291
9   Id, 289; & wikipedia.org/wiki/Franco-Prussian_War

CENTURY FIVE

1   *Avant venue de ruyne Celtique,*
Dedans le temple deux parlamenteront:
Pognard cœur d'vn monté au coursier & pique,
Sans faiauire:re bruit le grand enterront.

2   *Sept coniurés au banquet feront tire.luyre,*
Contre les trios le fer hors de nauire:
L'vn les deux classes au grand fera conduire.
Quant par le mal Denier au front luy tire.

3   *Le successeur de la duché viendra:*
Beaucoup plus oultre que la mer de Toscane,
Gauloise branche le Florence tiendra,
Dans son giron d'accord nautique Rane.

oultre (OF) besides; que (OF) in part; tiendra (OF) retain; giron (OF) lap, breast, *also* (*anagram & paragram* 'T' for 'g') Torin'
(Italian) Torino; nautique (L. nautic\us) nautical;

                  The successor of the Duchy (**LORRAINE**) will arrive: 1737
                  Many more besides: in part, the sea of Tuscany,
                  The Gallic branch will retain Florence,
                  In his lap (**TURIN**) by agreement, the nautical Frog (**LOUIS NAPOLEON**).

The successor of the Duchy will arrive

After the death of Grand Duke Gian Gastone in 1737, the last of the Medicis, and the member of a family that had ruled the duchy of Tuscany since 1537, "Lorraine became managed by France under terms resulting from the War of the Spanish Succession. Francis and House of Lorraine received the Grand Duchy of Tuscany in the peace treaty that ended that war." [1]

Many more besides: in part, the sea of Tuscany

Many more besides Francis I, came to be dukes of Tuscany, up until 1859, when it became incorporated into the newly unified Italy. Before then …

> At his death in 1765 Tuscany passes to his son Peter Leopold [Leopold II], who has been an enlightened politician. When he becomes Emperor in 1790, his son Ferdinand III takes the power. He is forced to leave the Grand Duchy during the French occupation, [but] comes back after the Congress of Vienna in 1815. The last Grand Duke of Lorraine is Peter Leopold II [Leopold III]. He rules till 1859, when he abdicates because of Tuscany's annexation to [the] Italian Kingdom. [2]

It was during the French Revolution in 1789 that Ferdinand III lost control of his duchy. [2] and was later removed by Napoleon Bonaparte, who seized Tuscany and renamed it Etruria. Even so, "For a brief period, 1809 -1814, Napoleon's sister, Elisa, was the Duchess of Tuscany." [3] Napoleon's involvement in the duchy therefore explains why the sea of Tuscany is included in the prophecy. Elba is part of the Archipelago in the Tuscan Sea. It also became the island empire of Bonaparte in exile, when Ferdinand's rule was reinstated by the Congress of Vienna in 1814.

> After Napoleon's overthrow, the Congress of Vienna gave Tuscany again to Ferdinand and added to it Elba, Piombino, and the Stato degli Presidi. [4]

The Gallic branch will retain Florence

Ferdinand III, to whom the duchy of Tuscany was restored in 1814, died in 1824. His son Leopold II succeeded him until his own death in 1860. "The administration of his son Leopold II (1824-60) was long considered the most liberal in Italy, although he reigned as an absolute sovereign." [5] But when war broke out between Sardinia-Piedmont and Austria, it triggered revolutions in Tuscany, causing Leopold II to take flight. When later, the duchy was returned to him, his reign became subject to Italy's unification programme. As a result of this, Tuscany was incorporated into the kingdom of Italy (21 July 1859). Leopold thereupon abdicated in favour of his son, Ferdinand IV, who declined the title. Change was taking place "In the 1860s Florence became the capital of Italy, and King Vittorio Emmanuele II took up residence in the city." [6]

In his lap (Turin) by agreement

The end of the Habsburg-Lorraine rule in Florence coincided with the arrival of Victor Emanuel II, King of Piedmont-Sardinia, and now the ruler of a united Italy. His first act was to choose Florence for his capital. But to maintain a unified Italy, Victor Emmanuel needed help from the French. With the aid of Count Camillo Benso di Cavour, his prime minister, Victor Emmanuel sought the aid he required from Napoleon III.

On 24 March 1860, the Treaty of Turin was signed by Cavour and Talleyrand. This placed Napoleon in such a commanding position that he held the King of Sardinia in his lap—so to speak. Napoleon was therefore able to make territorial demands upon the King in return for French aid. This resulted in Italy being forced to hand over Savoy and Nice to France.

> With Austria vindictive and powerful, and in a threatening strategic position; with the Pope outraged and desperate, and in control of an army which attached to itself a large share of the fanaticism of Europe, there was no hope for struggling Italy but in a firmer alliance with France. In this fact alone is to be found an explanation of the willingness of the Sardinian government to part with so considerable a portion of its territory. [7]

The nautical frog

Napoleon III was born on 20 April 1808 in Paris, the capital city of the French Empire. As a Parisian, he was therefore a 'frog'. "Frenchmen, properly *Parisians.* So called from their ancient heraldic device, which was three frogs or three toads." (Brewer)

> To carry out his new overseas projects, Napoleon III created a new Ministry of the Navy and the Colonies, and appointed an energetic minister, Prosper de Chasseloup-Laubat, to head it. A key part of the enterprise was the modernization of the French Navy; he began the construction of fifteen powerful new battle cruisers powered by steam and driven by propellers; and a fleet of steam powered troop transports. The French Navy became the second most powerful in the world, after that of Great Britain. [8]

When placed side-by-side, these two facts explain an otherwise obscure phrase.

Summary: *The final line of this prophecy indicates how the seer thinks when he conceals the identity of his subject. As for the prophecy itself, it is really an extended history of the most powerful House in Europe, with a longstanding association to France. The facts all appear in chronological order, but the extensive time period of 123 years for its complete fulfilment can only be appreciated in retrospect. The fact that this quatrain follows those numbered 1 and 2 to become 3, may therefore be deliberate.*

4   *Le gros mastin de cité descassé,*
      Sera fasché de l'estrange alliance:
      Apres aux camps auoir le chef chassé,
      Le Loup & l'Ours se donront defiance.

5   *Soubz vmbre faincte d'oster de seruitude,*
      Peuple & cité, l'vsurpera luy mesme:
      Pite fera par fraulx de ieune pute,
      Liuré au champ lisant le faulx proësme.

6   *Au roy l'Agur sus le chef la main mettre,*
      Viendra prier pour la paix Italique:
      A la main gauche viendra changer le septre,
      De Roy viendra Empereur pacifique.

7   *Du triumuir seront trouvez les oz,*
      Cherchant profound tresor ænigmatique,
      Ceulx d'alentour ne seront en repoz,
      De concauer marbre & plomb metalique.

8   *Sera laissé le feu vif mort caché,*
      Dedans les globes horrible espouentables,
      De nuict à classe cité en pouldre lasché,
      La cité à feu l'ennemy fauorable.

9   *Iusques aux fondz la grand arq demolue,*
          Par chef captif l'amy anticip:
          Naistra de dame front face cheuelue,
          Lors par astuce duc à mort attrapé.

10   *Vn chef Celtique dans le conflit blessé,*
          Aupres de caue voyant siens mort abatre:
          De sang & playes & d'ennemis pressé,
          Et secourz par incogneuz de quatre.

11   *Mer par solaires seure ne passera,*
          Ceulx de Venus tiendront toute l'Affrique:
          Leur regne plus Sol, Saturne n'occupera,
          Et changera la part Asiatique.

N.B., 'Sol' in the third line is omitted in some editions

12   *Aupres du lac Leman sera conduite,*
          Par garce estrange cité voulant trahir:
          Auant son murtre à Auspurg la grand suitte,
          Et ceulx du Ryn la viendront inuahir.

13   *Par grand fureur le roy Romain belgique,*
          Vexer vouldra par phalange barbare:
          Fureur grinsant chassera gent libique,
          Despuis Pannons iusques Hercules la hare.

14   *Saturne & Mars en Leo Espaigne captiue,*
          Par chef Lybique au conflict attrapé:
          Proche de Malthe, Heredde prinse viue,
          Et Romain sceptre sera par Coq frappé.

captiuer (OF) to restrain liberty; libique (OF *syncope*) lib[urn]ique – a swift ship used by pirates; attrapé (OF) caught, apprehended; viue (AF vivant) living; sceptre (OF) absolute rule; frappé (OF) smitten

Saturn and Mars in Leo, Spain restrains liberty,   1566
Through the pirate ship chief, caught in the conflict
Close to Malta, **HEYREDDIN**, a living capture,
And the Roman rule will be smitten by the Cock.

Saturn and Mars in Leo

In the year 1566, three weeks after the death of the Seer, Saturn was in the constellation of Leo for its duration (24 July to 23 August). Mars also occupied Leo, but only for three days, 24th to the 26th of July.

Spain restrains liberty

At the same time, there was public disquiet at Philip II's occupation of the Spanish Netherlands. This came to a head in August 1566 with rioting.

> Churches - seen as the bastion of the rich - were wrecked, as were churches and monasteries. The riots spread quickly and much religious property was damaged. The magnates and the lesser nobility feared that property in general would be attacked and they were appalled at the fury of the mob.[1]

Margaret of Parma, daughter of Charles V, was Philip II's regent for the area, and she responded to the riots by appealing to Spain for troops to be sent, while also recruiting mercenaries from Germany.

Apart from the rioters, there was also intense civil unrest between the Catholic Spanish and the Calvinists of the Netherlands, which erupted into armed conflict in March 1567. Five months later the Duke of Alba arrived in the Spanish Netherlands with 9,000 men, and orders from Philip that "The towns must be punished for their rebelliousness with the loss of their privileges everyone must be made to live in constant fear."[2]

Through the pirate ship chief

This concerns Turgut Reis, a contemporary of de Nostredame, whose death occurred one year before that of the Seer.

> Turgut Reis (1485 – 23 June 1565) was a famous Ottoman admiral and privateer who successfully operated in the waters of the Mediterranean and Black Sea. [...] He successfully fought against Venetians in the famous 1538 Battle of Preveza. He raided cities across Sicily, Italy, Spain, Albania, and most notably captured the city of Castelnuovo from the Venetians. [3]

Caught in the conflict, close to Malta

In 1565, Sultan Sulieman ordered an attack on Malta. On 31 May, Turgut arrived at the island accompanied by an armed force of between 1600 and 3000 troops and a flotilla of fifteen ships, but discovered Malta had already been placed under siege by Piyale Pasha. After taking up position to isolate the Maltese stronghold of Fort Elmo, on the island's peninsula, he came under fire from Fort Angelo nearby. On 17 June, during a fierce bombardment, a near miss from cannon fire burst into fragments, some of which caught Turgut Reis, seriously wounding him.

Heyreddin, a living capture

Turgut suffered his wounds for six days, but died on 23 June. The Seer leaves no doubt for who was intended by his prophecy. For Turgut Ries had, in a manner of speaking, once belonged to Heyreddin.

> [Heyreddin Barbarossa was a] Greek Turkish pirate and admiral in the service of the Ottoman Empire. He and his brother Arj, sons of a Turk from Lesbos, hated the Spanish and Portuguese for their attacks on North Africa and took up piracy on the Barbary Coast in hopes of seizing an African domain for themselves. [...] Appointed admiral in chief of the Ottoman Empire (1533), he conquered all of Tunisia. [4]

In 1520 Turgut joined the fleet of Heyreddin Barbarossa, who became his protector and best friend. When, in 1540, Turgut was captured, it was Heyreddin who enforced those holding him to negotiate for his freedom, by laying siege to Genoa where he was held. Heyreddin then agreed to lift the siege and pay 3,500 ducats in gold for Turgut's release. "After Barbarossa's death in July 1546, Turgut succeeded him as supreme commander of Ottoman naval forces in the Mediterranean." [5] In this sense, Turgut was *a living capture* of the deceased *Heyreddin*.

And the Roman rule will be smitten by the Cock

The Roman rule (sceptre) will refer to Pope Pius IV, who was Bishop of Rome at the time.

> On 18 January 1562 the Council of Trent, which had been suspended by Pope Julius III, was convened by Pius IV for the third and final time. Great skill and caution were necessary to effect a settlement of the questions before it, [...] and by judicious management – and concession – brought the council to a termination satisfactory to the disputants and favourable to the pontifical authority. Its definitions and decrees were confirmed by a papal bull ("*Benedictus Deus*") dated 26 January 1564. [6]

France (the Cock), guided by the humanist Michel de L'Hôpital, refused to concede to it.

> It was also under L'Hôpital's influence that the royal council in 1564 refused to authorize the publication of the anti-Protestant acts of the Council of Trent, on account of their inconsistency with the Gallican liberties. [7]

> In July, 1561, he [L'Hôpital] caused all prosecutions for religious opinions to be suspended until a "council" should be assembled. [...] By another edict (January 15, 1562) he granted to the Protestants liberty of worship outside of cities, and recognized their right to hold meetings in private houses, even within the limits of cities.

> [Further] measures touching the Church, taken by L'Hôpital at the same time, gave the Holy See good reason for uneasiness. He caused a thesis on the pope to be denounced before the Parliament, because it seemed to him too ultramontane; he opposed the monitorium by which Pius IV had invited Jeanne d'Albret to appear in France before the Inquisition. At last Pius IV in 1562 requested of the French Court that the chancellor be dismissed. [8]

This prophecy, in reverse chronological order, concludes with papal authority being *smitten* by France's chancellor, L'Hôpital, between 1561 and 1564, because of his humanistic views.

Summary: *This prophecy, which is dated astronomically, was partially fulfilled during the final years of the Seer's life, although it appeared in print eleven years before his death. It is of interest because it names Heyreddin. Although he died in 1546, his successor, Turgut Ries, owed his freedom to the ransom paid byHeyreddin, and this identifies Turgut as the subject of the second and third lines.*

During the same band of five years in which this prophecy came to be fulfilled, the Spanish Netherlands was pacified after an uprising in 1566, and the reigning influence of Pius IV, who had finally completed the decrees set out by the Council of Trent, was obstructed upon several occasions by the French chancellor, Michel de L'Hôpital.

15   *En nauigant captif prins grand pontife,*
        Grand apretz faillir les clercz tumultuez:
        Second esleu absent son bien debise
        Son fauory bastard à mort tué.

16   *A son hault pris plus la lerme sabee,*
        D'humaine chair par mort en cendre mettre:
        A l'isle Pharos par croisars perturbee,
        Alors qu'a Rodes paroistra dur spectre.

17   *De nuict passant le roy pres d'vne Andronne,*
        Celuy de Cipres & principal guetto:
        Le roy failly la main fuict long du Rosne
        Les coniurés l'iront à mort metre.

18   *De dueil mourra l'infelix proflige,*
        Celebrera son vitrix l'heccatombe:
        Pristine loy franc edict redigé,
        Le mur & Prince au septiesme iour tombe.

19   *Le grand Royal d'or, d'œrain augmenté,*
        Rompu la pache, par ieune ouuerte guerre:
        Peuple affligé par vn chef lamenté,
        De sang barbare sera couuerte terre.

ærain (OF) brass; pache (OF) contract, agreement; barbare (Greek), foreign tongue.

The great golden Royal (**GOLDEN LOUIS**) augmented by brass,   1640
The agreement (**VERVINS**) broken, open warfare by a young man (**ENGHIEN**):
People afflicted by a lamented chief (**LOUIS XIII**),
The ground will be covered with foreign blood.

The great golden Royal

In 1640, Louis XIII decided to overhaul France's monetary system. To do this, he introduced *the golden louis*, or *louis d'or*, designed by Jean Varin, and worth 20 francs.

Hence, the Royal applies to both the King and to the unit of money he introduced.

Augmented by brass

Amongst the other denominations of French coinage established at the same time were those of two, four, eight and ten francs, also the demi-louis. The higher denominations were therefore *augmented by* adding values in *brass* coins, which measured their value in francs. [1]

The agreement broken

In 1643, Louis XIII became seriously ill and his demise seemed inevitable. Spain sought to take advantage of the King's failing health by sending an army into France from the Netherlands: the intention being to occupy Paris. Spain's action therefore *broke the agreement* made between the two countries—Peace of Vervins, 2 May 1598. It was this peace treaty, signed by Henri IV and Philip II [2] that had successfully brought an end to the French Wars of Religion.

Open warfare by a young man

On 19 May 1643, at Rocroi in northern France, the twenty-one-year-old Duke of Enghien (the great Condé) rode at the head of his country's cavalry to confront the Spanish army, which numbered 19,000 infantry and 8000 horse, including its dreaded *tercios*. In the battle that ensued, Enghien's cavalry cut its way through the Spanish force, inflicting defeat upon the army before reinforcements could arrive.

People afflicted by a lamented chief

Five days before the battle of Rocroi the Court's worst fears were confirmed: Louis XIII breathed his last. Whilst reigning, the King had possessed that rare "gift of appearing at ease with the common people:" [3] for which he received the cognomen of 'Le Juste'. It was this 'common touch' that was later reflected by the people's affliction through the loss of their much lamented chief. [4]

Several days before Louis expired, an event of some interest occurred, which was noted at the time. Apparently, the King suddenly awoke from his sick bed, and addressing the Prince of Condé, he said:

> I was dreaming that your son, the Duc d'Enghien, had engaged the enemy: that the fighting was fierce and persistent, and that victory hung long in the balance, but that after a severe struggle it remained with our forces who achieved the mastery of the field of battle. [5]

The ground will be covered with foreign blood

Louis did not live long enough to learn that his dream had been prophetic.

After invading France from the north, Spain's commander-in-chief, Francisco de Melo, suffered appalling losses. Those who survived were forced to escape by fleeing into the marshes. Only the resolute *tercios* stood their ground, but to no purpose for they were killed where they stood; [6] *the ground, covered with foreign blood.*

Spain lost eight thousand men killed and almost another seven thousand captured. [7] Added to this, France's victory filled the treasury with enough *louis d'or* to pay the army for a month.

Summary: *This prophecy captures two events that occurred in the last three years of Louis XIII's life—his revision of French currency, and the valour of the 21-year-old duc d'Enghien who achieved at Rocroi, one of the greatest victories in France's military history. These two events are followed by the death of the King, timed to coincide with the defeat of the Spanish. Many times, the seer exhibits his foreknowledge of when the subject of his prophecy will die, which emphasises the advice given by Jesus, "So don't be afraid; you are worth more than many sparrows." (Matthew 10: 31)*

20   *Dela les Alpes grand armee passera,*
        Vn peu deuant naistra monstre vapin:
        Prodigieux & subit tournera,
        Le grand Toscan à son lieu plus propin.

21   *Par le trespas du moarque latin,*
        Ceulx qu'il aura par regne secouruz:
        Le feu luyra, diuisé le butin,
        La mort publique aux hardis incoruz.

22   *Auant qu'a Rome grand aye rendu l'ame,*
        Effrayeur grande à l'armee estrangiere:
        Par esquadrons, l'embusche pres de Parme,
        Puis les deux roges ensemble feront chere.

aye (AF vertu) virtue; effrayeur (OF effroy) astonishment, fright; embusche (OF) waylaying, ambush, laying in wait; chere (AF amitié) friendship. This prophecy precedes No. 3 above with the Treaty of Vienna.

> Before, when at Rome, a great man of virtue rendered up his soul (**CLEMENT XII**), 1734
> A great scare at the foreign army:
> The waylaying by squadrons close to Parma,
> Afterwards, the two reds together will make a friendship.

Before, when at Rome, the great man of virtue has rendered up his soul

Clement XII, who reigned from 1730 to 1740, fits the timeframe for this prophecy. He was also a virtuous person, whose good deeds earned him a statue from the people of Ancona. And when he was elected to the papacy, the people of Rome celebrated: although his election was actually a compromise between two warring sides—of which, more later. His time in office began at the age of 78. Although by then, already infirm,

> ... in the second year of his pontificate he became totally blind; in his later years he was compelled to keep to his bed, from which he gave audiences and transacted affairs of state. [...] He demanded restitution of ill-gotten goods from the ministers who had abused the confidence of his predecessor. [..] Clement surrounded himself with capable officials, and won the affection of his subjects by lightening their burdens, encouraging manufacture and the arts, and infusing a modern spirit into the laws relating to commerce.
> Clement, also poured into his treasury an annual sum amounting to nearly a half million of SCUDI (dollars), enabling him to undertake the extensive buildings which distinguish his reign. He began the majestic façade of St. John Lateran and built in that basilica the magnificent chapel of St Andrew Corsini. He restored the Arch of Constantine and built the governmental palace of the Consulta on the Quirinal. He purchased [...] for 60,000 SCUDI the fine collection of statues, inscriptions, etc. with which he adorned the gallery of the Capitol. He paved the streets of Rome and the roads leading from the city, and widened the Corso. He began the great Fontana di Trevi, one of the noted ornaments of Rome. [...] His activity in the spiritual concerns of the Church was equally pronounced. His efforts were directed towards raising the prevalent low tone of morality and securing discipline, especially in the cloisters. [1]

Although successfull in so many ways, "he was unable to maintain the rights of the Holy See over the Duchies of Parma and Piacenza." [2] The oracle therefore concerns the fate of Italy.

A great scare at the foreign army

In February 1733, King Augustus II of Poland died. His death led to two separate elections taking place for his successor: both greatly influenced by competing powers. France supported Stanislaw Leszczynski, whereas the Habsburg Emperor favoured Frederick Augustus I.

On 10 October, France declared war on Austria and Saxony: having obtained military support from Sardinia. This *foreign army* then entered northern Italy, which was part of the Habsburg Empire, causing *a great scare* among the people as Milan was taken by the 3rd November.

> Starting in October 1733, a combined Franco-Sardinian army, numbering over 40,000 and led by Charles Emmanuel, rapidly took control of Milanese territory without significant opposition from the roughly 12,000 Austrian troops defending the duchy. [3]

The waylaying by squadrons close to Parma

"In response to the allied seizure of Milan, Austria organized a relief army." [4] By April the Austrian force had grown to 55,000, and in May the army began to push the French and Sardinian squadrons back towards Parma.

> Marshal Coigny determined to make a stand at Parma, and on June 28 established a strong position outside the city walls. Anchoring his left flank to the city's defences, he placed the right at the village of Crocetta, where it was further protected by swampy areas of the Taro River. The road between Crocetta and Parma ran on a causeway, and Coigny had deep trenches dug on either side of the road. [4]

At about 10 o'clock on the morning of 29 June 1734,

> The Battle of San Pietro, also known as the Battle of Crocetta or the Battle of Parma was [...] fought [...] between France and Sardinia on one side, and Habsburg-Austrian troops on the other, as part of the War of Polish Succession, between the village of La Crocetta and the city of Parma, then in the Duchy of Parma. Austrian troops assaulted an entrenched Franco-Sardinian position, and were ultimately repulsed. [...] Both sides suffered significant casualties in the battle, which lasted for most of the day. [5]

The War of the Polish Succession ended in 1735 with the drafting of the Treaty of Vienna (1738). "The Treaty of Vienna was the peace treaty that ended the War of the Polish Succession. It was signed by France and Austria. The other parties involved in the war agreed to the terms of this treaty in 1739." [6] Importantly, within the context of this prophecy, "Spain had gained Austrian-ruled Lombardy, Naples, and Sicily, while Austria received the duchies of Parma and Piacenza." [7] The treaty therefore united Parma and Piacenza under Austrian rule in the year before Clement XII died.

Afterwards, the two reds together will make a friendship

This prophecy began with the papacy of Clement XII. "The Conclave of 1730 was long, contentious, and sometimes disgraceful. It lasted four and a half months." [8] The cause of the friction was because, apart from the Zelanti and Sardinians, "There was also an Imperial party [...] and a French party, allied with the Spanish." [9]

The opposition between these two sides became evident in the voting, and it was the reason why Clement XII eventually received the two-thirds majority for his election. He was not the first choice. It was Cardinal Giuseppe Imperiali who received 35 of the 36 votes required for appointment. With one more vote needed, Cardinal Cornelio Bentivoglio applied the Spanish veto, which had been ordered by King Carlos I.

The next person to get close to the two-thirds majority of 36 votes was Cardinal Pier Corrodini, who obtained 30 votes. With the possibility that he might find the extra 6 votes at the next ballot, Cardinal Alvaro Cienfuego stepped forward and applied the Austrian veto, as ordered by Emperor Charles VI. It was from this position of stalemate that Lorenzo Corsini, aged 78, infirm and almost blind, received 52 votes to become elected as Clement XII. [10]

The two cardinals – *the two red ones* – who vetoed each other's candidate, lived long enough to see the Treaty of Vienna restore a new *friendship* between Spain and Austria.

Summary: *Most of these prophecies refer to the political quest for power that develops into conflict. In this prophecy, one of the more enlightened popes to rule the Catholic Church, Clement XII, has been linked to a war involving, principally, France and Spain combating the interests of the Austrian Habsburgs in the War of the Polish Succession. Pope Clement's reign lasted a decade and included within it this drawn out conflict for the right to rule Poland. It ended with a peace treaty that was finally accepted by all parties in 1739, the year before Clement XII, 'the great man of virtue rendered up his soul.'*
Once again, his time of death is apparently known to the seer, even though this oracle was published 97 years before Lorenzo Corsini was born. But this is merely a further example of what already appears in the Bible: "Before I formed you in the womb I knew you, before you were born I set you apart." (Jeremiah I: 5). How many reading this were ignorant of the biblical truth that links their birth and being to God?

23   *Les deux contens seront vnis ensemble,*
        Quant la pluspart à Mars seront conionct:
        Le grand d'Affrique en effraieur & tremble,
        DUUMUIRAT par la classe desioinct.

24   *Le regne & loy soubz Venus esleué,*
        Saturn aura sur Iupiter empire:
        La loy & regne par le Soleil leué,
        Par Saturnins endurera le pire.

25   *Le prince Arabe, Mars, Sol, Venus, Lyon,*
        Regne d'Eglise par mer succombera:
        Deuers la Perse bien pres d'vn million,
        Bisance, Egipte ver. serp invadera.

The next occasion when the Sun, Mars and Venus will be in Leo is 12 – 23 August 2019

26   *La gent esclaue par vn heur martial,*
        Viendra en hault degré tant esleuee:
        Changeront prince, naistre vn prouincial,
        Passer la mer copie aux montz leuee.

copie (L copi\a) army; esleuee (OF) raised; degree (OF) place of honour; naistre (OF) born, bred.
This prophecy follows Century One. No. 14.

The slavish people through a martial hour: 1917
He will arrive, raised to such a high place of honour,
They will change the prince (**LVOV**): one born a provincial (**LENIN**),
Crossing the sea; an army raised at the mounts.

The slavish people

The word slavish – 'servily following or conforming' – is derived from the Old French word 'esclave', originally a Slav. (Chambers English Dictionary). In Medieval Latin it is, 'Sclavus':

from which we get the word Slav – people of Russia; OED. Hence, "The Russian people have long been inured to tyranny." (Refer Century One N°. 14) [1]

Through a martial hour

The 'October Revolution' (it was called this, because according to the Julian calendar then in use inside Russia, it occurred on 25/26 October 1917) took place in Petrograd. It began on the 6th November (N.S.) and by the end of the next day, *through a martial hour*, it was all over.

The uprising was directed by the Bolshevik Military-Revolutionary Committee headed by Lenin. The Committee had actually planned its moves several weeks earlier. The first act was to order Trotsky's Red Guards to secure control of the post and telegraph offices; this was followed by securing the railway stations, and finally the military garrisons. Only then was the Winter Palace – 'the home of the Provisional Government' – placed under siege. [2]

He will arrive, raised to such a high place of honour

"Lenin was a fanatical visionary whose effective power was multiplied threefold by an inner conviction that he was designed by fate to be the commander of a victorious Russian Revolution." [3] After the overthrow of the government inside the Winter Palace, the delegates voted overwhelmingly to accept full power and "elected Lenin as chairman of the Council of People's Commissars, the new Soviet Government. [...] Overnight, Lenin had vaulted from his hideout as a fugitive to head the Revolutionary government of the largest country in the world." [4]

They will change the prince

From July that year, Alexander Kerensky had been allowed control over *Prince* Lvov's Provisional Government; this arrangement provided the *Prince* with time to give more attention to the Soviets; that is, the elected bodies that stood for workers' rights. But, on November 7th, Lenin seized this power for himself, effectively taking control of *Prince* Lvov's government.

Realizing that he had not the manpower to withstand the Bolsheviks, Prime Minister Kerensky secretly vacated the Winter Palace in disguise. Hours later, in a united assault, Lenin's forces were able to break through the Palace defences and arrest the remaining government officers. This final act completed their *coup d'état*, and they were able to *change the Prince* for a government headed by Lenin, which would thereafter be based upon the political philosophy of Karl Marx. [5]

One born a provincial, crossing the sea

Lenin was born a provincial. His real name was Vladimir Ilyich Ulyanov, and he was raised in the country town of Simbirsk. The town was founded in 1648, and stands aside the Volga River amidst agricultural surroundings. It is now called Ulyanovsk in honour of its famous son. [6]

During the months preceding the uprising that brought Lenin to power, he had been forced to seek refuge abroad, spending time in Helsinki. But, with the prospect of overthrowing the Provisional Government becoming increasingly probable: due mainly to Kerensky's mounting problems with the First World War, he secretly left Finland, returning across the sea to Russia. Once on home soil, sympathisers in Petrograd concealed his presence until it was time to strike. [7]

An army raised at the mounts

Lenin's rise to power was not without opposition. A small *army* of Cossacks in favour of returning Kerensky to power was *raised* under the command of General Pyotr Krasnov, an anti-Bolshevik army officer who had previously served in the Imperial Guard. Fully armed, the men advanced towards Petrograd.

Soldiers belonging to Lenin's newly formed Sovnarkom (a Russian acronym for the Council of People's Commissars) rallied to defend their leader, and the two opposing armies met at the *'Pulkovo Heights'*, which overlook the capital. The subsequent defeat of the Cossacks, and the capture of Krasnov, removed the final obstacle to Lenin's control of Russia, and he continued as Premier, until his death in 1924. [8]

Summary: This prophecy represents another step in the prophetic chain of events that the seer has predicted for Russia. On this occasion it concerns the October Revolution that brought Lenin to power. His provincial background is remarked upon in contrast to that of Prince Lvov, whom he replaced. The circumstances surrounding his rise to power have also been indicated and the attempted counter revolution on the 'mounts' at the Pulkovo Heights has been predicted in the final line.

27   *Par feu & armes non loing de la mer negro,*
          Viendra de Perse occupier Trebisonde:
          Trembler Pharos, Methelin, Sol allegro,
          De sang Arabe d'Adrie couuert vnde.

28   *Le bras pendu & la iambe liee,*
          Visaige, passé au seing poignard caché,
          Trois qui seront iurés de la meslee,
          Au grand de Gennes fera le fort lasché.

29   *La liberté ne sera recouuree,*
          L'occupera noir fier villain inique:
          Quant la matiere du pont sera ouuree,
          D'Hister, Venise faschee la republique.

noir (AF livide, triste: *Fig.* Noir, par opposition à blanc, se dit, en parlant des personnes, de la noirceur morale. Also, anagram & paragram: roi (AF règle) ruler; villain (AF - laid moralement) morally ugly; fier (OF) cruel; Quant (AF dans le temps où) in the time when; matiere; (OF) material, matter,; ouvrée (OF) laboured; Hister (as before) Hitler. Refer, C.II: 24; C.IV: 68.

Liberty will not be recovered,   1940
A ghastly (ruler) will occupy it: cruel, wicked and morally ugly,
In the time when the material of the (**REMAGEN**) bridge will be laboured
By Hister (**HITLER**): Venice having displeased the (**SALO**) REPUBLIC.

Liberty will not be recovered

France lost her liberty during the Second World War when the country was invaded by Hitler's

Nazi Germany. The occupation commenced in 1940, with the German army having marched across Holland and Belgium to invade France. Paris was captured in June. Thereafter, *liberty would not be recovered* until august 1944 [1] when, Normandy, Toulon and Paris were among the first to be freed.

It is noteworthy that, "the Convention at the end of September 1792 decreed that the Seal of State should include a 'Liberty figure'. Modestly attired, and now wearing a crown of seven rays, Liberté still appears on the French Seal of State seated and holding a fasces in her right hand." [2]

LIBERTY HOLDING A FASCES

A ghastly (ruler) will occupy it, cruel, wicked and morally ugly

During the entire time that the French nation was occupied, war raged across Europe. Historians hold Hitler responsible for the many millions of civilian and military deaths, which his insatiable ambition for conquest caused, quite apart from the millions more who became victims of his extermination camps. [3]

Having produced a recognizable description of Hitler, as *cruel, ghastly, and wicked,* the oracle predicts the events leading to his end. It begins, appropriately enough, in the month before his death, with a prediction of the Rhine crossing. Once this obstacle had been overcome, the way was then clear for the Allies to press deeper into Germany and eventually reach Berlin. Occupation of the German capital would then bring the war in Europe to an end.

In the time when the material of the bridge will be laboured by Hitler

The railway bridge that spanned the Rhine at Remagen played a crucial part in speeding up the fall of Germany. It had been overlooked when Hitler ordered all bridges across the Rhine to be destroyed: his intention being to hinder the allied advance into Germany.

On 7 March 1945, during the battle for Germany, it was captured by an armoured patrol of
Hodges First US Army, when the Germans failed to destroy it. This gave the Allies a great
psychological, as well as military advantage for it enabled more than 8,000 troops, supported by
tanks and self-propelled guns, to cross in under 24 hours. [...] Hitler was furious at the bridge's
capture. [...] The German officer charged with destroying it was, along with four others,
summarily shot and V-2 rockets were even fired at it.

But the bridge remained intact for some time, despite the laboured efforts made by Hitler's
command to destroy it. Finally, it collapsed into the Rhine on 17 March 1945. [4]

Six weeks after the Remagen bridge affair (30 April), and with Soviet troops entering Berlin from
the east, as well as American and British troops approaching from the west, Hitler committed
suicide inside his Berlin bunker. His end had, however, been cryptically indicated by the Seer,
using the liberation of Venice as a timing event.

Venice having displeased the Republic

As American troops moved steadily northwards across Italy, "Both corps of the Eighth Army began to
cross the Po on 24th April against no opposition, and by the 29th they were over the Adige also, advancing
rapidly thereafter, reaching Venice on 29th April." [5] Venice surrendered next day with minimum
opposition, thereby having displeased the Salo Republic, which ruled northern Italy.

The Salo *Republic* was "the Italian Social Republic, a last-ditch Fascist regime based in Salò on Lake
Garda." [6] Its purpose was to maintain control of German occupied northern Italy, which had
been placed under the control of Mussolini. But the news of the Duce's death on 28 April 1945,
and the liberation of northern Italy, made grim news for Hitler. And, on the same day that
Venice capitulated (30 April 1945), the Nazi Führer committed suicide. [7]

Summary: *This is the third and final oracle that names Hitler by dissimilating it from Hister—the river of his
            boyhood. The oracle accurately foretells events in the weeks before his death. Moreover, Hitler's character is
            also foretold with a harshness that those who suffered under his rule will be unlikely to dispute. But the
            religious implications are profound, due to the obvious fact that Hitler is yet another figure within these
            oracles whose character was known to the seer centuries before 1889, the year of his birth. Christian
            ministers are not alone in feeling the need to reject prophecies that foretell the future of people before they
            are born. But one cannot have a timeless God that doesn't know the future. Apart from being a
            contradiction, it diminishes the omniscience of the LORD. Instead, the so-called 'block universe' heralds a
            new beginning to the world. Adhere to the two greatest commandments given by Jesus in Matthew 22: 37,
            and there will be no further need for any dire predictions of character.*

30   *Tout à entour de la grande cité,*
            Seront soldartz loges par champs & ville:
            Donner l'assault Paris, Rome incité,
            Sur le pont lors sera faicte grand pille.

pille (OF & *apocope*, pillerie) havoc, devastation; faicte (OF) done, wrought

            All around the great city (**PARIS**),   1871
            Soldiers will be quartered in fields and town,
            Paris giving the assault, Rome incited,
            Over the bridge (**PONT ROYAL**) at that time, great havoc will be wrought.

This concerns the second siege of Paris (the great city) The Prussian army had conducted the first
siege as a strategic follow-up to their victory at Sedan in September 1870. But after the armistice
signed in January, and departure of Napoleon III, an attempt was made to fill the political void
by the Communards. This was a party of anti-religious, left-wing, socialists who seized power in
March 1871. Their final revolt in Paris was dramatised by Victor Hugo in *Les Misérables*.

All around the great city soldiers will be quartered in fields and town

From his base at Versailles, Adolphe Thiers – the displaced head of the French government –
deployed the prisoners-of-war released by Bismarck to lay siege to Paris. Hence, all around the
great city were the soldiers who had recently fought in the Franco-Prussian War. Thiers's plan
necessitated billeting the men close to the capital, which meant that some were quartered in the
town of Versailles, while others occupied camp sites set-up in the fields outside Paris. [1]

Paris giving the assault

On 22 May, 70,000 French troops poured through a breach in the city wall to the southwest of Paris, and, street-by-street, the insurgent *'Versaillais'* began retaking the capital. [2]

Rome incited

> On 2 April, soon after the Commune was established, it voted a decree accusing the Catholic Church of 'complicity in the crimes of the monarchy.' The decree declared the separation of church and state, confiscated the state funds allotted to the church, seized the property of religious congregations, and ordered Catholic schools to cease religious education and become secular. Over the next seven weeks, some two hundred priests, nuns and monks were arrested, and twenty-six churches were closed to the public. [...] More extreme elements of the National Guard carried out mock religious processions and parodies of religious services. Early in May, some of the political clubs began to demand the immediate execution of Archbishop Darboy and the other priests in the prison. The Archbishop and a number of priests were executed during Bloody Week. [3]

Over the bridge at that time great havoc will be wrought

Meanwhile, the battle for Paris continued, with the fiercest fighting taking place on the other side of the river Seine; that is, *over* "the new Pont Royal, linking the Tuileries to the Left Bank." There, the Communards were in deadly combat with government troops. "On the Left Bank, Communards fought at Montparnasse Station until their ammunition ran out. [...] At the other end of the front, the Versailles troops were advancing rapidly towards Montmartre." Estimates of those killed vary, from 6,500 to 40,000. After Thiers had put down the revolt, Paris descended into a strange quietness. "Théophile Gautier noted the city's oppressive silence, and was particularly struck by the Rue de Lille, on the Left Bank [...] 'it seemed to be deserted throughout its length, like a street of Pompeii.'" [4]

Among the more prominent buildings that suffered destruction from the fighting were, "the Tuileries, a large part of the Palais Royal, the Palais de Justice, the Prefecture of Police and the Conseil d'Etat. Whole sections of streets were set ablaze; so was the Ministry of Finance." Even the great column in the *Place Vendôme*, erected to celebrate Napoleon's victories of 1805, was knocked down. [5]

Summary: *This is a straightforward prophecy of a significant event in the history of Paris. There can be no doubt that the wording of the oracle is descriptive of the events that took place, both martial and religious, during the uprising of 1871.*

> 31   *Par terre Attique chef de la sapience,*
>   *Qui de present est la rose du monde:*
>   *Pont ruyné & sa grand preeminence,*
>   *Sera subdite & nayfragé des vndes.*

Attique. (L. Attic\a) region of Athens; subdite (L. subdit\us) subdued, brought under, plunged under.

> By reason of the Athens region, master of wisdom,
> Which at present is the rose of the world:
> The pontifical ruined & his great pre-eminence,
> It/He will be subdued & shipwrecked from the waves.

There is also a reference to 'the rose' in Century Two N°. 95: and again in N°. 96 below. In this prediction, 'the rose' is identified as a person of wisdom in the Athenian tradition. This places him close to Plato, who came from Athens, where he founded his academy for the study of philosophy and mathematics. The remaining lines concern the Catholic Church: and, as in Century Two N°. 95, the papacy fares badly, since it is the bark of St. Peter. Hence, 'the shipwreck' is likely to be metaphorical, as too are the 'waves'. As this book goes to print, Athens is in revolt against the restrictions imposed by its bankrupt situation within the European Union.

> 32   *Ou tout bon est, tout bien Soliel & Lune,*
>   *Est abondant sa ruyne s'approche:*
>   *Du ciel s'aduance varier ta fortune,*
>   *En mesme estat que la septiesme roche.*

33   Des principaulx de cité rebellee,
       Qui tiendront fort pour liberté rauoir:
       Detrencher masles infelice meslee,
       Crys, hurlemens à Nantes, piteux voir.

infelice (L infelic\o) unhappy, wretched; detrencher (OF destrancher) to hack, mangle, chop in pieces

Concerning the principals of the city that rebelled (LYONS)   1793
Who will strongly hold out for recovering liberty:
Males cut in pieces, a wretched fray,
Shrieks, yelling at NANTES, pitiful to witness.

Concerning the principals of the city that rebelled

In contrast to the sans-culottes, whose name has since become synonymous with the French
Revolution, it was not they who rebelled inside Lyons in May 1793, but the professional elite:
'the principals of the city', "men who considered themselves the natural political and cultural leaders of
the city." [1]

Who will strongly hold out for recovering liberty

For five months the citizens of Lyons held out under siege conditions, against troops sent by the
Paris Convention to restore order. The principal citizens were protesting against the diminution
of their former liberty, which had been reduced by recent revisions made to the Constitution. [2]

Males cut in pieces

In retribution for what the Paris government saw as a counter-revolution, the Convention took
revenge on some of the greatest people of the city. These included many of the Lyonnais elite.
All were executed. But the severest measure taken against the citizens of Lyons was the act of
savagery inflicted upon their young *men* who were *cut in pieces*.

> What happened [in Lyon] was far worse than the Paris terror [...] the volleys on the plain of
> Brotteaux, where on the 14th Frimaire, [4th December] sixty-four young men, all firmly bound,
> were mown down by grape shot and then dispatched with sword thrusts. [3]

A wretched fray

> Fouché remained in Lyons till he had murdered 2000 persons 'whose blood-stained corpses,' he
> writes 'cast into the Rhône. [...] inspire a feeling of terror and a picture of omnipotence of the
> people on either bank.'" [4]

The final line of this oracle continues the theme of counter-revolution, but switches attention to
Nantes. Like Lyons, Nantes was also the scene of a revolt against the Paris government, but with
motives more aligned with those who were fighting for the royalist cause in the Vendée.

Shrieks, yelling at Nantes, pitiful to witness

In October 1793, the siege at Nantes was broken after the Republican Army surrounding the city
had been heavily reinforced by regiments transferred from the Grand Army at Mainz.
Retribution swiftly followed: "The most notorious massacres were at Nantes, where. [...] Jean-Baptiste
Carrier supplemented the guillotine with what he called 'vertical deportations' in the river Loire." In
short, guillotining was accompanied by mass drowning.
Nantes was a slave port, and there was an abundance of shallow boats on the Loire, which had
been used to convey their human cargo down river. These boats gave Carrier the idea for his
'noyades'. Men and women that had been sentenced for execution were first stripped naked
(victims' clothes were considered a perquisite), then bound together *vis-à-vis* in what were termed
'Republican Marriages'. In this state they were put on board the boats. Once the vessels were far
enough from the shore, they were scuttled, and the occupants of the boat sank beneath the
waves: the river finally silencing the terrified *shrieks* and *yelling*, which the Seer had found so
pitiful to witness. [5]

Summary: *In 1793 the French Revolution was well underway. This oracle concentrates upon two counter revolutions: both of which were savagely put down. At Lyons, a two-month siege took place, led by the professional classes who resented their loss of liberty under the revised Constitution. They were brutally put down by government troops, buildings were pulled down and the guillotine ended a great many lives apart from the example made to the rebel citizens by the deaths of the young men slaughtered by cannon fire. At Nantes, the rebellion was organized by a royalist faction. It, too, was viciously suppressed with mass drowning giving meaning to 'noyades'. Both at Lyon and at Nantes, a nearby river was used to dispose of the many corpses. Interestingly, the seer speaks of actually witnessing the event some 240 years before it reached the pages of history. This would imply the sense data for the event already existed in the mid-sixteenth century.*

34   *Du plus profond de l'occident Anglois,*
        Ou est le chef de l'isle Britannique:
        Entrera classe dans Gyrande par Blois,
        Par vin & sel, feuz. caché aux barriques.

N.B. Blois, in ancient French has several meanings, one of which is privé.

35   *Par cité franche de la grand mer Seline,*
        Qui porte encores à l'estomach la pierre:
        Angloise classe viendra soubz la bruine,
        Vn rameau prendre du grand ouerte guerre.

36   *De sœur le frère par simulate faintise,*
        Viendra mesler rosee en myneral:
        Sur la plancente donne à vielle tardisue,
        Meurt le goustant sera simple & rural.

37   *Trois cens seront d'vn vouloir & accord,*
        Que pour venir au bout de leur attainte:
        Vingtz moys après tous & recordz,
        Leur roy trahir simulant haine faincte.

38   *Ce grand monarque qu'au mort succedera,*
        Donnera vie illicit & lubrique:
        Par nonchalance à tous concedera,
        Qu'à la parfin fauldra à la loy Salique.

lubrique (L lubric\us) slippery, deceitful; à la parfin (OF) in the end; fauldra (future tense of falloir)

That great monarch (**LOUIS XIV**), whom he will succeed at death,   1715
He will give way to a life illicit and deceitful (**LOUIS XV**):
Through nonchalance he will concede to everything,
That, in the end, the Salic law will be necessary.

That great monarch whom he will succeed at death

That great monarch, "Louis Le Grand" *whom* his great-grandson *will succeed at his death*,[1] invites a comparison between the two monarchs. For example, Louis XV's "personal rule (1743-74) made ministerial inability a permanent feature of the rest of the reign." In this, he was the complete opposite of his great-grandfather, who made the rule of France his full-time profession.

He will give way to a life illicit and deceitful

Part of the reason for Louis XV's ineptitude may have begun with the man who became regent during his minority. Philippe II duc d'Orléans proved to be no exemplar of morality. By the time he became regent he had already acquired the reputation for: 'irreverence, habitual drunkenness, and licentious behaviour'. It is not surprising therefore that upon reaching adulthood, and with such a role model, the King followed the regent's example. To add his addiction for gambling and alcohol, he gave way to a life of illicit sex with young girls, whom he maintained in his 'birdcage' until pregnancy made it necessary for them to be replaced.[2]

The oracle also describes the King as *deceitful*. This can be explained as a reference to his 'cabinet noir': a group of men who, among other practices, had devised a means for opening letters and resealing them without detection. Louis XV became totally addicted to reading the salacious

gossip and intimate secrets of his courtiers, especially those of the clergy and the nobility, who were unwise enough to entrust secrets of a sexual nature to letters sent through the *Paris Poste*. [3]
The King also began a policy, which he set up in or about 1748, involving a complex system of underhand diplomacy known as 'le Secret du roi'. French spies were stationed in major European capitals and ordered to pursue, in secret, political objectives that were frequently opposed to Louis' own publicly acclaimed policy.

Through nonchalance, he will concede to everything

Louis XV's ineptitude for government was another of his failings. He had neither the interest nor the energy required for dealing with the day-to-day affairs of running the country. Instead, he preferred to fill the day with hunting, and the night by attending to his mistresses.
His nonchalance regarding state affairs caused a power vacuum to occur. And it allowed his ministers to form into factions, often with opposing viewpoints. This negligent attitude towards government, with a willingness to *concede everything* to others [4] further identifies Louis XV.

That, in the end, the Salic law will be necessary

The final line refers to the 'Salic law'. This operated in France and was designed to prevent the succession of the monarchy passing into female hands.

> [After] Fleury died, aged eighty-eight, in 1742, the King allowed himself – and France – to be ruled by his mistresses, first Mme de Pompadour for two decades, then after her demise, by the much hated vulgarian Mme du Barry. [5]

Madame de Pompadour (aka Mistress of France), "exerted her influence over appointments, promotions, honours, and preferment's of all kinds." She was therefore able to manipulate the course of France's affairs, both foreign and military. In addition, she gave regular audiences to visiting ambassadors. At the palace of Versailles, it was said she virtually achieved the position of Queen. [6]
The *Salic law* was intended to prevent women from becoming enthroned as queen. The oracle predicts how this came to be overturned in all but name, since the manner in which the King's mistresses had taken over the office of government, effectively bypassed this law.

Summary: *This prophecy is another that accurately foretells the character of its main subject 155 years before he was born. Louis XV did indeed succeed to the throne following the death of his great-grandfather, Louis XIV (the Great Monarch). And, as predicted, the Sun King's great-grandson became known for his licentious behaviour and deceitfulness with his 'cabinet noir'. His reign reflected his lax hand at governing France's affairs, causing state matters to be placed in the hands of his ministers, which caused factions to emerge. As the oracle predicted, it was left to his mistresses in the end to govern France, per pro the King.*

39   *Du vray rameau de fleur de lys issu,*
       Mis & logé heritier d'Hetrurie:
       Son sang antique de longue main issu,
       Fera Florence florit en l'armoirie.

heritier (OF) heir, inheritor; longue (*apocope*, longueue) extent in time; main (AF puissance) power; armoirie (OF) coat of arms

> Issued from the true branch of the fleur-de-lys (**FERDINAND III**),   1803
> Inheritor of Etruria, taken and lodged:
> His ancient blood (**LEOPOLD II**) issued from a long-time power,
> Will cause Florence to blossom on the coat of arms.

Issued from the true branch of the fleur-de-lys, inheritor of Etruria

> Ferdinand III was born in Florence, Tuscany, into the House of Habsburg-Lorraine. He was the second son of Leopold, then Grand-Duke of Tuscany. [...] When his father was elected Emperor of the Holy Roman Empire, Ferdinand succeeded him as Grand Duke of Tuscany, officially taking the office on 22 July 1790. [1]

Six years later, in 1796, the Duchy of Parma was occupied by French troops. Republicanism spread to Florence and in 1799, Ferdinand fled from Tuscany to seek refuge in Vienna. Two years later, when Napoleon came to power, he sought to obtain Spain as an ally against England. To accomplish this, he compensated the House of Bourbon for their loss of the Duchy of Parma by granting them the 'Kingdom of Etruria'. This was a new state that he had created from the Grand Duchy of Tuscany. As a result of this new creation, in 1801 Ferdinand III renounced his title.

Taken and lodged

Ferdinand was compensated by being given the Dukedom and Electorate of Salzburg, the secularized lands of the Archbishop of Salzburg, as Duke of Salzburg. He was also made a Prince - elector of the Holy Roman Empire, both on 26 December 1802. [2]

On 25 December 1805, Ferdinand had to give up Salzburg as well, which by the Treaty of Pressburgh was annexed by his older brother, Emperor Francis II. Ferdinand was then made Duke of Würzburg, a new state created for him from the old Bishopric of Würzburg, remaining an Elector. With the dissolution of the Empire in 1806 he took the new title of Grand Duke of Würzburg. [3]

From 1806 up until 1814, Napoleon's sister, Elisa, was made Duchess of Tuscany. But after Bonaparte's exile to Elba, the Congress of Vienna returned the title to Ferdinand III. He resumed his seat in Tuscany's main city, Florence, on 30 May 1814.

His ancient blood issued from a long-time power

The House of Lorraine, the main and now only remaining line known as Habsburg-Lorraine, was one of the most important and longest-reigning royal houses in the history of Europe. [...] In 1736 Emperor Charles arranged the marriage [of his daughter, Maria Theresa,] to Francis of Lorraine who agreed to exchange his hereditary lands for the Grand Duchy of Tuscany. [4]

After the death of Ferdinand III in Florence (18 June 1824), his son Leopold II became the inheritor of his father's title and with it, the duchy of Tuscany—formerly, if only briefly, known as Etruria. In fact, the name was revived by Napoleon from the ancient name given to that region of Italy, which it partly covered by what are now Tuscany, Lazio and Umbria.

Leopold II was born in Florence on 3 October 1797.

He succeeded his father on 18 June 1824. During the first twenty years of hi s reign he devoted himself to the internal development of the state. His was the mildest and least reactionary of all the Italian despotisms of the day, and although always subject to Austrian influence he refused to adopt the Austrian methods of government, allowed a fair measure of liberty to the press, and permitted many political exiles from other states to dwell in Tuscany undisturbed. [5]

Will cause Florence to blossom on the coat of arms

Florence remains the capital and most important city in Tuscany; it was also the residential home

of its dukes. Despite the political and revolutionary unrest in Italy at that time: "Tuscany under Ferdinand III of Habsburg-Lorraine," became a centre for the arts. Intellectual life positively *blossomed in* the city of *Florence* particularly with the establishment of the *Gabinetto di Lettura* ('Literary Club'), which boasted several famous writers amongst its members. [6]

The oracle does, however, refer to a coat of arms blossoming. This was perfectly true at that time.

Pope Leo XI was born in Florence in 1535. In March 1 573, Gregory XIII appointed him, "Archbishop of Florence and he rebuilt the Bishop's Palace in Piazza del Duomo. A gigantic coat of arms celebrates this fact." [7] (See figure, for the 3 blossoms and the inscription commemorating Leo XI.) Displayed on the coat of arms are three gold *fleurs-de-lis* on a blue background – 'symbols of Florence,'– for together, with "three roses and the motto, 'Sic Floruit' (he blossomed in this way. Refer picture), they provide reference to the fact that Leo XI was pope for less than four weeks. Elected on April 1, 1605, he died on April 27."

In 1823, one year before Ferdinand's death, Leo XII became Pope. Because "His father's family had been ennobled by Leo XI in 1605," Leo chose the same regnal name to honour the memory of his family's benefactor. Thus, under Ferdinand III, Florence *blossomed* once again *on the coat of arms*, with the memory of Leo XI refreshed by the election of Leo XII. [8]

Summary: *This is an interesting prophecy for French and Italian historians that takes a more focused look at the events predicted in No. 3 above, concerning the House of Lorraine. We may deduce from this that the seer's previsions required more than just one quatrain to include all that he thought worthy of report. This is also evident in other prophecies. The final line of the quatrain provides another of his intriguing predictions wrapped in a riddle. But, once this is unwrapped, its meaning becomes clear.*

40   *Le sang royal sera si tresmeslé,*
       Constraint seron Gaulois de l'Hesperie:
       On attendra que terme soit coulé,
       Et que memoire de la voix soit perie.

41   *Nay soubs les vmbres & iournee nocturne,*
       Sera en regne & bonté souueraine:
       Fera renaistre son sang de l'antique vrne,
       Renouuelant siècle d'or pour œrain.

42   *Mars esleué en son plus hault beffroy,*
       Fera retraire les Allobrox de France:
       La gent Lombarde fera si grand effroy,
       A ceux de l'Aigle comprins soubs la balance.

beffroy (AF befroi – ouvrage militaire) military performance; retraire (OF éloigner) draw back; Allobrox (L) 1. people of S.E. Gaul, 2. Savoy; effroy (OF) fright, dread; comprins (OF) contained within the compass (or limit); balance (AF chance) chance, good fortune.

The war god elevated by his highest military performance,   1800
He will make the Allobroges draw back from France,
The Lombardy people will cause such great fear
To those of the Eagle (**NAPOLEON**), contained within the compass under chance.

The war god elevated by his highest military performance

By the end of the eighteenth century, Napoleon had reached the very height of his military performance. In his First Italian Campaign he destroyed the Piedmontese army at the battles of Montenotte and Mondovi; defeated the Austrian armies at Castiglione, Bassano and Arcole; and after routing Alvinczi at Rivoli, he crossed into Austria, and by 7 April 1797 he was threatening Vienna, having reached within two days march of the city.

Thereafter, by the time he set sail for Egypt in 1798, Bonaparte had not only demonstrated his tactical brilliance as a military commander by forcing the Austrians to withdraw from Italy, but he had also laid the ground for empire, by occupying northern Italy.

In Egypt, at the head of his 'Army of the Orient' he took Alexandria, Cairo, and was victorious at the battles of the Pyramids, and at Salheyer, Sédiman, the Siege of Jaffa, Nazareth, Cana, and at Abukir, before returning to France. Then within weeks of arriving back in Paris, Napoleon sprang his *coup d'état* to become First Consul of France and its *de facto* ruler.

He will make the Allobroges draw back from France

After his elevation as First Consul of France, Napoleon began forming plans to defeat Austria and recover French territorial losses suffered during his absence in Egypt. On 15 May, inspired by the feat of Hannibal, Napoleon led his Army of the Reserve, numbering 50,000 men, on a perilous journey across the snow-covered Alps into Italy. It was this military operation that caused the Seer to refer to the *Allobrox*.

The first reference to the Allobroge tribe of Gaul is made by the Greek historian, Polybius, who, between 150 and 130 BC, recounted the Carthaginian general, Hannibal's crossing of the Alps in 218 BC. The Allobroges attempted to prevent him crossing when he entered the first passes but were defeated. [1]

The Allobroge tribes have long since disappeared from this region. But at the turn of the 18th century it was the Austrians, guarding the passes into Italy that had replaced them. Nevertheless, "By the 21st [May] the Austrians had been driven out of most of the villages," and three days later, Bonaparte was able to write to his brother Joseph, "The enemy did not expect us and still seem scarcely able to believe it." [2] The Austrians were completely taken by surprise and had been *forced to draw* back *from* the onslaught of *the French*: who, afterwards, were able to march triumphantly into Milan and be greeted as conquerors of the Austrian occupiers.

The Lombard people will cause such great fear to those of the Eagle (Napoleon)

According to the Lombard historian Paul the Deacon, [who] wrote in the *Historia Langobardorum* that the Lombards descended from a small tribe called the *Winnili*. [...]. By the end of the 5th century they had moved into the area roughly coinciding with modern Austria north of the Danube river. [3]

Concluded from this, the Austrians are referred to by a name taken from ancient history—'Lombard people'. While Napoleon had been busy conquering Egypt. Austria had been recovering most of the territory it had lost to France during Bonaparte's First Italian Campaign. Only Genoa and the Ligurian coast to Nice remained in French hands. But in April 1800, Austria's General Melas besieged the French at Genoa. Napoleon responded by ordering General Masséna to hold the city until he arrived with reinforcements.

It is notable that again, the Seer is referring to Napoleon as 'the Eagle'. He did so previously in Century One N°. 23; Century Three N°. 37, and Century Four N°. 70.

On 14 June, outside the village of Marengo, 'the Lombard people', numbering 30,000 imperial troops, led by General Melas, met *the Eagle* at the head of 18,000 French, marching on their way to Genoa, which had capitulated (2 June), after Masséna had been starved into submission.

It is conceivable that no other battle, until Waterloo, was so crucial for Bonaparte's career as that which decided this second Italian campaign. In order to justify his assumption of control over the French war effort, the first consul *had* to win—and he very nearly lost. [...] By mid-afternoon the battle seemed sure to end in victory for Melas, defeat for Bonaparte. [4]

Bonaparte and his officers feared the battle was lost: Melas having already handed over command to General Zach to complete the victory.

Contained within the compass under chance

It was not to be; the battle was saved for France by the timely arrival of General Desaix with his reinforcements, and by chance. As Desaix led his men forward to attack the Austrian grenadiers –

an ammunition wagon exploded, and a moment of consternation paralyzed the Austrian ranks in their turn. Seizing a fleeting opportunity, the younger Kellerman wheeled his 400 horsemen for a bold, spontaneous charge into the stunned left flank of Zach's 6,000-strong column. It was the moment of truth which converted near-defeat into crushing victory. "A minute earlier, or three minutes later, and the thing would not have succeeded, but the timing was perfect, and North Italy was recovered in that moment for the French Republic." [5]

Summary: *This oracle is another in the long list of those pertaining to the Napoleonic Era. Once again, he is identified as 'the Eagle'. On this occasion the prophecy follows him across the Alps to fight the Austrians at the Battle of Marengo. Against superior numbers, the French were losing the battle up until the arrival of Desaix's reinforcements. But it was the 'chance' explosion that swayed the outcome in Bonaparte's favour. Einstein was correct when he said; 'God does not play dice.' Hence, there is no such thing as 'chance'. Quantum theorists oppose this idea. But actions which take place at the quantum level do not occur 'outside' of time. And since space, time and motion are inseparable at any instant within a block universe; it follows that quantum events are defined by relativistic considerations.*

43   *La grand ruyne des sactés ne esloigne,*
        Prouence, Naples, Secile, Seez & Ponce:
        En Germanie, au Ryn & à Colonge,
        Vexés à mort par tous ceulz de Magonce.

44   *Par mer le rouge sera prins des pyrates,*
       La paix sera par son moyen troublee:
       L'ire & l'auare commettra par fainct acte,
       Au grand Pontife sera l'armee doublee.

45   *Le grand Empire sera tost desolé,*
       Et translaté pres d'arduenne silue:
       Les deux bastardz par l'aisné decollé,
       Et regnera Aenobarbe nay de milue.

46   *Par chapeaux rouges querelles & nouueaux scismes,*
       Quant on aura esleu le Sabinois:
       On produira contre luy grans sophisms,
       Et sera Rome lesee par Albanois.

Through the red hats, quarrels and fresh schisms,   1700
When men will have elected the **SABINE**:
Men will produce great cavils against him,
And **ROME** will be wounded by the Albanian (**ALBANI**).

The subject matter of this prophecy concerns the election of a pope amidst quarrels and division during the conclave. This reduces the number of popes to whom it can apply. We are then told this pope is known for his connexion to the region of Sabina, which limits the search still further. Next, we learn that his reign will be noted for the cavils made against him, and that Rome will suffer because of 'Albanois'. In fact, every single prophetic link in this chain of clues applies to Pope Clement XI, whose family name, Albani, had been handed down on his father's side from his Albanian forefathers who settled in Urbino in the 15th century.

Through the red hats, quarrels and fresh schisms
A cardinal's robe is red, as is his hat. In October 1700, following the death of Innocent XII, fifty-seven cardinals met in a conclave to decide their next leader.

> Pope Innocent XII (Pignatelli) died on September 27, 1700, at the worst possible time for Europe. The impending Spanish succession was promising to embroil France, Spain, the Empire and many others in a bloody struggle. Innocent had finally pronounced in favour of Philippe de Bourbon, Duke of Anjou, grandson of Louis XIV. This was contrary to the interests of the Empire, whose candidate, the Archduke Charles of Austria (Emperor Charles VI, 1711-1740), would by no means give way.
> Trouble had already broken out in the Duchy of Milan (a Spanish possession) in March 1700, between French and Spanish forces on the one hand, and Imperial forces, led by Prince Eugene, on the other. The mediation of a strong pope would be useful; the struggle to obtain a compliant pope would produce great difficulties. The Conclave of 1700 began on October 9, and lasted a total of 46 days. [1]

The French faction consisted of seven cardinals, led by César d'Estrée, whereas the Spanish faction, led by Cardinal Francesco de' Medici, could count upon only four, but was also able to rely upon votes from the Milanese and Neapolitans.

To complicate matters further, Venice had five cardinals and was demanding that they elect a pope who would promote Italian liberty. Genoa also had five cardinals, but the city was noted for its frequent opposition to the wishes of Venice. Set among these was the Duke of Savoy, a pretender to the Spanish throne. Although he had no power of veto, he had the ear of Carlo Barberini, who favoured the conclave's eventual choice. Mention must also be made of Marcello Durazzo, who had strong monetary support from Vienna.

In the event, Cardinal Galeazzo Marescotti was the electors' first choice. He was a Roman, and already greatly experienced in papal government. But his election was blocked by Louis XIV's veto. Other front runners were Cardinals Bandino Panciatici, Leandro Colloredo and Giambattista Spinola; the last named having come within ten votes of being elected. [2]

When men will have elected the Sabine

The fractious quarrelling by the conclave was interrupted on November 1st when news arrived that Charles II of Spain had died without an heir. The political implications were apparent to those assembled, and the cardinals settled down to find a neutral candidate. Their choice fell upon Cardinal Albani who had been advisor to both Alexander VIII and Innocent XII. After some modest protests from their choice, he received a unanimous vote, and chose Clement XI as his regnal title.

The oracle's reference to 'Sabine' directs attention to "Sabina, the region in the Sabine Hills of Latium named for the Sabines, is the ancient territory that today is still identified mainly with the North-Eastern Province of Rome and the Province of Rieti, Lazio."[3]

Before Giovanni Albani was elected, he had been, "at the age of twenty-eight made a prelate, and governed successively Rieti, Sabina, and Orvieto, everywhere acceptable on account of his reputation for justice and prudence."[4] Rieti "was originally a major site of the Sabine nation."[5]

Therefore, together with Sabina, the references made to the election of 'the Sabine' have acquired the background evidence needed for Clement XI to continue fulfilling this prophecy.

Men will produce great cavils against him

The year after his election, Clement became embroiled in a dispute over the right of the Church to bestow royal titles. The Elector of Brandenburg had assumed the title King of Prussia, without regard to papal authority, despite Prussia belonging, by ancient right, to the ecclesiastic-military institute of the Teutonic Order.

In the War of the Spanish Succession, Clement's intention had been to remain neutral, but he soon found himself entrapped between the wiles of Philip V and those of Emperor Archduke Charles: both of whom claimed to be receiving the Pope's support.[6]

As a result of these contrary claims, Clement's voice and that of his nuncio were ignored during the negotiations that were then underway for the Peace of Utrecht. As a direct consequence of their mute voice, Rome lost Sicily to Victor Amadeus II of Savoy, who then excluded the Pope from exercising control over the Church in Sicily. Clement's response was to issue an interdict, but this caused the banishment from the island of all priests loyal to the Holy See.

And Rome will be wounded by the Albanian (Albani)

Clement XI (Giovanni Francesco Albani) was descended from an Albanian family that had moved to northern Italy in the fifteenth century. But, despite the good report one reads from his biography, one issue stands out as probably the most disastrous to Rome ever made by a pontiff.

In the 16th and 17th centuries, great advances had been made by missionaries sent from Rome to China for the conversion of the country to the Christian faith. And in 1692, the Emperor, Kangxi issued an edict for the toleration of Christianity.

> The Europeans are very quiet; they do not excite any disturbances in the provinces, they do no harm to anyone, they commit no crimes, and their doctrine has nothing in common with that of the false sects in the empire, nor has it any tendency to excite sedition. [...] We decide therefore that all temples dedicated to the Lord of heaven, in whatever place they may be found, ought to be preserved, and that it may be permitted to all who wish to worship this God to enter these temples, offer him incense, and perform the ceremonies practised according to ancient custom by the Christians. Therefore let no one henceforth offer them any opposition.[7]

Conversion had been achieved by the Society of Jesus having united Chinese Confucianism with Christian teaching. But when other religious orders arrived in China and discovered that the people had not discarded their ancestral customs, they protested to Rome. When Clement XI became Pope in 1700, he listened to these protests, and began the task of imposing his high-minded attitude upon the Chinese people, with his anti-rites decree *Cum Deus optimus* (20 November 1704). Thereafter the situation in China slowly began to deteriorate. Until in March

1715, Clement XI issued a Papal bull, *Ex Illa Die,* which officially condemned Chinese ancestry rites—and with his declaration, the promotion of Christianity in China came to an abrupt end. [8] When the Emperor learned of the Papal bull, he issued his own decree. All missionaries were to be banished; churches destroyed and converts ordered to renounce their faith. Only Europeans useful to the welfare of the Chinese people were permitted to remain in the country. The wound done to Rome through the loss of China has ever since remained unhealed, although in 1939, Pope Pius XII attempted to lessen the damage inflicted by Clement XI's rashness, by relaxing the tone of his condemnation.

Summary: *This is another prophecy for the Vatican to digest. It provides a further example of a Pope that has been named in a publication 94 years before he was born. Only God has that knowledge. Clement XI's reign was noted for the contention that existed in the conclave before it was resolved by his election. His twenty-one years in office also brought with it a plethora of demands from across Europe, in what the Catholic Encyclopedia says was caused by "the age of selfishness and infidelity." The final line of the oracle adds to the detail that has gone before. By inserting the identity of the Pope in a manner that befits no other pope, and naming him from the land of his ancestry, the oracle connects with the condemnation he imposed upon Chinese culture, which so wounded the conversion process of that country.*

47   *Le grand Arabe marchera bien auant,*
          Trahy sera par les Bisantinois:
          L'antique Rodes luy viendra au deuant,
          Et plus grand mal par austre Pannonois.

48   *Apres la grande affliction du sceptre,*
          Deux ennemis par eulx seront deffaictz:
          Classe d'Affrique aux Pannons viendra naistre,
          Par mer & terre feront horrible faictz.

49   *Nul de l'Espagne mais de l'antique France,*
          Ne sera esleu pour le tremblant nacelle:
          A l'ennemy fera faicte fiance,
          Qui dans son regne sera peste cruelle.

50   *L'an que les frères du lys seront en aage,*
          L'vn d'eulx tiendra la grande Romanie:
          Trembler les monts ouuert Latin passaige,
          Pache marcher contre fort d'Armenie.

51   *La gent de Dace, d'Angleterre & Palonne,*
          Et de Bohesme feront nouuelle ligue:
          Pour passer oultre d'Hercules la colonne,
          Barcins, Tyrrens dresser cruelle brigue.

52   *Vn Roy sera qui donra l'opposite,*
          Les exilez esleuez sur le regne:
          De sang nager la gent caste hyppolite,
          Et florira long temps soubs telle enseigne

53   *La loy du Sol, & Venus contendens,*
          Appropriant l'esprit de prophetie.
          Ne l'un ne l'autre ne seront entendens,
          Par Sol tiendra la loy de grand Messie.

          The law of the Sun, and Venus at variance,
          Appropriating the spirit of prophecy.
          Neither the one nor the other: they will not be understood,
          By reason of the Sun, he will maintain the law of the great Messiah.

The law of the Sun and Venus is the law of gravity. If gravity is at variance with expectation, it explains the second line. The gospels foretell the end of the world will be preceded by the power of the heavens being shaken. Human nature will then turn to biblical prophecies and doubtless to these oracles also. The third line appears to be saying that even in this late age, neither gravity nor prophecy has yet been understood by science. The final line suggests that a world leader of that age will maintain order, by reason of the Sun's predicted, gravitational change: using it as a reminder of what the great Messiah foretold would happen..

54   *Du pont Euxine, & la grand Tartarie,*
Vn roy sera qui viendra voir la Gaule:
Transpercera Alane & l'Armenie,
Et dans Bisance lairra sanglante gaule.

55   *De la felice Arabie contrade,*
Naistra puissant de loy Mahometique:
Vexer l'Espaigne conquester la Grenade,
Et plus par mer à la gent lygustique.

56   *Par le trespass du tresuieillart pontife,*
Sera esleu Romain de bon aage:
Qu'il sera dict que le Siege debiffe,
Et long tiendra & de picquant ouuraige.

viellart (OF) a very aged man; debiffe (OF debiffé) torn in pieces;

Through the decease of the very aged pontiff (**GREGORY XVI**)   1846
A Roman will be elected of favourable age (**PIUS IX**):
When it will be said that the Seat is torn in pieces,
Also, long will he hold, and with nettling work.

Through the decease of the very aged pontiff
This first line is very general; it could apply to many Roman pontiffs. But as the clues unfold, one is left in no doubt that the oracle is directing its opening words at one 'very aged pontiff' in particular, Gregory XVI. He was born in September 1765 and died 1 June 1846, aged eighty. [1]

A Roman will be elected of favourable age
The pope elected to succeed him was Pius IX (Giovanni Maria Mastai-Ferretti) who, at fifty-four, was of a favourable age. Had the Austrian veto arrived earlier, a different pope would have been elected, and this prophecy would likely have failed its fulfilment.

The conclave that followed Pope Gregory's death was held in troubled times, and it commenced with only 46 of the available 62 cardinals present. As had happened in previous elections, there was deadlock between the two front runners. Mastai-Ferretti's election removed the block, but the result came at nightfall and was not immediately announced. [...] When the Austrian government was informed next morning, it instantly rejected the appointment, but its official 'Right of Exclusion' arrived too late. [2]

When it will be said that the Seat is torn in pieces
In 1848, Pius IX became caught up in the revolutions sweeping across many parts of Europe. The popular outcry was for liberal reform, especially in the Papal States, where repression was at its severest.

Riot followed riot, the pope was denounced as a traitor to his country, his Prime Minister Rossi was stabbed to death while ascending the steps of the Cancelleria, whither he had gone to open the parliament, and on the following day the pope himself was besieged in the Quirinal. Palma, a papal prelate, who was standing at a window, was shot, and the pope was forced to promise a democratic ministry. With the assistance of the Bavarian ambassador, Count Spaur, and the French ambassador, Duc d'Harcourt, Pius IX escaped from the Quirinal in disguise, 24 November, and fled to Gaëta where he was joined by many of the cardinals. Meanwhile Rome was ruled by traitors and adventurers who abolished the temporal power of the pope, 9 February 1849, and under the name of a democratic republic terrorized the people and committed untold outrages. [3]

Pius IX became the last pope to rule as a Sovereign of the Papal States. These were transferred to the Italian nationalists in 1870, and afterwards, incorporated into the Kingdom of Italy.

Also, long will he hold
Appeals for assistance by the Pope were made to France, Austria, Spain and Naples. And on 29

June, French troops, acting under General Oudinot, restored order in the papal territories. But Pius IX was only able to return to his Seat at the Vatican with French and Austrian troops on permanent guard. He was therefore apt to regard himself as 'The Prisoner of the Vatican'.

Pope Pius died on 7 February 1878 from a heart attack brought on by epilepsy. After 32 years in office, he had become the longest serving pope in the history of the papacy: [4] longer than that of Leo XIII (1878-1903) and John Paul II (1978-2005). Hence, the opening line of this oracle, which particularly refers to a 'very aged pope'.

And with nettling work

Pius had begun his term of office with liberal views. But bitter experience subsequently forced upon him to adopt a different realism; to wit, that giving way to liberal thought only serves to lower standards of public behaviour and morality, and this will ultimately undermine the foundations of the very system that allowed it—lessons that present-day western leaders have failed to learn, and have still to come to terms with.

In response to this realization, Pius became the implacable enemy of political reform. Moreover, his irritation became infused within the content of his allocutions published in 1850, 1852, 1853 and 1855, in which he made known the numerous injustices committed against the Church. His "liberal stance was now discarded, and [...] he set up a paternalistic regime in the Papal States which alienated the educated and frowned on national aspirations." But this led to a division between Church and State. And so, in a desperate attempt to consolidate Catholic thought, "he published (8 Dec. 1864) the encyclical Quanta cura, with the 'Syllabus of Errors' attached, which denounced 'the principal errors of our times.'"

N.B. Pius IX also introduced the dogma of Papal Infallibility, and made known the Church's teaching regarding Mary's Immaculate Conception. [5]

Summary: *Here we have yet another oracle directed at the history of the Vatican. This time it involves Pius IX. It was his misfortune to reign at a time when Italy was violently intent upon political reform. In the frenzied outburst that occurred, Pius was forced to flee to Gaëta for his personal safety. While he was absent, the papal throne in Rome remained under the control of political nationalists. While this dramatic event clearly identifies Pius IX, who suffered under it, there are also additional facts that serve to confirm his part in the fulfilment of this prophecy; to wit, the longevity of his reign, the age of his predecessor, and the 38 encyclicals that he published. Many were not written with the intention of explaining matters of faith, but rather to sting those guilty of committing errors into a realization of their offence.*

57   *Istra du mont Gaulfier & Auentin,*
Qui par le trou aduertira l'armee:
Entre deux rocz fera prins le butin,
De Sext. mansol faillir la renommee.

Istra (AF istre –hors de) outside of; mont Gaulfier (*dissimulation*, mont G[o]lfier) Montgolfier; Aventine (anag. + parag.) VI entent (AF) seize suddenly; advertira (OF) give intelligence unto; roc (*synonym* pierre) rock, Peter, i,e,pope; Sext. (L. *abbreviation* – Sext\us) the sixth; mansol (AF mansor - qui sert de residence) & (L *portmanteau*, man+sol – i.e. man\eo +sol\us) endure alone.

Outside of **MONTGOLFIER** and Aventine (**VI SEIZED SUDDENLY**)   1794
That which by the orifice, one will give intelligence to the army:
Between two popes (**PIUS VI & PIUS VII**) the booty will be taken,
For the Sixth (**PIUS VI**), he endures alone, failing his renown.

Outside of Montgolfier

The name *Montgolfier* is easily recognizable as the surname of two brothers: Joseph Michel and Jacques Etienne. Both men were co-inventors of the hot air balloon, for which the first publicly demonstrated flight took place in Paris as early as 1783. [1] The Seer looks beyond the inventors (*outside* of them) to predict its military potential.

And Aventine (VI seized suddenly)

Aventine is one of the Seven Hills of Rome, and the location of the Vatican. Pope Pius VI vacated the Aventine in 1798, when France invaded Rome and the pontiff was taken captive. Incidentally, of the Seven Hills of Rome *Aventine* is the one that describes the Pope's situation.

When the letters are rearranged as a paragram, with 't' replacing 'A', the result can be written as 'VI entent'—in Modern French, *VI attaqué*. This translates as 'the Sixth seized suddenly'.

His captives being uncertain what to do with Pius, other than remove him from the attention his presence inside the Vatican was attracting, caused the Directory to send the Holy Father through Italy and into France on an extended journey lasting eighteen months. The Pope's travels took him through Siena, Florence, Parma, Piacenza, Turin, Briancon, Grenoble, and finally to Valence, where he died under extreme duress *outside* Rome.

That which by the orifice, one will give intelligence to the army

BATTLE OF FLEURUS

Ten years after the Montgolfier brothers' discovery of the hot air balloon, its military potential for aerial observation purposes was investigated. It was first tried at Maubeuge in 1794 at the battle of Fleurus.

"A French reconnaissance balloon, *l'Entreprenant*, continuously informed the General of Division, Jean-Baptiste Jourdan, about Austrian movements." [3]

The orifice is, of course, the inlet for the hot air required to raise the balloon off the ground.

Between two popes

The two popes referred to in the oracle are Pius VI and Pius VII. Pius VI died in August 1799, but it was not until March 1800 that his successor, Pius VII was elected.

The booty will be taken

During the half year interval *between* these *two popes*, both Rome and the Vatican were plundered of their treasures; that is, *the booty was taken*.

Palaces, galleries and churches were stripped; antique sculptures, Renaissance paintings, tapestries, and precious stones and metals were packed up and lo aded on to wagons. [...] On one day gold and silver bars worth 15 000 000 scudi were carried off; on another 386 diamonds, 333 emeralds, 692 rubies, 208 sapphires and numerous other precious stones and pearls, many of them prized off papal tiaras, were sent to Paris. [4]

For the Sixth (Pius VI), he endures alone

After Rome was invaded in 1798, Pope Pius (the *Sixth* to choose that regnal title) was separated from the Vatican and its officers, and sent on an eighteen-month coach journey – which served him as a temporary residence, as he travelled under guard between towns. All the while, the Directory in Paris remained undecided upon what next to do with him.

Failing his renown

Pius VI was elected Pope on 15 February 1775. By 1798, he had also become *renowned* in the Christian world as the longest serving pope since the commence ment of the papacy, having then reigned for 23 years. But *his renown failed* to extend beyond another year. [5] On 29 August 1799, inside the citadel at Valence, his frail health finally gave way, and he died aged 82. His record for the longevity of his reign was later surpassed by Pius IX, Leo XIII and John Paul II.

Summary: *The outstanding feature of this oracle is the less than subtle naming of Montgolfier ('au' and 'o' are audibly indistinguishable in the French tongue). Another 'Mont', this time Aventine, which accompanies the inventors of the hot air balloon, directs attention to the Vatican. At this time, Pius VI was the reigning Pope, and the number of his regnal title is given in the oracle, together with his approaching death: he having been the longest serving pontiff up until then. The military function of th e hot air balloon is clearly predicted. But less obvious is the 'booty' between two 'rocks', until one realizes that the 'rocks' are biblical synonyms for Peters, who are the popes that came after the apostle Peter. Thus between Pius VI and Pius VII there was a gap of six full months: during which, Rome and the Vatican's treasure was plundered.*

58   *De l'archeduc d'Vticense, Gardoing,*
        Par la forest & mont inaccessible:
        Emmy du pont fera tasché au poing,
        Le chef Nemans qui tant sera terrible.

59   *Au chef Anglois à Nymes trop seiour,*
        Deuers l'Espaigne au secours Aenobarbe:
        Plusieurs morront par Mars ouuerte ce iour,
        Quant en Artoys faillir estoille en barbe.

60   *Par test rase viendra bien mal eslire,*
        Plus que sa charge ne porte passera:
        Si grand fureur & raige fera dire,
        Qu'a feu & sang tout sexe trenchera.

eslire (OF) choose; passer (OF) s'acquitter; trencher (OF thwite) to whittle away. Cross-reference: teste rase, C.I: 88; C.VII: 13

> Through the crop head (**NAPOLEON**), he will come to choose much evil,   1795
> Not bearing more than his burden, he will acquit himself:
> He will express such great fury and rage
> That in fire and blood he will whittle away an entire sex.

Through the crop head

Napoleon Bonaparte has previously been identified as 'Le Tondu' [1] *the crop head*, as he became known to his soldiery. In an age that flaunted elaborate hairstyles, the Emperor of the French chose instead to wear his hair close cut.

He will come to choose much evil

Napoleon rose to the forefront of his military and political career in 1795, when he successfully put down a group of Parisians who were rioting against "the new 'Constitution of the Year III' which placed power in the hands of an executive Directory of Seven and further prolonged the life of the notorious Convention." [2] The crowd was suppressed when Napoleon placed his guns in the streets leading to the Tuileries, and under his command, "several salvoes of grapeshot tore into the crowd at point-blank range, killing at least 200 and probably wounding twice as many more. The crowd stunned by this ruthless action, hesitated, turned and fled." [3] As a reward for his action, Bonaparte was made Commander in Chief, with a responsibility for law and order across France.

This atrocity was the first step to an era in history that became known as 'Napoleonic'. His name soon became synonymous with this age after achieving a string of victories during the First Italian Campaign. It ended abruptly with his defeat at Waterloo in 1815, and subsequent exile.

In Century One N°. 15, the oracle predicted that this period would result in 70 battles. The cost of this in lives lost has been estimated at one and three-quarter million: a great evil.

Incidents of great evil can never be eliminated from warfare. But if we exclude the arrest of Pope Pius VII, and concentrate only upon those committed under military rule, it commences with Bonaparte's First Italian Campaign, in which he ordered the burning of Binasco, the shooting of its men folk, together with the freedom he gave his men in Pavia, to loot, rape and destroy at leisure (Century Three N°. 37).

In Egypt, it will be recalled that he reneged on an agreement to spare the lives of 3000 men who had agreed to surrender, by afterwards ordering their execution, and then adding a further 1400 to their number (Century One N°. 60). And, while in Egypt, he ordered the mercy killing of his sick and wounded at Acre, so they would not delay his return to France (Century Three N°. 75).

His retreat from Russia revealed this same inhuman streak, when he ruthlessly ordered the bridges over the river Berezina to be burnt, after first ensuring the main strength of his army had reached safety. The result was that it "left behind some thousands of unarmed or wounded men, with many women and children who had followed the army from Moscow, to perish on the bridges or breaking ice. [...] Perhaps 10,000 never came back alive." [4]

Not bearing more than his burden, he will acquit himself

Napoleon was also a liar. Sometimes his falsehoods were deliberate misrepresentations, and sometimes they were acts of self-deception, but they were always designed *to lessen his burden*. Even when he had given written instructions for an action to take place, he was quite capable of *acquitting himself* from any involvement, particularly if the consequences turned out to be unpopular. In which case, blame for failure would be explained away as the fault of his underlings. [5]

He will express such great fury and rage

Bonaparte's fits of *rage* also need to be considered when assessing his character. These were moments when the Emperor lost his composure and gave way to 'hystero-epileptic attacks'. These episodes have been well documented. At times he would use his riding whip to thrash unfortunate servants, and even officers if they angered him. On one occasion, while in a fit of rage, he hammered Marshal Berthier's head against a stone wall. On another occasion he kicked a minister of State in the stomach. [6]

That in fire and blood he will whittle away an entire sex

The final line of this oracle acknowledges *the fire and blood* accompanying the numerous battles and conflicts fought during the Napoleonic Era. War on the scale fought by France required a continuous supply of men to serve in the field. It has been estimated that between March 1804 and April 1815, that is, after his *election* as Emperor, as many as 'two million native-born Frenchmen saw active service in his successive armies'.

There were also 'no less than thirty-two levies on the various classes over the same period'. [7] Yet still this failed to take account of the millions more pressed into service from other countries. Without the least shadow of doubt, the Napoleonic wars gave rise to the largest armies the world had ever seen. And to accomplish it, *he whittled away an entire sex*.

Summary: *This oracle provides another pen portrait of Napoleon I's character. It serves to remind us that outside of our perception of space and time, there exists a timeless region in which everyone's character has already been woven into the timeless fabric of that tapestry we call a block universe. Yet, at the same time, our ability to will the outcome of events under our control is ever present. The union between freewill and determinism can only be resolved by the union between time and eternity, when understood as a dual aspect overseen by an omniscient Creator. Bonaparte's freely chosen preferences, foreseen by God, were therefore made part of the tapestry of the temporal world. Two centuries before then, the seer of Salon was privileged to record them for posterity. This was so that one day, people in the world would come to understand this same dual aspect also applies to their lives, however seemingly insignificant they may appear by comparison.*

61   *L'enfant du grand n'estant à sa naissance,*
        Subiuguera les haultz monts Appenis:
        Fera trembler tous ceulx de la balance,
        Et des monts feux iusques à mont Senis.

62   *Sur les rochers sang on verra plouuoir,*
        Sol Orient, Saturne Occidental:
        Pres Orgon guerre, à Rome grand mal voir,
        Nefz parfondrees & prins le Tridental.

63   *De vaine emprise l'honneur indue plaincte,*
        Gallotz errants par Latins froid, faim, vagues:
        Non loing du Tymbre de sang terre taincte,
        Et sur humains seront diuerses plagues.

64   *Les assemblés par repos du grand nombre,*
        Par terre & mer conseil contremandé:
        Pres de l'Automne, Gennes, Nice de l'ombre,
        Par champs & villes chef contrebandé.

65   *Subit venu l'effrayeur sera grande,*
        Des principaulx de l'affaire cachés:
        Et dame en braise plus ne sera en veue,
        De peu à peu feront les grans saschés.

66   Soubz les antiques edifices vestaulx,
      Non esloignez d'aqueduct ruyné:
      De Sol & Luna sont les luisans metaulx.
      Ardante lampe Traian d'or buriné.

67   Quant chef Perouse n'osera sa tunique,
      Sens au couuert tout nud s'expolier:
      Seront prins sept faict Aristocatique,
      Le pere & fils mors par poincte au colier.

68   Dans le Danube & du Rin viendra boire,
      Le grand Chameau ne s'en repentira:
      Trembler du Rosne & plus fort ceux de Loire:
      Et pres des Alpes coq le ruynera.

69   Plus ne sera le grand en faulx sommeil,
      L'inquietude viendra prendra repoz:
      Dresser phalange d'or, azur, & vermeil,
      Subiuguer Affrique la ronger iusques aux oz.

70   Des regions subiectes à la Balance,
      Feront troubler les monts par grande guerre:
      Captif tout sexe deu & toute Bisance,
      Qu'on criera à l'aube terre à terre.

71   Par la fureur d'vn qui attendra l'eaue,
      Par sa grand raige tout l'exercite esmeu:
      Chargé des nobles à dixsept basteulx,
      Au long du Rosne tard messagier venu.

72   Pour le plaisir d'Edict voluptueux,
      On meslera la poison dans l'aloy:
      Venus sera en cours si vertueux.
      Qu'obfusquera du Soleil tout aloy.

73   Persecutee sera de Dieu l'eglise,
      Et les sainctz temples seront expoliez:
      L'enfant la mere mettra nud en chemise,
      Seront Arabes aux Polons raliez.

74   De sang Troyé naistra cœur Germanique,
      Qu'il deuiendra en si haulte puissance:
      Hors chassera gent estrange Arabique,
      Tournant l'eglise en pristine preeminence.

75   Montera hault sur le bien plus à dextre,
      Demourra assis sur la pierre quarree:
      Vers le midy posé à la fenestre,
      Baston tortu en main, bouche ferree.

76   En lieu libere tendra son pauillon,
      Et ne voldra en cités prendre place:
      Aix, Carpen l'Isle Volce, mont Cauaillon,
      Par tous les lieux abolira la trasse.

77   Tous les degrés d'honneur ecclesiastique,
      Seront changez en dial quirinal:
      En Martial quirinal flaminique,
      Vn roy de France le rendre vulcanal.

dial (OF - diale) devil; in Latin, Diale is either the god Jupiter, or the priest of Jupiter; quirinal (L) belonging to the deified Romulus; Martial (L. – Martialis) a priest of Mars, god of war; flaminique (L - flaminica) the wife of a flamen—priest of one particular deity; alternatively, 'flaminium', the office or dignity of a flamen; or possibly, 'flaminia' the dwelling of the flamen Dialis. ["Festus enumerates from the highest flamen, that of Jupiter, to the lowest, that of Pomona, fifteen of these priests; in the times of the emperors, the deified emperors and other deified persons also had their separate flamens assigned to them:" (Lewis & Short). vulcanal (L. – vulcanis) of or belonging to the fire-god, Vulcan, the son of Jupiter and Juno.

      All the ranks of Ecclesiastical honour
      Will be changed by the priest serving the deified Romulus:
      As a priest of Mars in that office, belonging to a god,
      A king of France rendering him volcanic.

After sixteen prophecies that appear to refer to the years ahead – although it is very possible that some among these sixteen have already been fulfilled, but bypassed through a lack of awareness concerning the historical event(s) they predicted, this present prophecy seems to foretell the reign of the biblical Antichrist. The Seer is exemplary for choosing his words carefully, and in this case, the key words are implied by the Latin language: e.g. Jupiter, the god over all; Romulus, associated with Rome; Mars with its connexion to wars, conflicts and battles.

> 78   *Les deux vnys ne tiendront longuement,*
> *Et dans treze ans au Barbare strappe:*
> *Aus deux costés feront tel perdement:*
> *Qu'on benira la barque & sa cappe.*

> 79   *La sacree pompe viendra baisser les œsles,*
> *Par la venue du grand legislateur:*
> *Humble haulsera vexera les rebelles,*
> *Naistra sur terre aucun œmulateur.*

æsles (OF) wings; venue (OF venuë) arrival; æmulateur (OF emulateur) emulator, imitator

The sacred pomp will proceed to let fall its wings,   1800
Through the arrival of the great legislator (**NAPOLEON**):
He will raise the humble; he will vex the rebellious,
Not one emulator will be born on earth.

The sacred pomp will proceed to let fall its wings

Pius VII entered Rome as the newly elected Pope on 3 July 1800, and was immediately confronted by a proposed draft of a Concordat. This contained Napoleon's preferred ideas concerning the relationship which he thought should exist between Church and State.

The document demanded from the Pope that all French bishops be directed to give up their sees; the number of dioceses be reduced, and the Papacy must cease to claim back the booty taken from the Vatican following Pius VI's arrest (refer N°. 57 above). The State would then accept responsibility for paying the clergy their wages.

Negotiations took a year, during which 'ten successive drafts' were argued over before the Pope eventually signed the agreement (15 July 1801). But in April of the following year, Napoleon withdrew the concessions, which he had used as an inducement to persuade Pius to accept his proposals. In their place, he issued a set of Organic Articles; these tightened the State's control over the Church, and restricted papal intervention in France. [1]

Further humiliation followed in 1804, when the Pope was persuaded to attend the Emperor's coronation in his official capacity as the Church's spiritual leader. At the critical moment in the ceremony, Napoleon snatched the crown from Pius's hands, and placed it on his own head: repeating this for the crowning of the Empress Joséphine.

Thus, the Catholic Church with its centuries-old traditions and high-flying *sacred pomp* had been publicly shown to have *let fall its wings*.

Through the arrival of the great legislator

That Bonaparte was *the great legislator* referred to in this oracle is further advanced by his part in framing the Code Civil—often presiding over the council as it debated the future course of French law. His work led to the Civil Code being produced in 1804, and, two years later, to the Code of Civil Procedure. From 1807 onwards, these Codes became known as 'Code Napoléon' and they still form the basis of much that comprises French law. [2]

He will raise the humble

This part of the prophecy became fulfilled when Napoleon *raised* men born in the most *humble* of circumstances to the peerage. Pierre Augereau, the son of a stonemason became duke of Castiglione; André Masséna, an orphan and former cabin boy, became prince of Rivoli; Joachim Murat, the son of an innkeeper became king of Naples; Michel Ney, the son of a blacksmith became prince of Moscowa; Jean de Bernadotte, a private soldier, became king of Sweden; Louis-Alexandre Berthier, an engineer, became prince of Wagram; Jean-Baptiste Bessières, a cavalry trooper, became duke of Istria; Armand-Augustin-Louis Caulaincourt, another cavalry trooper, became duke of Vicenza &c. [3]

He will vex the rebellious

Ever since the beginning of the Revolution, rebel forces had been operating inside France, particularly in both the west of the country and in the southern parts. These small bands of rebels were mostly composed of monarchist sympathizers and were often backed by recalcitrant priests. On 28 December 1800, Napoleon issued a proclamation that was intended to bring to an end all rebellious dissent. In the document, he drew attention to original grievances that had since been redressed, and offered a pardon to those who agreed to end their struggle. In the same breath, he threatened punishment for all those who continued to rebel. Within weeks, a full scale mopping-up operation had begun, which included his threat to execute any "villagers carrying arms or preaching rebellion." In the south, the rebels were dealt with by reorganizing the gendarmerie into brigades a hundred strong. They were then ordered to clear the region of its rebels and brigands. [4]

Not one emulator will be born on earth

No other career seems to embody quite so strikingly the dynamism of what Oswald Spengler was later to call 'Faustian man' – tireless in his activity, at once intelligent and unscrupulous in his choice of means, ruthless in his egoistic will to power.[5]

He forgot that a man cannot be God. [6]

Summary: *The clash between Pope Pius VII and Napoleon Bonaparte is confirmed by Pius's first contact with the 'great legislator', and his subsequent treatment at his coronation in Notre Dame Cathedral: which, together, resulted in the humbling of the papacy. Moreover, the titles of the nobility given by Napoleon to men who were born in lowly circumstances, stands out as unique in modern history. Finally, while the last line must await the still distant future, it seems very unlikely that Napoleon will ever be emulated by another.*

80   *Logmion grand Bisance approuchera,*
       Chassé sera la barbarique ligne:
       Des deux loix l'vne estinique lechera,
       Barbare & franche en perpetuelle brigue.

Logmion (L'Ogmion?); ligne (ligue?)

81   *Le oiseau royal sur la cité solaire,*
       Sept moys deuant fera nocturne augure:
       Mur d'Orient cherra tonnaire, esclaire,
       Sept iours aux portes les ennemis à l'heure.

82   *Au conclud pache hors de la forteresse,*
       Ne sortira celuy en desespoir mys:
       Quant ceux d'Albois, de Langres, contre Bresse,
       Auront monts Dolle bouscade d'ennemis.

conclud (OF – conclu) determined, resolved; pache (OF) agreement, capitulation; contre (OF) towards; bouscade (OF *apheresis*, i.e. [em]bouscade) ambuscade, to waylay;

At the agreement, determined outside of the fortress: 1678
The one placed in despondency (**LEOPOLD 1**) will not depart,
Notwithstanding those of Arbois, of Langres: towards Bresse
They will possess the mountains; Dôle waylaid by enemies.

At the agreement, determined outside of the fortress

The agreement referred to in the oracle refers to the Treaty signed in Nijmegen by the Netherlands on 10 August 1678, and by Spain nine days later. This ended the Franco-Dutch War and gave Louis XIV legal control over the region of the Franche-Comté in eastern France. The French victory had come after the besieged fortress at Ypres (in Flanders) fell. Louis XIV's army had first taken Ghent on 12 March, and then moved on to take Ypres two weeks later.

Ypres had been fortified since the middle ages and the fortifications had recently been strengthened in anticipation of a French attack. These included a number of demi-lunes and a strong pentagonal citadel, which had been built recently in anticipation of a French attack. [1]

On 25 March, the garrison defending Ypres was forced to capitulate, having learned that the French had found a way into the fortress, thereby rendering their position hopeless. "Peace talks began the following month, resulting in the signing of the Treaty of Nijmegen in August." [2]

The one placed in despondency will not depart

The Holy Roman Emperor, Leopold I, had at first sought to restrict Louis XIV's territorial ambitions, but in the process he suffered several military defeats. "The Emperor was accused of a wavering attitude and lack of initiative, and these character traits were indeed partly responsible for the failure of his policies." [3] To add to this indictment, Leopold had further reason to feel despondent. His first alliance, aimed at defending the United Provinces, had collapsed and his second alliance with Spain, Netherlands and Lorraine, had also failed with the recent fall of Ypres. Despite this, he refused to abandon his opposition to the Sun King. And it was not until the following year that "The Holy Roman emperor Leopold I finally accepted French terms on Feb. 5, 1679, keeping Phillipsburg but giving up Freiburg im Breisgau to France and granting free access through his territory to it from Breisach (French since 1648)." [4]

Notwithstanding those of Arbois, of Langres

These two named cities are situated in the region known as Franche-Comté, which Louis XIV legally acquired by the Treaty of Nijmegen. *Those of,* which is again employed in this prophecy, refers not to the resident population, but to those occupying it: which was the French. In fact, France had earlier invaded this region and taken it by force, when it "was captured by France in 1668 but returned under the Treaty of Aix-La-Chapelle. It was conquered a second time in 1674, and was finally ceded to France in the Treaty of Nijmegen (1678)." [5]

In the same year, Louis XIV ordered that the castle in *Arbois,* which was built in 1270, be razed to the ground. Some of its foundations still survive as a tourist attraction. [6]

As for *Langres,*

> The occupation of the Lorraine (1670-1698) and the integration of the Franche-Comté (1678) brought a lasting peace, but tolled the knell of the Langroise fortified town. The creation of the Dijon's diocese in 1731 at the expense of Langres, contributed to the decline of the city which saw its population stagnate. [7]

Towards Bresse, they will possess the mountains

> Bresse extends from the Dombes on the south to the Doubes River on the north, and from the Saône eastwards to the Jura Mountains, measuring some 60 miles in the former, and 20 miles in the latter direction. [8]

Bresse and Jura are both in the Franche-Comté, which was acquired by Louis XIV in 1668. The Jura Mountains form a chain of defence against invasion.

Dôle waylaid by enemies

"Dole was the capital of Franche-Comté until Louis XIV conquered the region; he shifted the *parlement* from Dole to Besabçon." [9] Voltaire described Louis XIV's capture of Dôle – which afterwards led to the entire capitulation of Franche-Comté – as follows.

> In person, he next laid siege to Dôle, a place reputed very strong, in which the count of Montrevel commanded; a man of distinguished valour. [...] His garrison consisted of no more than four hundred soldiers and the inhabitants of the place, and yet he bravely resolved to defend it. The trenches were not carried on in form; for no sooner were they opened than a crowd of young volunteers, who had followed the king, flew to attack the counterscarp, on which they made a lodgement. [10]

Greatly outnumbered by the French, the siege at Dôle lasted only four days. Louis XIV was therefore able to profess that "in less than three weeks the whole province of Franche-Comté was reduced." (Ibid)

Summary: *This oracle focuses upon an important event in French history, which became fulfilled during the reign of*
Louis XIV. The signing of the Peace of Nijmegen, following the fall of the fortress at Ypres, gave the Sun
King control of the Franche-Comté. The places named in the prophecy, and which, in their own way,
formed part of the history relating to Louis' conquest of this region, therefore provide the oracle with a more
detailed account of the events accompanying his victory. The details also confirm the comprehensive nature of
the seer's foreknowledge.

83   *Ceulx qui auront entreprins subuertir,*
       Nompareil regne puissant & inuincible:
       Feront par fraude, nuictz trois aduertir,
       Quand le plus grand à rable lira Bible.

84   *Naistra du gouffre & cité immesuree,*
       Nay de parens obscurs & tenebreux:
       Qui la puissance du grand Roy reueree,
       Vouldra destruire par Rouan & Eureux.

85   *Par les Sueues & lieux circonuoisins,*
       Seront en guerre pour cause des nuees:
       Camp marins locusts & confins,
       Du Leman faultes seront bien desnuees.

Sueues (L – Suev\i) People of N.E. Germany; pour (OF) because; Camp (AF - pays plat) flat country; nuee (OF) cloud; locuste
(L. & *epenthesis* locus[t]es) locations; confin (OF) adjoining; Leman (L. – Leman\nus lacus) Geneva. Cross-refer'ces: camp,

Through the people of Germany and circumjacent places,   1940
They will be at war, for a cause out of the clouds:
Flat country, marine locations, and near neighbours,
At Geneva, the faults will be very bare.

N.B. Du Rosne, who published the original version of this prophecy in 1557, printed *Camp* and *confins*, as given above. Rigaud,
who published a copy in 1568, printed cousins instead of confins (an inverted 'n' with 's' for 'f').

Through the people of Germany and circumjacent places

The Sueves were a Germanic people who occupied the land to the east of Hamburg, and whose
central tribe was situated in what is now Brandenburg: a region lying to the west of Berlin. [1]
The circumjacent places are therefore identified as the countries that surround the German
heartland, namely: Austria, Poland, Czechoslovakia, France, England, Belgium, Netherlands,
Denmark and Norway.

They will be at war, for a cause out of the clouds

Between 1939 and 1945, it was precisely these countries adjoining Germany that had cause to be
at war with their militant neighbour. The action began, as predicted, from the clouds.

> There were, of course numerous hazards inherent in airborne operations, but until now the
> Germans had known only successes. Their use of paratroopers in Norway, Belgium and Holland
> during 1940 had brought striking results. [...] The Luftwaffe's airborne supremo was Kurt Student,
> a World War I fighter pilot and squadron leader. He had keenly studied the potential of airborne
> techniques in Russia. [...] Not only did he have troops leaping from flying aircraft but also
> equipment-bearing soldiers carried in gliders, and 'air mobile' forces, men trained in the art of
> going into action straight from the door of a landed plane. [2]

On 10 May 1940, the German air force bombed "Dutch and Belgian airfields while airborne troops
landed ahead of ground forces." During the next four days "Airborne troops attacked The Hague and
secured bridges near Rotterdam." At the same time, "glider-borne troops captured the Fort of Eban
Emael and bridges over the Albert Canal." But most importantly, it was *from the clouds* that the first
ever parachute battalion invaded another country. On 9 April 1940, German parachutists
captured the airfields at Oslo and Stavanger during Hitler's invasion of Norway. [3]

Flat country

After having predicted the means by which this new type of warfare would be waged; that is from
the clouds, the Seer lists three areas that would be among the first to be caught up in the war.

The *flat country*, known also as the lowlands of Belgium and Holland, became Germany's first target in its plan of conquest. Hitler's armed forces were able to cross into the Low Countries by circumventing France's Maginot Line: a fortified stretch of armed sections that extended along the French bank of the Rhine, but which stopped at the Belgian frontier.

> The invasion of Belgium and Holland on 10 May 1940 opened seven weeks of 'lightning war' (Blitzkrieg) in which penetration by German tank columns ('panzers') and use of air power encompassed the fall of the Netherlands and Belgium by the end of May, and of France by 22 June. [4]

Marine locations

On 13 October 1939 a German submarine penetrated the defences at Scapa Flow in the Orkneys and sank HMS Royal Oak with the loss of 833 lives. On 13 December the battle of the River Plate took place at Uruguay. On 16 March 1940 it was the Luftwaffe's turn to bomb the naval base at Scapa Flow. On 5 April, the RAF retaliated with a strike at German shipping in the Kiel Canal. On the 10th and 13th of April, two naval battles were fought at Narvik in Norway between the Royal Navy and the Kriegsmarine.

On the Continent, the soldiers of the British Expeditionary Force, which had been sent to assist France, were forced to retreat: "driven back through Belgium and north-western France, forcing their eventual evacuation from several ports along the French northern coastline. [...] The most notable evacuation was from the Dunkirk region." [5] Other coastal towns involved in the fighting of 1940 took place at Boulogne (battle of Boulogne) and at Calais (siege of Calais). Much farther along the coast, Cherbourg, Le Havre and St Nazaire were also involved in transporting troops back to Britain: mostly, against fierce opposition and with considerable loss to life.

And near neighbours

By the time these events took place German troops had already marched into Czechoslovakia (15 March 1939), occupying Bohemia, and establishing a protectorate in Slovakia. On that same evening, Hitler was able to make his triumphant arrival into Prague.

The German invasion of Poland commenced on September 1, 1939. After one month of brutal fighting against overwhelming odds, the Polish forces were suppressed.

Czechoslovakia and Poland had, however, previously signed defence treaties with France and Britain respectively. Hence, it was Hitler's disinterest in observing these treaties that provided the reason for a state of war to be declared against Germany by Britain and France.

At Geneva, the faults will be very bare

The prophecy ends with a condemnation of the League of Nations, which had its headquarters *at Geneva*. [6] The League had been formed after the First World War as a means of preventing disagreements between countries escalating out of control. But the United States Congress refused to ratify the Treaty of Versailles and disassociated itself from the League. Thereafter, in the 1930s, the fragile agreement between member nations began breaking down. Japan invaded China; Italy invaded Ethiopia; Germany invaded the Rhineland. In each of these cases the League did no more than make a token protest of disapproval.

In the midst of this international lack of effective response, a disarmament conference was convened in which Germany failed to achieve the parity it was seeking. Attempts made to remedy the situation were ineffective. And by the time they reached the table for further discussion, Hitler was already Chancellor of the German Reich. On 14 October 1933, the Chancellor formally withdrew Germany's support for the League. Japan too, withdrew. The remaining member of the Axis, Italy, pulled out in 1937. Soon afterwards, the League disbanded — 'the faults having been made very obvious.' [7]

Summary: *The phrase, 'out of the clouds' and 'warfare' dates this prophecy to a time of aerial combat. If we add to this 'the people of Germany' and the 'countries surrounding' it, the Second World War comes to mind as the most likely fulfilment for this prophecy. Further phrases, such as: 'flat country' and 'marine locations', quickly fall into place, since both were evident during the opening stages of WW II. Finally, the fault of the League of Nations, centred in the city of Geneva, where countries were meant to resolve their differences, were laid bare by its abject failure to prevent the outbreak of the Second World War.*

> 86   *Par les deux testes & trios bras separés,*
>   *La cité grande par eaues sera vexee:*
>   *Des grans d'entre eulx par exil esgarés,*
>   *Par teste Perse Bisance fort pressee.*

> 87   *L'an que Saturne sera hors de seruage,*
>   *Au franc terroir sera d'eaue inondé:*
>   *De sang Troyen sera son mariage.*
>   *Et sera seur d'Esaignolz circonder.*

N.B 'Saturn out of bondage' implies a gravitational anomaly in the Solar system. This in turn would affect the tides; hence, the inundation of waters. The New Testament has more to say on this.

> 88   *Sur le sablon par vn hideux deluge,*
>   *Des autres mers trouué monstre marins:*
>   *Proche du lieu sera faict vn refuge,*
>   *Tenant Sauone esclaue de Turin.*

> 89   *Dedans Hongrie par Boëme, Nauarre,*
>   *Et par banniere sainctes seditions:*
>   *Par fleurs de lys pays pourtant la barre,*
>   *Contre Orleans sera esmoutions.*

et (OF) likewise; banniere (O.Fr. – bannie) confiscation of goods; saincte (OF) religious; pourtant (OF) notwithstanding; contre (OF) towards

> Within Hungary, by reason of Bohemia: Navarre   1618
> Likewise, through confiscation of goods, religious seditions:
> For the fleur-de-lys land: notwithstanding the bar,
> There will be emotions against (**DUKE OF**) **ORLEANS**

The Thirty Years' War (1618–1648) was a series of wars principally fought in Central Europe [...] It was one of the longest continuous wars in modern history. Initially, religion was a motivation for war as Protestant and Catholic states battled it out even though they all were inside the Holy Roman Empire. Changing the relative balance of power within the Empire was at issue. [1]

Within Hungary, by reason of Bohemia

Hungary entered the Thirty Years' War when Royal (Habsburg) Hungary joined the Catholic side of the new Austrian monarch, Ferdinand II. He was attempting to unify Germany and re-catholicize it. But his aim was met with fierce opposition from the Protestants, who were intent upon defending the country's Lutheranism and Calvinism.

Bohemia became the trigger when Ferdinand sent two Catholic councillors to Prague to rule in his absence. Their arrival on 23 May 1618 was to start 'The Bohemian Revolt', which led to the outbreak of the Thirty Years' War. It began when both councillors were seized by an Assembly of Protestants, and together, with their secretary, all three were hurled out of the window of Hradcany Castle. They survived the drop of 23 yards (21 metres), but not without serious injury.

> Soon afterward, the Bohemian conflict spread through all of the Bohemian Crown [Czech Crown lands] including Bohemia, Silesia, Upper and Lower Lustia, and Moravia. Moravia was already embroiled in a conflict between Catholics and Protestants. The religious conflict eventually spread across the whole continent of Europe, involving France ... [2]

Navarre likewise, through confiscation of goods

Linking Navarre with Bohemia has an unlikely ring to it. Nonetheless, the reason for this connexion occurred because the Bohemian Revolt (1618-21) coincided with a similar outbreak in France during that same period, and this was also caused by dissention between Catholics and Protestants.

The dispute in France had a history, and it came to a head in Louis XIII's reign. "Louis's grandmother, Jeanne d'Albret, Queen of Navarre, a Protestant, had, in her friendship for her co-religionists, confiscated the churches and revenues of the people of the Béarn province in Southern France." However, in 1593, when Henri IV converted to the Catholic religion, "Clement VIII made it an indispensable condition of the absolution from heresy that the inhabitants of Lower Navarre and the Béarn provinces should be allowed free enjoyment of their religion. [...] An article of the Edict of Nantes also provided for the restitution of th e temporal goods of the deprived Catholic churches." [3]

Religious seditions

Unfortunately, part of this article contained clauses that were disputed by the Protestants, and it was left to Louis XIII to enforce them. In 1620, the King issued an edict commanding the restitution of all confiscated Catholic goods and estates, and a commissioner was sent to insist this was carried out. But seditions followed.

> So much opposition did this commissioner encounter from the Hugu enot governor and others that Louis, who was then in Poitiers, decided to go and see the matter carried through in person. [...] Louis came first to St Julien, where the garrison wa s under the Duc de Soubise. [...] The king commanded the duke to give up the keys and to resign his command. This Soubise ref used to do, saying that he was under the orders of his brother the Sieur de Rohan. [...]. A council was held, and next day, June 3, 1621, a siege was laid to the recalcitrant stronghold. [4] (Refer Century 7 N°. 11.)

For the fleur-de-lys land

The *fleur-de-lys land* is France under Bourbon rule. The royal coat of arms consists of three gold lilies against an azure background. But, at the time this oracle was written, France was ruled by the Valois dynasty. This became succeeded by the House of Bourbon against severe opposition in 1590: twenty-four years after the Seer's death.

Notwithstanding the bar, there will be emotions against Orleans

In 1616 Louis XIII suffered a fit, and became so ill that it was feared he would die. This caused

thoughts of the succession to become a matter of immediate concern, since he was still childless. The King's brother Gaston was next in line for the throne, but he was unmarried. Hence, should anything also happen to him, the succession would fall to the 'Princes of the Blood'. Among these was Henri de Bourbon, Prince of Condé. He had been heir to the throne (9 May 1590 — 27 September 1601) prior to the birth of Henri IV's son, Louis XIII.

HENRI PRINCE OF BOURBON
COAT OF ARMS WITH BAR

Condé could not put away the remembrance of his own nearness in the succession. Did not a bend alone in his Bourbon coat distinguish his arms from those of the reigning family? *Barre-à-bas!* Had this not been one of the catch-words of the seditious hour which came before the Bastille and Vincennes? In the defect of sons, a nephew is the forced resource of rulers. [5]

But the hopes of Condé were threatened when it became known that plans for Gaston to marry Mademoiselle Montpensier, heiress to the duchies of Orléans, were being prepared. "The Condé faction had pricked their ears at this suggested union which might, if carried out, be a new barrier between them and the throne." [6] The marriage between Gaston d'Anjou and Marie de Montpensier took place in the King's closet and was performed by Cardinal Richelieu on 5 August 1626. "Gaston was given the title of Orléans but was not officially allowed to be styled as the *Duke of Orléans* till his marriage with the heiress Marie de Bourbon, Duchess of Montpensier in her own right." [6]

In the weeks leading up to the proposed marriage, Ornano and the Comte de Chalais, both of whom served as attendants to Orléans, had been meeting with him at night in secret. A plot to assassinate both the King and Richelieu, and then marry the widowed Queen to Gaston was later alleged. Both Ornano and Chalais were arrested and imprisoned. Under questioning, Chalais implicated the Queen, which led to her being questioned. For a time thereafter, she earned the mistrust of the King. Chalais was beheaded for treason two weeks after Orléan's marriage, having begged pardon from the Queen. His death was particularly gruesome because it took almost thirty strokes of the axe to decapitate him, while his mother stood watching her son die.

Summary: *This is a rather detailed prophecy concerning events centred on and around the year 1618. It introduces the 'Thirty Years War' with brief but lucid details relating to Hungary and Bohemia. It then switches to the religious unrest in France at that time, which involved Louis XIII. His illness in 1616 led to plans for the succession, since he was then childless. The King's brother, named by the seer as Orléans (it was the ducal title he acquired from his wife's lands after their marriage), then became the centre for a plot against the King and Cardinal Richelieu. He escaped punishment, but his hirelings were executed.*

90   Dans les cyclades, en perinthe & larisse,
         Dedans Sparte tout le Pelloponnesse:
         Si grand famine, peste, par faulx connisse,
         Neuf moys tiendra & tout le cherrouesse.

91   Au grand marché qu'on dit des mensongers
         Du bout Torrent & champ Athenien:
         Seront surprins par les cheuaulx legiers,
         Par Albanois Mars, Leo, Saturn vn versie.

The planets date this prophecy to a time when Mars is in Leo and Saturn is retrograde (AF verse)

92   Apres le siege tenu dixsept ans,
         Cinq changeront en tel reuolu terme:
         Puis sera l'vn esleu de mesme temps,
         Qui des Romaines ne sera trop conforme.

tel (OF) resembling; trop (OF) more than needed.

After the seat is held for seventeen years (**PIUS XI**),   1939
Five will change, as resembling a time completed:
Afterwards, there will be one elected (**JOHN XXIII**) from the same time,
Who, for the Romans, will not conform more than needed.

After the seat is held for seventeen years

Precognitive interest in the papacy continues throughout these prophecies. In this prediction, three popes are identified in succession, with a unique fact applying to each one in turn.

From the time this prophecy first went into print in 1557, up until the time of Pope Francis' election in 2013, only *one pope has held the seat* of St Peter *for seventeen years*, and that is Pius XI. Ambrogio Damiano Achille Ratti was born on 31 May 1857. On 6 February 1922, after fourteen ballots, making it the longest conclave of the 20th century, he was elected to the papal throne. *Seventeen years* and four days later, on 10 February 1939, he suffered a third heart attack in as many months and died aged 81.

Five will change, as resembling a time completed

His successor was Eugenio Maria Giuseppe Giovanni Pacelli, born on 2 March 1876. He was elected to office on 2 March 1939 after only three ballots: it being also his 63rd birthday, and he chose Pius XII for his regnal title. Before his first year at the Vatican had elapsed, world events had already begun to cast a shadow over his reign; Poland was invaded in September, causing England and France to respond by declaring war on the aggressor, Germany.

The five years of change predicted in the oracle encompass the worst atrocities of the Second World War. For the Pope, these began in 1940 and continued until the middle of 1945. "During his time in office, he would learn of the death camps, the Nazi gas chambers, the bombing of civilian populations, and the occupation of much of Europe." [1]

Fortunately, it has been Gordon Thomas's book – *The Pope's Jews: The Secret Plan to Save Jews from the Nazis* – in which the author (a Protestant researcher) has revealed the full extent of Pius XII's role during the war. While openly avowing the Vatican's neutrality in the War, Pius XII was heavily involved in secret operations. Thomas describes —

> ... how priests were instructed to issue baptism certificates to Jews who were in hiding across Italy, concealed behind the closed doors of convents and monasteries. In Hungary, more than 2000 Jews were given false documents to certify they were practising Catholics. [2]

Assisting Pius XII at the Vatican during the War was Mother Pacalina Lehnert, a German nun. She had served the Pope's household for more than forty years, and in 1959 she recorded her memories of the War in *Ich durfte Ihm Dienen, Erinnerungen an Papst Pius XII*. It was published in 1982, and it recounts what happened in 'neutral' Vatican City.

> Inside the Vatican [she] was in charge of housing, clothing and food for as many Jewish refugees as the walls could hold. By the end of the war no less than 200,000 Jews had been sheltered and fed inside the Holy City under her supervision [...] in addition to this, 12,000 packages were delivered to the children of Rome alone, many of which were handed over by Pope Pius XII himself. [3]

Pinchas Lapide, an Israeli diplomat in Milan as well as being a Jewish theologian, wrote that Pius XII "was instrumental in saving at least 700,000 but probably as many as 860,000 Jews from certain death at Nazi hands." (*Three Popes and the Jews*) [4] By the end of the war, the passing of the past *five years* must have *resembled a time completed*: one in which the years spent in the Vatican had brought about a considerable change to its normal routine.

Afterwards, there will be one elected from the same time

Pius XII died on 9 October 1958 from heart failure: brought on – for so it was said – by overwork. He was succeeded by John XXIII, who was elected on 28 October 1958.

Angelo Giuseppe Roncalli was an Italian, born on 25 November 1881: a mere five years after his predecessor, Pius XII. Both popes were therefore from the same period of time. His election, shortly before his 77th birthday was intended to be a stop-gap measure. After eleven ballots, and with no clear indication that this situation would alter, Roncalli was chosen because of his age, and the short time it was anticipated he would be in office. [5]

Who, for the Romans, will not conform more than needed

John XXIII's reign actually lasted four and a half years. He died from stomach cancer on 3 June 1963, but not before he had surprised the Roman conformists who never believed he would do other than sit-out his time at the Vatican as a caretaker pope.

> One of his first acts was to annul the regulation of Sixtus IV limiting the membership of the College of Cardinals to 70; within the next four years he enlarged it to 87 with the largest international representation in history.
> Less than three months after his election he announced that he would hold a diocesan synod for Rome, convoke an ecumenical council for the universal Church, and revise the Code of Canon Law. The synod, the first in the history of Rome, was held in 1960; Vatican Council II was convoked in 1962; and the Pontifical Commission for the Revision of the Code was appointed in 1963. [6]

Summary: *It may well surprise the Vatican (although it should not) to be reassured that God knows who will be pope, centuries before the conclave meets to affirm His 'will be done.' In the present case, the predicted span of 17 years service on the papal throne has only ever been completed by Pius XI. He was succeeded by Pius XII who immediately became faced with the outbreak of WW II: during which, for 5 turbulent years, the Vatican was changed into an undercover refugee camp. The third pope to be elected in order of succession was John XXIII. Instead of conforming to the expectations of those who had elected him as a short-term, caretaker pope, John spent his four years and seven months in office, restructuring the Church.*

93   *Soubz le terroir du rond globe lunaire,*
       Lors que sera dominareur Mercure:
       L'isle d'Ecosse fera vn luminaire,
       Qui les Anglois mettra à desconfiture.

94   *Translatera en la grand Germanie,*
       Brabant & Flandres, Gand, Bruges, Bologna,
       La tresue faincte le grand duc d'Armenie
       Assaillira Vienne & la Cologne

       He will transfer thither great Germany,
       Brabant & Flanders, Ghent, Bruges, Bologna,
       The truce dissembled, the great duke of Armenia,
       He will assail Vienna and Cologne.

95   *Nautique rame inuitera les vmbres,*
        Du grand Empire lors viendra conciter:
        La mer Egee des lignes les encombres,
        Empeschant l'onde Tyrrene deflottez.

96   *Sur le millieu du grand monde la rose,*
        Pour nouueaux faictz sang public espandu:
        A dire vray on aura bouche close,
        Lors au besoing viendra tard l'attendu.

        In the midst of the great world, the rose,
        In respect of new/rare/unheard of actions/propositions, public blood spilled:
        To speak true, men will have a closed mouth,
        In that time if need be/at the distress, the one awaited will arrive late.

This is the third prophecy to mention 'the rose'. In which case, Centuries Two Nº. 97 and Five Nº. 31 may complement what has been foretold in this oracle. There also exists some evidence to indicate that the prediction in line three has already begun to be fulfilled. If that should be true, then the remainder of this prophecy may be less than a generation away.

97   *Le nay difforme par horreur suffoqué,*
        Dans la cité du grand Roy habitable:
        L'edict feuere des captifz revoqué,
        Gresle & tonnerre Condom inestimable.

98   *A quarante huict degré climaterique,*
        A fin de Cancer si grande seicheresse:
        Poisson en mer fleuve, lac cuit hectique,
        Bearn, Bigorre par feu ciel en detresse.

This prophecy portends global warming having reached an intense degree.

99   *Milan, Ferrare, Turin, & Aquilloye,*
        Capue, Brundis vexés par gent Celtique,
        Par le Lyon & phalange aquilee,
        Quant Rome aura le chef vieux Britanique.

100   *Le bout-feu par son feu attrapé,*
        De feu du ciel à Carcas & Cominge:
        Foix, Aux, Mazeres haut viellart eschapé,
        Par ceulx de Hasse, des Saxons & Turinge.

References Century 5

Nº. 3

1 wikipedia.org/wiki/Francis_I,_Holy_Roman_Emperor
2 discovertuscany.com/tuscany-history-and-culture/great-tuscans/house-of-lorraine.html
3 florencewebguide.com/history-of-florence.html
4 tuscany-toscana.co.uk/history_of_tuscany.htm#.UycXUc5qHs0
5 http://www.tuscany-toscana.co.uk/history_of_tuscany.htm#.VPjLo47LLQs
6 http://www.italyheaven.co.uk/tuscany/florence/history.html
7 wikipedia.org/wiki/Treaty_of_Turin
8 wikipedia.org/wiki/Napoleon_III#Prelude_to_the_Italian_Campaign

Nº. 14

1 historylearningsite.co.uk/revolt_of_spanish_netherlands.htm
2 Ibid
3 thewayofthepirates.com/famous-pirates/turgut-reis.php
4 answers.com/topic/barbarossa#ixzz2wQHkwA56
5 wikipedia.org/wiki/Turgut_Reis
6 wikipedia.org/wiki/Pope_Pius_IV#Council_of_Trent
7 wikipedia.org/wiki/Michel_de_l'Hôpital
8 http://oce.catholic.com/index.php?title=Michel_de_L%27Hospital

Nº. 19

1 Ian Littlewood, *The Rough Guide Chronicle France*, 148; & *Grand Larousse Encyclopedique*, Louis Ancienne pièce d'or
2 K. Patmore, *The Court of Louis XIII*, 310-1; 313; 315; 322
3 E.N. Williams, *Dictionary of English and European History 1485–1789*, 264
4 Patmore, 338-40
5 Ibid 336
6 *Chronicle of the World* (ed.) Derrik Mercer, 542
7 Ian Dunlop, *Louis XIV*, 5

Nº. 22

1 newadvent.org/cathen/04030a.htm
2 Ibid
3 wikipedia.org/wiki/Battle_of_San_Pietro
4 Ibid
5 Ibid
6 http://www.emersonkent.com/historic_documents/treaty_of_vienna_1738.htm
7 encyclopedia.com/topic/War_of_the_Polish_Succession.aspx
8 http://www.csun.edu/~hcfll004/SV1730.html
9 Ibid
10 saint-mike.org/library/papal_library/clementxii/biography.html

Nº. 26

1 Jonathan White, *Russia 1905 – 1941*, 9–10
2 Robert Service, *A History of Twentieth-Century Russia*, 62
3 H.A.L. Fisher, *A History of Europe*, 1288
4 Lenin, *Encyclopædia Britannica 2001*: CD-ROM
5 White, 35; & Prince Lvov, *Encyclopædia Britannica 2001*: CD-ROM
6 Lenin, Ibid
7 Service, 58-9
8 Krasnov, *Encyclopædia Britannica 2001*: CD-ROM; & Service, 67

Nº. 29

1 World War II, Italy's Entry into the War, and the French Armistice, *Encyclopædia Britannica 2001*: CD-ROM
2 languedoc-france.info/06141204_liberty.htm
3 Norman Davies, *Europe A History*, 969-70
4 I.C.B. Dear (ed.) *The Oxford Companion to the Second World War*, 944
5 Field Marshal Lord Carver, *War In Italy 1943 – 1945*, 290
6 Mussolini, Role in World War II, *Encyclopædia Britannica 2001*: CD-ROM
7 Hitler, *Encyclopædia Britannica 2001*: CD-ROM

Nº. 30

1 Ian Littlewood, *The Rough Guide Chronicle France*, 254
2 Stephen Badsey, *The Franco-Prussian War 1870 – 1871*, 85–6
3 wikipedia.org/wiki/Paris_Commune#The_Commune_and_the_Catholic_Church
4 Ibid 159
5 Ibid 309

Nº. 33

1 Simon Schama, *Citizens*, 779

2   Ibid 727
3   Louis Madelin, *The French Revolution*, 376
4   Ibid 376
5   Schama, 789

N°. 38

1   E.N. Williams, *Dictionary of English and European History 1485–1789*, 274
2   Louis XV, *Encyclopædia Britannica 2001*, CD-ROM; & Margaret Crosland, *Madame de Pompadour*, 110–1
3   Christine P. Algrant, *Madame de Pompadour*, 95, 130
4   Williams, 276
5   The Salic Law, *Encyclopædia Britannica 2001* CD-ROM
6   Ibid Louis XV; Alistair Horne, *Seven Ages of Paris*, 167

N°. 39

1   wikipedia.org/wiki/Ferdinand_III,_Grand_Duke_of_Tuscany
2   Ibid
3   Ibid
4   wikipedia.org/wiki/House_of_Lorraine
5   wikipedia.org/wiki/Leopold_II,_Grand_Duke_of_Tuscany
6   Italy, the Restoration Period, Ibid; & Florence, cultural life, Ibid
7   Internet: members.tripod.com/romeartlover/Granduca.html (for photographs of heraldic devices)
8   Ibid & *The Catholic Encyclopedia*

N°. 42

1   http://hannibalbarca.webspace.virginmedia.com/Allobroges.htm
2   David Chandler, *The Campaigns of Napoleon:* 279-80, 281
3   http://en.wikipedia.org/wiki/Lombards
4   Franklin L. Ford *Europe 1780-1830:* 192
5   Chandler, 296

N°. 46

1   http://www.csun.edu/~hcfll004/SV1700.html
2   Ibid
3   http://en.wikipedia.org/wiki/Sabina_%28region%29
4   http://www.newadvent.org/cathen/04029a.htm
5   http://en.wikipedia.org/wiki/Rieti
6   http://www.nndb.com/people/214/000094929/
7   wikipedia.org/wiki/Chinese_Rites_controversy
8   Ibid

N°. 56

1   Gregory XVI – *Encyclopædia Britannica 2001* - CD-ROM
2   David L. Roper, *The Popes of Saint Malachy:* 232
3   *Catholic Encyclopedia – Pius IX*
4   Pius IX, *Encyclopædia Britannica 2001* - CD-ROM
5   J. Kelly, *The Oxford Dictionary of Popes*, 309, 310

N°. 57

1   Montgolfier, *Encyclopædia Britannica 2001* - CD-ROM
2   Ibid Seven Hills of Rome
3   Ibid History of transportation – the balloon; & Norman Hampson, *The First European Revolution: 1776-1815*, 104;
     wikipedia.org/wiki/Battle_of_Fleurus_(1794)
4   Harrison Smith, *The Illness of Pius VI and its Effect on the Maltese Question*, 409; & C R Cheney (ed.) *Handbook of
     Dates For Students of English History*, 39; & Christopher Hibbert, *Rome*, 231–2
5   Hibbert, 234

N°. 60

1   Bonaparte, *Encyclopædia Britannica 2001* - CD-ROM
2   David Chandler, *The Campaigns of Napoleon*, 39
3   Ibid
4   J.M. Thompson, *Napoleon Bonaparte:* 337
5   Franklin L Ford, *Europe 1780-1830*, 168
6   Chandler, xxix; xxxvii
7   *Cambridge Modern History*, vol. ix, 345; & Ford, 229, quoting: A. Meynier, cited in Bruun, 72; & Chandler, xxix

N°. 79

1   J.M. Thomson, *Napoleon Bonaparte*, 174
2   Ibid 179–80; & Franklin L Ford, *Europe 1780-1830*, 173
3   The Imperial Nobility – Appendix J, David Chandler, *The Campaigns of Napoleon*, 1122–5
4   Thompson, 158
5   Franklin L. Ford, *Europe 1780-1830*, 167
6   Thomson, book cover reverse side

Nº. 82

1   fortified-places.com/sieges/ypres1678.html
2   Ibid
3   britannica.com/EBchecked/topic/336625/Leopold-I/4157/The-struggle-with-France
4   britannica.com/EBchecked/topic/415163/Treaties-of-Nijmegen
5   wikipedia.org/wiki/Franche-Comté
6   wikipedia.org/wiki/Arbois
7   tourisme-langres.com/langres-city-of-art-and-history-a-city-a-history_en_01_01.html
8   wikipedia.org/wiki/Bresse
9   wikipedia.org/wiki/Dole,_Jura
10 Voltaire, *The Works of Voltaire, Volume XII.* 131 (translated by William F. Fleming)

Nº. 85

1   N.G.L. Hammond and H.H. Scullard (ed.) *The Oxford Classical Dictionary:* 2nd edition, 1020
2   Karen Farrington, *Handbook of World War II*, 188-9
3   Parachute, *Encyclopædia Britannica 2001:* CD-ROM; & World War II, Invasion of Norway, Ibid; & Peter Furtado, *World War II 1939 – 1945*, 28
4   World War II, Invasion of the Low Countries, *Encyclopædia Britannica 2001:* CD-ROM; & Farrington, 19, 253, 254; & A. Palmer, *Dictionary of Twentieth-Century History 1900-1982*, 402
5   wikipedia.org/wiki/British_Expeditionary_Force_(World_War_II)
6   League of Nations, *Encyclopædia Britannica 2001:* CD-ROM
7   Ibid

Nº. 89

1   wikipedia.org/wiki/Thirty_Years'_War
2   Ibid
3   K.A. Patmore, *The Court of Louis XIII:* 117-18
4   Ibid 118
5   Ibid 87-8
6   Ibid 90

Nº. 92

1   David L. Roper, *The Popes of Saint Malachy:* 246
2   Ibid
3   Ibid
4   Ibid
5   wikipedia.org/wiki/Pope_John_XXIII
6   vatican.va/holy_father/john_xxiii/biography/documents/hf_j-xxiii_bio_16071997_biography_en.html

CENTURY SIX

1   *Avtour des monts Pirenees grand amas,*
De gent estrange, secourir roy noueau:
Pres de Garonne du grand temple du Mas,
Vn Romain chef le caindra dedans l'eau.

2   *En l'an cinq cens octante plus & moins,*
On attend le siècle bien estrange:
En l'an sept cens & trois cieulx en tesmoins,
Que plusieurs regnes vn à cinq feront change.

    En l'an sept cens et neuf cieux seront tesmoings,
Que pour de l'or en bled non sans peine il change.

siècle (AF) a long period of time; cieulx (modern) cieux; regne (AF pays, fief) region; bled (blé) corn, wheat

In the year '**580** plus and minus,	1580
One awaits truly, the strangest period:	
In the year '**703**, the skies as testimony,	1703
Then several reigns, one to five, will change.	
In the year '**709** the skies will be testimony,	1709
When, in respect of gold for corn, not without grief, he exchanges.	

In 1568, two years after the death of Michel de Nostredame, Jean Aimes de Chavigny, acting in the capacity of executor, appears to have overseen the publication of the Seer's prophetic works. The result was published that year by Benoist Rigaud at Lyons, but it was not until 1605 that a number of adjustments made by the Seer were included (presumably under the direction of César de Nostredame). The second ending to N°. 2 above, is among those adjustments.

In 1867, Anatole Le Pelletier reproduced the 1568 edition in a two-volume scholarly edition of the Seer's works, which included, "un essai de rectification fait sur les manuscrits laissés par Nostredame." These 'rectifications' included the adjustment to lines 3 and 4 noted above.

In the year 1580 plus and minus

1580 was the year when France reached halfway in its Wars of Religion. These began in 1562 and came to an end in 1598. The year halfway between them is ½(1562 + 1598) = 1580. Hence, 1580 ± 18 = 1598 and 1562: exactly those years that marked the beginning and end of the French Wars of Religion.

One awaits, truly, the strangest period

1580 was also the year of 'the Lovers' War'. In April, the Huguenots of Montauban launched an offensive, which they claimed was prompted by an affair between Henri of Navarre's wife, Marguerite, and the vicomte de Turenne. [1]

> As a result of quarrels with his unworthy wife, and the unwelcome intervention of Henri III, he [Henri of Navarre] undertook the seventh war of religion, known as the 'war of the lovers' (*des amoureux*), seized Cahors on the 5th of May 1580, and signed the treaty of Fleix on the 26th of November 1580. [2]

The conflict began after some offensive remarks were made by Henri III about his sister Marguerite, and it continued for more than seven months. Although relatively minor, the skirmishes were classified as the 7th War of Religion.

France's Wars of Religion were fought intermittently for 38 years, and they did mark *a truly strange period* in the history of France.

> Town was divided against town, village against village, family against family. Armed affrays and assassinations were committed out of religious fanaticism, others in pursuit of private vengeance, others, as in all times when the hideous taint of espionage infects the body politic out of a sense of terror. [3]

In the year 1703, the skies in testimony

"The Great Storm of 1703" (26 November OS) was the worst natural disaster ever recorded in the South of England. "The storm, unprecedented in ferocity and duration, was generally reckoned by witnesses to represent the anger of God – in recognition of the 'crying sins of this nation'." [4]

In London, approximately 2,000 massive chimney stacks were blown down. The lead roofing was blown off Westminster Abbey. [...] On the Thames, around 700 ships were heaped together in the Pool of London [port area] [...] HMS Vanguard was wrecked at Chatham. [...] [And] HMS Association was blown from Harwich to Gothenbrg in Sweden.

There was extensive and prolonged flooding in the West Country [...] Hundreds of people drowned in flooding on the Somerset Levels, along with thousands of sheep and cattle, and one ship was found 15 miles (24 km) inland.

At sea, many ships (some of which were returning from helping Archduke Charles, the claimed King of Spain, fight the French in the War of the Spanish Succession were wrecked [...] with about 1,500 seamen killed [...] Between 8,000 and 15,000 lives were lost overall. The first Eddystone Lighthouse off Plymouth was destroyed, [...] A ship torn from its moorings in the Helford River in Cornwall was blown for 200 miles (320 km) before grounding eight hours later on the Isle of Wight. The number of oak trees lost in the New Forest alone was 4,000. [5]

The year 1703 also takes us to the War of the Spanish Succession, fought by Louis XIV.

Then several districts, one to five, will change, the skies in testimony

On 18 May 1703, following eleven days of fighting, John Churchill 1st Duke of Marlborough finally took Bonn, defeating Louis XIV's ally, the Archbishop of Cologne, and depriving him of his territorial rule along the Rhine. [6]

In 1703 Villeroi took command of French troops in Flanders, where he frustrated Marlborough's attempt to take Antwerp although the Allies managed to seize Huy. [7]

Louis ordered Villars to make the enemy pay for as much as 40 percent of his campaign by imposing contributions on enemy German populations. Villars and Max Emanuel defeated an imperial army under Styrum at the battle of Höchstädt on 20 September. [...] Meanwhile, French operations back along the Rhine went well in 1703, as the duke of Burgundy and Marshal Tallard took Breisach in September. Tallard next besieged Landau, and when a German army approached to relieve the fortress, Tallard came out from his lines and defeated the Germans at the battle of Speyer on 15 November. Landau was soon in French hands again. [8]

In 1703, Bonn, Huy, Höchstädt, Breisach and Landau, five districts, changed reigns.

In the year 1709, the skies will be testimony

This prediction of "The Great Winter of 1709": [9] was subsequently added to complement the "Great Storm of 1703". It occurred, when France suffered its worst winter on record.

When, in respect of gold for corn, not without grief, he exchanges

The terrible winter of 1709 brought grief to so many as both cold and hunger killed thousands of people from both famine and the icy weather that spread across the land. Bonfires had to be lit in the town squares to alleviate suffering, and the rivers Loire and Rhine froze over to form a bridge of ice. This caused consternation among villagers dwelling along the banks, for the people feared it would invite invasion. While in the cemeteries, the dead lay unburied because the frozen ground had become too solid for digging.

On 19 April, the Paris *Parlement* ordered every city and every parish to accept responsibility for the poor in their area. It also directed that a proportion of every person's income (approximately 3%) be paid monthly to either the *Bureau de Bienfaisance* or the *Comité de Charité* to compensate for the damaged harvest. Even the King, Louis XIV, was not exempted from this tax, and he had to pay '4,220 livres' from his own purse. The total revenue was then exchanged for corn from abroad, most notably from Dalmatia and North Africa. [10]

Summary: *The seer appears to be firmly in touch with the years ahead in this oracle. Three times he names a year to accompany an historical event that is to happen that year, and each time he speaks truly. Yet, there is no obvious connexion between 1580 and 1703, 1709. The first marks the halfway point in France's Wars of Religion, which he identifies by plus and minus. The other two prophecies were fulfilled during the reign of Louis XIV and the War of the Spanish Succession. France and England were both involved in that conflict and both were struck by the severest weather on record: for which, incredibly, the respective years in which they occurred has been precisely predicted. The science of weather forecasting can never match such an accurate prediction. So, once again, only a block universe explains such certainty.*

3   *Fleuue qu'esproue le nouueau nay Celtique,*
       Sera en grande de l'Empire discord:
       Le ieune prince par gent ecclesiastique,
       Oftera le sceptre coronal de concorde.

4   *Le Celtique fleuue changera de riuaige,*
       Plus ne tiendra la cité d'Aripine:
       Tout transmué ormis le viel langaige,
       Saturne, Leo. Mars, Cancer en rapine.

5   *Si grand famine par vnde pestifere,*
       Par pluye longue de long du polle artique:
       Samarobryn cent lieux de l'hemispere,
       Viuront sans loy, exemp de pollitique.

Samarobryn (L Samarabria) people of India: *alternatively* (L Samarobriva) Amiens: Also, hybrid word - Samar (OF Samarré *see* Chamarré) studded, set thick with studs; brin (A.Fr. – bruit, cri, orgueil) outcry, clamour, arrogance. The French *lieue* – at different times – existed in several variants: 10,000, 12,000, 13,200 and 14,400 French feet, about 3.25 km to about 4.68 km.

Such great hunger through a pestiferous wave,
Through continual rain, the extent of the Arctic Pole:
'Samarobryn' one hundred leagues from the hemisphere,
They will live without law, exempt from politics.

It is difficult to escape the conclusion that by speaking of 100 leagues (325 to 468 km) from the hemisphere, the oracle is referring to a view from space. The present "International Space Station maintains an orbit with an altitude of between 330 km (205 mi) and 435 km (270 mi)." (Wikipedia)

The space station, including its large solar arrays, spans the area of a U.S. football field, including the end zones, and weighs 924,739 pounds. The complex now has more liveable room than a conventional six-bedroom house, and has two bathrooms, a gymnasium and a 360-degree bay window. (NASA)

6   *Apparoistra vers le Septentrion,*
       Non loing de Cancer l'estoille cheuelue:
       Suze, Sienne, Boece, Eretrion,
       Mourra de Rome grand, la nuict disperue.

7   *Nor neigre & Dace, & l'Isle Britanique,*
       Par les vnis frères feront vexes:
       Le chef Romain issu de sang Gallique,
       Et les copies aux forestz repoulsees.

'Nor neigre' is otherwise written as Norneige, and thought to be Norway (Latin, Norvegia). An alternative possibility is that *nor* is an apocope of *nord* (north) or *Noroi* (AF. for Norway) in which case, *neigre* may suggest snow. Between the time of Paul IV (1555 – 1559) and the reign Pope Francis there have been no popes issued from Gallic blood.

8   *Ceulx qui estoient en regne pour scavoir,*
       Au Royal change deuiendront apouuris:
       Vns exiles sans appuy, or n'auoir,
       Lettés & lettres ne seront à grans pris.

9   *Aux sacres temples seront faictz escandales,*
       Comptés seront par honneurs & louanges:
       D'vn qu' on graue d'argent d'or les medalles,
       La fin sera en tourmens bien estranges.

This came close to fulfilment during the French Revolution. Medals of silver were engraved with the head of Louis XVI, and of Marie Antoinette in a tumbrel. Also, churches were desecrated sacrilegiously at the time. But there was no gold medal, nor does the final line seem particularly appropriate.

10   *Vn peu temps les temples des couleurs*
       De blanc & noir des deux entre meslee:
       Roges & iaunes leur embleront les leurs,
       Sang, terre, peste, faim. feu, d'eaue affolée.

11   *Des sept rameaulx à trois seront reduictz,*
      Les plus aisnés seront surprins par mort:
      Fratricider les deux seront seduictz,
      Les coniurés en dormant seront mort.

conjuré (OF) earnestly sought; dormant, napping; also, a *paragram* for Dormans.

Of the seven branches, they will be reduced to three: 1575
The oldest will be intercepted by death:
The two (**HENRI III & ALENÇON**) will be seduced to commit fratricide,
Those earnestly sought caught napping (at **DORMANS**) will be slain.

Of the seven branches they will be reduced to three

During the reign of Henri II and Catherine de' Medici, the Queen gave birth to ten children of which seven survived into adulthood: the age of majority at that time being fourteen. But by 1575, the seven royal children; that is, 'the seven branches', had been reduced by death to three.[1] They were, Henri III, Marguerite of Navarre, and Hercule, duc d'Alençon.

The oldest will be intercepted by death

The births and deaths of the seven Valois children were as follows:

	BIRTH	DEATH BY 1575	DEATH AFTER 1575
FRANCIS	1544	1560	
ELISABETH	1545	1568	
CLAUDE	1547	1575	
CHARLES	1550	1574	
HENRI	1551		1589
MARGUERITE	1553		1615
HERCULE	1555		1584

Princess Claude married Charles III, Duke of Lorraine, but died from childbirth on 21 February 1575.[2] Her death reduced the number of Valois children to three.

Interestingly, the mathematical probability of specifying that it will be the four most senior of the seven who will die first is one chance in thirty-five. In other words, if the Seer had been using guesswork, there were thirty-four opportunities of guessing incorrectly, and only one chance that he would be right.

The two will be seduced to commit fratricide

In September 1575, *the two* surviving brothers, Henri III and the duc d'Alençon became *fratricidal*. Henri III had decided to keep his two remaining siblings apart, so that he could exercise better control over their political aspirations. In particular, he was suspicious of the confidences shared between his brother and sister, and her husband, Henri of Navarre. In an attempt to divide them, he first spread the false tale of a love affair involving Marguerite and a courtier. Next, he engaged the services of the beautiful Charlotte, Baroness de Sauve. She was instructed to *seduce* Navarre and Alençon, so as to set them against each other in the single pursuit of her sexual favours.

Because of the tensions produced by this love triangle, Alençon secretly left Court: raging against his brother. His destination was Dreux, where he joined Henri III's enemies, the *Huguenot-Politiques*. Furious, at Alençon's treachery, the King, too, became *fratricidal*. He put together a squadron of loyal officers, ordering them to bring back his brother "dead or alive."[3]

Those earnestly sought caught napping (at Dormans) will be slain

At the time when the repercussions to Henri III's court intrigues were taking place, an armed force of German mercenaries, led by Guillaume de Thoré entered France. Thoré was the fifth son of Anne de Montmorency, Constable of France under Henri II. Thoré had also been colonel of the King's cavalry between 1572 and 1574; but became opposed to the regime whilst witnessing the massacre of Protestants on St Bartholomew's Day. Thereafter, he was involved in plotting against the King. Together with his brother, he travelled to Germany to hire troops to assist the Protestant cause in France's fifth war of religion.

In the month following Alençon's escape from Paris, Thoré's German troops invaded northern France in an attempt to unite with the Protestants in the south. But *at Dormans* (10 October 1575), they were met by Henri duc de Guise and his Catholic army, which had been searching for them. Thoré and his mercenaries were ill-prepared for the encounter – caught napping – and Guise imposed a heavy defeat upon them, leaving most of their number dead. [4]

Summary: *The seer had known the seven 'branches' referred to in this prophecy since their childhood, and he also knew when the four older ones would die. His clever choice of words is also apparent. The fratricidal hatred that existed between the King and his brother is cleverly referred to by the word 'seduced', since seduction played a key role in enflaming their hatred for each other. The German invaders who were caught 'napping' (dormant in French), were attacked and killed at Dormans, thus allowing a paragram to play its part when describing the oracle's fulfilment.*

12   *Dresser copies monter à l'Empire,*
      Du Vatican le sang Royal tiendra:
      Flamans, Anglois, Espaigne auec Aspire,
      Contre l'Italie & France contendra.

Dresser (OF) train up; monter (AF - servir) to be of service; tenir (OF) govern; Aspire (aspire), also anagram Persia.

Training up armies to be of service to the Empire,   1808
The blood Royal will govern for the Vatican,
Flemish, English Spanish with (PERSIA) aspire,
Italy in opposition and France will contend.

Training up armies to be of service to the Empire

Under Napoleon, the French Empire expanded its boundaries from the Mediterranean to the Baltic and from the Atlantic to the western borders of Austria and Prussia. A constant input of men was therefore required for maintaining the country's position of dominance. In 1808, Bonaparte, "disposed of some 300,000 troops in Spain, 100,000 in France, 200,000 in the Rhineland, and 60,000 in Italy." It has been calculated that during the entire time in which Bonaparte remained Emperor of the French, the number of men called to serve in his armies reached 2 million. [1]

By using the word *Empire*, the oracle has foreseen the decree made on 18 May 1804 by the *Sénatus-Consulte*. This placed the Republic in the hands of an Emperor. The decision was not made to follow a precedent set by the Roman Empire, but as a practical means of keeping the French Emperor apart from Royalist plots intent upon returning France to a monarchist state.

The blood royal will govern for the Vatican

In 1808, French troops entered Rome. Napoleon, now *King of Italy*, [2] ordered General Miollis to seize the Vatican, mount guard over the entrances to the papal palace *and take control of the government* Napoleon's plan was to annex the Papal States, and incorporate them into France's expanding, political system: thereby adding to "his passionate aim to be Rex Totius Italiae [King of all Italy]." [3] In the early hours of the morning of 6 July, "detachments of troops with scaling-ladders, forced their way into the Quirinal, broke down door after door in the dark, echoing palace." The Pope was at last found seated at a table attended by five cardinals. "I am sent by His Majesty the Emperor Napoleon to ask whether your Holiness is disposed to agree to the treaty whose terms have been presented to him." The Pope replied that he was unable to comply. "'Then', said the General, 'I must put you under arrest.'" [4] Pius VII was then taken to Savona, leaving Bonaparte in overall control.

Flemish, English, Spanish with (Persia) aspire

Since 5 June 1806, Napoleon's third brother Louis had become King of both Belgium and Holland, in what was then Flanders. A problem arose when Napoleon decreed on 18 February 1808 that a further increase to his infantry was required.

This included troops from the Netherlands. Louis, confronted by his brother's demand, refused point-blank. Napoleon then accused Louis of putting Dutch interests above those of France, and removed most of the French forces in Holland for the coming war in the east, leaving only about 9,000 garrison soldiers in the country.[5]

In Britain this was seen as an opportunity to launch an attack on the Netherlands. In the summer of 1809, an army commanded by the 2nd Earl of Chatham, and supported by ships under the command of Sir Richard Strachan, reached the Dutch coast at the island of Walcheran. And, although "the British captured Flushing, after a ferocious bombardment, and surrounding towns on 15 August,"[6] the expedition failed. An outbreak of Malaria contracted from the swamps of Walcheran, together with the arrival of French forces commanded by Jean-Baptiste Bernadotte, who had been sent from Paris to defend the Netherlands, were sufficient to overcome British aspirations.

The year, 1808 also saw the commencement of the Peninsula War, and a build-up of troops. "Early in 1808 there were 20,000 in Portugal, 40,000 in northern Spain, and 12,000 in Catalonia."[7]

In April, the *Spanish* royal family was summoned to Bayonne, and forced to abdicate in favour of Napoleon's brother Joseph. But, by the time summer arrived, Spain was in revolt against their new King, and Joseph was forced to flee from Madrid.

Britain saw Spain's uprising as an opportunity to establish a bridgehead in Portugal. Towards the end of the year, an army was dispatched under the command of Sir Arthur Wellesley (later Duke of Wellington) to achieve this objective.

In the third line of the quatrain, *Aspire* has been given a capital letter. This usually signals a second meaning is involved; and, as an anagram of Persia, this is rather more than coincidental.

In 1808, Napoleon was still engaged in an attempt to persuade the *Shah of Persia* to join him in an offensive against Georgia. The Emperor had sent General Gardanne to see the Shah, carrying with him a promise of material aid if the plan he had in mind was undertaken. Accompanying the promise was Bonaparte's agreement to equip the Shah with, "4,000 infantry, commanded by chosen and experienced officers, 10,000 muskets and 50 pieces of cannon." But in the event, very little aid was sent.[8]

Italy in opposition and France will contend

Prior to 1808, the kingdom of Italy comprised only the northern and eastern plains of the peninsula from Lombardy to the Adriatic. But in 1808 this was extended, when France added the March of Ancona down to the border of Naples. Pius VII naturally remained opposed to the occupation of Rome and to the seizure of the Papal States.

The irritation between France and the Vatican increased so rapidly that on the 2nd of February 1808 Rome was occupied by General Miollis; a month later the provinces of Ancona, Macerata, Fermo and Urbino were united to the Kingdom of Italy, and diplomatic relations between Napoleon and Rome were broken off; finally, by a decree issued from Schönbrunn on the 17th of May 1809, the emperor united the papal states to France. Pius retaliated by a bull excommunicating the invaders. [...] The palace on the Quirinal was broken open during the night of July 5th, and, on the persistent refusal of Pius to rescind the bull of excommunication and to renounce his temporal authority, he was carried off, first to Grenoble, thence after an interval to Savona on the Gulf of Genoa.[9]

Summary: *This is a straightforward oracle detailing events that happened in 1808. Especially noticeable is the reference made to the Empire and the armies needed to maintain it. This included taking troops from Flanders in preparation for combating the Anglo-Spanish alliance made that year. The occupation of Rome, also in 1808, and the seizure of the Papal States, completes the prophecy, with Italy opposing the French who were maintaining their position and rights as conquerors. Even distant Persia received a mention due to Napoleon's plan to arm the Shah.*

13   *Vn dubieux ne viendra loing de regne,*
     La plus grand part le vouldra soustenir:
     Vn capitol ne vouldra point qu'il regne,
     Sa grande charge ne pourra maintenir.

14   Loing de sa terre Roy perdra la bataille,
      Prompt eschappe poursuiuy suivant prins,
      Ignare prins soubz la doree maille,
      Soubz sainct habit & l'ennemy surprins.

15   Dessoubz la tombe sera trouué le prince,
      Qu'aura le pris par dessus Nuremberg:
      L'Espaignol Roy en Capricorne mince,
      Fainct & trahy par le grand Vitemberg.

16   Ce que rauy sera du ieune Milue,
      Par les Normans de France & Picardie:
      Les noirs de temple du lieu Negresilue,
      Feront aulberge & feu de Lombardie.

17   Apres leslimes bruslez les asiniers,
      Constrainctz seront changer habitz diuers:
      Les Saturnins bruslez par les musniers,
      Hors la pluspart qui ne sera couuers.

18   Par les physiques le grand Roy delaissé,
      Par sort non art ne l'Ebrieu est en vie:
      Luy & son genre au regne hault poulsé,
      Grace donnee à gent qui Christ envie.

19   La vraye flame engloutira la dame,
      Que vouldra metre les Innocens à feu:
      Pres de l'assault l'exercite s'enflamme,
      Quant dans Seuille monstre en bœuf sera veu.

20   L'vnion saincte sera peu de duree,
      Des vns changés reformés la pluspart:
      Dans les vaisseaux sera gent enduree,
      Lors aura Rome vn nouveau liepart.

21   Quant ceulx de polle artique vnis ensemble,
      En Orient grand effaieur & crainte:
      Esleu nouueau soustenu le grand temple,
      Rodes, Bisance, de sang Barbare taincte.

22   Dedans la terre du grand temple celique,
      Nepueu à Londres par paix faincte meurtry:
      La barque alors deuiendra scimatique,
      Liberte faincte sera au corn& cry.

temple (OF - *anatomical*) temple; celique (OF) celestial; meurtry (AF tuer) to butcher

Within the land of the great celestial temple (**NEWTON**),   1685
Nephew in London, through feigned peace, butchered (**MONMOUTH**):
The barque at that time will become divided;
Feigned liberty will be in the hue & cry.

Within the land of the great celestial temple

In both the French and English language, the word 'temple' is a homonym. One definition points to a place of worship; the other definition indicates a part of the cranium enclosing the brain. The Seer's use of 'celestial' as a defining adjective would tend to indicate a religious interpretation is required. But the intelligence behind these prophecies is subtle, cryptic and of a different order. Just once in the history of England – and London is referred to in the second line – 'celestial temple' was capable of taking its alternative meaning.

This occurred in 1687, when England's great scientific genius, Isaac Newton, published his famous *Principia*. It was a book that contained the single law that described the movement of every 'celestial' body in the universe. And it had been worked out in the 'temple' of its inventor. Hence, England is understood to be the land of Isaac Newton and his 'celestial temple': within which, he formulated the motion of the heavenly bodies. [1] Once this is understood, everything else in the oracle follows from it.

Nephew in London

James Scott Duke of Monmouth, the illegitimate son of Charles II, was by birth *the nephew* of King James II. But he also believed himself to be legitimate, and the rightful heir to the English throne. In June 1685, in pursuit of this goal, he landed at Lyme Regis in Dorset at the head of a rabble army. Several days later, at Taunton in Somerset, he proclaimed himself King of England. His 'reign' was short-lived. On 6 July, John Churchill, future Duke of Marlborough, intercepted him and his troops on their way to London. The rebel army was swiftly defeated, and after a brief flight Monmouth was taken captive and imprisoned *in the Tower of London.* [2]

Through feigned peace, butchered

Inside his prison cell, Monmouth wrote a contrite letter to his uncle. It was full of remorse, begging the King to be lenient and to overlook his past disloyalty, which he accompanied by the promise to repay him with his total allegiance. [3] (The Victorian artist John Pettie has painted a dramatic canvas of Monmouth's penitent appeal). The King's response was to allow his nephew the impression of being won over, and Monmouth was re-admitted to court. However, this move towards peace proved to be no more than a ruse, through which the King hoped to discover information concerning Monmouth's accomplices. This came to light when Monmouth refused to divulge their names: whereupon, he was returned to his cell in the Tower. [4]

It was *through* the failure of this *feigned peace* that Monmouth was *beheaded* a few days later (15 June 1685); his butchered death is referred to in Century 4 N°. 89.

The barque at that time will become divided

The barque of Saint Peter represents the Church, which brings us to the next part of the oracle. Before succeeding to the throne, James II had converted to the Catholic faith. Whereupon, soon after becoming King (6 February 1685), he set about returning England to the Catholic fold. But his religious fervour quickly met with opposition, and the attempts he made to achieve his goal opened up a religious divide. England, by this time, had become a predominantly Protestant nation, with little sympathy for Catholic France held tightly under the reign of Louis XIV.

Prominent amongst James' more divisive schemes was the appointment of Catholics to military commands. Parliament objected to this policy, but the courts upheld the King's right to make the appointments. James also tried to gain admission for pro-Catholic administrators to the universities. This, too, was met with strenuous opposition. Another of his objectives was the *Declaration of Indulgence*, which suspended the penal code against Catholics. This incited bishops across the country even more, and many refused to announce it to their congregations. For this act of defiance they were arrested and imprisoned.

The dissention caused by a Catholic King ruling a predominantly Protestant country inevitably resulted in a division occurring within the Church. [5] And in 1688, James II was driven out of the country because of his pro-Catholic bias.

Feigned liberty will be in the hue and cry

The Glorious Revolution that followed James II's deposition, and which placed William III on the throne, heralded an air of change amid the *hue and cry* that took place at the time. William reversed the policies of James II by replacing the Catholics with Protestants. And in May 1689, the *Toleration Act* was passed. Despite its name, it was a *feigned liberty*, since the proclamation failed to provide complete liberty for Catholics by denying them the right of full citizenship. [6]

The Act allowed freedom of worship to Nonconformists who had pledged to the oaths of Allegiance and Supremacy and rejected transubstantiation, i.e., Protestants who dissented from the Church of England such as Baptists and Congregationalists but not to Catholics.
Nonconformists were allowed their own places of worship and their own teachers, if they accepted certain oaths of allegiance [...] It purposely did not apply to Catholics, nontrinitarians and atheists [... However] Catholics and Unitarians were not hunted down after the Act was passed but they still had no right to assemble and pray. [7]

Summary: *This oracle foresees a piece of English history at the time of Sir Isaac Newton, to whom it cryptically makes reference. Politically, it was a time of turmoil, with a Catholic King governing a Protestant country, and causing dissent and division by his ruling. Amidst this commotion, The King's nephew arrived from abroad with a small army to claim the throne for himself, but his intended revolt landed him in prison with a rather nasty execution to follow. All these events are neatly predicted in this oracle, and easily confirmed from historical records.*

23   D'esrit de regne munismes desreiees,
  Et seront peoples esmeuz contre leur Roy:
  Paix, faict nouueau sainctes loix empires,
  Rapis onc fut en si tresdur arroy.

Munismes (L. - munis) ready to serve; Rapis (*anagram*) Paris: *also* (L Rapio) seize by force; onc (OF) never; empirer (OF) to make worse; tresdur (OF) very harsh; arroy (OF) order, array.

Concerning the spirit of the reign, a readiness to serve decried,   1789
Also, people will be stirred up against their King (**LOUIS XVI**),
Peace, a new act, sacred laws made worse;
Seized by force (**PARIS**) had never been in such very harsh array.

After the fall of the Bastille in 1789, the King's position became increasingly precarious. He no longer commanded enough power to defend his friends and family. On the other hand, the move towards a republic had been too fast. Its supporters had yet to come to terms with the role of the monarch in this new power shift. Their solution was a new constitution. Louis would be known only as King of the French. He would also be allowed a veto in the Assembly, valid for four years.

Concerning the spirit of the reign, a readiness to serve decried
It was the King's reply concerning the new arrangements to his reign that fulfils the opening line of this oracle. For, although Louis XVI declared himself to be in full agreement with "the spirit" [1] of the document's intentions, he qualified his readiness to serve under the constitution with a small number of reservations. It was these personal preferences that were to be the cause of his response being *decried*, for they were considered unnecessarily querulous. [2]

Also, people will be stirred up against their King
The Press responded to the King's pettiness by mounting a continuous attack against him. By 2 October 1789, these outbursts had descended to the level of character assassination. With the Press's power to circulate its political bias, *via* the printed word, the people were soon stirred up against their King. [3] Louis' situation had begun to look increasingly perilous.

Peace
Concerned at the international attention France was now receiving, the Assembly moved to calm the growing fears by announcing to the world (22 May 1790) its resolve for *peace*. France – so members of the Assembly declared – would never wage war, nor would they seek conquest, or use military might against the freedom of any people. [4]

A new act
A month later, on 19 June, the Assembly passed *a new act*. This ended the nobility's right to pass on their titles and coats of arms to their children. [5] This was a direct blow against the privileges enjoyed by the Ancient Regime. And, as the Abbé Maury cleverly pointed out: "If there is no nobility, there is no monarchy." Time was beginning to run out for the royal family.

Sacred laws made worse
On 12 July 1790, it was the turn of the Church to come under attack. The Assembly announced that priests and bishops were to be elected, and all men of the cloth were to become civil servants. To pay for the clergy's upkeep, the Church's assets, including its vast lands, would be placed under state control. Moreover, there would also be a reduction in the number of dioceses, so as to bring them into line with the number of departments. [6]

Seized by force

In June 1791 a new drama unfolded. The government announced to the people that the King had been *kidnapped*, but that he had been rescued before he could be taken out of the country. [7] In fact Louis XVI and Marie Antoinette had attempted to leave Paris secretly, and escape across the Belgian frontier. But at Varennes, just forty kilometres from safety, they were recognized and detained. Under guard, the royal couple were brought back to the capital. The report of their kidnap was just a cover story to avoid the embarrassment of admitting publicly, that the King had tried to escape the restrictions imposed upon him by this new government.

Paris had never been in such very harsh array

As a result of the King and Queen's attempt to leave secretly for Belgium, and with the cover story of their kidnap still only partly believed, the King and Queen were brought back to Paris. Their return from Varennes is described in Century One N°. 5.

It was at this time that Paris had never been is such very harsh array. "The streets were lined with National Guards, their arms reversed as though for a funeral procession." The crowd was huge, but in obedience to a government decree, the onlookers remained utterly silent, as the King and Queen were driven through the streets to their palace. Notices were everywhere on display – "Whoever applauds the King shall be flogged. Whoever insults him shall be hanged." [8]

Summary: *This prophecy returns to the French Revolution shortly after it began. The King is still King, but with reduced powers. Swayed by his wife's fear for their safety, because of Press attacks and crowd abuse, the royal couple took their children out of Paris and then made their way towards the Belgian border, but were seized at Varennes. Their arrival back in the capital is described in the final line. The oracle also includes other events that were happening during this period. Externally, France issued a declaration of Peace toward other countries, while internally; a new act was passed reducing the power and influence of the Church.*

24   *Mars & le sceptre se trouuera conioinct,*
      Dessoubz Cancer calamiteuse guerre.
      Vn peu après sera nouueau Roy oingt,
      Qui par long temps pacifiera la terre.

se trouvera (OF) to appear; oingt (OF oindre) anoint; pacifier (OF) to calm,

Mars and Jupiter will appear conjoined,   1812
Under Cancer (**JUNE 1812**): a calamitous war (**FRANCE INVADES RUSSIA**)
A little while after a new King will be anointed, (**LOUIS XVIII**)
Who, for a long time, will calm the land.

Mars and Jupiter will appear conjoined under Cancer

It was on the 22nd of June 1812 that Napoleon reached the banks of the River Niemen in what is now Lithuania. There, he surveyed the prospect of crossing the river and taking his *Grande Armée* into Russia to wage war against Czar Alexander. For the remainder of June, his army and provisions were engaged in crossing the Nieman: while in the sky above, Mars and Jupiter approached their closest point, with less than a degree separating them on 28 June. [1]

Those familiar with horoscopes will know that the period *under Cancer*, extends from 22 June to 22 July: the exact period of time when this activity in the heavens and on land began.

A calamitous war

In the event, France's war against Russia proved to be *calamitous*. The Battle of Borodino, fought on 7 September 1812, was to be the most costly of all France's victories. At its close 30,000 Frenchmen perished, although the loss to the Russian Army was greater, totalling approximately 58,000 dead.

And when Bonaparte finally reached Moscow, he met only disappointment. The city had been torched to deny his troops both provisions and shelter. Moreover, any hope he had had of establishing a treaty with Czar Alexander came to nothing. The Czar ignored his proposals.

Gloomily, Napoleon was forced to retrace his steps back to Poland, having accomplished nothing, except the deaths of nearly a 100,000 men.

Even the retreat was disastrous, for it coincided with the fierce onset of a Russian winter, and many thousands among Napoleon's starving men fell dead from malnutrition and hypothermia, or else as victims of a Cossack skirmish against the straggling party at the tail end of the French army. [2]

A little while after a new King will be anointed

Sixteen months after re-crossing the river Niemen, *en route* for France, with what was left of his *Grande Armée*, Napoleon's reign came to an ignominious end. [3] Replacing him was *a new King*, Louis XVIII: thereby signalling the country's return to its former system of rule by a monarchical government. [4] But the King deemed it wiser to forego a coronation and instead was anointed. He thus avoided antagonising the pro-republicans. It was Charles X, who succeeded him in 1824, who reinstated the coronation ceremony in full, holding it at Reims on 29 May 1825.

Who, for a long time will calm the land

From 1792 until 1815, France had been almost continuously at war. But in 1815, Louis XVIII was able to agree peace terms with those countries that had previously been its enemies. Based upon treaties signed in Vienna (9 June 1815) and in Paris (20 November 1815), France was able to enjoy an extended period of peace. "Under Louis, French industry prospered, the Army was reformed, and France recovered international confidence after suppressing a revolt in Spain (1823)."

Louis XVIII died in 1824, leaving France's interior in peace until 1854, when the country joined with England against Russia in the Crimean War. [5]

Summary: *The astronomical dating of this prophecy is perfectly accurate, and it is used to signal the disastrous war France waged against Russia in 1812. It was this that preceded the end of the Napoleonic era: except for a brief intermission in 1815. The prophecy also foretells the re-establishment of the monarchy in France, with the reign of Louis XVIII, which brought with it a period of calmness that replaced the wars and revolution of the previous 25 years.*

25   *Par Mars contraire sera la monarchie.*
         De grand pescheur en trouble ruyneux:
         Ieune noir rouge prendra la hierarchie,
         Les proditeurs iront iour bruyneux.

Mars (god of war); contraire (OF) contrary, adverse; noir (AF livide - Littré. *Fig.* se dit, en parlant des personnes, de la noirceur morale.); hierarchie (OF) sacred government; proditeurs (L - prodit\ors) traitors; bruyneux (OF) hot mists.

Through war, the monarchy will be contrary.   1792
Concerning the great fisherman (**PIUS VI**), for him ruinous trouble
The young man ghastly and red will seize the priestly government;
The traitors will act on a day of mists (**18 BRUMAIRE**).

Through war, the monarchy will be contrary

In 1792, Louis XVI and Marie Antoinette were still nominally King and Queen of the French, but they were under mounting pressure from those who wanted to see France become a republic. The royal couple's plight was recognized abroad, causing the King's two brothers, Provence and Artois, together with their sister, to urge Austria to invade France. But despite agitating for this, it was actually France that declared war on Austria (April 1792).

Although opposed to war with the country of his wife's birth (the monarchy will be contrary), even though its aim was to restore him to his former power, Louis XVI "felt compelled to give way to the demands for war which were now almost universal." His brothers had told him, if you make this declaration we will know that you have been forced to do so.

The disastrous beginning of the war led to the most violent demonstrations in the capital: rumours of counter-revolution were rife, the King and Queen were accused of conspiring with the enemy and an 'Austrian Committee' at the Tuileries was supposed to be betraying military intelligence to Vienna. [1]

Concerning the great fisherman, for him ruinous trouble

The great fisherman is an aptronym for the pope. It dates back to St. Peter, the fisherman who followed Christ as a disciple to become a fisher of men's souls. The Roman Church adopted Peter as its first pope. At the time of this prophecy's fulfilment, Pius VI was Pope, and his accumulation of trouble began when he condemned the French Assembly for issuing the Civil Constitution of the Clergy, with its anti-Christian content.

> The Pope's eventual condemnation of the Civil Constitution led to violent disturbances in Paris where anti-clericalism was fostered both by political clubs and by theatres which presented plays about the horrors of the Inquisition, the tribulations and hypocrisy of monastic and convent life, and the alleged greed and dissipation of the leaders of the Roman Catholic Church. Effigies of the Pope were set alight on bonfires, revolutionary slogans were plastered on church doors, convents were invaded and nuns assaulted. [2]

The young man ghastly and red will seize the priestly government

The young man described as both black and red is a description of Napoleon Bonaparte. In June 1796 he was still 26 years of age. The year previously, he had already proved himself to be of both colours when, on the 5th of October, he fought on the side of the Revolution (the Reds) against the royalists assembled in the street outside the Tuileries. These were men agitating for a return of the monarchy. His *whiff of grapeshot*, which he directed at them, was to add to the reputation he had begun to acquire for himself as both single-minded and ruthless—a blackening of his character. Pius VI was soon to discover this for himself.

> The pope's co-operation with the Allies against the French Republic, and the murder of the French attaché, Basseville, at Rome, brought on by his own fault, led to Napoleon's attack on the Papal States. At the Truce of Bologna (25 June, 1796) Napoleon dictated the terms: twenty-one million francs, the release of all political criminals, free access of French ships into the papal harbours, the occupation of the Romagna by French troops etc. At the Peace of Tolentino (19 Feb. 1797) Pius VI was compelled to surrender Avignon, Venaissin, Ferrara, Bologna, and the Romagna; and to pay fifteen million francs and give up numerous costly works of art and manuscripts. [3]

The traitors will act on a day of mists

In 1799, a group of politicians discontented with the nation's affairs suggested to Napoleon that he might 'purge' the Assembly. He agreed, and a plot was put together. The action took place inside the Orangery at St. Cloud. Troops who served under Bonaparte cleared the hall at bayonet point allowing a *coup d'état* to be completed. The successful outcome placed Napoleon in the position of First Consul of France. "All through France the *coup d'état* of Brumaire (November 9) was acclaimed as the dawn of a new era." [4]

The Revolutionary calendar which replaced the Christian, Gregorian calendar began with Year One in 1793. It continued up until Napoleon abolished it on 1 January 1806. Instead of twelve months, it divided the year into the four seasons, each having three 30-day periods named after seasonal scenes of the year. "Brumaire (Month of Mist)": [5] began on 22 October and ended on 20 November. *A day of mists* therefore dates the time when *the traitors acted* (9 November) to bring about their *coup d'état*—as predicted in the oracle.

Summary: *The oracle predicts the month named by the Revolutionary calendar of 1793, which dates the coup d'état that put Napoleon in power. The oracle also refers to Bonaparte as 'young', 'black' and 'red', which is a fitting description for the 26-year-old man who helped defeat the royalists that were planning to restore the monarchy to France. And it justifies the manner in which Napoleon dealt with the ageing Pope Pius VI, after successfully invading the Papal States and forcing him to sign the Treaty of Tolentino. These events were preceded by the seer having also predicted that France would engage in a war for which the monarchy was contrary, and which would then be followed by torment for the Pope.*

26   *Quatre ans le siege quelque peu bien tiendra,*
        Vn suruiendra libidineux de vie:
        Rauenne & Pyse, Veronne soustiendront,
        Pour esleuer la croix de Pape enuie.

enuie (OF) spite; suruenir (OF) step in unlooked for; soustenir (AF sostenir – réparer) make amends for.

Four years the seat will hold little good whatsoever (**PAUL IV**),   1555
One of a libidinous life (**PIUS IV**) will step in unlooked for:
Ravenna and Pisa will make amends for Verona,
Instead of elevating the Cross, spite by the Pope.

Four years the seat will hold little good whatsoever

Gian Petro Carafa was 78 years of age when, in May 1555, he became Pope Paul IV. His reign is notable for his having lost England to the Holy See; for his detestation of Spain, and for his use of the Inquisition against heresy, in which "The inquisitors were now sentencing to death fornicators, sodomites, actors, buffoons, lay folk who failed to keep the Lenten fast, even a sculptor who had carved a crucifix judged to be unworthy of Christ." [1] The Pope also introduced the *Index of Prohibited Books*, which included the banning of works by Protestants. Furthermore, he was openly hostile to the Jews; and used his position to enrich his family members. He died on 18 August 1559.

One of a libidinous life will step in unlooked for

Giovanni Angelo de' Medici was 60 years of age when he became Pope Pius IV. Before his elevation to the papacy he had been absent from Rome. This was the result of a disagreement with Paul IV concerning his anti-Spanish bias. In August 1559, following Paul's death, Giovanni de' Medici arrived at the Vatican in order to participate in the election for a successor. But, as the months went by with neither the French nor the Austro-Spanish cardinals prepared to give way, the conclave decided to elect a compromise candidate: *one unlooked for*. On 25 December, Giovanni de' Medici was offered the nomination. This was a surprise choice, because "Prior to his election, he had fathered three illegitimate children." [2] Nevertheless, he agreed to accept the nomination, and having received the required majority, chose Pius IV for his title.

Ravenna and Pisa will make amends for Verona

The same year in which Paul IV died and Pius IV was elected marked the time in which the Italian Wars came to an end: brought about by the signing of the Peace of Cateau-Cambrésis (3 April). It signalled the end of a conflict between France and Spain, for control of Italy.

> With this treaty, France gave up on the dream of controlling Italy. The House of Savoy began the slow process of Italian expansion that resulted in national unification in the 19th century. Venice maintained its policy of neutrality and continued its losing battle against the Turks in defence of its overseas empire. Milan, Tuscany, Naples, and the Papal States were formally independent but under the direct or indirect control of Spain. The Italian states, unable to defend themselves against the greater powers, gained the protection of Spain. [3]

The oracle names three cities that were affected by this peace treaty. "Ravenna was ruled by Venice until 1509. [...] After the Venetian withdrawal, Ravenna was again ruled by legates of the Pope as part of the Papal States." Ravenna therefore received the protection of Spain. And, since "Pisa is a city in Tuscany," [4] it too came under the protection of Spain.

Verona, however, was under the protection of Venice, to which it had succumbed in 1405. And, apart from a brief interlude under Maximilian I (1509 – 1517), it remained under the rule of Venice until it fell to invasion by Napoleon I. Venice had already suffered several wars with the Ottomans: the most recent having taken place between 1537 and 1540, and which had resulted in several important captures by the Ottomans. But Venice still retained the island of Cyprus

> After concluding a prolonged war with the Habsburgs in 1568, the Ottomans were free to turn their attention to Cyprus. Sultan Selim II had made the conquest of the island his first priority already before his accession in 1566.
> On the Venetian side, Ottoman intentions had been clear, and an attack against Cyprus had been anticipated for some time. A war scare had broken out in 1564–1565, when the Ottomans eventually sailed for Malta, and unease mounted again in late 1567 and early 1568. [5]

The fears of the Venetians were well grounded, for two years later Cyprus was captured by the Ottomans in July 1570, and with further conquests threatened in the Mediterranean coastal areas Venice sought help. Aid came from Spain and the Papal States in the form of the Holy League, which defeated the Ottoman navy (7 October 1571) at the Battle of Lepanto.

Instead of elevating the Cross, spite by the Pope

Pius IV was Pope during this period (1566-1572), and was later elevated to sainthood. His austere character, his denouncement of nepotism, his humility before the poor, and his dedication to the sacred word earned for him a reputation not too unlike that of the Pharisees— ever obedient to the word of God, but lacking in the understanding of Jesus's humanity. It is this 'spitefulness' in his nature that has been criticized by historians. For example:

> The rules governing the Inquisition were sharpened; old charges, long suspended, were revived; rank offered no protection but rather exposed its possessor to fiercer attack. None was pursued more relentlessly than the intellectuals, among whom many of the Protestant doctrines had found acceptance. Princes and states withdrew their protection of heretics and courted the favour of the Holy See by surrendering distinguished offenders [...] In March 1571 the special Congregation of the Index, a list of books condemned as dangers to faith and morals, was established distinct from the Inquisition, and hundreds of printers took flight to Switzerland and Germany. The regret of Pius was that he had sometimes been too lenient. He encouraged Philip II of Spain to use the most ruthless tyranny to preserve his Dutch subjects in the Catholic faith and sent troops to France to help Catherine de Médicis repress the Huguenots; he protested against the tolerance shown by the Holy Roman emperor Rudolf II. [6]

Summary: *This oracle begins the foretelling of many popes who were to occupy the Vatican during the coming centuries. Its date coincides with the year in which Paul IV was elected, and in the space of four lines introduces two other popes that followed after his reign. Each one of the three popes has been characterised by a fact that is particularly relevant to him. The political climate in Italy at that time is also foretold in relationship to the Peace of Cateau-Cambrésis, and the Holy League: the latter having been created by the third mentioned pope, Pius V. In this respect it is interesting to note that the divine oracle refers to Pope Pius V not by any saintly characteristic, but, instead, is rather critical of his time in office.*

27   *Dedans les isles de cinq fleuues à vn,*
         Par le croissant du grand Chyren Selin:
         Par les bruynes de l'aër fureur en l'vn,
         Six eschapes cachés fardeaux de lvn.

28   *Le grand Celtique entrera dedans Rome,*
         Menant amass d'exilés & bannis:
         Le grand pasteur mettra à mort tout homme
         Qui pour le coq estoient aux Aples vnys.

29   *Le vesue saincte entendant les nouuelles,*
         De ses rameaus mis en perplex & trouble:
         Qui sera duict appaiser les querelles,
         Par son pourchas des razes sera comble.

30   *Par l'apparence de faincte saincteté,*
         Sera trahy aux ennemis le siege:
         Nuict qu'on cuidoit dormir en seureté,
         Pres de Brabant marcheront ceulx du Liege.

31   *Roy trouuera ce qu'il desiroit tant,*
         Quant le Prelat sera reprins à tort:
         Responce au duc le rendra mal content,
         Qui dans Milan mettre plusieurs à mort.

desiroit (conditional tense of désirer); à tort (OF) unjustly; duc (AF chef de guerre) head of warfare, also, Italian *apocope* – Duce. Cross-references: duc, C.IX: 80, C.IX: 95; C.X: 64.

> The King (**VICTOR IV**) will obtain that which he would have so much wished: 1943
> As for the Prelate (**CARDINAL SHUSTER**), he will be unjustly accused:
> A reply to the chief (**IL DUCE**) will render him dissatisfied,
> Who, in Milan, sending several to death.

The King will obtain that which he would have so much wished

Victor Emmanuel III of Italy had bowed to public pressure when appointing Benito Mussolini as Italy's Prime Minister. It was an action the King had not wished to take, but the Duce had been too powerful at the time to ignore. This changed soon after the outbreak of the Second World

War. A number of political and military failures diminished Mussolini's support amongst the Italian people, and the opportunity presented itself for the King to dismiss Mussolini from office. A Council meeting held on 24 July 1943 voted for the Prime Minister to be dismissed. Next morning, *the King was able to obtain that which he had so much wished for.* [1]—Mussolini's arrest.

As for the prelate, he will be unjustly accused

The Prelate referred to is Cardinal Alfredo Shuster, Archbishop of Milan. His relationship with Mussolini and the belief that Italy's occupation of Ethiopia in 1935 would bring Christianity to its people had led to a widespread belief that he was a fascist. In a letter written to Fr David Maria Turoldo in 1938 by the director of the Catholic paper *L'Italia,* this was corrected: "Schuster was neither a fascist nor anti-fascist and was not even neutral. Schuster was a monk and a just man. A monk is one that only has God inside his head: a 'monk in battle' after being a 'soldier in the monastery'." [2]

This prophecy serves to bring Cardinal Shuster into the next part of the oracle.

A reply to the chief will render him dissatisfied

Eighteen months after Mussolini's dismissal by King Victor Emmanuel, and after he had escaped into German occupied Italy to become head of its Salo Republic, *the Duce* attended a meeting inside Cardinal Schuster's palace in Milan; present were Italy's Resistance leaders. During the meeting, "Mussolini asked if the Resistance and the Allied commanders would guarantee his life and the lives of his ministers and their families if they surrendered."

The Duce was replied to in no uncertain terms. He was told: "anyone guilty of war crimes would be put on trial." Mussolini retorted that he would prefer to discuss this with his German allies. But, the reply he received immediately confirmed that the German Commander had already agreed to surrender, and had done so without seeing any need to consult him: quite apart from which, the Allied forces would never agree to the proposal put forward by the Duce.

Reports from those present at the meeting said *the reply showed him badly pleased,* as "Mussolini violently denounced the Germans for their treachery." [3]

Who, in Milan, sending several to death

Some months before attending the meeting inside Cardinal Schuster's palace in Milan, Mussolini had sanctioned the deaths of fifteen partisans who were residents of the city. Earnest pleas for clemency had been made to the Duce at the time, but he had ignored these. "When it was a question of dealing with the Partisans, Mussolini was as pitiless as any of the Germans [...] and ordered that captured Partisans must always be shot."

After his own death, several days later, his body was hung up for display in Milan where the partisans had earlier been shot. "Many of those who kicked and spat [... were] the mothers of young partisans who had been captured and shot [...] by Mussolini's Fascist militia." [4]

Summary: *This prophetic episode was fulfilled by Mussolini from the time he was deposed as 'Il Duce' to the eve of his capture and death, after leaving Cardinal Shuster's palace in Milan (see Century 10 No. 64). Cardinal Shuster is briefly introduced to confirm his identity: as too is King Victor Emmanuel, who began Mussolini's downfall. Significant detail of the meeting that led to Mussolini taking the final step towards his death is given in the oracle. Prophecy, like history, is composed of the biographies of those who make both possible. It is the logical outcome of a timeless universe in which both are one, but seen from opposite views.*

32 Par trahysons de vers gens à mort battu,
    Prins surmonté sera par son desordre:
    Conseil friuole au grand captive sentu,
    Nez par sureur quant Begich viendra mordre.

'vers gens' is written elsewhere as verges

33 Sa main derniere par Alus sanguinaire,
    Ne se pourra par la mer guarantir:
    Entre deux fleuues caindre main militaire,
    Le noir l'ireux le sera repentir.

34 *De feu volant la machination.*
  Viendra troubler au grand chef assigés:
  Dedans sera telle sedition,
  Qu'en desespoir seront les profligés.

35 *Pres de Rion, & proche à blanche laine,*
  Aries, Taurus, Cancer, Leo la Vierge:
  Mars, Iupiter, le Sol ardre grant plaine,
  Boys & cités, lettres cachés au cierge.

36 *Ne bien ne mal par bataille terrestre,*
  Ne paruiendra aux confins de Perouse:
  Rebeller Pise, Florence voir mal estre,
  Roy nuict blessé sus mulet à noire house.

37 *L'œuure ancient se paracheuera,*
  Du toict cherra sur le grand mal ruyne:
  Innocent faict mort on accusera:
  Nocent caiché, taillis à la bruyne.

38 *Aux profligés de paix les ennemis,*
  Apres auoir l'Italie supperee:
  Noir sanguinaire, rouge sera commis,
  Feu, sang verser, eaue de sang couloree.

There are similarities to the Napoleonic Era but the correlation is not complete.

39 *L'enfant du regne par paternelle prinse,*
  Expolié sera pour deliurer:
  Aupres du lac Trasimen l'azur prinse,
  La trope hostaige pour trop fort s'enyurer.

40 *Grand de Magonce pour grande soif esteindre,*
  Sera privé de sa grand dignité:
  Ceux de Cologne si fort le viendront plaindre
  Que le grand groppe au Ryn sera getté.

Magonce (L – Mogontiacum) Mainz; soif (AF - haie) line; esteindre (OF) abolish; plaindre (OF) bemoan; groppe (Italian groppo = groupe; in French – and as a *paragram*: croupe) rump; getté (OF – getter, as iecter, *also* AF geter) to draw,

 The great man of Mainz (**DALBERG**), in respect of abolishing the great line, 1801
 Will be deprived of his great authority:
 Those of Cologne will so strongly come to bemoan it,
 Then the great rump will be drawn to the Rhine.

The great man of Mainz

Karl Theodor Anton Maria von Dalberg was Archbishop of Mainz, Arch-Chancellor of the Holy Roman Empire, Prince-Primate of the Confederation of the Rhine, Prince of Regensburg and Grand Duke of Frankfurt. Consequently, as the Archbishop-Elector of Mainz he was ranked first among ecclesiastical and secular princes of the Empire, and second only to the Emperor himself.

In respect of abolishing the great line

On 9 February 1801, the Treaty of Luneville consolidated the territorial gains made in Germany by the French Republic in 1794. Article VI confirmed the loss to Dalberg of Worms, Constance and Mainz.[1] It also meant that *the great line* dividing German held territory from France was abolished to release the gains made by France..

> His majesty the emperor and king, as well as in his own name as in that of the Germanic empire, consents that the French republic shall possess henceforth in complete sovereignty, and as their property, the country and domains situated on the left bank of the Rhine, and which formed part of the Germanic empire: so that, in conformity with what had been expressly consented to at the congress of Rastadt, by the deputation of the empire, and approved by the emperor, the towing path of the Rhine will henceforth be the limit between the French republic and the Germanic empire; that is to say , from the place where the Rhine leaves the Helvetic territory, to that where it enters the Batavian territory.[2]

Will be deprived of his great authority

Because Mainz had now been annexed by France, Dalberg's archiepiscopal see was transferred to Regensburg. His eastern territories became known as the Principality of Regensburg. In 1803, the archbishopric of Mainz was actually secularized, and in 1806 the Holy Roman Empire was dissolved altogether. Karl von Dalberg therefore became the last elector of Mainz along a line of successive electors dating back to 1356.

Those of Cologne

As in other prophecies, the phrase *those of* invariably means an occupying force, rather than the people of that locality. In this oracle, the phrase therefore points to the French.

> The French Revolutionary Wars resulted in the occupation of Cologne and the Rhineland in 1794. In the following years the French consolidated their presence. In 1798 the city became an arrondissement in the newly created Département de la Roer. [...] . In 1801 all citizens of Cologne were granted French citizenship. [3]

Will so strongly come to bemoan it

> The position of the established Roman Catholic Church in Germany, the *Reichskirche*, was not only diminished, it was nearly destroyed. The Church lost its constitutional role in the Empire; most of the Catholic universities were closed, as well as thousands of monasteries; and many Catholic foundations closed down. [4]

Among those closed down was the University of Cologne, established in 1388 as the fourth university in the Holy Roman Empire. It had first begun teaching on 6 January 1389. But, in 1798, the university was closed down by the French. It was not reopened until May 1919.

It was not only the university that caused the citizens of Cologne to bemoan their loss. There was, in addition, an enormous cost to the Church as a result of secularizing the city. Pope Pius VII was to acknowledge this deficit after the city was visited by Archbishop Dalberg.

> [T]he seizure of ecclesiastical property was permitted in 1803 by the Imperial Deputation at Ratisbon. The measure resulted in enormous loss for the Church, but the pope was powerless to resist its execution. [5]

Then the great rump will be drawn to the Rhine

After achieving the secularization of cities along the French bank of the Rhine, Napoleon's next move was one of consolidation. On 12 July 1806, the Treaty of the *Confederation of the Rhine* was signed. This drew together sixteen states from present-day Germany into a confederation or *rump*: that is "a contemptible remnant of a parliament or similar body:" OED. It was also able to provide Napoleon with soldiers and supplies for his armed forces.

> Instead of a monarchical head of state, as the Holy Roman Emperor had been, its highest office was held by Karl Theodor von Dalberg, the former Arch Chancellor, who now bore the title of a Prince-Primate of the confederation. As such, he was President of the College of Kings and presided over the *Diet of the Confederation*, designed to be a parliament-like body though it never actually assembled. After Prussia lost to France in 1806, Napoleon cajoled most of the secondary states of Germany into the Rheinbund. Eventually, an additional 23 German states joined the Confederation. It was at its largest in 1808, when it included 36 states—four kingdoms, five grand duchies, 13 duchies, seventeen principalities, and the Free Hansa towns of Hamburg, Lübeck, and Bremen. [6]

Summary: *This oracle concerns the political aftermath of Germany having succumbed to Napoleon's empire building. The Archbishop of Mainz was indeed a great man of that time, and the political effects felt by him are correctly predicted. Cologne is also picked out for the effect which the French occupation had upon the city. Furthermore, two treaties are indicated but not overtly mentioned. Yet their effects proved to be the driving force which brought this prophecy to its fulfilment.*

41   *Le second chef du regne Dannemarc.*
      Par ceulx de Frise & l'isle Britannique,
      Fera despendre plus de cent mille marc,
      Vain exploicter voyage en Italique.

42   *A l'Ogmyon sera laissé le regne.*
       Du grand Selin qui plus fera de faict:
       Par les Italies estendra son enseigne,
       Regi sera par prudent contrefaict.

Ogmyon *for* Ogmios; Selin *for* Selene, the goddess of the moon, which symbolises Turkey. Caliph Selim is therefore a paragram from Selin; contrefaict (OF) a simulation

For the Ogmios (**SULEYMAN**), the reign will be relinquished   1566
For the great **SELIM**, who will do more by achievement:
Through the Italies, he will extinguish his ensign,
It will be governed by prudent simulation.

For the Ogmios the reign will be relinquished

We know from the Roman satirist Lucian, writing in the second century A.D. that Ogmios resembled the Greek god Hercules. Both gods were known for their leonine strength, which was illustrated by the lion skins they wore. But Ogmios also possessed great wisdom, together with the power to employ it as a leader of men. For, it was said, that his eloquence had such persuasive power, it infected all who heard him. And he used this gift to fill men's minds with the desire to follow him to the ends of the earth. [1]

Compare these descriptive terms with those of Suleyman the Magnificent, who died on 7 September 1566, thus outliving the Seer by two days short of ten weeks.

> Süleyman the Magnificent [...] his chest was broad and his arms were long and muscular. He resembled a lion with his majestic bearing and had a beautiful and clear voice. He was heroic, determined, and powerful, and was blessed with good fortune and luck for both for himself and for those around him. [...] Suleyman's poetry is among the best poetry in Islam, and he sponsored an army of artists, religious thinkers, and philosophers that outshone the most educated courts of Europe. [2]

For the great Selim, who will do more by achievement

After Suleyman's death, the reign of the Ottoman Empire was given over to Selim II, his eldest son, aged forty-two. Selim's reign lasted eight years. He died on 5 December 1574. His misfortune was to slip on the wet floor of the bathroom inside the Topkapi palace and injure his head. Nevertheless, during his reign, it is known from existing Ottoman Archives: Muhimme Defteri Vol 7 No 721, that he foresaw the need to join the Mediterranean with the Red Sea.

In the archives it is also recorded that he brought together all the experts in architecture and engineering to investigate the land between the seas, so that a canal might be built. Another of his architectural projects was to build the Selimye Mosque designed by Mimar Sinan at Edirne (Adrianople). Lady Mary Wortley, the wife of the British ambassador to Turkey in the 18th century, declared it to be "The noblest building I ever saw." Sultan Selim also continued his father's involvement with Mecca, where the work he put into the task gave the great mosque its distinctively Ottoman appearance, which it retains today.

> This was a Sultan who ruled by the foundations of Islam such that they literally stand to this day, and that itself is testimony to the righteousness of Sultan Selim II. With all of the information of his personal pursuits such as his love of archery, his political activities, his architectural projects and plans, and considering the short time of his rule, it is impossible to buy into the Kinrossian picture of a disinterested drunk perpetuated by his book (Hasha Astaghfirullah). [3]

Selim II also maintained the territorial gains made by his influential father. In 1568 he negotiated with Maximilian II the *Treaty of Adrianople* 17 February 1568 (also called *Treaty of Edirne*). This concluded the Austro-Turkish War (1566-1568) and it brought with it a period of peace between these two Empires. In this respect, it will be noted that the oracle prefixes *Selim* with the word *great*. This is in contrast to the much quoted reference to Selim made by Lord Kinross, who saw Selim as a debauched, drunk with no ability to rule. Presumably, this nobly titled author had overlooked the fact that consumption of alcohol is forbidden by Islam. Suffice to say, the Seer's prophecy originated from a supremely higher LORD.

Through the Italies, he will extinguish his ensign

"The Fourth Ottoman–Venetian War, also known as the War of Cyprus (Italian: *Guerra di Cipro*) was fought between 1570 and 1573. It was waged between the Ottoman Empire and the Republic of Venice." [4] Italy in the 16th century was confined to separate regions, hence, the plurality of the phrase in the prophecy. With Venice threatened by Selim II's quest for more territory, and with its island of Cyprus lost to the Ottomans, Pius V formed a Holy League (25 May 1571) to combat the Turkish menace, and diminish the threat of further land loss. When the League was completed, it included *the Italies*—"the Papal States, the Habsburg states of Naples and Sicily, the Republic of Venice, the Republic of Genoa and the Grand Duchy of Tuscany." [5] The oracle's plurality of Italy to Italies is therefore fully justified.

A fleet was formed by these regions and combined with ships and men from Spain, Savoy and Malta. Under the command of Don Juan, it met Selim's armada at the battle of Lepanto (7 October 1571). The defeat suffered by the Turks during this battle was so serious that for many years afterwards, it totally *extinguished the* Turkish *ensign* from the Mediterranean Sea.

It will be governed by prudent simulation

Unlike his father Suleyman the Magnificent, Selim II was not a warrior. He preferred to govern his empire through consultations with his viziers. Chief among these advisors was Sokollu Mehmed Pasha who had served under Suleyman, and who would go on to serve under Murad III, until his assassination in 1579. But for more than fourteen years, "he was *de facto* ruler of the Ottoman Empire." [6] Eight of those years having been spent behind the scenes in service to Selim II, who remained the figurehead and spokesman for the Ottoman Empire.

Summary: *This is a prophecy about Moslems for Islam to consider. The source of the prophecy is obviously the same as for the overtly Judaic and Christian oracles that are included among these accurate forecasts. Although there are three major religions, there is only one God. And that one God saw fit to reveal the future of the world to a Judaic Christian, and He has done so to cement understanding of His Creation, which stretches into a time zone that we refer to as the 'future'. In this oracle, Suleyman the Magnificent was followed by Selim, whose reign occurred shortly after the death of the seer. The prophecy therefore includes the Battle of Lepanto and the Holy League referred to in No. 26 of this chapter, and in Century Nine, No. 42. Selim's achievements and his method of government have also been correctly predicted.*

43   Long temps sera sans estre habitee,
        Ou Seine & Marne autour vient arrouser:
        De la Tamise & martiaulx temptee,
        Deceuz les gardes en cuidant reposer.

44   De nuict par Nantes L'yris apparoistra,
        Des artz marins susciteront la pluye:
        Arabique gouffre grand class parfondra,
        Vn monster en Saxe naistra d'ours & truye.

45   Le gouuerneur du regne bien scauant,
        Ne consenter voulant au faict Royal:
        Mellile classe par le contraire vent,
        Le remettra à son plus desloyal.

46   Vn iuste sera en exil renuoyé,
        Par pestilence aux confins de Nonseggle:
        Response au rouge le sera a desuoyé,
        Roy retirant à la Rane & à l'aigle.

47   Entre deux monts les deux grands assemblés,
        Delaisseront leur simulte secrete:
        Brucelles & Dolle par Langres accablés,
        Pour à Malignes executer leur peste.

48   La saincteté trop faincte & seductiue,
        Accompaigne d'vne langue diserte:
        La cité vieille & Palme trop hastiue,
        Florence & Sienne rendront plus desertes.

49   *De la partie de Mammer grand Pontife,*
Subiuguera les confins du Dannube:
Chasser les croix par fer raffe ne riffe,
Captifz, or, bagues plus de cent mille rubes.

N.B. rube, possibly a syncope for rub(l)e; an Italian weight of about 600 lbs, having 12 ozs to the pound.

50   *Dedans le puys seront trouués les oz,*
Sera l'incest commis par la maratre:
L'estat changé on querra bruit & loz,
Et aura Mars ascendant pour son astre.

51   *Peuple assemblé voir noueau expectacle,*
Princes & Roys par plusieurs assistans:
Pilliers faillir, murs, mis comme miracle,
Le Roy sauué & trente des instans.

52   *En lieu du grand qui sera condemne,*
De prison hors son amy en sa place:
L'espoir Troyen en six moys ioinct mort nay,
Le Sol à l'vrne seront prins fluues en glace.

53   *Le grand Prelat Celtique à Roy suspect,*
De nuict par cours sortira à hors du regne:
Par duc fertile à son grand roy Bretaigne,
Bisance à Cipres & Tunes insuspect.

This interval of eleven prophetic quatrains appears to contain no fulfilments, up to the present time. It recalls a longer interval in Century Five (see No. 77), in which an antichrist (if not the Antichrist) was foretold. This next oracle, too, includes an important scriptural reference.

54   *Au point du iour second chant du coq,*
Ceulx de Tunes, de Fez, & de Bugie:
Par les Arabes captif le roy Maroq,
L'an mil six cens & sept de Liturgie.

At daybreak, the second crowing of the cock,   1578
Those of Tunis, of Fez, and of Bougie:
By reason of the Arabs, the King (**SEBASTIAN**) captive, Morocco:
The year **1607** by Liturgy.

At daybreak, the second crowing of the cock

These oracles do not waste words. The first line must therefore have meaning. In fact, it is the opening line is from the Gospel of Saint Mark 14: 30. It concerns the prediction made by Jesus to the Apostle Peter on the night of his betrayal and arrest. "Truly I tell you," Jesus answered, "today—yes, tonight—before the rooster crows twice you yourself will disown me three times." These words were uttered on the eve of Christ's crucifixion. Their importance will emerge below.

Those of Tunis, of Fez, and of Bougie

The three towns mentioned above are located in North Africa: each one being situated in a different country; that is, Tunisia, Morocco and Algeria. Bougie is the former name of Bejaïa. At the time this prediction was fulfilled, Murad III was Sultan of Turkey and he controlled all three towns. [1] In 1578, the deposed Moroccan Caliph al-Mutawakkil, joined forces with King Sebastian of Portugal in a bid to conquer the whole of Morocco. Portugal already held the northern half of the country, having first taken Ceuta, opposite Gibraltar in 1415. King Sebastian was therefore already titular *King of Morocco*, and he believed it to be his divine mission in life to conquer the whole of that country and convert its Moslem population to Christianity.

Opposition to the invasion came from an Arab section and from Caliph Abd al-Malik, who had deposed King Sebastian's ally, al-Mutawakkil, in 1576: when, with the aid of 10,000 Ottomans from Algeria, he seized Fez. Tunis had previously been seized by Ottoman Turks in 1574, after the country briefly fell to Don Juan of Austria in the afterglow of his victory at the battle of Lepanto. Consequently, *those of Tunis, Fez, and Bougie* in 1578 were under Ottoman rule.

By reason of the Arabs

The reference to an *Arab* involvement is historically correct. Between 1525 and 1554, the Sa'dids had established their rule over Morocco by taking control of the southern part of the country. The Sa'dids were of *Arab* origin, and claimed to be sharifs; that is, descendants of the prophet, Muhammad. [2] As Moslems, they were therefore opposed to becoming Christian converts.

The King captive, Morocco

On 4 August 1578, the combined forces of Abd al-Malik and his Sa'did Moroccans met the troops of King Sebastian and al-Mutawakkil at Ksar el-Kebir. In the ensuing conflict known as the 'Battle of the Three Kings', the Portuguese were defeated. Forced into retreat, Sebastian reached only as far as the Wadi al-Makhazin, which was in full flow. Trapped between the water's edge and Abd al- Malik, Sebastian and al-Mutawakkil surrendered. *The King* had become *a captive in Morocco*.

Exactly what happened afterwards is undocumented. It is known only that the bodies of both King Sebastian and al-Mutawakkil were later discovered drowned in the Wadi. [3]

The year 1607, by liturgy

The oracle names the year this happened as 1607, and then qualifies it: adding, 'by Liturgy'. The Catechism of the Catholic Church defines a 'Liturgical Year' as "The celebration throughout the year of the mysteries of the Lord's birth, life, death, and Resurrection in such a way that it becomes a 'year of the Lord's grace.'" (p. 886). It is therefore to the first line of this oracle that we must return.

'The second crowing of the cock' occurred on the morning after Jesus was arrested. *By Liturgy* is therefore referring to his death. From this, it follows that the oracle is providing Christians and the world in general with the actual year in which Jesus died and was resurrected.

To explain this is a simple matter. The year 1607 *by* Liturgy means that we must take the year 1607, and instead of counting the years from Year One, we instead count the years from the crucifixion – which is according to Liturgy – until we arrive at 1607.

To do this involves an equation in one unknown. We do not know for certain the year in which the Crucifixion occurred, so we refer to it as x. The equation is therefore, $x + 1578 = 1607$. Whence, $x = 29$. Jesus was therefore crucified in the year 29 AD. Alternatively, in the year 1607, dating from the year in which Jesus was crucified, the year in question becomes 1578.

According to the Jewish calendar this date coincides with the 13th of Nissan, 3789: equivalent to Friday 13th of April 29 AD. The reason for this is because the Crucifixion occurred on the day before Passover, which commenced at sundown on the 14th of Nissan. Jesus would therefore have been thirty-three years of age at the time of his death. This calculation coincides with the gospel of *St John* (19:31-36), which states that the crucifixion took place on Preparation Day (i.e., preparation for celebrating the Passover). [4]

The orthodox Jew, having rejected Jesus as the Messiah, has reason to be greatly concerned by this. The Seer was himself Jewish, and his prophecies being without error, therefore strongly imply that their source came from the same God that is worshipped in the Judaic religion.

Further Jewish unease may be expected when the Seer adopts the same strategy to confirm the year in which Jesus was born. It coincides exactly with the year prophesied by Daniel for the birth of the 'Anointed One'.

Summary: *This is an intriguing prophecy for the way it refers to the Christian, Moslem and Judaic religions. King Sebastian's attempt to convert Moslem Morocco to Christianity failed disastrously in 1578. But, by counting this number of years from the date of the Crucifixion of Jesus, carried out by order of the Sanhedrin in Jerusalem, up to the year given in the oracle, the exact date of the Crucifixion can be determined. But note also, this is the first occasion that the seer has gone back in time to the past.*

55   *Au chalmé Duc en arrachant l'esponce,*
          Voille arabesque voir, subit descouuerte:
          Tripolis, Chio. & ceulx de Trapesconce,
          Duc prins, Marnegro, & sa cité deserte.

chalmé (AF chaume) stubble; arrachant (OF) tearing away; esponce (OF) forgoing; arabesque (OF) Arabian-like.

The Duke, at the stubble through the violent tearing away of foregone land,   1914
Seeing Arabian-like sails, an unexpected detection:
Tripoli, Chios, and those of Trabzon:
The Duke (**NICHOLAS**) seized, Black Sea, and his city (**TRABZON**) abandoned.

The Duke at the stubble through the violent tearing away of foregone land

The Duke, to whom this opening line refers, historically speaking, was Grand Duke Nikolay
Nikolayevich Romanov of Russia. At the onset of World War One, he was made Commander–
in-Chief of the Russian armies that were fighting against Germany, Austro-Hungary and Turkey.
It was in this capacity that he issued his Manifesto to the Polish people (14 August 1914), in
which he promised, "that though 'a hundred and fifty years ago the living body of Poland was torn to
pieces, [...] her soul survived and she lived in hope that for the Polish people would come an hour of
regeneration and reconciliation with Russia'. Nicholas promised the re-unification of the Polish lands
under the aegis of the Russian Czar and autonomy to the Poles." [1]

Nicholas was referring to Poland having been divided up - "torn to pieces" - during the land
seizures that took place in 1772, 1793 and 1795, for the benefit of Austria, Prussia and Russia:
thus leaving behind the 'stubble'. Nicholas's intention, after so much had been lost, was to
remove the fears of the Polish people, and assure them that Russia would reunite their country,
and give them autonomy. His proclamation was met with wide approval by the Polish citizens.

Seeing Arabian-like sails

In 1915, the Tsar replaced Nicholas as Commander-in-Chief of the Russian armies that were
fighting against Germany and Austro-Hungary, and appointed him Commander-in-Chief and
Viceroy of the Caucasus. This was where the Russian army was engaged in fighting against the
Ottoman Empire. It was also where he came to see Arab-like ships.

> The Caucasus Campaign extended from the Caucasus to the Eastern Asia Minor region, reaching
> as far as Trabzon, Bitlis, Mus and Van. The land warfare was accompanied by the Russian navy in
> the Black Sea Region of the Ottoman Empire. [2]

The Black Sea is bounded by Europe, Anatolia (the Arabian part of Turkey where Asia and
Europe meet) and the Caucasus. The Sea became a significant location for naval battles during
World War I. Before then, it had been used as the Ottoman Empire's "Navy Lake". This dated
back to when the Crimea was seized from Genoa in 1479.

An unexpected detection

On 10 January 1916, under the command of Duke Nicholas, "General Yudenich launched a major
winter offensive" against one of the strongest fortresses in Europe. And it resulted in the Russian
army successfully capturing the fortress at Erzurum and the city port Trabzon.

> The Battle of Erzurum was a major winter offensive by the Imperial Russian Army on the Caucasus
> Campaign that led to the capture of the strategic city of Erzurum [... The] Ottoman High
> Command did not expect any Russian operations during winter, Mahmut Kamil was in Istanbul,
> and his chief of staff, Colonel Felix Guse, was in Germany. [3]

Tripoli, Chios

Before the commencement of hostilities leading to World War One, both Tripoli and Chios
were part of the Ottoman Empire. Both locations were liberated from Ottoman rule by naval
battles, and both places subsequently became the scenes of crimes against humanity.

> Italy had long claimed that Tripoli fell within its zone of influence and that Italy had the right to
> preserve order within the state. Under the pretext of protecting its own citizens living in Tripoli
> from the Ottoman Government, it declared war against the Ottomans on 29 September 1911, and
> announced its intention of annexing Tripoli. On 1 October 1911, a naval battle was fought at
> Prevesa, Greece, and three Ottoman vessels were destroyed. [4]

After the First World War ended, the Treaty of Lausanne confirmed that Italian sovereignty in
Tripoli was to be officially acknowledged by Turkey.

Chios rejoined the rest of independent Greece after the First Balkan War (1912). The Greek Navy liberated Chios in November 1912 in a hard fought but brief amphibious operation. [5]

One year later, Turkey was forced to acknowledge Greece's annexation of Chios and the other Aegean islands by the Treaty of London (1913).

From 1551 until 1911, Tripolitania (the region surrounding the city of Tripoli) was ruled by the Ottoman Empire. But On 3 October 1911 this changed when Italian troops occupied *Tripoli*, claiming that it was liberating the region. Thereafter, terrible, inhuman brutality was perpetrated against Italians that were captured during this incursion.

On 23 October 1911, Italian troops were attacked by a Turkish-Arab force while marching through the Mechiya oasis and were heavily defeated: 500 bersaglieri were massacred at Sciara Scia. They were attacked mainly by local Arabs, who killed all the soldiers made captives with tortures and cruelty. [6]

I saw in one mosque seventeen Italian crucified with their bodies reduced to the status of bloody rags and bones, but whose faces still retain traces of hellish agony. It has passed through the neck of these wretched a long barrel and arms resting on this rod. They were then nailed to the wall and died for a slow fire between untold sufferings. In a corner another body is crucified, but as an officer he was to have refined his sufferings. The eyes are stitched. All the bodies were mutilated and castrated; so indescribable was the scene and the bodies appeared swollen as shapeless carrion. But that's not all! In the cemetery of Chui which served as a refuge from the Turks and whence pulled from afar we could see another show. Under the same door in front of the Italian trenches five soldiers had been buried up to their shoulders, their heads emerged from the black sand stained of their blood: heads horrible to see, and there you could read all the tortures of hunger and thirst. [7]

Chios is the fifth largest of the Greek islands in the Aegean Sea, situated 4 miles off the Anatolian coast. It was also the birthplace of the poet Homer. "The Ottoman government regarded it as one of the most valuable provinces of the Empire." [8]

Chios was affected by the population exchanges after the Greco-Turkish War of 1919-1922, the incoming Greek refugees settling in Kastro (previously Turkish) and in new settlements hurriedly built south of Chios Town. [9]

In the Treaty of Lausanne, which also affected Tripoli: Greece and Turkey agreed to an exchange of populations. As a result, two million people were uprooted in an enforced deportation.

Some 1.5 million Greeks who lived in Turkey had to move to Greece and about 500.000 Turks were sent from Greece to Turkey. Many spoke little or none of their ancestral language, and most were regarded with intense hostility in their new homelands. [...] To this day Greece is dotted with towns with such names as Nea Smyrni and Nea Chios (New Smyrna and New Chios) reminders of this forced migration. [10]

And those of Trabzon

Trabzon is the Turkish name for Trebizond. And, as with Tripoli and Chios, it was also part of the Ottoman Empire before being captured in 1916 by an invading force. At the same time, "Trabzon [became] a major Armenian extermination centre during the Armenian Genocide." [11]

The city was the site of one of the key battles between the Ottoman and Russian armies during the Caucasus Campaign of World War I which resulted in the capture of Trabzon by the Russian Caucasus army under command of Grand Duke Nicholas and Nikolai Yudenich in April 1916. [12]

Trabzon was retaken by Turkey in the following year, when Russia retreated from the city and the whole of eastern and north-eastern Anatolia, due to the outbreak of the Russian Revolution.

In 1915, leaders of the Turkish government set in motion a plan to expel and massacre Armenians living in the Ottoman Empire. Though reports vary, most sources agree that there were about 2 million Armenians in the Ottoman Empire at the time of the massacre. By the early 1920s, when the massacres and deportations finally ended, some 1.5 million of Turkey's Armenians were dead, with many more forcibly removed from the country. [13]

Cemal Azmi (1868-1922), also spelled Jemal Azmi, was an Ottoman politician and governor of the Trabzon province during World War I and the final years of the Ottoman Empire. He was one of the perpetrators of the Armenian genocide and was mainly responsible for the liquidation of Armenians in the Trabzon province. He was known as the "butcher of Trabzon". [...] Azmi, along with the collaboration of Nail Bey, ordered the drowning of thousands of women and children in the Black Sea. [14]

"Many of the children were loaded into boats and taken out to sea and thrown overboard." The Italian consul of Trabzon in 1915, Giacomo Gorrini, writes: "I saw thousands of innocent women and children placed on boats which were capsized in the Black Sea." [15]

The Duke seized

The oracle now returns to Duke Nicholas. Upon leaving the Caucasus at the time of the Russian Revolution in 1917, the Grand Duke ...

was appointed by the Emperor, in his last official act, as the supreme commander in chief, and was wildly received as he journeyed to headquarters in Mogilev; however, within 24 hours of his arrival, the new premier, Prince Georgy Lvov, cancelled his appointment. Nicholas spent the next two years in the Crimean Peninsula, sometimes under house arrest. [16]

Black Sea

The Black Sea, which was the graveyard of Armenian orphans, women and others considered undesirable by the Turkish administration, was also the scene of naval warfare at the time.

As 1916 opened, the Russian navy focused on supporting army operations on the Caucasus front. There they built up Batum as a base for small warships [...] It is a measure of the leadership of Ebergard and Kolchak that the fleet's sailors were among the last to give way to the November revolution, which swept the Bolsheviks into power and triggered the great Russian Civil War. As a result, the Russians continued to dominate the Black Sea throughout the year. [17]

And his city abandoned

His city is a euphemism for Trabzon, since it was captured by Grand Duke Nicholas. Under the Treaty of Lausanne, Trabzon was returned to Turkish rule. It then became abandoned by the mass exodus of Greeks, forced into exile to rebuild their lives anew.

Following the Turkish War of Independence and the annulment of the Treaty of Sèvres (1920) which was replaced by the Treaty of Lausanne (1923), Trabzon again became a part of Turkey. In the early 1920s there was a mass exodus of Greeks from Trabzon. [18]

Summary: *This oracle focuses upon World War in the Caucasus. It begins with Grand Duke Nicholas of Russia, who issued his Manifesto to Poland at the beginning of WW I, before taking command in the Caucasus. Tripoli, Chios and Trabzon were part of the Ottoman empire, but within a few years of each other their rule changed hands, and all three became scenes of crimes against humanity. The prophecy concludes with the Duke returning to Russia, and a mass exile of Greeks from Trabzon.*

> 56   *La crainte armee de l'ennemy Narbon,*
>   *Effrayera si fort les Hesperiques:*
>   *Perpignan vuide par l'aueuglé d'arbon,*
>   *Lors Barcelon par mer donra la piques.*

> 57   *Celuy qu'estoit bien auant dans le regne,*
>   *Ayant chef rouge proche à la hierarchie:*
>   *Aspre & cruel, & se sera tant craindre,*
>   *Succedera à sacree monarchie.*

The one that was forward in the reign,   1585
Having a red principal (**CARDINAL GHISLIERI**) close to the holy government:
Severe and unmerciful, likewise he will himself fear so many:
He will succeed to the sacred monarchy (**SIXTUS V**).

The one that was forward in the reign

Felice Peretti di Montalto became a novice at the age of twelve and was ordained thirteen years later. At the age of twenty-eight, he was appointed rector of his convent at Siena: and then, in 1553, as rector of San Lorenzo at Naples. Three years later he was made rector of the convent of the Frari at Venice. And in 1557, Pius IV appointed him counsellor to the Inquisition in Venice. After his recall to Rome, in quick succession he became counsellor to the Holy Office, professor at the Sapienza, and finally general procurator and vicar Apostolic of his Franciscan order.

In 1565, Pius IV sent him on a mission to Spain, where he was to investigate a charge of heresy against Archbishop Carranza of Toledo. Upon his return one year later, Pius V created him Bishop of Naples, and chose him as his confessor. After which, the Pope raised him to Cardinal. [1]

Having a red principal close to the holy government

Cardinal Montalto first come to the notice of the Vatican because of the Lenten sermons he was preaching at the Church of the Twelve Apostles. It was alleged that these were blasphemous, and he was initially charged with heresy.

The case came before Cardinal Ghislieri, who had been made *principal* inquisitor by Pope Julius III, after his having served as inquisitor at Como and Bergamo. At the hearing, Cardinal Ghislieri completely exonerated Montalto of any heresy: and, as a result, he was recommended to Paul IV, who invited him to join the commission for reforming the Roman Curia.

Montalto now had the powerful backing of Ghislieri, whose closeness to the holy government would make him a candidate for the papacy. "From that time his advancement was assured." [2]

Severe and unmerciful

Montalto had already displayed the severity of his character in Venice, where he served as inquisitor for three years. It was because of this that his, "severity and highhandedness in dealing with the cases brought before him caused his recall." [3] That same severity was exposed after he became Pope. In his papal bull, *Effraenatum* (1588), "He said all abortions for whatever reason were homicide and were penalized by excommunication reserved to the Holy See." [4]

His successor, Gregory XIV realized that this "view was too severe" and he reversed it. (Ibid) Montalto's attempt to impose the death penalty upon those found guilty of adultery did not make the statute book either.

Another commentator upon Montalto's extreme views was Count Olivares, Spain's ambassador to Rome. At the time when the Pope was threatening to place the work of theologian Vittorio, together with Robert Bellermine's book *Conroversies,* on the *Index of Prohibited Books*, Olivares wrote to Philip II, reporting in a mocking tone that the cardinals of the Congregation of the Index were too fearful of his Holiness to tell him that these two works were based upon that of the saints, "for fear Sixtus might give them a taste of his sharp temper and perhaps put the saints themselves on the Index." [5] Sixtus V also showed unnecessary cruelty in the punishments he administered. At the time of his election, "Four youngsters who had attended the papal procession carrying weapons were arrested and put to death. For some time the sight of bodies hanging from gallows or of beheaded heads at the top of pikes became common in Rome." [6] After his election as Pope, "Sixtus proceeded with an almost ferocious severity against the prevailing lawlessness" of his time. [7] The Catholic Encyclopedia has exposed the cruelty with which his punishments were carried out.

> Thousands of brigands were brought to justice: Having obtained the co-operation of the neighbouring states, he exterminated, often with excessive cruelty, the system of brigandage which had reached immense proportions.

Likewise, he will himself fear so many

Sixtus V "restored peace and safety by harsh and repressive means, but his extreme measures in dealing with bandits created many enemies." [8] But it was not only repercussions from these quarters that he feared. During the pontificate of his predecessor, Gregory XIII whom he detested, Sixtus had retired to his villa on the Esquiline Hill, where he began preparing plans to extend his home; but this created even more anger against him from those he displaced.

> The first phase (1576–80) was enlarged after Peretti became pope and was able to clear buildings to open four new streets in 1585–6. The villa contained two residences, the *Palazzo Sistino* or "di Termini" ("of the Baths") and the casino, called the *Palazzetto Montalto e Felice*.
>
> Displaced Romans were furious, and resentment of this act was still felt centuries later, when the decision was taken to build the central pontifical railroad station (begun in 1869) in the area of the Villa, marking the beginning of its destruction. [9]

He will succeed to the sacred monarchy

Since the lines above have contained examples of Sixtus V's severity, cruelty and the reaction it caused, it seems superfluous to include this line of prophecy, for it is already implied by what has gone before; but there is a purpose to it. Montalto's election to the sacred monarchy was controversial; and that is why it has been included.

Peter de Rosa, a former Catholic priest and Professor of Metaphysics and Ethics at Westminster Seminary, who became Dean of Theology at Corpus Christie College in London, had this to say about Sixtus V before his election to the papacy.

> At the rare meetings of the Sacred College which he was obliged to attend, he coughed continuously as if he were in the final stages of consumption. To whatever was proposed he meekly bowed his big tonsured head in assent. He was too weak to argue [...] An English visitor to Rome chanced to catch a rare glimpse of his Eminence bent over his fire and wrote home about this "most crouching, humble cardinal that was ever lodged in an oven."

> Pope Gregory died in 1585. Montalto appeared at the conclave, hollow-cheeked, dull-eyed, with wrinkles carefully applied. His gait was snail-like, his voice scarcely audible. He walked on crutches, and so round-shouldered was he that his head nearly touched the ground.[10]

His election to the throne is therefore not without interest. It began on Easter Sunday (21 April 1585) and it became immediately clear that the next pope would be decided by Ferdinando de' Medici and Ludovico d'Este. By Wednesday that week, the two cardinals had gathered enough promises to elect Peretti.

> When the cardinals finally assembled in the Paoline Chapel, d' Este declared that it was not necessary to proceed to a ballot, since it was obvious who the new pope was. Without opposition the cardinals proceeded to do homage ('adoration') to Felice Cardinal Peretti, OFM, "Cardinal Montalto," though, immediately afterwards, a vote was conducted by asking each cardinal to cast his vote aloud. The vote was unanimous.[11]

"According to his biographer Leti, he straightened up, threw his crutches away with the cry, 'Now I am Caesar,' before intoning the *Te Deum* with a voice of thunder."[12] There are many who decline to take this account seriously. Presumably, that is why attention is drawn to what otherwise would be an unnecessary line of prophecy.

Summary: *Yet again the seer has provided a brief pen picture of a recognizable pope. This time, a mere thirty years before his election; he has also drawn attention to the unusual nature of the manner in which it was accomplished: and to his favoured situation as a protégé of a 'red principal', namely, Cardinal Ghislieri, who became Pius V in 1566. An apocryphal story exists that the seer chanced to meet Peretti as a young man travelling among a group of monks, and recognized him by falling upon his knees before him. When asked to account for his action, the seer replied that he had recognized a future pope. This story is plausible since it is known that Peretti travelled from one monastery to another across northern Italy during his younger days and that de Nostredame, too, had once been the proverbial 'Wandering Jew', with visits to Italy.*

58   *Entre les deux monarquese esloignés,*
        Lors que le Sol par Selin clair perdue:
        Simulte grande entre deux indignés,
        Qu'aux isles & Sienne la liberté rendue.

59   *Dame en fureur par raige d'adultere,*
        Viendra à son prince coniurer non de dire:
        Mais bref cogneu sera le vitupere,
        Que seront mis dix sept à martire.

60   *Le prince hors de son terroir Celtique,*
        Sera trahy deceu par interprete:
        Rouan, Rochelle par ceulx d'Armorique,
        Au port de Blaue deceuz par moine & prestre.

61   *Le grand tappis plié ne monstrera,*
        Fors qu'à demy la pluspart de l'histoire:
        Chassé du regne loing aspre apparoistra,
        Qu'au fait bellique chascun le viendra croire.

62   *Trop tard tous deux, les fleurs seront perdues,*
      Contre la loy serpent ne vouldra faire:
      Des liguers forces par gallots confondues
      Sauone, Albinge par Monech grand martire.

63   *La dame seulle au regne demouree,*
      L'vnic estaint premier au lict d'honneur:
      Sept ans sera de douleur exploree,
      Puis longue vie au regne par grand heure.

seulle (AF seul *adj.*) alone; demouree (AF demorer) to remain; vnic (L. unic\us) unique, *also anagram and paragram*, L'vn(o)c for Luçon; estaint (OF estainct) come to nought; lict d'honneur *for* lit de justice

N.B. It is noteworthy that the Seer has written *L'vnic*. Elsewhere, as in Century 8 Nos. 7 and 32 the word is spelt 'unique', according to convention.

> The woman alone in the reign that remained (**MARIE DE MEDICI**),   1617
> The unique (**LUÇON**) foremost, come to nought at the *lit de justice*,
> Seven years she will be explored by sorrow,
> Then a long life in the realm through great happenstance.

The woman alone in the reign that remained

The woman can only be Marie de' Médicis, the widow of Henri IV, who immediately after his death and "in accordance with his wishes, the boy King and the *Parlement* of Paris pronounced her Regent in a *lit de justice.*"[1] The Queen-mother's appointment was intended to continue Henri's reign in a smooth manner. This was in contrast to the lengthy interregnum that had preceded her husband's succession.[2] But with no man by her side, and faced with hostility and revolt from the Princes of the Blood who coveted her position as regent, she was forced to *reign alone.*[3]

The unique Luçon foremost

It was during her term as regent that the Queen-mother made a significant appointment. She engaged the Bishop of Luçon as France's Secretary of State (25 November 1616).[4]
This politically astute prelate would later become known as Cardinal Richelieu. From the very outset of his political career, *Luçon* achieved a position of considerable responsibility. His position as one of the Queen-mother's chief ministers placed him *foremost* at the King's *lit de justice*. The *lit* was a traditional seat of government where the King and his ministers met to discuss impending issues. It consisted of a pile of cushions on which the monarch traditionally reclined.[5]

Come to nought at the lit de justice

Despite his eminence's progress, Richelieu's political career came to an abrupt and indefinite end (24 April 1617). The Queen-mother's role as Regent to Louis XIII was terminated by a *coup d'état* which the King, himself, had approved. At a stroke, the Queen-mother's governing council was replaced by those of her son.

> It is said that in their bewilderment they hid themselves in the royal stables. It is difficult to believe that the Bishop of Luçon, though his nervous faculties were highly developed, would long skulk in so undignified a shelter. At any rate he soon resolved to appear before the king, where he at once learned that his political career was to be suspended.[6]

Seven years she will be explored by sorrow

Thus it was, on that same day, Marie de' Médicis' role as the effective head of state came to an unexpected end, brought about by the assassination of her chief minister Concini. "God help me!" cried the Queen-mother; "I have reigned for seven years; now the only crown to which I can look forward will be a heavenly one."[7]
For *seven years,* Marie de' Médicis had retained control of the government, although often *in a state of sorrow*. Her period in office began with tears she shed in 1610, following the assassination of her husband, and her natural anxiety as to how she would cope as regent. Her office ended in 1617 as tearfully as it began, with the murders of her two Florentine companions, Concino

Concini and his wife Leonora Galigai. Their deaths coincided with her own exile to the castle at Blois, with her departure observed by her son Louis XIII, as she wept profusely. [8]

Then a long life in the realm

During her seven years in power, the Queen-mother had had to contend with the aspirations of the Princes of the Blood, which several times escalated into open revolt; also, the defiant attitude of the Huguenots, who seized every opportunity to take action against her authority; and the increasing antipathy of her son, the King. [9] This hostility would eventually lead to open warfare between mother and son. Yet, despite the many trials and tribulations she endured, although it must be said the attraction of political power was the cause of her problems, she survived into her seventieth year. This was deemed to be *a long life* for the age in which she lived, where life expectancy fell short of fifty. Her death came on 3 July 1642, in the reign of her son, whose own end followed ten months later on 14 May 1643.

Through great happenstance

The Queen-mother's survival can be explained by her great good fortune of possessing an enduring maternal relationship with the King, even though it underwent many trials. Without that relationship, she would undoubtedly have ended her days, prematurely, on the executioner's block. For despite her involvement in several plots against her son, committed on the behalf of her second son Gaston, Louis XIII could never bring himself to order the execution of his own mother.

Instead, he settled for exiling her: at first to Blois, and then to Compiègne, from where she later fled to Flanders. Her final days were spent in the Spanish Netherlands in the company of Gaston, both of whom were still plotting to overthrow the King. [10]

Summary: *This oracle has a clarity that befits its fulfilment in an age that credited the seer with prescient knowledge. Five years after Louis XIII exiled his mother, and established himself as King of France and Navarre, he visited Salon to pay his respects at the tomb of de Nostredame. The inclusion of Cardinal Richelieu in this and in Century Eight No. 68, born on 9 September 1585, and presently identified by his former diocese at Luçon, again confirms the seer's prescient knowledge of persons born long after his own decease in 1566. Such knowledge is wholly incompatible with Darwin's atheistic theories concerning evolution, but not with Einstein's 'block universe'.*

64   *On ne tiendra pache aucune arresté,*
       Tous receuans iront par tromperie:
       De paix & tresue terre & mer protesté:
       Par Barcelone classe prins d'industrie.

65   *Gris & bureau, demie ouuerte guerre,*
       De nuict seront assaillis & pillés:
       Le bureau prins passera par serre,
       Son temple ouert deux au plaster grilles.

66   *Au fondement de la nouuelle secte,*
       Seront les oz de grand Romain trouués:
       Sepulcre en marbre apparoistra couuerte,
       Terre trembler en Auril, mal ensouetz.

67   *Au grand empire paruiendra tout vn autre,*
       Bonté distant plus de felicité:
       Regi par vn issu non loing du peaultre,
       Corruer regnes grande infelicité.

68   *Lors que souldartz fureur seditieuse,*
       Contre leur chef feront de nuict fer luire
       Ennemy d'Albe soir par main furieuse,
       Lors vexer Rome & principaulx seduire.

69   *La pitié grande sera sans loing tarder,*
        Ceulx qui donnoient, seront constraints de prendre:
        Nudz affamez de froit, soif, soy bender,
        Les monts passer faisant grand esclandre.

pitié (AF piété) godliness; donner (OF) to minister; bender (AF bander) to bind; faisant (OF) causing; esclandre (OF) uproar.

The great godliness will be without delaying long,   1702
Those that were ministering will be constrained from conducting:
Nude, starved by cold, thirsty, binding oneself,
Departing from the mountains: causing great tumult.

The great godliness will be without delaying long

In October 1685, Louis XIV issued the Edict of Fontainebleau. It was a decree that reversed his grandfather's Edict of Nantes, signed in 1598, which had been instrumental in ending the French Wars of Religion and enabling Catholics and Protestants to live and worship peacefully, without interference. Louis XIV's edict was designed to compel Protestants to convert to Catholicism: if not willingly, then by forcing objectors to feed and host his troops at their expense—the so-called *Dragonnades*. In the Cévennes: a region in south-central France, this enforcement would be challenged, not so much politically, but spiritually and physically.

> On 3 February 1688, Isabeau Vincent [aged 15], a young unlettered shepherdess of Dauphinée, was heard calling for repentance and announcing the imminent judgement of God. She was apparently sound asleep. On the night of the 23rd she again spoke in her sleep and her words were recorded. What was astonishing was that, instead of speaking in the local dialect, the *lang d'oc,* which was the only language known to her, she proclaimed her message 'en fort bon français'. [...] Her condition was infectious; the infection soon reached the proportion of an epidemic [...]those possessed spoke, like Isabeau Vincent, in a French which was not their language; sometimes they spoke 'with tongues' [...] 'convulsionaries' heard voices and received instructions which they never doubted were the dictation of the Holy Ghost. [1]

Without a long delay, the movement increased until in 1702, it erupted in an outbreak of violence. Before then, there had been many attempts to re-convert the rebellious Camisards to Catholicism. "The King had sent missionaries, who have preached and urged those people to come and listen. They came. They have received instructions. But that was never brought about by violence." [2]

Nevertheless, in May 1702, the Camisards, driven by the fanaticism of the Mandagout commune and the dreams of Abraham Mazel, finally gave way to violence.

> The program of the Camisards was to sack and burn churches and drive off or even kill priests. [...] The Camisards fought successfully, even to the point of holding royal armies in check. Their tactics of ambush and night attacks, their knowledge of the mountains in which they operated, and the support of the local populace all were factors in their favour. [3]

Those that were ministering will be constrained from conducting

The Edict of Fontainebleau had created a state of affairs in France where only the Catholic religion was legally tolerated. The Edict of Nantes, which had guaranteed religious toleration since 1598, had effectively ceased to operate for the time being.

Contained within Louis XIV's Edict were the following restrictions. Worship of the alleged Reformed religion (*Religion prétendue réformée*) was banned; pastors who did not want to convert were to be sentenced to serve in the galleys; all Protestant schools were prohibited; members of the Reformed religion were ordered to have their children baptised and educated in the Catholic faith; members of the Reformed religion who had left the country and then failed to return after four months would have their possessions confiscated by the State; those emigrating would be sentenced to the galleys, or in the case of women, to prison, and those who had converted to the Catholic faith but returned to the Reformed religion would be severely punished.

Consequently, those who had been ministering in the Reformed church were now legally prevented from doing so, and were required instead to convert to Catholicism. In the Cévennes, where the Reformed religion was flourishing, steps were taken to enforce the law.

The Camisards were many of them prepared to give their lives for their faith. [...] Fulcran Rey, tortured and condemned to the gallows, wrote to his father just before his execution: "Oh what happiness it would be to me if I could be one of those whom the Lord has set aside to pronounce his praise and to die for his cause!" He and many others like him, walked with light–hearted step to enrol their names in the noble army of martyrs.[4]

"Lilian Crété states that nearly a thousand Camisards were condemned to the galleys and some seventy, five of whom were women, were hanged or broken on the wheel."[5]

Nude, starved by cold, thirsty, binding oneself

Elsewhere, others who were still free and determined to resist conversion suffered a different fate.

Convinced that the only way to stop the rebellion was to cut off its supplies, royal officials finally resorted to burning some five hundred villages in the mountains and conducting murderous military pogroms aimed principally at the civilian population.[6]

The thought of losing their home, neighbourhood, means of employment, and food, had the effect of fulfilling this line of prophetic verse. For it resulted in many of those affected, binding themselves together, either to become actively engaged in an uprising, or else to choose exile, and be numbered among the "prodigious number of people proscribed, naked, fugitive, [that] wandered, innocent of any crime, seeking asylum far from their native land." (Refer Century Two N°. 7)

Departing from the mountains: causing great tumult

On September 11, 1702, the forces of the Camisards met royal troops in a battle at Champ-Domergue. Neither side was clearly victorious, but the fact that these villagers stood before trained troops of the strongest army in Europe was an indication that Louis' army was not going to rout the Camisards. On October 22 of the same year the forces met again at Télémac. This encounter brought two men to prominence in the leadership of the Camisards: Jean Cavalier, and Pierre Laporte whose nom de guerre was "Roland." They were 21 and 22 years of age respectively. Cavalier and Roland led the Camisards in what greatly resembled a modern guerrilla war.[7]

Not everyone stayed to fight. The rugged mountainous terrain of the Cévennes saw the departure of many of its inhabitants as a result of the violence. And they were among the "large number of Protestants — estimates range from 210,000 to 900,000 — that left France over the next two decades."[8]

[U]nder the direction of the administrator of Languedoc, Nicolas Lamoignon de Bâsville, over 2,000 churches were burned; their pastors and worshippers were captured and later exiled, killed, tortured or sent to the galleys. [...] Reformed worship and private Bible reading were outlawed. [...] Many of the Huguenots fled to neighbouring countries who gladly received them. Once Louis realized that many of his most talented artisans and craftsmen had fled, he closed the borders.[9]

Summary: *This oracle concerns the uprising in the Cévennes by the Reformed Church of the Camisards. For more than a decade it caused Louis XIV a great deal of concern. It began following a protest against the Edict of Fontainebleau, which required Protestants everywhere in France to convert to Catholicism, but in the Cévennes, the protest against it was energised by the supernatural revelations of an uneducated shepherdess. Eventually, anger against the Edict turned to violence, with many atrocities committed by both sides. To escape the violence, and the hated Dragonnades, large numbers of Camisards fled from France for the safety of more tolerant countries. The prophecy alludes to this in sufficiently recognizable detail for it to be acknowledged as events that occurred in the Cévennes during the reign of Louis XIV.*

70   *Au chef du monde le grand CHYREN sera,*
        PLVS OVLTRE après aymé, craint, redoubté:
        Son bruit & loz les cieulx surpassera,
        Et du seul tiltre Victeur fort contenté.

Chyren (anag. L. Henric\us); après (OF) following; redoubté (OF) awed; fort (OF adj. & adv. puissant) mightily

At the head of the world will be the great Chyren,
More beyond following, beloved, feared, awed:
His fame and praise will surpass the heavens,
Also from the single title Victor, mightily contented.

Apart from this quatrain, the Seer has used '*the great Chyren*' before, in Century Two N°. 79: and in N°. 27 above: also in Century Eight N°. 54: as well as in Century Nine N°. 41. Added to which, it was also employed – but with King replacing the prefix *great* – as an anagram for Henri II in Century Four N°.34.

Henri II reigned for barely two years after the publication of this oracle, and although his father, Francis I, had a naval agreement with the Turks, there appears to be no obvious connexion between this reference to the great Chyren and Henri II.

Henri IV would be a much better choice, since he was nicknamed "Henry the Great". The French artist, Toussaint Dubreuil (c.1561-1602) also painted the King's portrait in the pose of Hercules vanquishing the Lernaean Hydra: presumably to celebrate Henri IV's victory over the Catholic League. By identifying this king with Hercules, it forms a link with the words '*plvs oultre*'. For it was said these same words appeared on the Pillars of Hercules. "Renaissance tradition says the pillars bore the warning *Nec plus ultra* (also *Non plus ultra*, "nothing further beyond", serving as a warning to sailors and navigators to go no further." (Wikipedia – Pillars of Hercules)

As for the reason why the Seer resorted to the use of capital letters, this may be due to the interest taken in his predictions by Queen Catherine de' Medici. She was fiercely loyal to her husband, and spitefully vengeful towards any lack of deference to him. But she looked kindly upon the Seer for as long as he told her what she wanted to hear. In order to retain her favour, which also protected him, the Seer knew she would view this prophecy as a reflection of her own personal regard for the King. In point of fact, most of the qualities above best fitted Henri IV, although describing him as '*chef du monde*' could be argued as excessive.

Finally, if '*the great Chyren*' is one and the same person that appears in 2/79, 6/27, 8/54 and 9/41, as well as in this oracle, then it must surely rule out Henri IV. Which means the world must await a more fitting candidate to fulfil the information contained in this prophecy.

> 71   *Quand on viendra le grand Roy parenter,*
> *Auant qu'il ait du tout l'ame rendue:*
> *Celuy qui moins le viendra lamenter,*
> *Par lyons d'aigles croix, cororne vendue.*
>
> *[On le verra bien tost apparenter*
> *D'Aigles, Lions, Croix, Couronne vendue]*

Lines 5 and 6 appear in the 1605 edition, replacing lines 3 and 4 in the 1557 edition.

> 72   *Par fureur faincte d'esmotion diuine.*
> *Sera la femme du grand fort violee:*
> *Iuges voulant damner telle doctrine,*
> *Victime au peuple ignorant immolee.*

> 73   *En cité grande vn moyne & artisan,*
> *Pres de la porte logés & aux murailles:*
> *Contre Modene secret, caue disant,*
> *Trahis saisant soubz couleur d'esposailles.*

> 74   *Là deschassee au regne tournera,*
> *Ses ennemis trouués des coniurés:*
> *Plus que iamais son temps triomphera,*
> *Trois & septante à mort trop asseurés.*

Là (OF) yonder; dechasser (OF) expelled; asseurer (OF) to lay up in a safe place.

> The expelled yonder, he will return to the realm (**LOUIS NAPOLEON**)   1848
> His enemies discovered composed of plotters:
> More than ever his time will triumph,
> Seventy-three at death, too much laid up.

The expelled yonder

After Napoleon's defeat at the battle of Waterloo, and the restoration of the monarchy in 1815, the former Emperor's closest relatives were expelled from France. Charles Louis-Napoleon, though only a child at the time, was taken by his mother to Switzerland and lodged in their new castle home at Arenberg. He would reside there for the next decade.

In 1836, by then a young man, he became fired with political ambition. He saw himself as the natural heir to the French throne. In pursuit of this goal, Louis-Napoleon sought to win over the Strasbourg garrison as a first step towards displacing the reigning king. But the attempt failed and he found himself expelled again, this time at the mercy of Louis Philippe, who sent him to the United States.

A year later, his mother suffered a serious illness, and he returned to Switzerland to be with her. From there, in 1838, he was taken into custody, and again expelled. This time he was sent to England. But, two years later, overcome by restlessness, he returned to France for another attempt at dislodging Louis Philippe. Once more, he was arrested: this time his sentence was life imprisonment inside the fortress at Ham in northern France. However, in May 1846, he managed to escape from the castle disguised as a mason. From France, he fled to England, where he remained in wait for some new opportunity to arise that would enable him to seize power. [1]

He will return to the realm

In 1848, news of an uprising against Louis Philippe was brought to Louis Napoleon from across the Channel. Seeing this as another prospect for achieving power, he quickly travelled to Paris, only to discover that a provisional government had taken control. The opportunity seemed lost, especially when he received orders to return to his exile in England. But help was at hand; a group of supporters nominated him for a place in the Constituent Assembly.

During the September elections that followed, five *départements* voted for him, and this allowed Louis-Napoleon– *the expelled* – *to return to the realm* permanently as an elected member of the Assembly. Moreover, he was now eligible to run for the presidency.

His name and popularity with the people, combined with the fact there was little opposition, won him the vote. From President, he became Prince-President, and in 1852 he took over the reign of France as Emperor Napoleon III. [2]

His enemies discovered, composed of plotters

Louis-Napoleon's reign was not without *enemies*. These were mostly members of the Legitimist Party of royalists. They were divided into two groups, one supporting a Bourbon succession, the other preferring Orleans.

The Republican Party, too, opposed Louis-Napoleon, and during the first four years of his presidency they met privately in groups across France: sometimes even using voluntary organizations to mask their political activities. In the crackdown that followed, thousands of these political *plotters* were *discovered*, and either jailed or sent to Algeria. In 1852, Prince-President Napoleon even became forced to take action against members of the Orleans family, as a safeguard against their secretive *plotting*. A decree was issued, and they were banished from France. [3]

More than ever his time will triumph

Napoleon III's Second Empire enjoyed unprecedented prosperity. Gold flooded into the country from French owned mines in California and South Africa. Railways were built, bringing the Riviera within reach of Parisians. Industrial production doubled; foreign trade did the same. Paris was reborn as a new city. The decaying remnants of former times were replaced with the great boulevards, mansions, stores and public buildings that brought the city into line with modern thinking. Under direction from the Emperor, Baron Haussmann created much that was to make Paris one of the most beautiful cities in the world. The humanities also flowered with a great blossoming of talent, in music, in literature and in the visual arts. To the world at large, it must have seemed that Napoleon III's Second Empire represented the summit of prosperity, gaiety and culture: *more than ever his time triumphed.* [4]

Seventy-three at death, too much laid up

Louis Napoleon, otherwise Napoleon III died on 9 January 1873. For many years he had been suffering excruciating pain from bladder stones. With the weight of power lifted from his shoulders, following his defeat and brief period of captivity during the Franco-Prussian War, he left France for England, where he agreed to have the gallstones removed. But having survived two operations, he died while being prepared for further surgery—too much laid up. [5]

It is noteworthy that this prophecy succeeds by nine days, for had he died during an earlier operation, the prediction of (eighteen) *seventy-three* would have failed.

Summary: *Everything predicted in this oracle concerns Napoleon III. Restricted though it is to four lines, it reports several major facts that clearly identify him as the subject of the prophecy. And, yet again, it is to be observed that the year of his death has been accurately foreseen: even though it occurred more than three centuries after it was predicted. Furthermore, the seer has deliberately chosen a word that describes Napoleon's condition at the time of death—so that even this was foreknown. The implications of such foresight indicate the distinctive nature of the conscious self as being essentially different from the temporal order of animate life. The former is timeless, therefore indestructible, whereas, the latter is temporal, having a created beginning and end. Everyone should therefore expect the survival of their conscious self after death.*

> 75   *Le grand pillot par Roy sera mandé,*
>   *Laisser la classe, à plus hault lieu attaindre:*
>   *Sept ans apres sera contrebandé,*
>   *Barbare armee viendra Venise craindre.*

classe (L class\is) army; haut (OF) élevé; contrebandé (anag. + paragram) Condé trepan; barbare (Greek), foreign tongue.

The great Pilot (**COLIGNY**) will be sent for by the King (**CHARLES IX**),   1571
Leaving the army to attain to a higher position:
Seven years after, he will be contraband (**CONDÉ TREPANNED**):
The foreign army will arrive, Venice fearing.

The great pilot

Gaspard de Coligny became Admiral of France in 1552; hence, *the great Pilot*. [1] Although the title of admiral appears nautical, in France it can also refer to a commander on land. It was while languishing in captivity for two years, following his capture at the battle of St Quentin that Coligny decided to convert to the Protestant faith. It was a decision which would play a major part in the final years of his life.

In March 1562, as a result of the massacre of Protestants at Vassy and the occupation of Paris by the Catholic Duke of Guise, Coligny left Court to join Louis de Bourbon, 1st Prince of Condé at Meaux. Together, they joined forces to capture the city of Orleans. It was a conquest that began the religious wars, which were to continue across France until the end of the century.

Will be sent for by the King

By the end of the 1560s, Coligny had become leader of the Huguenot party's political wing and Commander–in-Chief of its army. Such was the power and influence he wielded, particularly across the south and west of France, that it became impossible for the King to ignore him. After conferring with the Huguenot leader, albeit at a distance, Coligny was *sent for by the King*.

Leaving the army to attain to a higher position

"On 12 September 1571 Gaspard de Coligny arrived to join the Court at Blois [...] armed with a promise of safe conduct signed by the King, Anjou and Catherine." [2] His return to Court began an ambitious campaign to reunite France. The country would combat the might of Spain in the Netherlands by allying France with William I of Orange and Queen Elizabeth I of England. This high-minded idea meant that by *leaving the* Huguenot-Politiques and the Protestant *army* for service to the Crown, he had *attained to a higher position* as a councillor, and advocate to the King. [3]

Seven years after he will be contraband (Condé trepanned)

This line predicts the fate of Condé, who Coligny replaced to become leader of the Huguenots.

When Coligny left court in 1562, he joined up with the Prince of Condé to capture the city of Orleans. Condé, too, had left Court during that same year to take his place as leader of the Huguenots. But *seven years later Condé was trepanned*—alternatively, *he was contraband*.

Again the Seer has chosen the right word. This time it is *'contreband'*, which provides two pieces of prescient information. Firstly, the word likens the Prince to an unlawful commodity. On the other hand, by anagram and paragram, the letters name Condé and explain his death.

Condé was killed by a shot to the head on 13 March 1569,[4] (refer, Century Three N°. 41). As a Prince of the Blood, it was his legal right to stand trial before his peers, and have them determine his punishment, but by deliberately murdering him, it denied him his legal right.

The foreign army will arrive, Venice fearing

In the final line of this quatrain, the Seer provides further evidence of his timing ability. In the spring of 1570, one year after Condé's assassination, and one year before Coligny was sent for by the King, foreign ships appeared in the Mediterranean. The fleet was Turkish, and composed of three squadrons.[5] To disguise their intention, the ships crisscrossed the Aegean Sea before heading for the southern coast of Cyprus, where an occupation force disembarked to seize control of the island. Up until that time, Cyprus had been part of the Republic of Venice. But with *Venice fearing* that the loss of its island would encourage further attacks against other territory it owned, the city joined forces with the Holy League established by Pope Pius V[6] The intention of the League was to resist Turkey from making further conquests. And it achieved this goal with victory over the Ottoman Turks at the Battle of Lepanto in 1571.

Summary: *This oracle is at one with events that took place between 1569 and 1571 inclusive, involving Admiral Coligny and Louis, Prince of Condé. Both men at different times were leaders of the Huguenot Church's political wing and its armed forces. Coligny's recall to court, after the murder of Condé by order of the King's brother, caused the Admiral to seek assurances for his safety before returning to Court. In the event, they proved useless (See, Century Four No. 47). Another important event during these years was the seizure of Cyprus by the Ottomans, since it led to their defeat as a naval force in the Mediterranean (See Century Nine No. 42). The references supporting these prophecies provides confirmation of their validity.*

76   *La cité antique d'antenorée forge,*
     Plus, ne pouuant le tyran supporter:
     Le manche feïnct au temple couper gorge,
     Les siens le peuple à mort viendra bouter.

77   *Par la victoire du deceu fraudulente,*
     Deux classes vne, la reuolte Germaine,
     Le chef meurtry & son fils dans la tente,
     Florence, Imole pourchassez dans Romaine.

78   *Crier victoire du grand Selin croissant,*
     Par les Romains sera l'Aigle clamé,
     Ticcin, Milan & Gennes ny consent,
     Puis par eux mesmes Basil grand reclamé.

79   *Pres du Tesin les habitans de Loyre,*
     Garonne & Saone, Seine, Tain, & Gironde,
     Outre les monts dresseront promontoire,
     Conflict donné, Pau granci, submergé onde.

promontoire (OF) promontory; high ground, elbow like that juts out (usually into the sea etc.); Pau (AF petit) short, also diminutive of Na[pau]leon; granci (Italian, grancire, *also*, grancio. See also Tuscan dialect, grancito) grab, seize, hook,
Cross-references: Pau, C.II: 33; C.II: 94; C.III: 75; C.IV: 70; C.VIII: I; also, 'dresseront promontoire', C.I: 77.

Near the Ticino, the inhabitants of Loire,   1796
Garonne, and Saône, Seine, Tarn, and Gironde:
Over the mountains, they will lay out a promontory,
Conflict given, Pau (**NAPOLEON**) grabbed, submerged in water.

Near the Ticino

During Napoleon's Italian Campaign, begun in April 1796, Milan was his first objective. "But to reach Milan he would have to cross the most formidable river of Italy, the Po: and also its left hand tributary, the Ticino, and each crossing would be disputed by Beaulieu's army." [1]

The inhabitants of Loire, Garonne, and Saône, Seine, Tarn and Gironde

"Bridges and rivers were apparently of prime importance in the Italian campaign." [2] The oracle reflects this by referring *to the inhabitants of the different river regions across France*, each of which would be from where many soldiers of his Army of Italy had been drawn.

> The dominating natural feature [of the First Italian Campaign] was the great River Po with its series of Alpine tributaries – the Sestia, Ticino, Adda, Oglio and Mincio watercourses, and beyond them the rivers Adige and Brenta, flowing independently into the Adriatic. [...] A series of smaller streams similarly linked the Apennines with the Po. [3]

Over the mountains they will lay out a promontory

Having taken his liberating army *across the mountains* that divide France from Italy, [4] Bonaparte literally drove a wedge – that is to say, he *laid out a promontory* – between the combined forces of the opposition, the Piedmontese and the Austrians. [5] This strategy proved extremely successful, and resulted in King Victor Amadeus III of Sardinia-Piedmont being forced to cede the transalpine provinces to France. It also required him to grant safe passage to the French armies at the *Peace of Paris* (1796).

Napoleon's divisive strategy in achieving this victory is still considered a textbook classic in military warfare. It is noteworthy that a similar strategy of dividing the opposition by '*laying out a promontory*' was later employed by the English navy at the Battle of Trafalgar; and for which, the Seer used the same phrase (Century One N°. 77), when predicting Admiral Nelson's victory.

Conflict given

It was during Napoleon's first Italian campaign that a dramatic incident occurred: one, which had the outcome been different, would have changed the entire future of European history. In November 1796, while still in the process of subduing Northern Italy, Napoleon reached the town of Arcola on the River Alpone. It was there that a fierce *conflict broke out* between the French and an Austrian detachment that had positioned itself in defence of the bridge. Further advance was temporarily brought to a standstill by the gunfire from both sides.

Napoleon grabbed

Impatient at the delay, and believing that a joint charge across the bridge would solve the problem, Napoleon seized a flag and began to lead a party of men across the canal. A volley of gunfire met his appearance. [6]

The charge forward had proved to be a serious blunder. One of Bonaparte's men quickly saw the peril in which the Commander had placed himself, and *grabbed* hold of Napoleon, urging that he take cover. But Bonaparte resisted. (Note the use of the Tuscan word for 'grabbed' to foretell that the action will take place in Tuscany.)

Submerged in water

In the ensuing "confusion the commander fell into the deep dyke at the side:" and being *submerged in water*, was in real danger of drowning. Two aides-de-camp, Louis Bonaparte and Antoine Marmont, dived into the water to rescue their Commander, and Napoleon was brought safely but spluttering to the bank. [7] Had it not been for this quick intervention, as well as the reaction of the officer on the bridge, who was shot dead a moment later, the Napoleonic era could never have begun.

Summary: *The use of 'Pau' to identify Napoleon, offers a convenient way of cross-referencing the various incidents that occurred in his life with those predicted in these oracles. The incident at the bridge, which was a small matter in the wider issue of France's conquest of northern Italy, is nevertheless important; because, had the outcome been different, from the hail of bullets that met Bonaparte's charge against the Austrians defending the bridge, the future history of every country in the world would have been affected: and the world would have taken a different course to that which is now the present time.*

80 *De Fez le regne paruiendra à ceux d'Europe,*
    Feu leur cité, & lame trenchera:
    Le grand d'Asie terre & mer à grand troupe,
    Que bleux, pers, croix, à mort dechassera.

81 *Pleurs, cris & plaincts, hurlemens, effrayeurs,*
    Cœur inhumain, cruel, noir, & transy:
    Leman, les Isles, de Gennes les maieurs,
    Sang espancher, frofaim, à nul mercy.

frofaim (hybrid, fro + faim; fro, A.Fr. land uncultivated and abandoned; faim, famine)

82 *Par les deserts de lieu, libre, & farouche,*
    Viendra errer nepueu du grand Pontife:
    Assommé à sept auecques lourde souche,
    Par ceux qu'apres occuperont le cyphe.

83 *Celuy qu'aura tant d'honneur & caresse,*
    A son entrée en la Gaule Belgique:
    Vn temps apres fera tant de rudesse,
    Et sera contre à la fleur tant bellique.

fleure (abbreviation for *fleure-de-lis*, which is a metonymy for France).

The one that will have so much honour and welcome,   1578
At his passage into Belgian France:
One time afterwards, he (**PARMA**) will cause such great austerity;
Also, he will be in opposition to France, warlike as well.

The one that will have so much honour

The historical facts pertaining to this oracle indicate that Alexander Farnese, Duke of Parma, is the intended subject.

> Alessandro was the son of Duke Ottavio Farnese of Parma, a grandchild of Pope Paul III. [...] His mother was the half-sister of Philip II of Spain and John of Austria. He led a significant military and diplomatic career in the service of Spain under the service of his uncle the King. He fought in the Battle of Lepanto (1571). [1]

And welcome at his passage into Belgian France

On 1 October 1578, Don John, Governor of the Netherlands, died and was succeeded by the Duke of Parma. At the time of his succession, the Dutch Revolt was taking place.

> The Dutch Revolt (1566 or 1568–1648) was the successful revolt of the northern, largely Protestant Seven Provinces of the Low Countries against the rule of the Roman Catholic King Philip II of Spain, who had inherited the region (Seventeen Provinces) from the defunct Duchy of Burgundy [2]

Among the Seventeen Provinces was a region in northern France containing Arras and Lille.

> Belgium's formation [...] can be traced back to the 'Seventeen Provinces' within the Burgundian Netherlands. These were brought together under the House of Valois-Burgundy. [3]

This explains the Seer's reference to '*Belgian France*', and to *the welcome* received by the Duke of Parma at his passage into the region: especially when, from 1581 onwards, he effectively answered the appeal made to him by the wealthy citizens living in this former French duchy.

> When theocratic Calvinist militants seized control of the chief Flemish towns, including Ypres, Ghent, and Bruges, the middle classes flocked to Parma. Divided, the towns fell, and, by the end of 1584, Parma was able to lay siege to Antwerp. [4]

> The seven northern provinces, controlled by Calvinists, responded with the Union of Utrecht, where they resolved to stick together to fight Spain. Farnese secured his base in Hainault and Artois, then moved against Brabant and Flanders. City after city fell: Tournai, Maastricht, Breda, Bruges, and Ghent opened their gates. [5]

One time afterwards, he will cause such great austerity

Parma's next conquest would fulfil the prediction made above. It took place when he laid siege to the seaport of Antwerp, which was then the major city of the Seventeen Provinces. Parma first constructed a pontoon bridge made of boats, which he strung across the River Scheldt, over a distance of approximately 760 meters. This prevented access to or from the sea. Despite several attempts to destroy the bridge, it remained intact. Finally, on 17 August 1585, the city was at last starved into submission. After suffering siege conditions that lasted for more than a year – *such great austerity* – survivors left the city *en masse*: perhaps as many as 60% of the population never returned.

Also, he will be in opposition to France: warlike as well

After the assassination of Henri III in 1589, his successor, the Protestant Henri of Navarre, had to fight Catholic opposition to gain recognition as Henri IV. It was during France's interregnum that the future French King laid siege to Paris (May 1590), causing Parma to invade France.

> The siege of Paris, which lasted from 7 May until 30 August, inflicted terrible hardships on the inhabitants. Some 13,000 of the 30,000 victims of the siege allegedly died of hunger. [...] One foreign observer who feared that Paris might fall into Protestant hands was the king of Spain, Philip II. He ordered Alexander Farnese, duke of Parma (his commander in the Low Countries) to invade northern France with 14,000 Spanish veterans. [6]

The Catholic duke of Mayenne, with 10,000 French troops and a cavalry of 2,000 met Parma and his army at Meaux, and together they captured the town of Ligny, thereby enabling food supplies to reach Paris, and thus break the siege. Henri withdrew his forces without confronting Parma, who then besieged and captured Corbeil before returning to the Low Countries on 16 October 1590.

Summary: *European history concerning the sixteenth century may appear of little interest after the passing of the centuries. But it was of immense importance to those living in that age. In this oracle we have the seer's prognostication of the Duke of Parma's affect upon the people of the Netherlands, and afterwards of France. Parma was a contemporary of de Nostredame, but the events foretold in this oracle occurred several decades after the seer's death, and, in any case, could not be foreseen by human intelligence. Parma's subsequent invasion of France, for example, was entirely due to the assassination of Henri III and the lack of a Catholic successor capable of thwarting Henri of Navarre's claim to the throne. When this oracle was first published, Henry III was little more than a toddler, and Henry IV was still in his pram.*

84   Celuy qo'en Sparte Claude ne peut regner,
      Il sera tant par voye seductiue:
      Que du court, long, le sera araigner,
      Que contre Roy sera sa perspectiue.

85   La grand cité de Tharse par Gaulois
      Sera destruicte, captifz tous à Turban:
      Secours par mer, du grand Portugalois,
      Premier d'esté le iour du sacré Vrban.

86   Au grand Prelat vn iour apres son songe,
      Interpreté au rebours de son sens:
      De la Gascogne luy suruiendra vn monge,
      Qui fera eslire le grand Prelat de Sens.

87   L'eslection faicte dans Frankfort,
      N'aura nul lieu Milan s'opposera:
      Le sien plus proche semblera si grand sort,
      Que oultre le Ryn és marestz chassera.

88   Vn regne grand demoura desolé,
      Aupres de l'Hebro se seront assemblees:
      Monts Pyrenees le rendront consolé,
      Lors que dans May seront terres tremblées.

89 *Entre deux cimbes piez & mains estachés,*
  De miel face oingt & de laict substanté:
  Guespes & mouches, fitine amour faschés,
  Poccilateur faulcer, Cyphe temptee.

90 *L'honnissement puant abhominable,*
  Apres le faict sera felicité:
  Grand excusé pour n'estre fauorable,
  Qu'à paix Neptune ne sera incité.

91 *Du conducteur de la guerre n aualle,*
  Rouge effrené, seuere, horrible grippe,
  Captif eschappé de l'aisné dans la basle:
  Quant il naistra du grand vn filz Agrippe.

92 *Prince de beauté tant venuste,*
  Au chef menee le second faict trahy:
  La cite au glaisue de pouldre, face aduste,
  Par trop grand meurtre le chef du Roy hay.

tant (OF) as well as; venuste (L venust\us) beautiful; aduste (L adust\us) scorched.

A Prince of loveliness, as well as beautiful (**LOUIS-CHARLES**):   1793
Conducted to (**CHAMBON**) the principal, betrayed at the second act:
The city at the blade: the face scorched with powder (**QUICKLIME**),
Through an excessively great murder, the head of the King (**LOUIS XVI**) despised.

A Prince of loveliness, as well as beautiful

PRINCE LOUIS CHARLES

By the time Louis Charles's features had developed, it was obvious that the dauphin had inherited the attractive looks of his mother, Queen Marie Antoinette. The oracle's words have never been more appropriate to a prince of France than to her son.

It is also noticeably that the oracle specifically refers to him as *a Prince*. This is especially apt, because after the dauphin had been placed inside the Temple prison, an order was passed decreeing that in future, he must be referred to as the 'Prince Royal'. [1]

Conducted to the principal

The structure of this oracle is similar to that of Century Seven N° 11, which concerns another royal child, Louis XIII. It, too, begins with a prediction for the royal child, before abruptly changing to the senior adult of the realm. Such openings act as a timing device. When this occurs, it is a sign that the rest of the prophecy will follow. In the present instance, the child's senior was his father, Louis XVI, and it is to this King that the remainder of the oracle refers.

On the morning of 11 December 1792, Louis XVI was *conducted* from his prison quarters inside the Temple *to the principal* – Citizen Aubin-Begorre Chambon, Mayor of Paris. [2] The purpose of this enforced meeting was to submit the King to a lengthy period of questioning before an assembled tribunal, so that a way might be found to bring a prosecution against him. It was therefore as a direct result of this meeting that Louis XVI was brought to trial later that month.

For the sake of appearances, the King was granted permission to engage a legal representative. This proved ineffective. And by a unanimous vote the King was found guilty of treason.

Betrayed at the second act

Trying the King for treason against the State, and then finding him guilty as charged was only the first of three acts in this courtroom drama. *The second act* required a vote to be taken in order to determine the nature of his sentence; the options available were death, detention or exile. It was during *the second act* that the King was *betrayed*. The duc d'Orléans, a cousin of Louis XVI, but now calling himself Philippe Égalité was among those who voted for the King's death. [3] Louis later confessed how much Orléans betrayal had grieved him.

The city at the blade

On 21 January 1793, the entire city of Paris was drawn to a single focal point, the *Place de la Révolution*, where *the blade* of the guillotine hung menacingly in the air. Surrounding the scaffold was a "great sea of twenty thousand faces," awaiting the arrival of the King.

> The Commune had turned Paris into an immense garrison. The city gates had been shut; a special escort of twelve hundred guards had been assigned to accompany Louis' coach to the scaffold, and the streets were lined four deep with soldiers. [4]

The King arrived at his final destination at ten o'clock. After dismounting from his carriage, both hands were tied behind his back, and his hair quickly cut short above the neck. He then climbed the steps to the platform above, whereupon his body was strapped upon a plank and his head held braced beneath the iron blade above. A deadly hush filled the square, to be broken by a momentary swish of metal between the worn wooden grooves of the two upright columns, and France's hereditary monarch was no more.

The face scorched with powder

Immediately after the execution, the King's severed head, together with his decapitated body were conveyed to the cemetery of the Madeleine. A deep pit had been dug to receive the remains. The head and torso were then "laid in a coffin, which was put in the grave, and immediately covered with quicklime." [5] That is to say, *the face* was *scorched with powder*. This may be contrasted with the *beauty* of Louis XVI's son, with which the prophecy began.

Through an excessively great murder

The world stood amazed: aghast at the beheading of Louis XVI. London referred to it a: "the foulest and most atrocious act the world has ever seen." The oracle called it simply: *an excessively great murder*. The courts of Europe were vociferous in condemning those responsible: and whom they labelled, the 'assassins of Paris' [6]

The head of the king despised

Immediately after the execution, Louis' head was held aloft for the watching crowd to bear witness. They greeted the spectacle with an enormous, derisory cheer. Soon afterwards, pictures of the King's severed *head* appeared on prints and on crockery as a crude reminder *of the King* they had so much *despised*. [7]

MATTER FOR REFLECTION
FOR THE CROWNED
JUGGLERS

Summary: *The legal execution of a king by his subjects will always be sensational. In sixteenth century France, where this prophecy began, it would have been too outrageous to have ever been thought possible. Because of this, the seer devotes several quatrains to foretelling the different aspects of the drama that unfolded to his foreknowledge. In this prophecy, the steps leading up to the trial and execution are foretold, and the application of quicklime to the face of the deceased King at his burial is also included. The beauty of his son's face therefore makes a suitable timing device for the fulfilment of this prophecy.*

93   *Prelat auare, d'ambition trompé,*
        Rien ne fera que trop viendra cuider:
        Ses messagiers & luy bien attrapé,
        Tout au rebours voir, qui le bois fendroit.

94   *Vn Roy iré sera aux sedifragues,*
        Quant interdictz seront harnois de guerre:
        La poison taincte au sucre par les fragues,
        Par eaux meurtris, mors disant terre, terre.

95   *Par detracteur calumnié à puis nay,*
      Quant istront faictz enormes & martiaulx:
      La moindre part dubieuse à l'aisnay,
      Et tost au regne seront faictz partiaulx.

detracteur (OF) disparager; calumnié (OF) malicious charge; puis nay (OF puisné) younger; quand (OF) seeing that; dubieuse (L dubi\us) moving in two directions; aisnay (AF aîné) senior; tost *as* tôt; partiaul (OF partial) unsociable

A malicious charge for the younger (DE GAULLE) by a disparager (PÉTAIN)   1940
Seeing that enormous and martial deeds will proceed:
The lesser part with the elder moving in two directions,
And swiftly in the realm they will be made unsociable.

A malicious charge for the younger by a disparager

The two persons referred to in the opening line are understood to be Charles de Gaulle, aged 49 in the summer of 1940, and Marshal Philippe Pétain, aged 84. Both men had fought with distinction during the First World War, although de Gaulle had been badly injured at the battle of Verdun and was taken captive. Pétain, however, emerged as the 'Hero of Verdun'. The oracle's emphasis upon 'younger' indicates an awareness of someone notably older.

The Battle of France, which began on 10 May 1940, ended with the nation's defeat against the might of the German army. Adolf Hitler entered Paris on 14 June to commence his occupation of the country. Four days later negotiations began between their respective governments for an armistice agreement. This was signed on 22 June; and it divided France into three parts.

> Germany would occupy the north and west, Italy would control a small Italian occupation zone in the southeast, and an unoccupied zone, the *zone libre* [free zone], would be governed by the newly formed Vichy government led by Marshal Pétain. [1]

Just prior to signing the armistice agreement, General de Gaulle, who was serving as liaison officer with the British government, attempted to persuade the French Prime Minister, Paul Reynaud, to adopt the offer of a Declaration of Union, which would merge France with the UK, rendering it into a single political fighting force. But Reynaud was unable to persuade his government to adopt de Gaulle's suggested union, and he resigned. Pétain was more vociferous in denouncing the idea altogether, believing that Germany would soon overrun the UK. He told the British Prime Minister, Winston Churchill, "In three weeks, England will have its neck wrung like a chicken," and that joining France to Britain would be like "fusion with a corpse." [2]

This was undeniably *a malicious charge* made by a much older *disparager* who was intent upon rejecting the proposal made by *the younger* de Gaulle.

Seeing that enormous and martial deeds will proceed

This far, the prediction is entirely consistent with *the enormous military events* of the Second World War, which *proceeded* after the fall of France. The Russian invasion of Estonia, Latvia and Lithuania; the Battle of Britain; the London Blitz; Submarine warfare in the Battle of the Atlantic; Siege of Malta; the war in North Africa; German invasion of Yugoslavia and Greece; invasion of the Soviet Union by Germany, Italy and Romania; First Battle of Kharkov and the Kiev offensive; invasion of Iran; siege of Leningrad; attack on Pearl Harbour; Battle of Hong Kong; Japan and Thailand conquer Burma, Malaya, the Dutch East Indies, Singapore and Rabaul; the US captures the Philippines; Battle of Kursk; Battle of Changde; D-Day Landings; Battle of the Bulge and the nuclear bombs that fell on Hiroshima and Nagasaki.

The lesser part with the elder moving in two directions

When de Gaulle heard that Reynaud had resigned as prime minister and had been replaced by Marshal Pétain who was seeking an armistice with Germany, he and several fellow officers flew to Britain. From there, with the help of the allies, he was able to organize the Free French Forces, and "in September 1941, de Gaulle formed the Free French National Council, with himself as president. [...] By early 1942, the 'Fighting French' movement, as it was now called, gained rapidly in power and influence." [3]

In May 1940, Philippe Pétain – then aged 84 – requested an armistice with Germany, for which he was appointed "chief of state, with absolute powers." The armistice gave Germany control over the north and west of France, including Paris, but left the southern and eastern part (except for a small corridor of land, which was given to Italy) as a separate regime under the rule of Pétain with its capital at Vichy. De Gaulle and Pétain were now moving in opposite directions.

And swiftly in the realm they will be made unsociable

In their separate roles as Prime Minister of Vichy, and leader of the 'Fighting French', de Gaulle and Pétain *swiftly* became *unsociable* and eventually enemies. De Gaulle's broadcasts, rallying French resistance, so irritated Pétain that, "At a court-martial in Vichy, on 2 August 1940, de Gaulle was condemned to death for treason."[4] Whereas, in London ...

> The legitimacy of Vichy France and Pétain's leadership was constantly challenged by the exiled General Charles de Gaulle, based in London, who claimed to represent the legitimacy and continuity of the French nation. The overseas French colonies were originally under Vichy control, but it lost one after another to de Gaulle's Free French movement.[5]

Summary: *In 1940, France was overrun by Hitler's Germany. As a result, two men with an age difference of 34 years came to the fore. The elder, Philippe Pétain, formed an alliance with the Nazis and became ruler of Vichy France. Charles de Gaulle, the younger man, flew to Britain and organized the resistance to the German occupation. The oracle foreshadows the disagreement between these two, with easily recognizable incidents that are unique to this period of history.*

96   *Grande cité à souldartz abandonnee,*
          Onques ny eust mortel tumult si proche,
          O quel hideuse calamité s'approche,
          Fors vne offence n'y sera pardonnee.

abandonner (OF) release; fors (OF) without doors

> The great city (**PARIS**) released to soldiers,   1871
> Never, nor was mortal tumult so close,
> Oh, what hideous calamity draws near,
> Out of doors, not one offence will be forgiven there.

The great city (Paris) released to soldiers

The events of 1871 that fulfil this prophecy were seeded by the defeat of Louis Napoleon III in the Franco-Prussian War. The Emperor had been captured, but then released to leave France and find sanctuary in England. The government of France was therefore a vacuum waiting to be filled. A government of National Defence took over, and this elevated Adolphe Thiers to leadership. On 8 February 1871, he was made Chief Executive of the French Republic. It was while forming his government that an opposition party sprang to the fore: one that pronounced itself as the true representative of the people—and the National Guard supported its claim.

> During the night of 18–19 March, the National Guard occupied the empty offices vacated by the government; they quickly took over the Ministry of Finance, the Ministry of the Interior, and the Ministry of War. At eight in the morning on the 19th, the Central Committee was meeting in the Hotel de Ville. By the end of the day 20,000 national guardsmen were camped in triumph in the square in front of the Hotel de Ville, with several dozen cannon, and a red flag was hoisted over the building.
> The extreme left members of the Central Committee, led by the Blanquists [followers of the socialist revolutionary, Louis Blanqui], demanded an immediate march on Versailles, to disperse the Thiers government and to impose their authority on all of France.[1]

The mutinous National Guardsmen were joined by many thousands of manual workers, which became recognized as the first socialist, working-class uprising in the world. Together, they became known as the Communards. For two months and ten days they ruled Paris.

At Versailles, Thiers began making plans to regain control of the city.

Thiers had estimated that he would need 150,000 soldiers to recapture Paris, and he had only about twenty thousand reliable first-line soldiers, plus about five thousand gendarmes. He worked rapidly to assemble a new and reliable regular army. Most of the soldiers were prisoners of war who had just been released by the Germans, following the terms of the armistice. Others were sent from military units in all of the provinces. To command the new army Thiers chose Patrice Mac-Mahon. [2]

The Communards had in the meantime been busy establishing their defences of the city, and these had been successful in preventing Thiers' attempt to enter Paris with his armed troops. But on 21 May, part of the city wall at the Pont-du-Jour was left unattended by the National Guard. Attention to this was drawn to Mac-Mahon's invading force gathered outside the city "By dawn on the 22nd, Marshal MacMahon had already poured 70,000 troops through five gaping breaches in the walls between the Portes of Passy and Saint-Cloud. They had been welcomed warmly in this predominantly bourgeois arrondissement," [3] *thus, releasing the great city to the soldiers.*

Never, nor was mortal tumult so close
In a belated attempt to respond to this surprise attack, the Communards began building barricades across the streets. It marked the beginning of '*La Semaine sanglante*' "The Bloody Week". It would last for seven tumultuous days, and terminate only after the bodies of 20,000 comrades in arms lay dead—the Communards who had gallantly mounted the barricades against Thier's soldiers to defend their political beliefs on the streets of Paris, although greatly outnumbered by a ratio of five to one.

Oh, what hideous calamity draws near
By Tuesday, the soldiers were making visible progress in clearing street by street. "Some forty-nine captured Communards were collected at random and summarily shot in the Rue de Rosiers." Dr Herbert, a witness to the events, reported how "we saw the insurgents retreat from the different barricades and cross the Place. The troops then came in. A few scenes of horrid massacre and bloodshed, and then the streets were occupied by the regular troops." Elsewhere, "Marine sharpshooters positioned in the top storey of surrounding buildings directed a devastating fire down on to the Communards exposed behind their barricades." [4] In response, Paul-Antoine Brunel ordered the buildings to be burnt to the ground. By Wednesday evening Edwin Child, observing Paris from the east, wrote, "It seemed literally as if the whole town was on fire and as if all the powers of hell were let loose." The list of important buildings destroyed included the Tuileries Palace, the Palais Royal, the Palais de Justice, the Prefecture of the Police, part of the Louvre, and the Hôtel de Ville. [5]

> Friday, 26 May was a day of savage killing on both sides, in which the battle became a ruthless mopping-up operation [...] the dashing Marquis de Gallifet, now secured for himself a reputation for barbarity that Paris would never forget [...] with his mistress on his arm, pointing out who should die and who should live, he is described as 'making caustic jests as he did so'. Troops under Gallifet's orders treated the captured Communards with particular brutality, many never surviving the journey to Versailles.

And when the mutilated body of Archbishop Georges Darboys was discovered: a victim of the hostage-taking ...

> The Versailles troops marched 147 of the captured Communards out to Père Lachaise and summarily shot them against a wall of the cemetery. Inside La Roquette, which held such grim memories for the hostages of the Commune, some 1,900 prisoners are said to have been shot in two days, and at the Mazas prison another 400. [6]

The Seer's mention that this event 'draws near' is relative to the timescale of his prophetic range. Compare these 316 years with his entire set of 1000 oracles, which ranges over 2,242 years. This means the Paris revolt occurred after only 14% of this time period had lapsed.

Out of doors, not one offence will be forgiven there
"Having supported the Commune in any way was a political crime, of which thousands could be, and were, accused." [7] Not even one offence was pardonable.

Some prisoners who had been captured with weapons in their hands or gunpowder on their hands had been shot immediately. Others were taken to the main barracks of the army in Paris, after summary trials, were executed there.[8]

Summary: *Because this uprising, referred to as 'Bloody Week', occurred in Paris, it is rightly one of the seer's more dramatic prophecies. Yet, in the wider context of history's blood-soaked past, can it be said to be other than just another example of that 'sound and fury', which in the end 'signifies nothing'? Politicians need to take special note when they attempt to use their personal beliefs as an example for ruling others. It rarely lasts longer than the generation to which they belong, yet in their pride they ignore its failures, exterminate, or otherwise censor those who disagree with their politics, and blithely imagine nothing will ever change in the future. Here, in this prophecy, is a terrible example of secular socialism's ideals drenched in blood.*

97   *Cinq & quarante degrés ciel bruslera,*
       Feu approcher de la grand cité neufue,
       Instant grand flamme esparse saultera,
       Quant on voudra des Normans faire preuue.

98   *Ruyné aux Volsques de peur si fort terribles,*
       Leur grand cité taincte, faict pestilent:
       Pillier, Sol, Lune, & violer leurs temples,
       Et les deux fleuues rougir de sang coulant.

99   *L'ennemy docte se tournera confus,*
       Grand camp malade, & deffaict par embusches,
       Montz Pyrenées & Pœnus luy seront fait refus,
       Proche du fluue descourant antiques oruches.

100   *Fille de l'Aure, asyle du mal sain,*
       Où iusqu'au ciel se void l'amphitheatre,
       Prodige veu, ton mal est fort prochain,
       Seras captiue, & des fois plus de quatre.

LEGIS CAVTIO CONTRA INEPTOS CRITICOS

(CHOOSE CAUTION AGAINST INEPT CRITICS)

Qui legent hosce versus, maturé censunte:
Prophanum vulgus & inscium ne attrectato:
Omnesque Astrologi, Blenni, Barbari procul sunto,
Qui aliter faxit, is rité sacer esto.

They who read these verses, assess maturely,
The profane, the vulgar and the ignorant touch not.
All astrologers, simpletons, and barbarians are at a great distance.
Whoever acts differently, he is rightly accursed.

In this extra quatrain, the Seer categorically denies that the verses composed in these 'Centuries' have any connection with astrology. During his lifetime, he did draw up horoscopes, as did Johannes Kepler and Isaac Newton: both of whom were born many years after the death of de Nostredame. The importance of these two mathematicians' contribution to knowledge has allowed their astrological work to be overlooked. There is no reason to deny de Nostredame the same privilege, since he has denounced the practice quite vehemently: whereas, Newton and Kepler defended it.

It must also be understood that de Nostredame was not the originator of these prophecies. Instead, he acted as a scribe: an intermediary between mankind and the heavenly messenger sent by God. The purpose of this divine intervention was to deflate the pride of the counterfeiters by negating physical *causes* and their *effects*: replacing them by coexisting, temporal events perceived sequentially. Nevertheless, the method by which the seer achieved these communications is open to question but then, so is the manner in which the biblical prophets obtained their contact with the divine.

References Century 6

Nº. 2

1 E.N. Williams, *Dictionary of English and European History 1485–1789*, 167
2 NNDB.COM/PEOPLE/836/000093557/
3 H.A.L. Fisher, *A History of Europe*, Vol. 1, 572
4 en.wikipedia.org/wiki/Great_Storm_of_1703
5 Ibid
6 Williams, 167
7 Lynn, 62
8 Ibid 62-3
9 Ian Dunlop, *Louis XIV*, 210, 419
10 Ibid. 397, 422

Nº. 11

1 Leonie Frieda, *Catherine de Medici*, 325
2 Ibid. 61
3 Ibid. 326-7, 329
4 Ibid. 330

Nº. 12

1 Franklin L Ford, *Europe 1780-1830*, 228–9
2 Alan Palmer, *An Encyclopaedia of Napoleon's Europe*, 157
3 J.M. Thompson, *Napoleon Bonaparte*, 262
4 Ibid 263
5 wikipedia.org/wiki/Louis_Bonaparte
6 wikipedia.org/wiki/Walcheren_Expedition
7 Thompson, 243
8 David Chandler, *The Campaigns of Napoleon*, 528
9 http://www.nndb.com/people/518/000088254/

Nº. 22

1 Norman Davies, *Europe A History*, 598
2 Neil Grant, *Kings and Queens*, 1883 William H. Mountague, *A New and Universal History of England*: Vol. 2, 219
4 Ibid 219
5 Ibid 221
6 Ibid 231; & E.N. Williams, *Dictionary of English and European History 1485-1789*, 387
7 wikipedia.org/wiki/Act_of_Toleration_1689

Nº. 23

1 Simon Schama, *Citizens*, 458
2 Ibid 458–9
3 Ibid 459, 460
4 Jean Favier (ed.) *Chronicle of the French Revolution*, 152
5 Ibid 155
6 Ibid 158, 181
7 Norman Davies, *Europe A History*, 699
8 Christopher Hibbert, *The French Revolution*, 130

Nº. 24

1 Planets – *RedShift* 4 CD-ROM, Maris Mutimedia Ltd; & Franklin L Ford, *Europe 1780 – 1830*, 219; & David Chandler, *The Campaigns of Napoleon*, 770
2 J.M. Thompson, *Napoleon Bonaparte*, 329, 333–8; & Norman Davies, *Europe - A History*, 742; Alan Palmer, *An Encyclopaedia of Napoleon's Europe*, 197
3 H.A.L. Fisher, *A History of Europe*, 950
4 Louis XVIII, *Encyclopædia Britannica 2001* - CD-ROM
5 Palmer, 183; & Davies, 1287

Nº. 25

1 Christopher Hibbert, *The French Revolution*, 142-5
2 ————— *Rome The Biographu of a City*, 230
3 newadvent.org/cathen/12131a.htm
4 Thompson, 141; & Fisher, 916
5 Franklin L Ford, *Europe 1780-1830*, 121; & Norman Davis, *Europe –A History*, 698

Nº. 26

1 Peter de Rosa, *Vicars of Christ*: 173
2 http://www.archelaos.com/popes/details.aspx?id=263
3 Roland Sarti, *Italy: A Reference Guide from the Renaissance to the Present*. 189
4 wikipedia.org/wiki/Ravenna; wikipedia.org/wiki/Pisa
5 wikipedia.org/wiki/Ottoman–Venetian_War_(1570–73)

6   britannica.com/EBchecked/topic/462344/Saint-Pius-V

N°. 31
1   Derrik Mercer (ed.) *Chronicle of the Second World War*, 429
2   translate.google.co.uk/translate?hl=en&sl=it&u=http://it.wikipedia.org/wiki/Alfredo_Ildefonso_Schuster &prev=search
3   Jasper Ridley, *Mussolini*, 364-5
4   Ibid 355, 368

N°. 40
1   wikipedia.org/wiki/Karl_Theodor_Anton_Maria_von_Dalberg
2   http://www.napoleon-series.org/research/government/diplomatic/c_luneville.html
3   wikipedia.org/wiki/History_of_Cologne
4   wikipedia.org/wiki/Reichsdeputationshauptschluss
5   http://www.newadvent.org/cathen/12132a.htm
6   wikipedia.org/wiki/Confederation_of_the_Rhine

N°. 42
1   wikipedia.org/wiki/Ogmios
2   http://www.theottomans.org/english/family/suleyman1.asp
3   http://www.yursil.com/blog/2007/11/a-taste-of-the-real-sultan-selim-ii/
4   wikipedia.org/wiki/Ottoman–Venetian_War_(1570–1573)
5   wikipedia.org/wiki/Holy_League_(Mediterranean)
6   Imamović, Mustafa (1996). Historija Bošnjaka. Sarajevo: BZK Preporod. ISBN 9958-815-00-1

N°. 54
1   *Encyclopædia Britannica 2001* CD-ROM, Turkey and Eastern Europe; Bejaïa; & Murad III
2   Ibid Morocco Under Sharifian Dynasties; & D Fage, *A History of Africa*, 177
3   Ibid The Battle of the Three Kings
4   Ibid The Sufferings and Death of Jesus in Jerusalem

N°. 55
1   wikipedia.org/wiki/Manifesto_to_the_Polish_Nation
2   wikipedia.org/wiki/Caucasus_Campaign
3   wikipedia.org/wiki/Erzurum_Offensive
4   wikipedia.org/wiki/Tripoli#Late_Ottoman_era
5   wikipedia.org/wiki/1911/Chios#Modern_period
6   wikipedia.org/wiki/1911_Tripoli_massacre
7   wikipedia.org/wiki/Massacre_of_Italians_at_Sciara_Sciat Gaston Leroud , Matin Journal august 23, 1917
8   wikipedia.org/wiki/Chios#Ottoman_period
9   Ibid
10 John S. Bowman, Sherry Marker, Peter Kerasiotis, *Greek Islands,* (6th edition)
11 wikipedia.org/wiki/Trabzon
12 Ibid
13 www.history.com/topics/armenian-genocide
14 wikipedia.org/wiki/Cemal_Azmi
15 *Toronto Globe* (26 August 1915) & *World War I* by Wikipedians, p. 386
16 wikipedia.org/wiki/Grand_Duke_Nicholas
17 http://britishbattles.homestead.com/files/naval/The_Black_Sea_in_World_War_One.htm
18 wikipedia.org/wiki/Trabzon

N°. 57
1   http://www.newadvent.org/cathen/14033a.htm
2   wikipedia.org/wiki/Pope_Sixtus_V
3   David L. Roper, *The Popes of Saint Malachy:* 175
4   Peter de Rosa, *Vicars of Christ:* 524
5   Ibid 302
6   http://www.romeartlover.it/Storia23.html
7   wikipedia.org/wiki/Pope_Sixtus_V
8   http://www.britannica.com/EBchecked/topic/547156/Sixtus-V
9   wikipedia.org/wiki/Pope_Sixtus_V
10 Rosa, 301
11 http://www.csun.edu/~hcfll004/SV1585.html
12 Rosa, 301-2

N°. 63
1   E.N. Williams, *Dictionary of English and European History 1485-1587*, 295
2   *Encyclopædia Britannica 2001*, CD-ROM, Marie de Médicis
3   K.A. Patmore, *The Court of Louis XIII*, 26
4   Ibid 243; & *Encyclopædia Britannica*, History of France, Louis XIII
5   R. Mousnier, *The Assassination of Henry IV* (trans. Joan Spencer), 391
6   Patmore, 59

7   Ibid 58
8   Ibid 58
9   Ibid 15, 16, 63
10 Williams, 296

Nº. 69

1   Ian Dunlop, *Louis XIV*: 369
2   Ibid 373
3   britannica.com/EBchecked/topic/91022/Camisard
4   Dunlop, 373-4
5   Ibid 373
6   http://www.answers.com/topic/camisard-revolt
7   Doug Schlegel – www.leben.us/volume-4-volume-4-issue-4/264-the-camisards
8   wikipedia.org/wiki/Edict_of_Fontainebleau
9   Doug Schlegel

Nº. 74

1   E.N. Williams, *Dictionary of English and European History 1485-1587*, 216–7
2   Ibid
3   Roger Price, *A Concise History of France*, 182; & Derrik Mercer (ed.) *Chronicle of the World*, 814, 815
4   Alistair Horne, *Seven Ages of Paris*, 26
5   Napoleon III – Last Years, *Encyclopædia Britannica 2001*: CD-ROM

Nº. 75

1   E.N. Williams, *Dictionary of English and European History 1485-1587*, 101
2   Ibid 101; & Leonie Frieda, *Catherine de Medici*, 234
3   R .J. Knecht, *Catherine de' Medici*, 88
4   Williams, 104; Robert J. Knecht, *The French Religious Wars 1562–1598*, 41–3
5   Cyprus History: Ottoman Period; Microsoft Internet Explorer, reference B Rogerson (1994), *Cyprus*.
6   Williams, 352

Nº. 79

1   General Sir James Marshall-Cornwall, *Napoleon*, 58
2   Dr Enzo Orlandi (ed.) *The Life and Times of Napoleon*, 10
3   Ibid & David Chandler, *The Campaigns of Napoleon*, 60-1
4   H.A.L. Fisher, *A History of Europe*, 910
5   Arthur Bryant, *The Years of Endurance 1793-1802*
6   Napoléon Bonaparte, *Encyclopædia Britannica 2001*: CD-ROM
7   Chandler, 106, 107–8; & John Holland Rose, *The Life of Napoleon I*: 125

Nº. 83

1   wikipedia.org/wiki/Alexander_Farnese,_Duke_of_Parma
2   wikipedia.org/wiki/Dutch_Revolt
3   wikipedia.org/wiki/History_of_Belgium
4   http://www.answers.com/topic/alexander-farnese-duke-of-parma
5   wikipedia.org/wiki/Alexander_Farnese,_Duke_of_Parma
6   Robert J. Knecht, *The French Religious Wars*: 65

Nº. 92

1   Meade Minnigerode, *The Son of Marie Antoinette*, 28; & *Citizens*, Simon Schama, 654
2   Simon Schama, *Citizens*: 658
3   Ibid 662; & Bernard Faÿ, *Louis XVI* (trans. Patrick O'Brien), 402
4   Schama, 669
5   Ibid 673; & S K Padover, *The Life and Death of Louis XVI*, 334
6   Schama, 687; & Franklin L Ford, *Europe 1780-1830*, 121–2; & Christopher Hibbert, *The French Revolution*, 193
7   Padover, 334

Nº. 95

1   wikipedia.org/wiki/Battle_of_France
2   Winston Churchill, *Their Finest Hour*: 187
3   wikipedia.org/wiki/Charles_de_Gaulle#The_Battle_of_France
4   wikipedia.org/wiki/Charles_de_Gaulle
5   wikipedia.org/wiki/Vichy_France

Nº. 96

1   wikipedia.org/wiki/Paris_Commune
2   ibid
3   Alistair Horne, *Seven Ages of Paris*: 307
4   ibid 308
5   id 309 - 10
6   id 310-11
7   newworldencyclopedia.org/entry/Paris_Commune#The_Commune_in_retrospect
8   wikipedia.org/wiki/Paris_Commune#Prisoners.2C_trials_and_exiles

CENTURY SEVEN

1   *L'Arc du thresor par Achilles deceu.*
    Aux procrees sceu la quadrangulaire:
    Au faict Royal le comment sera sceu,
    Corps veu pendu au veu du populaire.

Arc (OF) vault: also (L – arc\a,) state treasure: & (*anagrammatic-paragram*: [n]e Arc) Ancre; thresor (OF) king's revenue; par (AF durant), during; deceu (OF) deceived, overwrought; procréer (OF) to procreate, make; sceu (OF) known, understood.

  The vault (**ANCRE**) for the king's revenue, during **ACHILLE** deceived,   1611
  The quadrangular known to the made ones:
  At the Royal deed, the explanation will be understood,
  The body (**CONCINI**) seen hung to the view of the common people.

The vault (Ancre) for the king's revenue

Concino Concini, Marquis d'Ancre, was a native of Florence. When Marie de Médici travelled to France for her wedding to Henri IV, Concini accompanied the royal party, and subsequently married Leonora Dori (known as *Galigai*), the new Queen's lady-in-waiting and foster sister.

In 1610, Concini purchased the marquisate of Ancre, which permitted him to become 'First Gentleman-in-waiting'. It is at this point that Concini enters the pages of history. On 14 May 1610, Henri IV was assassinated by François Ravaillac. The crown then passed to his eight-year-old son Louis XIII, with the Queen acting as Regent, and Concini aiding her as chief advisor.

The death of the King also brought to an ended the position held by Maximilien de Béthune, first Duke of Sully. Under his administration, and "by his honest, rigorous conduct of the country's finances, he was able to save, between 1600 and 1610, an average of a million *livres* a year." [1]

> The political role of Sully effectively ended with the assassination of Henry IV on 14 May 1610. Although a member of the Queen's council of regency, his colleagues were not inclined to put up with his domineering leadership, and after a stormy debate he resigned as superintendent of finances on 26 January 1611. [2]

Concini, in his capacity as advisor to the Queen-regent and the husband to her childhood friend, suddenly found himself in a position to advise upon matters of state expenditure. During his six years in office, which gave him overall control of the state treasury and the *King's revenue* – it is why he is described in the oracle as the vault – Ancre amassed a vast fortune. [3]

During Achille deceived

The Seer concludes the first line of this prophecy by revealing a second name: that of Achille de Harlay, Count of Beaumont, and President of Parliament at the time of Henri IV's murder. In fact, it was Harlay who was the judge at Ravaillac's trial for regicide. And this takes us to the timing of the predicted event in this first line.

Following Henri IV's assassination, the enquiry into his death ended with Achille being deceived.

> In 1611, charges were laid against the Duke of Épernon, Jean-Louis Nogaret de La Valette, about his involvement in the assassination of the King Henri IV. The accuser, Miss Jacqueline Escoman, Lady-in-waiting to the marchioness de Verneuil, implicated her mistress and accused her of having organized the killing with the complicity of Épernon. A trial conducted by a tribunal in which Achille de Harlay was first Chairman, heard the witnesses, including Verneuil and Epernon. The first (and only) order made by the tribunal, ultimately, was the continued detention of mademoiselle Escoman. Fifteen days after the order, Harlay retired. On 30 July, his successor condemned Escoman to prison for life for calumny. [4]

It was explained that Achille d'Harlay had been deceived by Jacqueline Escoman's story of her mistress, the marchioness de Verneuil, and the duke of Épernon's complicity in the killing of the King. In fact, Ravaillac had acted alone, and the trial had therefore been an embarrassment to Harlay and Èpernon. Harlay therefore resigned his chairmanship, and the 'witness' for the prosecution, Jacqueline Escoman, was jailed for life by the incoming chairman.

The quadrangular known to the made ones

The position held by Concini and his wife only became possible because of their relationship with the Queen-regent. By the spring of 1617, Louis XIII was still only fifteen-years-of-age; but he had come under increasing pressure from external sources to start ruling the country. Concini unwisely ignored what was happening: mistakenly believing that Louis' mother would continue to keep her son under control. But young Louis had grown to resent Concini's arrogance; and this resentment was shared by many other people.

Charles d'Albert, the royal falconer and a favourite of the King was quick to take advantage of the deterioration in Concini's relationship with Louis. He realised that a *coup* would not only please his royal master, but it would also help promote his own political ambitions. Acting under the King's authority, Baron Vitry, the captain of the royal bodyguard, was approached with a plan for removing d'Ancre.

On the morning of 24 April 1617, Concini crossed the Pont Neuf, accompanied by his retinue, and entered the square – *quadrangular* – leading to "the great door facing on to Saint-Germain l'Auxerrois." It was to be for the last time. Unbeknown to him, a warrant for his arrest had been made out. Vitry approached d'Ancre with the words: "The King has commanded me to seize your person." As the Marshal turned, three shots were heard from the guards accompanying Vitry, and Concini fell to the ground, shot through the head. [5]

News of what had just taken place in the square quickly became *known to* Concini's wife. She and her husband had, quite literally been *made* (procreated) by the Queen-mother: they both having "risen from a humble rank to arrogant enjoyment of riches and nobility."

Upon hearing of her husband's murder, the marchioness retreated to her apartment where she was arrested while attempting to conceal her jewellery inside a mattress. [6] After being put on trial and found guilty of witchcraft, she was beheaded at the Place de la Grève (8 July 1617). "What a lot of people to see a poor woman die," were her final words. Her body was then publicly burnt.

At the royal deed, the explanation will be understood

The facts relating to the King's involvement in the murder of Concini soon became public knowledge, but the reason for it was also understood.

> [T]he King had organized the assassination of the Queen-mother's minister, Concini. [...] Louis had now reached the point when he was determined to rid himself of the Maréchal. Few were in his secret. 'You are to confer with De Luynes,' were the king's command to Vitry, the captain of the body-guard, 'and do as he tells you.' [7]

The body seen hung to the view of the common people

After Concini's murder, his body was secretly taken to the church of St. Germain l'Auxerrois. Following the briefest of ceremonies, it was interred inside a cavity that had been specially prepared beneath the church organ. The site was then plastered over so that it might pass unnoticed. But, next day, the crowd went in search of the body, and its hiding place was revealed. [8] The anger of the mob drove them to rip open the concealed cavity, and after cutting down bell ropes from the church tower, with which to harness the body, it was dragged through the streets to the gallows, which Concini had only recently erected on the Pont Neuf. There, *the body* was *hung* upside down *to the view of the people.* [9]

Summary: This oracle names two men, Ancre and Achille, both of whom were involved in separate events following immediately after, and because of, the assassination of Henri IV. Concini's role in history occurred because he acted as chief advisor to the Queen–regent. Her appointment came about immediately after the death of her husband, and was meant to terminate when her son came of age. But she failed to let go her grip on power. The King was therefore persuaded to sanction the murder of his mother's chief councellor, in order to take his place as King. Achille was a member of the nobility who oversaw the trial of the King's assassin. But upon doing so, he was deceived by one of the witnesses, and resigned his office once this became evident.

2   Par Mars ouuert Arles ne donra guerre,
      De nuict seront les soldats estonnez:
      Noir, blanc à l'inde dissimulé en terre,
      Sous la saincte ombre traistre verrez & sonnez.

3   Apres de France la victoire nauale,
      Les Barchinons, Sallinons, les Phocens,
      Lierre d'or, l'enclume serré dedans la balle,
      Ceux de Prolon au fraud seront contens.

4   Le duc de Langres asiegé dedans Dolle,
      Accompaigné d'Ostun & Lyonnois:
      Geneue, Auspurg ioinct ceulx de Mirandole,
      Passer les monts contre les Anconnois.

5   Vin sur la table en sera espandu,
      Le tiers n'aura celle qu'il pretendoit:
      Deux fois du noir de Parme descendu,
      Perouse à Pize fera ce qu'il cuidoit.

6   Naples, Palerme, & toute la Secile,
      Par main barbare sera inhabitee,
      Corsicque, Salerne & de Sardaigne l'isle,
      Faim, peste, guerre, fin de maulx intentee.

      Naples, Palermo, and the whole of Sicily   1943
      Through barbarous possession, will be inhabited:
      Corsica, Salerno and for the island of Sardinia,
      Dearth, infection, warfare: the end of evils commenced.

main (AF metaphor) possession; intenter (OF) to commence

Naples

The events in this quatrain predict the Allied invasion of Italy during the Second World War. The goal was Rome, but before it could be reached, Naples and the islands named in the oracle had first to be overcome.

> Naples was the most bombed Italian city in World War II. There were about 200 air strikes between 1940 and 1944 by Allied forces, with 180 raids on the city in 1943. Estimates of civilian casualties vary between 20,000 and 25,000 killed.
> In Naples, the primary targets were the port facilities at the extreme eastern end of the Port of Naples as well as the rail, industrial and petroleum facilities in the eastern part of the city and the steel mill to the west, in Bagnoli. [1]

Palermo and the whole of Sicily

> During World War II, Palermo was untouched until the Allies began to advance up Italy after the allied invasion of Sicily in 1943. In July, the harbour and the surrounding quarters were heavily bombed by the allied forces and were all but destroyed. [2]

On 10 July 1943, 2,590 naval vessels had taken part in the invasion of German-held Sicily, with British and US forces landing at different parts of the island. Code named Operation Husky, "the fall of Palermo on 22 July damaged the Italian morale tremendously, giving those in Italy, who opposed Mussolini's pursuit of war, an opportunity to seek an armistice." [3]

> Operation Husky, was a major World War II campaign, in which the Allies took Sicily from the Axis Powers (Italy and Nazi Germany). It was a large scale amphibious and airborne operation, followed by six weeks of land combat. It launched the Italian Campaign. [4]

Through barbarous possession, will be inhabited

The oracle predicts the possession of Sicily and Naples by the German army. Although it does not actually name the occupying force, it does call them *barbarous*, which not only means cruel, but also foreign. It should be understood that at the time these events were taking place, the Nazi death camps were busily exterminating Jews from the occupied countries.

Corsica

In November 1942, Corsica, which was then part of Vichy France, had become placed under the occupation of 85,000 Italian troops.

> In July 1943, following the imprisonment of Mussolini, 12,000 German troops came to Corsica. They formally took over the occupation on 9 September 1943, the day after the armistice between Italy and the Allies. Following the Allied landings in Sicily and the Italian surrender, these German troops were joined by the remnants of the African Division of the German army [...] with about 40,000 men, which crossed over from Sardinia. [5]

When Italy joined the Allies against Germany, following Mussolini's arrest, Corsica was one of the few locations where Italy's *Regio Esercito* was able to resist the German army. By 4 October, after the arrival of French reinforcements at Ajaccio, the German army evacuated the island, and Corsica was liberated.

Salerno

With the conquest of Sicily accomplished, the way was clear for the Allied land force to begin fighting its way towards Naples. However, it was because the city was too far from the Allies newly established air base on Sicily that a decision was taken to invade Salerno, fifty miles south of Naples: where the air force could more easily operate from. In a pre-dawn invasion planned for 9 September, a fleet of some 450 ships arrived at the coast of Salerno for Operation Avalanche.

> U.S. Rangers hit the beach unopposed at 0310, twenty minutes in advance of the main assault force, moving quickly inland to seize their objectives. British Commandos captured the town of Salerno against light opposition. [6]

By 0610, all troops were ashore, some under heavy fire, as the Germans, awakened to the unexpected onslaught, and began a defensive operation.

> During 12 to 14 September, the Germans attacked the entire Allied Salerno front, searching for weaknesses, hoping to throw the beachhead into the sea before it could link with the Eighth Army. Although heavy casualties were endured by the thinly spread Allied units, the German efforts were unsuccessful. [7]

Against heavy fire power from the Allies, the German army defending Salerno were ordered to destroy key bridges, all means of transportation, and fall back to form a line of defence.

> Realizing the Germans were pulling back, British and American troops of US Fifth Army began marching toward Naples on 19 Sep. By the end of the month, the southern portion of Italy was under Allied control, including the major airfield complex near Foggia, which was captured on 27 Sep. [8]

And for the island of Sardinia

During the Second World War, Sardinia became an important air and naval base for the German and Italian coalition. Because of its strategic significance, the cities of Cagliari and Alghero were heavily bombed by the Allies. This ended, when ...

> German troops left the island on 8 September 1943, a few days after the Armistice of Cassibile [the total capitulation of Italy, approved by both King Victor Emanuel III and Prime Minister Pietro Badoglio], and retired to Corsica without fighting and bloodshed, after a bilateral agreement between the general Antonio Basso (Commander of the Armed Forces of Sardinia) and the German Karl Hans Lungerhausen. [9]

Dearth, infection, warfare: the end of evils commenced

The Seer ends his insight vision of the Allied invasion of Italy in 1943, with the familiar, social features of hardship that accompany prolonged warfare: namely food shortages and an increase in the rates of infection. But he also signals by his foreknowledge that the end of the Second World War had commenced. The US 5th Army reached Naples in October 1944 and the battle of

Monte Cassino in January 1944 preceded the battle of Anzio and the fall of Rome on 5 June. Pockets of resistance continued in northern Italy, which remained in German hands under the leadership of Mussolini's Salo Republic. This came to an end with the continued advance of the US army completing the liberation of Italy. "General Heinrich von Vietinghoff... signed the instrument of surrender on behalf of the German armies in Italy on 29 April, formally bringing hostilities to an end on 2 May 1945." [10]

Summary: *The final words of the oracle – the end of evils commenced – is what this prophecy foretells. It would take*
              the whole of the following year and a few months of the year after, to accomplish in its entirety what had
              begun. The oracle picks out the affected areas, as it foretells the approaching end of the Second World War,
              which began with the allied landing forces invading Italy from the south and moving ever upwards through
              Italy to drive the German army into retreat.

> 7   *Sur le combat des grands cheuaux legers,*
>   *On criera le grand croissant confond.*
>   *De nuict tuer mont, habits de bergers,*
>   *Abismes rouges dans le fossé profond.*

> 8   *Flora, fuis, fuis le plus proche Romain,*
>   *Au Fesulan sera conflict donné:*
>   *Sang espandu, les plus grands prins à main,*
>   *Temple ne sexe ne sera pardonné.*

> 9   *Dame à l'absence de son grand capitaine,*
>   *Sera priée d'amour du Viceroy,*
>   *Faincte promesse & mal'heureuse estreine,*
>   *Entre les mains du grand Prince Barroys.*

fainct (OF *also* feinct) feigned; estreine (OF) corrected; entre (OF entré) begun in.

> The woman at the absence of her great captain (**CHARLES IV**)   1635
> Will be entreated by love of the viceroy (**CANTECROIX**):
> A feigned vow and unhappiness corrected,
> Begun in the hands of the great Prince of Bar.

The woman

The woman in this prophecy is Béatrix de Cusance: once described by Pope Alexander VII as the most beautiful woman of the 17th century. She was born in Franche-Comté at Belvoir, in 1614, to Claude-François de Cusance, baron de Belvoir and de Saint-Julien, and his wife Ernestine van Witthem, Countess van Walhain (to whom he was introduced while serving as a military officer in the Spanish Netherlands). But he died in 1627, when Béatrix was aged thirteen.

Béatrix was raised by her grandmother Beatrix de Vergy at her home in Besançon. Later, as a young adult, she attended court at Brussels, which was then under the government of Philip III's half-sister Isabella Eugenia and her husband, Albert of Austria. [1]

It was at the court of Isabella: "the court of the Archdukes, as they were known" that at the age of nineteen or twenty Béatrix fell in love, and became the mistress of Charles IV, Duke of Lorraine and of Bar. (He previously appeared in Century Three N°. 98).

Charles, however, was already married to Nicole of Lorraine: their marriage having been conducted on 21 May 1621. It was actually an arranged marriage that had been planned by their respective fathers to ensure that the dukedom held by Henri of Lorraine would pass to his daughter Nicole. René II had imposed the Salic law on the title, which forbade a female from inheriting it. To everyone's misfortune, this marriage of convenience failed to stay its course. Nicole remained barren, and in 1631, Charles sought to escape his bond of matrimony by accusing the priest, who conducted the ceremony, of witchcraft. It failed. In 1635, he petitioned Pope Urban VIII to annul the marriage, but again, without success. In the year before seeking this annulment, Charles had taken Béatrix as his mistress.

At the absence of her great captain

Two years before that, Charles had become involved in a plot contrived by Gaston of Orleans,

Louis XIII's brother, and this had earned him the enmity of the King. It also caused him to abdicate his title and join the Imperial army in the Thirty Years War.

> In the Thirty Years' war, which began about 1620, Charles fought for the German empire, contributed to the victory over the Swedes at Nordlingen in 1634, and as an ally of Spain fought against the French in several ensuing campaigns. [2]

Will be entreated by love of the viceroy

In the absence of Charles IV, Béatrix's great captain (with whom she had since joined, and "who was at the time in the service of Spain"), her mother sought "To avoid a scandal" by finding a suitable husband for her daughter. The young nobleman who became captivated by Béatrix's beauty, and who soon afterwards entreated her to become his wife was Leopold-Eugène Perrenot de Granvelle, Prince de Cantecroix. [3] Their wedding was celebrated in Brussels on 6 March 1635. And on 15 January 1636, Béatrix gave birth to a daughter, who sadly lived only a few months.

> The Prince of Cantecroix [was] the last heir of the ancient House of Châlon, former counts of Burgundy and princes of Orange. Cantecroix himself was the son of a natural daughter of Emperor Rudolf II, and was heir to the immense wealth of the Cardinal de Granville, first minister of Philip II. [4]

The Seer has referred to Prince Cantecroix as 'Viceroy', having deliberately used a capital 'V' to draw attention to this. Why? In actual fact it serves as an extra prophecy. When 'Viceroy' is split into the two most obvious words of 'vice' and 'roy', they take on a different meaning. In ancient French, 'vice' meant 'défaut'. In English this translates as 'absence': while 'roy', as an adjective in ancient French, means 'raide' in modern French. This translates into English as 'rapid'. Putting these two words together we obtain, 'rapid absence'. Prince Cantecroix died on 6 February 1637, 23 months after his marriage to Béatrix. He was 22 years of age.

A feigned vow

On 2 April, two months after Leopold's death in Besançon, his widow entered into a second marriage. This time it was to her lover, Charles—even though he was still legally married to Nicole of Lorraine. The wedding *vow* Charles made was therefore *feigned*.

Six months after the ceremony, Béatrix gave birth to a son, whom Charles acknowledged was his. However, for 25 years, the birth was legally contested by Councils in Flanders and in Malines.

> His marriage to Béatrice de Cusance was not deemed valid by the Roman Catholic Church, which had not authorised his divorce from Nicole. The couple separated in April 1642 following his excommunication, which was the consequence of his second marriage; it was also the month in which she bore a son whom Charles recognised. [5]

The son, whom they named François, de Lorraine, died in February 1638. In the following year, Béatrix gave birth to Charles' daughter, Anne de Lorraine, who lived to the age of 81. The couple also had a third child born in 1649: Charles-Henri, Prince of Vaudémont who lived to be 74.

The excommunication was lifted after three years, although they were still not allowed to marry. They separated soon afterwards, but renewed their love affair at occasional intervals.

And unhappiness corrected

On 2 February 1657, Charles IV's legitimate wife, Nicole of Lorraine died in Paris aged 48. It was where she had spent the final years of her life. Six years later, "on 20 May 1663, Charles married Béatrice de Cusance a second time, to allow legitimation of their children. She died two weeks after this second marriage." [6] In fact, Béatrix had been dying from the effects of peritonitis at the time. Prior to her illness, Charles had rejected any thought of renewing his marriage. [7]

Begun in the hands of the great Prince of Bar

This prophecy is one of sadness for all concerned. Yet the seeds of this misfortune were planted by the Great Prince of Bar, René II, by his denying the inheritance of titles to females.

René II (2 May 1451 – 10 December 1508) was Count of Vaudémont from 1470, Duke of Lorraine from 1473, and Duke of Bar from 1483 to 1508. He claimed the crown of the Kingdom of Naples and the County of Provence as the Duke of Calbria 1480–1493 and as King of Naples and Jerusalem 1493–1508. He succeeded his uncle John of Vaudémont as Count of Harcourt in 1473, exchanging it for the county of Aumale in 1495. He succeeded as Count of Guise in 1504. [8]

"Madame Nicole de Loraine Dvchesse de Loraine et du Barrois"[9] had been denied the inheritance of her father's title by a clause in the testament of René II, which decreed that by Salic Law the duchy could not bypass the male lineage A way round this was planned by Francis, Count Vaudémont, who took the title himself before marrying his eldest son, Charles IV, to Nicole. He then abdicated his title, and passed it over to Charles, who then became Duke of Lorraine and Bar, and his wife Duchess of Lorraine and of Bar. This dual title occurred because "In his final testament published in 1506, René decreed that the two duchies [Lorraine and Bar] should never be separated. The two duchies remained joined in personal union permanently."[10]

Summary: *In this oracle, the seer foretells the deceit and betrayal to lives that unfold when attempts are made to facilitate selfish desires. The minor members of the nobility in this episode during the reign of Louis XIII appear to have left no lasting mark upon the history of their country, yet in their own way they have emphasised that the wiles they became involved in, imprint a lasting impression within the universe, of which they are (in block time) an inescapable part. Everything exists in the Mind of God, yet it is also where the life and loves of those He created, freely plan for themselves a future wrought by their own will.*

10   *Par le grand Prince limitrophe du Mans,*
        Preux & vaillant chef de grand exercite:
        Par mer & terre de Gallois & Normans,
        Caspre passer Barcelonne pillé Isle.

11   *L'enfant Royal contemnera la mere,*
        Oeil, piedz blesses, rude, inhobeissant:
        Nouuelle à dame estrange & bien amere,
        Seront tués des siens plus de cinq cens.

des siens (OF) of his side; amere, bitter *also* à mere – to mother.

The Royal child (**LOUIS XIII**) will despise his mother.   1617
Eye, the feet injured, boorish, not dutiful unto:
News for the foreign lady (**MARIE DE MEDICI**), and very bitter,
More than the five hundred of his (**TOIRAS**) own side will be killed.

The Royal child will despise his mother

To members of Louis XIII's court, this opening line would have instantly brought recognition. The Royal child did despise his mother, not least because "the mother of Louis XIII seems throughout to have sought the subjection of her son, and to have maintained him in a state of pupilage most detrimental to his career, either as man or monarch."[1]

Louis had succeeded to the throne after the assassination of his father Henri IV. But because he was only eight-years of age at the time, it was left to his mother, Marie de' Médicis to administer the affairs of France. Her role as regent had officially ended when the King reached maturity (October 1614); but, "It was hinted [...] that the favourite combined with Marie de Médicis to keep Louis from any participation in affairs."[2] The favourite was the Queen-mother's chief counsellor, Concini.

Unsurprisingly, as the King grew older his resentment increased; he was also especially sensitive to any lack of deference to his position as head of state—as Concini would soon discover to his peril, when Louis finally turned against his mother, by exiling her, and ordering the 'removal' of her chief councellor.

Eye, the feet injured

The assassination of Concini was carried out on 24 April 1617 when Concini was stopped outside the *Palais de Louvre* and shot through the head.[3] As previously remarked when discussing the murder of Condé (Century Three: N°. 41), the Seer always refers to the eye when predicting a victim's death by a shot to the head. In his view, it is as if the shot has opened up an extra socket in the skull. The same reference to the 'eye' is encountered again when commenting upon the death of Mussolini, where 'eye' is expressed in the plural to account for the several shots to the head that killed *Il Duce*.

After Concini's murder, his body was stripped: "one of the clogs, worn to protect the shoes, was dragged off the foot, and no time was lost by the underlings in rifling the dead ."[4] The absence of his footwear meant that when a harness was made for the body to be dragged through the streets, the corpse was barefoot, causing the feet to become injured.

Boorish, not dutiful unto

The King's decision to rid himself of Concini was probably made one November day in 1616, inside the great gallery of the Louvre. The King was idly standing near one of the windows overlooking the Seine when Concini appeared. Without once acknowledging Louis' presence – not being dutiful to his King – the Marshal went over to another window "and received obeisance from a hundred persons who had accompanied him and who doffed their headgear in his honour ."[5]

Concini's boorish attitude was to be the final reason which persuaded an inwardly, seething King to be rid of this man. It was also prompted by his favourite, Charles d'Albert, whom he afterwards raised to Duke of Luynes. The assassination of Concini was therefore set in motion, and it took place in the palace courtyard on 24 April 1617.[6]

News for the foreign lady, and very bitter

Noise from the shots that ended Concini's life penetrated into the palace. The Queen-mother's dresser, Cathérine, "leaned from the window, and, seeing, Vitry, called to him and asked what was the matter. ' The Maréchal d'Ancre is dead,' was the curt reply. Breathless, Cathérine repeated the news to Marie de' Médicis. 'God help me!' cried the queen-mother."[7]

The news did, indeed, prove very bitter for the 'foreign lady' (Marie de' Médicis was the daughter of Grand Duke Francesco de' Médicis of Tuscany and Joanna of Austria). It meant her power had ceased, and her exile was to follow. "She was to leave behind her favourite son, Gaston Duc d'Anjou, and her young daughters, Christine and Henriette-Marie. Blois was to be her place of exile."[8] At her departure, the Queen-mother's self-composure finally broke down: "leaning against the wall between the windows, she wept most bitterly. The courtiers kissed her dress, their eyes streaming with compassion, but she could neither speak nor see them through her blinding tears ."[9] It is noteworthy that Concini's wife, Leonora Galigai was also a foreign lady, but the King's mother is implied by the French word *amere* (*à mere*).

More than the five hundred of his own side will be killed

In 1620, Louis XIII issued an edict commanding the return of estates held by Huguenots to their original Catholic owners. As a result of mounting tension between Catholics and Protestants "the Île de Rhé, a Protestant stronghold on the west coast of France, was kept in hand and garrisoned by royal troops."[10] (See also Century 5 N° 89.)

Benjamin de Rohan, duc de Soubise, a Huguenot and commander of the garrison at Saint Julien, appealed to Protestant England for aid. James I responded with a squadron dispatched to lay siege at La Rochelle. This was later withdrawn by the Treaty of Montpellier.

Strength	
Siege Army: 22,001	La Rochelle: 27,000
Toiras:1,200	civilians and soldiers
	Buckingham:80 ships
	7,000 soldiers
Casualties and losses	
Siege Army: ?	La Rochelle:22,000 killed
Toiras:500 killed	Buckingham: 5,000 killed

"In June 1627 Buckingham organised a landing on the nearby island of Île de Ré with 6,000 men in order to help the Huguenots."[11]

In defence of the Île de Ré was Jean d'Aduze, Marquis de Toiras, in command of 1200 men.

> Toiras famously sustained the 3-month Siege of Saint-Martin de Ré in Île de Ré by the Duke of Buckingham in 1627. After three months of combat, Toiras managed to repel the Duke of Buckingham, who was forced to withdraw in defeat."[12]

Of Toiras' own side, 500 were killed,[13] with more dead from the siege army that was sent to help. As a reward for his victory, Louis XIII made Toiras governor of the Île de Ré.

Summary: The oracle begins with the rift between Louis XIII and his mother, who acted as regent during his
             minority, and then attempted to prolong her office after he had reached the age of maturity. As regent, the
             Queen-mother had relied upon Concini, the husband of her Florentine and childhood friend Leonora Dori
             (Galigai). But his pride and self-importance, combined with a lack of reverence for the young King, became
             his undoing. It led to his assassination, the execution of his wife and the exile of the Queen-mother.
             The final line includes one of the major events that occurred shortly after Louis XIII assumed the role of
             King. The religious conflict between Catholics and Protestants had still to heal, especially at the Huguenot
             stronghold at La Rochelle. The Duke of Buckingham's attempt to attack La Rochelle from the Île de Ré was
             thwarted by Marshal Toiras, who withstood the siege for the loss of 500 men under his command.

> 12   Le grand puisné sera fin de la guerre,
>   Aux Dieux assemble les excusés:
>   Cahors Moissac iront long de la serre,
>   Reffus Lestore, les Agennois razés.

> 13   De la cité marine & tributaire,
>   La teste raze prendra la satrapie:
>   Chasser sordide qui puis sera contraire,
>   Par quatorze ans tiendra la tyrannie.

teste (OF) tête; raze (OF) tondre de près; satrapie (L satrap\es) satrap. Cross-reference: teste raze, C.I: 88; C.V: 60

> From the maritime city and tributary,   1798
> The crop head (**NAPOLEON**) will capture the satrapy:
> Pursuing the sordid one (**DJEZZAH PASHA**) who then will be contrary,
> For fourteen years he will hold the tyranny.

From the maritime city and tributary

The 'maritime city' is Alexandria, described today as "an oriental Marseilles". When Bonaparte
arrived in the summer of 1798, little of the old city remained.[1] After successfully launching an
attack on Alexandria and securing it for occupation, Napoleon took a detachment of 25,000
men, and began a march to Cairo. "From Alexandria [...] an old canal led past Damanhour into the
western branch of the Nile at El-Ramanieh. The natural line of the march was along this canal."[2]
The oracle identifies this canal as a tributary from the marine city, which, it actually was. And it
was by following this waterway that Napoleon's army was led directly into Egypt's capital city.

The crop head

"Bonaparte, now 30 years old, [i.e. in 1799] was thin and short and wore his hair cut close - le petit tondu,
the 'little crop-head,' as he was called."[3]

Will capture the satrapy

In ancient times, Egypt had been a *satrapy* of Persia. "After Alexander's death in 323 [...] [Ptolemy]
became satrap of Egypt." The Seer has used this definition to emphasize its importance to the
oracle. From Alexandria, Cairo was promptly reached and the city taken, but only after a
particularly bloody encounter, which cost 6,000 Mamelukes their lives, for the loss of only 10
French. As victor, Napoleon (the crop head), lost no time in proclaiming himself to be the new
governor of this former satrapy.[4]

Pursuing the sordid one

The French army's next goal took them towards Syria: occupying the towns of El-Arish, Gaza
and Jaffa, as they made their way eastwards. The governor of Syria was Djezzah Pasha, also
known by his nickname, "The Butcher": a name derived from his sadistic and sordid practices.
Relentlessly, Napoleon pursued him from one town to the next, until eventually Pasha was
driven back to the fortress at Acre: the last secure foothold in his increasingly diminishing
dominion.[5]

Who then will be contrary

It was at Acre that Djezzah Pasha became a counter force in Bonaparte's plan of conquest. His resistance to the French onslaught would eventually compel the invading army to retreat. In the course of his defiant opposition he resisted eight direct assaults.

It was also at Acre that evidence of his sordid nature became apparent. In order to motivate his troops to their greatest effort, Djezzah Pasha promised a reward for every French head brought to him. This gruesome operation then had the effect of both delaying and disrupting the fighting, because each time a French soldier was killed, his assailant would stop to cut through the man's neck, and take the severed head to Pasha for payment. By next morning the scene in the gardens outside the Syrian governor's seraglio was littered with the corpses of headless French soldiers. [6]

For fourteen years he will hold the tyranny

After his failure to take Acre, and upon learning of the political unrest in France, Napoleon led his army in retreat, back to Cairo; whereupon, he returned secretly to France, abandoning his army to find their own way back. Within a month of his arrival in France, he had engineered a *coup d'état* that would make him First Consul of the nation and then Emperor of an increasing number of occupied countries.

The oracle has also provided the exact number of years in which Napoleon was destined to remain at the head of France's government. From the time of his *coup* in November 1799, up until his abdication on 6 April 1814, he held office – commonly seen as a tyrannical dictatorship – for 14 years, 4 months and 28 days. [7]

Summary: *This oracle appends the same nickname to Napoleon as that given to him by the soldiers who served in his arnies, It also predicts the exact number of years he ruled over France as First Consul and then as Emperor. His arrival at a maritime city with a tributary describes his march from Alexandria to Cairo: a city that was once a Satrap, and which he captured. The inclusion of the 'sordid one' provides an apt description of Djezzah Pasha, who was pursued by Napoleon to his fortress at Acre, where he proved to be contrary to Bonaparte's military plans for the further expansion of France's empire.*

14   *Faux exposer viendra topographie,*
       Seront les cruches des monuments ouuertes:
       Pulluler secte, saincte philosophie,
       Pour blanches, noires, & pour antiques vertes.

Faux (Byname) 'Louis le Faux'; cruches (AF coquilles); monument (OF) sepulchre, tomb,

     The error (**LOUIS XVI**) will come to make known topography;   1791
     The casings of sepulchral monuments will be opened:
     A sect multiplying, a philosophy sanctified:
     Instead of whites, blacks, and in lieu of ancient greens.

The error

'Faux' was the derisory nickname given to Louis XVI by a Paris newspaper after his ill advised attempt to flee Paris on 20 June 1791. The name quickly caught the public imagination, and the King became identified as, "the man whom Père Duchesne now habitually called 'Louis le Faux'-or sometimes just 'le Faux-Pas'," [1] *Le Père Duchesne* was Jacques-René' Hébert's Paris newspaper. It specialised in ridiculing the monarchy, as *Charlie Hebdo* mocks religion in the present age.

Will come to make known topography

During the French Revolution, the names of the old provinces – Aquitaine, Burgundy, Lorraine &c – were consigned to history. In their place, the country became divided into departments (*départements*): the names of which were incorporated into the Constitution of 1791. On 14 September, "Louis [came] to the Constituent [...] to swear 'to maintain it at home and defend it against attacks from abroad and to use all the means which it places in my power to execute it faithfully.'" [2]

Included within the new Constitution was the division of France into departments. By swearing to uphold it, the King agreed to make known this new topography to the nation.

The casings of sepulchral monuments will be opened

Before the revolution, the royal families of France had been interred inside the mausoleum at Saint-Denis. On 1 August 1793, a decree, passed by the Convention, authorised the opening of the outer casings of the royal tombs in order to transfer the remains of the bodies to a communal grave. For several days afterwards, tombs were opened "in churches, temples and other parts of the Republic:" particularly at Saint-Denis, where the desecration of the mausoleum took place in what can only be described as a macabre pantomime. The skeletal remains of the nation's former kings, queens and princes were gruesomely displayed, even toyed with, before being thrown unceremoniously into a common pit close by. [3]

It is of some interest to note that in the midst of this grisly scene, the embalmed body of Louis XIII was extricated from his tomb and observed to be almost unaffected by the time that had elapsed since his burial. (Century Eight N°. 68 specifically emphasises his embalming).

A sect multiplying, a philosophy sanctified

After religion had effectively been abolished in France (the movement to achieve this began gathering force during the first days of revolutionary fervour), and the de-Christianising of the country was almost complete, it became apparent that a new philosophy was needed to replace what had been lost. The sect that quickly grew to fill this void was the cult of the Federation, which included oaths sworn to liberty, temples of concord, and festivals of celebration. [4]

Intellectually, the mainspring of this new revolutionary creed was Jean-Jacques Rousseau's treatise of 1762, 'Du Contrat Social'. Festivals were held across the country to celebrate France's new Constitution, in which high priests of the Federation swore to uphold it. At the same time, effectively mimicking the priesthood, they sanctified Rousseau's philosophy, [5] by allowing it to become the country's new gospel.

Instead of whites, blacks and in lieu of ancient greens

Another feature of the Ancient Regime that became subject to replacement was the importance formerly given to coloured cockades. White (blanche) [6] was the traditional colour of the Bourbon dynasty to which Louis XVI belonged. Black was the colour adopted by the Queen. [7] This led to her followers becoming dubbed "les noires". And green was the colour which the dukes of Artois had chosen for their cockade. [8] The duc d'Artois was Louis XVI's youngest brother who became King Charles X in 1824. Once the revolution was underway, a new cockade was required to announce the change that was taking place; displaying the new cockade was almost obligatory. Green had been the revolutionaries' first choice: until it was realized this was the colour of d'Artois' cockade. Hence, it was *in lieu of ancient greens* that the *tricolour* was adopted.

Summary: *In the previous oracle, Napoleon was identified by his nickname. If sceptics believe this to be a coincidence, then the seer has anticipated their disbelief by repeating his precognitive ability. This time it is Louis XVI's nickname which the seer has foreseen; and it was employed during the French Revolution. The oracle confirms this timing by listing the changes that took place once the Revolution had begun. Among these changes, he includes the new topography, the desecration of tombs belonging to the nobility, the sanctifying of Rousseau's philosophy, the cult of the Federation and the replacement of aristocratic cockades. Whatever had once been identified as part of the Ancient Régime was extinguished and replaced by a new authority.*

> 15 *Deuant cité de l'Insobre contrée,*
> *Sept ans sera le siege deuant mis:*
> *Le tresgrand Roy y fera son entrée,*
> *Cité puis libre hors de ses ennemis.*

> 16 *Entrée profonde par la grand Royne faicte;*
> *Rendra le lieu puissant inaccessible:*
> *L'armée des trois Lyons sera deffaicte,*
> *Faisant dedans cas hideux & terrible.*

England has a national badge that depicts three lions, mostly for sporting events.

17 *Le prince rare de pitié & clemence,*
Par grand repos le regne trauaillé,
Viendra changer par mort grand cognoissace,
Lors que le grand toit sera estirillé.

18 *Les assiegés couloureront leurs paches,*
Sept iours apres feront cruelle issue:
Dans repousés, feu sang, sept mis à l'ache,
Dame captiue qu'auoit la paix tissue.

19 *Le fort Nicene ne sera combatu,*
Vaincu sera par rutilant metal:
Son faict sera vn long temps debatu,
Aux citadins estrange espouuental.

20 *Ambassadeurs de la Tosquane langue,*
Auril & May Alpes & mer passer:
Celuy de veau exposera l'harangue,
Vie Gauloise ne venant effacer.

21 *Par pestilente inimitié Volsicque,*
Dissimulée chassera le tyran:
Au pont de Sorgues se fera la traffique,
De mettre à mort luy & son adherant.

22 *Les citoyens de Mesopotamie,*
Yréz encontre amis de Tarraconne,
Geux, ritz, banquetz, toute gent endormie
Vicaire au Rosne, prins cité, ceux d'Ausone.

23 *Le Royal sceptre sera contrainct de prendre,*
Ce que ses predecesseurs auoient engaigé:
Puis par l'aneau on fera mal entendre,
Lors qu'on viendra le palays saccager.

l'aneau (O.Fr. anneau) link, also *paragram*, (B)'an(r)eau, and *anagram*, Barnave – *u* and *v* are interchangeable in Latin script.

The Royal sceptre will be restrained from receiving   1791
That which its predecessors had engaged.
Then, through the link (**BARNAVE**), men will make a bad understanding,
After that, people will arrive to ransack the palace.

The Royal sceptre will be restrained from receiving that which its predecessors had engaged

The sceptre is a staff of royal or imperial authority. In this quatrain, the oracle predicts that it will be forcibly held back, restrained. Since no other country is indicated, attention turns to France, and the year in which the monarchy was overturned.

In 1774 Louis XV died and his grandson Louis XVI received the royal sceptre, and with it the title King of France and Navarre. The line of succession linking France to Navarre extended back through his predecessors to Henri IV in the sixteenth century. Before then, the royal sceptre had been in the hands of the Valois dynasty as kings of France. Even before then, one can trace the French monarchy back to Hugh Capet, whose dynasty commenced in 987 AD.

In 1791, Louis XVI's royal powers were restrained, and his title was changed to King of the French. Essentially, his kingship had been reduced to that of an executive position in which he was allowed to sit in on governmental procedures, for which he was given permission to issue a veto under certain conditions.

His fall from grace had come after the failed attempt he made in June 1791, to escape with his family from the oppressive revolutionary mood in Paris. He was apprehended at Varennes, and returned under guard to the capital. Thereafter, for one year, Louis held the position of 'chief executive', while political forces gathered around him: as yet indecisive as to their next step.

Then through the link (Barnave)

After the royal family had been detained at Varennes, the government sent a young man, Antoine Barnave, to escort the coach and it occupants back to Paris. During that time, two days were spent inside the coach, and at stopping places, often in conversation with the Queen. A friendship developed between the two, which was encouraged by his courteous demeanour and "most animated and captivating eloquence;" it made a lasting impression upon Marie Antoinette. Afterwards, as the turmoil in her life grew worse, the Queen felt able to turn to him for advice. Secret coded letters passed between them, carried by the husband of her lady-in-waiting, the Chevalier François Regnier Jarjayes, so that "Throughout the summer and autumn, the Queen was in constant communication with Barnave." [1]

> Barnave's most significant letter was written on 25 July. In this he outlined a new and happier future for Marie Antoinette. [...] He told her that she had misunderstood the nature of the Revolution so far, not realizing that it could actually be helpful to her position. [...] But with her courage and character she could overcome this. [...] [Her] convictions hostile to recent political developments – would now work to her advantage. If she openly supported the Constitution, she would be believed to be equally sincere. [2]

Barnave was a politician from Grenoble and deputy of the Dauphiné. He was highly esteemed for his oratory, and because of his attachment to the Queen, for which he received scurrilous comments, he provided an important *link* between the royal family and the National Assembly.

The Seer appears to have deliberately employed the words *l'aneau* to identify Barnave as 'the link', which for a short time helped to keep the monarchy in par with the Assembly. Thus, Barnave remained convinced that "the monarchical principle [was] profoundly and solidly rooted." [3]

Men will make a bad understanding

Barnave retained this political belief throughout the autumn of 1791, as he attempted to present the Queen in a favourable light, also coaching her in what to say and what not to say.

> He counselled her to forswear, forever and in good faith, any kind of flirtation with armed counter-revolution; to make sure her brother the Emperor withdrew support from the émigrés; and to have the King persuade his brothers to return to France. In return for this he was prepared to work for the revision of the constitution so that it would strengthen the role of the executive. [4]

> Though a passionate lover of liberty, he hoped to secure the freedom of France and her monarchy at the same time. [...] Barnave was the most powerful orator of the Assembly. [...] In one of his most powerful speeches he maintained the inviolability of the king's person. [5]

Unfortunately, neither Barnave's oratory inside the Assembly hall nor his popularity among the deputies were sufficient to outsway the waves of revolution and republican fervour that had gripped France. His plan to use his influence to save the monarchy ended in failure.

After that, people will arrive to ransack the palace

The first wave of violence directed at the Tuileries Palace occurred on 20 June 1792: coming as the result of an intended celebration to mark the third anniversary of the Oath of the Tennis Court. During this gathering a group of disgruntled citizens among the crowd decided to turn the celebration into a political rally, and air their grievances before the King.

Upon arriving at the palace, the marchers succeeded in breaking down the door, and were equally successful in confronting Louis XVI with their demands; but they were dispersed when the National Guard arrived. Six weeks later, after the arrival of the five-hundred from Marseilles: and then inflamed by a speech from Danton, the Palace once again came under attack. This time it was completely ransacked. The royal family was fortunate enough to be removed to the safety of the Assembly hall before the attack began. Those who remained behind were left to suffer.

> The mob poured into the palace, cutting down everyone they found, ushers, pages, doorkeepers, cooks, maidservants as well as soldiers, and the Dauphin's sub-governor. They threw the bodies out of the windows, pocketed jewellery and ornaments and scattered papers over the floors. Fugitives who tried to escape were struck down as they ran across the garden and hacked down

under the trees and beside the fountains. Some clambered up the monuments but were prodded down with pikes and bayonets by the assailants who, forbearing to fire for fear lest they injure the marble, stabbed them as they fell at their feet. [6]

Summary: *In this oracle the overthrow of the French monarchy is seen from a different perspective. The attempt made by Antoine Barnave to incorporate the monarchy into the spirit of the Revolution by grooming the Queen to become an acceptable part of it failed, due to his misunderstanding. And with the failure of his plan came the consequences. The palace was ransacked twice, in fairly quick succession. On the second occasion, the King and Queen had to be given political protection for their safety, but this led to their captivity, and later, their execution.*

24   *L'enseuely sortira du tombeau,*
       Fera de chaines lier le fort du pont:
       Empoysoné auec œuf de barbeau,
       Grand de Lorraine par le Marquis du Pont.

       The interred one will depart from his sepulchre;
       He will fetter with chains the stronghold of the bridge:
       Poisoned with the egg of (the little beard or a barbell),
       The great man of Lorraine, through the Marquis du Pont.

Henry Prince of Lorraine Marquis du Pont (8 Nov. 1563 – 31 Jul. 1624) was the son of Charles III, Duke of Lorraine and Claude de Valois, daughter of Henri II and Catherine de' Medici. Charles III was known as 'the Great'. He was also made Lieutenant-General of France by Charles IX (Century Two N° 88 refers). This appears to be one of a very few prophetic quatrains in which history repeats itself in a futuristic setting (see also Century Ten, N° 64).

25   *Par guerre longue tout l'exercité expuise,*
       Que pour souldartz ne trouueront pecune:
       Lieu d'or, d'argent, car on viendra cuser,
       Gaulois œrain, signe croissant de Lune.

26   *Fustes & Galees autour de sept nauires,*
       Sera liuree vne mortelle guerre:
       Chef de Madric receura coup de vires:
       Deux eschapees & cinq menees à terre.

27   *Au cainct de Vast la grand caualerie,*
       Proche à Ferrare empeschee au bagaige,
       Pompt à Turin seront tel volerie,
       Que dans le fort rauiront leur hostaige.

cainct. (A. Fr. ceint – see ceindre) girdle or surround

28   *Le capitaine conduira grande proye,*
       Sur la montaigne des ennemis plus proche:
       Enuironné, par feu fera telle voye,
       Tous eschapez, or trente mis en broche.

29   *Le grand duc d'Albe se viendra rebeller,*
       A ses grans peres fera le tradiment:
       Le grand de Guise le viendra debeller:
       Captif mené & dressé monument.

grans (Spanish) great; tradiment (L trad\o), to betray; debeller (L debell\o), to end a war; dresser (OF) to direct; mené (*paragram*, Mé(r)é

       The great **DUKE OF ALBA** will himself come to rebel,   1559
       He will make the betrayal to his grandfathers:
       The great man of **GUISE** will agree it, ending the war,
       Captive (**MÉRÉ**) led away, and a memorial directed.

The great Duke of Alba

The great Duke of Alba was known in the 16th century as Fernando Alvarez de Toledo. "After the Peace of Cateau-Cambrésis (1559), Alba became one of Philip II's two leading ministers." [1]

Alba was born into a wealthy Spanish family, which had also enjoyed a long tradition of having served the kings of Castile. In Alba's own time, he achieved notoriety for the ruthless manner in which he put down rebellions, chiefly by executing their leaders. Particularly gruesome was his setting up of the 'Council of Blood', which resulted in 1105 executions or deportations. It was also, "In the last phase of the Franco-Spanish War in Italy [that] he out manoeuvred the Duke of Guise and forced Pope Paul IV to come to terms with Spain (1557)." [2]

Will, himself, come to rebel

The fighting between France and Spain had brought Alba and Guise, the two great men mentioned in this oracle, together at the close of the war. But it was to be several years later, in 1572, while serving in the Netherlands that Alba reached an impasse, and was unable to make further military progress. This "failure and the intrigues of the Gómez party at court induced Philip to recall him (1573)." [3] It was the first step towards the duke, himself, coming to rebel. [4]

Alba's rebellion became a reality when his son decided to marry. Philip sensed this could become a threat to his position as King, if the proposed union went ahead—and so he forbade it. But Alba ignored the King's ban, and his son's marriage took place as planned. Because of this act of defiance against a royal command, "Alba was placed under house arrest on his estates after his son had married against the king's wishes." [5]

He will make the betrayal to his grandfathers

The marriage, which lay at the heart of Alba's betrayal, involved his second son, Fadrique Álvarez de Toledo y Enríquez de Guzmán.

> Fadrique had in fact in 1566 promised to marry Magdalena de Guzman, lady of Queen Anne of Austria, but resiled from it, costing him arrest and imprisonment. [...] The following year he was released so he could go abroad to fight. In 1578 Philip II ordered the case reopened against Fadrique, during which it was discovered that in order to prevent the marriage with Magdalena de Guzman, Fadrique had secretly become married by proxy to María de Toledo, daughter of García Alvarez de Toledo and Osorio IV Marquis of Villafranca del Bierzo, with the permission of his father the Duke of Alba, in contravention of the provisions of the King. Fadrique was again confined in the Castillo de la Mota and his father was banished from the court. [6]

Fadrique's defiance of his king was a blemish on the House of Alba's previous history of service to Spain. Amongst his ancestry were his grandfather, Diego Enríquez de Guzmán 3rd Count of Alba de Liste, his great grandfather Fadrique Álvarez de Toledo y Enríquez, 2nd Duke of Alba, and his great-great grandfather, Garcia Álvarez de Toledo, 1st Duke of Alba.

> The House of Alba is a prominent Spanish aristocratic family that derives from the 12th century. [...] Their claim to Alba goes back to 1429, when the first *Alvarez de Toledo* was made Lord of the City of Alba de Tormes. In 1492, it was a member of this family, the second Duke of Alba, who signed the capitulation of the city of Granada. [7]

The great man of Guise will agree it, ending the war

The treaty of Cateau-Cambrésis negotiated between France, Spain, and England, with different interests dividing the three parties, was signed on separate days in April 1559. It finally ended France's sixty year dream of conquest in Italy, for which much blood and treasure had been spent. Henri II directed the Cardinal of Lorraine – the great man of Guise – to agree it. The Cardinal being at that time: [8] "one of the foremost members of the powerful Roman Catholic house of Guise and perhaps the most influential Frenchman during the middle years of the 16th century. He was intelligent, avaricious, and cautious." He was also the King's chief negotiator for ending the war with Spain. [9]

Captive (Méré) led away

The House of Guise was staunchly Catholic, and Francis, 2nd Duke of Guise, was intent upon opposing the Huguenots led by Louis, Prince of Condé. But, on the 18th February 1563, Jean Poltrot de Méré, a young nobleman and Huguenot sympathiser, concealed himself behind some bushes during the Siege of Orléans, and shot the Duke from behind. Guise died six days later.

He [Méré] was captured the next day, and following torture and a trial, he was sentenced to be drawn and quartered. The punishment, carried out on 18 March 1563, was botched; the horses having failed to rend his limbs, swords were used to finish the job. [10]

N.B. It is to be observed that as in N° 23 above, the Seer has again chosen a word that allows a paragram to be formed, thereby allowing the name of the person involved to be identified.

And a memorial directed

On the day after Méré's execution, the burial of the Duke of Guise took place. [11]

In remembrance of the Duke's service to France, his funeral was performed in a regal manner,

[with] the cortège, composed of twenty-two town criers ringing bells, important citizens carrying burning torches, and representatives of the Church and nobility all processed through Paris. A large troop of armed militiamen accompanied them. Thousands of mourners lined the streets. [12]

Summary: *Both Alba and Guise are openly identified by name in this oracle. For this reason, the predicted events that they were later to fulfil have not only been separated by a span of fourteen years, but the timing has also been inverted to obscure a premature understanding. Both men were contemporaries of the seer at a time when his prophecies were being circulated, thus adding to the need for extra security. Even so, Alba's part in this prophecy did not commence until seven years after the seer's death. To add to the prophecy, the death of Guise is indicated by the inclusion of a paragram revealing the name of his assassin.*

30   *Le sac s'aproche, feu, grand sang espandu,*
Po, grand fleuues, aux bouuiers l'entreprinse,
De Gennes, Nice, apres long attendu,
Foussan, Turin, à Sauillan la prinse.

31   *De Languedoc, & Guienne plus de dix*
Mille voudront les Alpes repasser:
Grans Allobroges marcher contre Brundis,
Aquin & Bresse les viendront rechasser.

Allobroges, - The territory of the Allobroges later became named Savoy.

Concerning Languedoc and Guyenne, more than ten   1944
Thousand will wish to recross the Alps,
The great Savoyards proceeding in opposition to Brindisi:
Aquino and Bresse will want to repel them.

Concerning Languedoc and Guyenne

After the surrender of France to Germany in WWII, the country was partitioned into three parts. Germany occupied the northern half, including the Atlantic coastline down to the border with Spain, and Italy was given control of a small section adjoining its mountain frontier with France. In between was the Vichy regime, or Free France, which covered the ancient provinces of Languedoc and Guyenne.

In May 1944, following the appointment of Gerd von Rundstedt as Commander-in-Chief in the West, Johannes Blaskowitz was appointed head of Army Group G. This comparatively small command, consisting of the 1st Army and the 19th Army, was given the task of defending southern France from the imminent Allied invasion. [1]

More than ten thousand will wish to recross the Alps

Operation Dragoon was the Allied invasion of southern France on 15 August 1944, during World War II. The invasion was initiated via a parachute drop by the 1st Airborne Task force, followed by an amphibious assault by elements of the U.S. Seventh Army, followed a day later by a force made up primarily of the French First Army. The landing caused the German Army Group G to abandon southern France and to retreat under constant Allied attacks to the Vosges Mountains. [2]

Operation Dragoon took place against a weakened German resistance; moreover, despite Hitler's orders for the defence – 'to the last man' – of the strategic seaports of Marseilles and Toulon, both cities were captured and liberated.

"While Marseille and Toulon were liberated, the German retreat continued": reaching the small city of Montélimar on the banks of the river Rhone. A fierce battle took place outside the city as the Allied forces attempted to block the German retreat.

> Over the next days a stalemate emerged, with the Allies unable to block the retreat route and the Germans unable to clear the area of the Allied forces. Both sides however became increasingly frustrated during the fighting. [...] Finally from 26–28 August, the majority of the German forces was able to escape and on 29 August the Allies captured Montélimar.[3]

Although the German army was able to continue its retreat to the Vosges Mountains—a range of mountains extending along the Rhine valley, covering 150 miles from Basel to Mainz that forms a frontier between France and Germany—"The Germans suffered 2,100 battle casualties plus 8,000 POWs"[4] at Montélimar. Whence, *more than 10,000 wishing to recross the 'alps'* were left behind.

The great Savoyards proceeding, in opposition, to Brindisi

From September 1943 onwards, with the signing of Italy's armistice agreement, and up until February 1944, Brindisi operated as the *de facto* capital of Italy.

The arrival of King Vittorio Emanuele III and Queen Elena on 10th September was followed by the King, "hosting Savoy Royalty."[5] This came about as a result of Italy having occupied Savoy in November 1942. After the occupation, it helped the cause of a number of fascist groups to begin claiming that nearly 10,000 Italian Savoyards wanted unification with Italy. These "Italian irredentists were citizens of Savoy who considered themselves to be Italian and who claimed Savoy had ties with the Savoy dynasty."[6] But the King opposed their demand, and the matter was dropped.

Aquino and Bresse will want to repel them

Aquino is a town in Italy, while Bourg-en-Bresse was part of Bresse province in France. The connexion between the actual place names occurs because they each, but separately, played a small, yet historical role in attempts made by the German Army to repel the Allied invasion force in Italy and in France. Furthermore, Bourg-en-Bresse was once part of the kingdom of Savoy: while Aquino and Brindisi were both situated within the kingdom of Two Scillies.

> In the spring of 1944, the Germans still held the line of defence north of Ortona, as well as the mighty bastion of Monte Cassino which blocked the Liri corridor to the Italian capital. Determined to maintain their hold on Rome, the Germans constructed two formidable lines of fortifications, the Gustav Line, and 14.5 kilometres behind it, the Adolf Hitler Line.
> The Adolf Hitler line was a German fallback position a few kilometres north of the Gustav line. Its strong points were at Aquino and Piedimonte.[7]

The Adolf Hitler Line was breached on 24 May 1944. Eight months earlier in France, *Operation Dragoon* had reached Lyons, from where the German Army had retreated.

> On 3 September Lyon was liberated by French units, but the Germans had already escaped. The Allies made a last-ditch attempt to cut the Germans off with an offensive towards Bourg-en-Bresse by the 45th Division and the 117th Cavalry Squadron from the original Taskforce Butler. However, the 45th Division was not able to overcome the German defences near Bourg-en-Bresse. The 117th Cavalry Squadron had more success, bypassing Bourg-en-Bresse and taking Montreval and Marboz north of Bourg-en-Bresse instead. By 3 September Montreval was taken.[8]

Summary: *The place names mentioned in this prophecy all came together in 1944-5 as the Second World War drew to an end. Each location has its own story to tell, but they all have one thing in common, namely the retreat suffered by the German armies occupying France and Italy. Apart from the defeated German troops wanting to recross the Alps to their homeland, the oracle also refers to the attempt made by those of Savoy who wanted to reunite with Italy, after the country's release from its coalition with Germany.*

32   *Du mont Royal naistra d'vne casane,*
      Qui caue, & comte viendra tyranniser,
      Dresser copie de la marche Millane,
      Fauene, Florence d'or & gents expuiser.

33 *Par fraulde regne, forces expolier,*
  La classe obsesse, passaiges à l'espie:
  Deux faincts amys se viendront rallier,
  Esueiller hayne de long temps assopie.

34 *En grand regret sera la gent Gauloise,*
  Cœur vain, legier, croit à temerité:
  Pain, sel, ne vin, eaue, venim ne ceruoise,
  Plus grand captif, faim, froit, necessité.

35 *La grande pesche viendra plaindre, plorer,*
  D'auoir esleu, trompés seront en l'aage:
  Guiere auec eulx ne vouldra demourer:
  Deceu sera par ceulx de son langaige.

36 *Dieu le ciel tout le diuin verbe à l'vnde,*
  Pourté par rouges sept razes à Bisance.
  Contre les oingz trois cens de Trebisonde,
  Deux loix mettront, borreur, puis credence.

37 *Dix enuoyés, chef de nef mettre à mort,*
  D'vn aduerty, en classe guerre ouuerte:
  Confusion de chef, l'vn se picque & mord,
  Leryn, stecades nefz, cap dedans la nerte.

38 *L'aisné Royal sur coursier voltigeant,*
  Picquer viendra si rudement courir:
  Gueule, lypee, pied dans l'estrein pleigant,
  Trainé, tiré, horriblement mourir.

39 *Le conducteur de l'armee Francoise,*
  Cuidant perdre le principal phalange:
  Par sus paué de l'auaigne & d'ardoise,
  Soy parfondra par Gennes gent estrange.

parfonder (AF - approfondir) s'appliquer exagérément à; auaigne (AF – aveine) oats

40 *Dedans tonneaux hors oingz d'huril & gres,*
  Seront vingt vn deuant le port fermés:
  Au second guet par mort feront proüesse,
  Gaigner les portes, & du guet assommés.

41 *Les oz des piedz & des mains enserrés,*
  Par bruit maison long temps inhabitee:
  Seront par songes concauant deterrés,
  Maison salubre & sans bruyt habitee.

42 *Deux de poyson saisiz, nouueaux venus,*
  Dans la cuisine du grand Prince verser:
  Par le soüillard tous deux au faict cogneus,
  Prins qui cuidoit de mort l'aisné vexer.

Unlike the other nine centuries, when the seventh was published it ended at No. 40. In the following year, Nos. 41 and 42 were added with a note affixed to say they had been received and sent for printing on 3 November (1568). They then became part of an edition published in 1643 together with two more, Nos. 43 and 44. Prior to this, Nos. 41, 42, 43, and 44 had been published elsewhere, as seems to have been the case, between 1605 and 1625.

In 1650, Pierre Leffen of Leyden printed the entire prophecies, which included the life of the Seer, plus four further quatrains belonging to century seven; these were numbered 73, 80, 82, and 83. He also added one further quatrain, unnumbered, against which he placed the following note: "Adjousté depuis l'impression de 1568" [Added since the edition of 1568]. This is important, because this additional oracle is dated 1660 (old style). Its publication therefore preceded its fulfilment by a decade.

It would appear that Leffen's publication was intended to collect together everything associated with de Nostredame's prophetic output. For, on the title page he writes, "Reveües & corrigées suyvant les premieres Editions imprimées en Avignon en l'an 1556. & à Lyon en l'an 1558. Avec la vie de l'Autheur." [Reviewed and amended following the first Editions printed in Avignon in the year 1556, and at Lyon in the year 1558. With the life of the Author].

Leffen's collection also included other oracles, allegedly written by the Seer, but which are of an unknown origin. Among these are 58 totally worthless sixains, and 141 monthly presages. These appear to be from almanacs that de Nostredame may or may not have published during his lifetime—plagiarism was rife in France at that time, as it was in England. Whatever predictive insights these had once held would have expired on the last day of the month assigned to them.

Past commentators have pointed to phrases contained in the presages and in the sixains which are said to be prophetic: which it is to say they contain some historical accuracy. However, in each case cited, the 'predicted' event occurred *before* the relevant prediction appeared in print.

Century Seven therefore concludes with Nos. 43 & 44, together with the four extra oracles published in 1650 by Pierre Leffen, and the unnumbered one added after 1568, marked 'X'.

43   *Lors qu'on verra les deux licornes,*
         L'une baissant l'autre abaissant,
         Monde au mileu, pilier aux bornes
         S'en fuira le neveu riant.

44   *Alors qu'un bour sera tort bon,*
         Portant en soy les marques de justice,
         De son sang lors portant son nom
         Par fuite injuste recevra son supplice.

bour (OF syncope) bour[sal]) a younger brother; tort (AF acte contraire au droit) bon (OF) courageous

That time when a younger (**BOURBON**) brother will be courageous, contrary to law. 1793
Carrying within himself the signs of justice,
Bearing then his name from his lineage (**LOUIS CAPET**),
Through an unjust flight, he will receive his punishment.

That time when a younger Bourbon brother

Before becoming king, Louis XVI was the Duke of Berry. He was also a grandson of Louis XV, and the third son of the then Dauphin, which made him a younger brother. In addition to this, Louis was a member of the Bourbon dynasty, which had taken the throne of France from the House of Valois after the death of Henri III in 1589; this was twenty-three years after the Seer's death. It is of particular note, therefore, that the Seer has indicated his foreknowledge of this change in House, because he has managed to include *bour* and *bon* into the opening line; thus, indicating the time period of the Bourbon dynasty, when this prophecy will be fulfilled. [1]

Will be courageous, contrary to law

Louis' surviving older brother and heir apparent, Louis duc de Bourgogne, died at the age 9 in 1761. And so, on 20 December 1765, after his father died of tuberculosis, Louis became dauphin at the age of 11. Consequently, when Louis XV, expired on 10 May 1774, Louis XVI was crowned King of France and Navarre.

This oracle, however, is set for the end time of his reign, when his position as King was seriously weakened. The Revolution had occurred, and with it had come two attacks made on the palace. For this reason, Louis and his family were confined to rooms inside the Temple Tower. It was while there, in December 1793, that Louis was accused of treason, and brought to trial.

In the end, after many voting complications, the death penalty was passed on 16 January 1793 by a narrow majority. The newly named Philippe Égalité, Louis' cousin and his closest adult male relative in France, was among those who voted for execution. [...] When Louis was told of the verdict on the following day, it was the behaviour of his cousin that visibly pained him. [2]

The King accepted the verdict calmly, and remained quite composed when he was aroused from his sleep before dawn on 20 January 1793 to be told he was to be executed the next day.

The next morning he was woken at five o'clock, and after attending Mass and receiving Communion, he heard the clatter of drums. The Irish-born priest, Henry Essex Edgeworth [...] said that his own blood froze in his veins at the sound of the hollow rhythmic tapping. But Louis retained his composure, remarking in a matter-of-fact tone, "I expect it's the National Guard beginning to assemble."[3]

There was a large green carriage waiting, and beyond it stretched line upon line of National Guardsmen and citizens with muskets and pikes on their shoulders. The King walked towards the carriage, "turning once or twice towards the tower, as if to say a last goodbye," so Edgeworth thought, "to all that he held dear to the world. His every movement showed that he was calling up all his reserves of strength and courage."[4]

Carrying within himself the signs of justice

The case brought against the King had gone to trial between December 1792 and January 1793. "The verdict as to the King's guilt was never in doubt, indeed it was given unanimously." During the whole of that time, the King stood before the court appearing quite unruffled: "showing the calmness of a man who actually believes he is irreproachably in the right." Each time an accusation was made against him, he responded by, "flatly denying that he had done anything illegal either before or after 1791."[5] Thus, at all times, carrying by his demeanour, the signs of justice.

Bearing then his name from his lineage

Before being taken from the Temple to face trial, the Mayor of Paris, Aubin-Bigore Chambon, had arrived with a summons for the man named Louis Capet. "I am not Louis Capet," retorted the King indignantly; "My ancestors had that name but I have never been called that."[6] It was, nevertheless, a fulfilment of the Seer's prediction; for he had foretold that at the time set for its fulfilment, the subject of his foresight would then be bearing the name of his lineage.

Through an unjust flight, he will receive his punishment

It was through Louis XVI's attempt to flee from France in June 1791 that proved to be most injurious. Not only did it end in ignominious failure, when he was stopped, arrested, and brought back to Paris under guard: but also, he had unwisely left letters behind, explaining his dissatisfaction with the treatment he had received from the Assembly.[7] Both actions were deemed treasonable against the State and punishable by death.

After a verdict of guilty was pronounced, and the death sentence passed, Louis XVI received his punishment beneath the blade of the guillotine (21 January 1793).[8]

Summary: *The subject of the prophecy is alluded to by the name of his dynasty, which has been deliberately split between 'bour' and 'bon'. The events predicted leave no genuine room for doubt as to which of the Bourbons this oracle alludes to, since Louis XVI was a younger brother, and was also the subject of an unjust trial, which he suffered courageously. Moreover, he was forced to respond to the name Capet, which had been that of his ancestors. And, finally, with the tide of public opinion having turned against the King, after he decided to flee Paris for the safety of Belgium, it took less than two years for him to be dethroned and punished—terminally.*

73   *Renfort de sieges manubis & maniples*
        Changez le sacre & passé sur le prosne,
        Prins & captives n'arreste les prez triples,
        Plus par fonds mis, eslevé, mis au trosne.

        An abundance of seats, money obtained from plunder, Eucharistic garments,
        The Church dedication changed & priestly announcements passed over:
        The seized and captives not resolved, the triples nearby,
        More taken through fonts, the glorified, placed on the throne.

80   *L'Occident libres les Isles Britanniques,*
        Le recogneur passer le bas, puis haut:
        Ne content triste Rebel. corss. Escotiques,
        Puis rebeller par plus & par nuict chaut.

recogneu (OF) recognized, acknowledged; passer (OF) surmount; haut (OF) chief; triste (OF) grave; Rebel. (*abbrev.* Rébellion); corss. (*abbrev.* corsairs) pirates; puis (AF *ensuite*) then; chaut (OF *homonym*, chaude) warm, *or* violent assault.

The West, the British Isles free,   1775
The acknowledged one (**WASHINGTON**) surmounting the low point, afterwards chief:
Not satisfied, grave, Rebellion, Scottish pirates (**JOHN PAUL JONES**),
Then rebelling, by addition, and by a violent night assault.

The West, the British Isles free

The focus of attention is upon 'The West'; that is to say, North America.

The British Isles was wrenched free from its North American colony as a result of the American War of Independence. This was fought between 1775 and 1783, with America ultimately achieving independence from the British Isles. The Treaty of Paris was signed 3 September 1783.

The acknowledged one

After war broke out in April 1775 at Lexington, George Washington, attired in military uniform, presented himself before Congress, indicating that he was ready to do battle.

> Washington had the prestige, the military experience, the charisma and military bearing, the reputation of being a strong patriot, and he was supported by the South, especially Virginia. Although he did not explicitly seek the office of commander and even claimed that he was not equal to it, there was no serious competition. Congress created the Continental Army on June 14, 1775; the next day. [...] Washington was appointed Major General and elected by Congress to be Commander-in-Chief. [1]

Surmounting the low point

By the end of the following year, the newly appointed Commander-in-Chief found himself having to surmount the lowest point of his fight for American independence.

> [He was] desperately short of men and supplies. Washington almost despaired. He had lost New York City to the British; enlistment was almost up for a number of the troops, and others were deserting in droves; civilian morale was falling rapidly; and Congress, faced with the possibility of a British attack on Philadelphia, had withdrawn from the city. [2]

Nevertheless, for the remainder of the war against the British, his force of character and strength of personality compensated for any lack of greatness as a general, although this appears to have contributed to his earlier setbacks in battle. Instead, it was through his charisma that he proved instrumental in keeping the Revolution active, right up until the point where victory was finally achieved: although it could not have been won without assistance from the French.

Then chief

Following independence from Britain, Washington resigned from the army on 23 December 1783 to begin retirement. But four years later, he was persuaded to attend the Constitutional Convention, whereupon he was elected to the office of President of the Convention. "Such was his prestige that agreement over a chief executive was reached only because he agreed to fill the position." [3]

On 30 April 1789 he became the first President of the United States, and the only president to receive 100% of the electoral votes. In fact, "The delegates designed the presidency with Washington in mind, and allowed him to define the office once elected." He was returned to office in the elections of 1792, but declined a third period in office.

Not satisfied, grave, rebellion

The American Revolutionary War (1775 – 1783) began out after ten years of increasing division between Britain and, primarily, thirteen Atlantic seaboard colonies. This was largely due to a growing dissatisfaction among the colonials caused by British attempts to impart greater regulations over their affairs: not least of which was taxation.

> The French and Indian War between 1755 and 1762 [...] left Britain with considerable debt. The British government considered the American colonies should contribute to the reduction of that debt and many of the measures that brought about the Revolutionary War were to that end. [4]

On 1 February 1775, a provisional congress was held in Cambridge Massachusetts that voted to prepare for war. As the situation grew evermore grave, the Massachusetts' governor was ordered to enforce British legislation "and suppress 'open rebellion' among the colonists by all necessary force." In April, seven hundred British redcoats were dispatched to Concord, where it was believed weapons had been concealed.

> At dawn on April 19 about 70 armed Massachusetts militiamen stand face to face on Lexington Green with the British advance guard. An unordered 'shot heard around the world' begins the American Revolution. A volley of British rifle fire followed by a charge with bayonets leaves eight Americans dead and ten wounded. The British regroup and head for the depot in Concord, destroying the colonists' weapons and supplies. [5]

On 17 June 1775, British and American troops engage in the first major battle at Boston's Bunker Hill. Eighteen days later, King George III declares the Americans to be in open rebellion.

Scottish pirates

John Paul Jones was born 6 July 1747 at Kirkcudbright on the southern coast of Scotland, where he learned his seamanship as a boy. Later, he emigrated to America, which thereafter became his adopted home.

At the time of the Revolutionary War, America had no navy, and needed to acquire one quickly. In December 1775, Jones became America's Continental Navy's very 1st Lieutenant aboard the frigate USS Alfred, with orders to attack British merchant ships. "During this six week voyage, Jones captured sixteen prizes and created significant damage along the coast of Nova Scotia." Despite this success, his disagreement with higher authority led to him being assigned a smaller command.

> After making the necessary preparations, Jones sailed for France on November 1, 1777 with orders to assist the American cause however possible. [...] Throughout the mission, the crew, led by Jones's second-in-command Lieutenant Thomas Simpson, acted as if they were aboard a privateer, not a warship. [6]

Indeed, "in Britain at this time, he was usually referred to as a pirate." [7]

Then rebelling by addition, and through a violent night assault

The American Revolution began with the colonials wanting self-government and freedom from the regulations imposed upon them by British rule. From a preliminary discussion to the actual preparation for a full-scale rebellion, led next to a planning stage that occupied the first months of 1775. The flashpoint came through the killings at Lexington, when British soldiers marched through the night to Concord, in order to seize weapons that had been hoarded there.

> By 1775 mutual intransigence and increasing turmoil had created a highly volatile situation; it exploded in April when British soldiers killed several militiamen at Lexington, Massachusetts. [8]

With the Battles of Lexington and Concord, the war had begun. [9]

Summary: *This oracle follows the example set by other prophecies that have contributed to the establishment of a nation's history. In this instance it is the War of Independence fought in North America by the colonists. It therefore precedes Century One No, 50, which referred to Thanksgiving Day. The oracle selects three major incidents for content. The part played by George Washington, the first steps taken to establish a navy, which involved the Scottish born corsair, John Paul Jones; and thirdly, the march by British soldiers through the night to Lexington, where the villagers were waiting to attack the approaching British army. This battle began the American Rebellion.*

> 82   *La stratagem simulte sera rare,*
> *La mort en voye rebelled par contrée,*
> *Par le retour du voyage Barbare,*
> *Exalteront la protestante entrée.*

> 83   *Vent chaut, conseil, pleurs, timidité.*
> *De nuict au lit assail sans les armes,*
> *D'oppression grande calamite,*
> *L'epithalame converti pleurs & larmes.*

The next quatrain was discovered without a number. It has therefore been allocated a position in Century Seven, in which 52 verses have been lost. The seer offered no explanation for those that were missing, and neither did he make any effort to reprint them.

> X   Quand le fourchu sera soustenu de deux paux,
>   Avec six demy cors, & six sizeaux ouvers:
>   Le trespuissant Seigneur, heritier des crampaux,
>   Alors subjuguera, sous soy tout l'univers.

pau (OF) stake; sizeaux as ciseaux.

> When the fork shall be supported by two stakes,   1661
> With six half horns, & six open scissors (**1660**):
> The exceedingly powerful Lord (**LOUIS XIV**), inheritor of the toads (**VERSAILLES**):
> Then he will subjugate, beneath him the entire universe.

When the fork shall be supported by two stakes

The first line of this quatrain invites the reader to construct a pictograph, so that what has been said can be seen. Thus, a fork supported by two stakes resembles the letter **M**.

With six half horns & six open scissors

The pictograph can now be further illustrated by adding **C C C C C** and **X X X X X**. When these are placed together in a row, they provide Latin numerical symbolism for the year 1660. When dealing with the matter of dating, it is well to remember that when this oracle was written, New Year's Day officially fell on 25 March. Consequently, according to present-day reckoning, the year 1660 would have extended from 25 March 1660 to 24 March 1661.

The exceedingly powerful Lord

On 9 March 1661; that is, 1660 (O.S.), Cardinal Jules Mazarin, the virtual ruler of France, died at Vincennes. His death allowed Louis XIV to begin his reign with uninterrupted freedom. "Only then," the King wrote in his memoirs, "did it seem to me that I was King: born to be King." And, eventually, as history would show, he became ruler of "the most absolute monarchy in Europe." [1]

Inheritor of toads

Louis XIV's reign has since become inseparable from the palace he ordered to be built for himself at Versailles. He inherited the site from his father, Louis XIII, who had used a small building in the vicinity of Versailles as a hunting lodge and retreat.

On 25 October 1660, Louis XIV, accompanied by his wife, Maria Theresa, had visited the Val de Galie next to the hamlet of Versailles in order to assess its potential. The King was clearly satisfied by what he saw, for upon returning to Paris he decided to construct a new palace on the site. However, the ground was low-lying and consisted mostly of marshland: an ideal habitat for amphibians. Hence, '*the inheritor of toads*'—more dark humour from the Seer.

Consequently, before any building work could begin, the land had to be drained. Thereafter, by the time of its completion in 1687, the Palace of Versailles had become – "one of the most massive architectural statements of political power in French history." [2]

Then he will subjugate

Louis XIV's sovereignty became notable for the fact that he desired above all other considerations to make his reign glorious. He therefore made it known that:

> All power, all authority, resides in the hands of the king, and there can be no other in his kingdom than that which he establishes. The nation does not form a body in France. It resides entire in the person of the king. [3]

Beneath him the entire universe

During the time of the Sun King's 'effective' reign (1661 – 1703), France made important progress in every field of political, economic, scientific, philosophic, and artistic development, until eventually – "Louis XIV appeared the most prosperous and powerful monarch in the world." [4]

By a series of wars, he was able to extend France's borders and acquire new territories. It was by this means that he spread his 'gloire' across half the civilized world.

> The king was at this time at the height of his greatness. Victorious since he had begun his reign, having besieged no place which he had not taken, superior in every way to his united enemies, for six years the terror of Europe [...] in 1680 the Council of Paris conferred the title of *Great* upon him. [5]

There is no contradiction in using the word 'universe'. In the 17th century, the Copernican system was still in the throes of replacing the ancient belief that the earth was a stationary body at the centre of the universe.

Summary: *The oracle begins with the year 1660 (O.S.), and this introduces the commencement of Louis XIV's reign. The Palace of Versailles, which he caused to be built, stands as a monument to his quest for 'gloire'. But his personal glory also attracted to his court sycophants: in other words 'toads'. The seer therefore makes clever use of this homonym, since both meanings apply to the prophecy.*
His reign was also period that elevated France to a point when the only way forward after his death was downwards—Louis XV was debauched and Louis XVI was overthrown and beheaded.

References Century 7

Nº. 1

1 wikipedia.org/wiki/Maximilien_de_Béthune,_duc_de_Sully
2 Ibid
3 *Encyclopædia Britannica 2001*, CD-ROM, Concini, Concino; & *Grand Larousse Encyclopedique*, Concini
4 http://fr.wikipedia.org/wiki/Achille_de_Harlay
5 Alistair Horne, *Seven Ages of Paris*, 105; & K.A. Patmore, *The Court of Louis XIII*, 58
6 Patmore, 60-1
7 Ibid 58
8 Id 59
9 Id

Nº. 6

1 wikipedia.org/wiki/Allied_invasion_of_Sicily
2 wikipedia.org/wiki/History_of_Palermo
3 http://ww2db.com/battle_spec.php?battle_id=53
4 wikipedia.org/wiki/Allied_invasion_of_Sicily
5 wikipedia.org/wiki/History_of_Corsica
6 http://olive-drab.com/od_history_ww2_ops_battles_1943soitaly.php
7 Ibid
8 http://ww2db.com/battle_spec.php?battle_id=307
9 wikipedia.org/wiki/Sardinia#History
10 wikipedia.org/wiki/Italian_Campaign_(World_War_II)

Nº. 9

1 wikipedia.org/wiki/Béatrice_de_Cusance
2 Jonathan Spangler, *The Secrets of Princes:* 243
3 wikipedia.org/wiki/Béatrix_de_Cusance
4 Joseph Thomas, *Universal Dictionary of Biography & Mythology:* 1453-54
5 wikipedia.org/wiki/Charles_IV,_Duke_of_Lorraine
6 wikipedia.org/wiki/Béatrix_de_Cusance
7 http://resources.huygens.knaw.nl/vrouwenlexicon/lemmata/data/Cusance
8 wikipedia.org/wiki/René_II,_Duke_of_Lorraine
9 wikipedia.org/wiki/Nicole,_Duchess_of_Lorraine
10 wikipedia.org/wiki/Duchy_of_Bar

Nº. 11

1 K.A. Patmore, *The Court of Louis XIII*, 25; *Encyclopædia Britannica 2001* CD-ROM, Louis XIII
2 Patmore, 24
3 Ibid 58
4 Id 58
5 Id 57
6 Id 58
7 Id 58
8 Id 62
9 Id 63
10 Id 123
11 en.wikipedia.org/wiki/Siege_of_La_Rochelle
12 en.wikipedia.org/wiki/Jean_Caylar_d'Anduze_de_Saint-Bonnet
13 en.wikipedia.org/wiki/Siege_of_La_Rochelle

Nº. 13

1 J.M. Thompson, *Napoleon Bonaparte*, 111-2
2 Ibid 114
3 Napoleon I – the consulate, *Encyclopædia Britannica 2001:* CD-ROM
4 Alan Palmer, *An Encyclopaedia of Napoleon's Europe*, 63; & Egyptian Satrap - Ptolemy, *Britannica 2001*
5 Palmer, 265; & David Chandler, *The Campaigns of Napoleon*, 237–8; & Thompson, 127
6 Palmer, 3; & Thompson, 129; & Chandler, 237-8
7 Palmer, 208

Nº. 14

1 Simon Schama, *Citizens*, 604
2 Ibid 477, 568, 573; & French Revolution – new regime, *Encyclopedia Britannica 2001:* CD-ROM
3 Jean Favier (ed.) *Chronicle of the French Revolution*, 357
4 Schama, 502–3, 509

5   J. Black and R. Porter (ed.) *A Dictionary of Eighteenth-Century History*, 271; & Favier, 163; & Schama,511

6   Favier, 123

7   Schama, 459

8   Christopher Hibbert, *The French Revolution*, 90

Nº. 23

1   Antonia Fraser, *Marie Antoinette the Journey:* 422

2   Ibid

3   id 423

4   Simon Schama, *Citizens:* 575

5   Encyclopædia Britannica 1911 ed. Vol III

6   Christopher Hibbert, *The French Revolution:* 160

Nº. 29

1   *Encyclopaedia Britannica*, Alba, Fernando Álvarez de Toledo y Piment

2   Ibid

3   id

4   id

5   id

6   wikipedia.org/wiki/Fadrique_Álvarez_de_Toledo_y_Enríquez_de_Guzman

7   wikipedia.org/wiki/House_of_Alba

8   Encyclopaedia Britannica 2001 CD-ROM, 'Lorraine, 2e. Cardinal de...'

9   E.N. Williams, *Dictionary of English and European History 1485-1789*, 196; & R.J. Knecht, *Catherine de' Medici*, 55

10 wikipedia.org/wiki/Jean_de_Poltrot

11 Leonie Frieda, *Catherine de Medici*, 169

12 *Encyclopaedia Britannica*, Alba, Fernando Álvarez de Toledo y Piment

Nº. 31

1   wikipedia.org/wiki/Johannes_Blaskowitz

2   wikipedia.org/wiki/Operation_Dragoon

3   Ibid

4   Id

5   comune,brindid.it/turismo/index.php?option=com_content&view=category&layout=blog&id=10&Itemid=13&lang=en

6   wikipedia.org/wiki/Italian_irredentism_in_Savoy

7   http://www.canadaatwar.ca/page30.html

8   wikipedia.org/wiki/Operation_Dragoon#Final_German_retreat_towards_the_Vosges_Mountains

Nº. 44

1   Louis XVI, *Encyclopædia Britannica 2001:* CD-ROM

2   Antonia Fraser, *Marie Antoinette the Journey:* 476

3   Christopher Hibbert, *The French Revolution:* 185, 186

4   Ibid 187

5   Simon Schama, *Citizens*, 658

6   Ibid 658

7   Hibbert, 133

8   Ibid 188–9

Nº. 80

1   wikipedia.org/wiki/George_Washington

2   http://sc94.ameslab.gov/TOUR/gwash.html

3   *A Dictionary of Eighteenth Century History*, ed. J. Black and R. Porter, 778

4   http://www.britishbattles.com/american-revolution.htm

5   http://faculty.washington.edu/qtaylor/a_us_history/am_rev_timeline.htm

6   http://en.wikipedia.org/wiki/John_Paul_Jones

7   Ibid

8   *A Dictionary of Eighteenth-Century History:* ed. Jeremy Black & Roy Porter, 23

9   Wikipedia, *The American Revolution* (last visited 2009)

Nº. X

1   Ian Dunlop, Louis XIV: 67; also H.A.L. Fisher, A History of Europe: 674-5

2   C. Jones, Cambridge Illustrated History of France: 162

3   T. Wallbank, A, Taylor, N. Balkey, Civilization Past and Present: 419

4   Ibid

5   Voltaire, The Age opf Louis XIV (trans. Martyn P. Pollack), 126

CENTURY EIGHT

1   *PAV, NAY, LORON plus feu qu'à sang sera,*
        Laude nager, fuir grand aux surrez.
        Les agassas entrée refusera:
        Pampon, Durance les tiendra enserrez.

surrez (L surr\exi *from* surgo) raising-up; agassa (OF.pie) magpie *or* Pius; Pampon (Gk. *Syncope,* Pamp[an]on, παμπ[αν]ον) possessing all; enserrez (OF) restrain. For cross-references, see below.

        NAPOLEON ROY will be more fire than from blood,   1804
        Swimming in praise, shunning a great man (**PIUS VII**) at the raisings-up:
        He will refuse the **PIUSES** entrance,
        Possessing all, the **DURANCE** will hold them restrained.

Napoleon Roy

Pau, Nay and Oloron-Saint-Marie are three communes located in the Pyrénées-Atlantiques department in south-western France. They contribute to this prophecy not by their geographical location, but through their names, which form an anagrammatic paragram for Napoleon Roy.
Pau – as observed in previous oracles; viz, Century Two N°s 33 & 94; Century Three N^O 75; Century Four N^O 70, and Century Six N^O 79 – provides the diminutive identifier for Napoleon (the French pronunciation for pau is po). Also, Ney, as a paragram of Nay identifies Michel Ney, Duke of Elchingen and Prince of the Moskowa, who was also a marshal in Napoleon's army. Loron, as spelt in the oracle, is another paragram, this time for Loren: an anagram for Erlon. This identifies Count Jean-Baptiste Drouet d'Erlon: he served as a general in Napoleon's army. All three fought at the Battle of Waterloo.

He will be more fire than from blood

The French word 'sera' is in the third person singular; it cannot therefore refer to the three names that precede it. It could, conceivably, refer to Erlon, except that his military history does not fit the description. It does, however, fit Napoleon in every respect. It is therefore fitting that the three communes named in the first line, which are also paragrams for Po, Nay and Erlon, combine as an anagrammic paragram with 'O' replacing 'V' and 'E' replacing 'A' to produce, NAPOLEON ROY. The line can then be read as a fulfilment of Napoleon's fiery character; it even acknowledges his title as King of Italy and Emperor of France.
A previous commentator of this quatrain, the Victorian classical scholar, Charles Ward, made an apt observation that the *Dictionnaire de Trévoux* contained an entry under *Anagramme*, which stated that an exchange of a single letter in a word was permitted. However, paragrams are also admissible. But this does raise an interesting point. Did the Seer *hear* the names whispered to him, which he then spelt according to their phonetic structure? This would then account for the need to use paragrams. Or, did he construct them himself?
Napoleon was not, of course, descended from the Blood Royal: as the Seer correctly predicted, but he was, by nature, a fiery individual. "Miot de Melito, who met him at Brescia on June 5th [1796] described in his Mémoirs [...] his strong features, keen questioning look and quick decisive gestures revealed a flame-like spirit (âme ardente)." [1]

Swimming in praise

Three times, in 1800, in 1802, and in 1804, he sought and obtained authority from the people. In quick succession the popular voice made him First Consul for ten years, Consul for life, and finally Emperor. No European monarch could claim so good a title. [2]

Shunning a great man at the raisings-up

Pope Pius VII had been persuaded, although not without difficulty, to officiate at Napoleon's coronation in Paris. Eventually, he agreed to attend, but with a full understanding that it would be he, alone, who placed the crown upon the Emperor's head. It was not to be. As the critical point in the coronation ceremony approached, when the crown was to be placed upon the Emperor's head, Bonaparte realised this was an act of submission to higher authority. His vanity would not allow it. Seizing hold of the crown himself, he placed it upon his own head: crowning his wife Joséphine Empress of France immediately afterwards. Pius VII– the great man of this oracle – seething with annoyance at having been brought to Paris to officiate, and then shunned at the crowning moment: that is, at the raisings-up (plural from *aux*), was forced to step back and retake his seat amongst the other guests, having been thoroughly humiliated. [3]

He will refuse the Piuses entrance

This heading correctly predicts the exile of the two Piuses (Pius VI and Pius VII) by Napoleon. In February 1798, Pius VI was taken into custody and removed from Rome. Thereafter, he spent the remainder of his life journeying from town to town until he finally died inside the citadel at Valence. Ten years later (July 1809), Pius VII was also removed from the Vatican. He spent the next five years in exile at Savona on the Italian coast. Both Piuses [4] were therefore refused entrance to Rome and to the Vatican by order of Bonaparte. [5]

Possessing all

By the terms laid out in the *Treaty of Tilsit* (July 1807), Napoleon was able to establish control of the western and central mainland of Europe. In July of the following year, he re-entered Rome; this time, with the intention of adding the papal lands to his list of occupied territories, so that he might then possess all. [6]

The Durance will hold them restrained

Pius VII objected in the strongest terms to Napoleon's proposed acquisition of the Papal States, and responded by ex-communicating the French soldiers who were carrying out the annexation order. Napoleon retaliated by seizing the Pope and transporting him to Avignon, a city inside the fluvial curve of the River Durance. It was from there that he was subsequently sent to Savona. Ten years earlier it had been Valence, also inside the fluvial curve of the Durance, where Pope Pius VI had been taken under guard, and where, soon afterwards, he died. [7]

Summary: By encrypting the name and title, Napoleon Roy, from his diminutive nickname, Pau – together with the names of two of his commanders – marks this achievement as outstanding. The history that follows then presents a perfect support structure for the name. At the same time it confirms not only that de Nostredame possessed foreknowledge of Napoleon's name, as well as those of his marshals, Ney and Erlon, but he also knew the names of the two Popes, Pius VI and Pius VII, who would reign during the Napoleonic age.

     The events predicted in this quatrain occurred two and a half centuries after it was published: hence, the probability of a chance occurrence of this alone, without even considering the several thousand other predictions contained within these chapters, places it in contention with the biological sciences and the probability associated with the conception of a single human being.

     For instance, each sperm and each egg is genetically unique; whence, each baby at its conception is the result of the fusion of one particular egg with one particular sperm. On average, women have about 100,000 eggs during their lifetime, while men produce approximately 12 trillion sperm over the same period. But this figure can be reduced to – let it be supposed – 4 trillion: to tie in with one female's pre menopausal period of fertility. Nevertheless, the probability of one particular sperm uniting with one particular egg is still in the region of $10^{45,000}$.

     The reason why this conflict of probabilities between prophecy and biology disappears when seen as part of the 'Book of God', is because in eternity, probabilities have no place. The end and the beginning, as understood in this temporal world, do not exist in a timeless setting, because they are coeval.

     It is therefore sufficient for a perfect Creator's fiat of will to unfold the universe He created for us to perceive. Any probability calculated to predict a 'future' event within this temporal setting is therefore irrelevant to the event, since that event already exists in wait for the conscious awareness of those individuals living at the time it is perceived.

2 *Condon & Aux & autour de Mirande,*
   Je voy du ciel feu qui les enuironne.
   Sol Mars conioint au Lyon, puis Marmande,
   Foudre, grand gresle, mur tombe dans Garonne.

3 *Au fort chasteau de Vigilanne & Resuiers*
   Sera serré le puisnay de Nancy:
   Dedans Turin seront ards les premiers,
   Lors que de dueil Luon sera transy.

4 *Dedans Monech le coq sera receu,*
   Le Cardinal de France apparoistra:
   Par Logarion Romain sera deceu,
   Foiblesse à l'Aigle, & force au Coq naistra.

Monech (L Monœcis) Monaco; apparoistra (OF apparoir) show it/him/her self; Logarion (Gk. λογάριον) a small account book for keeping records); Foiblesse (OF - faiblesse); force (OF) power; Aigle (as before, aptronym for Napoleon; Cross-references: Aigle: C.l: 23; C.lll: 37; C.IV: 70; C.Vlll: 46; Cock & Aigle: C.Vlll: 46

Inside Monaco the Cock will be received,   1793
The Cardinal of France (**JOSEPH FESCH**) will show himself,
The Roman will be deceived by the record book,
Weakness by the Eagle (**NAPOLEON**), & power will be issued to the Cock.

Inside Monaco the Cock will be received

Prior to 1861, Monaco occupied more than twice the land it now covers. The reduction in size occurred under Prince Charles III, who sold off half the Principality to France in exchange for independence. This opening line concerns Monaco before the sell-off. "On 15th February, 1793, the Convention decided upon the incorporation of the Principality into France." The Cock was therefore received into Monaco for a period that extended from the French Revolution up until the close of the Napoleonic Era, when territorial acquisitions were restored to their former boundaries. [1]

The Cardinal of France will show himself

Cardinal Joseph Fesch, Archbishop of Lyon, was France's representative at the Vatican: he was also Napoleon's uncle. [2] Bonaparte's confrontation with Pope Pius VII, resulting from the annexation of the Papal States and the excommunication of those involved, had led to the Pope's exile at Savona. This was to develop into an even more divisive issue: but on this occasion it occurred between the Emperor of France and his uncle, the Cardinal of France.

Napoleon's objective was to force Pius into conceding to a new Concordat: one that included a provision enabling him to appoint bishops. Pius completely refused: that is, until in 1811, when he remained silent at a given point in the discussion. This was construed as agreement, and was quickly made public by the Emperor. Pius immediately protested his disagreement, having signed nothing. But Napoleon countered the Pope's objection by ordering his denial to be suppressed. Bonaparte then summoned the National Council and directed them to "endorse the decree embodying the Pope's concession." [3]

It was then that the Cardinal of France showed himself by rallying members of the Council into giving their support for the Pope in open defiance of the Emperor. Each member of the legation swore on oath their allegiance and obedience to Pope Pius, and to the Roman Catholic Church. [4]

The Roman will be deceived by the record book

Bonaparte's response to the clergy's act of defiance was to dissolve the Council and threaten each member separately, before presenting this record of agreement to Pius for his signature, The Pope (Bishop of Rome: hence, the Roman) agreed to sign, "but with reservations that Napoleon would not allow." [5]

Pius was then brought to Fontainebleau, while Napoleon embarked upon his disastrous war with Russia. Three months later, he was back in Paris, defeated in battle, but ready to make a fresh assault against Pius VI's continued intransigence.

At last Pius, who had always liked his enemy, and was sorry for him, consented to sign a document, which contained no more than the heads of a possible agreement, one of which was that after a delay of six months, investiture might be performed by the Metropolitan archbishop of Paris. But within twenty-four hours the Pope repented, as at Savona, of what he had done; and as at Savona, Napoleon tricked him by ignoring his change of mind, by publishing the provisional proposals [in the record book] as an agreed declaration, 'The Concordat of Fontainebleau' [...] The solemn retraction that Pius penned two months later was suppressed; and the Pope was once more subjected to almost solitary confinement. [6]

Weakness by the Eagle (Napoleon)

In 1814, following the Pope's fabricated submission to Napoleon's new Concordat – Bonaparte is referred to in this quatrain as the Eagle: this being his adopted emblem – began to show signs of weakness. It first became noticeable when he embarked upon his gravely misjudged invasion of Russia. It ended in complete failure, with the French forced into a decisive retreat from Moscow. One year later Bonaparte suffered another reversal, this time at Leipzig: a battle that freed Germany from French domination. And in 1814, Wellington pushed the French army back over the Pyrenees to free Spain and Portugal from the Eagle's grasp. [7]

And power will be issued to the cock

In Bonaparte's now weakened state, those poised against him were able to force him to abdicate, and accept exile on the island of Elba. In his place, Louis XVI's brother was invited to return to France and take his seat as Louis XVIII. A new period of monarchy had begun. And with it, the victorious nations that had opposed revolutionary France and the Napoleonic Empire met in September 1814, and "approved the final peace treaty with France limiting it to its 1792 borders." [8]

It marked the international recognition of the Gallic Cock, and the authority of its monarch.

Summary: *This oracle commences with the French occupation of Monaco, and ends with its liberation. In between times, the prophecy concentrates upon those who expressed opposition to Napoleon. Principally, this was led by Pope Pius VII and his refusal to sanction the Concordant of Fontainebleau. It was eventually passed by an act of duplicity, in which the draft proposal was published as a final agreement. This deception was also contested by Bonaparte's uncle, whom the Emperor had made Cardinal of France and ambassador to Rome. Although these were personal challenges to his authority, they were followed by deadly confrontations on the battlefield. These led to the loss of Germany, Spain and Portugal, combined with a disastrous retreat from a failed attempt to conquer Russia. In his weakened state, Bonaparte was deposed and power was restored to the French monarchy.*

5   *Apparoistra temple luisant orné,*
       La lampe & cierge à Borne & Bretueil,
       Pour la Lucerne le canton destorné,
       Quand on verra le grand Coq au cercueil.

6   *Clarté fulgure à Lyon apparante*
       Luysant, print Malte, subit sera estrainte,
       Sardon, Mauris traitera deceuante,
       Geneue à Londres à Coq trahison fainte.

7   *Verceil, Milan donra intelligence,*
       Dedans Tycin sera faite la playe.
       Courir par Seine eau, sang feu par Florence,
       Vnique cheoir d'hault en bas faisant maye.

8   *Prés de Linterne dans de tonnes fermez,*
       Chiuaz fera pour l'Aigle la menée,
       L'esleu cassé luy ses gens enfermez,
       Dedans Turin rapt espouse emmenée.

9   *Pendant que l'Aigle & le Coq à Sauone*
       Seront vnis, Mer, Leuant & Ongrie.
       L'armée à Naples, Palerne, Marque d'Ancone:
       Rome, Venise par Barbe horrible crie.

Whilst the Eagle and the Cock at Savona   1860
Will be united, Sea, Levant and Hungary:
The army at Naples, Palermo, Marche of Ancona:
Rome, Venice by the Bearded one (**GARIBALDI**), horrible outcry.

Whilst the Eagle and the Cock at Savona will be united

The Napoleonic Eagle and the French Cock were united by the Emperor Napoleon III between
the years 1852 and 1870. It was during this period that Savona was returned to France. The city had been annexed to the French Empire in 1805 by Napoleon Bonaparte, but after his downfall in 1815, the Congress of Vienna returned Savona to the Kingdom of Sardinia, who held it as part of the County of Nice—that is, until Napoleon III retook it.

The Emperor regained the County of Nice in 1860, during the Italian Wars of Independence.

Earlier, in 1858, by a secret agreement concluded at Plombières between Napoleon III of France and the Sardinian Prime Minister Count Camillo de Cavour, France agreed to support Piedmont in its war against Austria. The reason for the conflict was to free the provinces of Lombardy and Venetia from Austrian rule. As a reward

COAT OF ARMS SECOND
FRENCH EMPIRE
(1852-1870)

for French aid, Napoleon III was allowed to take formal possession of Nice on 12 June 1860.

This roused the Italian nationalist leader Giuseppe Garibaldi, who was born in Nice, to oppose the cession of his home city to France. He maintained that the County of Nice was essentially Italian and should not be sold as "a ransom" to French expansionism. [1]

Sea, Levant and Hungary

The opening line of this quatrain has timed the period for its prophetic content to become history. In doing so, it has pointed to Savona in the County of Nice, where the Italian nationalist Garibaldi was born (4 July 1807). The remaining lines of the oracle are focused upon this man's efforts to achieve a unified Italian state.

The Levant is a term "which first appeared in English in 1497, originally it meant the East in general or 'Mediterranean lands east of Italy'." [2]

> The Battle of Lissa (sometimes called *Battle of Vis*) took place on 20 July 1866 in the Adriatic Sea near the Dalmatian island of Lissa ("Vis" in Croatian) and was a decisive victory for an outnumbered Austrian Empire force over a numerically superior Italian force. It was the first major sea battle between ironclads and one of the last to involve deliberate ramming. [3]

At the same time, Hungary enters the prophecy through its unity with Austria.

> [After] The Italian regular forces were defeated at Lissa on the sea. [...] Garibaldi took up arms again in 1866, this time with the full support of the Italian government. The Austro-Prussian War had broken out, and Italy had allied with Prussia against Austria-Hungary in the hope of taking Venezia from Austrian rule (Third Italian War of Independence). Garibaldi gathered again his Hunters of the Alps, now some 40,000 strong, and led them into the Trentino. He defeated the Austrians at Bezzecca. [4]

The army at Palermo, Naples

Six years before this, the uprisings in Messina and Palermo had provided Garibaldi with the opportunity to conquer Sicily. Together with his army of volunteers – *i Mille* (the thousand) he landed on the island on 11 May 1860, and next day …

> [Garibaldi] declared himself dictator of Sicily in the name of Victor Emmanuel II of Italy. He advanced to Palermo, the capital of the island and launched a siege on 27 May. [...] Having conquered Sicily, he crossed the Strait of Messina with help from the British Royal Navy, and marched north. Garibaldi's progress was met with more celebration than resistance, and on 7 September he entered the capital city of Naples, by train. Despite taking Naples, however, he had not, to this point, defeated the Neapolitan army. [5]

Marche of Ancona

Ancona is one of the major seaports of the Adriatic, and situated in the Marche region. It is also the main demographic centre and economic heart of the region.

> The siege of Ancona (18-29 September 1860) was the last major action during the brief Piedmontese invasion of the Papal States in 1860, and saw the fall of the only port that might have been used by an Austrian expeditionary force, greatly reducing the risk of foreign intervention in the war. [6]

Cavour, Prime Minister of Piedmont, had instigated the invasion of the Papal States in a bid to unify Italy under the reign of Victor Emanuel II of Piedmont. His intention was to meet up with Garibaldi who, earlier in the month, had taken Naples, and was heading for Rome. After obtaining victory at the Battle of Castelfidardo, Cavour went on to take Ancona.

Rome, Venice, by the bearded one, horrible outcry

Garibaldi had already conquered Rome eleven years earlier in 1849, but the French army, under the future Emperor Napoleon III, had besieged Rome, forcing Garibaldi to flee the city. Now, in 1860, having taken Naples, his next target was to march again on Rome. "Garibaldi declared that he would enter Rome as a victor or perish beneath its walls." But he was denied that opportunity; the Italian government intercepted him, and he was held for a time under honourable arrest.

Venetia existed as a part of the Republic of Venice; "the Republic was annexed by the Austrian Empire, until it was ceded to the Kingdom of Italy in 1866, as a result of the Third Italian War of Independence." [7] Garibaldi's role in this war is referred to above, when he and his army of 40.000 followers were supported by the Italian government during the Austro-Prussian War against Austria-Hungary. After which, the horrible outcry of war was again heard, when …

THE BEARDED ONE
GIUSEPPE GARIBALDI

> In 1867, he again marched on Rome, but the Papal army, supported by a French auxiliary force, proved a match for his badly armed volunteers. He was shot and wounded in the leg in the Battle of Mentana, and had to withdraw out of the Papal territory. The Italian government again imprisoned and held him for some time, after which he returned to Caprera. [8]

Summary: The main subject of this oracle is Giuseppe Garibaldi and his part in freeing Italy during its Wars of Independence. The seer refers to him as 'the bearded one'. Since the oracle was not fulfilled until the 1860s and the prophecy was published in the 1550s (a time span of more than three centuries) such detailed accuracy concerning a person's visage can only be possible in a block universe. Einstein was therefore correct, and quantum theorists' counterfeit universes wrong. The oracle's precognitive content is further enhanced by its reference to Napoleon III, and his acquisition of Nice—Garibaldi' birthplace.

10 Puanteur grande sortira de Lausanne,
    Qu'on ne sçaura l'origine du fait.
    Lon mettra hors tout la gent loingtaine,
    Feu veu au ciel, peuple estranger deffait.

11 Peuple infiny paroistra à Vicence
    Sans force, feu brusler la basilique,
    Prés de Lunage deffait grand de Valence,
    Lors que Venise par mort prendra pique.

12 Apparoistra aupres de Buffalore,
    L'hault & procere entré dedans Milan:
    L'abbé de Foix auec ceux de sainct Morre,
    Feront la forbe habillez en vilain.

13   *Le croise frere par amour effrenée,*
       Fera par praytus Bellerophon mourir,
       Classe à mil ans la femme forcenée
       Beu le breuuage, tous deux apres perir.

14   *Le grand credit d'or & d'argent l'abondance,*
       Aueugler par libide l'honneur:
       Cogneu sera d'adultere l'offense,
       Qui paruiendra à son grand deshonneur.

libide (L llbid\o) sensual desire; cogneu (OF) avow, acknowledge

The great esteem for gold and the abundance of money,   2015 ±
Blinding honour through sensual desire:
The transgression of adultery will be acknowledged,
Which will rise in the world to its great disgrace.

The great esteem for gold and the abundance of money
In this present age, the admiration given to wealth has become so great that a person's value to society is not measured by their character, but assessed by the value of their assets. [1] It is therefore not for nothing that this generation is called 'The Consumer Society'.

The greatest esteem is given to multi-national companies, who increase their annual profits, and reward those at managerial level with multi-million bonuses, together with retirement packages of Midas proportions. Political parties, too, are affected; for, they seek votes by persuading the electorate that their promises for economic growth will personally enrich the voter. Sporting idols also benefit with massive prize money or multi-million salaries added to by advertising contracts. All else is secondary. But, for every credit there must be a debit, therefore pity the poor: for while credits increase to further enrich the prosperous, the debits proportionately impoverish by the same margin the needy. Hence, the gap between the rich and the poor widens for want of political correctness in matters of finance. [1]

The abundance of money in this current society is not only confirmed by the growing number of millionaires, even billionaires (whether they be in pounds, dollars, Euros or yen), but also by a country's National Debt. In the USA, this figure stands in excess of eighteen trillion dollars ($18,031,021,541,348, as at December 2014). In the UK, this figure is approaching 1.5 trillion pounds (£1,468,547,500,000). The accumulated National Debt, involving forty-nine major trading countries, totals $60.85 trillion dollars. For a comparison of this figure, imagine the age of the universe (13.7 billion years) repeating itself sixteen and a half times. You will then have arrived at the national debt of these forty-nine countries, with little to spare.

Blinding honour through sensual desire
The pursuit of riches in the entertainment world, by emphasising the freedom of expressing one's self sexually, increased during the twentieth century and became rampant in the twenty-first. One need only investigate the music industry to discover how it has affected pubescent and pre-pubescent children to emulate false idols: immersed in the wealth they sucked from the purses and pockets of those seeking to emulate them. Never before have children been so sexualised.

The acting profession once reviled and whipped out of towns and villages for fear of subverting people, by allowing the atheistic imaginings of playwrights to infiltrate the moral wellbeing of the community, now enjoy a total reversal of their antecedents' humiliation, with the reward of fame, wealth and noble titles. But professional success is very often accompanied by lewd performances, scripts punctuated by the language of a gutter-snipe, nudity, and open scenes of debauchery. Blinded by the snares and lures of Mammon, personal honour, dignity and decorum are abandoned to serve the lustful eyes of the paying public, who are led to believe it is 'progress'.

The transgression of adultery will be acknowledged, which will rise in the world
Adultery is now so prolific in western culture that those without knowledge of the Bible will probably fail to understand the meaning that was comprehended by societies up until the latter half of the 20th century. Once divorce became widely available to the general public by

government law, a floodgate was opened to the masses that would enter into a state of adultery. Yet the law of God is perfectly clear. The seventh commandment in Deuteronomy 5: 18 states, "You shall not commit adultery." Jesus enlarged upon this in the gospel of Mark 10: 11, 12: "Anyone who divorces his wife and marries another woman commits adultery against her. And if she divorces her husband and marries another man, she commits adultery." There are few exceptions to this decree.

At the time of writing (2015) the Seer's prophecy has now been fulfilled. On the World Wide Web, the "The Ashley Madison website has 37 million members around the world – including a claimed 1.2 million in the UK – with its tagline: 'Life is short. Have an affair.' [...] Ashley Madison [...] the 'Google of cheating' [...] hoped to float on the London stock Exchange later this year," [2]

A democratically, elected, secular government will ignore God, in the knowledge that more votes are to be won by allowing people the freedom to satisfy their desires than to legislate against them. Consequently, democratically-elected, secular governments sow the seeds of rebellion against their Creator. And because governments are democratically-elected, sinful laws become the responsibility of those whose votes make such legislation possible. Hence, in the 20th and 21st centuries, laws that transgress God's ruling have become increasingly apparent.

Step by step, in the space of just five decades the taboos of two thousand years of western culture have been overturned by laws deliberately aimed at contesting the teaching of God, through His prophets and anointed son Jesus Christ. Narcotics, alcohol, gambling, pornography, sadistic computer games, assisted suicides, euthanasia, abortion, eugenics and same-sex unions, have become design features for the 'brave new world', counterfeited by science.

Since scientists *do not* possess visual outlook, everything in their counterfeit universe is out of sight, and without guarantee it even exists. This means they are just as likely to be subject to the sense data arriving from the 'future' state of their own personal world-line—for which this oracle, no less than any other, provides valid evidence. Democracy will flourish within every society only when this lesson is sufficiently understood to become universally accepted. For, only then will the lamb lie down with the lion, while men beat their spears into ploughshares. Until then, as Moses soon discovered, disorder quickly spreads when a people are left without moral guidance. This occurred when he left his people to speak with God on Mount Sinai. Left to themselves, the people turned to idolatry (Exodus 32). This can happen to any nation, when it is left to make up its own moral laws. A semblance of the second law of thermodynamics will then cause it to self-destruct, until it is overrun or destroyed completely. But, if the entire western world self-destructs—what comes after?

To its great disgrace

The Seer's final statement is of special interest because he was not speaking as a person of the twenty-first century, but as someone who already knew its future. The English novelist, L. P. Hartley wrote, "The past is a foreign country: they do things differently there." [3] Historians are likely to agree: hindsight being their speciality. But consider; *we* are the past to every future generation. It is *we* who are the 'foreign country' to a future race of people. And it is *we* who are doing something different to those who come after us. Therefore, if the Seer retains the same 100% accuracy, which he has so far achieved, then it is this present generation who will wear the sackcloth of disgrace, and bequeath to a future age the ashes from its degradation.

15   *Vers Aquilon grands efforts par hommasse,*
      Presque l'Europe & l'vniuers vexer,
      Les deux eclypses mettra en telle chasse,
      Et aux Pannons vie & mort renforcer.

hommasse (OF - hommesse) virago, manly woman; mettra (AF imputer) chasse (AF – bannissement); Pannons (L Pannonia) Hungary; Cross-reference: vie & mort, C.II: 90.

Towards the North, great exertions by a manly woman (**CATHERINE THE GREAT**),   1762
Vexing nearly all Europe and the universe,
The two eclipses, thereof, she will ascribe as banishment (**PETER III & IVAN**),
Also, for the Hungarians, life and death increasing.

Towards the North

The 'north', having been set for the fulfilment of this oracle, takes us to Russia, the adopted country of German-born Catherine the Great, Empress, and the 'All-wise Mother of the Fatherland'. [1]

Great exertions

As the unopposed ruler of Russia, Catherine was free to exert her energy in the management of the country's state affairs exactly as she pleased. Her first accomplishment was to turn Russia into a prosperous and powerful state. She achieved this by establishing order and justice across the land. In the course of doing so, "she reformed the administrative system, plundered the Church, liberalized the economy, emancipated the nobility, and helped it absorb Western culture." She also made plans for improving the spread of education, and then set about creating a court that would rival Versailles. [2]

By a manly woman

As for the Empress's appearance, described by the Seer as being that of a manly woman: "Even Catherine's admirers sometimes noticed [...] that she looked her best in masculine attire." [3]

Vexing nearly all Europe and the universe

It was, however, her foreign policies that caused concern to Europe, and to many other parts of the world. This began with an extension of Russia's boundary to the west, taking in Poland, Lithuania, Byelorussia and Western Ukraine. To the south, she wrested the Crimea from Turkey's grasp, and to the east, brought Alaska into the Russian fold, thereby involving America. Few countries in Europe failed to feel the effects of Catherine's rule.

With the acquisition of the Crimea, Russia was able to exert its influence in the Mediterranean and reach Central and Western Europe. An alliance with Austria coupled with the renouncing of treaties made with Prussia and England; the division of Poland, between Russia, Austria and Prussia; an excursion into Persia to lay the foundations of her Empire in Central Asia; and an alliance with Denmark in the war against Sweden: [4] these were more than enough to fulfil the Seer's prediction that she would vex nearly most of Europe and the world. In 16th century civilization, when this was written, the world was understood to be at the centre of the universe.

The two eclipses, thereof, she will ascribe as banishment

Catherine initially came to Russia as the wife of Czar Peter III. But when her husband showed signs of feebleness, which he coupled with an open admiration for the Prussian army, thereby losing respect in the eyes of his subjects, she saw this as a means by which she could replace him. Her opportunity came when he further antagonised his subjects by attempting to cajole the Russian Orthodox Church into adopting Lutheran ideas.

In a *coup d'état* assisted by Grigory Orlov, and joined by other members of the guard, Peter III was seized and forced to abdicate (10 July 1762). He was then *banished* and sent to the village of Ropsha, where he was strangled a week later by Grigory's brother, Aleksey Orlov. This was the first eclipse that began as banishment.

A similar plight befell Ivan, Peter III's predecessor. In November 1741, the child-Emperor Ivan VI was seized by the Grand Duchess Elisabeth in a palace *coup*, and banished to Schlüsselburg. He remained there until July 1764, when a young officer, Vasily Mirovich, launched a rescue attempt designed to restore him to his rightful position as Emperor of Russia. But Catherine had previously given orders that if anyone tried to liberate the former Emperor, he was to be killed. Her orders were meticulously carried out, for when Mirovich found Ivan, he was already dying from multiple stab wounds. [5] This was the second eclipse that had been set as banishment.

Within the space of three years, two Czars, Ivan VI and Peter III were 'eclipsed': both men having been banished, and then murdered by order of the Empress.

Also, for the Hungarians death increasing

The final line of this oracle focuses upon Hungary. During the 18th century, the country then formed part of the Habsburg Empire: its territory having once been part of the Roman province known as Pannonia, hence, the classical reference to this part of the world by the Seer.

In the early part of the 18th century the Hungarian death toll had steadily been increasing as the country became rocked by "Fierce fighting that raged for decades." The cause of this death toll was due to the country's patriots, who were striving to free their land from Turkish control. In the event, their attempts at obtaining liberation brought in Austria, which too became locked in conflict with the Hungarian freedom fighters.

Life increasing

Exhausted by years of fighting the country welcomed the intervention of the Habsburgs and recovery thereafter was swift. "Hungary made an impressive recovery, both material and cultural, from the sorry state to which it had earlier been reduced. The population more than doubled, to reach 8 or 9 million by 1800." [6]

Most aptly, the prophecy has concluded with a prediction of 'life increasing'. It is a theme which commenced Century Two N° 90: a quatrain that continues foretelling the future of Hungary during the years that followed.

Summary: *The seer begins by describing a manly woman in the North. It is a description that aptly fits Catherine the Great. Her biography thereafter fulfils the prophecies made about her reign. Europe felt the full force of her territorial expansion. And her position as empress, in place of the two Czars that had ancestral rights to rulership, is foretold by their banishment and subsequent murder. The final line, concerning Hungary and the recovery of its falling population is historically correct in placing it at the time of Catherine's rule.*

16   *Au lieu que HIERON fait sa nef fabriquer*
      Si grand deluge sera & si subite,
      Qu'on n'aura lieu ne terres s'ataquer,
      L'onde monter Fesulan Olympique.

17   *Les bien-aisez subit seront desmis,*
      Par les trois freres le monde mis en trouble.
      Cité marine saisiront ennemis,
      Faim, feu, sang, peste, & de tous maux le double.

18   *De FLORE issuë de sa mort sera cause,*
      Vn temps deuant par ieusne & vieille bueyre.
      Car les trois lys luy feront telle pose,
      Par son fruit sauue comme chair cruë mueyre.

19   *A soustenir la grand cappe troublée,*
      Pour l'esclaircir les rouges marcheront,
      De mort famille sera presque accablée,
      Les rouges rouges le rouge assommeront.

soubstenir (OF soustenir) to uphold, tolerate; Cappe (anag. paragram.) cap[t]e – Capet, also, capper (OF) prendre; accabler (OF) overthrow; assomeront (OF, tuer) Cross-reference: la grande cappe, C.IV: II; C.IX: 20; C.IX: 26.

The great man taken (**CAPET**), troubled for upholding,   1791
As for explaining it, the reds will progress:
By death, the (**ROYAL**) family will have been well nigh overthrown.
The red, reds will kill (**DANTON**) the red one.

The great man taken (Capet), troubled for upholding

Louis XVI, the great man who was taken captive at Varennes during his attempt to escape the Revolution, and who was now addressed as Louis Capet, became greatly troubled after returning to Paris. [1] Unwisely, before leaving, he had written a letter (see Century Nine No. 26) upholding his reasons for abandoning the country. [2] When the letter was passed to the revolutionary government, its content made painful reading – even for the King's most loyal supporters.

As for explaining it

As for attempting to explain its content, there was little his followers could say that might placate the growing animosity against the King. For the letter continued to uphold the old traditions of monarchical rule. To make matters still worse, Louis admitted that the support he had given for the new order had been made under duress. And he questioned if there was any truth in the claim that Frenchmen really did want to replace fourteen hundred years of monarchical government with "anarchy and despotism" that was arising from the current political situation. [3]

The reds

'The reds' were the revolutionaries. The red flag they adopted emerged "in 1791, when the crowd attacking the Tuileries picked up a blood-soaked royal standard. Henceforth, 'red' and 'white' were the accepted colour codes for revolution and counter-revolution." [4]

Will progress

After the ignominy of his arrest at Varennes, and the embarrassment of having his grievances made known to his enemies, public support for Louis XVI dwindled, even amongst moderate politicians. In July, a petition began to circulate, which declared that Louis XVI had 'deserted his post' and, in effect, abdicated. Tom Paine, author of *Rights of Man*, claimed that the King's attempt to leave France had already 'instituted a Republic'. In this atmosphere of unrest, the political club known as the Cordeliers demanded that their members take a solemn vow of 'tyrannicide' to protect the liberty of France. To make matters worse, the failure to explain the contents of the King's letter as anything other than pique, allowed the reds to make further progress towards their aim, which was to abolish the monarchy altogether. [5]

By death, the family will have been well nigh overthrown

It was soon becoming evident that the reign of the King and Queen was approaching its end: all but crushed beneath the gathering weight of opposition to their existence. On 20 June 1792, a mob of armed rioters broke into the palace and threatened the King with violence if he did not obey their demands. He was rescued by the National Guard before any injury could be done to his person. Then, on 3 August, the Paris sections voted for the King's deposition. This was followed two weeks later by a mob of rioters, far more violent than before, who invaded the Tuileries, slaughtering the Swiss Guard and every palace worker that came within their reach. With no place of safety remaining for the royal family, they were forcibly taken to the Temple Tower. [6] By the end of the year, Louis XVI was standing trial for his life. He was executed on 21 January 1793. Nine months later, the Queen followed her husband to the guillotine. Their son, Louis-Charles died two years later from illness and neglect. Only their daughter survived.

The red reds will kill the red one

In 1793 Georges Danton, Minister of Justice during the September Massacres, received a new appointment to sit on the Committee of Public Safety. But ill health caused him to leave Paris, and spend time recuperating in the country. Nursed back to health by his sixteen-year-old wife Louise, his political views became more restrained. And it was with this fresh turn of mind that he returned to political life in Paris, with fresh appeals to his fellow revolutionaries for greater moderation in their ambition to distance France from its monarchical and Christian past.

However, in his absence, 'the reds' had become much redder in their desire to shed blood: seeing this to be the fastest means of furthering their objectives; which is to say, they were now *the red reds*. [7] They therefore rejected Danton's appeal for restraint, perceiving it as a weakness.

History has had little trouble in affirming, "the memory of Danton is red with violence." Brutal though he had been, and still politically 'a red', Danton now viewed the carnage taking place as excessive, and sought to find ways of reducing the bloodletting. The 'red reds' remained unmoved by his arguments: and his urge for moderation was ignored. Instead, they now viewed

Danton's plea as a betrayal of the Republic. Reaction was swift. On the night of 30 March 1794, Danton was arrested and charged on very weak evidence put together by Robespierre and Saint-Just. Three days later, the former Minister of Justice experienced the same fate he had meted out to so many unfortunates in the past. He was made to stand trial for his life. Revolutionary justice was swift, and he was executed on 5 April: [8] the red reds had killed the red one.

Summary: *The seer returns to the French Revolution for this oracle. It traces yet another step towards the deaths of the King and Queen. Once again, the seer identifies the attempted escape from France by Louis XVI and Marie Antoinette as the major cause of the events that led to the termination of the monarchy. This time, it is the letter that Louis left behind to explain his reasons for leaving France; its discovery simply added further fuel to a reputation that had already been damaged in the public mind through his bid to flee the country. Thereafter, the monarchy was slowly crushed by a series of anti-royalist rage attacks against the palace. The oracle then moves ahead in time to the year after the guillotining of the King, when it was Danton's turn to feel the blade on his neck.*

20   Le faux message par election fainte,
        Courir par vrben rompuë pache arreste,
        Voix aceptées, de sang chapelle tainte,
        Et à vn autre l'empire contraincte.

21   Au port de Agde trois fustes entreront
        Portant l'infect non foy & pestilence,
        Passant le pont mil milles embleront,
        Et le pont rompre à tierce resistance.

22   Gorsan, Narbonne, par le sel aduertir,
        Tucham, la grace Parpignan trahye,
        La ville rouge n'y vouldra consentir,
        Par haulte voldrap gris vie faillie.

Gorsan (*paragram*) Gorsa[s]; le sel (*anagrammatic paragram*) [t]e s[a]l – Stael; aduertir (L advert\o) turn; Tucham (*apocope*, Tu Cham[pi]; i.e., OF Champi = Bourbon): also (Greek) Tυχα[μ] chance; Parpignan (L *portmanteau* – Per + pign\us) by assurance *also* Perpignan; hault (OF) haughty, arrogant; faillie (OF – finir).finished.

GORSAS, NARBONNE, through the salt (STAEL) turning,   1793
TUI BOURBON chance, good will, Perpignan betrayed (BY ASSURANCE),
The red city (PARIS BLOODY) will not be willing to consent to it.
Through haughty flight, grey cloth, (LOUIS XVI'S) life finished.

Gorsas

ANTOINE-JOSEPH GORSAS

At the time of the French Revolution, Antoine-Joseph Gorsas was a journalist for the *Courrier de Paris à Versailles*. In September 1792 he was elected as deputy for Seine-et-Oise, which led to him joining the Mountain. But he soon dissociated from this group and became one of the few men willing to write articles in support of the monarchy. At the King's trial, he voted for detention and banishment in preference to execution. After which, he wrote a scathing condemnation of Jean-Paul Marat, which forced him to leave Paris for his personal safety. But, upon returning, he was quickly arrested, tried, and executed, all in a single day. [1] He was the first journalist to be guillotined. He died on 7 March 1793.

Narbonne, turning through the salt

Another person of note who was sympathetic to the King was the Comte de Narbonne-Lara, whom Louis XVI had appointed as Minister for War. Narbonne believed the King might be restored to favour by his subjects if he declared war against the *émigré*

LOUIS COMTE DE
NARBONNE-LARA

army, which had gathered at Coblenz; for he believed it would encourage an atmosphere of patriotism across the country. [2] But as the revolution progressed, he came increasingly under the influence of others: referred to as 'the salt'. This is a biblical reference (Matthew 5: 13), and it usually refers to the moral elite (see Century Nine No. 49 and Century Ten No. 7). In this particular case, 'le sel' can also be seen as a reference to Madame de Staël. Narbonne had planned to speak at the King's trial, but through the persuasive arguments of his mistress and mother of his child, Madame de Staël, he turned away from his resolve and remained silent. [3]

Tu! Bourbon

The subtle interplay between *tucham'* and *tu cham*pi is particularly noteworthy, for it employs both the paragram and an apocope. This word-play therefore enables Louis XVI to be identified by both his Bourbon name and *Tu*. This singular form of you is, in itself, prophetic. It was adopted by citizens at the time of the Revolution; viz. – "They had two principal goals: greater social equality and a secularization of the state. It was during this period that [...] tu replaced vous." [4]

Chance

> It was sheer bad luck that the political crisis should have coincided with a catastrophic harvest. Crops had suffered in the previous July from a hailstorm of quite exceptional extent and severity. The British Embassy reported men being killed on the roads by hailstones sixteen inches round. 'It is certain that a Country at least thirty leagues in circumference [around Rainbouillet] is entirely laid waste.' Farther to the north-east, the local Estates calculated that the damage in the province of Artois amounted to nearly two million livres (about £80,000). The inevitable result was that the price of bread [...] shot up to prohibitive heights. [5]

Chance, too, played an important role in the failure of Louis XVI to escape Paris. It was the *chance* observation made by Drouet, the postmaster in Sainte-Ménéhould, who caught sight of the King inside his stationary coach, causing the alarm to be raised. It was *chance* again that Drouet found his way to Varennes through miles of forest on a moonless night, which enabled him to arrive before the King left town for the final part of his bid to reach the Belgian border. It was also by *chance* that the dragoons, sent to escort the King's carriage to the safety of the Belgian border became lost in the forest before they could arrive to escort the royal family to safety.

Good will

After the King's enforced return to Paris, and in the wake of much debate, amends were made. A period of good will followed, in which Louis was restored to the throne in the reduced capacity of King of the French, but which did include the promise for his personal safety. [6]

Perpignan betrayed (by assurance)

Three months later in December, the pro-Royalist officers at the garrison in Perpignan mutinied, in an attempt to provide support for the monarchy. But the revolt foundered when large numbers of those who had given their assurance betrayed their trust and withdrew support. [7]

The red city

Following the elections of September 1791, Paris literally became the red city. It is not difficult to see why. "It was among the hundreds of 'new men' [...] that some of the most extreme revolutionaries were to be found." These 'new men' were far more revolutionary than their predecessors, and they were intent upon turning France into a republic as soon as possible. [8]

Will not be willing to consent to it

For the beleaguered monarchy, the situation became grim. The majority of politicians who had previously given the King their promise for his safety had been replaced by new deputies. And these were men of a different mettle. They were eager to build a new order upon the policies of the previous administration, and were not willing to consent to the safeguards given to the monarchy by the delegates they had replaced. [9]

Within a short time, their impatience to rid France of its monarchy found expression in mob violence. Gangs of revolutionaries twice overran the royal palace. On the second occasion, all pretension of a monarchy in France ceased, and the King and Queen were placed under guard inside the Temple Tower.

Through haughty flight, grey cloth
In telegraphic language, the oracle refers back to the major events that were responsible for what had occurred. It began with the King's flight from Paris and the haughty letter he foolishly left behind explaining his action. [10] The grey cloth worn by Louis XVI during his flight confirms the King's identity, for grey was the colour of the cloak, the breeches and the stockings he wore while disguised as a valet (refer Century Nine N°. 20).[11]

Life finished
Louis XVI's life ended beneath the guillotine as a result of the incidents outlined above. [12]

Summary: *The oracle commences with two names that were part of the French Revolution. One was a journalist, the other a former, titled minister of state; but both had the same objective in mind—to speak favourably on the King's behalf. On the other hand, both failed. The popular voice had voted during the September elections for republican deputies, and Louis' brief term as King of the French came to an end, preceded by a failed attempt to raise a monarchist army at Perpignan. The oracle is also of note for its covert reference to 'Bourbon', the family name of the King's dynasty. The oracle also correctly describes the colour of Louis' attire at the time of his capture in Varennes, when he adopted the disguise of a butler.*

23   *Lettres trouuées de la Royne les coffres,*
        Point de subscrit sans aucun nom d'autheur,
        Par la police seront cachez les offres,
        Qu'on ne sçaura qui sera l'amateur.

subscrit (L subscript\io) signature; police (OF) civil government; offres (OF) propositions, proposals; amateur (OF) lover.

Letters of the Queen (**MARY STUART**) found [in] the coffers,   1567
Place of signature without any name of author,
The proposals will be hidden by the civil government,
That one will not know who will be the lover.

Letters of the Queen found in the coffers
On the night of 9 February 1567, the body of Lord Darnley (aged 21), husband to Mary Queen of Scots, was found strangled in the grounds of Kirk o' Field, and his house destroyed by an explosion. The destruction of the house appeared to be a failed attempt at concealing the murder. The Scottish nobility was incensed by the crime, and ordered the arrest of Bothwell's servants. Among those detained was George Dalgleish. While undergoing torture, he confessed to his investigators that he knew where incriminating evidence might be found. This, he said, was inside a house in Edinburgh's Potterow. After a thorough search of the premises, a small coffer was found; inside, was a silver casket containing letters of the Queen. [1]

Place of signature without any name of author
The contents of the letters were disappointing. There was no signature. Furthermore, there was no date, and the letters had neither a proper beginning nor a proper ending. [2]

The proposals will be hidden by the civil government
Three weeks after Darnley's murder, the Earl of Bothwell was arrested for the crime and put on trial. He was also charged with a string of other offences relating to the content of the Casket Letters. Yet, remarkably, none of the letters were ever produced as evidence. In fact, the proposals in the letters, and their very existence remained hidden by the civil government for a full eighteen months after their discovery. [3]

As a further note to this affair, when going to his execution for participating in the crime, John Hay of Tallo, a kinsman of Bothwell, confided that the murder of Darnley was committed by Scottish nobles, who then tried to frame Bothwell and Mary for the crime. In which case, the letters would most likely have been incomplete forgeries, with at least one of the documents implicating the pair.

That one will not know who will be the lover

Mary, of course completely denied all knowledge of the letters. It was therefore thought unnecessary to show them to her, and the case against the Queen was not pursued. In the event, only copies of the letters now survive. And so, who wrote them, and who the lover was, continues to remain unknown, even to the present day. [4]

Summary: Mary Queen of Scots was a contemporary of the seer: she having married the Dolphin, Francis II, who became King in the summer of 1559 following the tragic death of his father, Henri II. In the following year, Francis too died. With no part to play in France, Mary returned to her native Scotland as the nation's Queen. Four years later she married Lord Darnley. The oracle takes up the Queen's story after the murder of Lord Darnley. The affair of the Casket Letters was a cause célèbre at the time and the seer devotes the entire quatrain to this subject.

24   *Le Lieutenant à l'entrée de l'huys*
Assommera le grand de Parpignan,
En se cuidant sauuer à Montpertuis.
Sera deceu bastard de Lusignan.

25   *Cœur de l'amant ouuert d'amour fertiue*
Dans le ruisseau fera rauir la Dame,
Le demy mal contrefera lassiue,
Le pere à deux priuera corps de l'ame.

26   *De Caton es trouuez en Barcelonne,*
Mys descouuers lieu retrouuez & ruyne,
Le grand qui tient ne tient voudra Pamplonne,
Par l'abbage de Montferrat bruyne.

es (AF Latin, ipsum, - adjective marking the identity) master, the self-same.

27   *La voye auxelle l'vn sur l'autre fornix,*
Du muy deser hor mis braue & genest,
L'escript d'empereur le fenix
Veu en celuy ce qu'à nul autre n'est.

28   *Les simulachres d'or et d'argent enflez,*
Qu'apres le rapt lac au feu furent iettez
Au descouuert estaincts tous & troublez,
Au marbre escripts, perscripts interiettez.

29   *Au quart pillier l'on sacre à Saturne.*
Par tremblant terre & deluge fendu
Sous l'edifice Saturin trouuée vrne,
D'or Capion rauy & puis rendu.

30   *Dedans Tholouse non loing de Beluzer*
Faisant vn puis loing, palais d'espectacle
Thresor trouué vn chacun ira vexer,
Et en deux locs tout & prés des vesacle.

31   *Premier grand fruict le Prince de Pesquiere:*
Mais puis viendra bien & cruel malin,
Dedans Venise perdra sa gloire fiere,
Et mis à mal par plus ioyeux Celin.

32   *Garde toy roy Gaulois de ton nepueu,*
Qui fera tant que ton vnique fils
Sera meurtry à Venus faisant vœu,
Accompagné denuict que trois & six.

33   *Le grand naistra de Veronne & Vincence,*
Qui portera vn surnom bien indigne.
Qui à Venise vouldra faire vengeance,
Luy mesme prins homme du guet & signe.

34   *Apres victoire du Lyon au Lyon,*
Sus la montagne de IVRA Secatombe,
Delues & brodes septiesme million,
Lyon, Vlme à Mausol mort & tombe.

35   *Dedans l'entrée de Garonne & Bayse;*
Et la forest non loing de Damazan
Du marsaues gelées, puis gresle & bize
Dordonnois gelle par erreur de Mezan.

36   *Sera commis conte oindre aduché*
De Saulne & sainct Aulbin & Belœuure
Pauer de marbre de tous loing espluché
Non Bleteran resister & chef d'œuure.

37   *La forteresse aupres de la Tamise,*
Cherra par lors le Roy dedans serré,
Aupres du pont sera veu en chemise:
Vn deuant mort, puis dans le fort barré.

cherra (OF cheoir) fall as an escheat; serré (OF) locked up; pont (L pont\o) ferryboat; barré (AF clouer) to fix or attach.

The fortress close by the Thames (**WINDSOR CASTLE**)   1649
Will fall as an escheat, through that time, once the King (**CHARLES 1**) is locked inside,
Close by the (**STANGATE**) ferryboat he will be seen in a shirt,
One before death: then barred within the fort.

The fortress close by the Thames will fall as an escheat

Discounting palaces, there are two fortresses on the banks of the river Thames; they are the Tower of London and Windsor Castle. The fortress close by the Thames at Windsor in Berkshire has been the home of the royal families of England ever since Edward III converted part of the building into royal apartments in 1348. It is this castle that is the focus of the present oracle. [1] Windsor Castle did in fact fall as an escheat during the time of the English Civil War, when it was captured by Oliver Cromwell's model army. It therefore did not pass on to Charles II after his father's death in 1649.

Through that time, once the king is locked inside

"Windsor Castle survived the tumultuous period of the English Civil War, when it was used as a military headquarters for Parliamentary forces and a prison for Charles I." [2] In December 1648, the King, who had been made a captive by Cromwell, was taken under guard from Hurst Castle on the Isle of Wight to Windsor Castle. He remained there as a prisoner until 19 January, when he was transferred to St. James's Palace at Westminster to stand trial for High Treason. [3] Before the month's end, the King would be dead and the English monarchy in the hands of Cromwell.

Close by the ferryboat

The complex of government buildings that run adjacent to the Houses of Parliament along Whitehall, and which occupy the site where Charles I was executed, can today be reached from the southern shore of the Thames by crossing Westminster Bridge. But in 1649, Westminster Bridge did not exist. In its place was the Stangate ferryboat, which crossed the Thames from Lower Marsh to Westminster.

> London's busiest crossing point other than at London Bridge was from Stangate, the ferry of Lambeth Marsh, to Westminster and near the point that the Romans crossed with a ford to link with Watling Street. [4]

Its main competitor was the Horse Ferry that crossed at a point farther upstream, outside Lambeth Palace. Today, Horseferry Road, running from Lambeth Bridge to Victoria, still bears the name of that particular crossing point.

He will be seen in a shirt: one before death

It was a grey, icy-cold January day in London when the King prepared to leave St. James's Palace for his execution. What follows is a story told many times by historians. The King requested permission to wear an extra shirt, lest the chill in the air should make him shiver, and this was misinterpreted as a tremble of fear. [5] His plea was granted, and Charles was then escorted to the scaffold, which had been set up outside the Banqueting Hall in Whitehall, near the ferryboat.

Then barred within the fort

After this act of legalized regicide, Charles's body was placed in a lead coffin and returned to Windsor Castle where it was interred within the fortress inside the Henry VIII vault. [6] It had been intended he would be buried inside Westminster Abbey, but Cromwell refused permission.

Summary: *This oracle features a fortress by the river Thames in which a king is locked inside. The history of England includes only one such event since the time this prophecy went to print, and that is the imprisonment of Charles I at Windsor Castle during the English Civil War. From there he was taken to London to stand trial at Westminster, close to where the Stangate ferry crossed the Thames from Southwark's Lower Marsh. The charge against him was crimes against the state, and he was sentenced to death. The seer latches onto the fact that the execution took place on a cold January day and Charles requested an extra shirt, lest his shivers be interpreted as trembling. After his death, the body was interred inside a lead coffin and returned to the chapel crypt at Windsor Castle, where it remains today.*

> 38   *Le Roy de Bloys dans Auignon regner*
>   *Vne autre fois le peuple emonopolle,*
>   *Dedans le Rosne par murs fera baigner*
>   *Iusque à cinq le dernier prés de Nolle.*

emonopolle (portmanteau – emono, (L) emon[et]o + polle, (L) polle[to]; both Latin words – *to admonish* & *strongly* - sare in the future active imperative tense, which is correct for this prediction); Nolle (L) unwilling).

> The King of Blois (**CHARLES IX**) reigning in Avignon:
> One other time he will strongly admonish the people,
> Within the Rhône, through walls, he will cause bathing,
> Even as far as to five: the vilest near to the Unwilling One.

The King of Blois

During the lifetime of the Seer, Blois Castle (Château Royal de Blois) was the much frequented residence of the Valois kings of France. But, in the context of this prophecy, it is Charles IX to whom this prophecy is directed. His reign began at the age of ten in 1560, with the death of his elder brother, Francis II.

It was as France's newly appointed King that the Seer first met Charles IX at Blois Castle. "[It] had taken place at Blois in 1560, where at Catherine's request she had asked Nostradamus to draw up Henri of Anjou's horoscope that predicted he would one day be King of France. This prophecy seemed to please the Queen Mother very much indeed. [1]

Reigning in Avignon

In 1564, Catherine de Medici decided to take Charles IX on a grand tour of his kingdom. It would last two years and four months. In the summer of that year the Court reached Avignon, having arrived via Roman, Valence, Montelimar and Orange. From there the royal party intended to visit the Seer in his home town of Salon. But the Court remained at Avignon for three weeks, while the King recovered from a cold that had developed into bronchitis.

> Charles IX passed through the city during his royal tour of France (1564-1566) together with his court and nobles of the kingdom: his brother the Duke of Anjou, Henry of Navarre the cardinals of Bourbon and Lorraine The court stayed for three weeks. [2]

One other time he will strongly admonish the people

Having 'personally' introduced the King as Charles IX, the Seer next moves forward to the St Bartholomew's Day Massacre that occurred in Paris in August 1572, but which also has connexions to Blois Castle.

In March 1572, several festivals in Blois were held for the arrival of Henry of Navarre concerning his engagement to Marguerite de Valois, sister of Charles IX, celebrated in April in the castle chapel. The marriage celebrated in Paris on August 18 established the prelude to the massacre of St. Bartholomew.[3]

The St Bartholomew's Day Massacre is predicted in Century Four N° 47. It was sparked by the assassination of Admiral Coligny, leader of the protestant Huguenot party, after the first attempt on his life resulted in just a slight wound. Catherine de Medici had planned his murder, and when it failed, she responded by so haranguing the King with false fears that he finally yielded to his mother and reportedly said: "**Then kill them all! Kill them all.**"[4] Charles IX was apparently referring to Coligny and his associates, but when word got out, it was construed as meaning all Huguenots. The death toll varies, but in Paris alone those slain totalled at the very least, 3,000. Alarmed at the outcome, which seemed unceasing, as it spread to other towns and cities, the King attempted to exert his authority by issuing a 'royal order' for the killing to cease.

Once the killing started, mobs of Catholic Parisians, apparently overcome with bloodlust, began a general massacre of Huguenots. Charles issued a royal order on August 25 to halt the killing, but his pleas went unheeded as the massacres spread.[5]

Within the Rhône, through walls, he will cause bathing.

"Lyons, Toulouse, Bordeaux, and Rouen all had their massacres. So many Lyonese corpses drifted down the Rhône to Arles that, for three months, the Arlesians did not want to drink the river water."[6]

In an attempt to save Protestant lives, the officials at Lyons attempted to shield the Huguenots behind the walls of the city's convent and jail. But their attempt was short-lived. "In Lyon, city officials placed Protestants under protective custody in the city's convents and jails on August 29. Two days later, crowds broke in and massacred the prisoners by sword, strangulation, and drowning. Witnesses reported that the Rhone River flowed red with several thousand mutilated corpses."[7]

Orléans was another city in which *the walls* and *bathing* became an active part in the massacre of hundreds of Protestants: although it was the River Loire into which corpses were dispatched:

In Orléans the massacres began on August 26. Catholic extremists herded Protestants to the city wall and slaughtered them, mocking their victims by chanting the opening verse of Psalm 43: "Vindicate me, O God [...] and rescue me from wicked men." In two days, around 1,000 men, women, and children were killed.[8]

Even as far as to five

The time span of each city's massacre varied across the provinces, but in general, the killing continued for a further five days.

Other massacres broke out in the provinces, but none were as brutal as the one in Paris; conflicting messages were coming from the king, some purporting to act on his behalf in attacking Huguenots, others heeding his later call to end the violence, and the subsequent killings in the provinces were more sporadic and less intense than those in Paris. Around 7,000 additional Huguenots were slain throughout the entire countryside over the next five days. By the time the killings ended on August 29th, around 10,000 people had been killed throughout the kingdom.[9]

The vilest near to the Unwilling One.

'Nolle – the 'Unwilling One' – has been given a capital letter: presumably, so that it will be treated as a proper noun, thereby representing an actual person. In which case, Charles IX fits this description. When approached by his mother, Catherine de Medici, and told that Coligny was plotting against him, Charles rejected the suggestion outright.

At first the King cried out that these were lies and 'The Admiral loves me as though I were his own son. He would never do anything to harm me.' Eventually the haranguing of his mother and the mournful affirmations of her supporters broke his spirit and drained his endurance. Feeling he had been betrayed by his trusted friend, he began to listen to Catherine as she outlined their plan to kill all the senior Huguenots in Paris, starting with the Admiral.[10]

The 'vilest' near to him were therefore 'Catherine de Medici' and 'her supporters'.

It is also true to say that having had his mind poisoned by his mother, Charles saw fit to engage in the killing that resulted from the lies he had been fed. Soon afterwards, when realizing the full extent of what was happening, he felt compelled to order the immediate cessation of the murders that were now spreading across his kingdom.

Summary: *The seer's son, César, later wrote that Charles IX held several private conversations with his father during the Court's visit to Salon, for which de Nostredame was appointed Physician and Councillor to the King. This oracle foretells Charles' tour of his kingdom, which led to those private interviews. It would have been too dangerous for the seer to have revealed the truth embedded within this quatrain, and so he speaks of the King's tour which had reached Avignon before arriving at Salon. If the King made this association, the knowledge that he would 'strongly admonish his people' would not have displeased him. But how the seer managed to evade the reason for this, and who would be 'Unwilling' is left to the imagination.*

39   *Qu'aura esté par prince Bizantin,*
      Sera tollu par prince de Tholose:
      La foy de Foix par le chef Tholentin,
      Luy faillira ne refusant l'espouse.

40   *Le sang du Iuste par Taur & la Dorade,*
      Pour se venger contre les Saturnins
      Au nouueau lac plongeront la maynade,
      Puis marcheront contre les Albanins.

41   *Esleu sera Renard ne sonnant mot,*
      Faisant le saint public viuant pain d'orge,
      Tyrannizer apres tant à vn cop,
      Mettant à pied des plus grands sur la gorge.

Renard (F) sly fellow, *also* paragram – Renar[t] (AF malice, ruse) spite.

A Reynard will be elected: not a word ringing out,   1792
Playing the public saint, living on barley bread (**ROBESPIERRE**),
Afterwards, tyrannizing so many at a blow,
Putting with foot on the neck of the greatest ones.

A Reynard

Renart in the ancient French language is a noun that means 'cunning', 'guile', 'spite', 'malice'. It befits a character in stories that date back to the twelfth century.

Reynard (French: Renart) is the main character in a literary cycle of allegorical French, Dutch, English and German fables. Those stories are largely concerned with Reynard, an anthropomorphic red fox and trickster figure. His adventures usually involve him deceiving other anthropomorphic animals for his own advantage, for revenge or by pure malice or trying to avoid retaliations from them. [1]

Before Maximilien Robespierre achieved power, he presented himself in a far different light to the person he later became. As William Pitt the Elder, and a contemporary of Robespierre, said, "Unlimited power is apt to corrupt the minds of those who possess it."

No one who knew him then pictured him as a revolutionary. He professed – and for several years continued to profess – his belief in the King as a 'young and wise monarch', part of whose 'august character' was a 'sacred passion for the happiness of the people.'

Once in public office, his attitude and opinions dramatically changed, portraying the slyness that had lain hidden in his former attitude. As one politician commented,

He possessed a truly Machiavellian skill [...] in dividing men and sowing differences between them, of enticing others to test the ground for him and then either abandoning them or supporting them as prudence or ambition dictated.

His spiteful nature also became apparent: – "he had for every dissenter from his narrow creed the one and simple remedy of the guillotine [...] which in Paris alone cost two thousand six hundred victims." [2]

Will be elected

Although Robespierre took no part in the attack on the Tuileries (10 August 1792), "that same afternoon his *section* (an administrative subdivision of Paris), Les Piques, nominated him to the insurrectional Commune." Three weeks later, the terrible September Massacres took place. And on 5 September, without having done more than excuse these crimes: "the people of Paris elected him to head the delegation to the national Convention." It was also as their representative that "The National Convention elected him president, on June 4, by a vote of 216 out of 220."

Not a word ringing out

It is on record that although Robespierre was the elected President of the National Convention, "His voice was weak" and he often struggled to make himself heard—not a word *ringing out*. [3]

Playing the public saint, living on barley bread

Despite the French Revolution's anti-Christian commitment, Robespierre publicly acknowledged the existence of a Supreme Being and for his own part he received the sobriquet: *The Incorruptible*. Later, in a display of sanctimonious passion, he organized the 'Festival of the Supreme Being' (8 June 1794), in which, he took the role of "true priest of the Supreme Being." Then, by *playing the pubic saint*, he delivered a sermon to the people, explaining to them, "the relations between moral and religious ideas with republican principles." [4]

Robespierre's sister Charlotte confirmed that her brother ate only "a meagre breakfast of bread and milk. [...] He seems to have been almost completely uninterested in food, living mainly on bread, fruit and coffee." Consequently, apart from fruit, his meals were, as described in the oracle. [5]

Afterwards tyrannizing so many at a blow

On July 27, 1793, Maximilien Robespierre was elected to the Committee of Public Safety, formed to oversee the government with virtual dictatorial control. Faced with pressures both from the outside and from within, the Revolutionary government instituted the Reign of Terror in September. In the next 11 months, 300,000 suspected enemies of the Revolution were arrested and more than 17,000 were executed, most by guillotine. In the orgy of bloodshed, Robespierre was able to eliminate many of his political opponents. [6]

Putting with foot on the necks of the greatest ones

Robespierre "entered the Committee of Public safety on July 28, 1793 [...] and for one amazing year [...] was the real ruler of France."

It was while in this position of power that he was able to put his foot on the necks of the great ones. The following names bear tragic witness to the accuracy of this prophecy: Marie Antoinette (16 October); the Girondin leaders (31 October); the duc d'Orléans (6 November); Madame Roland (8 November); Jean-Sylvain Bailly (11 November), Antoine Barnave (29 November); Jacques Hébert (24 March); Georges Danton, Camille Desmoulins, Charles Delacroix, Fabre d'Églantine, Hérault de Séchelles (5 April). [7]

The prophetic expression used in this line also appears to offer a metonymy for 'putting the *blade* on the necks of the greatest ones'.

Summary: *Without naming Robespierre, the oracle provides detail after detail that applies to this man. Without exception, each of these details has been factually recounted by historians writing independently of their prophetic fulfilment. For the person who cannot see time as being anything other than a succession of fleeting moments, this prophecy, like all others, is impossible to comprehend. But from the vantage point of a Creator existing in eternity, its comprehension presents no obstacle.*

> 42   *Par auarice, par force & violence*
> *Viendra vexer les siens chefs d'Orleans,*
> *Prés sainct Memire assault & resistance,*
> *Mort dans sa tante diront qu'il dort leans.*

> 43   *Par le decide de deux choses bastars,*
> *Nepueu du sang occupera le regne,*
> *Dedans lectoyre seront les coups de dards*
> *Nepueu par peur pleira l'enseigne.*

decide (L decid\o) cut off, put an end to; choses (OF affaires) matters; dard (OF arme de trait); Dedans (*anagram & paragram*) Se[d]dan – Sedan; lectoyre (*anagram & paragram*) Le Torcey, *also dissimulation* – (L) electare, to coax or worm out

Through the ending of two illegitimate matters,   1848
A nephew of the blood will occupy the realm:
Within (**SEDAN**) a coaxing out: (**LE TORCEY**) there will be blows from bolts:
The nephew (**NAPOLEON III**), through apprehension, will fold his ensign.

Through the ending of two illegitimate matters

The first 'illegitimate matter', relevant to this oracle, began in February 1848 with an uprising in
Paris that ended Louis Philippe's reign, and with it, a thousand years of French monarchy.

> Hardly had Louis-Philippe left than the mob invaded the Tuileries, just as they had done in the
> last days of Louis XVI [...] France, and Paris, were taken totally by surprise by the events of
> February 1848. With 350 dead over three days, it was the least bloody uprising of the century. [1]

The republican government that replaced the King did nothing to resolve the plight of the poor
and unemployed. As a result, within months of the recent outbreak of rioting, a second wave of
violence erupted in the city.

> On 23 June, rioting began once more in Paris, and by the evening the whole eastern half of the
> city was in the hands of the insurrectionists [...] But this time the government was ready for
> trouble. General Louis-Eugène Cavaignac, Minister of War [...] attacked, deploying his artillery
> without compunction against the barricades. [...] Official figures – though these were almost
> certainly a gross underestimate – put deaths at 914 among the government troops and 1,435 for
> the insurgents. A police commissioner counted fifteen large furniture vans piled high with
> corpses; many were 'shot while escaping', or summarily executed in the quarries of Montmartre
> or the Buttes-Chaumont in eastern Paris. The Rue Blanche reeked with rotting cadavers hastily
> interred in the Montmartre cemetery [...] thousands were arrested and transported to the
> colonies, or to Algeria, without trial. [2]

A nephew of the blood will occupy the realm

With order restored, France's Second Republic tottered to its close. Fresh elections took place
and this brought a new candidate onto the scene—"A dark horse in the shape of Louis Napoleon
Bonaparte, nephew of Napoleon I." Backed by the provinces and middle class, he swept to victory
with five and half million votes.

Three years later in 1851, Louis Napoleon overthrew this newly created republic and declared
himself to be the 'Prince-President'. [3] On 2 December, one year after he made himself Prince-
President, Louis Napoleon proclaimed France to be the Second Empire: taking for himself, as its
ruler, the title: Emperor Napoleon III. [4]

His hold on the realm was to last three months short of eighteen years. Its end came in 1870 as
the result of a war in which, as his famous uncle had done before him, he miscalculated the limit
of his ability.

Within (Sedan) a coaxing out: (Le Torcey) there will be blows from bolts

The Franco-Prussian War began in July 1870, and continued into August with four major battles
being fought. On 1 September the battle of *Sedan* commenced, with Napoleon III having joined
his men in the engagement. Three relatively small clashes took place by the side of the River
Meuse on 29 and 30 August. Nevertheless, the outcome persuaded the French marshal, Patrice
Mac-Mahon to order his troops into Sedan, where refuge was offered inside the town's fifteenth-
century fortress.

> The only part which its defences played, or might have played, in the ensuing battle lay in the
> strategic possibilities of the fine and roomy bridge-head of Torcy, covering the elbow bend of the
> Meuse whence the whole French army might have been hurled between the German III. [5]

Hence, the French, having deprived themselves of Le Torcey's strategic advantage, were forced to
seek cover within Sedan. Unfortunately, inside the fortress Mac-Mahon received an injury. At
the same time, the Emperor Napoleon was himself suffering excruciating pain from gallstones. In
the absence of a single, efficient commander and with the continuous bombardment of shells

exploding around them from the Prussian artillery – *there will be blows from bolts* – the French army fell into disarray. The only course of action was for soldiers to seek shelter from the barrage of exploding shells wherever cover could be found. [6]

The nephew, through apprehension, will fold his ensign

At about 5 o'clock in the evening, Napoleon III (*the nephew* of Napoleon Bonaparte) realizing that the battle was lost, and through genuine *apprehension* for his men's safety, for they were being slaughtered at an alarming rate, *folded his ensign,* and replaced it with a white flag, which he hoisted above the citadel. He then informed King Wilhelm I – "Having been unable to die in the midst of my troops, there remains nothing for me but to deliver my sword into your Majesty's hands. I am Your Majesty's true brother, Napoleon."

On 2 September 1870, at about 11 o'clock, Napoleon III signed the document prepared by Bismarck acknowledging his personal surrender. [7] He was then removed from the field of battle and held as captive by his German victor. He was later released to seek asylum in England: his role as Emperor having ended in defeat.

Summary: *The reign of Napoleon III coincided with the lifetime of Anatole Le Pelletier, who conducted an exhaustive research into these prophecies at that time. The result of his scholarship was published in Paris in 1867, and subsequently became the source of a book published by Charles A. Ward in England, in 1891. Pelletier recognized his Emperor, Napoleon III, as the subject of this prophecy, at least three years before the Franco-Prussian War began. But because the war had yet to commence, he was unable to comprehend the final two lines of the quatrain, and could only refer to their content as an enigma, later to be understood. These last two lines are, of course, incomprehensible until after the event. Why should it be suspected that 'dedans' will point to Sedan? And what secret does the unknown word, 'lectoyre' conceal? One cannot escape the thought that this difficulty was intended to prevent Le Pelletier forewarning the effect of France's future war.*

44   *Le procreé naturel d'ogmion,*
       De sept à neuf du chemin destorner
       A roy de longue & amy au my hom,
       Doit à Nauarre fort de PAV prosterner.

45   *La main escharpe & la iambe bandée,*
       Longs puis nay de Calais portera,
       Au mot du guet la mort sera tardée,
       Puis dans le temple à Pasques saignera.

46   *Pol mensolée mourra trois lieuës du rosne,*
       Fuis les deux prochains tarasc destroys:
       Car Mars fera le plus horrible trosne,
       De coq & d'Aigle de France freres trois.

Pol mensolee (Medieval Latin Pol\ita mensol\is); mourra (Littré - Être sur le point de mourir) to be dying; Fuis (OF *anagram & paragram* [P]ius, *also* fuis (imperative) flee, escape; tarasc (Medieval Latin – tarasc\us)
Cross-references: aigle, C.I: 23; C.III: 37; C.IV: 70; C.VIII: 4; cock, C.II: 42

      (**PIUS**) Citizen, Southerner of France, will be dying three leagues from the Rhône, 1799
      Flee the two (**PIUSES**) neighbours: a fabulous monster destroyed (**BUCENTAURE**),
      Because Mars will make the most horrible throne
      For the Cock and for the Eagle: **THREE BROTHERS** for France.

Citizen, Southerner of France

After Napoleon's Army of Italy invaded Rome in February 1797, under the command of General Berthier, Rome was declared a republic. Pope Pius VI, although old and very ill, was nevertheless ordered by the Paris Directory to be removed from Rome. This led to him being taken on an extended journey that finally ended with his death inside the citadel at Valence in south-eastern France. [1] "His obituary in the local registry read: 'Name: Citizen John Braschi. Trade: pontiff.'" [1]

Will be dying three leagues from the Rhône

It was while stopping over for the night at a town called Romans, which is exactly three leagues from the river Rhône that the Pope's already fragile health drastically deteriorated.

The Pope produced a lot of blood without in the least acknowledging any further discomfort: the medicine prescribed for his paralysis having prevailed upon his interior. To conclude the course of this last illness, the pulse not conspicuous at all from fever but beating naturally with extreme faintness. [...] The steward charged with his conveyance, without heeding to the requests of the inhabitants of Romans, who were hoping very much that the Pope would pass the following day in the midst of them, had decided that the departure would take place the next day at the most convenient hour so as to avoid the tumultuous mob. The Holy Father was thus transported on the 14 July from Romans to Valence. (Report by L'Abbé Baldassari). [2]

Flee the two (Piuses) neighbours

Pius VII, who was elected pope after the death of Pius VI, also became a victim of the French Republic. And, as his predecessor had failed to do before him, Pius VII, too, failed to heed the Seer's warning and flee from Napoleon's rage. His downfall came as the result of his refusal to sign Bonaparte's new Concord. For this display of steadfast opposition to the Emperor of France and King of Italy he was exiled to Savona: to be kept there until he changed his mind.

By coincidence, Pius VII was born in Cesana in the Romagna: the same town in which his predecessor, Pius VI, was born. [3] Moreover, the Braschi and the Chiarmonti were "family friends": which is why the oracle refers to Pius VI and Pius VII as *the two neighbours*. [4]

A fabulous monster destroyed

The French flag ship, the *Bucentaure* (βουξ + κενταυροξ) – half ox and half man – is the *fabulous monster* referred to in this oracle. The ship was commanded by Admiral Villeneuve, who led the French and Spanish fleets against Nelson's British squadron off Cape Trafalgar in October 1805. But during the battle, the *Bucentaure* was raked by cannon shot from Nelson's ship *Victory*, and it took no further part in the action. An attempt to salvage the wrecked vessel was made after the fighting ceased, but this failed, and the ship was destroyed when it sank while being taken to Cadiz. [5]

Because Mars will make the most horrible throne

Mars, the mythological god of war and strife, is used in this oracle as a metonymy for the French revolutionary wars and those of Napoleon's era: conflicts that occupied France: from 1792, when it waged war against Austria, up until the final battle fought against Britain and Prussia in 1815. Between these years the throne of both Louis XVI and Napoleon I was deluged with blood.

For the Cock

As for the 'Cock', Louis XVI and Marie Antoinette were both guillotined in 1793, leaving the throne vacant for ten years, during that decade the French Revolutionary Wars and the guillotine accounted for the horror predicted at this time.

The Cock had become the symbol of France during its revolution, since the Latin word *'Gallus'* translates as either Gaul or a cock. It can therefore be understood to represent the French Republic after the fall of the monarchy (see also Century Two N°. 42). [6]

And for the Eagle

The throne then passed to Napoleon I and the age of Napoleonic Wars that was to last from 1803 until 1815, apart from a short break in 1814, when he was exiled to Elba. [7]

The Eagle was adopted by Napoleon as the symbol of his power. (Refer, Century One N°. 23; Century Three N°. 37, and Century Four N°. 70). [8]

Three brothers for France

The three brothers predicted for France were the three Kings who lived during this troubled period of French history. They were Louis XVI, who was guillotined during the French Revolution, his brother, Stanislas Xavier, duc de Provence, who fled France until returning after Napoleon's exile to became Louis XVIII, and their brother, the Comte d'Artois, another exile who succeeded to the throne in 1824 as Charles X. The three brothers were grandsons of Louis XV, whose own son died before he could inherit the Crown. [9]

Summary: *This oracle is packed with information relevant to the Papacy, the Crown and the years between 1792 and*
              1815. The captivity of two popes, whose family members were neighbours, the destruction of the French
              flagship, named after a fabulous monster, a reference to the throne during its most horrible period, the Cock
              and the Eagle as metonymies for France and Napoleon, and three royal brothers, who wore the crown and
              were affected by the conflicts of that age, all these came together to fulfil this prophecy.
              It is another unique prophecy that occurred just once, and was foretold to prove the existence of a superior
              and knowledgeable Creator—a divine spirit who likewise knows the future of everyone alive today.
              Three thousand years ago, King David realized the same truth when he asked, "Where can I go from your
              spirit? Where can I flee from your presence?" (Psalm 139)

47   *Lac Transmenien portera tesmoignage,*
      Des coniurez serrez dedans Perouse
      Vn despolle contrefera le sage,
      Tuant Tedesq de sterne & minuse.

48   *Saturne en Cancer, Iupiter auec Mars,*
      Dedans Feurier Caldondon saluaterre.
      Sault Castallon assaily de trois pars,
      Pres de Verbiesque conflit mortelle guerre.

49   *Saturn au beuf iouë en l'eau, Mars en fleiche,*
      Six de Feurier mortalité donra,
      Ceux de Tardaigne à Bruge si grand breche,
      Qu'à Pontereso chef Barbarin mourra.

50   *La pestilence l'entour de Capadille,*
      Vne autre faim pres de Sagone s'appreste:
      Le cheualier bastard de bon senille,
      Au grand de Thunes fera trancher la teste.

51   *Le Bizantin faisant oblation,*
      Apres auoir Cordube à soy reprinse:
      Son chemin long repos pamplation,
      Mer passant proy par la Colongna prinse.

52   *Le roy de Bloys Auignom regner,*
      D'Amboise & seme viendra le long de Lyndre
      Ongle à Poytiers sainctes aisles ruyner
      Deuant Boni[eux viendra la guerre esteindre.]

The first line is repeated from N°. 38 above. The fourth line was incomplete, consisting of two
words: 'Devant Boni.' The 19th century French scholar Anatole Le Pelletier discovered an
undated edition of the prophecies in which the words above, inserted in parenthesis, appear.

53   *Dedans Bologne voudra lauer ses fautes,*
      Il ne pourra au temple du soleil,
      Il volera faisant chose si hautes,
      En hierarchie n'en fut oncq vn pareil.

54   *Soubs la couleur du traicté mariage,*
      Fait magnanime par grand Chyren Selene,
      Quintin, Arras recouurez au voyage
      D'espagnols fait second banc macelin.

selin (Selene) the moon goddess; second (AF secont – selon) according to; macelin (AF macel), butchery, carnage; banc (AF)
bench *also* "banc *n.* the judges' bench: in banc, in banco in full court. [Fr.] refer, Chambers English Dictionary 1988.

          Beneath the shadow of the marriage treaty,   1559
          A magnanimous act by the great **HENRI SELENE**.
          SAINT-QUENTIN: ARRAS recovered with the voyage:
          Action by the Spanish, according to the carnage bench.

Beneath the shadow of the marriage treaty

The Treaty of Cateau-Cambrésis brought to an end the war between France's ruling family, the
House of Valois, and Philip II of Spain. Included among the Treaty's clauses were two marriage
arrangements. Spain was to be united to France by the marriage of King Philip to thirteen-year-

old Elisabeth de Valois, daughter of Henri II. Also, Emmanuel Philibert, Duke of Savoy would marry Henry II's sister, Marguerite, Duchess of Berry, aged thirty-six. The two weddings were to be celebrated in Paris by a tournament held in June. It was at this spectacle, on Friday 30 June 1559, *under the shadow of the marriage treaty* that Henri II was fatally injured while jousting. The lance of his opponent, Gabriel count of Montgomery, shattered upon impact, and the splinters penetrated the King's eye and head.

A magnanimous act

Lowering him to the ground, they removed his armour. They found the visor half open and his face soaked in blood with wooden splinters 'of a good bigness' protruding from the eye and temple. "The King was 'very weak' [...] almost benumbed [...] he moved neither hand nor fote, but laye as one amazed." Seeing this, his young opponent begged his sovereign that his head and his hands be cut off, but: 'The good natured King who for his kindness had no equal in his time answered that he was not angry [...] and that he had nothing to pardon, since he had obeyed his King and carried himself like a brave knight.' [1]

By the great Henri Selene

Diane de Poitiers was Henri II's long term mistress. At the fatal tournament, the King had worn her colours, black and white, in preference to those of the Queen. Diane possessed a sharp intellect and was so politically astute that King Henry II trusted her to write many of his official letters, and even to sign them jointly with the one name HenriDiane. [2] This form of signature, "HenriDiane" is reflected in the prophecy as "Chyren selin" or "Henri Selene".

Selene, The moon-goddess; sometimes, but improperly called Diana, as Diana is always called the chaste huntress; but Selene had fifty daughters by Endymion, and several by Zeus. [...] Selene is represented in a chariot drawn by two white horses; she has wings and a sceptre in her hand. [3]

Diane de Poitiers actively encouraged this connexion to Selene. A portrait of her as *Diana goddess of the hunt* was displayed in the bedroom of Francis I at the Château de Chenonceau. After his death, the castle was given to Diane by Henri II. Her choice for a personal emblem was three crescent moons entwined, emphasising her connexion to Selene.

Saint-Quentin

The city of Saint-Quentin in northern France was the scene of a disastrous French defeat on 10 August 1557. Spain's ally, Emmanuel-Philibert Duke of Savoy, invaded France from the north and seized Saint-Quentin. Two years later, after looting the city, it was "Given back to France in 1559, [whereupon] it underwent intense fortification work: the medieval wall was protected by many new advanced fortifications, redesigned several times." [4]

It was the French defeat at Saint-Quentin which brought Henri II to the negotiating table, and from which the Peace of Cateau-Cambrésis resulted.

Arras recovered with the voyage

Arras is the capital 'chef-lieu' of the Pas-de-Calais department. It is part of the Nord-Pas-de-Calais region, France's fourth most populous region. [5]
Although Calais is by far the largest city in Pas-de-Calais, the department's capital is its third-largest city of Arras. [6]

After the humiliation of defeat at Saint-Quentin, Henri II resolved to recapture Calais from the English. It had been won from France during the Hundred Years War.

The plans for the reduction of Calais being thus formed, several bodies of troops were detached on various pretences towards the frontiers, and a strong squadron of ships was ordered to cruise in the channel under the colour of annoying the trade in England. These precautions being taken, the several detachments suddenly assembled, and the duke of Guise marched at the head of the army towards Calais. The ships made the first attack on the risbank which guarded the entrance of the harbour; and during the cannonade, three thousand harquebusiers assaulted the castle of St Agatha, with so much fury, that the garrison, though they made a vigorous defence, were soon obliged to abandon the place, and retreat towards Newnam bridge, which was immediately besieged.[7]

"Lord Wentworth, the governor," upon seeing the impossibility of maintaining a defence of the city and having lost two hundred men after Guise had breached the castle wall, "capitulated to the duke of Guise, and delivered Calais into the hands of the French, after it having been for above two hundred years under the English government." (Ibid)

> By the Treaty of Cateau-Cambrésis (Apr 1559) Henry abandoned French claims in Italy, but kept the three Bishoprics , as well as Calais, which he had taken from Queen Mary of England in January 1558.[8]

Action by the Spanish according to the carnage bench

The judicial meaning of 'bench' is here implied. At the time in which the earlier part of this prophecy entered history, the Spanish Inquisition was operating—hence, the carnage bench. It had been operating since 1478, when it sat in judgement of heresy committed by *conversos*—Jews and Moslems who had been compelled by law to convert to the Catholic faith, but had later lapsed. Now, its new target was the elimination of Protestantism.

> The first trials against Lutheran groups, as such, took place between 1558 and 1562, at the beginning of the reign of Philip II, against two communities of Protestants from the cities of Valladolid and Seville numbering about 120. The trials signalled a notable intensification of the Inquisition's activities. A number of *autos-de-fé* were held, some of them presided over by members of the royal family and around 100 executions took place. The *autos-de-fé* of the mid-century virtually put an end to Spanish Protestantism. [...] After 1562, though the trials continued, the repression was much reduced.[9]

Summary: *This is another prophecy that foretells events that were to occur soon after the publication of this quatrain. It begins with the accidental death of Henri II, and his forgiveness of Count Montgomery (ignored by his wife, Catherine de' Medici – refer Century Three No. 30). It then refers back in time to the taking back of St Quentin and Calais, which had been lost to France, but were recovered by Henri before the publication of these oracles. The verse concludes with a condemnation of Spain's revival of its infamous heresy trials, in which those accused were tried before a bench of judges (the Inquisition) and, if guilty, were executed.*

55   *Entre deux fleuues se verra enserré,*
     Tonneaux & caues vnis à passer outre,
     Huict ponts rompus chef à tant enferré,
     Enfans parfaicts sont iugulez en oultre.

56   *La bande foible le tertre occupera*
     Ceux du haut lieu feront horribles cris,
     Le gros troupeau d'estre coin troublera,
     Tombe pres D. nebro descouuers les escris.

57   *De souldat simple paruiendra en empire,*
     De robe courte paruiendra à la lonque
     Vaillant aux armes en eglise ou plus pyre,
     Vexer les prestres comme l'eau faict l'esponge.

parvenir (OF atteindre le but) attain his end; vaillant (OF de grande valeur); esponge (AF homonym) sponge, *also* free arbitrator *or* free will (libre arbiter).

> From a simple soldier he will attain his end in empire,   1804
> From a short robe, he will attain to the long one,
> Valiant at arms: in church, where, much worse,
> Vexing the priests, as water does the sponge (**NAPOLEON**).

From a simple soldier

Napoleon Bonaparte began his military career as a second lieutenant stationed at Valence in the *Régiment de la Fère du corps royal d'artillerie.*[1]

He will attain his end in empire

It was later, through military action at Toulon and again in Paris that he came to the notice of the Directory. This led to his appointment as Commander-in-Chief of the Army of Italy. Thereafter, through a succession of victories in Italy, and later in Egypt, he secured the adoration of the French people. In November 1799, he sprang a *coup* to remove the corrupt Directory and seize control of the government as its Consul. Five years later, he was able to proclaim himself Emperor of the French. [2]

From a short robe, he will attain to the long one

Before the Revolution, '*Noblesse de Robe*' referred to magistrates who had attained their title of nobility through having bought or inherited it. By contrast, the short robe indicated a person who was not of that order. For good measure, the artist, Jacques-Louis David, when painting those present at Napoleon's coronation, showed the Emperor in a long robe. François Gérard also painted a portrait of Napoleon in his long coronation gown. [3]

Valiant at arms

The oracle correctly predicts Bonaparte's valour on the battlefield. Legends surrounded his victories, "and he encouraged it. The legend of Lodi, the legend of the Pyramids, the legend of St. Bernard, the legend of Marengo." [4]

In church, where, much worse

Despite Napoleon's achievements in government and on the battlefield, he was never able to repeat this success when dealing with the Church, except by force. In 1796 Pope Pius VI was compelled to bow to Napoleon's military supremacy and agree the terms set out in the Treaty of Tolentino. This cost the papacy the cities of Ferrara, and Bologna as well as a collection of very valuable manuscripts. Five years later, Pius VII, too, was forced into submission when he agreed under pressure to the Concordat of 1801. This required the papacy: "to accept the revolutionary reforms in clerical matters, including the abolition of tithes, the sale of church property and the suppression of many dioceses." (Sutherland). Eight years later, Bonaparte confiscated the papal territories completely, and exiled Pius VII because he refused to accede to their annexation. [5]

Vexing the priests

Bonaparte's "studies left him attached to a sort of Deism, an admirer of the personality of Christ, a stranger to all religious practices, and breathing defiance against 'sacerdotalism' and 'theocracy'."[6]. He believed a nation required religion, but he had no intention of allowing it to interfere with his ambitions. And his conflict with both Pope Pius VI and especially Pius VII bears adequate witness to this.

After Pius VII had languished for three years in exile at Savona, Bonaparte ordered the Pope to be brought to Fontainebleau. The Emperor had recently become irritated at his failure to obtain Pius' signature to an agreement he was preparing (the *Concordat of Fontainebleau*). The Pope's arrival failed to ease the situation. Instead, it began many long, drawn out periods of argument, in which Napoleon vexed the priests with his proposals, but which Pius steadfastly refused to consider. "Day after day cardinals, bishops, and state officials repeated in his ears arguments he had grown tired of refuting." [7]

As water does the sponge

"Sponges are multicellular organisms that have bodies full of pores and channels allowing water to circulate through them." Hence, vexing a sponge is to fill it with water and then squeeze it dry. Napoleon's favours, which he first bestowed upon the Church, and then later withdrew, provide the analogy.

> But it was Napoleon's desire that, in the new society which was the issue of the Revolution, the Church should have a place, and consciences should be set at rest. The Concordat with the Holy See was signed on 17 July, 1801; it was published, together with the Organic Articles, as a law, 16 April, 1802. The former of these two acts established the existence of the Church in France, while the other involved the possibility of serious interference by the State in the life of the Church. [8]

The Organic Articles were never accepted by the Church, and not long afterwards, Napoleon also began to disregard the Concordat by legalizing divorce. The distance between the Emperor and the Pope rapidly grew. And in February 1808, Bonaparte ordered the occupation of Rome, so that he could unite Italy under his rule. His next assault against the Pope occurred when he attempted to force Pius VII to sign a new Concordat: one which would grant greater powers to French bishops at Rome's expense. Pius's rejection of the new Concordat brought about his exile from Rome.

N.B. 'Esponge', in ancient French, means 'libre arbitre' (free arbitrator). Hence the sub-heading above could read, *as water does the free arbitrator*. In which case, the 'water' would then point to the palace of Fontainebleau, originally called by its fall name, *Fontaine Belle Eau*.

Summary: *This oracle takes the form of a short biographical snapshot of Napoleon Bonaparte's rise to power, from a simple soldier to Emperor. It correctly refers to his prowess on the battlefield, while contrasting it with his lack of success in spiritual and religious matters. There is particular reference to his vexatious attitude when confronting and then exiling Pius VII, in order to overcome his opposition to the 'Organic Articles', which he wished to impose upon the Church.*

58   *Regne en querelle aux freres diuisé,*
      Prendre les armes & le nom Britannique
      Tiltre d'Anglican sera tard aduisé,
      Surprins de nuict mener à l'air Gallique.

Prendre (AF se terminer) terminate; aduisé (AF aviser) endorse; nom (AF titre) title.

The kingdom in dispute with the brothers (**DAVID & ALBERT**) disunited,   1936
Terminating the armorial bearings and the British title,
The English title (**DUKE OF WINDSOR**) will be endorsed later,
At night, unexpectedly steering to the French air.

The kingdom in dispute

On 20 January 1936, King George V died, and a crisis hit the British monarchy. The King's eldest son, the Prince of Wales, known familiarly as David in royal circles, was the natural heir. Unfortunately, at least from his family's point of view, and the government's, he had met and subsequently fallen passionately in love with a twice-married American woman, Mrs. Wallace Simpson. This complicated matters, because England's heir to the throne intended to marry her: that is, as soon as the lady's second divorce had been legalized. A constitutional crisis followed, and one that placed *the kingdom in dispute*.

As King Edward VIII of England, and ruler of its remaining Empire, he would also be the Church of England's Defender of the Faith. This made his intended marriage to a divorcee unacceptable, for the Church's ruling forbade this type of remarriage. Moreover, according to tradition, Wallace Simpson, although having no aristocratic pedigree, would nevertheless become Queen of England if the marriage took place.

The British people at once began to take sides in their future King's affair, and the country; that is, the *kingdom*, became *divided* over the issue. "Small crowds gathered outside No. 10 waving placards inscribed 'Hands Off Our King' and 'Abdication Means Revolution'." But, Parliament and the Royal family remained true to the Christian faith. The King must renounce his intention to marry Wallace Simpson, or he must abdicate.[1]

With the brothers disunited

It was the fallout from this dispute that led to disunity between the two brothers, and "By the end of 1937, they were no longer on speaking terms."[2] Albert, was David's natural successor, but it was not a position that he relished occupying, or felt comfortable with. And when Edward VIII resolved to abdicate, rather than separate from the woman he loved, the ramifications led to a split between the brothers. Their quarrel began the same week in which the abdication took place, and concerned *disputes* involving the precise amount of the proposed financial settlement.

Terminating the armorial bearings and the British title

On 11 December 1936, Edward VIII publicly announced over the radio that he was abdicating, and passing the British title to his brother. The oracle refers to the British crown in terms of armorial bearings, that is, the Royal Coat of Arms; this accords with the custom in England, which was introduced in the reign of Queen Victoria. During her period of rule, the monarch increasingly became a figurehead of the State, rather than a decision-making office. The Royal Coat of Arms therefore came to represent the public face of the British monarchy. It is of some interest to note that by abdicating, which the King did on the day prior to his public announcement; Edward VIII became the only monarch ever to have voluntarily given up the crown of England. [3]

Previously, in July 1911, as the eldest son of George V, David had been invested with the title, 'Prince of Wales'. He retained this distinction until the death of his father, whereupon he became, "King of Great Britain and Ireland and British Dominions Overseas, Emperor of India." This was the official title by which he was known for the entire eleven months of his reign.

The English title will be endorsed later

After relinquishing the crown and the titles that went with it, David was given the title: 'Duke of Windsor'. This was endorsed by King George VI, on 12 December 1936, after all his non-English titles had expired or been removed. His new title was now, of course, wholly English. [4]

At night, unexpectedly steering to the French air

Edward was soon to be surprised at the rapid development of events following his abdication. He had expected to remain in England with Wallace Simpson at Fort Belvedere, near Sunningdale in Berkshire. The 18th century manor house had been a gift from his father George V, and he had renovated it and made it a home. But his popularity in the country contrasted too well against the nervousness of his younger brother, now King George VI; therefore, to avoid competition between these two among the population, England and Fort Belvedere were denied him.

Instead of enjoying married life in Berkshire, the duke of Windsor found himself unexpectedly ushered out of the country. He was escorted from his home at night, and put on board HMS Fury. The ship left Portsmouth harbour during the early hours of Saturday 12 December, steering for the French coast and the French air, with the former king about to begin the life of an exile. "For the next two years the duke and duchess lived mainly in France." [5]

Summary: This oracle is another that tracks the fortune of the English monarchy. The scandal attached to Edward VIII's succession to the throne, brought on by his insistence to marry the woman he loved, but who also happened to have been twice married before, rocked the nation at the time. It also caused friction within the House of Windsor, and even threatened to end the monarchical system in England. The seer points to key moments in Edward's abdication, which are easily recognizable, and help to identify the prophecy's true fulfilment.

59   Par deux fois haut, par deux fois mis à bas
        L'orient aussi l'occident foiblira
        Son aduersaire apres plusieurs combats,
        Par mer chassé au besoing faillira.

60   Premier en Gaule, premier en Romanie,
        Par mer & terre aux Anglois & Paris
        Merueillex faits par celle grand mesnie
        Violant, terax perdra le NORLARIS.

Romanie (L Roman\us) Rome, Romans; mesnie; (AF armée) army; terax (Gk Τερας *in the concrete sense*) a monster; Violant (L viol\o) to violate an agreement; NORLARIS (*portmanteau & paragram*) nor[d] + lar[r]is (OF) north + uncultivated land, *also* lariz (AF – tertre) hillock, *and, as an anagrammatic paragram,* Lorrain[e]. Cross reference; norlaris, C.IX: 50

                Foremost in France, foremost in Rome (**NAPOLEON**),   1804-15
                Through sea and land by the English, and Paris:
                Marvellous deeds by that great army:
                Violating an agreement, the monster will lose the north uncultivated hillock (**LORRAINE**)

Foremost in France, foremost in Rome

The prophecy commences by introducing Napoleon as the man who, in 1804, became foremost in France. [1] He had rejected the title of King because of its revolutionary connotation. Instead, he chose the title Emperor, thereby following the tradition of the Romans. After subjugating Rome, then declaring himself King of Rome, he demanded from Pius VII that he hand over the Papal States. By then, Bonaparte had obtained such "a concentration of power comparable only to that of the Roman Caesars, of Charlemagne and of the Holy Roman Emperors." [2]

Through sea and land by the English

Napoleon's reign in France was dominated by war at sea and on land. He was opposed militarily, principally by the English: a nation that quickly became his chief adversary.

The War of the Second Coalition, led by the English, involved the battle of the Pyramids (21 July 1798); the Nile (1 August 1798); Marengo (14 June 1800), and Hohenlinden (3 December 1800). The War of the Third Coalition, again led by the English, involved battles at Ulm (20 October 1805), Trafalgar (21 October 1805), and Austerlitz (2 December 1805). The War of the Fourth Coalition, also led by the English, involved the battles of Jena and Auerstedt (14 October 1806), Eylau (8 February 1807), and Friedland (14 June 1807). Between 1808 and 1815 Napoleon's occupation of Spain and Portugal resulted in the Peninsula War, in which Wellington led a coalition of English, Spanish and Portuguese that slowly drove the French back across the Pyrenees. [3]

And Paris

After so many years of opposition from the English, by land and sea, the final overthrow of Napoleon came with the fall of Paris. In the third week of March 1814, Russian troops entered the suburbs of the capital from the east. Napoleon had made a brave and strategic defence of the city. "But no amount of skill could do more than postpone defeat." By the last day of the month, Paris was forced to capitulate. Inside the city, Talleyrand's "opportunity had come to free France from the tyranny of Napoleon. [...] On the morning of the 31st [...] he drafted a Declaration, which was approved by Alexander and published the same night." This confirmed the occupation of Paris by allied forces, and that no negotiations with Napoleon would be undertaken.

On 6 April, Bonaparte, while still resident at Fontainebleau and having found himself without support, "signed an unconditional abdication." [4]

> On a beautiful spring day, 31 March, the victorious Allies had marched into Paris led by the Cossacks of the Imperial Guard. [...] Military grandees, bearing white cockades of the Bourbons on their hats, pranced down on horseback to meet them. [...] By now thoroughly disenchanted with Paris and its inhabitants, a censorious Stendhal recorded the 'fickle delight' with which the Parisian crowd greeted its conquerors. The almost universal enthusiasm struck some as positively indecent. [5]

Marvellous deeds by that great army

"La Grande Armée – Officially came into existence in September 1805." The marvellous deeds accomplished by it are well known.

> The *Grande Armee* was the trenchant instrument with which Napoleon reshaped both Europe and the art of war. Swift marching, furious in the attack, grimly enduring, high-hearted, stubborn in disaster, it still ranks among the few greatest of the great. It also was many men of many different nations - many heroes, not a few cowards, and the multitude who were neither but did their duty as they saw it. Probably no armies in all history have fought such a variety of enemies in so short a space of time as did the French soldiers under Napoleon Bonaparte. –
>
> *Colonel John Elting, US Army* [6]

Its end came "After Napoleon had sacrificed the whole of the Grande Armée in Russia in 1812, abandoning its shattered remnants as he scurried home to a disbelieving and restive Paris." And with its end came another defeat in October 1813, in the Battle of Nations at Leipzig, "in the bloodiest encounter Europe would know until 1914." [7] Bonaparte's abdication and his exile to Elba came less than six months later, with the fall of Paris.

Violating an agreement
"The Treaty of Fontainebleau, signed on April 12th by the representatives of Russia, Austria Prussia, and France (but not England), provided for the future of the deposed Bonapartes." A clause in this *agreement* stipulated: – "For Napoleon the island of Elba was to 'form during his lifetime a separate principality which he shall possess in full sovereignty and property.'" [8] But Bonaparte violated the agreement by escaping from his exile on Elba as soon as the opportunity arose. [9]

The monster will lose the north uncultivated hillock (Lorraine)
Napoleon's covetousness for empire and his reputation as a conqueror had by the time of his exile earned him the widely known sobriquet of *'Ogre'*, or *'the Corsican Ogre'*. This "image lingered well into the Victorian period. English mothers, for instance, reputedly chastened their recalcitrant offspring with the dire threat that 'Boney will come and get you.'" [Confirmed by the author's Victorian great-grandmother]. [10]

The end of Napoleon's reign came on 18 June 1815, at the Battle of Waterloo. Wellington had positioned his army of British and allied forces on the Mont-Saint Jean escarpment – the oracle refers to it as *larris*, which is old French for uncultivated land, while *lariz* is ancient French for a hillock. The oracle also places it in the *north*, particularly citing it as an anagram of *Lorraine*.

> Mont-Saint-Jean is a hamlet located in the province of Walloon Brabant, Belgium, south of Waterloo [...] Mont-Saint-Jean is on the reverse slope of the escarpment where the Battle of Waterloo was fought, and is the name Napoleon Bonaparte gave to the battle (*la bataille de Mont-Saint-Jean*). [11]

Lorraine was not always part of France. In the 9th century, Charlemagne divided his empire into three parts, Lorraine, like today's Luxembourg, Holland and Belgium, was situated in part of the middle Empire, between France in the west and Germany in the east. This middle section of the Carolingian empire was bequeathed to Charlemagne's grandson Lothair, and was thus known as Lotharingia, which has given us the modern name Lorraine. [12]

> Wallonia is the predominantly French speaking southern region of Belgium. It is governed as the Walloon Region, which makes up 55% of the territory of Belgium. [13]

Summary: *This oracle spreads itself across the reign of Napoleon Bonaparte. It commences at the pinnacle of his career, signalling the fact that he was Emperor of the French and King of Italy. It concludes by indicating its end in Paris, having been brought about, principally, by the English. In between his rise and fall, the oracle correctly identifies the part played by Napoleon's Grand Army. The prophecy ends with a telegraphic use of words: which, nevertheless, does well to identify the location of where the Battle of Waterloo was fought. It even indicates Napoleon, by referring to his well-known nickname of the Corsican Ogre.*

61   *Iamais par le descouurement du iour*
         Ne paruiendra au signe sceptrifere
         Que tous ses sieges ne soient en seiour,
         Portant au coq don du TAG amifere.

62   *Lors qu'on voirra expiler le saint temple*
         Plus grand du rosne leurs sacrez profaner:
         Par eux naistra pestilence si ample.
         Roy fuit iniuste ne fera condamner.

63   *Quand l'adultere blessé sans coup aura*
         Meurdry la femme & le fils par despit,
         Femme assoumée l'enfant estranglera:
         Huict captifs prins, s'estouffer sans respit.

64   *Dedans les Isles les enfans transportez,*
         Les deux de sept seront en desespoir:
         Ceux de terroüer en seront supportez,
         Nom pelle prins des ligues fuy l'espoir.

deux (Cassells French Dictionary) second (of the month); sept (L sept\em) from which we get Septem[ber]; terroüer (Middle Ages - terrouer) soil plotter; pelle (AF *dissimulation* pel) lance, boar-spear; prins (OF) apprehended

Within the (**BRITISH**) Isles, the children transported (**EVACUATED**),   1939
The second of September, they will be in despair.
Those of the soil plotters will be supported within,
Title spear apprehended (**GRAF SPEE**), the hope of the confederacies gone.

Within the Isles, the children transported

The Isles is a term which the seer has frequently applied to the British Isles in the past, and the present case is no exception. At the outbreak of the Second World War, children living in the major towns and cities of England and within range of German bombers were, quite literally, transported: either across the sea to America, to Canada, to South Africa, or else by rail to remote rural locations in mainland Britain.

> 1939: London, 3 September. The mass evacuation of children from cities to the reception areas considered safe from air attacks has been proceeding for three days. By tonight nearly 1,500,000 will have been moved. [1]

The second of September, they will be in despair

War between England and Germany was declared on 3 September 1939. The oracle, however, refers to the day before; that is, 2 September. It was on this day that the British Parliament waited in despair for a reply to their ultimatum sent to Hitler. If the German Chancellor failed to concede to proposals made in the government's compromise formula, war would be inevitable. "September 2 [...] The Cabinet met that afternoon without Churchill. Its members were unanimous that an ultimatum should be sent to Germany, to expire at midnight." But, the German Chancellor ignored Neville Chamberlain's offer of peace, and a state of war was declared between the two countries next morning. [2]

Those of the soil plotters will be supported within

With children from the big cities evacuated, their parents and the people who remained behind were now left as targets for aerial bombing. Government support was therefore offered to every household in the form of an underground shelter: nicknamed, collectively, as dugouts. For those living in apartments (blocks of flats) a communal shelter was built underground, close by, but with brick sides above ground, and a thick concrete slab on top for cover; fatal to all inside if the shelter suffered a direct hit.

The need for these dugouts had been anticipated some months earlier. On 5 April 1939, the British House of Commons was told by the minister in charge that 279,435 shelters for use underground had already been delivered to houses in the city, giving cover for one and a half million people, and another 80,000 were being made weekly. Since February 1939, these Anderson shelters (named after the Home Secretary) had been delivered to homes within the metropolitan boroughs of London and other provincial towns and cities thought to be at risk. In order to erect an underground shelter ...

> one began by digging a hole 7ft. 6in. long by 6ft. wide [...] to a depth of 4ft. into which were inserted six curved steel sheets, bolted together at the top to form an arch. At either end were flat steel plates. [...] Outside, an Anderson had to be covered with at least fifteen inches of earth. [3]

Once a plot of ground in the house owner's garden had been chosen, the soil would be removed and the shelter erected in the hole 'dug out'. This gave some protection for those sheltering against the possibility of a bomb exploding nearby.

Title, spear, apprehended

In the same year, on 13 December 1939, whilst on patrol in the South Atlantic, three British cruisers apprehended the German battleship *Admiral Graf Spee*. What followed became known as the battle of the River Plate, and it resulted in serious damage being inflicted upon the German battleship, causing it to dock and seek repairs

After taking temporary refuge in Montevideo, the *Graf Spee* was expelled by the Uruguayan government, and the ship was forced to return to sea. In wait was a British cruiser squadron under the command of Commodore Harwood. On 17 December, under orders from Hitler, the German commander, Admiral Langsdorff scuttled the *Graf Spee* rather than face defeat. [4]

Quite often within these oracles, the final line of a quatrain has been is deliberately written in a cryptic mode. Once an explanation has been given, all becomes clear. *Graf* in the German language is a *title* of nobility, comparable to *Comte* in French, or *Earl* in English. *Speer*, on the other hand, is the German word for 'spear'. Hence, *Admiral Graf Spee* is equivalent to 'title' 'spear' in English, which can then be translated cryptically into French as *Nom pel*.

The hope of the confederacies gone
The oracle concludes by predicting that the treaties and alliances formed after the First World War, and which were designed to prevent further warfare breaking out, would prove ineffective; that is, *the hope of the confederacies gone*. Between 1925 and 1939 there were at least ten pacts or peace treaties made between the major countries of Europe. [5] Yet, despite the hope these had initially held for peace, none were sufficient to avert the world war that broke out in 1939.

Summary: *The events predicted in this oracle were all fulfilled during the beginning of the Second World War. The 'transportation' of children in the British Isles implies the existence of a reason. Aerial bombing was the reason, but impossible to envisage when the prophecy was written four centuries earlier. Yet, the very next line states the month and the day when this prophecy would become history. There is also a reference to those in the affected districts who were left behind; they would be provided with their own means of support. The final line refers to the failure of the peace treaties that existed to prevent war, and to the encounter between ships of the Royal Navy and the Admiral Graf Spee, which is cryptically named.*

65   *Le vieux frustré du principal espoir,*
         Il paruiendra au chef de son empire:
         Vingt mois tiendra le regne à grand pouuoir,
         Tiran, cruel en delaissant vn pire.

empire (AF) jurisdiction; Tiran (AF tyran) tyrant; delaissant (AF delaissier) to hand over

The old man (**PÉTAIN**) disappointed with his principal hope,   1940
He will attain to the head of his dominion:
Twenty months he will hold authority with great force:
Tyrant, through relinquishing to one worse (**DARNAND**).

The old man
Henri Philippe Benoni Omer Joseph Pétain (24 April 1856 – 23 July 1951), otherwise known as Marshal Philippe Pétain, was 84 years old in 1940, when he was appointed Premier of France by President Lebrun at Bordeaux. He therefore ranks as France's oldest head of state.

Disappointed with his principal hope
"On 5 June, following the fall of Dunkirk [...] Prime Minister Reynaud brought Pétain, Weygand, and the newly promoted Brigadier-General de Gaulle [...] into his War Cabinet." [1] Throughout the month of June, the government discussed the future of France in the light of the German invasion. The question was whether or not to negotiate an armistice with Germany. Pétain believed this to be the only hope for France, and argued for its acceptance.

> Several ministers were still opposed to an armistice, and Weygand immediately lashed out at them for even leaving Paris. Like Pétain, he said he would never leave France. [...] Reynaud proposed an alternative compromise: Complete surrender, and the army (after laying down its arms) to leave the country and continue the fight from abroad. Weygand exploded and he and Pétain both said that such a capitulation would be dishonourable. The Cabinet was now split almost evenly. Camille Chautemps said the only way to get agreement was to ask the Germans what their terms for an armistice would be and the cabinet voted 13 – 6 in agreement. [2]

On the next day, the French government received two setbacks: each damaging to their decision to seek an armistice agreement with Germany: both were to add to Pétain's disappointment.

From America, President Roosevelt wrote to Reynaud admitting that he could do nothing without the agreement of Congress. Britain replied that it would only agree to an armistice "if the French fleet was immediately sent to British ports. In addition, the British Government offered joint nationality for Frenchmen and Englishmen in a Franco-British Union." [3]

This caused a rift in the French government. "Reynaud and five ministers thought these proposals acceptable. The others did not, seeing the offer as insulting and a device to make France subservient to Great Britain, in a kind of extra Dominion." [4]

The result of this difference in opinion was that Reynaud resigned as Prime Minister, and Pétain was appointed Chief of State so that he could commence negotiations with Germany for an armistice agreement.

> Adolf Hitler had a number of reasons for agreeing to an armistice. He wanted to ensure that France did not continue to fight from North Africa, and he wanted to ensure that the French Navy was taken out of the war. In addition, leaving a French government in place would relieve Germany of the considerable burden of administering French territory, particularly as he turned his attentions toward Britain. Finally, as Germany lacked a navy sufficient to occupy France's overseas territories, Hitler's only practical recourse to deny the British use of them was to maintain France's status as a supposedly independent and neutral nation. [5]

Consequently, the armistice negotiations did not go as Pétain had hoped. Hitler was intent upon humiliating the French in the same manner that France had humiliated Germany after the First World War. The negotiations were held at the same location, and even in the same railway carriage that was used in 1918.

> The armistice terms imposed on France were harsher than those imposed on Germany in 1918. They provided for German occupation of three-fifths of France north and west of a line through Geneva, Tours and the Spanish border so as to give the German Navy access to all French Channel and Atlantic ports. All persons who had been granted political asylum had to be surrendered and all occupation costs had to be borne by France, to the tune of 400 million French francs a day. [...] The French delegation – led by General Charles Huntziger – tried to soften the harsher terms of the armistice, but [General Wilhelm] Keitel replied that they would have to accept or reject the armistice as it was. Given the military situation that France was in, Huntziger had "no choice" but to accede to the armistice terms. [6]

He will attain to the head of his dominion

On 10 July 1940, the armistice agreement was ratified. On the day following, Pétain formally assumed near-absolute powers as "Head of State" with authority to rule Vichy France; "officially the French State (*État français*), was the government during the regime of Marshal Philippe Pétain, during France's occupation by Nazi Germany during World War II. From 1940 to 1942, though it was officially the government of France as a whole, Vichy only fully controlled the unoccupied zone (*zone libre*) in Southern France, while Germany occupied Northern France." [7]

Twenty months he will hold authority

Pétain's hold on power lasted from 10 July 1940 up until 18 April 1942. If we count the complete number of months that elapsed between these two dates, we arrive at twenty months. "When, in April 1942, the Germans forced Pétain to take Laval back as premier, he himself withdrew into a purely nominal role." [8]

Pétain had previously dismissed Laval in December 1940, because of his advocacy for increased collaboration with Germany. Consequently, by reinstating him, Petain became viewed by most people as a puppet of the Third Reich.

With great force

Despite Pétain's short time in power,

> His regime soon took on clear authoritarian—and in some cases, fascist—characteristics. The republican motto of '*Liberté, égalité, fraternité*' was replaced with '*Travail, famille, patrie*' ('Work, family, fatherland'). He issued new constitutional acts which abolished the presidency, gave him full power to appoint and fire ministers and civil service members, pass laws through the

Council of Ministers, indefinitely adjourned parliament and designate a successor (he chose Laval). By January 1941 Pétain possessed almost all legislative, executive, and judicial power; one of his advisors commented that he had more power than any French leader since Louis XIV. [9]

Tyrant

As soon as it had been established, Pétain's government took measures against the so-called "undesirables": Jews, métèques (immigrants), Freemasons, Communists — inspired by Charles Maurras' conception of the "Anti-France", or "internal foreigners", which Maurras defined as the "four confederate states of Protestants, Jews, Freemasons and foreigners" — but also Gypsies, homosexuals, and, in a general way, any left-wing activist. Vichy imitated the racial policies of the Third Reich and also engaged in natalist policies aimed at reviving the "French race", although these policies never went as far as the eugenics program implemented by the Nazis. [10]

The new government [also] used its new powers to order harsh measures, including the dismissal of republican civil servants, the installation of exceptional jurisdictions, the proclamation of anti-Semitic laws, and the imprisonment of opponents and foreign refugees. Censorship was imposed, and freedom of expression and thought were effectively abolished with the reinstatement of the crime of "felony of opinion." [11]

Cruel through relinquishing to one worse

The appointment of Joseph Darnand caused Petain to relinquish his overall control of the Vichy regime. "In joining the SS, Darnand took a personal oath of loyalty to Adolf Hitler, receiving a rank of *Sturmführer* (Lieutenant) in the Waffen SS in August 1943. In December 1943, he became head of police and later secretary of the interior." [12]

The police in Vichy France proceeded to round up those considered to be decadent. The police helped the Germans round up Jews who were sent east to the death camps. [13] Within six months, 60,000 non-French citizens had been interned in thirty concentration camps that had sprung up in France with alarming speed and efficiency. [14]

Summary: *This oracle proceeds from the one before, by foretelling the situation that developed after the occupation of Paris, during the Second World War. France became a divided country with the aged Marshall Petain having been given authority to rule the Vichy government in 'free France', but under the watchful eye of Hitler. As it has done so many times before, the oracle foresees the thoughts and activities of the person who is the subject of this prophecy, despite the four centuries that intervene. Not only were the events predicted fulfilled, but the exact number of months that Petain would occupy his role as chief was also correctly foretold.*

66   *Quand l'escriture D. M. trouuée,*
        Et caue antique à lampe descouuerte,
        Loy, Roy & Prince Vlpian esprouuée,
        Pauillon Royne & Duc sous la couuerte.

67   *PAR. CAR. NERSAF, à ruine grand discorde,*
        Ne l'vn ne l'autre n'aura election,
        Nersaf du peuple aura amour & concorde,
        Ferrare, Collonne grande protection.

68   *Vieux Cardinal par le ieune deceu,*
        Hors de sa charge se verra desarmé,
        Arles ne monstres double soit aperceu,
        Et Liqueduct & le Prince embaumé.

monstres (OF) disclosures; aperceu (AF connaître) understood; Liqueduct (*portmanteau*) Lique\sco + duct\or, also (L paragram) l'aquaduct\io.

The aged Cardinal (**RICHELIEU**) deceived by the young man (**CINQ MARS**),   1642
Outside of his employment, he will see himself disarmed,
Arles, no disclosures: the duplicate well and truly understood,
The leader wasting away (**LED BY WATER**), also the Prince (**LOUIS XIII**) embalmed.

The aged Cardinal

When nearing the end of his life, Cardinal Richelieu − by then an *aged cardinal* − appointed a young man, Henri Coiffier de Ruzé Marquis de Cinq-Mars, as a personal attendant to Louis

XIII. Cinq-Mars was just 17 years of age, but so successful was this arrangement that by the age of 21 he had risen to the office of King's Grand Écuyer (Master of the Horse). It was a position that entitled him to be addressed as Monsieur le Grand; and his appetite for further advancement was whetted. But Richelieu's response to any further advancement was dismissive.

Deceived by the young man

Louis XIII's brother, Gaston d'Orléans, was always on the lookout for resentment against Richelieu and he saw in Cinq-Mars fertile ground for yet another plot aimed at ending the Cardinal's influence over the King. Together with the duc de Bouillon, M. Le Grand was drawn into a devious plot of deception and betrayal against Richelieu, which also contained a plan for military intervention by Spain. [1]

Outside of his employment, he will see himself disarmed

At Narbonne, where Louis XIII was a guest of the Archbishop, a message was secretly conveyed to Cinq-Mars urging him to flee, as the plot he was involved in had been uncovered and his life was now in great danger.

The young conspirator lost no time in leaving his employment. In great haste, he hurried outside, making for the city gates, but found them barred. In desperation, he sought refuge in a farm worker's cottage where the occupant's two nieces were living, and with one of whom he had recently been intimately acquainted. But his effort to escape was short-lived. The owner returned unexpectedly, having heard the commotion caused by the search. Cinq-Mars's whereabouts was quickly made known, and he was arrested and *disarmed* by the guards who had been hastily summoned by the farmer to his cottage. [2]

The disarming of Cinq-Mars is not without further interest, because the young captive made a big issue about giving up his sword. This weapon was part of a gentleman's attire: without it, those in the street would quickly recognize his disgrace. "'Let me at least keep my sword as we pass through the streets,' begged the proud Frenchman." [3] And the sword was returned to him.

Arles, no disclosures

The plot to assassinate Richelieu and then ally Spain with France had been uncovered while examining Spain's diplomatic box. Inside was a secret document that revealed the conspirators' intentions. It had been written in the form of a treaty between those named in the plot and the Spanish government.

After its discovery the document was replaced, but not before a duplicate had been made. The Secretary of State, Chavigny, then sent the copy to Arles. [4] But at Arles, it was decided the conspiracy should not be disclosed until the text had been thoroughly examined, and a properly formed case had been made against the conspirators.

The duplicate well and truly understood

Silence was therefore maintained as Richelieu began completing a court case against de Bouillon, Cinq-Mars and his friend de Thou. Once the duplicate was well and truly understood, a charge of treason was brought against the three conspirators. [5] The King's brother again evaded arrest.

The leader wasting away, led by water

At the time of Cinq-Mars betrayal, Richelieu was fifty-seven, and the years had taken their toll. France's leader was wasting away. "His body devoured by rodent ulcers, one of which paralysed his right arm; parchment faced, wasted to a skeleton, he seemed to be living by will-power alone." [6]

It was because of his failing health that the Cardinal decided it would ease his discomfort if he travelled from Arles to Lyons for the forthcoming trial, using the French waterways. In preparation for the trip: "His Eminence lay in a bed hung with purple taffeta. Before him, went a little boat to mark the fairway, and immediately behind it a boatload of arquebusiers and their officers." [7]

We may now take note of the oracle's ingenious use of the word *liqueduct*. This single hybrid word has allowed information to be conveyed that relates to both the Cardinal's means of travel; that is, "led by water", and the poor state of his health, "wasting away". He died in Paris on 4 December 1642, eighty-three days after the execution of Cinq Mars.

Also, the prince embalmed

Louis XIII died five months later, on 14 May 1643. Throughout his reign he had relied upon others to rule in his name. "His reign can be studied under the names of those who ruled for him – Marie de Medici, Luynes, Richelieu." In this sense he was more Prince than King. [8]
In Century Nine N°. 18, Louis XIII is described as 'the Man from Dauphiné', rather than King. There is also a further, interesting fact about Louis XIII's death. Before his interment, the body was so carefully embalmed that when his coffin was smashed open one hundred and fifty years later, during the French Revolution, his remains were discovered to be still in a remarkably good state of preservation (refer Century Seven N°. 14).

Summary: *This prophecy involves the connexion between two members of Louis XIII's court: Cardinal Richelieu and Cinq-Mars. The former of the two was by then, old, and nearing the end of his time in office. Cinq-Mars, on the other hand, was still a young man with ambition to secure a higher position at court. Lured by the promises made to him by the King's brother, his betrayal is foretold in this oracle. The death of Richelieu soon after the execution of Cinq-Mars, and then followed by the death of Louis XIII, together make a noteworthy conclusion to this oracle.*

       69   *Aupres du ieune se vieux Ange baisser,*
               Et le viendra sur monter à la fin:
               Dix ans esgaux aux plus vieux rabaisser,
               De trois deux l'vn huictiesme Seraphin.

       70   *Il entrera vilain, meschant, infame,*
               Tyrannisant la Mesopotamie:
               Tous amis faict d'adulterine dame:
               Terre horrible noir de phisonomie.

entrer (OF) to step in; meschant (OF) wicked; Mesopotamie (Mesopotamia) Modern-day Iraq.

       He will step in, villainous, wicked, infamous,   1979
       Tyrannising Iraq (**SADDAM HUSSEIN**)
       Everyone made friends of the adulterine lady (**STATUE OF LIBERTY**):
       The land horrible, black in aspect.

He will step in

Although of peasant upbringing, [1] by 1968, Saddam Hussein had managed to achieve the first of his ambitions: that of leading the Ba'ath Socialists. He was also involved in a *coup* that brought the Party back to power under the presidency of Ahmad Hassan al-Bakr. When al-Bakr resigned in 1979, Hussein stepped in to occupy the seat of power in Iraq.

Villainous, wicked

Saddam Hussein joined the Ba'th Socialist Party in 1957 aged 20. It took just two years before he committed the first of his many infamous acts; this was the attempted assassination of the Iraqi Prime Minister, Abdal-Karim Qasim.
After taking power in Iraq, Hussein set about suppressing all opposition to his rule. To achieve this, he used an extensive secret police operation. The incarceration, torture and disappearances of his political opponents was the result.

[He] put on trial his former communist associates in the government, twenty-two of whom were executed [...] [I]n April 1980 he ordered the Shia Ayatollah and his sister to be hanged. [...] "I knew then just how dangerous the Ba'ath party was," Dr Shal-am explained: – "I had seen what had happened to Iraqi soldiers who had deserted their posts during the American invasion. They had their ears cut off. And those who spoke against Saddam usually had their tongues cut out." [2]

Infamous, tyrannising Iraq

There is no doubt that Saddam Hussein was guilty of tyrannising Iraq. "Saddam's government repressed movements that it deemed threatening, particularly those of ethnic or religious groups that sought independence or autonomy." [3] Many thousands of Iraqis were murdered under his infamous regime, and it was only after he had been overthrown in 2003, that their unmarked graves began to be unearthed. "The Kurds and other non-Arabs living in the North were subjected to Iraq's worst instance of minority persecution in 1987-89. [...] Anywhere from 100,000 to 182,000 were massacred in a genocidal offensive." [4]

Everyone made friends

In August 1990, Saddam Hussein took a step too far when he embarked upon an invasion of Kuwait. The United States objected to the attack, and from then onwards, President George H. W. Bush headed a United Nations campaign against Saddam Hussein's aggression. Unwisely, the Iraqi leader ignored the warnings, resolutions and deadlines set by the U.N. and this led directly to the Persian Gulf War, which commenced, 16 January 1991.

From that moment onwards, Iraq found itself under attack from every direction, and from every major country in the world. Gathered behind the US and offering it their total support were: Argentina, Australia; Belgium; Bulgaria; Canada; Czechoslovakia; Denmark; Finland; France; Germany; Greece, Hungary; Italy; Japan; Luxembourg; Netherlands; New Zealand; Norway; Philippines; Poland; Portugal; Romania; Saudi Arabia; Sierra Leone Singapore; South Korea; Spain; Sweden; Turkey; United Kingdom; USSR, and the United Arab Emirates. *Everyone*, it seemed, had *made friends* with the United States in its campaign against Saddam Hussein. [5]

Of the adulterine lady

Why, then, has the US been called an *adulterine lady?* The adjective refers to an adulterous relationship; it is also one that has been used in the Bible for the same purpose, which is that of defining countries that renege on political agreements in order to unite with another country. In the present case, the US had earlier formed a close alliance with Iraq: to the extent of supporting Saddam's war against Iran. It later abandoned this association after an estimated million people lost their lives. Instead, it formed a new relationship with Kuwait: Iraq's enemy.

> The US restored formal relations with Iraq in November 1984, but the US had begun, several years earlier, to provide it with intelligence and military support (in secret and contrary to this country's official neutrality) in accordance with policy directives from President Ronald Reagan. [...] [O]n December 20, 1983, Donald Rumsfeld [...] the US Secretary of Defence, met with Saddam Hussein during the first of Rumsfeld's two now-famous visits to Baghdad. [6]

Furthermore, "The White House and State Department pressured the Export-Import Bank to provide Iraq with financing, to enhance its credit standing and enable it to obtain loans from other international financial institutions. The US Agriculture Department provided taxpayer-guaranteed loans for purchases of American commodities, to the satisfaction of US grain exporters." [7] However, in 1990, the US deserted Iraq in order to join forces with other nations in attacking its former associate in what became known as the Persian Gulf War.

> Vowing to free Kuwait, Bush rallied the United Nations, the U.S. people, and Congress and sent 425,000 American troops. They were joined by 118,000 troops from allied nations. After weeks of air and missile bombardment, the 100-hour land battle dubbed Desert Storm routed Iraq's million-man army. [8]

America's abandonment of Hussein, and thereafter joining forces with Kuwait, at war with Iraq, explains why the oracle refers to the country as adulterine, [9] but not why it is called a *lady.*

That reason abides with the female colossus standing on Liberty Island in Upper New York Bay, and which is known throughout the world as the Statue of Liberty. It is a symbol, uniquely and proudly representing the United States of America.

For the oracle to have designated this female figure as a personification of the country, with which it has become uniquely associated, is not without precedent. The same symbolic strategy was used for Britain in order to personify Britannia – 'the dame of antiquity' – with the British people (refer Century Two N°s. 51 and 53). "It was perhaps Athena, Greek goddess and wise warrior-queen who set the pattern for the powerful female figures who, like Britannia, personify the traits and characteristics of the nations they represent." [10] For Britannia, no less for the Statue of Liberty, both *ladies* represent the people of the nation that adopted them.

The land horrible, black in aspect

In the aftermath of operation Desert Storm: the name given to the UN-led invasion against Iraq, the country was laid waste over a six week period (January and February of 1991). The amount of destruction was appalling—the land was horrible to witness, said one United Nations observer who saw the devastation: declaring it to be "far worse than anything one could have imagined."

To add to the scene of desolation, and with the intention of preventing the occupying army from accessing Iraq's fuel supply, Saddam Hussein ordered the firing of seven hundred oil wells. Thereafter, the skies over Kuwait remained darkened as the thick black smoke from the burning oil covered the country and cut out the light from the sun. This blackened aspect covered the land and lingered on for up to three months afterwards. [11]

Summary: *At the time of writing, the ultimate fate of Iraq remains in the balance. The oracle has correctly traced a broad outline of Saddam Hussein's power in Iraq, up until the time of his defeat by the US led coalition. Century Three No. 61 also referred to Iraq under the reign of Hussein, and Century Ten No. 72 has an even more disconcerting prophecy involving Iraq's future. Yet, the real lesson contained in this prophecy, as with the others, is that a person's freewill is not unknown outside the temporal dimension in which it is exercised. It has consequences, all of which are known to the Creator of the universe. When democracy works for the people, it will be a time when elected politicians finally understand their commitment to a vastly greater intellect than they can ever imagine. For, only then will the people of the world cease suffering the plight of war-torn countries like Iraq; which, of course, is just one of many, from the past up until the present-day. It is therefore totally fitting that the next oracle in line should be about Jesus Christ,*

    71   *Croistra le nombre si grand des Astronomes*
            Chassez, bannis & liures censurez,
            L'an mil six cens & sept par sacre glomes,
            Que nul aux sacres ne seront asseurez.

glomes (L glom\us) a clue; asseurer (OF) to assure

                The number of astronomers will grow so great,   1612
                Pursued, banned and books censured,
                The year **1607** by sacred clue,
                When none at the sacraments will be assured.

The number of astronomers will grow so great

Interest in astronomy was revitalised by Copernicus following the publication of his theory that the Earth revolved around the Sun (*De revolutionibus orbium coelestium*, 1543). The interest this received enjoyed a further boost when Kepler published *Mysterium cosmographicum* in 1596: a book concerned with the structure of the heavens. Kepler's ideas also became a forerunner to the discovery of his 'first law' (1605), which described the motion of the planets as elliptical. His major work, *Astronomia Nova*, which introduced his second law, proved that the radius between a planet and the sun sweeps out equal areas in equal time, and was published in 1609.

The interest which these theories generated caused the number of astronomers to increase, and it brought to the forefront Galileo Galilei, a mathematical professor at the University in Pisa. His telescopic observations of the night sky were to change mankind's view of the universe forever. [1]

Pursued, banned and books censured

Official opposition to Galileo's ideas first began to emerge in the spring of 1612, when the Archbishop decided that his talk concerning the motion of the Earth was so blasphemous that it could be denounced from the pulpit. In fact ...

> By December of 1612 Galileo had virtually completed his career as a practising scientist. Every important discovery that he was going to make he had now made. [...] He continued to work on the tables of Jupiter's moons, but he stopped exploring the heavens. [2]

In the following year, Galileo was compelled to issue a public letter in defence of his work and his person. But by 1616, he had become such a nuisance to the Church, that he was even excluded from making contact with the papacy's official astronomers.

On 5 March 1616, the Congregation of the Index finally took punative action and suspended Copernicus's book – which had been the first to promote the idea that the earth orbited the sun – declaring the idea to be contrary to Holy Scripture.

Another book was similarly censured; that of Fr. Paolo Antonio Foscarini, who had attempted to reconcile the Bible with Copernicus. His book was condemned. Catholics were prohibited from reading it, and an order was made for the book to be destroyed. Even the hapless printer from Naples was arrested: while Fr. Foscarini died very suddenly and unexpectedly; some will have it that he died under suspicious circumstances. Galileo's book: *A Dialogue Concerning the Two Chief World Systems, Ptolemaic & Copernican,* was likewise condemned and would remain on the Index of Forbidden Books (*Librorum Prohibitorum*) until 1835.

> Galileo's increasingly overt Copernicanism began to cause trouble for him [...] the tide in Rome was turning against the Copernican theory, and in 1615, when the cleric Paolo Antonio Foscarini (c. 1565-1616) published a book arguing that the Copernican theory did not conflict with scripture, Inquisition consultants examined the question and pronounced the Copernican theory heretical. Foscarini's book was banned, as were some more technical and non-theological works, such as Johannes Kepler's *Epitome of Copernican Astronomy.* Copernicus's own 1543 book, *De revolutionibus orbium coelestium libri vi* ('Six Books Concerning the Revolutions of the Heavenly Orbs'), was suspended until corrected. [...] An improperly prepared document placed in the Inquisition files at this time states that Galileo was admonished 'not to hold, teach, or defend' the Copernican theory 'in any way whatever, either orally or in writing'. [3]

The year 1607 by sacred clue

Let it now be recalled that in Century Six N°. 54, the same year, 1607, was predicted as a means of identifying the date of Jesus's crucifixion ("The year 1607, from Liturgy"). This time, we are required to understand the meaning of 1607 when it is attached to "sacred clue".

Since the first two lines of this oracle refer to an astronomical view of the starlit sky, it is to the heavens that one should first look for a solution to the present puzzle. This immediately suggests that the Star of Bethlehem provides the answer. It is a *sacred* symbol; it is an astronomical event and it offers a possible *clue* to discovering Jesus's date of birth. If so, it would then reinforce the validity of his date of execution; since the same strategy, together with the same year, will have led to the discovery of the two most important dates in the Christian calendar.

Working upon this basis, the calculation is a simple one. The year 1612 is to be understood as 1607 when dated from the sacred clue. Therefore, this five year difference 'pushes' the calendar back from the year 1 AD to 5 BCE (there was no Year 0). The sacred clue (the Star of Bethlehem) can therefore be dated as having shone in 5 BCE. But is there any record of anything resembling an unexpected light in the sky during that year?

In fact, there is. By consulting the astronomical records for 5 BCE, it is possible to discover there was a brief appearance of a new star that rose in the east and shone for ten weeks. "Ancient Chinese astronomers recorded this as an unusually bright star that appeared in the eastern sky for 70 days." [4] This star, which is likely to have been a nova, appeared during late February, the whole of March and early April, and was located in the constellation of Aquila, just below Altair. By computer simulation it would have appeared to observers in Jerusalem as if it were suspended above Bethlehem. (A nova is a star that suddenly increases in its brightness by as much as ten magnitudes, then declines gradually over a period of months. It is not to be confused with a supernova.)

The evidence for Jesus's birth occurring in 5 BCE is perfectly consistent with the death of Herod one year later. The gospel of Matthew, Chapter 2, records how Herod and all Jerusalem were disturbed upon learning that the Messiah, which had been promised to the Jewish nation, would be born in Bethlehem, and that his 'star' had appeared over the city. Herod's response was to order the deaths of all boys born in that city who were under the age of 2. Consequently, since Herod died in 4 BCE, apparently at the time of a lunar eclipse, it follows that Jesus was born before the time of his death. There were actually two lunar eclipses in 4 BCE. The first occurred on 13 March, and the second on 5 September.

Further evidence that 5 BCE is the correct date can be determined from the prophet Daniel. At the time of his exile to Babylon, he predicted that his captive nation would be released, and the Temple, which had been destroyed by Nebuchadnezzar c.586 BCE, would be rebuilt.

> Know and understand this: from the time the word goes out to restore and rebuild Jerusalem until the Anointed One, the ruler, comes, there will be seven "sevens", and sixty-two "sevens". It will be rebuilt with streets and a trench, but in times of trouble. After the sixty-two "sevens"; the Anointed One will be put to death and will have nothing. (Daniel, 9:25, 26)

The date intended for the arrival of the Messiah, who will later be executed, can be calculated from the clues provided in this piece of text, taken from the Old Testament.

Cyrus, who was named by the prophet Isaiah as the conqueror of Babylon, did as predicted in 538 BCE: allowing the Jewish captives to return to Judah and rebuild their Temple. This was completed in 516 BCE under the reign of Darius. However, the city itself remained in ruins. It is with this that we turn to the Book of Nehemiah, cup-bearer to Artaxerxes I, the King of Persia in the twentieth year of his reign (2: 1). The King's sovereignty extended from 465 to 425 BCE, therefore the year in question is 446 BCE. This was the year when Nehemiah returned to Judah with published letters of authority from Artaxerxes for the rebuilding of Jerusalem and the acquisition of materials to accomplish the task.

It is now possible to apply Artaxerxes' decree of 446 BCE for the rebuilding of Jerusalem to the prophetic timetable given to Daniel by the angel Gabriel. The 'weeks' referred to in the prophecy are *years* and *week-years*, which explains their separation. Therefore seven weeks is actually seven years. But Daniel is told to add to this a further sixty-two 'week-years'. The total then stands at $441=(7 + 62 \times 7)$. The prophet is told that this is the time that must elapse before the appearance of the Messiah, the Anointed One. Therefore, commencing at 446 BCE, (when word went out to restore Jerusalem) and allowing a further 441 years to pass, we arrive at 5 BCE; which, is the year predicted by Daniel for the Messiah to make his appearance in the world. It also coincides with the new star (a nova) that appeared in the east during February-March-April of that year.

In which case—is there any evidence to support the birth of Jesus having occurred during this time of the year? There is, and it occurs in the gospel of Luke, chapter 2.

> And there were shepherds living out in the fields nearby, keeping watch over their flocks at night. An angel of the Lord appeared to them, and the glory of the Lord shone around them, and they were terrified. But the angel said to them, 'Do not be afraid. I bring you good news that will cause great joy for all people. Today in the town of David a Saviour has been born to you; he is the Messiah, the Lord.' (Luke, 2: 8-11)

At what time of the year would shepherds be watching over their flocks at night? The lambing season most surely is the likeliest answer; and, what better time for the Lamb of God to be born? Therefore, in the time scale available, late March or early April coincides with the available facts.

> Lacking any scriptural pointers to Jesus's birthday, early Christian teachers suggested dates all over the calendar. Clement [...] picked November 18. Hippolytus [...] figured Christ must have been born on a Wednesday. [...] An anonymous document believed to have been written in North Africa around A.D. 243, placed Jesus's birth on March 28.[5]

The fact is that our Seer not only claimed to know the exact dates of all his prophecies; but the evidence so far acquired does support his claim. In which case, he would have known the day and the month as well as the year when Jesus was born.

How then, would this information most likely be conveyed within the oracles? It must surely be by concealing the date in another quatrain and marking it 1607, so as to coincide with the other two quatrains dated 1607. It is therefore to Century Three N° 56 that we return (p. 174). The final two lines of the verse read:

De Paris pont, Lyon mur, Montpellier,	Bridge for Paris, Lyon wall, Montpellier,
Depuis six cent & sept. xxiij pars.	For 1607, 23 parts *or* divisions.

When compared with other prophecies – the more so, those he dates – this statement is trivial; it refers to the 23 provinces that Henri IV had jurisdiction over in 1607, because in that year, Foix had been added to the other 22. But if we take the cryptic course, and note that 1607 has been used to determine, firstly the death and then the birth of Jesus Christ, and that the only part missing from these prophecies is the day and month of the year 5 BCE in which the birth of our Lord occurred, then 'XXIIJ divisions' is just right: especially since the same oracle precedes these two lines with *à fin de Mars* (at the end of March). Thus, Jesus was born on 23 March 5 BCE.

When none at the sacraments will be assured

The fears nursed by the Church, which were made manifest in 1612 and continued thereafter, were to reflect the dismay felt at man's unique position in the universe coming under threat. Aristotle's teaching had earlier been brought into line with Catholic theology, but this was now being overturned. And the Bible, the Word of God, seemed in danger of becoming superseded by the discoveries made in astronomy. Poetry, plays, and literature, during the first half of the seventeenth century, were also being written to reflect the "confusion and dismay" of the people: because none at the sacraments could any longer be certain, concerning the Church's teaching. [6]

Summary: *This quatrain, naming the year 1607, is the third of three oracles bearing that date. Each one contributes to providing the exact day of the year in which Jesus Christ was born and died. We can therefore say with total confidence, since only God would know the truth, that His Son was born to Mary on Sunday 23rd March in 5 BCE, and that he was crucified on Friday 13th April in 29 CE. Jesus was therefore 33 years of age when his bodily death occurred. To have constructed these prophecies so that they would reveal the two most important dates in the history of the Christian calendar is a brilliant piece of intellectual cryptology. Those who cannot countenance this would do well to sit in the corner and suck their thumb until they do.*

72   *Champ Perusin ô l'enorme deffaite*
      Et le conflict tout aupres de Rauenne,
      Passage sacre lors qu'on fera la feste,
      Vainqueur vaincu cheual manger l'auenne.

73   *Soldat Barbare le grand Roy frappera,*
      Iniustement non eslongné de mort,
      L'auare mere du faict cause sera,
      Coniurateur & regne en grand remort.

74   *En terre neufue bien auant Roy entré*
      Pendant subges luy viendront faire acueil,
      Sa perfidie aura tel rencontré,
      Qu'aux citadins lieu de feste & recueil.

75   *Le pere & fils seront meurdris ensemble,*
      Le prefecteur dedans son pauillon:
      La mere à Tours du fils ventre aura enfle,
      Cache verdure de fueilles papillon.

76   *Plus Macelin que Roy en Angleterre,*
      Lieu obscur nay par force aura l'empire:
      Lasche sans foy sans loy seignera terre.
      Son temps s'aproche si pres que ie souspire.

Macelin (L Macellin\us); empire (OF) government; Lasche (OF lâche, also *anagrammatic paragram* Lasche[r] Charles.

More like **MACELLINUS** than a king in England,   1649
Born in an obscure place, by force he will have the government (**CROMWELL**):
Shameful (**CHARLES**) without faith, without law, the land will bleed,
His time approaches so near that I sigh.

More like Macellinus than a king in England

Macellinus was an epithet for Marcus Opilius Macrinus. He had formerly been an army officer, but became Rome's Emperor after initiating the death of the reigning Emperor, Caracalla. [1]

In England, Oliver Cromwell exhibited similarities to Macellinus. That is to say, Cromwell, too, began his career as an army officer. Likewise, in 1649 – as Macrinus did in 217 AD – Cromwell initiated the death of the reigning king, Charles I. Thereafter, for eleven years, there would be no further kings in England. Instead, Cromwell became the nation's Lord Protector: preferring this title to that of King or Emperor. [2]

Born in an obscure place

On 25 April 1599, Elizabeth Steward, wife of Robert Cromwell, gave birth to her second son Oliver. His arrival in the world took place inside a very ordinary house, in an obscure place that lay on the main High Street of a small town called Huntingdon. [3]

By force, he will have the government

Between 1640 and 1646, Cromwell made his mark as a member of parliament, and from then onwards he rose to become the most successful commanding officer in the Parliamentary army. It was from this power base, achieved by force during the English Civil War, that he was able to influence the House of Commons into putting the King on trial for treason.

After a verdict of guilty was read out, Charles I was sentenced to death. His execution took place in January 1649, leaving the way open for Cromwell to replace him as head of the British Commonwealth. [4]

Shameful (Charles)

The oracle now inserts a few brief, descriptive words that are meant to portray the character of Cromwell, although their negative connotations will not please his admirers. For example, was Cromwell's treatment of Charles I shameful? The oracle leaves no doubt that it was.

> As one of the generals on the parliamentary side in the English Civil War against King Charles I, Cromwell helped to bring about the overthrow of the Stuart monarchy.

To complete the King's overthrow, Charles I was made to stand trial. He was accused of "high treason [... and] other high crimes against the realm of England." On January 27, the court reached their verdict. The King was declared "a tyrant, traitor, murderer, and public enemy." He was executed two days later. [5]

Without faith

Upon matters of religion, Cromwell remained independent: lacking the faith of either Anglicans or Roman Catholics. When questioned upon matters of religion, he replied that it was easier to say what he was against than what he was for.

Although he declared belief in God, this did not prevent him killing Catholic priests, ejecting Anglican clergy from their parishes, proscribing the Prayer book, and forbidding the December celebration of Jesus Christ's nativity. [6]

Without law

The oracle is correct in predicting the absence of law during Cromwell's reign. By announcing the abolition of the monarchy, and then declaring that England would become a Free State, or Commonwealth, he distanced the nation from its "last tenuous link with legality."

The Rump Parliament that gained prominence in Britain represented no more than a few eccentrics, and it operated entirely without constitutional respectability. It was followed by the

Barebones Parliament, consisting of Cromwell's handpicked supporters. But even they were unable to agree with Cromwell, and so he disbanded them, explaining his illicit action with the terse words: "Necessity hath no law." [7]

The land will bleed

The English Civil War is referred to in the oracle as a time when the land will bleed. In the conflict between King and Parliament, Cavalier and Roundhead, Cromwell's model army quickly raised their commander to prominence. Victorious in more than thirty battles fought during the nine years between 1642 and 1651, he delivered a convincing and decisive blow against the royalist armies opposing him. These victories paved the way for his final and political overthrow of the English monarchy. [8]

His time approaches so near that I sigh

Cromwell's life span extended from 25 April 1599 to 3 September 1658. The Seer's own life ended thirty-three years before Cromwell's birth, therefore justifying his sigh, and the reference he made to the time he foresaw approaching, when Cromwell would be born into the world to fulfil this prophecy.

Summary: *This is another of the oracles that predicts the future by its close resemblance to an historical event. Macellinus and Cromwell had the same military background; both men became the first to rule their respective countries without connexions to the ruling class. Both men were implicated in the murder of their respective Emperor and King, and both men were confirmed as heads of state by their respective senates. That said, the oracle then confirms what came to be a historically correct assessment of Cromwell's character traits. Finally, against a broad sweep of prophecies covering more than two thousand years, the seer announced the approach of Cromwell's time on earth. It began just thirty-six years after his death.*

77 L'antechrist trois bien tost annichilez,
    Vingt & sept ans sang durera sa guerre,
    Les heretiques morts, captifs exilez,
    Son corps humain eau rougie gresler terre.

78 Vn Bragamas auec la langue torte
    Viendra des dieux le sanctuaire,
    Aux heretiques il ouurira la porte
    En suscitant l'eglise militaire.

79 Qui par fer pere perdra nay de Nonnaire
    De Gorgon sur la fera sang perfetant,
    En terre estrange fera si tout de taire,
    Qui bruslera luy mesme & son entant.

80 Des innocens le sang de vefue & vierge.
    Tant de maux faicts par moyen se grand Roge,
    Saincts simulachres trempez en ardant cierge:
    De frayeur craincte ne verra nul que boge.

81 Le neuf empire en desolation,
    Sera changé du pole aquilonaire,
    De la Sicile viendra l'emotion,
    Troubler l'emprise à Philip tributaire.

82 Ronge long, sec faisant du bon vallet,
    A la parfin n'aura que son congie,
    Poignant poyson, & lettres au collet,
    Sera saisi eschappé en dangie.

83 Le plus grand voile hors du port de Zara,
    Prés de Bisance fera son entreprise.
    D'ennemy perte & l'amy ne sera,
    Le tiers à deux fera grand pille & prise.

84   *Paterne orra de la Sicile crie,*
      Tous les aprests du goulphre de Trieste,
      Qui s'entendra iusque à la Trinacrie,
      De tant de voiles fuy, fuy l'horrible peste.

aprest (OF apprest) preparation; Trinacrie (L Trinacria) Sicily; voiles (OF) sails of ships; this can be shortened to just ships.
(*Cotgrove*); fuy (OF) gone, escaped; peste (OF) a pestiferous fellow

Paterno will hear the outcry of Sicily,   1943
All preparations at the Gulf of Trieste,
Which will be comprehended as far as Sicily:
Gone from so many ships: the horrible pestiferous fellow escaped.

Paterno will hear the outcry of Sicily

With the Axis defeat in North Africa foreseen, the invasion of Sicily was decided upon by
Roosevelt and Churchill at the Casablanca Conference in January 1943. [...] The plan called for
British troops to land in the south-eastern region near Syracuse (Siracusa), with American forces
controlling a landing zone westward in the Gulf of Gela. [1]

The attack began on the night of July 9th. By dawn next morning the southern coastal areas of
Sicily around Gela and Licata were under Allied occupation. The surprise element had been
completely successful, and it was not until "morning [that] the Axis command near Palermo knew of
the landings." [2]

The town of Paterno, situated to the south-east of Palermo and to the north of Syracuse, sits on
the edge of the Plain of Catania. "The Gerbini airfields on the Plain of Catania were targeted early in
the campaign, to be captured or—if necessary—destroyed." [3] Syracuse to the south of Paterno was
also captured on the first day of the invasion, against little opposition, and then used as a base by
the Royal Navy.

All preparations at the Gulf of Trieste

The successful assault on Sicily, which was used as a stepping stone to the mainland, and Italy's
subsequent surrender on 8 September to the Allies, announced by Victor Emmanuel III, had
repercussions in the German high command. Hitler tightened his grip upon the country by
creating the Salo Republic in the northern half of Italy. Its purpose was to counter the Allied
forces that were fighting their way towards Rome. His second strategy was the creation of OZAK
(*Operationszone Adriatisches Küstenland*), with its headquarters in Trieste.

Operational Zone of the Adriatic Littoral OZAK was established, with its headquarters in Trieste,
on 10 September 1943, by Adolf Hitler as a response to the Italian capitulation (8 September
1943) following the Allied invasion of Italy. It comprised the provinces of Udine, Gorizia, Trieste,
Pula (Pola), Rijeka (Fiume) and Ljubljana (Lubiana). [4]

The Gulf of Trieste is a shallow bay, part of the Adriatic Sea in the extreme northern half of the
Mediterranean Sea. It forms part of the Gulf of Venice and is shared by Italy, Slovenia and
Croatia. In fact, the entire Slovenian coastline is located on the Gulf of Trieste.

Once the signing of the armistice was announced on 8 September, German troops quickly
disarmed the Italian forces and took over critical defensive positions. [...] This included Italian-
occupied south-eastern France and the Italian-controlled areas in the Balkans. [5]

Which will be comprehended as far as Sicily

The fall of Sicily to the Allies and the capitulation of the Italian government, which led to the
dismissal and arrest of Benito Mussolini, attracted the immediately response of OZAK at Trieste.
Thus from one end of Italy to the other, the repercussions were comprehended. Consequently,
while the allied forces were making progress northwards towards Rome, the Germans, aided by
approximately 94,000 Italian soldiers that had opted to remain loyal to Hitler, were stubbornly
resisting the approaching forces aimed at liberating their country.

Gone from so many ships

The successful outcome of the operation had begun with the invasion of Sicily, when "On the night of 9-10 July, almost half a million Allied soldiers, sailors and airmen, with an armada of 2590 vessels, began the assault on Sicily, using various transport ships and even gliders." [6] This led to the evacuation of defeated German and Italian troops—gone from Sicily to the mainland.

On 10 July 1943, a combined force of American and British Commonwealth troops invaded Sicily. German generals again took the lead in the defence and, although they lost the island after weeks of bitter fights, they succeeded in ferrying large numbers of German and Italian forces safely off Sicily to the Italian mainland. [7]

The horrible pestiferous fellow escaped

Another major outcome that resulted from the fall of Italy was the dismissal and arrest of the Fascist leader, Benito Mussolini. "On 25 July, the Grand Council of Fascism voted to limit the power of Italian dictator Benito Mussolini and handed control of the Italian armed forces over to King Victor Emmanuel III. The next day Mussolini met with the King, was dismissed as prime minister, and was then imprisoned." [8] But after several weeks of captivity he escaped, aided by a German task force.

About two months after he was stripped of power, Benito Mussolini was rescued by the Germans in Operation Eiche ("Oak"). The Germans re-located Mussolini to northern Italy where he set up a new Fascist state, the Italian Social Republic (*Repubblica Sociale Italiana* or RSI). [9]

Summary: *This prophecy found its fulfilment in the massive operation to liberate Italy during the Second World War. The facts concerning the planning that went into the operation are fairly represented in this oracle. They began with a surprise invasion of Sicily, which had repercussions in Trieste and the north of Italy. The German army holding Sicily was forced to flee to the mainland, pursued by the Allied forces of the US and UK, which fought their way towards Rome. With the capitulation of the Italian government, and its abandonment of support for Hitler, the country sided with the Allies; Mussolini was therefore arrested and imprisoned, but later escaped, aided by the German army. He then became Hitler's puppet leader in the new Salo Republic of northern Italy.*

85   *Entre Bayonne & à sainct Iean de Lux,*
        Sera pose de Mars la promottoire :
        Aux Hanix d'Aquilon Nanar hostera lux,
        Puis suffoqué au lict sans adiutoire.

86   *Par Arnani Tholoser Ville Franque,*
        Bande infinie par le mont Adrian,
        Passe riuiere, Hutin par pont la planque,
        Bayonne entrer tous Bichoro criant.

87   *Mort conspirée viendra en plein effect,*
        Charge donnée & voyage de mort.
        Esleu, creé, receu, par siens deffaict:
        Sang d'innocence deuant soy par remort.

88   *Dans la Sardaigne vn noble Roy viendra,*
        Qui ne tiendra que trois ans le Royaume,
        Plusieurs couleurs auec soy conioindra,
        Luy mesme apres soin sommeil marrit scome.

soy (3rd person reflexive); conioindra (OF unir) unite; soin (OF soigner) provided for; marrit (OF) sad; scome, (L scomma) taunt;

A noble King (**CHARLES EMMANUEL**) will arrive in Sardinia   1798
Who, but for three years, will not hold the kingdom:
He will unite several colours with himself,
The same He, afterwards, provided for, sleepy, sad, taunted.

A noble King will arrive in Sardinia

Sardinia became a kingdom of the House of Savoy only in 1720. Before then it had been a Spanish possession. The change resulted from the *Treaty of London* (1718), which compelled Victor Amadeus II to surrender Sicily to Austria. In exchange, he received Sardinia. Importantly, it was only after 24 August 1720 that "he and his successors were known as kings of Sardinia."

Charles Emmanuel IV, whose biographical details fit this oracle, became King of Sardinia and Piedmont on 14 October 1796, following the death of Victor Amadeus III. His accession coincided with the French Revolution, to which he was bitterly opposed. In the following year, the uprising in France intruded into his kingdom, and he responded by executing the insurgents, including many Jacobins who were intending to introduce their revolutionary ideas to his people. At the time of Charles Emmanuel's succession, Piedmont was allied with Austria. But his kingdom became diminished when, during a strategically brilliant ten-day campaign, Napoleon divided the two armies, taking Piedmont, and scuttling the Austrians. Further losses occurred on 9 December 1798, when the French general, Barthélemy-Catherine Joubert, forced the King to surrender all his mainland possessions to France.

In the following year Naples, too, was overrun and Charles was forced to concede that all hope of recovering his possessions had now vanished. Bowed down by these losses, King Charles Emmanuel retired to the island of Sardinia: the only part of his kingdom that remained free from Napoleon's grasp. [1]

Who, but for three years, will not hold the kingdom

For the next three and a half years, Charles remained King of Sardinia. But the death of his wife Marie Clotilde, daughter of the French dauphin, who died on 2 March 1802 so grieved the King that three months later he abdicated in favour of his brother Victor Emmanuel. [2]

There is an interesting postscript to this part of the prophecy: for although Charles Emmanuel held the Kingdom for just over three years, *he retained the title of King* until the end of his life.

He will unite several colours with himself

The loss of Piedmont occurred in April 1796, six months before the death of Victor Amadeus III. He and his forty-year-old son had allowed the Piedmontese to *unite* with the Austrians under General Colli. And it was during their combined battle with the French that Napoleon achieved his great victory: driving a wedge between their two armies (refer Century Six N°. 79).

By 25 April 1796, Cherasco, too, had been captured, and the King of Sardinia-Piedmont was forced to admit the total defeat of his armies in the field. Paris was quickly notified of these successes, and its streets were thronged with cheering onlookers when General Andoche Junot entered the city: "carrying a trophy of twenty-one captured flags." These were the *several colours* which the King of Piedmont-Sardinia had united with. [3]

The same He, afterwards, provided for

By emphasizing the same 'He', the seer has acknowledged that sometimes, when writing these quatrains, he changes from one subject's identity to another, as one line changes to the next. But, we are assured, this strategy does not apply in the present case. It was after abdicating in 1802 that Charles Emmanuel became a novitiate of the Jesuits in Rome. He remained there, provided for, until his death on 6 October 1819, aged sixty-eight. [4]

Sleepy, sad, taunted

The stress of past defeats, the death of his beloved wife, and the loss of his kingdoms appear to have played upon the King's mind. In his new life with the Jesuits, he would sometimes give special heed to the need for piety. In this state, he would leave his cell in a state of drowsiness and wander into the streets begging for alms. [5] It was a sad, and much lamented end for a king descended from the noble House of Savoy. [6]

Summary: *This oracle presents a biographical sketch of one of the kings of Sardinia. It has been chosen, so one may assume, because it includes the unique instance of a king encountering the reversal of everything that he had been brought up to accept. It differs from other kings who have suffered the loss of their kingdom in respect that after his downfall, Charles Emmanuel freely chose to follow a path of humility in a Jesuit monastery. Apart from this, the oracle includes the unity of the Piedmontese with the armed forces that opposed the French as well as citing the three full years that Charles remained, effectively, King of Sardinia.*

89   *Pour ne tomber entre mains de son oncle,*
    Qui ses enfans par regner trucidez:
    Orant au peuple mettant pied sur Peloncle
    Mort & traisné entre cheuaux bardez.

90   *Quand des croisez vn trouué de sens trouble*
    En lieu du sacre verra vn bœuf cornu
    Par vierge porc son lieu lors sera comble,
    Par Roy plus ordre ne sera soustenu.

91   *Frimy les champs de Rodanes entrées*
    Où les croisez seront presque vnis,
    Les deux brassierez en pisces rencontrées,
    Et vn grand nombre par deluge punis.

92   *Loin hors du regne mis en hazard voyage*
    Grand ost duyra, pour soy l'occupera,
    Le Roy tiendra les siens captif, ostage,
    A son retour tout pays pillera.

93   *Sept mois sans plus obtiendra prelature*
    Par son decez grand scisme fera naistre:
    Sept mois tiendra vn autre la preture,
    Pres de Venise paix vnion renaistre.

94   *Deuant le lac où plus cher fut getté*
    De sept mois, & son ost desconfit
    Seront Hispans par Albannois gastez,
    Par delay perte en donnant le conflit.

95   *Le seducteur sera mis en la fosse,*
    Et estaché iusques à quelque temps,
    Le clerc vny le chef auec sa crosse
    Pycante droite attraira les contens.

96   *La Synagogue sterile sans nul fruit*
    Sera receuë entre les infideles
    De Babylon la fille du poursuit
    Misere & triste luy trenchera les aisles.

97   *Aux fins de VAR changer le Pompotans,*
    Prés du riuage les trois beaux enfans naistre,
    Ruyne au peuple par aage competans
    Regne au pays charger plus voir croistre.

fin(AF finance, argent) finance; VAR (*abbreviation. and transposition* of AVR); Alexandrina Victoria Regina; Pompotans
(L *portmanteau* - pomp + potens) ostentatious masters; ruyne (OF ruine) desolation; Cross-reference: Pompotans, C.X: 100

With the finances of **VAR**, the ostentatious masters changing,   1837
Close to the river (**WINDSOR**), three fine children born (**VICKY, ALFRED, LEOPOLD**).
Dreary sorrow for the people by a competent age:
The reign in the country burdening: more to see increasing.

With the finances of VAR

Victoria **A**lexandrina **R**egina (she dropped the name Alexandrina after her succession to the monarchy.[1]) was Queen of England, ruler of the British Empire and Empress of India. It was also her privilege to reign at a time when the imperial power, fame and reputation of Great Britain were at its greatest. The nation's coffers were bursting from trade with member nations, which enabled massive changes to take place.

Upon the whole, a confidant hope is entertained, that on the strictest examination the aggregate property of the British empire, amounting to the enormous sum of £4,081,630,805, will be found to fall considerably short of its real value. It exhibits in glowing colours the proud height to which this great empire has arrived in the scale of nations. It proves incontestably the incalculable resources of the State, and the rapid growth of the wealth of the people. And what is of more importance, the facility and power of rendering this wealth productive to a greater extent than prevails in any other nation in the world.[2]

The ostentatious masters changing

By using the hybrid word *Pompotans,* to describe the British people, the oracle catches the character of the British Empire in the Victorian age. Its people were, indeed, masters of the world, and the pomp and ceremony that attended both royal and formal occasions were then at their height; and they linger still, discernible in those events where an ostentatious display of historical costume and pageantry have earned a traditional place. [3]

Under Queen Victoria's rule, Great Britain saw more changes than at any other time in its history. The monarchy was transformed: brought about by delegating power to Parliament; this has since become a standard model for the system presently in place within the U.K. Apart from this, Victoria's reign was an era of massive progress which …

> has lengthened life; it has mitigated pain; it has extinguished diseases; it has increased fertility of the soil; it has given new securities to the mariner [...] it has spanned great rivers and estuaries with bridges of form unknown to our fathers [...] it has enabled man to descend to the depths of the sea, to soar into the air, to penetrate securely into the noxious recesses of the earth, to traverse the land in cars which whirl along without horses, and the ocean in ships which run ten knots an hour against the wind. [4]

Close to the river

Standing close to the River Thames in Berkshire is Windsor Castle. It has been the home of the royal families of England ever since 1348, when Edward III converted part of the fortress into royal apartments. Queen Victoria lived there at the beginning of her reign, but she later removed her court to Buckingham Palace in London. Despite this change of abode, she retained Windsor as an occasional residence. [5]

Three fine children born

Queen Victoria's first child was a daughter who took her mother's name, Victoria, and became known as 'Vicky': — "Windsor, 21 November 1840. The queen gave birth to a princess here today, three weeks prematurely." Four years later, Alfred arrived: – "Windsor, 6 August 1844. Queen Victoria's expanding brood gained a new member today with the birth, at Windsor Castle, of a new prince. He will be christened Alfred Ernest Albert." Last of the three to be born at Windsor was Leopold, born in 1853. This birth was remarkable because Victoria opted to be given chloroform during delivery. This was administered by Dr John Snow.

> The decision of the queen to use chloroform during the birth of Prince Leopold, on 7 April has done a great deal to popularise what has hitherto been a controversial form of medication [...] knowing full well the suffering of giving birth, she welcomed the arrival at Windsor of the famous Dr. John Snow. [6]

Of Victoria's other children, all six were born at Buckingham Palace.

Dreary sorrow for the people

The wealth of the British Empire during Victoria's reign is contrasted with the plight of the working class. Those familiar with the novels of Charles Dickens will have read his pen pictures, describing the desolation found among the poor of the land. In fact, the term *working class* was invented to describe the wage earners of that time. Rates of pay were low, and to supplement a living wage, families were forced to send their children to work. Child labour was rife, with infants employed to climb and sweep chimneys, or they were sent into the mines where the stronger ones hauled trucks and the weaker ones stood for hours, ankle deep in water, while they operated the pumps.

> Many of the Victorian poor were people who had no hope of ever doing more than picking up a few days' or a few weeks' money here and there, existing in the intervals as best they could. [...] And so they jolted down an uneven road of poverty to old age in the workhouse, if they lived so long. [7]

Large numbers of both skilled and unskilled people were looking for work, so wages were low, barely above subsistence level. [...] Many cases of death caused by starvation and destitution were reported. One example of such a report will suffice. In 1850 an inquest was held on a 38 year old man whose body was reported as being little more than a skeleton, his wife was described as being 'the very personification of want' and her child as a 'skeleton infant'. [...] 'In 1848 Lord Ashley referred to more than thirty thousand 'naked, filthy, roaming lawless and deserted children, in and around the metropolis'. [...] In his book *The Victorian underworld*, Kellow Chesney gives a graphic description of the conditions in which many were living: 'Hideous slums, some of them acres wide, some no more than crannies of obscure misery, make up a substantial part of the, metropolis [...] big, once handsome houses, thirty or more people of all ages may inhabit a single room.'[8]

By a competent age

As the prophecy correctly states, this was a competent age. The British Empire was at its pinnacle, bringing in wealth from the lands it ruled. Industry expanded beyond all expectation, and literature, science and the arts flourished as never before.[9]

The increased scale of industry and oversees trade, together with the expansion of empire fuelled the proliferation of commerce and finance such as banks, insurance companies, shipping and railways. This system needed administrating by clerks, managers and salaried professionals. The expansion of cities, towns and the economy produced new spaces that needing regulating and running. The Victorian period witnessed the massive expansion of local government and the centralised state, providing occupations for a vast strata of civil servants, teachers, doctors, lawyers and government officials as well as the clerks and assistants which helped these institutions and services to operate.[10]

The reign in the country burdening

"One of the most glaring abuses of the labour of English women and children was the agricultural 'gang labour' system prevalent in East Anglia and the Midlands." Agricultural workers were often employed on a sub-contractual basis. This meant that the money paid by the landowner was given to a gang leader, who took his commission and then passed over the little that remained to those who had actually worked the fields. Once again, children became part of the labour force in order to add to the meagre wages that a hard day's work brought home.

In 1867, the government's conscience was partially touched by the necessity of child labour, which was a burden to people living in the country, and a law – *The Gangs Act* – was passed, forbidding the employment of any child below the age of eight.[11]

More to see increasing

Queen Victoria [...] ruled over an era of tremendous change. [...] Photography, moving pictures, electric light, the motorcar and the telephone have transformed people's view of the world.

Rail travel should also be included. In short, there was *more to see*, and this had been increasing throughout her reign, whether through the speed of travel or with new inventions involving light.[12]

Summary: Queen Victoria and the age in which she reigned witnessed the British Empire reaching its most prestigious period. It was also an age of large families, with the Queen giving birth to nine children, of which the seer refers to the three who were born at Windsor Castle. Yet, despite the country's huge success, Charles Dickens was still able to write novels with characters that were poor and oppressed, thus reflecting the society into which they had been born. The oracle also points to the state of agricultural workers who laboured for the profit of their gang master. Significantly, however, the oracle manages to indicate the huge change within society that took place during the Victorian age.

98   *Des gens d'Eglise sang sera espanché,*
    Comme de l'eau en si grande abondance
    Et d'vn long temps ne sera restranché
    Ve, vë au clerc ruyne & doleance.

99   *Par la puissance des trois Roys temporels,*
        En autre lieu sera mis le saint siege:
        Où la substance de l'esprit corporel,
        Sera remis & receu pour vray siege.

100   *Pour l'abondance de l'arme respanduë*
        Du haut en bas par le bas au plus haut
        Trop grande foy par ieu vie perduë,
        De soif mourir par habondant deffaut.

References Century 8

N⁰. 1

1 Franklin L Ford, *Europe 1780 – 1830*, 167; & J.M. Thompson, *Napoleon Bonaparte*, 69–70; & David Chandler, *The Campaigns of Napoleon*, xxv–xxvi, xxviii.
2 Thompson, 135-6; & H.A.L. Fisher, *A History of Europe*, 293
3 Thompson, 214; & Georges Lefebvre, *Napoleon from 18 Brumaire to Tilsit* (trans. Henry F Stockold), 185
4 Pie VI, pape de 1775 à 1799, *Petit Larousse* 1966 (Librarie Larousse) Paris; & Pie VII, pape de 1800 à 1823, Ibid
5 Harrison Smith, *The Illness of Pius VI and the Effect on the Maltese Question* (Estratto da Studi Romagnoli XIX, 1968) Faenza, 409; & Pius VII, *Encyclopædia Britannica 2001:* CD-ROM
6 Tilsit, Ibid; & Pius VII, Joseph N. Scionti, *McGraw-Hill Encyclopedia of Names*; & Thompson, 262
7 Durance, *Encyclopædia Britannica 2001:* CD-ROM; & Scionti; & Ford, 178

N⁰. 4

1 J.M. Thompson, *Napoleon Bonaparte*, 264; & *History of Monaco*, anon. published by Gale Force of Monaco
2 Thompson, 177, 273
3 Thompson, 273
4 Ibid
5 id
6 id 274
7 Alan Palmer, *Dictionary of Modern History 1789-1945*, 208
8 John Belcham & Richard Price (ed.) *A Dictionary of Nineteenth – Century History*, 649

N⁰. 9

1 wikipedia.org/wiki/county_of_nice
2 wikipedia.org/wiki/Levant
3 wikipedia.org/wiki/Battle_of_Lissa_(1866)
4 wikipedia.org/wiki/Giuseppe_Garibaldi
5 Ibid
6 J. Rickard, Siege of Ancona, 18-29 (September 1860) historyof war.org/articles/siege_ancona.html (15 Feb. 2013)
7 wikipedia.org/wiki/Venetia_(region)
8 wikipedia.org/wiki/Giuseppe_Garibaldi#Expedition_against_Rome

N⁰. 14

1 Evidence for the fulfilment of this prophecy can be found in most news outlets in any single week.
2 Katherine Rushton, *Dail Mail,*Thursday, July 21, 2015, 13
3 J.P. Hartley, *The Go-Between*, 1

N⁰. 15

1 Saint Petersburg – foundation and early growth, *Encyclopædia Britannica 2001:* CD-ROM
2 Catherine II – early years as empress, Ibid; & E.N. Williams, *Dictionary of English and*European History *1485 – 1789:* 54-5
3 Nicholas V. Riazanovsky, *A History of Russia*, 256; & Simon Sebag Montefiore, *Prince of Princes The Life of Potemkin*, 46
4 *A Dictionary of Eighteenth-Century History*, Jeremy Black and Roy Porter (ed.) 127; & Influence of Potemkin, *Encyclopædia Britannica 2001:* CD-ROM; & Montefiore, 233
5 Montefiore, 50, 59
6 Black and Porter, 339

N⁰. 19

1 Norman Davies, *Europe - A History*, 699; & Simon Schama, *Citizens*, 604
2 Schama, 558–60
3 Ibid 560–1
4 Davies, 710
5 Schama, 566-7
6 Christopher Hibbert, *The French Revolution*, 149
7 H.A.L. Fisher, *A History of Europe*, 897, 904
8 Ibid 897; & Jeremy Black & Roy Porter (ed.) *Dictionary of Eighteenth Century History*, 186

N⁰. 22

1 Louis Madelin, *The French Revolution*, 197
2 Ibid 229
3 Gorsas, *Grand Larousse Encyclopédique*; & Simon Schama, *Citizens*, 683
4 Ian Littlewood, *The Rough Guide Chronicle France:* 208
5 Norman Hampson, *The French Revolution: A Concise History*, 57
6 S.K. Padover, *Life and Death of Louis XVI*, 239
7 *Chronicle of the French Revolution*, see 6 December 1791, Perpignan (ed.) Jean Favier
8 Norman Davies, *Europe - A History*, 710; & Franklin L. Ford, *Europe 1780-1830*, 119
9 H.A.L. Fisher, *A History of Europe*, 891–2; & Schama, 581
10 Schama, 891

11 Alexandre Dumas, *The Flight to Varennes* (trans. A. Craig Bell), 84
12 Christopher Hibbert, *The French Revolution*, 332

Nº. 23

1 Antonia Fraser, *Mary Queen of Scots*, 405
2 Ibid 465
3 Id 405
4 Id 345

Nº. 37

1 *Encyclopædia Britannica 2001*, CD-ROM, Windsor Castle
2 wikipedia.org/wiki/Windsor_Castle
3 D.R. Watson, *The Life and Times of Charles I*, 175–6
4 Graham Gibberd, *On Lambeth Marsh*, 45, 71
5 Watson, 186; & Charles I, Execution of the King, *Encyclopædia Britannica*
6 Ibid

Nº. 38

1 Frieda, Leoni. *Catherine de Medici*. 187
2 Miquel, Pierre (1980). *Les guerres de religion* (in French). Paris: Fayard. 1980, p.254
3 chateaudeblois.fr/?CHARLES-IX
4 Frieda, 266
5 history.com/this-day-in-history/saint-bartholomews-day-massacre
6 Catholic Encyclopedia: Saint Bartholomew's Day Massacre
7 ctlibrary.com/ch/2001/issue71/1.8.html
8 Ibid
9 unamsanctamcatholicam.com/history/79-history/255-bartholomew-day-massacre-death-toll.html
10 Freida, 266

Nº. 41

1 wikipedia.org/wiki/Reynard
2 Christopher Hibbert, *The French Revolution*, 205, 210; & H.A.L. Fisher, *A History of Europe*, Vol. 2: 905
3 Hibbert, 208; & Leadership of the Jacobins: *Encyclopædia Britannica 2001:* CD-ROM
4 Simon Schama, *Citizens;* 831
5 Hibbert, 207
6 www.biography.com/people/maximilien-de-robespierre-37422#entering public-service&awesm=~oGuDbVlmVlWZ9e
7 Leadership of the Jacobins: *Encyclopædia Britannica 2001:* CD-ROM; & Hibbert, 333, 486, 491

Nº. 43

1 Alistair Horne, *seven Ages of Paris*, 258
2 Ibid 259-60
3 Napoleon III, *Encyclopædia Britannica 2001:* CD-ROM
4 Ibid
5 Sedan (article by Colonel Maude) *Encyclopædia Britannica*
6 Stephen Badsey, *The Franco-Prussian War 1870-1871*, 50-1
7 Ibid 51-2

Nº.46

1 Peter de Rosa, *Vicars of Christ*, 177
2 L'Abbé Baldassari, *Histoire de l'enlèvement et de la captivité De Pie VI* (Vanderborght, Bruxelles, 1840), 478
3 Pius VI, *The New Catholic Encyclopedia*; & J.M. Thompson, *Napoleon Bonaparte*, 263-4
4 Alan Palmer, *An Encyclopaedia of Napoleon's Europe*, 221
5 Palmer, 274
6 'The 'Red Cock', M. Liebman, *The Russian Revolution*, 142.
7 Jeremy Black and Roy Porter (ed.) *A Dictionary of Eighteenth-Century History*, 870-4; & *Europe A History*, 1286-7
8 Davies, 157
9 Black and Porter, 427; & John Belcham and Richard Price (ed.) *A Dictionary of Nineteenth-Century History*, 111

Nº.54

1 Leonie Frieda, *Catherine de Medici:* pp. 4, 5
2 wikipedia.org/wiki/Diane_de_Poitiers
3 E. Cobham Brewer, *The Dictionary of Phrase and Fable:* (Classic Edition) p. 1119
4 wikipedia.org/wiki/Saint-Quentin,_Aisne
5 wikipedia.org/wiki/Arras#History
6 wikipedia.org/wiki/Calais
7 William Henry Mountague, *A New and Universal History of England*, vol. I, p. 569
8 E.N. Williams, *Dictionary of English and European History*
9 wikipedia.org/wiki/Spanish_Inquisition

Nº. 57

1 J.M. Thompson, *Napoleon Bonaparte*, 10
2 Norman Davies, *Europe - A History*, 275

3   Thompson, 191; & 'Napoleon in Coronation Robes' painted by François Gérard at Versailles; (B.B.C. Hulton Picture Library, 178*f*), Ibid
4   Francine Barker, *Napoleon: The First European*, 14, 15, The Observer 26/1/1969
5   Thompson, 270; & Jeremy Black and Roy Porter (ed.) *A Dictionary of Eighteenth-Century History*, 543; & 451
6   http://home.newadvent.org/cathen/10687a.htm
7   Thompson, 273;
8   http://ww.newadvent.org/cathen/10687a.htm

Nº. 58

1   Kirsty McLeod, *Battle Royal – Edward VIII & George VI Brother Against Brother*, 172
2   Ibid 176-7, 193
3   Edward VIII, *Encyclopædia Britannica 2001:* CD-ROM
4   McLeod, 181
5   Edward VIII, *Encyclopædia Britannica 2001:* CD-ROM

Nº. 60

1   David Chandler, *The Campaigns of Napoleon*, 307, 318
2   Alistair Horne, *Seven Ages of Paris*, 196; & J.M. Thompson, *Napoleon Bonaparte*, 252
3   Norman Davies, *Europe A History*, 1286-7
4   Thompson, 355-6; & Horne, 232
5   Horne, 232
6   http://www.napolun.com/mirror/napoleonistyka.atspace.com/
7   Horne, 231
8   Thompson, 358
9   Ibid 371
10 Chandler, xxv, 1011
11 wikipedia.org/wiki/Mont-Saint-Jean, Belgium
12 http://about-france.com/regions/lorraine.htm]
13 wikipedia.org/wiki/Wallonia

Nº. 64

1   Derrik Mercer (ed.) *Chronicle of the Second World War*, 17, 91, 130
2   Martin Gilbert, *Churchill A Life*, 620-1
3   Norman Longmate, *How We Lived Then*, 121-2
4   World War II – The war in the west, September 1939 — June 1940, *Encyclopædia Britannica 2001:* CD-ROM
5   For a full list of treaties, see Norman Davies, *Europe: A History*, 1322

Nº. 65

1   wikipedia.org/wiki/Philippe_Pétain#France_and_World_War_II
2   Ibid
3   id
4   id
5   wikipedia.org/wiki/Second_Armistice_at_Compiègne
6   Ibid
7   wikipedia.org/wiki/Vichy_France
8   britannica.com/EBchecked/topic/453539/Philippe-Petain
9   wikipedia.org/wiki/Philippe_Pétain#France_and_World_War_II
10 www.jewishvirtuallibrary.org/jsource/Holocaust/VichyRegime.html
11 historylearningsite.co.uk/marshal_philippe_petain.htm
12 wikipedia.org/wiki/Joseph_Darnand
13 wikipedia.org/wiki/Philippe_Pétain
14 historyinanhour.com/2010/07/23/philippe-petain-and-vichy-france-summary/

Nº. 68

1   Maland, D. *Europe in the Seventeenth Century 2nd edition*, 189–90; & *The New Cambridge Modern History*, (ed.) J P Cooper, 493
2   K.A. Patmore, *The Court of Louis XIII*, 314–5
3   Ibid 315
4   C. Wedgwood, *Richelieu and the French Monarchy*, 179–80
5   Ibid 178-80
6   Wedgwood, 178
7   Ibid 182
8   Patmore, 337-8

Nº. 70

1   Hussein, *Encyclopædia Britannica 2001:* CD-ROM; & Andrew Cockburn and Patrick Cockburn, *SaddamHussein An American Obsession*, 68
2   Hussein, *Encyclopædia Britannica 2001:* CD-ROM; & Burhan Wazir, The Guardian, S April 12 2003, 11
3   Hussein, Ibid
4   Iraq, the People – Kurds, Ibid; & www.geocities.com/Athens/Ithaca/3291/page1.html

5   UN coalition and ultimatum, *Encyclopædia Britannica 2001:* CD-ROM; & Bruce W. Watson (ed.) *Military Lessons of the Gulf War,* 221-2
6   www2.gwu.edu/~nsarchiv/NSAEBB/NSAEBB82/]
7   www.thirdworldtraveler.com/Ronald_Reagan/Shaking_Hands_Saddam.html
8   whitehouse.gov/about/presidents/georgehwbush
9   Statue of Liberty, (Liberty Enlightening The World), *Encyclopædia Britannica 2001:* CD-ROM; & The Independent, Saturday 5 April 2003; & www.whitehouse.gov/history/presidents/gb41.html
10   Royal Mint, *A New Britannia for 2005*
11   *The Independent,* Saturday 5 April 2003, 19

N⁰. 71

1   *Encyclopædia Britannica,* 2001 CD-ROM, Galileo's Copernicanism and Physical Science, Astronomy
2   David Wootton, *Galileo Watcher of the Skies:* 134
3   Ibid Galileo's Condemnation; and Galileo's Copernicanism
4   Star of Bethlehem website of the National Maritime Museum at the Royal Observatory Greenwich. (Dr Peter Andrews, Institute of Astronomy, University of Cambridge.)
5   Joseph L. Sheler, *U.S. News & World Report ,* "In Search of Christmas," Dec. 23, 1996, 58
6   *Encyclopædia Britannica,* 2001 CD-ROM History of Europe – The Role of Science and Mathematics; also History of France, Cultural Transformation

N⁰. 76

1   Lewis and Short, *A Latin Dictionary;* & Macrinus, *Longmans English Larousse,* 217–8.
2   *Collins Gem Encyclopedia,* ed. Ian Crofton, 256
3   Antonia Fraser, *Cromwell Our Chief Of Men,* 3
4   *Encyclopædia Britannica 2001:* CD-ROM, Oliver Cromwell
5   Peter Young & Richard Holmes, *The English Civil War,* 292
6   *Encyclopædia Britannica 2001:* CD-ROM, Cromwell in Parliament
7   H.A.L. Fisher, *A History of Europe,* 667; & Maurice Ashley, *England in the Seventeenth Century,* 97
8   *Collins Gem Encyclopedia,* 216

N⁰. 84

1   http://www.bestofsicily.com/ww2.htm
2   Ibid
3   id
4   wikipedia.org/wiki/Operational_Zone_of_the_Adriatic_Littoral
5   wikipedia.org/wiki/Military_history_of_Italy_during_World_War_II#Allied_invasion_of_Sicily. 2C_Fall_of_Mussolini_and_Armistice
6   http://www.bestofsicily.com/ww2.htm
7   Same as reference 5
8   Ibid
9   id

N⁰. 88

1   Charles Emmanuel IV, *Encyclopædia Britannica 2001:* CD-ROM
2   Ibid
3   J.M. Thompson, *Napoleon Bonaparte,* 64-5
4   http://www.djhooker.com/48/22801.htm
5   'He reached such a state of detachment from the world that one saw this old King become blind and infirm ...' B. Grasset, *Histoire de Savoie.*
6   'Sometimes he would leave his cell and extend his hand to passers-by for alms. For the descendent of such a proud race ... this was really carrying too far the need of humiliation and the heroism of voluntary poverty.' Ibid

N⁰. 97

1   Derrik Mercer (ed.) *Chronicle of the Royal Family,* 400, 474
2   Patrick Colquoun, *A Treaty on the Wealth, Power and Resourcesof the British Empire* (1814), 54
3   Neil Grant, *Kings & Queens,* 218
4   Thomas Babington Macaulay, *The History of England, from the Accession of James II,* (1848),
5   Windsor Castle, *Encyclopædia Britannica 2001:* CD-ROM
6   Mercer, 400, 406, 409, 410, 413, 420, 424
7   Nicolas Bentley, *The Victorian Scene: 1837-1901,* 42, 204, 212; & John Belcham and Richard Price (ed.) *A Dictionary of Nineteenth Century History,* 665
8   Barbara Daniels, *Poverty and Families in the Victorian Era* (March 2003) 'Hidden Lives Revealed 1881 -1981'
9   Bentley, 212; & Mercer, 470; & Victoria, *Compton's Encyclopedia 2000:* CD-ROM
10   http://www.bbc.co.uk/history/british/victorians/middle_classes_01.shtml
11   Belcham and Price, 119; & Bentley, 220
12   Mercer, 475

CENTURY NINE

1   *Dans la maison du traducteur de Bourc*
     Seront les lettres trouuées sur la table,
     Borgne, roux blanc, chenu tiendra de cours,
     Qui changera au nouueau Connestable.

2   *Du hault du mont Auentin voix ouye,*
     Vuidez, vuidez de tous les deux costez,
     Du sang des rouges sera l'ire assomie,
     D'Arimin Prato, Columna debotez.

3   *La magna vaqua à Rauenne grand trouble,*
     Conduicts par quinze enserrez à Fornase:
     A Rome naistra deux monstres à teste double,
     Sang, feu, deluge, les plus grands à l'espase.

4   *L'an ensuyuant descouuerts par deluge,*
     Deux chefs esleuz, le premier ne tiendra
     De fuyr ombre à l'vn d'eux le refuge,
     Saccagée case qui premier maintiendra.

5   *Tiers doibt du pied au premier semblera*
     A vn nouueau Monarque de bas haut
     Qui Pyse & Luques Tyran occupera
     Du precedent corriger le deffault.

6   *Par la Guyenne infinité d'Anglois*
     Occuperont par nom d'Anglaquitaine
     Du Languedoc Ispalme Bourdelois.
     Qu'ils nommeront apres Barboxitaine.

7   *Qui ouurira le monument trouué,*
     Et ne viendra le serrer proprement,
     Mal luy viendra, & ne pourra prouué
     Si mieux doit estre Roy Breton ou Normand.

8   *Puisnay Roy fait son pere mettre à mort,*
     Apres conflict de mort tres-inhonneste:
     Escrit trouué soubson donra remort,
     Quand loup chassé pose sur la couchette.

9   *Quand lampe ardente de feu inextinguible*
     Sera trouuée au temple des Vestales,
     Enfant trouué, feu, eau passant par crible:
     Nismes eau perir. Tholose cheoir les hales.

10   *Moyne moynesse d'enfant mort exposé,*
     Mourir par ourse & rauy par verrier.
     Par Fois & Pamyes le camp sera pose
     Contre Tholose Carcas dresser forrier.

11   *Le iuste à tort à mort l'on viendra mettre*
     Publiquement, & du milieu estaint:
     Si grande peste en ce lieu viendra naistre,
     Que les iugeans fouyr seront contraints.

estaint (OF estainct) extinguished, naistre (OF) to take beginning; iugean (AF – jugier – to pronounce judgement) judgments;
fouyr (OF *syncope* – fouyer) hearth; constraint (AF ému) affected.
Cross-references: iuste, C.II: 53; C.II: 51; mettra à mort, C.IX: 49

The 'Just One' (**CHARLES 1**) to injustice; men will arrive to put him to death   1649
Publicly, and extinguished in the social surrounding:
Such great pestilence (**PLAGUE**) within this place will arrive to take beginning,
That the hearth judgements (**FIRE OF LONDON**) will be affected.

The Just One

Charles I was the legitimate King of England, therefore the 'Just One'. This has become part of the Seer's nomenclature for the English monarch who was unjustly executed in 1649.

To injustice

As the English Civil War drew to a close and with Charles I in captivity on the Isle of Wight, it was decided by Parliament that he should stand trial for treason and other high crimes. Without support from the House of Lords, the House of Commons was forced to appoint a High Court to try the King. But Charles responded to this injustice by refusing to acknowledge either the legitimacy of the tribunal, or the lawfulness of the charges brought against him. The government being made aware of its own dubious legality, and with the Lords mounting a protest at their exclusion from all further proceedings relating to the trial, the Commons prorogued further consultations, and summarily declared the monarchy abolished. [1]

Men will arrive to put him to death

At his trial, Charles was charged with high treason and "other high crimes against the realm of England." But when he refused to plead, Cromwell decided to accept the trial as an act of justice, and signed the death warrant. [2]

Publicly, and extinguished in the social surrounding

The execution was scheduled to take place publicly, outside the Banqueting Hall of Whitehall Palace at Westminster: the spectacle having been arranged, as it were, in the social milieu.

The venue soon filled up with an unrestricted gathering of onlookers who were keen to witness the beheading of a king. Situated inside the actual Banqueting Hall were soldiers, privileged visitors, and foreign ambassadors – "[an] abundance of men and women [...] to behold the saddest sight England ever saw." Outside the Hall, on the roofs of adjacent buildings, other onlookers had scrambled to find a position. And on the ground, massed around the scaffold, were several ranks of foot soldiers. To the rear of them were more troops on horseback, and then throngs of spectators behind barricades, all drawn to the scene. At 2 pm on 30 January 1649, the axe fell and the life of Charles I was extinguished in fulfilment of this prophecy. [3]

Such great pestilence within this place will arrive to take beginning

Sixteen years passed by, during which time the resumption of the monarchy had taken place. The Plague, however, was never far away, and in 1665 such great pestilence arrived in the city of London to commence its beginning that for the space of eleven months, close to 100,000 people perished. [4]

That the hearth judgements will be affected

In 1666, the year after the Great Plague of London, the capital suffered another blow, when a fire broke out in the *hearth* of Thomas Farrynor's cook-room in Pudding Lane (N.B. 'fuyer de galere' is old French for a cook-room). The flames quickly spread, covering an area from the Tower of London to Temple Church. For three days, London was affected as the fire spread, threatening to engulf the entire capital. During that time, "eighty churches, several of the city gates, and thirteen thousand two hundred dwelling houses [were destroyed]. The ruins covered a space of four hundred and twenty six acres." [5]

For many church-goers in London, the *Great Fire*, following within a year of the *Great Plague* caused the faithful to believe that the two disasters were divine retribution for having violated Holy Scripture by executing the King. For, biblical text stated that a monarch ruled by divine right. [6] Also, to add to their worries, were London's relaxed attitude to the liberal pleasures that had been ushered in by Charles II, after England reverted back to monarchical rule. [7] "Charles II was popularly known as the *Merry Monarch*: [8] in reference to both the liveliness and hedonism of his court." The titles given to the offspring of Charles II's mistresses have survived into the present age: most famous of which, are probably those descended from Nell Gwynne.

The oracle's reference to *judgements* would seem to have connotations with the *book of Judges* in the Bible. This refers to Israel having abandoned God and then been punished for its sinfulness. The connexion between England having abandoned God by executing its King, and afterwards suffering two disasters in quick succession, appeared ominous. Thus, "Some even saw the fire as a punishment from God." [9] The judgements voiced, surrounding the fire that began in the hearth of Thomas Farrynor, were therefore conditioned by the Plague that arrived in the previous year.

Summary: *The beheading of King Charles I is explicitly predicted in N°. 49 below: even to the month and day. This oracle adds to it by describing the scene of the execution, and connecting it to the Great Plague of London and to the Great Fire of London, which occurred one year apart (Century Two Nos. 51 & 53 refer). As with other predictions that were contrary to the time in which the seer lived, he devotes several quatrains to the King's execution. For instance, in Century Eight No. 37, the extra shirt requested by the King to prevent him shivering is implied: together with the place of execution, which was close to the Stangate ferryboat, later replaced in the 1740s by Westminster Bridge.*

12   *Le tant d'argent de Diane & Mercure*
        Les simulachres au lac seront trouuez:
        Le figulier cherchant argille neufue
        Luy & les siens d'or seront abbreuuez.

13   *Les Exilez autour de la Solongne*
        Conduicts de nuict pour marcher en l'Auxois,
        Deux de Modene truculent de Bologne,
        Mis descouuerts par feu de Burançois.

14   *Mis en planure chaulderon d'infecteurs,*
        Vin, miel & huyle, & bastis sur fourneaux
        Seront plongez, sans mal dit mal facteurs
        Sept. fum. extaint au canon des borneaux.

15   *Prés de Parpan les rouges detenus,*
        Ceux du milieu parfondrez menez loing:
        Trois mis en pieces, & cinq mal soustenus,
        Pour le Seigneur & Prelat de Bourgoing.

16   *De castel Franco sortira l'assemblée,*
        L'ambassadeur non plaisant fera scisme:
        Ceux de Ribiere seront en la meslée,
        Et au grand goulphre desnieront l'entrée.

castel (Spanish syncope) castel+lano – Castilian, hence Castile; Ribiere (OF *Epenthesis*, Riviere) riverside *also* (Spanish *anag.* & *parag.*) Rivera; desnier (AF - denier) refuse

Concerning Castile, **FRANCO** will depart from the ruling body,   1936
The ambassador (**ROSENBERG**), not being pleased, he will make a schism:
Those of the riverside (**RIVERA**) will be in the conflict,
And at the great gulf, they will refuse entrance.

Concerning Castile

This oracle describes events that took place before and during the Spanish Civil War. Although the revolt started in Morocco, and then spread to garrisons on the mainland: "The Civil War took place because the rising was successful only in Old Castile." [1]

Franco will depart from the ruling body

The oracle pinpoints the precise event that was to bring about the Spanish Civil War. It was Franco's departure from mainland Spain to become Military Commander and Governor of the Canary Islands. The move was meant to remove him from political influence amongst members of the ruling body, but it had the opposite effect. On 18 July 1936, "while serving as Governor of the Canary Islands, he led the anti-Socialist revolt which began the Spanish Civil War." [2]

The ambassador

The ambassador referred to in the oracle was a Russian diplomat, Marcel Rosenberg. One month after civil war broke out, Spain agreed to resume diplomatic relations with Russia, and an ambassador was sent to Madrid from Moscow. Rosenberg's arrival in Spain coincided with Franco's rise to prominence. [3]

Not being pleased, he will make a schism

Franco soon became deeply suspicious of the Russian ambassador's growing influence amongst Spain's socialists. He therefore ordered Moscow to recall Rosenberg. The ambassador was clearly not pleased at receiving this sudden recall. Consequently, before leaving Spain, he devised a plot involving key members of the opposition parties. [4]

"Skilfully, Rosenberg, while he was still in Valencia [...] cultivated good relations with Largo Caballero's great socialist rival, Indalecio Preto." This relationship eventually caused the predicted schism, with its mass resignations that followed.

"On 13th May [1937] the Spanish Communist Party brought matters to a crisis." Two of the party members who held government office demanded that Cabellero dissolve the PUOM. The demand was refused and the two ministers walked out of the cabinet meeting. This appears to have been a prearranged signal because, "Simultaneously, the Russians let it be known that they would not provide aircraft for an offensive in Extremadura, which Largo Caballero had long been planning." A ministerial crisis immediately followed in which moderate socialists, who had been backing Caballero, went over to the Communists. With his party *divided*, that is, the predicted schism having been brought about, "Largo Caballero was forced out of office." [5]

Those of the riverside (Rivera) will be in the conflict

José Antonio Rivera was the founding-leader of a political party called the 'Falange Espanola'. The party's intentions were initially peaceful, but this failed to prevent its members becoming involved in the fighting. "José Antonio had lost all ability to steer his followers away from the path of violence [...] Though it was not the Falangists who had started the firing, they continued it with a vengeance." [6]

Added to this, during the civil war the River Manzanares, which flows through Madrid, became the scene of a desperate, bloody and heroic stand by the citizens of the city. On 8 November: "the Army of Africa suffered casualties on a scale hitherto unknown as it battled to cross the Manzanares." The opposition were ordinary citizens, those of Madrid, who, being armed only with old rifles and little ammunition, were still able to position themselves on the riverside and halt the Nationalist forces as they fought to cross the river. [7]

And at the great gulf, they will refuse entrance

The great gulf describes a bird's-eye view of the Mediterranean Sea. This had to be crossed by Franco from Morocco to mainland Spain in order to supply his forces with the large shipments of armaments needed for the war. However, all attempts to carry these arms into Spain by ship were opposed. The Republican Navy had set up a blockade, refusing entrance to the mainland.

> One by one, the ships of the Republican Navy, led by the battleship Jaime I, were steaming towards Tangier. Once anchored there, they might make it impossible for the Army of Africa to cross the Strait. [8]

The blockade proved to be so efficient that Franco was forced to convey his armaments by air.

Summary: *The names of both Franco and Rivera can be read from this oracle, both of whom were combatants in the Spanish Civil War. Added to this, the content of the verse correctly describes several major events in that conflict. These were: the success of its beginning in Old Castile, the part played by the ambassador, Marcel Rosenberg, the importance of the Manzanares riverside, and the refusal of mainland Spain to allow Franco use of the Mediterranean for the transportation of his armaments.*

17   *Le tiers premier pis que ne fit Neron,*
Vuidez vaillant que sang humain respandre
R'édifier fera le forneron,
Siècle d'or, mort, nouueau Roy grand esclandre.

vuidez (OF) exempted from; vaillant (AF de grande valeur) of great worth; r'edifier (AF) re-edifying; forneron (OF fornier) a baker, hence, fourneron: baker's boy; siècle (OF) age, time season; esclandre (OF scandale) scandal, disgust.

The third (**ESTATE**) foremost: worse than Nero did;   1793
Exempted from great worth, as human blood pours out:
It will act to re-edify the **BAKER'S BOY**,
The season of 'dor', death, a new king (**LOUIS XVIII**), a great scandal.

The third foremost

In France during the *Ancien Regime* the reigning monarch ruled by divine right. It was therefore his prerogative to summon together the Estates General to discuss any pressing problems that had arisen, but only when it was considered necessary. There were three estates: the first was the clergy, the second the nobility and the third was reserved mostly for professional men.

In 1788, a fiscal crisis occurred in France, and it was decided, for the first time since 1614, to convene the Estates General. They met at Versailles in June 1789; but because of the disruption that occurred during this convention, the seeds of the French Revolution were sewn.

Once the overthrow of the monarchy had been achieved, the abolition of the nobility followed, and the Second Estate disappeared. At the same time a programme of de-Christianising France swept through the land, and this brought to an end the power of the First Estate. With the first and second estates removed from power, the *Third* Estate became *foremost*.[1]

Worse than Nero did

The catalogue of crimes committed by the Third Estate against the nobility, the clergy and ordinary citizens, is far too long to be contained in a single paragraph. For brevity, one may simply call to mind the September Massacres of 1792, in which many hundreds of priests, nuns and novices were put to the sword, or to the mass drowning that was carried out at Nantes, where 'Republican Baptisms' involved locking priests into the belly of a boat before sinking it in the river Loire.

At Gonnord, thirty children were deliberately buried alive. Sentences of death were passed for the most trivial of reasons; and trials, if they can be called that, made Justice hide her head in shame.

> Hundreds of innocent people suffered [...] some of them through clerical and administrative errors, or even because their accusers chose not to spare them. Others were sentenced on the strength of denunciations by jealous or vindictive neighbours.[2]

Nero has acquired a much deserved reputation from historians for brutality against Christians.

> Nero had begun the persecution of Christians (daubing them with pitch and burning them alive as torches for his nightly garden parties or sewing them in the skins of wild animals to be hunted by dogs) [although] this was limited in duration and location.[3]

Exempted from great worth, as human blood pours out

In the midst of this heinous carnival of judicial carnage were the atheist politicians who, being exempt from any great qualities, especially justice, finally yielded to poetic justice, and handed out death sentences to each other: thus causing even more human blood to pour out from those caught up in this frenzy of inhuman, political insanity.

> ... day after day, the guillotining continued. Unsuccessful generals suffered with fallen politicians, men convicted of publishing counter-revolutionary writings or of airing royalist opinions with deserters and traitors [...] Throughout the autumn and winter of 1793 the Terror was maintained unabated. [...] Nearly 3,000 executions took place in Paris; about 14,000 in the provinces.[4]

It will act to re-edify the baker's boy

Inside the Temple Tower, at the time it held the royal family captive, was the heir to the French throne: the eight-year-old prince, Louis Charles. He had begun life as the younger brother of the next in line for the throne, but his brother Louis Joseph died, 4 June 1789, and so Louis Charles became the new Dauphin. By then he had already received a preliminary education in writing, drawing and natural history from his tutor, the Abbé d'Avaux who, "filled him full of moral maxims and classical anecdotes."

But during his incarceration inside the Temple, it was decided "to retrain – or brainwash – the former Dauphin. [...] The Commune's prosecutor, Chaumette, had declared the previous year: 'I wish to give him [Louis Charles] some education. I will take him from his family to make him lose the idea of rank.'" The tutor appointed to re-edify the little boy was Antoine Simon, a cobbler. "Dirty books, rowdy songs, blasphemy and brandy—that was the regime which Simon found perfectly natural for his pupil, since it was his own." [5]

Louis-Charles is identified in this prophecy as 'The Baker's Boy'. The Dauphin actually obtained this nickname from the 'poissardes'. These were the market women and fishwives who marched to Versailles demanding that the royal family relocate to the centre of Paris and take up residence in the *Palais de Tuileries* (5 October 1789). The Baker's Boy is also the heading of Chapter Two in the Dauphin's biography, *The Son of Marie Antoinette*, by Meade Minnigerode.

It was during the royal family's enforced journey to the capital that the cheering women, who were celebrating their triumph at removing Louis XVI, Marie Antoinette and Louis Charles from Versailles, sang that they were bringing "the baker, the baker's wife and 'the baker's boy' to Paris." [6] This emphasis on baking was due to the shortage of bread at that time caused by a poor harvest.

A season of 'dor'

The final line of this quatrain is a further example of the cryptic clues embedded within these prophecies, for while this phrase appears to speak of a golden age (*Siecle d'or*), the time of the French Revolution was quite the opposite.

What the oracle is secretly alluding to is the Republican Calendar, in which each month was renamed according to one of the four seasons. We therefore discover that 'dor' occurred in the summer months of Messi**dor**, Thermi**dor** and Fructi**dor**. [7] And, it was during this season in 1795 that the fulfilment of the last part of this prophecy occurred.

Death

In the summer of 1795, ten-year-old Louis-Charles, *the baker's boy*, died from tuberculosis; his death was "exacerbated by conditions that were at best neglectful, at worst brutal." [8]

A new king

After the death of Louis Charles (nominally Louis XVII), the Comte de Provence, who at that time was in exile in Verona, at once declared himself to be the new king, taking the title, Louis XVIII "He [also] announced that on his return to the throne he would restore the traditional three orders in France." [9]

A great scandal

Plans were soon underway for the restoration of the monarchy. On 27 June 1795 (9 Messidor III) an émigré army financed by English money, and aided by Chouan forces from the Vendée, landed on the southern coast of Brittany. But General Lazare Hoche and his Republican Army had already arrived to meet the insurgent army.

In the fierce battle between the two sides, seven hundred combatants, including ennobled members of the Ancient Regime, were taken prisoner. It was then that a great scandal took place. The captives, together with many titled members of the nobility, were executed by firing squad for high treason. The repercussions this caused in Europe were to continue for many years, further blackening the revolutionary movement. [10]

Summary: One of the most outstanding statements in this oracle is the seer's reference to 'The Baker's Boy'. This actually forms the title of Chapter Two in Meade Minnigerode's biography of Louis Charles, which he called 'The Son of Marie Antoinette' (published by Jarrolds of London in 1935). The base attempt at re-educating the little prince by the Third Estate is accompanied by a more general description of the baseness to which its members had descended. The timing of the events has also been encoded, and with it the oracle ends by predicting the boy's death and the reinstatement of his uncle as the new King. The attempt made at re-engaging the nobility by returning the émigrés to France, concluded instead with their execution, thereby heaping further scandal upon the Third Estate.

18   *Le lys Dauffois portera dans Nansi,*
      Iusques en Flandres Electeur de l'Empire,
      Neufue obturée au grand Montmorency,
      Hors lieux prouuez deliure à clere peyne.

Dauffois (syncope) Dauph[in]ois = person of Dauphiné; obturee (L obtur\o), to close, to seal; neufve (OF) new, unused; clere (AF assuré, certain) fixed *also* 'clere peyne', Clerepeyne.

The Man of Dauphiné (**LOUIS XIII**),will carry the lily into Nancy   1632
Even into Flanders: Elector of the Empire (**VON SÖTERN**),
Unused, enclosed for the great **MONTMORENCY**,
Outside the premises approved, delivered to a fixed punishment (**CLEREPEYNE**).

The man of Dauphiné

Dauphin was the title given to the eldest son of the French king. It was derived from the province of Dauphiné, which was ceded to Philip de Valois by Humbert III in 1349, but on the condition that it would always belong to the eldest Prince of the realm. After the death of Francis II in 1560, France had to wait until the birth of Louis XIII in 1601 before the title could again be applied to a male heir.

Although Louis XIII became king in his ninth year, and had abundant time to learn the profession of kingship, he never truly took the reins of power himself, preferring instead to allow others to act in his name. "He was well aware that he lacked the ability and application to rule France, and he left the tedious detail to others." [1]

The first of the surrogate rulers was Louis' mother, Marie de' Medicis. She was followed by a favourite of the King, the duc de Luynes. Finally, Cardinal Richelieu took over as head of state. In this sense, Louis XIII remained a Prince throughout his life, never really making the transition from Dauphin to King. It was, therefore, in this sense that he fulfilled the role predicted in the oracle—the Man of Dauphiné. [2]

Will carry the lily into Nancy

In 1632, Louis XIII carried his royal standard, the Fleur-de-Lys – the lily – into Nancy. This was in response to his brother Gaston having married the Duke of Lorraine's sister, without having obtained royal approval. [3] In the brief conflict that followed, Lorraine's troops suffered a heavy defeat and the Duke was forced to concede terms to the King. Gaston, however, simply fled, seeking refuge in Brussels.

The voluntary exile of the King's brother to the Spanish Netherlands, where his mother later joined him, posed a new threat to France. Louis therefore sought some form of justification for invading Flanders, so that he could remove the troublesome danger posed by his brother. He eventually found the excuse he was seeking, and took action. "May 19 1635, – France declares war on Spain on the pretext of Spaniards carrying off the Elector of Trèves."

Even into Flanders

"The old international rule of declaring war by a herald was still in use. Louis XIII was the last to observe this custom, when in 1635 he sent a herald-at-arms to Brussels to declare war on Spain." Carrying the lily into Flanders in order to declare war was therefore the last opportunity for this oracle to be fulfilled. [4] Flanders was then part of the Spanish Netherlands and its capital was Brussels.

Elector of the empire

Louis XIII's excuse for invading Flanders came when Philip Christoph von Sötern was forcibly removed to Tervuren in Flanders, and later imprisoned. [5] Sötern was "elected elector-archbishop of Trier in 1623." [6] "Initially, there were seven electors: the Count Palatine of the Rhine, the King of Bohemia, the Duke of Saxony, the Margrave of Brandenburg, and the Archbishops of Cologne, Mainz, and Trier." [7] (Wikipedia – Holy Roman Empire). Philip Sötern was also a Francophile, and his support for Cardinal Richelieu in the Thirty-Years-War had resulted in his abduction in 1635 by Spanish Hapsburg troops.

Unused, enclosed for the great Montmorency

Three years earlier in Languedoc, Henri, II duc de Montmorenci, its governor since 1614, who had been made Grand Admiral that year and appointed Marshal of France in 1630, was captured during the final stages of the battle of Castelnaudary (1 October 1632). This immensely popular figure, known locally as the great Montmorency – "the greatest nobleman of France outside the royal family itself," [8] – had been inveigled by the King's brother, Gaston, to raise a rebellion in the south against the King. The uprising was intended to coincide with Gaston's own insurrection in Lorraine, but the Prince's part in the plan failed when he was defeated and forced to flee to Brussels. When news of the uprising in Languedoc reached Louis, a detachment of the King's army left Nancy and marched south to engage the rebels.

Once again, the army of Louis XIII was victorious, and Montmorency was captured. However, because of his rank and title, he was not thrown into a common gaol, but enclosed under guard inside Toulouse's newly constructed, and as then unused, *Hôtel de Ville*, where he awaited trial for his treason. [9]

As an interesting aside, before his capture, and when Montmorency saw the battle was lost, he continued to fight single-handed, so that he might die with honour in full armour. His efforts failed; instead of death he received only dreadful wounds. Had he succeeded in his effort to die on the battlefield, this prophecy would have failed, or more than likely, never have been made.

Outside the premises approved

On 30 October, the Duke mounted the scaffold to meet his death. The execution was no longer a public affair. "It was thought safer to carry out the sentence in private." Fearing the violence of the crowd and with deference to a request made by the condemned man's noble family, the venue was changed from the Place de Salin, and the scaffold was instead erected outside the newly approved premises, which was "in the quadrangle of the Parliament House, the Capitol of Toulouse." [10] Armed troops lined the streets outside the building, and even ringed the raised platform on which the beheading was to take place. The verdict of guilty had not been well received, and the sentence of execution evoked such an outcry, even from countries outside France, that had it not been for Richelieu's intractable opposition to a reprieve, Louis XIII would have spared the condemned man's life.

Delivered to a fixed punishment

Before the day of execution, an agreement had been reached that this disgraced nobleman from one of the most illustrious families in France be spared his death blow at the hands of a common headsman. It was for this reason that a soldier, a serving officer from the King's regiment, was chosen to carry out the sentence. Moreover, because of the rebellious mood amongst large sections of the crowd, it was decided that the execution be carried out in private.

A contemporary print of Montmorency at the point of his beheading confirms the status of his executioner. It displays this person attired in the finery of a gentleman, quite possibly from the *gardes du corps*. [11] And, no less importantly, "The duke of Montmorency was not beheaded by the axe but by a kind of slightly scimitar curve. This weapon is retained at the Capitol of Toulouse in a sheath of portfolio lined with velvet." [12]

Clerepeyne

Seventeen years after Étienne Jaubert, a physician from Amiens, published his interpretation of

this prophecy, in which Clerepeyne was named as executioner of Montmorency, the Chevalier de Jant, a knight in service to Philippe I, Duke of Orleans, King Louis XIV's brother, had became so interested in this prophecy and its interpretation that he made the long journey down to Toulouse in order to check the facts for the Court. It was there that he discovered Montmorency's executioner had indeed been Clerepeyne, an officer of the King who was attached to the royal army sent by Louis XIII to restore order in the district. [13]

EXECUTION OF HENRI II DUC DE MONTMORENCI

It so happens that Clerepeyne's name is fully attested by Étienne Jaubert and by the Chevalier de Jant, both contemporary with the event. Further than this, M. Motret has brought to light, after minute historic research, that the family, by solicitation of the King, could obtain only two concessions of mere formality – that the execution should be with closed doors, and by a soldier in lieu of the common headsman. [14] (Engraving from cabinet des Estampes showing "exécution de Henri II MONTMORENCY" — Grand Larousse Encyclopedique).

In this matter it should not be overlooked that Jaubert wrote in 1656, "All France recounts diverse events predicted by the Author, but not wishing to write anything without being assured about it, I omit them." Neither should it be overlooked that the oracle has deliberately avoided rhyming *clere* with *empire* in order to affirm that the word order, 'clere peyne' is to be understood.

Summary: *As with No. 16 above, this oracle also contains two names: those of Montmorenci and his executioner , Clerepeyne. The first half of the oracle sets the scene at the time of Louis XIII, and refers to the trouble he endured from his envious brother, who repeatedly plotted against him. Gaston was also the cause of Montmorenci losing his life, as yet another of his plots failed. A further clue to the timing of this oracle is found in the ceasing of the manner in which declarations of war were made. Louis XIII was the last to use the ancient method of carrying a royal standard into the enemy's capital to declare war. Noticeably, this also corresponds in time with the kidnapping of the Elector of the Empire, Philip Sötern.*

19   Dans le milieu de la forest Mayenne,
      Sol au Lyon la foudre tombera,
      Le grand bastard yssu du grand du Maine,
      Ce iour Fougeres pointe en sang entrera.

20   De nuict viendra par la forest de Reines,
      Deux pars voltorte Herne la pierre blanche,
      Le moine noir en gris dedans Varennes
      Esleu cap. cause tempeste, feu, sang tranche.

de Reines (*anag. parag.*) d[a] Ren[n]es, Ardennes; pars (AF égal) alike; voltorte (*portmanteau*, vol+torte: (OF flight + wrong) N.B. vaulter, volter (AF - changer de route; also. *Fencing term:* Changer de place pour éviter les coups de l' adversaire; see Dictionnaire de L'Academie français; moine (AF religieux) religious; Herne (folklore) The Woodland Hunter; noir (as before) *also* [n]roi; cap. (*abbrev.*) Cap[et]. Cross-references: cap, C.IV: 11; C.VIII: 19; C.IX: 26.

By night there will come through the forest of Queens (**ARDENNES**),   1791
Two alike, wrong flight, the Woodland Hunter, the white stone,
LEMOINE: the religious (**KING**) ghastly, in grey inside **VARENNES**.
Elected chief (**CAPET**), causes storm, passion, blood slice.

By night there will come through the forest of queens (Ardennes), two alike

During the French Revolution, the royal family's bid to flee Paris was planned for the night of 20 June 1791. Shortly after midnight, clinging to the shadows, the King and Queen of France secretly made their way out of the palace to an awaiting coach. A short ride took them to the luxurious *berline de voyage* that was to carry them to the French border with Belgium.

All through the night of the 20th and the next day, the royal party made its way unrecognised and unimpeded through the French countryside, where wayside inns in little towns and villages provided them with fresh horses. This far, all seemed to be going according to plan.

By the night of June 21, the *berline* had reached the vast area of woodland that was once part of the ancient forest of Ardennes. This was the route chosen by the Queen when planning the direction for their escape. Ambassador Mercy had already written to Vienna explaining: "Marie Antoinette was arranging the whole thing." Hence, the Ardennes forest was the Queen's choice. [1]

But, on the night of the 21st the escape plan faltered, and the scene was set for one of the most dramatic events in the history of France. [2]

Unbeknown to the occupants inside the *berline*, a chase through the surrounding woodland had just begun. The King had allowed himself to be recognized at their last stop. And the success or failure of the ensuing pursuit would result in either their capture or their freedom. Either way, the future of France was at issue.

Wrong flight

"The route they had chosen [...] was less frequented than the main way through Chateau Thierry and Epernay." It also avoided Rheims where the King was known by sight. [3] Despite the care taken, it would eventually lead to their downfall.

When the coach reached Sainte-Ménéhould, the King carelessly allowed himself to be seen at the carriage window. The postmaster standing close by, an ex-dragoon named Jean-Baptiste Drouet, who had been eying the coach with suspicion, thought he recognized the face, and reported what he had seen to the local mayor. Plans were hastily made. Drouet was to ride ahead and raise the alarm in the next town so that the identities of those inside the *berline* could be verified.

Once in the saddle, Drouet took with him a local innkeeper named Gillaume, and together they set off towards Verdun in pursuit of the coach. But, after galloping some miles, without gaining sight of their quarry, it began to occur to Drouet that they were on the wrong road. He now suspected that the coach must have turned off at the crossroads some way back, and was heading for Varennes.

Woodland hunter

It was at this point in the pursuit that Drouet became the *woodland hunter*. [4] He left the road, with or without Guillaume (one account says that Guillaume rode on to Verdun in case the coach was still on the road ahead), and headed for a shortcut that he knew, which led through the forest to Varennes. It was a moonless night, but not yet completely dark. The chase had begun. Drouet must reach *Varennes* before the coach ahead left town.

The white stone

As Drouet galloped hastily through the forest, the next part of the prophecy became fulfilled. Ahead of him, the *woodland hunter* saw "the glimmer of a known white stone, a landmark." Drouet "sheered down a ride to the right: the wood ended abruptly, and they [*sic*] saw below [...] the lights of Varennes [5] Had *the white stone* been missed, Drouet would have become lost in the forest, and the *berline* would have continued on its uninterrupted journey to the frontier. But, there, still in town, was his prey – the *berline* – with its occupants quite unaware of the great drama that was about to unfold.

Lemoine

Meanwhile, in Paris, Louis XVI's senior valet: a man named *Lemoine* was the first person to discover that the King had left. "It was 7 a.m. precisely at the Tuileries when the royal manservant, Lemoine, drew the curtains of the bed to wake the King up. The bed was empty!" [6] Louis had, of course, escaped in the night *disguised as his valet.*

> Since the Revolution was in the process of reducing them to common citizens, how fitting it would be to depart reversing roles with their servants. [...] the King, in round hat, wig and plain coat, was to play the valet. [7]

The religious (King) ghastly

The Seer has used *noir* before, when describing Charles IX's part in the St. Bartholomew's Eve Massacre (Century Four No. 47). On this occasion, Louis XVI's flight to Varennes was arguably the gravest and most ghastly error he ever made. It lost him valuable support from the public, and cost him his life, as well as those of the Queen, his sister Elisabeth, and his son.

The oracle also refers to the King's devotion to his religious faith – hence *the religious king*. For, as his biographer indicated, "he never ceased praying to God [...] for Louis XVI Christ was an immediate reality [...] he was at one with [...] the thousands of loyal priests." [8]

In grey, inside Varennes

But now, inside Varennes, Drouet having caught up with the *berline* quickly raised the alarm. The bridge leading out of town was quickly blocked by a cart, and the procurator was summoned to the scene. A crowd soon gathered around the royal party, whose travel papers were being examined in the light of glowing lanterns. The King, still incognito as the valet, stood in the lantern light dressed *in grey* – "a grey coat, satin waistcoat, grey breeches and stockings, shoes with buckles and a three-cornered hat." [9]

> At that period, when it took six or seven days by diligence to go from Varennes to Paris, it was a remarkable thing to see the King. [...] And thus there was great stupefaction when Louis XVI showed himself [...] pale, fat and silent, with a dull eye, a hanging lip, a shabby wig and a grey coat. [10]

Elected chief, (Capet)

Within the hour, Louis XVI was identified by a former courtier living in Varennes, and his bid to escape came to an abrupt end. Next day the coach was turned round, and under guard, Louis XVI and Marie Antoinette were returned to Paris. The King was then suspended while both the Assembly and the nation argued amongst themselves concerning the monarchy's future.

Finally, on 3 September 1791, Louis XVI was given another chance to take an active role in government, this time as the nation's constitutional head. The Assembly *elected* him as France's *Chief* Executive. [11] But this did not prevent criticism. In the Press, as elsewhere, Louis XVI began to be called by the derogatory title, "Louis Capet", [12] sometimes even "Citizen Capet". (The name, Capet, was obtained from his ancestors, but he personally deplored its use).

Causes storm, passion

For the three months following his return to Paris, the King had remained suspended from office while the Assembly debated in private what the country continued to discuss publicly – Was the King a traitor to his people? As a result, France "seethed like a sea in a storm," [13] while the monarchy, now virtually powerless, tottered towards its inevitable destruction.

Inside parliament, "Passionate debates tore the Assembly asunder." [14] While outside, protests were repeatedly voiced aloud, condemning the King as a traitor to his country. Eventually, on 10 August 1792, the intensity of emotion boiled over, and a band of revolutionaries, inspired by the oratory of Danton marched towards the royal palace intent upon murder.

Blood slice

Outside the Tuileries, a company of Swiss bodyguards were on duty. Previously, news had been brought to the King of the threatened strike against the royal palace. For his family's safety, he and they were given refuge inside a small room in the Assembly Hall. Secure behind the walls of the building, Louis sent a written message to the Swiss guards, ordering them not to fire on the people. The order proved to be a further error by this already blackened King.

> The Swiss were massacred and then cut to slices. Their heads and arms were severed from their bodies. [...] Eight hundred Swiss and gentlemen lost their lives because Louis XVI could not bear the thought of violence [15]

Summary: *As France's celebrated novelist, Alexandre Dumas wrote, after trying his hand at history, "Nobody spoke*
of Varennes before June 21st 1791. On the 22nd, Varennes was the subject of the whole world's talk;
all Europe had its eyes fixed on it. Varennes lived a fevered life for twelve hours. During these twelve
hours an event of immense importance took place within its walls… never again will an event of this
importance occur to efface the remembrance of this one." [16] *The seer names Varennes and describes the*
colour of the King's disguise at the time of his arrest, having also named his valet, whose attire he copied.
Drouet's dash through the forest at night is indicated in some detail, in which the landmark known as the
'white stone' played an important role in guiding the horseman to Varennes in time to denounce the King.
Following Louis' arrest and his ignominious return to Paris, the furore he caused across the country, and the
name he came to be called, Capet, when his role as Chief Executive became known, are correctly foretold;
as, too, is the slicing to pieces of the palace's Swiss guard, which brought to an end Louis XVI's reign.

21   Au temple haut de Bloys sacre Salonne,
        Nuict pont de Loyre, Prelat, Roy pernicant:
        Curseur victoire aux marestz de la Lone,
        D'où prelature de blancs abormeant.

22   Roy & sa court au lieu de langue halbe,
        Dedans le temple vis à vis du palais:
        Dans le iardin Duc de Mantor & d'Albe,
        Albe & Mantor poignard langue & palais.

halbe (OF syncope, halb[ard]e) halberd; Mantor (L portmanteau, [Mant\o + or\a] awaiting + end, *also* de Mantor (*reverse syllables*
& paragram) d[i]e Man[n]or – Normandie: N.B. Manto\r was the name of a prophetess; Albe (Late Latin, Alb) white *or* (L albeo),
to become white; palais (AF *homonym*,) palace, *also*, public

                    King and his court at the place of the halberd language (**TEMPLE TOWER**),   1792
                    Inside the temple, face to face with the palace,
                    In the garden, **DUKE NORMANDY** (awaiting the end) and **BLANCH**,
                    Blanch and Normandy, dagger language and in public.

King and his court at the place of the halberd language

After the Tuileries Palace had been ransacked, and the Swiss guardsmen murdered in a frenzy of
killing, which also included many of the palace staff, the King and Queen were taken to the
Temple. Accompanying them were their two children and the King's sister. It was a dark, sombre
building in which two floors had been assigned to the royal party. Attending them was a catering
staff of thirteen and a valet. In effect, this was now *the place of the King and his court.*

No longer was there any privacy. Armed guards (hence the halberds) occupied the tower at all
times, and the crudity of their *tongue* became a frequent means of insulting the royal party, who
were now powerless to respond. [1]

Inside the Temple, face to face with the palace

The Temple, which had now become their prison, had once been a medieval keep. When Louis
and his family arrived there, several days after the sacking of the Tuileries, they had expected to
be lodged inside the palace: a part of the building that had formerly housed the King's brother,
the duc d'Artois. [2] Instead, the King and his family were given rooms *inside the Temple* Tower. It
was a building situated directly *opposite to the palace.* [3]

In the garden, Duke Normandy awaiting the end, and Blanch

On 27 March 1785, at the time of his baptism, Louis Charles had been proclaimed Duke of
Normandy. He therefore became "the first son of France to bear that title in three hundred years." [4]
But now, aged only eight, he was confined behind the Temple walls, a child prisoner of the State.
For some time he was not seen by those visiting the Temple, causing the Committee to become
aware of rumours that he was no longer inside the keep.

After that, his guardian, Antoine Simon, was told to take him for regular walks *in the garden.* [5]
He would eventually die inside his prison cell from neglect and disease. His little life ending at
the age of ten (8 June 1795): twenty months after the execution of his mother.

The Duke of Normandy's mother, Marie Antoinette is appropriately referred to in this oracle as 'Blanch': this was because her hair had turned white as a result of her ordeal – "blanchis par la douleur".[6] Although separated from her son, and confined to her room, the Queen managed to find a crack in the woodwork of the turret, and there she would stand for hours every day, peeping through in the hope of catching just a glimpse of her little son in the garden below.

Sadly, like her son, she, too, would soon meet her end. On 3 August 1793, Marie Antoinette was removed from the Temple and taken to the Conciergerie. The time had arrived for the Queen to be tried for treason. But for such an important event: one with international consequences, a legal case had first to be made against her.

Blanch and Normandy, dagger language and in public

In an attempt to defame Marie Antoinette to the fullest possible extent, her chief prosecutor devised a story in which the Queen stood accused of an incestuous relationship with her eight-year-old son. The oracle's phrase: *dagger language* is sexual innuendo for this piece of calumny.[7] Robespierre, to his credit, rejected the story completely, and the Committee of Public Safety ordered it to be suppressed. But a juror demanded that it be read out in court. The accusation of incest (*dagger language*) between *Blanch and Normandy* was therefore made *public*.[8]

Summary: Once again the seer returns to the French Revolution. On this occasion he takes up the story of the royal family's imprisonment inside the Temple Tower. It begins with the 'halberd language' of the prison guards, who were now free to insult the King and Queen without fear of reprisal. Having described the place of their captivity, the oracle foretells the end of both the Queen and her son: both having been deliberately set apart from each other after the King's execution. The future heir to the throne, Louis Charles, has also been named by the ducal title he bore, which had not been used for more than 300 years, thus adding emphasis to its prescient reference. The oracle concludes by exposing the calumny endured by the Queen when she stood accused of sexual intercourse with her little son.

23　　*Puisnay ioüant au fresch dessous la tonne,*
　　　Le haut du toit du milieu sur la teste:
　　　Le pere Roy au temple sainct Solonne,
　　　Sacrifiant sacrera fum de feste.

puisnay (OF puisné) the one born after; ioüant (OF *imperative* of iouër) representing; fresche (OF - fres) coolness; tonne (*apocope*, tonne[rre]) tun & Tonnerre; toit (AF forteresse) fortress; teste (L test\ae) broken bricks; Solonne (Spanish, Solanne) Solano; fum (L fum\us) empty promises, *also* (AF fumée) dreams. Cross-reference: milieu, C.I: 65.

Representing the one born after, in the coolness, under the tun (**TONNERRE**), 1789
The summit of the fortress (**BASTILLE**) with the milieu upon the broken bricks,
THE FATHER KING at the temple: **SAINT SOLANO (14 JULY)**,
Offering a sacrifice, he will dedicate the empty promises of the festival.

Representing the one born after

This prophecy once again takes the reader to the French Revolution. On this occasion it is to its commencement. In 1789 Louis XVI was still King of France. He was also the eldest surviving member of three brothers. The, one born after him was the Duke of Provence.[1] Consequently, Provence represents *the one born after* the King. But, in terms of the concealed fashion in which these oracles have been constructed, it is not Provence the person who is intended as the subject, but the region of Provence in south-east France.

In the coolness

At the beginning of 1789, Provence suffered its worst winter for eighty years, and it led to a shortage of bread. The water had frozen in the icy conditions and the mills ceased to operate, which meant they were unable to grind the flour to make bread.[2] The conditions of famine had begun.

This icy winter had also coincided with recent elections across France, in which Aix-en-Province acquired a new person as its representative in Paris.

Under the tun (Tonnerre)

Honoré-Gabriel Riqueti, Comte de Mirabeau was the newly elected representative for Aix-en-Provence. The Seer has punned on the Count's nickname, *Tonnerre:* this being the aptronym by which he had become known: *viz:* "Mirabeau–Tonnerre". [3] "Sheer size singled out Mirabeau: a mountain of flesh and muscle crammed with difficulty into black coat and hose." [4]

It was through his election in January that the people of Provence came under Mirabeau-Tonnerre's governance. And, it is an interesting fact that the people of Marseilles had also wanted him as their representative, but he had chosen Aix-en-Provence. Had he chosen Marseilles, this prophecy would have been written differently.

One of Mirabeau's first tasks, as representative of the people of *Provence* was to issue a report to the Assembly in Paris concerning the dreadful weather conditions in the south, and the effect it was having upon his constituents.

The summit of the fortress, with the milieu, upon the broken bricks

In the summer of that year, on 14 July 1789, the great Parisian *fortress* known as the Bastille, and which formed part of the old city walls was invaded by an angry mob. In the midst of the affray, the governor was killed, the prisoners released, and the building torn down, brick by brick. The scene is described in the painting by Pierre Antoine Demachy: 'The Demolition of the Bastille'. It shows the invading mob clambering over the brickwork (*sur la teste*) at the top (*le hault*) of the fortress (*du toict*), while in the process of demolishing it. [5]

The mob that raided the Bastille was acting on the assumption that the King was bringing armed troops into Paris to disband the newly constituted National Assembly. Seizing the Bastille was meant to diminish the fortress's importance, and to send a warning to the King. It achieved its purpose. Louis ordered his troops to withdraw. He also agreed to accept the 'new constitutional development'.

The Father King

Three days later, on 17 July, Louis XVI was asked to attend the *Hôtel de Ville* in Paris and accept the Assembly's formal approval of his willingness to comply with the new political order. The King left Versailles under heavy escort and arrived in Paris amidst cheers from the people and cries of: "Our King, our father!" When Louis reached his destination at the centre of Paris, he saw the chants had been confirmed in writing. For in large letters above the archway ran the slogan: LOUIS XVI; FATHER OF THE FRENCH; THE KING OF A FREE PEOPLE. [6]

At the Temple

In the summer of 1790, within many towns and regions across France, festivals began celebrating the new political order. Paris decided it too would hold a celebration of its own, choosing July 14th to commemorate the fall of the Bastille.

In less than a month the Champ de Mars to the west of the city had been transformed into what was called a "Temple to the Federation". At the centre was a large raised dais. This was to be the Altar of the Fatherland, where political oaths would be sworn before a bishop of the Revolution. Encircling this were the enclosures needed to seat the congregation. At the far end of the field, a tall triple arch eighty feet high had been erected with a platform for spectators. Beneath it, the King had been allocated his own seat *at the Temple*; but it was one that had been deliberately placed amongst other invited guests. [7]

Saint Solano

Saint Solano has no obvious connection with the French Revolution, for he had acquired his reputation as a miracle worker in Peru during the sixteenth century, His inclusion in this oracle, especially at the temple, is because his feast day, 14 July, coincides with 'Bastille Day' which is also 'July 14th'. [8] Quite remarkably, we therefore have a prophecy within a prophecy, for *Solano* was not beatified until long after the author of this quatrain was dead. The Seer therefore had no way of knowing, by ordinary means, that *Solano* would be beatified, nor had he any normal means of knowing that the date selected for his feast day would be on Bastille Day, which, at the time when he lived, was still 230 years into the future.

Offering a sacrifice, he will dedicate the empty promises of the festival

At the temple to the Federation, Louis XVI was required to approve the vows given at the ceremony with a personal declaration of support for the new constitution. He did this by raising his hand and swearing that as, "King of the French [...] [he would] use the power entrusted to him by the constitutional law of the State, to maintain and see the decrees of the National Assembly were upheld." [9] Essentially, what Louis XVI had done was to sacrifice his royal power by sanctifying the smoke – the *fumum vendere* (empty promises) – of the festival.

Summary: *The name of Saint Solano dominates this oracle because his feast day in the Catholic Church is 14 July, Bastille Day. The prophecy commences with the election of Mirabeau in the same year that the Bastille was razed to the ground, in an act of violence which augured scenes that were soon to follow. Three days later, the King confirmed his willingness to comply with the government's new order, and was received with great acclamation as the country's 'Father King': an appellation that was foretold in the prophecy. One year later, and in line with the prophetic word, Paris celebrated Bastille Day by building a temple in the Champ de Mars, where a quasi-religious ceremony was held for the King to sanctify the new constitution.*

24   *Sur le palais au rochier des fenestres*
           Seront rauis les deux petits royaux,
           Passer aurelle Luthece Denis cloistres,
           Nonnain, Mallods aualler verts noyaux.

'Le palais des fenestres' would seem to indicate the Palace of Versailles, which did not exist when this was written.

25   *Passant les Ponts venir prés des rosiers,*
           Tard arriué plustost qu'il cuydera,
           Viendront les noues Espagnols à Besiers,
           Qui icelle chasse emprinse cassera.

26   *Nice sortie sur nom des lettres aspres,*
           La grande cappe fera present non sien:
           Proche de Vultry aux murs de vertes capres
           Apres plombim le vent à bon essien.

Nice (AF niais) foolish; aspres (OF) churlish; cappe *(anagrammatic-paragram:* Cap[t]e) Capet, *also* c[h]appe (OF) a churchman's cape; present (OF) in sight, in view; de Vultry *(anagrammatic-paragram:* [a]e V[o]ltry)– Voltayre, *also* Vultry (Gk. βολτα) walk; plombin (L plumb\um) lead, bullet; vent (OF) rumour, report; à bon essien (à bon escient) knowingly. Cross-reference: La grande cappe, C.IV: 11; C.VIII: 19; C.IX: 20.

N.B. 'Vultry' is spelt with a small 'v' in the Rigaud edition of 1568, but with a capital 'V' in the 1558 Lyon edition, which was reproduced at Leyden in 1650. Note, too, that the town of Nice is spelt Nisse in Century Ten No. 87.

A foolish departure by the name (**LOUIS XVI**) on the churlish letters,   1791
The great cloak (**CAPET**) will place in view, not his own:
Adjoining the walk (**VOLTAYRE**) at the walls by the green shrubs,
Afterwards lead; the rumour knowingly.

A Foolish departure

This oracle begins with a reference to Louis XVI's *foolish departure* from Paris, which was the subject of N°. 20 above. The flight ended with his arrest at Varennes and his return to Paris. It also marked the beginning of the monarchy's downfall. [1]

By the name on the churlish letters

The churlish letters were those Louis XVI signed *by name*, and left behind when he fled Paris. In the letters, he reproached those who had taken away his powers.
The King anticipated that his escape to the border would be successful, and he was quite candid when explaining the reasons for his unannounced departure. But the escape failed, and the letters were discovered. In these letters, Louis accused the political clubs of promoting anarchy; he also

admitted that his devotion to the revolution was made under extreme duress. And, furthermore, his stipend had been totally insufficient to maintain the honour and dignity of his position. The recriminations resulting from these missives were never forgotten, and they added greatly to his disgrace. [2]

The great cloak (Capet)

Capet was the derogatory name given to Louis XVI after his arrest at Varennes. The name had belonged to his ancestry, but it soon caught on amongst the revolutionaries, and thereafter he became referred to as 'Citizen Capet', or plain 'Louis Capet'. [3] The anagram used for this purpose is concealed by 'the great cloak', which, for the monarchy, refers to the King's coronation robe.

Will place in view, not his own

After the debacle of his departure and subsequent arrest, Louis XVI remained suspended from office until the Constitution had been completed. By 14 September 1791, the document was ready, and the King was called upon by the Constituent Assembly to swear to uphold and defend it; that is, to *make his view known* to the nation by publicly swearing to support it. But, as the oracle clearly indicates, the instrument of government to which Louis was required to swear was *not his own*. Although he remained King, he had not been allowed any part in its preparation. [4]

Adjoining the walk (Voltayre) at the walls by the green shrubs

The oracle next contrasts Louis XVI's ignominious return to Paris from Varennes with the triumphant arrival of Voltaire's body. Although the writer had been dead for thirteen years, his remains were to be re-interred inside the Pantheon, alongside those of Descartes.

Voltaire's coffin began its journey to Paris from Romilly-sur-Seine during the second week of July 1791, and was attended by a huge procession (walk), estimated to be close to a million people; it also included the National Guardsmen. The cortège reached the outskirts of the city on the 11th July. And from there, Voltaire's body was first taken to *the walls* of the Bastille. [5] Although the major part of these fortifications had been reduced to rubble in 1789, during the storming of the fortress, it was still considered to be an important stopping point, because Voltaire had been imprisoned there in 1717, and again in 1726.

Upon reaching the site of this former fortress, "The coffin was then placed behind a barrier of poplars and cypresses" (*the green shrubs*). [6] An address was then read. This declared that Voltaire had endured, whereas the walls that once enclosed him had not. Finally, at 10 o'clock that evening, his body made its final stop at the Pantheon where it was laid to rest.

Afterwards, lead

Five days afterwards, on 16 July, the people of Paris were invited to put their names to a petition on the 'Altar of the Patrie' at the Champ de Mars. On the following day, a confrontation occurred between a crowd of demonstrators, numbering about 50,000, and the National Guardsmen that had been sent to restore order. Stones were thrown at the guards who responded with a hail of bullets—*lead*. [7] As many as fifty people died in the resulting gunfire.

The rumour knowingly

The petition, to which the people had been invited to sign, was an expression of an earlier rumour that had since become knowingly accepted. It described how Louis XVI "had deserted his post" and through his "perjury" had effectively abdicated. It went on to state that unless the nation indicated otherwise, Louis should no longer be recognized as King.

The petition was effectively calling for the abolition of the monarchy. [8]

Summary: *Yet again, we have a further quatrain that refers to the French Revolution. It takes up the story beginning with the King's flight to Varennes and his arrest. Before leaving, the King had felt compelled to explain his reasons. Alas for him, he was detained before reaching the Belgian border and his letters were used to undermine his position on the throne. Despite their discovery, events were moving too fast for the abolition of the monarchy, and Louis was given a chance to redeem his position, by swearing to adhere to the new Constitution. Just prior to this, Voltaire's body had been brought to Paris for interment in the Pantheon. It was followed by a petition calling for the resignation of the King, harking back to his secret departure. In the event, it caused the deaths of about fifty people who were shot by the National Guard while trying to restore order.*

27   *De bois la garde, vent clos rond pont sera,*
      Haut le receu frappera le Dauphin,
      Le vieux teccon bois vnis passera,
      Passant plus outre du Duc le droict confin.

28   *Voille Symacle pour Massiliolique,*
      Dans Venise port marcher aux Pannons:
      Partir du goulfre & Synus Illyrique,
      Vast à Socille, Ligurs coups de canons.

29   *Lors que celuy qu'à nul ne donne lieu,*
      Abandonner voudra lieu prins non prins:
      Feu nef par saignes, bitument à Charlieu,
      Seront Quintin Balez reprins.

30   *Au port de PVOLA & de sainct Nicolas,*
      Peril Normande au goulfre Phanatique
      Cap. de Bisance rues crier helas,
      Secours de Gaddes & du grand Philippique.

31   *Le tremblement de terre à Mortara,*
      Cassich sainct Georges à demy perfondrez,
      Paix assoupie, la guerre esueillera,
      Dans temple à Pasques abysmes enfondrez.

32   *De fin porphire profond collon trouuée*
      Dessous la laze escripts capitolin:
      Os poil retors Romain force prouuée,
      Classe agiter au port de Methelin.

33   *Hercules Roy de Rome & d'Annemarc,*
      De Gaule trois Guion surnommé,
      Trembler l'Itale & l'vnde de sainct Marc,
      Premier sur tous Monarque renommé.

34   *La part soluz mary sera mittré,*
      Retour conflict passera sur la thuille:
      Par cinq cens vn trahyr sera tiltré,
      Narbon & Saulce par coutaux auons d'huille.

La part (OF côte) rib of a body, [Adam's rib – wife]; also see No. 20 above - deux pars, hence, la part: wife; soluz (L solum) alone; mittré (OF), to mitre; retour (OF) returning; thuille (OF *apocope* – tuile[rie] tile works: that later became the site of the Tuileries Palace; Narbon (*apocope*) Narbon[ne]; Saulce (*epenthesis*) Sauce; auons (ellipsis: nous avons) Cross-reference: part, C.IX: 20.

The wife (**MARIE ANTOINETTE**) alone, the husband (**LOUIS XVI**) will be mitred: 1792
Returning conflict will pass over the tile works (**TUILERIES**):
Through **FIVE-HUNDRED**: a betrayer will be titled (**duc d'ORLÉANS**),
NARBONNE by knives, and **SAUCE**, we have oil.

The wife alone

On 20 June 1792, a crowd that had earlier gathered together in Paris to celebrate the Oath of the Tennis Court suddenly turned violent. With their anger whipped up by the revolutionary spirit that permeated the French capital at the time, a decision was made to confront the King personally with their demands. The mob thereupon lost no time in making its way to the palace grounds, and by force of number, it was allowed to enter. Chaos immediately broke out. Armed with pikes, hatchets, knives, clubs, and even a cannon (which was later abandoned on the staircase, causing immense damage as it fell back to the ground), the mob led by Antoine

Santerre, hacked its way through room after room in an effort to locate the King. Louis was eventually found alone in the *Oeil de Boeuf*, a room overlooking the courtyard and garden.

Others in the crowd had been searching for the Queen. But Madame Elisabeth, the King's sister, allowed herself to be mistaken for Marie Antoinette by staying close to her brother.

The Queen, "had originally wished to take her place at the King's side, telling those who tried to stop her that they were trying to damage her reputation." [1] But from this she was dissuaded by her duty to her children, and so she escaped through a secret exit to the Council room, whereupon, furniture was hurriedly heaped up against the door to prevent the mob from entering.

The husband will be mitred

Louis remained impassive as the mob approached him. Having cornered their prey, the leaders were slightly at a loss as to what they should do next. First there was abuse; next came the demands. "The demonstrators crowded in front of him, shouting in unison with the people in the courts below, 'No aristocrats! No veto! No priests!'"

These last two demands referred to the King having vetoed legislation that priests who refused to swear an oath of allegiance to France should be exiled. Then, taking a red revolutionary cap (*Bonnet Rouge*) offered to him at the end of a pike, the King allowed it to be placed on his head. Having defended the priests, Louis' reward was to be mitred for his effort. In fact, wearing the bonnet was also an important gesture showing support for the people. The bonnet had a long history, dating back to its appearance on Roman coins. But during the French Revolution it became a popular emblem as well as a simple item of clothing.

When the National Guardsmen eventually arrived to rescue the King, he was found safe, but perspiring, and with the red cap still askew on his powdered hair. Critics among the nobility later described it as his 'Crown of Thorns'. [2]

Returning conflict will pass over the tile works (Tuileries)

For the whole of July the King and Queen inside the *Palais de Tuileries* were left alone, and during those few weeks some semblance of normality was established. But on the 10 August 1792, in blistering heat, the violence returned as a fresh wave of conflict surged over the Tuileries: [3] eventually drowning the monarchy in its swell.

It was during this orgy of violence and murder that the gallant Swiss guardsmen, together with many of the palace servants were cut to pieces (see No. 20). "Some of the men were still continuing the slaughter; others were cutting off the heads of those already slain; while the women, lost all sense of shame, were committing the most indecent mutilations on the dead bodies from which they tore pieces of flesh and carried them off in triumph." [3] A wall plaque commemorating more than five hundred gallant Swiss guards and a further sixty who were captured and later massacred was erected in Geneva, where it can still be seen.

The history of the Tuileries dates back to the 16th century.

> After the death of Henry II of France in 1559, his widow Catherine de' Medici (1519–1589) planned a new palace. She began building the palace of Tuileries in 1564, using architect Philibert de l'Orme. The name derives from the tile kilns or *tuileries* which had previously occupied the site. [4]

Through five hundred

The disaster that befell those at the *Palais de Tuileries* on 10 August can be traced to the arrival of the 500 from Marseilles. "Upon the evening of Sunday, the 29th of July the dusty 500 of Marseilles with their guns, crossing the bridge at Charenton, saw the distant towers of Notre Dame above the roofs of Paris." [5] Eager to participate in the overthrow of the monarchy, the spark which ignited their fury rose from the inflammatory speeches urging a republic during the days after their arrival.

The royal family had been forewarned of the attack and had been given shelter inside the press room attached to the Assembly Hall. Unable to return to the palace, they were taken to the Convent of the Feuillants while a permanent place of protection could be found for them. From there they were escorted to the Temple Tower. Except for their daughter, this was to be the family's final residence.

On 21 September, France declared itself a Republic. Thereafter, with no further use for a king, it was decided that Louis should be tried for treason. By December of that year, the court proceedings were under way.

A betrayer will be titled

Louis XVI's cousin, the Duke of Orleans, had seen the Revolution in France as an opportunity for obtaining political power. Using the sobriquet Philip Égalité he had been elected to the Assembly. Now, seated at the trial of the King, he was to become his cousin's *betrayer*.

The death penalty was passed on 16 January 1793. "The newly named Philip Égalité, Louis' cousin and his closest adult male relative in France, was among those who voted for execution. [...] When Louis was told of the verdict on the following day, it was the behaviour of his cousin that visibly pained him"[6]

> The Duc d'Orléans was greeted with cries of a very different type. On the preceding evening he had voted for the King's death: when he advanced, the sweat standing on his brow, and mumbled his 'No' to the question of the reprieve, the Right yelled mercilessly at him: 'We cannot hear you!' and Égalité had to repeat his 'No'.[7]

Narbonne by knives

Prior to the King's trial and execution, Louis, Comte de *Narbonne-Lara*, whom Louis XVI had made Minister of War (7 December 1791), sought to raise the King's esteem in the public eye by directing the country's patriotism toward the monarchy. "Instead of holding the line at peace, he began to prepare actively for war."[8]

Par coutaux (by knives), indicates Narbonne's role as War Minister; the phrase: *aiguiser ses couteaux*, means 'sharpening knives', and is used in French to mean: 'preparing for war'. But when Narbonne was sacked from the Ministry, as a result of his intrigues, the Catholics accused him of "handing over the monarchy to the demagogues.'"[9]

And Sauce we have oil

Sauce, on the other hand, was to earn his place in history as the man who did, quite literally, hand over the King to his enemies. Jean-Baptiste Sauce was the Procurator of Varennes, and the official to whom Drouet made his approach after galloping through the forest to overtake the royal coach. Sauce was also the town's chandler and the owner of a small oil shop that sold candles and similar merchandise; hence, 'we have oil'.

It was in an upper bedroom of Sauce's shop that the King and Queen were persuaded by the owner to spend the night of June 21st. On the following day, envoys arrived from Paris to detain the King, and upon their arrival Sauce handed over the royal family to the National Guard.[10]

Summary: *Sauce, the oil seller; Narbonne, the minister for war; Philip Égalité, the titled betrayer of the King; the 500 from Marseilles; the returning conflict over the Tuileries; a husband who was 'mitred' during the first conflict; and his wife alone during that first onslaught: put them all together and we have another insight to a number of major events and their participants during the French Revolution. The fact that historians record these incidents during that Revolution, exactly as they were predicted to happen more than 230 years before, confirms the type of universe in which this is possible—a block universe, complete with an intelligent Creator who exists outside of time.*

35   *Et Ferdinand blonde sera descorte,*
        Quitter la fleur, suyure le Macedon,
        Au grand besoing defaillira sa routte,
        Et marchera contre le Myrmiden.

Et (OF) and, also, likewise; blonde (OF susceptible) capable; descorte (AF en discord) in discord; Macedon (L Macedonia); fleur (ellipsis) fleur-de-lis; besoing (AF combat) combat; defaillira (OF) to fail; Myrmidon (L Myrmidones) follower of Achilles: N.B. Achilles was the son of the mortal Peleus, king of the Myrmidons, a people occupying Thessaly].

Likewise, capable **FERDINAND** will be in discord,
Leaving the fleur-de-lis to pursue Macedonia,
At the great combat, his route will fail;
He will also proceed against the holder of Thessaly.

Likewise, capable Ferdinand

It appears from this opening sentence that the thoughts of the seer carried over from the previous prophecy, to predict further discord, this time at the court of Ferdinand.

When Russia engineered the removal of Prince Alexander of Battenberg from his seat of power in Bulgaria, the regency, which had been set up to rule in place of the Prince, found great difficulty in obtaining a suitable candidate to replace him. This was because of a fear that Russian hostility would be similarly aimed at Prince Alexander's successor.

Thus, when Ferdinand agreed to accept the throne, it had already been declined by the princes in Denmark and the Caucasus, also by the King of Romania. Eventually, the invitation to rule Bulgaria fell to Ferdinand, the son of Prince August of Saxe-Coburg-Gotha. He accepted the appointment, and the Grand National Assembly elected him Prince of Bulgaria in July 1887.

> His accession was greeted with disbelief in many of the royal houses of Europe. Queen Victoria, his father's first cousin, stated to her Prime Minister, "He is totally unfit [...] delicate, eccentric and effeminate [...] and should be stopped at once." [1]

But, to the amazement of his titled detractors, Ferdinand proved himself to be the very opposite. He demonstrated his capability to rule, especially during the first two decades of his reign.

Will be in discord

Initially, Ferdinand's appointment as Bulgaria's Prince had been met with considerable discord and a barrage of opposition.

> Russia accused Ferdinand of being a usurper, while Europe simply refused to recognize his appointment, even the bishops of the Holy Synod declined to pay him homage; everywhere, it seemed, conspiracies were flourishing. [2]

Despite the antagonism he encountered, Ferdinand was able to prove his ability when dealing with those who had opposed his nomination; even though this resentment to him came not only from Russia, but also from within Bulgaria itself. Eventually, it subsided, and "in March 1896 Ferdinand finally received international confirmation of his rule." [3]

Leaving the fleur-de-lys

Ferdinand I of Bulgaria was the son of Princess Clementine of Orleans and Prince Auguste; he was therefore the maternal grandson of the French King, Louis Philippe. Consequently, when Ferdinand quit France to take the throne of Bulgaria, he also left the fleur-de-lis behind. Nevertheless, his attachment to the French royal family and to his own ancestry was very evident, even from his table setting.

> On every fork and spoon, on every piece of the massive silver plate was engraved the French fleur-de-lys. They marked the descent of the royal couple; the prince as grandson of Louis Philippe, [his wife] the Princess Marie Louise as granddaughter of Charles X. [4]

To pursue Macedonia

In 1903, the Macedonian people rose up in protest against their Ottoman rulers in what became known as the St. Elijah's Day Uprising. But the revolt was brutally suppressed. Ferdinand had always been keen to pursue the recovery of Macedonia for Bulgaria, but on this occasion he was compelled to bide his time.

Five years later, a new opportunity arose with the activities of the 'Young Turks' (ideologists and discontented members of the 3rd Army Corps in Macedonia). Their discontent gave Ferdinand the chance he had been waiting for, and together with other Balkan states, he decided the time was ripe to free Macedonia from Turkish rule. On 8 October 1912, joined by an alliance with Serbia, Greece and Montenegro, Ferdinand declared war against the Ottoman Empire, [5].

At the great battle, his route will fail

The result of the *great battle* fought between the Balkan States and the Ottoman Empire was that the Alliance won a resounding victory, leaving Turkey to sue for peace (3 December 1912). But the victors were not satisfied. Ferdinand, in particular, urged the Bulgarian army to continue with its assault on the defeated Turkish Empire and occupy Constantinople. [6] It was an error of judgement. Ferdinand was stopped short in his tracks: "the assault on the Çatalca line failed, leaving the Bulgarian army in a weakened state."

This had political repercussions at the peace table. Because the Prince's route to Constantinople had ended in failure, his negotiating power during the peace deliberations suffered, causing him to receive a reduction in his share of the spoils of war. [7]

At the negotiating table Turkey was forced to concede almost all of its European territory. But, because of Ferdinand's weakened position, the way was left open for Serbia and Greece to claim the greater part of Macedonia. Ferdinand's annoyance at the terms of this settlement became the cause of a political quarrel with his former allies. And it was Bulgaria's inability to resolve these differences that eventually led their King to embark upon his next venture.

He will also proceed against the holder of Thessaly

On the night of 29 June 1913, King Ferdinand ordered his troops to proceed against Greece and Serbia (Second Balkan War). His plan was to attack the Greek and Serbian armies who were occupying territory they had recently captured. Three days earlier, Greece had taken control of the Macedonian capital Salonika; that is, Thessaloniki (named after Thessalonike, a half-sister of Alexander the Great). *Thessalo-nikē* means 'victory over the Thessalians'. Consequently, once having taken control of Salonika, Greece automatically became *the holder of Thessaly*.

In the battle that ensued, both the Greek and Serbian armies fiercely resisted the Bulgarian army's attempt to displace them. At the same time, neighbouring Romania, together with Turkey joined the quarrel by marching on Sofia. Amidst this political conflict and military upheaval, Bulgaria was defeated. In the new peace settlement, which was devised to resolve past grievances, the top half of Macedonia was given to Serbia, and the southern half to Greece, leaving Ferdinand with just a fraction of his former territory. [8]

Summary: *In the previous quatrain, the seer named M. Sauce and the Comte de Narbonne. In this quatrain, he names King Ferdinand of Macedonia. The enthronement of Ferdinand is correctly foretold, together with the initial opposition which his election caused. Although Ferdinand is a name that is not unique amongst the crowned heads of Europe, this Ferdinand's French ancestry sets him apart from the rest, especially when combined with his interest in retaking Macedonia. His failure to take Constantinople is also identified, and it was to cause in him the anguish that led to the Second Balkan War.*

36   *Vn grand Roy prins entre les mains d'vn ioyne*
     Non loing de Pasque, confusion, coup cultre,
     Perpet. captifs temps que fouldre en la husne
     Lors que trois freres lors se blesseront, & murtre.

ioyne (AF joyne - jeune); cultre (L. culter) knife; Perpet. (Medieval Latin, *abbrev.* – Perpet[uatio]) continuation; la husne (*naut.* hune) top, *also* (anagrammatic-paragram) l' [y]usne - Luynes; murtre (OF) homicide.

> A great King (**HENRI IV**) taken between the hands of (**RAVAILLAC**) a young man,   1610
> Not far from Easter, a knife blow, confusion,
> Continuation: captives, a time when a thunderbolt at the top (**LUYNES**),
> From that time when three brothers will give offence to themselves, and a homicide.

A great king

Henri III and Henri IV were both assassinated by a knife thrust, but only Henri IV is considered by historians to have been a 'great king'. [1]

> Henry IV died a victim of the fanaticism he wanted to eradicate. [...] Too often misunderstood during his lifetime, his tragic end seemed finally to have opened the eyes of his people. They soon bestowed on him the appellation Henry the Great. [2]

Taken between the hands of a young man

Henri IV met his death at the hands of a young man named François Ravaillac. The assassin had formerly been a schoolmaster in Touvre near Angoulême. [3] At the time of the crime, he was aged about twenty-nine or thirty, and had recently become incensed at the King's "traffic with heretics".

Not far from Easter

The assassination took place on Friday 14 May 1610, not far from Easter (33 days in fact, and 2 days before Rogation Sunday). In the year 1610, Easter Sunday fell on 11 April. [4] The Christian festival of Easter was, in those days, celebrated over many weeks, and it was inside the church where the King's body had been laid out that "the flowers left over from the Easter celebrations were just beginning to fade."

A knife blow

The murder occurred while the King was travelling by coach along the Rue de la Ferronnerie in Paris. A runaway pig had caused a hold-up in the flow of traffic, and the King's carriage was brought to a halt just long enough for the assassin to act. It was by sheer coincidence that Ravaillac was standing nearby. He climbed onto the wheel, leaned through the window, and thrust a knife into the King's chest. [5]

Confusion

So sudden was the murder that for a few seconds there was total confusion. [6] Henri's companions remained rooted to their seats, unable to comprehend what had just happened: even the assassin seemed frozen to the wheel. Unlike Jacques Clément, who had been slain on the spot and thrown from the window after knifing Henri III, Ravaillac was captured. He was then put to torture, and subsequently executed in a most gruesome fashion.

Continuation

The succession to the throne by the King's elder son followed within hours. Arrangements for the continuation of the monarchy had been made necessary by the long, drawn-out interregnum that took place after Henri III's death. This had proved to be a bloody and acrimonious affair. [7] To overcome any repetition of a similar occurrence, the King had made prior arrangements for the Queen to become regent during the minority of their son, if the need ever arose. This also insured the efficient continuation of any policies that were then being negotiated at the time. Consequently, just one day after the death of her husband, a very tearful Marie de' Médicis, was pronounced regent to Louis XIII by the *Paris Parlement*.

Captives, a time when a thunderbolt at the top (Luynes)

The Queen-mother continued her regency until 1614, when the King was judged to have come of age. Nevertheless, for a further three years after that, she continued to govern through her minister, Concini, the Marshal d'Ancre. But then a 'thunderbolt' fell, striking at the top, and bringing with it a sudden, dramatic change in government.

Louis XIII had decided to sweep aside his mother's administration and take control of the country himself. Acting at a time when France's ministers were all behind bars [8] (captives), Charles d'Albert ordered the murder of Concini.

Proceeding with full authority from the King, d'Ancre was shot dead, and the Queen-mother was sent to the castle at Blois as an exile.

As a reward for his services to Louis XIII, d'Albert was made duc de Luynes, Governor of Picardy, Constable of France and Keeper of the Seals. In effect he became France's new ruler. [9]

From that time when three brothers will give offence to themselves

It was also during this period that a new figure emerged on the political landscape – Armand Jean du Plessis, Bishop of Luçon, and known to the future as Cardinal Richelieu. Luynes and his spies watched this particular bishop, and his family members, with growing concern: especially Luçon's interest in the activity surrounding the Queen-mother, who remained under house arrest inside the Château de Blois.

On 7 April 1618, fearing that a *coup* was about to be sprung against him, Luynes persuaded Louis XIII to issue a royal directive exiling Richelieu and his associates. The King obliged, and three brothers, Richelieu, Henri, and their brother-in-law, René de Pont-Courlay, having brought offence upon themselves, were sent to Avignon where they would cease to pose a threat to Luynes. [10]

And a homicide

By the following year, Richelieu had not only contrived to obtain his release from exile, he had also managed to manipulate his brother Henri into the position of Governor at the Castle of Angers. The appointment proved to be a death sentence. The former governor, the Marquis de Thémines took umbrage at this act of nepotism and deliberately provoked a quarrel with his successor. A fight broke out between the two men, during which Henri Richelieu was killed. [11]

Summary: *This oracle predicts the period of French history that followed from the death of Henri IV. His widow's taste for power as Regent of France exceeded the age of majority of her son. Louis XIII's annoyance at being ignored then took a sinister turn, resulting in the assassination of his mother's chief councillor and her exile. This brought the King's boyhood favourite to power, whom he made duc de Luynes. It was also a time when Cardinal Richelieu was beginning to exercise his political abilities, and he, together with his brother and brother-in-law, are given a place in the prophecy.*

> 37   *Pont & molins en Decembre versez,*
>   *En si haut lieu montera la Garonne:*
>   *Murs, edifices, Tholose renuersez,*
>   *Qu'on ne sçaura son lieu autant matronne.*

Pont (*apocope*: Pont[iff]) Pope; molins (OF moulins) mills; lieu (AF estime), esteem; monter (AF être utile) to be useful; sçaura (OF future tense of savoir) to know.

> Pope and mills reversed in December: 1560
> Through such high esteem, the Garonne will be useful:
> Walls, buildings, Toulouse overturned,
> That one will not know his place, the matron (**JEANNE D'ALBRET**) as well.

Pope and mills reversed in December

Jeanne d'Albret, Queen of Navarre from 1555 to 1572 was a promoter of religious freedom. Five years after the death of her father, from whom she inherited Navarre in her own right, Jeanne attended a meeting of the Estates at Orléans, arranged by Catherine de Medici, acting as regent for her ten-year-old son, Charles IX. The meeting began on 13 December, with the purpose of discussing religious issues.

> As the meeting of Estates continued in their deliberations, Navarre's Queen Jeanne declared Calvinism her new religion and the official religion of Navarre on Christmas Day of 1560. She commissioned the translation of the Bible into the native language of Basque and Béarnese. (Queen Jeanne would soon banish Catholic priests and nuns from Navarre, destroy Catholic churches and outlaw all Catholic rituals in her land.) [1]

As a result of this, the Edict of Orléans, which resulted from the Estates meeting, granted Protestants freedom of conscience in the hope of maintaining peace in France. However,

> In addition to having to face the extension of toleration to Protestants by the Edict of Orleans, the Catholic Church's position also seemed shaken by the abolishment of the arrangement made between the papacy and the French crown. [2]

Two years later, growing antagonism between the Catholic Church and the Reformed Church of France would mark the start of the French Wars of Religion, which also gave impetus in the same year to the 'Riots of Toulouse' in the south of France.

The conflict in Toulouse had been inspired by Louis I de Bourbon, Prince of Condé, leader of the Huguenot army. He suggested that the *capitoul* (municipal officers in the city of Toulouse) seize the Town Hall for the Protestants. This was successfully achieved by secretly housing soldiers in the city before making the attack. But after having installed themselves in a defensive position inside the Town Hall and other strategic sites, the embedded Protestants found they were cut off from their food supply.

> Even before the riots there had been a shortage of grain supplies throughout the town and as the days of rioting stretched on, the Reformed Church members within the *Hôtel de ville* and at their strongholds in the university colleges began to run out of food. [...] The Protestants had never been able to control the river [Garonne] and so were cut off from the mills alongside it. [3]

In brief, the implications of the Estates meeting held at Orléans in December 1560 had reversed the situation in France, with regard to the special relationship existing between crown and pope. While in Toulouse, it caused a siege that separated the Calvinists from the mills.

Through such high esteem, the Garonne will be useful

With the Town Hall in Protestant hands, Catholic councillors from the Toulouse *Parlement* in their red robes of office strode through the streets calling for citizens to take up arms against members of the Reformed Church. It was out of such high esteem for the Catholic Church that citizens were given special dispensation to murder heretics: having been told that they could "Pillage, kill boldly, with the approval of the pope, (Pius IV), of the king, and of the court."

> On the Catholic side all Protestants were viewed in the same light as those holed up in the *Hôtel de ville* - being viewed as not only heretics but open traitors. Those not in the *Hôtel de ville* were seized in their homes, thrown from windows, or dragged to the Garonne River and thrown in. Even Protestants being taken to prison by town constables were massacred by mobs of angry Catholics. Still the majority of those arrested did make it to prison and the arrests of Protestants were so numerous that those in jail for merely criminal charges but who were not charged with heresy were released to make more room for captured Reformed Church members. [...] When the prisons were filled to capacity, those arrested on suspicion of Protestantism were stripped naked and thrown into the river – those attempting to swim were shot with arquebuses. [4]

> Also on May 15, Reformed Church members began using the ancient Roman sewer that ran to the Garonne river to move around or to find shelter. Catholics flushed the system with a large amount of water and capturing twenty five Protestants threw them from a bridge into the Garonne river where they drowned. [5]

Walls, buildings, Toulouse overturned

Between 3,000 and 8,000 Catholic citizens responded to the Toulouse Parlement's call, and joined in the street fighting. Amongst these were "the town guard, a supplementary militia of around 400, private troops garrisoned in wealthy homes, and the Catholic knights and their retinues." Opposed to these were some 2,000 Protestants, most of whom were either members of the militia or students. Although outnumbered, the Protestants were much better armed with weapons and ammunition that had secretly been brought into the city. "Urban warfare gripped Toulouse and events quickly descended into chaos." [6]

> All contemporary sources hold that more were slain outside the walls than in the streets of Toulouse. It is estimated that around 3,000 to 5,000 people had died in the continuous days of rioting and the massacre outside the walls, with the vast majority being Protestants. [7]

Inside the city, the Huguenots made use of buildings with upper levels that overhung the street below. From this vantage point, musket fire and stones targeted the Catholics at street level. They also used their own homes as thoroughfares to connect their armed detachments of fighters. In response to these tactics, Catholics began setting fire to the houses.

On Friday, May 15 [1562], frustrated by the standoff, the Catholic leadership attempted to both dislodge the Reformed Church members, remove cover for any escape route, and end street fighting in that area by setting fire to all Protestant homes in the Saint-Georges quarter (where the *Hôtel de ville* was located). The *Parlement* declared anyone attempting to extinguish the flames would be guilty of a capital offense, which resulted in some Catholic homes burning as well. In the end, more than 200 homes were burnt to the ground. [8]

"Inside Toulouse, revenge killing continued." When the Seigneur de Montluc arrived with armed troops to put down the insurrection, he reported that "up to 400 Protestants were slain, by his own armored and mounted troops or by mobs of Catholic peasants, while trying to escape Toulouse." [9] The situation of the Protestants inside the Town Hall had also become grim.

The morale of the Reformed Church members quickly sunk when they realized that there was little hope of additional reinforcements. Relying heavily on their captured canons and having failed to capture the eighteen casks of powder and mills at the Porte du Bazâcle, their military supplies of gunpowder were also soon as scarce as their food supplies. [10]

Under truce conditions, men, women and children agreed to leave the safety of the Town Hall and made their way to the Villeneuve Gate. But, once out in the open, the tocsin bells rang, drawing mobs of angry Catholics from the churches. Seizing hold of weapons, and with cries of 'Long Live the Cross', they began slaughtering the defenceless Protestants. Chased through the streets of Toulouse by this bloodthirsty mob, those who passed outside the city walls were still not safe. They were met by Catholics who "had forced a violation of the truce terms by ordering the city guards at gunpoint to open another gate so they could intercept the fleeing Protestants. [...] Many slain outside the walls would lay their half-eaten on the roadsides until identified and collected by the capitaine de la santé." [11]

That one will not know his place

On 19 March 1563, Catherine de Medici signed the Edict of Pacification at the Château of Amboise. The treaty was designed to bring religious peace to France "by guaranteeing the Huguenots religious freedoms." However, this was not recognized in Toulouse, for which no place was made available for worship.

The protestants of Toulouse no longer had the right to worship in their own city but were assigned a *lieu du culte* first at Grenade, then Villemur, both over twenty kilometres away. There is no evidence that they retained the service of a pastor, but a consistory was still active in 1564, hoping to reconstitute the church. By September 1567, those who wished to attend the *cêne* had to travel to Montauban; in 1572, Toulousian Protestants can be found at Villemur and trying to worship at Castanet, just outside the city, where the *seigneur* claimed the right to hold services. [12]

The matron as well

In 1562, the joint rulers of Navarre, Jeanne and her husband, Antoine de Bourbon, were at the French Court amidst a power struggle for control of France's religious direction. It was then and there that Antoine decided to support the Catholic faction headed by the duc de Guise. Its immediate consequence was that Antoine,

... threatened to repudiate Jeanne when she refused to attend Mass. Catherine de' Medici, in an attempt to steer a middle course between the two warring factions, also pleaded with Jeanne to obey her husband for the sake of peace but to no avail. Jeanne stood her ground and staunchly refused to abandon the Calvinist religion, and continued to have Protestant services conducted in her apartments. [13]

In fear of her husband, and of the Queen-regent, who had appointed Antoine Lieutenant General of France, "Jeanne left Paris in March 1562 and made her way south to seek refuge in Béarn." [14] Meanwhile, her husband was blaming her for recent Huguenot atrocities that were perpetrated at his ducal home in Vendôme, and he ordered her to be arrested and brought back to Paris, where he had arranged for her to be confined in a Catholic convent. But she evaded those sent to arrest her and journeyed safely into Béarn.

Having been separated from her husband, who was fatally injured one year later at the Siege of Rouen, she is identified as the *matron* figure described in the oracle.

Summary: *The seer who penned this prophecy was alive when it became fulfilled, but the prophecy had already been committed to print by that time. It is because of the nearness in time to its fulfilment that the facts have been disguised by the use of ancient French. A modern interpretation would therefore fail to unravel the oracle's hidden meaning, as is evident from other commentators who have remarked upon this quatrain. But even this provides a valuable lesson. These oracles were never intended to be understood until the events they predicted had revealed their true meaning by becoming conscious moments of history.*

> 38   *L'entrée de Blaye par Rochelle & l'Anglois,*
>   *Passera outre le grand Aemathien,*
>   *Non loing d'Agen attendra le Gaulois,*
>   *Secours Narbonne deceu par entretien.*

Æmathien (Gk paronym) Amythaon – Unspeakably Great, *also* Amethea (one of the horses of the Sun); passer (OF) proceed; deceu (OF. decevoir) betrayed; de Agen (*anagrammatic-paragram*) [U]e [E]gen = Eugene; attendre (OF) look for, attend. Cross-references: Aemathien, C.IX: 64; C.IX: 93; C.X: 7; C.X: 58; entretien, C.X: 58; Narbonne, C.IX: 64.

     The entrance of Blaye, by reason of Rochelle and the English,   1700
     The great Amythaon (**LOUIS XIV**) will proceed beyond:
     Not far from Agen (**EUGENE**), he will attend to the Frenchman,
     Assistance, Narbonne betrayed by the conference.

The entrance of Blaye

Blaye is a town 45 kilometres north of Bordeaux, standing on the estuary of the rivers Garonne and Dordogne. Overlooking the entrance to the estuary at Blaye is an imposing fortification built by Vauban for Louis XIV. Plans for the work outlining this construction were proposed to the King in a memoir dated 30 October 1685. The stronghold was finally completed in the autumn of 1689 at a cost of more than a million livres. Its purpose was to shield the approach to Bordeaux, which is situated further inland. [1]

By reason of La Rochelle and the English

The reason for the King's sudden urge to construct a fortification at the entrance of Blaye was because of La Rochelle and the English. La Rochelle had been the centre and stronghold of the Huguenots ever since Calvin's Protestant religion was introduced into France. Louis' fear was that the English might attack La Rochelle in an attempt to support, perhaps even repatriate, the Huguenot population that had fled France after having been denied legal representation under the newly decreed Edict of Fontainebleau (see N° 7 Century 2). Consequently, in the same year that Louis revoked the Edict of Nantes, he found it necessary to fortify the entrance at Blaye. [2]

The great Amythaon will proceed beyond

It was at Blaye on 30 December 1700 that Louis XIV's young grandson arrived on his journey to Bordeaux; later passing beyond the fortress town *en route* for the French frontier and the Spanish crown, which he was to accept under the guidance and rule of his grandfather, Louis XIV, the Sun King.

Spain's King, Charles II had died without a natural successor, and Louis XIV's grandson had been nominated to succeed him as Philip V.

> Europe at first seemed lost in surprise, and unable to bestir itself when it saw the Spanish monarchy become subject to France, whose rival it had been for over three hundred years. Louis XIV. seemed the most fortunate and powerful monarch in the world. He saw himself, at the age of sixty-two, surrounded with a numerous posterity, and one of his grandsons going to rule, under his orders, the kingdom of Spain, America, one half of Italy, and the Low Countries. [3]

It was therefore through the rule of his sixteen-year-old grandson, that Louis XIV – the great Amythaon – was able to extend his power and influence well beyond Iberia and into other parts of Europe, as well as across the Ocean to America. It also became the principal cause of the War of the Spanish Succession, to which reference now turns.

Not far from Agen (Eugene)

Agen is not the actual place where the event predicted in the third line occurred, but it did take place *not far from Agen*. This leaves open a suggestion that the town has been specially mentioned to convey a precognitive truth. This appears to have been the case, since *d'Agen* forms an anagrammatic paragram for Eugene. Moreover, Agen is situated on the river Garonne, which flows down from Blaye, thus linking it to the previous part of the prediction. Importantly, too, it lies to the west of Provence in southern France, where this part of the oracle was fulfilled.

> [W]hile the grandson of Louis XIV. was thus deprived of Naples, the grandfather was on the point of losing Provence and Dauphiny. The duke of Savoy and Prince Eugene had already entered those provinces by the narrow pass of Tenda; and Louis XIV. had the mortification of seeing that very duke of Savoy, who a twelvemonth before had hardly anything left but his capital, and Prince Eugene, who had been brought up at his court, on the point of stripping him of Toulon and Marseilles. [4]

> Eugene enhanced his standing during the War of the Spanish Succession, where his partnership with the Duke of Marlborough secured victories against the French on the fields of Blenheim (1704), Oudenarde (1708), and Malplaquet (1709); he gained further success in the war as Imperial commander in northern Italy, most notably at the Battle of Turin (1706). [5]

He will attend to the Frenchman

Since this oracle is centred upon France, there can be only one reason why emphasis has been given to *the Frenchman;* it is because this person would be recognized by that description.

> The first general to put a check to the superiority of the French arms was a Frenchman, for so we should call Prince Eugene, though he was the grandson of Charles Emanuel, duke of Savoy: his father, the count de Soissons, had settled in France, where he was lieutenant-general of the king's armies, and governor of Champagne, and had married Olympia Mancini, one of the nieces of Cardinal Mazarin. From this match, so unfortunate in other respects, was born this prince, who afterward proved so dangerous an adversary to Louis XIV., and was so little known to him in his youth. [6]

Nevertheless, on 22 August 1707, *the Amythaon attended to the Frenchman* when Louis XIV broke the siege of Toulon. This provided him with the necessary means to secure Provence and liberate the Dauphiny.

> A sickness, which made great havoc in the enemy's army, proved favourable to Louis XIV. The siege of Toulon was raised, and soon afterward the enemy evacuated Provence, and Dauphiny was out of danger; so seldom does an invasion prove successful, unless there is intelligence with the people of the country. [7]

Assistance, Narbonne betrayed by the conference

Prior to the Conference held on the Isle of Pheasants in 1659, which resulted in the signing of the *Peace of the Pyrenees*, Narbonne, the former capital of Gaul had been under the protection of the fortress at Carcassonne. But when Roussillon became annexed to France, as part of the 1659 Peace treaty, the frontier fortress was left to fall into disrepair. The consequences of this are made plain in the final part of this prophecy.

Roussillon originally formed part of the Roman province of Gallia Narbonensis, and Narbonne is still known as 'the crossroads of southern Europe': it having also been the capital of Languedoc. But *the city was betrayed* by the 'Atlantic Ocean Conference', OF 1659 which gave Roussillon to France. [8] The acquisition of this region was considered at the time to be a triumph. But the downside was that the fortress at Carcassonne became neglected, since maintaining it no longer appeared necessary. This later proved to be a mistake when the city found itself unable to provide *assistance* to Louis XIV in his war against *the Frenchman*. For, Toulon, which was then under siege, is a naval port inside the *Golfe du Lion*, which shares the same stretch of coastline that was controlled by *Narbonne:* its former medieval capital.

Summary: *Louis XIV, the Sun King, was the greatest monarch of his age, and the name given to him by the seer, 'THE AMYTHAON', reflects the general recognition of his greatness, not only at the time he lived, but by historians ever since. Blaye and La Rochelle have been cleverly mentioned at the beginning of the oracle, since they are not only of historical importance, but it was from there that Louis XIV's grandson, Philip, set off for Spain as its new King, and which, thereafter, began the War of the Spanish Succession. This involved Prince Eugene of Savoy, one of the most successful military commanders in modern European history, who was actually a Frenchman, having been born and brought up in Paris. The remainder of the oracle concerns the war taking place against Austria in the south of France, and events involving the Siege of Toulon in 1706.*

> 39   *En Arbissel à Veront & Carcari,*
>   *De nuict conduicts par Sauone attraper,*
>   *Le vif Gascon Turby, & la Scerry,*
>   *Derrier mur vieux & neuf palais gripper.*

> 40   *Prés de Quintin dans la forest bourlis,*
>   *Dans l'Abbaye seront Flamans tranches:*
>   *Les deux puisnais de coups my estourdis,*
>   *Suitte oppressée & garde tous achés.*

> 41   *Le grand CHYREN soy saisir d'Auignon,*
>   *De Rome lettres en miel plein d'amertume*
>   *Lettre ambassade partir de Chanignon,*
>   *Carpentras prins par duc noir rouge plume.*

> 42   *De Barcelonne, de Gennes & Venise,*
>   *De la Secille peste Monet vnis,*
>   *Contre Barbare classe prendront la vise,*
>   *Barbar poulsé bien loing iusqu'à Thunis.*

pester (OF pétrir) to form, mould; vise (AF rusé) guile; Monet (L Monet\a) Surname of Juno (*anagrammatic-paragram*) Jun[a] - Juan, *also,* mone\t: (L mone[res] vessels with a single bank of oars: i.e., galleys; Barbare (Gk.) foreign tongue; poulsé: (OF) driven

From Barcelona, from Genoa & Venice,   1571
From Sicily, galleys (**JUAN**) forms, unites:
Against a foreign fleet they will embrace guile,
Foreign tongues (**OTTOMAN SEAMEN**) driven well away, even at **TUNIS**.

From Barcelona, from Genoa and Venice
In preparation for the battle to come, ships from Venice and Genoa, [1] many of which were galleys similar to the full size replica on display at the Maritime Museum in Barcelona [2] (from where the Spanish fleet set sail), reached Messina on 24 August 1571. The fleet numbered 206 galleys. Spain had provided 80, and Venice 109. These were accompanied by a further 6 Venetian galleasses carrying substantial armoury.

From Sicily galleys, Juan forms, unites
With the fleet made ready for action, the ships departed from Sicily bound for Corfu. [3] They arrived off the coast on 15 September.
The fleet belonged to the Holy League's coalition force; it had been placed under the leadership of Don Juan of Austria, [4] the half-brother of Philip II. Under his command, the quarrelsome admirals with their different opinions were quickly formed into a united fighting force ready for the sea battle that lay ahead. [5]

Against a foreign fleet they will embrace guile
From Corfu, the ships of the Holy League advanced against the foreign fleet that lay in the Gulf of Petros, near Lepanto (Návpaktos). [6] The battle began with Christian guile.

> The left and centre galleasses had been towed half a mile ahead of the Christian line. When the battle started, the Turks mistook the galleasses for merchant supply vessels and set out to attack them. This proved to be disastrous; with their many guns, the galleasses alone were said to have

sunk up to 70 Ottoman galleys before the Ottoman fleet left them behind. Their attacks also disrupted the Ottoman formations. [7]

After a battle lasting five hours, Ali Pasha's loss had mounted to 50 ships sunk and another 137 captured. Of his fighting force, 20,000 men were killed, wounded or captured, and 10,000 Christian galley slaves were set free.

Foreign tongues driven well away, even at Tunis
The victory of the Holy League's alliance brought to an end the myth of Ottoman invincibility. The Ottoman navy was never again seen as an efficient fighting force, having been driven from the Mediterranean. The battle of Lepanto also made its impact on European morale in the years that followed Turkey's defeat. [8]

The loss of Tunis to Turkey occurred two years after Lepanto. Don Juan having been fired by success became anxious to engage in further campaigns. But Philip was wary of his half-brother's motives, and allowed him only one further operation. This was to be an assault against the Turkish held city of Tunis, which Don Juan conquered in 1573. [9]

Summary: *The Battle of Lepanto is the subject of this oracle. It occurred in the autumn of 1571, and was fought against the Turks by countries that had united under Pope Pius V to form a Holy League. At the time, Turkey, was threatening Christian occupied lands. The fleet was led by Don Juan, the half-brother of King Philip of Spain. His victory over the Turkish armada rid the Mediterranean of Ottoman domination, and, as the oracle foretold, Don John was able to further his victory by invading and subduing Tunis.*

43   *Proche à descendre l'armée Crucigere,*
        Sera guettée par les Ismaëlites,
        De tous costez batus par nef Rauier,
        Prompt assaillis de dix galeres eslites.

44   *Migrés, migrés de Genesue trestous,*
        Saturne d'or en fer se changera,
        Le contre RAYPOZ exterminera tous,
        Auant là ruent le ciel signes fera.

Migrés (L migr\o) migrate; Saturne (OF used by alchemists as a word for lead); RAYPOZ (*portmanteau* – RAY + POS); (AF rai) beam poz (AF *apocope*, pos[er] – s'arrêter) to stop; ruent (AF ruer – lancer violemment) shoot forth violently, *syncope* – ru[em]ent.

       Migrate; migrate from Geneva, absolutely everyone!
       Lead for gold will change itself into iron
       The opposite beam arrested will exterminate everything.
       Before the violent shooting forth, the sky will make signs.   2015≤?

The Large Hadron Collider (LHC) that lies buried between 50 and 175 metres beneath the outskirts of Geneva extends as far as the Swiss-French border. It is part of the CERN nuclear laboratory and consists of a 27-kilometre circular tunnel.

1232 powerful magnets have been installed throughout the tunnel, each one designed to bend a beam of protons travelling in opposite directions at a speed close to that of light. Upon reaching an energy level of approximately 14 trillion electron volts, they then collide into each other releasing a cloud of particles. The magnets used to guide the protons are so powerful that they generate a magnetic field that is 150,000 times stronger than Earth's magnetic field.

The prophecy in the second line indicates that an experiment will one day go out of control and cause a nuclear disaster beyond anything that could ever be imagined.

During the time of the alchemists, attempts were made to turn base metal into gold. They failed, because iron (mentioned in the oracle), has only 26 protons, whereas gold contains 79. In order to transform iron into gold, a temperature far hotter than that of the Sun would be needed, especially since our Sun's temperature permits transmutations only as far as nickel with its 28 protons. Despite this, the oracle reads as if gold is stripped of protons to become iron.

However, this phrase is followed by two words, *Le contre* (the opposite), which may mean *iron converting into gold* —the alchemists' dream, hence the word, *Saturne*. But it would require a temperature much greater than the Sun. In 2012, when the Higgs boson was discovered, the LHC was running at 7 tera-electron volts. This power has now been increased to run at 13 tera-electron volts (13TeV). Researchers have already booked use of the LHC for experiments that will smash new high-powered proton beams into their respective targets. Of particular note for the coming programmes is the Compact Muon Solenoid (CMS) experiment, involving one of two large general-purpose particle physics detectors built onto the (LHC). The CMS experiment is investigating a number of projects. These include exploring physics at the TeV scale; investigating properties of the newly discovered Higgs boson particle and looking for evidence of supersymmetry and dimensions above the four that are already known.

Of further interest, the oracle mentions lead. This is used in the CMS experiment. Every time the CMS detector's lead tungstate crystals are hit by a particle beam, they emit light. These are analysed to identify which particles were responsible.

Another experiment of interest at CERN is Alpha-2, the second phase of an existing study. This will allow scientists to explore antimatter at a greater depth by accelerating beams of protons at a speed close to that of light and then smashing them into a block of metal. The resulting burst of energy is intended to produce paired protons, one consisting of matter the other of antimatter. The antiproton is then magnetically separated from its 'twin' and when combined with positrons it will generate an atom of antihydrogen.

The planned resumption of experiments at CERN in 2015 began in the Spring. Scientists have restarted the magnets. When these are fully operational, they will produce collisions on a scale never before achieved by any accelerator in the past, equivalent to 154 tons of TNT. It is hoped this will re-create the conditions just after the Big Bang and provide fundamental answers to questions of science regarding the theoretical origin of the universe.

The final line of the prophecy will only become evident at the time of the predicted catastrophe. Insofar as the sky will show signs—were this to happen in 2015—then any time before or after 28th September would fulfil the oracle, since this date coincides with the final appearance of the four blood moons; (a rare event when it also coincides with four Jewish religious festivals).

There is also the repeated use of 'Migrate' to consider, especially when the migration of hundreds of thousands of refugees across Europe is creating daily headlines around the world. The Seer's choice of words are always more meaningful to those for whom his prophecy is intended.

Despite these experiments, the existence of matter remains a mistaken interpretation for the flow of sense data that is perceived as 'matter' at different times along its world-line. Its *esse* is *percipi* as Berkeley correctly inferred. Consequently, pursuit of the impossible by the means proposed at CERN, can only end in disaster, and the termination of physics as it is presently understood.

> 45   *Ne sera soul iamais de demander,*
> *Grand MENDOSVS obtiendra son empire*
> *Loing de la court fera contremander,*
> *Piedmont, Picart, Paris Tyrren le pire.*

Soul (Littré: pleinement repu); MENDOSVS (Latin) the faulty one, also (*transposition-paragram*) VENDOSM[E]; Picart (*apocope*); empire (Littré: autorité souveraine); Tyrren (L Tyrrhen\ia) Etruria; Cross-references: MENDOSVS, C.IX: 50; Vendosme, C.X: 18.

> He will not ever be entirely replete from demanding,   1594
> The great faulty one **VENDOME** will obtain his sovereign authority:
> Far from court he will begin countermanding:
> Piedmont, Picardy, Paris, Etruria the worst.

He will not ever be entirely replete from demanding

Once Henri IV became accepted by the people of France as their lawful King, he lost little time in establishing his authority: for which his efforts were subsequently rewarded by the title, Great. Under his sovereignty anarchy was reduced, agriculture promoted, commerce encouraged, peace restored, public works accomplished, marshlands reclaimed, roads improved, revenue increased, and the national debt decreased. [1]

"Consulting daily with his *Conseil des Affaires* (a strong inner ring of ministers), he issued oral as often as written orders, and insisted on being obeyed." [2] In short: he never grew sick of making demands for the benefit of his people and the common good of France.

The great faulty one Vendome will obtain his sovereign authority

Great Vendome, *the faulty one*, confirms the subject of this oracle to be Henri IV: king from 1589 to 1610. Henri IV was title-holder of the duchy of Vendôme, later transferring it to his illegitimate son, César.

In 1589, when Henri III was assassinated, Vendôme was already King of Navarre, and although he was the rightful heir to the vacant throne—through his descent from King Louis IX—he did not immediately obtain sovereignty. This was because of his *one great fault*. He was, in the eyes of French Catholics, a Huguenot, a Protestant heretic. To win their acceptance and unify France, it was required that he renounce his heresy by publicly converting to the Roman religion. [3] With his famous declaration that 'Paris is worth a Mass;' he converted to the faith on 25 July 1593 and his coronation followed in February 1594.

Far from court he will begin countermanding: Piedmont

Militarily, Henri IV soon began countermanding: that is to say, he began restoring the territorial losses to the kingdom, which occurred during the French Wars of Religion. In 1588, during 'The War of the 3 Henris', Charles Emmanuel I Duke of Savoy had captured the French held fortress of Saluzzo in Piedmont. This had once been France's gateway into Italy. But in 1600, Henri IV responded to the loss by invading Savoy, and forcing the Duke to return the fortress. [4] Century Ten N° 37 refers to Henri's war with Savoy in more detail.

Picardy

Five years earlier (January 1595), Henri had declared war on Spain, but Spanish forces swiftly responded by marching south from the Netherlands and occupying Doullens and Cambrai in Picardy.

Two years later, in March 1597, the region's historic capital, Amiens, was also taken by the Spanish. It took another ten months before Henri IV was able to successfully regroup, and recover Amiens: driving the enemy out of Picardy and bringing Spain to the negotiating table. Peace was eventually restored in 1598 by the treaty of Vervins. [5]

Paris

It is, perhaps, curious to see Paris described as 'far from court'. But at the time of Henri III's death, the Catholic League controlled the French capital, and it refused to acknowledge Henri of Navarre as the country's lawful king. Thus, although Henri was widely accepted as the rightful King, this was not the case in Paris, which barred his entry. [6]

Consequently, after his coronation at Chartres, Henri began preparations to invade his capital. In the event, this proved unnecessary. The governor, Charles de Crossé-Brissac, together with the mayor, secretly arranged for two gates to be opened. [7] Henri was therefore able to enter Paris unopposed on 22 March 1594.

Etruria the worst

Etruria was the ancient region of northwest Italy that once covered Tuscany and part of Umbria. Through expansion, the Etruscans occupied much of the central-northern part of the country. In 1610, Henri IV signed the 'treaty of Brussolo' with the Duke of Savoy. Together they intended to march into northern Italy– old *Etruria*– and liberate the duchy of Milan from its Spanish master. Henri was about to embark upon this undertaking when François Ravaillac, a religious fanatic, fatally stabbed him.[8] It is in this context that Etruria was the worst enterprise of Henri's military career, because it marked the time when his reign, and indeed his life, came to an end.

Summary: *This oracle outlines the reign of Henri IV: one of France's greatest kings. It identifies him by his ducal territory, and by the fault that prevented his acceptance as King of France; that is, until he had remedied it by converting to the Catholic faith. His untiring workload is also predicted; as, too, are the names of the places that he reclaimed for his country. His reign ended, as the oracle has covertly predicted, at the time he was about to invade northern Italy.*

46   *Vuydez, fuyez de Tholose les rouges*
         Du sacrifice faire expiation,
         Le chef du mal dessous l'ombre des courges
         Mort estrangler carne omination.

47   *Les soulz signez d'indigne deliurance,*
         Et de la multe auront contre aduis,
         Change monarque mis en perille pence,
         Serrez en cage se verront vis à vis.

48   *La grand' cite d'Occean maritime,*
         Enuironnée de marets en cristal:
         Dans le solstice hyemal & la prime,
         Sera tentée de vent espouuantal.

49   *Gand & Bruceles marcheront contre Enuers,*
         Senat de Londres mettront à mort leur Roy,
         Le sel & vin luy seront à l'enuers,
         Pour eux auoir le regne en desarroy.

Enuers (Anvers) Antwerp; marcher (Littré: aller selon un certain progrès en bien ou en mal, en parlant des personnes) proceeding according to a certain development whether good or bad when speaking of people; Cross-references: sel & vin, C.X: 7; à l'enuers, C.I: 3. (This expression is consistent with its use in describing the political opposition to both Charles 1 and Louis XVI at the time of their show trials and subsequent beheading.) Note also the number of this quatrain is given as 49.

Ghent & Brussels will proceed contrary to Antwerp;   1648
The governing body in London will put their king (**CHARLES 1**) to death,
The salt and wine will be on the wrong side of him,
Because of them, having the kingdom in disarray.

Ghent and Brussels will proceed contrary to Antwerp

The date, 30 January 1648 proved to be auspicious. It was exactly one year to the very day before *the government in London would put their king to death.* And it is the incidence of these two dates that provides the reason for this opening line of prophecy.

TREATY OF PEACE concluded on January 30th of this present year 1648 in the city of Münster in Westphalia, between his Most Serene and Mighty Prince PHILIP, fourth of the name, King of Spain, etc., on the one side and the High, Mighty Lords States General of the United Netherlands, on the other.

Under the terms of the treaty, the main waterways connecting Antwerp were to be closed to navigation.

The recognition of the independence of the United Provinces by the treaty of Münster in 1648 carried with it the death-blow to Antwerp's prosperity as a place of trade for one of its clauses stipulated that the Scheldt should be closed to navigation.

The boats that had been transporting goods to and from the seaport of Antwerp were no longer able to serve Brussels and Ghent, as well as a number of less well known towns. As a consequence of the treaty, citizens of the places affected were forced to seek alternative routes for their trade.[1]

The governing body in London will put their King to death

In the aftermath of the English Civil War, and with Charles I held in captivity, the House of Commons decided the King should stand trial for his life. In the days following this decision,

Charles was brought to London and charged with treason. He was then tried before a tribunal, found guilty, and on 30 January 1649, *the governing body in London put their King to death*.[2]

EXECUTION OF CHARLES 1   30 JANUARY 1649

The salt and wine will be on the wrong side of him

Salt and *wine* are the same two biblical metaphors that later occur in Century Ten N°. 7. They therefore provide a neat cross-reference to what was occurring in France during the middle of the 17th century. The *salt* of the earth refers to the moral elite: people, by whose standards of behaviour, the conduct of the world is held in check. The *wine* represents new principles of government. These biblical metaphors are entirely consistent with this period of English history, in which politics and religion had become intensely interwoven. "For twenty years, from 1640 to 1660, religious enthusiasm and political idealism so swept English thought that by comparison for the following twenty years they seemed almost to disappear."[3]

In the middle of the 17th century, the nation's moral elite – the salt (see, Matthew v: 13) – turned against its divinely ordained king. By taking this stand, *the salt* agreed to a set of new political ideas – the wine (see, Matthew ix.17) – which a caucus of politicians deemed to be justification for their anti-royalist attitude.[4] From this, it follows that the *salt* and *wine* were positioned on the wrong side of the King.

Because of them, having the kingdom in disarray

It was therefore *becasue of them* (the salt and wine) that the kingdom was brought into a state of disarray. "The nation [became] divided along a series of irregular jagged lines which defy simple interpretation in clear-cut social, religious, geographical, or economic terms."[5]

The English gentry were just as equally split, some expressing allegiance to the King, and others to Parliament; even members of the same family might be found in disagreement. "In general, in most areas there were two parties – one supporting the King and the other Parliament."[6]

Summary: *This particular prophecy is frequently mentioned (even without the first line having dated it) as an example of the seer's ability to predict the future: it being unquestionably accurate and without any attempt to conceal its meaning before the event. These prophecies were, in fact, known in England at the time, for they were discussed in Elizabethan England more than fifty years earlier. The sceptic must therefore dismiss it as 'chance'. For, if it were so, the same argument would apply to all, including those that are still to come.*

50   *Mendosvs tost viendra à son haut regne,*
        Mettant arriere vn peu le Norlaris:
        Le Rouge blesme, le masle à l'interregne,
        Le ieune crainte & frayeur Barbaris.

Mendosus (as No. 45) Norlaris (*anagrammatic-paragram*) Lorrain[e], *also* (portmanteau) Nor' + laris (OF) north land; Barbaris (Gk.) Βαρβαρος: foreign tongue. Cross-references: Mendosus, C.IX: 45; Norlaris, C.VIII: 60.

The faulty one **VENDOME** will soon come to his high reign, 1593
Putting behind a little the North land (**LORRAINE**):
The Red One pale (**Cardinal Bourbon**); the male (**Mayenne**) at the interregnum,
The young man (**Guise IV**), apprehension, and the foreign tongue (**Philip II**), dread.

The faulty one Vendôme will soon come to his high reign

"Henry de Bourbon-Navarre was the son of Antoine de Bourbon, Duke de Vendôme, and Jeanne d'Albret, Queen of Navarre from 1555." As we have seen previously, from N°. 45 above, Henri IV, King of Navarre and France, inherited the duchy of Vendôme from his father, and in 1598, he presented it to his illegitimate son César, born 1594.

Henri was also at fault in the eyes of Catholic France. His imperfection lay in the fact that he was a Huguenot: a person who protested against papal authority. But after the League had suffered several military defeats at the hands of Henri IV (or Vendôme), it was compelled to concede his right to take the crown.

The King in waiting was therefore able to come to his high reign, as had been predicted many years before at Salon, when Henri was still a pre-pubescent cousin of Char;es IX. Nevertheless, concessions were required. In order to obtain the League's full approval, the King had to agree to convert to Catholicism. This was achieved on 25 July 1593 in the abbey of St Denis. It was only later that Henri was reported to have said – "Paris is worth a Mass." [1]

Putting behind a little the north land (Lorraine)

Before Vendôme rose to power, the House of Lorraine had been seen as first in line to provide the next king of France. (Lorraine is a region in the north of France and shares its border with Germany, Belgium and Luxembourg.) But, this ambition was abruptly cut short by the duc de Guise's assassination in December 1588—at a time when the duke had already become known by the assumed title, 'King of Paris'.

The loss of Guise as the principal contender, followed by defeats on the battlefield at the hands of Vendôme, reduced the House of Lorraine's aspirations to provide the next king. But there were still other members of the family that were considered suitable contenders for the crown. [2]

The red one pale

Chief amongst these contenders at the time had been Cardinal de Bourbon, a prince of the blood, and already seen by Catholics as the future Charles X. His merit lay in the fact that Sixtus V had previously agreed to his appointment. He is therefore described in the oracle as *the red one*, because it is the colour of a cardinal's robes.

But Charles was also *pale*, for he had not long to live His health rapidly declined after his arrest, which occurred on the same day that the duke of Guise was cut down. Henri III ordered him to be arrested and he was imprisoned inside the château at Chinon. The Cardinal was never released and he died there in 1590, aged sixty-seven. [3]

The male at the interregnum

In their search to replace Charles X, the League chose Mayenne. He was from the House of Lorraine, and brother of the two murdered men. But his military losses in two major battles at Arques and Ivry, combined with the internal bickering in the League, weakened his claim. In the oracle he is referred to as the male, which implies competition from a female contender.

> Mayenne curbed the extremists who sought to put the Spanish Infanta Isabella on the French throne; in 1593 he summoned a meeting of the States General in Paris, which upheld the principles of the Salic law of succession against Isabella's claim. [4]

Mayenne eventually agreed to Vendome's right of succession, but not until September 1595.

The young man, apprehension

Charles of Lorraine 4th duc de Guise was aged seventeen when his father was murdered. His arrest quickly followed and he was "transferred to the Château of Tours, in which he was imprisoned for three years, escaping in 1591."⁵ After arriving inside the capital city, which the League still held: "He was welcomed with enthusiasm by the Paris mob, which hoped he would wed the Infanta of Spain and, with the help of Philip II, secure for himself the throne of France."⁶ But Mayenne strongly opposed this plan: believing that it would open the door to Spain's ambitions. The young man shared this apprehension and withdrew his support for the arrangement.⁷

And the foreign tongue, dread

Nevertheless, Spain continued to remain a contender for the throne. Philip II had married Elisabeth, eldest daughter of Henri II and Catherine de' Medici in 1560 as part of the Cateau-Cambrésis treaty. Their child, the Infanta Isabella Clara Eugenia was therefore proposed as Queen of France. But Spain was still France's ancient enemy, and the Salic law forbidding female succession to the throne also prevailed. Antagonistic as the Leaguers were to the accession of Vendôme, the alternative, a foreign tongue, filled them with even greater dread: believing, as they did that it was Spain's intention to secure France as a satellite nation.⁸

In the end, it was Henri IV's conversion to the Catholic faith in July 1593 that enabled the excommunication placed upon him in September 1585, by Pope Sixtus V, to be removed. His coronation took place on 27 February 1594.

Summary: The assassination of Henri III in 1589 was followed by an interregnum that was not completely resolved until 1594. The House of Lorraine had been the chief contender to provide a successor for the French crown, since Henri III was childless and the last of the Valois. But the joint assassination of the Duke of Guise and the Cardinal of Lorraine diminished the family's prospects. While Spain argued for the Infanta, and Mayenne battled unsuccessfully, Guise's son withdrew at his uncle's suggestion and the Pope's choice for France's next king died in custody at Chinon. The seer hints at all of these contenders "at the interregnum" but declares that Henri of Vendome will be the one to achieve the honour. In fact, he had already said this when Charles IX visited him at Salon, and the old seer remarked to the attendant of Henri's household that in time to come, Henri would become King of France and Navarre.

51   *Contre les rouges sectes se banderont,*
        Feu, eau, fer, corde par paix se minera,
        Au point mourir, ceux qui machineront,
        Fors vn que monde sur tout ruynera.

banderont (OF lier) bind, join; se minera (AF décrôitre) wane, decrease; point (AF endroit déterminé) determined place; Fors (OF hors); machineront (OF organiser un complot)

Sects will join against the reds: 1795
Fire, water, iron, rope, through peace, will wane:
Those that will organize a conspiracy, dying at the place decided,
Except for one (**NAPOLEON**) who will lay ruin upon the whole world.

Sects will join against the reds

The death of Robespierre brought to an end the reign of terror. All across France people began to rise up against the excessive brutality that had made victims of so many. In Paris, deprived of their leaders, the Jacobins became disorganized and different sects: such as the Monarchists, Federalists, Girondists were among those who joined in loose coalitions¹ against the reds.²

Fire, water, iron rope, through peace, will wane

The end of the 'Terror', which had gripped France for more than half a decade, brought with it a decline in the means by which so many lives had been terminated. For example:

Throughout 1794 the 'infernal columns' of the Republic wreaked revenge on the rebel villages. Tens of thousands were shot, guillotined, burned in their barns or their churches. At the harbour of Rochefort, several thousand non-juror priests were slowly starved to death on the decks of prison huks. At Angers, thousands of prisoners were shot out of hand. At Nantes, thousands more were systematically drowned.³

Rope needs little explanation; even less to those unfortunate enough to hear the blood-curdling yells directed at them: 'à la lanterne' (lamp-posts served as gibbets during the early part of the Revolution).

Those that will organize a conspiracy, dying at the place decided

At this time, there was also an opportunist attempt at organising a conspiracy to re-establish the monarchy. It was put together soon after the death of Robespierre. Royalists intended to seize power for a renewal of the monarchy by taking advantage of a distracted administration. But their attempt was countered by stiff opposition from troops still loyal to the revolution.

In a bloody battle that took place outside the *Palais de Tuileries* on 5 October 1795 – 'journées de Vendémiaire' – the royalists came under massive firepower, many dying on the spot. By evening: "when two or three hundred men had been killed or wounded on both sides, the fighting was over." Napoleon Bonaparte, who had been appointed second in command under General Barras, later wrote: "We killed a large number of them. They killed thirty of our men, and wounded sixty." [4]

Except for one who will lay ruin upon the whole world

The 'excepted one' who survived the street battle was Napoleon Bonaparte. Here, for the first time, history brings to notice France's future emperor: a man whom the Seer says will 'lay ruin upon the whole world'. Bonaparte's famed 'whiff of grapeshot', which he afterwards claimed had scattered the insurrectionists and restored order, quickly brought him to the notice of the Directory. Three weeks later, he was put in charge of France's internal affairs. From this position, he advanced to command the army that drove the Austrians out of Italy. And his subsequent conquest enabled him to dictate to Pope Pius VI the terms laid down at the treaty of Tolentino.

Summary: *This oracle predicts the end of the French Revolution, which wound down after the death of Robespierre. Bereft of their leader, the Revolution began to flounder, allowing smaller sects to vie to fill the vacant leadership. Chief among these were the monarchists, keen to restore a king to France's government. But the attempt proved bloody, and brought onto the scene Napoleon, whose cannon fire against the monarchists proved deadly, but earned him the respect of the Directory. Having won the governing body's favour and a position of authority, Bonaparte's next appointment was to make him Commander of the army that he would take into Italy, and, from thereon, to an immortal fame that would shake the world.*

52   *La paix s'approche d'vn costé, & la guerre*
        Oncques ne feut la poursuitte si grande,
        Plaindre homme, femme, sang innocent par terre
        Et ce sera de France à toute bande.

53   *Le Neron ieune dans les trois cheminées*
        Fera de paiges vifs pour ardoir ietter,
        Heureux qui loing sera de tels menées,
        Trois de son sang le feront mort guetter.

54   *Arriuera au port de Corsibonne,*
        Prés de Rauenne qui pillera la dame,
        En mer profonde legat de la Vlisbonne
        Sous roc cachez rauiront septante ames.

55   *L'horrible guerre qu'en Occident s'appreste,*
        L'an ensuiuant viendra la pestilence,
        Si fort horrible, que ieune, vieil, ne beste,
        Sang, feu, Mercure, Mars, Iupiter en France.

appreste (AF appresser – opprimer) to oppress; ensuivant (OF) following; vieil (OF) old, aged

The horrific war that in the west oppresses (**WW 1**):   1918
The following year, the pestilence (**SPANISH FLU**) will arrive,
So powerful, horrifying, whether young or old, but not beasts:
Blood, fire, Mercury, Mars, Jupiter in France.

The horrific war that in the west oppresses

On 3 August 1914, Germany declared war on France, while at the same time invading Belgium. Great Britain, under obligation to beleaguered Belgium, declared war on Germany. The next day, Austria-Hungary declared war on Russia and, the day after, Serbia declared war on

Germany. Montenegro then declared war on Austria-Hungary, and five days later extended this declaration to include Germany. France and Great Britain responded by declaring war on Austria-Hungary. On the 23rd of the month, Japan joined in the fray by declaring war against Germany. Austria-Hungary responded by declaring war on Japan, and two days later, on the 25th, it declared war against Belgium. [1] Thereafter, the war was at its bloodiest and most deadly. "Everyone expected the decisive campaign to be in the west; and they were right," the killing was to continue for four long years, and "was virtually unprecedented in the slaughter, carnage, and destruction it caused." [2]

The following year, the pestilence will arrive

Hostilities finally came to an end on 11 November 1918. In the year following, there "came the biggest pandemic visited on Europe since the Black Death. The 'Spanish Flu' killed more Europeans than the War did." The first spate of this new strain of influenza virus was comparatively mild when it appeared in July 1918, and exacted only a minor death toll. In October, it reappeared, but with greater severity. Finally, in February 1919, the virus mutated with deadly consequences. [3]

So powerful, horrifying, whether young or old, but not beasts

The infectious disease proved to be so powerful, so horrifying, that "Altogether an estimated 30 million persons throughout the world perished." No one was immune from the contagion, whether young or old: although cattle were not affected by the disease. The elderly, with their weakened immune system were always vulnerable; but the epidemic also "specialized in prime young adults, particularly women [...] about half the deaths were among 20-to-40-year-olds, an unusual age pattern for influenza." [4]

Blood, fire

For the final line, the oracle returns to its first subject, the war in France. It commences with the bloodletting, which occurred on a scale unprecedented by comparison with past conflicts. The reason for this was entirely due to the increased firepower brought about by technological advances in the machinery of death and destruction. [5]

Mercury, Mars, Jupiter, in France

By referring to these three planets in conjunction, quite a rare occurrence, the Seer has provided a form of astronomical dating for the timing of the oracle's fulfilment. A conjunction occurs when two planets have the same (or very nearly the same) right ascension, as seen from Earth. On 11 January 1913, Mars, Mercury and Jupiter were in the constellation of Sagittarius. The right ascension of these planets were, respectively, 18hrs 02' 41"; 18hrs 07' 12"; 18hrs 08' 26" [6]

On 9 June 1917 the same three planets came together again, this time in the constellation of Taurus. The right ascensions of Mercury, Mars and Jupiter were, then, 03hrs 35' 58"; 03hrs 36' 56"; 03hrs 33' 57".

On the first occasion when these three planets came together, Raymond Poincaré, who had been elected President of the French Republic that same year, ordered all military service to be extended for three years. On 1st August 1914, he further decreed that a general mobilization must begin in preparation for war. This followed the assassination of Archduke Franz-Ferdinand of Austria on 28th June. Interestingly, the triple conjunction occurred during two other triples!

> Decades of international tension had divided the major European powers into two rival camps: on the one side, the Triple Alliance of Germany, Austria-Hungary and Italy; on the other the Triple Entente of France, Russia and Great Britain. No more than a spark — Franz Ferdinand's assassination — was needed to set the continent alight. [7]

On the second occasion that Mercury, Mars and Jupiter came together, the First World War had already been in progress for three years; during the course of which, the conjunction of these planets coincided with the battle of Messines Ridge (7th – 17th June 1917), which led to

Passchendaele—a name wrought with horror. It began in July after the success at Messines Ridge and lasted until November. In the course of the battles that took place, the Allied casualties amounted to somewhere between 200,000 and 448,614, while German losses were numbered between 217,000 and 410,000.

> The Ypres Salient was one of the most intensely fought over sections of the Western Front. Early in 1917, the British high command laid down plans to seize control of the area once and for all. The starting point was the capture of the Messines Ridge, to the south of Ypres. [...] The huge volume of shelling around Ypres not only devastated the landscape and smashed up pathways, but caused a high death toll. [...] Passchendaele was remembered by most of its veterans as one of the worst periods of their war service. [8]

Summary: *The First World War cost more human lives than any previous war had done. But even this number was exceeded by the pandemic that followed one year after the conflict ended. The seer correctly refers to the connexion between the War and the outbreak of disease. Then, to ensure there is no ambiguity, he times the outbreak of war to follow the triple conjunction of Mars, Mercury and Jupiter in Sagittarius; whereafter, the same triple conjunction recurred in Taurus, when it preceded the end of the war.*

56   *Camp pres de Noudam passera Goussan ville,*
        Et à Maiotes laissera son enseigne,
        Conuertira en instant plus de mille,
        Cherchant les deux remettre en chaine & legne.

57   *Au lieu de DRVX vn Roy reposera,*
        Et cherchera loy changeant d'Anatheme,
        Pendant le ciel si tresfort tonnera,
        Portée neufue Roy tuera soy-mesme.

58   *Au costé gauche à l'endroit de Vitry,*
        Seront guettez les trois rouges de France
        Tous assoumez rouge, noir non meurdry,
        Par les Bretons remis en asseurance.

59   *A la Ferté prendra la Vidame,*
        Nicol tenu rouge qu'auoit produit la vie,
        La grand Loyse naistra que fera clame.
        Donnant Bourgongne à Bretons par enuie.

Vidame (OF) Originally, an officer of a bishop that later became a title for a lord, by altering his office into a fief, held for the bishopric he was attached to; Nicol (*apocope*) Nicolas; tenu (OF) supported; produire (OF) to furnish with lechery; naistra (OF) proceed; clame (AF réclamation en justice) request for justice; donnant (OF) delivering up

        At La Ferté he (**FERRIÈRES**) will take the title Vidame,   1560
        NICOL supported the red one (**Cardinal Lorraine**) who had furnished life with lechery:
        The great **LOUISE** will proceed when she will make a claim for justice:
        Burgundy delivering up to the Bretons through envy.

At La Ferté he will take the title Vidame

"A château has existed at La Ferté-[Arnault, but later renamed] Vidame since 985 AD. In 1374, the domain was acquired by the Vendôme family who rebuilt the Castle. This family [held] the prestigious title of vidame of Chartres." [1] The title *vidame* is an odd feudal relic, of which some half-dozen examples survived to the end of the France's Ancient Regime. [2]

The title passed down the blood line of the Vendôme who were Princes of Chabanais only until: "François de Vendôme, Vidame of Chartres, Prince of Chabanais, Seigneur of La Ferté-Arnaud, Born in 1522 (or 25?), François de Vendôme, the last male descendant of the house of the Counts of Vendôme." [3]

In December 1560, Vendôme died suddenly in Paris after being released from the Bastille. With no natural heir, the title 'Vidame of Chartres' went to his first cousin, Jean de Ferrières, at his domain in La Ferté-Vidame. "Ferrières inherited from his cousin both 'immense riches' and the title of Vidame de Chartres." [4]

During Ferrières' life and career, he made many contributions of outstanding importance, both politically and in the French Wars of Religion. The oracle appears to have used this prediction as a simple timing device to mark the year 1560.

Nicholas supported the red one that had furnished life with lechery

This timeframe now acts as a pointer to *Nicholas of Lorraine* (16 October 1524 – 23 January 1577), He was the second son of Antoine, Duke of Lorraine and Renée de Bourbon.

> He was originally destined for an ecclesiastical career, being made bishop of Metz in 1543 and of Verdun in 1544. In June 1545, he became joint "tutor and administrator" for his nephew, Charles III. Duke of Lorraine, with his sister-in-law Christina of Denmark. However, the Estates of Lorraine, in November 1545, removed him in favour of Christina as sole regent. He opposed her pro-Imperial policies. Resigning his dioceses in 1548 in favour of his uncle Jean, Cardinal of Lorraine, he took the title *Count of Vaudémont.*[5]

In this manner, *Nicholas* gave his support to the *Red One,* Cardinal Jean de Lorraine (1498 – 1550). He was the younger brother of Antoine Duke of Lorraine, and had received the appointment of cardinal-deacon at the age of twenty from Pope Leo X. Thereafter he held a large number of benefices as Administrator, although not all at once. These included the bishoprics of Metz, Toul and Verdun, together with those of Albi Agen, Luçon, Nantes, Thérouanne and Valence. He was appointed Archbishop of Reims, Lyon and Narbonne. Yet, despite his noble background and religious authority "He is considered a corrupt ruler who before he died squandered most of the wealth which he had derived from these and other benefices [...] he was disgraced in 1542, and retired to Rome."[6]

By 1542, the cardinal's activities had come under the suspicion of Francis I, who regarded him as "dissolute and extravagant, lavishing vast sums of money on entertainments at the Hôtel de Cluny, his Paris residence."[7] This, of course, is not prophecy, but history of a scandalous nature that would have reached the ears of the Seer: as he makes clear by using the past tense.

In 1567, one year after the Seer's death, the Holy Roman Emperor, Maximilian II, appointed *Nicholas of Lorraine* a hereditary and independent Prince of the Empire. He was also created a knight of the Order of Saint Esprit. But the purpose of introducing Nicholas, insofar as this prophecy is concerned, exists in the fact that he was father to the Queen of France.

The great Louise will proceed when she will make a claim for justice

Louise of Lorraine was born on 30 April 1553, five years before this quatrain was published. She was the fourth child born to Nicolas Comte de Vaudémont and Marguerite d'Egmont his first wife. Shortly before Louise's twenty-second birthday, she became Queen of France, following her marriage to Henri III on 14 February 1575—one day after her husband's coronation at Riems: hence, 'the great Louise'.

However, it was not until the assassination of the King at the hands of Jacques Clément in August 1589 that Louise emerged to fulfil this prediction. Details of the assassination appear in Century One N°. 97, where it will be recalled how Clément had been groomed by the Duke of Guise's sister, and her cohorts, into believing that his divine mission was to kill the King. Louise saw it as a duty to her deceased husband to bring the perpetrators of the crime to justice. As a staunch Roman Catholic, and now dowager Queen of France, she entreated both Henri IV and the Pope to punish those responsible.

Unfortunately, Henri was King by nomination only. As a Protestant, he did not have the backing of French Catholics. Moreover, at the Vatican, Sixtus V had already excommunicated Henri IV to prevent him becoming King; and then, on 27 August 1590, the Pope had died. His successor, Pope Urban VII, also died a mere twelve days after his election. He was succeeded by Gregory XIV, who was elected on 5 December 1590. But ten months later he, too, died. Innocent IX reigned next, but expired after just two months on the papal throne (30 December 1591). It therefore fell to Clement VIII to deal with the French succession.

After Henri IV agreed to convert to Catholicism, the Pope removed the excommunication. Since this helped to bring the French Wars of Religion to a close, the Pope appears to have taken care not to incite members of the Guise family into action, by excommunicating one of their family. Thus, "Louise also failed in her attempts to convince the king and the pope to punish both the Duke of

Mayenne, believed to have ordered the assassination of Henri III, and the Jacobin order to which the assassin belonged." [8]

Burgundy delivering up to the Bretons through envy

After the assassination of her husband, the King, "Louise retired to Chenonceau, which Catherine de' Medici had bequeathed to her in January 1589. She suffered severe financial hardship, particularly as Gabrielle d'Estrées was determined to get her hands on the property by negotiating with the creditors of both Catherine and Louise.

In the end, Louise handed Chenonceau over to her niece, daughter of the Duke of Mercoeur, when the duke joined Henri IV's camp and negotiated the betrothal of his daughter to César de Vendôme, the son of Gabrielle and Henri IV." [9] The new beneficiary of Chenonceau, Françoise de Lorraine-Mercœur was the daughter of Emmanuel de Lorraine, Duke of Mercœur, and her husband was the son of Gabrielle d'Estrées, one of the Bretons mentioned in the oracle. This was because …

> In 1582 he [Mercœur] was made governor of Brittany by Henry III of France, who had married his half-sister [Louise]. In 1588 Mercœur put himself at the head of the League in Brittany, and had himself proclaimed protector of the Roman Catholic Church in the province. His wife's family, the House of Penthièvre, were descendants of the House of Dreux as Dukes of Brittany. [...] Mercœur endeavoured to make himself independent in that province, and organized a government at Nantes, calling his son "prince and duke of Brittany" [...] [But] Henry IV assured his control of Brittany through the marriage of his illegitimate son to Mercœur's daughter Francoise. [10]

César and Françoise were married in 1608, when they were 16 and 15 years of age respectively, and became the new owners of Chenonceau. Louise retired to her château at Moulins, which was in "Bourbonnais [...] a historic province in the centre of France that corresponded to the modern *département* of Allier, along with part of the *département* of Cher. Its capital was Moulins." [11] Bourbonnais was acquired by the "House of Burgundy [...] in 1249 during a crusade." [12]

Thus, a transfer of property that began with envy was concluded when Burgundy – a metonymy – for Louise, delivered Chenonceau to the Bretons – a metonymy for César and his family.

Summary: *This oracle bridges the time between the seer, while living, and long after his death. It rather suggests that Nostredame's curiosity surrounding the House Lorraine, while he was alive, led him to discover the outcome of what began with the scandalous behaviour of Cardinal Nicholas of Lorraine. Thereafter, by following the trail of time it led to the birth of Louise of Lorraine who eventually became Henri III's Queen, and then his widow. The trail ends with Henry IV's son, by his mistress Gabrielle d'Estrées, marrying the dowager Queen's niece. Louise then transferred the beautiful château at Chenonceaux to the envious mistress's son who was also the husband of her niece. But Gabrielle did not live to enjoy it; she died in 1599 at the age of 25 or 26.*

> 60   *Conflict Barbar en la Cornere noire,*
>   *Sang espandu trembler la d'Almatie,*
>   *Grand Ismaël mettra son promontoire,*
>   *Ranes trembler, secours Lusitanie.*

> 61   *La pille faite à la coste marine,*
>   *Incita noua & parenz amenez,*
>   *Plusieurs de Malte par le fait de Messine,*
>   *Estroit serrez seront mal guerdonnez.*

> 62   *Au grand de Cheramon agora*
>   *Seront croisez par ranc tous attachez,*
>   *Le pertinax Oppi, & Mandragora,*
>   *Raugon d'Octobre le tiers seront laschez.*

> 63   *Plainctes & pleurs, crys & grands vrlemens*
>   *Prés de Narbon à Bayonne & en Foix*
>   *O quel horrible calamitz changemens,*
>   *Auant que Mars reuolu quelques foys.*

64   *L'Aemathion passer montz Pyrennees,*
       En Mars Narbon ne fera resistance,
       Par mer & terre fera si grand menee,
       Cap. n'ayant terre seure pour demeurance.

Æmathion (refer No. 38); passer (AF & OF) depart from; menée (Littré: a feudal right; e.g. AF - Exploit symbolique par lequel un seigneur fait sommer son vassal de satisfaire à ses devoirs) Symbolic feat by which a Lord summons his vassals to fulfil their duties; grand (OF) stately; seure (AF qui a de l'assurance) which has assurance; Cap. (L abbrev. – Cap\ut) chief.

The Amythaon (**LOUIS XIV**) departing from the Pyrenean Mountains,   1659
In warfare, Narbonne will not make resistance:
By sea and land, he will so much enforce a stately feudal right:
The chief (**FOUQUET**) not having land that has assurance for dwelling.

The Amythaon departing from the Pyrenean Mountains

On 7 November 1659 Louis XIV signed the *Peace of the Pyrenees*: a treaty that took its name from the mountains separating France from Spain. It was in their shadow that Louis XIV – the Amythaon, [1] – reached a favourable settlement with Philip IV to end the war between them, which had lasted since 1639. He departed, having gained Roussillon, Artois, together with parts of Luxembourg and Flanders. And a new border with Spain west of the Pyrenees was drawn. [2]

> However, the treaty stipulated only that all villages north of the Pyrenees should become part of France. For that reason there is an exclave of Spain in this part of France, the town of Llívia, considered a town and not a village, which remains under Spanish control and is part of the *comarca* of Baixa Cerdanya, the Spanish province of Girona. [...] On the western Pyrenees a definite borderline was drawn and decisions made as to the politico-administrative affiliation of bordering areas in the Basque region—Baztan, Aldude, Valcarlos. [3]

In warfare, Narbonne will not make resistance

Among the gains made by Louis XIV was the province of Roussillon. It was because of this acquisition that Carcassonne, the former capital of Languedoc, together with nearby Narbonne, were no longer considered frontier towns. From then onwards, the fortifications at Carcassonne were left to fall into decay. Consequently, in warfare, Narbonne, which had once been the capital of that region ("The Romans made it the capital of their first colony in Gaul, Gallia Narbonensis, and it was a vital port both then and later in the Middle Ages," [4]) was no longer able to make resistance against a future invasion. It was Narbonne's inability to defend the province that later became a critical issue in the Sun King's reign. (See N°. 38 above for details.)

By sea and land, he will so much enforce a stately feudal right

Two years after the Peace conference, the oracle turns attention to events across the Channel. In July 1661, Britain's newly installed King Charles II sent a request to the French and Spanish ambassadors, asking that they not attend the arrival of the diplomatic party from Venice. The appeal was made because of what was known as 'the rights of passage' (*céder le pas*); Charles wanted to avoid a confrontation between Spain and France as to which of these two nations' ambassadors would take precedence in the parade through London.

When Louis XIV received news from England that his ambassador had agreed to this request and had stood down, he was furious. And, in August, his injured pride was made known to Charles II in London. England was to be left in no doubt as to the pre-eminence of France when appearing on parade. Charles II was even criticized for intervening in French affairs.

On 30 September, the French ambassador to England, d'Estrades, saw an opportunity to regain favour with his King. The Swedish ambassador was due to arrive in London, and the opportunity for French carriages to take a leading position in the parade presented itself. Unfortunately, the Spanish ambassador had a similar idea. And to serve his purpose, he imported into England several thousand Spanish soldiers as 'servants'. The French had only five hundred. Therefore, when a fight broke out in this charged atmosphere, "a number of French dead were left on the city streets."

Louis was outraged when details reached him at Fontainebleau, and he vowed he would oblige all countries, "to yield to my ambassadors the precedence in all the courts of Europe." The French ambassador was recalled from Madrid, and Spain's ambassador in France was ordered to leave the country. Negotiations concerning the future of the Low Countries were also broken off, and a renewal of the war with Spain was threatened.

Louis XIV's displeasure lasted well into the next year, until on 24 March 1662 the Comte de Fuentes arrived in Paris on a special embassy. His mission was to offer Spain's apologies, and provide assurances that Spanish ambassadors would never again compete against the precedence of France.

Hardly had one diplomatic incident been resolved when another arose. On 2 June 1662, Louis' ambassador to Rome, the duc de Créqui, arrived at the French Embassy and found it situated close to the barracks housing Pope Alexander VII's Corsican guards. On 20 August, an argument developed between three Frenchmen and three of the Pope's men. Soon, swords were drawn and a fight began. In the excitement, others from the garrison, armed with harquebuses, joined the Corsicans and they began shooting at anyone suspected of being French. When de Créqui appeared on the balcony to see what had caused the commotion, a volley of gunfire greeted him. He survived, but Louis' outrage, hardly quelled since the previous incident, now extended to the Pope, and an immediate apology was demanded for the behaviour of his guards.

The Pope vacillated for several days, allowing thirty-two Corsicans to leave Rome and avoid punishment. Ten days after the affray, Louis wrote to the Pope withdrawing his ambassador, and declaring "that no one who concerns my dignity should remain any longer exposed to outrages such as have been unequalled even by the barbarians themselves." He then ordered the papal nuncio to leave Paris and commanded that his army seize the papal state of Avignon.

This further injury to Louis' pride was eventually pacified by the *Treaty of Pisa* (12 February 1664), in which Pope Alexander finally yielded to Louis XIV's demands. [5]

The chief not having land that has assurance for dwelling

The final line of this oracle covers the same period of time, and concerns Nicolas Fouquet who served under Cardinal Mazarin and continued to see himself as First Minister in charge of finances. But the ambitious Jean-Baptiste Colbert dissembled Fouquet's accounts before the King, and demonstrated several inaccuracies. This led to Fouquet's arrest, and he was charged with lèse-majesté. [6]

As France's finance minister during Louis XIV's regency, Fouquet had acquired some expensive properties. Among these was his house at Saint Mandé adjoining the park at Vincennes; another was a château on Belle-Isle at the mouth of Quiberon Bay. But the most extravagant, and architecturally grand was his mansion known as Vaux-le-Vicomte.

> On 2 August 1656, he signed an agreement with Louis Le Vau. [...] Early in 1657 a task force of 18,000 was set to work. Levelling the ground for the immense gardens and laying the foundations for the château and its palatial outbuildings. Within a year the shell of masonry was completed. [7]

The entire construction was finally finished in 1661. It was magnificently furnished, complete with '143 tapestries' designed by Le Brun and manufactured in a special factory created for the occasion. But on 3 September, Fouquet was arrested. For the next three years, this former chief finance minister of France – now without any certainty of his property being available for dwelling – was put on trial for embezzlement. In December 1664 he was finally sentenced. Initially his punishment had been banishment, but Louis subsequently altered this to perpetual imprisonment. Fouquet was sent to the castle at Pignerolo on the borders of Piedmont, where he remained until his death twelve years later. [8]

Summary: *This oracle, which again introduces the Amythaon, provides a further example of the cross-referencing that remains fairly consistent in these oracles. Hister (Hitler); le Duc (the Duce); the 'crop head', 'the eagle' and 'Po' (Napoleon), also 'Cap' or 'Faux' (Louis XVI) are other examples of aptronyms befitting the person intended. The present oracle concerns the reign of Louis XIV during a brief span of years between 1659 and 1664. It commences with the important Peace of the Pyrenees and then foretells the personal gloire of the French King in compelling other monarchs – even the Pope – to respect his feudal rights abroad. It ends with the downfall of Nicholas Fouquet, who enriched himself as chief minister during the King's minority.*

65   *Dedans le coing de luna viendra rendre,*
          Où sera prins & mys en terre estrange,
          Les fruitz immeurs seront à grand esclandre,
          Grand vitupere à l'vn grande louange.

66   *Paix, vnion sera & changement,*
          Estatz, offices, bas hault, & hault bien bas.
          Dresser voiage, le fruict premier, torment:
          Guerre cesser, ciuil proces debatz.

67   *Du hault des montz à l'entour de Lizer*
          Port à la roche Valen. cent assemblez
          De chasteau neuf pierre late en donzere,
          Contre le crest Romans foy assemblez.

68   *Du mont Aymar sera noble obscurcie,*
          Le mal viendra au ioinct de sonne & rosne,
          Dans bois caichez soldatz iour de Lucie,
          Qui ne fut onc vn si horrible throsne.

A[y]mar(*epenthesis*) Amar: *also* Aymar (*anagrammatic paragram*, 't' for 'y' - Atmar) Marat.

Of the Mountain, **AMAR** (**MARAT**), the high born will be obscured: 1793
The evil will come at the junction of the Saône and Rhône (**LYONS**),
Soldiers hidden in woodland (**VENDÉANS**): day of **LUCY**,
That which was not at any time, one such horrible throne.

Of the Mountain, Amar

During the French Revolution, 'the Mountain' was the name given to the political body that occupied seats high above the floor of the Assembly Hall. [1] "Across the assembly in the high seats on the far left which gave them the nickname of 'The Mountain', sat Robespierre, Danton and their Jacobin cohorts." [1] Seated also among the arrivals to the newly constituted Convention was André Amar, an "enthusiastic Terrorist and dechristianizer" (Schama p.839), but also the representative for Isère. He took his seat beside fellow members of the Mountain.

> In Paris thousands of people went out regularly to witness the operations of what the deputy, J.A.B. Amar, called the red 'Mass' performed on the 'great altar' of the 'holy guillotine'. They took their seats around the scaffold with the *tricoteuses,* buying wine and biscuits from hawkers while they waited for the show to begin. [2]

In this sense, Amar's sanguinary, antichristian vocabulary had much in common with that of Jean Paul Marat, the editor of *L'Ami du Peuple*—with whom Amar has been linked.

(Marat)

> On September 9, Marat was elected one of the twenty-four Paris deputies. [...] He was supported by the Jacobin Club [...] the Mountain had to show a united front [...] and Marat's now known and firmly established influence with the lower classes was too great for them to disregard. [...] To add to the strength of Marat's position there was the weight of his paper. Since the opening of the Convention he had distributed gratis six or seven hundred copies of it daily. [...] These went almost entirely to members of the Mountain. [3]

Marat was by then well known for his bloodthirsty rhetoric. But there was another, significant link that brought the names of Amar and Marat together. After the murder of Marat by Charlotte Corday, Amar was chosen by the Convention to investigate and prepare an official report detailing those implicated in his murder.

The highborn will be obscured

On 19 March 1793, just six months after Marat and Amar had taken their seats in the newly constituted Convention; the Mountain demanded the proscription of all noblemen. Thereafter, in rapid succession, on 28 March and again on 5 April, all émigrés were sentenced to perpetual banishment.

> These eighteen months were again filled with the movement of the 'Emigration'. The movement was of course, the departure of many of the more prominent of the privileged order and of a crowd of humbler nobles, as also of a few ecclesiastics, from France. [4]

The evil will come at the junction of the Saône and Rhône

Lyons lies *at the junction of the Saône and Rhône*. The city has not been named in the oracle, but its location is unmistakeable. Quite possibly, this omission was deliberate, and intended to signal the city's forthcoming loss of its name. Lyons had earlier rebelled against the new constitution. An irate Convention in Paris responded by dispatching troops to restore order. Once this had been accomplished, Couthon declared that the name Lyons should be wiped off the map, and a column was erected to declare – LYON N'EST PLUS (Lyons is no more). Thereafter, the city was renamed: Ville-affranchie (Freed City).

As a more exacting mark of the Convention's anger, Lyons was forced to endure a Terror that is regarded, still, to have been even worse than that suffered in Paris. As the oracle recounts – the evil will come at the junction of the Saône and Rhône.

Joseph Fouché was put in charge of executing the city's rebels, and he remained in Lyons until 2,000 of its citizens had been executed; some of these were young men that he bound together and used as targets for cannon fire, having loaded the barrels with grape-shot. [5]

Soldiers hidden in woodland

In that same year, 1793, another rebellion broke out, this time in the Vendée, part of western France. The bocages or *woodland*, mostly comprised of copses and groves, proved to be an excellent battleground for the armed guerrillas who were fighting for the royalist cause. "[T]he Vendéans spontaneously practised tactics suitable for such improvised troops: sharpshooting or ambush, then a mass attack upon a disorganized enemy." These militants, known as Chouans, would conceal themselves amongst the trees; that is, *soldiers hidden in woodland*: and from there, they were able to ambush the republican forces sent to confront them. [6]

Day of Lucy

At first these guerrilla tactics were enormously successful. But in October, the Vendéan rebels were falsely led to believe that a ship was arriving at Granville with an army of *émigré* volunteers. 30,000 armed men, followed by more than a 100,000 citizens of all ages, made their way to the Normandy port to greet the arrivals. It was a trap. There was no ship. Realizing they had been the victims of a cruel deception, this huge flock of people began to straggle back the way they had come. Alas, there was an army in wait for them. During their 120-mile trek, the Vendéan rebels, including women and children, were raped, robbed and killed without mercy.

> The last confused horde of La Vendée had been driven from the walls of Granville in Normandy, to which it had erred and drifted rather than retreated. At Mans on 13th December it was cut to pieces. [7]

In the Roman Catholic Calendar of Saints, 13th December is Saint Lucy's Day – day of Lucy. [8] The Seer has now dated three prophecies by stating the name of a saint whose feast day falls on the same day as the fulfilment of a particular prophecy; they are Saint Solano (14 July, Bastille Day), Saint Agnes (21 January, beheading of Louis XVI) and now Saint Lucy (13 December).

That which was not at any time, one such horrible throne

1793 began in January with the guillotining of Louis XVI. Before the end of the year, the Queen, too, would go to the guillotine. Both their children, the heir to the throne, ten-year-old Louis-

Charles and his sister Marie-Thérèse, were kept separate from each other, orphaned, locked away and alone inside the Temple prison.

The little Prince would soon die from tuberculosis and neglect. His sister remained alone inside the Temple Tower until her release in December 1795. The oracle's description of this period in French history is surely incontestable: There never was ever one such horrible throne, as that which occurred in 1793.[9]

Summary: *This is a very informative prophecy. It begins by revealing a clever conjunction between the names of Amar and Marat—both of who were members of the Mountain, which is also named. It ends by foretelling the exact day of this same year, 1793, when the people of the rebellious Vendée were slaughtered. Accompanying these events during that same year was the enforced exile of France's nobility, and Fouché's heinous act of slaughtering 2000 citizens in Lyon. The oracle's final prediction correctly foretells that these things would happen at a time unprecedented in French history, when the throne would be at it most horrible. Although unstated in this oracle (but not in others), the beheading of the King and Queen fulfilled this prediction.*

69   *Sur le mont de Bailly & la Bresle*
Seront caichez de Grenoble les fiers,
Oultre Lyon, Vien. eulx si grand gresle,
Langoult en terre n'en restera vn tiers.

70   *Harnois trenchant dans les flambeaux cachez*
Dedans Lyon le iour du Sacrement,
Ceux de Vienne seront trestous hachez
Par les cantons Latins Mascon ne ment.

71   *Aux lieux sacrez animaux veu à trixe,*
Auec celuy qui n'osera le iour:
A Carcassonne pour disgrace propice,
Sera posé pour plus ample seiour.

72   *Encor seront les saincts temples pollus,*
Et expillez par Senat Tholossain,
Saturne deux trois circles reuollus,
Dans Auril, May, gens de nouueau leuain.

73   *Dans Fois entrez Roy ceiulee Turban,*
Et regnera moins euolu Saturne,
Roy Turban blanc Bizance cœur ban,
Sol, Mars, Mercure prés la hurne.

74   *Dans la cité de Fertsod homicide,*
Fait & fait multe beuf arant ne macter,
Retour encores aux honneurs d'Artemide,
Et à Vulcan corps morts sepulturer.

75   *De l'Ambraxie & du pays de Thrace,*
Peuple par mer mal & secours Gaulois,
Perpetuelle en Prouence la trace,
Auec vestiges de leur coustume & loix.

76   *Auec le noir Rapax & sanguinaire,*
Yssu du peaultre de l'inhumain Neron,
Emmy deux fleuues main gauche militaire,
Sera murtry par Ioyne chaulueron.

77   *Le regne prins le Roy conuiera,*
La dame prinse à mort iurez à sort,
La vie à Royne fils on desniera,
Et la pellix au fort de la consort.

convier (AF *syncope* or *misprint* – conveier) convey; sort (AF suffrage) vote; desnier (OF) say no to; pellix (L pellex) concubine.

The reign seized, it will convey the King (**LOUIS XVI**),   1793
The captive wife (**MARIE ANTOINETTE**) to a death sworn by vote:
The life of the Queen and son (**LOUIS-CHARLES**), men will say no to,
And the concubine (**Mme du BARRY**) to the stronghold of the consort.

The reign seized

In the summer of 1792, the monarchy's long reign in France was finally brought to an inglorious end. The revolutionary government had seized control of the country, and the First French Republic came into existence. [1] This oracle foretells the consequences that befell Louis XVI, his consort Marie Antoinette, and their son, Prince Louis Charles.

It will convey the King

On 11 December 1792, Louis XVI was taken from the Temple Tower, where he and his family had been confined for the past four months, and brought before the Convention to hear the indictment made against him. The full trial began at the close of the month. By 15 January the 749 deputies were preparing to proceed with the sentencing. Voting took place next day. "As dawn came up it was apparent that the death sentence would be passed." [2] It was to be carried out on the 21 January at the square renamed *Place de la Révolution,* and which is now called *Place de la Concorde.*

On the morning of the 21st the King awoke early and prepared himself for the ordeal of his execution. "Outside a light rain had begun to fall from a grey sky. There was a large green carriage waiting, and beyond it stretched line upon line of National Guardsmen and citizens with muskets and pikes on their shoulders." The significance of the 'carriage' is that it represents the only occasion in which a tumbrel was not used to convey a condemned prisoner to the site of the guillotine. The King alone was conveyed by carriage. Everyone else, even the Queen, made the journey in an open dung cart. "At about half-past nine the carriage arrived at the Place de la Révolution where Louis saw the platform which had been set up [...] On the platform stood Charles Sanson, the city's executioner [...] Above Sanson loomed the instrument of execution, the guillotine." [3] In accordance with custom, after the beheading, the severed head dripping with warm blood was held aloft before the crowd.

The captive wife to a death sworn by vote

Marie Antoinette, as consort to Louis XVI was the captive wife. At two o'clock on the morning of 2 August 1793, she was taken from her place of confinement inside the Temple Tower, and transferred to a cell inside the Conciergerie, situated on the Île Saint Louis. There, she was to remain while her trial was prepared. Evidence was being put together to prove that she had performed acts of treason against the state. [4]

The trial began on Monday 14 October, with the charges made against the Queen put before fifteen jurors. The second and final session took place on the following day. At its conclusion, the jury retired to cast their votes: aware no doubt of Hébert's demand to the Convention, "I must have the head of Antoinette." A verdict of guilty was duly given, and the former Queen was sentenced to death. She was executed on the following morning (16 October 1793). [5]

The life of the Queen and son, men will say no to

Three months before her execution, on the evening of 3 July, six Municipals arrived at the Temple to address the Queen. Their mission was to remove her son and place him in the care of Antoine Simon. Marie Antoinette became defiant. "She stood in front of his bed, and she said 'never' [...] they could kill her but she would never consent." But the child was removed, "and all night long and for two whole days he cried for his mother." But he never saw her again. [6] She was executed three months after their separation.

Two years later, alone, ill and under-nourished inside his prison room, Louis Charles was allowed to slip from this life: health and recovery having been denied him. It was thought provident at the time to allow the child's illness to take its natural course.

And the concubine to the stronghold of the consort

Seven weeks after the execution of Marie Antoinette, the beheading of Marie Jeanne du Barry took place. She had been a prostitute who subsequently became the concubine of Louis XVI's grandfather, Louis XV. [7] Her inclusion in this prophecy is not insignificant, nor unconnected with Marie Antoinette. The two women had been bitter enemies at court.

The curve of destiny had brought the one time enemies together again at the end of their lives. They had entered history within a year of one another; they were to die upon the same scaffold within a few months. [8]

"On December 4th, Madame Du Barry was transferred [...] to the grim prison of the Conciergerie." [9] After her trial, "Madame du Barry, back in her cell at the Conciergerie, must have suffered a hundred times over the death that awaited her in the morning." [10] She was guillotined on 8 December 1793 amidst appalling scenes of hysteria.

Summary: Except for the death of Louis Charles, the son of Louis XVI and Marie Antoinette, which occurred in 1795, and the reign of the monarchy which was seized to become transformed into a republic in 1792, the events described in this oracle occurred in 1793. These concern three deaths: those of the King and Queen, and that of the mistress of the King's grandfather, Louis XV. All three were guillotined that year. The King and Queen are referred to by title, and the terminology identifying them is a matter of historical record: as is that of the Queen's enemy at court, the mistress of Louis XV. The oracle is a part of the tapestry we call the universe. These events have all been 'embroidered' into a pattern of incidents that were foreseen two and a half centuries before they became known to a public that shared the timeframe of those whose lives were foretold. This tells us that our own lives could also have been foretold, centuries before we were born, had there been reason for doing so. Think about it!

78   La dame Grecque de beauté laydique,
      Heureuse faicte de procs innumerable,
      Hors translatee au regne Hispanique,
      Captiue prinse mourir mort miserable.

79   Le chef de classe par fraude stratageme,
      Fera timides sortir de leurs galleres,
      Sortis murtris chef renieur de cresme,
      Puis par l'embusche luy rendront les saleres.

80   Le Duc voudra les siens exterminer,
      Enuoyera les plus forts lieux estranges,
      Par tyrannie Pize & Luc ruiner,
      Puis les Barbares sans vin feront vendanges.

Duc (AF chef de guerre) head of war, also apocope; Duce. Note the capital 'D' indicating a name or title; estrange (OF) outlandish; Pize (syncope) Pi[acen]ze; Luc (apocope Luc[ca]; Barbares (Gk βαρβαρος) foreign speaking.
Cross-references: Duc, C.VI: 31; C.IX: 95; C.X: 64.
N.B. "Barbarians is certainly not derived from the Latin barba (a beard), as many suppose. It is, instead a Greek word, and has many analogous meanings. The Greeks and Romans called all foreigners barbarians; meaning they were babblers:" men who spoke a language not understood by them.

THE DUCE (head of war) will want to exterminate his own kind (SOCIALISTS); 1921
The most powerful ones he will send to outlandish places,
Ruining Piacenza and Lucca by tyranny,
Then, the foreign speakers (GERMANS), without wine, will go grape gathering.

The Duce (head of war)

The Duce (Benito Mussolini) was brought up as the member of a staunchly, socialist family. In his youth he was a ready convert to his father's socialism, and while still young, became actively involved in arguing for socialist policies. Only later did political ambition overcome his working-class background, and he began to reject the socialist philosophy of his upbringing. In its place, he turned his attention to fascism. It was this policy that eventually led to him becoming the fascist dictator of Italy. It also raised him to the position of Head of Warfare. And he was the instigator of Italy's invasion and occupation of Abyssinia (1936-41), thus verifying his title. [1]

Will want to exterminate his own kind

Mussolini's rise to the rank of leadership in Italy was obtained at a heavy price. In order to secure his position from attacks by the opposition; he was forced to allow gangs of black-shirted "Squadristi" to murder his former socialist colleagues; which is to say, the Duce will want to exterminate his own kind.

They made fifty-seven raids between January and March 1921 and burned down twenty-five buildings. They killed twelve Socialists [...] and as Mussolini relied on the Fascists, and had no alternative but to rely upon them, he implicitly at least, allowed them to murder. [2]

The most powerful ones he will send to outlandish places

The Duce's initial response to attempts that were made against his life was to place the blame on the socialists. But after gaining power in 1922, he lost little time in sending the leading members of the socialist party into exile: transporting them to some of the remotest parts of the country. The victims of his purge, the "confine" –

were originally interned in the Isle of Lipari off the north coast of Sicily. In later years, places of internment were opened on the Isles of Tremiti off the Adriatic coast and of Ponza and Ventotene in the Gulf of Gaeta, and on the mainland at Amalfi, Cava dei Tirreni and elsewhere. [3]

Ruining Piacenza and Lucca by tyranny

Piacenza, on the banks of the River Po was to become the scene of repeated, murderous attacks at night, perpetrated against members of the socialist farm-workers' union who were objecting to Mussolini's policies. [4]

In Lucca, the citizens also came to experience the tyranny that essentially identified Mussolini's brand of Fascism. This was exemplified by the Fascist Party activists who targeted the Catholic People's Party. [5] Before then, the CPP had enjoyed full support from the majority of Lucca's population. But this sharply declined as a direct result of the repeated attacks made against its members. [6]

Then the foreign speakers, without wine, will go grape gathering

In this final line, the Seer provides another example of his cryptic humour. *The foreign speakers* are the Germans who, as part of the peace negotiations that followed World War I, were forced to relinquish the 30-mile wide zone known as the Rhineland. The region has been made famous for its grapevines. Hence, the Germans, *the foreign speakers*, were – apropos the oracle's humour – *without wine*. But in 1936, Adolf Hitler saw an opportunity to recover the Rhineland.

World attention was at that time firmly focused upon the Duce and his invasion of Abyssinia. Seizing this opportunity, and in defiance of both the 'Versailles' and the 'Locarno' treaties, Hitler ordered his troops to occupy the Rhineland; or, as the Seer predicted, with tongue in cheek, *the foreign speakers will go grape gathering.* [7]

Summary: *The rise of Il Duce, Benito Mussolini, is predicted in this oracle by describing the tyrannical manner in which he achieved high office: even to the extent of sanctioning the murders of socialists who held principles that he, too, had once supported. The outlandish places to which many others of those opposed his rule were sent is also predicted. Moreover the manner of his despotic rule is affirmed by naming two of the cities affected, Lucca and Piacenza. The final line of prophecy, which refers to foreign speakers, was fulfilled when Mussolini's ally in the Second World War, Adolf Hitler, retook the Rhineland, while Italy was involved in occupying Abyssinia.*

81   *Le Roy rusé entendra ses embusches*
        De trois quartiers ennemis assaillir,
        Vn nombre estrange larmes de coqueluches
        Viendra Lemprin du traducteur faillir.

82   *Par le deluge & pestilence forte*
        La cité grande de long temps assiegee,
        La sentinelle & garde de main morte,
        Subite prinse, mains de nul oultragee.

83   *Sol vingt de Taurus si fort terre trembler.*
        Le grand theatre rempli ruinera:
        L'air, ciel & terre obscurcir & troubler,
        Lors l'infidele Dieu & sainctz voguera.

84   *Roy exposé parfaira L'hecatombe,*
        Apres auoir trouué son origine,
        Torrent ouurir de marbre & plomb la tombe
        D'vn grand Romain d'enseigne Medusine.

85   *Passer Guienne, Languedoc & le Rosne,*
        D'Agen tenans de Marmande & la Roole,
        D'ouurir par foy parroy, Phocen tiendra son trosne,
        Conflit aupres sainct Pol de Manseole.

86   *Du bourg Lareyne paruiendront droit à Chartes*
        Et feront pres du pont Anthoni panse.
        Sept pour la paix cautelleux comme martres:
        Feront entree d'armee à Paris clause.

panse (n), panser (v) or pause?

87   *Par la forest du Touphon essartee,*
        Par hermitaige sera posé le temple,
        De Duc d'Estampes par sa ruse inuentee,
        Du mont Lehori prelat donra exemple.

Touphon (Arabic means 'deluge') but touphon (τουφα) in Greek means bunch, cluster

88   *Calais, Arras secours à Theroanne,*
        Paix & semblant simulera l'escoutte,
        Soulde d'Alobrox descendre par Roane
        Destornay peuple qui deffera la routte.

89   *Sept ans sera PHILIP. fortune prospere,*
        Rabaissera des BARBARES l'effort.
        Puis son midy perplex, rebours affaire,
        Ieune ognion abysmera son fort.

PHILIP. (*apocope*) Philip[pe]; rabaisser (OF) abate - Dictionnaire de français: Littré - *Fig.* Réduire à un degré plus bas) reducing to a degree more lower; rebours (OF) wayward; perplex (OF) vexed; BARBARES; (Gk βαρβαρος) foreign tongues; ognion - Ogmios – the Gallic Hercules; abysmer (OF) to cast into a bottomless pit / hell; fort (AF *apocope* – fort[iz]) fortress.

N.B. Some early editions print *Arabes l'effaict* in place of *Barbares l'effort.*

SEVEN YEARS it will be PHILIPPE: his fortune prospers;   1715
The effort of the foreign tongues will reduce to a lower degree.
Furthermore, his midi (NEW ORLEANS) vexed, a wayward affair,
Young Gallic HERCULES will cast his stronghold into hell.

Seven years it will be Philippe

The period of seven years and five months that passed between September 1715 and February 1723, marked the time that Philippe duc d' Orléans acted as Regent to Louis XV. "His rakish friends turned the seven years of his regency into a disorderly reaction against the sad, stiff austerity which characterised the last years of his uncle's, Louis XIV, reign." [1]

His fortune prospers

Upon becoming regent, Orléans' first act was to remove the little King from Versailles and house him at the *Palais de Tuileries* in the heart of Paris. From this base, and with the circumstances favourable for reform, he set about transforming the capital into a thriving success. "His regency, unlike most preceding ones, passed off in relative tranquillity."

> An application of money and energy stimulated the development of an entire new district of the city, the faubourg Saint-Germain, where the nobility, freed from the constraints of life at Versailles, began to build elegant new town houses; Parisian society turned to the pursuit of pleasure, buying beautiful clothes and objets de luxe, discovering the delights of fine cuisine and lavish entertaining, and all the joys of la vie mondaine. [2]

The effort of the foreign tongues will reduce to a lower degree

This line of prophecy leaves open the question of exactly what it is that will abate. Is it the effort of foreign tongues? Or is it an unfinished sentence, leaving undeclared what exactly the effort of

foreign tongues will abate? The seer is intent to leave the answer to history, having made it clear
that Philippe and foreign tongues will be involved in the fulfilment. We now know the answer is
the French empire, and that the foreign tongues were those of the Prussians, English and Dutch,
including Austria's allies, the Swedes and the Russians. Even the Indian nation was involved.

> For France [...] Louis XV was a loser. He [...] impoverished the country by his wars (though he
> hated battles). [...] In the first war (of the Austrian Succession), the French army found itself
> having to fight a terrible mid-winter retreat from Prague; in the second it was roundly defeated.
> [...] In both conflicts Prussia emerged with net gains. [...] Worse still, in the course of the bitter
> Seven Years War, which was almost a first world war, France lost her empire in Canada, the
> Mississippi territory and India. [...] As French historians accept, the Peace of Paris signed in 1763
> was one of the saddest in French history. [3]

Furthermore, his Midi vexed

France's Midi – 'Midi (de la France)' – refers to the South of France (Cassell's Dictionary). From
this, it is but a single step to understand that 'his midi' is Philippe's Midi, which was situated in
America. For it was in the state of Louisiana, in the 'Deep South', that New Orleans [4] was named
after Philippe d'Orléans. In this sense, New Orleans is understood as being 'his Midi'.

In 1720, Paris was in uproar. A Scottish financier named John Law, with the Regent's approval,
had started a commercial bank (later the *Banque Royale*), using the innovative idea of paper
money. People were being encouraged to bring their gold and silver to the bank and exchange it
for banknotes. The precious metal received this way was then invested, to enable the exploitation
of America's resources.

Law's company had by then obtained exclusive rights to develop the vast French territories in the
Mississippi river valley of North America. As part of the enterprise the Mississippi Company had
been established in 1717, primarily to deal with investments following the founding of New
Orleans. But the venture collapsed, causing vexation amongst everyone involved. "Those who had
invested in the 'Mississippi' saw their savings gone, their security vanished, their hopes destroyed." John
Law wisely fled to Brussels to escape their wrath. [5]

A wayward affair

At its high point before the collapse, 500-livres shares were being exchanged for 18,000 livres,
and an open-air stock market in the centre of Paris was conducting business amidst frenzied
scenes of buying and selling. When the bank eventually collapsed, the Regent, who had made
John Law France's Controller-General of Finance, took fright at this wayward affair [6] and he
quickly removed Louis XV to the safety of Versailles.

Young Gallic Hercules

The oracle now turns its attention to the King.

> In May 1715, a few months before the Sun-King's death, Fleury became tutor to Louis' great-
> grandson and heir, and in spite of a seeming lack of ambition, he acquired an influence over the
> child that was never broken, fostered by Louis' love and confidence. [7]

This appointment continued to be approved by the regent, Philippe d'Orléans, after the Sun
King's death. Some years later, in June 1726, Louis decided to reward his old tutor, then aged
73, by firstly appointing him Minister of State, and then by arranging for his election to the
College of Cardinals.

Sometimes, a special relationship will occur when a pupil receives the sobriquet of the master he
learned to copy from. For example, Louis XV might easily have been called 'young Fleury'.
Because, "Fleury was the only father he had known," and the child had grown-up totally under his
influence. Instead, with his preference for classical literature, the Seer refers to him as 'Young
Ogmios' – Young Gallic Hercules.

What makes this sobriquet so appropriate? The solution is that Louis XV was *young*, he was *Gallic*, and the full name of his tutor, and surrogate father, was André-*Hercule* de Fleury.

Interestingly, in Greek literature, Ogmios is portrayed as a balding, wrinkled old man, gifted with eloquence. It was therefore a perfectly apt description of the 73-year-old Hercule de Fleury, the King's minister of state and former educator.

Will cast his stronghold into hell

The deliberate use of *abysmera* in this quatrain (a verb derived from the abyss) provides an accurate, if religiously, moralistic prophecy of Louis XV's reign. The reason behind this is that the monarch had become addicted to gambling, alcohol, and fornication, but with no preference as to order. "Louis XV drank beyond measure so that his royal majesty was sometimes compromised upon leaving the table." Also, Madame de Pompadour, in later life: "did everything she could to divert him from his passion for gambling but could not manage it."

It was, however, his sexual appetite for teenage virgins, who he installed in his 'Birdcage' until they became pregnant, as almost invariably they did. This established for him a reputation for licentiousness. "The Parc-aux-Cerfs at Versailles visited nightly by Louis for assignations arranged by Pompadour gained an infamous reputation."[8] The Palace of Versailles was the King's stronghold; it was where he had been taken for safety at the time of the Mississippi Company's crash, and, as predicted in the oracle, Louis XV abased his stronghold by engaging in sins of the flesh.

Summary: *This oracle describes the period in French history that began after the death of Louis XIV (the Amythaon or Sun King). Since the heir to the throne was a boy of five, a regent was needed. Hitherto, regents had always been the child's mother, but for Louis XV, the death of his parents had deprived him of that possibility, and Philippe of Orleans made it his task to undertake that responsibility. The Seer actually provides the regent's forename, and the number of years he required to complete this undertaking. He also signals the name of the King's educator, while alluding to New Orleans as a pun on the Regent's titled name. But what is most likely to disconcert an age that believes it lives in total freedom of both God and religion is that the oracle attests to the King's vice in biblical language. Yet, denial of this eludes a reality in which God is eternal. He has no future because there is no time in which it could exist. Hence, God always knows everything. And since He created our temporal dimension, complete with our freewill, we then prove to Him, by our preferences, that He knew us before we were born into His world: one, which is ordered by time to obey our wishes. There is irony, too, in this fact: because oracle No. 38 in Century Five, which also concerns the reign of Louis XV, is equally open as to its meaning. The irony is that both prophecies openly predict events that occurred at a time when the Enlightenment – the Age of Reason – was gathering force, and its champions were busily ridiculing religion and the supernatural.*

90   *Vn capitaine de la grand Germanie,*
       Se viendra rendre par simulé secours:
       Vu Roy des roys ayde de Pannonie
       Que sa reuolte fera de sang grand cours.

91   *L'horrible peste Perynte & Nicopolle,*
       Le Chersonnez tiendra & Marceloyne,
       La Thessalie vastera l'Amphipolle,
       Mal incogneu, & le refus d'Anthoine.

92   *Le Roy vouldra dans cité neufue entrer,*
       Par ennemys expugner l'on viendra:
       Captif libere faulx dire & perpetrer,
       Roy dehors estre, loin d'ennemys tiendra.

93   *Les ennemis du fort bien eslongnez,*
       Par chariots conduict le bastion,
       Par sur les murs de Bourges esgrongnez,
       Quand Hercules battra l'Hæmathion.

eslongnez (OF esloingner) set far back; conduict (OF) manage; sur (sûr) surety; esgrongnez (AF. es+groignier - gronder); ['es' is a preposition set before a word in the plural denoting 'in the', 'at the', 'into or unto the'] into a rumble; Hæmathion (Gk) Amythaon, also Amethea; battre (Dictionnaire de français Littré – ébranler, en parlant de la mer) unsettle, when speaking of the sea; Cross-reference: Hæmathion, C.IX: 38; C.IX: 64; C.X: 7; C.X: 58.

> The enemies of the fortress set far back:
> The bastion managed by wagons;
> For surety, the walls of Bourges into a rumble,
> When Hercules will unsettle the Amythaon (**LOUIS XIV**).

The enemies of the fortress set far back

The interesting point about this particular prophecy is that it concerns some of the major building and structural operations undertaken during the reign of Louis XIV. Sebastien Le Prestre de Vauban was the engineering genius of that era, and a man who specialized in both making and breaking fortifications.

In 1672, the fortress at Maastricht housed a garrison of six thousand troops fighting for the United Provinces. The enemies of the fortress were the French, who had taken Maastricht in the preceding year, but had omitted to secure the fortress. The obligation to retake it therefore fell to Vauban.

> At the siege of Maastricht (1673) he used a complete system of 'parallels'—*i.e.,* trenches dug parallel or concentric to the perimeter of the defences and connected by radical zigzag trenches that made the approach comparatively safe from the defenders' artillery fire.

On the night of 17 June, the sappers who were now placed out of danger from the enemy's artillery "opened the attack trenches." Three days later, on 30 June, the fortress surrendered to Vauban who had been directing the siege. [1]

The bastion managed by wagons

In the spring of 1678, Vauban completed another great defence system. This was the fortification of Dunkirk, which Louis had acquired from Charles II in 1661.

> In November 1670 Louvois allocated a task force of 22,000 men to accelerate the prodigious earthworks at Dunkirk, Tournai and Ath. The transport of earth from the excavations to the parapets was achieved by each soldier carrying a hod-load. [...] Vauban applied for a large number of barrows [...] Louvois immediately rejected the idea [...] But Vauban's quiet persistence won the day, and 2,000 barrows were provided.

On 10 May Colbert wrote to Vauban to congratulate him upon his achievement. Vauban had re-designed the fortification at Dunkirk, in order to defend it and protect the vessels sailing in and out of the port: the major part of the work having been achieved by the use of wagons.

> I have no doubt that you would consider this job as one of the finest things which you have ever done so far. [...] it seems that you have given to Dunkirk a port which will be capable of receiving vessels of up to 700 or 800 tons, so that the King could keep here a squadron as large as he pleases and, greatly increase his maritime strength. [2]

For surety, the walls of Bourges into a rumble

On 8 October 1651, Louis XIV entered *Bourges*, receiving great acclaim from the people. The Governor of the city, the Prince of Condé, had recently begun negotiations with France's enemy, King Philip of Spain, and this had opened up the Second *Fronde*. At the same time, Condé's brother, the Prince of Conti had been stirring up the people of *Bourges* against the King. But the people's attitude dramatically changed when Louis XIV entered the city, for his presence quickly won them over.

As reward for their show of loyalty, Louis ordered that the walls of the *Grosse Tour* (a donjon at Bourges), be razed to the ground. [3] The tower had for long been a hated symbol of subjugation amongst the townsfolk, but after the Sun King's command, it was destroyed.

> In November, 1651, the explosion of a first mine could only crack the building in two. The scars of the torsion which took place then upon the foundations are still visible on the relics at the foot of the tower: retained in the second basement of the underground parking lot, located under the town hall of Bourges. Kerbstones were jostled and torn off from their foundation.

A new attempt took place in December of the same year. The contrivance caused a better calculated explosion than previously: so strong, that half of the donjon collapsed, killing and injuring several dozen witnesses, who were crushed by the stony blocks projected by the blast from the powder. The last relics of the donjon were carefully left on site, but disappeared later.[4]

The use of the word 'rumble' to describe the collapse of the *Grosse Tour* is an appropriate choice, when the cause is attributed to an explosive device – 'in its groin' – as was the case at Bourges. The destruction of the city's hated tower also quelled the rebellion being stirred up among the population by the Prince of Conti: for the people now had strong evidence – a surety –of the King's good favour towards them.

When Hercules will unsettle the Amythaon

The final line of this prophecy involves a building project of a different kind. It refers to "The Strait of Gibraltar – Latin, FRETUM HERCULEUM", which is an existing channel "connecting the Mediterranean Sea with the Atlantic Ocean."[5]

This Strait, shortened to 'Hercules', had unsettled the Amythaon (Louis XIV) during France's war with the United Provinces. At the battle of Stromboli (8 January 1676), French losses reached a total of 400 killed, compared with an estimated eighty casualties suffered by the Dutch. Louis realised that to be a force in the Mediterranean, his ships on the west coast would have to avoid the 2,000-mile detour through the Strait of Gibraltar that was required to reach the heart of the Mediterranean. The Sun King's solution was to plan the construction of a waterway that would eliminate the need to sail around the Spanish coastline. The engineer chosen for this massive enterprise was Pierre-Paul Riquet.

Riquet's solution was the construction of a channel running between the Atlantic Ocean and the Mediterranean Sea. This took the form of a canal between the River Garonne and the *Golfe du Lion*. The result of this enormous exercise in engineering was the *Canal des Deux Mers* or *Canal de Languedoc*. It measures 279 kilometres in length, 20 metres in breadth and 2 metres in depth; it was finally completed in 1681: nine years after Vauban's defence structure at Maastricht.

Summary: *This oracle reintroduces the Amythaon, namely Louis XIV. Among those he assembled to serve him in his bid to make his reign great were engineers like Sebastien Vauban and Pierre Riquet. This oracle predicts some of their major achievements. The use of explosives to bring down the walls of the hated tower in Bourges is also not without interest, since it helped prevent a rebellion that was brewing inside the city. The oracle also reveals that prophecies may equally apply to the destruction of buildings, as with the Bastille (Century Nine No. 23) and to the construction of engineering products, such as the Suez Canal (Century Ten No. 89), for both destruction and construction figure in this prophetic quatrain.*

94   *Foibles galeres seront vnies ensemble,*
      Ennemis faux le plus fort en rampart:
      Faible assaillies Vratislaue tremble,
      Lubecq & Mysne tiendront barbare part.

foible (OF) powerless; galères (plural) imprisoned with hard labour; faux (OF) fauls) treacherous; rampart (AF rampant – Qui se tient debout) who holds himself upright; Mysne (named after the small river Mysna) Meissen; barbare (foreign speakers).

The powerless imprisoned with hard labour will be united together,   1940
The enemies treacherous, the strongest of them holding themselves upright:
The weak assaulted, Bratislava trembles:
Lübeck and Meissen will hold the foreign share.

The powerless imprisoned with hard labour will be united together

The powerless referred to in this oracle, and who were brought together, were those made captive during the Second World War. In occupied Europe, these fell into two main groups, prisoners of war and civilians. Prisoners of war were usually questioned before being sent to a concentration camp, where they were detained indefinitely. Interestingly, concentration camps were unknown when this prophecy was written, and would remain so for several centuries afterwards.

The majority of civilians who were rounded-up were Jewish. They were then united together in communities and placed in ghettos.

> Ghettos isolated Jews by separating Jewish communities from the non-Jewish population and from other Jewish communities. The Germans established at least 1,000 ghettos in German-occupied and annexed Poland and the Soviet Union alone. [...] The largest ghetto in Poland was the Warsaw ghetto, where more than 400,000 Jews were crowded into an area of 1.3 square miles. Other major ghettos were established in the cities of Lodz, Krakow, Bialystok, Lvov, Lublin, Vilna, Kovno, Czestochowa, and Minsk. Tens of thousands of western European Jews were also deported to ghettos in the east. [1]

In 1941, a plan to empty the ghettos began. "German SS and police authorities deported a small minority of Jews from ghettos to forced-labour camps and concentration camps." [2] By the turn of the year 1942, forced labour had become a mass phenomenon. This was part of the *Final Solution* decreed by Hitler, and it was intended to exterminate the Jewish population.

Some would be transported to death camps, others to concentration camps until either they or their usefulness had been exhausted.

> The largest number of foreign labourers in the area of the Reich was registered in August 1944 at 7,615,970. Among these were about 1.9 million prisoners of war and 5.7 million civilians. Of the 7.6 million, 2.8 million were from the Soviet Union, 1.7 million from Poland, and 1.3 million from France. Altogether, during World War II, up to 13.5 million men, women, and children were brought to the Reich and forced to labour. [3]

The enemies treacherous

> Germany's war in the East was based on Hitler's long-standing view that Jews were the great enemy of the German people and that *Lebensraum* was needed for Germany's expansion. Hitler focused his attention on Eastern Europe, aiming to defeat Poland, the Soviet Union and remove or kill the resident Jews and Slavs in the process. [...] Plans for the total eradication of the Jewish population of Europe—eleven million people—were formalised at the Wannsee Conference on 20 January 1942. Some would be worked to death and the rest would be killed in the implementation of *Die Endlösung der Judenfrage* (the Final Solution of the Jewish Question. [4]

The implementation of these orders was carried out with the assistance of officials in the countries occupied by the Nazis, which made them 'enemies'.

The strongest of them holding themselves upright

The seer, here, appears to have previewed a stereotype of the highly disciplined German officer standing straight-backed, heel-clicking, and saluting 'Heil Hitler', with arm rigidly outstretched before him: as was then the case with the strongest members of the German military.

> The *Oberkommando des Heeres* (OKH) was Germany's Army High Command from 1936 to 1945. In theory the *Oberkommando der Wehrmacht* (OKW) served as the military General Staff for the German Reich's armed forces, coordinating the *Wehrmacht* (Army *Heer*, Navy *Kreigsmarine*, and the Air Force Luftwaffe) operations. In practice OKW acted in a subordinate role as Hitler's personal military staff, translating his ideas into military plans and orders, and issuing them to the three services. However, as the war progressed the OKW found itself exercising increasing amounts of direct command authority over military units, particularly in the west. This created a situation where by 1942 the OKW was the *de facto* command of Western Theatre forces while the Army High Command (OKH) served Hitler as his personal command Staff on the Eastern Front. [5]

There is also a deeper meaning to this prophetic statement. Adolf Hitler and his Nazi party, ascribed to the Darwinian belief of survival by the fittest. This led to belief that those of Aryan birth were a stronger, superior race of people. It was 'natural' – for so they supposed – that those who were racially inferior, or physically imperfect, should be systematically eliminated. This would allow the world's diminishing resources to be available only to those fittest to benefit from them. "Under Hitler's leadership and racially motivated ideology, the regime was responsible for the genocide of at least 5.5 million Jews, and millions of other victims whom he and his followers deemed racially inferior." [6]

The weak assaulted, Bratislava trembles

The oracle now returns to the plight of the Jews, describing them once again as powerless. In this instance, the Seer particularly pinpoints Bratislava, in south-west Slovakia.

> Bratislava was declared the capital of the first independent Slovak Republic on March 14, 1939, but the new state quickly fell under Nazi influence. In 1941–1942 and 1944–1945, the new Slovak government cooperated in deporting most of Bratislava's approximately 15,000 Jews; they were transported to concentration camps, where most were killed or died before the end of the war. [7]

The people of Bratislava also had good reason to tremble after the second deportation of Jews. "Bratislava was bombarded by the Allies, occupied by German troops in 1944, and eventually taken by the Soviet Red Army on April 4, 1945." [8]

Lübeck and Meissen will hold the foreign share

In this final line of prophecy, the oracle names two more places where concentration camps were situated; one of them was for prisoners of war and the other held Jews.

> Oflag X-C was a German World War II prisoner of war camp for officers (*Offizierlager* in Lübeck in northern Germany. The camp was located on the corner of *Friedhofsallee* and *Vorwerkstrasse*, close to Lübeck's border with the town of Schwartau (now Bad Schwartau), and is often cited as being located in Schwartau rather than Lübeck.
>
> The camp was opened in June 1940 for French officers captured during the Battle of France. In June 1941 British and Commonwealth officers from the Battle of Crete and the North African Campaign arrived. During 1941 and 1942 many Allied air crews that had been shot down were taken to Lübeck. [9]

"At the time of National Socialism in Meissen, the Jewish families living in the city were driven out of the country or were deported to extermination camps." [10] This is not particularly remarkable, considering the policy of the NS party. But what is really to the point is that during "World War II, a subcamp of Flossenbürg concentration camp was located at Meissen." [11]

> The Flossenbürg concentration camp was established in Bavaria in May 1938. It was established to provide forced labourers to factories in the region. In later years, it became the centre of an extensive network of branch camps for forced labourers. During its existence, approximately 100,000 prisoners arrived in Flossenbürg the majority of whom perished. Jews from Hungary, Czechoslovakia, and Poland arrived from the east in late 1944 and early 1945. [12]

Summary: *Except for the fact that Bratislava, Meissen and Lübeck share the content of this prophecy, one might look elsewhere for its fulfilment. But since these cities are mentioned, and they share a presence in the Second World War, it is to this event that one must look for history's report, and it is then obvious that the oracle has the Jews in mind. This becomes clear when the same word 'powerless' at the commencement of the prophecy is repeated when referring to Bratislava, which was responsible for transporting Jews to their deaths. Further references to locations within Lübeck and at Meissen confirm these were also where concentration camps were located, initially for non-Jews. The characterisation of Hitler's racial conceit further confirms the oracle's 20th century fulfilment.*

95   *Le nouueau faict conduyra l'exercite,*
       Proche apamé iusques au pres du riuage,
       Tendant secour de Milannoile eslite,
       Duc yeux priué à Milan fer de cage.

conduire (AF – Servir de sauf conduit) to serve as safe passage; exercite (L exercit\us) army; proche (AF proche en temps) near in time; apamé (Gk απαμαω) to cut off; ravage (OF) waterside; tendant (OF) reaching for; succour (secours) assistance; Milannoile – Milanese; Duc (as before) Duce, chef de guerre. Cross-reference: Duc, C.IX: 80; C.VI: 3; C.X: 64.

> The recent action will avail the army safe passage,   1945
> Nigh cut off, as far as by the waterside,
> Reaching for assistance from the Milanese select few,
> War chief (**DUCE**), eyes deprived at Milan, cage of iron.

The recent action will avail the army safe passage

With the successful invasion of Europe by the Allied forces almost complete, the Second World War was drawing to a close. "Around 25 April 1945, Mussolini's republic came to an end. In Italy, this day is known as *Liberation Day*. On this day a general partisan uprising alongside the efforts of Allied forces, during their final offensive in Italy, managed to oust the Germans from Italy almost entirely."[1] At Como, a German convoy was on the point of departure, when it was approached by Mussolini.

Upon leaving Milan, where he had attended a meeting with Cardinal Schuster and the resistance leaders, Mussolini had learned there that the Germans were vacating Italy, and he realized that he, too, must now seek his own safety. After arriving at Como, the German Commander agreed to allow Mussolini to accompany the army as far as the Swiss border.[2] Feeling assured of a safe passage out of Italy, the Duce promptly adopted the disguise of a German trooper and joined the soldiers at the rear of the convoy.[3]

Nigh cut off, as far as by the waterside

As the retreating convoy left Como, it slowly made its way along the side of the lake in the direction of the Swiss border; but the journey was soon cut off. Upon reaching Dongo, a small settlement of shops and houses situated by the lake side, a group of armed partisans emerged to stop the line of vehicles. Mussolini was immediately recognized, and removed from the truck.[4] The convoy was then allowed to proceed, leaving the Duce in the hands of the partisans.

Reaching for assistance from the Milanese select few

"He immediately raised his hands, vainly begging for mercy," as he was bustled away at gun point to a nearby farmhouse, where he was made to await the arrival of the resistance leaders from Milan. As soon as news of the Duce's capture reached the city, General Raffaele Cordona of the Royal Italian Army, together with a few select members of the Milanese resistance, hurried over to the farmhouse where Mussolini was being held. Cordona had represented the Council in Milan when he met the Duce at Cardinal Schuster's palace. According to historian David Mason: "[Mussolini] might have been safe but for the bitterness of a small Communist caucus within the partisan movement." Had this been the case, he would have been kept alive and handed over to the Allies for war crimes.[5]

War chief (the Duce), eyes deprived, at Milan

Instead, "After a quick and expedient trial, which included cries of 'Let me live and I will give you an empire!' the once seemingly invincible dictator was shot." A Tommy gun was used for his execution, and when the corpse was put on show in public, the head could be seen riddled with bullet holes. In this, the Seer has been consistent throughout these oracles by calling each bullet wound an 'eye', when predicting that someone would be shot in the head (refer to Condé, Century Three N°. 41, and to Concini, Century Seven N°. 11). In the present case, *eye* has been pluralized to mark the use of many bullet holes: *viz.* "A yellowing disfigured face and a head riddled with bullets capped the corpses atop a pile of bodies in Milan. The decaying carcass belonged to 'the Father of Fascism', Benito Mussolini.[6]

Cage of iron

At the farmhouse near Dongo, after the Duce had been shot, his corpse was "flung into a removal van"; that is, a pantechnicon-van – a *cage of iron* – and driven to Milan. In the same square, where some months earlier a group of partisans had been shot, his body was strung up by the heels beneath an iron girder above a petrol station;[7] (another possible meaning for an iron cage). It is noteworthy that Mussolini's final 'inverted' form is consistent with the oracle's description, for the relevant phrase has also been inverted, so that 'cage of iron', reads: *fer de cage – iron of cage.*[8]

Summary: *This oracle describes the events leading to the death of Benito Mussolini. It is one of the rarer oracles that describe a single event spread over a very short period of time. To those familiar with the events leading to the Duce's capture and execution, the seer's choice of words are remarkably apt. (The present author having once passed through Dongo to hear the story of Mussolini's capture retold.)*

96   *Dans cité entrer exercit desniée,*
        Duc entrera par persuasion,
        Aux foibles portes clam armée amenée,
        Mettront feu, mort, de sang effusion.

desniée (AF denier: empêcher) hinder; exercit (L exercit\us) a troop; clam (*apocope:* clam[eur]) clamour; foible (OF) feeble.

Inside the city (**PARIS**), a troop is denied entering,   1588
The Duke (**GUISE**) will enter through persuasion,
At the feeble gates, clamour, forces prevailed upon,
They will employ fire, death, with effusion of blood.

Inside the city, a troop is denied entering

On 11 May 1588, at the request of Henri III, Swiss troops began entering the city of Paris, accompanied by soldiers drawn from the royal army,[1] but they were rapidly prevented by the Parisians: their arrival serving only to inflame an already aggravated populace.[2]

For centuries Paris had jealously guarded its ancient right to defend itself. But the King had been advised that a *coup* was about to be sprung. For this reason he summoned the Swiss troops to Paris for his protection: his action overriding a tradition that had been upheld by the Parisians.

> The citizens were outraged when they saw the soldiers being deployed around the city. [...] During the night the citizens erected barricades of huge barrels filled with rocks and stones to block the streets.[3]

The erection of these temporary barriers served as *gates*; their strength lying not in their *feeble* structure, but in the resolution of the volunteers guarding them.

The Duke will enter through persuasion

The King's anxiety at the threat of a *coup* first began when he learned that the Duke of Guise had been invited by the League's Committee of Sixteen to enter Paris with an armed escort. Henri's response was to order Guise to stay away. If the Duke had any reservations concerning the King's order, they were removed by Catherine de' Medici. She sent an envoy to Guise, convincing him that he must come to Paris. This decided the matter, and *the Duke entered through persuasion.*[4]

The underlying reason for the Duke's invitation does appear to have been Catherine de' Medici's desire to become regent of France again, for she saw in Guise a strong man who would do her bidding.

At the feeble gates, clamour, forces prevailed upon

With the barricades (or feeble gates) in place, only those considered friendly to the League were allowed to pass through. Catherine de' Medici was one permitted to bypass the barriers on her way to Mass at the Saint-Chapelle. Another at the barricades was the Duke of Guise who received the acclamation: "'Vive Guise!' 'To Rheims, we must bring Monsieur to Rheims!' "[5] This was a clear indication that the citizens of Paris were already viewing Guise as the next king of France, since Rheims was the traditional city for the coronation of its monarchs.

Those men at arms loyal to Henri III who confronted the bourgeois members of the League and the students from the Sorbonne, who were manning the barricades, received a very different reception. They were prevailed upon "with stones and a few troops [... were] killed by snipers."[6]

They will employ fire, death, with effusion of blood

The number of troops killed on the 'Day of the Barricades' was given as sixty. Later that day, after a number of incidents involving firepower, death and an effusion of blood, Guise wrote to the Governor of Orleans, "I have defeated the Swiss, cut to pieces part of the guards of the King and I am holding the Louvre so closely invested that I shall give a good account of those within it."[7]

One of those within it was the King, and he was seething with rage. The chain of events that followed are given in the prophecies above, which predict the Duke's assassination (by order of Henri III); but which then led to Jacques Clément being groomed by the Duke's sister to assassinate Henri. (Refer Century One N°. 97).

Summary: *The Day of the Barricades set in motion a series of events that rocked France. The nation had become divided into religious halves—the traditional Catholics supporting the Pope as head of the Christian Church, and the Protestant Huguenots, who refused to accept papal authority. Henri III was unable to unite the two halves, whereas Guise, as Head of the Holy League, desired only to suppress the dissident half. Paris supported him and the King was seen to be weak. To make matters worse, Guise was already being promoted as the future King of France. On 12 May 1588, 30 years after this was published, Paris erupted in a spontaneous show of support for Guise against the King, causing him to flee the capital, in fear for his life. The next part of this continuing saga is foretold in Century Three No. 51, followed by Century One No. 85.*

97   *De mer copies en trois parts diuisees,*
       A la seconde les viures failleront,
       Desesperez cherchant champs Helisees,
       Premiers en breche entrez victoire auront.

98   *Les affligez par faute d'vn seul taint,*
       Contremenant à partie opposite,
       Aux Lygonnois mandera que contraint
       Seront de rendre le grand chef de Molite.

99   *Vent Aquilon fera partir le siege,*
       Par murs geter cendres, chauls, & pousiere:
       Par pluye apres qui leur fera bien piege,
       Dernier secours encontre leur frontiere.

100   *Naualle pugne nuict sera superee,*
       Le feu, aux naues à l'Occident ruine:
       Rubriche neufue, la grand nef coloree,
       Ire à vaincu, & victoire en bruine.

Nº 11

1   Graham Edwards, *The Last Days of Charles I*, 132-3
2   Ibid 174
3   Ibid 178
4   William Henry Mountague, *A New and Universal History of England*, 181; & *Encyclopaedia Britannica 2001* CD-ROM, Mediation and the Second Civil War
5   Ibid Great Fire of London
6   Robert Gray, *A History of London*, 168
7   John Bedford, *London's Burning* (From Samuel Pepys Diary)
8   wikipedia.org/wiki/Charles_II_of_England
9   nationalarchives.gov.uk/education/resources/fire-of-london/

Nº 16

1   Alan Palmer, *Dictionary of Twentieth-Century History 1900-1982*, 156; & *Encyclopædia Britannica, Vol. 17: 15th edition*, 441
2   Brian Crozier, *Franco*, 150, 161, 170; & Palmer, 156
3   Stanley G Payne, *The Spanish Revolution*, 234
4   Ibid 260
5   Ibid 260
6   Crozier, 135, 164
7   Paul Preston, *Franco*, 2-4
8   Crozier, 192, 193, 194

Nº 17

1   Simon Schama, *Citizens*, 290
2   Christopher Hibbert, *The French Revolution*, 227; & F.L. Ford, *Europe 1780-1830*, 137
3   Nero, *Encyclopædia Britannica 2001: CD-ROM*; & D. Pawson, *Unlocking the Bible*, 1267
4   Hibbert, 223, 225
5   Meade Minnigerode, *The Son of Marie Antoinette*, 184–5; & Antonia Fraser, *Marie Antoinette The Journey*, 493-4
6   Minnigerode, CHAPTER TWO THE BAKER'S BOY, 46
7   Hibbert, 231
8   Ibid 280
9   Ibid 281
10   Ibid 281

Nº 18

1   E N Williams, *Dictionary of English and European History 1485-1789*, 264
2   Ibid 264
3   *Encyclopædia Britannica 2001*, CD-ROM, Fleur-de-Lys, or Fleur- de- Luce ('lily flower'); & K A Patmore, *The Court of Louis XIII*, 150-1
4   Ibid 151
5   Neville Williams, *Chronology of the Expanding World 1492-1762*; & Voltaire, *The Age of Louis XIV*, (trans. Martyn P. Pollack), 16
6   A. Horne, *Seven Ages of Paris*, London, 2003, 108
7   David M. Luebke, *The Counter Reformation*, p. 166).
8   Wikipedia – Holy Roman Empire
9   C. Burckhardt, *Richelieu and His Age* (trans. Bernard Hoy), 71
10   Ibid 89; and Patmore, 159; & D Pennington, *Seventeenth Century Europe*, 269
11   Patmore, 159; & C Jant, *Prédictions tirées des Centuries de Nostradamus*; & *Grand Larousse Encyclopedique*, Montmorenci, Henri II; & Contemporary print of the execution reproduced from the original owned by *Cabinet des Estampes*; & Charles Ward, *The Oracles of Nostradamus*, 126
12   *Prédictions tirées des Centuries de Nostradamus*: 1673
13   www.nemausensis.com/personnages/Montmorency.htm
14   Ward, 126, also Étienne Jaubert, *Eclaircissement des veritable Quatrains de Maistre Michel Nostradamus, Docteur et Professeur en Medecine. Conseiller et Medecin ordinaire des Roys Henry II, François II & Charles IX*, 1656.

Nº 20

1   Ardennes, Forest of - *New Century Cyclopedia of Names*: Appleton-Century-Crofts, Inc; & S.K. Padover, *The Life and Death of Louis XVI*
2   Ibid 209
3   S. Hopewell, *Europe from Revolution to Dictatorship*, 12; & Christopher Hibbert, *The French Revolution*, 121 & H. Belloc, *Marie Antoinette*, 261-6
4   Louis Madelin, *The French Revolution*, 161
5   Belloc, 278
6   Jean Favier (ed.) *Chronicle of the French Revolution*, 218
7   Simon Schama, *Citizens*, 551–2
8   Bernard Fäy, *Louis XVI* (trans. Patrick O'Brien) 61, 105, 134, 139

9   John Hearsey, *Marie Antoinette*, 137
10 Alexandre Dumas, *The Flight to Varennes* (trans. A Craig Bell), 84
11 Padover, 239, 241
12 Schama, 560, 604, 658
13 Padover, 267
14 Ibid 266
15 Ibid 277; & Madelin, 271
16 Dumas, 93

Nº 22

1   S K Padover, *The Life and Death of Louis XVI*, 292
2   Meade Minnigerode, *The Son of Marie Antoinette*, 133
3   Ibid 125-7
4   Ibid 22-3
5   Ibid 178
6   Ibid 179; & Antonia Fraser, *Marie Antoinette*, 327
7   Simon Schama, *Citizens*, 799; & Minnigerode, 191
8   Minnigerode, 192

Nº 23

1   Simon Schama, *Citizens,* 25
2   Ibid 305
3   Mirabeau – Election to the States General, *Encyclopædia Britannica 2001:* CD-ROM
4   Schama, 339
5   Colin Jones, *Cambridge Illustrated History of France*, 183
6   Schama, 424
7   Ibid 508-9
8   John J. Delaney, *Dictionary of Saints*
9   Schama, 509-11

Nº 26

1   Alistair Horne, *Seven Ages of Paris*, 176
2   Simon Schama, *Citizens*, 560
3   Ibid 604; & Norman Davies, *Europe - A History*, 699
4   Schama, 573-4
5   Ibid
6   Id 564
7   Id 566-7
8   Id 566

Nº 34

1   Antonia Fraser, *Marie Antoinette – The Journey:* 440-1; Christopher Hibbert, *The French Revolution:* 148-9
2   Hibbert, 149-50; Annunziata Asquith, *Marie Antoinette*, 184-5; F.A. Mignet, *History of the French Revolution*,
    133, 138; Louis Madelin, *The French Revolution:* 332; & Simon Schama, *Citizens*, 607
3   Madelin, 271
4   wikipedia.org/wiki/Tuileries_Palace
5   Hilaire Belloc, *Marie Antoinette*, 343
6   Fraser, 476
7   Madelin, 318, 323
8   Schama, 587-8
9   Madelin, 232, & Stanley Loomis, *The Fatal Friendship*, 165; Thomas Carlyle, *The French Revolution* vol. 2;
    P. Huisman and M Jallut, *Marie Antoinette*
10 Fraser, 406-7

Nº 35

1   wikipedia.org/wiki/Ferdinand_I_of_Bulgaria
2   *Prince Ferdinand's Rule,* Ibid
3   Bulgaria – the Principality, *Encyclopædia Britannica 2001:* CD-ROM
4   Alexandre Hepp, *Ferdinand, King of Bulgaria*
5   Bulgaria – Foreign Policy under Ferdinand, *Encyclopædia Britannica 2001:* CD-ROM
6   The First Balkan War, *Encyclopædia Britannica 2001:* CD-ROM
7   Bulgaria - The Balkan Wars, Ibid
8   Ibid; & Dr J Lemprière, *Lemprières Classical Dictionary:* third edition, 394

Nº 36

1   *Royalty, Peerage and Nobility of the World,* Vol. 91 Henry IV (Le Grand) 1589–1610, 383
2   *Encyclopædia Britannica 2001*, CD-ROM Henry IV - Assessment
3   Ibid; & *New Century Cyclopedia of Names*, François Ravaillac
4   *Butchers Ecclesiastical Calendar*, 1610
5   R. Mousnier, *The Assassination of Henry IV* (trans. Joan Spencer),
6   Ibid

7   E N Williams, *Dictionary of English and European History 1485-1789*, 264
8   D. O'Connell, *Richelieu*, 50
9   G. Treasure, *Seventeenth Century France*, 77; & Williams, 287
10 K.A. Patmore, *The Court of Louis XIII*, 72; & O'Connell, 54
11 Patmore, 162; & O'Connell, 59–60

N° 37

1   wikipedia.org/wiki/1562_Riots_of_Toulouse
2   Ibid
3   The Anatomy of a Religious Riot in Toulouse in May 1562. *The Journal of Ecclesiastical History* 34: 367–391.
4   Ibid *also*, G. de Felice (1853), *History of the Protestants of France, from the commencement of the Reformation to the present time.*
5   The Anatomy of a Religious Riot in Toulouse in May 1562". *The Journal of Ecclesiastical History* 34: 367–391.
6   Ibid
7   wikipedia.org/wiki/1562_Riots_of_Toulouse
8   Felice (1853)
9   Joan Davies (March 1979). "Persecution and Protestantism: Toulouse, 1562-1575". *The Historical Journal Vol. 22, No. 1*: 31–51
10 The Anatomy of a Religious Riot in Toulouse in May 1562: *The Journal of Ecclesiastical History* (CUP) 34: 367–391
11 Ibid
12 Joan Davies 31–51.
13 wikipedia.org/wiki/Jeanne_d'Albret
14 Ibid

N° 38

1   *Biblioteque Blaye* - Imposante et majestueuse, la citadelle surplombe l'Estuaire avec ses 33 hectares située au coeur de la ville de Blaye. Fortifiée par Vauban à partir de 1685. &, Blaye - *Petit Histoire* (anon.) *30 octobre 1685* - Mémoire de Vauban mettant définitivement au point le plan de construction de la Citadelle de Blaye.
2   La Rochelle, *Encyclopædia Britannica 2001*, CD-ROM
3   Voltaire, The Works of Voltaire. A Contemporary Version. A Critique and Biography by John Morley, notes by Tobias Smollett, trans. William F. Fleming (New York: E.R. DuMont, 1901). In 21 vols. Vol. XII. Refer, http://oll.libertyfund.org/titles/2132#Voltaire_0060.12_533
4   Voltaire_0060.12_642
5   wikipedia.org/wiki/Prince_Eugene_of_Savoy
6   Ibid. Voltaire_0060.12_551
7   Ibid. Voltaire_0060.12_642
8   Roussillon, *Encyclopædia Britannica, 2001*, CD-ROM

N° 42

1   *Encyclopædia Britannica 2001*, CD-ROM, Turkey and Eastern Europe
2   Ibid Barcelona - Cultural Life
3   Ibid Battle of Lepanto
4   *The Oxford Classical Dictionary*: second edition (ed.) N Hammond and H Scullard, 698; & *Encyclopædia Britannica*, Juan de Austria
5   Juan de Austria, Ibid
6   Battle of Lepanto and the Age of Galley Warfare, Ibid
7   wikipedia.org/wiki/Battle_of_Lepanto
8   Juan de Austria, Ibid
9   Ibid

N° 45

1   H.A.L. Fisher, *A History of Europe*, 583; & *Encyclopædia Britannica*, Henry IV, The Achievements of the Reign
2   E.N. Williams, *Dictionary of English and European History 1485–1789*, 217
3   *Encyclopædia Britannica 2001*, CD-ROM, Henry IV Assessment
4   Ibid
5   Williams, 217
6   Ibid 174; & *Encyclopædia Britannica*, Henry IV
7   Robert J Knecht, *The French Religious Wars 1562–1598*, 84
8   Williams, 217; & Knecht, 84

N° 49

1   E.J. Brill, *The Low Countries in Early Modern Times* (trans. Herbert H Rowan), 30–60; & *Encyclopædia Britannica*, Vol II 13th Edition, 156
2   Peter Young, Richard Holmes, *The English Civil War*, 292
3   Maurice Ashley, *England in the Seventeenth Century*, 106
4   *Matthew v.13 & ix.17*; & OED 4th edition; & Holmes and Young, 25
5   Holmes & Young, 27–8
6   Ibid 28

N° 50

1   Robert J. Knecht, *The French Religious Wars 1562-1598*, 83–4

2   Ibid 62-3, 66
3   Ibid 83
4   *Encyclopædia Britannica, 2001*, CD-ROM, Mayenne, Charles de Lorraine, duc de
5   *Encyclopædia Britannica*, Guise, Charles de Lorraine 4e duc de
6   Ibid
7   Ibid
8   E.N. Williams, *Dictionary of English and European History 1485-1789*, 354; & D. Seward, *The First Bourbon*, 97

Nº 51

1   Jean Favier (ed.) *Chronicle of the French Revolution*, 500
2   Norman Davies, *Europe - A History*, 710
3   Ibid 705
4   C. Hibbert, *The French Revolution*, 283–8; & J M. Thompson, *Napoleon Bonaparte*, 54-5

Nº 55

1   World War I, the outbreak of war, *Encyclopædia Britannica 2001*: CD-ROM; & A.J.P. Taylor, *The First World War*, 25
2   World War I, The years of stalemate, *Encyclopædia Britannica 2001*: CD-ROM
3   Ibid Influenza Epidemic
4   Norman Davies, *Europe A History*, 777
5   Verdun, *Encyclopædia Britannica 2001*: CD-ROM; & Davies, 1328
6   11 January 1913, Object information – Planets, *RedShift 4*: CD-ROM, Maris Mutimedia Ltd
7   Triple Alliance, *Encyclopædia Britannica 2001*: CD-ROM; & Ian Littlewood, *The Rough Guide Chronicle France*, 275, 277; & A Palmer, *Dictionary of Modern History 1789-1945*, 230
8   iwm.org.uk/history/podcasts/voices-of-the-first-world-war/podcast-31-passchendaele

Nº 59

1   http://fr.wikipedia.org/wiki/Ch%C3%A2teau_de_La_Fert%C3%A9-Vidame
2   wikipedia.org/wiki/La_Ferté-Vidame
3   http://racineshistoire.free.fr/LGN/PDF/Vendome.pdf *also* "Testament of François de Vendome Visdame of Chartres 1560"
4   wikipedia.org/wiki/Jean_de_Ferrieres
5   wikipedia.org/wiki/Nicholas,_Duke_of_Mercœur
6   wikipedia.org/wiki/Jean,_Cardinal_of_Lorraine
7   http://universalium.academic.ru/276920/Lorraine%2C_Jean_de_Lorraine%2C_1st_cardinal_de
8   http://www.siefar.org/dictionnaire/en/Louise_de_Lorraine
9   Ibid
10 wikipedia.org/wiki/Philippe_Emmanuel,_Duke_of_Mercœur
11 wikipedia.org/wiki/Bourbonnais
12 Ibid

Nº 64

1   R. Graves, *The Greek Myths*, Vol.2, 379
2   http://www.encyclopedia.com/topic/Peace_of_the_Pyrenees.aspx
3   wikipedia.org/wiki/Treaty_of_the_Pyrenees
4   *Encyclopædia Britannica*, Roussillon; & Carcassone, Ibid
5   Ian Dunlop, *Louis XIV*, 97–101
6   *Encyclopædia Britannica*, Fouquet, also Dunlop, 98
7   Dunlop, 87
8   *Encyclopædia Britannica*, Vaux-le-Vicomte

Nº 68

1   Franklin L. Ford, *Europe 1780-1830*, 120
2   Christopher Hibbert, *The French Revolution:* 229
3   Louis R. Gottschalk, *Jean Paul Marat*, 128, 183
4   Hilaire Belloc, *The French Revolution:* 195
5   Lyon, *Encyclopædia Britannica* - Vol. VI. 15th edition 417; & Louis Madelin, *The French Revolution:* 376
6   Georges Lefebvre, *The French Revolution 1793-1799* (trans. John Hall Stewart & James Friguglietti), 46–7
7   Hilaire Belloc, *The French Revolution*, 203; also Norman Davies, *Europe A History*, 705
8   Lucy, Saint, *Encyclopædia Britannica* - Vol. VI. 15th edition, 375
9   Christopher Hibbert, *The French Revolution*, 332-3

Nº 77

1   Louis Madelin, *The French Revolution*, 307
2   Christopher Hibbert, *The French Revolution*, 186–7
3   Ibid 187
4   Id 211
5   H. Belloc, *Marie Antoinette*, 394
6   Meade Minnigerode, *The Son of Marie Antoinette*, 176–7
7   Simon Schama, *Citizens*, 800; & Stanley Loomis, *Du Barry*, 260
8   Loomis, 250

9   Ibid 255
10 Id 262

Nº 80

1   I.C.B. Dear (ed.) *The Oxford Companion to the Second World War*, 766-7; & Jasper Ridley, *Mussolini*, 208
2   Ridley, 106, 146, 163
3   Ibid 202
4   G.M.D. Howat (ed.) *Dictionary of World History*, 1186; & George Holmes (ed.) *The Oxford Illustrated History of Italy*, 169
5   Ridley, 104
6   Holmes, 274
7   Alan Palmer, *Dictionary of Twentieth-Century History 1900-1982*, 325

Nº 89

1   Derrik Mercer (ed.) *Chronicle of the World*, 607; & E.N. Williams, *Dictionary of English and European History 1485 – 1789*, 274
2   Jeremy Black and Roy Porter (ed.) *A Dictionary of Eighteenth-Century History*, 532
3   Alistair Horne, *Seven Ages of Paris*, 169
4   New Orleans, *Encyclopædia Britannica 2001*, CD-ROM, and Christine Pevitt Algrant, *Madame de Pompadour*, 4-5
5   Williams, 275
6   Mississippi Bubble, *Encyclopædia Britannica*
7   wikipedia.org/wiki/André-Hercule_de_Fleury' &, Fleury, *Encyclopædia Britannica*; &*Lemprière's Classical Dictionary 3rd ed.*, 420; & Maria Leach (ed.) *The Standard Dictionary of Folklore Mythology and Legend*, 816
8   Algrant, 137, 163; & Alistair Horne, *Seven Ages of Paris*, 167

Nº 93

1   *Encyclopædia Britannica 2001*, CD-ROM, Vauban – Innovations in Siege Craft; & Voltaire, *The Age of Louis XIV* (trans. Martyn Pollack), 81
2   Ian Dunlop, *Louis XIV*, 165-6; & Vauban, Innovations in siege craft, *Encyclopædia Britannica 2001*,
3   Dunlop 23; & Colin Jones, *Cambridge Illustrated History of France*, 162
4   http://berry.medieval.over-blog.com/article-le-donjon-royal-dit-grosse-tour-de-bourges-18-59568333.html
5   *Encyclopædia Britannica*, The Strait of Gibraltar – Latin: Fretum Herculeum; & Dunlop, 131

Nº 94

1   http://www.ushmm.org/wlc/en/article.php?ModuleId=10005059
2   Ibid
3   http://www.jewishvirtuallibrary.org/jsource/judaica/ejud_0002_0007_0_06611.html
4   wikipedia.org/wiki/Nazi_Germany#Persecution_of_Jews
5   wikipedia.org/wiki/German_Army_(Wehrmacht)
6   wikipedia.org/wiki/Adolf_Hitler
7   wikipedia.org/wiki/Bratislava#History
8   Ibid
9   wikipedia.org/wiki/Oflag_X-C
10 http://de.wikipedia.org/wiki/Mei%C3%9Fen
11 wikipedia.org/wiki/Meissen
12 http://www.jewishgen.org/databases/holocaust/0141_Flossenburg.html

Nº 95

1   wikipedia.org/wiki/Italian_Social_Republic
2   Jasper Ridley, *Mussolini*, 365
3   Ibid 365
4   Ibid
5   Mussolini, Role in World War II, *Encyclopædia Britannica 2001*: CD-ROM; & David Mason, *Who's Who In World War II*, 219; & 1945, April 28. *20th Century Day By Day*: CD-ROM
6   Ibid
7   I.C.B. Dear (ed.) *The Oxford Companion to the Second World War*, 771
8   Mason, 219

Nº 96

1   E.N. Williams, *Dictionary of English and European History 1485-1789*, 172; Leonie Frieda, *Catherine de Medici*, 367–8
2   Frieda, 368
3   Ibid 368
4   M. Freer, *Henry III: King of France and Poland*
5   Frieda, 369
6   Ibid 368
7   Ibid 3

CENTURY TEN

1   *A l'ennemy l'ennemy foy promise*
Ne se tiendra, les captifs retenus:
Prins preme mort, & le reste en chemise,
Damné le reste pour estre soustenus..

The final line in Leffen's edition has an alternative: ending; viz. 'Donnant le reste pour estre secourus.'

2   *Voile gallere voil de nef cachera,*
La grande classe viendra sortir la moindre,
Dix naues proches le torneront poulser,
Grande vaincue vnies à soy ioindre.

3   *En apres cinq troupeau ne mettra hors*
Vn fuytif pour Penelon l'aschera,
Faulx murmurer secours venir par lors,
Le chef le siege lors habandonnera.

4   *Sus la minuict conducteur de l'armee*
Se sauvera, subit esvanouy,
Sept ans apres la fame non blasmee,
A son retour ne dira oncq ouy.

Sus (AF sur pied) on foot; esvanouy (OF) slipped out of sight; oncq (AF - oncques: jamais) never

The leader of the army on foot at midnight   1651
Will save himself, unexpectedly slipping out of sight (**CHARLES II**):
Seven years afterwards his reputation not blamed,
To his return, never will one not say yes.

The leader of the army

In 1651, England was a Commonwealth: not a monarchy. Charles I had been executed in 1649, leaving the country to be ruled by Parliament under the protection of Oliver Cromwell. But there were still monarchists who wanted to reverse this situation. These were led by the future Charles II, the son of the executed King. Matters came to a head on 3 September at Worcester, where Charles, leading his army of royalists, fought against Cromwell's Model Army.

> Cromwell attacked Worcester with an army of above forty thousand men, and meeting with little resistance, broke in upon the disordered royalists. The streets of the city were soon strewed with dead bodies. According to the best accounts two thousand royalists were cut in pieces, and upwards of seven thousand taken prisoners.[1]

On foot at midnight, will save himself, unexpectedly slipping out of sight

At 6 o'clock in the evening, seeing all was lost, Charles, together with fifty or sixty of his friends, fled the city by the northern gate, to secure their own safety. But, upon realizing that travelling with so large a company would attract attention, "he left them without communicating his intentions to any other than lord Derby, by whose direction he went to Boscobel, a low house on the borders of Staffordshire, inhabited by one Penderell a farmer, and his wife."[2] Upon reaching their destination in Shropshire, it was decided it would be safer to take refuge at White Ladies Priory close by.

The journey, which they began on the evening before, took them through the night across country, and it was not until "the early hours of 4 September"[3] that they arrived at White Ladies Priory. Thereafter, following almost six weeks of evasive action and many adventures, Charles eventually secured a passage aboard ship at Shoreham in Sussex, which sailed for Normandy. He arrived in France on 15 October.

Seven years afterwards

The Battle of Worcester was fought on 3rd September 1651 between Charles II and Oliver Cromwell in a failed royalist bid to reinstate the monarchy. On 3 September 1658– seven years to the day after the battle – the Lord Protector, Oliver Cromwell, died from natural causes.

As with the loss of any charismatic leader, those left behind found themselves in a state of flux. Neither one of Cromwell's two remaining sons was anxious to follow in their father's footsteps and they soon renounced any ambition toward that goal. Throughout 1659, Parliament sought and failed to establish a firm foundation for the rule of the Commonwealth. Finally, after many altercations between different factions, including some from the military, General George Monck, commander-in-chief of the English army in Scotland, crossed the border, arriving in London during February 1660, with the firm intention of resolving the issue.

His reputation not blamed

On 1 May, with the House of Commons reassembled, General Monck was invited to read the declaration he had received: sent by Charles from across the Channel.

> Without one moment's delay, or a contradictory vote, a committee was appointed to prepare an answer; and on the eighth of May both houses attended, while the king was, with great solemnity, proclaimed in Palace-yard, at Whitehall, and at Temple-bar [...] and a committee of lords and commons was dispatched to invite his majesty to return and take possession of his dominions. [4]

To his return, never will one not say yes.

Charles II returned to England and made his public entry into London on 29 May: it being also his date of birth. As Lord Clarendon remarked, "One could not but wonder where those people dwelt, who had done all the mischief, and kept the king so long from enjoying the comfort and support of such excellent subjects." To which the King then responded, "It must certainly have been his own fault that he had not sooner taken possession of the throne, since everybody was so zealous for restoring him to it." [5]

Summary: *Three previous oracles foretell the execution of King Charles I (Century Eight No. 37, and Century Nine Nos. 11 & 49). This oracle takes up the story of the English monarchy by predicting the future of Charles II, the son of the executed King. Seven years to the day after losing at the battle of Worcester and escaping to France, Oliver Cromwell died. With no competent successor among his heirs, the monarchy in Britain was re-established and Charles II was recalled to the throne.*

5   *Albi & Castres feront nouuelle ligue,*
        Neuf Arriens Lisbon & Portugues,
        Carcas, Tholosse consumeront leur brigue,
        Quand chief neuf monstre de Lauragues.

6   *Sardon Nemans si hault desborderont,*
        Qu'on cuidera Deucalion renaistre:
        Dans le collosse la plus part fuyront,
        Vesta sepulchre feu estaint apparoistre.

7   *Le grand conflit qu'on appreste à Nancy,*
        L'Æmathien dira tout ie soubmetz,
        L'isle Britanne par vin, sel en solcy,
        Hem. mi. deux Phi. long temps ne tiendra Metz.

appreste (OF) prepare, make ready; L'Æmathien (Gk) The Amythaon, *also* Amethea; solcy (AF souci); Hem. (L *abbreviation:* Hem[erodromus] express courier; mi. (L *abbreviation:* mi[litia] war; Hem + mi. (*portmanteau paragram*) (H)emmi (OF - au milieu de) in the midst of; Phi. (*abbreviation:* Phi[lippe]; vin, sel (biblical references). Cross-references: (i) Æmathien, C.IX: 38; C.IX: 64; C.IX: 93; C.X: 58. (ii) vin, sel, C.IX: 49.

The great conflict that one makes ready at Nancy,   1659
The Amythaon (**LOUIS XIV**) will say, 'I subjugate everything,'
The British Isle in anxiety through wine & salt,
Express courier, war amid **TWO PHILIPS**, a long time he will not occupy Metz.

The great conflict that one makes ready at Nancy

The *Peace of the Pyrenees* in 1659 (see also N°. 58 *infra*) contained a number of clauses to ensure that France and Spain would continue to live peacefully together. As part of the insurance that these terms would be honoured, Louis XIV agreed to take the Infanta Marie-Thérèse for his wife.

Another clause stipulated that swift action was to be taken jointly, by both parties to the treaty, against Charles IV Duke of Lorraine.

Despite both Spain and France having been at war with each other, Louis XIV and Philip IV had much to complain about regarding Lorraine's recent involvement in their affairs. Initially, the Duke had received money from Spain to take his troops into Paris, but he had then accepted a larger sum from France not to march them into Paris. As an act of reprisal against Charles, but moderated by a concession: "France restored to him his estates, but razed Nancy to the ground." [1]

The Amythaon will say, "I subjugate everything"

Louis XIV resolved from the very beginning of his reign to make the monarchy his profession. In the belief that kingship was a divine office, and its incumbent had been appointed by God, he positioned himself at the pinnacle of every state department. Ministers were appointed for their brains, and Louis used their talents and intellect for his own purpose, while always making the final decision his own. Consequently, when the Seer predicted that the Amythaon would declare, "I subjugate everything." he presumably had in mind Louis XIV's famous dictum, 'L'Etat C'est Moi'. (I am the State). [2]

Interestingly, as indicated previously, the appellation *Amythaon,* given by the oracle to Louis XIV, translates as *unspeakably great.* It therefore forms an appropriate cognomen for a monarch whose subjects called him *'Louis le Grand'* (Louis the Great) and *'Le Roy Soleil'* (the Sun King). This second by-name, acquired its significance from the inscription engraved on coins minted in 1638 to celebrate Louis' birth. In Greek Mythology, each day began with *Amethea* making its appearance in the east as it pulled the Sun across the sky on its daily journey to the west. And so, "In 1638 the Mint struck a coin with the zodiacal sign of September 5, 1638, and the inscription Orbus Solis Gallici (Thus Rises the Sun of France.)" [3]

The British Isle in anxiety through wine and salt

One decade before the *Peace of the Pyrenees* was signed (1659, the British Isle committed regicide by beheading Charles I. [4] The monarchy was overthrown and a republic, or commonwealth, became the new political order under the leadership of Oliver Cromwell. At the same time, the nation was passing through a phase in which politics and religion had become more integrated than during any other period in its history. The oracle reflects this union between politics and religion by referring to wine and salt. These biblical metaphors (*Matthew* ix. 17 and v. 13) serve to denote firstly, the new style of government introduced into Britain by Oliver Cromwell, and secondly the moral elite. The latter is represented by members of the Church who were most troubled by Parliament's act of regicide. They believed it placed people like themselves, whom Jesus had referred to as the *salt* of the earth, in direct opposition to biblical teaching. Thus, many people came to develop a state of anxiety concerning possible retribution by God. This was much in evidence when London was struck by the Great Plague of 1665, followed one year later by the Great Fire of London.

Express courier, war

In France, in 1651 – the year that coincided with Cromwell's rule in Britain, following the defeat of Charles II at the Battle of Worcester (see N°. 4 *supra* – an unfortunate incident took place that plunged the country into a renewed state of civil war.

The Prince of Condé had been threatening to upset the fragile peace in France by raising insurrections in Guienne, Poitou and Anjou. He was also begging help from Spain. [5] In an effort to placate the Prince, and avoid a fresh outbreak of civil war, the Queen-mother, acting as regent for Louis XIV, dispatched an *express courier* to Angerville with terms favourable to Condé.

But the courier blundered, and instead of going to Angerville, where the prince was, arrived at Augerville. The message came too late. Condé said that had he received it sooner, he would have accepted the peace proposals. Thus through the error of a courier and the sheer caprice of the prince, France was again plunged into civil war. [6]

Amid two Philips

At the commencement of Louis XIV's reign, Philip IV was King of Spain (1621 – 1665). At the end of Louis XIV's reign, Philip V had become King of Spain (1700 – 1746, except for a brief intermission in 1724). Between the reigns of these two Philips, there was a gap of 35 years, during which Charles II occupied the Spanish throne. It was in the midst of Charles's reign; that is, during the period commencing 10 August 1678 and ending on 2 October 1679 that the six treaties of Nijmegen were signed.

A long time he will not occupy Metz

The importance of these treaties to France resided in the fact that Louis XIV was finally able to acquire Metz. This city had originally been ceded to France in 1552 during the reign of Henri II, under terms agreed by the *Treaty of Chambord*. But it was not until the *Peace of Westphalia* in October 1648 that the transfer was finally confirmed. This delay in agreement had occurred because of disputes as to where the boundary lines lay. Attempts at resolving these difficulties were begun many times, but fresh outbreaks of war always intervened. Consequently, it was not until 1679 – *between two Philips* – that questions involving the precise location of these boundaries were finally resolved, allowing France to occupy Metz legally. [7]

Summary: *The Amythaon reappears in this oracle as an aptronym for Louis XIV. Once again the content of the prophecy proves to be correct when foreseeing that the Sun King would act against Lorraine's capital, Nancy. It also correctly refers to Louis' famous dictum, 'I am the State'. Noticeably, too, is the fact that during this timeframe, there was deep anxiety in Britain caused by 'wine and salt'. These biblical metaphors also appear in Century Nine No. 49, where the oracle predicts the death of Charles I. And they appear here, too. This serves to confirm a single period of time for the fulfilment of both prophecies.*
The reign of Louis XIV preceded the Age of Reason, consequently not only did Louis pay homage to the seer by visiting Salon, his subjects actively searched for prophecies that applied to their King. Hence, the freedom of expression given to these prophecies during the reign of Louis XV, at the time of the Enlightenment, is found lacking during the reign of his great-grandfather. In its place, by ingenious acts of cryptology to avoid meanings becoming understood in advance of their happening, events that could be changed by an act of freewill have instead been carefully concealed.

8   *Index & poulse parfondera le front*
         De Senegalia le Conte à son filz propre
         La Myrnamee par plusieurs de prin front
         Trois dans sept iours blesses mors.

perfondera (L perfunder\e) to wet *or* moisten; propre (Dictionnaire de français Littré - En parlant des personnes, qui a l'aptitude, les qualités nécessaires pour quelque chose.) Myrnamee (*portmanteau & paragram* - Myr[m]+ a[r]mée), i.e. Myrm[idon] army; prin (OF) piercing.

Fore-finger and thumb will wet the forehead,   1792
For the **COUNT OF SENIGAGLIA**, on his special son (future **PIUS IX**):
The Myrmidon army, through a great number at the piercing front,
Three within seven days, casualties, deaths.

Fore-finger and thumb will wet the forehead

The opening line to this oracle introduces the fact that a baptism is to be understood. It therefore signals a connexion with the Church, for which baptism is the first and chief sacrament that unites the baptized person to Christ.

For the Count of Senigaglia, on his special son

The baptism must therefore be that of a 'special' child who will one day make history. Since we know from the prophecy that the child is also the son of a count living in Senigaglia (old Italian name for Senigallia, which became part of the Papal States after 1624) a small commune and port on the Adriatic coast, a quick search reveals that its most celebrated native, since these prophecies were written, was Pope Pius IX. He was born on 13 May 1792 at "Senigaglia: ninth child of Count Girolamo Mastai Ferretti and Caterina Sollazzi. Baptized on the same day of his birth." [1]

Fifty-four years later, Giovanni Maria Mastai-Ferretti – this 'special' infant baptised in Senigaglia –became Pope Pius IX.

> Despite having shunned honours, on the evening of 16 June 1846 Mastai [...] was elected Pope and took the name Pius IX. He had a difficult pontificate, but precisely because of that he was a great Pope, certainly one of the greatest. Thoroughly aware of being the "Vicar of Christ" and responsible for the rights of God and of the Church, he was clear, simple consistent. He combined firmness and understanding, fidelity and openness. [2]

> Pope John Paul II declared him venerable on 6 July 1985, and beatified him on 3 September 2000 (his commemoration is 7 February). [3]

The seer devotes quatrain N°. 56 in Century Five to the reign of Pope Pius IX. Here, he confirms the Pope's identity by naming his father at his baptism. This also has the effect of dating the present prophecy as beginning in 1792: the year in which the French Revolutionary Wars began, with France declaring war on Austria.

The Myrmidon army

> THE MYRMIDONS were the soldiers of Achilles, in the Trojan War. From them all zealous and unscrupulous followers of a political chief are called by that name, down to this day. [4]

The Seer uses his classical knowledge in this quatrain to compare France's army of Italy with the Myrmidons. The army, to which Napoleon was appointed as Commander-in-Chief, was formed in 1792 (the year Pius IX was born). It originally consisted of 106,000 men: but "desertion, sickness and casualties in action" had reduced the number to 63,000. On 27 March 1796, when Bonaparte took command, the men were already being compared "To the motley collection of hungry scarecrows, who bore a closer resemblance to brigands than to trained soldiers." [5]

But, also, in terms of similarity to the Myrmidons, Napoleon was 'zealous', 'unscrupulous', as well as being a 'political chief', and his men swiftly became infected by the first two of these traits. This was made clear by Masséna, who wrote of Bonaparte's first meeting with his generals.

> He asked us where our divisions were stationed, how they were equipped, what was the spirit and fighting value of each corps; he gave us our marching orders, and announced that tomorrow he would inspect the whole army, and the day after tomorrow it would march and deliver battle against the enemy. He spoke with such dignity, preciseness and competence that his generals retired with the conviction that at last they had a real leader. [6]

Through a great number at the piercing front

In the spring of 1796, Napoleon in his new role as Commander-in-Chief, led the army of Italy, although little more than a rag-tag band of men, across the mountains into Italy. The Sardinian army was the first to fall: defeated in a matter of weeks. At Lodi, on 10 May, it was the Austrian army that was defeated. Five days later, Napoleon led his now fully revitalized soldiers into Milan, declaring it to be a satellite conquest of the French Republic.

With the Austrians driven out of the northern part of Italy, Napoleon's army began the siege of Mantua, which he finally took on 2 February 1797. During the intervening months, his forces also fought and won battles at Lonato (3-4 August) and Castiglione (5 August).

Three within seven days, casualties, deaths

In February 1797, having successfully taken Mantua, Napoleon received fresh instructions from the Directorate in Paris. He was to "deal with Rome; and they had given him full powers to make an armistice with the Pope, or even to conclude the treaty of peace which had been hanging fire all the summer." He was further told, "If the Pope refuses to sign, he may take military measures and march on Rome." [7]

Acting under these instructions, Napoleon led his men into the Papal States. With characteristic boldness he warned the towns and villages, through which he intended to pass, not to sound the alarm, to avoid attacking any Frenchman, and for priests to behave according to Gospel teaching. Those who disobeyed would either be shot or severely dealt with, and their village burnt. Despite this warning, there were casualties and some deaths were reported. Further deaths and injuries also occurred in the seven days of conquests that followed.

Napoleon then set off from Sant' Antonio, reaching and then subduing Faenza and Forli on "3 February". Next day he took Rimini, "demanding that the Republic of San Marino should surrender its bishop, who had taken refuge there." On "7 February", Pesaro fell to his command, and finally, on "10 February", he reported the capture of the port at Ancona, "together with £350,000 worth of treasure from Loretto, and the friendly welcome given to the French troops by people tired of Papal misrule." [8] (In 1532 this major port on the Adriatic Sea had become an important city in the Papal States, with the symbol of papal authority residing in its massive Citadel).

Thus, in the space of just *seven days* commencing with day 'three' – the 3rd February and concluding his conquests on day 'ten' the 10th of February, Napoleon numbered among his conquests Faenza, Forli, Rimini, Pesaro Senigaglia and Ancona. It is noteworthy that Senigaglia was taken on 9 February: it being the birthplace of Pope Pius IX.

Summary: *This prophecy commences with the birth of Pope Pius IX, thereby acting as a signal for the time period. No attempt has been made to disguise the title of the father, which helps to identify the name of the child. The year also coincides with that in which the Army of Italy was formed, and which became Napoleon Bonaparte's means of achieving his destiny. Thereafter, apart from the description of his army, the predicted 'seven days' in which Bonaparte achieved total victory over towns in the Papal States, beginning with 'three' for the 3rd of February is yet another significant feature of this prophecy. Interestingly, too, is the fact that this prophecy began and concluded with events at Senigaglia.*

9   *De Castillon figuieres iour de brune,*
       De feme infame naistra souuerain prince
       Surnon de chausses perhume luy posthume,
       Onc Roy ne fut si pire en sa prouince.

10   *Tasche de murdre, enormes adulteres,*
       Grand ennemy de tout le genre humain
       Que sera pire qu'ayeulx, oncles, ne peres
       En fer, feu, eau, sanguin & inhumain.

11   *Dessoubs Ionchere du dangereux passage*
       Fera passer le posthume sa bande,
       Les monts Pyrens passer hors son bagaige
       De Parpignam courira duc à tende.

12   *Esleu en Pape, d'esleu sera mocqué,*
       Subit soudain esmeu prompt & timide,
       Par trop bon doulx à mourir prouocqué,
       Crainte estainte la nuit de sa mort guide.

subit (OF) swift; esmeu (AF) émotion; doulx (OF doux) pleasing; à (OF before infinitive) for to; estainte (OF estaincte) extinguished.

Elected as Pope (**SIXTUS V**), by the elected he will be mocked,   1590
Swift, sudden emotion, ready at hand and timorous:
For to die provoked, through too much good natured pleasing:
The night of his death leads to fear extinguished.

Elected as Pope

Sixtus V was elected to office on 24 April 1585. [1] Three years into his reign the Pope was shown an edited adaptation of the Vulgate Bible. What he read caused him such huge disappointment that he decided to produce an edition of his own. At first sight it appeared to be an enormous undertaking. Nevertheless, despite the many difficulties, after just eighteen months he succeeded in preparing for publication an edition of his own, and by the beginning of May 1590, the Bible was ready for sale. A papal Bull accompanied its launch, *Aeternus Ille* (March 1590). This declared the new Bible "true, lawful, authentic and unquestioned in all public and private discussions, readings, preachings and explanations." Anyone contravening the Bull would be excommunicated.

By the elected he will be mocked

After the Pope's Bible, the *Editio Sixtina,* had been dissected by those who had elected him to the papal chair, the Vatican must have reverberated from the shock at what was being discovered, as error after error became revealed. The disdain for Sixtus's lack of care in issuing his Bible had become a cause for mockery: albeit in subdued tones of dignified concern. [2]

Swift, sudden, emotion, ready at hand and timorous

In the middle of April, just two weeks prior to the Bible's public distribution, the first priority copies were delivered to the cardinals. It was then that a swift, sudden emotion gripped those who had received their advanced copy. Unbelievably, Pope Sixtus V's Bible was "so full of blunders that it had to be withdrawn after his death." Although ready at hand, timidity prevented the clergy from making them known.

Working from the *Louvain* text, Sixtus had felt free to add sentences for clarification, to translate difficult words according to personal whim, and to change the references that had previously been put together by Robert Stephanus in 1555: replacing them with those of his own. Even some titles to the Psalms were altered, and an entire verse here and there omitted. But fear of excommunication caused the clergy to remain silent. As the Spanish ambassador, Count Olivares pointed out in a letter addressed to Philip II: it is through their *timidity* that the cardinals have preferred to stay silent, "for fear Sixtus might give them a taste of his sharp temper." [3]

For to die provoked, through too much good natured pleasing

As Olivares' letter indicated, the cardinals' timorous attitude had allowed the Pope too much leeway for his personal whims. Some of these were quite extraordinary. Apart from re-editing the Vulgate Bible, "He entertained fantastic ambitions, such as the annihilation of the Turks, the conquest of Egypt, the transporting of the Holy Sepulchre to Italy (and) the accession of his nephew to the throne of France." [4] But his threat of excommunication for objectors [5] sheltered him from the abundant criticisms that became known only after his death. And so, while Sixtus lived, those who served under him did so without confronting "the iron pope" with his errors.

Sixtus V died on 27 August 1590, after suffering successive attacks of malaria. However, his death had more to do with the provocation he was subjected to by Spain's ambassador, who insisted the Pope continue to excommunicate France's future King, Henri IV. But Sixtus resisted this demand by good naturedly pleasing the French, having learned that Henri was preparing to convert to the Catholic faith. Instead, "He preferred to call a Jubilee Year to pray for the restoration of a Catholic king on the French throne, rather than financially support Philip II in sending an army against Henri." [6] The "acrimonious confrontations" that followed this decision led to his early death.

The night of his death leads to fear extinguished

On 27 August Sixtus V died suddenly, and on 5 September the College of Cardinals stopped all further sales [of Sixtus's Bible, and] bought and destroyed as many copies as possible. [7]

After his death Robert Bellarmine warned that his work was an embarrassment, and great danger to the church. [8]

The fear to the Church having been extinguished, Sixtus's Bible was subsequently reprinted three times, under direction from Pope Clement VIII, in 1592, 1593 and 1598, during which "about six thousand on matters of detail, and a hundred that were important," [9] needed correction.

Summary: *This oracle has a great deal of relevance for those at the Vatican during any era. It is one among a number of prophecies directed at the Church of Rome, in order to confirm that God is very much aware of the content existing on the world's time dimension, both past and future; in consequence to which, neither the Pope nor those who serve the Catholic Church are exempt. In the present oracle, the reign of Sixtus V proved to be an enormous embarrassment, which he brought upon himself by undertaking a task for which he was ill-equipped, by character, to perform. The fact that he became pope did not change the character of the man he had been before his enthronement, but it gave him the ability to express his character in a manner that would not have been possible before then.*

13   *Soulz la pasture d'animaux ruminant*
        Par eux conduicts au ventre herbipolique
        Soldatz caichez les armes bruit menant,
        Non loing temptez de cité Antipolique.

herbipolique (L *portmanteau* & *syncope*, i.e., herbi[dus] + pol[it]ique); menant (*syncope* men[aç]ant); temptez (AF chercher à atteindre; Antipolique (AF *portmanteau* & *syncope*) Anti + pol [it] ique: anti (AF antique), ancient. Cross-reference: par eux, C.ll: 1

Beneath the pasture for ruminant animals,   1914
For the sake of them brought to the grassy administrative belly:
Soldiers hidden, the weapons noisy, menacing,
Not far, having sought to reach the ancient administrative city.

Beneath the pasture for ruminant animals

The French farming country that runs from Armentières to Lens, with its meadows and pasture land for cattle – *ruminant animals* – is indicated by the opening line of this oracle. During the First World War, this tract of land became part of the Western Front. Both sides in the conflict dug their own, massive systems of interconnecting trenches *beneath this pasture.* [1]

For the sake of them brought to the grassy administrative belly

Troops were regularly shipped over from England and then transported by train to within marching distance of the battlefield. Upon arrival, the soldiers took up positions in the trenches that had previously been dug for the sake of them *brought to the grassy* battlefield.

The trenches on both sides soon developed into a labyrinth of intercommunicating passageways. First, there were the main fire trenches, with perhaps a shorter advance line to the forward position. Several alleys then led back to another trench running parallel with the first one. This was used for command, communications and support. Behind these were further trenches for supplies and a reserve force. At the centre of each complex was an *administrative belly*. It was there that orders were received from 'high command': generals who were running the war at a safe distance, using 'cigar butt ideas', intelligence reports and 'trial and error' judgments. [2]

Soldiers hidden

Both the Germans and the Allied forces were engaged in a conflict that placed soldiers out of sight, below ground level where they were hidden from the enemy's sight and from the sniper's bullet. Trench warfare was quite unlike any other major battle that had been fought in the past. [3]

The weapons noisy, menacing

Noise, terrible at times, was a fairly unremitting feature of the Great War, and it often resulted in soldiers returning to their homeland 'shell-shocked'. In the end, "Artillery did not win the war, but the noise and surreal landscape it produced defined war on the Western Front. Nothing like it had ever occurred before."

The weapons employed were those developed in line with the approach of the technological age. Rifles could be loaded and fired in seconds. Machine guns, with their loud, seemingly incessant nattering, could fire seven or eight rounds every second. Howitzers were also firing shrapnel shells, timed to explode in mid-air so as to scatter hundreds of lead balls in every direction. *The weapons* were, as predicted in the oracle, *noisy* and very *menacing.* [4]

Not far, having sought to reach the ancient administrative city

Paris was the goal of the enemy's 'Schlieffen Plan'; it being Germany's intention to secure the French capital as part of its invasion strategy. Led by General Moltke at command headquarters, Alexander von Kluck's forces arced their way across northern France towards the capital. On 5

September 1914, they crossed the River Marne and reached Meaux, about 20 miles from Paris; that is, not far from the outskirts of the capital. [5]

During the First World War, Paris, apart from being *ancient* (archaeological evidence shows that the site of Paris has been occupied by man since between 9800 and 7500 BC), it had also become an *administrative city*. At the start of the First World War, developments in radio and telephone communications had already reached a stage when battle plans and strategies could be relayed by wire from one administration centre to another, as implied by this oracle.

Fortunately for Paris, the rear of Kluck's assault party had been left unguarded, and after a successful counterattack by the French, the Germans were forced to retreat. [6]

Summary: *This oracle peers more than three and a half centuries into the future to foresee, in detail, the trench warfare, with its menacing new artillery that defined the First World War. Radio technology also allowed the war to be directed far from the battlefield, and this is implied by the effort involved in constructing the portmanteau (or hybrid syncope) 'anti\que, plus poli\que, condensed to 'antipolique' to describe the administrative orders sent from the ancient city of Paris to the battlefield.*

> 14   *Vrnel Vaucile sans conseil de soy mesmes,*
> *Hardit timide par crainte prins vaincu,*
> *Accompagné de plusieurs putains blesmes:*
> *A Barcellonne aux chartreux conuaincu.*

> 15   *Pere duc vieux d'ans & de soif chargé,*
> *Au iour extreme filz desniant les guiere*
> *Dedans le puis vif mort viendra plongé,*
> *Senat au fil la mort longue & legiere.*

> 16   *Heureux au regne de France, heureux de vie,*
> *Ignorant sang mort fureur & rapine,*
> *Par mon flateur seras mys en enuie,*
> *Roy desrobé trop de foy en cuisine.*

> Happy in the reign of France, happy with life,   1830
> Ignorant of blood, death, fury and plundering:
> By my flattering you will be placed in envy (**KING LOUIS-PHILIPPE**),
> King disrobed, too much faith in cuisine.

Happy in the reign of France, happy with life

Louis Philippe was proclaimed King of the French on 9 August 1830, following the abdication of Charles X. He immediately set about popularising himself. [1] In this endeavour, he became the "Citizen-King"; always ready with a cheery word to rich and poor alike, and regularly to be seen strolling along the Paris boulevards with an umbrella on his arm. People would sometimes gather beneath his window and call for him to appear. The King would then emerge with his family, wave a tricolour and sing the Marseillaise. Everyone loved him for his charm and good humour. [2]

Ignorant of blood, death, fury and plundering

Louis Philippe was born in Paris on 6 October 1773, but was able to avoid the atrocities of the French Revolution; which is to say, he was *ignorant of the blood, death, fury and plundering* that marked the worst excesses of the French Revolution: and to a lesser extent, the French wars under Napoleon. He was spared these acts of violence by choosing exile, and thereafter serving in the Austrian army. Later, he moved to Switzerland, where he occupied himself as a tutor.

In a restless mood, he travelled to America, spending two years there before returning to Europe in 1800. For a short while he stayed in England; and it was from where he later left to join the Neapolitan royal family in Sicily. During this visit he met and subsequently married Marie-Amélie, the daughter of King Ferdinand IV. But it was not until the abdication of Napoleon and the restoration of the monarchy in 1815 that he felt it safe to return to France. [3]

By my flattering you will be placed in envy

It is of especial note to see how the sixteenth-century Seer has addressed his subject by employing the 2nd person singular, '*seras*'. This familiarity of address is customarily restricted to family, close friends and small children. Yet, the Seer addresses the King of France across the centuries in this familiar way. This, at any other time in French history would have been unacceptable, even insolent. Nevertheless, of all French monarchs, it was the final one, Louis Philippe who would have been perfectly content to be addressed with this familiarity, for he openly and actively encouraged it. "He called workmen 'my friends', and the National Guardsmen 'my comrades'." [4]

But, despite these flatteries, and the king being placed in envy of less fortunate monarchs in the past, the verse concludes by predicting his abdication. It also gives the cause; and, once again, the last line is not without a hint of that dark humour for which the Seer was noted.

King disrobed

In 1848, Louis Philippe was forced to abdicate. The reason was entirely political. The first sign of trouble began in 1846, with poor harvests, industrial unrest and peasant protests. The mood of the country was also made worse by a large number of bankruptcies. And on 23 February, under pressure from his sons, the King abdicated. [5]

The disrobing of the King became necessary as a result of the growing unrest in the country. In his attempt to curb this, Louis-Philippe placed a banning order on public meetings. But this only led to the political opposition retaliating by arranging 'banquets', which were seen as a legitimate means of getting-together. At these functions, diners could meet freely to vent their discontent.

Too much faith in cuisine

"It is I," said the King, "I personally whom the banquets are aimed against. We shall see who is the strongest." The King's trust in his ability to withstand the stratagems of his opponents was soon put to the test. A banquet had been arranged for 22 February 1848, but at the last minute it was cancelled. Louis Philippe received the news with raised spirits. "Didn't I tell you it would all end in smoke? It is a regular April Fool's Day."

He was mistaken; the King had placed *too much faith in cuisine* as the only means open to the protesters. On the day of the banquet, crowds of people paraded through the streets, waving banners and shouting their protests. Next day, the barricades went up. And when soldiers fired into protesters, killing some twenty men and women, the mob howled for vengeance. Louis Philippe attempted to make his way to the safety of Saint-Cloud but the National Guardsmen barred his way. Under pressure, he was forced to abdicate. [6]

Summary: *Three centuries passed between the year when these prophecies were first printed and the time when the last king to rule France stepped down from the throne. For every one of these kings, during those three hundred years, the seer has recognized the monarch by his inclusion in at least one oracle. The kings were - Henri II; Francis II; Charles IX; Henri III; Henry IV; Louis XIII; Louis XIV; Louis XV; Louis XVI; Napoleon Bonaparte; Louis XVIII; Charles X and Louis-Philippe. Louis XVII was never proclaimed king, but features in several oracles. This present oracle is very apt in describing the friendly character of the 'Citizen King', Louis Philippe, also the cause of his abdication, which finally ended the monarchy in France.*

17   *La royne Ergaste voiant sa fille blesme,*
      Par vn regret dans l'estomach encloz,
      Crys lamentables seront lors d'Angolesme,
      Et au germain mariage fort clos.

Ergaste (L ergastulum) prisoner, also (2 *anagrammatic paragrams*: gaster[e] & (AF dévaster) devastate, & estra[n]ge (OF) foreign; regret (OF) grief; enclos (AF enceinte) enclosure *also* pregnant; fort (AF difficile) difficult; clos (OF) accomplished.

(**MARIE ANTOINETTE**) the foreign queen (prisoner, devastated.) seeing her daughter pale: 1793
Through a grief, during the stomach enclosure,
Distressing wails will subsist at the time of **ANGOULÊME**,
And for the cousin (**MARIE THÉRÈSE**), a difficult marriage accomplished.

The prisoner Queen (devastated, foreign)

By presenting 'Ergaste' with a capital 'E', it emphasizes the word's importance. It is therefore not surprising to discover that it offers three key words that each describe the situation of Marie Antoinette during the months before her execution. The French Queen was Austrian by birth, hence foreign. She was being held under guard inside the Temple Tower, therefore a prisoner. And on 16 January 1793 she had every reason to be devastated, for on that day her husband, Louis XVI had received the death sentence. He was to be guillotined. [1]

Seeing her daughter pale

On the evening of 20 January, the night before the execution, the King was allowed to visit his family for one last time. It was during this final farewell that the emotional stress of their parting proved too traumatic for the Queen's daughter, Marie Thérèse, and the little princess became pale. The climax came just as the King was on the point of leaving the room, at which point, "the Princesse Royale, the King's daughter, suddenly threw herself at her father and collapsed in a dead faint. Bringing her round was the family's last embrace." [2]

Through a grief during the stomach enclosure

From the moment of the King's death onwards, Marie Antoinette remained bowed down with a grief that went too deep for words. [...] She wanted suitable mourning clothes [... and] asked for [and received] a black taffeta cloak, fichu, skirt and gloves.

She also asked for black curtains and a black coverlet but these were refused. This particular phrase in the prophecy does, however, conceal a further prediction that is remarkably subtle. This is because the words: '*a grief during the stomach enclosure*' provides the exact date of Marie Antoinette's own execution.

When her period of grief is timed from news of her husband's death sentence on 16th January, and is allowed to continue for exactly nine months until her own death on 16 October, it covers a period of precisely nine months, which is the time of the 'stomach enclosure' (*enceinte*) during pregnancy. [3] The word 'enclos' in ancient French actually meant the period of pregnancy.

Distressing wails will subsist at the time of Angoulême

The French Revolution began in 1789 and ended in 1799: from whence came the distressing wails during that decade. But, at the same time, it also marked *the time of Angoulême*. [4]

In 1789 at Versailles, Louis XVI's enforced removal to Paris signalled to his brother, the duc d'Artois, that it was time to leave the country. The Duke did so with little delay, taking with him his wife and two sons, the dukes of Angoulême and Berri.

Unfortunately, the King's' daughter, Marie Thérèse, who had been promised in marriage to Louis Antoine, Duke of Angoulême, was compelled to remain in Paris with her parents. She was then forced to accompany them inside the Temple Tower, where she remained for several years after the execution of her parents. It was not until 26 December 1795 that she was released. Her freedom was granted in exchange for French prisoners held by Austria.

Four years later, the Princesse Royale married her cousin, the Duke of Artois' son, and became the Duchesse d'Angoulême. Thus, *Angoulême's* departure from France coincided with the start of the Revolution, and his marriage to the Princess Royal corresponded with his return to France at the end of the Revolution with its distressing wails.

And for the cousin, a difficult marriage accomplished

Angoulême might well marry his first cousin, the daughter of Louis XVI who left the prison of the Temple for Vienna in December 1795. [...] Finally, on 10 June 1799 she was married to the Duc de Angoulême at Mittau. [5]

Summary: *This oracle begins with the imprisonment of Marie Antoinette and her daughter in the Temple Tower. It correctly predicts the nine months that passed between the death sentence imposed upon Louis XVI and the Queen's day of execution, by using an old French word for enceinte, which is still in use. The remaining part of the prophecy focuses upon the royal couple's daughter, Madame Royale. Her pallid complexion at the final parting between her and her father on the night before his execution, when she fell into a faint, makes it appear that the seer was also present, despite a time gap of 235 years. Her release from the Temple and the marriage to her cousin, which had been proposed before the Revolution, and through which she became the Duchess of Angoulême, forms the last part of an obviously successful prophecy.*

18   *Le ranc Lorrain fera place à Vendosme,*
      Le hault mis bas & le bas mis en hault,
      Le fils d'Hamon sera esleu dans Rome,
      Et les deux grands seront mys en deffault.

ranc (AF. *apocope:* ranc[or] – ressentiment) resentment; esleu (OF) chosen; Hamon (*biblical name*) Haman; deffault (OF) in want of appearance before a judge.

The **LORRAINE** resentment will give place to **VENDÔME**,   1588
The high placed low, and the low placed on high,
The son of **HAMAN** will be chosen inside Rome,
Also, the two great ones (**GUISE & LORRAINE**) will be placed in want of appearance.

The Lorraine resentment will give place to Vendôme

After the death of Charles IX in 1574, with the King having left no legitimate heir, his younger brother Edouard, changed his name to Henri before taking his place on the vacant throne. This line of inexperienced youths, which began with Francis II, was the principal reason why Henri of Lorraine, 3rd Duke of Guise, Prince of Joinville, and his brother Louis, Cardinal of Lorraine, were able to exercise so much power in the affairs of France. So effective were they politically that ultimately they came to be seen as the virtual rulers of the country. The effect this had on Henri III's self esteem has previously been noted, especially in Century Three N°. 51.

The oracle, however, predicts *resentment* within the House of Lorraine; and this came about when Guise and his brother were both murdered by order of the King. Their deaths were intended to remove the two obstacles that had been interfering with Henri's rule of France. What it did, instead, was to cause such terrible resentment against the King within the House of Lorraine that a plan to assassinate him was hatched by the brothers' sister, the duchess Montpensier. Her plan succeeded, and Henri III was himself struck down by Jacques Clément.

> Understanding all too well that he had not many hours left to live, the King [...] first addressed the assembled nobles. Holding out his hand to Navarre, he said, 'You see my brother, how my subjects have treated me! [...] It is now for you, my brother, to wear that crown which I have striven to preserve for you; justice and the principle of legitimacy demand that you should succeed me in the realm.' [1]

Navarre was the King of that province. Later he also became Henri IV of France. But in this oracle, he is referred to by the name of his duchy—Vendôme.

The high placed low and the low placed on high

Up until their deaths in December 1588, Henri duc de Guise and Cardinal Lorraine had been at the very peak of political power. Both men had risen to such a high degree through the influence of the Holy Catholic League that they were already seen as the real power in France. But at a conference held in Henri III's château at Blois, both men were placed low – quite literally – having been struck down by the assassin's knife. [2]

Henri of Navarre, whom the Seer calls Vendôme (Henri's father had been the Duke of that duchy. And when Henry later became King, he passed the title on to his illegitimate son) was the second cousin of Henri III. This blood relationship with the murdered King legitimized his succession to the throne. But he had also been labelled a heretic on account of his Protestant faith. In 1585, Pope Sixtus V excommunicated him for this, which effectively barred him from ever becoming anointed King of France. Nonetheless, after the deaths of the Guise brothers, the opportunity presented itself for Vendôme to renew his challenge for the crown. And when he converted to the Catholic religion in July 1593, he also converted those who had opposed his succession. On 27 February 1594, he was finally crowned King of France at Chartres Cathedral.

The son of Haman will be chosen inside Rome

From the time of Charles IX (1560-74) up until the assassination of his brother, Henri III (1589), The Wars of Religion had turned Catholic France into a divided nation, with large parts of the country coming under Protestant administration. In the eyes of Rome, a heretic state was now operating inside a Catholic state, and it was conducting its affairs according to the tenets of its own principles of faith. [3]

A similar situation had occurred many years before in Susa, where the *Book of Esther* recounts what happened there, and how King Xerxes had restored order His solution had been to elect a man named *Haman* and place him in office, with the understanding that he would purge the kingdom of its heretics.

When Sixtus V ratified the secret Treaty of Joinville (31 December 1584), and acknowledged Cardinal Bourbon as the future king of France, it was as if he had chosen a son of Haman inside Rome. For, upon taking the crown, Charles X was to model his reign on that of *Haman*. So that with the assistance of the Holy Catholic League, France would purge the country of its heretics, and the kingdom would again become wholly Catholic. [4]

Also, the two great ones will be placed in want of appearance

Things did not go according to plan. In December 1588, both Henri duc de Guise and his brother Cardinal Lorraine were summoned to a meeting of the Estates-General at the Château de Blois. And there, on the 23rd and 24th of the month, the *two great ones* were assassinated; which, it may be said, *placed them in want of appearance* at the assembly. [5]

Summary: *As with Angoulême in the previous oracle, identified as Duke Louis Antoine, Lorraine is identified as the Duke of Guise and Vendôme as Henri IV. The prophecy foretells how the expectations of the House of Lorraine to succeed Henri III were crushed by the murders of Guise and his brother at the King's command. It also disrupted the plans of the Pope, who had chosen Cardinal Bourbon as France's new king, so that he might purge the country of its heretics, and restore religious unity in France. The seer likens the situation at this time, in a religiously divided France, to one described by the Bible in the Book of Esther. Hence, he introduces Haman, who was expected to purge Susa of its Jewish heretics and restore religious unity across the country. In fact, the Cardinal chosen by the Pope died before he could mount a challenge for the throne, as did Guise, who was cut down. Vendôme was therefore left to be placed on high as Henri III's successor, which occurred after Henri was, himself, assassinated in a revenge attack organised by Guise's sister.*

19   *Iour que sera par royne saluee,*
         Le iour apres le salut, la priere:
         Le compte fait raison & valbuee,
         Par auant humble oncques ne feut si fiere.

valbuee (*metathesis & paragram 'e' for 'b'* – [e]valuee) evaluated *also* val[b]uee; (OF) worth; compte (OF) an unlikely tale; raison (AF sujet d'une conversation;) subject of a conversation; humble (*apocope* – humble[ment]) humbleness; oncques, (OF une fois) one time; fiere (AF orgueilleux) a proud and haughty person.

The day that she (**EUGENIE**) will be bowed to as Queen,   1853
The day after the salutation, the prayer:
The unlikely tale made a subject of conversation and evaluated worth,
From previous humbleness, at any time, was never a person so proud.

The day that she will be bowed to as Queen

The civil wedding ceremony between Eugenia and Napoleon III was conducted in Paris on the evening of 29 January 1853, and took place inside the Tuileries Palace. The bride later wrote to her sister describing how "[she] felt she was acting in a play when people addressed her as 'Your Majesty'." For almost an hour after the marriage ceremony, and having been proclaimed Empress, Eugénie was bowed to by each member of the French government and from the elite of society. [1]

The day after the salutation, the prayer

The day after the salutation, "Eugénie (no longer Eugenia)" together with her husband, Napoleon attended the Cathedral of Notre Dame for the religious ceremony to bless their marriage.

> The service is taken by the archbishop of Paris Monseigneur Sibour. [...] During the wedding Lady Cowley has sketched the new empress inside her prayer book. Kneeling at a prie-dieu [praying stool], Eugénie's chin rests pensively on her hand. [2]

The unlikely tale made a subject of conversation

The marriage between Napoleon III and Eugénie had been such an unlikely tale that it became the subject of frequent conversation. In fact, "the emperor had changed the date from 10 February on account of so much opposition to the marriage." As late as early January, "Many people at the highest level were still convinced that the marriage would never happen." The London ambassador to Paris, Lord Cowley reported: "It was, of course, ill received in Paris even by the emperor's friends, and it has set all the women against him. Clergy and army disapprove." Gossip about the marriage had also caused news of the impending wedding to travel across the Channel, where it was reported in the *Illustrated London News:* "alas for the gallantry of Frenchmen [...] they find nothing better to do than repeat the scandals originating in the boudoirs of the fairer part of creation." [3]

And evaluated worth

In London, the foreign secretary responded to Lord Cowley's opinion of Eugénie by referring to her as "an adventuress": and with similar aloofness, remarked: "to put this 'intrigante' on the throne is a lowering of the imperial dignity with a vengeance." Napoleon, realising how his wife was being evaluated, was forced into diffusing the growing apprehension with a distinctly positive attitude. At the Tuileries on the eve of his wedding, he called together the Council of State and Assembly to hear a speech he had prepared concerning his marriage, "copies of which were distributed throughout France. [...] His future wife, he told them was of high birth, French by education and a devout Catholic. He promised she would bring back 'the virtues' of his grandmother, Empress Joséphine." Not everyone was convinced, as one learns from Baron Hübner's report, sent to his masters in Vienna. "However democratic people may be, they would have preferred a princess." [4]

From previous humbleness

In complete contrast to what would be normally expected of an Empress of the French, Eugénie's early childhood was very humble. Although descended from a noble Spanish family, the financial circumstances of her father had initially been poor. At one time, while under house arrest, he had even faced bankruptcy. Eugénie's mother was from the merchant class: the daughter of a Scottish fruit and wine merchant who had settled in Malaga and then lost his money in a failed business venture. The contrast between the expectations of France for its charismatic Emperor, and the background of the woman he had chosen for his wife, is therefore evident. [5]

At any time was never a person so proud

After the wedding ceremony at the Tuileries, Eugénie described in a letter to her sister how: "For three-quarter of an hour they filed past her, cardinals, generals and ministers bowing, ladies curtseying." Then, on the next day, she appeared at Notre Dame Cathedral, elegantly dressed ...

> in white velvet sewn with diamonds; her full three-layered skirt is trimmed with priceless old English lace, her tight bodice is sewn with sapphires and orange blossom, and around her waist is Empress Marie-Louise's sapphire girdle—her three-quarter length sleeves reveal long, jewel-studded gloves. Her red hair has been arranged by the famous coiffeur Félix, curls flowing down the neck from the chignon to which her veil is fastened, and she wears the diamond and sapphire tiara that Empress Joséphine had worn at her coronation in 1804. [6]

Summary: The wedding of Emperor Napoléon III to Eugenia de Montijo in January 1853 is the subject of this prophecy. Once again, the descriptive words and passages are so apt that it might appear the seer was reading from reports made at the time of the marriage, 295 years after the prophecy was published. The fact is that these repeated displays of prescient knowledge continue to accumulate, and will likely to do so until the second coming of Jesus Christ: at which point, any remaining doubt as to the veracity of prophecy will be irrelevant.

> 20 Tous les amys qu'auront tenu party,
> Pour rude en lettres mys mort & saccagé,
> Biens publiez par sixe grand neanty,
> Onc Romain peuple ne feut tant outragé.

tenu (OF) supported; neanty,(OF *apocope:* - neanty[se]) baseness; lettres (OF) decrees from a governing person; onc (AF - une fois) at one time.

All the friends that will have supported the party,   1945
Put to death and ransacked for the brutishness of decrees:
A huge baseness by six, completely manifest:
Not ever were the Roman people outraged in such a manner.

All the friends that will have supported the party

The context of this quatrain from start to finish runs parallel to events occurring in April 1945, following the capture of Benito Mussolini by Italian partisans.

Mussolini's mistress, Claretta Petacci, had attempted to follow his escape route, but she and her brother Marcello were stopped and taken captive. They were then both taken to join the Duce at Mezzegra, where he had been taken after his capture at Dongo. They were not alone in their captivity; a group of Fascist party supporters, friends of the Duce, had also been rounded-up in their bid to join up with their leader. Together, the prisoners were held in wait for a decision as to their fate, which was to be decided by the communist led National Liberation Committee. [1]

Put to death and ransacked

In the farmhouse outside Dongo, where Mussolini had been taken after his capture, the order for his execution was apparently made by Togliatti, the secretary of the Communist Party and Vice-Premier of Italy. Colonel Valerio was entrusted to carry out the sentence. But when he arrived at Dongo with this news, an argument broke out between the communists and the partisans. To settle the matter, Colonel Valerio took the list of prisoners and selected from it fifteen names for execution.

Then, taking Mussolini and his mistress aside, with a promise for their safety, he drove them to the Villa Belmonte, about a mile away, where they were both shot; a guard was then placed over their bodies while Valerio returned to Dongo. Upon arriving, he arranged a firing squad for the execution of the fifteen men selected from the list. Claretta Petacci's brother was among them, and was shot while trying to escape. [2]

After Mussolini's death and the end of occupation in Italy, large numbers of Fascist sympathizers immediately became targets for revenge killings. "The Musocco Cemetery in Milan contains more than 1,008 Fascists that were executed in the purges at the end of the war, including the 15 mentioned above. Most of these graves are dated April 28, 29 or 30." [3]

For the brutishness of decrees

After marching on Rome in October 1922, and then being given power to form a government, Mussolini had been able to tighten his grip on Italy. "He bullied the Italian Parliament into giving him emergency powers that allowed him to shut down other parties, censor the press, and end other civil liberties. By 1925, Italy was a fascist dictatorship." [4]

All Italians were expected to obey Mussolini and his Fascist Party. Authority was enforced by the use of the Blackshirts – the nickname for the Fasci di Combattimenti. Those men in this unit were usually ex-soldiers and it was their job to bring into line those who opposed Mussolini. It was the Blackshirts who murdered the socialist Matteotti – an outspoken critic of Mussolini. [5]

SIX COMPLETELY MANIFEST

A huge baseness by six completely manifest

The bodies of the fifteen shot at Dongo, together with those of Mussolini and Claretta Petacci, were then taken to the Piazzale Loreto, a square in Milan, and laid out on the ground in an open display for the public to gaze upon.

Six corpses, including those of the Duce and his mistress, were then selected and suspended by their feet from a girder supporting the roof of a nearby petrol station.

The other four bodies joining this grizzly display were Francesco Barracu, an undersecretary to the cabinet; Alessandro Pavolini, editor of Rome's *Messagero*; Fernando Mezzasomma, a government propagandist, and Paolo Zerbino, the Minister of the Interior. [6]

A seventh body was later added to those suspended. This was the corpse of Achille Starace, the Secretary of the Fascist Party. He was not among those captured in Dongo, but had been recognized and shot in Milan. His body was then added to those in the Piazzale Loreto. "Others and not only Fascists, were disgusted by the gory spectacle, and the bodies were hastily taken down and buried." [7]

Not ever were the Roman people outraged in such a manner

The 'Roman people' in this case, and at that time, were those in Milan.

> Soldiers guarding the bodies were unable to prevent an immense crowd from taking out their anger on the exposed corpses. People spat at them, kicked them, and even pumped more bullets into them. These scenes were filmed by US troops, and postcards of the event became macabre mementoes treasured by thousands of anti-Fascists. [8]

One woman was reported to have fired five shots into Mussolini's body, according to Milan Radio, and shouted: "Five shots for my five assassinated sons!" The anger of the Milanese people had been incensed by the recent killings of partisans in this same square, on orders issued by *Il Duce*.

Summary: *This oracle foretells the aftermath of Mussolini's capture. Numbered among the incidents following his arrest are his friends that were rounded-up while attempting to join him, their deaths, and the deaths and ransacking that was directed against others who had given their support to Fascist policies. Also included is a reference to the harshness of Mussolini's dictatorial powers. Of special note, too, is the grizzly end to Mussolini's time in power, when he was placed among the six suspended upside down from a girder, in full sight of the public. The prophecy ends with the outburst of pent up rage exacted against Mussolini's corpse and his party members by the Italian people.*

21   *Par le despit du Roy soustenant moindre,*
      Sera meurdry luy presentant les bagues,
      Le pere au filz voulant noblesse poindre
      Fait comme à Perse iadis feirent les Magues.

22   *Pour ne vouloir consentir au diuorce,*
      Qui puis apres sera cogneu indigne,
      Le Roy des Isles sera chassé par force,
      Mis à son lieu que de roy n'aura signe.

cogneu (OF) perceived; indigne (OF) undeserving; signe (L sign\um) seal.

1688

For not wishing to consent to the divorce,
Who, then afterwards, will be perceived as undeserving,
The King of the Isles (**JAMES II**) will be expelled by force,
Put in his place, for which a king (**WILLIAM III**), will not have the seal.

In 1685 Charles II died without leaving a legitimate heir, although the Duke of Monmouth (see Century Four N°. 89) did declare that Charles had secretly married his mother, Lucy Walters, thereby legitimising his claim to the throne. This was ignored, and the crown passed to Charles's brother, who became James II.

For not wishing to consent to the divorce

Unhappily for English Protestants, before taking over the reign, James had converted to the Catholic faith, and was therefore one of a number who was still unwilling to consent to the legitimacy of Henry VIII's divorce in the previous century. The divorce had been the cause of England's break with Rome. Consequently, like other practising Catholics, James believed that Henry's divorce remained illegal, and that England had become a Protestant nation under a false pretence. His reign therefore began with an ambition to return the nation to its Catholic roots. [1]

But his ambitious project soon encountered opposition from both Whigs and Tories, especially when the King systematically began dismissing Protestants from positions of authority, and then replacing them with Catholic sympathisers.

Further antagonism arose from across the Channel, when Louis XIV repealed the legislation that gave Huguenots freedom to practise their religion. Thousands of refugees began to arrive in England. And this encouraged fear within the public that James would follow Louis' example. Protestant anxiety finally reached crisis point when, on 10 June 1688, the Queen gave birth to a male heir, James Edward, thus signalling a Catholic succession to the throne.

Who then afterwards will be perceived as undeserving

Historical appraisals of James II have tended to agree with the oracle; that is, after his succession, he will be recognized by his subjects as undeserving. What most antagonised his subjects was James's persistent belief that the Bible asserted the absolute power of the monarch; moreover, he set about implementing this in a way that was considered to be obstinate, short-sighted, and mulish. And, although Pope Innocent XI counselled greater caution, and to beware of alienating the very people he wished to win over, this good advice was ignored. Further still, quite apart from James's preference to place Catholic favourites in positions of power, he also dissolved Parliament (July 1687): his intention being to reopen it with men sympathetic to his aims. [2]

Powerful forces at once united to oppose the King's intention. Emerging from among these dissenting voices was a decision that many fell into agreement with; it was to permit Prince William of Orange to invade England.

When this resolution was put to Parliament and then received the backing of members, James II panicked and tried to reverse the measures that had brought this about. But it was too late. Realizing his error, he fled for the safety of France and the protection of Louis XIV. But at Faversham in Kent, he was apprehended and brought back to Whitehall.

The King of the Isles will be expelled by force

The prophecy now focuses upon Prince William, to whom the throne of England was offered, so that it might be shared jointly with his wife Mary. Before this could be legitimised, James II, despite everything, was still legally the King of England and Scotland – that is, King of the Isles and it was imperative that he be removed. He was therefore ordered to leave the country. On 23 December 1688, under guard, James was expelled by force. At Rochester in Kent, he was placed on board a ship heading for the French coast. Upon arriving in Picardy, he was granted sanctuary and the protection of Louis XIV. [3]

Interestingly, at the time this oracle was written in the middle of the 16th century, there was no 'King of the Isles'. The people of England and Scotland each had their own monarch. This did not change until Queen Elizabeth's death in 1603, when James VI of Scotland was invited to take the English crown as James I.

Of equal interest is the fact that James II was the first, and so far only King of England and its associated territories to be *expelled* from the country *by force*. His expulsion left the way clear for his replacement to be elected into office.

Put in his place

> Seven eminent Englishmen, among them the Tory Earl of Danby and Henry Compton, bishop of London, [had written] inviting William of Orange to come over with an army to redress the nation's grievances.

When news of this invitation reached the Prince in Friesland, he accepted the offer subject to certain conditions being met. Thereafter, in a successful, and unopposed invasion that took place in November 1688 (the Glorious, or Bloodless Revolution), William arrived in England to take his place as King, alongside his sovereign wife Mary. [4]

For which a king will not have the seal

The oracle concludes with an interesting piece of prophecy. During King James' moment of panic; that is, before taking flight from the capital, he first burnt all the writs he had made for electing his new Catholic parliament. Then, taking the great *seal of England* with him, he threw it into the River Thames. Consequently, when William III replaced James II *as King*, he discovered that *he did not have the seal*. This lay somewhere in the mud, at the bottom of the river Thames near Vauxhall. [5]

Summary: *An important piece of English history is foreseen in this oracle. The legitimate succession of James II was absolved by Parliament on the grounds of the monarch's affection for the Catholic faith. Protestants were able to gather enough political 'clout' to safeguard their interests. As a result, a new line of succession was introduced to the English monarchy, which replaced the direct line of the Stuarts. This brought William of Orange and his wife Mary to the throne and with it, the preservation of Protestantism in England. The loss of the great seal of England is another prophetic gem, because it is specific, yet of minor significance to the greater drama of which it was a part.*

23   *Au peuple ingrat faictes les remonstrances,*
        Par lors l'armée se saisira d'Antibe,
        Dans l'arc Monech feront les doleances,
        Et à Freius l'vn l'autre prendra ribe.

se saisir (OF) lay hands on; l' arc (L arc\us) curve, & *anagrammatic paragram:* Ne aNc - Canne; Monech (L Monoecis) Monaco; doleance (OF) complaining; autre (OF) different; ribe (OF) rive) coast *or* shoreline.

The remonstrances made by the ungrateful people,   1815
In that time, the army will lay hands on Antibes:
Within the curve (Cannes), Monaco: they will make complaints,
And to Fréjus, the one (**NAPOLEON**) will take the different shoreline.

On 3 May 1814 Louis XVIII entered Paris. The monarchy had been restored in France and Napoleon Bonaparte was an exile on the island of Elba. The end of the Napoleonic period was expected to herald a period of relief after almost two decades of continuous warfare.

The remonstrances made by the ungrateful people

Instead, there were protests. These came predominantly from the country folk. The French Revolution had driven out the nobles, and divided up the land amongst the people. But with the return of the monarchy came talk of land reform, and this was accompanied by fear that the government might reverse the gains made by the people. Some became resentful, harking back to an earlier time of French greatness, and the man who had ruled them. To add to this, the huge armies employed by Napoleon had since been reduced for economic reasons, and many soldiers, with years of service behind them, suddenly found themselves unemployed, unwanted, and very hungry. Paris soon became a hotbed of dissent, especially amongst disaffected officers on half-pay, who were airing their grievances to each other.

On 27 February 1815, Napoleon, having been informed of the rising level of dissent, left Elba and secretly headed for the French coast and one last gamble at regaining his lost empire. When news of his escape reached Paris a plethora of painted slogans went on display: 'Down with the Priests!' 'Down with the nobles!' 'Death to the Royalists!' 'Bourbons to the Scaffold!' These protests by people, ungrateful at the restoration of peace in France, were viewed to be so life-threatening that Louis XVIII was forced to make a hurried exit from Paris, and he fled to Ghent. [1]

In that time, the army will lay hands on Antibes

On 1 March, Napoleon's flotilla dropped anchor in the *Golfe Jouan*, which lies between *Antibes* and *Fréjus*. Captain Lamouret, accompanied by a party of twenty soldiers, set off to capture an observation post outside Antibes. Captain Henri Bertrand followed this up by entering the town to deliver Bonaparte's proclamation and collect passports. It was a misjudgement. Inside Antibes, the military commander lost little time in arresting Bertrand and taking him away for interrogation. This led to Lamouret taking his troop into Antibes and seizing the garrison. But the local commander responded by quickly surrounding the fortress, leaving the French soldiers penned up inside. It was a poor start to Napoleon's ambitions, especially since, "efforts to free the soldiers under arrest in Antibes [...] proved nugatory." [2]

Within the curve (Cannes), Monaco

After coming ashore, and being advised of the advance party's arrest, Bonaparte headed away from *Antibes*, along the coast to Cannes, where he set up camp among the dunes. Cannes lies on the crescent coastline of the Gulf of Napoule, and the curve of its sandy shoreline has given distinction to an excellent promenade (*Promenade de la Croisette*) lined with palm trees. [3]

It was while Napoleon was encamped outside Cannes that Prince Honoré IV of Monaco passed by in his carriage. Napoleon at once summoned him to his tent and invited the Prince to join his expedition. But the Prince warily replied that he was going home. To which Napoleon replied, – "So am I." [4]

They will make complaints

A further incident occurred while Napoleon's men were encamped outside Cannes. A local butcher had apparently devised a plot to murder Bonaparte. Armed with a musket, he declared that he would assassinate the former Emperor. But the citizens of Cannes became fearful that the attempt might result in terrible repercussions, even in deaths and their houses burnt down. After hearing their complaints, the would-be assassin relented, and gave up the idea. [5]

And to Fréjus, the one will take the different shoreline

Napoleon's arrival back in France in 1815 was that of a wanted man, threatened with arrest. His journey after disembarking at "Juan Bay, between Fréjus and Antibes" began in the direction of Antibes. But the arrest of his two captains Lamouret and Bertrand inside the town, forced him to change direction and he headed, instead, to Fréjus, taking the shoreline to Cannes.

By "purposely avoiding Marseilles and the department of Provence with its traditional royalist sympathies," he moved inland to Grasse, then on to Castellane, Gap, and Laffrey, before entering Grenoble. By then, it seemed to him that he had regained the acceptance of the people. "Before Grenoble I was an adventurer;" he said. "At Grenoble I was a ruling prince." [6]

Summary: *This prophecy addresses the post-Napoleonic period, during which France attempted to adjust to its former monarchical rule. But the people grew restless, and when Napoleon, while in exile on the island of Elba, learned of their unrest, he gambled on returning to power. This oracle foretells the chain of incidents that met his return to the French mainland. By including the Prince of Monaco in the oracle, it serves to emphasise that the future is not just composed of major events, but that day-to-day incidents also have their place on each person's biographical time line.*

24   *Le captif prince aux Italles vaincu,*
       Passera Gennes par mer iusqu'à Marseille,
       Par grand effort des forens suruaincu:
       Sauf coup de feu barril liqueur d'abeille.

25   *Par Nebro ouurir de Brisanne passage,*
       Bien eslongnez el tago fara muestra,
       Dans Pelligouxe sera commis l'outrage
       De la grand dame assise sur l'orchestra.

26   *Le successeur vengera son beau frere,*
       Occuper regne souz vmbre de vengeance,
       Occis ostacle son sang mort vitupere,
       Long temps Bretaigne tiendra auec la France.

27   *Par le cinquieme & vn grand Herculés*
       Viendront le temple ouurir de main bellique,
       Vn Clement, Iule & Ascans reculés,
       Lespe, clef, aigle n'eurent onc si grand picque.

28   Second & tiers qui font prime musique
      Sera par Roy en honneur sublimee,
      Par grasse & maigre presque à demy eticque
      Raport de Venus faulx randra deprimee.

29   De Pol MANSOL dans cauerne caprine,
      Caché & prins extrait hors par la barbe:
      Captif mené comme beste mastine,
      Par Begourdans amenee pres de Tarbe.

30   Nepueu & sang du sainct nouueau venu,
      Par le surnom soustient arcs & couuert
      Seront chassez mis à mort chassez nu,
      En rouge & noir conuertiront leur vert.

31   Le saint empire viendra en Germanie,
      Ismaelites trouueront lieux ouuerts.
      Anes vouldront aussi la Carmanie:
      Les soustenens de terre tous couuerts.

Line 3 reads: 'Asses will also want Carmania.' This refers to a region situated to the east of Fars province, equivalent to Kerman, and is mentioned in Alexander's conquests. It is interesting to note that the people of Carmania used donkeys when they fought battles. (*Encyclopædia Iranica*)

32   Le grand empire chacun an deuoir estre,
      Vn sur les autres le viendra obtenir,
      Mais peu de temps sera son regne & estre,
      Deux ans aux naues se pourra soustenir.

33   La faction cruelle à robbe longue
      Viendra cacher souz les pointus poignars
      Saisir Florence le duc & lieu diphlongue,
      Sa descouuerte par immeurs & flangnards.

34   Gauloys qu'empire par guerre occupera,
      Par son beau frere mineur sera trahy,
      Par cheual rude voltigeant traynera,
      Du fait le frere long temps sera hay.

Gaulois (OF) of France, French, a Frenchman; voltigeant (OF) curvetting; Cross-reference: Gaulois, C.IV: 37.

The Frenchman (**NAPOLEON**) that will occupy the empire by war,   1814
By his lesser brother-in-law (**MURAT**), he will be betrayed,
He will languish for a rough curvetting horse,
The brother will be hated a long time for the deed.

The Frenchman

Napoleon was born a Frenchman through the fortunate circumstance of Corsica having been acquired by the Genoese two weeks before his birth. It was this legal nicety that bestowed French citizenship upon him. By doing so, it qualified him for the military education in France that was to lead eventually to him becoming Emperor and conqueror of much of mainland Europe.

That will occupy the empire by war

Napoleon's reign as Emperor of France lasted from 1804 until 1814. During that period, and a little before, when he was appointed First Consul, five separate coalitions opposed the Empire by war. The nations that took part in these were drawn from Britain, Austria, Russia, Turkey, Naples, Portugal, Prussia, Sweden, Saxony and Spain. As a result of these coalitions, France was compelled to fight a great many battles, which afterwards became household names; e.g., Pyramids, Nile, Marengo, Hohenlinden, Ulm, Trafalgar, Austerlitz, Jena, Eylau, Friedland, Aspern, Wagram, Smolensk, Borodino; and these are given without a mention of those fought in the Peninsula War. Understandably, the expression 'Napoleonic Wars' soon became a recognized generalization for this period in history, for the conflicts were "massive in their geographic scope, ranging [...] over all of the five continents." [1]

By his lesser brother-in-law

In 1800 Napoleon's youngest sister, eighteen-year-old Caroline, married the dashing cavalry leader Joachim Murat. Seven years later, the Emperor rewarded his sister and *brother-in-law* with the throne of Naples. Whence, it follows that King Joachim of Naples was a *lesser brother-in-law* than the Emperor, who bestowed the title upon him. [2]

He will be betrayed

The betrayal referred to in this oracle occurred in 1814. It also became the motivation for a book *The Betrayers: Joachim and Caroline Murat*, by historian Hubert Cole. " 'Sire, I have just concluded a treaty with Austria,' " Joachim wrote to Napoleon on January 15, 1814. " 'He, who for so long fought at your side, your brother-in-law, your friend, has signed an act which appears to give him a hostile attitude towards you.' " Murat was referring to a treaty he had entered into with Austria at the time he and his wife were King and Queen of Naples. The treaty was intended to unify central and southern Italy by bringing the Neapolitans into Rome at the expense of evacuating Napoleon's occupying forces inside the eternal city. But Murat realised, far too late to remedy the situation, that he had been outmanoeuvred by the wily Austrians. [3]

He will languish for a rough curvetting horse

Although a king, Murat had become despondent through this change in occupation, and he began to dwell upon his former life as a cavalry leader, and victor of many memorable battles. Instead of activity, he was now languishing as a politician and administrator in the Court of Naples " 'The King appears to be extremely bored and seeks every opportunity to escape from the inactivity which wearies him to death,' reported Aubusson." It may be noted, in passing, that the Louvre in Paris owns a huge portrait of Joachim Murat astride a prancing cavalry horse. [4]

The brother will be hated a long time for the deed

When Napoleon heard what had happened, he raged against *his brother-in-law's betrayal*, and never forgave him for his treachery, refusing even to call upon him for aid when the Emperor's need was at its greatest. Even, "the allies showed little consideration for Murat, who in their eyes was still only the defaulting henchman of Bonaparte." [5]

Summary: *The betrayal of Joachim Murat at a time when he was the Emperor Napoleon's brother-in-law is well documented in history. The fact that he is also foreseen languishing for a cavalry type of horse confirms his status as a horse rider. This prophecy apparently caused a flurry of interest in the New York Times of 4 January 1942. According to author Stewart Robb, Professor Jacques Barzun, who later became dean and provost of Columbia University, had felt a need to give serious attention to these prophecies, based upon the strength of this one prediction. Another academic was associate mathematician, Professor Siceloff. He considered the probability of these predictions combining in the manner they had, solely by chance, was so close to zero that it could be discounted.*

35   *Puysnay royal flagrand d'ardant lIbide,*
      Pour se iouyr de cousine germaine
      Habit de femme au temple d'Arthemide:
      Allant murdry par incognu du Marne.

36   *Apres le Roy du soucq guerres parlant,*
      L'isle Harmotique le tiendra à mespris:
      Quelques ans bons rongeant vn & pillant
      Par tyrannie à l'isle changeant pris.

37   *L'assemblee grande pres du lac de Borget,*
      Se ralieront pres de Montmelian:
      Marchans plus oultre pensifz feront proget,
      Chambry, Moriane combat sainct Iulian.

assemblee (OF) an encounter of two armies; marchans,(OF – marchand) marching; proget (projet) a plan.

The huge encounter of two armies close to Lake Bourget:
They will rally close to Montmélian:
Marching beyond, thoughtful, they will make a plan,
Chambéry, Maurienne a conflict, SAINT JULIAN.

The huge encounter of two armies close to Lake Bourget

Henri IV of France had obtained his kingdom during the French Wars of Religion. In 1598, he signed the Edict of Nantes, which brought the Wars to an end by granting Huguenots religious freedom. But his discontent with the Duke of Savoy, who had taken advantage of the civil unrest in France, caused him to declare war on Savoy, which he did on 11 August 1600. (Century Nine N°. 45 refers to this war.)

> The French troops, who at first numbered 8,000 men quickly increased to double that number. The Master of French artillery, the Marquis de Rosny directed the commissaires from Lyonnais and Dauphine, as well as commissioned officers from Burgundy, Provence and Languedoc with their best cannon, which provided, in a very short time, a considerable amount of artillery with abundant ammunition. On August 11, the war was declared, and the king of France ordered Marshals Biron and Lesdiguières to enter the Duchy of Savoy. [1]

The campaign against Savoy began with Marshal Biron capturing Bourg-en-Bresse on 13 August. This was followed by the conquest of Bresse, Bugey and Gex.

Lake Bourget is approximately 12 kilometres from Chambéry, which in turn is barely 5 km from Montmélian: both of which are included in this prophecy. It therefore forms a focal point for the conflict between the armies of France and Savoy.

They will rally close to Montmélian

At the beginning of the war, the Duke of Savoy …

> took no concern because he relied upon the strength of his squares and the assistance of allies to defeat the King of France. [2] However, the fortresses of which the Duke of Savoy was so proud began to fall, one after the other.

Only "the citadel town of Montélian still resisted."

> François de Bonne Lesdiguières had been charged with the responsibility for the valleys of Maurienne and of Tarentaise: which permitted the dividing of all the reinforcements arriving. [3]

Before beginning the siege of the citadel, which was considered impregnable The French troops of Marshal Lesdiguières attacked the city of Montmélian

French historian Jean-Pierre Babelon wrote that the town of Montmélian fell to Lesdiguières on 17 August, after two days of fighting. [4]

> Charles II Créquy, colonel of the regiment, and Abel Berenger Morges, captain of the French Guards, both serving under Marshal Lesdiguières, began their attack on the city from different sides. Créquy laid an explosive at the door of the Capuchins, where it made a big enough gap to allow 7 companies into town. The explosive used by Morges was insufficient to make more than a small hole, and a cannon had to be used to break down the door. After two days of fighting the city of Montmélian fell. With the city taken, the French commander perceiving it would not be easy to take the citadel divided his forces into two bodies, leaving several forces to block it. [5]

Marching beyond, thoughtful, they will make a plan

Although Montmélian had been taken with little difficulty, the citadel posed a more difficult problem. It was built on rock, well armed, and one of the most famous in Europe. In command of the citadel was Count Brandis, who said with confidence it would become "the graveyard of the French." Nevertheless, the citadel was placed under siege, while the main body of French troops under Lesdiguières continued their conquest by *marching beyond* Maurienne into Tarantaise. But after returning from the Tarentaise and having chased the Savoyard troops beyond the col du Petit-Saint-Bernard, Lesdiguières took up position at Moutiers to await troops for the task of overcoming the citadel at Montmélian. The Duke of Sully then sought and received permission from the King to use his artillery against the citadel.

Sully, who was commander-in-chief of the Royal artillery, began by completing a full survey of the fortress and its surrounds. Having satisfied himself of the difficulty, he began implementing *his plan*. Under the cover of night, he concealed behind the trees 31 guns in 7 batteries. "A battery of four cannons was then installed on the hillside, and another battery of five guns placed at the *Maison Rouge*." With similar precision, he placed a battery of five cannons inside the city itself, and another four, also inside the city, pointing at the nearby castle of Perugia. A further four cannons were emplaced on the banks of the river Isère, aimed at the walls of the citadel.

On 14 October the bombardment began. One month later, on 16 November Count Brandis surrendered the citadel, which had been under siege since the city was taken on 17 August. [6]

Chambéry

The troops of Louis des Balbes Berton de Crillon, which were composed of French Guards, the Swiss Guard and the Regiment of the Bourg de Lespinasse then invested Chambéry. The French stormed the outskirts of the Recluse and Montmélian, which constitutes the suburbs of Savoy's capital Chambéry (the suburb called Montmélian should not be confused with the town of the same name located 17 km from Chambéry).

However during the night two French companies, believing they were fighting the enemy, fought with such fury that the ground was strewn with dead and wounded, which delayed the taking of the city on August 17. The Savoy garrison, under the command of Count Chabod Jacob, sought refuge in the fortified castle of Chambéry, where he surrendered upon the arrival of Henri IV, on 23 August. [7]

Maurienne, a conflict

After the castle at Conflans surrendered to the French on 27 August, there only remained the fortress Charbonniã Res, which, as Henri IV foresaw, was "une place dont on n'aurait pas bon marché." (A place that one would not possess cheaply). It stood on the top of a rock and was inaccessible except via a narrow path to the gatehouse. It was therefore a "key defence of the Maurienne defended by some companies of Piedmont Bindi regiment under the command of Governor Humbert de Saix, lord of Arnens." [8]

On August 28, French troops invaded the place, but their first difficulty was the approach, within range of the guns. Their only way was along a very narrow conduit, bordered on one side by the river Arc, which met the pathway: while on the other side were inaccessible rocks. [9]

Realizing the difficulty, the Duke of Sully reconnoitred the area during nightfall. Next day he ordered the bombardment of the fortress, compelling its surrender. On 10 September 1600, "the French troops of Marshal Lesdiguières took the castle Charbonniã res." [10]

The taking of Charbonniã res opened the way for Lesdiguières to occupy the top of the valley of the Arc. Accompanied by a thousand men, he was able to take Saint-Jean-de-Maurienne and Saint-Michel de-Maurienne. By 18 September, the French army had completely conquered the Maurienne valley. [11]

Saint Julian

Saint Julian of Auvergne was a "Martyred officer of the Roman army, also called Julian of Brioude. He was from France. [...] he died 304 AD." [12] "Saint Julian's feast day" is celebrated on "28 August".

It was on the 28th August that the conflict against the besieged castle Charbonniã res began. It is therefore noteworthy that this is the fourth example of the Seer having employed the name of a saint whose feast day coincides with the event predicted. The other three examples are Saint Solano (14 July, 'Bastille Day'); Saint Lucy (13 December, 'Massacre of La Vendée'), and Saint Agnes (21 January, 'Beheading of King Louis XVI).

As this final chapter of oracles draws to a close, it is to be recalled that the fulfilment of these prophecies, and more especially those that include the date of their fulfilment, is intended to establish the promised proof from history that we—by which I mean all of mankind—are living in a block universe, as was also concluded mathematically by Einstein, and by physicists of the modern age—although they remain loath to admit it. Acknowledgment would deprive scientists of *cause* and *effect*, and with it their authority as explicators of nature and the universe.

The author of these oracles had reached the same conclusion about the universe, for he admitted in his letter to Henri II, dated 27 June 1558. "Had I wished to give every quatrain its detailed date, it could easily have been done, but it would not have been agreeable to all, no less interpreting them."

In a previous letter addressed to his infant son César, dated 1 march 1555, the Seer gave the biblical reason for not having done so; it is the same reason which Jesus gave to his disciples. "It is not for you to know the times or dates the Father has set by his own authority." (Acts I: 7).

In the same letter, the Seer also declared that "past, present and future are clasped in one eternity", where "Nothing in all creation is hidden from God's sight. Everything is uncovered and laid bare before the eyes of him to whom we must give account." (Hebrews IV: 13). Insofar as what has been written in these ten chapters, the Seer spoke truly.

Summary: *Although this oracle was first published some forty years before the events it predicted were fulfilled, it accurately describes Henri IV's war of 1600-01 against the Duke of Savoy. The places named were all locations of conflict in Savoy, where the war took place. And, even the exact date of one battle fought during that war has been stated. How foolish, therefore, are the politicians who, ignorant of God, blind to the reality of His Creation, and brainwashed by scientism into believing the imperceptible, counterfeit universe, cobbled together by different and conflicting theories from separate disciplines, is superior to the greater and consistent truth of God. As we see from this oracle all wars once existed in the future, were fought in the present and then receded into history— full of sound and fury, signifying nothing other than their truth.*

38   *Amour alegre non loin pose le siege,*
      Au sainct barbar seront les garnisons,
      Vrsins Hadrie pour Gaulois feront plaige,
      Pour peut rendus de l'armée aux Grisons.

39   *Premier fils vefue mal'heureux mariage,*
      Sans nuls enfans deux Isles en discord,
      Auant dixhuict incompetant eage,
      De l'autre prés plus bas sera l'accord.

vefue (OF veufve),widow; eage (OF) age; prés OF) nigh unto; bas (OF) abject;

The first son (**FRANCIS II**), widow (**MARY STUART**), an unfortunate marriage,   1560
Without children, not any: two Isles in discord (**ENGLAND & SCOTLAND**),
Before eighteen, an incompetent age,
Of the other nigh unto (**CHARLES IX**), harmony will be much less.

The first son, widow

The first son of France, [1] up until the death of Henri II was the dauphin, François. After his father's fatal accident, and not yet sixteen, he became King Francis II. His wife, Mary Stuart, whom he married in April 1558, was history's tragic queen, popularly known as Mary Queen of Scots. She became a widow upon the death of her young husband in December 1560. [2]

Incidentally, this is the fourth quatrain recognized for its accuracy by historian Norman Davies, and mentioned in his book, *Europe A History* (1997). It is also referred to for its importance by another historian, Ian Wilson.

Its significance has arisen from a previous objection that this prophecy may not have been in print until after the event, which would cast doubt upon its precognitive content. This is because no known copy of the 1558 edition has survived. However, Wilson has made available the following salient facts in his 2002 biography of the

FRANCIS II

Seer: *Nostradamus The Evidence* (p. 200).

Firstly, Queen Elizabeth's ambassador to France, Sir Nicholas Throckmorton, reported that on 29 November, the court believed the King would not recover from his illness. "Whereupon there immediately broke out amongst Throckmorton's fellow ambassadors talk of a quatrain in the third and final section of Nostradamus's *Prophecies*. This has to refer to the 1558 edition [...] which must have already existed, and been in circulation, because of the ambassadors' very discussion of it." This is also backed up by the Venetian ambassador to France, Michele Surano. He "reported back to Venice in a dispatch sent from Orléans on November 20, 1560."

> 'And they [the court] discussed also a prophecy made by the astrologers, to the effect that he [Francois II] would not reach the eighteenth year of his age.' [...] at the same time another Venetian ambassador, Giovanni Michieli, even quoted the exact chapter and verse for the prophecy, thereby confirming that the tenth and last 'Century' must have been in print; 'Each courtier remembers the thirty-ninth quatrain of *Century X* of Nostradamus and comments upon it under his breath.'"

Unfortunate marriage, without children, not any

The marriage did, indeed, prove to be unfortunate, and without children. Francis was ill-conditioned for matrimony. Sickly from childhood, it was said that he had still to reach puberty, even into his seventeenth year. [3] *Not any* is also subtly prophetic. It distinguishes between legitimate and illegitimate children. Both Charles IX and Henri III, who succeeded Francis, produced offspring that were illegitimate, but neither fathered a legitimate heir to the throne.

Two Isles in discord

In November 1558, Elizabeth I succeeded to the English throne, but only amidst controversy. Some wanted a Catholic queen, and Mary Stuart was the popular choice to fulfil that role. In fact, Mary Queen of Scotland actually proclaimed herself 'Queen of England', thus potentially uniting England and Scotland. But in 1559, the Scottish nobles rose up in revolt against the English, and the two kingdoms in the British Isles were placed in discord. [4]

From 1560 onwards, as a result of the disagreement between England and Scotland, John Knox was able to establish a Calvinist regime north of the border. This further added to the religious divisions of that time.

Before eighteen

Meanwhile, across the English Channel, the death of sixteen-year-old Francis II meant that Mary's role as Queen of France was of short duration. The young King died on 5 December 1560, just three days before Mary's 18th birthday—a widow before eighteen. And, with Francis having reigned for a little *less than eighteen* months, the significance of this number is doubled. [5] The predicted death of Francis was also referred to by the Tuscan ambassador, Niccolò Tornabuoni in a letter sent to the Duke of Cosimo on 3 December 1560.

> The King's state of health remains ever uncertain [...] This is what the people are saying. And in particular Nostradamus, by prophecy, for his predictions for this month he says 'One most young will lose the monarchy because of an unexpected illness.' [6]

An incompetent age

The years immediately following Henri II's fatal accident in 1559 became the prelude to an age of political incompetence. [7] First in line for the throne had been Francis II, a sickly boy of fifteen, who became easy prey for the powerful and influential Guise family. His ten-year-old brother, Charles IX, was next on the throne. But, being fatherless, young and without political judgement he, too, was easily influenced by the power-hungry factions surrounding him. The unrest this caused in the country would, before long, turn to civil war.

Of the other nigh unto, harmony will be much less

The youthful inexperience of these royal juveniles allowed their adult seniors, the 'princes of the blood', to compete for power in the political vacuum caused by the want of a strong leader to keep them in their place. This became evident in 1560, during the reign of Francis II, when the discord between Catholics and Protestants erupted into the 'Tumult of Amboise'.

Determined to stop the persecution and have Protestantism officially recognised, a group of noblemen planned the Amboise conspiracy to overthrow the government and give power to the Princes of the Blood, who supported the new religion. The conspirators planned to take over the palace with the help of the royal guard, abduct the king, then eliminate the Guises if they offered any resistance. A substantial external military deployment was intended to secure the operation. [8]

The plan failed when "two hundred men tried to storm one of the city gates at the foot of the castle." [9] They were repelled and pursued without mercy. "More than a hundred were executed, some even hanged from the ramparts of the castle. The retaliation continued for several weeks, and almost twelve hundred people died." [10]

After Francis II's death, Charles IX, his younger brother ('the other nigh unto'), succeeded to the reign under the regency of his mother, Catherine de' Medici. [11] Powerful and opposing forces were again prominent, ready to go to war for control of the weakened throne. Within two years of Charles's succession, France had succumbed to the iron grip of its Wars of Religion, in which the accord between Catholics and Protestants descended to its nadir.

In May 1574, Charles IX died: already a broken man, and not yet twenty-four years of age. [12] He never recovered from the Massacre of St Bartholomew's Eve.

The massacre began in the night of 23–24 August 1572 (the eve of the feast of Bartholomew the Apostle) [...] The king ordered the killing of a group of Huguenot leaders, including Coligny, and the slaughter spread throughout Paris. Lasting several weeks, the massacre expanded outward to other urban centres and the countryside. Modern estimates for the number of dead across France vary widely, from 5,000 to 30,000. [13]

Summary: *The importance of this oracle exists in the fact that letters sent from the French court by foreign ambassadors during the life and death of Francis II, confirm that this oracle was known to them. Thus extinguishing all doubt as to the true provenance of the seer's later 'Centuries'. But even more than this, it also confirms the seriousness attending these oracles at the time, particularly by learned men. They recognized the truth of what they read, and were free from the scientific brainwashing that in the present age, would have rinsed it clear of intelligent acceptance. The facts relating to Francis II and Mary – a widow 'before 18' – are undeniable, and although the young King's delicate nature would have been recognized by the seer, the future outcome could not have been predicted with certainty, unless it had been divinely inspired.*

40   *Le ieune nay au regne Britannique,*
       Qu'aura le pere mourant recommandé,
       Iceluy mort LONOLE donra topique,
       Et à son fils le regne demandé.

iceluy,(OF) the same man; LONOLE (*anagram & paragram:* OLE NOL) OLD NOL; donra (*syncope:* donnera); topique (OF) remedy

The young man born to the Britannic reign (**CHARLES 1**),   1625
Who, the father, (**JAMES 1**) departing this life, will have recommended:
The same man dead, **OLD NOL** will offer a remedy,
Thus, to his (**JAMES'S**) son, the reign is demanded.

The young man born to the Britannic reign

The young man, to whom this oracle refers, is Charles I. The clue to his identity exists in the word 'Britannic'. Charles was born on 19 November 1600 to James I of England—also James VI of Scotland. James succession to the crown in 1603 united Scotland with England.

In the Renaissance tradition, Britannia came to be viewed as the personification of Britain, in imagery that was developed during the reign of Elizabeth I. With the death of Elizabeth in 1603 came the succession of her Scottish cousin, James VI, King of Scots, to the English throne. He became James I of England, and so brought under his personal rule the Kingdoms of England (and the dominion of Wales), Ireland and Scotland. On 20 October 1604, James VI and I proclaimed himself as "King of Great Brittaine, France and Ireland," a title that continued to be used by many of his successors. [1]

Who, the father departing this life, will have recommended

It was shortly after James concluded the marriage arrangements with Louis XIII of France, which involved the betrothal of the French princess to his son the Prince of Wales that he fell ill.

He was seized with a tertian ague; and after some fits found himself extremely weakened. He sent for the Prince of Wales, and gave him instructions for his future conduct, with regard to public and domestic affairs. He exhorted him to bear a tender affection for his wife, but to preserve a constancy in religion: to protect the Church of England, and to extend his care to the palatine's unhappy family. He then prepared himself with courage and decent resignation to meet the king of terrors, and died on the twenty-seventh of March, in the forty-ninth year of his age, and the twenty-third of his reign. [2]

The same man dead, Old Nol will offer a remedy

After the death of his father James I (the same man dead), the Prince of Wales became King Charles I. His coronation took place on 2 February 1626. In the course of his reign, the British parliament, at first little more than an advisory council, grew in strength until it became an instrument of power and a divisive cause between those supporting the King's right to rule and Parliament's right to decide law. The English Civil War (1642-51) was the outcome.

It was this conflict that brought Oliver Cromwell (Old Noll) to the forefront of the political scene. "(Noll. *Old Noll.* Oliver Cromwell was so called by the Royalists. Noll is a familiar contraction of Oliver—*i.e.* Ol' with an initial liquid.)" [3] Hence, by transposing the first two letters of LONOLE, we obtain OLNOLE, from which, OLD NOL' with 'D' replacing 'E' forms a paragram, or Ol' Nol.

Cromwell's opportunity came after the King had been captured and placed under protective custody on the Isle of Wight, thus effectively depriving him of his power.

> In 1647-8 he argued in favour of a settlement with the king that would require him to accept Cromwell's political allies as his ministers and which would guarantee rights of religious liberty for all sincere protestants. This brought him into conflict with those in Parliament who wanted to replace the old Church of England, with a new 'Presbyterian' Church based on the teachings of Calvin and the experience of Geneva and Scotland, but also with more radical voices that wanted a much more democratic system of government - the right of all adult males to vote, for example. For too long, Cromwell trusted in the King's willingness to agree to his proposals. When, instead, he escaped from army custody and launched a second civil war, Cromwell rounded on him and hounded him to death. [4]

> The king's alliance with the Scots and his subsequent defeat in the Second Civil War convinced Cromwell that the king must be brought to justice. He was a prime mover in the trial and execution of Charles I in 1649 and subsequently sought to win conservative support for the new republic by suppressing radial elements in the army. [5]

Thus, to his son, the reign is demanded

When Charles II heard of his father's execution, he immediately took the title of King and returned to Britain prepared to raise troops from Scotland and the English Presbyterians, but found neither of these sources willing to take up arms against Cromwell. In response, Parliament, at the instigation of Cromwell issued an *Act* "forbidding the abetting of Charles Stuart or any of his adherents, on pain of high treason. They ordered the militia of the several counties to be drawn out to oppose his march." [6] The end came at the battle of Worcester on 3 September 1651 (see p.476), when Cromwell defeated the royalists, forced Charles into exile, and took the reign for himself.

Summary: *Names given in these prophecies always attract remark—as if it were somehow possible that the events predicted could be fulfilled without those who made them history having taken part. In this case, the first two letters of Oliver (Ol, a recognized abbreviation for Oliver) have been combined with the word (noll) defined as "Crown of) head" (OED) to make OL NOLL. The seer's familiar strategy of combining an anagram with a paragram results in LONOLE, which is signalled for special attention by his use of capital letters. Apart from this, the accompanying prophecy confirms the period in which it came to be fulfilled. The dying speech by James I recommending his son as King is a matter of historical record: as, too, is the action initiated by Cromwell to rid England of Charles I. After which, it was then necessary to prevent the dead King's son from inheriting the Crown, which he accomplished at Worcester.*

41   *En la frontiere de Caussade & Charlus,*
         Non guieres loing du fonds de la valee,
         De ville Franche musicque à son de luths,
         Enuironnez combouls & grand myttee.

42   *Le regne humain d'Anglique geniture,*
      Fera son regne paix vnion tenir,
      Captiue guerre demy de sa closture,
      Long temps la paix leur fera maintenir.

43   *Le trop bon temps, trop de bonté royalle:*
      Fais & deffais prompt, subit, negligence,
      Legier croira faux d'espouse loyalle.
      Luy mis à mort par sa beneuolence.

fais (AF - peine) anxiety, trouble; deffaict (AF defait – mal, malheure) evil; legier (OF) readily; lui (OF) the same man.

(**For MARIE ANTOINETTE**), the too many good times, too much royal bounty,   1785
An evil & rapid anxiety (**over the DIAMOND NECKLACE**), unexpected, negligence:
Readily, he (**LOUIS XVI**) will believe false, concerning his loyal wife.
The same man put to death (**GUILLOTINED**) through his benevolence.

The too many good times

Marie Antoinette's entry into the social whirl of French court life soon drew notice, and was to set the standard by which her 'too many good times' were becoming judged. Elaborate hairstyles, parties, the latest fashion, dancing, masked balls, and visits to the opera and theatre, which were often preceded by attendance at race meetings held in the Bois de Boulogne.

The Queen had also become addicted to gambling, and her participation in card games would go on through the night, with her losses paid out of the King's purse, while her winnings were collected for herself, from distraught courtiers. At Versailles, a little village was even constructed for her pleasure, set amidst meandering streams and rustic bridges, where she was able to dwell in a sylvan paradise constructed from her personal fantasies. [1]

Too much royal bounty

By 1776, the Queen's dress allowance had grown from 150,000 livres to half a million. "The King paid up 'at her very first word' according to Mercy. Again when she bought a pair of diamond bracelets for 400,000 livres, she had to borrow from the King, who did not complain." Added to these extravagances were those of the Queen's household: it was a privilege of the maids at that time to acquire her "garments once discarded but hardly worn." [2]

An evil and rapid anxiety

Charles Auguste Böhmer and his partner Paul Bassenge were the official Court Jewellers. Some time prior to 1785, they had produced "an elaborate, many-looped diamond necklace [...] It consisted of 647 diamonds, gemstones of the highest quality; its weight was 2800 carats." [3] The necklace, worth between one-and-a-half and two million francs, was offered for sale to Marie Antoinette, but she declined to buy it. Thereafter, a maze of confused assumptions followed.

Cardinal Rohan, who was descended from one of the more illustrious families of France, received a letter, allegedly from the Queen, requesting that he purchase the necklace for her. In fact, a woman, Nicole d'Oliva – *aka* le Guay – had impersonated the Queen. And in doing so, had successfully duped the Cardinal into believing he was to act secretly as Marie Antoinette's agent.

The Cardinal happily obliged, thinking to enjoy royal favour as a reward. Unaware of what was happening behind her back, Marie Antoinette was surprised to receive a letter from Böhmer, who had lately become worried that the Queen had not yet worn the necklace, nor had he been repaid the money promised to him (12 July 1785). Unable to comprehend the content of this letter, the Queen dismissed it, and impulsively used it as a lighter to melt the wax on her correspondence. [4]

When Böhmer received no reply to his letter, and subsequently learned that it had been burnt, he angrily remonstrated with Madame Campan (First Lady of the Bedchamber) "That's impossible! The Queen knows she has money to pay me!" [5]

Thereafter, the story slowly began to emerge. Marie Antoinette had obviously been made the innocent victim of a conspiracy to defraud Böhmer. Behind it was the Comtesse, Jeanne de

Lamotte Valois (impoverished, but claiming to be descended from Henri II). She had forged the signature of Marie Antoinette on the letter she sent to Cardinal Rohan, requesting that he purchase the necklace on the Queen's behalf.

Unexpected, negligence

The affair of the Diamond Necklace had been so completely unexpected that when the letter from Böhmer arrived 'out of the blue', the Queen's negligence in dealing with it at the very outset had allowed the matter to grow into a monster of the moment. "The Queen's complete surprise and shock is well attested, as is the way she persistently underrated the seriousness of what was happening in the months to come." [6]

Readily he will believe false, concerning his loyal wife

"Louis XVI's instinctive and honourable support of his wife was the next key element in the affair." [7] At noon on 15 August, Louis XVI took action. He summoned the Queen and Cardinal Rohan to his inner cabinet. There, the full truth was disclosed. The Cardinal had been duped into believing the signature of the Queen was genuine, and from thereon, he had acted improperly, hoping to ingratiate himself in the eyes of the Queen. The King was outraged.

> The letter was neither written nor signed by the Queen. How could a prince of the House of Rohan, the Grand Almoner himself, ever think that the Queen would sign 'Marie Antoinette de France'? All the world knew that queens signed only their baptismal names. The Cardinal did not answer. Pale and bewildered, he felt unable to speak further in the royal presence...
> The forged signature 'Marie Antoinette de France' turned out to be a key element in the Diamond Necklace Affair because it prejudiced Louis XVI against the Cardinal. Breathing royal etiquette since birth, the King simply could not understand how a courtier, and above all a Rohan, a member of a family keen on the details of status, could make such a mistake. [8]

Cardinal Rohan was made to stand trial for his part in the duplicity, and imprisoned, albeit comfortably in the Bastille. After his release, he suffered banishment. Jeanne de Lamotte Valois was dealt with more harshly. She was stripped naked, with a hangman's noose about her neck, and whipped by the public executioner before a red-hot iron accidentally branded her breast instead of her shoulder with 'V' (voleuse—thief), She was then sent to Salpêtrière with a life sentence, but later escaped and fled to London.

The same man put to death through his benevolence

The oracle concludes with the fate of Louis XVI: even though, "at the very centre of it all, unavoidably, was Marie-Antoinette. It was her transformation in public opinion from innocent victim to vindictive harpy, from Queen of France to the 'Austrian whore' (putain autrichienne), that damaged the legitimacy of the monarchy to an incalculable degree." [9] The consequence of this was that despite the kindness and goodwill shown by the King, it would later contribute towards his eventual death at the hands of the revolutionaries.

> Louis XVI (23 Aug 1754–21 Jan 1793) King of France (1774), whose kind heart and good intentions proved inadequate to deal with the mounting crisis of the Ancien Regime. [...] He was guillotined in Paris. [10]

Summary: *Before the French Revolution, the reign of Louis XVI and his pretty young wife, Marie Antoinette, showed great promise for the future. It therefore came as a great shock when the early details of the 'Affair of the Diamond Necklace' reached the public ear. The finger of suspicion turned to point at the Queen as being the one at fault. This oracle foretells the basic details that led to the development of the scandal. And, although the Queen was an innocent victim in what happened, public attention nevertheless became far more focused upon the frivolity of her life style. Thereafter, it took a mere four years to the storming of the Bastille that opened the gateway to a full-blooded revolution. The oracle actually connects the diamond necklace affair to the bloodshed that followed, by predicting the execution of the King, at the same time noting, particularly, his benevolent character.*

44   *Par lors qu'vn Roy sera contre les siens,*
      Natif de Bloys subiuguera Ligures:
      Mammel, Cordube & les Dalmatiens,
      Des sept puis l'ombre à Roy estrennes & lemure s.

45   *L'ombre du regne de Nauarre non vray,*
      Fera la vie de sort illegitime:
      La veu promis incertain de Cambray,
      Roy Orleans donra mur legitime.

veu (OF) vow; promis (OF) covenanted.

The shadow of **NAVARRE**'s reign not true,   1619
It will make the life of destiny unlawful,
The covenanted vow of Cambrai uncertain;
The King will give **ORLEANS** a legitimate wall.

The shadow of Navarre's reign not true

Henri IV's reign as King of France and Navarre began the dawn of his country's revival after the devastation caused by the French Wars of Religion. This was achieved militarily, politically and socially: but his assassination in 1610 placed the kingdom in the hands of his widow and her underage son, Louis XIII. Plans had previously been put in place for the smooth continuation of Henri's reign, should he die, but attempts to follow what the King had worked so hard to achieve were soon replaced by circumstances that his wife, Marie de' Medici was unable to control. "During [Louis XIII's] minority, his mother, Marie de Medici dissipated practically all the authority and treasure that his father Henry IV, had built up after the French Wars of Religion." [1]

> Incapable of dominating the competing forces that divided France [...] [And] as only a Regent and a foreigner, she was unable to withstand the demands of Condé and his followers except by bribes and offices, which bankrupted the treasury and threatened to break up France into a confederation of provinces. [2]

The pretence of continuing Navarre's reign also failed in another way. Apart from the illegal practices that diminished the treasury, the regency came to its own abrupt end through a *coup*. The murder of the Queen-regent's chief minister, the Marshal d'Ancre, propelled Charles d'Albert, Louis XIII's favourite, into the vacant office, and for which he was granted the title, duc de Luynes [3]. In this capacity he became the virtual ruler of France: but, "He was to prove an increasingly pernicious influence on Louis."

It will make the life of destiny unlawful

Predestination is, in other words, *a life of destiny*, and this became the doctrine that Calvin advocated. It was his belief that there existed an 'Elect, ordained by God', who were predestined for heaven. In 1619, at the Synod of Dort in the Netherlands, this became an important tenet, central to Calvinism and one that was adopted by the Protestant Huguenots.

Contrarily, with overall control of the government, Luynes set about removing every vestige of Huguenot influence from the land.

> At home, he embarked on the policy of liquidating the independence of the [...] Huguenots [...] Against the Huguenots, preliminary measures had already been taken in June 1617, when Luynes decreed that [...] Kingdoms of Navarre and Béarn in the Pyrenees were united with France [...] this order entailed the restoration of Roman Catholic worship and the restoration of Church lands. [4]

Inevitably, military action followed this decree; two-thirds of the Huguenot "state-within-a-state" were re-conquered and restored to Catholicism. Thus, a life of destiny became unlawful because it was a tenet of Calvinism, in what had become once again, predominantly, Catholic France. [5]

The covenanted vow of Cambrai uncertain

The peace settlement of 1559, signed by France, Spain, the Holy Roman Empire and England at Le Cateau-Cambrésis, took place fourteen miles outside Cambrai. [6] It brought to an end the

Franco-Habsburg War, begun by Henri II in a vain attempt to subjugate Italy. Sixty years later, in the reign of Louis XIII, the promise of peace, settled by the covenanted vow made at Cambrai, looked uncertain: it having come under threat from the Thirty Years War, which broke out on 23 May 1618. "Ferdinand II in alliance with Spain revived the apprehensions of France, and inaugurated another stage in the long Franco-Habsburg power-struggle." [7]

The King will give Orleans a legitimate wall

In April 1624, three years after the death of Luynes, Richelieu received his long-awaited recall to the King's Council. And by the following August, he had converted this appointment to one of supreme authority. Louis XIII's brother Gaston, over-ambitious for power, was moved to jealousy by the Cardinal's office, and the spark of rebellion began smouldering inside him. In 1626, this spark ignited into a blaze when Gaston openly refused to obey Louis' wish that he marry Marie de Bourbon-Montpensier. To make matters worse, Gaston then conspired with the Marquis de Chalais to assassinate Richelieu.

The plot was uncovered before it could be implemented and Chalais was executed. Gaston, however, who was still heir to the throne, received only a reprimand. But to assuage his hurt, and to help motivate his sense of responsibility, he was made *duc d'Orléans*.

In a further bid to encourage his brother to adopt a conciliatory attitude towards the realm, the King put Orléans in charge of redesigning the classical wing at the Château Blois: completed in 1635 by François Mansard. [8] The oracle emphasises the legality of this new wall because four years earlier, a series of illegal activities by Louis Le Barbier had surrounded the demolition and rebuilding of *the wall* on the right bank of the Seine: built originally by Charles V.

> Richelieu was in a hurry to build the new wall on the Right Bank [...] because the old one obscured the view from his Palais Cardinal. A contract was signed in October 1631, but the contractors [...] were as unreliable as Le Barbier – whose front-men they turned out to be. Virtually nothing was ever completed [...] Given the treatment meted out to the likes of Concini, he and his accomplices were lucky to escape with their lives. [9]

The oracle has therefore contrasted the illegal operations surrounding the Paris wall with the perfectly legal order given to Orléans for the construction of walls to the new wing at Blois.

Summary: *In line with the oracle's intention to follow the future history of France, this oracle broadly covers events that stood out following the assassination of Henri IV. Once again, the seer has used the strategy of identifying individuals by their title. Navarre is therefore Henri IV, King of France and Navarre, hence Orleans is Gaston, the King's brother, having received his title in 1626. The mention of a 'legitimate wall' during this same period is most apt, as is the threat to the peace treaty signed at Cambrai, and the counter measures taken against Calvinism.*

46   Vie sort mort de L'OR vilaine indigne,
        Sera de Saxe non nouueau electeur:
        De Brunsuic mandra d'amour signe,
        Faux le rendant au peuple seducteur.

47   De Bourze ville à la dame Guyrlande,
        L'on mettra sus par la trahison faicte,
        Le grand prelat de Leon par Formande,
        Faux pellerins & rauisseurs defaicte.

48   Du plus profond de l'Espaigne enseigne,
        Sortant du bout & des fins de l'Europe,
        Troubles passant aupres du pont de Laigne,
        Sera deffaicte par bandes sa grand troppe.

49   Iardin du monde aupres de cité neufue,
        Dans le chemin des montaignes cauees,
        Sera saisi & plongé dans la Cuue,
        Beuuant par force eaux soulfre enuenimées.

lardin (*ellipsis*) Garden *State;* monde (*ellipsis*) *new* world; cauees (OF) hollowed; saisi (Mod. Fr.) struck; Cuue (Dictionnaire de français Littré - Grand vase en pierre, en marbre, en bronze destiné à contenir de l'eau, tel que les baignoires) large vessel in stone, marble or bronze purposed for containing water, such as in sort bathtubs; beuvant (OF bevant) drinking to excess; enuenimees (AF enveniner - imprègner de venin) impregnated with venom.

> GARDEN (STATE) of the (NEW) WORLD, close to the new city (NEW YORK),   2001
> In the path of the hollowed mountains (WORLD TRADE CENTER),
> It will be struck, and plunged into the BATHTUB,
> By force, consuming to excess, sulphurous streams, impregnated with malice.

Garden (State)

New Jersey is one of the original 13 States of the USA and known across the world by its official designation, the Garden State.

> Abraham Browning of Camden is given credit for giving New Jersey the nickname the Garden State. According to Alfred Heston's 1926 two-volume book *Jersey Wagon Jaunts*, Browning called New Jersey the Garden State while speaking at the Philadelphia Centennial exhibition on New Jersey Day (August 24, 1876). [1]

Of the New World

The New World is the historic name for the Americas.

> The New World is one of the names used for the American continents and adjacent islands collectively, since the 16th century [the actual century when this prophecy was written]. The Americas were at that time new to the Europeans, who previously thought of the world as consisting only of Europe, Asia, and Africa [...] America is always described as 'New World'. [2]

Close to the new city

New Jersey, the Garden State of the New World is situated *close to the new city;* that is, *New* York City. On 11 September 2001, America was struck by a disaster of catastrophic proportions. It not only brought with it a tragic loss of human life numbering several thousand, but the political repercussions from what happened that day in Lower Manhattan were felt around the world. Two hijacked airliners crossed New Jersey and impacted, one after the other, with the twin towers of the World Trade Center. [3]

In the path of the hollowed mountains

By studying the flight paths of the two hijacked airliners, it can be established that after leaving Boston bound for Los Angeles, one of the planes deviated from its course north of Albany, and headed south towards New York City. The other aircraft headed in a south-westerly direction, passing well to the south of Albany, and north of New York City. It then turned in a south-south-easterly direction, finally veering northeast, to take it back to New York and the World Trade Center. Both planes passed over New Jersey's air space *in the path* leading to the giant twin towers.

There is also a second, and perhaps coincidental, meaning attached to 'the path'. *Path* was the acronym given to the Port Authority Trans-Hudson Corporation, which was instrumental in the construction of the World Trade Center. [4] The association existing between the WTC and the PATH Corporation therefore serves as a possible addition to the prophecy.

The phrase, *hollowed mountains*, is actually a very apt description of the World Trade Center's two towers. It not only identifies the *mountainous* nature of these skyscrapers, but also their *hollow* structure. Each tower rose to "a height of 417 metres." Moreover, their interior was designed in the form of interconnecting rooms and office suites, so that "Office spaces will have no interior columns:" [5] the overall effect was both open and spacious—in a word, hollow.

It will be struck

The first attack on the World Trade Center came at 8.48 AM: "when American Airlines flight 11, bound from Boston to Los Angeles and carrying 92 people, flew into the World Trade Centre's north tower. It punched a gaping hole and set off a firestorm that soon consumed the top third of the tower." [6]

Within minutes, and while onlookers were still gaping in disbelief at this dreadful spectacle, "a second plane, a United Airlines Boeing-707, carrying 56 passengers and nine crew and also heading for Los Angeles from Boston, plunged into the other tower, sending flames blasting out of the other side. " [7]

With huge numbers of people trapped in the upper floors of the two buildings, cut off from the stair wells and elevators by scorching flames, and unable to exit the stricken buildings, the next part of the tragedy unfolded.

And plunged into the Bathtub

"[B]oth towers, where thousands of business people and city employees worked, collapsed devastating the

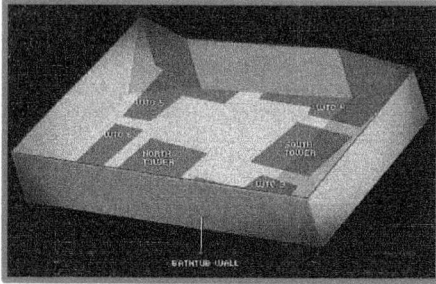

THE BATHTUB

New York City skyline." [8] One after the other, both towers collapsed *and plunged into the Bathtub* below.

In the days and weeks that followed this tragic, terrible, violent incident, "108,342 truckloads of debris were removed from the site before the bathtub was cleared." [9] It is therefore important to note that 443 years before this deliberate act of terrorism was carried out, the surround to the World Trade Center was already known as — *"the Bathtub"*.

The World Trade Center straddled the border between solid ground and late less stable additions. A reinforced enclosure had to be built around the foundations to secure the buildings and stop flooding. This became known as the bathtub. [10]

"The bathtub, built along the western side of the World Trade Centre site is five stories deep, containing a subway tunnel, water, gas and utility lines." [11] It was bordered by Vesey Street, West Street and Liberty Street. It is also to be noted that the word 'Cuve' is spelt with a capital letter, so as to draw particular attention to its name and intended importance.

By force, consuming to excess sulphurous streams

The *force* of the impact upon the buildings caused both planes to disintegrate. This caused the towers *to consume* the full load of aircraft diesel carried in the shattered fuel tanks. Both flights "were fully loaded with fuel. Security experts believe that this may have been part of the plan of attack, as the fuel would guarantee a much larger and more extensive explosion than would have otherwise happened."

Since diesel was not a word that existed in the vocabulary of the sixteenth-century (the name is taken from its German inventor), the fuel is described according to the qualities it has in common with sulphur—both being 'fluid', 'yellowish', 'pungent', 'fusible', and 'inflammable'.

The fuel ignited instantly upon impact, causing a raging inferno to engulf the upper regions of the towers. The excess of burning material further weakened the already damaged structure of the buildings, and this led to the collapse of both towers, *plunging them into the Bathtub* below.

THE TWIN TOWERS

"It was the fire that killed the buildings – nothing on Earth could survive those temperatures with that amount of fuel burning." [12]

Impregnated with malice

Whatever else may be said, the oracle has unequivocally identified, with the most apposite words, the intense hatred felt against America by the assailants who planned and executed this appalling crime. It involved not only the hijacking of two passenger aircraft, but a great many months of training in order to pilot these planes. And when that was accomplished, their final act was to commit suicide by impregnating their malice into the two aircraft they used as missiles. For, upon striking the World Trade Center, a sulphurous stream of diesel fuel was released, which ignited to contribute to the collapse of the towers. The perpetration of this disaster not only took the lives of those, whose great misfortune it was to be passengers on these two aircraft, but also several thousand other people working in the towers at the time they were struck.

Summary: *The entire prophecy is devoted to that momentous event in world history known as 9/11. On 11 September 2001, the World Trade Center in New York was completely destroyed. Two airliners had been hijacked, and were then flown into each of the two towers, which together formed the WTC. This oracle, using subaudition in its opening line, so as to include America, the state of New Jersey and the city of New York, confining it to just ten syllables, then pinpoints the actual area bounded by the three streets, where this disaster was to take place. The act was carried out by an Islamic group operating under the name of al-Qaeda, and which is totally infused with malice towards the USA; that malice was also predicted in the oracle. It is also noteworthy that in 1941, Rolfe Boswell published Nostradamus Speaks in which he correctly identified this quatrain as referring to America, New Jersey and New York (pp. 349-50). But this did nothing to prevent the fulfilment of the prophecy, because the predicted event was, at the time, unimaginable: the more so, since neither the World Trade Center nor the Bathtub existed until construction began in the 1970s (it was opened in 1973).*

50   *La Meuse au iour terre de Luxembourg,*
      Descouurira Saturne & trois en l'urne.
      Montaigne & pleine, ville, cité & bourg:
      Lorrain deluge trahison par grand hurne.

51   *Des lieux plus bas du pays de Lorraine,*
      Seront des basses Allemaignes vnis,
      Par ceux du siege Picards, Normans, du Maisne,
      Et aux cantons ce seront reunis.

52   *Au lieu où LAYE & Scelde se marient,*
      Seront les nopces de long temps maniees,
      Au lieu d'Anuers où la crappe charient,
      Ieune vieillesse conforte intaminee.

53   *Les trois pellices de loing s'entrebatron,*
      La plus grand moindre demeurera à l'escoute;
      Le grand Selin n'en sera plus patron,
      Le nommera feu pelte blanche routte.

54   *Née en ce monde par concubine fertiue,*
      A deux hault mise par les tristes nouuelles,
      Entre ennemis sera prinse captiue,
      Et amené à Malings & Bruxelles.

55   *Les malheureuses nopces celebreront,*
      En grande ioye mais la fin malheureuse:
      Mary & mere nore desdaigneront,
      Le Phybe mort, & nore plus piteuse.

56   *Prelat royal son baissant trop tiré,*
      Grand fleux de sang sortira par sa bouche,
      Le regne Anglicque par regne respiré,
      Long temps mort vif en Tunys comme souche.

57   *Le subleué ne cognoistra son sceptre,*
      Les enfans ieunes des plus grands honnira:
      Oncques ne fut vn plus ord cruel estre,
      Pour leurs espouses à mort noir bannira.

58   *Au temps du dueil que le felin monarque,*
            Guerroyera le ieune Aemathien:
            Gaule bransler, perecliter la barque,
            Tenter Phossens au Ponant entretien.

dueil (deuil); felin (F. *also* Spanish *paragram:* 'p' for 'n' Felip) Philip; Æmathien (Gk *as before*); pérecliter (F. pericliter); Tenter (AF chercher à atteindre) endeavouring to attain; Phossens (Gk *syncope:* Phoss[at]ens – Φοσσατονς) boundaries, *also* Greek *anagrammatic paragram,* - phossens - Φασ[ι]ανος — (Pheasants). Cross-references: Æmathien, C.IX: 38; C.IX: 64; C.IX: 93; C.X: 7.

At the time of mourning when the feline (**FELIPE IV**) monarch   1643
Will make war upon the young Amythaon (**LOUIS XIV**):
France shaking, the ship in jeopardy:
Endeavouring to attain boundaries (pheasants) at the **ATLANTIC OCEAN** conference.

At the time of mourning

At the time when the Court in France was mourning the death of Louis XIII in May 1643, Philip IV of Spain seized this moment for a surprise attack against its old enemy.[1] Victory had seemed assured, because France had just come under the rule of a four-year-old boy king, with his mother acting as regent.

When the feline monarch (Felipe)

Philip IV is referred to in the oracle as a monarch with feline tendencies: cat-like being a term of contempt for a human being (OED). The Venetian ambassador reported that Philip had fathered 32 bastards by actresses procured for him through a network of agents. He was also prone to bouts of sexual debauchery, followed by religious remorse. On one occasion, he even appealed to the abbess at the convent of Àgreda to pray for him to be relieved of his lechery, but she was unsuccessful.[2]

Will make war upon the young Amythaon

On 19 May 1643, Spain prepared for its assault on Paris, but was repelled by the duc d'Enghien at the battle of Rocroi in the Ardennes. The conflict actually took place on the day of Louis XIII's funeral.

Hence, at the time France was mourning the death of Louis XIII, Philip IV, the feline monarch, began waging war upon the young Amythaon, but lost up to 8,000 men dead, and almost another 7,000 captured. France suffered fewer casualties, with 2,000 killed and as many again captured. The battle of Rocroi is frequently referred to as one of France's greatest victories.[3]

France shaking

Louis XIV's reign began with the triumph of Enghien's victory at Rocroi.[4] He had not long to wait for this piece of good fortune to suffer a reversal. In 1648 there began the first of the French civil wars known collectively as the *Fronde*.

Such was the turmoil inside France, resulting from these civil wars that it "threatened to shake the fabric of the state to its foundations."[5] The First *Fronde* concerned the Revolt of the *Parlements* (1648-49), and was aimed against the extremism of Cardinal Mazarin as adviser to the Regent Anne of Austria. The Second *Frond* known as The Fronde of the Princes (1651-52) was "a series of riots, and skirmishes involving Paris, the provinces and the Spanish."

The ship in jeopardy

At the time of this civil unrest, and for some years afterwards, the Catholic Church experienced a rise in Jansenism. The movement was a puritan division of orthodox Catholicism, mainly aimed at independent thinkers, and like Calvinism it accepted the doctrine of predestination. It soon took a tight hold on French intellectual life during the early part of Louis' reign: even threatening the power of the Jesuits and their influential position close to the King. Moreover, it played a role amongst those who took part in the *Fronde*, thereby earning the detestation of Louis XIV. But in 1653 Pope Innocent X, perceiving the Church – *the bark* of Saint Peter – to be *in danger*, publicly condemned Jansen's *Augustinus* by issuing his papal Bull, *Cum Occasione*.[6]

Endeavouring to attain boundaries (pheasants) at the Atlantic Ocean conference
This oracle began with a war between France and Spain. It ends with the restoration of peace between both countries. In November 1659, Louis XIV was finally able to force Philip IV of Spain to the negotiating table. The *Peace of the Pyrenees*, as it became called, took place on the border between France and Spain, where the River Bidassoa divides the two countries.

It was in the middle of this river, on the *Ile de Faisans* (Island of *Pheasants*), just a few miles upstream from the Atlantic Ocean that the delegates held a conference to decide the exact boundaries defining France's recent acquisitions. As a result of these negotiations, Louis obtained almost all of Artois, the Flemish towns Gravelines and Landrecies, some places in Hainault and Luxembourg, notably Thionville by the Moselle, and Moyenvic and Stenay. Roussillon, in the south, was also acquired by France.[7]

One may also presume, in line with the occasional humorous remark found in the final line of these oracles that the delegates tasted pheasant during their time away from the negotiating table.

Summary: *This successfully predicts the war made against young Louis XIV by Philip IV on the day of Louis XIII's funeral; followed by the civil wars that shook France, and the threat posed to the Catholic Church by Jansenism. It concludes with the western Conference, on the Isle of Pheasants, which redefined France's borders with Spain. Predestination refers to God's timeless knowledge of His Creation. Freewill refers to mankind's discovery of the implications that attend his/her temporal choices. It therefore characterises the person by the way he or she thinks; and is therefore - from a scriptural point of view - a perfect way of judging each person upon the evidence of their personal thoughts and the implications arising from them.*

59   *Dedans Lyon vingtcinq d'vne alaine,*
        Cinq citoyens Germains, Bressans, Latins:
        Par dessous noble conduiront longue traine,
        Et descouuers par abbois de mastins.

60   *Ie pleure Nisse, Mannego, Pize, Gennes,*
        Sauone, Sienne, Capue, Modene, Malte:
        Le dessus sang & glaiue par estrennes,
        Feu, trembler terre, eau, malheureuse nolte.

61   *Betta, Vienne, Emorre, Sacarbance,*
        Voudront liurer aux Barbares Pannone:
        Par picque & feu, enorme violance,
        Les coniurez descouuers par matrone.

62   *Prés de Sorbin pour assaillir Ongrie.*
        L'heraut de Bude les viendra aduertir:
        Chef Bizantin, Sallon de Sclauonie,
        A loy d'Arabes les viendra conuertir.

63   *Cydron, Raguse, la cité au sainct Hieron,*
        Reuerdira le medicant secours,
        Mort fils de Roy par mort de deux heron,
        L'Arabe, Ongrie feront vn mesme cours.

64   *Pleure Milan, pleure Luques, Florence,*
        Que ton grand Duc sur le char montera,
        Changer le siege pres de Venise s'aduance,
        Lors que Colomne à Rome changera.

Duc (AF chef de guerre, *also*, Italian *paragram* – Duc[e]); pres; (AF dans le voisinage) in the vicinity; s'aduance (AF. s'avancer – sortir) depart; lors (OF) in the time; Cross-reference: Duc, C.IX: 80; C.VI: 3; C.IX: 95.

Weep Milan, weep Lucca, Florence,   1945
When your great war leader (**the DUCE**) shall climb into the vehicle,
Changing his seat in the vicinity of Venice, he departs:
At the time when Colonna will change in Rome.

Weep Milan, weep Lucca, Florence
Milan,[1] Lucca,[2] and Florence,[3] are three major cities in northern Italy: each one of which gave

encouragement and support to Mussolini during his time in power. Their reason for weeping occurred on 28 April 1945: the date on which their great Duce was shot dead by order of the communist partisans who made him captive at Dongo. By employing the second person singular for you; that is, *ton*, the Seer has injected an air of familiarity into this oracle. This was especially poignant for the sadness felt by the Duce's followers when his death was announced.

When your great war leader (the Duce) shall climb into the vehicle

As recorded in previous oracles, when the Second World War drew to a close, Mussolini's failure to agree terms regarding his surrender to the Allies impelled him to seek an escape route. From Cardinal Schuster's palace in Milan, where he had previously been talking to the Resistance, *the Duce* made his way to the lakeside town of Como, where the commencement of his final hours were set to unfold.

With northern Italy already falling into Allied hands, the German armed forces stationed in Como were making hasty preparations to depart for neutral Switzerland. Mussolini arrived in Como just in time to receive permission to join the convoy. After climbing up into one of the vehicles and seating himself at the rear, he was given part of a German uniform as disguise. But *en route*, the convoy was stopped by partisans, at which point he was quickly recognised. After being removed from the convoy and interrogated, he was shot. [4]

Changing his seat

The expression: *'changing his seat'* is used for its double meaning, since it provides a pun on the word 'seat'. As head of the Salo Republic, Mussolini had occupied his *seat* of government at its headquarters near Lake Garda. But, when he departed this seat, it was to exchange it for a *seat* in one of the German vehicles leaving Como for Switzerland. [5]

In the vicinity of Venice

Como is situated in Lombardy. It was during the expansion of the Republic of Venice that "Lombardy lost territory to the Swiss, Venetians, and other neighbours in the early 16th century." Since this was also the time when the author of these prophecies lived, it helps to explain why Como is described as being *in the vicinity of Venice*. More importantly, however, it draws attention to that city. This is of particular importance because American soldiers arrived in Venice to liberate it from German occupation *on the same day* that Mussolini made his fatal journey. "The Corps of the 8th Army began to cross the Po on 24 April against no opposition, and by the 27th they were over the Adige also, reaching Venice on 29 April." [6]

He departs

Mussolini's final journey was in company with the German army departing from Como. But, at Dongo, on the lakeside road leading to the Alps, resistance fighters stopped the German vehicles and took Mussolini captive. After several hours of deliberation, he was executed. "Mussolini is executed as the Allies take Milan and Venice." [7]

At the time when Colonna will change in Rome

The final line refers to Pompeo *Colonna*, a contemporary of the sixteenth-century seer. It is often said that 'history never repeats itself', but parallels do occasionally occur. In the commentary below, it will be shown that an episode in Rome's history runs parallel to an event that occurred in the city's future. History has therefore been used by the Seer as a mirror to reflect that event as a future prophecy.

The incidents that specifically affected Colonna in Rome, [8] and which later invited parallels with those of Mussolini in Rome – hence the *change* from Colonna to Mussolini – were as follows:

[1] *Colonna* raised troops to march on Rome because he wanted power. Mussolini did the same in October 1922. [2] In trepidation, Pope Clement VII pardoned *Colonna*. Likewise, with similar apprehension, King Victor Emmanuel III pardoned Mussolini; and fearful of his growing

popularity with the public, he made him Prime Minister. [3] "As soon as he could, Pope Clement broke the treaty, sent papal troops to ravage the Colonna estates, [and] declared the family outlaws." Victor Emmanuel responded in a similar fashion. "25 July [1943] Mussolini who led the country into a disastrous war, was stripped of his office [...] by King Victor Emmanuel III," and imprisoned at Campo Imperatore: a fortress in the Apennines. [4] *Colonna* allied himself with the powerful German army, the Landsknecht, against Rome. In a similar fashion, Mussolini allied himself with the powerful German army, the Wehrmacht, against Rome. [5] On 6 May 1527, soldiers of the Landsknecht attacked Rome.

> The inevitable attack began at about four o'clock in the morning of 6 May 1527 [...] The number of people killed in the Sack of Rome was never determined. 'We took Rome by storm,' one of the German invaders reported laconically.

On 5 September 1944, soldiers of the Wehrmacht attacked Rome.

> The German High Command ordered its troops in the neighbourhood of Rome [...] After a brief, bravely conducted but badly commanded resistance, the Italian defences of Rome crumbled [...] over 2,000 were arrested in raids and deported to Germany in conditions of terrible, brutality.[9]

Summary: *This successfully predicts the end of the Duce by naming him and the cities where he rose to power: also to Venice, which was liberated on the day of his death, It adds to the prediction by referring to five important events involving Rome and Pompeo Colonna during the sixteenth-century. Each one of these five events was repeated with recognizable similarity 500 years later; this time involving Rome and Benito Mussolini. The prophecy also provides a further example of the seer's intriguing and enigmatic last lines that is no less prophetic for the manner of its construction.*

65   *O vaste Rome ta ruyne s'approche,*
     Non de tes murs, de ton sang & substance:
     L'aspre par lettres fera si horrible coche,
     Fer poinctu mis à tous iusques au manche.

     Oh mighty Rome, your ruin advances,
     Not of your walls, but of your blood and substance:
     The harshness through letters/decrees will make such a terrible gash,
     Pointed iron put to all, even to the haft.

66   *Le chef de Londres par regne l'Americh,*
     L'isle d'Escosse t'empiera par gelee:
     Roy Reb auront vn si faux antechrist,
     Que les mettra trestous dans la meslee.

     The chief of London through the reign in America:
     The Scottish isle will transform you (like stone) through frost:
     The Reb rule will have one, such a falsifying antichrist,
     That it will put them — very much all — into the conflict.

67   *Le tremblement si fort au mois de May,*
     Saturne, Caper, Iupiter, Mercure au bœuf:
     Venus aussi, Cancer, Mars en Nonnay,
     Tombera gresse lors plus grosse qu'vn œuf.

68   *L'armée de mer deuant cité tiendra,*
     Puis partira sans faire longue allee:
     Citoyens grande proye enterre prendra,
     Retourner classe reprendre grande emblee.

69   *Le fait luysant de neuf vieux esleué,*
     Seront si grands par midi aquilon:
     De sa seur propre grande alles leué,
     Fuyant murdry au buisson d'ambellon.

70   *L'œil par obiect fera telle excroissance,*
     Tant & ardante que tombera la neige,
     Champ arrousé viendra en descroissance,
     Que le primat succumbera à Rege.

71   *La terre & l'air gelleront si grand eau,*
       Lors qu'on viendra pour ieudy venerer:
       Ce qui sera iamais ne feut si beau,
       Des quatre pars le viendront honnorer.

72   *L'an mil neuf cens nonante neuf sept mois,*
       Du ciel viendra vn grand Roy d'effraieur
       Resusciter le grand Roy d'Angolmois,
       Auant apres Mars regner par bon heur.

Angoulmois (OF) Angoulême; bon heure (Provençal) good fortune

The year **1999**, month SEVEN,   1999
From the sky will come a great King of terror:
Resuscitating the great King of Angoulême
In advance; afterwards the god of war reigning by good fortune.

The year 1999, month seven

As a part of the Seer's concealment strategy, he dates the months according to the old style, in which each year commenced on 25 March: bringing it in line with the nine month pregnancy of Mary, the mother of Jesus, who traditionally gave birth on 25 December (although we now have credible information that the Lord's date of birth was actually 23 March 5 BCE). Because of the OS dating, 'sept mois' becomes the month of September (from the Latin word for seven).

This quatrain is also the last one that has been explicitly dated by the Seer. His reference to the year 3797, when his oracles cease, appears in a letter addressed to his son César, and it does not directly figure in these oracles. It should therefore strike the reader as curious that having named the correct year for the following quatrains – **1580** [6:2]; **1607** [3:56], [6:54], [8:71]; **1609** [10:91]; **1660** [7:X]; **1666** [2:51]; **1700** [1:49]; **1703** & **1709** [6:2]), and **1727** [3:77], he then dates only one more, **1999**, before leaving the following 1797 years without recording a single one: even though there remain close to 700 quatrains relating to the future; any one of which could have been connected to a stated year. The reason, I suggest, is because of the Seer's commitment to secrecy. In 3:94 he predicted that in this, the twenty-first century, his oracles will demonstrate their truth. Once that happens, any future year he named would cause the content of the prophecy to come under such intense scrutiny worldwide, that the temptation to comprehend it and prove it false would become a major objective in the minds of dissenters, anxious to discredit his work. The Seer would then have placed himself unnecessarily at the focal point of activities intent upon usurping the future in order to destroy confidence in his prophetic work.

From the sky will come a great King of terror

As for the question, 'who is this King of terror that descends from the sky?' the answer is surely derived from the scholarship of the Seer. Who would a post-medieval scholar identify in this manner, if not a god from Greek mythology?

"In Greek mythology [...] Ouranos [is] the sky god," [1] he was also *a great King of terror*. Uranus (modern spelling of Ouranos) was father to the Furies and rightly famed for spreading fear and apprehension in the minds of mortals. Moreover, being already at home in the clouds, Uranus was well placed to descend *from the skies*, should the occasion arise. And such an occasion did arise, and it occurred in September 1999.

Because of Uranus's mythological ancestry, his name has been given to the deadly radioactive substance uranium; that is, "uranus + -ium" (OED). If this fell from the sky in sufficient quantity, as would be expected to occur after a nuclear explosion, then it would fulfil this line of prophecy; that is, assuming it fell in September 1999.

It is said, everyone remembers where they were when they heard that President Kennedy had been shot. This author certainly remembers where he was on 30 September 1999, when news broke confirming what he had for several years suspected—a nuclear incident would occur in September 1999. Even as this news broke, uranium was falling from the sky over a wide area at 15,000 times above the level of safety. The following news report appeared next day.

The world's worst nuclear accident since Chernobyl rocked Japan yesterday after an explosion took place at a nuclear fuel plant, threatening 300,000 people living within a six-mile radius of the disaster. When the plant was evacuated radiation levels were reported 2km from the site to be 15,000 times the normal level. [...] The disaster began as workers at the JCO plant were attempting to dissolve 16kg of enriched uranium in nitric acid – almost enough to make a nuclear bomb. It is considered dangerous to process more than 2.4kg at one time. This set off an uncontrolled chain reaction, resulting in a 'blue flash' at the processing plant in Tokai village. A hole was punched through the roof of the building, radiation began spewing into the atmosphere, and radiation levels went up to 4,000 times normal levels within a minute. [2]

Resuscitating the great King of Angoulême in advance

The year 2000 quickly arrived, and with it came the presidential elections in America. It was with the change of president in the USA that the next part of the oracle was brought to fulfilment. George W. Bush, son of the victorious President during the Gulf War, became the new commander-in-chief of America's armed forces, and he brought with him an agenda to spread western style democracy across the world, commencing with the work his father had left unfinished. War-like sounds were soon emanating from the White House; firstly directed against Afghanistan and then against the Iraqi leader, Saddam Hussein.

In the UK, Prime Minister Tony Blair worked feverishly to win the British people over to America's martial programme. And for week after week it seemed impossible to find a single day when some politician did not repeat the politically motivated mantra of 'Iraq's Weapons of Mass Destruction'. In fact, Iraq possessed no such weapons, as was confirmed by the U.N. weapons inspectorate. But the odious WMD phrase lingered on and stuck in the mind, until eventually it succeeded in frightening enough people to support Britain joining the US in declaring war against Iraq. Those who understood this oracle were left in no doubt, this was the war foreseen by the Seer, which was to occur after the nuclear incident in September 1999.

Referring back to the time when the author of this oracle lived, and Francis I was King of France, the monarch was "the son of Charles of Valois-Orléans, Count of Angoulême," and in 1515, he became "the first king in the Valois-Angoulême line."

Of the four kings descended from him, whose reigns extended until the death of Henri III, none were greater than he: in fact, most were pathetic. Francis I must therefore be the King to whom the oracle refers. With this in mind, a brief look at the salient parts of his reign includes an intriguing fact. This French monarch had stood up against an "over-mighty Emperor; recruited allies from all quarters, and had common cause with [Moslem powers]." [3]

As the threat of war between Iraq and the US led forces drew closer, it was France's President, Jacques Chirac who emerged to reprise the role of Francis I, the great King of Angoulême.

Like Francis, Chirac was the ruler of France at the time war began. And, whereas the King had once opposed the Holy Roman Emperor Charles V, leader of all Christendom, Jacques Chirac opposed President George Bush, leader of the most powerful nation in the world, and the chief spokesman for the west. Whereas Francis I had allied himself with leaders from 'all quarters', even to the extent of finding 'common cause' with Turkey, a Moslem nation: President Chirac likewise recruited support from many countries, even enjoying support from Moslem nations.

There's no doubt that the French president is going down a storm at home. [...] Chirac's determination to halt (or at least delay) Washington's march to war may have made him a hero in the Arab world, pretty popular in Africa and something of a wow even in Asia, but it is doing untold damage to Franco-US [relations] [...] encouraged by the popular support for his stance, and the backing of such heavyweights as Germany, Russia and China, Chirac is now prepared to ignore even the US argument that if Paris fails to fall in with the American line, it will be the UN the very source of France's veto – wielding influence – that suffers most. [4]

Afterwards, the god of war reigning by good fortune

On Tuesday 18 *March* 2003, less than two weeks after this report on President Chirac's stand against the America's foreign policy, the final part of this prophecy began.

In a televised address effectively amounting to a declaration of war, the US president, George

Bush, gives President Saddam and his sons 48-hours to leave Iraq or face war 'at a time of our choosing'. He warns Iraqi troops not to fight for a 'dying regime'."

The third war in the Persian Gulf, in little more than twenty years, was about to commence, and the newspaper presses were humming with the events taking place.

19 March: Military hostilities start when US forces bomb sites near Baghdad University where Saddam Hussein and his sons are believed to be sleeping. 20-21 March: Ground war begins when thousands of American and British troops cross the Kuwait-Iraq border. [...] Night of 21 March: Baghdad is ablaze after a massive bombing campaign titled Operation Shock and Awe is launched on the city.

Fighting continued in the fortified regions of Iraq at Najaf, Nasiriyah, Basra, Tikrit and Baghdad, with the Fedayeen proving very effective. Baghdad was regularly lit by massive air strikes. After three weeks, and believing that his goal had been achieved, President Bush claimed the war was won. He was manifestly mistaken.

The 'good fortune' enjoyed by Mars did not cease in 2003. Instead, the legacy left to Iraq by the conflict to oust Saddam Hussein and replace his dictatorship with western style democracy became just a shadow of what was intended. In the many years that have now passed, since war was declared, the number killed had already passed one million, even by 2008. Since then, the deaths from car bombs and internecine conflicts have steadily increased that number.

By the second half of 2014, a new wave of atrocities began with the appearance of fighters calling themselves I.S. (Islamic State), and which has drawn the US back into the fray, together with promises of assistance from other western powers. In short, the good fortune of the war god Mars seems set to continue. But is there worse to come? The opening line augured war by affixing the month and year to a nuclear fallout. Until peace is restored in Iraq, the question that will not go away is this; 'was the first line of the oracle also an omen?'

Summary: *This dated prophecy was fulfilled by the nuclear accident which occurred in the month of the year foretold; it also heralded the commencement of the Iraq War, indicated by Mars. In between these events it foretold the action taken by President Chirac who repeated the stand made by Francis I in the sixteenth century. Although this is the final dated prophecy in these oracles, there is still quatrain 91, in which the year of its fulfilment is also given, albeit earlier than 1999, but with religious implications.*

73   *Le temps present auecques le passé*
        Sera iugé par grand Iouialiste,
        Le monde tard luy sera lassé,
        Et desloial par le clergé iuriste.

74   *Au reuolu du grand nombre septiesme,*
        Apparoistra au temps Ieux d'Hecatombe,
        Non esloigné du grand eage milliesme,
        Que les entres sortiront de leur tombe.

75   *Tant attendu ne reuiendra iamais*
        Dedans l'Europe, en Asie apparoistra
        Vn de la ligue yssu du grand Hermes,
        Et sur tous roys des orientz croistra.

76   *Le grand senat discernera la pompe,*
        A l' vn qu'apres sera vaincu, chassé:
        Des adherans seront à son de trompe,
        Biens publiez ennemy deschassez.

77   *Trente adherans de l'ordre des quyretres,*
        Bannys, leurs biens donnez ses aduersaires,
        Tous leurs bienfais seront pour desmerites,
        Classe espargie deliurez aux corsaires.

78   *Subite ioye en subite tristesse,*
        Sera à Romme aux graces embrassees:
        Dueil, cris, pleurs, larm. sang excellant liesse :
        Contraires bandes surprinses & troussees.

79   *Les vieux chemins seront tous embelys,*
          L'on passera à Memphis somentrée,
          Le grand Mercure d'Hercules fleur de lys
          Faisant trembler terre, mer & contree.

80   *Au regne grand du grand regne regnant,*
          Par force d'armes les grands portes d'airain,
          Fera ouurir, le roy & duc ioignant,
          Port demoly nef à fons iour serain.

81   *Mys tresor temple citadins Hesperiques,*
          Dans iceluy retiré en secret lieu,
          Le temple ouurir les liens fameliques.
          Reprens rauys, proye horrible au milieu.

82   *Cris, pleurs, larmes viendront auec coteaux,*
          Semblant fouyr donront dernier assault:
          L'entour parques planter profons plateaux,
          Vifs repoulsez & meurdrys de prinsault.

83   *De batailler ne sera donné signe,*
          Du parc seront contraint de sortir hors,
          De Gand lentour sera cogneu l'ensigne,
          Qui fera mettre de tous les siens à mors.

84   *Le naturelle à si hault hault non bas,*
          Le tard retour fera martis contens,
          Le Recloing ne sera sans debatz,
          En empliant & perdant tout son temps.

85   *Le vieil tribung au point de la trehemide,*
          Sera pressee captif ne desliurer,
          Le veuil non veuil le mal parlant timide
          Par legitime à ses amys liurer.

86   *Côme vn gryphon viendra le Roy d'Europe,*
          Accompagné de ceux d'Aquilon,
          De rouges & blancz conduira grand troppe
          Et iront contre le roy de Babilon.

87   *Grâd roy viendra prendre port pres de Nisse,*
          Le grand empire de la mort si enfera:
          Aux Antipolles posera son genisse,
          Par mer la Pille tout esuanoira.

enferer (AF garnir de fer) to furnish with iron; si (AF autant) so much; poser (AF cesser) break off, *also* (Mod. F) to lay down; Pille (*apocope:* Pille[ur]); pillager; esuanoira (AF esvanuira – disparaître) disappear.

A great king will arrive (**NAPOLEON**), taking the port close to Nice,   1815
The great empire, from its death, he will furnish with so much iron,
At the Antipodes, his heifer will break off (lay down):
Through the sea, the Pillager and everything will disappear.

A great King will arrive, taking the port close to Nice

On 1 March 1815, Napoleon arrived back in France, having secretly left Elba, and accompanied by a small army of men who had been his entourage during his period of exile. The party landed at Juan Bay, *a port close to Nice*. And with the taking of the port, "The imperial invasion of France was about to begin." [1] From there, the once great king began his long march towards Paris. By the time he arrived, the numbers supporting him had swelled to a multitude. Wisely, King Louis XVIII hurriedly left Paris to seek sanctuary in Ghent.

The great empire, from its death,

From the moment of his arrival on French soil, Napoleon revived the title, 'Empereur des Français'. He then issued a manifesto declaring: "his abdication had been a voluntary retirement, and that he returned by invitation. [...] In future, the aim of all my thoughts will be the happiness and the consolidation of the French Empire."

After Bonaparte's exile to Elba, a medal had been struck by the Allied powers with the motto, 'Gallia reddita Europae' (France restored to Europe). The medal was intended to mark the death of France's great empire, but that was soon to change, with Bonaparte intending to revive it and bring it back from its death. [2]

He will furnish with so much iron

Realising that Europe would oppose his voluntary release from exile Napoleon began preparing his newly assembled *Armée du Nord* for war: a project that involved furnishing his fighting force with so much iron; i.e., weaponry.

> Every week a million and a half cartridges were manufactured; every day the Paris workshops produced 1,250 uniforms. Arsenals and depots were ransacked for firearms, however ancient, and teams of ordnance experts worked night and day to adapt the old weapons and refurnish them.

Manpower had also been a problem. But, within two months of arriving in France: "a force of 280,000 soldiers was produced [... with] a prospect of a further 150,000 once the Class of 1815 had been re-conscripted and put back in uniform." [3]

It was to prove but a brief moment of glory. England, Austria, Prussia and Russia quickly formed a new alliance, determined to rid Europe of the 'Corsican Ogre'. A collision course between the two was inevitable, and the clash of wills was resolved on a field to the south of Brussels where the battle of Waterloo took place (see Century One N°. 23).

At the Antipodes

After losing at Waterloo, Napoleon was again forced to accept exile; this time it was to be the remote rocky island of St Helena in the South Atlantic Ocean. Upon arriving in the southern hemisphere, he was settled in an old farmhouse that had been made ready for his dwelling: this was "Longwood House, the damp, unhealthy, rat-infested wooden farmhouse that became Napoleon's home." [4] It had once been joined to a cattle stall, hence the verbal connection to 'heifer'.

His heifer will break off (lay down)

Heifer refers to "a young cow that has not had calf." It also provides an unflattering but rather deserved description of Bonaparte's young wife. At the time they were married (11 March 1810), Marie-Louise had only just celebrated her eighteenth birthday, and with her upbringing as a princess of the royal Austrian household, she was therefore untouched: [5] unlike Napoleon's first wife, who had already given birth to two children when they married. But after Napoleon's removal from power, the Empress Marie-Louise broke off her marital relationship, in order to live with Count Neipperg as his mistress.

The Seer's acidic reference to the empress as *his heifer* is therefore another example of the bitter wit, for which he was known. After Bonaparte's first exile to Elba, Prince Metternich sent Count Neipperg to escort Marie-Louise back to Vienna. This led to an amorous relationship forming between Neipperg and the Austrian princess, subsequent to which, she allowed herself to *lay down* with the Count. He subsequently fathered four children by her: two at least, and possibly three, being sired while her legal husband was on St Helena. [6]

Through the sea, the pillager and everything will disappear

It was through the South Atlantic Ocean – the sea – that Napoleon Bonaparte was separated from all further involvement in the affairs of France. The Seer refers to him as 'the Pillager' by capitalising 'Pille': an apt description, with its association to gain from warfare. [7] It also provides an unflattering image of Napoleon and the battles he fought to build an empire. But, with the reinstatement of the monarchy in France the First French Republic came to an end, and with its cessation the territorial gains made under Bonaparte were returned to their former boundaries. With the countries of Europe once more behind their pre-war borders, and the 'Pillager' exiled in the Antipodes, everything that had come about during the recent past swiftly disappeared. [8]

Summary: *This prophecy was fulfilled by the return to France of its former emperor, Napoleon, in 1815. It correctly*
refers to the preparations made for his final battle, and it follows this up by predicting the break-up of his
marriage to Marie-Louise, during his exile on the other side of the equator. The return of France to its
former state is also indicated by referring to the disappearance of everything acquired under Bonaparte. As a
further remark, it is important to note that the Seer adopts the religious view of marriage by referring to
Napoleon's wife, and mother of his son, as a 'heifer'. Some people have disputed the seer's Christian faith,
but the evidence at hand lends this benighted opinion no genuine support. His biblical references, his
interest in providing the precise dates for Jesus's birth and death, his vision of the Valois in hell, and his
contempt for the lechery of Louis XV, all point to a religiously, motivated man of exemplary character.

88   *Pieds & Cheual à la seconde veille,*
       Feront entree vastient tout par la mer,
       Dedans le poil entrera de Marseille,
       Pleurs, crys, & sang, onc nul temps si amer.

89   *De brique en marbre seront les murs reduits,*
       Sept & cinquante annees pacifiques,
       Ioie aux humains, renové L'aqueduict,
       Santé, grandz fruicts, joye & temps melifique.

marbre (OF *homonym:* - caillou, marbre) small stones, marble; reduit (OF) brought back; melifique (L mellif\er) honey-making.

From brick into marble (small stones), the walls will be brought back,   1853
Seven and fifty pacific years,
Joy to mankind, the Aqueduct (**SUEZ CANAL**) resumed,
Health, abundant results, happiness and a mellifluous time.

From brick into marble (small stones) the walls will be brought back

After winning the presidential election of 10 December 1848, Louis-Napoleon Bonaparte took the first step toward realizing his dream. "I want to be a second Augustus," he had earlier declared, "because Augustus made Rome a city of marble." [1] With the aid of Georges-Eugène Haussmann: "Paris became one immense building site of mud, dust and rubble." [2]

In the centre of the city 20,000 houses were pulled-down and twice that number rebuilt. The old alleys and side streets gave way to great boulevards: which, with their wrought iron balcony-fronted mansions, they soon became homes for the Paris bourgeoisie. The *marble* halls of the Louvre were finally completed; a new *Palais d'Industie* was built, and massive renovations were made to the Hôtel de Ville. [3]

Before the arrival of Haussmann, Paris had been a semi-medieval city; after his period of renewal the capital that emerged from the brick dust reflected both the commercial needs and social requirements of a modern society, much of which remains in evidence today.

Seven and fifty pacific years

In March 1814, during the reign of Napoleon I, 170,000 allied troops, drawn from Prussia, Austria and Russia entered the outskirts of Paris, with the intention of unseating the Emperor. On the 30th, the capital came under cannon fire, and the city capitulated. The conquering armies that marched into Paris were headed by Czar Alexander of Russia, King Frederick-William of Prussia, and Prince Schwartzenberg of Austria. Napoleon I abdicated on 6 April.

Fifty-seven years later, a similar scene unfolded inside Paris. On 1 March 1871, 30,000 German troops, marching to the sound of kettle drums, paraded in front of the Arc de Triomphe to celebrate the victory of Prussia over France in the Franco-Prussian War. Then, in the afternoon, the triumphant German army repeated its march. [4]

Between 1814 and 1871, France did engage in warfare, but always outside its borders. In 1821, seven years after Napoleon was exiled to Elba, he died on the island of St Helena. His final bid to power had ended with defeat at Waterloo, in Belgium. During the next fifty years the French intervened in Spain to restore authority to Ferdinand VII (1823); blockaded Algeria before occupying and colonizing it (1830-1); entered into a twelve-years conflict in Algeria (1835); occupied several islands in the Pacific, including Tahiti (1842); defeated Moroccan forces at Isly

(1844); united with England in declaring war against Russia (1854); occupied Saigon and took control of parts of Indo-China. France also declared war on Austria (1859); sent an expeditionary force to Mexico to protect its interests (1861), while Cambodia also came under French control in 1863. But when France declared war on Prussia in 1870, and soon afterwards, on 28 January 1871, was forced to surrender to Germany, the the fifty-seven years without a foreign invasive force occupying Paris came to its predicted end.

Joy to mankind

During the reign of Napoleon III, Parisian society became a veritable joy to mankind. It was a period particularly noted for the introduction of nineteenth-century gaiety within the capital. Masked balls, opera and the theatre became frequent leisure activities for those caught up in the social whirl. Art prospered too, with works from Monet, Delacroix, Berlioz, Chopin, Offenbach, Gounod, Balzac, Stendhal, Dumas, Flaubert, and many others. [5]

The aqueduct resumed

Napoleon III also revived the idea of uniting the Mediterranean Sea with the Red Sea. His uncle, Napoleon I, had earlier discovered the previous excavation attempts made to achieve this during his Egyptian Campaign in 1798-9. In 1849, plans for redeveloping the Aqueduct were resumed. After ten years of construction work under the direction of Ferdinand de Lesseps, the Empress Eugénie was able to open the Suez Canal on 16 November 1859. [6]

Health

Health was another issue that came under the Emperor's gaze, so that: "By the end of the reign the number of free hospitals in France had grown from 9,332 in 1852 to 13,278, of laying-in hospitals from 44 to 1,860." In addition to this, the streets, the Gothic alleyways of old medieval Paris were "horribly unhealthy [...] filthy open drains ran down the middle of each thoroughfare. There was no proper water supply, everyone drinking from dubious wells: thousands died in the cholera epidemics of the 1830s." Napoleon III's response was to have Haussmann "install modern drainage". This considerably reduced the incidence of disease in the city. [7]

Abundant results, happiness and a mellifluous time

By the time the Emperor's plans were near completion, the results of his industry were abundant. Chief amongst many were:

> ... the rue de Rivoli, then [...] the avenue Napoleon III (now avenue de l'Opéra) [...] then came the 'grands boulevards' radiating out from the great squares [...] Among the tall, white buildings that went up were the huge markets of Les Halles, the Polytechnique, the Ecole des Beaux Arts and such government offices as the Ministry of Foreign Affairs. [...] The Louvre was completed, the Bibliothèque Nationale rebuilt and a new opera house begun. Two vast parks were laid out at each end of the city. [...] Paris also acquired its first department store, the Bon Marché, which opened in 1853. [8]
>
> In Paris nothing characterized the mood of the epoch more than those masked balls so cherished by Louis Napoleon. [...] Each ball was more sumptuous than the last and throughout the reign [...] took place with such regularity that they almost resembled a never-ending carnival.

Elsewhere in the Second Empire, society became as keen as ever to follow the ways of their 'pleasure-loving Emperor'.

For the working man, Louis Napoleon introduced beneficial social reforms. These included – "institutions of maternal welfare, societies of mutual assistance, workers' cities and homes for injured workers; he proposed shorter working hours and health legislation; and he got rid of the degrading prison hulks." The Great Exposition of 1867 completed the picture. It attracted crowds from around the world, and contributed towards the Emperor's so-called, 'bread and circuses' regime. [9]

Summary: This prophecy was fulfilled when, in response to Napoleon III's intention to modernise his capital city, Baron Haussmann pulled down the old houses and alleys of medieval Paris, replacing them with broad tree-lined avenues, balconied villas and a number of public buildings. The accuracy of the prophecy is *further identified by the exact number of 57 years having been predicted between two armed incursions into Paris: both as the result of lost battles. The first was caused by the downfall of Napoleon I, and the second occurred after the defeat of Napoleon III. It was also under Napoleon III that the great aqueduct, the Suez Canal, was completed. Improvements in the health of Parisians and a gayer attitude in society also became accessible: all of which is predicted in this oracle.*

90   *Cent foys mourra le tyran inhumain.*
        Mys à son lieu scauant & debonnaire,
        Tout le senat sera dessoubz sa main,
        Faché sera par malin themeraire.

foys, (OF fois — "Il signifie aussi dans une certaine occasion, à une certaine époque." *Dictionnaire français Littré*) It also signifies a certain occasion, in a certain epoch) a time, a course; mourir (ibid: Ne pas s'achever) to achieve nothing himself; mys (OF) brought; scavant (OF) learned, person of great experience;.debonnaire (AF de bonne race) of good ancestry, *also* Mod. Fr. affable; main, (AF pouvoir) authority.

One hundred times, the inhuman tyrant (**NAPOLEON**) will achieve nothing himself. 1815
Brought to his seat, one learned and of good ancestry (**LOUIS XVIII**):
All the senate will be under his authority;
He will be angered by (**LOUVEL**) a malignant, reckless person.

One hundred times the inhuman tyrant will achieve nothing himself

The inhuman tyrant is a description that found fulfilment in the public outcry: "the Devil is unchained." This chorus of outrage was taken up across the whole of Europe when it was learned that Bonaparte had escaped from Elba, and was back in Paris.
Napoleon's now famous 'One Hundred Days' [1] were spent in the vain attempt to re-establish himself as Emperor of France.

> During the Hundred Days both the Coalition nations and Napoleon I mobilised for war. [...] By the end of May the total armed forces available to Napoleon had reached 198,000 with 66,000 more in depots training up but not yet ready for deployment. By the end of May Napoleon had formed L'Armée du Nord (the "Army of the North") which, led by himself, would participate in the Waterloo Campaign. [2]

After Bonaparte's defeat at Waterloo, and the refusal of America to grant him asylum, he was again exiled. This time it was to the rocky outpost of St. Helena in the South Atlantic. He remained there until his death on 5 May 1821.

Brought to his seat, one learned and of good ancestry

Louis-Stanislas-Xavier, Comte de Provence, brother of the executed Louis XVI, and uncle to his deceased nephew who died aged ten, imprisoned inside the Temple—assumed the title Louis XVIII upon the child's death.
As a young boy, "His education was supervised by the devout duc de la Vauguyon, but his own taste was for the writings of Voltaire and the encyclopaedists." In adult life, he was the author of a number of political pamphlets: but, "At the same time he cultivated literature, entertaining poets and writers both at the Luxembourg and at his château of Brunoy, and gaining a reputation for wit by his verses and *mots* in the salon of the charming and witty comtesse de Balbi, one of Madame's ladies." [3]
It may also be added that among Louis XVIII's forefathers were two of France's greatest kings, Henri IV and Louis XIV: he was therefore Bourbon by birth and *of good ancestry.*
After Bonaparte's second exile, France was able to resume its return to a monarchical system of government; thus, on 8 July 1815, Louis-Stanislas-Xavier returned to Paris as King Louis XVIII.

> It may be said that the king's policy throughout his reign was one of prudence and common sense. His position was more passive than active, and consisted in giving his support as far as possible to the ministry of the day. While Decazes was still in power, the king's policy to a large extent followed his, and was rather liberal and moderate, but after the assassination of the duc de Berry (1820), when he saw that Decazes could no longer carry on the government, he sorrowfully acquiesced in his departure, showered honors upon him, and transferred his support to Richelieu, the head of the new ministry. [4]

All the senate will be under his authority

During the reign of Louis XVIII, France began to experiment with a new parliamentary system of government. The King was given full executive powers, and this placed the governing body under his authority—*Sénatus-Consulte* was the actual name given to this governing body. It consisted of 141 members: they being men who had opposed Napoleon in April 1814. Under this revised system of government, laws continued to be passed by parliament, and budgets were still subject to its approval; but, with such a strong monarchist support, the King was able to exercise full control over affairs of State. [5]

He will be angered

The anger felt by Louis XVIII was initially caused by the murder of his nephew, the duc de Berry. It was then further exacerbated by the resignation of his favourite, Élie Decazes, whom the King had only just appointed as France's Premier. Decazes was forced to submit his resignation five days after the duc de Berry's murder, because of repeated censures by the ultra-royalists. They had directed blame for the duke's assassination on his 'too liberal attitude'. [6]

By an evil, reckless person

De Berry's murderer was "a little weasel-faced mongrel," named Louis-Pierre Louvel a saddler by trade and a Bonapartist by persuasion. On 13 February 1820 he mortally wounded the Duke as he was leaving the *Paris Opéra*, and he died next day. [7]

Summary: *This prophecy foretells the time of Napoleon's 'One Hundred Days'. After that time had expired, France adopted a revised form of monarchical government headed by Louis XVIII. The oracle correctly describes the King's character, and his anger, brought about by the murder of his nephew. This also caused a disruption to his government, which further displeased him. Moreover, unlike the fanatical but otherwise intelligent assassin that usually commits a political murder, the duc de Berry met his death at the hands of a person from the underclass. This man's character, too, is predicted.*

91   *Clergé Romain l'an mil six cens & neuf,*
       Au chef de l'an feras election:
       D'vn gris & noir de la Compagne yssu,
       Qui onc ne feut si maling.

Compagne (*a double paragram:* Compagni), *also* (Campagne) the fields.

Clergy! The Roman year **1609**:   1564
At the head of the year (**7 JANUARY**), you will make an election:
Of one grey and black, issued from the fields (**COMPAGNI – GREGORY XIII**),
Who, at one time, was never so malicious.

Clergy, Roman, the year 1609

This quatrain completes the set of those within these *Centuries* that specifically names a year. It can be seen from this, the lengths to which the Seer has gone to provide a date, and yet conceal its true meaning.

For example, '1580 plus and minus' meant nothing until 18 was added and subtracted, whereupon 1562 and 1598 marked the beginning and end of the French Wars of Religion. With equal bafflement, 1607 was stated three times. Twice the prophecy led to nothing. However, once it was read as '1607 by sacred clue', and on the second occasion, '1607 by liturgy' the prophecies could be seen to date, the birth of Jesus, and secondly his crucifixion. On the third occasion when 1607 was mentioned together with XXIII, it could be construed as the day of the month on which Christ was born. It is a strange mind that does not find the repeated usage of this year to determine two otherwise unknown dates – concerning the birth and death of our Saviour – as incredibly ingenious.

It is with these examples in mind that attention is drawn to 1609 adjacent to the word 'Roman'. This suggests that the Roman calendar, inaugurated by Julius Caesar in March 45 BC, should be consulted. In which case, the year 1609 – commencing not at Year One but at 45 BC – becomes

1564 AD.[1] (There was no year zero.) Suddenly the prophecy becomes alive with potential, since 1564 proved to be a year of outstanding importance to the Roman Catholic Church.

Between 13 December 1545 and 4 December 1563, the Council of Trent was busy re-defining Christian doctrine and exploring new ways of ridding the Church from the abuses that had accumulated in the past. The Clergy was also intent upon answering many serious points in theology. These were ones raised by Protestants, particularly those by Luther and Calvin. On 26 January 1564 (the Roman year 1609), Pius IV was finally able to announce in public the decrees arrived at by the Council of Trent.[2] These were to provide the clergy with a new framework of "doctrinal clarity and ecclesiastical discipline," which would last for many centuries to come. Six months later, on 30 June 1564, Pius IV published *Benedictus Deus*, which confirmed the doctrine in formal terms. 1609, according to the Roman style of dating was therefore a milestone that marked the theological deliberations of the Roman Catholic Church.

You will make an election at the head of the year

Pius IV died in December of the following year. After nine days of mourning, the cardinals met in conclave to choose his successor. *At the head of the year* (7 January) *they made an election*. Their choice was Antonio Michele Ghislieri who became Pope Pius V.

Look again at the timing of the election, 'at the head of the year'. No pope, either before or since, has ever been elected earlier than 7 January, the first week of the New Year. Also, it immediately followed the declaration of the Council of Trent, dated 1609: according to the 'Roman' calendar.

Of one grey and black, brought forth from the fields

The oracle then refers to the elected pope as being 'of one grey and black'. The Pope's surname was Ghislieri which allows an anagrammatic paragram to be formed by exchanging 'I' for a 'C', *viz.* GHISLIER(C). This is an anagram for 'HIC GRISLE' (He Grey). 'Grisle', is an ancient French word for 'grey', and 'hic' is Latin for 'he'. Whence, Ghislieri can be expressed as 'he grey'.

As for 'black', this refers to Ghislieri's entry into a religious order. At the age of fourteen, he changed his name from Antonio to Michele and became a Dominican. Dominicans are known as 'Black Friars'.[3] The sobriquet is derived from the *black* mantle and *black* scapula that they wear.

Finally, Antonio Ghislieri was born into humble circumstances. Before entering the Dominican Order, he worked in *the fields* "as a shepherd."[4] And it was *from the fields* that he was *brought forth* to a new life in service of the Church.

Compagni

The word 'Compagne', with its capital letter, suggests that a name or proper noun is to be understood. But for Pope Pius V, this does not apply. Moreover, the word is unusual in that it allows two paragrams to be formed. The first, 'Campagne', followed by 'yssu' allowed the translation: 'brought forth from the fields', and this was true of Michele Ghislieri.

However, the second paragram, 'Compagni', followed by 'yssu' allows the translation: brought forth from the Compagni, which means born of the Compagni family. This enables it to be prophetic, especially in conjunction with the final line of the oracle. The reason for this is because the successor to Pius V, who died in 1572, was *issued* or *brought forth* from the 'Bon-compagni' family. Ugo Bon-compagni became Pope Gregory XIII on 14 May 1572.[5]

At one time was never so malicious

One does not have to look far into the history of Bon-compagni's reign to discover that at one time, he was never so malicious: for it was Gregory XIII who celebrated one of the bloodiest events in European history with a *Te Deum*.

"Gregory XIII had publicly rejoiced at the St Bartholomew's day massacre of Huguenots on 24 August 1572 by attending a service of thanksgiving at the French church of San Luigi in Rome."[6] He also ordered that a medal be struck to commemorate the many thousands of Huguenots who had been butchered in the streets of Paris. Historians have rightly denounced his response, describing the murders that took place in France as, "one of the bloodiest massacres in European history." Pope Gregory's one-time, malicious act was therefore a direct fulfilment of this prophecy.

There is also a deeper level to this prophecy. It commences with a date taken from the calendar introduced by Julius Caesar, from which the Julian calendar acquired its name. It concludes with a prophecy concerning Pope Gregory XIII. It was this Pope who revised the Julian calendar, and by doing so, gave his papal name to the Gregorian calendar, which is in use today.

Furthermore, it is noteworthy that unlike other quatrains, the author has made no attempt to set this particular verse to rhyme. Observe how the final line ends abruptly after only seven syllables. A possible reason for this is that the verse was never edited. It is a suggestion that finds additional support in the haphazard way it is presented. Each subject seems to fuse in with the one that follows, and this has caused past commentators to give up at ever understanding it: preferring, instead, to write it off as a failure. Yet, factually, everything is superbly correct: although this only becomes apparent when clear separations are shown between the several subjects contained in its construction.

A possibility also exists that these four lines represent a unique example of an oracle written down in its original form, from which the seer then had to compose as a rhyming quatrain.

Summary: *This oracle is one for the Vatican to contemplate. It commences with the year in which the decisions arising from the Council of Trent were made public. It then indicates the name, Ghislieri, belonging to the pope who would succeed Pius IV. It also predicts the religious order to which Pope Pius V belonged and the time of his election. Next, the oracle foretells the name of a second pope who would reign after Pius V: once again predicting his family name, Compagni, and foreseeing that there would be one blemish of malign influence to his time in office. This was fulfilled when the Pope celebrated the massacre of Protestants on St Bartholomew's Day.*

92   *Deuant le pere l'enfant sera tué:*
        Le pere apres entre cordes de ionc,
        Geneuois peuple sera esuertué,
        Gisant le chief au milieu comme vn tronc.

93   *La barque neufue receura les voyages,*
        Là & aupres transfereront l'empire:
        Beaucaire, Arles retiendront les hostages,
        Pres deux colomnes trouuees de porphire.

94   *De Nismes, d'Arles, & Vienne contemner,*
        N'obey tout à l'edict Hespericque:
        Aux labouriez pour le grand condamner,
        Six eschappez en habit seraphicque.

95   *Dans les Espaignes viendra Roy trespuissant,*
        Par mer & terre subiugant or midy:
        Ce mal fera, rabaissant le croissant,
        Baisser les æsles à ceux du vendredy.

96   *Religion du nom des mers vaincra,*
        Contre la secte fils Adaluncatif,
        Secte obstinee deploree craindra,
        Des deux blessez par Aleph & Aleph.

97   *Triremes pleines tout aage captif,*
        Temps bon à mal, le doux pour amertume:
        Proye à Barbares trop tost seront hastifs,
        Cupid de veoir plaindre au vent la plume.

98   *La splendeur claire à pucelle ioyeuse,*
        Ne luira plus long temps sera sans sel:
        Auec marchans, russiens, loups odieuse,
        Tous pesle mesle monstre vniuersel.

99   *La fin le loup, le lyon, beuf: & l'asne,*
        Timide dama seront auec mastins,
        Plus ne cherra à eux la douce manne,
        Plus vigilance & custode aux mastins.

100   *Le grand empire sera par Angleterre,*
        Le pempotam des ans plus de trois cens:
        Grandes copies passer par mer & terre,
        Les Lusitains n'en seront pas contens.

Pempotan (Gk *portmanteau*: Πεμπω + ταν - Pempo – sending forth, convoying, as applied to troops + tan – a form of address to several persons, e.g. 'Mark you! or, Look! Refer: *Liddell & Scott*); copies, (L copi\a) armies; Lusitains (L Lusitan\ia) Lusitanians. Cross-reference: Pempotan, C.VIII: 97.

The great empire will be from England.   1914
Mark you, the convoying, for more than three hundred years:
Great armies crossing by sea and land,
The Lusitanians will not be pleased thereof.

The great empire will be from England

"Queen Victoria reigned over a worldwide empire, which at its peak in 1914 included about one-fifth of the world's land surface and one-quarter of its population." Yet, when this prophecy was written, which was more than thirty years before England withstood Spain's great armada of 1588, there was no reason whatever to suspect that at some future date, one quarter of the world's population would be under the rule of England's great empire. [1]

Mark you, the convoying, great armies crossing by sea and land

The maintenance of a *great empire* can only be sustained by the occupation of great armies within the countries it governs. The enormous number of troops crossing by sea and land – the convoying – that was required to accomplish this end can only be imagined. [2]

> The story of the British Army in the 19th Century is the story of the Empire's wars. The army fought Chinese, Afghans Abyssinians, Maoris, Zulus and Sudanese, Boers and Canadians. Its battle-honours are nothing less than a roll-call of Empire; or more prosaically a gazetteer of Africa, the Near East and Asia. Indeed the British professional army owes its very existence to the growth of the British Empire. [3]

For more than 300 years

> The British Empire consisted of various territories all over the world conquered or colonized by Britain from about 1600. [...] The Empire faded gradually into the Commonwealth from the 1930s onward. [4]

The calculation of 'more than 300 years' is therefore confirmed.

The Lusitanians will not be pleased thereof

In the fifteenth century, Pope Alexander VI issued a Bull, *Inter Caetera* (May 1493), which divided the New World between Spain and Portugal: *Lusitania* was the name given to a major part of the two countries. "By the time the British began colonizing overseas, the Portuguese and Spaniards had already divided a considerable part of the earth's land surface between them." But the subsequent emergence of England as a naval power greatly threatened the territorial ambitions of these two countries, especially after the buccaneering exploits of Elizabeth I's navy, which included a resounding victory over the Spanish armada in 1588. The Lusitanians therefore had good reason to be displeased, as England's formidable sea power began to lay the foundations for its empire. [5]

After three centuries of empire building, in which Britannia proudly ruled the waves, the first dent in its invincibility occurred. On 7 May 1915, during the First World War, the German Navy successfully sank the RMS Lusitania, killing 1200 passengers and crew. To mark this event, the German government struck a special medal commemorating the sinking of the Lusitania:

aware that the British Navy was now vulnerable. In little more than a decade after this incident, the British Empire began to diminish in size as it gradually evolved into a Commonwealth. [6]

Summary: This final oracle completes the intended set of 1000. It began with a prediction of the French Revolution: an event that set in motion massive changes to the world in which we live. The oracles end with a prediction of the British Empire: the greatest empire the world has ever known. And which, in its own way, introduced massive changes across the world. In making this prediction, the oracle correctly foresees the length of time it will endure; the massive movement of armies across the sea, and overland in the countries that it occupied; also, the effect it had upon Lusitania, which holds a double meaning concerning the beginning and end of the empire. But why did the seer choose to end his oracles with this prophecy? His oracles are mostly directed towards France, why conclude them with an English oracle?

One possible reason proposed is that just as the French Revolution heralded a massive change developing in the future of western societies, so will England, after the end of the British Empire. In the letter he addressed to his King, the seer included a change in the direction that society will take. "Then there will issue from the stock, so long in time barren, proceeding from the 50th degree, one who will renovate the Christian Church. A great peace, union and concord will then spring up between some of the children of the races, long opposed to each other and separated by diverse kingdoms. Such a peace will be set up, that the Instigator and promoter of military faction by means of diversity of religions, shall dwell attached to the bottom of the abyss, and united to the kingdom of the furious, who shall have counterfeited the wise."

Since the final quatrain of these oracles refers to England, which happens to be cut by the 50th degree of latitude in the vicinity of Truro, Falmouth and Penzance, thoughts turn to John Wesley (1703 – 1791), as the last great English Christian, evangelist who was of a stock that has long since been barren. Wesley visited Cornwall numerous times to preach the Gospel, and Gwennap Pit, also on the 50th degree, is one of the locations where he preached on 18 occasions.

The Bible also predicts that Satan will be chained to the abyss for a thousand years, to bring a millennium of peace to the world. The seer states the 'Instigator' will be accompanied by the kingdom of the furious who counterfeited the wise. How long will it be before this prophecy, too, is fulfilled?

This concludes the prophetic evidence, rigorously confirmed by history, for the existence of a block universe existing as a huge and magnificent thought in the Mind of God. As such, it brings to the fore a passage from the New Testament: "For he chose us in him before the creation of the world [...] In him we were also chosen, having been predestined according to the plan of him who works out everything in conformity with the purpose of his will." (Ephesians, I: 4, 11). That is precisely the story of these past ten chapters.

References Century 10

Nᵒ 4

1 William Henry Mountague, *A New and Universal History of England:* vol, II 164
2 Ibid 164-5
3 wikipedia.org/wiki/Escape_of_Charles_II
4 Mountague, 176
5 Ibid

Nᵒ. 7

1 Voltaire, *The Age of Louis XIV*, (trans. Martyn P Pollack) 40
2 T. Wallbank, A. Taylor, N Bailkey, *Civilization Past and Present*, 419
3 R. Graves, *The Greek Myths*, Vol. 2, Amythaon, 379
4 E.N. Williams, *Dictionary of English and European History 1485 –1789*, 111; & H.A.L. Fisher, *History of Europe*, 667
5 Voltaire, 40
6 Ibid 40
7 R. Hatton, *Louis XIV and His World*, 75

Nᵒ. 8

1 http://www2.fiu.edu/~mirandas/bios1839-iii.htm#Mastai
2 http://www.vatican.va/news_services/liturgy/saints/ns_lit_doc_20000903_pius-ix_en.html
3 wikipedia.org/wiki/Pope_Pius_IX
4 Thomas Bullfinch, *The Age of Fable – Stories of Gods and Fables:* XII.b 'The Myrmidons'
5 David Chandler, *The Campaigns of Napoleon*, 53
6 J.M. Thompson, *Napoleon Bonaparte:* 62
7 Ibid 80
8 Ibid 81

Nᵒ. 12

1 J. Kelly, *The Oxford Dictionary of Popes*, 271
2 Peter de Rosa, *Vicars of Christ*, 303–5
3 Kelly, 272; Rosa, 302
4 http://www.nndb.com/people/332/000095047/
5 Rosa, 302, 304
6 http://www.romeartlover.it/Storia23.html
7 Bruce M. Metzer, *The Early Versions of the New Testament*, 348
8 Roberto Bellermino, *Spiritual Writings*, 15
9 Félix Bungener, *History of the Council of Trent* (1855) 92

Nᵒ. 13

1 Alan Palmer, *Dictionary of Modern History 1789–1945*, 308; & Tony Ashworth, *TrenchWarfare*, 3; & Neil Demarco, *Britain and the Great War*, 11
2 Ibid 5-6
3 Ian Littlewood, *The Rough Guide Chronicle France*, 283
4 Demarco, 19; & Peter Furtado, *World War I*, 120
5 A.J.P. Taylor, *The First World War – An Illustrated History*, 33
6 Ibid 34; & Palmer, 257

Nᵒ. 16

1 André Maurois, *A History of France*, (trans. Henry L Buisse), 368
2 Ibid 368
3 Ibid 368
4 Lesley A Robertson, Lorna A Sinclair, *French Grammar*, 164
5 Maurois, 378
6 J. Lucas-Dubreton *The Restoration and the July Monarchy*, (trans. E F Buckley), 354

Nᵒ. 17

1 Ian Crofton (ed.) *Collins Gem Encyclopedia*, 71; & H Belloc, *Marie Antoinette*, 343; & Simon Schama, *Citizens*, 662,
2 Christopher Hibbert, *The French Revolution*, 185; & Schama, 668
3 Antonia Fraser, *Marie Antoinette The Journey*, 481-2
4 Hibbert, 225-6
5 Jean Favier (ed.) *Chronicle of the French Revolution*, 636; & Hibbert, 314; & Jeremy Black & Roy Porter (ed.) *A Dictionary of Eighteenth-Century History*, 271–2; & Philip Mansel, *XVIII*, 105

Nᵒ. 18

1 Leonie Frieda, *Catherine de Medici:* 384-5
2 A. Pettegree, *Europe in the Sixteenth Century*, 161–5
3 E.N. Williams, *Dictionary of English and European History 1485–1789*, 172, 215; & Book of Esther
4 Williams, 216
5 Robert J. Knecht, *The French Religious Wars 1562 – 1598*, 60–1

Nº. 19

1 Desmond Seward, *Eugénie The Empress and Her Empire*, 40
2 Ibid xii, 41
3 Ibid 39
4 Ibid 38-39
5 Ibid 1-2
6 Ibid xi-xii

Nº 20

1 http://www.custermen.com/ItalyWW2/ILDUCE/Mussolini.htm
2 http://www.custermen.com/ItalyWW2/ILDUCE/Mussolini.htm
3 Ibid
4 http://www.flowofhistory.com/units/etc/20/FC133
5 http://www.historylearningsite.co.uk/life_in_fascist_italy.htm
6 http://www.custermen.com/ItalyWW2/ILDUCE/Mussolini.htm
7 http://www.historytoday.com/john-foot/dead-duce
8 Ibid

Nº. 22

1 E.N. Williams, *Dictionary of English and European History 1485–1789*, 239-40
2 Ibid 240–1; & H.A.L Fisher, *A History of Europe:* Vol. I, 682
3 William Henry Mountague, *A New and Universal History of England* Vol. 2, 228–30
4 Williams, 387
5 Mountague, 229; and Neil Grant, *Kings & Queens*, 189

Nº. 23

1 David Chandler, *The Campaigns of Napoleon*, 1012
2 Stephen Coote, *Napoleon and the Hundred Days*, 126
3 Cannes, *Encyclopædia Britannica 2001:* CD-ROM
4 Coote, 127
5 J.M. Thompson, *Napoleon Bonaparte*, 372
6 Thompson, 371; & Chandler, 1011

Nº. 34

1 Alan Palmer, *Dictionary of Modern History 1789-1945*, 208; & History of the United
   Kingdom – Napoleonic Wars, *Encyclopædia Britannica 2001:* CD-ROM
2 Murat – John G. Gallagher, *The McGraw-Hill Encyclopedia of World Biography*
3 Hubert Cole, *The Betrayers: Joachim and Caroline Murat*, 116-7; & Christopher Hibbert,
   Rome The Biography of a City, 242
4 Cole, 117; & Murat, *Encyclopædia Britannica 2001:* CD-ROM
5 David Chandler, *The Campaigns of Napoleon*, 950; & *Encyclopædia Britannica* Vol. 15 - 14th Edition, 1003

Nº. 37

1 http://fr.wikipedia.org/wiki/Guerre_franco-savoyarde_(1600-1601)
2 Ibid
3 http://fr.wikipedia.org/wiki/Siège_de_Montmélian_(1600)
4 Ibid
5 id
6 id
7 id
8 http://fr.wikipedia.org/wiki/Siège_du_château_de_Charbonnières_(1600)
9 Ibid
10 id
11 id
12 http://www.catholic.org/saints/saint.php?saint_id=4111

Nº. 39

1 E.N. Williams, E. *Dictionary of English and European History 1485–1789*, 154
2 Antonia Fraser, *Mary Queen of Scots*, 143
3 Ibid 192-4
4 A. Pettegree, *Europe in the Sixteenth Century*, 144
5 Fraser, 32, 141
6 Ian Wilson, *Nostradamus The Evidence*, 201
7 Pettegree, 154; & R.J. Knecht, *Catherine de' Medici*, 68
8 wikipedia.org/wiki/Francis_II_of_France
9 Ibid
10 Id
11 Knecht, 72
12 Williams, 85
13 wikipedia.org/wiki/St._Bartholomew's_Day_massacre

Nº. 40

1 wikipedia.org/wiki/Britannia
2 William Henry Mountague, *A New and Universal History of England* Vol. 2, 106
3 E. Cobham Brewer, *Dictionary of Phrase and Fable:* (classic edition).894
4 http://www.bbc.co.uk/history/british/civil_war_revolution/cromwell_01.shtml
5 http://www.bbc.co.uk/history/historic_figures/cromwell_oliver.shtml
6 Mountague, 164

Nº. 43

1 Antonia Fraser, *Marie Antoinette: The Journey*, 131, 167-8
2 Ibid 177-8
3 id 270
4 id 271
5 id 273
6 id 281
7 id 279
8 id 276
9 Simon Schama, *Citizens:* 205
10 E.N. Williams, *Dictionary of English and European History 1485-1789*, 279-83

Nº. 45

1 E.N. Williams, *Dictionary of English and European History 1585-1789*, 264
2 Ibid 295
3 Ibid 287
4 Ibid 287-8
5 *Encyclopædia Britannica 2001*, CD-ROM, Calvinism; & Williams, 288; & R.J. Knecht, *The French Religious Wars 1562–1598*, 91
6 Wikipedia – Cateau-Cambrésis
7 William H. Mountague, *A New and Universal History of England*, vol. 1, 496; & Williams, 426
8 *Encyclopædia Britannica*, Gaston, duc de Orléans; & Blois, Ibid
9 Alistair Horne, *Seven Ages of Paris*, 111

Nº. 49

1 The Official website for the State of New Jersey
2 Wikipedia
3 Guardian Unlimited, Special Report, Rebuilding Manhattan New York
4 The PATH to the World Trade Center, Cohen
5 great buildings online
6 Guardian, 12 September 2001
7 Ibid
8 Ibid
9 Ibid
10 Guardian Unlimited, Special Report, Rebuilding Manhattan New York
11 Ibid
12 Chris Wise: Structural Engineer: BBC News/Americas/How the World Trade Center Fell

Nº. 58

1 K.A. Patmore, *The Court of Louis XIII*, 338–9
2 *Historians History of the World*, Vol. X, 271; & E.N. Williams, *Dictionary of English and European History 1485 – 1789*, 357
3 Voltaire, *The Age of Louis XIV*, (trans. Martyn P. Pollack); & Ian Dunlop, *Louis XIV*, 5
4 H.A.L. Fisher, *A History of Europe*, 639; & R. Graves, *The Greek Myths*, Vol. 2, 379; & *Longmans English Larousse*, 685
5 Fisher, 638–9
6 Ibid 698; & *Encyclopædia Britannica*: 15th edition, Jansenism
7 G. Treasure, *Seventeenth Century France*, 185–6; & D. Ogg, Europe *in the Seventeenth Century*, 9th edition, 225

Nº. 64

1 George Holmes (ed.) *The Oxford Illustrated History of Italy*, 269
2 Jasper Ridley, *Mussolini*, 104
3 Holmes, 271
4 Ridley, 365
5 Derrik Mercer (ed.) *Chronicle of the Second World War*, 445
6 Ibid 620; & Field Marshal Lord Carver, *War in Italy 1943 – 1945*, 290; & *Penguin Atlas of World History*, Vol. 1, Hermann Kinder and Werner Hilgemann, (trans. Ernest A. Menze with maps designed by Harold and Ruth Bukor), 182
7 Ridley, 365
8 Christopher Hibbert, *Rome The Biography of a City*, 154, 157, 160, 286, 287; & Alan Palmer, *Dictionary of Twentieth-Century History 1900-1982*, 276; & Derrik Mercer (ed.) *Chronicle of the Second World War*, 429; & Ridley, 300–2, 342–3
9 Hibbert, 161; & Mercer, 521

Nº. 72

1   *The Encyclopedia of World Mythology:* Arthur Cotterell & Rachel Storm, 44
2   The Guardian, Friday October 1, 1999
3   Norman Davies, *Europe A History*, 544-5; & see commentary for further references
4   The Guardian, March 6, 2003

Nº. 87

1   J.M. Thompson, *Napoleon Bonaparte*, 371–2
2   Ibid 373-3; & David Chandler, *The Campaigns of Napoleon*, 1010 & 1012
3   Chandler, 1014–5
4   Franklin L. Ford, *Europe 1780-1830*, 223
5   Thompson, 304–5; & Stephen Coote, *Napoleon and the Hundred Days*, 287
6   Thompson, 305
7   Ibid 387
8   H.A.L. Fisher, *A History of Europe*, 960; & Ford, 257–8

Nº. 89

1   Alistair Horne, *Seven Ages of Paris*, 265
2   Ibid 266
3   Ian Littlewood, *The Rough Guide Chronicle France*, 247
4   Horne, 232, 300
5   Ibid 274
6   Suez Canal, *Encyclopædia Britannica 2001:* CD-ROM; & Littlewood, 252
7   Desmond Seward, *Eugénie The Empress and her Empire*, 118-19
8   Ibid 119-20
9   Napoleon III, Domestic policy as Emperor, *Encyclopædia Britannica 2001:* CD-ROM; & Horne, 274-77

Nº. 90

1   Alan Palmer, *An Encyclopaedia of Napoleon's Europe*, 150
2   wikipedia.org/wiki/Hundred_Days
3   nndb.com/people/834/000093555/
4   Ibid
5   Louis XVIII, *Encyclopædia Britannica 2001*, CD-ROM
6   Decazes, *Encyclopædia Britannica 2001*, CD-ROM
7   Berry, Charles-Ferdinand de Bourbon, Ibid; & Alistair Horne, *Seven Ages of Paris*, 242

Nº. 91

1   *Handbook of Dates for Students of English History*, (ed.) C.R. Cheney, 1
2   *Encyclopædia Britannica 2001*, CD-ROM, The Council of Trent
3   J. Kelly, *The Oxford Dictionary of Popes*, 268; *Collins Gem Encyclopaedia*, (ed.) I. Crofton, 296
4   Kelly, 268
5   Ibid 270-1
6   *Encyclopædia Britannica*, Massacre of St Bartholomew, and Gregory XIII, Ibid

Nº. 100

1   British Empire, *Encyclopædia Britannica 2001:* CD-ROM; & N. Grant, *Kings & Queens*, 218
2   British Empire, Ibid
3   British Empire, *Encyclopædia Britannica 2001:* CD-ROM &
    homepage.ntlworld.com/britway/guardiansofempire.html (last visited 28/2/2006).
4   http://www.atlasofbritempire.com/ (last visited 17/4/2015)
5   Portugal – History, *Encyclopædia Britannica 2001:* CD-ROM; & www.britishempire.info (last visited 28/2/2006).
6   British Empire, Ibid; & Lusitania, Ibid; & E.N. Williams, *Dictionary of English and European History 1485-1789*, 436

AFTERWORD

For those who have read the previous ten chapters, which provide historical confirmation for the presence of world-lines existing in a state of timelessness, and which contain the sense data from where these previous events acquired their recognizable form, many questions are likely to occur. For the most part, the required answers have already been provided in the prolegomena.

In brief, God, by His timeless nature, has created the perceptible universe as sensible data. It is this from which the events reported from history have taken form in the minds of those who received that data. It therefore coincides with the words of Isaiah, "I am God, and there is none like me. I make known the end from the beginning, from ancient times, what is still to come." (46: 8-10). Note the words of God: "I make known". 'Making known the world' is equivalent to relaying sense data to the minds of men, from which they are able to reproduce the creative thoughts of their Maker. From a Judæo-Christian point of view this completely vindicates the prophecies recorded in the previous ten chapters, as well as those in the Bible.

With regard to this present, prophetic presentation, not only has it been possible to show that the complete set of predictions, when counted singly, tops two thousand over a period of almost five hundred years, but they are all without a single error of fact: as would be expected from a divine source. This demonstrates an urgent need to understand that the attachment of this data to a timeless Creator, as their genesis and source, is a perfectly logical deduction to make.

The scientific response to this is nugatory. Of course, scientists can point to their Nobel laureates and the great discoveries that have won acclaim. But all such discoveries are intended to apply to the counterfeit world from which sense data supposedly originates. Not only is that world imperceptible to the senses: as it may be recalled, when Stephen Hawking indicated, "There is no model-independent test of reality." But also, if this other reality were to exist, then according to relativity theory, it would be timeless, therefore motionless—for motion to exist requires time. In which case, it is meaningless to talk about physical causes and their effects existing in this other reality. Further still, such a world would be *black* throughout. The illumination that pervades the world we inhabit, and which is experienced purely as a mental vision, exists only because it is consciously perceived—and the same can be said for colour, sound, tastes, aromas and tactility. The light that we daily see, but can never explain to a person born blind, does not exist anywhere but in the mental vision of a sentient being. This, too, is confirmed by biblical text. "And God said, 'Let there be light,' and there was light." (Genesis 1: 2). "I am the LORD, and there is no other. I form the light and create darkness, I bring prosperity and create disaster; I the LORD do all these things." (Isaiah 45: 6, 7). This explains that the light we experience is divine; it also explains the prediction of events that inevitably became recorded history.

How is it, therefore, that scientists explain so effectively the world in which we live? They speak with a forked tongue. One fork is well aware of the inadequacies imparted by their own theories, which deny direct access to a physical world. The other fork provides assurance by the feedback they obtain from observation, measurement and experiment. If the results agree with observation then some form of union has been obtained between the perceptible and the imperceptible; whereafter, the perceptible is conveniently substituted for the imperceptible when presenting their results for public attention. Essentially, the public are deceived by these pretensions, as it would seem are many scientists, who deceive themselves by overlooking the scientific fact that the perceived world is *not* the reality to which their theories are intended. This deception comes naturally to everyone, because all people behave like naïve realists, believing that the world in which they live and move is the only one that exists, and it is *directly* observable.

In fact, they are perfectly correct in believing this to be true, but for the wrong reason. Everything *is* directly observable, but its reality is a perceived reality. There is no imperceptible world. Everything perceived is composed from sense data, which includes light. It is this data that exists on world-lines that stretch through the eternity of the Mind of God. The future is therefore relative to the input of data at any point on a world-line. And since that data is timeless, foreknowledge at any point on a world-line is conceptually possible. The same cannot be said for an imperceptible world composed of motionless matter. The possibility of matter existing in a timeless universe while also exhibiting change is incomprehensible. Physical motion requires time: without which, nothng can move.

The world at large—there are no exceptions—is therefore presented with two alternatives. Each is offering to explain the world in which we dwell. Both accept that the immediate appearance of everything perceived is a mental construct—be it obtained by any one, or a combination from sight, sound, touch, taste or smell. The scientific model claims that these sensations originate from a non-mental cause called *matter*. This, they allege, exists independently in the vast, unilluminated, timelessness of an unknown space. The biblical model proposed in this book asserts, instead, that these same sensations originate from world-lines existing in the timeless Mind of God, and when decoded, they compose the one and only world perceived by the senses.

Stephen Hawking, whom I again mention as a leading figure within the scientific community, when writing his book, *The Grand Design,* acknowledged a certain frailty in the scientific model. The examples he gave – not those above – led him to the conclusion "there is no picture – or theory – independent concept of reality." (p. 38). In this absence, he and his followers have adopted "a view that [they ...] call model-dependent realism: the idea that a physical theory or world picture is a model (generally of a mathematical nature) and a set of rules that connect the elements of the model to observations. This provides a framework with which to interpret modern science." (Ibid).

The weakness of this initiative is that the final judgment depends upon *observation:* for the same may be admitted by those adhering to the biblical model. They have good reason to make the same assertion. Scientific theories are not unique to 'model-dependent realism'. The results obtained equally apply to the biblical model, on the grounds that both the biblical and the scientific model allow *theories* to be formed that predict the sequence of perceptions that are anticipated to emerge from the forward part of the world-line wherein true reality exists. The scientists will possibly seek to defend their reasoning by recourse to 'laws of nature', which they stress is the cause of their findings. The riposte to this is that the true cause of their findings is actually the Creator of the laws of nature to which they refer. As Einstein remarked, "The most incomprehensible thing about the universe is that it is comprehensible." It is comprehensible because it has been intelligently designed and has a law maker. If it were otherwise, everything would be of a random nature. Consequently, it is no more possible to apply intelligence to unintelligent structures, than it is fitting to submit unreason to an intelligent design.

Hawking appears aware of the 'thin ice' upon which the structure of scientific reasoning has been constructed: not least, perhaps, because of 'natural laws' in the absence of a law giver. For, he goes on to explain, "Most scientists would say they [natural laws] are the mathematical reflection of an external reality that exists independent of the observer who sees it. But as we ponder the manner in which we observe and form concepts about our surroundings, we bump into the question, do we really have reason to believe that an objective reality exists?" (*The Grand Design* p. 48)

The theologian has a ready response by denying the necessity of an external physical reality. If the future exists in the form of sense data that eventually becomes perceived as each percipient's mental reality, then 'matter' is a redundant notion and should be consigned to the history of science, alongside the ether and phlogiston. In its place are world-lines and the sense data they induce to present the world as it is perceived to exist—real to the senses and fully illuminated. Unlike the time when Bishop Berkeley came to this same conclusion, scientists have now been forced to ponder the inferences of their own discoveries, which lead to the same assumption.

NOTHING seems more real than the world of everyday objects, but things are not as they seem. [...] The scientific reductionist sets out to reduced the human mind to the activity of the brain, the brain to an assembly of interacting cells, the cells to molecules, the molecules to atoms, the atoms to subatomic particles, the subatomic particles to collections of space-time points [on world-lines] the collection of space-time points to sets of numbers, and the sets of numbers to pure sets. But at the very end of this reduction, we now seem to loop right back to where we came from : to the mental entities.

We encounter a similar curious loop in the most influential way of understanding quantum mechanics, the Copenhagen interpretation [...] In our search for foundations, we have gone round in a circle, from the mind, via various components of matter, back to the mind – or, in the case of the Copenhagen interpretation, from the macroscopic to the microscopic, and then back again to the macroscopic.   (*New Scientist*, special issue 'What *is* Reality?' 29 September 2012)

A version of this circular reasoning is also given in the Prolegomena (pages 2 & 22).

Circular reasoning is avoided for a universe created as a tapestry of world-lines in the Mind of God. Each thread carries sense data for the lesser minds of men. With each act of conscious perception this data transmutes into the world perceived by the senses. When the perception ceases, the data continues to exist as information subsisting in the timeless mind of its Creator.

Science is concerned with the observation, measurement, and experimentation of whatever exists within *the world perceived by sense*. Its practitioners believe the theories they devise from this exercise will simulate the existence of the source of their sense data. This source is inferred to be a physical universe, external to the one known by sense. It is therefore imperceptible: wherein, there exist archetypes of everything constructed by the activity of their *real* brain.

The superior credibility of the biblical model of the universe, authored by the Mind of God, comes at a critical time in the history of mankind. Ever since the early part of the second half of the 20th century there has been a growing movement to dispense with religion, especially Christianity, and replace it by the authority of science and its political advocates.

This combination has been seen as the way forward for laying a foundation in which mankind replaces the supernatural by rationality and science. It is a dangerous delusion: and one that year by year has been gathering force. It is simply not credible that a deity who has created the world will then allow it to desist, worldwide, from the bonds of morality that He deemed necessary to complete the perfection of His work. By the use of world-lines, He has the means and ability to demonstrate, by 'natural' causes, His reaction to a cultural rebellion aimed at disestablishing itself from His presence.

We may be reassured of the veracity attending this contention. For, in a world that has been created by sense data, existing in a timeless fashion, our present age has been known for its rebellion against God since the dawn of time. As this age drew nearer, God began preparing for it by privately displaying a panorama of future events that would grab national and international attention in the time they came to pass. His chosen vessel for reporting this prophetic display was Michael of Our Lady (in French Michel de Notre-dame). Prophecy was intended as the Deity's reminder to His people that He is the Lord, and only He knows the end from the beginning. Nor does this panorama of world events cease with the present age; instead, it remains as a constant reminder for generations yet to be born. They, too, will be mindful of the presence of God in their lives, by the fulfilment of prophecies that concern the era into which they are born.

There was also an added warning that He sanctioned for this present age. In 1634 Mary, the mother of Jesus, known as Our Lady of Good Success, appeared several times to Mother Mariana Francisca de Jesus Torres, a Conceptionist nun at the Royal Convent in Quito, Ecuador. On one occasion, Mary predicted the ordeal of a pope—Pius IX (r 1846-78). She correctly foretold that this pope would be 'persecuted and imprisoned inside the Vatican, because of an uprising orchestrated in the Papal States'. This was fulfilled when a wave of nationalism and liberalism swept across, Italy, besieging the Pope inside the Vatican, from which he eventually escaped by fleeing to Gaeta: (see Century Five N° 56 p. 267 for de Nostredame's prophecy of this event). Mary also predicted this same Pope would proclaim 'My Immaculate Conception' and 'Papal Infallibility'. Both were fulfilled in 1848 and 1870 respectively.

In the year before Mariana's death, Mary reappeared to her in a vision that provided a warning of the tribulations that were to befall the Church in the late 20th century: a time when Christianity would be more terribly riven than at any time in its previous history.

MARIANA FRANCISCA DE
JESUS TORRES

I make it known to you that from the end of the 19th century and shortly after the middle of the 20th century. [...] passions will erupt and there will be a total corruption of (moral) customs. [...] They will focus principally on the children in order to sustain this general corruption. Woe to the children of these times! It will be difficult to receive the Sacrament of Baptism, and also that of Confirmation. [...] As for the Sacrament of Matrimony [...] it will be attacked and deeply profaned. [...] Faith will gradually be extinguished. [...] Added to this will be the effects of secular education, which will be one reason for the dearth of priestly and religious vocations. [...] The Devil will try to persecute the ministers of the Lord in every possible way; he will labour with cruel and subtle astuteness to deviate them from the spirit of their vocation and will corrupt many of them. These depraved priests, who will scandalize the Christian people, will make the hatred of bad Catholics and the enemies of the Roman Catholic and Apostolic Church fall upon all priests. [...] Further, in these unhappy times, there will be unbridled luxury, which will ensnare the rest into sin and conquer innumerable frivolous souls, who will be lost. Innocence will almost n o longer be found in children, or modesty in women.   (Catholic Herald, 26 July 2012)

In 1906, after 271 years, Mother Mariana's tomb was opened and her body and habit were found to be whole and incorrupt. In 1986 A request and cause for the beatification of Mother Mariana began. Five years later, in response to a request from the Archbishop o f Quito, Rome agreed to the canonical coronation of Mary, Our Lady of Good Success, as Queen of Quito.

The reader is now invited to consider the complaints levelled against the second half of the twentieth century by Mary in her prophecy to Mother Mariana. Did the statements made above begin to emerge in the middle of the twentieth century? If they did, then why do you think they offend God? If you do not see why they should offend God, then why did Mary mention them as a warning? If you do understand why they offend God, what are you going to do about it? Life is short and the older you grow the shorter it becomes.

Take note of the prophecy regarding children. Are you not aware of the policies that prohibit or otherwise limit Christianity in the classroom, and which have developed only during the last half-century? Raise children as atheists. Silence biblical truth as 'hate crimes', and when the older generation has passed away, the world will be all but godless. The Satanic urge will have won, and death will have populated the lower regions of eternity, instead of the promised Heaven.

Prophecy in a timeless universe ensures everyone of that eternity. But how you spend eternity is qualified by the personal memories you take with you when you are reborn into conscious perpetuity. Without reconciling with the Creator, there is no appeal against the memories that accompany you when you leave this world. At the time of Judgment, so many condemn themselves by evidence from their memories. The best advice, surely, is to make certain this can never happen to you. Take action, before the wish has passed, and the bell tolls, 'Too late'.

INDEX

www.ingramcontent.com/pod-product-compliance
Lightning Source LLC
Chambersburg PA
CBHW060419100426
42812CB00030B/3243/J